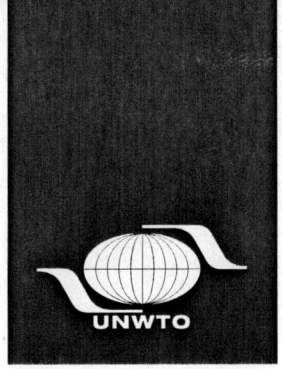

Yearbook

of Tourism Statistics

Data 2007–2011

2013 Edition

World Tourism Organization (UNWTO)
Calle Capitán Haya 42 · 28020 Madrid · Spain

FOREWORD

Decision making requires reliable information to guide adequate policies and development strategies. To support countries monitor and better understand the impact and evolution of tourism across their economies, the World Tourism Organization (UNWTO) systematically gathers tourism statistics from countries and territories around the world into a vast database that, each year, gives way to two key statistical publications: the *Compendium of Tourism Statistics* and the *Yearbook of Tourism Statistics*. Together, these two publications constitute the most comprehensive statistical information available on the tourism sector.

The UNWTO *Compendium of Tourism Statistics* provides data and indicators on inbound, outbound and domestic tourism, as well as on the number and types of tourism industries, the number of employees by tourism industries, and macroeconomic indicators related to international tourism. This data is complemented by the *Yearbook of Tourism Statistics* which focuses specifically on inbound tourism related data (total arrivals and overnight stays), broken down by country of origin.

The statistics presented in the 2013 Editions of the *Compendium* and the *Yearbook* give an insight into tourism's multiple facets and its ever growing importance and are an indispensible reference guide for all tourism stakeholders. Above all, they provide decision makers with the evidence for more informed policy-making and, as a result, more sustainable tourism development.

Taleb Rifai

UNWTO Secretary-General

AVANT-PROPOS

La prise de décision doit pouvoir s'appuyer sur des informations fiables permettant de définir des politiques et des stratégies de développement adéquates. Pour aider les pays à assurer le suivi de l'impact et de l'évolution du tourisme dans leurs économies et à en avoir une meilleure compréhension, l'Organisation mondiale du tourisme (OMT) procède à une collecte systématique de statistiques du tourisme auprès de pays et de territoires du monde entier. Ces statistiques sont rassemblées dans une vaste base de données qui permet, chaque année, de faire paraître deux publications statistiques clés : le *Compendium des statistiques du tourisme* et l'*Annuaire des statistiques du tourisme*. À elles deux, ces publications offrent les informations statistiques les plus complètes sur le secteur touristique.

Le *Compendium des statistiques du tourisme* préparé par l'OMT contient des données et des indicateurs sur le tourisme récepteur, émetteur et interne, sur le nombre et les types d'industries touristiques et le nombre de salariés par industrie touristique, ainsi que des indicateurs macroéconomiques liés au tourisme international. Ces données sont complétées par l'*Annuaire des statistiques du tourisme* qui se concentre spécifiquement sur les données liées au tourisme récepteur (nombre total d'arrivées et de nuitées), avec une ventilation par pays d'origine.

Les statistiques présentées dans les éditions 2013 du *Compendium* et de l'*Annuaire* apportent un éclairage sur les multiples facettes du tourisme et sur son importance croissante. Elles constituent un guide de référence incontournable pour toutes les parties prenantes du secteur touristique. Et par-dessus tout, elles fournissent aux décideurs les éléments d'appréciation dont ils ont besoin pour formuler des politiques en connaissance de cause et, partant, assurer un développement plus durable du tourisme.

Taleb Rifai

Secrétaire général de l'OMT

PRÓLOGO

La adopción de decisiones requiere información fiable que permita orientar adecuadamente las políticas y las estrategias de desarrollo. Con el fin de ayudar a los países a supervisar y entender mejor la incidencia y la evolución del turismo en su economía, la Organización Mundial del Turismo (OMT) compila sistemáticamente estadísticas de turismo de países y territorios de todo el mundo en una extensa base de datos que cada año da lugar a dos publicaciones estadísticas clave: el *Compendio de estadísticas de turismo* y el *Anuario de estadísticas de turismo*. Juntas, estas dos publicaciones constituyen la más completa información estadística disponible sobre el sector turístico.

El *Compendio de estadísticas de turismo* de la OMT proporciona datos e indicadores sobre turismo receptor, emisor e interno, sobre el número y los tipos de industrias turísticas, sobre el número de asalariados por industria turística y sobre aspectos macroeconómicos relacionados con el turismo internacional. Estos datos se complementan con el *Anuario de estadísticas de turismo* que se centra específicamente en los datos relacionados con el turismo receptor (totales de llegadas y de pernoctaciones) desglosados por país de origen.

Las estadísticas presentadas en las ediciones de 2013 del *Compendio* y del *Anuario* permiten explorar las múltiples facetas del turismo y su creciente importancia y son una guía de referencia indispensable para todos los agentes del turismo. Sobre todo, proporcionan datos fehacientes a los responsables públicos para que sus políticas tengan mayor fundamento y, como resultado, promuevan el desarrollo de un turismo más sostenible.

Taleb Rifai

Secretario General de la OMT

TABLE OF CONTENTS

TABLE OF CONTENTS

TABLE OF CONTENTS

TABLE OF CONTENTS

TABLE OF CONTENTS

INTRODUCTION

The *Yearbook of Tourism Statistics 2013 Edition* presents inbound tourism data for 199 countries and territories, broken down by country of origin. It is the 65th edition in a series initiated in 1947. It constitutes, together with the *Compendium of Tourism Statistics*, the World Tourism Organization's (UNWTO) main dataset and publications on annual tourism statistics, both under the responsibility of the Statistics and Tourism Satellite Account Programme.

The *Yearbook* contains data on total arrivals and overnight stays of international inbound tourism, broken down by country of origin for both arrivals and overnight stays.

> **Arrivals**

    A.   Border statistics
- Table 1. Arrivals of non-resident tourists at national borders
- Table 2. Arrivals of non-resident visitors at national borders

    B.   Statistics on accommodation establishments
- Table 3. Arrivals of non-resident tourists in hotels and similar establishments
- Table 4. Arrivals of non-resident tourists in all types of accommodation establishments.

When a person visits the same country several times a year, each visit is counted as one arrival. If a person visits several countries during the course of a single trip, his/her arrival in each country is also recorded separately. Consequently, *arrivals* are not necessarily equal to the number of persons travelling, as one person can generate several arrivals.

Arrivals data correspond to international visitors to the economic territory of the country of reference and include both tourists and same-day, non-resident visitors.

Data may be obtained from different sources: border statistics derived from administrative records (police, immigration, traffic counts, and other types of controls), border surveys and registrations at accommodation establishments.

> **Overnight stays**

- Table 5. Overnight stays of non-resident tourists in hotels and similar establishments
- Table 6. Overnight stays of non-resident tourists in all types of accommodation establishments.

Overnight stays refers to the number of nights spent by non-resident tourists in accommodation establishments (*guests*). If one person travels to a country and spends five nights there, that makes five tourist overnight stays (or person-nights).

In the 2013 hardcover edition of the *Yearbook*, the titles of the tables, names of countries, regions and sub-regions as well as the classification included in the tables are provided in English only, with notes in English, French and Spanish. Countries are classified according to the English alphabetical order. Data published originates from official sources and has undergone various checks by UNWTO's Statistics and Tourism Satellite Account Programme, which consults the reporting entity in the event that discrepancies are detected.

The 2013 Edition of the *Yearbook* reflects official data as entered in the UNWTO database as of 14 December 2012. Any corrections or changes in the tables received after this date will be included in the next edition of the *Yearbook*. Due to the rounding in the partial figures, the totals shown in the different tables of the *Yearbook* may not coincide with the totals shown in the basic indicators of the *Compendium of Tourism Statistics*.

INTRODUCTION

UNWTO wishes to express its gratitude to the national tourism administrations and national statistical offices for their valuable support, recognizing especially the crucial role of all contributing countries and territories for their continued commitment to the development and improvement of tourism statistics.

Madrid, January 2013

INTRODUCTION

L'édition 2013 de l'*Annuaire des statistiques du tourisme* présente des données sur le tourisme récepteur de 199 pays et territoires, ventilées par pays d'origine. C'est la 65ème édition d'une série lancée en 1947. L'Annuaire et le *Compendium des statistiques du tourisme* constituent à eux deux les principales réalisations de l'Organisation mondiale du tourisme (OMT) en termes de bases de données et de publications sur les statistiques annuelles du tourisme. Tous deux sont préparés sous la direction du programme Statistiques et compte satellite du tourisme.

L'*Annuaire* contient des données sur le nombre total d'arrivées et de nuitées du tourisme récepteur international, ventilées par pays d'origine pour les arrivées comme pour les nuitées.

> **Arrivées**

    A.   Statistiques aux frontières
- Tableau 1.   Arrivées de touristes non résidents aux frontières nationales
- Tableau 2.   Arrivées de visiteurs non résidents aux frontières nationales

    B.   Statistiques sur les établissements d'hébergement
- Tableau 3.   Nuitées de touristes non résidents dans les hôtels et établissements assimilés
- Tableau 4.   Nuitées de touristes non résidents dans tous les types d'établissements d'hébergement.

Lorsqu'une personne visite le même pays plusieurs fois dans l'année, chacune de ses visites est comptée séparément comme une arrivée. Si une personne visite plusieurs pays au cours d'un seul et même voyage, son arrivée dans chaque pays est elle aussi enregistrée séparément. Par conséquent, le nombre d'*arrivées* n'est pas forcément égal au nombre de personnes qui voyagent, étant donné qu'une personne peut donner lieu à plusieurs arrivées.

Les données des arrivées correspondent aux visiteurs internationaux sur le territoire économique du pays dont il s'agit, visiteurs qui comprennent à la fois les touristes et les visiteurs de la journée (excursionnistes) non résidents.

Ces données peuvent être obtenues de différentes sources : statistiques aux frontières tirées des registres administratifs (police, immigration, comptages de véhicules et autres types de contrôle), enquêtes aux frontières et registres des établissements d'hébergement.

> **Nuitées**

- Tableau 5. Nuitées de touristes non résidents dans les hôtels et établissements assimilés
- Tableau 6. Nuitées de touristes non résidents dans tous les types d'établissements d'hébergement.

Les *nuitées* correspondent au nombre de nuits que les touristes non résidents ont passées dans les établissements d'hébergement (en qualité de *clients*). Si une personne se rend dans un pays et y passe cinq nuits, on enregistre cinq nuitées de touriste (ou nuits-personne).

Dans l'édition 2013 reliée de l'*Annuaire*, les titres des tableaux, les noms des pays, des régions et des sous-régions ainsi que la classification incluse dans les tableaux apparaissent uniquement en anglais, tandis que les notes sont en anglais, espagnol et français. Les pays sont classés selon l'ordre alphabétique anglais. Les données publiées proviennent de sources officielles et ont fait l'objet de différentes vérifications de la part du programme de l'OMT Statistiques et compte satellite du tourisme, qui contacte l'entité déclarante si elle repère des divergences.

INTRODUCTION

L'édition 2013 de l'*Annuaire* reflète les données officielles telles qu'elles ont été saisies dans la base de données de l'OMT au 14 décembre 2012. Toutes les corrections ou modifications ayant été reçues après cette date apparaîtront dans l'édition suivante de l'*Annuaire*. En raison de l'arrondissement des données partielles, les totaux figurant dans les différents tableaux de l'*Annuaire* peuvent ne pas correspondre aux totaux des indicateurs de base du *Compendium des statistiques du tourisme*.

L'OMT exprime sa gratitude, pour leur aide précieuse, aux administrations nationales du tourisme et aux bureaux nationaux de statistique. Elle tient à saluer plus spécialement le rôle crucial joué par tous les pays et territoires ayant apporté leur contribution, témoignant de leur engagement constant à l'appui du développement et de l'amélioration des statistiques du tourisme.

Madrid, janvier 2013

INTRODUCCIÓN

La edición de 2013 del *Anuario de estadísticas de turismo* presenta datos sobre turismo receptor para 199 países y territorios, desglosados por país de origen. Constituye la 65ª edición de una serie que comenzó en 1947. El *Anuario* y el *Compendio de estadísticas de turismo* son los conjuntos de datos y publicaciones más importantes de la Organización Mundial del Turismo (OMT) sobre estadísticas anuales de turismo, siendo ambos responsabilidad del Programa de Estadísticas y Cuenta Satélite del Turismo.

El *Anuario* contiene datos sobre totales de llegadas y pernoctaciones del turismo receptor internacional, desglosados en ambos casos por país de origen.

> **Llegadas**

    A.   Estadísticas de fronteras
- Tabla 1.   Llegadas de turistas no residentes a las fronteras nacionales
- Tabla 2.   Llegadas de visitantes no residentes a las fronteras nacionales

    B.   Estadísticas en establecimientos de alojamiento
- Tabla 3.   Llegadas de turistas no residentes a los hoteles y establecimientos asimilados
- Tabla 4.   Llegadas de turistas no residentes a todo tipo de establecimientos de alojamiento

Cuando una persona visita un mismo país varias veces en un año, cada una de esas visitas se cuenta como una llegada. Si una persona visita varios países en el transcurso de un mismo viaje, cada llegada a uno de esos países se registra también por separado. Por lo tanto, el número de *llegadas* no coincide necesariamente con el número de personas que viajan, ya que una persona puede generar varias llegadas.

Los datos de llegadas se refieren a los visitantes internacionales que llegan al territorio económico del país de referencia, sean turistas o visitantes del día no residentes.

Los datos pueden proceder de diversas fuentes: estadísticas de fronteras basadas en registros administrativos (policía, inmigración, recuentos de circulación y otros tipos de controles), encuestas en las fronteras y registros en establecimientos de alojamiento.

> **Pernoctaciones**

- Tabla 5.   Pernoctaciones de turistas no residentes en hoteles y establecimientos asimilados
- Tabla 6.   Pernoctaciones de turistas no residentes en todo tipo de establecimientos de alojamiento

Las *pernoctaciones* se refieren al número de noches que pasan los turistas no residentes en establecimientos de alojamiento (*huéspedes*). Si una persona viaja a un país y pasa en él cinco noches, se contarán cinco pernoctaciones turísticas (o pernoctaciones/persona).

En la edición impresa de 2013 del *Anuario,* los títulos de las tablas, los nombres de los países, las regiones y las subregiones, así como la clasificación incluida en las tablas, figuran únicamente en inglés, mientras que las notas aparecen en español, francés e inglés. Los países aparecen siguiendo el orden alfabético en inglés. Los datos publicados proceden de fuentes oficiales y han sido comprobados por el Programa de Estadísticas y Cuenta Satélite de Turismo de la OMT, que consulta a la entidad en caso de que se detecten discrepancias.

INTRODUCCIÓN

La edición de 2013 del *Anuario* muestra los datos oficiales introducidos en la base de datos estadística de la OMT a 14 de diciembre de 2012. Por lo tanto, cualquier corrección o cambio en las tablas recibido después de esta fecha aparecerá en la siguiente edición del *Anuario*. Debido al redondeo de las cifras parciales, los totales que figuran en las distintas tablas del *Anuario* pueden no coincidir con los totales que aparecen en los indicadores básicos del *Compendio de estadísticas de turismo*.

La Organización Mundial del Turismo desea expresar su agradecimiento por su valioso apoyo a las administraciones nacionales de turismo y a las oficinas nacionales de estadística, y reconocer especialmente el papel crucial de todos los países y territorios que contribuyen con sus datos y mantienen su compromiso de desarrollar y mejorar las estadísticas de turismo.

Madrid, enero de 2013

Country tables
2007-2011

➢ <u>Arrivals</u>

   A.   Border statistics

        •   Table 1.   Arrivals of non-resident tourists at national borders

        •   Table 2.   Arrivals of non-resident visitors at national borders

   B.   Statistics on accommodation establishments

        •   Table 3.   Arrivals of non-resident tourists in hotels and similar establishments

        •   Table 4.   Arrivals of non-resident tourists in all types of accommodation establishments

➢ <u>Overnight stays</u>

        •   Table 5.   Overnight stays of non-resident tourists in hotels and similar establishments

        •   Table 6.   Overnight stays of non-resident tourists in all types of accommodation establishments

ALBANIA

2. Arrivals of non-resident visitors at national borders, by nationality

		2007	2008	2009	2010	2011	Market share 11	% Change 11-10
TOTAL	(*)	1,126,514	1,419,191	1,855,634	2,417,337	2,932,132	100.00	21.30
AFRICA		319	317	211	3,193	432	0.01	-86.47
Central Africa		10	56	23	12	12	0.00	
Democratic Republic of the Congo		10	56	23	12	12	0.00	
North Africa		124	133	164	3,041	252	0.01	-91.71
Morocco		61	68	78	2,924	139	0.00	-95.25
Sudan		36	22	33	54	39	0.00	-27.78
Tunisia		27	43	53	63	74	0.00	17.46
Southern Africa		185	128	24	140	168	0.01	20.00
South Africa		185	128	24	140	168	0.01	20.00
AMERICAS		51,881	60,978	59,945	61,878	70,291	2.40	13.60
Caribbean		22	28	50	782	263	0.01	-66.37
Dominican Republic			8	18	59	20	0.00	-66.10
Saint Lucia		22	20	32	723	243	0.01	-66.39
Central America		33	42	60	25	59	0.00	136.00
El Salvador		16	27	26	11	18	0.00	63.64
Honduras		10	7	24	13	32	0.00	146.15
Nicaragua		7	8	10	1	9	0.00	800.00
North America		51,207	59,996	57,875	59,941	67,529	2.30	12.66
Canada		7,342	9,511	9,243	10,301	11,468	0.39	11.33
Mexico		86	131	33	103	111	0.00	7.77
United States of America		43,779	50,354	48,599	49,537	55,950	1.91	12.95
South America		619	912	1,960	1,130	2,440	0.08	115.93
Argentina		109	192	140	294	293	0.01	-0.34
Brazil		264	566	1,660	609	1,871	0.06	207.22
Colombia		101	35	66	60	97	0.00	61.67
Peru		98	66	51	101	108	0.00	6.93
Uruguay		36	16	11	22	22	0.00	
Venezuela		11	37	32	44	49	0.00	11.36
EAST ASIA AND THE PACIFIC		9,674	15,419	28,433	11,361	17,418	0.59	53.31
North-East Asia		2,752	5,972	19,991	4,303	7,170	0.24	66.63
China		880	1,267	1,346	1,718	1,967	0.07	14.49
Japan		1,159	1,067	1,116	1,529	2,713	0.09	77.44
Korea, Republic of		713	3,638	17,529	1,056	2,490	0.08	135.80
South-East Asia		492	777	835	759	2,220	0.08	192.49
Malaysia		187	224	238	243	1,423	0.05	485.60
Philippines		206	207	439	397	547	0.02	37.78
Singapore		60	175	115	62	110	0.00	77.42
Thailand		39	171	43	57	140	0.00	145.61
Australasia		6,430	8,670	7,607	6,299	8,028	0.27	27.45
Australia		5,689	7,523	6,435	5,429	6,753	0.23	24.39
New Zealand		741	1,147	1,172	870	1,275	0.04	46.55
EUROPE		1,060,975	1,335,227	1,512,734	2,238,958	2,738,846	93.41	22.33
Central/Eastern Europe		52,589	60,038	60,880	63,722	82,418	2.81	29.34
Bulgaria		11,141	13,210	14,327	13,760	16,117	0.55	17.13
Czech Republic		7,077	7,029	7,000	7,006	8,165	0.28	16.54
Estonia		1,183	1,073	1,143	510	640	0.02	25.49
Hungary		4,660	5,709	4,697	5,939	6,319	0.22	6.40
Lithuania		1,113	793	984	889	1,312	0.04	47.58
Republic of Moldova		175	5	243	365	491	0.02	34.52
Poland		11,026	14,427	17,037	17,350	23,869	0.81	37.57
Romania		4,786	6,086	7,242	8,705	10,399	0.35	19.46
Russian Federation		6,690	7,331	4,555	5,657	9,752	0.33	72.39

ALBANIA

2. Arrivals of non-resident visitors at national borders, by nationality

	2007	2008	2009	2010	2011	Market share 11	% Change 11-10
Slovakia	2,714	2,348	2,456	2,133	2,861	0.10	34.13
Ukraine	2,024	2,027	1,196	1,408	2,493	0.09	77.06
Northern Europe	**68,655**	**79,553**	**79,931**	**85,463**	**109,924**	**3.75**	**28.62**
Denmark	2,029	2,408	2,831	3,186	4,068	0.14	27.68
Finland	2,749	3,146	3,094	3,299	4,671	0.16	41.59
Iceland	285	94	233	383	236	0.01	-38.38
Ireland	2,651	2,648	2,910	2,425	2,701	0.09	11.38
Norway	3,007	4,294	3,654	5,315	7,556	0.26	42.16
Sweden	5,016	6,920	6,073	8,604	14,673	0.50	70.54
United Kingdom	52,918	60,043	61,136	62,251	76,019	2.59	22.12
Southern Europe	**830,802**	**1,058,063**	**1,220,254**	**1,912,383**	**2,320,746**	**79.15**	**21.35**
Bosnia and Herzegovina	2,365	3,636	3,833	8,646	9,094	0.31	5.18
Croatia	8,372	10,237	11,824	26,438	20,734	0.71	-21.58
Greece	58,217	85,505	106,227	113,008	155,086	5.29	37.23
Holy See		17	8	14			
Italy	84,680	98,573	109,702	125,036	135,389	4.62	8.28
Malta	338	2,877	781	1,586	735	0.03	-53.66
Montenegro	105,636	120,125	128,547	123,833	159,838	5.45	29.08
Portugal	611	581	780	640	1,167	0.04	82.34
Serbia	60,802	59,557	40,873	43,940	48,029	1.64	9.31
Slovenia	7,414	7,513	9,745	9,834	11,283	0.38	14.73
Spain	2,499	2,870	3,573	3,813	4,288	0.15	12.46
TFYR of Macedonia	224,348	341,801	330,939	276,268	335,380	11.44	21.40
Other countries of Southern Europe	275,520	324,771	473,422	1,179,327	1,439,723	49.10	22.08
Western Europe	**85,207**	**101,616**	**116,030**	**141,187**	**186,531**	**6.36**	**32.12**
Austria	12,816	12,292	11,809	15,659	21,149	0.72	35.06
Belgium	7,764	8,197	9,609	11,094	14,973	0.51	34.96
France	16,527	18,369	20,165	25,651	30,410	1.04	18.55
Germany	31,181	38,428	48,408	55,919	73,102	2.49	30.73
Luxembourg	238	243	388	540	690	0.02	27.78
Netherlands	7,524	8,427	9,691	10,055	15,333	0.52	52.49
Switzerland	9,157	15,660	15,960	22,269	30,874	1.05	38.64
East Mediterranean Europe	**23,722**	**35,957**	**35,639**	**36,203**	**39,227**	**1.34**	**8.35**
Cyprus	473	1,140	733	850	890	0.03	4.71
Israel	1,437	2,242	4,337	1,809	2,121	0.07	17.25
Turkey	21,812	32,575	30,569	33,544	36,216	1.24	7.97
MIDDLE EAST	**1,262**	**1,115**	**1,313**	**1,247**	**1,178**	**0.04**	**-5.53**
Palestine	6	53	26	32	39	0.00	21.88
Iraq	22	19	26	24	17	0.00	-29.17
Jordan	127	88	82	72	83	0.00	15.28
Kuwait	103	75	94	41	29	0.00	-29.27
Libya	139	47	37	65	36	0.00	-44.62
Saudi Arabia	160	107	202	151	206	0.01	36.42
Syrian Arab Republic	106	147	171	138	152	0.01	10.14
Egypt	599	579	675	724	616	0.02	-14.92
SOUTH ASIA	**376**	**484**	**661**	**764**	**909**	**0.03**	**18.98**
Bangladesh	18	14	30	31	42	0.00	35.48
India	191	262	393	423	514	0.02	21.51
Iran, Islamic Republic of	144	161	150	196	265	0.01	35.20
Nepal		5	7	10	7	0.00	-30.00
Pakistan	23	42	81	104	81	0.00	-22.12
NOT SPECIFIED	**2,027**	**5,651**	**252,337**	**99,936**	**103,058**	**3.51**	**3.12**
Other countries of the World	2,027	5,651	252,337	99,936	103,058	3.51	3.12

ALGERIA

2. Arrivals of non-resident visitors at national borders, by nationality

		2007	2008	2009	2010	2011	Market share 11	% Change 11-10
TOTAL	(*)	1,743,084	1,771,749	1,911,506	2,070,496	2,394,887	100.00	15.67
AFRICA		157,554	194,403	257,936	310,684	554,380	23.15	78.44
North Africa		123,980	163,009	215,211	262,337	502,251	20.97	91.45
Morocco		15,101	14,852	17,300	17,115	17,218	0.72	0.60
Tunisia		108,879	148,157	197,911	245,222	485,033	20.25	97.79
West Africa		21,539	23,127	29,277	35,429	38,991	1.63	10.05
Mali		15,354	18,100	23,907	30,648	34,478	1.44	12.50
Mauritania		4,315	4,043	4,450	4,318	3,445	0.14	-20.22
Niger		1,870	984	920	463	1,068	0.04	130.67
Other Africa		12,035	8,267	13,448	12,918	13,138	0.55	1.70
Other countries of Africa		12,035	8,267	13,448	12,918	13,138	0.55	1.70
AMERICAS		10,271	10,939	13,120	10,495	12,265	0.51	16.87
North America		8,415	8,328	10,085	7,442	9,155	0.38	23.02
Canada		4,152	3,919	5,010	3,151	4,063	0.17	28.94
Mexico		232	282	380	370	393	0.02	6.22
United States of America		4,031	4,127	4,695	3,921	4,699	0.20	19.84
South America		797	878	857	898	733	0.03	-18.37
Argentina		360	377	273	376	275	0.01	-26.86
Brazil		437	501	584	522	458	0.02	-12.26
Other Americas		1,059	1,733	2,178	2,155	2,377	0.10	10.30
Other countries of the Americas		1,059	1,733	2,178	2,155	2,377	0.10	10.30
EAST ASIA AND THE PACIFIC		27,590	39,227	46,613	42,171	55,246	2.31	31.00
North-East Asia		3,613	4,208	4,468	3,325	23,725	0.99	613.53
China						20,153	0.84	
Japan		3,613	4,208	4,468	3,325	3,572	0.15	7.43
Australasia		786	683	662	775	832	0.03	7.35
Australia		635	585	560	667	687	0.03	3.00
New Zealand		151	98	102	108	145	0.01	34.26
Other East Asia and the Pacific		23,191	34,336	41,483	38,071	30,689	1.28	-19.39
Other countries of Asia		23,191	34,336	41,483	38,071	30,689	1.28	-19.39
EUROPE		270,881	267,552	283,843	241,637	218,629	9.13	-9.52
Northern Europe		13,784	11,757	12,968	10,688	11,023	0.46	3.13
Denmark		612	638	668	441	450	0.02	2.04
Finland		296	277	461	336	389	0.02	15.77
Norway		914	846	884	660	935	0.04	41.67
Sweden		1,125	1,293	1,580	1,227	1,257	0.05	2.44
United Kingdom		10,837	8,703	9,375	8,024	7,992	0.33	-0.40
Southern Europe		40,541	41,028	49,634	49,183	53,310	2.23	8.39
Greece		763	584	581	525	548	0.02	4.38
Italy		16,554	15,477	18,824	16,886	19,127	0.80	13.27
Portugal		3,476	4,967	6,483	6,139	5,584	0.23	-9.04
Spain		19,748	20,000	23,746	25,633	28,051	1.17	9.43
Western Europe		193,089	194,291	197,546	161,654	133,199	5.56	-17.60
Austria		1,167	1,095	1,253	1,037	1,121	0.05	8.10
Belgium		7,646	6,051	6,843	6,414	5,889	0.25	-8.19
France		170,233	170,538	171,314	140,129	112,241	4.69	-19.90
Germany		10,177	10,961	12,148	9,244	9,492	0.40	2.68
Luxembourg		152	134	176	193	93	0.00	-51.81
Netherlands			1,818	2,217	1,764	1,541	0.06	-12.64
Switzerland		3,714	3,694	3,595	2,873	2,822	0.12	-1.78
East Mediterranean Europe		11,314	11,323	12,140	9,783	9,653	0.40	-1.33
Turkey		11,314	11,323	12,140	9,783	9,653	0.40	-1.33

ALGERIA

2. Arrivals of non-resident visitors at national borders, by nationality

	2007	2008	2009	2010	2011	Market share 11	% Change 11-10
Other Europe	12,153	9,153	11,555	10,329	11,444	0.48	10.79
Other countries of Europe	12,153	9,153	11,555	10,329	11,444	0.48	10.79
MIDDLE EAST	44,892	44,576	54,298	50,000	61,122	2.55	22.24
Libya	13,523	13,940	16,359	19,313	28,615	1.19	48.16
Syrian Arab Republic					12,444	0.52	
Other countries of Middle East	31,369	30,636	37,939	30,687	20,063	0.84	-34.62
NOT SPECIFIED	1,231,896	1,215,052	1,255,696	1,415,509	1,493,245	62.35	5.49
Nationals Residing Abroad	1,231,896	1,215,052	1,255,696	1,415,509	1,493,245	62.35	5.49

ANDORRA

1. Arrivals of non-resident tourists at national borders, by country of residence

		2007	2008	2009	2010	2011	Market share 11	% Change 11-10
TOTAL	(*)	2,189,421	2,059,451	1,829,869	1,808,001	1,947,531	100.00	7.72
EUROPE		2,189,421	2,059,451	1,829,869	1,808,001	1,947,531	100.00	7.72
Southern Europe		1,628,528	1,555,475	1,409,868	1,414,298	1,507,111	77.39	6.56
Spain		1,628,528	1,555,475	1,409,868	1,414,298	1,507,111	77.39	6.56
Western Europe		450,780	402,299	332,783	310,800	327,250	16.80	5.29
France		450,780	402,299	332,783	310,800	327,250	16.80	5.29
Other Europe		110,113	101,677	87,218	82,903	113,170	5.81	36.51
Other countries of Europe		110,113	101,677	87,218	82,903	113,170	5.81	36.51

ANGOLA

1. Arrivals of non-resident tourists at national borders, by country of residence

	2007	2008	2009	2010	2011	Market share 11	% Change 11-10
TOTAL	194,730	294,258	365,784	424,919	481,207	100.00	13.25
AFRICA	33,193	37,219	46,476	72,519	147,903	30.74	103.95
East Africa	8,257	4,053	4,271	7,418	15,740	3.27	112.19
Burundi	23	58	21	34	37	0.01	8.82
Comoros	5	6	5				
Ethiopia	209	258	252	383	300	0.06	-21.67
Eritrea	102	146	366	351	467	0.10	33.05
Djibouti		2	1	6	6	0.00	
Kenya	165	249	326	411	516	0.11	25.55
Madagascar	37	31	48	91	77	0.02	-15.38
Malawi	38	129	98	96	113	0.02	17.71
Mauritius	89	83	104	43	63	0.01	46.51
Mozambique	6,227	1,400	1,550	3,089	1,577	0.33	-48.95
Rwanda	77	112	75	71	60	0.01	-15.49
Seychelles	1	1	9	7	3	0.00	-57.14
Somalia	4	5	10	16	120	0.02	650.00
Zimbabwe	537	573	598	1,317	1,176	0.24	-10.71
Uganda	45	57	67	70	157	0.03	124.29
United Republic of Tanzania	182	191	140	120	174	0.04	45.00
Zambia	516	752	601	1,313	10,894	2.26	729.70
Central Africa	4,467	6,429	5,414	9,387	23,203	4.82	147.18
Cameroon	397	658	633	3,405	556	0.12	-83.67
Central African Republic	22	44	22	21	18	0.00	-14.29
Chad	51	56	79	69	61	0.01	-11.59
Congo	945	954	728	568	9,436	1.96	1561.27
Democratic Republic of the Congo	1,058	1,108	890	446	10,241	2.13	2196.19
Equatorial Guinea	97	129	72	85	101	0.02	18.82
Gabon	162	437	294	956	142	0.03	-85.15
Sao Tome and Principe	1,735	3,043	2,696	3,837	2,648	0.55	-30.99
North Africa	284	693	2,956	9,364	967	0.20	-89.67
Algeria	104	262	2,589	3,460	327	0.07	-90.55
Morocco	56	123	115	2,762	295	0.06	-89.32
Sudan	5	81	72	30	96	0.02	220.00
Tunisia	119	227	180	3,112	249	0.05	-92.00
Southern Africa	14,389	17,306	27,238	32,872	100,467	20.88	205.63
Botswana	138	469	130	88	145	0.03	64.77
Lesotho	13	67	19	20	40	0.01	100.00
Namibia	887	1,174	1,225	3,506	37,834	7.86	979.12
South Africa	13,328	15,476	25,803	29,217	62,380	12.96	113.51
Swaziland	23	120	61	41	68	0.01	65.85
West Africa	5,796	8,738	6,597	13,478	6,321	1.31	-53.10
Cape Verde	1,145	2,049	1,085	821	957	0.20	16.57
Benin	102	111	90	1,134	47	0.01	-95.86
Gambia	370	597	327	230	303	0.06	31.74
Ghana	234	217	289	1,483	325	0.07	-78.08
Guinea	633	1,201	280	32	27	0.01	-15.63
Côte d'Ivoire	216	230	571	1,495	309	0.06	-79.33
Liberia	35	31	31	39	18	0.00	-53.85
Mali	561	514	532	1,839	392	0.08	-78.68
Mauritania	308	570	426	449	471	0.10	4.90
Niger	15	72	18	131	48	0.01	-63.36
Nigeria	1,254	2,205	2,038	2,996	2,528	0.53	-15.62
Guinea-Bissau	386	459	353	974	495	0.10	-49.18
Senegal	232	240	341	1,635	215	0.04	-86.85
Sierra Leone	211	111	91	56	70	0.01	25.00
Togo	28	50	57	63	70	0.01	11.11

ANGOLA

1. Arrivals of non-resident tourists at national borders, by country of residence

	2007	2008	2009	2010	2011	Market share 11	% Change 11-10
Burkina Faso	66	81	68	101	46	0.01	-54.46
Other Africa					**1,205**	**0.25**	
Other countries of Africa					1,205	0.25	
AMERICAS	**38,113**	**59,358**	**76,321**	**82,835**	**58,233**	**12.10**	**-29.70**
Caribbean	**1,676**	**3,236**	**5,674**	**4,811**	**4,454**	**0.93**	**-7.42**
Antigua and Barbuda		1		1			
Bahamas		1	7	4			
Barbados				8			
Cuba	1,256	2,754	5,045	4,113	4,058	0.84	-1.34
Dominica		3			6	0.00	
Dominican Republic	89	24	40	167	7	0.00	-95.81
Grenada			2				
Guadeloupe			1				
Haiti	3	4	8	3	2	0.00	-33.33
Jamaica	13	7	8	12			
Martinique		2		1			
Aruba		2	4	1			
Puerto Rico	7	2	3	4			
Trinidad and Tobago	308	436	556	497	381	0.08	-23.34
Central America	**155**	**320**	**407**	**554**	**273**	**0.06**	**-50.72**
Belize			5	4	7	0.00	75.00
Costa Rica	24	11	30	77	30	0.01	-61.04
El Salvador	4	5	33	15	9	0.00	-40.00
Guatemala	3	17	22	27	49	0.01	81.48
Honduras	110	248	225	154	162	0.03	5.19
Nicaragua	7	18	15	181	3	0.00	-98.34
Panama	7	21	77	96	13	0.00	-86.46
North America	**12,706**	**17,595**	**18,055**	**25,826**	**19,782**	**4.11**	**-23.40**
Canada	1,976	2,978	2,583	3,024	2,223	0.46	-26.49
Mexico	137	298	332	2,489	389	0.08	-84.37
United States of America	10,593	14,319	15,140	20,313	17,170	3.57	-15.47
South America	**23,576**	**38,207**	**52,185**	**51,644**	**33,683**	**7.00**	**-34.78**
Argentina	538	598	1,492	1,849	789	0.16	-57.33
Bolivia	50	102	126	133	134	0.03	0.75
Brazil	21,749	35,231	46,866	45,848	29,738	6.18	-35.14
Chile	176	469	326	471	167	0.03	-64.54
Colombia	385	548	665	779	602	0.13	-22.72
Ecuador	45	75	230	498	144	0.03	-71.08
Guyana	49	49	688	818	843	0.18	3.06
Paraguay	28	62	118	66	50	0.01	-24.24
Peru	132	223	595	353	388	0.08	9.92
Uruguay	87	142	193	149	141	0.03	-5.37
Venezuela	337	708	886	680	687	0.14	1.03
Other Americas					**41**	**0.01**	
Other countries of the Americas					41	0.01	
EAST ASIA AND THE PACIFIC	**28,299**	**59,051**	**66,492**	**80,515**	**87,626**	**18.21**	**8.83**
North-East Asia	**20,887**	**46,126**	**54,056**	**62,336**	**71,241**	**14.80**	**14.29**
China	18,500	43,035	51,900	60,577	69,907	14.53	15.40
Taiwan, Province of China	125	58	103	98	119	0.02	21.43
Japan	537	580	759	904	800	0.17	-11.50
Korea, Dem. People's Republic of		476	461	246	135	0.03	-45.12
Korea, Republic of	1,722	1,953	821	504	279	0.06	-44.64
Macao, China		4	11	7	1	0.00	-85.71
Mongolia	3	20	1				
South-East Asia	**6,140**	**11,534**	**11,021**	**15,538**	**15,210**	**3.16**	**-2.11**
Myanmar	202		3				

ANGOLA

1. Arrivals of non-resident tourists at national borders, by country of residence

	2007	2008	2009	2010	2011	Market share 11	% Change 11-10
Cambodia	1	9	2	5	1	0.00	-80.00
Indonesia	580	977	1,536	1,336	948	0.20	-29.04
Malaysia	409	598	844	836	789	0.16	-5.62
Philippines	3,488	7,043	6,096	8,414	7,452	1.55	-11.43
Timor-Leste	8	4	3	9	33	0.01	266.67
Singapore	108	125	295	299	225	0.05	-24.75
Viet Nam	1,270	2,657	2,062	4,351	5,449	1.13	25.24
Thailand	74	121	180	288	313	0.07	8.68
Australasia	**1,272**	**1,391**	**1,415**	**2,638**	**1,175**	**0.24**	**-55.46**
Australia	1,075	1,120	1,197	1,473	944	0.20	-35.91
New Zealand	197	271	218	1,165	231	0.05	-80.17
Melanesia				**3**			
Solomon Islands				3			
EUROPE	**89,351**	**129,838**	**161,169**	**170,381**	**170,488**	**35.43**	**0.06**
Central/Eastern Europe	**6,000**	**8,158**	**9,545**	**10,412**	**7,837**	**1.63**	**-24.73**
Azerbaijan	80	155	167	144	152	0.03	5.56
Armenia	75	66	57	22	36	0.01	63.64
Bulgaria	217	364	322	229	262	0.05	14.41
Belarus	114	127	251	165	242	0.05	46.67
Czech Republic	131	191	168	846	127	0.03	-84.99
Estonia	6	33	21	28	14	0.00	-50.00
Georgia	13	50	20	23	28	0.01	21.74
Hungary	42	89	146	77	56	0.01	-27.27
Kazakhstan	86	118	129	95	86	0.02	-9.47
Kyrgyzstan		28	31	2			
Latvia			46	36	85	0.02	136.11
Lithuania		249	242	186	249	0.05	33.87
Republic of Moldova	41	51	837	1,381			
Poland	877	1,772	1,395	1,949	1,803	0.37	-7.49
Romania	804	786	814	1,934	975	0.20	-49.59
Russian Federation	2,414	2,477	2,694	1,484	1,737	0.36	17.05
Slovakia	53	43	51	53	62	0.01	16.98
Tajikistan			14	2	4	0.00	100.00
Turkmenistan	14	3	20	6	18	0.00	200.00
Ukraine	938	1,500	1,994	1,670	1,794	0.37	7.43
Uzbekistan	95	56	126	80	107	0.02	33.75
Northern Europe	**19,469**	**24,869**	**20,613**	**22,586**	**36,398**	**7.56**	**61.15**
Denmark	528	720	1,332	957	939	0.20	-1.88
Finland	184	151	71	90	712	0.15	691.11
Iceland	25	51	14	24	10	0.00	-58.33
Ireland	442	493	544	485	555	0.12	14.43
Norway	2,272	2,282	2,269	1,728	1,836	0.38	6.25
Sweden	578	747	513	536	414	0.09	-22.76
United Kingdom	15,440	20,425	15,870	18,766	31,932	6.64	70.16
Southern Europe	**43,329**	**61,115**	**97,328**	**109,916**	**94,454**	**19.63**	**-14.07**
Albania	8	41	11	8	7	0.00	-12.50
Andorra	4		180	4	2	0.00	-50.00
Bosnia and Herzegovina			24	34	23	0.00	-32.35
Croatia	686	1,103	1,119	947	1,147	0.24	21.12
Greece	99	121	105	116	109	0.02	-6.03
Italy	2,308	3,324	4,259	3,854	4,133	0.86	7.24
Malta	74	83	77	69	54	0.01	-21.74
Portugal	37,905	53,658	86,330	100,645	84,755	17.61	-15.79
Serbia			12	40	16	0.00	-60.00
Slovenia	77	56	115	88	70	0.01	-20.45
Spain	2,044	2,593	5,007	4,052	4,138	0.86	2.12
TFYR of Macedonia	11	16	21	46			

ANGOLA

1. Arrivals of non-resident tourists at national borders, by country of residence

	2007	2008	2009	2010	2011	Market share 11	% Change 11-10
Serbia and Montenegro	113	120	68	13			
Western Europe	**18,995**	**33,682**	**30,343**	**25,003**	**27,801**	**5.78**	**11.19**
Austria	180	141	246	234	201	0.04	-14.10
Belgium	1,469	1,654	1,650	1,472	1,458	0.30	-0.95
France	13,305	26,649	21,760	18,243	20,884	4.34	14.48
Germany	1,790	2,551	3,361	2,334	2,254	0.47	-3.43
Luxembourg		6	9	17	5	0.00	-70.59
Monaco				1			
Netherlands	1,762	2,180	2,910	2,098	2,324	0.48	10.77
Switzerland	489	501	407	604	675	0.14	11.75
East Mediterranean Europe	**1,558**	**2,014**	**3,340**	**2,464**	**2,454**	**0.51**	**-0.41**
Cyprus			8	7	15	0.00	114.29
Israel	1,460	1,899	3,081	2,183	2,036	0.42	-6.73
Turkey	98	115	251	274	403	0.08	47.08
Other Europe					**1,544**	**0.32**	
Other countries of Europe					1,544	0.32	
MIDDLE EAST	**1,491**	**2,682**	**4,404**	**8,639**	**2,946**	**0.61**	**-65.90**
Palestine		3	40	43	31	0.01	-27.91
Iraq	4	3	8	138	7	0.00	-94.93
Jordan	83	116	129	147	152	0.03	3.40
Kuwait	7	2	6	6	2	0.00	-66.67
Lebanon	916	1,530	2,291	2,701	1,315	0.27	-51.31
Libya	25	56	17	972	24	0.00	-97.53
Oman		6	19				
Qatar	3		17	3	1	0.00	-66.67
Saudi Arabia	17	8	8	274	2	0.00	-99.27
Syrian Arab Republic	48	154	168	1,147	184	0.04	-83.96
United Arab Emirates	1	12	49	2	10	0.00	400.00
Egypt	381	784	1,634	3,177	1,181	0.25	-62.83
Yemen	6	7	15	14	37	0.01	164.29
Other countries of Middle East		1	3	15			
SOUTH ASIA	**4,283**	**6,110**	**10,922**	**10,030**	**14,011**	**2.91**	**39.69**
Afghanistan	3	3	13	3	9	0.00	200.00
Bangladesh	87	103	308	211	231	0.05	9.48
Sri Lanka	28	45	75	70	73	0.02	4.29
India	3,768	5,262	9,517	8,831	12,741	2.65	44.28
Iran, Islamic Republic of	13	18	70	51	38	0.01	-25.49
Maldives				12	8	0.00	-33.33
Nepal	24	106	125	224	84	0.02	-62.50
Pakistan	360	573	814	628	827	0.17	31.69

ANGUILLA

1. Arrivals of non-resident tourists at national borders, by country of residence

		2007	2008	2009	2010	2011	Market share 11	% Change 11-10
TOTAL	(*)	**77,652**	**68,284**	**57,891**	**61,998**	**65,783**	**100.00**	**6.11**
AMERICAS		**63,792**	**57,024**	**49,029**	**53,136**	**56,606**	**86.05**	**6.53**
Caribbean		**15,425**	**14,748**	**12,924**	**11,851**	**10,954**	**16.65**	**-7.57**
Puerto Rico		765	838	724	346			
Other countries of the Caribbean		14,660	13,910	12,200	11,505			
All countries of the Caribbean						10,954	16.65	
North America		**48,367**	**42,276**	**36,105**	**41,285**	**45,652**	**69.40**	**10.58**
Canada		2,393	2,074	2,032	2,403	2,823	4.29	17.48
United States of America		45,974	40,202	34,073	38,882	42,829	65.11	10.15
EUROPE		**10,795**	**8,943**	**7,457**	**7,544**	**7,523**	**11.44**	**-0.28**
Northern Europe		**4,568**	**3,816**	**2,947**	**2,914**	**3,118**	**4.74**	**7.00**
United Kingdom		4,568	3,816	2,947	2,914	3,118	4.74	7.00
Southern Europe		**1,792**	**1,583**	**1,312**	**1,449**	**1,226**	**1.86**	**-15.39**
Italy		1,792	1,583	1,312	1,449	1,226	1.86	-15.39
Western Europe		**2,982**	**2,237**	**2,083**	**2,215**	**372**	**0.57**	**-83.21**
Austria		110	105	69	82			
Belgium		111	77	83	86			
France		1,775	1,410	1,404	1,425			
Germany		759	449	425	478	372	0.57	-22.18
Luxembourg		2	8	1	2			
Switzerland		225	188	101	142			
Other Europe		**1,453**	**1,307**	**1,115**	**966**	**2,807**	**4.27**	**190.58**
Other countries of Europe		1,453	1,307	1,115	966	2,807	4.27	190.58
NOT SPECIFIED		**3,065**	**2,317**	**1,405**	**1,318**	**1,654**	**2.51**	**25.49**
Other countries of the World		3,065	2,317	1,405	1,318	1,654	2.51	25.49

ANGUILLA

2. Arrivals of non-resident visitors at national borders, by country of residence

	2007	2008	2009	2010	2011	Market share 11	% Change 11-10
TOTAL	164,067	127,861	112,115	118,411	123,558	100.00	4.35
AMERICAS	127,182	99,785	88,459	93,584	97,166	78.64	3.83
Caribbean	33,458	29,087	25,976	25,103	23,626	19.12	-5.88
Puerto Rico	1,028	1,016	909	559			
Other countries of the Caribbean	32,430	28,071	25,067	24,544			
All countries of the Caribbean					23,626	19.12	
North America	93,724	70,698	62,483	68,481	73,540	59.52	7.39
Canada	7,111	4,970	5,110	5,982	7,141	5.78	19.37
United States of America	86,613	65,728	57,373	62,499	66,399	53.74	6.24
EUROPE	30,682	23,584	20,412	20,260	20,451	16.55	0.94
Northern Europe	8,039	5,730	4,667	4,471	4,557	3.69	1.92
United Kingdom	8,039	5,730	4,667	4,471	4,557	3.69	1.92
Southern Europe	3,178	2,552	2,385	2,278	2,139	1.73	-6.10
Italy	3,178	2,552	2,385	2,278	2,139	1.73	-6.10
Western Europe	14,835	10,942	9,831	10,369	1,024	0.83	-90.12
Austria	212	214	157	213			
Belgium	503	476	195	381			
France	12,063	8,864	8,220	8,148			
Germany	1,479	1,001	931	1,239	1,024	0.83	-17.35
Luxembourg	15	27	13	22			
Switzerland	563	360	315	366			
Other Europe	4,630	4,360	3,529	3,142	12,731	10.30	305.19
Other countries of Europe	4,630	4,360	3,529	3,142	12,731	10.30	305.19
NOT SPECIFIED	6,203	4,492	3,244	4,567	5,941	4.81	30.09
Other countries of the World	6,203	4,492	3,244	4,567	5,941	4.81	30.09

ANTIGUA AND BARBUDA

1. Arrivals of non-resident tourists at national borders, by country of residence

		2007	2008	2009	2010	2011	Market share 11	% Change 11-10
TOTAL	(*)	261,802	265,844	234,410	229,943	241,331	100.00	4.95
AMERICAS		140,823	151,785	138,489	137,254	145,556	60.31	6.05
Caribbean		46,464	48,954	41,546	37,505	37,887	15.70	1.02
Bahamas		173	262					
Barbados		4,035	4,455					
Bermuda		312	362					
British Virgin Islands		1,829	1,827					
Cayman Islands		166	123					
Cuba		344	277					
Dominica		5,858	5,890					
Dominican Republic		894	1,174					
Grenada		809	898					
Guadeloupe		1,765	1,149					
Haiti		111	98					
Jamaica		6,093	5,832					
Martinique		336	296					
Montserrat		3,704	3,527					
Aruba		32	66					
Bonaire		4	6					
Curaçao		148	116					
Puerto Rico		919	955					
Saint Kitts and Nevis		3,626	4,150					
Anguilla		813	1,014					
Saint Lucia		2,849	2,831					
Sint Maarten		1,347	1,480					
Saint Vincent and the Grenadines		1,337	1,444					
Trinidad and Tobago		6,653	7,019					
Turks and Caicos Islands		47	78					
United States Virgin Islands		2,073	3,446					
Other countries of the Caribbean		187	179					
All countries of the Caribbean				41,546	37,505	37,887	15.70	1.02
Central America		451	491	488	333	434	0.18	30.33
Belize		70	75					
Other countries of Central America		381	416	488	333	434	0.18	30.33
North America		89,187	97,221	95,015	99,416	107,235	44.43	7.86
Canada		10,489	13,189	12,947	17,818	22,403	9.28	25.73
United States of America		78,698	84,032	82,068	81,598	84,832	35.15	3.96
South America		4,721	5,119	1,440				
Argentina		109	222					
Brazil		167	245					
Colombia		124	136					
Guyana		3,680	3,740					
Suriname		109	185					
Venezuela		369	361					
Other countries of South America		163	230	1,440				
EUROPE		115,454	110,266	93,442	88,945	92,097	38.16	3.54
Northern Europe		100,075	93,150	73,251	66,623	69,184	28.67	3.84
Denmark		216	346					
Ireland		1,947	1,949					
Norway		355	511					
Sweden		756	830					
United Kingdom		96,801	89,514	73,251	66,623	69,184	28.67	3.84
Southern Europe		6,781	8,027	7,726	10,180	11,048	4.58	8.53
Greece		63	90					
Italy		6,147	7,212	7,726	10,180	11,048	4.58	8.53

ANTIGUA AND BARBUDA

1. Arrivals of non-resident tourists at national borders, by country of residence

	2007	2008	2009	2010	2011	Market share 11	% Change 11-10
Portugal	114	121					
Spain	457	604					
Western Europe	**7,437**	**7,558**	**5,319**	**5,000**	**4,646**	**1.93**	**-7.08**
Austria	233	301					
Belgium	297	313					
France	1,841	1,710	1,567	1,661	1,747	0.72	5.18
Germany	3,480	3,597	3,752	3,339	2,899	1.20	-13.18
Luxembourg	20	27					
Netherlands	768	589					
Switzerland	798	1,021					
Other Europe	**1,161**	**1,531**	**7,146**	**7,142**	**7,219**	**2.99**	**1.08**
Other countries of Europe	1,161	1,531	7,146	7,142	7,219	2.99	1.08
NOT SPECIFIED	**5,525**	**3,793**	**2,479**	**3,744**	**3,678**	**1.52**	**-1.76**
Other countries of the World	5,525	3,793	2,479	3,744	3,678	1.52	-1.76

ARGENTINA

1. Arrivals of non-resident tourists at national borders, by nationality

	2007	2008	2009	2010	2011	Market share 11	% Change 11-10
TOTAL	4,561,743	4,700,492	4,307,666	5,325,130	5,704,650	100.00	7.13
AMERICAS	3,608,724	3,710,497	3,392,017	4,367,985	4,760,388	83.45	8.98
North America	445,410	445,407	395,376	404,770	360,616	6.32	-10.91
Canada, United States	445,410	445,407	395,376	404,770	360,616	6.32	-10.91
South America	2,662,506	2,800,113	2,580,176	3,544,037	3,898,602	68.34	10.00
Bolivia	157,626	147,846	164,406	184,697	231,636	4.06	25.41
Brazil	742,232	873,794	718,203	1,196,832	1,282,374	22.48	7.15
Chile	987,290	940,496	820,128	1,076,372	1,101,337	19.31	2.32
Paraguay	354,906	391,217	389,619	432,200	627,620	11.00	45.22
Uruguay	420,452	446,760	487,820	653,936	655,635	11.49	0.26
Other Americas	500,808	464,977	416,465	419,178	501,170	8.79	19.56
Other countries of the Americas	500,808	464,977	416,465	419,178	501,170	8.79	19.56
EUROPE	737,634	765,962	721,622	751,331	738,778	12.95	-1.67
Other Europe	737,634	765,962	721,622	751,331	738,778	12.95	-1.67
All countries of Europe	737,634	765,962	721,622	751,331	738,778	12.95	-1.67
NOT SPECIFIED	215,385	224,033	194,027	205,814	205,484	3.60	-0.16
Other countries of the World	215,385	224,033	194,027	205,814	205,484	3.60	-0.16

ARMENIA

1. Arrivals of non-resident tourists at national borders, by country of residence

	2007	2008	2009	2010	2011	Market share 11	% Change 11-10
TOTAL	510,622	558,443	575,284	683,979	757,935	100.00	10.81
AFRICA	496	643	443	215	603	0.08	180.47
East Africa	64	98	83		19	0.00	
Ethiopia	45	70	65		14	0.00	
Zimbabwe	19	28	18		3	0.00	
Zambia					2	0.00	
Central Africa	49	60	30		29	0.00	
Cameroon	49	60	30		29	0.00	
North Africa	330	430	330	215	365	0.05	69.77
Algeria	190	250	180	215	211	0.03	-1.86
Morocco	140	180	150		154	0.02	
Southern Africa	28	30			182	0.02	
All countries of Southern Africa	28	30			182	0.02	
West Africa	25	25			8	0.00	
Liberia	25	25			8	0.00	
AMERICAS	127,155	135,550	134,940	135,673	144,632	19.08	6.60
Caribbean	45	50		31	22	0.00	-29.03
Cuba	45	50		30	22	0.00	-26.67
Puerto Rico				1			
Central America	90	110		60	70	0.01	16.67
El Salvador				4	3	0.00	-25.00
Guatemala	30	40		1	9	0.00	800.00
Honduras	10	15			2	0.00	
Nicaragua	50	55		55	56	0.01	1.82
North America	89,326	95,860	95,000	97,760	103,715	13.68	6.09
Canada	28,969	32,110	30,200	30,350	32,807	4.33	8.10
Mexico	1,125	1,500	1,700	1,650	1,992	0.26	20.73
United States of America	59,232	62,250	63,100	65,760	68,916	9.09	4.80
South America	37,694	39,530	39,940	37,822	40,825	5.39	7.94
Argentina	25,654	26,450	26,600	24,350	26,414	3.48	8.48
Brazil	9,490	10,110	10,500	10,490	11,203	1.48	6.80
Chile	160	190		180	178	0.02	-1.11
Colombia				25	27	0.00	8.00
Ecuador				18	10	0.00	-44.44
Guyana				2	2	0.00	
Peru	250	260	200	217	218	0.03	0.46
Uruguay	1,780	2,140	2,240	2,170	2,411	0.32	11.11
Venezuela	360	380	400	370	362	0.05	-2.16
EAST ASIA AND THE PACIFIC	23,005	24,365	24,600	25,584	29,222	3.86	14.22
North-East Asia	18,625	19,925	20,300	21,008	23,510	3.10	11.91
China	7,780	8,100	8,400	8,450	9,713	1.28	14.95
Taiwan, Province of China	250	155		54	191	0.03	253.70
Japan	10,150	11,110	11,900	11,730	12,973	1.71	10.60
Korea, Republic of	275	350		733	591	0.08	-19.37
Mongolia	170	210		41	42	0.01	2.44
South-East Asia	215	220		236	357	0.05	51.27
Cambodia					13	0.00	
Indonesia				21	49	0.01	133.33
Malaysia	30			50	98	0.01	96.00
Philippines	120	140		127	128	0.02	0.79
Viet Nam				2	14	0.00	600.00
Thailand	65	80		36	55	0.01	52.78
Australasia	4,165	4,220	4,300	4,340	5,355	0.71	23.39

ARMENIA

1. Arrivals of non-resident tourists at national borders, by country of residence

	2007	2008	2009	2010	2011	Market share 11	% Change 11-10
Australia	4,150	4,200	4,300	4,340	5,224	0.69	20.37
New Zealand	15	20			131	0.02	
EUROPE	**278,209**	**308,266**	**311,268**	**350,926**	**375,195**	**49.50**	**6.92**
Central/Eastern Europe	**191,346**	**212,479**	**215,198**	**240,223**	**253,639**	**33.46**	**5.58**
Bulgaria	3,450	3,780	3,950	3,915	4,506	0.59	15.10
Czech Republic	1,290	1,540	1,720	1,745	1,825	0.24	4.58
Estonia	210	250					
Hungary	640	660		489	572	0.08	16.97
Latvia	569	640		761	970	0.13	27.46
Lithuania	210	250		750	919	0.12	22.53
Poland	1,230	1,340	1,200	2,350	3,351	0.44	42.60
Romania	750	850		890	899	0.12	1.01
Slovakia	410	519		513	619	0.08	20.66
Commonwealth Independent States	182,587	202,650	208,328	228,810	239,978	31.66	4.88
Northern Europe	**11,740**	**12,880**	**11,900**	**14,013**	**14,308**	**1.89**	**2.11**
Denmark	850	890	990	1,071	1,263	0.17	17.93
Finland	510	590	710	826	826	0.11	
Iceland				16	31	0.00	93.75
Ireland	150	170	250	765	416	0.05	-45.62
Norway	810	890	940	975	917	0.12	-5.95
Sweden	755	890	910	1,640	1,727	0.23	5.30
United Kingdom	8,665	9,450	8,100	8,720	9,128	1.20	4.68
Southern Europe	**19,406**	**21,540**	**20,600**	**21,415**	**25,151**	**3.32**	**17.45**
Albania				55	48	0.01	-12.73
Bosnia and Herzegovina	986	1,110	950	985	1,034	0.14	4.97
Croatia	40	50		235	270	0.04	14.89
Greece	8,950	9,940	8,700	8,930	11,765	1.55	31.75
Italy	6,230	7,580	7,900	7,945	8,722	1.15	9.78
Malta				95	48	0.01	-49.47
Portugal	750			730	729	0.10	-0.14
Serbia		70					
Slovenia	410	550	700	760	762	0.10	0.26
Spain	1,490	1,590	1,650	1,680	1,773	0.23	5.54
Serbia and Montenegro	550	650	700				
Western Europe	**51,222**	**55,967**	**57,070**	**58,854**	**65,013**	**8.58**	**10.46**
Austria	5,012	5,120	5,200	5,270	6,137	0.81	16.45
Belgium	4,250	4,680	4,800	4,830	5,122	0.68	6.05
France	22,210	23,500	24,100	24,250	24,735	3.26	2.00
Germany	16,120	18,780	18,970	19,120	22,193	2.93	16.07
Netherlands	2,100	2,297	2,300	3,604	4,814	0.64	33.57
Switzerland	1,530	1,590	1,700	1,780	2,012	0.27	13.03
East Mediterranean Europe	**4,495**	**5,400**	**6,500**	**16,421**	**17,084**	**2.25**	**4.04**
Cyprus	1,115	1,250	1,800	1,930	2,143	0.28	11.04
Israel	1,920	2,250	2,500	2,834	3,124	0.41	10.23
Turkey	1,460	1,900	2,200	11,657	11,817	1.56	1.37
MIDDLE EAST	**40,849**	**43,800**	**44,690**	**46,470**	**49,598**	**6.54**	**6.73**
Iraq	150	290		398	911	0.12	128.89
Jordan				358	363	0.05	1.40
Kuwait	20			44	97	0.01	120.45
Lebanon	19,790	22,200	23,100	23,330	24,171	3.19	3.60
Libya					18	0.00	
Qatar	90	110		120	121	0.02	0.83
Saudi Arabia	55	50		80	73	0.01	-8.75
Syrian Arab Republic	19,890	20,210	21,000	21,340	23,001	3.03	7.78
United Arab Emirates	355	390		185	246	0.03	32.97
Egypt	499	550	590	615	597	0.08	-2.93

ARMENIA

1. Arrivals of non-resident tourists at national borders, by country of residence

	2007	2008	2009	2010	2011	Market share 11	% Change 11-10
SOUTH ASIA	**40,908**	**45,819**	**59,343**	**125,111**	**158,685**	**20.94**	**26.84**
Afghanistan	578	750			4	0.00	
Bangladesh	70	150			6	0.00	
Sri Lanka				15	27	0.00	80.00
India	2,590	3,970	4,100	4,180	4,311	0.57	3.13
Iran, Islamic Republic of	37,450	40,699	55,243	120,863	154,278	20.36	27.65
Nepal				15	23	0.00	53.33
Pakistan	220	250		38	36	0.00	-5.26

ARUBA

1. Arrivals of non-resident tourists at national borders, by country of residence

	2007	2008	2009	2010	2011	Market share 11	% Change 11-10
TOTAL	771,822	826,677	812,623	824,330	870,287	100.00	5.58
AMERICAS	703,367	748,922	735,339	745,723	786,249	90.34	5.43
Caribbean	30,182	26,939	24,554	26,457	29,699	3.41	12.25
Dominican Republic	2,287	931	839	1,028	1,273	0.15	23.83
Netherlands Antilles	22,452	21,992	21,536	23,363	25,827	2.97	10.55
Puerto Rico	3,007	1,660	119	86	19	0.00	-77.91
Trinidad and Tobago	1,288	1,175	873	953	1,285	0.15	34.84
Other countries of the Caribbean	1,148	1,181	1,187	1,027	1,295	0.15	26.10
North America	547,511	572,310	563,308	574,533	573,036	65.84	-0.26
Canada	25,668	32,530	33,856	37,643	40,511	4.65	7.62
Mexico	1,545	1,407	1,348	1,223	1,298	0.15	6.13
United States of America	520,298	538,373	528,104	535,667	531,227	61.04	-0.83
South America	125,674	149,673	147,477	144,733	183,514	21.09	26.79
Argentina	3,602	4,195	5,486	6,365	10,325	1.19	62.22
Brazil	7,480	8,745	10,594	20,235	22,423	2.58	10.81
Chile	980	1,689	1,345	1,840	2,432	0.28	32.17
Colombia	13,214	13,439	15,685	15,004	16,936	1.95	12.88
Ecuador	1,197	2,316	1,186	2,532	3,572	0.41	41.07
Peru	940	1,181	1,092	1,372	1,397	0.16	1.82
Suriname	1,867	2,376	3,651	3,556	4,243	0.49	19.32
Venezuela	92,157	112,986	105,063	90,709	118,068	13.57	30.16
Other countries of South America	4,237	2,746	3,375	3,120	4,118	0.47	31.99
EAST ASIA AND THE PACIFIC	148	157	158	152	118	0.01	-22.37
North-East Asia	148	157	158	152	118	0.01	-22.37
Japan	148	157	158	152	118	0.01	-22.37
EUROPE	67,446	73,772	75,000	76,077	81,204	9.33	6.74
Central/Eastern Europe	231	247	272	285	446	0.05	56.49
Russian Federation	231	247	272	285	446	0.05	56.49
Northern Europe	14,232	13,719	16,018	21,477	21,859	2.51	1.78
Denmark	530	349	305	166	350	0.04	110.84
Finland	1,047	996	826	766	964	0.11	25.85
Norway	423	593	613	617	808	0.09	30.96
Sweden	2,639	2,810	2,762	5,398	5,853	0.67	8.43
United Kingdom	9,593	8,971	11,512	14,530	13,884	1.60	-4.45
Southern Europe	5,857	6,231	8,148	4,065	7,927	0.91	95.01
Italy	2,012	3,885	6,369	2,869	6,520	0.75	127.26
Portugal	338	316	200	165	244	0.03	47.88
Spain	3,507	2,030	1,579	1,031	1,163	0.13	12.80
Western Europe	43,845	50,163	47,885	47,573	47,722	5.48	0.31
Austria	432	325	347	407	369	0.04	-9.34
Belgium	1,680	2,016	2,161	2,377	2,430	0.28	2.23
Germany	3,137	5,125	3,357	3,568	3,498	0.40	-1.96
Netherlands	37,841	41,874	41,211	40,294	40,336	4.63	0.10
Switzerland	755	823	809	927	1,089	0.13	17.48
Other Europe	3,281	3,412	2,677	2,677	3,250	0.37	21.40
Other countries of Europe	3,281	3,412	2,677	2,677	3,250	0.37	21.40
NOT SPECIFIED	861	3,826	2,126	2,378	2,716	0.31	14.21
Other countries of the World	861	3,826	2,126	2,378	2,716	0.31	14.21

ARUBA

3. Arrivals of non-resident tourists in hotels and similar establishments, by country of residence

	2007	2008	2009	2010	2011	Market share 11	% Change 11-10
TOTAL	688,080	728,119	719,347	727,590	756,993	100.00	4.04
AMERICAS	641,074	675,830	664,735	672,653	697,022	92.08	3.62
Caribbean	16,756	13,769	13,273	15,068	16,527	2.18	9.68
Dominican Republic	1,309	308	328	387	313	0.04	-19.12
Netherlands Antilles	11,131	10,578	11,502	13,284	14,647	1.93	10.26
Trinidad and Tobago	796	802	642	748	976	0.13	30.48
Other countries of the Caribbean	3,520	2,081	801	649	591	0.08	-8.94
North America	523,299	542,489	534,620	542,173	535,117	70.69	-1.30
Canada	23,799	29,995	31,274	34,496	36,784	4.86	6.63
Mexico	1,294	1,043	1,050	1,026	990	0.13	-3.51
United States of America	498,206	511,451	502,296	506,651	497,343	65.70	-1.84
South America	101,019	119,572	116,842	115,412	145,378	19.20	25.96
Argentina	3,354	3,972	5,283	6,167	9,945	1.31	61.26
Brazil	6,537	8,328	10,115	19,558	21,303	2.81	8.92
Chile	912	1,612	1,288	1,778	2,334	0.31	31.27
Colombia	10,769	10,269	11,470	11,804	12,885	1.70	9.16
Ecuador	867	2,001	805	2,236	3,235	0.43	44.68
Peru	769	884	797	1,086	1,119	0.15	3.04
Suriname	656	1,032	1,627	1,728	1,990	0.26	15.16
Venezuela	75,441	89,333	81,467	67,455	89,167	11.78	32.19
Other countries of South America	1,714	2,141	3,990	3,600	3,400	0.45	-5.56
EAST ASIA AND THE PACIFIC	118	136	126	108	100	0.01	-7.41
North-East Asia	118	136	126	108	100	0.01	-7.41
Japan	118	136	126	108	100	0.01	-7.41
EUROPE	46,341	50,708	52,819	54,415	58,703	7.75	7.88
Central/Eastern Europe	143	112	140	187	253	0.03	35.29
Russian Federation	143	112	140	187	253	0.03	35.29
Northern Europe	13,216	12,838	14,895	20,381	20,155	2.66	-1.11
Denmark	462	272	215	126	229	0.03	81.75
Finland	976	911	756	699	801	0.11	14.59
Norway	312	422	495	483	703	0.09	45.55
Sweden	2,461	2,646	2,641	5,172	5,534	0.73	7.00
United Kingdom	9,005	8,587	10,788	13,901	12,888	1.70	-7.29
Southern Europe	3,545	5,230	7,236	3,252	6,886	0.91	111.75
Italy	1,557	3,889	5,972	2,383	5,856	0.77	145.74
Portugal	193	179	158	134	205	0.03	52.99
Spain	1,795	1,162	1,106	735	825	0.11	12.24
Western Europe	25,722	29,872	28,493	28,583	28,968	3.83	1.35
Austria	364	265	294	321	313	0.04	-2.49
Belgium	1,300	1,590	1,641	1,869	1,934	0.26	3.48
Germany	2,557	3,508	2,877	2,952	2,785	0.37	-5.66
Netherlands	20,914	23,867	23,017	22,718	23,111	3.05	1.73
Switzerland	587	642	664	723	825	0.11	14.11
Other Europe	3,715	2,656	2,055	2,012	2,441	0.32	21.32
Other countries of Europe	3,715	2,656	2,055	2,012	2,441	0.32	21.32
NOT SPECIFIED	547	1,445	1,667	414	1,168	0.15	182.13
Other countries of the World	547	1,445	1,667	414	1,168	0.15	182.13

ARUBA

5. Overnight stays of non-resident tourists in hotels and similar establishments, by country of residence

	2007	2008	2009	2010	2011	Market share 11	% Change 11-10
TOTAL	4,904,177	5,169,616	5,138,557	5,272,565	5,410,538	100.00	2.62
AMERICAS	4,433,264	4,647,484	4,595,415	4,697,020	4,815,346	89.00	2.52
Caribbean	96,105	54,633	51,214	56,565	62,345	1.15	10.22
Dominican Republic	35,902	1,219	1,538	1,785	2,188	0.04	22.58
Netherlands Antilles	40,266	37,629	41,718	47,684	53,087	0.98	11.33
Trinidad and Tobago	4,465	4,605	3,588	3,794	4,176	0.08	10.07
Other countries of the Caribbean	15,472	11,180	4,370	3,302	2,894	0.05	-12.36
North America	3,784,541	3,946,339	3,894,317	3,956,611	3,915,897	72.38	-1.03
Canada	201,585	248,060	261,918	285,358	301,434	5.57	5.63
United States of America	3,582,956	3,698,279	3,632,399	3,671,253	3,614,463	66.80	-1.55
South America	552,618	646,512	649,884	683,844	837,104	15.47	22.41
Argentina	28,512	32,797	43,811	50,572	82,214	1.52	62.57
Brazil	41,698	52,664	63,805	120,697	133,011	2.46	10.20
Chile	5,865	11,216	8,842	12,752	16,257	0.30	27.49
Colombia	67,858	63,853	72,056	73,261	75,380	1.39	2.89
Ecuador	4,257	9,015	5,329	11,778	16,278	0.30	38.21
Peru	5,459	6,100	6,354	7,556	6,800	0.13	-10.01
Suriname	4,136	5,234	8,090	7,658	10,011	0.19	30.73
Venezuela	377,611	448,485	421,498	378,816	472,433	8.73	24.71
Other countries of South America	17,222	17,148	20,099	20,754	24,720	0.46	19.11
EAST ASIA AND THE PACIFIC	424	584	586	381	350	0.01	-8.14
North-East Asia	424	584	586	381	350	0.01	-8.14
Japan	424	584	586	381	350	0.01	-8.14
EUROPE	460,734	499,879	533,300	567,032	584,640	10.81	3.11
Central/Eastern Europe	1,541	1,062	1,327	1,983	2,090	0.04	5.40
Russian Federation	1,541	1,062	1,327	1,983	2,090	0.04	5.40
Northern Europe	151,181	147,437	180,769	251,231	236,427	4.37	-5.89
Denmark	4,069	2,616	2,063	952	1,760	0.03	84.87
Finland	8,638	7,864	7,325	7,410	8,128	0.15	9.69
Norway	2,741	4,357	5,108	4,863	7,208	0.13	48.22
Sweden	24,324	26,507	30,218	63,992	67,857	1.25	6.04
United Kingdom	111,409	106,093	136,055	174,014	151,474	2.80	-12.95
Southern Europe	39,328	36,748	57,499	25,447	56,250	1.04	121.05
Italy	13,283	28,312	47,652	19,028	48,886	0.90	156.92
Portugal	1,295	1,383	1,335	855	1,364	0.03	59.53
Spain	24,750	7,053	8,512	5,564	6,000	0.11	7.84
Western Europe	250,209	288,406	275,891	270,810	268,819	4.97	-0.74
Austria	3,981	2,528	3,033	3,471	3,265	0.06	-5.93
Belgium	12,100	14,899	15,785	17,094	16,773	0.31	-1.88
Germany	27,318	34,662	32,206	29,323	29,202	0.54	-0.41
Netherlands	200,978	230,003	218,619	214,323	212,145	3.92	-1.02
Switzerland	5,832	6,314	6,248	6,599	7,434	0.14	12.65
Other Europe	18,475	26,226	17,814	17,561	21,054	0.39	19.89
Other countries of Europe	18,475	26,226	17,814	17,561	21,054	0.39	19.89
NOT SPECIFIED	9,755	21,669	9,256	8,132	10,202	0.19	25.45
Other countries of the World	9,755	21,669	9,256	8,132	10,202	0.19	25.45

ARUBA

6. Overnight stays of non-resident tourists in all types of accommodation establishments, by country of residence

	2007	2008	2009	2010	2011	Market share 11	% Change 11-10
TOTAL	5,879,377	6,268,072	6,172,913	6,466,217	6,725,828	100.00	4.01
AMERICAS	5,075,070	5,383,932	5,270,446	5,539,453	5,778,994	85.92	4.32
Caribbean	227,662	167,815	141,274	157,940	191,650	2.85	21.34
Dominican Republic	66,001	11,764	9,363	18,508	32,954	0.49	78.05
Netherlands Antilles	127,761	125,845	113,347	120,034	127,527	1.90	6.24
Puerto Rico	14,211	10,357	609	617	95	0.00	-84.60
Trinidad and Tobago	11,280	9,972	6,876	6,883	9,062	0.13	31.66
Other countries of the Caribbean	8,409	9,877	11,079	11,898	22,012	0.33	85.01
North America	4,042,572	4,251,499	4,191,931	4,286,388	4,280,415	63.64	-0.14
Canada	225,586	280,012	295,177	325,361	346,406	5.15	6.47
Mexico	12,922	11,499	8,498	9,058	8,700	0.13	-3.95
United States of America	3,804,064	3,959,988	3,888,256	3,951,969	3,925,309	58.36	-0.67
South America	804,836	964,618	937,241	1,095,125	1,306,929	19.43	19.34
Argentina	31,296	35,923	46,072	53,291	86,634	1.29	62.57
Brazil	46,792	56,279	67,939	127,293	141,924	2.11	11.49
Chile	6,588	11,886	9,341	13,530	17,270	0.26	27.64
Colombia	120,879	130,998	128,743	145,143	174,911	2.60	20.51
Ecuador	9,137	13,682	10,236	18,022	23,101	0.34	28.18
Peru	8,311	11,475	11,348	14,233	13,828	0.21	-2.85
Suriname	20,489	23,566	32,114	29,295	36,918	0.55	26.02
Venezuela	515,368	655,480	612,030	670,662	780,321	11.60	16.35
Other countries of South America	45,976	25,329	19,418	23,656	32,022	0.48	35.37
EAST ASIA AND THE PACIFIC	576	702	739	562	540	0.01	-3.91
North-East Asia	576	702	739	562	540	0.01	-3.91
Japan	576	702	739	562	540	0.01	-3.91
EUROPE	795,880	847,336	884,079	906,628	919,542	13.67	1.42
Central/Eastern Europe	1,954	2,171	2,282	2,654	2,872	0.04	8.21
Russian Federation	1,954	2,171	2,282	2,654	2,872	0.04	8.21
Northern Europe	164,423	160,821	195,808	267,813	259,731	3.86	-3.02
Denmark	4,740	3,410	2,987	1,343	2,682	0.04	99.70
Finland	9,601	9,814	8,320	8,487	12,555	0.19	47.93
Norway	4,704	7,339	7,377	6,906	8,903	0.13	28.92
Sweden	26,201	28,648	31,780	67,185	72,342	1.08	7.68
United Kingdom	119,177	111,610	145,344	183,892	163,249	2.43	-11.23
Southern Europe	47,646	48,154	68,960	38,159	69,749	1.04	82.79
Italy	18,967	34,024	52,893	25,680	56,443	0.84	119.79
Portugal	2,569	1,808	1,997	1,259	1,772	0.03	40.75
Spain	26,110	12,322	14,070	11,220	11,534	0.17	2.80
Western Europe	555,174	605,296	591,452	571,025	555,714	8.26	-2.68
Austria	4,970	3,221	3,922	4,242	3,818	0.06	-10.00
Belgium	18,264	20,945	23,548	25,045	23,320	0.35	-6.89
Germany	34,292	49,172	39,523	37,778	38,021	0.57	0.64
Netherlands	487,906	522,524	515,662	494,926	480,764	7.15	-2.86
Switzerland	9,742	9,434	8,797	9,034	9,791	0.15	8.38
Other Europe	26,683	30,894	25,577	26,977	31,476	0.47	16.68
Other countries of Europe	26,683	30,894	25,577	26,977	31,476	0.47	16.68
NOT SPECIFIED	7,851	36,102	17,649	19,574	26,752	0.40	36.67
Other countries of the World	7,851	36,102	17,649	19,574	26,752	0.40	36.67

AUSTRALIA

2. Arrivals of non-resident visitors at national borders, by country of residence

	2007	2008	2009	2010	2011	Market share 11	% Change 11-10
TOTAL (*)	5,644,076	5,585,826	5,584,076	5,885,101	5,875,068	100.00	-0.17
AFRICA	85,553	93,195	83,999	89,170	91,650	1.56	2.78
East Africa	18,070	19,962	18,867	21,707	21,271	0.36	-2.01
Burundi	20	37	41	8	36	0.00	350.00
Comoros	45	19			15	0.00	
Ethiopia	137	264	235	338	248	0.00	-26.63
Eritrea	32	35	28	22	18	0.00	-18.18
Djibouti	27	18			17	0.00	
Kenya	2,254	2,504	2,790	2,966	2,956	0.05	-0.34
Madagascar	116	144	98	168	99	0.00	-41.07
Malawi	211	217	177	155	202	0.00	30.32
Mauritius	5,447	6,976	6,304	7,270	7,378	0.13	1.49
Mozambique	264	287	201	299	344	0.01	15.05
Reunion	3,428	3,391	3,855	4,941	3,802	0.06	-23.05
Rwanda	43	45	51	98	145	0.00	47.96
Seychelles	585	458	371	531	398	0.01	-25.05
Somalia	253	60	21	73	89	0.00	21.92
Zimbabwe	3,029	3,250	2,619	2,563	2,510	0.04	-2.07
Uganda	485	442	333	556	633	0.01	13.85
United Republic of Tanzania	856	798	869	781	1,040	0.02	33.16
Zambia	838	1,017	874	938	1,341	0.02	42.96
Central Africa	436	687	394	494	697	0.01	41.09
Angola	159	273	108	352	170	0.00	-51.70
Cameroon	42	45	105	32	123	0.00	284.38
Central African Republic	3	3					
Chad	4	31	56	10	146	0.00	1360.00
Congo	202	254	73	64	109	0.00	70.31
Democratic Republic of the Congo	16	36	13	21	15	0.00	-28.57
Equatorial Guinea	3	3	35	3	3	0.00	
Gabon	7	39	4	12	126	0.00	950.00
Sao Tome and Principe		3			5	0.00	
North Africa	622	559	719	1,120	1,005	0.02	-10.27
Algeria	202	143	213	256	357	0.01	39.45
Morocco	161	132	275	416	317	0.01	-23.80
Sudan	194	200	162	263	100	0.00	-61.98
Tunisia	65	84	69	185	231	0.00	24.86
Southern Africa	64,581	69,816	61,584	63,608	65,817	1.12	3.47
Botswana	662	557	625	726	719	0.01	-0.96
Lesotho	44	27	60	77	47	0.00	-38.96
Namibia	304	673	435	446	520	0.01	16.59
South Africa	63,428	68,460	60,291	62,198	64,370	1.10	3.49
Swaziland	143	99	173	161	161	0.00	
West Africa	1,844	2,171	2,435	2,231	2,764	0.05	23.89
Cape Verde		4		3	4	0.00	33.33
Benin	30	8	5	10	5	0.00	-50.00
Gambia	8	25	14	12	30	0.00	150.00
Ghana	385	431	513	523	590	0.01	12.81
Guinea	19	121	31	175	114	0.00	-34.86
Côte d'Ivoire	11	55	57	61	24	0.00	-60.66
Liberia	61	111	46	44	78	0.00	77.27
Mali	14	19	114	43	44	0.00	2.33
Mauritania	298	287	309	193	108	0.00	-44.04
Niger	28	21	80	26	192	0.00	638.46
Nigeria	850	958	1,169	1,006	1,294	0.02	28.63
Guinea-Bissau		3			3	0.00	
Senegal	94	63	53	74	77	0.00	4.05

AUSTRALIA

2. Arrivals of non-resident visitors at national borders, by country of residence

	2007	2008	2009	2010	2011	Market share 11	% Change 11-10
Sierra Leone	34	33	31	37	136	0.00	267.57
Togo		16	7	6	33	0.00	450.00
Burkina Faso	12	16	6	18	32	0.00	77.78
Other Africa				**10**	**96**	**0.00**	**860.00**
Other countries of Africa				10	96	0.00	860.00
AMERICAS	**628,773**	**644,163**	**670,055**	**661,819**	**645,830**	**10.99**	**-2.42**
Caribbean	**3,035**	**2,977**	**2,992**	**3,193**	**2,687**	**0.05**	**-15.85**
Antigua and Barbuda	38	13	11	13	13	0.00	
Bahamas	335	148	290	162	236	0.00	45.68
Barbados	241	96	225	270	144	0.00	-46.67
Bermuda	691	474	604	511	545	0.01	6.65
British Virgin Islands	15	7		44			
Cayman Islands	358	319	428	626	337	0.01	-46.17
Cuba	143	90	161	239	224	0.00	-6.28
Dominica	31	101	47	18	47	0.00	161.11
Dominican Republic	123	115	43	86	54	0.00	-37.21
Grenada	35	43	66	57	153	0.00	168.42
Guadeloupe	43	34	69	22	30	0.00	36.36
Haiti	23	52	15	62	73	0.00	17.74
Jamaica	275	359	324	298	255	0.00	-14.43
Martinique	11	54	46	77	12	0.00	-84.42
Montserrat	4	12	5	28	4	0.00	-85.71
Netherlands Antilles			19		9	0.00	
Aruba	36	9	56		38	0.00	
Puerto Rico	242	570	192	273	48	0.00	-82.42
Saint Kitts and Nevis		38	7	12	19	0.00	58.33
Anguilla	24	6	19				
Saint Lucia	55	25	22	27	26	0.00	-3.70
Saint Vincent and the Grenadines	13	14	12	12	18	0.00	50.00
Trinidad and Tobago	289	322	328	356	360	0.01	1.12
Turks and Caicos Islands		43	3		42	0.00	
United States Virgin Islands	10	33					
Central America	**868**	**1,417**	**1,129**	**1,134**	**954**	**0.02**	**-15.87**
Belize	21	82	34	15	10	0.00	-33.33
Costa Rica	281	458	430	341	311	0.01	-8.80
El Salvador	166	271	163	184	113	0.00	-38.59
Guatemala	117	282	128	254	119	0.00	-53.15
Honduras	83	122	71	98	89	0.00	-9.18
Nicaragua	23	63	27	28	124	0.00	342.86
Panama	171	139	264	210	185	0.00	-11.90
Other countries of Central America	6		12	4	3	0.00	-25.00
North America	**581,403**	**586,622**	**609,770**	**600,570**	**580,188**	**9.88**	**-3.39**
Canada	114,636	124,637	123,330	121,870	117,636	2.00	-3.47
Mexico	7,034	7,477	6,685	6,578	6,384	0.11	-2.95
Saint Pierre and Miquelon			11				
United States of America	459,733	454,444	479,744	472,122	456,156	7.76	-3.38
Other countries of North America		64			12	0.00	
South America	**43,467**	**53,147**	**56,164**	**56,922**	**62,001**	**1.06**	**8.92**
Argentina	5,977	5,832	8,607	8,611	9,389	0.16	9.03
Bolivia	187	264	178	221	207	0.00	-6.33
Brazil	19,600	25,010	25,846	26,904	29,203	0.50	8.55
Chile	8,444	10,268	10,156	9,538	10,483	0.18	9.91
Colombia	4,278	5,799	6,197	6,140	6,552	0.11	6.71
Ecuador	382	513	423	430	733	0.01	70.47
Falkland Islands, Malvinas	78	76		26			
French Guiana		30	22				
Guyana	27	35	39	59	68	0.00	15.25

AUSTRALIA

2. Arrivals of non-resident visitors at national borders, by country of residence

	2007	2008	2009	2010	2011	Market share 11	% Change 11-10
Paraguay	133	303	103	198	175	0.00	-11.62
Peru	2,138	2,378	2,325	2,255	2,564	0.04	13.70
Suriname	29	36	23	17	36	0.00	111.76
Uruguay	925	1,122	877	1,042	1,080	0.02	3.65
Venezuela	1,257	1,440	1,357	1,469	1,508	0.03	2.65
Other countries of South America	12	41	11	12	3	0.00	-75.00
EAST ASIA AND THE PACIFIC	**3,386,801**	**3,244,422**	**3,226,010**	**3,515,746**	**3,566,095**	**60.70**	**1.43**
North-East Asia	**1,426,815**	**1,257,717**	**1,162,638**	**1,321,624**	**1,328,607**	**22.61**	**0.53**
China	357,557	356,428	366,362	453,738	542,123	9.23	19.48
Taiwan, Province of China	92,680	77,646	98,538	87,136	84,458	1.44	-3.07
Hong Kong, China	146,958	143,956	156,892	163,930	166,400	2.83	1.51
Japan	573,031	457,257	355,421	398,151	332,573	5.66	-16.47
Korea, Dem. People's Republic of	16	10	52	3	3	0.00	
Korea, Republic of	253,311	218,311	180,878	214,118	197,825	3.37	-7.61
Macao, China	2,784	3,478	3,784	3,448	3,830	0.07	11.08
Mongolia	478	631	711	1,100	1,395	0.02	26.82
South-East Asia	**682,547**	**714,565**	**789,968**	**861,954**	**896,909**	**15.27**	**4.06**
Brunei Darussalam	7,492	7,942	7,832	7,783	8,142	0.14	4.61
Myanmar	1,126	1,390	1,627	1,626	2,068	0.04	27.18
Cambodia	3,696	4,300	5,443	5,277	5,089	0.09	-3.56
Indonesia	89,075	94,265	108,738	123,890	140,372	2.39	13.30
Lao People's Democratic Republic	1,903	1,907	2,025	1,660	1,684	0.03	1.45
Malaysia	159,414	171,019	211,545	237,018	241,181	4.11	1.76
Philippines	42,442	46,898	47,418	51,440	56,667	0.96	10.16
Timor-Leste	4,003	3,225	3,243	3,892	3,826	0.07	-1.70
Singapore	263,819	270,900	285,342	307,994	318,546	5.42	3.43
Viet Nam	26,535	33,180	34,937	37,227	33,913	0.58	-8.90
Thailand	83,042	79,539	81,804	84,147	85,421	1.45	1.51
Other countries of South-East Asia			14				
Australasia	**1,138,019**	**1,113,313**	**1,110,456**	**1,161,658**	**1,172,726**	**19.96**	**0.95**
New Zealand	1,138,019	1,113,313	1,110,456	1,161,658	1,172,726	19.96	0.95
Melanesia	**119,321**	**133,824**	**141,680**	**148,332**	**144,160**	**2.45**	**-2.81**
Solomon Islands	7,344	8,282	7,389	8,212	7,917	0.13	-3.59
Fiji	26,306	29,732	32,462	33,370	32,352	0.55	-3.05
New Caledonia	41,363	45,817	45,669	45,808	41,677	0.71	-9.02
Vanuatu	8,032	8,347	9,980	9,738	10,416	0.18	6.96
Norfolk Island	3,093	2,895	2,551	2,349			
Papua New Guinea	33,183	38,751	43,629	48,855	51,798	0.88	6.02
Micronesia	**5,081**	**5,518**	**5,369**	**4,477**	**4,582**	**0.08**	**2.35**
Kiribati	1,406	1,301	1,345	943	1,148	0.02	21.74
Guam	1,233	1,797	1,744	1,671	1,124	0.02	-32.73
Nauru	1,690	1,666	1,524	1,233	1,614	0.03	30.90
Northern Mariana Islands	16	76	17	11	3	0.00	-72.73
Micronesia, Federated States of	264	304	267	258	290	0.00	12.40
Marshall Islands	220	141	215	177	154	0.00	-12.99
Palau	252	233	257	184	249	0.00	35.33
Polynesia	**14,802**	**19,114**	**15,653**	**17,592**	**18,574**	**0.32**	**5.58**
American Samoa	11	42	122	100	75	0.00	-25.00
Cook Islands	1,096	1,814	1,473	1,859	1,799	0.03	-3.23
French Polynesia	5,137	5,754	4,438	3,777	3,522	0.06	-6.75
Niue	210	371	209	180	62	0.00	-65.56
Tokelau	49	86	84	4	41	0.00	925.00
Tonga	3,463	5,460	4,507	5,969	7,587	0.13	27.11
Tuvalu	221	204	250	213	171	0.00	-19.72
Wallis and Futuna Islands	230	374	329	241	376	0.01	56.02
Samoa	4,385	5,009	4,241	5,249	4,941	0.08	-5.87

AUSTRALIA

2. Arrivals of non-resident visitors at national borders, by country of residence

	2007	2008	2009	2010	2011	Market share 11	% Change 11-10
Other East Asia and the Pacific	**216**	**371**	**246**	**109**	**537**	**0.01**	**392.66**
Other countries of Oceania	216	371	246	109	537	0.01	392.66
EUROPE	**1,355,280**	**1,381,169**	**1,362,172**	**1,347,469**	**1,291,198**	**21.98**	**-4.18**
Central/Eastern Europe	**40,982**	**46,982**	**45,277**	**46,061**	**47,057**	**0.80**	**2.16**
Azerbaijan	181	178	94	110	155	0.00	40.91
Armenia	117	109	73	87	142	0.00	63.22
Bulgaria	846	1,011	1,255	1,033	963	0.02	-6.78
Belarus	277	210	269	353	256	0.00	-27.48
Czech Republic/Slovakia	3,449	4,063	5,368	1,879	1,681	0.03	-10.54
Czech Republic	1,881	2,488	1,740	4,921	4,947	0.08	0.53
Estonia	1,439	1,867	2,238	2,190	2,388	0.04	9.04
Georgia	115	4,014	112	40	78	0.00	95.00
Hungary	4,638	30	4,055	3,718	3,752	0.06	0.91
Kazakhstan	617	667	647	904	897	0.02	-0.77
Kyrgyzstan	73	83	102	90	73	0.00	-18.89
Latvia	981	968	1,005	785	798	0.01	1.66
Lithuania	654	973	753	760	843	0.01	10.92
Republic of Moldova	52	71	85	135	86	0.00	-36.30
Poland	8,505	10,517	8,393	8,752	8,745	0.15	-0.08
Romania	1,194	1,579	1,493	1,452	1,112	0.02	-23.42
Russian Federation	11,738	12,795	12,436	13,631	14,494	0.25	6.33
Slovakia	2,057	2,150	2,237	2,343	2,368	0.04	1.07
Tajikistan	28	72	37	28	20	0.00	-28.57
Turkmenistan	10	9	20	4	9	0.00	125.00
Ukraine	1,858	2,739	2,533	2,597	3,052	0.05	17.52
USSR (former)	96	178	68	14			
Uzbekistan	176	211	264	235	198	0.00	-15.74
Northern Europe	**842,699**	**828,369**	**813,499**	**788,626**	**753,707**	**12.83**	**-4.43**
Denmark	22,709	24,036	24,118	23,047	22,079	0.38	-4.20
Faeroe Islands	51	96	42	94	21	0.00	-77.66
Finland	11,697	11,336	11,935	11,929	11,979	0.20	0.42
Iceland	647	905	627	442	518	0.01	17.19
Ireland	67,331	68,155	62,546	52,961	58,711	1.00	10.86
Norway	16,191	17,353	17,615	19,125	17,884	0.30	-6.49
Sweden	35,123	34,352	32,816	34,354	34,264	0.58	-0.26
United Kingdom	687,665	670,919	661,442	645,155	606,926	10.33	-5.93
Channel Islands	368	623	1,513	1,085	872	0.01	-19.63
Isle of Man	917	584	809	434	453	0.01	4.38
Other countries of Northern Europe		10	36				
Southern Europe	**97,446**	**109,820**	**99,319**	**103,642**	**100,656**	**1.71**	**-2.88**
Albania	201	261	259	183	190	0.00	3.83
Andorra	102	196	139	107	100	0.00	-6.54
Bosnia and Herzegovina	491	631	638	713	689	0.01	-3.37
Croatia	2,129	3,296	2,187	2,118	2,085	0.04	-1.56
Gibraltar	131	98	96	221	125	0.00	-43.44
Greece	7,935	6,944	6,813	8,094	7,452	0.13	-7.93
Holy See		16					
Italy	53,617	58,730	55,106	56,399	54,956	0.94	-2.56
Malta	2,927	2,730	2,659	2,773	2,748	0.05	-0.90
Portugal	3,630	4,388	3,673	3,748	3,498	0.06	-6.67
San Marino	32	43	25	45	24	0.00	-46.67
Slovenia	2,145	2,494	2,369	2,315	2,388	0.04	3.15
Spain	20,729	26,243	22,054	23,007	22,654	0.39	-1.53
TFYR of Macedonia	1,166	1,476	1,383	1,482	1,311	0.02	-11.54
Serbia and Montenegro	2,211	2,274	1,918	2,437	2,436	0.04	-0.04
Western Europe	**352,053**	**373,558**	**382,470**	**386,273**	**369,012**	**6.28**	**-4.47**
Austria	17,815	17,083	16,704	16,244	14,080	0.24	-13.32

AUSTRALIA

2. Arrivals of non-resident visitors at national borders, by country of residence

	2007	2008	2009	2010	2011	Market share 11	% Change 11-10
Belgium	14,064	13,762	14,646	16,240	15,588	0.27	-4.01
France	73,657	85,650	93,290	97,280	93,951	1.60	-3.42
Germany	151,583	160,717	161,334	160,350	153,839	2.62	-4.06
Liechtenstein	87	135	89	87	23	0.00	-73.56
Luxembourg	1,197	1,109	1,276	1,056	926	0.02	-12.31
Monaco	517	431	495	517	532	0.01	2.90
Netherlands	51,206	54,643	51,462	49,989	47,593	0.81	-4.79
Switzerland	41,927	40,028	43,174	44,510	42,480	0.72	-4.56
East Mediterranean Europe	**22,002**	**22,297**	**21,574**	**22,836**	**20,724**	**0.35**	**-9.25**
Cyprus	2,421	1,933	2,150	2,095	1,990	0.03	-5.01
Israel	15,198	15,500	14,249	14,485	12,283	0.21	-15.20
Turkey	4,383	4,864	5,175	6,256	6,451	0.11	3.12
Other Europe	**98**	**143**	**33**	**31**	**42**	**0.00**	**35.48**
Other countries of Europe	98	143	33	31	42	0.00	35.48
MIDDLE EAST	**62,743**	**74,695**	**79,610**	**87,140**	**81,594**	**1.39**	**-6.36**
Bahrain	2,539	2,142	2,462	2,373	1,674	0.03	-29.46
Iraq	433	566	843	1,143	1,088	0.02	-4.81
Jordan	1,018	1,285	1,270	1,108	1,177	0.02	6.23
Kuwait	3,567	3,053	2,343	3,017	2,936	0.05	-2.68
Lebanon	5,602	6,097	5,779	5,276	5,245	0.09	-0.59
Libya	170	170	258	660	237	0.00	-64.09
Oman	2,344	2,701	2,237	2,616	2,353	0.04	-10.05
Qatar	2,576	3,032	3,664	4,646	5,151	0.09	10.87
Saudi Arabia	7,536	10,883	13,015	13,663	13,575	0.23	-0.64
Syrian Arab Republic	419	860	751	600	368	0.01	-38.67
United Arab Emirates	33,777	41,132	44,130	48,774	45,001	0.77	-7.74
Egypt	2,580	2,676	2,654	3,026	2,634	0.04	-12.95
Yemen	85	30	116	184	37	0.00	-79.89
Other countries of Middle East	97	68	88	54	118	0.00	118.52
SOUTH ASIA	**124,690**	**148,089**	**162,022**	**183,526**	**195,896**	**3.33**	**6.74**
Afghanistan	319	176	312	293	301	0.01	2.73
Bangladesh	4,018	4,230	5,495	6,457	7,351	0.13	13.85
Bhutan	151	178	194	262	263	0.00	0.38
Sri Lanka	12,095	13,309	13,917	16,652	17,148	0.29	2.98
India	95,214	116,001	124,888	138,705	148,191	2.52	6.84
Iran, Islamic Republic of	4,509	4,625	4,890	7,481	8,538	0.15	14.13
Maldives	374	486	460	574	460	0.01	-19.86
Nepal	3,165	3,840	5,090	5,192	4,767	0.08	-8.19
Pakistan	4,845	5,244	6,776	7,910	8,877	0.15	12.23
NOT SPECIFIED	**236**	**93**	**208**	**231**	**2,805**	**0.05**	**1114.29**
Other countries of the World	236	93	208	231	2,805	0.05	1114.29

AUSTRIA

3. Arrivals of non-resident tourists in hotels and similar establishments, by country of residence

		2007	2008	2009	2010	2011	Market share 11	% Change 11-10
TOTAL	(*)	15,348,001	16,091,160	15,520,385	16,169,935	16,972,143	100.00	4.96
AFRICA		36,005	35,565	34,631	40,676	47,141	0.28	15.89
Southern Africa		16,886	16,376	12,764	17,099	17,533	0.10	2.54
South Africa		16,886	16,376	12,764	17,099	17,533	0.10	2.54
Other Africa		19,119	19,189	21,867	23,577	29,608	0.17	25.58
Other countries of Africa		19,119	19,189	21,867	23,577	29,608	0.17	25.58
AMERICAS		684,537	599,728	546,539	638,867	664,935	3.92	4.08
North America		609,360	518,240	468,770	543,442	536,997	3.16	-1.19
Canada		75,694	75,940	69,227	77,923	84,364	0.50	8.27
United States of America		533,666	442,300	399,543	465,519	452,633	2.67	-2.77
South America					3,407	43,453	0.26	1175.40
Brazil					3,407	43,453	0.26	1175.40
Other Americas		75,177	81,488	77,769	92,018	84,485	0.50	-8.19
Other countries of the Americas		75,177	81,488	77,769	92,018	84,485	0.50	-8.19
EAST ASIA AND THE PACIFIC		688,663	642,244	582,651	668,022	820,794	4.84	22.87
North-East Asia		496,712	445,074	418,173	477,455	603,608	3.56	26.42
China		165,313	147,364	147,417	173,116	245,340	1.45	41.72
Taiwan, Province of China		30,696	28,559	29,332	35,588	54,566	0.32	53.33
Japan		220,108	200,791	191,321	206,217	220,691	1.30	7.02
Korea, Republic of		80,595	68,360	50,103	62,534	83,011	0.49	32.75
South-East Asia		35,663	42,826	39,072	47,799	67,930	0.40	42.12
All countries of South-East Asia		35,663	42,826	39,072	47,799	67,930	0.40	42.12
Australasia		108,265	111,997	89,781	99,269	107,836	0.64	8.63
Australia		94,315	97,768	78,521	87,742	96,316	0.57	9.77
New Zealand		13,950	14,229	11,260	11,527	11,520	0.07	-0.06
Other East Asia and the Pacific		48,023	42,347	35,625	43,499	41,420	0.24	-4.78
Other countries of Asia		48,023	42,347	35,625	43,499	41,420	0.24	-4.78
EUROPE		13,563,555	14,350,098	13,964,009	14,405,592	15,009,758	88.44	4.19
Central/Eastern Europe		1,279,113	1,634,118	1,516,356	1,635,813	1,832,305	10.80	12.01
Bulgaria		45,314	54,015	50,093	50,052	56,949	0.34	13.78
Czech Republic		235,181	302,131	318,086	332,214	360,611	2.12	8.55
Estonia		11,463	15,760	12,805	15,805	13,293	0.08	-15.89
Hungary		285,310	311,619	283,542	291,622	310,792	1.83	6.57
Latvia		18,733	18,848	11,640	11,322	12,844	0.08	13.44
Lithuania		17,754	20,578	13,937	14,383	15,722	0.09	9.31
Poland		162,006	220,801	206,416	228,861	247,051	1.46	7.95
Romania		211,235	280,007	238,325	223,919	236,469	1.39	5.60
Russian Federation		164,112	243,778	208,613	275,932	359,348	2.12	30.23
Slovakia		67,655	85,157	89,048	97,499	106,142	0.63	8.86
Ukraine		37,390	53,711	56,623	60,041	75,288	0.44	25.39
Other countries Central/East Europe		22,960	27,713	27,228	34,163	37,796	0.22	10.63
Northern Europe		1,270,465	1,281,341	1,117,272	1,182,644	1,152,609	6.79	-2.54
Denmark		198,032	206,458	199,532	205,901	200,370	1.18	-2.69
Finland		58,992	63,153	68,630	68,690	73,418	0.43	6.88
Iceland		10,365	7,793	5,441	6,525	6,823	0.04	4.57
Ireland		63,524	66,085	52,473	48,052	42,994	0.25	-10.53
Norway		57,865	62,511	57,437	68,649	73,605	0.43	7.22
Sweden		145,177	169,067	139,883	164,721	158,229	0.93	-3.94
United Kingdom		736,510	706,274	593,876	620,106	597,170	3.52	-3.70
Southern Europe		1,454,676	1,477,196	1,434,049	1,483,900	1,561,456	9.20	5.23
Croatia		78,748	99,228	83,348	79,825	80,470	0.47	0.81
Greece		86,420	90,445	83,145	73,029	59,856	0.35	-18.04
Italy		902,319	882,436	895,285	907,257	918,415	5.41	1.23

AUSTRIA

3. Arrivals of non-resident tourists in hotels and similar establishments, by country of residence

	2007	2008	2009	2010	2011	Market share 11	% Change 11-10
Malta	4,733	5,309	3,632	5,048	5,172	0.03	2.46
Portugal	28,114	27,864	26,231	28,212	30,014	0.18	6.39
Slovenia	66,156	71,314	70,358	73,650	81,001	0.48	9.98
Spain	246,183	251,683	222,329	246,217	294,456	1.73	19.59
Serbia and Montenegro	42,003	48,917	49,721	70,662	92,072	0.54	30.30
Western Europe	**9,471,281**	**9,854,942**	**9,792,268**	**9,978,470**	**10,315,476**	**60.78**	**3.38**
Belgium	347,476	354,566	353,483	353,391	373,709	2.20	5.75
France	388,652	395,148	397,979	414,677	434,953	2.56	4.89
Germany	7,000,727	7,341,427	7,258,959	7,394,154	7,547,399	44.47	2.07
Luxembourg	42,957	43,338	44,468	46,863	49,262	0.29	5.12
Netherlands	855,600	888,748	875,811	853,187	864,402	5.09	1.31
Switzerland	835,869	831,715	861,568	916,198	1,045,751	6.16	14.14
East Mediterranean Europe	**88,020**	**102,501**	**104,064**	**124,765**	**147,912**	**0.87**	**18.55**
Cyprus	6,187	8,790	8,310	9,029	7,677	0.05	-14.97
Israel	51,514	53,445	58,826	65,551	73,296	0.43	11.82
Turkey	30,319	40,266	36,928	50,185	66,939	0.39	33.38
MIDDLE EAST	**86,643**	**95,226**	**89,519**	**109,523**	**142,173**	**0.84**	**29.81**
All countries of Middle East	86,643	95,226	89,519	109,523	142,173	0.84	29.81
SOUTH ASIA	**44,423**	**44,840**	**45,482**	**57,368**	**79,891**	**0.47**	**39.26**
All countries of South Asia	44,423	44,840	45,482	57,368	79,891	0.47	39.26
NOT SPECIFIED	**244,175**	**323,459**	**257,554**	**249,887**	**207,451**	**1.22**	**-16.98**
Other countries of the World	244,175	323,459	257,554	249,887	207,451	1.22	-16.98

AUSTRIA

4. Arrivals of non-resident tourists in all types of accommodation establishments, by country of residence

		2007	2008	2009	2010	2011	Market share 11	% Change 11-10
TOTAL	(*)	20,773,316	21,935,409	21,355,439	22,004,266	23,011,956	100.00	4.58
AFRICA		40,472	39,957	38,794	44,965	52,345	0.23	16.41
Southern Africa		20,546	19,418	15,699	19,874	20,479	0.09	3.04
South Africa		20,546	19,418	15,699	19,874	20,479	0.09	3.04
Other Africa		19,926	20,539	23,095	25,091	31,866	0.14	27.00
Other countries of Africa		19,926	20,539	23,095	25,091	31,866	0.14	27.00
AMERICAS		755,989	672,610	616,730	708,515	742,821	3.23	4.84
North America		668,951	572,513	523,314	596,125	594,679	2.58	-0.24
Canada		88,035	88,955	81,466	90,684	98,545	0.43	8.67
United States of America		580,916	483,558	441,848	505,441	496,134	2.16	-1.84
South America					3,918	50,796	0.22	1196.48
Brazil					3,918	50,796	0.22	1196.48
Other Americas		87,038	100,097	93,416	108,472	97,346	0.42	-10.26
Other countries of the Americas		87,038	100,097	93,416	108,472	97,346	0.42	-10.26
EAST ASIA AND THE PACIFIC		747,319	705,701	645,203	741,244	914,840	3.98	23.42
North-East Asia		526,131	475,655	445,635	512,054	654,442	2.84	27.81
China		171,123	156,190	155,179	182,282	259,944	1.13	42.61
Taiwan, Province of China		33,102	31,387	32,354	38,631	59,580	0.26	54.23
Japan		229,347	208,150	198,751	213,581	228,559	0.99	7.01
Korea, Republic of		92,559	79,928	59,351	77,560	106,359	0.46	37.13
South-East Asia		38,079	46,276	43,269	53,425	74,242	0.32	38.96
All countries of South-East Asia		38,079	46,276	43,269	53,425	74,242	0.32	38.96
Australasia		133,391	139,384	118,112	129,818	142,258	0.62	9.58
Australia		115,995	121,314	103,063	114,457	126,169	0.55	10.23
New Zealand		17,396	18,070	15,049	15,361	16,089	0.07	4.74
Other East Asia and the Pacific		49,718	44,386	38,187	45,947	43,898	0.19	-4.46
Other countries of Asia		49,718	44,386	38,187	45,947	43,898	0.19	-4.46
EUROPE		18,795,014	19,993,474	19,613,283	20,042,806	20,818,964	90.47	3.87
Central/Eastern Europe		1,777,503	2,242,687	2,131,821	2,279,602	2,519,532	10.95	10.53
Bulgaria		50,411	59,439	56,305	55,947	63,992	0.28	14.38
Czech Republic		412,101	522,680	556,073	569,279	603,581	2.62	6.03
Estonia		15,741	20,549	16,551	19,670	16,759	0.07	-14.80
Hungary		429,738	462,627	426,498	442,245	466,860	2.03	5.57
Latvia		25,265	25,252	15,634	15,766	18,371	0.08	16.52
Lithuania		26,212	31,075	23,766	23,007	25,417	0.11	10.48
Poland		245,583	335,141	317,222	346,582	372,924	1.62	7.60
Romania		239,658	316,235	273,225	261,439	275,722	1.20	5.46
Russian Federation		177,979	264,115	230,598	305,714	400,399	1.74	30.97
Slovakia		89,528	117,183	123,164	135,332	148,080	0.64	9.42
Ukraine		40,965	58,994	63,929	68,264	86,649	0.38	26.93
Other countries Central/East Europe		24,322	29,397	28,856	36,357	40,778	0.18	12.16
Northern Europe		1,554,154	1,595,397	1,403,027	1,478,706	1,447,011	6.29	-2.14
Denmark		301,474	318,612	312,734	321,642	313,013	1.36	-2.68
Finland		69,254	73,678	79,189	80,922	87,105	0.38	7.64
Iceland		11,179	8,788	6,198	7,613	7,912	0.03	3.93
Ireland		76,318	79,982	64,110	59,152	53,416	0.23	-9.70
Norway		67,885	73,703	67,775	79,838	84,951	0.37	6.40
Sweden		179,368	215,321	171,774	198,122	191,405	0.83	-3.39
United Kingdom		848,676	825,313	701,247	731,417	709,209	3.08	-3.04
Southern Europe		1,705,208	1,733,501	1,694,882	1,748,616	1,842,030	8.00	5.34
Croatia		105,311	129,338	109,903	105,712	105,184	0.46	-0.50
Greece		90,704	95,381	88,208	77,587	64,210	0.28	-17.24
Italy		1,058,113	1,033,306	1,056,491	1,067,721	1,086,957	4.72	1.80

AUSTRIA

4. Arrivals of non-resident tourists in all types of accommodation establishments, by country of residence

	2007	2008	2009	2010	2011	Market share 11	% Change 11-10
Malta	5,063	5,732	4,086	5,424	5,877	0.03	8.35
Portugal	32,999	31,514	30,082	32,051	33,846	0.15	5.60
Slovenia	93,481	101,944	102,126	106,520	117,740	0.51	10.53
Spain	273,242	283,271	249,384	274,651	326,091	1.42	18.73
Serbia and Montenegro	46,295	53,015	54,602	78,950	102,125	0.44	29.35
Western Europe	**13,657,717**	**14,306,248**	**14,263,593**	**14,392,893**	**14,841,017**	**64.49**	**3.11**
Belgium	449,127	462,822	461,299	461,784	488,810	2.12	5.85
France	465,255	473,235	478,747	499,894	521,955	2.27	4.41
Germany	10,164,758	10,709,251	10,622,835	10,706,153	10,929,670	47.50	2.09
Luxembourg	48,985	50,444	51,164	53,804	57,004	0.25	5.95
Netherlands	1,559,796	1,650,134	1,654,959	1,617,692	1,644,620	7.15	1.66
Switzerland	969,796	960,362	994,589	1,053,566	1,198,958	5.21	13.80
East Mediterranean Europe	**100,432**	**115,641**	**119,960**	**142,989**	**169,374**	**0.74**	**18.45**
Cyprus	6,986	9,475	8,951	9,624	8,218	0.04	-14.61
Israel	61,136	63,587	71,678	80,296	89,834	0.39	11.88
Turkey	32,310	42,579	39,331	53,069	71,322	0.31	34.39
MIDDLE EAST	**91,354**	**102,099**	**97,053**	**120,055**	**160,005**	**0.70**	**33.28**
All countries of Middle East	91,354	102,099	97,053	120,055	160,005	0.70	33.28
SOUTH ASIA	**46,210**	**46,990**	**47,604**	**59,780**	**83,911**	**0.36**	**40.37**
All countries of South Asia	46,210	46,990	47,604	59,780	83,911	0.36	40.37
NOT SPECIFIED	**296,958**	**374,578**	**296,772**	**286,901**	**239,070**	**1.04**	**-16.67**
Other countries of the World	296,958	374,578	296,772	286,901	239,070	1.04	-16.67

AUSTRIA

5. Overnight stays of non-resident tourists in hotels and similar establishments, by country of residence

		2007	2008	2009	2010	2011	Market share 11	% Change 11-10
TOTAL	(*)	57,881,542	60,468,710	57,798,255	58,314,787	59,147,120	100.00	1.43
AFRICA		132,890	123,372	108,776	128,883	149,633	0.25	16.10
Southern Africa		72,106	66,071	50,416	59,254	62,914	0.11	6.18
South Africa		72,106	66,071	50,416	59,254	62,914	0.11	6.18
Other Africa		60,784	57,301	58,360	69,629	86,719	0.15	24.54
Other countries of Africa		60,784	57,301	58,360	69,629	86,719	0.15	24.54
AMERICAS		1,676,595	1,448,208	1,342,812	1,524,758	1,568,231	2.65	2.85
North America		1,504,960	1,262,868	1,159,958	1,313,600	1,283,178	2.17	-2.32
Canada		190,044	185,771	170,513	190,823	205,616	0.35	7.75
United States of America		1,314,916	1,077,097	989,445	1,122,777	1,077,562	1.82	-4.03
South America					7,924	96,380	0.16	1116.30
Brazil					7,924	96,380	0.16	1116.30
Other Americas		171,635	185,340	182,854	203,234	188,673	0.32	-7.16
Other countries of the Americas		171,635	185,340	182,854	203,234	188,673	0.32	-7.16
EAST ASIA AND THE PACIFIC		1,250,823	1,183,238	1,096,782	1,214,144	1,418,535	2.40	16.83
North-East Asia		827,597	752,997	727,575	795,424	955,351	1.62	20.11
China		231,523	217,115	206,576	249,334	340,655	0.58	36.63
Taiwan, Province of China		47,425	44,372	50,874	61,272	80,270	0.14	31.01
Japan		433,448	390,347	387,987	393,431	417,538	0.71	6.13
Korea, Republic of		115,201	101,163	82,138	91,387	116,888	0.20	27.90
South-East Asia		66,348	79,496	74,191	89,710	122,214	0.21	36.23
All countries of South-East Asia		66,348	79,496	74,191	89,710	122,214	0.21	36.23
Australasia		248,862	256,457	212,390	235,320	251,823	0.43	7.01
Australia		219,346	226,153	187,649	208,685	225,447	0.38	8.03
New Zealand		29,516	30,304	24,741	26,635	26,376	0.04	-0.97
Other East Asia and the Pacific		108,016	94,288	82,626	93,690	89,147	0.15	-4.85
Other countries of Asia		108,016	94,288	82,626	93,690	89,147	0.15	-4.85
EUROPE		53,867,483	56,567,773	54,267,191	54,438,114	54,940,288	92.89	0.92
Central/Eastern Europe		3,993,838	5,146,585	4,817,482	5,050,336	5,547,838	9.38	9.85
Bulgaria		104,123	128,090	119,747	123,252	137,444	0.23	11.51
Czech Republic		686,528	890,714	970,092	992,854	1,066,545	1.80	7.42
Estonia		36,218	55,108	43,394	51,130	42,431	0.07	-17.01
Hungary		884,975	986,308	878,544	873,197	918,744	1.55	5.22
Latvia		64,379	60,416	37,803	34,040	37,172	0.06	9.20
Lithuania		61,992	72,457	51,068	45,664	47,798	0.08	4.67
Poland		553,205	748,703	729,691	752,794	801,360	1.35	6.45
Romania		529,384	736,540	662,774	627,184	645,438	1.09	2.91
Russian Federation		680,312	954,639	802,394	981,242	1,217,496	2.06	24.08
Slovakia		198,248	262,316	281,003	295,712	313,888	0.53	6.15
Ukraine		127,986	172,307	166,819	178,530	217,819	0.37	22.01
Other countries Central/East Europe		66,488	78,987	74,153	94,737	101,703	0.17	7.35
Northern Europe		5,466,390	5,578,304	4,772,415	4,803,177	4,615,983	7.80	-3.90
Denmark		883,973	924,429	884,510	888,454	849,192	1.44	-4.42
Finland		202,967	213,363	233,717	225,430	241,533	0.41	7.14
Iceland		42,456	34,498	19,335	21,327	24,939	0.04	16.94
Ireland		306,013	319,568	250,742	211,253	182,739	0.31	-13.50
Norway		188,696	204,430	191,839	223,083	234,757	0.40	5.23
Sweden		532,943	619,118	523,827	584,509	579,911	0.98	-0.79
United Kingdom		3,309,342	3,262,898	2,668,445	2,649,121	2,502,912	4.23	-5.52
Southern Europe		3,831,187	3,897,326	3,751,722	3,805,545	3,867,238	6.54	1.62
Croatia		228,609	271,907	241,935	219,400	209,847	0.35	-4.35
Greece		248,528	260,044	231,312	201,413	163,446	0.28	-18.85
Italy		2,419,295	2,375,772	2,367,675	2,372,913	2,352,974	3.98	-0.84

AUSTRIA

5. Overnight stays of non-resident tourists in hotels and similar establishments, by country of residence

	2007	2008	2009	2010	2011	Market share 11	% Change 11-10
Malta	20,169	20,911	15,008	19,697	18,590	0.03	-5.62
Portugal	72,734	72,799	73,430	74,792	76,836	0.13	2.73
Slovenia	158,294	171,512	177,879	182,082	201,087	0.34	10.44
Spain	590,636	610,853	528,346	573,381	642,134	1.09	11.99
Serbia and Montenegro	92,922	113,528	116,137	161,867	202,324	0.34	24.99
Western Europe	**40,301,308**	**41,627,063**	**40,605,574**	**40,398,966**	**40,467,243**	**68.42**	**0.17**
Belgium	1,830,563	1,874,394	1,848,562	1,793,325	1,860,265	3.15	3.73
France	1,379,740	1,413,693	1,414,698	1,445,896	1,484,696	2.51	2.68
Germany	29,565,273	30,740,151	29,851,032	29,701,628	29,329,241	49.59	-1.25
Luxembourg	223,071	232,320	232,605	240,851	254,089	0.43	5.50
Netherlands	4,291,161	4,448,949	4,276,323	4,091,901	3,999,153	6.76	-2.27
Switzerland	3,011,500	2,917,556	2,982,354	3,125,365	3,539,799	5.98	13.26
East Mediterranean Europe	**274,760**	**318,495**	**319,998**	**380,090**	**441,986**	**0.75**	**16.28**
Cyprus	17,774	25,561	24,770	27,261	22,238	0.04	-18.43
Israel	172,109	187,735	199,474	227,075	256,823	0.43	13.10
Turkey	84,877	105,199	95,754	125,754	162,925	0.28	29.56
MIDDLE EAST	**282,962**	**303,292**	**270,280**	**327,847**	**409,365**	**0.69**	**24.86**
All countries of Middle East	282,962	303,292	270,280	327,847	409,365	0.69	24.86
SOUTH ASIA	**82,102**	**90,224**	**90,103**	**103,892**	**145,647**	**0.25**	**40.19**
All countries of South Asia	82,102	90,224	90,103	103,892	145,647	0.25	40.19
NOT SPECIFIED	**588,687**	**752,603**	**622,311**	**577,149**	**515,421**	**0.87**	**-10.70**
Other countries of the World	588,687	752,603	622,311	577,149	515,421	0.87	-10.70

AUSTRIA

6. Overnight stays of non-resident tourists in all types of accommodation establishments, by country of residence

		2007	2008	2009	2010	2011	Market share 11	% Change 11-10
TOTAL	(*)	88,442,873	92,839,547	89,864,164	89,857,167	90,705,554	100.00	0.94
AFRICA		159,409	147,641	130,413	152,378	177,467	0.20	16.46
Southern Africa		94,619	84,317	66,412	74,114	79,954	0.09	7.88
South Africa		94,619	84,317	66,412	74,114	79,954	0.09	7.88
Other Africa		64,790	63,324	64,001	78,264	97,513	0.11	24.59
Other countries of Africa		64,790	63,324	64,001	78,264	97,513	0.11	24.59
AMERICAS		1,881,217	1,642,552	1,531,406	1,723,910	1,788,074	1.97	3.72
North America		1,682,924	1,423,529	1,317,648	1,472,085	1,449,928	1.60	-1.51
Canada		224,572	224,884	207,190	229,015	246,821	0.27	7.78
United States of America		1,458,352	1,198,645	1,110,458	1,243,070	1,203,107	1.33	-3.21
South America					9,371	113,007	0.12	1105.92
Brazil					9,371	113,007	0.12	1105.92
Other Americas		198,293	219,023	213,758	242,454	225,139	0.25	-7.14
Other countries of the Americas		198,293	219,023	213,758	242,454	225,139	0.25	-7.14
EAST ASIA AND THE PACIFIC		1,391,412	1,337,593	1,244,356	1,382,262	1,634,091	1.80	18.22
North-East Asia		887,582	816,142	784,816	863,947	1,057,035	1.17	22.35
China		245,126	236,433	222,225	267,483	369,718	0.41	38.22
Taiwan, Province of China		52,204	50,058	57,620	67,250	90,533	0.10	34.62
Japan		455,817	409,001	407,112	412,494	437,949	0.48	6.17
Korea, Republic of		134,435	120,650	97,859	116,720	158,835	0.18	36.08
South-East Asia		72,244	88,129	84,200	101,781	136,251	0.15	33.87
All countries of South-East Asia		72,244	88,129	84,200	101,781	136,251	0.15	33.87
Australasia		318,021	332,893	285,489	315,130	343,338	0.38	8.95
Australia		279,035	292,188	250,998	279,417	304,430	0.34	8.95
New Zealand		38,986	40,705	34,491	35,713	38,908	0.04	8.95
Other East Asia and the Pacific		113,565	100,429	89,851	101,404	97,467	0.11	-3.88
Other countries of Asia		113,565	100,429	89,851	101,404	97,467	0.11	-3.88
EUROPE		83,859,097	88,336,909	85,776,665	85,388,146	85,806,605	94.60	0.49
Central/Eastern Europe		6,257,690	7,937,810	7,745,592	8,091,969	8,838,267	9.74	9.22
Bulgaria		120,813	147,606	145,774	150,509	168,678	0.19	12.07
Czech Republic		1,390,841	1,778,581	1,955,027	1,972,457	2,078,822	2.29	5.39
Estonia		51,817	74,626	60,901	68,219	59,150	0.07	-13.29
Hungary		1,510,896	1,641,621	1,499,474	1,510,379	1,597,850	1.76	5.79
Latvia		95,359	88,530	59,085	55,052	62,767	0.07	14.01
Lithuania		104,443	128,062	105,013	93,384	97,039	0.11	3.91
Poland		1,036,999	1,389,296	1,385,970	1,422,764	1,518,525	1.67	6.73
Romania		636,110	898,885	841,457	822,928	853,549	0.94	3.72
Russian Federation		786,592	1,105,921	969,166	1,195,360	1,501,355	1.66	25.60
Slovakia		295,448	388,827	424,182	464,825	499,057	0.55	7.36
Ukraine		149,919	203,501	209,856	226,260	282,264	0.31	24.75
Other countries Central/East Europe		78,453	92,354	89,687	109,832	119,211	0.13	8.54
Northern Europe		6,980,554	7,226,117	6,306,276	6,369,751	6,166,919	6.80	-3.18
Denmark		1,444,801	1,523,212	1,501,450	1,514,888	1,464,303	1.61	-3.34
Finland		247,784	257,353	279,429	280,480	303,829	0.33	8.32
Iceland		45,948	40,122	23,427	26,001	30,121	0.03	15.85
Ireland		363,769	386,959	308,291	269,442	235,490	0.26	-12.60
Norway		236,132	253,482	240,005	271,184	282,148	0.31	4.04
Sweden		710,612	846,633	689,808	754,680	746,684	0.82	-1.06
United Kingdom		3,931,508	3,918,356	3,263,866	3,253,076	3,104,344	3.42	-4.57
Southern Europe		4,874,671	4,952,813	4,837,856	4,903,684	4,995,293	5.51	1.87
Croatia		368,947	424,858	387,895	351,491	333,806	0.37	-5.03
Greece		270,163	284,383	255,116	221,551	183,410	0.20	-17.22
Italy		3,055,505	2,979,137	3,015,873	3,020,992	3,013,847	3.32	-0.24

AUSTRIA

6. Overnight stays of non-resident tourists in all types of accommodation establishments, by country of residence

	2007	2008	2009	2010	2011	Market share 11	% Change 11-10
Malta	21,736	23,011	17,177	21,815	21,891	0.02	0.35
Portugal	97,871	85,427	90,141	94,320	90,226	0.10	-4.34
Slovenia	269,868	306,447	310,055	317,008	354,656	0.39	11.88
Spain	677,973	710,340	616,697	665,925	741,009	0.82	11.28
Serbia and Montenegro	112,608	139,210	144,902	210,582	256,448	0.28	21.78
Western Europe	**65,417,073**	**67,846,928**	**66,494,567**	**65,559,316**	**65,267,644**	**71.96**	**-0.44**
Belgium	2,495,023	2,563,793	2,530,232	2,464,985	2,565,423	2.83	4.07
France	1,701,614	1,733,339	1,739,002	1,785,956	1,834,629	2.02	2.73
Germany	48,167,380	50,144,306	48,856,862	48,155,743	47,389,531	52.25	-1.59
Luxembourg	260,098	280,882	274,864	284,358	301,951	0.33	6.19
Netherlands	9,089,463	9,562,516	9,451,747	9,071,437	8,899,263	9.81	-1.90
Switzerland	3,703,495	3,562,092	3,641,860	3,796,837	4,276,847	4.72	12.64
East Mediterranean Europe	**329,109**	**373,241**	**392,374**	**463,426**	**538,482**	**0.59**	**16.20**
Cyprus	21,172	29,085	28,388	30,235	24,764	0.03	-18.09
Israel	214,467	230,032	257,619	295,279	337,004	0.37	14.13
Turkey	93,470	114,124	106,367	137,912	176,714	0.19	28.14
MIDDLE EAST	**326,892**	**365,598**	**331,139**	**410,128**	**527,108**	**0.58**	**28.52**
All countries of Middle East	326,892	365,598	331,139	410,128	527,108	0.58	28.52
SOUTH ASIA	**88,524**	**98,688**	**96,857**	**110,442**	**158,686**	**0.17**	**43.68**
All countries of South Asia	88,524	98,688	96,857	110,442	158,686	0.17	43.68
NOT SPECIFIED	**736,322**	**910,566**	**753,328**	**689,901**	**613,523**	**0.68**	**-11.07**
Other countries of the World	736,322	910,566	753,328	689,901	613,523	0.68	-11.07

AZERBAIJAN

2. Arrivals of non-resident visitors at national borders, by country of residence

	2007	2008	2009	2010	2011	Market share 11	% Change 11-10
TOTAL	1,332,701	1,898,936	1,830,367	1,962,906	2,239,141	100.00	14.07
AFRICA	835	1,630	1,732	2,056	1,781	0.08	-13.38
East Africa	89	247	140	165	189	0.01	14.55
British Indian Ocean Territory		6	2				
Burundi		4	3	2	5	0.00	150.00
Comoros		2	1	9	12	0.00	33.33
Ethiopia	19	30	36	30	22	0.00	-26.67
Eritrea		1	2	1	4	0.00	300.00
Djibouti		3	2	6	4	0.00	-33.33
Kenya		34	12	37	22	0.00	-40.54
Madagascar		2	3	1	4	0.00	300.00
Malawi	4	6	3	3	4	0.00	33.33
Mauritius	6	37	19	15	32	0.00	113.33
Mozambique	5	7	6	7	6	0.00	-14.29
Reunion		52	15				
Rwanda		10	2	6	15	0.00	150.00
Somalia	23	2	1	3	1	0.00	-66.67
Zimbabwe	4	8	13	8	17	0.00	112.50
Uganda	9	27	12	13	21	0.00	61.54
United Republic of Tanzania	18	9	8	15	13	0.00	-13.33
Zambia	1	7		9	7	0.00	-22.22
Central Africa	44	181	142	63	109	0.00	73.02
Angola	6	47	24	9	14	0.00	55.56
Cameroon	27	42	47	40	55	0.00	37.50
Central African Republic		1			1	0.00	
Congo	11	12	6	1	11	0.00	1000.00
Democratic Republic of the Congo		10	5	9	9	0.00	
Equatorial Guinea		1					
Gabon		28	28	4	19	0.00	375.00
Sao Tome and Principe		40	32				
North Africa	246	405	557	634	506	0.02	-20.19
Algeria	64	137	213	229	180	0.01	-21.40
Morocco	40	123	196	155	183	0.01	18.06
Sudan	52	63	50	98	47	0.00	-52.04
Tunisia	90	82	98	152	96	0.00	-36.84
Southern Africa	226	464	553	728	567	0.03	-22.12
Botswana		1	2	9	4	0.00	-55.56
Lesotho		3			4	0.00	
Namibia		6		2	8	0.00	300.00
South Africa	226	453	549	716	550	0.02	-23.18
Swaziland		1	2	1	1	0.00	
West Africa	230	333	340	466	410	0.02	-12.02
Benin		2	2	6	7	0.00	16.67
Gambia	1	6	3	17	9	0.00	-47.06
Ghana	6	13	37	38	64	0.00	68.42
Guinea		15	7	16	7	0.00	-56.25
Côte d'Ivoire	5	24	10	12	29	0.00	141.67
Liberia	1	6	7	7			
Mali	6	9	3	12	19	0.00	58.33
Mauritania	6	6	9	53	4	0.00	-92.45
Niger		3	6	5	7	0.00	40.00
Nigeria	183	209	218	223	178	0.01	-20.18
Guinea-Bissau	4	1	4	3	1	0.00	-66.67
Senegal	17	28	25	45	43	0.00	-4.44
Sierra Leone		4	1	12	33	0.00	175.00
Togo		3	1	11	2	0.00	-81.82

AZERBAIJAN

2. Arrivals of non-resident visitors at national borders, by country of residence

	2007	2008	2009	2010	2011	Market share 11	% Change 11-10
Burkina Faso	1	4	7	6	7	0.00	16.67
AMERICAS	**11,021**	**17,329**	**15,445**	**15,789**	**15,532**	**0.69**	**-1.63**
Caribbean	**140**	**261**	**346**	**386**	**484**	**0.02**	**25.39**
Bahamas		1	2	3	4	0.00	33.33
Barbados		6	3	3	4	0.00	33.33
Cayman Islands		1			2	0.00	
Cuba	24	26	32	88	81	0.00	-7.95
Dominica		1	2	2	8	0.00	300.00
Dominican Republic		2	12	13	33	0.00	153.85
Grenada	1	6	9	1	3	0.00	200.00
Haiti		1	1		1	0.00	
Jamaica		3	3	2	8	0.00	300.00
Montserrat		1					
Aruba		22	13				
Anguilla		3					
Trinidad and Tobago	115	168	253	274	336	0.02	22.63
Turks and Caicos Islands		20	16		4	0.00	
Central America	**22**	**40**	**25**	**56**	**92**	**0.00**	**64.29**
Belize	3	5	1	6	3	0.00	-50.00
Costa Rica	6	6	6	11	18	0.00	63.64
El Salvador	2	9	2	4	7	0.00	75.00
Guatemala	3	5	7	6	15	0.00	150.00
Honduras		7	5	15	20	0.00	33.33
Nicaragua		1	1	7	14	0.00	100.00
Panama	8	7	3	7	15	0.00	114.29
North America	**10,415**	**15,780**	**13,833**	**14,134**	**13,465**	**0.60**	**-4.73**
Canada	1,319	2,356	2,036	2,050	1,851	0.08	-9.71
Mexico	59	110	134	98	171	0.01	74.49
United States of America	9,037	13,314	11,663	11,986	11,443	0.51	-4.53
South America	**444**	**1,248**	**1,241**	**1,213**	**1,491**	**0.07**	**22.92**
Argentina	60	140	97	71	159	0.01	123.94
Bolivia	18	62	27	53	36	0.00	-32.08
Brazil	97	255	399	434	500	0.02	15.21
Chile	16	35	13	28	35	0.00	25.00
Colombia	116	364	349	332	417	0.02	25.60
Ecuador	10	63	44	37	89	0.00	140.54
Guyana		1	1	1	2	0.00	100.00
Paraguay	12	35	12	11	7	0.00	-36.36
Peru	9	47	43	31	54	0.00	74.19
Suriname		1		2			
Uruguay	4	95	47	26	18	0.00	-30.77
Venezuela	102	150	209	187	174	0.01	-6.95
EAST ASIA AND THE PACIFIC	**8,391**	**16,190**	**13,839**	**14,730**	**15,092**	**0.67**	**2.46**
North-East Asia	**4,940**	**11,180**	**9,680**	**10,405**	**11,060**	**0.49**	**6.30**
China	2,458	7,138	6,322	5,846	6,224	0.28	6.47
Taiwan, Province of China	125	78	108	29	186	0.01	541.38
Hong Kong, China	1	2	1				
Japan	1,036	1,434	1,076	1,809	2,098	0.09	15.98
Korea, Dem. People's Republic of	22	5	4	15	3	0.00	-80.00
Korea, Republic of	1,294	2,446	2,082	2,647	2,461	0.11	-7.03
Macao, China		6	3		1	0.00	
Mongolia	4	71	84	59	87	0.00	47.46
South-East Asia	**2,447**	**3,345**	**2,763**	**2,898**	**2,539**	**0.11**	**-12.39**
Brunei Darussalam	8	14	6	9	4	0.00	-55.56
Myanmar	17	15	24	39	13	0.00	-66.67
Cambodia	1	15	14		7	0.00	

AZERBAIJAN

2. Arrivals of non-resident visitors at national borders, by country of residence

	2007	2008	2009	2010	2011	Market share 11	% Change 11-10
Indonesia	282	378	314	353	440	0.02	24.65
Lao People's Democratic Republic	3			2	8	0.00	300.00
Malaysia	538	802	603	550	402	0.02	-26.91
Philippines	906	1,505	1,216	1,153	1,003	0.04	-13.01
Singapore	317	254	246	316	203	0.01	-35.76
Viet Nam	138	53	95	178	252	0.01	41.57
Thailand	237	309	245	298	207	0.01	-30.54
Australasia	**1,003**	**1,656**	**1,390**	**1,419**	**1,485**	**0.07**	**4.65**
Australia	769	1,276	1,109	1,122	1,129	0.05	0.62
New Zealand	234	380	281	297	356	0.02	19.87
Melanesia	**1**	**2**	**1**		**1**	**0.00**	
Solomon Islands		1					
Fiji	1	1	1		1	0.00	
Micronesia		**4**	**2**	**1**	**1**	**0.00**	
Kiribati		2		1			
Palau		2	2		1	0.00	
Polynesia		**3**	**3**	**7**	**6**	**0.00**	**-14.29**
Tuvalu		2	2	4	4	0.00	
Samoa		1	1	3	2	0.00	-33.33
EUROPE	**1,104,267**	**1,541,306**	**1,454,046**	**1,568,063**	**1,786,808**	**79.80**	**13.95**
Central/Eastern Europe	**955,843**	**1,313,235**	**1,205,273**	**1,282,747**	**1,470,964**	**65.69**	**14.67**
Bulgaria	552	1,193	1,351	1,638	1,984	0.09	21.12
Belarus	2,011	4,660	5,308	5,479	5,724	0.26	4.47
Czech Republic	459	784	948	1,013	1,025	0.05	1.18
Estonia	409	794	606	566	559	0.02	-1.24
Georgia	403,677	607,875	529,613	491,942	573,063	25.59	16.49
Hungary	358	510	597	737	910	0.04	23.47
Kazakhstan	9,662	15,335	16,048	19,209	28,225	1.26	46.94
Kyrgyzstan	928	1,850	1,921	2,279	2,337	0.10	2.54
Latvia	786	1,101	1,281	1,295	1,536	0.07	18.61
Lithuania	426	1,063	1,133	1,372	1,557	0.07	13.48
Republic of Moldova	956	1,705	4,289	3,645	3,753	0.17	2.96
Poland	1,233	1,830	1,699	2,455	2,224	0.10	-9.41
Romania	3,149	885	1,039	1,296	1,417	0.06	9.34
Russian Federation	497,876	630,860	598,894	701,110	786,684	35.13	12.21
Slovakia	177	405	511	518	445	0.02	-14.09
Tajikistan	350	703	675	742	1,009	0.05	35.98
Turkmenistan	4,380	5,155	3,687	4,072	3,969	0.18	-2.53
Ukraine	22,388	28,420	28,606	31,500	40,030	1.79	27.08
Uzbekistan	6,066	8,107	7,067	11,879	14,513	0.65	22.17
Northern Europe	**23,432**	**35,604**	**31,508**	**30,488**	**30,666**	**1.37**	**0.58**
Denmark	560	682	688	745	870	0.04	16.78
Finland	399	973	1,098	1,041	699	0.03	-32.85
Iceland	748	64	219	170	384	0.02	125.88
Ireland	602	838	757	961	919	0.04	-4.37
Norway	1,163	2,300	1,921	2,054	1,874	0.08	-8.76
Sweden	1,106	1,385	1,126	1,357	1,274	0.06	-6.12
United Kingdom	18,854	29,362	25,699	24,160	24,646	1.10	2.01
Southern Europe	**3,779**	**8,885**	**9,851**	**10,025**	**10,138**	**0.45**	**1.13**
Albania	84	116	159	136	177	0.01	30.15
Andorra		2	1	6	5	0.00	-16.67
Bosnia and Herzegovina	70	901	1,301	276	179	0.01	-35.14
Croatia	276	519	415	497	730	0.03	46.88
Greece	325	680	736	729	832	0.04	14.13
Holy See	5	9	14	17	13	0.00	-23.53
Italy	1,654	3,762	4,066	4,732	4,857	0.22	2.64

AZERBAIJAN

2. Arrivals of non-resident visitors at national borders, by country of residence

	2007	2008	2009	2010	2011	Market share 11	% Change 11-10
Malta	26	37	30	61	68	0.00	11.48
Portugal	477	867	976	948	414	0.02	-56.33
San Marino		1	3	1	2	0.00	100.00
Serbia				655	907	0.04	38.47
Slovenia	227	247	254	237	265	0.01	11.81
Spain	367	697	936	1,074	1,388	0.06	29.24
TFYR of Macedonia	40	254	175	292	221	0.01	-24.32
Other countries of Southern Europe	228	793	785	364	80	0.00	-78.02
Western Europe	**15,756**	**19,341**	**23,431**	**23,781**	**26,616**	**1.19**	**11.92**
Austria	767	1,392	1,801	2,513	3,021	0.13	20.21
Belgium	2,104	1,980	2,389	2,233	2,299	0.10	2.96
France	2,911	3,833	3,994	4,128	4,799	0.21	16.25
Germany	6,909	8,740	10,695	10,602	11,927	0.53	12.50
Liechtenstein		39	1	3	4	0.00	33.33
Luxembourg	906	154	527	378	316	0.01	-16.40
Monaco		1		8	5	0.00	-37.50
Netherlands	1,326	2,180	2,595	2,689	2,999	0.13	11.53
Switzerland	833	1,022	1,429	1,227	1,246	0.06	1.55
East Mediterranean Europe	**105,457**	**164,241**	**183,983**	**221,022**	**248,424**	**11.09**	**12.40**
Cyprus	44	181	159	82	147	0.01	79.27
Israel	3,876	6,233	6,516	6,346	5,671	0.25	-10.64
Turkey	101,537	157,827	177,308	214,594	242,606	10.83	13.05
MIDDLE EAST	**1,854**	**3,716**	**3,095**	**3,581**	**3,932**	**0.18**	**9.80**
Bahrain	28	78	80	87	97	0.00	11.49
Palestine	21	34	42	25	68	0.00	172.00
Iraq	330	677	476	549	679	0.03	23.68
Jordan	191	576	299	392	379	0.02	-3.32
Kuwait	95	158	149	322	324	0.01	0.62
Lebanon	185	239	282	270	308	0.01	14.07
Libya	52	45	38	36	27	0.00	-25.00
Oman	11	48	67	63	26	0.00	-58.73
Qatar	12	89	131	83	123	0.01	48.19
Saudi Arabia	257	416	290	312	284	0.01	-8.97
Syrian Arab Republic	243	375	492	390	426	0.02	9.23
United Arab Emirates	154	346	270	412	469	0.02	13.83
Egypt	219	541	407	559	663	0.03	18.60
Yemen	56	94	72	81	59	0.00	-27.16
SOUTH ASIA	**205,242**	**316,514**	**339,949**	**356,590**	**414,045**	**18.49**	**16.11**
Afghanistan	372	443	303	194	270	0.01	39.18
Bangladesh	116	294	453	576	439	0.02	-23.78
Bhutan		2			3	0.00	
Sri Lanka	81	102	86	96	215	0.01	123.96
India	2,110	4,236	3,721	3,755	3,715	0.17	-1.07
Iran, Islamic Republic of	201,109	308,650	329,913	349,960	407,576	18.20	16.46
Maldives		1	5	4	5	0.00	25.00
Nepal	8	48	52	56	79	0.00	41.07
Pakistan	1,446	2,738	5,416	1,949	1,743	0.08	-10.57
NOT SPECIFIED	**1,091**	**2,251**	**2,261**	**2,097**	**1,951**	**0.09**	**-6.96**
Other countries of the World	1,091	2,251	2,261	2,097	1,951	0.09	-6.96

AZERBAIJAN

3. Arrivals of non-resident tourists in hotels and similar establishments, by country of residence

	2007	2008	2009	2010	2011	Market share 11	% Change 11-10
TOTAL	153,053	224,112	208,868	212,356	257,987	100.00	21.49
AMERICAS	10,352	13,357	11,622	15,013	7,947	3.08	-47.07
North America	10,352	13,357	11,622	15,013	7,947	3.08	-47.07
Canada	328	570	272	548	630	0.24	14.96
United States of America	10,024	12,787	11,350	14,465	7,317	2.84	-49.42
EAST ASIA AND THE PACIFIC	9,758	6,762	5,087	6,913	5,669	2.20	-18.00
North-East Asia	9,350	5,406	4,499	6,167	5,669	2.20	-8.08
China	7,518	4,285	3,545	5,037	3,761	1.46	-25.33
Japan	1,203	696	950	782	777	0.30	-0.64
Korea, Dem. People's Republic of	629	425	4	348	1,131	0.44	225.00
South-East Asia	274	951	275	431			
Malaysia	154	597	56	269			
Philippines	120	354	219	162			
Australasia	134	405	313	315			
Australia	134	405	313	315			
EUROPE	56,469	141,327	138,817	139,139	168,791	65.43	21.31
Central/Eastern Europe	24,344	50,542	39,420	43,052	56,111	21.75	30.33
Belarus	930	510	523	1,181	1,449	0.56	22.69
Georgia	3,091	7,677	8,210	2,435	3,701	1.43	51.99
Kazakhstan	1,085	2,366	1,841	2,070	3,856	1.49	86.28
Latvia	103	63	108	394	424	0.16	7.61
Poland	638	444	80	500	946	0.37	89.20
Romania	537	120	67	195	495	0.19	153.85
Russian Federation	14,106	34,253	23,261	29,570	36,503	14.15	23.45
Ukraine	3,854	5,109	5,330	6,707	8,737	3.39	30.27
Northern Europe	6,619	55,342	26,823	17,077	29,904	11.59	75.11
Finland	336	589	123	227	225	0.09	-0.88
Norway	1,071	2,660	1,451	2,209	3,285	1.27	48.71
Sweden	391	1,179	522	448	880	0.34	96.43
United Kingdom	4,821	50,914	24,727	14,193	25,514	9.89	79.76
Southern Europe	697	2,514	4,534	4,914	5,248	2.03	6.80
Greece	52	166	87	161			
Italy	605	1,695	4,021	4,005	3,706	1.44	-7.47
Spain	40	653	426	748	1,542	0.60	106.15
Western Europe	6,640	9,121	11,729	12,508	16,229	6.29	29.75
Austria	109	726	1,195	912			
Belgium	340	626	269	840	651	0.25	-22.50
France	2,563	2,759	3,512	3,696	4,767	1.85	28.98
Germany	3,393	3,842	5,903	6,115	9,903	3.84	61.95
Netherlands	235	1,168	850	945	908	0.35	-3.92
East Mediterranean Europe	18,169	23,808	56,311	61,588	61,299	23.76	-0.47
Israel	618	1,969	2,935	3,305	1,431	0.55	-56.70
Turkey	17,551	21,839	53,376	58,283	59,868	23.21	2.72
MIDDLE EAST	437	57	2	387			
United Arab Emirates	437	57	2	387			
SOUTH ASIA	11,717	12,073	31,255	19,423	23,158	8.98	19.23
India	490	560	1,162	485	743	0.29	53.20
Iran, Islamic Republic of	10,736	10,657	29,798	18,775	21,779	8.44	16.00
Pakistan	491	856	295	163	636	0.25	290.18
NOT SPECIFIED	64,320	50,536	22,085	31,481	52,422	20.32	66.52
Other countries of the World	64,320	50,536	22,085	31,481	52,422	20.32	66.52

AZERBAIJAN

5. Overnight stays of non-resident tourists in hotels and similar establishments, by country of residence

	2007	2008	2009	2010	2011	Market share 11	% Change 11-10
TOTAL	573,090	636,678	561,343	568,056	673,811	100.00	18.62
AMERICAS	27,207	37,316	25,071	25,627	15,560	2.31	-39.28
North America	27,207	37,316	25,071	25,627	15,560	2.31	-39.28
Canada	1,328	2,020	458	937	1,148	0.17	22.52
United States of America	25,879	35,296	24,613	24,690	14,412	2.14	-41.63
EAST ASIA AND THE PACIFIC	55,133	11,677	12,013	16,198	11,156	1.66	-31.13
North-East Asia	35,826	7,907	10,388	12,457	11,156	1.66	-10.44
China	32,747	5,668	8,424	10,205	6,694	0.99	-34.40
Japan	2,048	1,211	1,952	1,874	2,391	0.35	27.59
Korea, Dem. People's Republic of	1,031	1,028	12	378	2,071	0.31	447.88
South-East Asia	10,640	2,750	1,172	3,263			
Malaysia	4,956	336	104	2,833			
Philippines	5,684	2,414	1,068	430			
Australasia	8,667	1,020	453	478			
Australia	8,667	1,020	453	478			
EUROPE	160,546	249,279	292,247	421,195	489,685	72.67	16.26
Central/Eastern Europe	70,260	74,242	87,195	94,923	133,824	19.86	40.98
Georgia	6,700	10,773	13,301	4,748	6,465	0.96	36.16
Kazakhstan	5,411	4,699	8,726	5,787	12,719	1.89	119.79
Latvia	299	258	380	745	597	0.09	-19.87
Poland	1,222	1,886	794	763	1,685	0.25	120.84
Romania	3,691	403	302	786	605	0.09	-23.03
Russian Federation	42,913	43,660	51,411	66,894	84,323	12.51	26.05
Ukraine	10,024	12,563	12,281	15,200	27,430	4.07	80.46
Northern Europe	31,959	78,396	69,477	43,292	72,962	10.83	68.53
Finland	723	1,180	781	374	270	0.04	-27.81
Norway	2,125	6,055	2,649	2,624	3,736	0.55	42.38
Sweden	1,788	2,085	686	588	2,144	0.32	264.63
United Kingdom	27,323	69,076	65,361	39,706	66,812	9.92	68.27
Southern Europe	1,655	6,572	6,683	8,310	9,172	1.36	10.37
Greece	187	283	287	332			
Italy	1,328	5,580	5,770	6,639	6,798	1.01	2.39
Spain	140	709	626	1,339	2,374	0.35	77.30
Western Europe	14,924	21,832	24,145	21,645	25,200	3.74	16.42
Austria	238	1,019	1,499	1,508			
Belgium	585	2,910	479	1,084	800	0.12	-26.20
France	4,908	6,674	7,253	5,808	6,218	0.92	7.06
Germany	8,448	9,170	12,496	11,959	16,906	2.51	41.37
Netherlands	745	2,059	2,418	1,286	1,276	0.19	-0.78
East Mediterranean Europe	41,748	68,237	104,747	253,025	248,527	36.88	-1.78
Israel	1,078	2,545	3,622	4,133	1,969	0.29	-52.36
Turkey	40,670	65,692	101,125	248,892	246,558	36.59	-0.94
MIDDLE EAST	941	151	22	535			
United Arab Emirates	941	151	22	535			
SOUTH ASIA	26,629	23,843	52,079	48,079	49,322	7.32	2.59
India	4,585	1,153	1,767	1,289	2,960	0.44	129.64
Iran, Islamic Republic of	21,450	20,922	49,733	46,509	44,819	6.65	-3.63
Pakistan	594	1,768	579	281	1,543	0.23	449.11
NOT SPECIFIED	302,634	314,412	179,911	56,422	108,088	16.04	91.57
Other countries of the World	302,634	314,412	179,911	56,422	108,088	16.04	91.57

BAHAMAS

1. Arrivals of non-resident tourists at national borders, by country of residence

	2007	2008	2009	2010	2011	Market share 11	% Change 11-10
TOTAL	1,527,728	1,463,006	1,327,007	1,370,140	1,346,372	100.00	-1.73
AFRICA	1,812	1,785	1,778	1,654	1,733	0.13	4.78
East Africa	122	142	179	145	136	0.01	-6.21
Burundi	2		1	1			
Comoros	1		2				
Ethiopia	2	8	14	16	14	0.00	-12.50
Eritrea	1		3	2			
Djibouti			1	1			
Kenya	33	25	19	36	27	0.00	-25.00
Madagascar	2	2	11	1	1	0.00	
Malawi	6	3	6	2	1	0.00	-50.00
Mauritius	11	14	25	12	20	0.00	66.67
Mozambique	7	7	9	3	4	0.00	33.33
Rwanda	1	18	3	2			
Seychelles	3	8	8	8	4	0.00	-50.00
Somalia			2				
Zimbabwe	18	15	13	25	26	0.00	4.00
Uganda	9	11	22	21	8	0.00	-61.90
United Republic of Tanzania	12	15	23	8	9	0.00	12.50
Zambia	14	16	17	7	22	0.00	214.29
Central Africa	26	42	57	35	88	0.01	151.43
Angola	9	10	16	6	31	0.00	416.67
Cameroon	12	9	17	1	6	0.00	500.00
Central African Republic		1	2		2	0.00	
Chad	1	2	7	13	15	0.00	15.38
Congo	4	10	13	7	9	0.00	28.57
Equatorial Guinea					13	0.00	
Gabon		10	2	8	12	0.00	50.00
North Africa	80	86	138	82	76	0.01	-7.32
Algeria	4	22	1	2	10	0.00	400.00
Morocco	60	51	58	68	42	0.00	-38.24
Sudan	2	1	5		2	0.00	
Tunisia	14	12	74	12	22	0.00	83.33
Southern Africa	1,418	1,250	1,175	1,226	1,222	0.09	-0.33
Botswana	12	9	23	36	24	0.00	-33.33
Lesotho		1	7	8	1	0.00	-87.50
Namibia	17	10	21	16	11	0.00	-31.25
South Africa	1,356	1,213	1,090	1,127	1,169	0.09	3.73
Swaziland	33	17	34	39	17	0.00	-56.41
West Africa	166	265	229	166	211	0.02	27.11
Cape Verde	1	1	3	1	7	0.00	600.00
Benin		2	1				
Gambia	4	2	8	1	1	0.00	
Ghana	30	33	38	27	30	0.00	11.11
Guinea	2	19	10	3	7	0.00	133.33
Côte d'Ivoire	11	12	6	8	18	0.00	125.00
Liberia	1		3	1	2	0.00	100.00
Mali		1	1	5	1	0.00	-80.00
Mauritania		2	3	2	1	0.00	-50.00
Niger				4	1	0.00	
Nigeria	88	173	128	95	121	0.01	27.37
Senegal	21	8	15	18	12	0.00	-33.33
Sierra Leone	5	10	6	3	6	0.00	100.00
Togo	3	2	1	1			
Burkina Faso			2	1	4	0.00	300.00
AMERICAS	1,404,001	1,331,022	1,213,309	1,255,707	1,230,533	91.40	-2.00

BAHAMAS

1. Arrivals of non-resident tourists at national borders, by country of residence

	2007	2008	2009	2010	2011	Market share 11	% Change 11-10
Caribbean	**22,111**	**22,066**	**18,463**	**18,048**	**17,458**	**1.30**	**-3.27**
Antigua and Barbuda	129	157	122	131	169	0.01	29.01
Barbados	897	1,129	852	1,052	943	0.07	-10.36
Bermuda	925	958	1,009	857	805	0.06	-6.07
British Virgin Islands	100	155	99	119	91	0.01	-23.53
Cayman Islands	1,857	2,279	1,964	1,699	1,458	0.11	-14.18
Cuba	305	252	365	365	455	0.03	24.66
Dominica	87	137	166	117	138	0.01	17.95
Dominican Republic	456	547	578	493	540	0.04	9.53
Grenada	70	100	76	55	74	0.01	34.55
Haiti	3,999	3,243	1,318	556	491	0.04	-11.69
Jamaica	7,830	6,966	6,207	6,831	6,888	0.51	0.83
Martinique	29	31	57	41	50	0.00	21.95
Montserrat	9	13	19	16	9	0.00	-43.75
Netherlands Antilles	32	53	23	33	22	0.00	-33.33
Aruba	75	94	106	78	117	0.01	50.00
Curaçao	116	164	137	153	164	0.01	7.19
Puerto Rico	251	227	226	252	270	0.02	7.14
Sint Eustatius	7	5	4	4	6	0.00	50.00
Saint Kitts and Nevis	82	124	144	127	100	0.01	-21.26
Anguilla	61	58	29	50	23	0.00	-54.00
Saint Lucia	204	238	197	199	199	0.01	
Sint Maarten	88	145	75	68	114	0.01	67.65
Saint Vincent and the Grenadines	105	88	74	72	85	0.01	18.06
Trinidad and Tobago	1,618	1,752	1,453	1,693	1,759	0.13	3.90
Turks and Caicos Islands	2,703	3,031	3,080	2,946	2,433	0.18	-17.41
United States Virgin Islands	27	32	30	22	16	0.00	-27.27
Other countries of the Caribbean	49	88	53	19	39	0.00	105.26
Central America	**1,895**	**1,770**	**1,987**	**1,851**	**2,819**	**0.21**	**52.30**
Belize	109	120	123	117	122	0.01	4.27
Costa Rica	526	401	372	334	490	0.04	46.71
El Salvador	167	214	257	126	209	0.02	65.87
Guatemala	344	228	312	295	356	0.03	20.68
Honduras	215	179	194	196	254	0.02	29.59
Nicaragua	82	82	90	97	79	0.01	-18.56
Panama	452	546	639	686	1,309	0.10	90.82
North America	**1,369,103**	**1,295,824**	**1,179,664**	**1,219,999**	**1,187,547**	**88.20**	**-2.66**
Canada	100,340	114,960	107,041	119,321	124,166	9.22	4.06
Greenland	5	3	2	3	1	0.00	-66.67
Mexico	5,078	3,590	3,895	3,524	4,698	0.35	33.31
United States of America	1,263,680	1,177,271	1,068,726	1,097,151	1,058,682	78.63	-3.51
South America	**10,892**	**11,362**	**13,195**	**15,809**	**22,709**	**1.69**	**43.65**
Argentina	1,683	2,050	2,579	3,167	4,992	0.37	57.63
Bolivia	139	83	158	113	141	0.01	24.78
Brazil	3,240	3,863	4,309	5,310	6,595	0.49	24.20
Chile	469	537	548	637	1,106	0.08	73.63
Colombia	1,147	809	1,281	1,720	4,155	0.31	141.57
Ecuador	471	544	487	529	547	0.04	3.40
Guyana	360	366	306	373	433	0.03	16.09
Paraguay	35	194	250	620	838	0.06	35.16
Peru	801	800	807	879	1,027	0.08	16.84
Suriname	55	96	87	97	88	0.01	-9.28
Uruguay	141	194	230	323	405	0.03	25.39
Venezuela	2,351	1,826	2,153	2,041	2,382	0.18	16.71
EAST ASIA AND THE PACIFIC	**6,861**	**6,902**	**6,232**	**7,143**	**6,707**	**0.50**	**-6.10**
North-East Asia	**2,452**	**2,544**	**2,081**	**2,527**	**2,045**	**0.15**	**-19.07**
China	206	265	486	384	682	0.05	77.60

BAHAMAS

1. Arrivals of non-resident tourists at national borders, by country of residence

	2007	2008	2009	2010	2011	Market share 11	% Change 11-10
Taiwan, Province of China	88	171	66	470	78	0.01	-83.40
Hong Kong, China	300	358	205	283	277	0.02	-2.12
Japan	1,563	1,424	1,018	874	776	0.06	-11.21
Korea, Dem. People's Republic of	1	1		1	2	0.00	100.00
Korea, Republic of	290	323	298	514	228	0.02	-55.64
Mongolia	4	2	8	1	2	0.00	100.00
South-East Asia	**837**	**887**	**760**	**947**	**764**	**0.06**	**-19.32**
Brunei Darussalam	6	5	2	5	2	0.00	-60.00
Myanmar	2		4	2	3	0.00	50.00
Cambodia	1	1	4	3	6	0.00	100.00
Indonesia	85	55	65	73	58	0.00	-20.55
Lao People's Democratic Republic			3				
Malaysia	78	100	59	165	99	0.01	-40.00
Philippines	281	347	315	297	232	0.02	-21.89
Singapore	246	251	201	293	280	0.02	-4.44
Viet Nam	10	10	21	25	17	0.00	-32.00
Thailand	128	118	86	84	67	0.00	-20.24
Australasia	**3,540**	**3,390**	**3,328**	**3,634**	**3,871**	**0.29**	**6.52**
Australia	2,855	2,778	2,758	3,075	3,267	0.24	6.24
New Zealand	685	612	570	559	604	0.04	8.05
Melanesia	**10**	**58**	**30**	**12**	**16**	**0.00**	**33.33**
Solomon Islands	7	45	3	2	3	0.00	50.00
Fiji	2	9	17	7	8	0.00	14.29
Vanuatu	1	2	6	1	1	0.00	
Papua New Guinea		2	4	2	4	0.00	100.00
Micronesia	**10**	**7**	**11**	**5**	**3**	**0.00**	**-40.00**
Kiribati	1		5		1	0.00	
Nauru	1	3					
Micronesia, Federated States of	8	3	4	4	2	0.00	-50.00
Marshall Islands			2	1			
Palau		1					
Polynesia	**12**	**16**	**22**	**18**	**8**	**0.00**	**-55.56**
French Polynesia	9	12	13	13	5	0.00	-61.54
Tonga	1	2	3				
Samoa	2	2	6	5	3	0.00	-40.00
EUROPE	**87,931**	**94,560**	**79,648**	**78,900**	**78,929**	**5.86**	**0.04**
Central/Eastern Europe	**1,874**	**2,359**	**2,934**	**4,156**	**4,347**	**0.32**	**4.60**
Azerbaijan	9	4	15	4	19	0.00	375.00
Armenia	1	4	11	7	3	0.00	-57.14
Bulgaria	87	81	113	166	144	0.01	-13.25
Belarus	12	13	11	15	13	0.00	-13.33
Czech Republic	181	197	303	407	330	0.02	-18.92
Estonia	45	31	120	96	85	0.01	-11.46
Georgia	18	24	19	21	21	0.00	
Hungary	212	278	289	369	334	0.02	-9.49
Kazakhstan	36	26	12	52	18	0.00	-65.38
Kyrgyzstan	1		6	8			
Latvia	25	31	55	76	59	0.00	-22.37
Lithuania	53	47	33	74	85	0.01	14.86
Republic of Moldova	8	3	5	19	7	0.00	-63.16
Poland	370	674	574	785	924	0.07	17.71
Romania	193	261	253	398	334	0.02	-16.08
Russian Federation	398	414	822	1,203	1,582	0.12	31.50
Slovakia	96	128	166	276	235	0.02	-14.86
Tajikistan	8		3				
Turkmenistan	2	1	3	4			
Ukraine	119	142	112	173	149	0.01	-13.87

BAHAMAS

1. Arrivals of non-resident tourists at national borders, by country of residence

	2007	2008	2009	2010	2011	Market share 11	% Change 11-10
Uzbekistan			9	3	5	0.00	66.67
Northern Europe	**45,882**	**41,106**	**32,057**	**28,791**	**28,679**	**2.13**	**-0.39**
Denmark	961	1,039	1,007	933	921	0.07	-1.29
Faeroe Islands	4	5	4	2	14	0.00	600.00
Finland	529	725	751	696	584	0.04	-16.09
Iceland	179	149	70	75	100	0.01	33.33
Ireland	1,427	1,501	1,184	970	638	0.05	-34.23
Norway	1,069	1,358	1,088	1,337	1,228	0.09	-8.15
Sweden	1,452	1,762	1,552	1,599	1,698	0.13	6.19
United Kingdom	40,261	34,567	26,401	23,179	23,496	1.75	1.37
Southern Europe	**11,420**	**14,341**	**12,421**	**13,899**	**13,589**	**1.01**	**-2.23**
Albania	26	4	16	10	10	0.00	
Andorra	34	25	30	20	9	0.00	-55.00
Bosnia and Herzegovina	5	4	8	18	6	0.00	-66.67
Croatia	67	98	98	124	119	0.01	-4.03
Greece	358	444	392	450	472	0.04	4.89
Italy	8,201	10,866	9,269	10,228	9,853	0.73	-3.67
Malta	59	54	55	52	77	0.01	48.08
Montenegro	1	1	5	3	6	0.00	100.00
Portugal	529	531	402	629	505	0.04	-19.71
San Marino	11	18	15	7	21	0.00	200.00
Serbia	7	69	66	61	80	0.01	31.15
Slovenia	65	89	67	99	111	0.01	12.12
Spain	2,018	2,122	1,979	2,180	2,295	0.17	5.28
TFYR of Macedonia	8	8	17	17	25	0.00	47.06
Serbia and Montenegro	31	8	2	1			
Western Europe	**27,573**	**35,570**	**31,033**	**30,747**	**31,158**	**2.31**	**1.34**
Austria	1,175	1,657	1,533	1,461	1,439	0.11	-1.51
Belgium	1,298	1,752	1,436	1,466	1,355	0.10	-7.57
France	12,081	14,423	13,667	12,495	13,190	0.98	5.56
Germany	7,244	10,526	8,236	8,632	7,973	0.59	-7.63
Liechtenstein	27	30	40	22	54	0.00	145.45
Luxembourg	168	183	202	207	178	0.01	-14.01
Monaco	174	173	184	133	154	0.01	15.79
Netherlands	1,815	2,657	1,924	2,075	1,835	0.14	-11.57
Switzerland	3,591	4,169	3,811	4,256	4,980	0.37	17.01
East Mediterranean Europe	**1,182**	**1,184**	**1,203**	**1,307**	**1,153**	**0.09**	**-11.78**
Cyprus	114	115	109	93	114	0.01	22.58
Israel	709	725	774	742	684	0.05	-7.82
Turkey	359	344	320	472	355	0.03	-24.79
Other Europe					3	0.00	
Other countries of Europe					3	0.00	
MIDDLE EAST	**644**	**670**	**708**	**593**	**708**	**0.05**	**19.39**
Bahrain	35	52	31	52	22	0.00	-57.69
Palestine		1	2	2			
Iraq		1	3	4			
Jordan	13	27	28	15	16	0.00	6.67
Kuwait	38	55	77	65	93	0.01	43.08
Lebanon	55	43	28	22	37	0.00	68.18
Libya	3			2			
Oman	6	7	13	8	9	0.00	12.50
Qatar	27	44	38	25	31	0.00	24.00
Saudi Arabia	149	156	155	113	214	0.02	89.38
Syrian Arab Republic	2	9	10	7	6	0.00	-14.29
United Arab Emirates	255	207	249	202	211	0.02	4.46
Egypt	61	66	74	76	66	0.00	-13.16
Yemen		2			3	0.00	

BAHAMAS

1. Arrivals of non-resident tourists at national borders, by country of residence

	2007	2008	2009	2010	2011	Market share 11	% Change 11-10
SOUTH ASIA	**580**	**696**	**526**	**666**	**494**	**0.04**	**-25.83**
Afghanistan	3		5	2	2	0.00	
Bangladesh	12	12	6	18	15	0.00	-16.67
Bhutan		1	3	2	1	0.00	-50.00
Sri Lanka	19	31	39	39	41	0.00	5.13
India	506	605	435	561	398	0.03	-29.06
Iran, Islamic Republic of	5	6	7	9	6	0.00	-33.33
Maldives	4	1	3		1	0.00	
Nepal	8	15	16	15	13	0.00	-13.33
Pakistan	23	25	12	20	17	0.00	-15.00
NOT SPECIFIED	**25,899**	**27,371**	**24,806**	**25,477**	**27,268**	**2.03**	**7.03**
Other countries of the World	25,899	27,371	24,806	25,477	27,268	2.03	7.03

BAHAMAS

6. Overnight stays of non-resident tourists in all types of accommodation establishments, by country of residence

		2007	2008	2009	2010	2011	Market share 11	% Change 11-10
TOTAL	(*)	10,054,187	9,678,609	9,039,234	9,127,653	9,123,171	100.00	-0.05
AFRICA		21,979	23,455	21,000	22,515	22,984	0.25	2.08
East Africa		1,317	1,674	2,124	1,444	1,178	0.01	-18.42
Burundi		6		4	30			
Comoros		8		9				
Ethiopia		20	46	114	122	147	0.00	20.49
Eritrea		30		12	16			
Djibouti				5	3			
Kenya		297	226	123	362	145	0.00	-59.94
Madagascar		5	33	54	3	7	0.00	133.33
Malawi		34	16	36	10	5	0.00	-50.00
Mauritius		208	502	652	124	332	0.00	167.74
Mozambique		82	98	31	15	22	0.00	46.67
Rwanda		8	103	12	6			
Seychelles		98	64	104	87	45	0.00	-48.28
Somalia				7				
Zimbabwe		246	176	94	184	195	0.00	5.98
Uganda		83	119	397	317	71	0.00	-77.60
United Republic of Tanzania		73	54	286	128	71	0.00	-44.53
Zambia		119	237	184	37	138	0.00	272.97
Central Africa		262	258	277	213	580	0.01	172.30
Angola		148	70	44	44	105	0.00	138.64
Cameroon		67	69	81	5	193	0.00	3760.00
Central African Republic			2	10		15	0.00	
Chad		3	16	34	91	111	0.00	21.98
Congo		44	71	96	20	28	0.00	40.00
Equatorial Guinea						56	0.00	
Gabon			30	12	53	72	0.00	35.85
North Africa		710	484	817	513	671	0.01	30.80
Algeria		13	39	2	4	132	0.00	3200.00
Morocco		541	330	297	469	335	0.00	-28.57
Sudan		37	4	21		6	0.00	
Tunisia		119	111	497	40	198	0.00	395.00
Southern Africa		18,365	19,471	16,192	19,163	18,327	0.20	-4.36
Botswana		131	115	530	237	286	0.00	20.68
Lesotho			5	39	29	7	0.00	-75.86
Namibia		147	118	185	122	66	0.00	-45.90
South Africa		17,783	19,041	15,183	18,587	17,706	0.19	-4.74
Swaziland		304	192	255	188	262	0.00	39.36
West Africa		1,325	1,568	1,590	1,182	2,228	0.02	88.49
Cape Verde		2	2	34	14	102	0.00	628.57
Benin			8	4				
Gambia		18	7	43	4	2	0.00	-50.00
Ghana		207	166	421	268	688	0.01	156.72
Guinea		6	58	67	13	39	0.00	200.00
Côte d'Ivoire		133	43	29	46	95	0.00	106.52
Liberia		5		13	2	14	0.00	600.00
Mali			2	4	25	7	0.00	-72.00
Mauritania			4	37	4	28	0.00	600.00
Niger				22		3	0.00	
Nigeria		656	1,144	804	631	1,115	0.01	76.70
Senegal		203	59	70	127	89	0.00	-29.92
Sierra Leone		86	67	31	21	28	0.00	33.33
Togo		9	8	3	2			
Burkina Faso				8	25	18	0.00	-28.00
AMERICAS		8,807,700	8,409,420	7,900,946	8,027,215	8,011,185	87.81	-0.20

BAHAMAS

6. Overnight stays of non-resident tourists in all types of accommodation establishments, by country of residence

	2007	2008	2009	2010	2011	Market share 11	% Change 11-10
Caribbean	**202,979**	**190,161**	**158,798**	**152,196**	**152,018**	**1.67**	**-0.12**
Antigua and Barbuda	827	971	1,283	865	1,393	0.02	61.04
Barbados	5,662	6,757	4,956	6,811	5,620	0.06	-17.49
Bermuda	6,024	7,902	8,069	6,170	5,306	0.06	-14.00
British Virgin Islands	1,850	919	1,123	1,288	765	0.01	-40.61
Cayman Islands	8,819	9,093	8,774	8,244	7,005	0.08	-15.03
Cuba	6,172	5,921	5,695	6,109	7,572	0.08	23.95
Dominica	710	1,226	1,063	657	1,291	0.01	96.50
Dominican Republic	3,014	2,964	4,958	3,078	3,519	0.04	14.33
Grenada	529	557	565	386	728	0.01	88.60
Haiti	53,438	49,281	20,919	7,817	5,670	0.06	-27.47
Jamaica	83,734	70,133	66,985	75,673	79,694	0.87	5.31
Martinique	261	133	288	212	370	0.00	74.53
Montserrat	120	95	153	179	64	0.00	-64.25
Netherlands Antilles	159	263	194	166	303	0.00	82.53
Aruba	427	560	586	404	940	0.01	132.67
Curaçao	517	794	798	837	798	0.01	-4.66
Puerto Rico	1,183	1,149	982	1,207	1,263	0.01	4.64
Sint Eustatius	38	23	11	23	55	0.00	139.13
Saint Kitts and Nevis	579	692	981	976	903	0.01	-7.48
Anguilla	432	264	171	252	106	0.00	-57.94
Saint Lucia	1,440	1,778	1,534	1,771	1,845	0.02	4.18
Sint Maarten	787	962	562	374	697	0.01	86.36
Saint Vincent and the Grenadines	999	946	973	606	847	0.01	39.77
Trinidad and Tobago	11,454	12,304	10,684	12,101	11,750	0.13	-2.90
Turks and Caicos Islands	13,419	13,916	15,758	15,725	12,887	0.14	-18.05
United States Virgin Islands	192	167	262	157	170	0.00	8.28
Other countries of the Caribbean	193	391	471	108	457	0.01	323.15
Central America	**13,143**	**11,322**	**13,297**	**14,136**	**19,125**	**0.21**	**35.29**
Belize	890	825	759	741	891	0.01	20.24
Costa Rica	4,256	3,343	2,373	2,983	3,058	0.03	2.51
El Salvador	704	1,145	2,123	1,247	1,726	0.02	38.41
Guatemala	2,015	1,610	1,928	2,509	2,921	0.03	16.42
Honduras	1,422	1,014	1,336	1,592	2,466	0.03	54.90
Nicaragua	466	378	761	489	401	0.00	-18.00
Panama	3,390	3,007	4,017	4,575	7,662	0.08	67.48
North America	**8,527,385**	**8,140,131**	**7,650,947**	**7,770,160**	**7,706,085**	**84.47**	**-0.82**
Canada	855,030	913,157	897,050	957,193	980,819	10.75	2.47
Greenland	45	42	6	27	4	0.00	-85.19
Mexico	31,143	21,594	26,254	21,607	27,329	0.30	26.48
United States of America	7,641,167	7,205,338	6,727,637	6,791,333	6,697,933	73.42	-1.38
South America	**64,193**	**67,806**	**77,904**	**90,723**	**133,957**	**1.47**	**47.65**
Argentina	9,721	11,860	14,351	17,534	30,298	0.33	72.80
Bolivia	695	392	793	637	866	0.01	35.95
Brazil	18,225	20,256	22,125	27,723	36,658	0.40	32.23
Chile	2,763	3,027	3,787	3,683	7,262	0.08	97.18
Colombia	7,169	5,501	8,547	10,242	23,209	0.25	126.61
Ecuador	2,618	3,264	3,265	3,589	3,819	0.04	6.41
Guyana	5,220	5,217	4,904	4,953	5,664	0.06	14.35
Paraguay	171	667	860	2,082	2,690	0.03	29.20
Peru	4,576	4,382	4,716	6,441	7,049	0.08	9.44
Suriname	265	468	1,374	452	491	0.01	8.63
Uruguay	1,252	3,233	1,805	2,596	3,173	0.03	22.23
Venezuela	11,518	9,539	11,377	10,791	12,778	0.14	18.41
EAST ASIA AND THE PACIFIC	**69,266**	**66,453**	**67,705**	**68,944**	**67,681**	**0.74**	**-1.83**
North-East Asia	**14,119**	**13,571**	**11,890**	**13,645**	**11,882**	**0.13**	**-12.92**
China	1,245	1,457	3,207	2,881	4,364	0.05	51.48

BAHAMAS

6. Overnight stays of non-resident tourists in all types of accommodation establishments, by country of residence

	2007	2008	2009	2010	2011	Market share 11	% Change 11-10
Taiwan, Province of China	369	683	354	2,199	361	0.00	-83.58
Hong Kong, China	3,142	2,636	1,045	1,698	1,606	0.02	-5.42
Japan	8,115	7,135	5,895	4,406	4,165	0.05	-5.47
Korea, Dem. People's Republic of	7	6		6	38	0.00	533.33
Korea, Republic of	1,198	1,649	1,354	2,448	1,256	0.01	-48.69
Mongolia	43	5	35	7	92	0.00	1214.29
South-East Asia	**8,831**	**9,304**	**7,965**	**10,822**	**8,705**	**0.10**	**-19.56**
Brunei Darussalam	29	18	8	17	14	0.00	-17.65
Myanmar	28		13	5	14	0.00	180.00
Cambodia	2	3	14	21	23	0.00	9.52
Indonesia	871	600	568	485	321	0.00	-33.81
Lao People's Democratic Republic			12				
Malaysia	804	1,134	414	975	731	0.01	-25.03
Philippines	4,883	4,803	4,514	6,102	3,899	0.04	-36.10
Singapore	1,218	1,790	1,138	2,261	2,626	0.03	16.14
Viet Nam	34	40	208	219	180	0.00	-17.81
Thailand	962	916	1,076	737	897	0.01	21.71
Australasia	**46,129**	**43,058**	**47,292**	**44,069**	**46,933**	**0.51**	**6.50**
Australia	34,883	32,120	36,009	33,712	35,512	0.39	5.34
New Zealand	11,246	10,938	11,283	10,357	11,421	0.13	10.27
Melanesia	**59**	**269**	**259**	**138**	**55**	**0.00**	**-60.14**
Solomon Islands	33	162	15	22	3	0.00	-86.36
Fiji	11	55	198	67	42	0.00	-37.31
Vanuatu	15	24	24	16	2	0.00	-87.50
Papua New Guinea		28	22	33	8	0.00	-75.76
Micronesia	**37**	**94**	**161**	**116**	**15**	**0.00**	**-87.07**
Kiribati			26		5	0.00	
Nauru	2	6					
Micronesia, Federated States of	35	74	15	26	10	0.00	-61.54
Marshall Islands			120	90			
Palau		14					
Polynesia	**91**	**157**	**138**	**154**	**91**	**0.00**	**-40.91**
French Polynesia	69	120	100	113	74	0.00	-34.51
Tonga	14	24	12				
Samoa	8	13	26	41	17	0.00	-58.54
EUROPE	**890,049**	**911,736**	**811,786**	**776,920**	**773,421**	**8.48**	**-0.45**
Central/Eastern Europe	**17,503**	**20,151**	**27,387**	**33,442**	**38,564**	**0.42**	**15.32**
Azerbaijan	176	16	85	13	140	0.00	976.92
Armenia	2	68	83	28	7	0.00	-75.00
Bulgaria	1,050	828	1,168	1,813	1,530	0.02	-15.61
Belarus	83	151	60	98	142	0.00	44.90
Czech Republic	1,848	2,018	2,535	2,295	2,737	0.03	19.26
Estonia	278	361	1,504	908	1,599	0.02	76.10
Georgia	105	176	129	138	222	0.00	60.87
Hungary	1,796	2,077	1,949	2,525	3,090	0.03	22.38
Kazakhstan	283	188	189	377	144	0.00	-61.80
Kyrgyzstan	2		199	42			
Latvia	253	363	385	439	442	0.00	0.68
Lithuania	680	509	339	562	672	0.01	19.57
Republic of Moldova	65	28	20	119	31	0.00	-73.95
Poland	3,474	5,567	5,823	7,226	8,257	0.09	14.27
Romania	1,958	2,571	2,566	3,863	3,763	0.04	-2.59
Russian Federation	3,300	3,273	6,756	8,805	12,330	0.14	40.03
Slovakia	810	837	1,766	2,250	1,705	0.02	-24.22
Tajikistan	98		15				
Turkmenistan	5	4	12	14			
Ukraine	1,237	1,116	1,768	1,911	1,735	0.02	-9.21

BAHAMAS

6. Overnight stays of non-resident tourists in all types of accommodation establishments, by country of residence

	2007	2008	2009	2010	2011	Market share 11	% Change 11-10
Uzbekistan			36	16	18	0.00	12.50
Northern Europe	**504,922**	**457,128**	**381,216**	**342,081**	**337,559**	**3.70**	**-1.32**
Denmark	8,452	9,050	10,017	8,099	8,836	0.10	9.10
Faeroe Islands	24	38	13	28	230	0.00	721.43
Finland	4,764	4,869	5,439	4,534	4,965	0.05	9.51
Iceland	2,161	2,094	1,474	1,114	1,503	0.02	34.92
Ireland	12,837	12,980	12,679	9,641	7,619	0.08	-20.97
Norway	9,391	11,055	9,685	12,561	11,939	0.13	-4.95
Sweden	13,344	14,853	15,051	14,620	14,772	0.16	1.04
United Kingdom	453,949	402,189	326,858	291,484	287,695	3.15	-1.30
Southern Europe	**91,601**	**108,907**	**98,237**	**102,583**	**103,360**	**1.13**	**0.76**
Albania	133	26	192	63	71	0.00	12.70
Andorra	208	345	708	301	59	0.00	-80.40
Bosnia and Herzegovina	32	34	46	105	65	0.00	-38.10
Croatia	739	814	969	1,051	1,387	0.02	31.97
Greece	3,262	3,210	2,789	3,467	3,860	0.04	11.34
Italy	66,706	82,947	72,381	73,854	73,297	0.80	-0.75
Malta	615	395	487	541	643	0.01	18.85
Montenegro	5	3	95	33	28	0.00	-15.15
Portugal	4,488	3,827	3,375	5,524	4,608	0.05	-16.58
San Marino	75	76	66	42	189	0.00	350.00
Serbia	61	794	802	1,042	1,425	0.02	36.76
Slovenia	447	701	438	788	813	0.01	3.17
Spain	14,504	15,525	15,745	15,439	16,573	0.18	7.35
TFYR of Macedonia	17	52	109	319	342	0.00	7.21
Serbia and Montenegro	309	158	35	14			
Western Europe	**268,549**	**318,315**	**296,150**	**289,175**	**285,620**	**3.13**	**-1.23**
Austria	12,495	15,682	17,033	15,378	14,033	0.15	-8.75
Belgium	10,763	14,355	12,957	13,883	13,482	0.15	-2.89
France	108,179	121,517	118,382	106,397	110,396	1.21	3.76
Germany	80,928	103,234	90,467	90,165	81,903	0.90	-9.16
Liechtenstein	264	240	230	251	412	0.00	64.14
Luxembourg	1,569	1,708	1,869	1,761	2,267	0.02	28.73
Monaco	2,118	1,654	2,141	1,487	1,376	0.02	-7.46
Netherlands	17,168	22,085	17,599	18,206	16,899	0.19	-7.18
Switzerland	35,065	37,840	35,472	41,647	44,852	0.49	7.70
East Mediterranean Europe	**7,474**	**7,235**	**8,796**	**9,639**	**8,318**	**0.09**	**-13.70**
Cyprus	696	714	625	463	582	0.01	25.70
Israel	5,036	5,022	6,538	6,636	6,057	0.07	-8.73
Turkey	1,742	1,499	1,633	2,540	1,679	0.02	-33.90
MIDDLE EAST	**4,921**	**4,481**	**4,562**	**4,098**	**5,676**	**0.06**	**38.51**
Bahrain	183	255	188	314	147	0.00	-53.18
Palestine		2	7	11			
Iraq		10	15	28			
Jordan	105	130	127	110	99	0.00	-10.00
Kuwait	218	285	441	452	463	0.01	2.43
Lebanon	340	341	167	119	243	0.00	104.20
Libya	24		8	12			
Oman	45	38	81	75	51	0.00	-32.00
Qatar	283	331	223	112	183	0.00	63.39
Saudi Arabia	1,607	1,587	1,310	865	2,871	0.03	231.91
Syrian Arab Republic	12	57	50	56	67	0.00	19.64
United Arab Emirates	1,691	1,072	1,484	1,431	1,172	0.01	-18.10
Egypt	413	362	461	513	366	0.00	-28.65
Yemen		11			14	0.00	
SOUTH ASIA	**4,709**	**6,617**	**5,302**	**4,532**	**4,957**	**0.05**	**9.38**
Afghanistan	18		23	12	18	0.00	50.00

BAHAMAS

6. Overnight stays of non-resident tourists in all types of accommodation establishments, by country of residence

	2007	2008	2009	2010	2011	Market share 11	% Change 11-10
Bangladesh	85	41	25	57	128	0.00	124.56
Bhutan		3	9	5	5	0.00	
Sri Lanka	71	473	249	370	705	0.01	90.54
India	4,217	5,739	4,367	3,771	3,691	0.04	-2.12
Iran, Islamic Republic of	63	34	126	79	43	0.00	-45.57
Maldives	28	21	22		4	0.00	
Nepal	81	138	432	164	175	0.00	6.71
Pakistan	146	168	49	74	188	0.00	154.05
NOT SPECIFIED	**255,563**	**256,447**	**227,933**	**223,429**	**237,267**	**2.60**	**6.19**
Other countries of the World	255,563	256,447	227,933	223,429	237,267	2.60	6.19

BAHRAIN

2. Arrivals of non-resident visitors at national borders, by nationality

		2007	2008	2009	2010	2011	Market share 11	% Change 11-10
TOTAL	(*)	7,833,609				6,731,974	100.00	
AFRICA		109,114				99,545	1.48	
East Africa		19,509				15,626	0.23	
Burundi		1				1	0.00	
Comoros		14				18	0.00	
Ethiopia		11,595				7,017	0.10	
Eritrea		2,429				2,155	0.03	
Djibouti		152				132	0.00	
Kenya		2,013				2,824	0.04	
Madagascar		25				20	0.00	
Malawi		32				60	0.00	
Mauritius		282				268	0.00	
Mozambique		13				13	0.00	
Rwanda		1						
Seychelles		490				478	0.01	
Somalia		1,613				1,505	0.02	
Zimbabwe		338				639	0.01	
Uganda		126				139	0.00	
United Republic of Tanzania		332				330	0.00	
Zambia		53				27	0.00	
Central Africa		305				604	0.01	
Angola		4				9	0.00	
Cameroon		70				171	0.00	
Central African Republic		4						
Chad		161				173	0.00	
Congo		38				213	0.00	
Democratic Republic of the Congo		1						
Equatorial Guinea						2	0.00	
Gabon		27				35	0.00	
Sao Tome and Principe						1	0.00	
North Africa		61,364				57,013	0.85	
Algeria		4,250				4,392	0.07	
Morocco		12,375				8,657	0.13	
Sudan		39,522				38,733	0.58	
Tunisia		5,217				5,231	0.08	
Southern Africa		23,846				22,026	0.33	
Botswana		54				27	0.00	
Lesotho		11						
Namibia		11				20	0.00	
South Africa		23,768				21,976	0.33	
Swaziland		2				3	0.00	
West Africa		4,090				4,215	0.06	
Cape Verde		4				1	0.00	
Benin		15				123	0.00	
Gambia		54				12	0.00	
Ghana		316				786	0.01	
Guinea		52				61	0.00	
Côte d'Ivoire		61				64	0.00	
Liberia		37				5	0.00	
Mali		157				101	0.00	
Mauritania		118				103	0.00	
Niger		136				99	0.00	
Nigeria		2,924				2,674	0.04	
Guinea-Bissau		6				13	0.00	
Senegal		128				123	0.00	
Sierra Leone		48				17	0.00	

BAHRAIN

2. Arrivals of non-resident visitors at national borders, by nationality

	2007	2008	2009	2010	2011	Market share 11	% Change 11-10
Togo	16				4	0.00	
Burkina Faso	18				29	0.00	
Other Africa					**61**	**0.00**	
Other countries of Africa					61	0.00	
AMERICAS	**267,496**				**291,253**	**4.33**	
Caribbean	**2,060**				**2,340**	**0.03**	
Antigua and Barbuda	4				6	0.00	
Bahamas	1				44	0.00	
Barbados	16				9	0.00	
Bermuda	1						
Cayman Islands					3	0.00	
Cuba	27				58	0.00	
Dominica	13				16	0.00	
Dominican Republic	36				29	0.00	
Grenada	1				4	0.00	
Haiti	5						
Jamaica	54				84	0.00	
Netherlands Antilles					4	0.00	
Sint Eustatius	1						
Saint Kitts and Nevis	2						
Saint Lucia	20				2	0.00	
Saint Vincent and the Grenadines	5				12	0.00	
Trinidad and Tobago	1,874				2,069	0.03	
Central America	**631**				**612**	**0.01**	
Belize	103				29	0.00	
Costa Rica	124				141	0.00	
El Salvador	21				37	0.00	
Guatemala	64				69	0.00	
Honduras	191				26	0.00	
Nicaragua	19				37	0.00	
Panama	109				273	0.00	
North America	**249,564**				**272,186**	**4.04**	
Canada	61,529				64,019	0.95	
Mexico	797				1,546	0.02	
United States of America	187,238				206,354	3.07	
Other countries of North America					267	0.00	
South America	**15,241**				**16,115**	**0.24**	
Argentina	1,940				1,633	0.02	
Bolivia	240				234	0.00	
Brazil	4,793				2,252	0.03	
Chile	190				167	0.00	
Colombia	3,529				3,701	0.05	
Ecuador	400				243	0.00	
Guyana	20				6	0.00	
Paraguay	5				2	0.00	
Peru	312				564	0.01	
Suriname	1						
Uruguay	48				90	0.00	
Venezuela	3,763				7,223	0.11	
EAST ASIA AND THE PACIFIC	**390,262**				**338,724**	**5.03**	
North-East Asia	**49,572**				**69,352**	**1.03**	
China	13,193				22,418	0.33	
Hong Kong, China	4,511				3,711	0.06	
Japan	17,979				17,129	0.25	
Korea, Dem. People's Republic of	31				107	0.00	
Korea, Republic of	13,840				25,908	0.38	

BAHRAIN

2. Arrivals of non-resident visitors at national borders, by nationality

	2007	2008	2009	2010	2011	Market share 11	% Change 11-10
Macao, China	3				1	0.00	
Mongolia	15				78	0.00	
South-East Asia	**296,713**				**234,081**	**3.48**	
Brunei Darussalam	108				88	0.00	
Myanmar	962				730	0.01	
Cambodia	422				14	0.00	
Indonesia	33,634				25,597	0.38	
Lao People's Democratic Republic	23				18	0.00	
Malaysia	19,637				20,218	0.30	
Philippines	225,562				175,775	2.61	
Singapore	4,226				3,915	0.06	
Viet Nam	277				479	0.01	
Thailand	11,862				7,247	0.11	
Australasia	**43,906**				**35,220**	**0.52**	
Australia	35,874				27,315	0.41	
New Zealand	8,032				7,905	0.12	
Melanesia	**51**				**46**	**0.00**	
Solomon Islands	8						
Fiji	43				42	0.00	
Papua New Guinea					4	0.00	
Micronesia	**9**				**3**	**0.00**	
Kiribati	1						
Nauru	7				1	0.00	
Marshall Islands					1	0.00	
Palau	1				1	0.00	
Polynesia	**11**				**22**	**0.00**	
American Samoa	1						
French Polynesia	2						
Tonga	5				10	0.00	
Tuvalu	3				12	0.00	
EUROPE	**506,891**				**513,232**	**7.62**	
Central/Eastern Europe	**18,091**				**27,396**	**0.41**	
Azerbaijan	455				992	0.01	
Armenia	55				79	0.00	
Bulgaria	1,791				1,064	0.02	
Belarus	633				805	0.01	
Czech Republic/Slovakia	14				8	0.00	
Czech Republic	1,443				1,552	0.02	
Estonia	250				198	0.00	
Georgia	288				213	0.00	
Hungary	1,086				1,062	0.02	
Kazakhstan	463				498	0.01	
Kyrgyzstan	107				108	0.00	
Latvia	185				234	0.00	
Lithuania	206				123	0.00	
Republic of Moldova	107				154	0.00	
Poland	1,940				1,866	0.03	
Romania	2,309				5,102	0.08	
Russian Federation	3,967				10,630	0.16	
Slovakia	577				633	0.01	
Tajikistan	89				26	0.00	
Turkmenistan	97				272	0.00	
Ukraine	1,274				1,322	0.02	
Uzbekistan	755				455	0.01	
Northern Europe	**294,586**				**281,029**	**4.17**	
Denmark	3,460				4,507	0.07	

BAHRAIN

2. Arrivals of non-resident visitors at national borders, by nationality

	2007	2008	2009	2010	2011	Market share 11	% Change 11-10
Finland	1,850				2,447	0.04	
Iceland	175				147	0.00	
Ireland	16,704				17,190	0.26	
Norway	3,982				2,697	0.04	
Sweden	4,731				3,490	0.05	
United Kingdom	263,684				250,551	3.72	
Southern Europe	**41,629**				**48,638**	**0.72**	
Albania	79				34	0.00	
Andorra	7						
Bosnia and Herzegovina	265				345	0.01	
Croatia	822				877	0.01	
Gibraltar	1						
Greece	6,462				6,320	0.09	
Italy	25,545				28,197	0.42	
Malta	238				235	0.00	
Montenegro					10	0.00	
Portugal	1,167				1,897	0.03	
San Marino	11				7	0.00	
Serbia					645	0.01	
Slovenia	109				101	0.00	
Spain	6,398				9,205	0.14	
TFYR of Macedonia	124				77	0.00	
Serbia and Montenegro	401				688	0.01	
Western Europe	**131,829**				**128,733**	**1.91**	
Austria	7,053				6,196	0.09	
Belgium	7,582				7,079	0.11	
France	38,009				38,742	0.58	
Germany	54,312				55,329	0.82	
Liechtenstein	29				11	0.00	
Luxembourg	326				150	0.00	
Monaco	7				7	0.00	
Netherlands	19,212				17,715	0.26	
Switzerland	5,270				3,504	0.05	
Other countries of Western Europe	29						
East Mediterranean Europe	**20,756**				**27,436**	**0.41**	
Cyprus	3,236				2,917	0.04	
Turkey	17,520				24,519	0.36	
MIDDLE EAST	**5,451,041**				**4,276,021**	**63.52**	
Palestine	22,951				34,004	0.51	
Iraq	12,225				7,122	0.11	
Jordan	125,991				132,041	1.96	
Kuwait	309,324				275,897	4.10	
Lebanon	97,928				61,128	0.91	
Libya	937				1,100	0.02	
Oman	46,705				39,452	0.59	
Qatar	167,457				96,214	1.43	
Saudi Arabia	4,366,574				3,320,188	49.32	
Syrian Arab Republic	68,964				74,078	1.10	
United Arab Emirates	61,630				42,789	0.64	
Egypt	116,176				130,916	1.94	
Yemen	54,179				61,092	0.91	
SOUTH ASIA	**1,108,805**				**1,213,199**	**18.02**	
Afghanistan	956				1,649	0.02	
Bangladesh	98,922				70,858	1.05	
Bhutan	6				16	0.00	
Sri Lanka	27,399				33,013	0.49	
India	718,415				837,514	12.44	

BAHRAIN

2. Arrivals of non-resident visitors at national borders, by nationality

	2007	2008	2009	2010	2011	Market share 11	% Change 11-10
Iran, Islamic Republic of	8,834				3,158	0.05	
Maldives	28				54	0.00	
Nepal	58,446				51,985	0.77	
Pakistan	195,799				214,952	3.19	

BARBADOS

1. Arrivals of non-resident tourists at national borders, by country of residence

	2007	2008	2009	2010	2011	Market share 11	% Change 11-10
TOTAL	574,533	567,667	518,564	532,180	567,724	100.00	6.68
AFRICA	3,331	1,389	954	1,284	1,175	0.21	-8.49
East Africa	303	187	108	175	193	0.03	10.29
Ethiopia	6	7	4	2	4	0.00	100.00
Kenya	73	71	38	72	61	0.01	-15.28
Malawi	8	11	2	1	3	0.00	200.00
Mauritius	37	24	10	9	22	0.00	144.44
Rwanda	4	3	1	3	4	0.00	33.33
Seychelles	6	5		2	10	0.00	400.00
Zimbabwe	65	13	15	44	28	0.00	-36.36
Uganda	45	23	13	16	16	0.00	
United Republic of Tanzania	42	19	17	15	13	0.00	-13.33
Zambia	17	11	8	11	32	0.01	190.91
Central Africa	8	15	4	19	15	0.00	-21.05
Angola	3	4	2	3	6	0.00	100.00
Cameroon	3	7	2	9	5	0.00	-44.44
Congo	2	4		7	4	0.00	-42.86
North Africa	27	17	20	24	31	0.01	29.17
Morocco	19	4	13	9	14	0.00	55.56
Sudan		5	1	3			
Tunisia	8	8	6	12	17	0.00	41.67
Southern Africa	2,719	554	446	690	420	0.07	-39.13
Botswana	39	33	13	18	22	0.00	22.22
Lesotho	1	8	5	2	1	0.00	-50.00
Namibia	11	9	7	11	8	0.00	-27.27
South Africa	2,659	501	413	652	366	0.06	-43.87
Swaziland	9	3	8	7	23	0.00	228.57
West Africa	274	616	376	376	516	0.09	37.23
Gambia	4	10		5	2	0.00	-60.00
Ghana	31	168	35	34	41	0.01	20.59
Guinea	7	4	1	4	2	0.00	-50.00
Liberia	1	1			3	0.00	
Mali	1		6	1	1	0.00	
Nigeria	226	423	329	326	462	0.08	41.72
Sierra Leone	4	10	5	6	5	0.00	-16.67
AMERICAS	303,404	309,043	292,435	312,551	336,920	59.35	7.80
Caribbean	93,404	96,777	88,302	85,573	94,722	16.68	10.69
Antigua and Barbuda	5,386	5,519	5,345	4,518	4,287	0.76	-5.11
Bahamas	1,080	1,092	916	921	971	0.17	5.43
Bermuda	1,963	1,496	1,482	1,424	1,220	0.21	-14.33
British Virgin Islands	2,091	2,316	2,132	1,800	1,630	0.29	-9.44
Cayman Islands	844	985	886	769	727	0.13	-5.46
Cuba	171	209	185	160	143	0.03	-10.63
Dominica	4,752	5,404	5,251	5,185	5,146	0.91	-0.75
Dominican Republic	433	298	322	360	391	0.07	8.61
Grenada	5,138	5,586	5,231	4,941	5,035	0.89	1.90
Guadeloupe	801	1,027	846	1,168	1,010	0.18	-13.53
Haiti	166	152	202	194	212	0.04	9.28
Jamaica	9,607	10,991	8,078	7,948	8,862	1.56	11.50
Martinique	1,857	2,612	2,692	2,975	2,844	0.50	-4.40
Montserrat	284	351	279	244	250	0.04	2.46
Netherlands Antilles	1,659	1,548	1,489	1,317	915	0.16	-30.52
Aruba	99	89	76	98	118	0.02	20.41
Curaçao	233	221	206	212	228	0.04	7.55
Puerto Rico		1,218	898	742	683	0.12	-7.95

BARBADOS

1. Arrivals of non-resident tourists at national borders, by country of residence

	2007	2008	2009	2010	2011	Market share 11	% Change 11-10
Saint Kitts and Nevis	3,325	3,532	3,928	3,589	3,000	0.53	-16.41
Anguilla	790	844	797	658	498	0.09	-24.32
Saint Lucia	10,456	10,539	9,421	8,451	8,199	1.44	-2.98
Sint Maarten					238	0.04	
Saint Vincent and the Grenadines	10,735	11,432	10,410	9,900	10,596	1.87	7.03
Trinidad and Tobago	30,694	28,451	26,510	27,292	36,825	6.49	34.93
Turks and Caicos Islands	235	275	200	243	238	0.04	-2.06
United States Virgin Islands	605	590	520	464	456	0.08	-1.72
Central America	**1,261**	**1,547**	**1,270**	**1,461**	**1,535**	**0.27**	**5.07**
Belize	371	574	502	508	573	0.10	12.80
Costa Rica	163	195	224	318	259	0.05	-18.55
El Salvador	25	61	35	41	45	0.01	9.76
Guatemala	172	161	86	136	131	0.02	-3.68
Honduras	47	55	31	36	46	0.01	27.78
Nicaragua	35	39	22	17	32	0.01	88.24
Panama	448	462	370	405	449	0.08	10.86
North America	**188,132**	**189,894**	**186,965**	**208,368**	**214,975**	**37.87**	**3.17**
Canada	53,335	57,398	63,826	72,434	71,953	12.67	-0.66
Greenland				1	1	0.00	
Mexico	384	512	434	444	607	0.11	36.71
United States of America	134,413	131,984	122,705	135,489	142,414	25.09	5.11
South America	**20,607**	**20,825**	**15,898**	**17,149**	**25,688**	**4.52**	**49.79**
Argentina	291	411	375	317	656	0.12	106.94
Bolivia	13	50	45	26	30	0.01	15.38
Brazil	466	523	504	2,354	4,842	0.85	105.69
Chile	102	139	116	86	131	0.02	52.33
Colombia	280	377	333	373	399	0.07	6.97
Ecuador	42	100	35	46	39	0.01	-15.22
French Guiana	68	170	58	96	97	0.02	1.04
Guyana	17,134	16,528	12,010	11,673	16,524	2.91	41.56
Paraguay	11	9	3	2	15	0.00	650.00
Peru	114	106	103	131	92	0.02	-29.77
Suriname	521	559	532	518	681	0.12	31.47
Uruguay	37	43	16	20	49	0.01	145.00
Venezuela	1,528	1,810	1,768	1,507	2,133	0.38	41.54
EAST ASIA AND THE PACIFIC	**10,450**	**4,147**	**3,325**	**4,107**	**3,723**	**0.66**	**-9.35**
North-East Asia	**896**	**752**	**891**	**728**	**799**	**0.14**	**9.75**
China	478	399	531	397	403	0.07	1.51
Taiwan, Province of China	34	54	21	20	9	0.00	-55.00
Hong Kong, China	119	77	103	82	71	0.01	-13.41
Japan	248	208	231	214	310	0.05	44.86
Korea, Republic of	17	14	5	15	6	0.00	-60.00
South-East Asia	**895**	**890**	**990**	**970**	**768**	**0.14**	**-20.82**
Brunei Darussalam	2	3		3	5	0.00	66.67
Indonesia	66	80	65	69	76	0.01	10.14
Malaysia	85	115	91	85	58	0.01	-31.76
Philippines	479	514	644	633	506	0.09	-20.06
Singapore	175	126	117	112	86	0.02	-23.21
Viet Nam	5	4	9	7	3	0.00	-57.14
Thailand	83	48	64	61	34	0.01	-44.26
Australasia	**8,628**	**2,486**	**1,431**	**2,390**	**2,139**	**0.38**	**-10.50**
Australia	7,777	2,102	1,169	1,971	1,765	0.31	-10.45
New Zealand	851	384	262	419	374	0.07	-10.74
Melanesia	**30**	**16**	**12**	**13**	**13**	**0.00**	
Fiji	23	11	4	8	11	0.00	37.50
Vanuatu	1	1	1	1			

BARBADOS

1. Arrivals of non-resident tourists at national borders, by country of residence

	2007	2008	2009	2010	2011	Market share 11	% Change 11-10
Papua New Guinea	6	4	7	4	2	0.00	-50.00
Polynesia	**1**	**3**	**1**	**6**	**4**	**0.00**	**-33.33**
Cook Islands					2	0.00	
Tonga		2		4	1	0.00	-75.00
Samoa	1	1	1	2	1	0.00	-50.00
EUROPE	**250,924**	**250,022**	**218,770**	**210,726**	**223,964**	**39.45**	**6.28**
Central/Eastern Europe	**1,967**	**2,963**	**2,497**	**3,094**	**4,204**	**0.74**	**35.88**
Azerbaijan	3	6	1	8	2	0.00	-75.00
Bulgaria	68	96	84	59	126	0.02	113.56
Belarus	22	28	15	30	41	0.01	36.67
Czech Republic/Slovakia	2			2	2	0.00	
Czech Republic	235	286	278	257	345	0.06	34.24
Estonia	121	104	98	168	514	0.09	205.95
Georgia	2	3	3	6	11	0.00	83.33
Hungary	171	162	163	195	196	0.03	0.51
Kazakhstan	32	31	12	49	41	0.01	-16.33
Latvia	59	105	31	52	71	0.01	36.54
Lithuania	29	29	14	47	68	0.01	44.68
Poland	242	485	343	407	491	0.09	20.64
Romania	82	150	128	149	144	0.03	-3.36
Russian Federation	713	1,116	1,024	1,217	1,718	0.30	41.17
Slovakia	50	141	97	133	161	0.03	21.05
Ukraine	136	221	206	315	273	0.05	-13.33
Northern Europe	**231,058**	**228,288**	**196,987**	**188,079**	**197,814**	**34.84**	**5.18**
Denmark	988	1,010	806	947	938	0.17	-0.95
Finland	219	318	381	426	612	0.11	43.66
Iceland	37	98	18	22	21	0.00	-4.55
Ireland	5,080	5,371	4,105	3,852	3,738	0.66	-2.96
Norway	643	877	694	1,016	1,056	0.19	3.94
Sweden	1,391	1,519	1,270	1,526	2,299	0.40	50.66
United Kingdom	222,700	219,095	189,713	180,290	189,150	33.32	4.91
Southern Europe	**5,120**	**5,914**	**5,940**	**5,507**	**5,972**	**1.05**	**8.44**
Albania	1	1	6	8	8	0.00	
Andorra	2	2	7	1	5	0.00	400.00
Bosnia and Herzegovina	4	4	1	4	5	0.00	25.00
Croatia	67	101	92	63	72	0.01	14.29
Gibraltar	54	37	39	49	29	0.01	-40.82
Greece	83	135	72	168	149	0.03	-11.31
Italy	3,631	4,004	4,421	3,944	4,426	0.78	12.22
Malta	40	58	60	54	37	0.01	-31.48
Montenegro			4	1	3	0.00	200.00
Portugal	183	228	157	222	161	0.03	-27.48
San Marino	6	27	7	12	25	0.00	108.33
Serbia			39	36	33	0.01	-8.33
Slovenia	57	150	78	82	95	0.02	15.85
Spain	992	1,167	953	863	924	0.16	7.07
Serbia and Montenegro			4				
Western Europe	**12,389**	**12,508**	**13,045**	**13,725**	**15,676**	**2.76**	**14.21**
Austria	688	529	710	857	916	0.16	6.88
Belgium	885	763	647	624	550	0.10	-11.86
France	2,896	2,875	2,416	2,524	3,167	0.56	25.48
Germany	5,569	6,111	7,038	7,300	8,401	1.48	15.08
Liechtenstein	16	14	12	26	22	0.00	-15.38
Luxembourg	194	177	105	155	172	0.03	10.97
Monaco	143	119	108	108	97	0.02	-10.19
Netherlands	583	510	412	310	357	0.06	15.16
Switzerland	1,415	1,410	1,597	1,821	1,994	0.35	9.50

BARBADOS

1. Arrivals of non-resident tourists at national borders, by country of residence

	2007	2008	2009	2010	2011	Market share 11	% Change 11-10
East Mediterranean Europe	**390**	**349**	**301**	**321**	**298**	**0.05**	**-7.17**
Cyprus	56	86	92	54	57	0.01	5.56
Israel	240	166	141	172	179	0.03	4.07
Turkey	94	97	68	95	62	0.01	-34.74
MIDDLE EAST	**481**	**337**	**299**	**344**	**305**	**0.05**	**-11.34**
Bahrain	20	27	15	14	13	0.00	-7.14
Jordan	38	59	9	6	19	0.00	216.67
Kuwait	31	9	9	6	11	0.00	83.33
Lebanon	7	16	10	9	28	0.00	211.11
Oman	7	9	12	4	7	0.00	75.00
Saudi Arabia	56	61	35	18	55	0.01	205.56
Syrian Arab Republic	4	6	6	3			
United Arab Emirates	277	139	188	260	152	0.03	-41.54
Egypt	41	8	13	24	19	0.00	-20.83
Yemen		3	2		1	0.00	
SOUTH ASIA	**3,538**	**1,113**	**1,082**	**1,634**	**1,440**	**0.25**	**-11.87**
Afghanistan		2	2	26			
Bangladesh	111	33	30	58	8	0.00	-86.21
Sri Lanka	217	35	30	99	61	0.01	-38.38
India	3,090	963	959	1,317	1,230	0.22	-6.61
Iran, Islamic Republic of	2	8	2	3	6	0.00	100.00
Maldives	3	2		1			
Nepal	15	10	9	8	16	0.00	100.00
Pakistan	100	60	50	122	119	0.02	-2.46
NOT SPECIFIED	**2,405**	**1,616**	**1,699**	**1,534**	**197**	**0.03**	**-87.16**
Other countries of the World	2,405	1,616	1,699	1,534	197	0.03	-87.16

BELARUS

1. Arrivals of non-resident tourists at national borders, by nationality

		2007	2008	2009	2010	2011	Market share 11	% Change 11-10
TOTAL	(*)	104,890	91,232	94,719	119,370	115,653	100.00	-3.11
AFRICA		499	73	138	101	39	0.03	-61.39
East Africa		12		2	8			
Ethiopia		4			8			
Somalia		7						
Zimbabwe				2				
Uganda		1						
Central Africa		4		3	4			
Angola		3		2	4			
Congo		1		1				
North Africa		64	10	11	11	8	0.01	-27.27
Algeria		2	2	3	7	3	0.00	-57.14
Morocco		22	3	5	1	5	0.00	400.00
Sudan		36	1		3			
Tunisia		4	4	3				
Southern Africa		27	11	67	24	19	0.02	-20.83
Namibia				5	4	2	0.00	-50.00
South Africa		27	11	62	20	17	0.01	-15.00
West Africa		392	52	55	54	12	0.01	-77.78
Ghana		218	17	26	1			
Guinea			1					
Nigeria		166	34	28	52	12	0.01	-76.92
Sierra Leone					1			
Togo		8		1				
AMERICAS		5,587	1,401	1,075	974	624	0.54	-35.93
Caribbean		5	2	4	1	2	0.00	100.00
Cuba		4	2	4				
Dominican Republic		1				2	0.00	
Jamaica					1			
Central America		1	6		2	1	0.00	-50.00
Guatemala						1	0.00	
Nicaragua					2			
Panama		1	6					
North America		5,466	1,292	963	820	567	0.49	-30.85
Canada		181	115	79	129	33	0.03	-74.42
Mexico		17	9	20	8	7	0.01	-12.50
United States of America		5,268	1,168	864	683	527	0.46	-22.84
South America		115	101	108	151	54	0.05	-64.24
Argentina		12	11	13	10	11	0.01	10.00
Bolivia				4				
Brazil		51	37	22	43	29	0.03	-32.56
Chile		14	16	12	5	3	0.00	-40.00
Colombia		3	6	6		1	0.00	
Ecuador						2	0.00	
Paraguay		1			1			
Peru		11	5	14	9	5	0.00	-44.44
Uruguay					1			
Venezuela		23	26	37	82	3	0.00	-96.34
EAST ASIA AND THE PACIFIC		2,386	1,054	963	1,040	4,249	3.67	308.56
North-East Asia		1,140	924	811	839	1,053	0.91	25.51
China		599	376	391	603	364	0.31	-39.64
Taiwan, Province of China		40	78	86	20	252	0.22	1160.00
Hong Kong, China					1	37	0.03	3600.00
Japan		372	393	235	197	269	0.23	36.55

BELARUS

1. Arrivals of non-resident tourists at national borders, by nationality

	2007	2008	2009	2010	2011	Market share 11	% Change 11-10
Korea, Dem. People's Republic of	39	1	34	1	2	0.00	100.00
Korea, Republic of	89	76	55	14	50	0.04	257.14
Mongolia	1		10	3	79	0.07	2533.33
South-East Asia	**80**	**52**	**57**	**52**	**46**	**0.04**	**-11.54**
Indonesia	3	14	3	4	4	0.00	
Malaysia	2	6	7	5			
Philippines	11	5	21	5			
Singapore	34	7	5	1			
Viet Nam	27	17	20	29	42	0.04	44.83
Thailand	3	3	1	8			
Australasia	**1,166**	**78**	**95**	**149**	**3,150**	**2.72**	**2014.09**
Australia	1,087	68	57	132	65	0.06	-50.76
New Zealand	79	10	38	17	3,085	2.67	18047.06
EUROPE	**95,003**	**87,752**	**91,778**	**116,342**	**109,929**	**95.05**	**-5.51**
Central/Eastern Europe	**60,331**	**61,514**	**69,271**	**94,218**	**94,751**	**81.93**	**0.57**
Azerbaijan	57	70	290	194	251	0.22	29.38
Bulgaria	94	173	143	50	63	0.05	26.00
Czech Republic	542	464	421	350	334	0.29	-4.57
Estonia	4,288	1,166	690	595	464	0.40	-22.02
Hungary	73	96	119	136	105	0.09	-22.79
Kyrgyzstan	11	7	29	8	12	0.01	50.00
Latvia	3,855	1,425	1,550	1,409	1,550	1.34	10.01
Lithuania	9,309	2,600	2,979	4,357	3,170	2.74	-27.24
Republic of Moldova	97	148	158	104	40	0.03	-61.54
Poland	3,337	2,832	3,729	4,006	2,983	2.58	-25.54
Romania	144	66	69	91	99	0.09	8.79
Russian Federation	36,492	50,444	56,547	80,881	83,843	72.50	3.66
Slovakia	118	125	124	118	144	0.12	22.03
Ukraine	1,914	1,898	2,423	1,919	1,693	1.46	-11.78
Northern Europe	**7,109**	**9,877**	**6,701**	**8,172**	**4,233**	**3.66**	**-48.20**
Denmark	516	164	185	230	267	0.23	16.09
Finland	605	962	610	770	560	0.48	-27.27
Iceland	36	37	6	59	476	0.41	706.78
Ireland	436	144	178	57	39	0.03	-31.58
Norway	358	302	156	192	133	0.11	-30.73
Sweden	745	594	604	644	346	0.30	-46.27
United Kingdom	4,413	7,674	4,962	6,220	2,412	2.09	-61.22
Southern Europe	**5,527**	**3,583**	**3,868**	**3,428**	**2,627**	**2.27**	**-23.37**
Albania	1	14	1	49			
Bosnia and Herzegovina	4	1	5	20	137	0.12	585.00
Croatia	212	227	195	89	108	0.09	21.35
Greece	121	41	162	83	49	0.04	-40.96
Italy	4,183	2,672	2,531	2,275	1,816	1.57	-20.18
Malta	1	5	8		5	0.00	
Montenegro	1		32		17	0.01	
Portugal	40	22	118	72	16	0.01	-77.78
Serbia	117	65	277	63	44	0.04	-30.16
Slovenia	115	156	238	136	38	0.03	-72.06
Spain	687	372	274	582	349	0.30	-40.03
TFYR of Macedonia	45	8	27	59	48	0.04	-18.64
Western Europe	**12,437**	**5,994**	**5,988**	**4,432**	**4,111**	**3.55**	**-7.24**
Austria	345	586	471	295	250	0.22	-15.25
Belgium	1,830	239	155	249	120	0.10	-51.81
France	1,154	1,257	1,114	808	754	0.65	-6.68
Germany	7,826	3,027	2,568	2,245	2,191	1.89	-2.41
Liechtenstein				2			
Luxembourg	18	19	19	12	53	0.05	341.67

BELARUS

1. Arrivals of non-resident tourists at national borders, by nationality

	2007	2008	2009	2010	2011	Market share 11	% Change 11-10
Netherlands	971	386	475	552	327	0.28	-40.76
Switzerland	293	480	1,186	269	416	0.36	54.65
East Mediterranean Europe	**9,599**	**6,784**	**5,950**	**6,092**	**4,207**	**3.64**	**-30.94**
Cyprus	1,202	206	314	460	272	0.24	-40.87
Israel	4,333	491	956	925	339	0.29	-63.35
Turkey	4,064	6,087	4,680	4,707	3,596	3.11	-23.60
MIDDLE EAST	**818**	**473**	**331**	**522**	**344**	**0.30**	**-34.10**
Iraq	56	30	16	16	22	0.02	37.50
Jordan	15	25	15	14	6	0.01	-57.14
Kuwait	8	12	6	10			
Lebanon	475	102	83	225	245	0.21	8.89
Libya	24	27	11	2	6	0.01	200.00
Saudi Arabia	52	19	19	50	9	0.01	-82.00
Syrian Arab Republic	70	103	21	8	3	0.00	-62.50
United Arab Emirates	44	131	130	137	23	0.02	-83.21
Egypt	69	24	26	53	30	0.03	-43.40
Yemen	5		4	7			
SOUTH ASIA	**597**	**479**	**434**	**391**	**468**	**0.40**	**19.69**
Afghanistan	21	7	1	7	2	0.00	-71.43
Bangladesh	3	1	1	1			
Sri Lanka	48	15	11	7			
India	229	221	154	73	97	0.08	32.88
Iran, Islamic Republic of	273	210	255	298	368	0.32	23.49
Nepal			5	5			
Pakistan	23	25	7		1	0.00	

BELGIUM

3. Arrivals of non-resident tourists in hotels and similar establishments, by country of residence

	2007	2008	2009	2010	2011	Market share 11	% Change 11-10
TOTAL	5,713,290	5,819,853	5,451,600	5,771,650	6,076,926	100.00	5.29
AFRICA	59,316	58,943	59,410	57,194	57,570	0.95	0.66
East Africa	7,018	7,630	9,575	8,734	8,573	0.14	-1.84
Burundi	511	513	430	450	530	0.01	17.78
Comoros	53	14	14	58	28	0.00	-51.72
Ethiopia	2,278	3,009	4,474	3,717	3,439	0.06	-7.48
Eritrea	110	86	38	66	92	0.00	39.39
Djibouti	60	79	148	138	93	0.00	-32.61
Kenya	799	807	931	799	874	0.01	9.39
Madagascar	187	270	323	313	283	0.00	-9.58
Malawi	84	75	63	69	76	0.00	10.14
Mauritius	207	216	251	227	314	0.01	38.33
Mozambique	181	155	158	132	186	0.00	40.91
Rwanda	816	708	687	819	735	0.01	-10.26
Seychelles	266	314	245	219	337	0.01	53.88
Somalia	101	109	166	111	175	0.00	57.66
Zimbabwe	530	458	451	573	509	0.01	-11.17
Uganda	319	387	555	424	358	0.01	-15.57
United Republic of Tanzania	448	357	530	483	417	0.01	-13.66
Zambia	68	73	111	136	127	0.00	-6.62
Central Africa	11,209	11,015	10,953	10,231	10,443	0.17	2.07
Angola	1,016	1,159	1,144	1,070	1,096	0.02	2.43
Cameroon	1,836	2,048	2,590	2,236	2,078	0.03	-7.07
Central African Republic	476	275	234	303	326	0.01	7.59
Chad	152	284	190	171	158	0.00	-7.60
Congo	2,480	2,339	2,730	2,713	2,494	0.04	-8.07
Democratic Republic of the Congo	4,173	3,485	2,975	2,795	3,220	0.05	15.21
Equatorial Guinea	56	37	29	126	79	0.00	-37.30
Gabon	962	1,342	1,012	775	950	0.02	22.58
Sao Tome and Principe	58	46	49	42	42	0.00	
North Africa	19,568	19,460	19,620	18,602	18,006	0.30	-3.20
Algeria	3,272	3,160	3,225	3,032	3,116	0.05	2.77
Morocco	13,133	13,038	13,295	12,218	11,239	0.18	-8.01
Sudan	353	299	282	389	396	0.01	1.80
Tunisia	2,810	2,963	2,818	2,963	3,255	0.05	9.85
Southern Africa	8,389	8,824	7,441	7,735	8,481	0.14	9.64
Botswana	148	96	94	125	145	0.00	16.00
Lesotho	107	39	44	56	47	0.00	-16.07
Namibia	290	1,298	736	561	402	0.01	-28.34
South Africa	7,246	6,362	5,657	6,036	7,090	0.12	17.46
Swaziland	598	1,029	910	957	797	0.01	-16.72
West Africa	13,132	12,014	11,821	11,892	12,067	0.20	1.47
Cape Verde	61	65	71	152	213	0.00	40.13
Benin	880	541	380	322	489	0.01	51.86
Gambia	296	236	235	265	250	0.00	-5.66
Ghana	502	455	493	648	674	0.01	4.01
Guinea	630	551	729	694	769	0.01	10.81
Côte d'Ivoire	1,516	1,032	1,107	1,155	1,186	0.02	2.68
Liberia	348	274	232	257	221	0.00	-14.01
Mali	870	632	628	702	622	0.01	-11.40
Mauritania	392	484	423	597	384	0.01	-35.68
Niger	2,107	2,389	2,213	1,198	1,269	0.02	5.93
Nigeria	2,062	1,792	1,841	1,870	2,041	0.03	9.14
Guinea-Bissau	49	65	38	85	98	0.00	15.29
Senegal	1,059	1,031	1,338	1,662	1,402	0.02	-15.64
Sierra Leone	1,518	1,762	1,339	1,573	1,481	0.02	-5.85

BELGIUM

3. Arrivals of non-resident tourists in hotels and similar establishments, by country of residence

	2007	2008	2009	2010	2011	Market share 11	% Change 11-10
Togo	490	323	256	242	290	0.00	19.83
Burkina Faso	352	382	498	470	678	0.01	44.26
AMERICAS	**385,078**	**357,017**	**333,104**	**388,039**	**442,620**	**7.28**	**14.07**
Caribbean	**8,091**	**6,060**	**2,620**	**2,665**	**2,543**	**0.04**	**-4.58**
Antigua and Barbuda	225	754	249	317	233	0.00	-26.50
Bahamas	220	575	105	374	131	0.00	-64.97
Barbados	6,078	3,188	579	242	201	0.00	-16.94
Cuba	423	498	240	298	276	0.00	-7.38
Dominica	151	94	159	113	175	0.00	54.87
Dominican Republic	335	295	306	429	418	0.01	-2.56
Grenada	105	104	208	108	109	0.00	0.93
Haiti	106	134	130	180	173	0.00	-3.89
Jamaica	289	238	308	369	569	0.01	54.20
Saint Kitts and Nevis	8	28	35	20	33	0.00	65.00
Saint Lucia	35	19	17	33	24	0.00	-27.27
Saint Vincent and the Grenadines	7	16	70	20	84	0.00	320.00
Trinidad and Tobago	109	117	214	162	117	0.00	-27.78
Central America	**3,229**	**3,641**	**3,127**	**3,860**	**4,529**	**0.07**	**17.33**
Belize	118	170	167	255	303	0.00	18.82
Costa Rica	1,213	1,280	1,215	1,475	1,330	0.02	-9.83
El Salvador	580	619	476	551	849	0.01	54.08
Guatemala	278	353	342	437	511	0.01	16.93
Honduras	225	338	247	230	475	0.01	106.52
Nicaragua	307	426	295	374	398	0.01	6.42
Panama	508	455	385	538	663	0.01	23.23
North America	**338,002**	**308,767**	**289,411**	**330,889**	**369,894**	**6.09**	**11.79**
Canada	40,399	37,752	33,353	40,746	47,127	0.78	15.66
Mexico	15,286	12,773	10,449	13,807	15,978	0.26	15.72
United States of America	282,317	258,242	245,609	276,336	306,789	5.05	11.02
South America	**35,756**	**38,549**	**37,946**	**50,625**	**65,654**	**1.08**	**29.69**
Argentina	5,867	5,405	6,768	8,968	11,944	0.20	33.18
Bolivia	412	364	488	353	445	0.01	26.06
Brazil	19,130	22,425	19,681	29,135	38,511	0.63	32.18
Chile	2,529	2,257	2,373	2,638	3,566	0.06	35.18
Colombia	3,147	3,169	3,007	3,732	3,865	0.06	3.56
Ecuador	820	832	1,052	891	1,083	0.02	21.55
Guyana	49	41	64	65	76	0.00	16.92
Paraguay	140	115	143	182	315	0.01	73.08
Peru	1,053	1,108	1,100	1,312	1,446	0.02	10.21
Suriname	192	214	209	285	450	0.01	57.89
Uruguay	985	696	1,100	1,317	1,668	0.03	26.65
Venezuela	1,432	1,923	1,961	1,747	2,285	0.04	30.80
EAST ASIA AND THE PACIFIC	**272,964**	**239,011**	**208,563**	**226,179**	**275,432**	**4.53**	**21.78**
North-East Asia	**218,864**	**185,352**	**160,141**	**168,188**	**208,499**	**3.43**	**23.97**
China	94,864	71,734	71,547	75,201	95,880	1.58	27.50
Taiwan, Province of China	6,666	6,549	6,092	5,093	11,469	0.19	125.19
Japan	103,429	94,948	74,509	75,976	86,778	1.43	14.22
Korea, Dem. People's Republic of	1,641	2,371	1,540	1,687	2,167	0.04	28.45
Korea, Republic of	12,153	9,623	6,272	10,094	11,930	0.20	18.19
Mongolia	111	127	181	137	275	0.00	100.73
South-East Asia	**20,298**	**20,014**	**18,317**	**22,282**	**27,101**	**0.45**	**21.63**
Brunei Darussalam	147	106	90	171	182	0.00	6.43
Myanmar	75	75	104	123	123	0.00	
Cambodia	97	64	134	122	123	0.00	0.82
Indonesia	2,020	2,039	2,353	2,699	3,250	0.05	20.41
Lao People's Democratic Republic	278	245	151	247	252	0.00	2.02

BELGIUM

3. Arrivals of non-resident tourists in hotels and similar establishments, by country of residence

	2007	2008	2009	2010	2011	Market share 11	% Change 11-10
Malaysia	3,616	3,176	2,565	3,232	4,289	0.07	32.70
Philippines	4,324	4,711	4,614	4,537	5,330	0.09	17.48
Timor-Leste	7	39	5	26	16	0.00	-38.46
Singapore	4,677	4,744	3,488	4,333	4,941	0.08	14.03
Viet Nam	1,325	1,289	1,407	1,883	1,956	0.03	3.88
Thailand	3,732	3,526	3,406	4,909	6,639	0.11	35.24
Australasia	**32,959**	**32,506**	**29,307**	**34,778**	**38,805**	**0.64**	**11.58**
Australia	26,314	26,858	25,458	30,250	34,238	0.56	13.18
New Zealand	6,645	5,648	3,849	4,528	4,567	0.08	0.86
Melanesia	**343**	**322**	**316**	**374**	**439**	**0.01**	**17.38**
Solomon Islands	100	102	93	128	114	0.00	-10.94
Fiji	121	85	102	150	171	0.00	14.00
Vanuatu	34	43	38	23	79	0.00	243.48
Papua New Guinea	88	92	83	73	75	0.00	2.74
Micronesia	**365**	**490**	**263**	**454**	**355**	**0.01**	**-21.81**
Kiribati	54	58	27	48	48	0.00	
Nauru	151	176	129	197	191	0.00	-3.05
Micronesia, Federated States of	57	132	54	161	78	0.00	-51.55
Marshall Islands	3	11	2	7	4	0.00	-42.86
Palau	100	113	51	41	34	0.00	-17.07
Polynesia	**135**	**327**	**219**	**103**	**233**	**0.00**	**126.21**
Tonga	60	200	86	79	72	0.00	-8.86
Tuvalu	49	92	105	11	26	0.00	136.36
Samoa	26	35	28	13	135	0.00	938.46
EUROPE	**4,807,118**	**4,923,917**	**4,675,581**	**4,974,321**	**5,192,869**	**85.45**	**4.39**
Central/Eastern Europe	**265,978**	**297,157**	**265,228**	**301,414**	**340,657**	**5.61**	**13.02**
Azerbaijan	489	696	527	655	1,018	0.02	55.42
Armenia	728	1,033	1,040	1,028	1,192	0.02	15.95
Bulgaria	13,561	15,348	14,063	15,205	15,905	0.26	4.60
Belarus	1,393	1,555	2,490	2,373	2,629	0.04	10.79
Czech Republic	23,258	25,197	26,154	28,363	28,356	0.47	-0.02
Estonia	5,660	6,156	5,221	6,291	6,791	0.11	7.95
Georgia	3,314	3,233	3,060	2,744	2,245	0.04	-18.19
Hungary	24,612	24,327	23,071	24,221	27,746	0.46	14.55
Kazakhstan	550	814	835	940	1,147	0.02	22.02
Kyrgyzstan	130	161	137	133	212	0.00	59.40
Latvia	4,924	6,128	5,529	8,297	9,487	0.16	14.34
Lithuania	13,389	13,933	10,967	13,938	14,805	0.24	6.22
Republic of Moldova	514	429	527	590	666	0.01	12.88
Poland	70,677	83,881	70,407	74,955	78,955	1.30	5.34
Romania	26,722	32,439	30,999	35,709	39,726	0.65	11.25
Russian Federation	57,301	60,914	50,435	66,511	87,055	1.43	30.89
Slovakia	9,238	10,099	9,816	10,314	11,539	0.19	11.88
Tajikistan	294	109	103	74	152	0.00	105.41
Turkmenistan	160	122	107	72	117	0.00	62.50
Ukraine	8,439	10,053	9,391	8,716	10,555	0.17	21.10
Uzbekistan	625	530	349	285	359	0.01	25.96
Northern Europe	**1,211,795**	**1,184,708**	**997,273**	**1,026,628**	**1,034,371**	**17.02**	**0.75**
Denmark	49,955	51,332	49,684	51,261	54,763	0.90	6.83
Finland	32,391	31,780	29,445	32,290	34,801	0.57	7.78
Iceland	6,199	5,253	3,678	6,311	5,715	0.09	-9.44
Ireland	39,522	41,087	38,497	38,810	40,749	0.67	5.00
Norway	30,864	32,489	29,322	33,407	36,869	0.61	10.36
Sweden	70,063	69,202	62,365	68,827	68,451	1.13	-0.55
United Kingdom	982,801	953,565	784,282	795,722	793,023	13.05	-0.34
Southern Europe	**569,933**	**589,889**	**575,843**	**646,412**	**703,119**	**11.57**	**8.77**

BELGIUM

3. Arrivals of non-resident tourists in hotels and similar establishments, by country of residence

	2007	2008	2009	2010	2011	Market share 11	% Change 11-10
Albania	5,462	2,764	3,547	3,021	4,249	0.07	40.65
Andorra	1,585	1,501	476	479	509	0.01	6.26
Bosnia and Herzegovina	1,571	1,862	1,903	1,675	1,971	0.03	17.67
Croatia	5,350	5,358	5,393	5,972	6,455	0.11	8.09
Greece	31,783	31,647	28,622	28,367	30,952	0.51	9.11
Holy See	73	84	74	89	45	0.00	-49.44
Italy	217,840	222,647	220,777	242,079	262,177	4.31	8.30
Malta	4,540	4,621	5,030	5,605	6,062	0.10	8.15
Montenegro	557	1,139	478	594	1,031	0.02	73.57
Portugal	36,446	37,552	35,810	37,418	36,588	0.60	-2.22
San Marino	104	99	179	68	128	0.00	88.24
Serbia	3,479	6,163	5,906	3,936	6,020	0.10	52.95
Slovenia	7,628	8,963	7,031	7,992	8,235	0.14	3.04
Spain	252,487	264,189	259,442	307,875	337,147	5.55	9.51
TFYR of Macedonia	1,028	1,300	1,175	1,242	1,550	0.03	24.80
Western Europe	**2,692,463**	**2,792,491**	**2,787,372**	**2,942,795**	**3,046,946**	**50.14**	**3.54**
Austria	33,009	32,886	32,368	34,259	36,789	0.61	7.38
France	862,438	903,081	921,253	963,845	1,008,316	16.59	4.61
Germany	608,025	621,934	607,863	640,451	664,550	10.94	3.76
Liechtenstein	2,771	2,790	2,302	2,000	1,236	0.02	-38.20
Luxembourg	62,056	65,182	68,150	72,813	80,702	1.33	10.83
Monaco	526	750	934	945	1,041	0.02	10.16
Netherlands	1,063,034	1,102,665	1,089,867	1,154,451	1,170,608	19.26	1.40
Switzerland	60,604	63,203	64,635	74,031	83,704	1.38	13.07
East Mediterranean Europe	**66,949**	**59,672**	**49,865**	**57,072**	**67,776**	**1.12**	**18.76**
Cyprus	4,869	4,741	4,739	5,284	6,722	0.11	27.21
Israel	34,822	29,237	22,224	25,603	28,224	0.46	10.24
Turkey	27,258	25,694	22,902	26,185	32,830	0.54	25.38
MIDDLE EAST	**19,515**	**21,624**	**19,519**	**24,981**	**30,100**	**0.50**	**20.49**
Bahrain	401	741	382	393	529	0.01	34.61
Palestine	66	89	47	63	108	0.00	71.43
Iraq	417	532	494	577	654	0.01	13.34
Jordan	906	1,225	1,673	1,441	1,364	0.02	-5.34
Kuwait	894	1,302	1,186	1,201	1,835	0.03	52.79
Lebanon	2,225	2,153	2,081	2,066	2,918	0.05	41.24
Libya	821	578	616	811	420	0.01	-48.21
Oman	299	328	324	447	559	0.01	25.06
Qatar	1,023	797	535	780	1,042	0.02	33.59
Saudi Arabia	2,748	3,300	2,827	3,997	4,057	0.07	1.50
Syrian Arab Republic	837	708	814	739	632	0.01	-14.48
United Arab Emirates	3,943	5,404	4,180	6,823	10,299	0.17	50.95
Egypt	4,816	4,232	4,155	5,536	5,444	0.09	-1.66
Yemen	119	235	205	107	239	0.00	123.36
SOUTH ASIA	**42,508**	**63,047**	**45,221**	**49,912**	**52,356**	**0.86**	**4.90**
Afghanistan	1,435	1,295	2,111	1,078	1,001	0.02	-7.14
Bangladesh	396	358	396	566	525	0.01	-7.24
Bhutan	38	34	80	22	61	0.00	177.27
Sri Lanka	317	356	234	287	350	0.01	21.95
India	33,504	53,951	34,711	40,447	42,709	0.70	5.59
Iran, Islamic Republic of	5,001	5,018	6,029	5,506	5,683	0.09	3.21
Maldives	66	39	49	28	58	0.00	107.14
Nepal	113	150	196	214	261	0.00	21.96
Pakistan	1,638	1,846	1,415	1,764	1,708	0.03	-3.17
NOT SPECIFIED	**126,791**	**156,294**	**110,202**	**51,024**	**25,979**	**0.43**	**-49.08**
Other countries of the World	126,791	156,294	110,202	51,024	25,979	0.43	-49.08

BELGIUM

4. Arrivals of non-resident tourists in all types of accommodation establishments, by country of residence

		2007	2008	2009	2010	2011	Market share 11	% Change 11-10
TOTAL	(*)	7,044,719	7,164,765	6,815,141	7,186,419	7,494,141	100.00	4.28
AFRICA		62,449	63,250	63,444	61,332	61,949	0.83	1.01
East Africa		7,164	7,921	9,778	9,171	8,912	0.12	-2.82
Burundi		530	630	456	469	545	0.01	16.20
Comoros		53	16	14	60	30	0.00	-50.00
Ethiopia		2,312	3,015	4,491	3,737	3,484	0.05	-6.77
Eritrea		112	89	43	76	97	0.00	27.63
Djibouti		60	83	149	142	116	0.00	-18.31
Kenya		819	835	946	813	890	0.01	9.47
Madagascar		206	292	328	338	315	0.00	-6.80
Malawi		88	77	63	75	84	0.00	12.00
Mauritius		210	229	265	257	331	0.00	28.79
Mozambique		182	157	173	132	186	0.00	40.91
Rwanda		826	745	700	942	762	0.01	-19.11
Seychelles		268	314	268	237	341	0.00	43.88
Somalia		109	114	172	123	178	0.00	44.72
Zimbabwe		543	485	499	698	593	0.01	-15.04
Uganda		329	396	560	437	372	0.00	-14.87
United Republic of Tanzania		449	366	533	498	458	0.01	-8.03
Zambia		68	78	118	137	130	0.00	-5.11
Central Africa		11,746	11,515	11,377	10,569	10,944	0.15	3.55
Angola		1,025	1,194	1,162	1,130	1,326	0.02	17.35
Cameroon		1,982	2,124	2,664	2,306	2,175	0.03	-5.68
Central African Republic		477	277	240	304	328	0.00	7.89
Chad		155	292	193	175	161	0.00	-8.00
Congo		2,518	2,404	2,763	2,747	2,533	0.03	-7.79
Democratic Republic of the Congo		4,500	3,786	3,245	2,940	3,323	0.04	13.03
Equatorial Guinea		56	41	29	135	84	0.00	-37.78
Gabon		975	1,349	1,022	789	970	0.01	22.94
Sao Tome and Principe		58	48	59	43	44	0.00	2.33
North Africa		20,228	20,318	21,058	19,512	19,261	0.26	-1.29
Algeria		3,489	3,587	3,789	3,272	3,543	0.05	8.28
Morocco		13,482	13,373	13,993	12,780	11,944	0.16	-6.54
Sudan		379	306	292	398	407	0.01	2.26
Tunisia		2,878	3,052	2,984	3,062	3,367	0.04	9.96
Southern Africa		9,585	10,328	8,790	9,267	9,786	0.13	5.60
Botswana		206	100	96	125	145	0.00	16.00
Lesotho		107	39	44	56	47	0.00	-16.07
Namibia		384	1,302	755	599	411	0.01	-31.39
South Africa		8,281	7,837	6,951	7,508	8,344	0.11	11.13
Swaziland		607	1,050	944	979	839	0.01	-14.30
West Africa		13,726	13,168	12,441	12,813	13,046	0.17	1.82
Cape Verde		62	70	72	152	214	0.00	40.79
Benin		885	568	394	326	500	0.01	53.37
Gambia		296	239	236	265	255	0.00	-3.77
Ghana		527	465	502	708	737	0.01	4.10
Guinea		633	555	740	700	785	0.01	12.14
Côte d'Ivoire		1,576	1,082	1,134	1,205	1,224	0.02	1.58
Liberia		350	276	233	269	228	0.00	-15.24
Mali		1,087	870	803	939	773	0.01	-17.68
Mauritania		408	496	428	598	391	0.01	-34.62
Niger		2,190	2,839	2,327	1,506	1,605	0.02	6.57
Nigeria		2,156	2,015	1,928	1,949	2,152	0.03	10.42
Guinea-Bissau		53	66	41	87	98	0.00	12.64
Senegal		1,093	1,108	1,374	1,711	1,480	0.02	-13.50
Sierra Leone		1,553	1,788	1,448	1,674	1,553	0.02	-7.23

BELGIUM

4. Arrivals of non-resident tourists in all types of accommodation establishments, by country of residence

	2007	2008	2009	2010	2011	Market share 11	% Change 11-10
Togo	498	339	273	245	305	0.00	24.49
Burkina Faso	359	392	508	479	746	0.01	55.74
AMERICAS	**420,845**	**399,047**	**374,791**	**429,439**	**488,577**	**6.52**	**13.77**
Caribbean	**8,199**	**6,225**	**2,840**	**2,898**	**2,833**	**0.04**	**-2.24**
Antigua and Barbuda	225	757	310	368	335	0.00	-8.97
Bahamas	231	598	124	429	204	0.00	-52.45
Barbados	6,079	3,254	638	274	228	0.00	-16.79
Cuba	466	521	255	306	282	0.00	-7.84
Dominica	151	101	165	122	180	0.00	47.54
Dominican Republic	362	321	340	462	470	0.01	1.73
Grenada	116	104	209	109	109	0.00	
Haiti	112	136	136	186	179	0.00	-3.76
Jamaica	290	241	327	399	582	0.01	45.86
Saint Kitts and Nevis	10	29	35	20	33	0.00	65.00
Saint Lucia	35	19	17	34	26	0.00	-23.53
Saint Vincent and the Grenadines	7	16	70	20	84	0.00	320.00
Trinidad and Tobago	115	128	214	169	121	0.00	-28.40
Central America	**3,454**	**3,888**	**3,479**	**4,329**	**5,008**	**0.07**	**15.68**
Belize	132	188	210	262	310	0.00	18.32
Costa Rica	1,322	1,396	1,344	1,664	1,567	0.02	-5.83
El Salvador	601	629	489	632	911	0.01	44.15
Guatemala	323	410	425	536	600	0.01	11.94
Honduras	229	355	273	250	501	0.01	100.40
Nicaragua	323	429	327	389	417	0.01	7.20
Panama	524	481	411	596	702	0.01	17.79
North America	**365,330**	**339,011**	**320,035**	**359,199**	**401,180**	**5.35**	**11.69**
Canada	48,517	46,616	41,905	48,517	55,159	0.74	13.69
Mexico	18,760	17,277	13,965	17,679	20,781	0.28	17.55
United States of America	298,053	275,118	264,165	293,003	325,240	4.34	11.00
South America	**43,862**	**49,923**	**48,437**	**63,013**	**79,556**	**1.06**	**26.25**
Argentina	7,379	7,804	9,334	12,106	15,259	0.20	26.04
Bolivia	496	480	556	424	565	0.01	33.25
Brazil	23,408	28,355	24,770	35,052	45,160	0.60	28.84
Chile	3,364	3,166	3,038	3,467	4,669	0.06	34.67
Colombia	3,791	4,098	3,932	4,855	5,181	0.07	6.71
Ecuador	995	1,120	1,255	1,160	1,394	0.02	20.17
Guyana	49	41	84	77	81	0.00	5.19
Paraguay	158	147	164	214	362	0.00	69.16
Peru	1,235	1,402	1,415	1,714	1,780	0.02	3.85
Suriname	196	216	226	310	510	0.01	64.52
Uruguay	1,202	873	1,334	1,601	2,091	0.03	30.61
Venezuela	1,589	2,221	2,329	2,033	2,504	0.03	23.17
EAST ASIA AND THE PACIFIC	**301,959**	**267,943**	**237,535**	**255,712**	**307,495**	**4.10**	**20.25**
North-East Asia	**235,880**	**201,018**	**173,728**	**183,800**	**225,765**	**3.01**	**22.83**
China	98,150	74,959	75,219	79,908	101,448	1.35	26.96
Taiwan, Province of China	7,319	7,342	6,939	5,922	12,557	0.17	112.04
Japan	109,902	100,712	80,093	81,026	91,414	1.22	12.82
Korea, Dem. People's Republic of	3,496	4,321	3,441	4,009	5,363	0.07	33.77
Korea, Republic of	16,897	13,550	7,853	12,788	14,658	0.20	14.62
Mongolia	116	134	183	147	325	0.00	121.09
South-East Asia	**21,617**	**21,250**	**20,633**	**24,436**	**29,397**	**0.39**	**20.30**
Brunei Darussalam	177	106	102	227	198	0.00	-12.78
Myanmar	75	76	105	130	127	0.00	-2.31
Cambodia	102	68	136	132	136	0.00	3.03
Indonesia	2,137	2,124	2,483	2,928	3,493	0.05	19.30
Lao People's Democratic Republic	278	248	159	251	256	0.00	1.99

BELGIUM

4. Arrivals of non-resident tourists in all types of accommodation establishments, by country of residence

	2007	2008	2009	2010	2011	Market share 11	% Change 11-10
Malaysia	3,807	3,405	2,982	3,712	4,732	0.06	27.48
Philippines	4,385	4,793	4,731	4,643	5,481	0.07	18.05
Timor-Leste	7	40	6	27	25	0.00	-7.41
Singapore	4,987	5,039	3,924	4,824	5,488	0.07	13.76
Viet Nam	1,479	1,458	1,635	2,084	2,207	0.03	5.90
Thailand	4,183	3,893	4,370	5,478	7,254	0.10	32.42
Australasia	**43,594**	**44,519**	**42,352**	**46,502**	**51,217**	**0.68**	**10.14**
Australia	35,062	37,084	36,684	40,480	45,026	0.60	11.23
New Zealand	8,532	7,435	5,668	6,022	6,191	0.08	2.81
Melanesia	**363**	**328**	**321**	**381**	**456**	**0.01**	**19.69**
Solomon Islands	102	103	94	130	122	0.00	-6.15
Fiji	125	87	105	154	178	0.00	15.58
Vanuatu	47	44	38	23	80	0.00	247.83
Papua New Guinea	89	94	84	74	76	0.00	2.70
Micronesia	**370**	**499**	**280**	**487**	**374**	**0.00**	**-23.20**
Kiribati	54	58	27	48	49	0.00	2.08
Nauru	153	181	132	225	208	0.00	-7.56
Micronesia, Federated States of	59	136	54	161	79	0.00	-50.93
Marshall Islands	3	11	2	12	4	0.00	-66.67
Palau	101	113	65	41	34	0.00	-17.07
Polynesia	**135**	**329**	**221**	**106**	**286**	**0.00**	**169.81**
Tonga	60	200	87	81	77	0.00	-4.94
Tuvalu	49	92	106	12	38	0.00	216.67
Samoa	26	37	28	13	171	0.00	1215.38
EUROPE	**6,061,187**	**6,187,002**	**5,956,385**	**6,310,386**	**6,522,652**	**87.04**	**3.36**
Central/Eastern Europe	**285,834**	**317,011**	**285,636**	**323,683**	**363,437**	**4.85**	**12.28**
Azerbaijan	524	716	547	694	1,068	0.01	53.89
Armenia	760	1,052	1,138	1,172	1,299	0.02	10.84
Bulgaria	13,933	15,980	14,623	15,874	16,221	0.22	2.19
Belarus	1,429	1,631	2,584	2,505	2,774	0.04	10.74
Czech Republic	25,770	27,834	29,339	31,311	31,368	0.42	0.18
Estonia	5,896	6,286	5,461	6,566	7,041	0.09	7.23
Georgia	3,348	3,252	3,158	2,803	2,261	0.03	-19.34
Hungary	28,131	27,259	24,985	26,633	30,643	0.41	15.06
Kazakhstan	565	822	866	961	1,197	0.02	24.56
Kyrgyzstan	130	170	143	147	218	0.00	48.30
Latvia	5,291	6,524	5,854	8,762	10,104	0.13	15.32
Lithuania	14,014	15,123	11,946	14,834	15,429	0.21	4.01
Republic of Moldova	541	463	539	601	684	0.01	13.81
Poland	78,952	90,916	78,976	84,115	87,733	1.17	4.30
Romania	28,172	34,113	32,291	37,186	41,399	0.55	11.33
Russian Federation	58,607	62,490	52,031	68,609	89,942	1.20	31.09
Slovakia	9,993	11,238	10,957	11,197	12,500	0.17	11.64
Tajikistan	303	114	106	82	174	0.00	112.20
Turkmenistan	164	160	115	108	118	0.00	9.26
Ukraine	8,664	10,333	9,605	9,234	10,879	0.15	17.81
Uzbekistan	647	535	372	289	385	0.01	33.22
Northern Europe	**1,301,401**	**1,285,095**	**1,089,227**	**1,117,879**	**1,135,286**	**15.15**	**1.56**
Denmark	57,708	58,914	57,206	58,283	62,073	0.83	6.50
Finland	34,155	34,042	31,312	34,238	36,665	0.49	7.09
Iceland	6,370	5,455	3,897	6,489	6,021	0.08	-7.21
Ireland	42,375	44,149	41,648	41,581	44,072	0.59	5.99
Norway	32,687	33,808	30,745	35,122	38,463	0.51	9.51
Sweden	73,908	72,722	65,776	72,647	72,161	0.96	-0.67
United Kingdom	1,054,198	1,036,005	858,643	869,519	875,831	11.69	0.73
Southern Europe	**612,530**	**642,122**	**633,603**	**702,088**	**756,201**	**10.09**	**7.71**

BELGIUM

4. Arrivals of non-resident tourists in all types of accommodation establishments, by country of residence

	2007	2008	2009	2010	2011	Market share 11	% Change 11-10
Albania	5,487	2,855	3,696	3,245	4,624	0.06	42.50
Andorra	1,593	1,520	546	523	637	0.01	21.80
Bosnia and Herzegovina	1,651	1,895	2,009	1,729	2,048	0.03	18.45
Croatia	5,705	5,768	5,729	6,830	6,787	0.09	-0.63
Greece	33,161	32,376	29,848	29,176	31,851	0.43	9.17
Holy See	76	85	81	91	46	0.00	-49.45
Italy	230,124	236,405	236,806	258,163	278,908	3.72	8.04
Malta	4,582	4,719	5,120	5,642	6,246	0.08	10.71
Montenegro	583	1,183	484	611	1,047	0.01	71.36
Portugal	38,324	39,705	38,170	39,429	39,065	0.52	-0.92
San Marino	104	100	185	68	129	0.00	89.71
Serbia	3,763	6,255	6,034	4,071	6,269	0.08	53.99
Slovenia	8,702	9,901	7,922	9,177	9,719	0.13	5.91
Spain	277,633	298,019	295,764	342,025	367,236	4.90	7.37
TFYR of Macedonia	1,042	1,336	1,209	1,308	1,589	0.02	21.48
Western Europe	**3,792,671**	**3,880,799**	**3,895,618**	**4,107,209**	**4,197,026**	**56.00**	**2.19**
Austria	36,036	35,959	36,272	37,623	40,897	0.55	8.70
France	1,032,899	1,079,638	1,096,341	1,153,949	1,211,281	16.16	4.97
Germany	771,204	775,172	770,258	814,684	838,287	11.19	2.90
Liechtenstein	2,774	2,804	2,321	2,025	1,270	0.02	-37.28
Luxembourg	74,989	78,012	80,116	83,906	93,689	1.25	11.66
Monaco	531	754	948	954	1,068	0.01	11.95
Netherlands	1,808,042	1,838,987	1,838,549	1,933,579	1,920,003	25.62	-0.70
Switzerland	66,196	69,473	70,813	80,489	90,531	1.21	12.48
East Mediterranean Europe	**68,751**	**61,975**	**52,301**	**59,527**	**70,702**	**0.94**	**18.77**
Cyprus	4,907	4,778	4,848	5,358	6,797	0.09	26.86
Israel	35,735	30,421	23,389	26,507	29,410	0.39	10.95
Turkey	28,109	26,776	24,064	27,662	34,495	0.46	24.70
MIDDLE EAST	**20,284**	**22,067**	**19,976**	**25,599**	**30,602**	**0.41**	**19.54**
Bahrain	402	785	389	422	565	0.01	33.89
Palestine	74	154	68	108	116	0.00	7.41
Iraq	434	585	561	669	753	0.01	12.56
Jordan	912	1,229	1,695	1,518	1,388	0.02	-8.56
Kuwait	922	1,342	1,211	1,232	1,850	0.02	50.16
Lebanon	2,295	2,181	2,116	2,148	2,962	0.04	37.90
Libya	837	583	628	818	432	0.01	-47.19
Oman	301	337	328	449	569	0.01	26.73
Qatar	1,040	806	539	780	1,052	0.01	34.87
Saudi Arabia	2,775	3,320	2,857	4,047	4,111	0.05	1.58
Syrian Arab Republic	852	710	841	780	659	0.01	-15.51
United Arab Emirates	3,986	5,467	4,240	6,910	10,350	0.14	49.78
Egypt	5,302	4,333	4,296	5,611	5,553	0.07	-1.03
Yemen	152	235	207	107	242	0.00	126.17
SOUTH ASIA	**43,785**	**64,480**	**46,950**	**51,726**	**54,726**	**0.73**	**5.80**
Afghanistan	1,471	1,439	2,184	1,337	1,417	0.02	5.98
Bangladesh	403	436	412	614	570	0.01	-7.17
Bhutan	38	35	80	23	79	0.00	243.48
Sri Lanka	327	386	254	308	365	0.00	18.51
India	34,391	54,838	35,730	41,554	44,195	0.59	6.36
Iran, Islamic Republic of	5,236	5,233	6,560	5,780	5,941	0.08	2.79
Maldives	66	40	51	28	71	0.00	153.57
Nepal	130	161	206	238	285	0.00	19.75
Pakistan	1,723	1,912	1,473	1,844	1,803	0.02	-2.22
NOT SPECIFIED	**134,210**	**160,976**	**116,060**	**52,225**	**28,140**	**0.38**	**-46.12**
Other countries of the World	134,210	160,976	116,060	52,225	28,140	0.38	-46.12

BELGIUM

5. Overnight stays of non-resident tourists in hotels and similar establishments, by country of residence

	2007	2008	2009	2010	2011	Market share 11	% Change 11-10
TOTAL	10,976,346	11,119,811	10,336,598	10,854,245	11,436,408	100.00	5.36
AFRICA	139,809	134,136	134,559	140,428	137,706	1.20	-1.94
East Africa	17,228	17,287	21,708	20,959	20,423	0.18	-2.56
Burundi	1,542	1,546	1,598	1,348	1,773	0.02	31.53
Comoros	89	88	35	99	55	0.00	-44.44
Ethiopia	4,927	4,149	6,413	6,651	5,349	0.05	-19.58
Eritrea	225	187	73	172	206	0.00	19.77
Djibouti	144	220	460	274	199	0.00	-27.37
Kenya	2,486	2,749	2,665	2,528	2,337	0.02	-7.56
Madagascar	473	768	824	685	672	0.01	-1.90
Malawi	266	209	201	218	205	0.00	-5.96
Mauritius	535	591	648	593	1,885	0.02	217.88
Mozambique	641	619	544	524	480	0.00	-8.40
Rwanda	1,907	1,566	1,768	2,331	2,127	0.02	-8.75
Seychelles	537	622	730	403	891	0.01	121.09
Somalia	164	198	482	425	297	0.00	-30.12
Zimbabwe	1,117	1,235	1,009	1,331	1,300	0.01	-2.33
Uganda	909	1,396	1,595	1,270	898	0.01	-29.29
United Republic of Tanzania	1,032	935	2,317	1,628	1,303	0.01	-19.96
Zambia	234	209	346	479	446	0.00	-6.89
Central Africa	23,935	24,728	23,486	25,971	26,088	0.23	0.45
Angola	1,819	2,142	2,391	2,911	3,038	0.03	4.36
Cameroon	3,533	4,229	4,679	5,228	4,841	0.04	-7.40
Central African Republic	927	829	680	1,040	785	0.01	-24.52
Chad	363	836	625	412	340	0.00	-17.48
Congo	5,872	5,093	6,378	6,772	6,171	0.05	-8.87
Democratic Republic of the Congo	8,940	8,356	6,500	7,616	8,562	0.07	12.42
Equatorial Guinea	195	274	92	264	156	0.00	-40.91
Gabon	2,119	2,815	2,030	1,626	2,099	0.02	29.09
Sao Tome and Principe	167	154	111	102	96	0.00	-5.88
North Africa	39,745	41,665	43,688	39,269	39,280	0.34	0.03
Algeria	9,699	10,373	9,904	8,473	7,711	0.07	-8.99
Morocco	22,067	23,921	25,863	22,978	23,036	0.20	0.25
Sudan	1,017	953	788	1,065	909	0.01	-14.65
Tunisia	6,962	6,418	7,133	6,753	7,624	0.07	12.90
Southern Africa	24,205	22,561	18,431	20,259	21,955	0.19	8.37
Botswana	491	329	232	412	352	0.00	-14.56
Lesotho	190	125	116	126	104	0.00	-17.46
Namibia	717	1,743	1,212	1,472	698	0.01	-52.58
South Africa	21,689	18,430	15,010	16,397	19,226	0.17	17.25
Swaziland	1,118	1,934	1,861	1,852	1,575	0.01	-14.96
West Africa	34,696	27,895	27,246	33,970	29,960	0.26	-11.80
Cape Verde	232	217	189	376	468	0.00	24.47
Benin	1,646	1,313	1,180	1,095	1,324	0.01	20.91
Gambia	670	606	703	1,125	653	0.01	-41.96
Ghana	1,263	1,364	1,231	2,237	1,958	0.02	-12.47
Guinea	1,315	1,141	2,619	2,675	1,682	0.01	-37.12
Côte d'Ivoire	3,416	2,495	2,579	2,847	2,786	0.02	-2.14
Liberia	750	566	427	573	514	0.00	-10.30
Mali	1,859	1,236	1,437	1,756	1,695	0.01	-3.47
Mauritania	720	1,218	1,044	1,486	934	0.01	-37.15
Niger	3,532	4,835	3,870	2,316	2,416	0.02	4.32
Nigeria	5,360	4,513	3,909	5,456	5,414	0.05	-0.77
Guinea-Bissau	111	218	67	283	236	0.00	-16.61
Senegal	2,648	2,693	3,347	4,753	3,430	0.03	-27.84
Sierra Leone	3,143	3,752	2,676	3,552	3,464	0.03	-2.48

BELGIUM

5. Overnight stays of non-resident tourists in hotels and similar establishments, by country of residence

	2007	2008	2009	2010	2011	Market share 11	% Change 11-10
Togo	7,029	814	667	1,697	716	0.01	-57.81
Burkina Faso	1,002	914	1,301	1,743	2,270	0.02	30.24
AMERICAS	**849,932**	**791,552**	**727,655**	**840,134**	**955,148**	**8.35**	**13.69**
Caribbean	**15,111**	**11,378**	**5,388**	**5,857**	**5,649**	**0.05**	**-3.55**
Antigua and Barbuda	491	1,130	469	634	505	0.00	-20.35
Bahamas	454	761	188	552	265	0.00	-51.99
Barbados	9,665	5,839	938	589	442	0.00	-24.96
Cuba	1,039	1,212	613	556	722	0.01	29.86
Dominica	260	167	378	291	342	0.00	17.53
Dominican Republic	975	689	771	1,127	957	0.01	-15.08
Grenada	242	211	281	356	219	0.00	-38.48
Haiti	406	408	334	537	423	0.00	-21.23
Jamaica	983	516	658	648	1,075	0.01	65.90
Saint Kitts and Nevis	16	51	66	53	143	0.00	169.81
Saint Lucia	121	50	83	174	109	0.00	-37.36
Saint Vincent and the Grenadines	15	38	145	37	146	0.00	294.59
Trinidad and Tobago	444	306	464	303	301	0.00	-0.66
Central America	**6,822**	**9,095**	**7,511**	**8,800**	**9,244**	**0.08**	**5.05**
Belize	229	281	291	449	507	0.00	12.92
Costa Rica	2,820	3,235	2,934	3,260	2,766	0.02	-15.15
El Salvador	1,168	1,328	1,098	1,214	1,607	0.01	32.37
Guatemala	562	871	870	1,118	1,037	0.01	-7.25
Honduras	481	1,223	703	675	1,048	0.01	55.26
Nicaragua	564	1,097	759	962	747	0.01	-22.35
Panama	998	1,060	856	1,122	1,532	0.01	36.54
North America	**751,620**	**687,833**	**638,070**	**724,173**	**805,749**	**7.05**	**11.26**
Canada	95,501	89,467	79,201	95,307	110,521	0.97	15.96
Mexico	26,974	24,085	18,833	25,267	29,144	0.25	15.34
United States of America	629,145	574,281	540,036	603,599	666,084	5.82	10.35
South America	**76,379**	**83,246**	**76,686**	**101,304**	**134,506**	**1.18**	**32.77**
Argentina	11,634	10,662	12,771	17,415	23,443	0.20	34.61
Bolivia	1,154	1,154	1,258	920	1,080	0.01	17.39
Brazil	40,631	47,729	39,403	57,118	79,664	0.70	39.47
Chile	5,604	5,176	4,893	5,580	7,493	0.07	34.28
Colombia	5,950	6,400	5,832	7,647	6,768	0.06	-11.49
Ecuador	1,925	1,727	2,395	1,851	2,148	0.02	16.05
Guyana	176	106	189	184	273	0.00	48.37
Paraguay	383	416	401	487	793	0.01	62.83
Peru	2,731	2,565	2,437	2,759	3,149	0.03	14.14
Suriname	486	721	774	706	1,409	0.01	99.58
Uruguay	2,253	1,604	2,401	3,037	3,382	0.03	11.36
Venezuela	3,452	4,986	3,932	3,600	4,904	0.04	36.22
EAST ASIA AND THE PACIFIC	**475,238**	**434,716**	**382,073**	**416,187**	**499,647**	**4.37**	**20.05**
North-East Asia	**364,139**	**324,118**	**282,435**	**296,213**	**357,350**	**3.12**	**20.64**
China	135,431	109,815	112,941	115,428	141,839	1.24	22.88
Taiwan, Province of China	10,230	9,378	9,250	8,022	15,131	0.13	88.62
Japan	194,312	183,631	144,168	150,866	172,833	1.51	14.56
Korea, Dem. People's Republic of	3,605	5,118	3,023	3,801	5,192	0.05	36.60
Korea, Republic of	20,338	15,896	12,768	17,813	21,782	0.19	22.28
Mongolia	223	280	285	283	573	0.01	102.47
South-East Asia	**43,426**	**42,293**	**36,588**	**46,355**	**55,553**	**0.49**	**19.84**
Brunei Darussalam	331	218	180	381	515	0.00	35.17
Myanmar	98	139	144	261	194	0.00	-25.67
Cambodia	286	292	329	367	379	0.00	3.27
Indonesia	4,303	4,330	4,736	6,554	6,546	0.06	-0.12
Lao People's Democratic Republic	620	492	295	459	504	0.00	9.80

BELGIUM

5. Overnight stays of non-resident tourists in hotels and similar establishments, by country of residence

	2007	2008	2009	2010	2011	Market share 11	% Change 11-10
Malaysia	6,875	7,075	5,380	6,436	8,500	0.07	32.07
Philippines	8,225	8,182	6,965	7,359	9,716	0.08	32.03
Timor-Leste	10	122	11	89	20	0.00	-77.53
Singapore	11,360	10,932	8,451	10,797	12,165	0.11	12.67
Viet Nam	2,680	2,803	2,622	4,114	4,315	0.04	4.89
Thailand	8,638	7,708	7,475	9,538	12,699	0.11	33.14
Australasia	**65,786**	**65,685**	**61,278**	**71,725**	**84,466**	**0.74**	**17.76**
Australia	51,455	53,499	53,178	62,640	73,046	0.64	16.61
New Zealand	14,331	12,186	8,100	9,085	11,420	0.10	25.70
Melanesia	**951**	**889**	**826**	**849**	**1,135**	**0.01**	**33.69**
Solomon Islands	223	222	167	265	316	0.00	19.25
Fiji	452	388	253	294	414	0.00	40.82
Vanuatu	56	85	74	63	192	0.00	204.76
Papua New Guinea	220	194	332	227	213	0.00	-6.17
Micronesia	**669**	**1,009**	**459**	**852**	**670**	**0.01**	**-21.36**
Kiribati	136	142	42	122	101	0.00	-17.21
Nauru	285	322	221	307	371	0.00	20.85
Micronesia, Federated States of	77	171	68	334	120	0.00	-64.07
Marshall Islands	3	15	4	7	8	0.00	14.29
Palau	168	359	124	82	70	0.00	-14.63
Polynesia	**267**	**722**	**487**	**193**	**473**	**0.00**	**145.08**
Tonga	116	381	240	156	168	0.00	7.69
Tuvalu	81	233	193	18	50	0.00	177.78
Samoa	70	108	54	19	255	0.00	1242.11
EUROPE	**9,121,573**	**9,261,233**	**8,728,486**	**9,182,019**	**9,593,960**	**83.89**	**4.49**
Central/Eastern Europe	**605,446**	**638,463**	**558,868**	**631,326**	**737,367**	**6.45**	**16.80**
Azerbaijan	1,495	1,905	1,713	1,847	2,761	0.02	49.49
Armenia	1,727	2,570	2,545	4,768	2,786	0.02	-41.57
Bulgaria	31,024	31,032	29,080	32,118	35,099	0.31	9.28
Belarus	3,029	2,714	4,238	3,853	4,918	0.04	27.64
Czech Republic	50,906	50,321	52,577	58,653	61,253	0.54	4.43
Estonia	10,094	11,214	9,919	11,334	12,026	0.11	6.11
Georgia	6,971	6,458	6,446	5,775	4,670	0.04	-19.13
Hungary	62,157	63,006	53,123	50,629	58,694	0.51	15.93
Kazakhstan	1,535	3,039	2,401	2,476	3,233	0.03	30.57
Kyrgyzstan	408	479	258	326	399	0.00	22.39
Latvia	9,616	11,421	9,534	14,080	15,971	0.14	13.43
Lithuania	25,321	25,942	21,231	25,782	27,571	0.24	6.94
Republic of Moldova	934	1,086	1,461	1,640	1,823	0.02	11.16
Poland	179,676	183,166	149,135	162,008	183,088	1.60	13.01
Romania	60,082	74,558	71,879	81,096	100,182	0.88	23.54
Russian Federation	114,175	119,895	102,914	133,000	172,752	1.51	29.89
Slovakia	26,074	28,043	21,453	22,510	26,688	0.23	18.56
Tajikistan	728	302	312	196	371	0.00	89.29
Turkmenistan	509	326	263	266	187	0.00	-29.70
Ukraine	16,532	19,496	17,425	18,140	21,994	0.19	21.25
Uzbekistan	2,453	1,490	961	829	901	0.01	8.69
Northern Europe	**2,424,033**	**2,364,275**	**1,962,570**	**1,992,823**	**2,003,730**	**17.52**	**0.55**
Denmark	91,363	94,834	92,088	95,219	101,083	0.88	6.16
Finland	63,347	60,837	54,459	61,678	68,671	0.60	11.34
Iceland	13,809	12,775	8,496	13,885	13,609	0.12	-1.99
Ireland	76,282	79,786	77,600	72,457	77,673	0.68	7.20
Norway	61,334	62,904	57,588	65,957	74,393	0.65	12.79
Sweden	132,249	128,929	113,129	127,844	127,462	1.11	-0.30
United Kingdom	1,985,649	1,924,210	1,559,210	1,555,783	1,540,839	13.47	-0.96
Southern Europe	**1,179,596**	**1,197,317**	**1,194,579**	**1,309,535**	**1,423,395**	**12.45**	**8.69**

BELGIUM

5. Overnight stays of non-resident tourists in hotels and similar establishments, by country of residence

	2007	2008	2009	2010	2011	Market share 11	% Change 11-10
Albania	10,002	5,481	13,770	7,244	8,139	0.07	12.36
Andorra	4,712	4,862	2,292	925	1,084	0.01	17.19
Bosnia and Herzegovina	3,331	4,171	3,698	3,773	4,147	0.04	9.91
Croatia	12,209	12,316	13,019	13,540	13,416	0.12	-0.92
Greece	71,708	70,789	65,140	62,938	66,501	0.58	5.66
Holy See	209	175	155	166	104	0.00	-37.35
Italy	441,782	441,199	447,082	486,592	522,022	4.56	7.28
Malta	10,470	10,806	10,954	11,669	12,982	0.11	11.25
Montenegro	1,297	2,279	1,404	1,361	2,368	0.02	73.99
Portugal	99,333	86,935	76,679	79,399	77,053	0.67	-2.95
San Marino	199	149	508	141	219	0.00	55.32
Serbia	7,807	13,055	13,660	10,403	14,438	0.13	38.79
Slovenia	18,140	17,891	15,314	16,236	16,951	0.15	4.40
Spain	496,044	524,277	528,284	612,194	680,499	5.95	11.16
TFYR of Macedonia	2,353	2,932	2,620	2,954	3,472	0.03	17.54
Western Europe	**4,766,183**	**4,930,806**	**4,902,867**	**5,126,293**	**5,285,997**	**46.22**	**3.12**
Austria	66,055	67,402	68,778	72,122	80,125	0.70	11.10
France	1,414,220	1,475,516	1,511,377	1,566,510	1,652,525	14.45	5.49
Germany	1,231,185	1,243,047	1,219,512	1,285,781	1,316,049	11.51	2.35
Liechtenstein	5,730	6,056	4,979	3,884	2,407	0.02	-38.03
Luxembourg	123,748	128,926	132,001	139,409	149,036	1.30	6.91
Monaco	1,105	1,466	1,810	1,895	1,951	0.02	2.96
Netherlands	1,806,434	1,884,428	1,838,111	1,919,062	1,924,846	16.83	0.30
Switzerland	117,706	123,965	126,299	137,630	159,058	1.39	15.57
East Mediterranean Europe	**146,315**	**130,372**	**109,602**	**122,042**	**143,471**	**1.25**	**17.56**
Cyprus	11,856	12,034	11,633	12,397	15,458	0.14	24.69
Israel	67,746	59,132	46,341	51,490	58,242	0.51	13.11
Turkey	66,713	59,206	51,628	58,155	69,771	0.61	19.97
MIDDLE EAST	**72,936**	**77,666**	**58,297**	**74,513**	**84,545**	**0.74**	**13.46**
Bahrain	1,078	1,577	1,081	1,202	1,684	0.01	40.10
Palestine	127	358	101	152	233	0.00	53.29
Iraq	1,234	1,533	1,771	2,077	1,713	0.01	-17.53
Jordan	2,670	3,234	4,084	3,752	3,535	0.03	-5.78
Kuwait	3,217	4,399	3,878	3,999	6,080	0.05	52.04
Lebanon	6,399	5,880	5,516	5,571	6,932	0.06	24.43
Libya	4,871	1,877	1,474	1,799	1,144	0.01	-36.41
Oman	1,412	1,161	1,057	1,587	1,980	0.02	24.76
Qatar	7,463	4,085	1,927	2,965	3,294	0.03	11.10
Saudi Arabia	8,250	10,149	8,731	11,118	12,755	0.11	14.72
Syrian Arab Republic	1,800	1,827	2,695	1,973	1,646	0.01	-16.57
United Arab Emirates	20,680	29,440	14,518	24,723	30,508	0.27	23.40
Egypt	13,402	11,561	10,919	13,274	12,505	0.11	-5.79
Yemen	333	585	545	321	536	0.00	66.98
SOUTH ASIA	**97,454**	**127,831**	**94,671**	**104,830**	**116,850**	**1.02**	**11.47**
Afghanistan	2,533	2,452	4,037	3,237	3,137	0.03	-3.09
Bangladesh	845	621	870	1,240	1,377	0.01	11.05
Bhutan	72	74	263	44	96	0.00	118.18
Sri Lanka	795	945	623	690	931	0.01	34.93
India	78,133	107,704	71,101	82,881	94,665	0.83	14.22
Iran, Islamic Republic of	11,029	11,349	14,087	12,287	12,434	0.11	1.20
Maldives	147	85	89	80	109	0.00	36.25
Nepal	314	291	401	401	519	0.00	29.43
Pakistan	3,586	4,310	3,200	3,970	3,582	0.03	-9.77
NOT SPECIFIED	**219,404**	**292,677**	**210,857**	**96,134**	**48,552**	**0.42**	**-49.50**
Other countries of the World	219,404	292,677	210,857	96,134	48,552	0.42	-49.50

BELGIUM

6. Overnight stays of non-resident tourists in all types of accommodation establishments, by country of residence

	2007	2008	2009	2010	2011	Market share 11	% Change 11-10
TOTAL (*)	16,271,311	16,360,702	15,452,987	16,169,676	16,723,867	100.00	3.43
AFRICA	148,330	143,531	144,605	151,982	150,181	0.90	-1.19
East Africa	17,703	17,938	22,257	22,281	21,175	0.13	-4.96
Burundi	1,638	1,808	1,686	1,401	1,798	0.01	28.34
Comoros	89	90	35	103	59	0.00	-42.72
Ethiopia	5,055	4,159	6,457	6,696	5,476	0.03	-18.22
Eritrea	227	192	83	191	212	0.00	10.99
Djibouti	144	228	461	278	258	0.00	-7.19
Kenya	2,535	2,816	2,701	2,564	2,368	0.01	-7.64
Madagascar	569	822	832	730	758	0.00	3.84
Malawi	271	222	201	228	215	0.00	-5.70
Mauritius	538	607	673	646	1,909	0.01	195.51
Mozambique	644	626	619	524	480	0.00	-8.40
Rwanda	1,938	1,649	1,803	2,808	2,165	0.01	-22.90
Seychelles	539	622	770	437	904	0.01	106.86
Somalia	179	203	500	458	317	0.00	-30.79
Zimbabwe	1,138	1,281	1,122	1,732	1,464	0.01	-15.47
Uganda	920	1,432	1,608	1,338	934	0.01	-30.19
United Republic of Tanzania	1,045	966	2,348	1,667	1,409	0.01	-15.48
Zambia	234	215	358	480	449	0.00	-6.46
Central Africa	25,884	25,818	25,049	27,000	27,333	0.16	1.23
Angola	1,831	2,211	2,453	2,989	3,327	0.02	11.31
Cameroon	4,068	4,499	5,217	5,446	5,041	0.03	-7.44
Central African Republic	928	832	694	1,041	788	0.00	-24.30
Chad	372	846	637	427	349	0.00	-18.27
Congo	6,020	5,322	6,481	6,864	6,294	0.04	-8.30
Democratic Republic of the Congo	10,107	8,838	7,290	8,203	9,137	0.05	11.39
Equatorial Guinea	195	280	92	275	161	0.00	-41.45
Gabon	2,196	2,830	2,044	1,648	2,138	0.01	29.73
Sao Tome and Principe	167	160	141	107	98	0.00	-8.41
North Africa	41,811	44,057	47,528	41,706	42,375	0.25	1.60
Algeria	10,079	11,094	10,942	8,929	8,519	0.05	-4.59
Morocco	23,348	25,279	27,927	24,688	24,737	0.15	0.20
Sudan	1,134	982	824	1,096	923	0.01	-15.78
Tunisia	7,250	6,702	7,835	6,993	8,196	0.05	17.20
Southern Africa	26,628	24,711	21,181	24,338	26,624	0.16	9.39
Botswana	773	333	234	412	352	0.00	-14.56
Lesotho	190	125	116	126	104	0.00	-17.46
Namibia	1,009	1,756	1,290	1,580	710	0.00	-55.06
South Africa	23,521	20,533	17,636	20,280	23,563	0.14	16.19
Swaziland	1,135	1,964	1,905	1,940	1,895	0.01	-2.32
West Africa	36,304	31,007	28,590	36,657	32,674	0.20	-10.87
Cape Verde	234	223	190	376	470	0.00	25.00
Benin	1,653	1,479	1,228	1,120	1,386	0.01	23.75
Gambia	670	610	705	1,125	662	0.00	-41.16
Ghana	1,299	1,417	1,266	2,485	2,123	0.01	-14.57
Guinea	1,323	1,147	2,640	2,683	1,712	0.01	-36.19
Côte d'Ivoire	3,507	2,557	2,618	2,972	2,872	0.02	-3.36
Liberia	754	568	429	593	522	0.00	-11.97
Mali	2,189	1,507	1,648	2,060	1,927	0.01	-6.46
Mauritania	765	1,237	1,049	1,487	946	0.01	-36.38
Niger	3,897	6,441	4,157	3,488	3,288	0.02	-5.73
Nigeria	5,739	5,133	4,249	5,835	5,760	0.03	-1.29
Guinea-Bissau	125	220	72	286	236	0.00	-17.48
Senegal	2,813	2,863	3,414	4,886	3,636	0.02	-25.58
Sierra Leone	3,265	3,810	2,852	3,789	3,598	0.02	-5.04

BELGIUM

6. Overnight stays of non-resident tourists in all types of accommodation establishments, by country of residence

	2007	2008	2009	2010	2011	Market share 11	% Change 11-10
Togo	7,046	848	740	1,700	771	0.00	-54.65
Burkina Faso	1,025	947	1,333	1,772	2,765	0.02	56.04
AMERICAS	**903,604**	**852,482**	**791,281**	**907,808**	**1,031,301**	**6.17**	**13.60**
Caribbean	**15,567**	**11,754**	**5,786**	**6,318**	**6,152**	**0.04**	**-2.63**
Antigua and Barbuda	491	1,133	597	712	633	0.00	-11.10
Bahamas	471	799	207	689	414	0.00	-39.91
Barbados	9,667	5,937	1,029	626	478	0.00	-23.64
Cuba	1,347	1,301	659	566	734	0.00	29.68
Dominica	260	175	392	302	351	0.00	16.23
Dominican Republic	1,041	733	823	1,178	1,042	0.01	-11.54
Grenada	277	211	283	359	219	0.00	-39.00
Haiti	419	424	344	560	460	0.00	-17.86
Jamaica	984	525	694	728	1,111	0.01	52.61
Saint Kitts and Nevis	22	53	66	53	143	0.00	169.81
Saint Lucia	121	50	83	178	111	0.00	-37.64
Saint Vincent and the Grenadines	15	38	145	37	146	0.00	294.59
Trinidad and Tobago	452	375	464	330	310	0.00	-6.06
Central America	**7,178**	**9,602**	**8,271**	**9,581**	**10,095**	**0.06**	**5.36**
Belize	253	320	380	466	531	0.00	13.95
Costa Rica	2,951	3,410	3,243	3,588	3,138	0.02	-12.54
El Salvador	1,196	1,339	1,115	1,368	1,727	0.01	26.24
Guatemala	614	946	996	1,244	1,195	0.01	-3.94
Honduras	491	1,262	777	710	1,102	0.01	55.21
Nicaragua	630	1,102	868	990	809	0.00	-18.28
Panama	1,043	1,223	892	1,215	1,593	0.01	31.11
North America	**792,981**	**731,882**	**685,622**	**771,286**	**858,657**	**5.13**	**11.33**
Canada	108,743	103,266	92,726	108,803	125,031	0.75	14.92
Mexico	31,661	29,424	23,473	30,545	35,751	0.21	17.04
United States of America	652,577	599,192	569,423	631,938	697,875	4.17	10.43
South America	**87,878**	**99,244**	**91,602**	**120,623**	**156,397**	**0.94**	**29.66**
Argentina	13,657	13,655	16,303	22,270	28,268	0.17	26.93
Bolivia	1,251	1,296	1,359	1,042	1,250	0.01	19.96
Brazil	46,707	56,454	46,531	66,453	90,458	0.54	36.12
Chile	6,953	6,498	5,812	6,797	9,468	0.06	39.30
Colombia	6,778	7,631	7,075	9,213	8,692	0.05	-5.66
Ecuador	2,172	2,118	2,741	2,371	2,581	0.02	8.86
Guyana	176	106	269	196	278	0.00	41.84
Paraguay	421	467	457	541	855	0.01	58.04
Peru	2,991	2,970	2,884	3,379	3,649	0.02	7.99
Suriname	492	724	812	754	1,575	0.01	108.89
Uruguay	2,593	1,840	2,732	3,480	4,020	0.02	15.52
Venezuela	3,687	5,485	4,627	4,127	5,303	0.03	28.50
EAST ASIA AND THE PACIFIC	**520,801**	**475,517**	**425,803**	**462,634**	**552,824**	**3.31**	**19.49**
North-East Asia	**389,927**	**346,108**	**302,506**	**318,948**	**383,230**	**2.29**	**20.15**
China	141,299	114,587	118,001	122,462	150,047	0.90	22.53
Taiwan, Province of China	11,194	10,669	10,651	9,358	16,991	0.10	81.57
Japan	205,174	192,322	152,694	158,383	180,330	1.08	13.86
Korea, Dem. People's Republic of	6,158	7,631	5,737	7,057	9,671	0.06	37.04
Korea, Republic of	25,867	20,611	15,135	21,393	25,411	0.15	18.78
Mongolia	235	288	288	295	780	0.00	164.41
South-East Asia	**46,165**	**44,066**	**41,388**	**49,866**	**59,317**	**0.35**	**18.95**
Brunei Darussalam	473	218	208	455	537	0.00	18.02
Myanmar	98	145	146	274	202	0.00	-26.28
Cambodia	295	296	338	383	396	0.00	3.39
Indonesia	4,523	4,442	4,974	6,979	6,863	0.04	-1.66
Lao People's Democratic Republic	620	501	308	463	508	0.00	9.72

BELGIUM

6. Overnight stays of non-resident tourists in all types of accommodation establishments, by country of residence

	2007	2008	2009	2010	2011	Market share 11	% Change 11-10
Malaysia	7,223	7,427	6,028	7,215	9,096	0.05	26.07
Philippines	8,341	8,366	7,112	7,601	10,162	0.06	33.69
Timor-Leste	10	124	12	90	34	0.00	-62.22
Singapore	11,988	11,328	9,098	11,518	13,092	0.08	13.67
Viet Nam	3,091	3,049	2,965	4,432	4,667	0.03	5.30
Thailand	9,503	8,170	10,199	10,456	13,760	0.08	31.60
Australasia	**82,636**	**82,618**	**80,027**	**91,847**	**107,831**	**0.64**	**17.40**
Australia	65,056	67,745	69,087	80,066	93,539	0.56	16.83
New Zealand	17,580	14,873	10,940	11,781	14,292	0.09	21.31
Melanesia	**1,128**	**925**	**844**	**861**	**1,176**	**0.01**	**36.59**
Solomon Islands	253	223	169	267	330	0.00	23.60
Fiji	456	390	267	301	434	0.00	44.19
Vanuatu	198	87	74	63	194	0.00	207.94
Papua New Guinea	221	225	334	230	218	0.00	-5.22
Micronesia	**678**	**1,076**	**549**	**915**	**706**	**0.00**	**-22.84**
Kiribati	136	142	42	122	106	0.00	-13.11
Nauru	291	385	284	363	401	0.00	10.47
Micronesia, Federated States of	79	175	68	334	121	0.00	-63.77
Marshall Islands	3	15	4	14	8	0.00	-42.86
Palau	169	359	151	82	70	0.00	-14.63
Polynesia	**267**	**724**	**489**	**197**	**564**	**0.00**	**186.29**
Tonga	116	381	241	158	174	0.00	10.13
Tuvalu	81	233	194	20	63	0.00	215.00
Samoa	70	110	54	19	327	0.00	1621.05
EUROPE	**14,288,650**	**14,375,789**	**13,703,740**	**14,362,734**	**14,728,013**	**88.07**	**2.54**
Central/Eastern Europe	**691,228**	**721,375**	**639,908**	**746,507**	**868,655**	**5.19**	**16.36**
Azerbaijan	1,592	1,947	1,749	1,969	2,825	0.02	43.47
Armenia	1,838	2,636	2,854	5,243	3,004	0.02	-42.70
Bulgaria	31,883	32,074	30,578	33,550	35,785	0.21	6.66
Belarus	3,144	2,909	4,487	4,130	5,155	0.03	24.82
Czech Republic	58,604	59,104	59,920	65,544	70,373	0.42	7.37
Estonia	10,588	11,574	10,401	11,953	12,490	0.07	4.49
Georgia	7,112	6,581	6,658	5,870	4,697	0.03	-19.98
Hungary	68,756	70,385	59,506	58,050	67,498	0.40	16.28
Kazakhstan	1,550	3,054	2,496	2,536	3,368	0.02	32.81
Kyrgyzstan	408	497	265	343	409	0.00	19.24
Latvia	10,602	12,160	10,122	15,004	17,328	0.10	15.49
Lithuania	26,610	29,020	23,512	27,420	29,032	0.17	5.88
Republic of Moldova	1,223	1,655	1,502	1,663	1,859	0.01	11.79
Poland	233,269	223,246	197,467	238,986	272,693	1.63	14.10
Romania	63,997	77,977	76,319	87,254	107,076	0.64	22.72
Russian Federation	117,634	125,937	107,530	138,376	179,392	1.07	29.64
Slovakia	31,524	37,969	25,032	28,062	31,420	0.19	11.97
Tajikistan	746	319	315	205	393	0.00	91.71
Turkmenistan	516	474	273	357	188	0.00	-47.34
Ukraine	17,151	20,355	17,894	19,158	22,615	0.14	18.04
Uzbekistan	2,481	1,502	1,028	834	1,055	0.01	26.50
Northern Europe	**2,699,880**	**2,654,036**	**2,217,800**	**2,247,665**	**2,286,958**	**13.67**	**1.75**
Denmark	114,145	117,574	114,196	116,335	123,655	0.74	6.29
Finland	66,971	68,878	59,134	66,162	73,064	0.44	10.43
Iceland	14,510	13,831	9,370	14,536	14,488	0.09	-0.33
Ireland	83,171	87,580	87,497	78,751	87,665	0.52	11.32
Norway	66,420	66,079	61,051	69,907	78,252	0.47	11.94
Sweden	139,919	137,572	121,646	138,103	138,595	0.83	0.36
United Kingdom	2,214,744	2,162,522	1,764,906	1,763,871	1,771,239	10.59	0.42
Southern Europe	**1,285,117**	**1,306,469**	**1,315,923**	**1,425,684**	**1,537,009**	**9.19**	**7.81**

BELGIUM

6. Overnight stays of non-resident tourists in all types of accommodation establishments, by country of residence

	2007	2008	2009	2010	2011	Market share 11	% Change 11-10
Albania	10,046	5,919	14,131	7,683	8,889	0.05	15.70
Andorra	4,728	4,885	2,424	979	1,307	0.01	33.50
Bosnia and Herzegovina	3,440	4,299	3,869	4,067	5,195	0.03	27.74
Croatia	12,909	13,237	13,691	23,165	14,384	0.09	-37.91
Greece	94,516	73,080	82,302	65,158	69,084	0.41	6.03
Holy See	212	186	169	170	105	0.00	-38.24
Italy	465,649	471,865	477,343	517,006	555,628	3.32	7.47
Malta	10,538	11,077	11,183	11,774	13,536	0.08	14.97
Montenegro	1,392	2,356	1,417	1,404	2,422	0.01	72.51
Portugal	105,079	95,452	85,378	83,964	84,060	0.50	0.11
San Marino	199	151	534	141	222	0.00	57.45
Serbia	8,416	13,291	13,816	10,731	14,994	0.09	39.73
Slovenia	20,584	20,980	17,336	20,768	27,785	0.17	33.79
Spain	545,038	586,498	589,606	675,582	735,857	4.40	8.92
TFYR of Macedonia	2,371	3,193	2,724	3,092	3,541	0.02	14.52
Western Europe	**9,461,258**	**9,557,507**	**9,414,937**	**9,814,878**	**9,884,862**	**59.11**	**0.71**
Austria	72,643	75,200	77,851	80,752	90,910	0.54	12.58
France	2,005,244	2,071,472	2,089,571	2,173,874	2,301,498	13.76	5.87
Germany	1,949,312	1,901,580	1,879,846	1,992,544	2,027,052	12.12	1.73
Liechtenstein	5,739	6,094	5,012	3,924	2,536	0.02	-35.37
Luxembourg	180,605	185,554	184,544	189,479	203,259	1.22	7.27
Monaco	1,117	1,470	1,933	1,910	2,039	0.01	6.75
Netherlands	5,114,679	5,175,164	5,035,124	5,220,042	5,081,035	30.38	-2.66
Switzerland	131,919	140,973	141,056	152,353	176,533	1.06	15.87
East Mediterranean Europe	**151,167**	**136,402**	**115,172**	**128,000**	**150,529**	**0.90**	**17.60**
Cyprus	12,079	12,166	11,888	12,580	15,788	0.09	25.50
Israel	70,776	62,858	49,272	54,224	62,349	0.37	14.98
Turkey	68,312	61,378	54,012	61,196	72,392	0.43	18.30
MIDDLE EAST	**74,716**	**79,053**	**59,874**	**77,266**	**85,920**	**0.51**	**11.20**
Bahrain	1,080	1,624	1,107	1,243	1,771	0.01	42.48
Palestine	140	626	242	696	246	0.00	-64.66
Iraq	1,294	1,638	1,987	2,451	1,972	0.01	-19.54
Jordan	2,687	3,247	4,176	4,283	3,617	0.02	-15.55
Kuwait	3,335	4,783	4,024	4,177	6,118	0.04	46.47
Lebanon	6,677	5,941	5,573	5,724	7,034	0.04	22.89
Libya	4,900	1,883	1,508	1,817	1,163	0.01	-35.99
Oman	1,414	1,188	1,085	1,589	2,008	0.01	26.37
Qatar	7,579	4,108	1,971	2,965	3,306	0.02	11.50
Saudi Arabia	8,283	10,188	8,812	11,291	12,966	0.08	14.83
Syrian Arab Republic	1,849	1,831	2,922	2,064	1,693	0.01	-17.97
United Arab Emirates	20,798	29,687	14,713	25,092	30,757	0.18	22.58
Egypt	14,281	11,724	11,207	13,553	12,730	0.08	-6.07
Yemen	399	585	547	321	539	0.00	67.91
SOUTH ASIA	**100,074**	**130,228**	**98,108**	**108,265**	**121,261**	**0.73**	**12.00**
Afghanistan	2,569	2,616	4,150	3,625	4,020	0.02	10.90
Bangladesh	858	716	908	1,303	1,441	0.01	10.59
Bhutan	72	76	263	46	118	0.00	156.52
Sri Lanka	807	1,010	644	721	957	0.01	32.73
India	79,763	109,055	72,852	85,089	97,323	0.58	14.38
Iran, Islamic Republic of	11,803	11,945	15,502	12,859	12,983	0.08	0.96
Maldives	147	101	91	80	122	0.00	52.50
Nepal	347	311	417	447	564	0.00	26.17
Pakistan	3,708	4,398	3,281	4,095	3,733	0.02	-8.84
NOT SPECIFIED	**235,136**	**304,102**	**229,576**	**98,987**	**54,367**	**0.33**	**-45.08**
Other countries of the World	235,136	304,102	229,576	98,987	54,367	0.33	-45.08

BELIZE

1. Arrivals of non-resident tourists at national borders, by nationality

	2007	2008	2009	2010	2011	Market share 11	% Change 11-10
TOTAL	251,422	245,026	232,249	241,919	250,263	100.00	3.45
AFRICA	491	512	668	577	472	0.19	-18.15
Other Africa	491	512	668	577	472	0.19	-18.15
All countries of Africa	491	512	668	577	472	0.19	-18.15
AMERICAS	201,679	195,645	188,240	195,568	203,128	81.17	3.87
Caribbean	2,595	2,307	2,388	2,505	2,049	0.82	-18.20
Jamaica	643	584	669	663	599	0.24	-9.70
Other countries of the Caribbean	1,952	1,723	1,719	1,842	1,451	0.58	-21.26
Central America	21,869	20,207	22,208	21,908	16,834	6.73	-23.16
Guatemala	14,130	11,674	12,957	12,448	7,423	2.97	-40.36
Honduras	2,928	3,105	3,506	3,680	3,731	1.49	1.40
Other countries of Central America	4,811	5,428	5,745	5,780	5,679	2.27	-1.75
North America	174,976	171,112	161,555	168,958	181,984	72.72	7.71
Canada	16,655	17,695	17,211	18,246	20,093	8.03	10.12
Mexico	5,752	5,763	4,783	4,840	5,598	2.24	15.66
United States of America	152,569	147,654	139,561	145,872	156,293	62.45	7.14
South America	2,239	2,019	2,089	2,197	2,261	0.90	2.92
All countries of South America	2,239	2,019	2,089	2,197	2,261	0.90	2.92
EAST ASIA AND THE PACIFIC	5,482	5,234	4,973	6,069	5,737	2.29	-5.48
Other East Asia and the Pacific	5,482	5,234	4,973	6,069	5,737	2.29	-5.48
All countries of Asia	3,280	2,774	2,459	2,937	2,995	1.20	2.00
All countries of Oceania	2,202	2,460	2,514	3,133	2,741	1.10	-12.49
EUROPE	34,175	34,269	29,603	30,025	30,142	12.04	0.39
Northern Europe	11,268	11,230	9,334	10,142	9,046	3.61	-10.81
Sweden	1,088	1,130	800	841	847	0.34	0.69
United Kingdom	10,180	10,100	8,534	9,301	8,199	3.28	-11.85
Southern Europe	4,508	3,998	3,151	3,412	3,657	1.46	7.18
Italy	2,702	2,371	1,679	1,877	2,218	0.89	18.12
Spain	1,806	1,627	1,472	1,535	1,440	0.58	-6.20
Western Europe	11,426	12,047	9,994	9,856	10,254	4.10	4.04
France	3,126	3,258	3,269	2,916	3,101	1.24	6.36
Germany	4,054	4,161	3,376	3,438	3,262	1.30	-5.12
Netherlands	3,496	3,915	2,607	2,461	2,869	1.15	16.59
Switzerland	750	713	742	1,041	1,021	0.41	-1.85
Other Europe	6,973	6,994	7,124	6,615	7,184	2.87	8.61
Other countries of Europe	6,973	6,994	7,124	6,615	7,184	2.87	8.61
MIDDLE EAST	435	588	400	863	628	0.25	-27.28
All countries of Middle East	435	588	400	863	628	0.25	-27.28
NOT SPECIFIED	9,160	8,778	8,365	8,817	10,157	4.06	15.20
Nationals Residing Abroad	9,160	8,778	8,365	8,817	10,157	4.06	15.20

BELIZE

2. Arrivals of non-resident visitors at national borders, by nationality

		2007	2008	2009	2010	2011	Market share 11	% Change 11-10
TOTAL	(*)	1,044,988	990,757	1,091,406	1,197,326	1,177,462	100.00	-1.66
AMERICAS		953,427	881,904	989,821	1,105,499	1,077,276	91.49	-2.55
Caribbean		5,129	7,906	9,067	7,823	7,646	0.65	-2.26
Cuba		831	904	1,170	1,165	1,121	0.10	-3.78
Jamaica		886	1,173	1,292	1,213	1,184	0.10	-2.39
Other countries of the Caribbean		3,412	5,829	6,605	5,445	5,341	0.45	-1.91
Central America		133,354	114,525	129,308	154,968	168,044	14.27	8.44
Costa Rica		1,084	1,210	1,230	1,235	1,056	0.09	-14.49
El Salvador		3,879	4,533	4,792	5,182	5,069	0.43	-2.18
Guatemala		119,662	102,090	116,123	141,083	154,954	13.16	9.83
Honduras		4,206	4,324	4,824	5,283	5,070	0.43	-4.03
Other countries of Central America		4,523	2,368	2,339	2,185	1,895	0.16	-13.27
North America		809,152	753,015	840,771	933,035	892,230	75.78	-4.37
Canada		47,746	53,102	60,503	63,971	67,257	5.71	5.14
Mexico		33,369	29,432	26,259	26,101	33,864	2.88	29.74
United States of America		728,037	670,481	754,009	842,963	791,109	67.19	-6.15
South America		5,792	6,458	10,675	9,673	9,356	0.79	-3.28
All countries of South America		5,792	6,458	10,675	9,673	9,356	0.79	-3.28
EAST ASIA AND THE PACIFIC		5,424	5,742	5,925	6,424	7,862	0.67	22.38
Other East Asia and the Pacific		5,424	5,742	5,925	6,424	7,862	0.67	22.38
All countries of Asia		5,424	5,742	5,925	6,424	7,862	0.67	22.38
EUROPE		80,463	95,572	86,247	75,690	84,038	7.14	11.03
Northern Europe		21,159	33,468	19,885	18,500	20,474	1.74	10.67
United Kingdom		21,159	33,468	19,885	18,500	20,474	1.74	10.67
Other Europe		59,304	62,104	66,362	57,190	63,564	5.40	11.15
Other countries of Europe		59,304	62,104	66,362	57,190	63,564	5.40	11.15
NOT SPECIFIED		5,674	7,539	9,413	9,713	8,286	0.70	-14.69
Other countries of the World		5,674	7,539	9,413	9,713	8,286	0.70	-14.69

BENIN

1. Arrivals of non-resident tourists at national borders, by country of residence

	2007	2008	2009	2010	2011	Market share 11	% Change 11-10
TOTAL	186,394	188,000	190,000	199,491	209,475	100.00	5.00
AFRICA	153,016	117,929	90,757	138,000	125,685	60.00	-8.92
East Africa	6,502	3,713	2,634	5,914	5,027	2.40	-15.00
Burundi	1,240	74	31	1,035	611	0.29	-40.97
Comoros	615	72	106	515	498	0.24	-3.30
Ethiopia	91	126	47	110	118	0.06	7.27
Eritrea	88			9			
Djibouti	110	46	30	120	200	0.10	66.67
Kenya	90	332	142	76	120	0.06	57.89
Madagascar	1,148	332	239	980	612	0.29	-37.55
Malawi	890	12	35	1,100	940	0.45	-14.55
Mauritius	66	42	1	33			
Mozambique	880	115	26	500	610	0.29	22.00
Rwanda	733	1,081	1,061	845	900	0.43	6.51
Seychelles	9	18	20	11	5	0.00	-54.55
Somalia	44	397	717	300	187	0.09	-37.67
Zimbabwe	21	67	30	17	11	0.01	-35.29
Uganda	192	66	60	54	47	0.02	-12.96
United Republic of Tanzania	135	715	78	88	150	0.07	70.45
Zambia	150	218	11	121	18	0.01	-85.12
Central Africa	64,771	38,570	24,163	58,494	50,263	23.99	-14.07
Angola	10,921	3,504	609	11,410	9,872	4.71	-13.48
Cameroon	11,600	7,244	5,357	10,620	12,500	5.97	17.70
Central African Republic	1,047	1,445	840	800	700	0.33	-12.50
Chad	1,932	1,481	1,900	2,007	1,800	0.86	-10.31
Congo	33,896	12,468	6,839	25,953	22,897	10.93	-11.78
Democratic Republic of the Congo	1,030	370	47	915	600	0.29	-34.43
Equatorial Guinea	89	1,740	253	200	87	0.04	-56.50
Gabon	4,244	10,287	8,313	6,589	1,807	0.86	-72.58
Sao Tome and Principe	12	31	5				
North Africa	2,881	3,361	2,526	2,697	2,500	1.19	-7.30
Algeria	680	750	966	850	740	0.35	-12.94
Morocco	291	869	416	600	700	0.33	16.67
Sudan	410	400	227	320	350	0.17	9.38
Tunisia	1,500	1,342	917	927	710	0.34	-23.41
Southern Africa	781	2,099	1,160	977	512	0.24	-47.59
Botswana	28	153	135	200	99	0.05	-50.50
Lesotho	36	22	47	55	36	0.02	-34.55
Namibia	81	74	63	57	20	0.01	-64.91
South Africa	624	1,850	915	663	346	0.17	-47.81
Swaziland	12			2	11	0.01	450.00
West Africa	78,081	70,186	60,274	69,918	67,383	32.17	-3.63
Cape Verde	300	440	700	540	410	0.20	-24.07
Gambia	2,560	234	545	180	200	0.10	11.11
Ghana	8,300	4,196	5,126	4,400	5,500	2.63	25.00
Guinea	1,967	1,740	422	1,800	918	0.44	-49.00
Côte d'Ivoire	14,745	12,940	7,550	18,937	15,813	7.55	-16.50
Liberia	241	291	178	300	340	0.16	13.33
Mali	1,400	1,729	1,273	1,945	2,600	1.24	33.68
Mauritania	230	446	445	333	260	0.12	-21.92
Niger	7,700	5,240	5,900	6,000	5,500	2.63	-8.33
Nigeria	22,900	21,150	13,184	15,975	17,614	8.41	10.26
Guinea-Bissau	50	177	116	200	325	0.16	62.50
Senegal	2,880	4,111	3,059	4,600	3,100	1.48	-32.61
Sierra Leone	350	225	525	186	223	0.11	19.89
Togo	9,988	6,667	11,551	5,400	7,600	3.63	40.74

BENIN

1. Arrivals of non-resident tourists at national borders, by country of residence

	2007	2008	2009	2010	2011	Market share 11	% Change 11-10
Burkina Faso	4,470	10,600	9,700	9,122	6,980	3.33	-23.48
AMERICAS	**2,299**	**3,926**	**5,104**	**3,173**	**3,066**	**1.46**	**-3.37**
Caribbean	**125**	**556**	**336**	**266**	**189**	**0.09**	**-28.95**
Cuba	19	97	117	57	28	0.01	-50.88
Dominican Republic	20		91	19	11	0.01	-42.11
Guadeloupe	9	67		7	10	0.00	42.86
Haiti	15	145	120	152	129	0.06	-15.13
Jamaica	22	165	8	11	6	0.00	-45.45
Netherlands Antilles	40	82		20	5	0.00	-75.00
Central America	**18**	**1**			**11**	**0.01**	
Honduras	7				3	0.00	
Nicaragua	11	1			8	0.00	
North America	**1,973**	**2,175**	**3,756**	**1,974**	**2,150**	**1.03**	**8.92**
Canada	672	652	952	612	840	0.40	37.25
Mexico	101	75	120	375	420	0.20	12.00
United States of America	1,200	1,448	2,684	987	890	0.42	-9.83
South America	**183**	**1,194**	**1,012**	**933**	**716**	**0.34**	**-23.26**
Argentina	17	344	604	500	422	0.20	-15.60
Bolivia	8			9	12	0.01	33.33
Brazil	92	850	360	407	120	0.06	-70.52
Chile	10			2	20	0.01	900.00
Colombia	20		48	11	89	0.04	709.09
Uruguay	5			3	13	0.01	333.33
Venezuela	31			1	40	0.02	3900.00
EAST ASIA AND THE PACIFIC	**780**	**1,633**	**860**	**800**	**1,126**	**0.54**	**40.75**
North-East Asia	**621**	**1,468**	**603**	**679**	**972**	**0.46**	**43.15**
China	300	1,073	410	371	580	0.28	56.33
Japan	199	196	174	200	240	0.11	20.00
Korea, Dem. People's Republic of	122	199	19	108	152	0.07	40.74
South-East Asia	**126**	**165**	**113**	**88**	**97**	**0.05**	**10.23**
Indonesia	20	101	45	13	25	0.01	92.31
Malaysia	4	9	19	6	2	0.00	-66.67
Philippines	3	22	12	7	5	0.00	-28.57
Singapore	60	33	1	12	12	0.01	
Viet Nam	21		14	9	19	0.01	111.11
Thailand	18		22	41	34	0.02	-17.07
Australasia	**29**		**144**	**33**	**55**	**0.03**	**66.67**
Australia	14		144	30	19	0.01	-36.67
New Zealand	15			3	36	0.02	1100.00
Melanesia	**4**				**2**	**0.00**	
Fiji	4				2	0.00	
EUROPE	**26,283**	**50,706**	**35,448**	**32,886**	**57,081**	**27.25**	**73.57**
Northern Europe	**552**	**1,554**	**3,856**	**610**	**2,903**	**1.39**	**375.90**
Denmark	397	23	1,538	291	300	0.14	3.09
Finland	19	6	578	22	30	0.01	36.36
Ireland	20	11	34	33	987	0.47	2890.91
Norway	50	639	358	45	800	0.38	1677.78
Sweden	66	875	1,348	219	786	0.38	258.90
Southern Europe	**887**	**5,820**	**6,224**	**2,897**	**4,855**	**2.32**	**67.59**
Bosnia and Herzegovina	7				2	0.00	
Greece	12	100	314	300	206	0.10	-31.33
Italy	500	3,066	3,237	1,438	3,074	1.47	113.77
Montenegro				1	7	0.00	600.00
Portugal	267	630	466	346	600	0.29	73.41

BENIN

1. Arrivals of non-resident tourists at national borders, by country of residence

	2007	2008	2009	2010	2011	Market share 11	% Change 11-10
Slovenia	1			5	15	0.01	200.00
Spain	100	2,024	2,207	807	950	0.45	17.72
Serbia and Montenegro					1	0.00	
Western Europe	**24,167**	**34,244**	**17,616**	**22,641**	**41,132**	**19.64**	**81.67**
Austria	1,745	295	222	600	200	0.10	-66.67
Belgium	3,900	1,910	2,162	4,670	3,600	1.72	-22.91
France	14,641	15,846	2,519	13,206	20,386	9.73	54.37
Germany	2,000	2,718	1,992	1,950	2,317	1.11	18.82
Luxembourg	99	182	30	81	229	0.11	182.72
Netherlands	870	4,127	4,120	900	8,900	4.25	888.89
Switzerland	912	9,166	6,571	1,234	5,500	2.63	345.71
East Mediterranean Europe	**34**	**252**	**142**	**108**	**202**	**0.10**	**87.04**
Israel	25	252	142	88	135	0.06	53.41
Turkey	9			20	67	0.03	235.00
Other Europe	**643**	**8,836**	**7,610**	**6,630**	**7,989**	**3.81**	**20.50**
Other countries of Europe	643	8,836	7,610	6,630	7,989	3.81	20.50
MIDDLE EAST	**1,762**	**291**	**367**	**2,388**	**2,670**	**1.27**	**11.81**
Palestine	66	55		20	17	0.01	-15.00
Iraq	33	13	30	19	11	0.01	-42.11
Jordan	11	5	20	33	7	0.00	-78.79
Kuwait	30	1		15	25	0.01	66.67
Lebanon	740	97	290	1,300	1,659	0.79	27.62
Libya	520			940	889	0.42	-5.43
Qatar	7		18	11	12	0.01	9.09
Saudi Arabia	90	120	9	3	5	0.00	66.67
Syrian Arab Republic	21			2	4	0.00	100.00
Egypt	244			45	41	0.02	-8.89
SOUTH ASIA	**2,254**	**691**	**453**	**845**	**1,147**	**0.55**	**35.74**
Afghanistan	111	20	181	81	58	0.03	-28.40
Bangladesh					2	0.00	
Sri Lanka					5	0.00	
India	898	634	212	707	1,037	0.50	46.68
Iran, Islamic Republic of	630	17	9	22	19	0.01	-13.64
Nepal	15	3	1	5	11	0.01	120.00
Pakistan	600	17	50	30	15	0.01	-50.00
NOT SPECIFIED		**12,824**	**57,011**	**21,399**	**18,700**	**8.93**	**-12.61**
Other countries of the World		12,824	57,011	21,399	18,700	8.93	-12.61

BERMUDA

1. Arrivals of non-resident tourists at national borders, by country of residence

		2007	2008	2009	2010	2011	Market share 11	% Change 11-10
TOTAL	(*)	305,548	263,613	235,860	232,262	236,038	100.00	1.63
AMERICAS		257,342	216,595	197,515	196,418	202,107	85.62	2.90
North America		257,342	216,595	197,515	196,418	202,107	85.62	2.90
Canada		27,844	27,207	24,867	30,402	29,217	12.38	-3.90
United States of America		229,498	189,388	172,648	166,016	172,890	73.25	4.14
EAST ASIA AND THE PACIFIC		714	795	811	1,088	1,058	0.45	-2.76
North-East Asia		205	386	336	385	367	0.16	-4.68
Japan		205	386	336	385	367	0.16	-4.68
Australasia		509	409	475	703	691	0.29	-1.71
Australia		509	409	475	703	691	0.29	-1.71
EUROPE		35,938	35,003	28,949	28,498	26,940	11.41	-5.47
Northern Europe		30,726	29,584	24,218	23,501	21,797	9.23	-7.25
Sweden		340	329	313	261	273	0.12	4.60
United Kingdom		30,386	29,255	23,905	23,240	21,524	9.12	-7.38
Southern Europe		1,114	1,544	1,253	1,244	1,184	0.50	-4.82
Italy		1,114	1,544	1,253	1,244	1,184	0.50	-4.82
Western Europe		3,034	2,963	2,516	2,760	2,870	1.22	3.99
Austria		118	171	135	168	176	0.07	4.76
France		1,007	954	754	711	698	0.30	-1.83
Germany		1,402	1,293	1,032	994	1,116	0.47	12.27
Switzerland		507	545	595	887	880	0.37	-0.79
Other Europe		1,064	912	962	993	1,089	0.46	9.67
Other countries of Europe		1,064	912	962	993	1,089	0.46	9.67
NOT SPECIFIED		11,554	11,220	8,585	6,258	5,933	2.51	-5.19
Other countries of the World		11,554	11,220	8,585	6,258	5,933	2.51	-5.19

BHUTAN

1. Arrivals of non-resident tourists at national borders, by nationality

		2007	2008	2009	2010	2011	Market share 11	% Change 11-10
TOTAL	(*)	21,094	27,642	23,480	27,210	37,478	100.00	37.74
AFRICA		65	77	48	102	92	0.25	-9.80
East Africa		2	5	7	6	20	0.05	233.33
Kenya			1	2	4	6	0.02	50.00
Mauritius		1	3	5	1	14	0.04	1300.00
Somalia			1					
Uganda		1			1			
North Africa		1		5				
Algeria		1						
Morocco				4				
Tunisia				1				
Southern Africa		62	71	36	74	63	0.17	-14.86
Namibia			5		1	1	0.00	
South Africa		62	65	32	70	62	0.17	-11.43
Swaziland			1	4	3			
West Africa			1					
Liberia			1					
Other Africa					22	9	0.02	-59.09
Other countries of Africa					22	9	0.02	-59.09
AMERICAS		6,653	8,240	5,743	6,506	8,055	21.49	23.81
Caribbean		1	1					
Cuba		1	1					
Central America		3	1	2	13	13	0.03	
Belize		2			1	1	0.00	
Costa Rica		1			10	1	0.00	-90.00
Guatemala				2		11	0.03	
Honduras			1		2			
North America		6,488	7,931	5,467	6,141	7,511	20.04	22.31
Canada		588	852	556	786	1,061	2.83	34.99
Mexico		127	138	125	166	224	0.60	34.94
United States of America		5,773	6,941	4,786	5,189	6,226	16.61	19.98
South America		161	307	274	338	486	1.30	43.79
Argentina		43	21	59	40	80	0.21	100.00
Brazil		79	249	178	229	304	0.81	32.75
Chile		5	15	8	18	45	0.12	150.00
Colombia		11	5	14	27	45	0.12	66.67
Ecuador		1			1			
Peru			7	6	19	12	0.03	-36.84
Uruguay				1	1			
Venezuela		22	10	8	3			
Other Americas					14	45	0.12	221.43
Other countries of the Americas					14	45	0.12	221.43
EAST ASIA AND THE PACIFIC		5,393	7,412	7,743	8,599	14,966	39.93	74.04
North-East Asia		2,817	4,072	4,412	4,827	8,147	21.74	68.78
China		504	1,069	1,143	1,494	2,896	7.73	93.84
Taiwan, Province of China		132	114	83	184	891	2.38	384.24
Japan		2,008	2,749	3,136	2,963	3,943	10.52	33.07
Korea, Dem. People's Republic of			43			3	0.01	
Korea, Republic of		172	97	49	182	407	1.09	123.63
Macao, China				1	3			
Mongolia		1			1	7	0.02	600.00
South-East Asia		1,267	1,636	2,239	2,277	4,878	13.02	114.23
Myanmar			5	5	1	3	0.01	200.00

BHUTAN

1. Arrivals of non-resident tourists at national borders, by nationality

	2007	2008	2009	2010	2011	Market share 11	% Change 11-10
Cambodia	3	1	2				
Indonesia	46	36	98	110	295	0.79	168.18
Malaysia	94	221	367	356	788	2.10	121.35
Philippines	42	72	59	119	128	0.34	7.56
Singapore	350	667	708	785	1,349	3.60	71.85
Viet Nam	25	7	25	31	80	0.21	158.06
Thailand	707	627	975	875	2,235	5.96	155.43
Australasia	**1,308**	**1,704**	**1,092**	**1,423**	**1,917**	**5.12**	**34.72**
Australia	1,181	1,524	970	1,318	1,773	4.73	34.52
New Zealand	127	180	122	105	144	0.38	37.14
Melanesia	**1**						
Fiji	1						
Other East Asia and the Pacific				**72**	**24**	**0.06**	**-66.67**
Other countries of Asia				72	24	0.06	-66.67
EUROPE	**8,929**	**11,778**	**9,861**	**11,883**	**14,164**	**37.79**	**19.20**
Central/Eastern Europe	**737**	**820**	**720**	**857**	**1,038**	**2.77**	**21.12**
Bulgaria	2	13	12	11	11	0.03	
Belarus		2	2	2	1	0.00	-50.00
Czech Republic	71	65	77	71	135	0.36	90.14
Estonia	37	54	14	31	2	0.01	-93.55
Hungary	112	54	49	65	45	0.12	-30.77
Kazakhstan		1	5				
Latvia	24	9	3	9	44	0.12	388.89
Lithuania	9	32	4	13	44	0.12	238.46
Poland	252	233	184	268	311	0.83	16.04
Romania	3	12	19	52	35	0.09	-32.69
Russian Federation	204	245	270	275	291	0.78	5.82
Slovakia	18	55	53	32	38	0.10	18.75
Ukraine	5	44	28	27	81	0.22	200.00
Uzbekistan		1		1			
Northern Europe	**2,784**	**3,473**	**2,521**	**2,690**	**4,025**	**10.74**	**49.63**
Denmark	170	127	153	412	430	1.15	4.37
Finland	76	191	161	174	245	0.65	40.80
Iceland	7	13			7	0.02	
Ireland	56	98	59	59	78	0.21	32.20
Norway	116	109	92	136	214	0.57	57.35
Sweden	166	177	88	137	256	0.68	86.86
United Kingdom	2,193	2,758	1,968	1,772	2,795	7.46	57.73
Southern Europe	**1,317**	**1,761**	**1,506**	**1,826**	**2,045**	**5.46**	**11.99**
Andorra			3	1	1	0.00	
Bosnia and Herzegovina			1		2	0.01	
Croatia		8	4	1	6	0.02	500.00
Greece	29	45	107	88	70	0.19	-20.45
Italy	614	751	759	1,028	1,014	2.71	-1.36
Portugal	208	91	116	116	214	0.57	84.48
Slovenia	21	63	30	64	11	0.03	-82.81
Spain	444	803	485	528	727	1.94	37.69
Yugoslavia, SFR (former)	1		1				
Western Europe	**3,845**	**5,549**	**4,899**	**6,272**	**6,686**	**17.84**	**6.60**
Austria	443	472	420	505	528	1.41	4.55
Belgium	291	432	364	404	539	1.44	33.42
France	738	1,402	1,189	1,454	1,585	4.23	9.01
Germany	1,456	1,717	1,587	2,250	2,287	6.10	1.64
Luxembourg	24	14	16	23	33	0.09	43.48
Netherlands	497	915	780	847	933	2.49	10.15
Switzerland	396	597	543	789	781	2.08	-1.01

BHUTAN

1. Arrivals of non-resident tourists at national borders, by nationality

	2007	2008	2009	2010	2011	Market share 11	% Change 11-10
East Mediterranean Europe	246	175	215	232	348	0.93	50.00
Cyprus		6	5	5	4	0.01	-20.00
Israel	152	78	159	127	278	0.74	118.90
Turkey	94	91	51	100	66	0.18	-34.00
Other Europe				6	22	0.06	266.67
Other countries of Europe				6	22	0.06	266.67
MIDDLE EAST	15	29	31	27	44	0.12	62.96
Jordan		2		1	21	0.06	2000.00
Kuwait	1	5		2	8	0.02	300.00
Lebanon	1	9		5	4	0.01	-20.00
Oman		4		1	2	0.01	100.00
Saudi Arabia	5	2			2	0.01	
United Arab Emirates	7	7		8	5	0.01	-37.50
Egypt	1		18	10			
Other countries of Middle East			13		2	0.01	
SOUTH ASIA	39	106	52	93	157	0.42	68.82
Bangladesh		1					
Sri Lanka	4	26	6	30	6	0.02	-80.00
Iran, Islamic Republic of	3			1	4	0.01	300.00
Nepal	31	78	41	60	145	0.39	141.67
Pakistan	1	1	5	2	2	0.01	
NOT SPECIFIED			2				
Other countries of the World			2				

BOLIVIA

1. Arrivals of non-resident tourists at national borders, by nationality

	2007	2008	2009	2010	2011	Market share 11	% Change 11-10
TOTAL (*)	572,815	593,727	671,227	807,137			
AFRICA	951	1,028	1,115	1,336			
Other Africa	951	1,028	1,115	1,336			
All countries of Africa	951	1,028	1,115	1,336			
AMERICAS	403,963	406,709	473,364	595,472			
North America	44,248	56,442	51,850	67,826			
Canada	9,969	10,981	11,682	15,434			
Mexico	26,095	36,316	30,577	40,923			
United States of America	8,184	9,145	9,591	11,469			
South America	344,202	337,968	403,336	503,904			
Argentina	93,817	81,204	109,935	134,184			
Brazil	49,394	38,361	57,880	63,579			
Chile	43,368	46,337	50,819	64,382			
Colombia	12,355	11,643	14,477	18,372			
Ecuador	5,702	5,598	6,682	11,178			
Paraguay	16,901	16,821	19,803	19,060			
Peru	111,385	127,317	130,521	170,936			
Uruguay	4,716	5,082	5,527	9,467			
Venezuela	6,564	5,605	7,692	12,746			
Other Americas	15,513	12,299	18,178	23,742			
Other countries of the Americas	15,513	12,299	18,178	23,742			
EAST ASIA AND THE PACIFIC	33,905	38,610	39,730	46,248			
North-East Asia	6,857	8,631	8,035	6,683			
Japan	6,857	8,631	8,035	6,683			
Other East Asia and the Pacific	27,048	29,979	31,695	39,565			
Other countries of Asia	11,914	12,502	13,961	17,774			
All countries of Oceania	15,134	17,477	17,734	21,791			
EUROPE	133,996	147,380	157,018	164,081			
Northern Europe	21,544	23,679	25,245	24,404			
Sweden	3,839	3,685	4,498	5,185			
United Kingdom	17,705	19,994	20,747	19,219			
Southern Europe	26,102	29,300	30,587	27,621			
Italy	8,857	10,915	10,379	11,310			
Spain	17,245	18,385	20,208	16,311			
Western Europe	59,125	64,096	69,284	70,996			
France	24,036	26,331	28,165	32,364			
Germany	21,924	22,575	25,691	24,036			
Netherlands	6,463	7,379	7,574	6,906			
Switzerland	6,702	7,811	7,854	7,690			
Other Europe	27,225	30,305	31,902	41,060			
Other countries of Europe	27,225	30,305	31,902	41,060			

BOLIVIA

3. Arrivals of non-resident tourists in hotels and similar establishments, by nationality

		2007	2008	2009	2010	2011	Market share 11	% Change 11-10
TOTAL	(*)	**486,913**	**490,783**	**505,704**	**530,860**			
AFRICA		**1,957**	**1,524**	**1,018**	**1,062**			
Other Africa		**1,957**	**1,524**	**1,018**	**1,062**			
All countries of Africa		1,957	1,524	1,018	1,062			
AMERICAS		**297,960**	**304,429**	**309,910**	**329,529**			
North America		**71,059**	**64,841**	**64,784**	**67,854**			
Canada		11,236	10,933	10,641	10,658			
Mexico		7,536	6,605	7,322	6,571			
United States of America		52,287	47,303	46,821	50,625			
South America		**219,166**	**233,905**	**237,922**	**253,263**			
Argentina		44,741	50,205	52,960	55,680			
Brazil		38,661	38,967	41,670	44,274			
Chile		27,628	23,352	23,536	25,769			
Colombia		10,578	10,231	11,088	11,119			
Ecuador		6,262	6,709	6,504	6,827			
Paraguay		4,048	4,571	4,204	4,944			
Peru		82,275	92,993	93,676	100,396			
Uruguay		2,192	2,848	2,408	1,488			
Venezuela		2,781	4,029	1,876	2,766			
Other Americas		**7,735**	**5,683**	**7,204**	**8,412**			
Other countries of the Americas		7,735	5,683	7,204	8,412			
EAST ASIA AND THE PACIFIC		**30,106**	**34,748**	**29,844**	**33,293**			
North-East Asia		**7,101**	**6,913**	**7,800**	**7,674**			
Japan		7,101	6,913	7,800	7,674			
Other East Asia and the Pacific		**23,005**	**27,835**	**22,044**	**25,619**			
Other countries of Asia		12,885	14,644	10,796	12,484			
All countries of Oceania		10,120	13,191	11,248	13,135			
EUROPE		**156,890**	**150,082**	**164,932**	**166,976**			
Northern Europe		**29,601**	**28,988**	**30,744**	**31,732**			
Sweden		3,634	3,957	2,762	3,420			
United Kingdom		25,967	25,031	27,982	28,312			
Southern Europe		**26,574**	**24,430**	**27,230**	**27,217**			
Italy		12,466	9,768	9,407	10,748			
Spain		14,108	14,662	17,823	16,469			
Western Europe		**76,158**	**71,617**	**79,632**	**80,404**			
France		32,573	29,888	27,762	30,925			
Germany		22,953	23,626	30,327	31,396			
Netherlands		10,600	8,285	11,176	8,414			
Switzerland		10,032	9,818	10,367	9,669			
Other Europe		**24,557**	**25,047**	**27,326**	**27,623**			
Other countries of Europe		24,557	25,047	27,326	27,623			

BOLIVIA

5. Overnight stays of non-resident tourists in hotels and similar establishments, by nationality

		2007	2008	2009	2010	2011	Market share 11	% Change 11-10
TOTAL	(*)	832,079	848,486	860,216	886,363			
AFRICA		2,847	1,248	2,083	2,040			
Other Africa		2,847	1,248	2,083	2,040			
All countries of Africa		2,847	1,248	2,083	2,040			
AMERICAS		515,178	527,027	540,532	553,609			
North America		103,252	109,892	107,618	111,105			
Canada		10,109	13,696	13,872	11,008			
Mexico		10,091	16,224	12,152	14,294			
United States of America		83,052	79,972	81,594	85,803			
South America		395,041	400,766	414,487	427,177			
Argentina		83,513	85,197	95,025	98,781			
Brazil		74,211	74,770	71,533	76,393			
Chile		36,234	40,347	39,188	42,501			
Colombia		23,082	19,271	25,583	22,815			
Ecuador		12,271	10,791	12,684	10,767			
Paraguay		13,807	12,084	13,414	12,935			
Peru		139,762	147,602	144,488	151,803			
Uruguay		7,292	5,739	6,678	5,995			
Venezuela		4,869	4,965	5,894	5,187			
Other Americas		16,885	16,369	18,427	15,327			
Other countries of the Americas		16,885	16,369	18,427	15,327			
EAST ASIA AND THE PACIFIC		58,093	65,142	64,170	59,651			
North-East Asia		16,537	16,865	17,079	12,653			
Japan		16,537	16,865	17,079	12,653			
Other East Asia and the Pacific		41,556	48,277	47,091	46,998			
Other countries of Asia		26,384	31,402	31,836	29,507			
All countries of Oceania		15,172	16,875	15,255	17,491			
EUROPE		255,961	255,069	253,431	271,063			
Northern Europe		44,848	44,035	46,364	48,660			
Sweden		6,058	5,329	7,123	5,567			
United Kingdom		38,790	38,706	39,241	43,093			
Southern Europe		46,416	48,180	49,704	51,181			
Italy		13,561	15,525	16,600	17,104			
Spain		32,855	32,655	33,104	34,077			
Western Europe		117,428	117,198	111,936	122,642			
France		39,008	42,323	41,187	40,436			
Germany		37,214	38,796	36,752	43,630			
Netherlands		20,942	17,112	17,349	24,081			
Switzerland		20,264	18,967	16,648	14,495			
Other Europe		47,269	45,656	45,427	48,580			
Other countries of Europe		47,269	45,656	45,427	48,580			

BONAIRE

1. Arrivals of non-resident tourists at national borders, by country of residence

	2007	2008	2009	2010	2011	Market share 11	% Change 11-10
TOTAL	74,309	74,342	66,998	70,539			
AMERICAS	42,191	43,112	36,260	31,226			
Caribbean	3,831	4,451	4,220	2,076			
Dominican Republic	84	69	129				
Aruba	3,159	3,928	3,560	2,076			
Other countries of the Caribbean	588	454	531				
North America	33,801	34,291	27,035	27,025			
Canada	1,716	2,024	1,799	2,115			
United States of America	32,085	32,267	25,236	24,910			
South America	4,559	4,370	5,005	2,125			
Brazil	826	1,038	839				
Colombia	305	340	444				
Ecuador	245	261	361				
Peru	247	46	133				
Venezuela	2,538	2,186	2,643	2,125			
Other countries of South America	398	499	585				
EUROPE	31,427	30,768	30,234	32,409			
Northern Europe	2,717	2,407	1,520				
Finland	200	115	79				
Norway	146	199	123				
Sweden	668	427	301				
United Kingdom	1,703	1,666	1,017				
Southern Europe	522	394	390				
Italy	522	394	390				
Western Europe	27,079	26,999	27,118	27,640			
Belgium	818	783	897				
France	382	333	307				
Germany	1,648	1,646	2,254	1,838			
Netherlands	23,692	23,732	23,093	25,802			
Switzerland	539	505	567				
Other Europe	1,109	968	1,206	4,769			
Other countries of Europe	1,109	968	1,206	4,769			
NOT SPECIFIED	691	462	504	6,904			
Other countries of the World	691	462	504	6,904			

BONAIRE

6. Overnight stays of non-resident tourists in all types of accommodation establishments, by country of residence

	2007	2008	2009	2010	2011	Market share 11	% Change 11-10
TOTAL	732,274	694,237	670,455				
AMERICAS	367,791	355,188	315,967				
Caribbean	21,240	22,567	24,332				
All countries of the Caribbean	21,240	22,567	24,332				
North America	308,789	297,760	252,401				
Canada	20,776	23,992	24,543				
United States of America	288,013	273,768	227,858				
South America	17,834	14,977	16,692				
Venezuela	17,834	14,977	16,692				
Other Americas	19,928	19,884	22,542				
Other countries of the Americas	19,928	19,884	22,542				
EUROPE	357,645	334,248	349,705				
Western Europe	274,301	257,418	270,951				
Netherlands	274,301	257,418	270,951				
Other Europe	83,344	76,830	78,754				
Other countries of Europe	83,344	76,830	78,754				
NOT SPECIFIED	6,838	4,801	4,783				
Other countries of the World	6,838	4,801	4,783				

BOSNIA AND HERZEGOVINA

4. Arrivals of non-resident tourists in all types of accommodation establishments, by country of residence

	2007	2008	2009	2010	2011	Market share 11	% Change 11-10
TOTAL	306,452	321,511	310,942	365,454	391,945	100.00	7.25
AMERICAS	10,341	8,862	8,126	10,389	10,411	2.66	0.21
North America	10,341	8,862	8,126	10,389	10,411	2.66	0.21
Canada	1,876	1,473	1,462	2,150	1,874	0.48	-12.84
United States of America	8,465	7,389	6,664	8,239	8,537	2.18	3.62
EAST ASIA AND THE PACIFIC	4,399	5,348	4,496	7,092	9,464	2.41	33.45
North-East Asia	2,521	2,842	2,379	3,741	5,445	1.39	45.55
China	497	534	478	770	2,244	0.57	191.43
Japan	2,024	2,308	1,901	2,971	3,201	0.82	7.74
Australasia	1,878	2,506	2,117	3,351	4,019	1.03	19.93
Australia	1,624	2,238	1,853	2,951	3,601	0.92	22.03
New Zealand	254	268	264	400	418	0.11	4.50
EUROPE	286,280	300,672	291,903	338,500	355,718	90.76	5.09
Central/Eastern Europe	23,440	26,311	27,370	34,236	41,324	10.54	20.70
Bulgaria	978	1,632	1,654	1,632	2,133	0.54	30.70
Czech Republic	3,653	3,472	3,171	3,366	3,557	0.91	5.67
Hungary	4,038	4,193	5,124	4,906	5,415	1.38	10.38
Poland	9,888	12,041	12,616	17,888	22,633	5.77	26.53
Romania	923	1,433	1,830	2,748	3,048	0.78	10.92
Russian Federation	1,541	1,549	1,526	2,140	2,567	0.65	19.95
Slovakia	2,419	1,991	1,449	1,556	1,971	0.50	26.67
Northern Europe	16,587	15,975	14,406	17,318	17,456	4.45	0.80
Denmark	1,565	1,992	1,637	1,776	1,507	0.38	-15.15
Finland	1,114	943	873	1,030	1,027	0.26	-0.29
Iceland	159	103	155	97	82	0.02	-15.46
Ireland	1,129	1,229	983	2,638	1,897	0.48	-28.09
Norway	2,389	2,311	2,332	2,493	2,438	0.62	-2.21
Sweden	4,018	3,804	3,349	3,608	4,551	1.16	26.14
United Kingdom	6,213	5,593	5,077	5,676	5,954	1.52	4.90
Southern Europe	179,146	190,234	179,763	202,443	210,812	53.79	4.13
Albania	567	958	1,916	3,996	1,732	0.44	-56.66
Croatia	50,208	53,512	50,838	56,100	64,028	16.34	14.13
Greece	1,326	1,459	2,214	2,824	3,623	0.92	28.29
Italy	17,599	16,090	15,443	23,749	26,379	6.73	11.07
Montenegro	6,613	8,129	7,848	8,392	7,679	1.96	-8.50
Portugal	1,184	840	840	961	1,119	0.29	16.44
Serbia	56,936	60,481	56,221	56,370	54,169	13.82	-3.90
Slovenia	36,353	36,596	34,580	40,246	41,267	10.53	2.54
Spain	4,568	7,618	5,053	5,155	5,662	1.44	9.84
TFYR of Macedonia	3,792	4,551	4,810	4,650	5,154	1.31	10.84
Western Europe	49,041	49,526	50,840	53,532	53,830	13.73	0.56
Austria	11,741	12,163	13,005	14,344	14,786	3.77	3.08
Belgium	2,282	2,419	2,401	2,110	1,835	0.47	-13.03
France	9,629	9,576	9,291	10,734	9,609	2.45	-10.48
Germany	17,761	17,201	17,813	17,281	18,220	4.65	5.43
Luxembourg	223	467	343	192	254	0.06	32.29
Netherlands	4,348	4,703	5,124	5,567	5,465	1.39	-1.83
Switzerland	3,057	2,997	2,863	3,304	3,661	0.93	10.81
East Mediterranean Europe	13,580	14,369	15,397	25,834	27,724	7.07	7.32
Israel	2,304	2,278	1,737	1,810	1,831	0.47	1.16
Turkey	11,276	12,091	13,660	24,024	25,893	6.61	7.78
Other Europe	4,486	4,257	4,127	5,137	4,572	1.17	-11.00
Other countries of Europe	4,486	4,257	4,127	5,137	4,572	1.17	-11.00

BOSNIA AND HERZEGOVINA

4. Arrivals of non-resident tourists in all types of accommodation establishments, by country of residence

	2007	2008	2009	2010	2011	Market share 11	% Change 11-10
MIDDLE EAST	252	330	313	624	937	0.24	50.16
Saudi Arabia	118	185	179	464	651	0.17	40.30
Egypt	134	145	134	160	286	0.07	78.75
SOUTH ASIA	233	151	206	253	167	0.04	-33.99
Iran, Islamic Republic of	233	151	206	253	167	0.04	-33.99
NOT SPECIFIED	4,947	6,148	5,898	8,596	15,248	3.89	77.38
Other countries of the World	4,947	6,148	5,898	8,596	15,248	3.89	77.38

BOSNIA AND HERZEGOVINA

6. Overnight stays of non-resident tourists in all types of accommodation establishments, by country of residence

	2007	2008	2009	2010	2011	Market share 11	% Change 11-10
TOTAL	694,507	718,750	671,128	772,754	836,005	100.00	8.19
AMERICAS	26,527	23,321	23,040	26,540	24,145	2.89	-9.02
North America	26,527	23,321	23,040	26,540	24,145	2.89	-9.02
Canada	4,675	3,475	3,496	4,159	3,599	0.43	-13.46
United States of America	21,852	19,846	19,544	22,381	20,546	2.46	-8.20
EAST ASIA AND THE PACIFIC	7,771	9,418	7,817	10,869	14,789	1.77	36.07
North-East Asia	4,135	5,298	4,210	5,523	8,438	1.01	52.78
China	1,015	1,322	934	1,255	3,874	0.46	208.69
Japan	3,120	3,976	3,276	4,268	4,564	0.55	6.94
Australasia	3,636	4,120	3,607	5,346	6,351	0.76	18.80
Australia	3,184	3,674	3,143	4,815	5,744	0.69	19.29
New Zealand	452	446	464	531	607	0.07	14.31
EUROPE	642,512	669,347	620,832	708,598	758,494	90.73	7.04
Central/Eastern Europe	76,478	73,837	71,731	95,613	116,052	13.88	21.38
Bulgaria	2,303	3,784	4,077	3,845	4,591	0.55	19.40
Czech Republic	12,476	11,414	9,744	10,387	11,015	1.32	6.05
Hungary	8,086	7,293	11,404	9,996	12,833	1.54	28.38
Poland	36,976	36,776	33,467	54,989	65,853	7.88	19.76
Romania	2,319	3,490	4,576	6,545	9,253	1.11	41.38
Russian Federation	5,917	4,526	4,889	6,300	7,699	0.92	22.21
Slovakia	8,401	6,554	3,574	3,551	4,808	0.58	35.40
Northern Europe	40,909	38,461	34,974	45,787	42,146	5.04	-7.95
Denmark	4,455	4,789	4,117	4,359	3,670	0.44	-15.81
Finland	2,666	1,895	1,984	2,046	2,428	0.29	18.67
Iceland	285	174	774	208	351	0.04	68.75
Ireland	2,748	2,974	2,667	13,440	8,296	0.99	-38.27
Norway	5,451	4,914	4,612	5,125	5,278	0.63	2.99
Sweden	10,394	10,179	8,943	9,185	9,939	1.19	8.21
United Kingdom	14,910	13,536	11,877	11,424	12,184	1.46	6.65
Southern Europe	377,802	405,861	358,304	392,490	421,745	50.45	7.45
Albania	1,097	1,943	3,183	7,236	3,201	0.38	-55.76
Croatia	108,142	108,233	93,601	104,863	130,326	15.59	24.28
Greece	3,707	3,916	4,718	8,128	6,625	0.79	-18.49
Italy	33,122	31,826	32,685	49,113	54,485	6.52	10.94
Montenegro	13,041	21,123	19,506	22,830	19,174	2.29	-16.01
Portugal	2,725	1,713	2,129	2,132	2,325	0.28	9.05
Serbia	131,537	142,811	120,850	113,840	114,424	13.69	0.51
Slovenia	68,308	68,493	60,762	64,959	69,960	8.37	7.70
Spain	8,671	16,547	11,337	10,398	10,429	1.25	0.30
TFYR of Macedonia	7,452	9,256	9,533	8,991	10,796	1.29	20.08
Western Europe	106,199	106,682	112,843	115,270	115,108	13.77	-0.14
Austria	22,544	21,920	22,734	25,229	27,885	3.34	10.53
Belgium	5,058	5,636	5,751	5,180	4,426	0.53	-14.56
France	19,515	25,881	24,835	28,476	24,882	2.98	-12.62
Germany	39,635	35,493	40,944	36,925	37,627	4.50	1.90
Luxembourg	498	1,221	693	396	810	0.10	104.55
Netherlands	10,685	10,607	11,840	12,531	12,142	1.45	-3.10
Switzerland	8,264	5,924	6,046	6,533	7,336	0.88	12.29
East Mediterranean Europe	32,789	34,580	34,837	48,795	53,893	6.45	10.45
Israel	3,670	3,499	2,900	3,446	3,483	0.42	1.07
Turkey	29,119	31,081	31,937	45,349	50,410	6.03	11.16
Other Europe	8,335	9,926	8,143	10,643	9,550	1.14	-10.27
Other countries of Europe	8,335	9,926	8,143	10,643	9,550	1.14	-10.27

BOSNIA AND HERZEGOVINA

6. Overnight stays of non-resident tourists in all types of accommodation establishments, by country of residence

	2007	2008	2009	2010	2011	Market share 11	% Change 11-10
MIDDLE EAST	726	1,358	1,048	1,689	2,762	0.33	63.53
Saudi Arabia	386	676	667	1,144	1,999	0.24	74.74
Egypt	340	682	381	545	763	0.09	40.00
SOUTH ASIA	2,042	425	580	577	526	0.06	-8.84
Iran, Islamic Republic of	2,042	425	580	577	526	0.06	-8.84
NOT SPECIFIED	14,929	14,881	17,811	24,481	35,289	4.22	44.15
Other countries of the World	14,929	14,881	17,811	24,481	35,289	4.22	44.15

BRAZIL

1. Arrivals of non-resident tourists at national borders, by country of residence

	2007	2008	2009	2010	2011	Market share 11	% Change 11-10
TOTAL	5,025,834	5,050,099	4,802,217	5,161,379	5,433,354	100.00	5.27
AFRICA	75,435	75,824	78,110	83,688	86,511	1.59	3.37
Central Africa	24,608	25,307	36,123	38,051	37,221	0.69	-2.18
Angola	24,608	25,307	36,123	38,051	37,221	0.69	-2.18
Southern Africa	30,823	29,429	23,132	21,311	22,754	0.42	6.77
South Africa	30,823	29,429	23,132	21,311	22,754	0.42	6.77
West Africa	8,100	7,540	6,108	5,391	5,993	0.11	11.17
Cape Verde	5,847	4,781	4,233	2,664	2,736	0.05	2.70
Nigeria	2,253	2,759	1,875	2,727	3,257	0.06	19.44
Other Africa	11,904	13,548	12,747	18,935	20,543	0.38	8.49
Other countries of Africa	11,904	13,548	12,747	18,935	20,543	0.38	8.49
AMERICAS	2,779,164	2,883,839	2,862,171	3,196,300	3,401,592	62.61	6.42
Caribbean	553	6,268	3,550	4,004	4,246	0.08	6.04
Cuba		6,268	3,550	4,004	4,246	0.08	6.04
Puerto Rico	553						
Central America	46,021	41,800	28,271	34,929	38,633	0.71	10.60
Costa Rica	8,341	10,548	8,539	9,792	10,125	0.19	3.40
Guatemala		6,294	3,725	5,136	5,453	0.10	6.17
Panama	9,047	8,148	5,153	6,424	7,344	0.14	14.32
Other countries of Central America	28,633	16,810	10,854	13,577	15,711	0.29	15.72
North America	818,536	765,380	734,998	773,181	729,756	13.43	-5.62
Canada	63,983	62,681	63,296	64,188	70,358	1.29	9.61
Mexico	58,804	77,193	68,028	67,616	64,451	1.19	-4.68
United States of America	695,749	625,506	603,674	641,377	594,947	10.95	-7.24
South America	1,914,054	2,070,391	2,095,352	2,384,186	2,628,957	48.39	10.27
Argentina	921,679	1,017,675	1,211,159	1,399,592	1,593,775	29.33	13.87
Bolivia	61,990	84,072	83,454	99,359	85,429	1.57	-14.02
Chile	260,439	240,087	170,491	200,724	217,200	4.00	8.21
Colombia	45,838	96,846	78,010	85,567	91,345	1.68	6.75
Ecuador	24,450	32,018	26,220	23,095	25,495	0.47	10.39
French Guiana	13,452	15,275	15,152	12,592	9,457	0.17	-24.90
Guyana	2,590	6,292	4,594	5,236	4,314	0.08	-17.61
Paraguay	212,022	217,709	180,373	194,340	192,730	3.55	-0.83
Peru	96,336	93,693	78,975	81,020	86,795	1.60	7.13
Suriname	3,128	4,699	3,626	2,930	3,952	0.07	34.88
Uruguay	226,111	199,403	189,412	228,545	261,204	4.81	14.29
Venezuela	46,019	62,622	53,886	51,186	57,261	1.05	11.87
EAST ASIA AND THE PACIFIC	205,730	256,271	208,379	210,582	260,642	4.80	23.77
North-East Asia	126,620	163,149	119,025	128,450	163,855	3.02	27.56
China	23,490	39,514	28,230	37,849	55,978	1.03	47.90
Japan	63,381	81,270	66,655	59,742	63,247	1.16	5.87
Korea, Republic of	39,749	42,365	24,140	30,859	44,630	0.82	44.63
Australasia	43,520	46,349	48,186	45,982	44,451	0.82	-3.33
Australia	34,912	37,034	38,756	36,846	35,642	0.66	-3.27
New Zealand	8,608	9,315	9,430	9,136	8,809	0.16	-3.58
Other East Asia and the Pacific	35,590	46,773	41,168	36,150	52,336	0.96	44.77
Other countries of Asia	35,590	46,122	41,059	35,830	52,130	0.96	45.49
Other countries of Oceania		651	109	320	206	0.00	-35.63
EUROPE	1,938,165	1,814,146	1,642,070	1,651,840	1,662,829	30.60	0.67
Central/Eastern Europe	24,169	46,666	35,913	40,224	50,601	0.93	25.80
Czech Republic		7,162	5,258	5,732	6,774	0.12	18.18
Hungary	7,103	6,989	5,525	4,854	5,045	0.09	3.93
Poland	17,066	18,665	15,092	13,775	16,427	0.30	19.25

BRAZIL

1. Arrivals of non-resident tourists at national borders, by country of residence

	2007	2008	2009	2010	2011	Market share 11	% Change 11-10
Russian Federation		13,850	10,038	15,863	22,355	0.41	40.93
Northern Europe	**310,292**	**321,566**	**297,534**	**280,480**	**267,938**	**4.93**	**-4.47**
Denmark	26,042	25,539	25,645	21,460	22,208	0.41	3.49
Finland	19,375	17,826	15,873	13,251	13,049	0.24	-1.52
Ireland	18,141	21,999	17,620	16,475	16,871	0.31	2.40
Norway	29,918	31,429	29,339	27,793	30,462	0.56	9.60
Sweden	39,846	43,594	36,414	34,146	35,784	0.66	4.80
United Kingdom	176,970	181,179	172,643	167,355	149,564	2.75	-10.63
Southern Europe	**778,650**	**701,274**	**619,318**	**621,433**	**610,027**	**11.23**	**-1.84**
Greece	12,636	10,368	7,550	7,537	6,423	0.12	-14.78
Italy	268,685	265,724	253,545	245,491	229,484	4.22	-6.52
Portugal	280,438	222,558	183,697	189,065	183,728	3.38	-2.82
Spain	216,891	202,624	174,526	179,340	190,392	3.50	6.16
Western Europe	**723,538**	**670,255**	**625,420**	**633,388**	**647,075**	**11.91**	**2.16**
Austria	24,557	26,506	24,185	26,603	26,560	0.49	-0.16
Belgium	30,545	31,940	31,526	34,030	32,773	0.60	-3.69
France	254,367	214,440	205,860	199,719	207,890	3.83	4.09
Germany	257,740	254,264	215,595	226,630	241,739	4.45	6.67
Netherlands	83,566	81,936	75,518	76,411	72,162	1.33	-5.56
Switzerland	72,763	61,169	72,736	69,995	65,951	1.21	-5.78
East Mediterranean Europe	**36,084**	**37,813**	**29,405**	**36,976**	**41,646**	**0.77**	**12.63**
Israel	36,084	37,813	29,405	36,976	41,646	0.77	12.63
Other Europe	**65,432**	**36,572**	**34,480**	**39,339**	**45,542**	**0.84**	**15.77**
Other countries of Europe	65,432	36,572	34,480	39,339	45,542	0.84	15.77
MIDDLE EAST	**25,967**						
Iraq	165						
Saudi Arabia	715						
Other countries of Middle East	25,087						
SOUTH ASIA		**19,456**	**11,361**	**18,829**	**21,530**	**0.40**	**14.34**
India		19,456	11,361	18,829	21,530	0.40	14.34
NOT SPECIFIED	**1,373**	**563**	**126**	**140**	**250**	**0.00**	**78.57**
Other countries of the World	1,373	563	126	140	250	0.00	78.57

BRITISH VIRGIN ISLANDS

1. Arrivals of non-resident tourists at national borders, by country of residence

	2007	2008	2009	2010	2011	Market share 11	% Change 11-10
TOTAL	358,068	346,035	308,792	330,343			
AMERICAS	306,911	296,230	263,466	280,233			
Caribbean	45,102	44,982	41,148	44,963			
Antigua and Barbuda	1,581	1,563	1,375	1,440			
Barbados	1,069	1,038	923	971			
Dominica	1,802	1,814	1,653	1,777			
Dominican Republic	974	945	830	880			
Grenada	576	564	503	532			
Haiti	97	52	80	64			
Jamaica	1,629	1,611	1,448	1,574			
Puerto Rico	17,317	16,764	14,890	15,628			
Saint Kitts and Nevis	3,352	3,326	2,950	3,107			
Saint Lucia	820	799	715	764			
Saint Vincent and the Grenadines	2,033	1,992	1,758	1,884			
Trinidad and Tobago	1,613	1,604	1,420	1,484			
Other countries of the Caribbean	12,239	12,910	12,603	14,858			
North America	258,445	248,057	219,510	232,221			
Canada	9,094	8,675	7,741	8,408			
United States of America	249,351	239,382	211,769	223,813			
South America	919	918	824	858			
Guyana	919	918	824	858			
Other Americas	2,445	2,273	1,984	2,191			
Other countries of the Americas	2,445	2,273	1,984	2,191			
EUROPE	43,389	41,728	37,591	41,184			
Northern Europe	21,482	20,598	18,417	20,004			
Sweden	703	667	589	632			
United Kingdom	20,779	19,931	17,828	19,372			
Southern Europe	4,811	4,840	4,549	5,146			
Italy	3,901	3,938	3,729	4,225			
Spain	910	902	820	921			
Western Europe	11,854	11,400	10,270	11,346			
France	6,158	5,933	5,347	5,901			
Germany	4,364	4,208	3,834	4,275			
Netherlands	1,332	1,259	1,089	1,170			
Other Europe	5,242	4,890	4,355	4,688			
Other countries of Europe	5,242	4,890	4,355	4,688			
NOT SPECIFIED	7,768	8,077	7,735	8,926			
Other countries of the World	7,768	8,077	7,735	8,926			

BRITISH VIRGIN ISLANDS

2. Arrivals of non-resident visitors at national borders, by country of residence

	2007	2008	2009	2010	2011	Market share 11	% Change 11-10
TOTAL	948,426	934,269	856,865	842,498			
AMERICAS	695,730	685,901	628,154	616,341			
Caribbean	32,879	32,939	30,691	30,565			
All countries of the Caribbean	32,879	32,939	30,691	30,565			
North America	654,221	644,458	589,792	578,303			
Canada	33,935	33,439	29,928	28,773			
United States of America	620,286	611,019	559,864	549,530			
South America	8,630	8,504	7,671	7,473			
All countries of South America	8,630	8,504	7,671	7,473			
EUROPE	235,420	231,849	215,017	212,248			
Other Europe	235,420	231,849	215,017	212,248			
All countries of Europe	235,420	231,849	215,017	212,248			
NOT SPECIFIED	17,276	16,519	13,694	13,909			
Other countries of the World	17,276	16,519	13,694	13,909			

BRUNEI DARUSSALAM

1. Arrivals of non-resident tourists at national borders, by nationality

		2007	2008	2009	2010	2011	Market share 11	% Change 11-10
TOTAL	(*)	178,540	225,757	157,474	214,290	242,061	100.00	12.96
AMERICAS		5,116	5,652	5,108	5,940	6,611	2.73	11.30
North America		5,116	5,652	5,108	5,940	6,611	2.73	11.30
Canada		2,057	2,244	1,940	2,199	2,411	1.00	9.64
United States of America		3,059	3,408	3,168	3,741	4,200	1.74	12.27
EAST ASIA AND THE PACIFIC		144,488	186,475	121,652	170,555	194,809	80.48	14.22
North-East Asia		39,779	53,277	23,637	33,055	41,397	17.10	25.24
China		28,252	27,652	15,800	24,579	32,853	13.57	33.66
Taiwan, Province of China		1,838	1,806	1,487	1,917	1,438	0.59	-24.99
Hong Kong, China		1,706	1,782	1,197	1,210	1,270	0.52	4.96
Japan		4,154	4,489	3,549	3,637	4,140	1.71	13.83
Korea, Republic of		3,810	17,548	1,604	1,712	1,696	0.70	-0.93
Macao, China		19						
South-East Asia		84,632	98,039	75,955	109,939	124,186	51.30	12.96
Myanmar		311		300	529	522	0.22	-1.32
Cambodia		105		133	251	227	0.09	-9.56
Indonesia		10,520		8,576	16,343	20,350	8.41	24.52
Lao People's Democratic Republic		93		44	106	123	0.05	16.04
Malaysia		44,906		38,193	54,127	61,470	25.39	13.57
Philippines		8,306		11,013	14,720	17,446	7.21	18.52
Singapore		14,173		14,221	15,973	16,221	6.70	1.55
Viet Nam		1,445		85	3,301	3,018	1.25	-8.57
Thailand		4,773		3,390	4,589	4,809	1.99	4.79
Asean countries			98,039					
Australasia		20,077	35,159	22,060	27,561	29,226	12.07	6.04
Australia		14,616	25,732	13,824	17,237	18,845	7.79	9.33
New Zealand		5,461	9,427	8,236	10,324	10,381	4.29	0.55
EUROPE		20,796	22,765	21,553	26,199	28,581	11.81	9.09
Central/Eastern Europe		687	290	705	989	1,009	0.42	2.02
Czech Republic		234		355	305	228	0.09	-25.25
Poland		113		155	297	352	0.15	18.52
Russian Federation		315	290	195	387	429	0.18	10.85
Slovakia		25						
Northern Europe		14,114	17,386	15,687	18,834	20,203	8.35	7.27
Denmark		182	327	276	343	363	0.15	5.83
Finland		123		129	145	151	0.06	4.14
Ireland		280	427	322	379	699	0.29	84.43
Norway		245		261	250	400	0.17	60.00
Sweden		358	440	313	301	368	0.15	22.26
United Kingdom		12,926	16,192	14,386	17,416	18,222	7.53	4.63
Southern Europe		936	674	847	1,162	1,293	0.53	11.27
Greece		47		40	91	81	0.03	-10.99
Italy		629	674	467	524	676	0.28	29.01
Portugal		119		107	184	218	0.09	18.48
Spain		141		233	363	318	0.13	-12.40
Western Europe		5,059	4,415	4,314	5,214	6,076	2.51	16.53
Austria		151		89	88	86	0.04	-2.27
Belgium		197		192	219	219	0.09	
France		1,140	1,350	1,195	1,315	2,301	0.95	74.98
Germany		2,056	1,693	1,520	1,713	1,819	0.75	6.19
Netherlands		1,293	1,035	1,081	1,127	1,332	0.55	18.19
Switzerland		222	337	237	752	319	0.13	-57.58
MIDDLE EAST		574		711	1,571	1,527	0.63	-2.80
Bahrain		14		42	51	34	0.01	-33.33

BRUNEI DARUSSALAM

1. Arrivals of non-resident tourists at national borders, by nationality

	2007	2008	2009	2010	2011	Market share 11	% Change 11-10
Kuwait	33		48	58	53	0.02	-8.62
Lebanon	1						
Oman	173		160	174	266	0.11	52.87
Qatar	14		14	19	20	0.01	5.26
Saudi Arabia	45		261	1,021	837	0.35	-18.02
United Arab Emirates	294		186	248	317	0.13	27.82
SOUTH ASIA	**5,195**	**5,317**	**4,451**	**7,241**	**7,573**	**3.13**	**4.59**
Bangladesh	508	430	387	844	1,004	0.41	18.96
Sri Lanka	215		228	289	388	0.16	34.26
India	3,402	3,540	2,879	4,904	4,616	1.91	-5.87
Nepal	574	801	483	597	986	0.41	65.16
Pakistan	496	546	474	607	579	0.24	-4.61
NOT SPECIFIED	**2,371**	**5,548**	**3,999**	**2,784**	**2,960**	**1.22**	**6.32**
Other countries of the World	2,371	5,548	3,999	2,784	2,960	1.22	6.32

BULGARIA

2. Arrivals of non-resident visitors at national borders, by country of residence

	2007	2008	2009	2010	2011	Market share 11	% Change 11-10
TOTAL	7,725,747	8,532,972	7,872,805	8,374,034	8,712,821	100.00	4.05
AFRICA	1,734	2,178	2,242	2,452	2,323	0.03	-5.26
East Africa	26	38	25	54	39	0.00	-27.78
Ethiopia	26	38	25	54	39	0.00	-27.78
North Africa	1,240	1,635	1,695	1,921	1,876	0.02	-2.34
Algeria	348	434	425	499	457	0.01	-8.42
Morocco	482	582	686	617	614	0.01	-0.49
Sudan	94	123	126	130	346	0.00	166.15
Tunisia	316	496	458	675	459	0.01	-32.00
West Africa	468	505	522	477	408	0.00	-14.47
Ghana	98	98	107	116	66	0.00	-43.10
Nigeria	370	407	415	361	342	0.00	-5.26
AMERICAS	89,790	91,956	82,101	83,617	87,722	1.01	4.91
Caribbean	376	322	402	334	279	0.00	-16.47
Cuba	376	322	402	334	279	0.00	-16.47
North America	85,803	87,642	77,406	78,787	82,095	0.94	4.20
Canada	13,266	14,228	13,262	14,260	14,849	0.17	4.13
Mexico	1,477	1,919	1,438	1,745	1,763	0.02	1.03
United States of America	71,060	71,495	62,706	62,782	65,483	0.75	4.30
South America	3,611	3,992	4,293	4,496	5,348	0.06	18.95
Argentina	914	1,004	1,155	980	995	0.01	1.53
Brazil	2,285	2,486	2,666	2,954	3,744	0.04	26.74
Venezuela	412	502	472	562	609	0.01	8.36
EAST ASIA AND THE PACIFIC	43,563	48,049	41,773	43,772	51,145	0.59	16.84
North-East Asia	24,567	24,810	22,571	25,604	30,257	0.35	18.17
China	5,148	6,207	6,165	6,438	6,638	0.08	3.11
Japan	12,154	9,830	8,458	9,969	10,236	0.12	2.68
Korea, Republic of	6,869	8,445	7,582	8,834	12,940	0.15	46.48
Mongolia	396	328	366	363	443	0.01	22.04
South-East Asia	4,720	5,693	4,593	4,116	3,869	0.04	-6.00
Indonesia	2,400	2,960	2,034	1,674	1,667	0.02	-0.42
Viet Nam	2,320	2,733	2,559	2,442	2,202	0.03	-9.83
Australasia	14,276	17,546	14,609	14,052	17,019	0.20	21.11
Australia	11,591	14,294	11,941	11,461	14,267	0.16	24.48
New Zealand	2,685	3,252	2,668	2,591	2,752	0.03	6.21
EUROPE	7,371,761	8,260,649	7,602,264	8,080,924	8,389,436	96.29	3.82
Central/Eastern Europe	2,630,098	3,042,840	2,705,690	2,875,306	3,058,269	35.10	6.36
Belarus	29,985	28,034	36,882	49,163	43,450	0.50	-11.62
Czech Republic	141,595	167,738	197,863	184,440	176,135	2.02	-4.50
Hungary	137,033	151,237	137,195	124,438	123,735	1.42	-0.56
Republic of Moldova	45,218	59,567	75,740	93,468	109,862	1.26	17.54
Poland	221,593	257,713	304,659	294,131	289,742	3.33	-1.49
Romania	1,541,006	1,769,194	1,398,694	1,445,342	1,499,415	17.21	3.74
Russian Federation	249,128	296,918	295,713	389,864	469,772	5.39	20.50
Slovakia	140,692	161,621	104,243	95,380	94,355	1.08	-1.07
Ukraine	123,848	150,818	154,701	199,080	251,803	2.89	26.48
Northern Europe	792,576	850,305	639,799	578,807	562,614	6.46	-2.80
Denmark	94,678	122,364	90,672	84,172	81,860	0.94	-2.75
Finland	76,477	77,021	57,057	45,527	43,620	0.50	-4.19
Iceland	6,857	6,647	4,294	2,131	2,055	0.02	-3.57
Ireland	62,594	67,090	46,102	33,089	29,941	0.34	-9.51
Norway	79,041	87,362	59,598	55,414	48,707	0.56	-12.10
Sweden	112,278	118,913	65,148	48,992	49,492	0.57	1.02

BULGARIA

2. Arrivals of non-resident visitors at national borders, by country of residence

	2007	2008	2009	2010	2011	Market share 11	% Change 11-10
United Kingdom	360,651	370,908	316,928	309,482	306,939	3.52	-0.82
Southern Europe	**1,486,106**	**1,763,094**	**1,732,575**	**2,022,288**	**2,257,849**	**25.91**	**11.65**
Albania	9,138	10,415	12,993	14,241	26,512	0.30	86.17
Bosnia and Herzegovina	18,707	20,140	18,626	16,972	38,551	0.44	127.14
Croatia	23,621	26,036	22,802	21,355	26,520	0.30	24.19
Greece	868,153	881,458	924,220	1,017,914	1,120,640	12.86	10.09
Italy	93,591	104,931	126,108	125,683	130,259	1.50	3.64
Malta		10,757	7,479	6,370	4,178	0.05	-34.41
Montenegro		1,831	5,237	11,515	14,401	0.17	25.06
Portugal	12,149	11,536	9,339	9,381	9,099	0.10	-3.01
Serbia		311,666	217,940	307,838	365,644	4.20	18.78
Slovenia	16,277	20,055	22,871	22,550	22,340	0.26	-0.93
Spain	39,977	40,869	54,847	58,499	60,026	0.69	2.61
TFYR of Macedonia	241,358	323,400	310,113	409,970	439,679	5.05	7.25
Serbia and Montenegro	163,135						
Western Europe	**1,239,148**	**1,357,524**	**1,578,158**	**1,508,192**	**1,489,738**	**17.10**	**-1.22**
Austria	141,123	157,027	182,075	181,577	186,438	2.14	2.68
Belgium	88,203	93,269	96,334	91,183	91,947	1.06	0.84
France	138,380	148,417	196,174	181,317	182,407	2.09	0.60
Germany	691,596	759,660	898,352	853,430	836,845	9.60	-1.94
Luxembourg	2,974	5,159	6,408	4,681	4,432	0.05	-5.32
Netherlands	152,040	165,231	157,485	156,436	149,193	1.71	-4.63
Switzerland	24,832	28,761	41,330	39,568	38,476	0.44	-2.76
East Mediterranean Europe	**1,223,833**	**1,246,886**	**946,042**	**1,096,331**	**1,020,966**	**11.72**	**-6.87**
Cyprus	24,561	24,324	22,557	22,050	21,361	0.25	-3.12
Israel	109,588	105,882	106,825	131,144	138,951	1.59	5.95
Turkey	1,089,684	1,116,680	816,660	943,137	860,654	9.88	-8.75
MIDDLE EAST	**18,823**	**21,875**	**21,352**	**25,413**	**23,972**	**0.28**	**-5.67**
Iraq	1,083	1,392	2,551	2,849	2,633	0.03	-7.58
Jordan	1,784	2,038	1,606	1,941	1,573	0.02	-18.96
Kuwait	1,458	1,352	998	1,685	2,977	0.03	76.68
Lebanon	4,941	5,056	4,794	5,543	4,997	0.06	-9.85
Libya	338	414	390	390	169	0.00	-56.67
Saudi Arabia	169	244	156	214	217	0.00	1.40
Syrian Arab Republic	7,141	9,286	8,837	10,962	9,368	0.11	-14.54
United Arab Emirates	235	228	172	196	136	0.00	-30.61
Egypt	1,674	1,865	1,848	1,633	1,902	0.02	16.47
SOUTH ASIA	**15,000**	**21,294**	**23,025**	**24,105**	**27,129**	**0.31**	**12.55**
Afghanistan	248	367	441	353	424	0.00	20.11
Bangladesh	94	120	178	180	128	0.00	-28.89
India	3,701	4,605	4,106	3,696	3,849	0.04	4.14
Iran, Islamic Republic of	10,543	15,714	17,782	19,299	22,026	0.25	14.13
Pakistan	414	488	518	577	702	0.01	21.66
NOT SPECIFIED	**185,076**	**86,971**	**100,048**	**113,751**	**131,094**	**1.50**	**15.25**
Other countries of the World	185,076	86,971	100,048	113,751	131,094	1.50	15.25

BULGARIA

3. Arrivals of non-resident tourists in hotels and similar establishments, by country of residence

	2007	2008	2009	2010	2011	Market share 11	% Change 11-10
TOTAL	2,205,624	2,204,650	1,931,258	2,064,167	2,387,427	100.00	15.66
AFRICA		1,379	796	674	808	0.03	19.88
Southern Africa		1,379	796	674	808	0.03	19.88
South Africa		1,379	796	674	808	0.03	19.88
AMERICAS	35,349	50,655	37,648	41,281	42,687	1.79	3.41
North America	35,349	36,309	30,668	34,935	39,646	1.66	13.49
Canada		7,247	4,197	5,076	5,936	0.25	16.94
United States of America	35,349	29,062	26,471	29,859	33,710	1.41	12.90
South America		14,346	6,980	6,346	3,041	0.13	-52.08
Brazil		14,346	6,980	6,346	3,041	0.13	-52.08
EAST ASIA AND THE PACIFIC	14,967	114,984	117,952	130,119	150,226	6.29	15.45
North-East Asia	14,967	17,301	16,007	21,335	24,928	1.04	16.84
China		2,574	3,851	3,847	5,439	0.23	41.38
Japan	14,967	12,185	9,942	13,332	12,749	0.53	-4.37
Korea, Republic of		2,542	2,214	4,156	6,740	0.28	62.18
Australasia		7,251	4,659	5,467	7,846	0.33	43.52
Australia		7,251	4,659	5,467	7,846	0.33	43.52
Other East Asia and the Pacific		90,432	97,286	103,317	117,452	4.92	13.68
Other countries of Asia		90,432	97,286	103,317	117,452	4.92	13.68
EUROPE	2,041,296	1,931,433	1,686,025	1,770,522	2,054,116	86.04	16.02
Central/Eastern Europe	467,802	576,504	589,654	667,050	872,086	36.53	30.74
Czech Republic	34,728	33,589	34,565	36,261	44,259	1.85	22.06
Estonia	4,832	7,902	5,193	5,004	6,172	0.26	23.34
Hungary	22,673	25,629	20,661	24,991	31,994	1.34	28.02
Latvia	5,112	6,055	4,423	3,677	4,868	0.20	32.39
Lithuania	4,450	5,590	4,890	4,044	7,014	0.29	73.44
Poland	44,086	56,772	61,427	83,997	110,661	4.64	31.74
Romania	157,088	192,585	243,253	259,225	332,740	13.94	28.36
Russian Federation	155,714	198,466	175,695	196,211	246,464	10.32	25.61
Slovakia	16,577	20,938	15,276	17,186	28,032	1.17	63.11
Ukraine	22,542	28,978	24,271	36,454	59,882	2.51	64.27
Northern Europe	483,779	383,487	281,152	274,242	283,446	11.87	3.36
Denmark	56,731	46,478	30,706	31,701	28,976	1.21	-8.60
Finland	44,030	37,190	26,434	25,262	25,463	1.07	0.80
Iceland		2,066	3,141	1,153	1,647	0.07	42.84
Ireland	32,969	24,983	15,386	11,349	11,527	0.48	1.57
Norway	49,201	39,325	31,011	31,602	40,778	1.71	29.04
Sweden	66,977	47,798	30,425	25,828	26,789	1.12	3.72
United Kingdom	233,871	185,647	144,049	147,347	148,266	6.21	0.62
Southern Europe	255,721	254,869	226,491	234,003	225,396	9.44	-3.68
Greece	135,086	144,685	123,084	139,868	126,586	5.30	-9.50
Italy	61,279	53,756	52,337	48,282	54,312	2.27	12.49
Malta	5,298	9,015	4,196	1,516	1,999	0.08	31.86
Portugal	9,943	9,177	6,889	7,870	5,903	0.25	-24.99
Slovenia	10,550	8,927	11,698	9,727	11,390	0.48	17.10
Spain	33,565	29,309	28,287	26,740	25,206	1.06	-5.74
Western Europe	637,399	613,024	495,853	484,213	544,773	22.82	12.51
Austria	34,533	34,818	28,912	30,900	35,206	1.47	13.94
Belgium	41,053	49,889	34,394	33,096	35,482	1.49	7.21
France	94,452	89,890	83,457	68,062	70,223	2.94	3.18
Germany	408,279	377,322	299,031	305,048	352,518	14.77	15.56
Luxembourg	2,608	3,293	2,902	1,975	2,655	0.11	34.43
Netherlands	37,903	42,124	35,658	34,110	34,259	1.43	0.44

BULGARIA

3. Arrivals of non-resident tourists in hotels and similar establishments, by country of residence

	2007	2008	2009	2010	2011	Market share 11	% Change 11-10
Switzerland	18,571	15,688	11,499	11,022	14,430	0.60	30.92
East Mediterranean Europe	**54,137**	**55,806**	**48,803**	**54,148**	**56,215**	**2.35**	**3.82**
Cyprus	12,063	10,775	8,198	6,486	6,484	0.27	-0.03
Turkey	42,074	45,031	40,605	47,662	49,731	2.08	4.34
Other Europe	**142,458**	**47,743**	**44,072**	**56,866**	**72,200**	**3.02**	**26.97**
Other countries of Europe	142,458	47,743	44,072	56,866	72,200	3.02	26.97
NOT SPECIFIED	**114,012**	**106,199**	**88,837**	**121,571**	**139,590**	**5.85**	**14.82**
Other countries of the World	114,012	106,199	88,837	121,571	139,590	5.85	14.82

BULGARIA

4. Arrivals of non-resident tourists in all types of accommodation establishments, by country of residence

	2007	2008	2009	2010	2011	Market share 11	% Change 11-10
TOTAL		2,226,185	1,948,000	2,084,300	2,422,524	100.00	16.23
AMERICAS		31,576	26,767	30,182	34,076	1.41	12.90
North America		31,576	26,767	30,182	34,076	1.41	12.90
United States of America		31,576	26,767	30,182	34,076	1.41	12.90
EAST ASIA AND THE PACIFIC		12,191	9,952	13,381	12,823	0.53	-4.17
North-East Asia		12,191	9,952	13,381	12,823	0.53	-4.17
Japan		12,191	9,952	13,381	12,823	0.53	-4.17
EUROPE		2,032,421	1,788,994	1,884,543	2,191,202	90.45	16.27
Central/Eastern Europe		583,538	595,205	674,367	887,229	36.62	31.56
Czech Republic		34,845	34,951	36,856	45,027	1.86	22.17
Estonia		7,921	5,207	5,027	6,224	0.26	23.81
Hungary		25,947	20,946	25,232	32,613	1.35	29.25
Latvia		6,119	4,435	3,707	4,935	0.20	33.13
Lithuania		5,623	4,904	4,082	7,055	0.29	72.83
Poland		57,786	62,207	84,953	111,637	4.61	31.41
Romania		193,306	243,902	261,118	336,177	13.88	28.75
Russian Federation		201,530	178,158	199,046	253,232	10.45	27.22
Slovakia		21,147	15,628	17,372	28,206	1.16	62.36
Ukraine		29,314	24,867	36,974	62,123	2.56	68.02
Northern Europe		385,232	280,534	275,400	285,440	11.78	3.65
Denmark		46,650	30,759	31,803	29,149	1.20	-8.35
Finland		37,222	26,467	25,301	25,738	1.06	1.73
Ireland		25,313	15,575	11,427	11,602	0.48	1.53
Norway		39,410	31,194	31,834	40,992	1.69	28.77
Sweden		48,097	30,741	26,005	27,069	1.12	4.09
United Kingdom		188,540	145,798	149,030	150,890	6.23	1.25
Southern Europe		298,362	266,724	288,174	292,260	12.06	1.42
Greece		145,133	123,856	140,804	127,800	5.28	-9.24
Italy		54,094	52,622	48,686	55,028	2.27	13.03
Malta		9,041	4,230	1,560	2,004	0.08	28.46
Portugal		9,197	6,946	7,985	6,005	0.25	-24.80
Serbia		17,451	15,592	22,725	26,054	1.08	14.65
Slovenia		9,099	11,763	9,790	11,548	0.48	17.96
Spain		29,449	28,589	27,096	25,774	1.06	-4.88
TFYR of Macedonia		24,898	23,126	29,528	38,047	1.57	28.85
Western Europe		618,474	499,804	488,291	551,242	22.75	12.89
Austria		35,121	29,120	31,117	35,542	1.47	14.22
Belgium		50,122	34,635	33,374	35,817	1.48	7.32
France		91,421	84,644	69,446	72,370	2.99	4.21
Germany		380,077	300,340	306,687	354,957	14.65	15.74
Luxembourg		3,301	2,933	1,980	2,659	0.11	34.29
Netherlands		42,665	36,549	34,613	35,293	1.46	1.96
Switzerland		15,767	11,583	11,074	14,604	0.60	31.88
East Mediterranean Europe		146,815	146,727	158,311	175,031	7.23	10.56
Cyprus		10,788	8,213	6,511	6,555	0.27	0.68
Israel		90,566	97,462	103,671	117,797	4.86	13.63
Turkey		45,461	41,052	48,129	50,679	2.09	5.30
NOT SPECIFIED		149,997	122,287	156,194	184,423	7.61	18.07
Other countries of the World		149,997	122,287	156,194	184,423	7.61	18.07

BULGARIA

5. Overnight stays of non-resident tourists in hotels and similar establishments, by country of residence

	2007	2008	2009	2010	2011	Market share 11	% Change 11-10
TOTAL	11,868,123	11,640,780	9,377,995	10,454,674	12,286,819	100.00	17.52
AFRICA		4,403	2,240	1,899	2,927	0.02	54.13
Southern Africa		4,403	2,240	1,899	2,927	0.02	54.13
South Africa		4,403	2,240	1,899	2,927	0.02	54.13
AMERICAS	91,846	225,467	146,207	142,309	110,531	0.90	-22.33
North America	91,846	112,212	95,580	96,701	99,095	0.81	2.48
Canada		13,047	10,157	13,462	14,338	0.12	6.51
United States of America	91,846	99,165	85,423	83,239	84,757	0.69	1.82
South America		113,255	50,627	45,608	11,436	0.09	-74.93
Brazil		113,255	50,627	45,608	11,436	0.09	-74.93
EAST ASIA AND THE PACIFIC	25,438	61,500	41,903	48,889	64,030	0.52	30.97
North-East Asia	25,438	41,086	30,141	37,105	45,360	0.37	22.25
China		6,739	7,719	8,205	13,582	0.11	65.53
Japan	25,438	26,686	18,757	21,953	20,644	0.17	-5.96
Korea, Republic of		7,661	3,665	6,947	11,134	0.09	60.27
Australasia		20,414	11,762	11,784	18,670	0.15	58.44
Australia		20,414	11,762	11,784	18,670	0.15	58.44
EUROPE	11,576,954	10,914,006	8,805,328	9,712,792	11,486,671	93.49	18.26
Central/Eastern Europe	2,791,419	3,312,419	3,058,719	4,001,282	5,220,334	42.49	30.47
Czech Republic	216,123	196,841	194,018	206,265	271,504	2.21	31.63
Estonia	26,049	44,544	29,559	29,930	35,373	0.29	18.19
Hungary	102,955	123,083	92,049	102,379	153,830	1.25	50.26
Latvia	20,406	35,224	26,241	18,112	27,151	0.22	49.91
Lithuania	22,409	29,524	40,233	23,196	39,481	0.32	70.21
Poland	284,167	394,354	422,449	552,650	738,158	6.01	33.57
Romania	556,728	693,671	814,994	1,024,323	1,344,116	10.94	31.22
Russian Federation	1,283,264	1,458,427	1,182,012	1,689,907	2,021,541	16.45	19.62
Slovakia	126,099	143,694	109,154	122,474	197,160	1.60	60.98
Ukraine	153,219	193,057	148,010	232,046	392,020	3.19	68.94
Northern Europe	3,118,367	2,459,141	1,679,111	1,636,183	1,725,908	14.05	5.48
Denmark	380,898	287,714	187,559	190,379	180,737	1.47	-5.06
Finland	283,509	241,346	166,021	151,093	157,388	1.28	4.17
Iceland		11,549	5,991	2,273	5,669	0.05	149.41
Ireland	203,996	152,610	74,184	54,060	59,664	0.49	10.37
Norway	362,892	292,151	218,108	221,828	300,114	2.44	35.29
Sweden	440,514	303,427	185,943	143,934	157,623	1.28	9.51
United Kingdom	1,446,558	1,170,344	841,305	872,616	864,713	7.04	-0.91
Southern Europe	553,621	562,584	508,133	519,154	496,042	4.04	-4.45
Greece	251,589	275,165	227,528	272,585	241,627	1.97	-11.36
Italy	137,851	126,511	122,537	113,966	129,987	1.06	14.06
Malta	22,907	26,200	25,812	4,372	6,192	0.05	41.63
Portugal	32,973	35,308	26,635	26,188	18,740	0.15	-28.44
Slovenia	39,668	37,374	41,025	39,732	47,811	0.39	20.33
Spain	68,633	62,026	64,596	62,311	51,685	0.42	-17.05
Western Europe	4,215,213	4,006,406	2,986,215	2,905,168	3,289,394	26.77	13.23
Austria	121,219	117,140	88,377	99,926	116,028	0.94	16.11
Belgium	224,349	312,633	183,207	177,382	186,123	1.51	4.93
France	355,754	349,777	296,842	231,324	219,726	1.79	-5.01
Germany	3,198,548	2,902,130	2,158,649	2,161,331	2,512,804	20.45	16.26
Luxembourg	16,995	21,182	16,994	10,795	15,222	0.12	41.01
Netherlands	208,124	232,628	200,092	187,193	191,668	1.56	2.39
Switzerland	90,224	70,916	42,054	37,217	47,823	0.39	28.50
East Mediterranean Europe	437,171	408,594	429,142	474,545	532,993	4.34	12.32

BULGARIA

5. Overnight stays of non-resident tourists in hotels and similar establishments, by country of residence

	2007	2008	2009	2010	2011	Market share 11	% Change 11-10
Cyprus	30,444	29,357	20,557	16,886	16,566	0.13	-1.90
Israel	311,356	269,838	322,539	367,271	414,753	3.38	12.93
Turkey	95,371	109,399	86,046	90,388	101,674	0.83	12.49
Other Europe	**461,163**	**164,862**	**144,008**	**176,460**	**222,000**	**1.81**	**25.81**
Other countries of Europe	461,163	164,862	144,008	176,460	222,000	1.81	25.81
NOT SPECIFIED	**173,885**	**435,404**	**382,317**	**548,785**	**622,660**	**5.07**	**13.46**
Other countries of the World	173,885	435,404	382,317	548,785	622,660	5.07	13.46

BULGARIA

6. Overnight stays of non-resident tourists in all types of accommodation establishments, by country of residence

	2007	2008	2009	2010	2011	Market share 11	% Change 11-10
TOTAL	12,022,090	11,802,017	9,472,345	10,565,210	12,461,275	100.00	17.95
AMERICAS	92,446	99,850	96,816	97,390	85,575	0.69	-12.13
North America	92,446	99,850	96,816	97,390	85,575	0.69	-12.13
Canada			10,220	13,567			
United States of America	92,446	99,850	86,596	83,823	85,575	0.69	2.09
EAST ASIA AND THE PACIFIC	25,480	26,692	18,767	22,011	20,743	0.17	-5.76
North-East Asia	25,480	26,692	18,767	22,011	20,743	0.17	-5.76
Japan	25,480	26,692	18,767	22,011	20,743	0.17	-5.76
EUROPE	11,400,154	11,028,841	8,867,048	9,792,302	11,616,363	93.22	18.63
Central/Eastern Europe	2,835,113	3,383,139	3,099,171	4,050,728	5,314,646	42.65	31.20
Czech Republic	222,301	202,321	195,421	207,897	275,231	2.21	32.39
Estonia	26,109	44,581	29,575	30,022	35,653	0.29	18.76
Hungary	106,797	125,209	92,831	103,146	155,692	1.25	50.94
Latvia	20,708	35,789	26,285	18,179	27,395	0.22	50.70
Lithuania	22,656	29,587	40,261	23,504	39,563	0.32	68.32
Poland	290,728	400,590	426,285	557,115	742,170	5.96	33.22
Romania	559,547	696,816	817,729	1,030,997	1,352,372	10.85	31.17
Russian Federation	1,309,060	1,504,039	1,206,505	1,719,881	2,083,019	16.72	21.11
Slovakia	126,615	145,895	111,339	123,773	197,981	1.59	59.95
Ukraine	150,592	198,312	152,940	236,214	405,570	3.25	71.70
Northern Europe	3,162,635	2,477,804	1,690,235	1,652,523	1,738,579	13.95	5.21
Denmark	383,118	288,709	187,739	190,953	181,296	1.45	-5.06
Finland	284,332	241,438	166,156	151,252	158,391	1.27	4.72
Ireland	208,761	155,677	75,310	54,550	59,827	0.48	9.67
Norway	363,994	292,918	219,266	223,309	301,560	2.42	35.04
Sweden	442,432	305,329	187,713	144,705	158,568	1.27	9.58
United Kingdom	1,479,998	1,193,733	854,051	887,754	878,937	7.05	-0.99
Southern Europe	699,908	716,164	639,827	691,398	707,583	5.68	2.34
Greece	252,715	275,937	229,429	274,294	243,808	1.96	-11.11
Italy	138,847	127,169	123,179	114,744	131,836	1.06	14.90
Malta	22,940	26,244	26,135	4,476	6,202	0.05	38.56
Portugal	33,067	35,331	26,859	26,569	19,213	0.15	-27.69
Serbia		72,979	60,121	86,581	98,667	0.79	13.96
Slovenia	40,998	37,694	41,154	39,819	48,258	0.39	21.19
Spain	69,170	62,286	65,670	63,518	53,598	0.43	-15.62
TFYR of Macedonia	61,471	78,524	67,280	81,397	106,001	0.85	30.23
Serbia and Montenegro	80,700						
Western Europe	4,254,987	4,041,316	3,006,838	2,921,514	3,319,203	26.64	13.61
Austria	123,824	118,346	88,934	100,933	117,062	0.94	15.98
Belgium	225,084	313,316	183,610	178,003	187,027	1.50	5.07
France	359,318	353,227	299,004	233,878	224,861	1.80	-3.86
Germany	3,225,406	2,926,449	2,166,644	2,171,123	2,528,594	20.29	16.46
Luxembourg	17,053	21,196	17,189	10,800	15,226	0.12	40.98
Netherlands	213,658	237,391	209,180	189,461	197,970	1.59	4.49
Switzerland	90,644	71,391	42,277	37,316	48,463	0.39	29.87
East Mediterranean Europe	447,511	410,418	430,977	476,139	536,352	4.30	12.65
Cyprus	30,516	29,376	20,598	16,984	16,713	0.13	-1.60
Israel	311,720	270,098	322,842	367,885	415,573	3.33	12.96
Turkey	105,275	110,944	87,537	91,270	104,066	0.84	14.02
NOT SPECIFIED	504,010	646,634	489,714	653,507	738,594	5.93	13.02
Other countries of the World	504,010	646,634	489,714	653,507	738,594	5.93	13.02

BURKINA FASO

3. Arrivals of non-resident tourists in hotels and similar establishments, by nationality

	2007	2008	2009	2010	2011	Market share 11	% Change 11-10
TOTAL	288,965	271,796	269,227	274,330	237,725	100.00	-13.34
AFRICA	121,174	112,702	119,243	128,237	117,337	49.36	-8.50
West Africa	85,715	92,608	98,238	102,591	96,848	40.74	-5.60
Benin	10,442	11,005	11,138	11,754	10,032	4.22	-14.65
Ghana	6,359	7,996	8,412	8,402	10,152	4.27	20.83
Guinea	3,707	4,046	4,747	4,922	5,103	2.15	3.68
Côte d'Ivoire	18,009	18,176	18,090	19,251	18,276	7.69	-5.06
Mali	12,512	12,258	14,474	15,643	14,846	6.25	-5.09
Mauritania	2,022	2,213	1,943	2,217	2,501	1.05	12.81
Niger	11,406	11,811	14,888	14,342	12,486	5.25	-12.94
Nigeria	4,010	5,079	5,561	4,297	4,045	1.70	-5.86
Senegal	9,584	10,481	9,875	10,638	9,570	4.03	-10.04
Togo	7,664	9,543	9,110	11,125	9,837	4.14	-11.58
Other Africa	35,459	20,094	21,005	25,646	20,489	8.62	-20.11
Other countries of Africa	35,459	20,094	21,005	25,646	20,489	8.62	-20.11
AMERICAS	20,473	18,016	17,509	20,154	17,333	7.29	-14.00
North America	17,275	16,129	15,026	17,927	14,697	6.18	-18.02
Canada	7,025	6,695	6,434	8,833	7,442	3.13	-15.75
United States of America	10,250	9,434	8,592	9,094	7,255	3.05	-20.22
Other Americas	3,198	1,887	2,483	2,227	2,636	1.11	18.37
Other countries of the Americas	3,198	1,887	2,483	2,227	2,636	1.11	18.37
EAST ASIA AND THE PACIFIC	11,563	6,045	7,253	7,313	8,180	3.44	11.86
North-East Asia	1,990	1,460	1,591	1,898	1,587	0.67	-16.39
China	1,990	1,460	1,591	1,898	1,587	0.67	-16.39
Other East Asia and the Pacific	9,573	4,585	5,662	5,415	6,593	2.77	21.75
Other countries of Asia	9,573	4,585	5,662	5,415	6,593	2.77	21.75
EUROPE	126,544	124,426	116,180	107,098	85,535	35.98	-20.13
Northern Europe	3,942	5,253	4,712	4,523	4,749	2.00	5.00
United Kingdom	3,942	5,253	4,712	4,523	4,749	2.00	5.00
Southern Europe	7,405	7,260	6,726	5,892	4,875	2.05	-17.26
Italy	7,405	7,260	6,726	5,892	4,875	2.05	-17.26
Western Europe	102,487	100,571	92,592	85,784	64,898	27.30	-24.35
Belgium	8,345	7,889	7,806	7,344	6,491	2.73	-11.61
France	80,054	75,528	67,866	63,715	42,296	17.79	-33.62
Germany	6,562	7,524	7,193	6,855	6,420	2.70	-6.35
Netherlands	3,657	4,656	4,536	3,645	5,545	2.33	52.13
Switzerland	3,869	4,974	5,191	4,225	4,146	1.74	-1.87
Other Europe	12,710	11,342	12,150	10,899	11,013	4.63	1.05
Other countries of Europe	12,710	11,342	12,150	10,899	11,013	4.63	1.05
MIDDLE EAST	2,066	2,015	1,572	1,355	1,795	0.76	32.47
Lebanon	2,066	2,015	1,572	1,355	1,795	0.76	32.47
NOT SPECIFIED	7,145	8,592	7,470	10,173	7,545	3.17	-25.83
Nationals Residing Abroad	7,145	8,592	7,470	10,173	7,545	3.17	-25.83

BURKINA FASO

5. Overnight stays of non-resident tourists in hotels and similar establishments, by nationality

	2007	2008	2009	2010	2011	Market share 11	% Change 11-10
TOTAL	925,811	814,217	792,843	815,196	707,944	100.00	-13.16
AFRICA	430,581	360,498	375,082	392,274	334,706	47.28	-14.68
West Africa	281,470	282,510	293,719	305,845	269,016	38.00	-12.04
Benin	32,790	32,984	34,132	36,638	29,374	4.15	-19.83
Ghana	20,223	21,401	21,263	21,589	23,036	3.25	6.70
Guinea	11,600	12,636	14,229	15,755	12,467	1.76	-20.87
Côte d'Ivoire	62,853	58,436	57,028	58,043	55,124	7.79	-5.03
Mali	40,912	37,389	44,645	46,189	40,983	5.79	-11.27
Mauritania	6,156	5,824	5,231	6,801	5,824	0.82	-14.37
Niger	32,883	34,363	42,360	38,899	31,823	4.50	-18.19
Nigeria	11,251	12,982	14,887	13,187	10,450	1.48	-20.76
Senegal	37,947	37,537	32,468	38,229	33,137	4.68	-13.32
Togo	24,855	28,958	27,476	30,515	26,798	3.79	-12.18
Other Africa	149,111	77,988	81,363	86,429	65,690	9.28	-24.00
Other countries of Africa	149,111	77,988	81,363	86,429	65,690	9.28	-24.00
AMERICAS	68,758	67,766	58,773	74,409	57,519	8.12	-22.70
North America	58,988	62,382	52,178	67,600	49,563	7.00	-26.68
Canada	25,375	23,542	20,890	29,056	24,562	3.47	-15.47
United States of America	33,613	38,840	31,288	38,544	25,001	3.53	-35.14
Other Americas	9,770	5,384	6,595	6,809	7,956	1.12	16.85
Other countries of the Americas	9,770	5,384	6,595	6,809	7,956	1.12	16.85
EAST ASIA AND THE PACIFIC	40,345	19,370	24,640	28,062	30,555	4.32	8.88
North-East Asia	7,362	5,534	4,978	8,001	6,391	0.90	-20.12
China	7,362	5,534	4,978	8,001	6,391	0.90	-20.12
Other East Asia and the Pacific	32,983	13,836	19,662	20,061	24,164	3.41	20.45
Other countries of Asia	32,983	13,836	19,662	20,061	24,164	3.41	20.45
EUROPE	365,948	340,751	312,750	293,932	266,094	37.59	-9.47
Northern Europe	10,629	13,453	12,476	11,020	10,988	1.55	-0.29
United Kingdom	10,629	13,453	12,476	11,020	10,988	1.55	-0.29
Southern Europe	26,607	21,483	20,810	16,702	15,447	2.18	-7.51
Italy	26,607	21,483	20,810	16,702	15,447	2.18	-7.51
Western Europe	283,660	273,482	244,159	234,284	204,979	28.95	-12.51
Belgium	25,933	35,630	22,330	22,515	20,794	2.94	-7.64
France	214,259	188,714	176,285	169,317	141,106	19.93	-16.66
Germany	21,076	23,158	20,374	19,612	20,619	2.91	5.13
Netherlands	10,660	11,959	11,032	10,064	9,875	1.39	-1.88
Switzerland	11,732	14,021	14,138	12,776	12,585	1.78	-1.49
Other Europe	45,052	32,333	35,305	31,926	34,680	4.90	8.63
Other countries of Europe	45,052	32,333	35,305	31,926	34,680	4.90	8.63
MIDDLE EAST	3,998	4,933	3,623	3,596	4,449	0.63	23.72
Lebanon	3,998	4,933	3,623	3,596	4,449	0.63	23.72
NOT SPECIFIED	16,181	20,899	17,975	22,923	14,621	2.07	-36.22
Nationals Residing Abroad	16,181	20,899	17,975	22,923	14,621	2.07	-36.22

BURUNDI

1. Arrivals of non-resident tourists at national borders, by nationality

		2007	2008	2009	2010	2011	Market share 11	% Change 11-10
TOTAL	(*)	192,191	201,795	211,884	142,311			
AFRICA		168,457	177,579	186,457	122,045			
Other Africa		168,457	177,579	186,457	122,045			
All countries of Africa		168,457	177,579	186,457	122,045			
AMERICAS		854	5,044	5,297	3,883			
Other Americas		854	5,044	5,297	3,883			
All countries of the Americas		854	5,044	5,297	3,883			
EAST ASIA AND THE PACIFIC		11,713	4,237	4,449	2,912			
Other East Asia and the Pacific		11,713	4,237	4,449	2,912			
All countries of Asia		11,713	4,237	4,449	2,912			
EUROPE		1,782	12,107	12,713	9,985			
Other Europe		1,782	12,107	12,713	9,985			
All countries of Europe		1,782	12,107	12,713	9,985			
NOT SPECIFIED		9,385	2,828	2,968	3,486			
Other countries of the World		9,385	2,828	2,968	3,486			

CAMBODIA

1. Arrivals of non-resident tourists at national borders, by country of residence

	2007	2008	2009	2010	2011	Market share 11	% Change 11-10
TOTAL	2,015,128	2,125,465	2,161,577	2,508,289	2,881,862	100.00	14.89
AFRICA	3,270	4,040	5,403	4,627	5,993	0.21	29.52
East Africa					582	0.02	
Kenya					283	0.01	
Uganda					299	0.01	
Central Africa	133	340	1,051	493	545	0.02	10.55
Cameroon	133	340	1,051	493	388	0.01	-21.30
Congo					157	0.01	
North Africa	6	38	32	37	48	0.00	29.73
Sudan	6	38	32	37	48	0.00	29.73
Southern Africa	1,798	2,180	2,104	2,459	3,216	0.11	30.78
South Africa	1,798	2,180	2,104	2,459	3,216	0.11	30.78
West Africa	783	1,131	1,724	1,272	1,278	0.04	0.47
Ghana	154	132	624	503	415	0.01	-17.50
Liberia					335	0.01	
Nigeria	629	999	1,100	769	528	0.02	-31.34
Other Africa	550	351	492	366	324	0.01	-11.48
Other countries of Africa	550	351	492	366	324	0.01	-11.48
AMERICAS	194,706	204,878	201,130	199,089	217,500	7.55	9.25
Central America					201	0.01	
Costa Rica					201	0.01	
North America	174,983	185,349	187,544	187,880	199,901	6.94	6.40
Canada	34,008	36,891	36,340	38,718	42,462	1.47	9.67
Mexico	3,436	3,379	2,722	3,157	3,486	0.12	10.42
United States of America	137,539	145,079	148,482	146,005	153,953	5.34	5.44
South America	5,622	6,682	7,541	8,803	14,711	0.51	67.11
Argentina	1,162	1,645	1,717	2,212	5,223	0.18	136.12
Brazil	1,585	2,058	2,204	2,490	3,616	0.13	45.22
Chile	1,580	1,639	1,943	2,240	2,633	0.09	17.54
Colombia	690	785	942	1,060	2,060	0.07	94.34
Ecuador					184	0.01	
Peru	336	388	422	468	483	0.02	3.21
Uruguay	269	167	313	333	512	0.02	53.75
Other Americas	14,101	12,847	6,045	2,406	2,687	0.09	11.68
Other countries of the Americas	14,101	12,847	6,045	2,406	2,687	0.09	11.68
EAST ASIA AND THE PACIFIC	1,384,443	1,436,249	1,467,406	1,788,814	2,084,540	72.33	16.53
North-East Asia	731,392	646,432	548,422	715,045	855,697	29.69	19.67
China	118,417	129,626	128,210	177,636	247,197	8.58	39.16
Taiwan, Province of China	118,180	83,000	72,119	91,229	98,363	3.41	7.82
Hong Kong, China	2,731	3,320	3,888	4,378	5,266	0.18	20.28
Japan	161,973	163,806	146,286	151,795	161,804	5.61	6.59
Korea, Republic of	329,909	266,525	197,725	289,702	342,810	11.90	18.33
Mongolia	182	155	194	305	257	0.01	-15.74
South-East Asia	552,693	676,492	808,661	962,570	1,101,111	38.21	14.39
Brunei Darussalam	340	356	406	460	481	0.02	4.57
Myanmar	1,781	2,461	2,316	2,614	4,199	0.15	60.64
Indonesia	8,543	9,198	9,585	12,636	15,817	0.55	25.17
Lao People's Democratic Republic	23,060	60,933	94,181	92,276	128,525	4.46	39.28
Malaysia	84,039	80,738	77,759	89,952	102,929	3.57	14.43
Philippines	29,534	39,294	49,079	56,156	70,718	2.45	25.93
Singapore	35,803	40,945	41,273	45,079	47,594	1.65	5.58
Viet Nam	125,442	209,516	316,202	514,289	614,090	21.31	19.41
Thailand	101,590	109,020	102,018	149,108	116,758	4.05	-21.70

CAMBODIA

1. Arrivals of non-resident tourists at national borders, by country of residence

	2007	2008	2009	2010	2011	Market share 11	% Change 11-10
Other countries of South-East Asia	142,561	124,031	115,842				
Australasia	**83,949**	**99,087**	**98,678**	**107,306**	**121,485**	**4.22**	**13.21**
Australia	71,616	84,957	84,581	93,598	105,010	3.64	12.19
New Zealand	12,333	14,130	14,097	13,708	16,475	0.57	20.19
Melanesia					**117**	**0.00**	
Fiji					117	0.00	
Other East Asia and the Pacific	**16,409**	**14,238**	**11,645**	**3,893**	**6,130**	**0.21**	**57.46**
Other countries East Asia/Pacific	16,409	14,238	11,645	3,893	6,130	0.21	57.46
EUROPE	**417,096**	**463,602**	**470,181**	**495,586**	**551,452**	**19.14**	**11.27**
Central/Eastern Europe	**21,881**	**30,219**	**34,457**	**54,401**	**93,538**	**3.25**	**71.94**
Bulgaria	1,605	322	384	445	470	0.02	5.62
Czech Republic	1,907	2,147	2,649	3,113	3,310	0.11	6.33
Estonia					954	0.03	
Hungary	2,246	2,193	2,184	2,740	2,585	0.09	-5.66
Kazakhstan					1,224	0.04	
Lithuania					1,238	0.04	
Poland	3,895	5,630	6,319	8,712	9,151	0.32	5.04
Romania	422	569	774	1,171	1,081	0.04	-7.69
Russian Federation	9,922	16,927	19,395	34,170	67,747	2.35	98.26
Slovakia	594	762	895	1,286	1,269	0.04	-1.32
Ukraine	1,290	1,669	1,857	2,764	3,788	0.13	37.05
Uzbekistan					721	0.03	
Northern Europe	**133,946**	**153,376**	**153,311**	**145,767**	**151,600**	**5.26**	**4.00**
Denmark	8,477	9,371	8,937	7,810	9,352	0.32	19.74
Finland	5,640	6,833	6,559	5,244	6,410	0.22	22.23
Iceland	214	274	183	229	355	0.01	55.02
Ireland	10,260	11,255	9,037	8,567	8,541	0.30	-0.30
Norway	6,631	7,875	7,017	7,774	8,128	0.28	4.55
Sweden	18,621	19,675	14,741	13,076	14,762	0.51	12.89
United Kingdom	84,103	98,093	106,837	103,067	104,052	3.61	0.96
Southern Europe	**40,357**	**42,831**	**38,405**	**44,082**	**49,023**	**1.70**	**11.21**
Croatia	216	355	313	470	532	0.02	13.19
Greece	1,291	1,441	1,406	1,395	1,168	0.04	-16.27
Italy	18,077	19,516	17,154	19,808	20,837	0.72	5.19
Portugal	2,542	2,284	2,481	2,554	3,081	0.11	20.63
Serbia					408	0.01	
Slovenia	639	891	740	692	874	0.03	26.30
Spain	17,592	18,344	16,311	19,163	22,123	0.77	15.45
Western Europe	**196,641**	**215,227**	**226,057**	**238,812**	**242,011**	**8.40**	**1.34**
Austria	6,795	7,276	8,681	8,547	7,601	0.26	-11.07
Belgium	12,038	13,179	12,980	14,295	13,905	0.48	-2.73
France	90,168	97,517	105,437	113,285	117,408	4.07	3.64
Germany	53,087	59,903	59,916	62,864	63,398	2.20	0.85
Luxembourg	489	486	472	639	497	0.02	-22.22
Monaco					82	0.00	
Netherlands	20,773	22,408	22,058	23,537	22,725	0.79	-3.45
Switzerland	13,291	14,458	16,513	15,645	16,395	0.57	4.79
East Mediterranean Europe	**8,091**	**8,095**	**7,179**	**9,238**	**9,929**	**0.34**	**7.48**
Israel	6,453	6,131	5,439	6,186	6,644	0.23	7.40
Turkey	1,638	1,964	1,740	3,052	3,285	0.11	7.63
Other Europe	**16,180**	**13,854**	**10,772**	**3,286**	**5,351**	**0.19**	**62.84**
Other countries of Europe	16,180	13,854	10,772	3,286	5,351	0.19	62.84
MIDDLE EAST	**1,059**	**947**	**1,144**	**1,071**	**1,565**	**0.05**	**46.13**
Palestine					34	0.00	
Iraq					91	0.00	

CAMBODIA

1. Arrivals of non-resident tourists at national borders, by country of residence

	2007	2008	2009	2010	2011	Market share 11	% Change 11-10
Kuwait	410	472	633	543	530	0.02	-2.39
Oman					107	0.00	
Qatar					62	0.00	
Saudi Arabia	93	52	48	64	78	0.00	21.88
United Arab Emirates					155	0.01	
Egypt	77	155	173	220	196	0.01	-10.91
Yemen					98	0.00	
Other countries of Middle East	479	268	290	244	214	0.01	-12.30
SOUTH ASIA	**14,554**	**15,749**	**16,313**	**19,102**	**20,812**	**0.72**	**8.95**
Afghanistan	33	40	126	180	113	0.00	-37.22
Bangladesh	659	708	925	1,658	1,316	0.05	-20.63
Bhutan					81	0.00	
Sri Lanka	700	731	757	1,031	1,097	0.04	6.40
India	11,454	12,467	12,461	13,542	15,240	0.53	12.54
Iran, Islamic Republic of	415	297	338	518	696	0.02	34.36
Nepal	730	929	908	1,081	1,156	0.04	6.94
Pakistan	563	577	798	1,092	1,113	0.04	1.92

CANADA

1. Arrivals of non-resident tourists at national borders, by country of residence

	2007	2008	2009	2010	2011	Market share 11	% Change 11-10
TOTAL	17,934,881	17,142,102	15,737,150	16,097,369	16,014,405	100.00	-0.52
AFRICA	75,525	79,927	75,717	81,277	85,902	0.54	5.69
East Africa	13,560	15,004	14,219	14,956	15,137	0.09	1.21
Burundi	259	235	254	269	318	0.00	18.22
Comoros	40	39	54	61	110	0.00	80.33
Ethiopia	971	1,265	1,182	1,296	1,284	0.01	-0.93
Eritrea	256	264	198	241	218	0.00	-9.54
Djibouti	56	117	66	195	112	0.00	-42.56
Kenya	3,455	3,494	3,430	3,441	3,509	0.02	1.98
Madagascar	497	674	600	662	693	0.00	4.68
Malawi	278	229	228	304	319	0.00	4.93
Mauritius	1,352	1,846	1,738	2,103	1,953	0.01	-7.13
Mozambique	230	257	255	265	330	0.00	24.53
Reunion	1,557	1,799	1,257	1,226	1,523	0.01	24.23
Rwanda	319	394	386	451	436	0.00	-3.33
Seychelles	126	91	63	70	42	0.00	-40.00
Somalia	86	75	195	215	217	0.00	0.93
Zimbabwe	773	706	750	738	812	0.01	10.03
Uganda	1,057	1,209	1,120	1,375	1,228	0.01	-10.69
United Republic of Tanzania	1,595	1,675	1,742	1,542	1,450	0.01	-5.97
Zambia	653	635	701	502	583	0.00	16.14
Central Africa	3,318	3,784	3,695	3,888	3,798	0.02	-2.31
Angola	293	459	307	395	382	0.00	-3.29
Cameroon	1,557	1,451	1,711	1,758	1,743	0.01	-0.85
Central African Republic	25	34	22	16	28	0.00	75.00
Chad	44	114	163	111	111	0.00	
Congo	190	123	85	84	176	0.00	109.52
Democratic Republic of the Congo	752	1,039	897	1,003	859	0.01	-14.36
Equatorial Guinea	56	26	37	22	11	0.00	-50.00
Gabon	398	538	473	495	488	0.00	-1.41
Sao Tome and Principe	3			4			
North Africa	20,281	20,881	21,666	22,909	24,919	0.16	8.77
Algeria	5,055	5,896	6,446	6,954	8,216	0.05	18.15
Morocco	11,149	10,907	10,832	11,471	11,760	0.07	2.52
Western Sahara				2			
Sudan	349	432	390	550	519	0.00	-5.64
Tunisia	3,728	3,646	3,998	3,932	4,424	0.03	12.51
Southern Africa	24,314	24,998	19,957	20,473	22,791	0.14	11.32
Botswana	482	605	571	598	558	0.00	-6.69
Lesotho	53	74	114	71	87	0.00	22.54
Namibia	435	441	420	707	1,193	0.01	68.74
South Africa	23,258	23,774	18,715	18,916	20,826	0.13	10.10
Swaziland	86	104	137	181	127	0.00	-29.83
West Africa	13,990	15,193	16,111	19,003	19,240	0.12	1.25
Cape Verde	17	45	10	21	13	0.00	-38.10
Benin	532	767	795	735	795	0.00	8.16
Gambia	159	70	164	138	148	0.00	7.25
Ghana	2,139	2,079	2,008	2,138	2,264	0.01	5.89
Guinea	641	633	495	540	657	0.00	21.67
Côte d'Ivoire	893	1,181	1,087	1,093	715	0.00	-34.58
Liberia	92	109	107	137	202	0.00	47.45
Mali	634	733	883	744	953	0.01	28.09
Mauritania	290	217	199	158	236	0.00	49.37
Niger	225	274	243	195	233	0.00	19.49
Nigeria	5,838	5,952	7,371	10,195	9,821	0.06	-3.67
Guinea-Bissau	12	2	10	27	2	0.00	-92.59

CANADA

1. Arrivals of non-resident tourists at national borders, by country of residence

	2007	2008	2009	2010	2011	Market share 11	% Change 11-10
Saint Helena	2				13	0.00	
Senegal	1,563	1,855	1,667	1,711	1,896	0.01	10.81
Sierra Leone	112	111	117	142	142	0.00	
Togo	279	310	257	271	378	0.00	39.48
Burkina Faso	562	855	698	758	772	0.00	1.85
Other Africa	**62**	**67**	**69**	**48**	**17**	**0.00**	**-64.58**
Other countries of Africa	62	67	69	48	17	0.00	-64.58
AMERICAS	**13,946,446**	**13,111,691**	**12,150,425**	**12,214,291**	**12,079,843**	**75.43**	**-1.10**
Caribbean	**137,015**	**136,707**	**128,036**	**134,944**	**134,975**	**0.84**	**0.02**
Antigua and Barbuda	1,768	1,768	1,373	1,408	1,605	0.01	13.99
Bahamas	9,681	9,446	9,284	9,139	8,932	0.06	-2.27
Barbados	11,909	11,192	10,822	11,897	11,462	0.07	-3.66
Bermuda	21,927	20,461	19,234	21,604	20,800	0.13	-3.72
British Virgin Islands	629	489	570	476	504	0.00	5.88
Cayman Islands	6,760	5,958	5,636	5,379	6,281	0.04	16.77
Cuba	5,546	5,860	5,554	5,281	5,172	0.03	-2.06
Dominica	481	480	513	641	706	0.00	10.14
Dominican Republic	4,189	4,319	4,114	5,330	5,087	0.03	-4.56
Grenada	1,269	1,174	965	944	894	0.01	-5.30
Guadeloupe	2,874	3,672	3,152	3,984	4,264	0.03	7.03
Haiti	7,004	6,481	6,659	6,230	6,725	0.04	7.95
Jamaica	23,691	25,413	24,323	26,077	25,147	0.16	-3.57
Martinique	2,219	2,587	2,394	2,806	2,921	0.02	4.10
Montserrat	39	32	33	59	19	0.00	-67.80
Netherlands Antilles	1,107	1,128	1,269	1,503	1,838	0.01	22.29
Puerto Rico	1,943	1,517	1,103	995	1,005	0.01	1.01
Saint Kitts and Nevis	983	786	863	832	872	0.01	4.81
Anguilla	174	162	140	213	159	0.00	-25.35
Saint Lucia	2,847	3,381	2,934	3,668	3,937	0.02	7.33
Saint Vincent and the Grenadines	3,531	3,839	2,898	3,351	3,257	0.02	-2.81
Trinidad and Tobago	24,744	24,883	22,779	21,778	22,004	0.14	1.04
Turks and Caicos Islands	1,620	1,629	1,349	1,281	1,337	0.01	4.37
United States Virgin Islands	80	50	75	68	47	0.00	-30.88
Central America	**18,984**	**19,813**	**19,045**	**19,926**	**19,448**	**0.12**	**-2.40**
Belize	831	1,048	825	946	1,017	0.01	7.51
Costa Rica	5,410	4,782	4,647	4,682	4,438	0.03	-5.21
El Salvador	2,857	2,770	2,326	2,160	1,770	0.01	-18.06
Guatemala	4,975	5,863	6,598	6,938	6,443	0.04	-7.13
Honduras	1,451	1,589	1,167	1,248	1,487	0.01	19.15
Nicaragua	882	896	894	949	896	0.01	-5.58
Panama	2,578	2,865	2,588	3,003	3,397	0.02	13.12
North America	**13,639,463**	**12,792,893**	**11,856,529**	**11,887,727**	**11,743,918**	**73.33**	**-1.21**
Greenland	158	335	213	406	267	0.00	-34.24
Mexico	247,106	266,295	168,724	120,499	132,217	0.83	9.72
Saint Pierre and Miquelon	16,998	22,383	20,359	18,008	16,071	0.10	-10.76
United States of America	13,375,201	12,503,880	11,667,233	11,748,814	11,595,363	72.41	-1.31
South America	**150,984**	**162,278**	**146,815**	**171,694**	**181,502**	**1.13**	**5.71**
Argentina	15,710	18,094	15,013	16,744	17,737	0.11	5.93
Bolivia	1,153	962	831	853	976	0.01	14.42
Brazil	66,134	71,619	61,829	80,188	87,904	0.55	9.62
Chile	13,398	14,336	13,602	18,255	17,336	0.11	-5.03
Colombia	17,314	17,397	16,568	16,267	18,762	0.12	15.34
Ecuador	3,955	4,115	3,716	3,792	3,633	0.02	-4.19
Falkland Islands, Malvinas	5	4	12	8	5	0.00	-37.50
French Guiana	104	195	182	185	238	0.00	28.65
Guyana	4,114	4,106	3,947	3,267	3,803	0.02	16.41
Paraguay	1,291	1,169	1,074	1,202	1,312	0.01	9.15

CANADA

1. Arrivals of non-resident tourists at national borders, by country of residence

	2007	2008	2009	2010	2011	Market share 11	% Change 11-10
Peru	9,529	9,460	8,016	10,119	9,470	0.06	-6.41
Suriname	201	339	262	283	262	0.00	-7.42
Uruguay	2,125	1,963	1,638	1,921	2,180	0.01	13.48
Venezuela	15,951	18,519	20,125	18,610	17,884	0.11	-3.90
EAST ASIA AND THE PACIFIC	**1,266,560**	**1,230,626**	**1,025,526**	**1,170,281**	**1,222,621**	**7.63**	**4.47**
North-East Asia	**877,689**	**810,261**	**654,969**	**763,735**	**787,524**	**4.92**	**3.11**
China	152,200	159,927	160,833	194,979	243,692	1.52	24.98
Taiwan, Province of China	80,167	61,545	50,000	52,813	57,683	0.36	9.22
Hong Kong, China	113,404	128,139	107,410	114,973	123,060	0.77	7.03
Japan	330,931	276,091	197,752	235,510	211,062	1.32	-10.38
Korea, Dem. People's Republic of	23	4	2	8			
Korea, Republic of	200,388	183,895	138,150	164,282	151,101	0.94	-8.02
Macao, China	112	107	151	181	157	0.00	-13.26
Mongolia	464	553	671	989	769	0.00	-22.24
South-East Asia	**123,701**	**130,776**	**121,165**	**124,704**	**146,489**	**0.91**	**17.47**
Brunei Darussalam	525	515	450	527	548	0.00	3.98
Myanmar	457	396	487	318	262	0.00	-17.61
Cambodia	638	571	566	502	762	0.00	51.79
Indonesia	11,418	10,814	11,117	12,428	15,142	0.09	21.84
Lao People's Democratic Republic	280	223	180	176	223	0.00	26.70
Malaysia	10,894	12,892	8,754	11,255	11,867	0.07	5.44
Philippines	57,652	61,758	61,473	54,946	59,674	0.37	8.60
Singapore	23,967	24,904	21,043	24,770	29,254	0.18	18.10
Viet Nam	4,554	5,455	5,676	6,585	7,308	0.05	10.98
Thailand	13,316	13,248	11,419	13,197	21,449	0.13	62.53
Australasia	**261,185**	**285,252**	**245,971**	**278,280**	**285,114**	**1.78**	**2.46**
Australia	219,592	238,802	204,383	232,855	242,430	1.51	4.11
New Zealand	41,593	46,450	41,588	45,425	42,684	0.27	-6.03
Melanesia	**2,446**	**2,756**	**2,122**	**2,122**	**1,940**	**0.01**	**-8.58**
Solomon Islands	47	21	24	28	31	0.00	10.71
Fiji	1,580	1,607	1,216	1,091	903	0.01	-17.23
New Caledonia	605	845	690	749	819	0.01	9.35
Vanuatu	64	58	52	69	49	0.00	-28.99
Papua New Guinea	150	225	140	185	138	0.00	-25.41
Micronesia	**147**	**106**	**150**	**112**	**109**	**0.00**	**-2.68**
Kiribati	8	4	13	18	26	0.00	44.44
Guam	42	11	35	22	18	0.00	-18.18
Nauru	4			12	4	0.00	-66.67
Northern Mariana Islands	12	9	4	4	6	0.00	50.00
Micronesia, Federated States of	59	65	62	47	41	0.00	-12.77
Marshall Islands	22	17	36	9	14	0.00	55.56
Polynesia	**1,342**	**1,459**	**1,135**	**1,312**	**1,437**	**0.01**	**9.53**
American Samoa	47	31	28	53	23	0.00	-56.60
Cook Islands	32	28	12	26	6	0.00	-76.92
French Polynesia	1,208	1,353	1,046	1,201	1,371	0.01	14.15
Tonga	43	19	31	12	22	0.00	83.33
Tuvalu				2	3	0.00	50.00
Wallis and Futuna Islands		2	8	4			
Samoa	12	26	10	14	12	0.00	-14.29
Other East Asia and the Pacific	**50**	**16**	**14**	**16**	**8**	**0.00**	**-50.00**
Other countries East Asia/Pacific	24	12	10	2			
Other countries of Oceania	26	4	4	14	8	0.00	-42.86
EUROPE	**2,443,093**	**2,497,509**	**2,262,129**	**2,375,518**	**2,355,777**	**14.71**	**-0.83**
Central/Eastern Europe	**109,494**	**136,840**	**122,740**	**128,378**	**127,616**	**0.80**	**-0.59**
Azerbaijan	364	364	408	455	476	0.00	4.62
Armenia	476	451	341	480	604	0.00	25.83

CANADA

1. Arrivals of non-resident tourists at national borders, by country of residence

	2007	2008	2009	2010	2011	Market share 11	% Change 11-10
Bulgaria	3,267	3,646	3,278	3,210	3,128	0.02	-2.55
Belarus	1,389	1,543	1,537	1,461	1,245	0.01	-14.78
Czech Republic	12,254	15,599	16,068	11,864	11,112	0.07	-6.34
Estonia	2,080	2,024	1,675	1,540	1,577	0.01	2.40
Georgia	326	201	214	378	283	0.00	-25.13
Hungary	8,564	11,131	11,752	12,284	12,878	0.08	4.84
Kazakhstan	1,755	1,938	2,004	2,116	2,158	0.01	1.98
Kyrgyzstan	170	244	283	245	261	0.00	6.53
Latvia	1,329	3,046	2,398	2,488	2,027	0.01	-18.53
Lithuania	1,018	1,886	1,461	1,715	1,871	0.01	9.10
Republic of Moldova	871	1,067	1,480	1,783	1,910	0.01	7.12
Poland	23,637	34,354	28,352	29,295	29,536	0.18	0.82
Romania	17,301	17,784	15,408	15,633	15,416	0.10	-1.39
Russian Federation	20,563	24,422	19,389	25,027	23,796	0.15	-4.92
Slovakia	4,690	6,228	6,516	7,567	7,320	0.05	-3.26
Tajikistan	59	60	65	80	64	0.00	-20.00
Turkmenistan	33	34	78	75	70	0.00	-6.67
Ukraine	9,166	10,599	9,755	10,406	11,675	0.07	12.19
Uzbekistan	182	219	278	276	209	0.00	-24.28
Northern Europe	**1,062,975**	**1,017,039**	**850,301**	**874,143**	**846,280**	**5.28**	**-3.19**
Denmark	27,728	30,866	26,654	33,085	38,179	0.24	15.40
Faeroe Islands	20	69	83	151	97	0.00	-35.76
Finland	15,846	17,400	14,742	16,791	14,706	0.09	-12.42
Iceland	6,077	6,613	3,450	4,244	5,087	0.03	19.86
Ireland	50,331	49,593	43,664	46,273	42,638	0.27	-7.86
Norway	21,841	23,147	20,329	24,723	24,691	0.15	-0.13
Sweden	32,326	34,947	30,866	37,187	41,054	0.26	10.40
United Kingdom	908,806	854,404	710,513	711,689	679,828	4.25	-4.48
Southern Europe	**211,751**	**218,802**	**208,326**	**219,305**	**215,140**	**1.34**	**-1.90**
Albania	1,389	1,504	1,349	1,330	1,156	0.01	-13.08
Andorra	290	273	327	364	281	0.00	-22.80
Bosnia and Herzegovina	1,768	1,748	1,487	1,529	1,389	0.01	-9.16
Croatia	3,666	4,084	4,569	5,248	5,273	0.03	0.48
Gibraltar	305	248	238	261	324	0.00	24.14
Greece	13,488	13,681	12,058	12,799	12,482	0.08	-2.48
Holy See	2	9	1	4	6	0.00	50.00
Italy	94,850	96,050	92,393	101,738	98,191	0.61	-3.49
Malta	2,266	1,958	2,090	1,892	1,875	0.01	-0.90
Portugal	21,556	20,955	18,108	19,556	20,879	0.13	6.77
San Marino	38	38	30	64	48	0.00	-25.00
Slovenia	3,168	3,611	2,979	3,702	3,212	0.02	-13.24
Spain	61,855	67,811	66,733	64,383	63,858	0.40	-0.82
TFYR of Macedonia	1,015	945	1,015	968	896	0.01	-7.44
Serbia and Montenegro	6,095	5,887	4,949	5,467	5,270	0.03	-3.60
Western Europe	**978,502**	**1,047,629**	**1,012,096**	**1,078,818**	**1,089,427**	**6.80**	**0.98**
Austria	31,128	33,032	32,949	38,086	36,925	0.23	-3.05
Belgium	44,811	49,798	48,057	52,600	54,848	0.34	4.27
France	374,785	420,895	407,653	435,465	459,140	2.87	5.44
Germany	306,638	319,895	309,684	332,086	315,901	1.97	-4.87
Liechtenstein	357	291	462	483	473	0.00	-2.07
Luxembourg	3,628	4,081	3,497	4,179	4,260	0.03	1.94
Monaco	1,123	1,152	1,204	1,286	1,315	0.01	2.26
Netherlands	121,651	121,050	109,133	109,208	105,842	0.66	-3.08
Switzerland	94,381	97,435	99,457	105,425	110,723	0.69	5.03
East Mediterranean Europe	**80,371**	**77,199**	**68,666**	**74,874**	**77,314**	**0.48**	**3.26**
Cyprus	1,920	2,002	1,535	1,853	1,712	0.01	-7.61
Israel	69,187	66,236	57,704	60,681	63,322	0.40	4.35
Turkey	9,264	8,961	9,427	12,340	12,280	0.08	-0.49

CANADA

1. Arrivals of non-resident tourists at national borders, by country of residence

	2007	2008	2009	2010	2011	Market share 11	% Change 11-10
MIDDLE EAST	**67,512**	**77,272**	**77,602**	**83,668**	**85,069**	**0.53**	**1.67**
Bahrain	1,411	1,454	1,553	1,671	1,696	0.01	1.50
Iraq	509	775	1,190	1,576	1,554	0.01	-1.40
Jordan	3,350	3,887	3,443	3,422	3,787	0.02	10.67
Kuwait	3,559	3,268	3,197	3,385	3,615	0.02	6.79
Lebanon	10,777	8,990	8,300	8,372	9,925	0.06	18.55
Libya	1,552	1,575	1,504	1,558	441	0.00	-71.69
Oman	1,428	1,285	1,300	1,536	1,387	0.01	-9.70
Qatar	3,148	3,563	3,740	4,072	4,803	0.03	17.95
Saudi Arabia	13,069	16,710	17,799	20,124	18,756	0.12	-6.80
Syrian Arab Republic	1,926	2,045	2,277	2,209	2,506	0.02	13.44
United Arab Emirates	17,822	23,837	23,904	25,000	27,378	0.17	9.51
Egypt	8,584	9,387	9,009	10,434	8,942	0.06	-14.30
Yemen	377	496	386	309	279	0.00	-9.71
SOUTH ASIA	**135,745**	**145,077**	**145,751**	**172,334**	**185,193**	**1.16**	**7.46**
Afghanistan	506	591	656	680	812	0.01	19.41
Bangladesh	3,341	4,213	4,120	5,455	5,138	0.03	-5.81
Bhutan	97	52	97	299	372	0.00	24.41
Sri Lanka	4,646	5,331	3,068	3,612	4,126	0.03	14.23
India	101,724	110,890	107,959	127,619	139,213	0.87	9.08
Iran, Islamic Republic of	8,805	8,201	11,830	15,616	14,329	0.09	-8.24
Maldives	43	37	53	44	73	0.00	65.91
Nepal	838	915	1,164	1,435	1,445	0.01	0.70
Pakistan	15,745	14,847	16,804	17,574	19,685	0.12	12.01

CANADA

2. Arrivals of non-resident visitors at national borders, by country of residence

		2007	2008	2009	2010	2011	Market share 11	% Change 11-10
TOTAL		30,373,400	27,370,200	24,695,500	24,669,200	25,066,500	100.00	1.61
AFRICA		76,400	80,400	76,300	81,800	86,500	0.35	5.75
Southern Africa		23,800	24,100	19,100	19,200	21,100	0.08	9.90
South Africa		23,800	24,100	19,100	19,200	21,100	0.08	9.90
Other Africa		52,600	56,300	57,200	62,600	65,400	0.26	4.47
Other countries of Africa		52,600	56,300	57,200	62,600	65,400	0.26	4.47
AMERICAS		26,272,700	23,220,000	21,014,000	20,684,700	21,035,300	83.92	1.69
Caribbean		138,200	137,300	128,700	135,700	135,900	0.54	0.15
Bermuda		22,000	20,500	19,200	21,600	20,800	0.08	-3.70
Jamaica		23,900	25,500	24,500	26,200	25,400	0.10	-3.05
Trinidad and Tobago		24,900	25,000	22,900	21,900	22,100	0.09	0.91
Other countries of the Caribbean		67,400	66,300	62,100	66,000	67,600	0.27	2.42
North America		25,962,400	22,899,100	20,718,200	20,355,700	20,696,800	82.57	1.68
Greenland		200	300	200	400	300	0.00	-25.00
Mexico		250,600	270,800	172,000	123,800	136,900	0.55	10.58
Saint Pierre and Miquelon		17,000	22,400	20,400	18,000	16,100	0.06	-10.56
United States of America		25,694,600	22,605,600	20,525,600	20,213,500	20,543,500	81.96	1.63
South America		152,800	163,600	147,900	173,200	182,900	0.73	5.60
Argentina		15,900	18,300	15,100	16,800	17,900	0.07	6.55
Brazil		66,700	72,100	62,200	80,800	88,500	0.35	9.53
Colombia		17,700	17,600	16,800	16,500	19,000	0.08	15.15
Venezuela		16,100	18,700	20,300	18,800	18,000	0.07	-4.26
Other countries of South America		36,400	36,900	33,500	40,300	39,500	0.16	-1.99
Other Americas		19,300	20,000	19,200	20,100	19,700	0.08	-1.99
Other countries of the Americas		19,300	20,000	19,200	20,100	19,700	0.08	-1.99
EAST ASIA AND THE PACIFIC		1,313,500	1,280,200	1,064,200	1,211,300	1,262,300	5.04	4.21
North-East Asia		910,400	846,100	680,000	787,800	809,500	3.23	2.75
China	(*)	156,200	166,400	166,900	201,000	249,700	1.00	24.23
Taiwan, Province of China		82,500	63,500	51,600	54,400	58,500	0.23	7.54
Hong Kong, China		115,600	132,400	111,800	119,400	126,800	0.51	6.20
Japan		343,500	287,200	205,600	243,000	218,800	0.87	-9.96
Korea, Republic of		212,600	196,600	144,100	170,000	155,700	0.62	-8.41
South-East Asia		120,200	125,600	116,800	120,100	142,700	0.57	18.82
Indonesia		11,800	11,000	11,500	12,900	15,800	0.06	22.48
Malaysia		11,100	13,200	9,000	11,500	12,200	0.05	6.09
Philippines		58,800	62,300	62,700	56,600	61,200	0.24	8.13
Singapore		24,800	25,600	21,900	25,600	30,800	0.12	20.31
Thailand		13,700	13,500	11,700	13,500	22,700	0.09	68.15
Australasia		272,300	296,800	256,400	291,400	297,300	1.19	2.02
Australia		228,700	248,700	213,700	244,200	253,300	1.01	3.73
New Zealand		43,600	48,100	42,700	47,200	44,000	0.18	-6.78
Other East Asia and the Pacific		10,600	11,700	11,000	12,000	12,800	0.05	6.67
Other countries of Asia		6,600	7,300	7,600	8,400	9,300	0.04	10.71
Other countries of Oceania		4,000	4,400	3,400	3,600	3,500	0.01	-2.78
EUROPE		2,500,900	2,560,200	2,310,900	2,427,400	2,403,400	9.59	-0.99
Central/Eastern Europe		114,100	142,000	127,000	133,300	132,200	0.53	-0.83
Czech Republic/Slovakia		17,400	22,200	23,000	19,600	18,700	0.07	-4.59
Estonia	(*)	4,400	7,000	5,600	5,800	5,500	0.02	-5.17
Poland		24,000	34,800	28,600	35,200	35,100	0.14	-0.28
Other countries Central/East Europe		32,600	36,700	33,800	29,600	29,800	0.12	0.68
Commonwealth Independent States		35,700	41,300	36,000	43,100	43,100	0.17	
Northern Europe		1,084,200	1,036,700	867,400	893,900	864,400	3.45	-3.30
Denmark	(*)	28,900	32,200	27,400	33,900	38,900	0.16	14.75

CANADA

2. Arrivals of non-resident visitors at national borders, by country of residence

		2007	2008	2009	2010	2011	Market share 11	% Change 11-10
Finland		16,300	17,700	15,000	17,000	15,000	0.06	-11.76
Iceland		6,100	6,600	3,500	4,300	5,200	0.02	20.93
Ireland		51,300	50,600	44,600	48,000	43,900	0.18	-8.54
Norway		22,300	23,600	20,600	25,200	25,000	0.10	-0.79
Sweden		33,400	35,800	31,600	37,700	41,500	0.17	10.08
United Kingdom		925,900	870,200	724,700	727,800	694,900	2.77	-4.52
Southern Europe		**222,200**	**234,200**	**218,700**	**226,700**	**223,000**	**0.89**	**-1.63**
Greece		14,000	14,000	12,300	13,100	12,800	0.05	-2.29
Italy	(*)	104,900	108,500	101,500	110,400	106,500	0.42	-3.53
Portugal		21,900	21,500	18,500	19,900	21,300	0.08	7.04
Spain		67,200	75,900	72,900	68,600	68,100	0.27	-0.73
Yugoslavia, SFR (former)		14,200	14,300	13,500	14,700	14,300	0.06	-2.72
Western Europe		**1,000,100**	**1,070,400**	**1,029,500**	**1,099,300**	**1,106,900**	**4.42**	**0.69**
Austria		31,400	33,600	33,400	38,800	37,300	0.15	-3.87
France	(*)	380,700	426,800	413,300	442,400	466,200	1.86	5.38
Germany		318,200	332,000	318,800	342,000	324,000	1.29	-5.26
Netherlands		124,400	123,900	110,700	111,000	107,100	0.43	-3.51
Switzerland	(*)	96,200	99,600	101,200	107,700	112,700	0.45	4.64
Belgium / Luxembourg		49,200	54,500	52,100	57,400	59,600	0.24	3.83
East Mediterranean Europe		**80,300**	**76,900**	**68,300**	**74,200**	**76,900**	**0.31**	**3.64**
Israel		70,900	67,900	58,800	61,800	64,400	0.26	4.21
Turkey		9,400	9,000	9,500	12,400	12,500	0.05	0.81
MIDDLE EAST		**79,200**	**88,400**	**92,100**	**102,200**	**102,400**	**0.41**	**0.20**
All countries of Middle East		79,200	88,400	92,100	102,200	102,400	0.41	0.20
SOUTH ASIA		**130,700**	**141,000**	**138,000**	**161,800**	**176,600**	**0.70**	**9.15**
All countries of South Asia		130,700	141,000	138,000	161,800	176,600	0.70	9.15

CANADA

6. Overnight stays of non-resident tourists in all types of accommodation establishments, by country of residence

		2007	2008	2009	2010	2011	Market share 11	% Change 11-10
TOTAL		123,862,700	126,067,400	114,888,500	119,745,200	122,528,300	100.00	2.32
AFRICA		1,695,000	1,888,100	1,689,300	1,952,400	2,472,100	2.02	26.62
Southern Africa		398,000	401,800	331,100	352,100	397,000	0.32	12.75
South Africa		398,000	401,800	331,100	352,100	397,000	0.32	12.75
Other Africa		1,297,000	1,486,300	1,358,200	1,600,300	2,075,100	1.69	29.67
Other countries of Africa		1,297,000	1,486,300	1,358,200	1,600,300	2,075,100	1.69	29.67
AMERICAS		62,866,500	60,777,100	55,439,100	55,226,800	55,770,900	45.52	0.99
Caribbean		1,910,400	1,890,900	1,610,500	2,167,400	2,159,600	1.76	-0.36
Bermuda		333,900	291,900	156,200	207,600	197,800	0.16	-4.72
Jamaica		433,300	377,200	357,000	603,600	604,900	0.49	0.22
Trinidad and Tobago		319,200	463,400	370,000	462,800	466,400	0.38	0.78
Other countries of the Caribbean		824,000	758,400	727,300	893,400	890,500	0.73	-0.32
North America		58,226,500	55,897,600	51,071,600	49,906,600	50,040,000	40.84	0.27
Greenland		1,000	2,500	2,200	2,900	2,000	0.00	-31.03
Mexico		4,211,800	5,105,400	3,622,000	2,584,400	2,885,500	2.35	11.65
Saint Pierre and Miquelon		59,500	147,000	82,500	71,900	81,200	0.07	12.93
United States of America		53,954,200	50,642,700	47,364,900	47,247,400	47,071,300	38.42	-0.37
South America		2,542,400	2,739,600	2,397,400	2,911,000	3,294,700	2.69	13.18
Argentina		206,800	247,200	200,500	250,600	301,400	0.25	20.27
Brazil		1,196,500	1,344,500	979,600	1,381,800	1,439,000	1.17	4.14
Colombia		302,500	321,300	313,900	415,200	536,200	0.44	29.14
Venezuela		210,800	265,500	350,600	275,400	317,700	0.26	15.36
Other countries of South America		625,800	561,100	552,800	588,000	700,400	0.57	19.12
Other Americas		187,200	249,000	359,600	241,800	276,600	0.23	14.39
Other countries of the Americas		187,200	249,000	359,600	241,800	276,600	0.23	14.39
EAST ASIA AND THE PACIFIC		21,150,600	21,494,200	19,924,400	22,529,200	24,454,200	19.96	8.54
North-East Asia		14,751,200	14,766,900	13,027,800	15,588,000	16,781,400	13.70	7.66
China	(*)	4,095,700	4,439,300	4,470,800	5,401,000	6,795,900	5.55	25.83
Taiwan, Province of China		1,171,100	1,029,600	858,900	950,700	1,277,700	1.04	34.40
Hong Kong, China		1,780,900	2,022,400	1,780,000	1,958,100	2,141,400	1.75	9.36
Japan		3,396,600	3,103,500	2,468,500	3,045,800	2,697,400	2.20	-11.44
Korea, Republic of		4,306,900	4,172,100	3,450,500	4,232,400	3,869,000	3.16	-8.59
South-East Asia		2,888,200	2,952,700	3,189,400	3,108,700	3,766,300	3.07	21.15
Indonesia		221,600	190,600	180,200	128,000	217,100	0.18	69.61
Malaysia		133,700	129,000	185,200	234,500	122,000	0.10	-47.97
Philippines		2,076,400	2,138,700	2,384,800	2,043,400	2,779,100	2.27	36.00
Singapore		261,700	308,900	234,700	293,700	349,600	0.29	19.03
Thailand		194,800	185,500	204,500	409,100	298,500	0.24	-27.03
Australasia		3,302,200	3,605,200	3,546,600	3,606,400	3,713,800	3.03	2.98
Australia		2,739,300	2,935,200	2,644,200	3,023,600	3,188,000	2.60	5.44
New Zealand		562,900	670,000	902,400	582,800	525,800	0.43	-9.78
Other East Asia and the Pacific		209,000	169,400	160,600	226,100	192,700	0.16	-14.77
Other countries of Asia		146,800	99,500	103,200	162,200	133,600	0.11	-17.63
Other countries of Oceania		62,200	69,900	57,400	63,900	59,100	0.05	-7.51
EUROPE		33,952,500	37,283,600	33,197,600	34,504,500	33,717,300	27.52	-2.28
Central/Eastern Europe		2,073,600	2,924,000	2,304,100	3,124,200	3,210,300	2.62	2.76
Czech Republic/Slovakia		348,500	509,800	425,200	377,100	519,100	0.42	37.66
Estonia	(*)	47,500	198,400	63,500	111,200	48,500	0.04	-56.38
Poland		313,900	641,300	502,200	594,600	773,300	0.63	30.05
Other countries Central/East Europe		550,500	612,700	680,900	782,500	860,300	0.70	9.94
Commonwealth Independent States		813,200	961,800	632,300	1,258,800	1,009,100	0.82	-19.84
Northern Europe		13,046,300	13,336,900	11,085,100	10,796,400	10,293,000	8.40	-4.66
Denmark	(*)	399,500	443,600	332,700	363,800	355,700	0.29	-2.23

CANADA

6. Overnight stays of non-resident tourists in all types of accommodation establishments, by country of residence

		2007	2008	2009	2010	2011	Market share 11	% Change 11-10
Finland		155,900	164,200	215,500	262,200	152,600	0.12	-41.80
Iceland		54,800	84,200	28,700	40,700	46,400	0.04	14.00
Ireland		496,100	570,900	453,400	559,900	635,900	0.52	13.57
Norway		238,400	229,000	230,800	280,700	303,200	0.25	8.02
Sweden		386,500	482,100	463,800	379,800	511,200	0.42	34.60
United Kingdom		11,315,100	11,362,900	9,360,200	8,909,300	8,288,000	6.76	-6.97
Southern Europe		**3,137,800**	**3,357,200**	**3,112,900**	**2,926,800**	**2,845,200**	**2.32**	**-2.79**
Greece		275,700	141,500	188,400	185,600	150,400	0.12	-18.97
Italy	(*)	1,296,500	1,343,600	1,196,600	1,270,800	1,212,800	0.99	-4.56
Portugal		282,000	358,200	347,600	243,800	223,500	0.18	-8.33
Spain		732,200	966,600	898,500	821,100	752,900	0.61	-8.31
Yugoslavia, SFR (former)		551,400	547,300	481,800	405,500	505,600	0.41	24.69
Western Europe		**14,838,100**	**16,790,300**	**15,845,000**	**16,872,700**	**16,413,100**	**13.40**	**-2.72**
Austria		384,500	455,900	530,000	601,400	397,200	0.32	-33.95
France	(*)	5,845,900	7,014,600	6,351,000	6,657,200	6,829,800	5.57	2.59
Germany		4,816,600	5,249,400	5,160,900	5,515,100	5,057,500	4.13	-8.30
Netherlands		1,691,500	1,847,400	1,579,400	1,565,500	1,482,200	1.21	-5.32
Switzerland	(*)	1,459,500	1,436,100	1,562,300	1,608,400	1,781,000	1.45	10.73
Belgium / Luxembourg		640,100	786,900	661,400	925,100	865,400	0.71	-6.45
East Mediterranean Europe		**856,700**	**875,200**	**850,500**	**784,400**	**955,700**	**0.78**	**21.84**
Israel		677,200	716,000	604,300	646,200	757,700	0.62	17.25
Turkey		179,500	159,200	246,200	138,200	198,000	0.16	43.27
MIDDLE EAST		**1,682,000**	**1,832,700**	**1,961,100**	**2,282,300**	**2,394,600**	**1.95**	**4.92**
All countries of Middle East		1,682,000	1,832,700	1,961,100	2,282,300	2,394,600	1.95	4.92
SOUTH ASIA		**2,516,100**	**2,791,700**	**2,677,000**	**3,250,000**	**3,719,200**	**3.04**	**14.44**
All countries of South Asia		2,516,100	2,791,700	2,677,000	3,250,000	3,719,200	3.04	14.44

CAPE VERDE

3. Arrivals of non-resident tourists in hotels and similar establishments, by country of residence

		2007	2008	2009	2010	2011	Market share 11	% Change 11-10
TOTAL		267,188	285,141	287,183	336,086	428,273	100.00	27.43
AFRICA		307	193	175	218	2,819	0.66	1193.12
Southern Africa		307	193	175	218	2,819	0.66	1193.12
South Africa		307	193	175	218	2,819	0.66	1193.12
AMERICAS		4,932	4,004	3,935	3,188	3,711	0.87	16.41
North America		4,932	4,004	3,935	3,188	3,711	0.87	16.41
United States of America		4,932	4,004	3,935	3,188	3,711	0.87	16.41
EUROPE		228,165	234,309	244,060	297,614	385,424	89.99	29.50
Northern Europe		46,688	51,680	57,011	72,019	90,481	21.13	25.63
United Kingdom		46,688	51,680	57,011	72,019	90,481	21.13	25.63
Southern Europe		114,455	116,690	98,891	108,508	135,858	31.72	25.21
Italy		46,324	48,956	42,628	40,717	56,378	13.16	38.46
Portugal		59,420	57,854	50,617	60,277	65,693	15.34	8.99
Spain		8,711	9,880	5,646	7,514	13,787	3.22	83.48
Western Europe		67,022	65,939	88,158	117,087	159,085	37.15	35.87
Austria		971	876	977	962	1,772	0.41	84.20
Belgium	(*)	7,879	8,632	22,091	21,655	24,169	5.64	11.61
France		23,646	21,057	22,675	43,496	66,641	15.56	53.21
Germany		31,329	32,705	40,138	48,920	60,495	14.13	23.66
Switzerland		3,197	2,669	2,277	2,054	6,008	1.40	192.50
NOT SPECIFIED		33,784	46,635	39,013	35,066	36,319	8.48	3.57
Other countries of the World		33,784	46,635	39,013	35,066	36,319	8.48	3.57

CAPE VERDE

5. Overnight stays of non-resident tourists in hotels and similar establishments, by country of residence

	2007	2008	2009	2010	2011	Market share 11	% Change 11-10
TOTAL	1,307,558	1,711,875	1,897,573	2,217,563	2,703,909	100.00	21.93
AFRICA	619	543	606	663	14,540	0.54	2093.06
Southern Africa	619	543	606	663	14,540	0.54	2093.06
South Africa	619	543	606	663	14,540	0.54	2093.06
AMERICAS	15,805	12,521	10,632	10,162	12,988	0.48	27.81
North America	15,805	12,521	10,632	10,162	12,988	0.48	27.81
United States of America	15,805	12,521	10,632	10,162	12,988	0.48	27.81
EUROPE	1,134,291	1,448,975	1,663,042	2,006,352	2,507,979	92.75	25.00
Northern Europe	284,691	423,350	517,655	610,465	766,740	28.36	25.60
United Kingdom	284,691	423,350	517,655	610,465	766,740	28.36	25.60
Southern Europe	564,313	651,021	556,055	609,939	794,378	29.38	30.24
Italy	305,609	339,693	290,662	278,261	397,473	14.70	42.84
Portugal	232,035	271,595	242,905	299,228	335,688	12.41	12.18
Spain	26,669	39,733	22,488	32,450	61,217	2.26	88.65
Western Europe	285,287	374,604	589,332	785,948	946,861	35.02	20.47
Austria	3,236	4,841	5,541	5,397	13,208	0.49	144.73
Belgium (*)	34,942	51,305	161,667	159,061	171,851	6.36	8.04
France	77,701	68,612	102,015	241,527	293,334	10.85	21.45
Germany	154,239	236,739	307,861	370,359	426,532	15.77	15.17
Switzerland	15,169	13,107	12,248	9,604	41,936	1.55	336.65
NOT SPECIFIED	156,843	249,836	223,293	200,386	168,402	6.23	-15.96
Other countries of the World	156,843	249,836	223,293	200,386	168,402	6.23	-15.96

CAYMAN ISLANDS

1. Arrivals of non-resident tourists at national borders, by country of residence

		2007	2008	2009	2010	2011	Market share 11	% Change 11-10
TOTAL	(*)	291,503	302,879	271,949	288,272	309,069	100.00	7.21
AFRICA		530	538	518	673	613	0.20	-8.92
East Africa		34	43	48	76	65	0.02	-14.47
Comoros			2	3	2			
Ethiopia		3	1		5			
Eritrea		1						
Djibouti		1						
Kenya		12	16	26	34	31	0.01	-8.82
Madagascar		2		1	1	1	0.00	
Malawi		1	1	3	1			
Mauritius		3	6	1	7	4	0.00	-42.86
Reunion						1	0.00	
Rwanda					3			
Seychelles		1				1	0.00	
Somalia						1	0.00	
Zimbabwe		8	13	8	18	12	0.00	-33.33
Uganda			1	1		2	0.00	
United Republic of Tanzania		2			1	5	0.00	400.00
Zambia			3	5	4	7	0.00	75.00
Central Africa		12	7	9	20	28	0.01	40.00
Angola			1					
Cameroon				2				
Chad		1	1		1			
Congo					1			
Gabon		1	1		1			
Sao Tome and Principe		10	4	7	17	28	0.01	64.71
North Africa		3	9	2	6	6	0.00	
Algeria				1		1	0.00	
Morocco		2	3		4	4	0.00	
Sudan		1	1	1	2	1	0.00	-50.00
Tunisia			5					
Southern Africa		455	452	420	547	464	0.15	-15.17
Botswana		11	10	7	8	10	0.00	25.00
Namibia		2	4	5		1	0.00	
South Africa		428	397	364	487	386	0.12	-20.74
Swaziland		14	41	44	52	67	0.02	28.85
West Africa		26	27	39	24	50	0.02	108.33
Cape Verde			1	3	1			
Gambia			1		1	1	0.00	
Ghana		1	6	8	6	6	0.00	
Côte d'Ivoire			4					
Liberia				1	1	1	0.00	
Mauritania				1		1	0.00	
Nigeria		17	11	19	10	35	0.01	250.00
Guinea-Bissau		1						
Saint Helena		3		3				
Senegal			1		1	1	0.00	
Sierra Leone			1		1	2	0.00	100.00
Togo		4	2	4	3	3	0.00	
AMERICAS		268,141	278,584	249,692	264,999	284,504	92.05	7.36
Caribbean		14,617	15,171	12,985	13,000	12,531	4.05	-3.61
Antigua and Barbuda		77	98	27	72	64	0.02	-11.11
Bahamas		809	732	717	1,048	830	0.27	-20.80
Barbados		575	541	446	478	460	0.15	-3.77
Bermuda		574	731	570	788	526	0.17	-33.25

130

CAYMAN ISLANDS

1. Arrivals of non-resident tourists at national borders, by country of residence

	2007	2008	2009	2010	2011	Market share 11	% Change 11-10
British Virgin Islands	138	126	72	97	98	0.03	1.03
Cuba	382	428	340	1,328	1,815	0.59	36.67
Dominica	19	39	14	23	19	0.01	-17.39
Dominican Republic	227	220	243	247	292	0.09	18.22
Grenada	26	37	24	37	22	0.01	-40.54
Guadeloupe	1	1	1	10	9	0.00	-10.00
Haiti	60	14	26	13	15	0.00	15.38
Jamaica	10,262	10,470	9,527	7,609	7,378	2.39	-3.04
Martinique				17	2	0.00	-88.24
Montserrat	24	17	6	11	7	0.00	-36.36
Netherlands Antilles	17	2	8	12	9	0.00	-25.00
Puerto Rico	66	83	67	76	58	0.02	-23.68
Saint Kitts and Nevis	29	27	26	47	39	0.01	-17.02
Anguilla	73	32	10	37	16	0.01	-56.76
Saint Lucia	105	115	80	81	73	0.02	-9.88
Sint Maarten	8	22	10	9	10	0.00	11.11
Saint Vincent and the Grenadines	58	40	35	47	38	0.01	-19.15
Trinidad and Tobago	837	876	609	758	632	0.20	-16.62
Turks and Caicos Islands	169	469	96	111	66	0.02	-40.54
United States Virgin Islands	81	51	31	44	53	0.02	20.45
Central America	**2,258**	**2,059**	**2,200**	**1,839**	**1,871**	**0.61**	**1.74**
Belize	105		107	99	107	0.03	8.08
Costa Rica	244	112	170	131	118	0.04	-9.92
El Salvador	18	187	18	21	55	0.02	161.90
Guatemala	40	12	56	66	9	0.00	-86.36
Honduras	1,455	1,392	1,418	1,277	1,310	0.42	2.58
Nicaragua	198	208	284	118	106	0.03	-10.17
Panama	198	148	147	127	166	0.05	30.71
North America	**249,659**	**259,446**	**232,705**	**248,343**	**268,035**	**86.72**	**7.93**
Canada	17,355	18,544	17,254	19,499	24,629	7.97	26.31
Mexico	439	440	409	383	477	0.15	24.54
United States of America	231,865	240,462	215,042	228,461	242,929	78.60	6.33
South America	**1,607**	**1,908**	**1,802**	**1,817**	**2,067**	**0.67**	**13.76**
Argentina	210	173	274	296	377	0.12	27.36
Bolivia	5	18	1	11	4	0.00	-63.64
Brazil	355	401	438	536	681	0.22	27.05
Chile	68	71	100	97	117	0.04	20.62
Colombia	459	543	421	355	286	0.09	-19.44
Ecuador	53	70	67	57	68	0.02	19.30
Falkland Islands, Malvinas		1	1	1			
French Guiana			1		1	0.00	
Guyana	184	312	244	194	194	0.06	
Paraguay	2	3		2	4	0.00	100.00
Peru	91	132	84	80	109	0.04	36.25
Suriname	11	6	6	6	36	0.01	500.00
Uruguay	11	6	19	28	19	0.01	-32.14
Venezuela	158	172	146	154	171	0.06	11.04
EAST ASIA AND THE PACIFIC	**1,720**	**1,626**	**1,816**	**1,872**	**1,836**	**0.59**	**-1.92**
North-East Asia	**405**	**197**	**312**	**280**	**347**	**0.11**	**23.93**
China	56	71	51	47			
Taiwan, Province of China	9	16	9	4	5	0.00	25.00
Hong Kong, China	68	58	50	51	81	0.03	58.82
Japan	244	24	193	153	261	0.08	70.59
Korea, Republic of	28	28	9	25			
South-East Asia	**241**	**220**	**276**	**212**	**153**	**0.05**	**-27.83**
Brunei Darussalam	1		4	1	2	0.00	100.00
Myanmar	2		3				

CAYMAN ISLANDS

1. Arrivals of non-resident tourists at national borders, by country of residence

	2007	2008	2009	2010	2011	Market share 11	% Change 11-10
Cambodia		1	2	2	1	0.00	-50.00
Indonesia	27	15	16	19	15	0.00	-21.05
Malaysia	25		42	35	34	0.01	-2.86
Philippines	106	134	147	85	32	0.01	-62.35
Singapore	63	59	46	66	61	0.02	-7.58
Viet Nam	3		6		1	0.00	
Thailand	14	11	10	4	7	0.00	75.00
Australasia	**1,065**	**1,206**	**1,223**	**1,369**	**1,332**	**0.43**	**-2.70**
Australia	810	922	942	1,118	1,069	0.35	-4.38
New Zealand	255	284	281	251	263	0.09	4.78
Melanesia	**3**	**1**		**5**	**1**	**0.00**	**-80.00**
Solomon Islands	1			2			
Fiji				1	1	0.00	
New Caledonia	1			1			
Vanuatu		1					
Papua New Guinea	1			1			
Micronesia	**4**	**1**	**5**	**5**	**2**	**0.00**	**-60.00**
Cocos (Keeling) Islands				1	1	0.00	
Kiribati		1		2			
Guam	1		2				
Nauru			1	1	1	0.00	
Micronesia, Federated States of	2		2				
Marshall Islands	1			1			
Polynesia	**2**	**1**		**1**	**1**	**0.00**	
French Polynesia	1						
Niue				1			
Tonga			1				
Samoa	1				1	0.00	
EUROPE	**20,432**	**21,419**	**19,262**	**20,081**	**21,314**	**6.90**	**6.14**
Central/Eastern Europe	**328**	**367**	**470**	**546**	**665**	**0.22**	**21.79**
Bulgaria	16	14	24	27	43	0.01	59.26
Belarus	2			3			
Czech Republic/Slovakia	54			79	43	0.01	-45.57
Czech Republic		72	129	79	120	0.04	51.90
Estonia	8	1	13	6	31	0.01	416.67
Georgia			1		1	0.00	
Hungary	51	43	82	95	95	0.03	
Kazakhstan			1		4	0.00	
Latvia	1	8	7	6	11	0.00	83.33
Lithuania	3	6	1	18			
Poland	43	68	70	71	136	0.04	91.55
Romania	41	43	63	65	88	0.03	35.38
Russian Federation	93	87	45	81	85	0.03	4.94
Slovakia			21				
Ukraine	16	25	13	16	8	0.00	-50.00
Northern Europe	**15,837**	**16,296**	**14,605**	**14,215**	**14,539**	**4.70**	**2.28**
Denmark	156	209	124	138	200	0.06	44.93
Faeroe Islands	1	1					
Finland	62	81	48	69	113	0.04	63.77
Iceland	15	24	2	9	13	0.00	44.44
Ireland	1,080	1,161	965	946	1,085	0.35	14.69
Norway	142	225	137	243	224	0.07	-7.82
Svalbard and Jan Mayen Islands					1	0.00	
Sweden	255	318	222	299	362	0.12	21.07
United Kingdom	14,126	14,277	13,100	12,503	12,534	4.06	0.25
Isle of Man			7	8	7	0.00	-12.50

CAYMAN ISLANDS

1. Arrivals of non-resident tourists at national borders, by country of residence

	2007	2008	2009	2010	2011	Market share 11	% Change 11-10
Southern Europe	**1,357**	**1,524**	**1,514**	**2,152**	**2,688**	**0.87**	**24.91**
Albania		2	1	1			
Andorra	149	122	61	82	67	0.02	-18.29
Bosnia and Herzegovina			4	1	3	0.00	200.00
Croatia	13	13	12	11	12	0.00	9.09
Gibraltar	5	16	20	10	4	0.00	-60.00
Greece	28	60	53	73	67	0.02	-8.22
Holy See	3	1		1			
Italy	715	879	960	935	1,104	0.36	18.07
Malta	7	7	3	2	7	0.00	250.00
Portugal	89	78	62	115	114	0.04	-0.87
San Marino			2	1			
Serbia			15	13	11	0.00	-15.38
Slovenia	21	21	19	36	32	0.01	-11.11
Spain	308	324	298	870	1,264	0.41	45.29
TFYR of Macedonia	3	1		1	3	0.00	200.00
Serbia and Montenegro	16		4				
Western Europe	**2,833**	**3,074**	**2,577**	**3,038**	**3,290**	**1.06**	**8.29**
Austria	241	235	187	248	245	0.08	-1.21
Belgium	153	162	106	131	155	0.05	18.32
France	516	623	501	603	639	0.21	5.97
Germany	871	991	913	1,106	1,174	0.38	6.15
Liechtenstein	5	2	2	1	7	0.00	600.00
Luxembourg	19	14	9	13	21	0.01	61.54
Monaco	4	5	5	5	13	0.00	160.00
Netherlands	485	500	404	440	490	0.16	11.36
Switzerland	539	542	450	491	546	0.18	11.20
East Mediterranean Europe	**77**	**158**	**96**	**130**	**132**	**0.04**	**1.54**
Cyprus	12	15	9	15	8	0.00	-46.67
Israel	42	102	60	99	105	0.03	6.06
Turkey	23	41	27	16	19	0.01	18.75
MIDDLE EAST	**116**	**99**	**88**	**98**	**118**	**0.04**	**20.41**
Bahrain		2	3	2	8	0.00	300.00
Iraq			1				
Jordan	2			4	2	0.00	-50.00
Kuwait	1	3	6	4	4	0.00	
Lebanon	10	12	4	4	2	0.00	-50.00
Oman	8	2	3	8	1	0.00	-87.50
Qatar	3	8		16	31	0.01	93.75
Saudi Arabia	70	50	44	41	42	0.01	2.44
Syrian Arab Republic	1	1			1	0.00	
United Arab Emirates	9	6	14	13	14	0.00	7.69
Egypt	11	15	12	5	13	0.00	160.00
Yemen	1		1	1			
SOUTH ASIA	**158**	**214**	**202**	**187**	**179**	**0.06**	**-4.28**
Afghanistan		2	1	1			
Bangladesh		2	1	1	1	0.00	
Sri Lanka	4	9	16	11	18	0.01	63.64
India	141	190	171	157	149	0.05	-5.10
Iran, Islamic Republic of	1	1		5	2	0.00	-60.00
Maldives	1						
Nepal	7	2	11	7	4	0.00	-42.86
Pakistan	4	8	2	5	5	0.00	
NOT SPECIFIED	**406**	**399**	**371**	**362**	**505**	**0.16**	**39.50**
Other countries of the World	406	399	371	362	505	0.16	39.50

CENTRAL AFRICAN REPUBLIC

1. Arrivals of non-resident tourists at national borders, by nationality

		2007	2008	2009	2010	2011	Market share 11	% Change 11-10
TOTAL	(*)	17,117	30,611	52,429	53,821			
AFRICA		8,306	16,038	26,984	26,684			
East Africa		223	498	2,052	2,284			
Rwanda		72	190	566	674			
Other countries of East Africa		151	308	1,486	1,610			
Central Africa		3,732	7,230	9,964	10,926			
Cameroon		1,604	2,895	4,125	2,861			
Chad		740	1,275	3,221	2,732			
Congo		622	1,107	734	1,845			
Democratic Republic of the Congo		300	795	588	1,124			
Gabon		306	912	695	762			
Other countries of Central Africa		160	246	601	1,602			
North Africa		288	604	1,884	2,184			
Sudan		69	154	886	577			
Other countries of North Africa		219	450	998	1,607			
Southern Africa		242	580	2,898	1,587			
South Africa		172	386	1,553	709			
Other countries of Southern Africa		70	194	1,345	878			
West Africa		2,841	5,826	8,795	8,737			
Benin		312	692	1,386	1,088			
Côte d'Ivoire		418	1,024	1,116	1,236			
Mali		188	276	1,052	924			
Nigeria		295	811	1,133	1,350			
Senegal		564	1,127	1,662	1,577			
Togo		199	298	1,124	736			
Other countries of West Africa		865	1,598	1,322	1,826			
Other Africa		980	1,300	1,391	966			
Other countries of Africa		980	1,300	1,391	966			
AMERICAS		944	1,300	3,171	5,074			
North America		773	984	2,443	3,287			
Canada		144	209	1,076	1,130			
United States of America		629	775	1,367	2,157			
Other Americas		171	316	728	1,787			
Other countries of the Americas		171	316	728	1,787			
EAST ASIA AND THE PACIFIC		529	2,174	3,888	5,035			
North-East Asia		292	400	2,656	3,319			
China		226	292	1,748	1,997			
Japan		66	108	908	1,322			
Other East Asia and the Pacific		237	1,774	1,232	1,716			
Other countries of Asia		237	1,774	1,232	1,716			
EUROPE		6,708	10,559	16,612	13,141			
Northern Europe		134	212	2,028	868			
United Kingdom		134	212	2,028	868			
Southern Europe		759	788	2,017	1,229			
Italy		759	788	2,017	1,229			
Western Europe		4,974	8,256	8,263	9,899			
Belgium		368	476	1,407	803			
France		4,096	6,975	4,431	7,661			
Germany		290	433	1,276	672			
Switzerland		220	372	1,149	763			
Other Europe		841	1,303	4,304	1,145			
Other countries of Europe		841	1,303	4,304	1,145			

CENTRAL AFRICAN REPUBLIC

1. Arrivals of non-resident tourists at national borders, by nationality

	2007	2008	2009	2010	2011	Market share 11	% Change 11-10
MIDDLE EAST	**560**	**448**	**1,257**	**2,747**			
Lebanon	346	387	712	1,484			
Other countries of Middle East	214	61	545	1,263			
NOT SPECIFIED	**70**	**92**	**517**	**1,140**			
Other countries of the World	70	92	517	1,140			

CHAD

1. Arrivals of non-resident tourists at national borders, by nationality

	2007	2008	2009	2010	2011	Market share 11	% Change 11-10
TOTAL	77,000	61,000	70,000	71,000			
AFRICA	36,000	41,000	16,000	34,000			
Other Africa	36,000	41,000	16,000	34,000			
All countries of Africa	36,000	41,000	16,000	34,000			
AMERICAS	4,000	3,000	11,000	6,000			
Other Americas	4,000	3,000	11,000	6,000			
All countries of the Americas	4,000	3,000	11,000	6,000			
EAST ASIA AND THE PACIFIC	2,000	3,000	9,000	3,000			
Other East Asia and the Pacific	2,000	3,000	9,000	3,000			
All countries East Asia/Pacific	2,000	3,000	9,000	3,000			
EUROPE	32,000	12,000	24,000	25,000			
Other Europe	32,000	12,000	24,000	25,000			
All countries of Europe	32,000	12,000	24,000	25,000			
MIDDLE EAST	2,000	1,000	10,000	2,000			
All countries of Middle East	2,000	1,000	10,000	2,000			
SOUTH ASIA	1,000	1,000		1,000			
All countries of South Asia	1,000	1,000		1,000			

CHAD

3. Arrivals of non-resident tourists in hotels and similar establishments, by nationality

		2007	2008	2009	2010	2011	Market share 11	% Change 11-10
TOTAL	(*)	24,794	21,871	31,169	14,298			
AFRICA		6,365	5,933	7,890	4,007			
East Africa		318	288	74	146			
All countries of East Africa		318	288	74	146			
Central Africa		1,475	1,332	2,389	990			
All countries of Central Africa		1,475	1,332	2,389	990			
North Africa		417	627	1,174	208			
All countries of North Africa		417	627	1,174	208			
West Africa		860	1,046	3,112	657			
All countries of West Africa		860	1,046	3,112	657			
Other Africa		3,295	2,640	1,141	2,006			
Other countries of Africa		3,295	2,640	1,141	2,006			
AMERICAS		5,002	2,395	3,553	1,440			
North America		3,180	1,741	3,091	1,311			
Canada		420	42	512	230			
United States of America		2,760	1,699	2,579	1,081			
Other Americas		1,822	654	462	129			
Other countries of the Americas		1,822	654	462	129			
EAST ASIA AND THE PACIFIC		1,427	1,039	1,124	457			
North-East Asia		120	114	536	113			
China		65	77	536	57			
Japan		50	33		21			
Korea, Republic of		5	4		35			
Other East Asia and the Pacific		1,307	925	588	344			
Other countries East Asia/Pacific		1,307	925	588	344			
EUROPE		11,250	12,251	16,348	8,170			
Northern Europe		781	756	518	281			
United Kingdom		781	607	518	281			
Scandinavia			149					
Southern Europe		152	421	484	224			
Italy		152	421	484	224			
Western Europe		6,988	7,294	7,253	6,435			
Belgium		326	491	335	198			
France		6,167	6,142	6,564	5,843			
Germany		290	298	285	243			
Netherlands		27	147	33	52			
Switzerland		178	216	36	99			
Other Europe		3,329	3,780	8,093	1,230			
Other countries of Europe		3,329	3,780	8,093	1,230			
MIDDLE EAST		750	253	2,254	224			
Lebanon		17	8	136	20			
Libya		24	12	827	7			
Saudi Arabia		8	1		22			
Syrian Arab Republic		1	5		4			
Egypt		20	23	190	30			
Other countries of Middle East		680	204	1,101	141			

CHAD

5. Overnight stays of non-resident tourists in hotels and similar establishments, by nationality

		2007	2008	2009	2010	2011	Market share 11	% Change 11-10
TOTAL	(*)	64,992			36,916			
AFRICA		20,366			13,913			
East Africa		382			251			
All countries of East Africa		382			251			
Central Africa		4,915			3,214			
All countries of Central Africa		4,915			3,214			
North Africa		869			866			
All countries of North Africa		869			866			
West Africa		2,958			2,184			
All countries of West Africa		2,958			2,184			
Other Africa		11,242			7,398			
Other countries of Africa		11,242			7,398			
AMERICAS		11,807			3,494			
North America		5,979			2,895			
Canada		747			670			
United States of America		5,232			2,225			
Other Americas		5,828			599			
Other countries of the Americas		5,828			599			
EAST ASIA AND THE PACIFIC		3,186			1,119			
North-East Asia		573			233			
China		432			183			
Japan		132			41			
Korea, Republic of		9			9			
Other East Asia and the Pacific		2,613			886			
Other countries East Asia/Pacific		2,613			886			
EUROPE		26,232			17,782			
Northern Europe		657			702			
United Kingdom		657			702			
Southern Europe		300			527			
Italy		300			527			
Western Europe		15,729			13,158			
Belgium		637			493			
France		13,828			11,433			
Germany		807			845			
Netherlands		82			111			
Switzerland		375			276			
Other Europe		9,546			3,395			
Other countries of Europe		9,546			3,395			
MIDDLE EAST		3,401			608			
Lebanon		35			38			
Libya		98			100			
Saudi Arabia		22			1			
Syrian Arab Republic		2			12			
Egypt		2			29			
Other countries of Middle East		3,242			428			

CHILE

1. Arrivals of non-resident tourists at national borders, by nationality

	2007	2008	2009	2010	2011	Market share 11	% Change 11-10
TOTAL	**2,506,756**	**2,698,659**	**2,749,913**	**2,766,007**	**3,069,792**	**100.00**	**10.98**
AFRICA	**4,286**	**5,080**	**4,130**	**4,486**	**4,408**	**0.14**	**-1.74**
East Africa	**76**	**105**	**132**	**125**	**84**	**0.00**	**-32.80**
Kenya	51	74	63	57	51	0.00	-10.53
Somalia	4				1	0.00	
Zimbabwe	21	31	69	68	32	0.00	-52.94
Central Africa	**158**	**89**	**59**	**28**	**52**	**0.00**	**85.71**
Angola	140	89	59	28	52	0.00	85.71
Democratic Republic of the Congo	18						
North Africa	**331**	**440**	**300**	**270**	**207**	**0.01**	**-23.33**
Algeria	125	243	151	94	55	0.00	-41.49
Morocco	150	157	122	145	122	0.00	-15.86
Tunisia	56	40	27	31	30	0.00	-3.23
Southern Africa	**3,098**	**3,793**	**3,227**	**3,430**	**3,642**	**0.12**	**6.18**
South Africa	3,098	3,793	3,227	3,430	3,642	0.12	6.18
West Africa	**82**	**111**	**75**	**144**	**97**	**0.00**	**-32.64**
Cape Verde	14	4	18	8	9	0.00	12.50
Ghana	26	23	17	47	24	0.00	-48.94
Nigeria	42	84	40	89	64	0.00	-28.09
Other Africa	**541**	**542**	**337**	**489**	**326**	**0.01**	**-33.33**
Other countries of Africa	541	542	337	489	326	0.01	-33.33
AMERICAS	**1,967,792**	**2,154,437**	**2,251,897**	**2,282,786**	**2,572,031**	**83.79**	**12.67**
Caribbean	**7,629**	**5,541**	**5,812**	**6,370**	**8,215**	**0.27**	**28.96**
Antigua and Barbuda	201	32					
Bahamas	714	89	58	25	88	0.00	252.00
Barbados	147	87	80	51	75	0.00	47.06
Bermuda	57			13			
Cuba	1,812	1,446	1,232	1,281	1,068	0.03	-16.63
Dominica	452	22	26	20	114	0.00	470.00
Dominican Republic	2,307	2,876	3,324	3,598	4,766	0.16	32.46
Grenada	801	11	23	15	32	0.00	113.33
Haiti	219	392	477	820	1,389	0.05	69.39
Jamaica	248	243	196	132	164	0.01	24.24
Puerto Rico	231	44	22	11	111	0.00	909.09
Saint Lucia	202	20	13	14	20	0.00	42.86
Saint Vincent and the Grenadines	50	26	27	7	19	0.00	171.43
Trinidad and Tobago	140	209	260	294	258	0.01	-12.24
Other countries of the Caribbean	48	44	74	89	111	0.00	24.72
Central America	**17,909**	**14,337**	**12,943**	**12,556**	**13,824**	**0.45**	**10.10**
Belize	148	63	64	39	49	0.00	25.64
Costa Rica	6,015	4,636	4,218	4,283	5,000	0.16	16.74
El Salvador	1,810	1,893	1,753	1,581	1,722	0.06	8.92
Guatemala	2,171	2,392	2,184	2,007	2,184	0.07	8.82
Honduras	1,216	1,115	879	936	1,102	0.04	17.74
Nicaragua	903	788	717	708	642	0.02	-9.32
Panama	5,646	3,450	3,128	3,002	3,125	0.10	4.10
North America	**290,356**	**301,678**	**286,863**	**252,273**	**253,308**	**8.25**	**0.41**
Canada	44,116	48,334	46,777	40,795	40,984	1.34	0.46
Mexico	41,702	37,021	31,495	31,261	35,875	1.17	14.76
United States of America	204,538	216,280	208,566	180,215	176,433	5.75	-2.10
Other countries of North America		43	25	2	16	0.00	700.00
South America	**1,651,089**	**1,832,866**	**1,946,279**	**2,011,587**	**2,296,684**	**74.82**	**14.17**
Argentina	760,708	868,999	1,003,126	1,007,070	1,121,372	36.53	11.35
Bolivia	271,934	307,902	309,445	307,504	321,490	10.47	4.55

CHILE

1. Arrivals of non-resident tourists at national borders, by nationality

	2007	2008	2009	2010	2011	Market share 11	% Change 11-10
Brazil	228,779	261,080	216,801	233,644	328,274	10.69	40.50
Colombia	46,605	47,300	48,938	53,375	68,228	2.22	27.83
Ecuador	23,691	23,170	23,245	23,700	27,942	0.91	17.90
Guyana	44	33	28	25	29	0.00	16.00
Paraguay	18,195	22,876	22,391	28,290	30,072	0.98	6.30
Peru	252,626	252,573	269,669	308,877	339,020	11.04	9.76
Suriname	89	47	70	16	47	0.00	193.75
Uruguay	29,018	27,296	30,332	30,924	37,011	1.21	19.68
Venezuela	19,400	21,589	22,233	18,159	23,199	0.76	27.75
Other countries of South America		1	1	3			
Other Americas	**809**	**15**					
Other countries of the Americas	809	15					
EAST ASIA AND THE PACIFIC	**90,673**	**87,960**	**79,089**	**78,332**	**82,756**	**2.70**	**5.65**
North-East Asia	**32,194**	**32,625**	**28,816**	**30,885**	**35,713**	**1.16**	**15.63**
China	8,516	6,738	6,456	6,978	10,526	0.34	50.85
Taiwan, Province of China	340	1,156	1,112	1,136	1,318	0.04	16.02
Hong Kong, China	75	352	113				
Japan	14,674	15,553	14,065	15,760	13,615	0.44	-13.61
Korea, Dem. People's Republic of	811	716	360	346	360	0.01	4.05
Korea, Republic of	7,750	8,066	6,688	6,638	9,870	0.32	48.69
Mongolia	28	44	22	27	24	0.00	-11.11
South-East Asia	**11,929**	**6,700**	**4,204**	**4,278**	**4,446**	**0.14**	**3.93**
Brunei Darussalam	8	9	4	2	20	0.00	900.00
Myanmar	335	102	53	46	39	0.00	-15.22
Cambodia	6	4		9	3	0.00	-66.67
Indonesia	734	845	426	760	815	0.03	7.24
Lao People's Democratic Republic	260		2				
Malaysia	618	753	796	701	781	0.03	11.41
Philippines	8,961	3,911	1,726	1,483	1,371	0.04	-7.55
Singapore	450	646	551	814	869	0.03	6.76
Viet Nam	152	74	293	122	125	0.00	2.46
Thailand	405	356	353	341	423	0.01	24.05
Australasia	**45,386**	**48,479**	**45,399**	**42,406**	**41,446**	**1.35**	**-2.26**
Australia	36,516	39,013	36,318	33,781	33,321	1.09	-1.36
New Zealand	8,870	9,466	9,081	8,625	8,125	0.26	-5.80
Polynesia	**152**	**29**	**5**	**5**			
Tuvalu	68	23	4				
Samoa	84	6	1	5			
Other East Asia and the Pacific	**1,012**	**127**	**665**	**758**	**1,151**	**0.04**	**51.85**
Other countries of Asia	367	22	420	670	1,097	0.04	63.73
Other countries of Oceania	645	105	245	88	54	0.00	-38.64
EUROPE	**436,770**	**446,575**	**410,982**	**396,588**	**406,565**	**13.24**	**2.52**
Central/Eastern Europe	**16,206**	**18,147**	**13,505**	**12,239**	**14,426**	**0.47**	**17.87**
Azerbaijan	170	9	6	9	16	0.00	77.78
Armenia	48	16	18	23	22	0.00	-4.35
Bulgaria	583	529	524	572	590	0.02	3.15
Belarus	141	93					
Czech Republic	1,219	2,666	185				
Estonia	254	236	243	216	262	0.01	21.30
Georgia	147	54	10	14	39	0.00	178.57
Hungary	1,051	1,331	1,008	802	812	0.03	1.25
Kazakhstan	10	68	48	47	31	0.00	-34.04
Kyrgyzstan	10	4	8	10	5	0.00	-50.00
Latvia	103	463	251	264	224	0.01	-15.15
Lithuania	451	497	485	266	327	0.01	22.93
Republic of Moldova	11	28	13	15	26	0.00	73.33

CHILE

1. Arrivals of non-resident tourists at national borders, by nationality

	2007	2008	2009	2010	2011	Market share 11	% Change 11-10
Poland	3,832	4,921	4,650	4,314	4,261	0.14	-1.23
Romania	1,387	1,247	990	953	1,190	0.04	24.87
Russian Federation	4,174	3,918	3,461	3,356	4,965	0.16	47.94
Slovakia	454	955	933	702	838	0.03	19.37
Tajikistan	47	1		4			
Turkmenistan	35						
Ukraine	2,013	1,101	659	664	810	0.03	21.99
Uzbekistan	66	10	13	8	8	0.00	
Northern Europe	**102,109**	**99,427**	**84,815**	**77,404**	**84,945**	**2.77**	**9.74**
Denmark	6,295	6,168	5,214	5,017	4,999	0.16	-0.36
Finland	3,427	3,360	3,124	2,909	3,164	0.10	8.77
Iceland	442	323	247	217	346	0.01	59.45
Ireland	7,547	7,081	5,153	4,350	3,918	0.13	-9.93
Norway	6,808	7,081	5,745	6,001	5,980	0.19	-0.35
Sweden	13,280	13,748	12,630	12,711	12,941	0.42	1.81
United Kingdom	64,310	61,666	52,702	46,199	53,597	1.75	16.01
Southern Europe	**107,672**	**100,831**	**92,334**	**88,790**	**93,413**	**3.04**	**5.21**
Albania	149	86	28	52	65	0.00	25.00
Andorra	277	87	138	92	103	0.00	11.96
Bosnia and Herzegovina	31	24	19	41	41	0.00	
Croatia	614	778	637	695	654	0.02	-5.90
Greece	2,028	1,890	1,481	1,324	1,232	0.04	-6.95
Holy See	45	4	3	4	2	0.00	-50.00
Italy	29,362	29,683	28,436	27,746	28,173	0.92	1.54
Malta	216	113	207	165	133	0.00	-19.39
Montenegro	5						
Portugal	5,366	5,294	3,877	4,275	5,061	0.16	18.39
San Marino	88	29	17	16	13	0.00	-18.75
Serbia	203	282	316	269	335	0.01	24.54
Slovenia	723	987	946	708	788	0.03	11.30
Spain	68,557	61,551	56,212	53,372	56,781	1.85	6.39
TFYR of Macedonia	8	23	17	31	32	0.00	3.23
Western Europe	**187,385**	**196,927**	**187,907**	**187,044**	**185,265**	**6.04**	**-0.95**
Austria	8,113	7,411	8,195	8,018	7,484	0.24	-6.66
Belgium	9,797	9,569	9,347	9,429	9,660	0.31	2.45
France	61,069	62,984	63,623	63,538	63,800	2.08	0.41
Germany	71,170	75,579	67,592	67,894	66,652	2.17	-1.83
Liechtenstein	42	59	37	52	43	0.00	-17.31
Luxembourg	483	359	358	331	307	0.01	-7.25
Monaco	41	18	50	19	24	0.00	26.32
Netherlands	16,245	21,464	20,050	18,967	18,391	0.60	-3.04
Switzerland	20,425	19,484	18,655	18,796	18,904	0.62	0.57
East Mediterranean Europe	**22,172**	**26,387**	**24,755**	**23,748**	**24,943**	**0.81**	**5.03**
Cyprus	61	69	294	124	90	0.00	-27.42
Israel	20,758	24,369	23,017	22,046	23,210	0.76	5.28
Turkey	1,353	1,949	1,444	1,578	1,643	0.05	4.12
Other Europe	**1,226**	**4,856**	**7,666**	**7,363**	**3,573**	**0.12**	**-51.47**
Other countries of Europe	1,226	4,856	7,666	7,363	3,573	0.12	-51.47
MIDDLE EAST	**1,297**	**504**	**577**	**509**	**490**	**0.02**	**-3.73**
Bahrain	2	6	5	4	6	0.00	50.00
Iraq	12	11	66	8	7	0.00	-12.50
Jordan	545	107	67	55	69	0.00	25.45
Kuwait	39	6	3	57	24	0.00	-57.89
Lebanon	180	122	100	76	91	0.00	19.74
Libya	6		5		3	0.00	
Oman	3	11	13	2	5	0.00	150.00
Qatar	1	5		28	5	0.00	-82.14

CHILE

1. Arrivals of non-resident tourists at national borders, by nationality

	2007	2008	2009	2010	2011	Market share 11	% Change 11-10
Saudi Arabia	11	10	30	27	60	0.00	122.22
Syrian Arab Republic	61	44	38	32	35	0.00	9.38
United Arab Emirates	126	33	87	104	15	0.00	-85.58
Egypt	97	119	81	90	119	0.00	32.22
Yemen	10	5	4	1	6	0.00	500.00
Other countries of Middle East	204	25	78	25	45	0.00	80.00
SOUTH ASIA	**4,410**	**3,957**	**3,173**	**3,249**	**3,395**	**0.11**	**4.49**
Afghanistan	33	30	29	11	12	0.00	9.09
Bangladesh	39	52	28	57	29	0.00	-49.12
Bhutan		1	1	2	2	0.00	
Sri Lanka	139	107	36	71	40	0.00	-43.66
India	3,505	3,376	2,673	2,612	2,906	0.09	11.26
Iran, Islamic Republic of	215	71	58	83	83	0.00	
Maldives	76	6		9			
Nepal	26	50	36	26	28	0.00	7.69
Pakistan	377	264	312	378	295	0.01	-21.96
NOT SPECIFIED	**1,528**	**146**	**65**	**57**	**147**	**0.00**	**157.89**
Other countries of the World	1,528	146	65	57	147	0.00	157.89

CHINA

2. Arrivals of non-resident visitors at national borders, by nationality

	2007	2008	2009	2010	2011	Market share 11	% Change 11-10
TOTAL	131,873,287	130,027,393	126,475,923	133,762,239	135,423,453	100.00	1.24
AFRICA	327,142	323,921	340,443	391,475	424,482	0.31	8.43
East Africa	66,419	72,955	77,544	96,882	111,792	0.08	15.39
Burundi	656	793	727	934	1,298	0.00	38.97
Comoros	288	418	443	733	781	0.00	6.55
Ethiopia	10,259	11,292	11,952	14,776	18,561	0.01	25.62
Kenya	10,147	11,656	11,169	13,051	15,158	0.01	16.14
Madagascar	4,107	4,485	6,308	8,377	9,392	0.01	12.12
Mauritius	14,078	14,734	15,084	17,465	18,289	0.01	4.72
Mozambique	1,266	1,473	1,732	2,280	3,195	0.00	40.13
Seychelles	1,134	1,157	1,145	1,346	1,385	0.00	2.90
Somalia	470	489	564	709	951	0.00	34.13
Zimbabwe	5,937	6,017	4,361	6,888	7,072	0.01	2.67
Uganda	4,844	6,464	7,742	10,821	14,456	0.01	33.59
United Republic of Tanzania	10,038	10,898	13,429	15,246	16,441	0.01	7.84
Zambia	3,195	3,079	2,888	4,256	4,813	0.00	13.09
Central Africa	21,510	19,175	19,971	24,087	26,540	0.02	10.18
Cameroon	5,816	6,265	6,886	6,871	7,052	0.01	2.63
Central African Republic	252	256	327	375	426	0.00	13.60
Chad	727	624	685	824	808	0.00	-1.94
Congo	13,619	4,528	4,409	4,408	5,111	0.00	15.95
Democratic Republic of the Congo	37	6,484	6,853	10,491	12,080	0.01	15.15
Gabon	1,059	1,018	811	1,118	1,063	0.00	-4.92
North Africa	49,247	49,725	55,396	61,910	62,376	0.05	0.75
Algeria	20,409	20,243	24,893	25,776	27,982	0.02	8.56
Morocco	11,336	11,756	12,434	14,034	13,810	0.01	-1.60
Sudan	9,609	9,052	9,928	11,475	11,944	0.01	4.09
Tunisia	7,893	8,674	8,141	10,625	8,640	0.01	-18.68
Southern Africa	60,284	57,042	53,847	68,899	72,201	0.05	4.79
Botswana	1,217	1,357	1,643	2,367	2,545	0.00	7.52
Lesotho	441	422	343	474	555	0.00	17.09
Namibia	687	801	892	1,327	1,438	0.00	8.36
South Africa	57,763	54,251	50,783	64,477	67,354	0.05	4.46
Swaziland	176	211	186	254	309	0.00	21.65
West Africa	111,886	104,997	108,684	110,067	119,111	0.09	8.22
Benin	3,684	3,970	3,887	4,694	4,993	0.00	6.37
Gambia	2,513	1,681	1,874	2,167	2,100	0.00	-3.09
Ghana	17,353	17,160	14,657	17,152	19,767	0.01	15.25
Guinea	8,989	8,030	8,005	9,068	9,868	0.01	8.82
Côte d'Ivoire	3,649	2,570	2,445	2,886	2,301	0.00	-20.27
Mali	20,761	14,293	12,230	14,389	15,038	0.01	4.51
Niger	4,502	5,090	5,457	6,465	6,890	0.01	6.57
Nigeria	40,492	43,515	50,567	41,372	45,440	0.03	9.83
Senegal	5,955	4,811	5,625	7,484	8,026	0.01	7.24
Sierra Leone	1,037	1,165	1,172	1,279	1,585	0.00	23.92
Togo	2,951	2,712	2,765	3,111	3,103	0.00	-0.26
Other Africa	17,796	20,027	25,001	29,630	32,462	0.02	9.56
Other countries of Africa	17,796	20,027	25,001	29,630	32,462	0.02	9.56
AMERICAS	2,721,034	2,581,855	2,491,190	2,995,397	3,201,031	2.36	6.86
Caribbean	15,199	14,107	12,548	13,805	13,857	0.01	0.38
Antigua and Barbuda	225	173	201	268	223	0.00	-16.79
Bahamas	576	651	401	586	623	0.00	6.31
Cuba	4,212	3,632	2,391	2,705	2,433	0.00	-10.06
Dominica	870	927	890	661	578	0.00	-12.56
Dominican Republic	3,630	2,818	2,593	3,036	2,943	0.00	-3.06

CHINA

2. Arrivals of non-resident visitors at national borders, by nationality

	2007	2008	2009	2010	2011	Market share 11	% Change 11-10
Haiti	221	304	203	270	336	0.00	24.44
Jamaica	3,118	3,258	3,627	3,978	4,612	0.00	15.94
Netherlands Antilles	11	7	3	4	1	0.00	-75.00
Puerto Rico	18	7	14	11	8	0.00	-27.27
Trinidad and Tobago	2,318	2,330	2,225	2,286	2,100	0.00	-8.14
Central America	**20,537**	**19,843**	**18,371**	**21,827**	**22,661**	**0.02**	**3.82**
Belize	4,716	4,002	3,474	3,186	3,225	0.00	1.22
Costa Rica	4,183	4,568	4,111	5,084	5,451	0.00	7.22
El Salvador	1,445	1,074	860	987	1,120	0.00	13.48
Guatemala	1,903	1,924	1,637	2,135	2,350	0.00	10.07
Honduras	2,867	2,648	2,459	2,780	2,709	0.00	-2.55
Panama	5,423	5,627	5,830	7,655	7,806	0.01	1.97
North America	**2,524,665**	**2,370,080**	**2,292,444**	**2,744,250**	**2,917,845**	**2.15**	**6.33**
Canada	577,220	534,712	550,333	685,304	747,981	0.55	9.15
Mexico	46,224	48,920	32,298	49,351	53,720	0.04	8.85
United States of America	1,901,221	1,786,448	1,709,813	2,009,595	2,116,144	1.56	5.30
South America	**159,493**	**176,335**	**166,294**	**213,441**	**244,915**	**0.18**	**14.75**
Argentina	18,083	19,158	16,767	23,084	25,656	0.02	11.14
Bolivia	2,741	3,451	4,083	5,252	6,470	0.00	23.19
Brazil	67,439	74,656	63,676	85,050	97,912	0.07	15.12
Chile	11,761	13,014	12,245	15,927	17,763	0.01	11.53
Colombia	18,097	21,186	20,441	26,870	31,792	0.02	18.32
Ecuador	5,345	5,159	4,893	6,271	7,211	0.01	14.99
Guyana	732	715	782	761	837	0.00	9.99
Paraguay	1,128	1,142	1,119	1,673	1,535	0.00	-8.25
Peru	9,999	10,537	10,910	12,798	14,190	0.01	10.88
Suriname	2,477	2,287	2,658	2,637	2,944	0.00	11.64
Uruguay	2,610	2,616	2,641	3,540	3,784	0.00	6.89
Venezuela	19,081	22,414	26,079	29,578	34,821	0.03	17.73
Other Americas	**1,140**	**1,490**	**1,533**	**2,074**	**1,753**	**0.00**	**-15.48**
Other countries of the Americas	1,140	1,490	1,533	2,074	1,753	0.00	-15.48
EAST ASIA AND THE PACIFIC	**120,956,213**	**119,584,350**	**117,588,819**	**122,889,279**	**123,828,043**	**91.44**	**0.76**
North-East Asia	**115,313,476**	**113,915,659**	**111,734,016**	**116,353,704**	**117,301,530**	**86.62**	**0.81**
Taiwan, Province of China	4,627,881	4,385,591	4,484,041	5,140,554	5,263,014	3.89	2.38
Hong Kong, China	77,948,908	78,350,129	77,335,996	79,321,851	79,357,701	58.60	0.05
Japan	3,977,479	3,446,117	3,317,459	3,731,200	3,658,169	2.70	-1.96
Korea, Dem. People's Republic of	113,674	101,824	103,880	116,382	152,300	0.11	30.86
Korea, Republic of	4,776,752	3,960,392	3,197,538	4,076,392	4,185,398	3.09	2.67
Macao, China	23,186,830	22,966,336	22,718,406	23,172,939	23,690,767	17.49	2.23
Mongolia	681,952	705,270	576,696	794,386	994,181	0.73	25.15
South-East Asia	**4,914,012**	**4,979,513**	**5,182,042**	**5,745,684**	**5,666,788**	**4.18**	**-1.37**
Brunei Darussalam	7,224	7,594	7,538	10,051	9,449	0.01	-5.99
Myanmar	320,419	508,995	607,737	493,400	191,038	0.14	-61.28
Cambodia	18,253	18,548	20,104	24,265	26,534	0.02	9.35
Indonesia	477,109	426,251	469,044	573,409	608,675	0.45	6.15
Lao People's Democratic Republic	8,465	8,754	9,674	11,927	14,186	0.01	18.94
Malaysia	1,061,965	1,040,494	1,059,004	1,245,160	1,245,092	0.92	-0.01
Philippines	833,009	795,255	748,943	828,284	894,309	0.66	7.97
Singapore	922,021	875,826	889,538	1,003,658	1,062,993	0.78	5.91
Viet Nam	653,932	743,521	828,630	919,991	1,006,468	0.74	9.40
Thailand	611,615	554,275	541,830	635,539	608,044	0.45	-4.33
Australasia	**716,096**	**676,718**	**661,980**	**777,394**	**847,082**	**0.63**	**8.96**
Australia	607,364	571,534	561,542	661,342	726,184	0.54	9.80
New Zealand	108,732	105,184	100,438	116,052	120,898	0.09	4.18
Melanesia	**2,713**	**2,662**	**2,788**	**3,805**	**3,710**	**0.00**	**-2.50**
Fiji	2,390	2,265	2,398	3,342	3,207	0.00	-4.04

CHINA

2. Arrivals of non-resident visitors at national borders, by nationality

	2007	2008	2009	2010	2011	Market share 11	% Change 11-10
Vanuatu	323	397	390	463	503	0.00	8.64
Micronesia	**2,817**	**2,908**	**1,988**	**2,289**	**2,652**	**0.00**	**15.86**
Kiribati	2,817	2,908	1,988	2,289	2,652	0.00	15.86
Polynesia	**1,428**	**1,345**	**1,183**	**1,139**	**1,379**	**0.00**	**21.07**
Tonga	1,428	1,345	1,183	1,139	1,379	0.00	21.07
Other East Asia and the Pacific	**5,671**	**5,545**	**4,822**	**5,264**	**4,902**	**0.00**	**-6.88**
Other countries of Asia	272	352	329	560	412	0.00	-26.43
Other countries of Oceania	5,399	5,193	4,493	4,704	4,490	0.00	-4.55
EUROPE	**6,936,600**	**6,688,442**	**5,131,487**	**6,365,849**	**6,771,977**	**5.00**	**6.38**
Central/Eastern Europe	**3,872,493**	**3,861,098**	**2,392,709**	**3,180,919**	**3,528,537**	**2.61**	**10.93**
Azerbaijan	16,123	17,453	15,122	18,605	18,202	0.01	-2.17
Armenia	4,435	4,364	3,528	4,684	5,347	0.00	14.15
Bulgaria	16,823	15,856	13,846	16,421	17,556	0.01	6.91
Belarus	8,031	8,701	7,458	10,914	10,939	0.01	0.23
Czech Republic	17,743	17,345	15,768	19,483	20,285	0.01	4.12
Georgia	5,052	6,308	5,178	5,355	6,719	0.00	25.47
Hungary	16,567	17,490	13,626	15,791	16,289	0.01	3.15
Kazakhstan	438,869	300,732	279,875	380,312	506,215	0.37	33.11
Kyrgyzstan	50,056	43,493	32,787	35,444	47,633	0.04	34.39
Latvia	6,095	5,970	5,066	5,708	5,747	0.00	0.68
Lithuania	6,206	6,646	5,821	7,000	7,508	0.01	7.26
Poland	61,914	60,958	53,718	62,109	67,986	0.05	9.46
Romania	31,257	32,168	27,760	33,232	36,290	0.03	9.20
Russian Federation	3,003,867	3,123,415	1,742,973	2,370,313	2,536,321	1.87	7.00
Slovakia	5,545	5,386	4,969	9,028	9,183	0.01	1.72
Tajikistan	22,830	22,123	17,480	23,398	26,441	0.02	13.01
Turkmenistan	6,918	9,160	11,647	14,836	15,590	0.01	5.08
Ukraine	104,196	105,556	86,553	105,711	120,248	0.09	13.75
Uzbekistan	49,966	57,974	49,534	42,575	54,038	0.04	26.92
Northern Europe	**1,008,941**	**929,552**	**874,363**	**978,140**	**1,007,792**	**0.74**	**3.03**
Denmark	89,601	81,033	77,340	86,718	84,637	0.06	-2.40
Finland	75,291	70,577	60,906	69,226	65,288	0.05	-5.69
Iceland	4,309	4,156	2,686	3,056	3,009	0.00	-1.54
Ireland	38,776	35,128	31,221	36,164	37,596	0.03	3.96
Norway	50,732	49,449	47,653	53,500	51,428	0.04	-3.87
Sweden	145,138	137,686	125,771	154,513	170,137	0.13	10.11
United Kingdom	605,094	551,523	528,786	574,963	595,697	0.44	3.61
Southern Europe	**476,603**	**423,710**	**415,259**	**485,354**	**491,243**	**0.36**	**1.21**
Albania	3,053	2,883	2,586	2,740	2,638	0.00	-3.72
Croatia	18,650	18,449	16,072	16,159	16,355	0.01	1.21
Greece	38,558	34,445	32,060	34,690	32,652	0.02	-5.87
Italy	215,212	194,362	191,357	229,233	235,041	0.17	2.53
Malta	1,899	1,725	1,563	1,934	1,833	0.00	-5.22
Montenegro	333	1,665	4,431	6,038	6,584	0.00	9.04
Portugal	48,273	43,917	43,634	47,678	47,033	0.03	-1.35
Serbia	1,922	5,738	6,236	8,448	9,231	0.01	9.27
Spain	136,731	112,224	114,485	138,255	139,876	0.10	1.17
Serbia and Montenegro	11,972	8,302	2,835	179			
Western Europe	**1,410,581**	**1,323,650**	**1,292,574**	**1,533,403**	**1,543,373**	**1.14**	**0.65**
Austria	63,300	56,273	56,223	67,289	66,922	0.05	-0.55
Belgium	65,760	61,398	60,770	76,249	70,400	0.05	-7.67
France	463,392	429,967	424,770	512,734	493,132	0.36	-3.82
Germany	556,663	528,858	518,533	608,621	637,015	0.47	4.67
Liechtenstein	213	256	251	378	300	0.00	-20.63
Luxembourg	2,404	2,451	2,446	4,471	2,692	0.00	-39.79
Monaco	176	144	118	237	88	0.00	-62.87

CHINA

2. Arrivals of non-resident visitors at national borders, by nationality

	2007	2008	2009	2010	2011	Market share 11	% Change 11-10
Netherlands	194,079	180,891	166,884	189,128	197,530	0.15	4.44
Switzerland	64,594	63,412	62,579	74,296	75,294	0.06	1.34
East Mediterranean Europe	**151,187**	**131,635**	**140,254**	**171,413**	**184,250**	**0.14**	**7.49**
Cyprus	3,099	2,926	2,884	3,569	3,229	0.00	-9.53
Israel	74,285	68,349	73,008	83,384	82,234	0.06	-1.38
Turkey	73,803	60,360	64,362	84,460	98,787	0.07	16.96
Other Europe	**16,795**	**18,797**	**16,328**	**16,620**	**16,782**	**0.01**	**0.97**
Other countries of Europe	16,795	18,797	16,328	16,620	16,782	0.01	0.97
MIDDLE EAST	**179,771**	**178,131**	**207,488**	**246,794**	**239,427**	**0.18**	**-2.99**
Bahrain	2,672	3,959	3,792	3,839	3,222	0.00	-16.07
Palestine	4,515	4,146	5,050	6,886	6,336	0.00	-7.99
Iraq	14,548	10,624	19,234	22,246	19,289	0.01	-13.29
Jordan	19,581	21,018	22,661	25,343	27,568	0.02	8.78
Kuwait	7,925	6,215	6,948	7,746	8,303	0.01	7.19
Lebanon	17,188	19,050	20,186	22,251	22,854	0.02	2.71
Libya	9,319	9,764	11,051	12,956	3,414	0.00	-73.65
Oman	2,142	3,423	3,619	4,739	4,630	0.00	-2.30
Qatar	2,283	2,086	1,876	2,940	2,431	0.00	-17.31
Saudi Arabia	17,282	13,649	19,030	27,223	34,635	0.03	27.23
Syrian Arab Republic	18,372	16,879	19,745	21,029	18,473	0.01	-12.15
United Arab Emirates	4,196	4,936	5,256	8,816	9,041	0.01	2.55
Egypt	42,680	44,716	49,665	59,119	60,880	0.04	2.98
Yemen	17,068	17,666	19,375	21,661	18,351	0.01	-15.28
SOUTH ASIA	**749,103**	**668,806**	**714,327**	**871,339**	**956,602**	**0.71**	**9.79**
Afghanistan	12,506	12,230	15,519	11,809	11,695	0.01	-0.97
Bangladesh	48,193	31,352	32,281	41,648	47,661	0.04	14.44
Bhutan	599	261	282	569	597	0.00	4.92
Sri Lanka	26,134	24,360	23,574	30,852	38,013	0.03	23.21
India	462,450	436,625	448,942	549,321	606,474	0.45	10.40
Iran, Islamic Republic of	70,008	68,025	87,636	116,999	125,077	0.09	6.90
Maldives	1,450	1,373	1,330	2,025	2,623	0.00	29.53
Nepal	30,245	21,726	23,272	30,796	31,944	0.02	3.73
Pakistan	97,518	72,854	81,491	87,320	92,518	0.07	5.95
NOT SPECIFIED	**3,424**	**1,888**	**2,169**	**2,106**	**1,891**	**0.00**	**-10.21**
Other countries of the World	3,424	1,888	2,169	2,106	1,891	0.00	-10.21

COLOMBIA

2. Arrivals of non-resident visitors at national borders, by nationality

		2007	2008	2009	2010	2011	Market share 11	% Change 11-10
TOTAL	(*)	1,195,443	1,222,966	1,353,700	1,474,863			
AFRICA		3,929	1,969	2,014	2,252			
East Africa		303	271	374	292			
British Indian Ocean Territory					8			
Burundi		4	1	7	7			
Ethiopia		34	45	51	25			
Eritrea		8	24	33	8			
Djibouti			3	3	5			
Kenya		132	93	113	73			
Madagascar		7	5	5	13			
Malawi		3	5	5	8			
Mauritius		9	7	11	15			
Mozambique		20	15	26	11			
Reunion		3			6			
Rwanda		12	9	14	12			
Seychelles		2			1			
Somalia			1					
Zimbabwe		22	10	26	27			
Uganda		14	45	40	37			
United Republic of Tanzania		25		27	21			
Zambia		8	8	13	15			
Central Africa		235	171	198	213			
Angola		43	88	78	53			
Cameroon		35	24	52	42			
Central African Republic		107	10	10	47			
Chad		5	2	8	10			
Congo			35	37	36			
Democratic Republic of the Congo		33		3				
Equatorial Guinea		7	6	6	12			
Gabon		5	5	4	11			
Sao Tome and Principe			1		2			
North Africa		173	158	186	583			
Algeria		51	31	49	371			
Morocco		95	87	101	89			
Western Sahara					1			
Sudan		6	11	16	7			
Tunisia		21	29	20	115			
Southern Africa		1,243	1,063	979	897			
Botswana		3		5	6			
Lesotho		4			1			
Namibia		4	3	5	8			
South Africa		1,232	1,060	969	882			
West Africa		285	306	277	267			
Cape Verde		9	2	6	13			
Benin		1	9	12	10			
Gambia		3	3	6	3			
Ghana		30	25	50	47			
Guinea		9	37	6	11			
Côte d'Ivoire		16	17	17	18			
Liberia		7	3	5	8			
Mali		7	13	7	2			
Mauritania		9	2	2	4			
Niger		4	2	5	12			
Nigeria		157	152	101	76			
Guinea-Bissau		1		4	5			
Saint Helena		2			2			

COLOMBIA

2. Arrivals of non-resident visitors at national borders, by nationality

	2007	2008	2009	2010	2011	Market share 11	% Change 11-10
Senegal	11	27	23	23			
Sierra Leone	1		7	7			
Togo	8	4	16	7			
Burkina Faso	10	10	10	19			
Other Africa	**1,690**						
Other countries of Africa	1,690						
AMERICAS	**943,562**	**969,075**	**1,063,828**	**1,140,129**			
Caribbean	**17,799**	**13,631**	**15,802**	**28,703**			
Antigua and Barbuda	34	35		39			
Bahamas	194	192	17	170			
Barbados	122	151	2	100			
Bermuda	17	35	78	57			
British Virgin Islands	1	6	150	3			
Cayman Islands	263	197	122	120			
Cuba	3,998	4,136	25	2,427			
Dominica	79	42	4,074	150			
Dominican Republic	6,757	6,991	50	8,682			
Grenada	26	33	44	25			
Guadeloupe		1	51	96			
Haiti	220	210		242			
Jamaica	510	451	233	426			
Martinique	1	1	149	78			
Montserrat			2				
Netherlands Antilles	616	4	3				
Aruba	2,491	50	498	5,270			
Curaçao	1,281	43		5,705			
Puerto Rico	284	135		3,951			
Saint Kitts and Nevis	13			17			
Anguilla		2	251	3			
Saint Lucia	36	40	8,820	41			
Saint Vincent and the Grenadines	23	49	13	30			
Trinidad and Tobago	829	826	48	1,064			
Turks and Caicos Islands	1	1	35	3			
Other countries of the Caribbean	3		1,137	4			
Central America	**71,088**	**65,553**	**68,785**	**80,082**			
Belize	172	138	156	170			
Costa Rica	21,326	21,179	20,184	22,588			
El Salvador	4,469	3,867	4,512	6,300			
Guatemala	7,837	7,020	7,693	7,795			
Honduras	4,115	3,359	3,657	4,078			
Nicaragua	1,710	1,611	1,627	1,329			
Panama	31,459	28,379	30,956	37,822			
North America	**354,270**	**351,192**	**400,489**	**452,734**			
Canada	28,279	27,632	28,157	30,388			
Mexico	60,340	59,107	57,474	64,886			
United States of America	265,651	264,453	314,858	357,460			
South America	**500,405**	**538,699**	**578,752**	**578,610**			
Argentina	50,632	51,057	61,358	77,495			
Bolivia	5,785	5,945	6,293	6,119			
Brazil	41,145	45,506	47,493	63,793			
Chile	29,371	29,716	36,168	42,976			
Ecuador	110,508	93,452	101,820	116,358			
French Guiana	15	26	25	25			
Guyana	123	138	130	112			
Paraguay	1,367	1,754	1,634	2,102			
Peru	58,332	66,313	77,733	74,093			
Suriname	265	285	409	361			

COLOMBIA

2. Arrivals of non-resident visitors at national borders, by nationality

	2007	2008	2009	2010	2011	Market share 11	% Change 11-10
Uruguay	5,999	7,178	7,611	7,558			
Venezuela	196,863	237,329	238,078	187,618			
EAST ASIA AND THE PACIFIC	**24,427**	**21,228**	**25,784**	**25,217**			
North-East Asia	**17,060**	**13,230**	**14,619**	**12,367**			
China	7,332	3,296	4,264	3,378			
Taiwan, Province of China	1,071	1,185	1,326	794			
Hong Kong, China	102	21	14	157			
Japan	4,870	5,302	4,987	4,312			
Korea, Dem. People's Republic of	256	2	3	203			
Korea, Republic of	3,423	3,415	4,015	3,510			
Mongolia	6	9	10	13			
South-East Asia	**1,722**	**1,921**	**2,704**	**2,974**			
Brunei Darussalam	8	3	8	12			
Myanmar	6	2	20	3			
Cambodia	4	4	1,728	12			
Indonesia	225	277	363	494			
Lao People's Democratic Republic	84	4	209	93			
Malaysia	211	196	4	281			
Philippines	842	1,153	9	1,591			
Singapore	209	190	210	306			
Viet Nam	25	6	112	60			
Thailand	108	86	41	122			
Australasia	**5,618**	**6,060**	**8,440**	**9,694**			
Australia	4,727	5,039	7,104	8,401			
New Zealand	891	1,021	1,336	1,293			
Melanesia	**15**	**11**	**7**	**101**			
Solomon Islands	3	2	1				
Fiji	5	7	2	5			
New Caledonia	7	1	1	76			
Vanuatu			1	12			
Papua New Guinea		1	2	8			
Micronesia	**5**	**4**	**9**	**15**			
Cocos (Keeling) Islands				2			
Kiribati		1	1	4			
Guam				3			
Midway Islands	3	1	1	3			
Nauru				1			
Northern Mariana Islands	1		1				
Micronesia, Federated States of	1		1				
Palau		1	4	2			
Wake Island		1	1				
Polynesia	**5**	**2**	**5**	**66**			
French Polynesia			1	59			
Tonga	1	1	4	6			
Wallis and Futuna Islands	4	1		1			
Other East Asia and the Pacific	**2**						
Other countries of Asia	2						
EUROPE	**219,810**	**226,803**	**257,649**	**232,355**			
Central/Eastern Europe	**5,102**	**5,862**	**8,023**	**7,310**			
Azerbaijan	9	7	7	28			
Armenia	14	13	20	8			
Bulgaria	150	196	51	120			
Belarus	36	41	214	189			
Czech Republic/Slovakia			477	1,111			
Czech Republic	628	681	132				

COLOMBIA

2. Arrivals of non-resident visitors at national borders, by nationality

	2007	2008	2009	2010	2011	Market share 11	% Change 11-10
Estonia	45	62	2,471	116			
Georgia	11	15	10	28			
Hungary	351	415	483	420			
Kazakhstan	98	40	43	31			
Kyrgyzstan	1	4	3	6			
Latvia	63	77	104	104			
Lithuania	120	203	216	168			
Republic of Moldova	14	13	1,668	19			
Poland	796	1,221	1,067	1,499			
Romania	547	659		591			
Russian Federation	739	1,572	10	2,079			
Slovakia	258	287	624	396			
Turkmenistan	1	3	2	93			
Ukraine	334	345	396	304			
USSR (former)	874						
Uzbekistan	13	8	25				
Northern Europe	**26,279**	**31,172**	**35,927**	**33,383**			
Denmark	1,836	1,744	2,032	1,761			
Finland	1,049	1,099	1,251	1,286			
Iceland	159	95	189	133			
Ireland	1,519	1,734	2,166	1,753			
Norway	2,372	2,032	2,161	2,395			
Sweden	4,671	4,378	4,830	4,372			
United Kingdom	14,071	17,112	18,947	20,055			
Isle of Man	602	2,978	4,351	1,628			
Southern Europe	**95,179**	**90,595**	**108,281**	**102,634**			
Albania	30	31	34	44			
Andorra	85	82	87	40			
Bosnia and Herzegovina	20	20	21	18			
Croatia	254	262	343	286			
Greece	822	893	827	731			
Holy See	13	7	6	8			
Italy	24,620	24,320	26,054	22,706			
Malta	50	51	67	40			
Montenegro			4				
Portugal	2,155	2,094	2,381	1,824			
San Marino	9	17	4	11			
Slovenia	303	498	406	324			
Spain	66,748	62,176	77,913	76,484			
TFYR of Macedonia	54	115	54	11			
Serbia and Montenegro	16	29	80	107			
Western Europe	**80,029**	**83,961**	**96,551**	**81,283**			
Austria	2,174	2,540	2,849	2,443			
Belgium	3,289	3,433	4,115	3,500			
France	27,611	27,381	30,366	29,897			
Germany	21,668	22,133	26,138	24,134			
Liechtenstein	20	24	27	20			
Luxembourg	118	129	154	144			
Monaco	9	14	15	26			
Netherlands	17,104	20,576	23,621	12,064			
Switzerland	8,036	7,731	9,266	9,055			
East Mediterranean Europe	**8,480**	**7,615**	**8,867**	**7,706**			
Cyprus	50	53	82	67			
Israel	7,743	7,016	8,036	6,808			
Turkey	687	546	749	831			
Other Europe	**4,741**	**7,598**		**39**			
Other countries of Europe	4,741	7,598		39			

COLOMBIA

2. Arrivals of non-resident visitors at national borders, by nationality

	2007	2008	2009	2010	2011	Market share 11	% Change 11-10
MIDDLE EAST	**1,339**	**1,188**	**1,311**	**908**			
Bahrain	6	6	6	20			
Palestine	35	32	27	26			
Iraq	9	4	7	9			
Jordan	93	57	63	55			
Kuwait	14	12	27	21			
Lebanon	948	843	808	359			
Libya	10	8	6	12			
Oman	3	4	5	1			
Qatar	2	3	16	9			
Saudi Arabia	32	27	48	69			
Syrian Arab Republic	39	39	34	23			
United Arab Emirates	9	16	81	98			
Egypt	133	132	179	200			
Yemen	6	5	4	6			
SOUTH ASIA	**2,292**	**2,492**	**2,924**	**3,375**			
Afghanistan	9	30	21	507			
Bangladesh	13	41	30	29			
Bhutan		1	5	1			
Sri Lanka	35	34	36	27			
India	1,911	2,038	2,483	2,533			
Iran, Islamic Republic of	187	224	206	167			
Maldives	4	3		2			
Nepal	17	22	41	30			
Pakistan	116	99	102	79			
NOT SPECIFIED	**84**	**211**	**190**	**70,627**			
Other countries of the World	84	211	190	70,627			

COMOROS

1. Arrivals of non-resident tourists at national borders, by nationality

		2007	2008	2009	2010	2011	Market share 11	% Change 11-10
TOTAL	(*)	15,173	14,753	11,306	15,300			
AFRICA		4,241	2,148	2,889	1,800			
East Africa		2,310	724	1,113				
Madagascar		818	210	206				
Mauritius		206						
Reunion		1,286	514	907				
Southern Africa		409						
South Africa		409						
Other Africa		1,522	1,424	1,776	1,800			
Other countries of Africa		1,522	1,424	1,776				
All countries of Africa					1,800			
AMERICAS		420	258	137				
Other Americas		420	258	137				
All countries of the Americas		420	258	137				
EAST ASIA AND THE PACIFIC		471	353	272				
Other East Asia and the Pacific		471	353	272				
All countries of Asia		382	157	183				
All countries of Oceania		89	196	89				
EUROPE		9,150	11,021	7,484	12,500			
Northern Europe		115	213	146				
United Kingdom		115	213	146				
Western Europe		8,768	10,575	7,074				
France		8,675	10,509	6,957				
Germany		93	66	117				
Other Europe		267	233	264	12,500			
Other countries of Europe		267	233	264				
All countries of Europe					12,500			
NOT SPECIFIED		891	973	524	1,000			
Other countries of the World		891	973	524	1,000			

CONGO

3. Arrivals of non-resident tourists in hotels and similar establishments, by country of residence

		2007	2008	2009	2010	2011	Market share 11	% Change 11-10
TOTAL	(*)	55,027	62,106	93,797	100,691			
AFRICA		27,733	25,780	38,327	41,122			
Central Africa		11,767	12,760	17,113	20,420			
Angola		2,837	2,134	3,193	3,352			
Cameroon		2,136	2,792	3,182	3,954			
Central African Republic		503	576	1,114	1,482			
Chad			191	630	625			
Democratic Republic of the Congo		4,154	5,224	7,052	8,712			
Gabon		1,689	1,629	1,763	2,116			
Other countries of Central Africa		448	214	179	179			
North Africa		2,658	2,105	9,406	6,332			
All countries of North Africa		2,658	2,105	9,406	6,332			
West Africa		6,459	6,046	8,507	10,203			
Benin		216	129	60	76			
Côte d'Ivoire		1,066	1,064	1,873	1,974			
Mali		152	546	1,265	1,505			
Senegal		627	845	1,092	1,421			
Togo		262	392	941	938			
Other countries of West Africa		4,136	3,070	3,276	4,289			
Other Africa		6,849	4,869	3,301	4,167			
Other countries of Africa		6,849	4,869	3,301	4,167			
AMERICAS		2,274	2,528	4,976	4,899			
North America		1,181	1,693	2,948	2,882			
Canada		291	322	792	733			
United States of America		890	1,371	2,156	2,149			
Other Americas		1,093	835	2,028	2,017			
Other countries of the Americas		1,093	835	2,028	2,017			
EAST ASIA AND THE PACIFIC		1,150	1,117	2,974	3,442			
North-East Asia			418	1,307	1,574			
China			349	994	1,351			
Japan			69	313	223			
Other East Asia and the Pacific		1,150	699	1,667	1,868			
Other countries of Asia			699	1,667	1,868			
All countries of Asia		1,150						
EUROPE		21,274	30,246	43,885	46,154			
Central/Eastern Europe		419	730	953	1,269			
Russian Federation		419	730	953	1,269			
Northern Europe		743	819	2,565	3,607			
United Kingdom		743	819	2,565	3,607			
Southern Europe		999	1,617	3,097	2,945			
Italy		999	1,617	3,097	2,945			
Western Europe		16,113	24,097	33,374	33,213			
Belgium		1,266	1,056	1,149	1,518			
France		14,466	22,473	30,343	30,181			
Germany		381	419	831	762			
Switzerland			149	1,051	752			
Other Europe		3,000	2,983	3,896	5,120			
Other countries of Europe		3,000	2,983	3,896	5,120			
NOT SPECIFIED		2,596	2,435	3,635	5,074			
Other countries of the World		2,596	2,435	3,635	5,074			

CONGO

5. Overnight stays of non-resident tourists in hotels and similar establishments, by country of residence

		2007	2008	2009	2010	2011	Market share 11	% Change 11-10
TOTAL	(*)	168,748	196,734	192,886	218,845			
AFRICA		80,233	82,142	75,426	94,226			
Central Africa		31,153	35,390	35,272	46,652			
Angola		6,678	5,719	6,000	9,641			
Cameroon		6,869	8,705	7,439	10,072			
Central African Republic		1,641	1,828	2,334	3,353			
Chad			591	1,078	1,116			
Democratic Republic of the Congo		9,005	11,416	14,286	16,615			
Gabon		5,524	6,317	3,703	5,217			
Other countries of Central Africa		1,436	814	432	638			
North Africa		6,727	5,740	13,506	10,019			
All countries of North Africa		6,727	5,740	13,506	10,019			
West Africa		22,486	22,877	17,609	25,544			
Benin		581	389	236	388			
Côte d'Ivoire		3,593	4,012	3,606	4,087			
Mali		336	1,361	2,390	3,163			
Senegal		2,947	4,159	1,750	3,040			
Togo		1,125	1,262	1,625	1,675			
Other countries of West Africa		13,904	11,694	8,002	13,191			
Other Africa		19,867	18,135	9,039	12,011			
Other countries of Africa		19,867	18,135	9,039	12,011			
AMERICAS		6,517	7,694	12,345	12,154			
North America		4,073	5,648	7,086	6,865			
Canada		870	1,660	1,717	1,627			
United States of America		3,203	3,988	5,369	5,238			
Other Americas		2,444	2,046	5,259	5,289			
Other countries of the Americas		2,444	2,046	5,259	5,289			
EAST ASIA AND THE PACIFIC		2,241	3,096	6,889	6,998			
North-East Asia			1,113	3,361	3,352			
China			941	2,547	2,917			
Japan			172	814	435			
Other East Asia and the Pacific		2,241	1,983	3,528	3,646			
Other countries of Asia			1,983	3,528	3,646			
All countries of Asia		2,241						
EUROPE		71,150	94,903	90,923	94,172			
Central/Eastern Europe		779	1,411	1,830	2,484			
Russian Federation		779	1,411	1,830	2,484			
Northern Europe		3,141	3,692	7,948	11,785			
United Kingdom		3,141	3,692	7,948	11,785			
Southern Europe		3,492	7,091	10,287	9,599			
Italy		3,492	7,091	10,287	9,599			
Western Europe		53,569	74,029	60,755	59,272			
Belgium		3,154	3,229	2,761	3,999			
France		49,176	69,245	54,777	52,536			
Germany		1,239	1,037	1,684	1,520			
Switzerland			518	1,533	1,217			
Other Europe		10,169	8,680	10,103	11,032			
Other countries of Europe		10,169	8,680	10,103	11,032			
NOT SPECIFIED		8,607	8,899	7,303	11,295			
Other countries of the World		8,607	8,899	7,303	11,295			

COOK ISLANDS

1. Arrivals of non-resident tourists at national borders, by country of residence

		2007	2008	2009	2010	2011	Market share 11	% Change 11-10
TOTAL	(*)	97,316	94,776	101,228	104,265	112,881	100.00	8.26
AMERICAS		6,958	5,674	6,066	6,995	6,910	6.12	-1.22
North America		6,958	5,674	6,066	6,590	6,494	5.75	-1.46
Canada		2,602	2,085	2,069	2,262	2,031	1.80	-10.21
United States of America		4,356	3,589	3,997	4,328	4,463	3.95	3.12
Other Americas					405	416	0.37	2.72
Other countries of the Americas					405	416	0.37	2.72
EAST ASIA AND THE PACIFIC		74,583	75,238	82,066	86,713	95,703	84.78	10.37
Australasia		71,557	72,641	78,331	84,328	93,518	82.85	10.90
Australia		12,363	11,229	14,795	16,841	18,492	16.38	9.80
New Zealand		59,194	61,412	63,536	67,487	75,026	66.46	11.17
Polynesia		1,354	1,090	1,120	838	665	0.59	-20.64
French Polynesia		1,354	1,090	1,120	838	665	0.59	-20.64
Other East Asia and the Pacific		1,672	1,507	2,615	1,547	1,520	1.35	-1.75
All countries of Asia		494	549	676	780	669	0.59	-14.23
Other countries of Oceania		1,178	958	1,939	767	851	0.75	10.95
EUROPE		15,350	13,471	12,448	10,557	10,268	9.10	-2.74
Northern Europe		9,553	8,579	7,040	5,126	4,704	4.17	-8.23
Denmark		335	315	214	174	171	0.15	-1.72
Finland		111	108	107	169	225	0.20	33.14
Norway		387	310	303	287	270	0.24	-5.92
Sweden		567	725	518	498	500	0.44	0.40
United Kingdom		8,153	7,121	5,898	3,998	3,538	3.13	-11.51
Southern Europe		704	630	762	935	908	0.80	-2.89
Italy		472	456	533	711	698	0.62	-1.83
Spain		232	174	229	224	210	0.19	-6.25
Western Europe		3,954	3,413	3,821	3,663	3,789	3.36	3.44
Austria		405	290	389	324	335	0.30	3.40
Belgium		55	56	80	74	77	0.07	4.05
France		189	206	236	213	245	0.22	15.02
Germany		2,469	2,215	2,466	2,296	2,246	1.99	-2.18
Netherlands		170	130	79	160	168	0.15	5.00
Switzerland		666	516	571	596	718	0.64	20.47
Other Europe		1,139	849	825	833	867	0.77	4.08
Other countries of Europe		1,139	849	825	833	867	0.77	4.08
NOT SPECIFIED		425	393	648				
Other countries of the World		425	393	648				

COSTA RICA

1. Arrivals of non-resident tourists at national borders, by nationality

	2007	2008	2009	2010	2011	Market share 11	% Change 11-10
TOTAL	1,979,789	2,089,174	1,922,579	2,099,829	2,192,059	100.00	4.39
AFRICA	1,621	1,852	1,631	1,823	1,898	0.09	4.11
Other Africa	1,621	1,852	1,631	1,823	1,898	0.09	4.11
All countries of Africa	1,621	1,852	1,631	1,823	1,898	0.09	4.11
AMERICAS	1,670,551	1,754,547	1,634,866	1,781,572	1,856,794	84.71	4.22
Caribbean	15,129	15,289	16,184	14,579	13,043	0.60	-10.54
Cuba	5,224	5,888	7,043	5,882	4,399	0.20	-25.21
Dominican Republic	5,615	6,077	5,836	5,094	5,199	0.24	2.06
Jamaica	937	616	725	752	719	0.03	-4.39
Puerto Rico	647	83	47	95	25	0.00	-73.68
Trinidad and Tobago	878	772	846	972	976	0.04	0.41
Other countries of the Caribbean	1,828	1,853	1,687	1,784	1,725	0.08	-3.31
Central America	592,840	648,586	588,739	642,517	670,271	30.58	4.32
Belize	901	928	975	843	838	0.04	-0.59
El Salvador	48,976	46,837	44,185	53,669	61,257	2.79	14.14
Guatemala	43,864	40,840	40,340	48,682	54,759	2.50	12.48
Honduras	35,673	31,714	31,324	34,043	35,598	1.62	4.57
Nicaragua	379,222	455,412	413,713	427,362	432,766	19.74	1.26
Panama	84,204	72,855	58,202	77,918	85,053	3.88	9.16
North America	953,812	976,561	920,371	1,005,309	1,044,569	47.65	3.91
Canada	102,061	109,854	102,471	119,654	133,033	6.07	11.18
Mexico	61,436	59,545	47,771	54,662	52,707	2.40	-3.58
United States of America	790,315	807,162	770,129	830,993	858,829	39.18	3.35
South America	108,770	114,111	109,572	119,167	128,911	5.88	8.18
Argentina	18,505	19,522	18,987	20,080	22,186	1.01	10.49
Bolivia	2,634	2,541	1,788	2,025	2,071	0.09	2.27
Brazil	10,726	12,340	11,617	13,121	14,449	0.66	10.12
Chile	9,397	9,350	7,682	8,504	9,129	0.42	7.35
Colombia	31,299	33,644	32,014	32,999	33,121	1.51	0.37
Ecuador	5,039	4,883	4,431	5,039	5,637	0.26	11.87
Paraguay	516	636	657	786	975	0.04	24.05
Peru	7,987	7,692	8,167	9,122	10,076	0.46	10.46
Uruguay	2,311	2,997	3,091	2,905	3,030	0.14	4.30
Venezuela	20,356	20,506	21,138	24,586	28,237	1.29	14.85
EAST ASIA AND THE PACIFIC	25,730	28,197	26,900	29,479	31,432	1.43	6.63
North-East Asia	13,400	13,730	13,256	14,411	14,591	0.67	1.25
China	2,157	2,992	3,346	3,589	4,525	0.21	26.08
Taiwan, Province of China	2,839	2,673	2,440	2,560	1,997	0.09	-21.99
Japan	5,438	5,368	4,746	5,026	4,758	0.22	-5.33
Korea, Republic of	2,966	2,697	2,724	3,236	3,311	0.15	2.32
Australasia	7,411	8,627	7,995	8,597	9,613	0.44	11.82
Australia, New Zealand	7,411	8,627	7,995	8,597	9,613	0.44	11.82
Other East Asia and the Pacific	4,919	5,840	5,649	6,471	7,228	0.33	11.70
Other countries of Asia	4,919	5,840	5,649	6,471	7,228	0.33	11.70
EUROPE	281,515	299,798	259,126	286,923	301,929	13.77	5.23
Central/Eastern Europe	6,253	6,727	5,826	6,832	7,342	0.33	7.46
Czech Republic	1,565	1,579	1,466	2,184	1,639	0.07	-24.95
Poland	1,774	2,208	1,926	2,085	2,425	0.11	16.31
Russian Federation	2,914	2,940	2,434	2,563	3,278	0.15	27.90
Northern Europe	56,666	63,076	47,640	53,744	55,841	2.55	3.90
Denmark	3,910	4,718	3,823	3,834	4,269	0.19	11.35
Finland	1,329	1,934	1,930	1,930	1,775	0.08	-8.03
Ireland	2,801	3,367	2,730	2,828	2,557	0.12	-9.58

COSTA RICA

1. Arrivals of non-resident tourists at national borders, by nationality

	2007	2008	2009	2010	2011	Market share 11	% Change 11-10
Norway	3,192	4,081	3,336	3,455	3,709	0.17	7.35
Sweden	7,854	8,726	6,939	6,952	7,842	0.36	12.80
United Kingdom	37,580	40,250	28,882	34,745	35,689	1.63	2.72
Southern Europe	**82,017**	**75,822**	**66,761**	**70,513**	**70,141**	**3.20**	**-0.53**
Italy	20,251	18,994	18,497	19,658	20,225	0.92	2.88
Portugal	2,677	2,799	1,807	2,363	2,134	0.10	-9.69
Spain	59,089	54,029	46,457	48,492	47,782	2.18	-1.46
Western Europe	**120,033**	**137,392**	**124,017**	**139,683**	**150,311**	**6.86**	**7.61**
Austria	5,778	6,124	5,504	5,863	6,348	0.29	8.27
Belgium	6,659	8,368	9,509	13,306	12,508	0.57	-6.00
France	25,939	34,622	30,737	35,266	38,290	1.75	8.57
Germany	40,285	44,705	40,918	44,539	49,225	2.25	10.52
Netherlands	28,014	30,615	25,006	26,373	27,731	1.27	5.15
Switzerland	13,358	12,958	12,343	14,336	16,209	0.74	13.07
East Mediterranean Europe	**9,884**	**10,419**	**8,972**	**9,511**	**11,210**	**0.51**	**17.86**
Israel	9,884	10,419	8,972	9,511	11,210	0.51	17.86
Other Europe	**6,662**	**6,362**	**5,910**	**6,640**	**7,084**	**0.32**	**6.69**
Other countries of Europe	6,662	6,362	5,910	6,640	7,084	0.32	6.69
NOT SPECIFIED	**372**	**4,780**	**56**	**32**	**6**	**0.00**	**-81.25**
Other countries of the World	372	4,780	56	32	6	0.00	-81.25

CROATIA

3. Arrivals of non-resident tourists in hotels and similar establishments, by country of residence

		2007	2008	2009	2010	2011	Market share 11	% Change 11-10
TOTAL	(*)	3,909,542	3,919,786	3,684,215	3,955,433	4,308,270	100.00	8.92
AMERICAS		164,927	146,835	115,723	133,053	145,742	3.38	9.54
North America		164,927	146,835	115,723	133,053	145,742	3.38	9.54
Canada		23,465	24,813	22,484	27,998	31,663	0.73	13.09
United States of America		141,462	122,022	93,239	105,055	114,079	2.65	8.59
EAST ASIA AND THE PACIFIC		128,958	189,565	180,905	180,589	183,799	4.27	1.78
North-East Asia		78,805	132,974	143,868	132,315	125,263	2.91	-5.33
Japan		78,805	132,974	143,868	132,315	125,263	2.91	-5.33
Australasia		50,153	56,591	37,037	48,274	58,536	1.36	21.26
Australia		43,484	49,601	31,510	41,439	51,889	1.20	25.22
New Zealand		6,669	6,990	5,527	6,835	6,647	0.15	-2.75
EUROPE		3,554,917	3,521,313	3,321,698	3,542,954	3,813,900	88.53	7.65
Central/Eastern Europe		665,306	707,059	611,022	671,586	741,519	17.21	10.41
Bulgaria		20,926	26,316	29,535	25,655	30,098	0.70	17.32
Belarus		2,748	2,990	1,672	1,524	1,928	0.04	26.51
Czech Republic		152,193	140,997	128,366	132,801	143,765	3.34	8.26
Estonia		6,791	5,532	3,731	2,038	2,845	0.07	39.60
Hungary		111,361	112,150	95,719	94,728	103,733	2.41	9.51
Latvia		9,029	7,476	3,995	4,006	4,821	0.11	20.34
Lithuania		15,189	17,842	10,526	8,709	7,874	0.18	-9.59
Poland		87,591	103,614	108,591	129,645	144,994	3.37	11.84
Romania		24,726	35,403	33,056	29,946	33,355	0.77	11.38
Russian Federation		131,182	144,909	95,660	128,827	138,529	3.22	7.53
Slovakia		80,288	84,786	74,309	78,210	90,587	2.10	15.83
Ukraine		23,282	25,044	25,862	35,497	38,990	0.91	9.84
Northern Europe		348,323	339,072	304,474	325,678	344,210	7.99	5.69
Denmark		26,623	24,281	20,992	22,441	21,476	0.50	-4.30
Finland		16,517	15,147	14,016	15,218	21,644	0.50	42.23
Iceland		3,013	2,068	1,232	1,134	1,507	0.03	32.89
Ireland		27,694	23,097	18,338	17,839	17,194	0.40	-3.62
Norway		41,818	42,419	38,662	48,956	52,202	1.21	6.63
Sweden		64,053	67,632	59,186	62,838	67,079	1.56	6.75
United Kingdom		168,605	164,428	152,048	157,252	163,108	3.79	3.72
Southern Europe		1,016,497	1,000,312	938,117	997,684	1,062,707	24.67	6.52
Bosnia and Herzegovina		87,930	95,516	86,799	89,328	94,267	2.19	5.53
Greece		8,588	10,542	16,241	30,065	30,491	0.71	1.42
Italy		467,583	423,672	427,513	417,452	421,637	9.79	1.00
Portugal		24,481	24,539	20,333	20,986	23,658	0.55	12.73
Slovenia		298,576	304,948	238,973	267,917	308,612	7.16	15.19
Spain		113,824	124,196	132,133	158,288	168,357	3.91	6.36
TFYR of Macedonia		15,515	16,899	16,125	13,648	15,685	0.36	14.93
Western Europe		1,412,191	1,358,535	1,359,383	1,415,957	1,517,096	35.21	7.14
Austria		384,407	367,003	416,271	440,930	486,521	11.29	10.34
Belgium		47,588	44,342	44,650	50,022	55,812	1.30	11.57
France		296,084	275,476	242,739	231,098	232,885	5.41	0.77
Germany		541,444	527,118	510,558	538,617	583,473	13.54	8.33
Luxembourg		1,604	1,621	2,244	2,353	2,453	0.06	4.25
Netherlands		80,347	83,237	82,965	82,109	79,597	1.85	-3.06
Switzerland		60,717	59,738	59,956	70,828	76,355	1.77	7.80
East Mediterranean Europe		41,536	38,131	38,093	58,292	65,299	1.52	12.02
Israel		29,917	24,991	21,140	25,437	26,539	0.62	4.33
Turkey		11,619	13,140	16,953	32,855	38,760	0.90	17.97
Other Europe		71,064	78,204	70,609	73,757	83,069	1.93	12.63
Other countries of Europe		71,064	78,204	70,609	73,757	83,069	1.93	12.63

CROATIA

3. Arrivals of non-resident tourists in hotels and similar establishments, by country of residence

	2007	2008	2009	2010	2011	Market share 11	% Change 11-10
NOT SPECIFIED	**60,740**	**62,073**	**65,889**	**98,837**	**164,829**	**3.83**	**66.77**
Other countries of the World	60,740	62,073	65,889	98,837	164,829	3.83	66.77

CROATIA

4. Arrivals of non-resident tourists in all types of accommodation establishments, by country of residence

		2007	2008	2009	2010	2011	Market share 11	% Change 11-10
TOTAL	(*)	8,558,685	8,664,581	8,693,796	9,110,742	9,926,674	100.00	8.96
AFRICA		11,650	10,801	9,904	11,293	13,399	0.13	18.65
Southern Africa		6,546	5,775	4,790	5,578	6,908	0.07	23.84
South Africa		6,546	5,775	4,790	5,578	6,908	0.07	23.84
Other Africa		5,104	5,026	5,114	5,715	6,491	0.07	13.58
Other countries of Africa		5,104	5,026	5,114	5,715	6,491	0.07	13.58
AMERICAS		231,978	214,128	179,685	208,417	250,418	2.52	20.15
North America		211,028	191,523	155,178	176,614	201,135	2.03	13.88
Canada		35,352	36,824	34,763	41,483	48,877	0.49	17.82
United States of America		173,347	151,346	118,996	132,751	150,831	1.52	13.62
Other countries of North America		2,329	3,353	1,419	2,380	1,427	0.01	-40.04
South America		5,903	7,821	9,836	14,015	22,083	0.22	57.57
Brazil		5,903	7,821	9,836	14,015	22,083	0.22	57.57
Other Americas		15,047	14,784	14,671	17,788	27,200	0.27	52.91
Other countries of the Americas		15,047	14,784	14,671	17,788	27,200	0.27	52.91
EAST ASIA AND THE PACIFIC		207,110	274,544	271,067	298,789	360,124	3.63	20.53
North-East Asia		106,436	161,979	181,114	178,797	187,260	1.89	4.73
China		6,381	6,302	7,534	13,195	22,459	0.23	70.21
Japan		86,313	143,608	163,173	147,119	131,630	1.33	-10.53
Korea, Republic of		13,742	12,069	10,407	18,483	33,171	0.33	79.47
Australasia		79,562	89,866	62,137	76,690	95,561	0.96	24.61
Australia		67,116	76,670	51,452	64,526	82,729	0.83	28.21
New Zealand		12,446	13,196	10,685	12,164	12,832	0.13	5.49
Other East Asia and the Pacific		21,112	22,699	27,816	43,302	77,303	0.78	78.52
Other countries of Asia		17,468	20,156	24,906	39,916	74,286	0.75	86.11
Other countries of Oceania		3,644	2,543	2,910	3,386	3,017	0.03	-10.90
EUROPE		8,107,947	8,165,108	8,233,140	8,592,243	9,302,733	93.71	8.27
Central/Eastern Europe		1,845,031	1,936,045	1,886,151	2,005,719	2,173,622	21.90	8.37
Bulgaria		24,325	29,961	34,678	29,586	36,699	0.37	24.04
Belarus		3,822	3,795	3,547	2,605	3,231	0.03	24.03
Czech Republic		636,475	588,911	578,517	605,732	638,036	6.43	5.33
Estonia		11,626	9,297	7,352	5,464	6,128	0.06	12.15
Hungary		346,762	338,007	298,359	297,667	328,106	3.31	10.23
Latvia		15,664	13,143	7,658	7,142	8,813	0.09	23.40
Lithuania		30,825	33,955	23,514	20,029	20,674	0.21	3.22
Poland		286,526	373,451	417,849	454,445	494,702	4.98	8.86
Romania		46,097	66,649	64,536	57,761	63,526	0.64	9.98
Russian Federation		148,081	165,569	121,971	164,999	182,203	1.84	10.43
Slovakia		266,512	282,982	292,450	310,031	335,021	3.37	8.06
Ukraine		28,316	30,325	35,720	50,258	56,483	0.57	12.39
Northern Europe		561,212	565,891	539,520	580,086	610,153	6.15	5.18
Denmark		74,962	80,130	76,068	77,412	73,975	0.75	-4.44
Finland		23,607	23,203	24,612	27,145	34,583	0.35	27.40
Iceland		3,494	2,537	1,638	1,562	2,317	0.02	48.34
Ireland		39,986	34,540	29,252	28,933	28,284	0.28	-2.24
Norway		68,349	71,192	66,269	85,135	92,276	0.93	8.39
Sweden		114,171	121,993	112,613	118,682	122,454	1.23	3.18
United Kingdom		236,643	232,296	229,068	241,217	256,264	2.58	6.24
Southern Europe		2,567,177	2,566,370	2,583,878	2,645,066	2,882,202	29.03	8.97
Bosnia and Herzegovina		221,467	238,549	212,505	217,051	222,978	2.25	2.73
Greece		10,050	12,840	18,570	32,567	33,068	0.33	1.54
Italy		1,081,603	1,008,598	1,057,893	1,018,375	1,150,311	11.59	12.96
Malta		1,086	1,208	1,485	1,265	1,358	0.01	7.35

CROATIA

4. Arrivals of non-resident tourists in all types of accommodation establishments, by country of residence

	2007	2008	2009	2010	2011	Market share 11	% Change 11-10
Montenegro	7,096	9,689	9,089	9,798	12,361	0.12	26.16
Portugal	29,291	31,759	26,087	28,171	29,319	0.30	4.08
Serbia	74,645	84,256	85,211	86,797	86,582	0.87	-0.25
Slovenia	964,880	984,807	962,604	1,016,572	1,099,919	11.08	8.20
Spain	151,361	165,101	180,013	211,094	220,957	2.23	4.67
TFYR of Macedonia	25,698	29,563	30,421	23,376	25,349	0.26	8.44
Western Europe	**3,054,658**	**3,021,215**	**3,156,404**	**3,265,719**	**3,521,052**	**35.47**	**7.82**
Austria	713,843	692,282	776,450	810,340	892,467	8.99	10.13
Belgium	93,533	91,925	93,913	103,341	119,916	1.21	16.04
France	456,463	423,098	393,192	388,320	394,482	3.97	1.59
Germany	1,411,262	1,404,832	1,463,281	1,525,133	1,661,346	16.74	8.93
Luxembourg	3,444	3,138	3,745	4,152	4,344	0.04	4.62
Netherlands	251,770	283,929	296,086	285,257	286,986	2.89	0.61
Switzerland	124,343	122,011	129,737	149,176	161,511	1.63	8.27
East Mediterranean Europe	**57,625**	**52,921**	**50,209**	**71,539**	**79,945**	**0.81**	**11.75**
Cyprus	3,037	2,051	1,194	1,292	1,505	0.02	16.49
Israel	39,813	33,120	28,421	32,657	34,162	0.34	4.61
Turkey	14,775	17,750	20,594	37,590	44,278	0.45	17.79
Other Europe	**22,244**	**22,666**	**16,978**	**24,114**	**35,759**	**0.36**	**48.29**
Other countries of Europe	22,244	22,666	16,978	24,114	35,759	0.36	48.29

CROATIA

5. Overnight stays of non-resident tourists in hotels and similar establishments, by country of residence

	2007	2008	2009	2010	2011	Market share 11	% Change 11-10
TOTAL (*)	17,988,240	17,675,115	16,085,143	17,011,494	18,054,427	100.00	6.13
AMERICAS	383,178	336,982	270,297	300,442	339,156	1.88	12.89
North America	383,178	336,982	270,297	300,442	339,156	1.88	12.89
Canada	57,757	58,299	54,242	65,110	73,497	0.41	12.88
United States of America	325,421	278,683	216,055	235,332	265,659	1.47	12.89
EAST ASIA AND THE PACIFIC	223,842	300,531	274,120	285,356	293,168	1.62	2.74
North-East Asia	118,972	184,961	195,926	183,752	172,514	0.96	-6.12
Japan	118,972	184,961	195,926	183,752	172,514	0.96	-6.12
Australasia	104,870	115,570	78,194	101,604	120,654	0.67	18.75
Australia	90,934	101,933	66,355	88,128	106,993	0.59	21.41
New Zealand	13,936	13,637	11,839	13,476	13,661	0.08	1.37
EUROPE	17,246,787	16,903,919	15,400,318	16,225,867	17,131,890	94.89	5.58
Central/Eastern Europe	4,037,681	4,250,320	3,493,424	3,879,788	4,186,799	23.19	7.91
Bulgaria	38,576	46,098	55,451	46,181	53,035	0.29	14.84
Belarus	12,831	16,195	8,339	9,819	10,005	0.06	1.89
Czech Republic	982,855	900,781	825,402	840,197	909,239	5.04	8.22
Estonia	20,444	16,737	10,985	7,046	10,865	0.06	54.20
Hungary	554,040	542,739	440,346	427,483	465,975	2.58	9.00
Latvia	23,923	18,203	11,627	11,741	16,915	0.09	44.07
Lithuania	42,089	42,925	30,544	24,425	22,512	0.12	-7.83
Poland	447,935	557,494	530,160	612,847	650,808	3.60	6.19
Romania	98,125	142,274	128,222	113,154	122,011	0.68	7.83
Russian Federation	1,133,370	1,242,375	804,646	1,048,374	1,097,479	6.08	4.68
Slovakia	518,304	539,632	473,104	496,353	561,659	3.11	13.16
Ukraine	165,189	184,867	174,598	242,168	266,296	1.47	9.96
Northern Europe	1,897,727	1,823,299	1,591,319	1,614,129	1,707,353	9.46	5.78
Denmark	160,611	141,294	111,402	120,757	113,135	0.63	-6.31
Finland	77,422	70,785	49,955	58,124	94,675	0.52	62.88
Iceland	19,145	12,389	3,190	2,762	4,584	0.03	65.97
Ireland	135,920	113,940	78,599	75,534	74,018	0.41	-2.01
Norway	235,338	240,732	210,419	266,199	285,399	1.58	7.21
Sweden	354,561	381,493	319,897	317,539	330,658	1.83	4.13
United Kingdom	914,730	862,666	817,857	773,214	804,884	4.46	4.10
Southern Europe	4,007,338	3,782,882	3,315,224	3,413,491	3,561,161	19.72	4.33
Bosnia and Herzegovina	288,788	308,155	292,519	288,596	309,914	1.72	7.39
Greece	20,068	20,829	34,463	62,625	55,248	0.31	-11.78
Italy	1,895,834	1,638,053	1,603,643	1,507,672	1,472,506	8.16	-2.33
Portugal	47,586	47,464	41,399	40,586	45,365	0.25	11.77
Slovenia	1,496,128	1,474,141	1,043,760	1,176,469	1,324,916	7.34	12.62
Spain	218,385	243,071	255,892	304,662	317,822	1.76	4.32
TFYR of Macedonia	40,549	51,169	43,548	32,881	35,390	0.20	7.63
Western Europe	7,015,641	6,750,876	6,689,689	6,945,842	7,279,935	40.32	4.81
Austria	1,797,394	1,702,116	1,897,595	1,993,975	2,148,567	11.90	7.75
Belgium	237,051	207,285	205,373	233,560	249,681	1.38	6.90
France	1,107,609	1,086,737	969,855	892,091	887,044	4.91	-0.57
Germany	3,192,667	3,076,621	2,954,812	3,142,763	3,313,031	18.35	5.42
Luxembourg	6,136	6,072	7,822	8,935	9,469	0.05	5.98
Netherlands	424,820	436,807	425,941	414,685	396,548	2.20	-4.37
Switzerland	249,964	235,238	228,291	259,833	275,595	1.53	6.07
East Mediterranean Europe	101,255	88,474	97,484	162,721	177,974	0.99	9.37
Israel	68,851	53,959	50,704	63,702	68,351	0.38	7.30
Turkey	32,404	34,515	46,780	99,019	109,623	0.61	10.71
Other Europe	187,145	208,068	213,178	209,896	218,668	1.21	4.18
Other countries of Europe	187,145	208,068	213,178	209,896	218,668	1.21	4.18

CROATIA

5. Overnight stays of non-resident tourists in hotels and similar establishments, by country of residence

	2007	2008	2009	2010	2011	Market share 11	% Change 11-10
NOT SPECIFIED	**134,433**	**133,683**	**140,408**	**199,829**	**290,213**	**1.61**	**45.23**
Other countries of the World	134,433	133,683	140,408	199,829	290,213	1.61	45.23

CROATIA

6. Overnight stays of non-resident tourists in all types of accommodation establishments, by country of residence

		2007	2008	2009	2010	2011	Market share 11	% Change 11-10
TOTAL	(*)	48,280,416	49,267,686	49,229,508	50,992,321	54,751,305	100.00	7.37
AFRICA		36,955	34,449	36,754	37,341	42,304	0.08	13.29
Southern Africa		15,215	13,736	13,938	14,056	16,306	0.03	16.01
South Africa		15,215	13,736	13,938	14,056	16,306	0.03	16.01
Other Africa		21,740	20,713	22,816	23,285	25,998	0.05	11.65
Other countries of Africa		21,740	20,713	22,816	23,285	25,998	0.05	11.65
AMERICAS		605,396	557,894	480,807	545,362	652,142	1.19	19.58
North America		549,281	498,579	417,470	463,931	534,071	0.98	15.12
Canada		101,794	102,831	98,933	114,692	134,288	0.25	17.09
United States of America		440,657	386,971	314,442	341,398	395,084	0.72	15.73
Other countries of North America		6,830	8,777	4,095	7,841	4,699	0.01	-40.07
South America		15,966	20,368	25,323	35,740	54,003	0.10	51.10
Brazil		15,966	20,368	25,323	35,740	54,003	0.10	51.10
Other Americas		40,149	38,947	38,014	45,691	64,068	0.12	40.22
Other countries of the Americas		40,149	38,947	38,014	45,691	64,068	0.12	40.22
EAST ASIA AND THE PACIFIC		415,400	505,000	475,070	547,070	643,828	1.18	17.69
North-East Asia		165,142	230,166	251,305	253,351	263,618	0.48	4.05
China		15,274	11,816	15,479	23,143	34,578	0.06	49.41
Japan		130,997	201,097	221,002	204,422	185,740	0.34	-9.14
Korea, Republic of		18,871	17,253	14,824	25,786	43,300	0.08	67.92
Australasia		192,325	214,335	155,878	186,405	225,283	0.41	20.86
Australia		162,321	183,851	128,472	157,872	194,777	0.36	23.38
New Zealand		30,004	30,484	27,406	28,533	30,506	0.06	6.91
Other East Asia and the Pacific		57,933	60,499	67,887	107,314	154,927	0.28	44.37
Other countries of Asia		49,117	54,246	61,726	99,967	149,079	0.27	49.13
Other countries of Oceania		8,816	6,253	6,161	7,347	5,848	0.01	-20.40
EUROPE		47,222,665	48,170,343	48,236,877	49,862,548	53,413,031	97.56	7.12
Central/Eastern Europe		11,810,733	12,513,238	12,031,352	12,920,632	13,936,471	25.45	7.86
Bulgaria		49,362	58,751	70,899	58,791	75,977	0.14	29.23
Belarus		20,166	23,579	20,001	17,986	19,210	0.04	6.81
Czech Republic		4,338,610	4,062,609	3,961,828	4,170,084	4,388,696	8.02	5.24
Estonia		35,987	29,946	24,159	19,860	24,141	0.04	21.56
Hungary		1,926,954	1,871,609	1,594,794	1,604,753	1,746,138	3.19	8.81
Latvia		45,353	40,129	24,460	23,749	31,368	0.06	32.08
Lithuania		105,154	109,128	82,665	70,692	73,438	0.13	3.88
Poland		1,786,518	2,451,471	2,685,037	2,895,162	3,134,012	5.72	8.25
Romania		215,437	309,448	294,486	253,556	270,523	0.49	6.69
Russian Federation		1,276,077	1,431,033	1,051,991	1,375,981	1,497,761	2.74	8.85
Slovakia		1,809,680	1,900,977	1,974,402	2,084,013	2,282,066	4.17	9.50
Ukraine		201,435	224,558	246,630	346,005	393,141	0.72	13.62
Northern Europe		3,146,421	3,177,956	2,997,092	3,104,617	3,251,431	5.94	4.73
Denmark		558,502	591,756	562,683	567,053	537,679	0.98	-5.18
Finland		105,814	105,243	95,110	108,557	151,599	0.28	39.65
Iceland		21,573	14,651	5,245	4,825	7,751	0.01	60.64
Ireland		190,766	165,238	126,881	124,131	119,384	0.22	-3.82
Norway		397,969	419,384	387,475	489,923	545,800	1.00	11.41
Sweden		645,949	704,352	628,127	637,408	652,363	1.19	2.35
United Kingdom		1,225,848	1,177,332	1,191,571	1,172,720	1,236,855	2.26	5.47
Southern Europe		12,801,408	12,726,630	12,587,745	12,783,262	13,582,233	24.81	6.25
Bosnia and Herzegovina		1,145,420	1,196,953	1,077,624	1,047,909	1,061,467	1.94	1.29
Greece		26,352	28,731	42,522	70,697	63,877	0.12	-9.65
Italy		5,211,602	4,834,063	4,925,252	4,731,832	4,994,547	9.12	5.55
Malta		5,278	4,212	6,490	5,544	5,702	0.01	2.85

CROATIA

6. Overnight stays of non-resident tourists in all types of accommodation establishments, by country of residence

	2007	2008	2009	2010	2011	Market share 11	% Change 11-10
Montenegro	27,249	41,159	31,960	29,917	31,352	0.06	4.80
Portugal	61,923	75,536	58,214	70,060	61,541	0.11	-12.16
Serbia	310,584	380,031	433,445	419,553	433,048	0.79	3.22
Slovenia	5,598,156	5,681,930	5,512,808	5,885,315	6,389,183	11.67	8.56
Spain	301,235	336,155	360,003	423,468	437,258	0.80	3.26
TFYR of Macedonia	113,609	147,860	139,427	98,967	104,258	0.19	5.35
Western Europe	**19,246,536**	**19,564,534**	**20,435,860**	**20,781,204**	**22,314,522**	**40.76**	**7.38**
Austria	3,985,977	3,903,820	4,258,338	4,420,058	4,836,232	8.83	9.42
Belgium	500,318	502,873	509,980	545,342	604,678	1.10	10.88
France	1,639,245	1,609,816	1,510,894	1,464,114	1,483,546	2.71	1.33
Germany	10,547,586	10,682,174	11,166,827	11,476,383	12,487,389	22.81	8.81
Luxembourg	15,488	13,421	15,630	17,345	18,941	0.03	9.20
Netherlands	2,011,000	2,313,619	2,424,071	2,244,521	2,223,874	4.06	-0.92
Switzerland	546,922	538,811	550,120	613,441	659,862	1.21	7.57
East Mediterranean Europe	**152,088**	**126,289**	**131,065**	**199,690**	**219,204**	**0.40**	**9.77**
Cyprus	11,682	5,512	3,692	3,738	4,471	0.01	19.61
Israel	89,216	70,782	66,167	80,293	86,284	0.16	7.46
Turkey	51,190	49,995	61,206	115,659	128,449	0.23	11.06
Other Europe	**65,479**	**61,696**	**53,763**	**73,143**	**109,170**	**0.20**	**49.26**
Other countries of Europe	65,479	61,696	53,763	73,143	109,170	0.20	49.26

CUBA

2. Arrivals of non-resident visitors at national borders, by country of residence

	2007	2008	2009	2010	2011	Market share 11	% Change 11-10
TOTAL	2,152,221	2,348,340	2,429,809	2,531,745	2,716,317	100.00	7.29
AFRICA	6,611	7,346	8,691	8,698	8,202	0.30	-5.70
East Africa	725	821	1,370	1,050	646	0.02	-38.48
All countries of East Africa	725	821	1,370	1,050	646	0.02	-38.48
Central Africa	1,293	1,514	1,757	2,558	3,180	0.12	24.32
Angola	833	997	1,440	2,307	2,838	0.10	23.02
Other countries of Central Africa	460	517	317	251	342	0.01	36.25
North Africa	1,212	1,480	1,935	1,882	1,789	0.07	-4.94
All countries of North Africa	1,212	1,480	1,935	1,882	1,789	0.07	-4.94
Southern Africa	1,522	1,463	1,385	1,223	1,355	0.05	10.79
All countries of Southern Africa	1,522	1,463	1,385	1,223	1,355	0.05	10.79
West Africa	1,859	2,068	2,244	1,985	1,232	0.05	-37.93
All countries of West Africa	1,859	2,068	2,244	1,985	1,232	0.05	-37.93
AMERICAS	1,172,933	1,380,232	1,535,853	1,664,043	1,799,074	66.23	8.11
Caribbean	212,202	245,741	315,039	389,766	413,409	15.22	6.07
Antigua and Barbuda	179	178	201	54	76	0.00	40.74
Bahamas	4,537	3,826	3,456	3,122	2,966	0.11	-5.00
Barbados	367	337	695	209	165	0.01	-21.05
Bermuda	163	109	210	143	99	0.00	-30.77
Cayman Islands	921	461	562	480	583	0.02	21.46
Dominica	637	404	521	138	112	0.00	-18.84
Dominican Republic	5,483	5,102	5,022	4,735	4,969	0.18	4.94
Grenada	242	119	110	93	81	0.00	-12.90
Guadeloupe	53	7	6	8			
Haiti	2,012	4,061	4,691	2,549	3,839	0.14	50.61
Jamaica	3,147	2,721	2,173	1,512	1,285	0.05	-15.01
Martinique	41	17	5	5	3	0.00	-40.00
Netherlands Antilles	24	84	49	51	86	0.00	68.63
Puerto Rico	78	50	64	19	10	0.00	-47.37
Saint Lucia	575	567	188	148	179	0.01	20.95
Saint Vincent and the Grenadines	304	117	94	141	102	0.00	-27.66
Trinidad and Tobago	592	724	811	855	892	0.03	4.33
Other countries of the Caribbean	192,847	226,857	296,181	375,504	397,962	14.65	5.98
Central America	27,637	30,356	29,801	26,695	29,075	1.07	8.92
Belize	505	478	800	211	230	0.01	9.00
Costa Rica	5,903	8,449	7,855	7,319	8,071	0.30	10.27
El Salvador	4,474	4,952	3,496	2,368	2,700	0.10	14.02
Guatemala	4,789	5,042	3,874	3,268	3,689	0.14	12.88
Honduras	2,010	1,793	1,819	1,686	1,950	0.07	15.66
Nicaragua	2,463	1,858	2,280	2,187	2,088	0.08	-4.53
Panama	7,493	7,784	9,677	9,656	10,347	0.38	7.16
North America	793,025	944,202	1,028,826	1,074,944	1,152,210	42.42	7.19
Canada	660,384	818,246	914,884	945,248	1,002,318	36.90	6.04
Mexico	92,120	84,052	61,487	66,650	76,326	2.81	14.52
United States of America	40,521	41,904	52,455	63,046	73,566	2.71	16.69
South America	140,069	159,933	162,187	172,638	204,380	7.52	18.39
Argentina	37,922	47,405	48,543	58,612	75,968	2.80	29.61
Bolivia	1,781	1,639	2,002	1,600	1,286	0.05	-19.63
Brazil	12,165	13,865	13,498	14,367	14,507	0.53	0.97
Chile	14,951	18,895	18,205	17,521	23,527	0.87	34.28
Colombia	18,594	22,178	21,287	20,624	24,873	0.92	20.60
Ecuador	7,717	9,391	9,473	7,011	6,964	0.26	-0.67
French Guiana	24	5	5	5			
Guyana	1,323	574	617	238	297	0.01	24.79
Paraguay	1,002	369	492	412	559	0.02	35.68

CUBA

2. Arrivals of non-resident visitors at national borders, by country of residence

	2007	2008	2009	2010	2011	Market share 11	% Change 11-10
Peru	6,179	9,598	14,708	16,049	15,188	0.56	-5.36
Suriname	1,273	114	114	106	106	0.00	
Uruguay	3,543	3,967	4,585	5,128	7,009	0.26	36.68
Venezuela	33,593	31,931	28,657	30,965	34,096	1.26	10.11
Other countries of South America	2	2	1				
EAST ASIA AND THE PACIFIC	**42,311**	**44,225**	**40,558**	**41,349**	**48,498**	**1.79**	**17.29**
North-East Asia	**22,986**	**22,270**	**20,887**	**21,811**	**25,403**	**0.94**	**16.47**
China	10,864	11,252	12,352	11,247	14,749	0.54	31.14
Taiwan, Province of China	312	469	305	449	468	0.02	4.23
Hong Kong, China	7	14	10	6	10	0.00	66.67
Japan	6,647	5,550	5,460	6,372	5,420	0.20	-14.94
Korea, Dem. People's Republic of	439	472	338	202	318	0.01	57.43
Korea, Republic of	4,582	4,452	2,382	3,481	4,352	0.16	25.02
Mongolia	69	56	36	46	78	0.00	69.57
Other countries of North-East Asia	66	5	4	8	8	0.00	
South-East Asia	**11,371**	**12,891**	**11,812**	**11,419**	**14,611**	**0.54**	**27.95**
Cambodia	26	27	19	17	19	0.00	11.76
Indonesia	402	766	562	990	1,277	0.05	28.99
Lao People's Democratic Republic	26	16	15	14	3	0.00	-78.57
Malaysia	308	292	253	387	299	0.01	-22.74
Philippines	9,067	10,567	9,478	8,721	11,561	0.43	32.57
Singapore	203	155	233	239	255	0.01	6.69
Viet Nam	829	832	1,000	867	1,031	0.04	18.92
Thailand	302	196	204	157	159	0.01	1.27
Other countries of South-East Asia	208	40	48	27	7	0.00	-74.07
Australasia	**7,830**	**8,910**	**7,763**	**8,076**	**8,423**	**0.31**	**4.30**
Australia	6,242	7,226	6,410	6,797	7,115	0.26	4.68
New Zealand	1,588	1,684	1,353	1,279	1,308	0.05	2.27
Melanesia	**18**	**16**	**19**	**18**	**41**	**0.00**	**127.78**
Fiji	11	14	7	16	15	0.00	-6.25
New Caledonia	1		1	1	20	0.00	1900.00
Vanuatu					5	0.00	
Papua New Guinea	6	2	11	1	1	0.00	
Micronesia	**26**	**20**	**30**	**18**	**13**	**0.00**	**-27.78**
All countries of Micronesia	26	20	30	18	13	0.00	-27.78
Polynesia	**68**		**20**	**7**	**7**	**0.00**	
All countries of Polynesia	68		20	7	7	0.00	
Other East Asia and the Pacific	**12**	**118**	**27**				
Other countries of Oceania	12	118	27				
EUROPE	**924,025**	**909,086**	**838,340**	**809,515**	**852,065**	**31.37**	**5.26**
Central/Eastern Europe	**75,355**	**101,478**	**85,081**	**100,070**	**127,179**	**4.68**	**27.09**
Bulgaria	1,722	1,940	1,663	1,517	1,832	0.07	20.76
Czech Republic	8,547	11,214	11,516	8,855	8,927	0.33	0.81
Estonia	836	855	494	383	527	0.02	37.60
Hungary	4,187	4,135	3,439	3,028	3,512	0.13	15.98
Latvia	799	823	529	607	691	0.03	13.84
Lithuania	1,215	1,494	866	1,180	1,279	0.05	8.39
Poland	11,598	21,730	13,501	12,793	13,972	0.51	9.22
Romania	3,145	3,416	2,693	2,705	3,023	0.11	11.76
Russian Federation	29,077	40,621	37,391	56,245	78,472	2.89	39.52
Slovakia	4,300	4,357	4,387	4,115	4,324	0.16	5.08
Ukraine	7,910	8,637	6,353	5,686	6,771	0.25	19.08
Uzbekistan	72	40	49	86	68	0.00	-20.93
Other countries Central/East Europe	1,947	2,216	2,200	2,870	3,781	0.14	31.74
Northern Europe	**251,267**	**235,441**	**206,188**	**207,119**	**210,758**	**7.76**	**1.76**

CUBA

2. Arrivals of non-resident visitors at national borders, by country of residence

	2007	2008	2009	2010	2011	Market share 11	% Change 11-10
Denmark	10,156	10,179	8,782	8,476	8,009	0.29	-5.51
Finland	5,445	5,779	5,265	4,935	5,756	0.21	16.64
Iceland	1,865	257	190	154	188	0.01	22.08
Ireland	8,301	8,586	6,592	5,638	5,171	0.19	-8.28
Norway	9,881	9,974	7,202	7,441	8,754	0.32	17.65
Sweden	7,470	6,720	5,837	6,131	7,055	0.26	15.07
United Kingdom	208,122	193,932	172,318	174,343	175,822	6.47	0.85
Other countries of Northern Europe	27	14	2	1	3	0.00	200.00
Southern Europe	**308,642**	**289,531**	**285,845**	**247,098**	**235,698**	**8.68**	**-4.61**
Albania	291	416	376	404	351	0.01	-13.12
Andorra	149	111	124	113	113	0.00	
Bosnia and Herzegovina	313	428	307	299	288	0.01	-3.68
Croatia	1,908	1,817	1,442	1,344	1,383	0.05	2.90
Greece	6,598	7,533	4,769	4,263	3,427	0.13	-19.61
Italy	134,289	126,042	118,347	112,298	110,432	4.07	-1.66
Malta	100	136	140	117	125	0.00	6.84
Montenegro	67	76	96	142	151	0.01	6.34
Portugal	25,442	25,542	26,055	18,762	13,733	0.51	-26.80
San Marino	138	132	145	119	111	0.00	-6.72
Serbia				1,683	1,669	0.06	-0.83
Slovenia	3,014	2,749	2,358	2,130	1,941	0.07	-8.87
Spain	133,149	121,166	129,224	104,948	101,631	3.74	-3.16
Serbia and Montenegro	982	1,292	1,430				
Other countries of Southern Europe	2,202	2,091	1,032	476	343	0.01	-27.94
Western Europe	**280,077**	**272,255**	**253,812**	**246,704**	**266,923**	**9.83**	**8.20**
Austria	14,492	13,450	12,004	11,486	11,803	0.43	2.76
Belgium	17,256	15,681	15,722	13,049	14,266	0.53	9.33
France	92,304	90,731	83,478	80,470	94,370	3.47	17.27
Germany	103,054	100,964	93,437	93,136	95,124	3.50	2.13
Liechtenstein	69	61	62	64	85	0.00	32.81
Luxembourg	685	647	613	598	693	0.03	15.89
Monaco	24	33	34	19	37	0.00	94.74
Netherlands	33,605	33,548	33,123	31,787	32,402	1.19	1.93
Switzerland	18,588	17,140	15,339	16,095	18,143	0.67	12.72
East Mediterranean Europe	**8,684**	**10,381**	**7,414**	**8,524**	**11,507**	**0.42**	**35.00**
Cyprus	408	537	367	282	344	0.01	21.99
Israel	3,549	3,945	3,306	3,926	5,327	0.20	35.69
Turkey	4,727	5,899	3,741	4,316	5,836	0.21	35.22
MIDDLE EAST	**1,734**	**1,981**	**1,810**	**2,053**	**1,814**	**0.07**	**-11.64**
Bahrain	19	15	17	22	22	0.00	
Palestine	117	71	96	71	56	0.00	-21.13
Iraq	160	63	54	67	78	0.00	16.42
Jordan	171	202	211	172	162	0.01	-5.81
Kuwait	40	20	23	153	52	0.00	-66.01
Lebanon	488	655	533	522	574	0.02	9.96
Libya	34	50	80	73	29	0.00	-60.27
Oman	18	26	56	27	19	0.00	-29.63
Qatar	18	58	17	34	7	0.00	-79.41
Saudi Arabia	57	66	115	185	210	0.01	13.51
Syrian Arab Republic	252	355	215	368	266	0.01	-27.72
Egypt	221	324	240	271	292	0.01	7.75
Yemen	100	58	76	52	32	0.00	-38.46
Other countries of Middle East	39	18	77	36	15	0.00	-58.33
SOUTH ASIA	**4,021**	**5,156**	**4,467**	**5,832**	**5,841**	**0.22**	**0.15**
Afghanistan	14	23	49	42	48	0.00	14.29
Bangladesh	111	69	80	118	91	0.00	-22.88
Sri Lanka	453	541	483	487	362	0.01	-25.67

CUBA

2. Arrivals of non-resident visitors at national borders, by country of residence

	2007	2008	2009	2010	2011	Market share 11	% Change 11-10
India	1,898	2,730	2,551	3,614	3,574	0.13	-1.11
Iran, Islamic Republic of	719	784	940	1,092	1,075	0.04	-1.56
Maldives	20	53	55	81	1	0.00	-98.77
Pakistan	687	867	179	208	185	0.01	-11.06
Other countries of South Asia	119	89	130	190	505	0.02	165.79
NOT SPECIFIED	**586**	**314**	**90**	**255**	**823**	**0.03**	**222.75**
Other countries of the World	586	314	90	255	823	0.03	222.75

CURAÇAO

1. Arrivals of non-resident tourists at national borders, by country of residence

		2007	2008	2009	2010	2011	Market share 11	% Change 11-10
TOTAL	(*)	**299,730**	**408,942**	**366,679**	**341,651**	**390,282**	**100.00**	**14.23**
AMERICAS		**174,261**	**264,986**	**210,790**	**170,818**	**210,185**	**53.85**	**23.05**
Caribbean		**39,831**	**41,154**	**36,637**	**39,107**	**41,616**	**10.66**	**6.42**
Barbados		786	754	862	1,144	928	0.24	-18.88
Dominican Republic		3,231	2,612	2,644	2,927	4,118	1.06	40.69
Haiti		1,730	1,770	1,811	1,914	2,279	0.58	19.07
Jamaica		9,397	9,591	7,064	5,109	5,155	1.32	0.90
Aruba		14,442	16,848	16,756	18,817	20,478	5.25	8.83
Puerto Rico		902	845	756	711	437	0.11	-38.54
Trinidad and Tobago		7,079	6,499	5,318	6,852	6,437	1.65	-6.06
Other countries of the Caribbean		2,264	2,235	1,426	1,633	1,784	0.46	9.25
North America		**53,097**	**50,924**	**42,560**	**56,449**	**71,616**	**18.35**	**26.87**
Canada		6,898	7,244	6,513	7,628	8,785	2.25	15.17
United States of America		46,199	43,680	36,047	48,821	62,831	16.10	28.70
South America		**81,333**	**172,908**	**131,593**	**75,262**	**96,953**	**24.84**	**28.82**
Argentina		583	762	709	929	1,289	0.33	38.75
Brazil		3,295	4,215	4,466	8,096	8,826	2.26	9.02
Colombia		4,796	5,359	6,260	6,280	8,249	2.11	31.35
Ecuador		3,147	3,081	1,744	2,319	2,632	0.67	13.50
Guyana		738	822	917	1,029	988	0.25	-3.98
Peru		395	606	288				
Suriname		5,106	6,220	9,218	9,440	9,987	2.56	5.79
Venezuela		60,966	148,890	105,932	44,350	61,582	15.78	38.85
Other countries of South America		2,307	2,953	2,059	2,819	3,400	0.87	20.61
EUROPE		**121,383**	**136,747**	**149,538**	**163,831**	**169,137**	**43.34**	**3.24**
Northern Europe		**6,863**	**6,908**	**5,316**	**5,448**	**5,730**	**1.47**	**5.18**
Denmark		544	501	446	299	464	0.12	55.18
Finland		1,083	1,191	887	747	667	0.17	-10.71
Norway		439	655	659	742	837	0.21	12.80
Sweden		1,996	1,667	1,236	1,480	1,225	0.31	-17.23
United Kingdom		2,801	2,894	2,088	2,180	2,537	0.65	16.38
Southern Europe		**1,829**	**2,554**	**1,819**	**2,332**	**2,993**	**0.77**	**28.34**
Italy		805	1,024	730	1,131	1,853	0.47	63.84
Portugal		283	502	248	249	229	0.06	-8.03
Spain		741	1,028	841	952	911	0.23	-4.31
Western Europe		**109,264**	**123,493**	**139,055**	**152,739**	**156,462**	**40.09**	**2.44**
Austria		257	350	340	367	474	0.12	29.16
Belgium		3,204	3,156	3,744	4,429	5,117	1.31	15.53
Germany		4,654	5,516	6,842	6,652	8,059	2.06	21.15
Netherlands		100,384	113,696	127,175	140,161	141,536	36.27	0.98
Switzerland		765	775	954	1,130	1,276	0.33	12.92
Other Europe		**3,427**	**3,792**	**3,348**	**3,312**	**3,952**	**1.01**	**19.32**
Other countries of Europe		3,427	3,792	3,348	3,312	3,952	1.01	19.32
NOT SPECIFIED		**4,086**	**7,209**	**6,351**	**7,002**	**10,960**	**2.81**	**56.53**
Other countries of the World		4,086	7,209	6,351	7,002	10,960	2.81	56.53

CURAÇAO

3. Arrivals of non-resident tourists in hotels and similar establishments, by country of residence

		2007	2008	2009	2010	2011	Market share 11	% Change 11-10
TOTAL	(*)	213,796	224,322	234,070	223,044	248,884	100.00	11.59
AMERICAS		132,347	171,083	140,072	117,250	144,713	58.14	23.42
Caribbean		26,873	21,051	18,313	23,834	22,673	9.11	-4.87
Barbados		633	494	672	793	663	0.27	-16.39
Dominican Republic		1,452	1,082	816	875	953	0.38	8.91
Haiti		764	203	844	893	1,093	0.44	22.40
Jamaica		7,378	4,914	3,344	3,369	2,099	0.84	-37.70
Aruba		8,184	7,951	7,072	10,763	11,163	4.49	3.72
Puerto Rico		750	662	469	558	320	0.13	-42.65
Trinidad and Tobago		6,286	4,638	4,263	5,586	5,140	2.07	-7.98
Other countries of the Caribbean		1,426	1,107	833	997	1,242	0.50	24.57
North America		44,682	36,275	32,781	46,925	57,240	23.00	21.98
Canada		6,020	4,835	5,436	6,567	7,185	2.89	9.41
United States of America		38,662	31,440	27,345	40,358	50,055	20.11	24.03
South America		60,792	113,757	88,978	46,491	64,800	26.04	39.38
Argentina		468	457	547	797	1,014	0.41	27.23
Brazil		2,756	2,762	3,704	7,413	7,423	2.98	0.13
Colombia		2,394	2,339	2,685	3,473	4,920	1.98	41.66
Ecuador		2,902	2,703	1,439	2,100	2,404	0.97	14.48
Guyana		469	334	461	581	587	0.24	1.03
Peru		259	240	142		82	0.03	
Suriname		2,287	2,226	3,325	843	4,362	1.75	417.44
Venezuela		47,528	100,855	75,154	29,349	42,163	16.94	43.66
Other countries of South America		1,729	1,841	1,521	1,935	1,845	0.74	-4.65
EUROPE		79,933	51,759	92,603	104,420	102,017	40.99	-2.30
Northern Europe		5,417	4,039	3,739	3,836	3,691	1.48	-3.78
Denmark		432	311	317	193	333	0.13	72.54
Finland		1,019	736	808	676	541	0.22	-19.97
Norway		313	292	462	489	555	0.22	13.50
Sweden		1,743	1,219	962	1,181	977	0.39	-17.27
United Kingdom		1,910	1,481	1,190	1,297	1,285	0.52	-0.93
Southern Europe		1,134	996	1,029	1,401	1,974	0.79	40.90
Italy		503	406	476	795	1,427	0.57	79.50
Portugal		181	169	147	150	95	0.04	-36.67
Spain		450	421	406	456	452	0.18	-0.88
Western Europe		71,511	45,235	86,277	97,525	94,417	37.94	-3.19
Austria		211	139	246	266	338	0.14	27.07
Belgium		2,230	1,802	2,389	3,094	3,285	1.32	6.17
Germany		3,424	2,516	4,588	4,443	5,211	2.09	17.29
Netherlands		65,051	40,012	78,385	88,885	84,674	34.02	-4.74
Switzerland		595	766	669	837	909	0.37	8.60
Other Europe		1,871	1,489	1,558	1,658	1,935	0.78	16.71
Other countries of Europe		1,871	1,489	1,558	1,658	1,935	0.78	16.71
NOT SPECIFIED		1,516	1,480	1,395	1,374	2,154	0.87	56.77
Other countries of the World		1,516	1,480	1,395	1,374	2,154	0.87	56.77

CURAÇAO

6. Overnight stays of non-resident tourists in all types of accommodation establishments, by country of residence

	2007	2008	2009	2010	2011	Market share 11	% Change 11-10
TOTAL	2,560,281	2,978,363	2,696,798	2,907,435	3,200,356	100.00	10.07
AMERICAS	1,031,218	1,277,791	1,028,550	1,063,734	1,303,411	40.73	22.53
Caribbean	214,363	208,523	180,228	213,512	251,473	7.86	17.78
Barbados	3,435	3,089	2,982	5,237	4,042	0.13	-22.82
Dominican Republic	39,483	25,763	24,222	34,200	62,157	1.94	81.75
Haiti	16,840	14,767	13,383	16,621	20,005	0.63	20.36
Jamaica	43,567	46,078	37,292	32,190	36,021	1.13	11.90
Aruba	65,562	77,766	72,310	83,351	90,905	2.84	9.06
Puerto Rico	3,727	3,880	3,187	2,930	1,902	0.06	-35.09
Trinidad and Tobago	26,824	23,463	19,120	27,823	26,221	0.82	-5.76
Other countries of the Caribbean	14,925	13,717	7,732	11,160	10,220	0.32	-8.42
North America	386,862	384,873	300,174	375,576	469,450	14.67	24.99
Canada	57,140	61,406	53,342	62,825	75,057	2.35	19.47
United States of America	329,722	323,467	246,832	312,751	394,393	12.32	26.10
South America	429,993	684,395	548,148	474,646	582,488	18.20	22.72
Argentina	3,876	4,666	3,923	5,730	7,569	0.24	32.09
Brazil	17,043	20,863	22,602	40,540	45,886	1.43	13.19
Colombia	98,597	77,967	81,107	87,177	108,327	3.38	24.26
Ecuador	13,342	13,486	7,589	12,179	12,244	0.38	0.53
Guyana	3,979	4,823	4,713	5,555	6,182	0.19	11.29
Peru	2,342	5,485			1,501	0.05	
Suriname	38,856	43,713	60,472	60,660	61,025	1.91	0.60
Venezuela	236,697	496,077	353,292	242,654	318,410	9.95	31.22
Other countries of South America	15,261	17,315	14,450	20,151	21,344	0.67	5.92
EUROPE	1,499,330	1,644,197	1,634,474	1,805,450	1,850,752	57.83	2.51
Northern Europe	68,114	66,445	52,081	54,611	51,459	1.61	-5.77
Denmark	5,699	5,153	4,113	2,999	4,213	0.13	40.48
Finland	9,879	10,765	8,037	6,910	5,153	0.16	-25.43
Norway	4,295	5,611	6,528	6,900	7,781	0.24	12.77
Sweden	19,245	15,968	11,899	15,023	11,661	0.36	-22.38
United Kingdom	28,996	28,948	21,504	22,779	22,651	0.71	-0.56
Southern Europe	19,540	20,954	16,812	19,570	25,566	0.80	30.64
Italy	6,749	6,305	5,730	9,103	14,549	0.45	59.83
Portugal	5,135	5,480	2,886	1,659	2,127	0.07	28.21
Spain	7,656	9,169	8,196	8,808	8,890	0.28	0.93
Western Europe	1,385,396	1,525,024	1,540,097	1,704,960	1,738,421	54.32	1.96
Austria	3,239	3,466	3,769	3,940	5,004	0.16	27.01
Belgium	36,968	38,583	40,101	45,585	50,378	1.57	10.51
Germany	60,418	72,424	81,164	78,149	94,222	2.94	20.57
Netherlands	1,277,420	1,403,478	1,406,180	1,566,903	1,576,224	49.25	0.59
Switzerland	7,351	7,073	8,883	10,383	12,593	0.39	21.28
Other Europe	26,280	31,774	25,484	26,309	35,306	1.10	34.20
Other countries of Europe	26,280	31,774	25,484	26,309	35,306	1.10	34.20
NOT SPECIFIED	29,733	56,375	33,774	38,251	46,193	1.44	20.76
Other countries of the World	29,733	56,375	33,774	38,251	46,193	1.44	20.76

CYPRUS

1. Arrivals of non-resident tourists at national borders, by country of residence

	2007	2008	2009	2010	2011	Market share 11	% Change 11-10
TOTAL	2,416,081	2,403,750	2,141,193	2,172,998	2,392,228	100.00	10.09
AFRICA	7,139	7,535	6,833	6,481	6,615	0.28	2.07
Southern Africa	5,506	6,249	5,623	4,816	5,793	0.24	20.29
South Africa	5,506	6,249	5,623	4,816	5,793	0.24	20.29
Other Africa	1,633	1,286	1,210	1,665	822	0.03	-50.63
Other countries of Africa	1,633	1,286	1,210	1,665	822	0.03	-50.63
AMERICAS	30,352	27,777	23,737	31,357	32,080	1.34	2.31
North America	29,369	26,629	22,619	29,541	31,012	1.30	4.98
Canada	5,625	5,512	4,698	6,822	5,180	0.22	-24.07
United States of America	23,744	21,117	17,921	22,719	25,832	1.08	13.70
Other Americas	983	1,148	1,118	1,816	1,068	0.04	-41.19
Other countries of the Americas	983	1,148	1,118	1,816	1,068	0.04	-41.19
EAST ASIA AND THE PACIFIC	16,548	16,567	15,060	19,093	16,535	0.69	-13.40
North-East Asia	2,030	1,446	1,520	2,377	2,049	0.09	-13.80
China	692	722	441	655	651	0.03	-0.61
Japan	630	354	560	1,194	694	0.03	-41.88
Korea, Republic of	136		60	144	292	0.01	102.78
Other countries of North-East Asia	572	370	459	384	412	0.02	7.29
Australasia	11,547	12,160	10,996	14,139	13,110	0.55	-7.28
Australia	10,742	11,506	10,523	13,282	12,455	0.52	-6.23
New Zealand	805	654	473	857	655	0.03	-23.57
Other East Asia and the Pacific	2,971	2,961	2,544	2,577	1,376	0.06	-46.60
Other countries of Asia	2,971	2,922	2,511	2,534	1,294	0.05	-48.93
Other countries of Oceania		39	33	43	82	0.00	90.70
EUROPE	2,304,366	2,299,530	2,039,961	2,055,439	2,278,934	95.26	10.87
Central/Eastern Europe	246,253	286,663	245,429	325,061	463,583	19.38	42.61
Bulgaria	10,088	10,675	8,922	8,905	10,247	0.43	15.07
Belarus	2,405	2,125	2,186	3,507	3,371	0.14	-3.88
Czech Republic	20,972	20,027	20,477	15,458	20,576	0.86	33.11
Estonia	894	1,884	2,077	970	2,074	0.09	113.81
Georgia	204	95	195	146	141	0.01	-3.42
Hungary	10,086	9,641	9,700	10,721	11,334	0.47	5.72
Latvia	3,183	2,150	1,538	1,825	1,934	0.08	5.97
Lithuania	3,181	2,294	1,423	2,546	2,182	0.09	-14.30
Poland	16,669	20,358	17,186	18,439	24,236	1.01	31.44
Romania	14,527	20,346	19,931	19,980	30,601	1.28	53.16
Russian Federation	145,921	180,926	148,740	223,861	334,083	13.97	49.24
Slovakia	5,179	5,048	3,719	5,061	5,030	0.21	-0.61
Ukraine	8,729	8,847	7,496	11,766	14,274	0.60	21.32
Other countries Central/East Europe	4,215	2,247	1,839	1,876	3,500	0.15	86.57
Northern Europe	1,549,656	1,525,535	1,318,879	1,243,031	1,277,048	53.38	2.74
Denmark	34,759	38,216	29,667	30,335	34,064	1.42	12.29
Finland	21,461	32,333	32,758	32,886	36,289	1.52	10.35
Iceland	257	281	223	144	88	0.00	-38.89
Ireland	35,875	23,632	18,537	10,527	9,662	0.40	-8.22
Norway	53,442	63,470	60,245	63,347	64,024	2.68	1.07
Sweden	120,989	124,948	108,253	109,746	112,212	4.69	2.25
United Kingdom	1,282,873	1,242,655	1,069,196	996,046	1,020,709	42.67	2.48
Southern Europe	172,502	162,722	162,546	154,782	172,168	7.20	11.23
Greece	139,815	133,015	131,875	127,667	138,721	5.80	8.66
Italy	19,225	16,859	15,604	12,992	16,828	0.70	29.53
Malta	3,266	3,421	6,154	4,358	4,511	0.19	3.51
Montenegro	174	68	104	168	86	0.00	-48.81

CYPRUS

1. Arrivals of non-resident tourists at national borders, by country of residence

	2007	2008	2009	2010	2011	Market share 11	% Change 11-10
Portugal	1,148	855	1,106	1,161	1,034	0.04	-10.94
Serbia	2,817	3,322	3,678	3,431	3,986	0.17	16.18
Slovenia	1,939	1,541	953	1,046	2,245	0.09	114.63
Spain	4,118	3,641	3,072	3,959	4,757	0.20	20.16
Western Europe	**300,106**	**290,362**	**280,455**	**292,856**	**333,038**	**13.92**	**13.72**
Austria	24,359	26,620	27,463	21,559	23,341	0.98	8.27
Belgium	23,174	26,368	22,966	24,125	27,346	1.14	13.35
France	41,394	36,099	26,187	28,749	34,363	1.44	19.53
Germany	138,451	132,058	131,161	139,190	157,890	6.60	13.43
Luxembourg	4,671	4,355	3,020	3,374	3,154	0.13	-6.52
Netherlands	26,650	26,302	30,996	34,212	41,631	1.74	21.69
Switzerland	41,407	38,560	38,662	41,647	45,313	1.89	8.80
East Mediterranean Europe	**34,451**	**32,169**	**31,480**	**38,197**	**32,174**	**1.34**	**-15.77**
Israel	34,205	32,034	31,364	37,876	31,910	1.33	-15.75
Turkey	246	135	116	321	264	0.01	-17.76
Other Europe	**1,398**	**2,079**	**1,172**	**1,512**	**923**	**0.04**	**-38.96**
Other countries of Europe	1,398	2,079	1,172	1,512	923	0.04	-38.96
MIDDLE EAST	**50,896**	**48,280**	**49,947**	**51,110**	**50,799**	**2.12**	**-0.61**
Bahrain	2,297	2,790	2,970	2,184	1,766	0.07	-19.14
Iraq	164	58	89	358	1,409	0.06	293.58
Jordan	3,567	3,071	4,040	3,575	4,184	0.17	17.03
Kuwait	5,546	4,049	2,544	1,480	1,268	0.05	-14.32
Lebanon	14,635	14,192	15,431	20,664	21,202	0.89	2.60
Libya	447	449	408	298	145	0.01	-51.34
Saudi Arabia	3,873	2,978	2,071	2,463	1,445	0.06	-41.33
Syrian Arab Republic	2,143	1,392	1,455	1,626	983	0.04	-39.54
United Arab Emirates	10,705	12,853	14,197	11,832	11,433	0.48	-3.37
Egypt	5,706	4,351	5,067	4,324	4,940	0.21	14.25
Other countries of Middle East	1,813	2,097	1,675	2,306	2,024	0.08	-12.23
SOUTH ASIA	**6,432**	**3,751**	**5,020**	**8,406**	**6,963**	**0.29**	**-17.17**
Iran, Islamic Republic of	2,731	1,799	3,627	4,336	5,742	0.24	32.43
Other countries of South Asia	3,701	1,952	1,393	4,070	1,221	0.05	-70.00
NOT SPECIFIED	**348**	**310**	**635**	**1,112**	**302**	**0.01**	**-72.84**
Other countries of the World	348	310	635	1,112	302	0.01	-72.84

CYPRUS

3. Arrivals of non-resident tourists in hotels and similar establishments, by country of residence

	2007	2008	2009	2010	2011	Market share 11	% Change 11-10
TOTAL	1,775,447	1,753,561	1,646,564	1,788,372	1,921,951	100.00	7.47
AFRICA	1,005	1,055	1,529	2,201	2,090	0.11	-5.04
Southern Africa	1,005	1,055	1,529	2,201	2,090	0.11	-5.04
South Africa	1,005	1,055	1,529	2,201	2,090	0.11	-5.04
AMERICAS	16,886	15,799	19,706	23,951	23,828	1.24	-0.51
North America	16,886	15,799	19,706	23,951	23,828	1.24	-0.51
Canada	6,929	6,059	9,155	10,709	9,917	0.52	-7.40
United States of America	9,957	9,740	10,551	13,242	13,911	0.72	5.05
EAST ASIA AND THE PACIFIC	6,067	7,378	8,535	9,616	8,247	0.43	-14.24
North-East Asia	3,230	2,609	3,585	4,339	4,199	0.22	-3.23
China	776	1,084	1,405	1,631	1,533	0.08	-6.01
Japan	2,454	1,525	2,180	2,708	2,666	0.14	-1.55
Australasia	2,837	4,769	4,950	5,277	4,048	0.21	-23.29
Australia	2,837	4,769	4,950	5,277	4,048	0.21	-23.29
EUROPE	1,647,166	1,637,978	1,517,681	1,642,363	1,768,517	92.02	7.68
Central/Eastern Europe	197,867	223,495	187,270	268,914	379,716	19.76	41.20
Bulgaria	4,234	3,734	3,726	3,971	4,357	0.23	9.72
Czech Republic	17,843	16,566	15,396	16,037	18,965	0.99	18.26
Estonia	1,641	1,051	1,985	1,381	1,579	0.08	14.34
Hungary	9,465	7,229	6,162	7,934	7,425	0.39	-6.42
Latvia	1,262	914	1,016	1,273	953	0.05	-25.14
Lithuania	1,672	929	2,043	3,051	1,176	0.06	-61.46
Poland	13,529	15,490	15,517	19,388	24,404	1.27	25.87
Romania	8,728	10,030	9,511	10,109	14,551	0.76	43.94
Russian Federation	136,838	163,831	128,174	201,250	302,423	15.74	50.27
Slovakia	2,655	3,721	3,740	4,520	3,883	0.20	-14.09
Northern Europe	1,044,099	1,038,101	943,525	941,827	946,180	49.23	0.46
Denmark	25,847	23,574	22,626	25,714	25,307	1.32	-1.58
Finland	17,262	25,532	28,168	30,466	33,941	1.77	11.41
Iceland	2,875	2,235	4,314	2,583	4,903	0.26	89.82
Ireland	17,087	13,518	14,293	12,076	10,106	0.53	-16.31
Norway	40,114	51,799	57,228	63,207	69,191	3.60	9.47
Sweden	91,547	105,019	101,245	104,324	108,476	5.64	3.98
United Kingdom	849,367	816,424	715,651	703,457	694,256	36.12	-1.31
Southern Europe	115,147	98,303	100,933	108,677	114,691	5.97	5.53
Greece	70,813	66,349	68,394	74,281	74,791	3.89	0.69
Italy	23,239	22,151	18,170	19,472	22,121	1.15	13.60
Malta	1,701	1,406	5,543	4,299	5,013	0.26	16.61
Portugal	13,529	2,081	2,523	2,514	2,921	0.15	16.19
Slovenia	1,277	1,875	1,533	1,595	2,411	0.13	51.16
Spain	4,588	4,441	4,770	6,516	7,434	0.39	14.09
Western Europe	290,053	278,079	285,953	322,945	327,930	17.06	1.54
Austria	17,631	18,643	20,036	21,459	19,477	1.01	-9.24
Belgium	18,322	19,989	20,850	24,017	25,434	1.32	5.90
France	54,224	46,227	36,571	47,785	50,169	2.61	4.99
Germany	142,313	139,640	147,826	159,998	155,843	8.11	-2.60
Luxembourg	2,348	2,505	3,625	3,248	2,654	0.14	-18.29
Netherlands	22,462	23,523	27,573	33,077	40,683	2.12	22.99
Switzerland	32,753	27,552	29,472	33,361	33,670	1.75	0.93
NOT SPECIFIED	104,323	91,351	99,113	110,241	119,269	6.21	8.19
Other countries of the World	104,323	91,351	99,113	110,241	119,269	6.21	8.19

CYPRUS

4. Arrivals of non-resident tourists in all types of accommodation establishments, by country of residence

	2007	2008	2009	2010	2011	Market share 11	% Change 11-10
TOTAL	1,784,735	1,761,777	1,671,864	1,814,328	1,947,446	100.00	7.34
AFRICA	1,005	1,068	1,655	2,347	2,220	0.11	-5.41
Southern Africa	1,005	1,068	1,655	2,347	2,220	0.11	-5.41
South Africa	1,005	1,068	1,655	2,347	2,220	0.11	-5.41
AMERICAS	16,939	15,816	20,054	24,394	24,223	1.24	-0.70
North America	16,939	15,816	20,054	24,394	24,223	1.24	-0.70
Canada	6,929	6,061	9,289	10,872	10,077	0.52	-7.31
United States of America	10,010	9,755	10,765	13,522	14,146	0.73	4.61
EAST ASIA AND THE PACIFIC	6,069	7,385	8,900	10,055	8,681	0.45	-13.66
North-East Asia	3,230	2,609	3,804	4,616	4,469	0.23	-3.18
China	776	1,084	1,508	1,760	1,656	0.09	-5.91
Japan	2,454	1,525	2,296	2,856	2,813	0.14	-1.51
Australasia	2,839	4,776	5,096	5,439	4,212	0.22	-22.56
Australia	2,839	4,776	5,096	5,439	4,212	0.22	-22.56
EUROPE	1,644,677	1,645,990	1,540,209	1,665,018	1,791,403	91.99	7.59
Central/Eastern Europe	198,046	223,693	189,726	272,261	383,165	19.68	40.73
Bulgaria	4,236	3,744	3,877	4,162	4,533	0.23	8.91
Czech Republic	17,871	16,599	15,637	16,330	19,240	0.99	17.82
Estonia	1,641	1,051	2,099	1,500	1,714	0.09	14.27
Hungary	9,479	7,242	6,332	8,139	7,613	0.39	-6.46
Latvia	1,268	914	1,117	1,381	1,054	0.05	-23.68
Lithuania	1,672	929	2,144	3,179	1,279	0.07	-59.77
Poland	13,540	15,510	15,733	19,654	24,667	1.27	25.51
Romania	8,755	10,049	9,733	10,375	14,857	0.76	43.20
Russian Federation	136,918	163,920	129,186	202,889	304,189	15.62	49.93
Slovakia	2,666	3,735	3,868	4,652	4,019	0.21	-13.61
Northern Europe	1,051,997	1,044,932	958,753	955,346	959,568	49.27	0.44
Denmark	25,952	23,915	22,908	26,262	25,739	1.32	-1.99
Finland	17,272	25,626	28,524	30,849	34,320	1.76	11.25
Iceland	2,879	2,237	4,489	2,713	5,066	0.26	86.73
Ireland	17,141	13,552	14,481	12,276	10,353	0.53	-15.66
Norway	40,280	52,139	57,889	63,828	70,261	3.61	10.08
Sweden	91,881	105,158	105,194	107,581	111,753	5.74	3.88
United Kingdom	856,592	822,305	725,268	711,837	702,076	36.05	-1.37
Southern Europe	103,634	98,416	102,381	110,235	116,239	5.97	5.45
Greece	70,842	66,396	68,936	74,873	75,314	3.87	0.59
Italy	23,278	22,212	18,449	19,850	22,487	1.15	13.28
Malta	1,701	1,406	5,709	4,477	5,219	0.27	16.57
Portugal	1,939	2,083	2,729	2,633	3,057	0.16	16.10
Slovenia	1,279	1,875	1,628	1,706	2,529	0.13	48.24
Spain	4,595	4,444	4,930	6,696	7,633	0.39	13.99
Western Europe	291,000	278,949	289,349	327,176	332,431	17.07	1.61
Austria	17,747	18,703	20,317	21,777	19,806	1.02	-9.05
Belgium	18,351	20,061	21,168	24,351	25,789	1.32	5.91
France	54,467	46,468	37,104	48,519	50,806	2.61	4.71
Germany	142,679	139,980	149,064	161,708	157,835	8.10	-2.40
Luxembourg	2,349	2,506	3,786	3,415	2,816	0.14	-17.54
Netherlands	22,549	23,647	28,042	33,621	41,286	2.12	22.80
Switzerland	32,858	27,584	29,868	33,785	34,093	1.75	0.91
NOT SPECIFIED	116,045	91,518	101,046	112,514	120,919	6.21	7.47
Other countries of the World	116,045	91,518	101,046	112,514	120,919	6.21	7.47

CYPRUS

5. Overnight stays of non-resident tourists in hotels and similar establishments, by country of residence

	2007	2008	2009	2010	2011	Market share 11	% Change 11-10
TOTAL	13,129,131	13,151,048	11,488,361	12,267,921	12,933,024	100.00	5.42
AFRICA	3,915	3,783	5,355	7,581	8,262	0.06	8.98
Southern Africa	3,915	3,783	5,355	7,581	8,262	0.06	8.98
South Africa	3,915	3,783	5,355	7,581	8,262	0.06	8.98
AMERICAS	70,629	66,888	87,796	92,594	99,121	0.77	7.05
North America	70,629	66,888	87,796	92,594	99,121	0.77	7.05
Canada	31,460	28,464	47,940	46,115	54,906	0.42	19.06
United States of America	39,169	38,424	39,856	46,479	44,215	0.34	-4.87
EAST ASIA AND THE PACIFIC	20,870	27,613	32,763	31,498	24,997	0.19	-20.64
North-East Asia	8,625	8,156	9,652	11,079	10,421	0.08	-5.94
China	2,896	4,391	4,388	4,974	4,764	0.04	-4.22
Japan	5,729	3,765	5,264	6,105	5,657	0.04	-7.34
Australasia	12,245	19,457	23,111	20,419	14,576	0.11	-28.62
Australia	12,245	19,457	23,111	20,419	14,576	0.11	-28.62
EUROPE	12,566,773	12,658,846	10,968,124	11,725,629	12,322,509	95.28	5.09
Central/Eastern Europe	1,463,562	1,705,779	1,389,566	2,023,462	2,708,095	20.94	33.83
Bulgaria	30,582	21,368	21,800	23,259	21,767	0.17	-6.41
Czech Republic	130,243	123,123	115,004	110,833	126,912	0.98	14.51
Estonia	8,814	6,876	11,952	7,592	8,054	0.06	6.09
Hungary	45,693	41,018	34,447	40,934	39,560	0.31	-3.36
Latvia	7,121	4,610	4,182	6,302	3,555	0.03	-43.59
Lithuania	8,993	5,276	11,251	18,392	4,501	0.03	-75.53
Poland	104,767	125,237	114,197	141,083	164,444	1.27	16.56
Romania	41,680	47,034	42,316	51,588	70,293	0.54	36.26
Russian Federation	1,069,021	1,304,608	1,009,963	1,594,304	2,244,688	17.36	40.79
Slovakia	16,648	26,629	24,454	29,175	24,321	0.19	-16.64
Northern Europe	8,633,647	8,473,944	7,145,584	7,033,697	6,894,782	53.31	-1.97
Denmark	183,356	173,196	166,314	184,340	177,212	1.37	-3.87
Finland	145,318	186,566	191,165	215,030	223,188	1.73	3.79
Iceland	15,707	15,070	33,531	15,771	40,591	0.31	157.38
Ireland	124,610	98,282	94,174	76,487	51,280	0.40	-32.96
Norway	434,121	511,293	430,975	519,232	530,107	4.10	2.09
Sweden	822,854	857,287	754,013	803,474	775,120	5.99	-3.53
United Kingdom	6,907,681	6,632,250	5,475,412	5,219,363	5,097,284	39.41	-2.34
Southern Europe	396,502	389,444	382,878	395,405	394,850	3.05	-0.14
Greece	236,850	222,743	237,930	234,997	232,519	1.80	-1.05
Italy	119,526	118,840	87,210	91,616	90,120	0.70	-1.63
Malta	8,327	6,342	22,334	21,081	22,393	0.17	6.22
Portugal	7,774	11,942	10,543	13,182	11,605	0.09	-11.96
Slovenia	6,671	11,419	8,672	9,115	12,613	0.10	38.38
Spain	17,354	18,158	16,189	25,414	25,600	0.20	0.73
Western Europe	2,073,062	2,089,679	2,050,096	2,273,065	2,324,782	17.98	2.28
Austria	128,500	144,870	142,865	155,367	142,150	1.10	-8.51
Belgium	127,825	144,906	147,207	171,904	166,798	1.29	-2.97
France	264,012	231,656	171,133	218,898	245,568	1.90	12.18
Germany	1,128,888	1,170,838	1,149,174	1,219,945	1,216,119	9.40	-0.31
Luxembourg	16,755	19,502	23,852	23,025	19,346	0.15	-15.98
Netherlands	149,636	154,421	182,201	221,999	275,127	2.13	23.93
Switzerland	257,446	223,486	233,664	261,927	259,674	2.01	-0.86
NOT SPECIFIED	466,944	393,918	394,323	410,619	478,135	3.70	16.44
Other countries of the World	466,944	393,918	394,323	410,619	478,135	3.70	16.44

CYPRUS

6. Overnight stays of non-resident tourists in all types of accommodation establishments, by country of residence

	2007	2008	2009	2010	2011	Market share 11	% Change 11-10
TOTAL	13,197,004	13,208,954	11,666,663	12,448,159	13,112,597	100.00	5.34
AFRICA	3,915	3,804	5,827	8,163	8,790	0.07	7.68
Southern Africa	3,915	3,804	5,827	8,163	8,790	0.07	7.68
South Africa	3,915	3,804	5,827	8,163	8,790	0.07	7.68
AMERICAS	70,629	66,974	89,289	94,657	100,766	0.77	6.45
North America	70,629	66,974	89,289	94,657	100,766	0.77	6.45
Canada	31,460	28,520	48,525	46,820	55,546	0.42	18.64
United States of America	39,169	38,454	40,764	47,837	45,220	0.34	-5.47
EAST ASIA AND THE PACIFIC	20,876	27,620	34,465	33,151	26,656	0.20	-19.59
North-East Asia	8,625	8,156	10,748	12,038	11,369	0.09	-5.56
China	2,896	4,391	4,766	5,486	5,262	0.04	-4.08
Japan	5,729	3,765	5,982	6,552	6,107	0.05	-6.79
Australasia	12,251	19,464	23,717	21,113	15,287	0.12	-27.59
Australia	12,251	19,464	23,717	21,113	15,287	0.12	-27.59
EUROPE	12,645,419	12,798,536	11,134,307	11,890,914	12,487,513	95.23	5.02
Central/Eastern Europe	1,475,801	1,789,421	1,405,506	2,046,319	2,729,730	20.82	33.40
Bulgaria	41,960	21,383	22,507	24,184	22,549	0.17	-6.76
Czech Republic	130,292	123,302	116,430	112,649	128,604	0.98	14.16
Estonia	8,814	6,876	12,519	8,199	8,699	0.07	6.10
Hungary	45,754	41,084	35,277	42,361	40,592	0.31	-4.18
Latvia	7,133	4,610	4,592	6,820	3,978	0.03	-41.67
Lithuania	8,993	5,276	11,731	18,999	4,908	0.04	-74.17
Poland	104,787	125,331	115,410	142,645	165,858	1.26	16.27
Romania	41,960	129,695	43,424	53,018	71,825	0.55	35.47
Russian Federation	1,069,436	1,305,211	1,018,545	1,607,554	2,257,729	17.22	40.44
Slovakia	16,672	26,653	25,071	29,890	24,988	0.19	-16.40
Northern Europe	8,695,022	8,525,033	7,268,409	7,141,690	7,000,579	53.39	-1.98
Denmark	183,892	175,193	167,784	187,791	179,754	1.37	-4.28
Finland	145,346	186,745	193,340	217,471	225,410	1.72	3.65
Iceland	15,747	15,072	34,385	16,338	41,247	0.31	152.46
Ireland	124,911	98,531	95,163	77,765	52,862	0.40	-32.02
Norway	434,895	514,070	435,388	523,564	539,137	4.11	2.97
Sweden	825,199	857,700	786,829	831,000	797,679	6.08	-4.01
United Kingdom	6,965,032	6,677,722	5,555,520	5,287,761	5,164,490	39.39	-2.33
Southern Europe	396,762	389,744	389,138	402,525	402,342	3.07	-0.05
Greece	236,990	222,674	240,230	237,444	234,764	1.79	-1.13
Italy	119,619	119,188	88,416	93,534	92,264	0.70	-1.36
Malta	8,327	6,342	23,036	21,963	23,309	0.18	6.13
Portugal	7,776	11,946	11,532	13,747	12,384	0.09	-9.91
Slovenia	6,673	11,419	9,126	9,683	13,137	0.10	35.67
Spain	17,377	18,175	16,798	26,154	26,484	0.20	1.26
Western Europe	2,077,834	2,094,338	2,071,254	2,300,380	2,354,862	17.96	2.37
Austria	129,475	145,002	144,525	157,408	144,218	1.10	-8.38
Belgium	127,880	145,214	149,130	173,863	168,537	1.29	-3.06
France	264,675	232,228	173,554	222,107	248,492	1.90	11.88
Germany	1,130,821	1,173,741	1,158,271	1,232,561	1,231,935	9.40	-0.05
Luxembourg	16,757	19,504	24,734	24,138	20,466	0.16	-15.21
Netherlands	150,333	154,927	184,973	225,595	279,000	2.13	23.67
Switzerland	257,893	223,722	236,067	264,708	262,214	2.00	-0.94
NOT SPECIFIED	456,165	312,020	402,775	421,274	488,872	3.73	16.05
Other countries of the World	456,165	312,020	402,775	421,274	488,872	3.73	16.05

CZECH REPUBLIC

3. Arrivals of non-resident tourists in hotels and similar establishments, by nationality

	2007	2008	2009	2010	2011	Market share 11	% Change 11-10
TOTAL	6,098,495	6,134,720	5,609,025	5,974,227	6,376,697	100.00	6.74
AFRICA	18,153	21,335	18,592	24,290	28,423	0.45	17.02
Southern Africa	3,827	5,257	4,068	5,163	6,039	0.09	16.97
South Africa	3,827	5,257	4,068	5,163	6,039	0.09	16.97
Other Africa	14,326	16,078	14,524	19,127	22,384	0.35	17.03
Other countries of Africa	14,326	16,078	14,524	19,127	22,384	0.35	17.03
AMERICAS	414,396	412,037	379,615	440,387	465,364	7.30	5.67
North America	365,529	349,305	317,828	367,084	380,253	5.96	3.59
Canada	44,325	43,836	42,793	50,930	54,163	0.85	6.35
Mexico	15,369	15,207	12,806	16,215	20,811	0.33	28.34
United States of America	305,835	290,262	262,229	299,939	305,279	4.79	1.78
South America	19,059	24,890	28,590	36,781	42,360	0.66	15.17
Brazil	19,059	24,890	28,590	36,781	42,360	0.66	15.17
Other Americas	29,808	37,842	33,197	36,522	42,751	0.67	17.06
Other countries of the Americas	29,808	37,842	33,197	36,522	42,751	0.67	17.06
EAST ASIA AND THE PACIFIC	477,172	479,744	465,479	568,741	657,245	10.31	15.56
North-East Asia	246,768	237,659	225,361	283,759	320,947	5.03	13.11
China	36,376	50,664	59,429	76,809	105,878	1.66	37.85
Japan	134,075	120,937	112,814	131,223	119,914	1.88	-8.62
Korea, Republic of	76,317	66,058	53,118	75,727	95,155	1.49	25.66
Australasia	47,053	54,376	49,562	62,352	70,335	1.10	12.80
Australia	41,111	48,102	43,906	56,021	63,076	0.99	12.59
New Zealand	5,942	6,274	5,656	6,331	7,259	0.11	14.66
Other East Asia and the Pacific	183,351	187,709	190,556	222,630	265,963	4.17	19.46
Other countries of Asia	180,230	181,880	185,660	217,234	260,872	4.09	20.09
Other countries of Oceania	3,121	5,829	4,896	5,396	5,091	0.08	-5.65
EUROPE	5,188,774	5,221,604	4,745,339	4,940,809	5,225,665	81.95	5.77
Central/Eastern Europe	1,081,383	1,300,779	1,137,156	1,304,962	1,535,280	24.08	17.65
Bulgaria	15,975	18,805	17,365	19,836	21,551	0.34	8.65
Estonia	16,551	18,422	12,665	11,431	15,523	0.24	35.80
Hungary	88,246	93,706	82,669	96,623	102,198	1.60	5.77
Latvia	20,136	19,720	9,488	8,100	9,383	0.15	15.84
Lithuania	55,754	60,936	41,511	40,552	45,460	0.71	12.10
Poland	253,647	329,189	299,525	313,918	338,014	5.30	7.68
Romania	32,624	45,174	46,185	49,199	56,227	0.88	14.28
Russian Federation	291,957	395,222	310,294	398,438	537,268	8.43	34.84
Slovakia	249,936	250,488	244,896	266,218	303,921	4.77	14.16
Ukraine	56,557	69,117	72,558	100,647	105,735	1.66	5.06
Northern Europe	895,191	827,233	688,439	688,224	626,261	9.82	-9.00
Denmark	96,997	96,653	89,481	101,251	89,329	1.40	-11.77
Finland	44,673	45,799	40,005	39,078	43,167	0.68	10.46
Iceland	3,970	4,211	3,455	3,398	3,466	0.05	2.00
Ireland	46,561	52,702	32,023	26,738	21,432	0.34	-19.84
Norway	79,688	75,150	83,501	75,919	69,917	1.10	-7.91
Sweden	71,922	80,732	77,632	82,417	78,400	1.23	-4.87
United Kingdom	551,380	471,986	362,342	359,423	320,550	5.03	-10.82
Southern Europe	808,537	781,685	700,884	673,630	717,798	11.26	6.56
Croatia	39,078	39,886	36,500	39,580	46,977	0.74	18.69
Greece	60,779	73,316	65,694	50,063	43,496	0.68	-13.12
Italy	397,695	362,496	344,667	323,854	328,612	5.15	1.47
Malta	3,147	2,040	1,766	1,869	2,346	0.04	25.52
Portugal	24,434	25,864	26,419	26,016	23,362	0.37	-10.20
Slovenia	20,896	24,027	24,037	23,007	24,318	0.38	5.70

CZECH REPUBLIC

3. Arrivals of non-resident tourists in hotels and similar establishments, by nationality

	2007	2008	2009	2010	2011	Market share 11	% Change 11-10
Spain	250,028	241,092	188,430	190,279	220,938	3.46	16.11
Serbia and Montenegro	12,480	12,964	13,371	18,962	27,749	0.44	46.34
Western Europe	**2,095,256**	**2,031,777**	**1,955,883**	**1,990,148**	**2,070,982**	**32.48**	**4.06**
Austria	168,711	162,387	169,803	183,098	177,819	2.79	-2.88
Belgium	72,625	79,199	80,144	78,195	80,078	1.26	2.41
France	222,154	222,388	209,956	240,675	272,209	4.27	13.10
Germany	1,384,781	1,337,372	1,278,621	1,258,852	1,303,329	20.44	3.53
Liechtenstein	852	746	811	896	901	0.01	0.56
Luxembourg	3,169	3,486	5,332	5,038	4,952	0.08	-1.71
Netherlands	166,303	161,627	146,862	151,359	159,089	2.49	5.11
Switzerland	76,661	64,572	64,354	72,035	72,605	1.14	0.79
East Mediterranean Europe	**93,917**	**99,320**	**119,407**	**135,419**	**136,255**	**2.14**	**0.62**
Cyprus	8,491	7,779	7,811	8,154	7,510	0.12	-7.90
Israel	52,149	56,570	78,561	81,980	80,716	1.27	-1.54
Turkey	33,277	34,971	33,035	45,285	48,029	0.75	6.06
Other Europe	**214,490**	**180,810**	**143,570**	**148,426**	**139,089**	**2.18**	**-6.29**
Other countries of Europe	214,490	180,810	143,570	148,426	139,089	2.18	-6.29

CZECH REPUBLIC

4. Arrivals of non-resident tourists in all types of accommodation establishments, by nationality

	2007	2008	2009	2010	2011	Market share 11	% Change 11-10
TOTAL	6,679,704	6,649,410	6,032,370	6,333,996	6,715,067	100.00	6.02
AFRICA	19,520	22,934	20,191	25,981	29,759	0.44	14.54
Southern Africa	4,224	5,566	4,445	5,365	6,184	0.09	15.27
South Africa	4,224	5,566	4,445	5,365	6,184	0.09	15.27
Other Africa	15,296	17,368	15,746	20,616	23,575	0.35	14.35
Other countries of Africa	15,296	17,368	15,746	20,616	23,575	0.35	14.35
AMERICAS	441,493	434,061	397,586	460,259	480,668	7.16	4.43
North America	388,747	368,699	333,235	384,163	393,061	5.85	2.32
Canada	49,893	47,518	45,549	54,004	56,615	0.84	4.83
Mexico	16,640	16,124	13,375	17,276	21,496	0.32	24.43
United States of America	322,214	305,057	274,311	312,883	314,950	4.69	0.66
South America	21,225	26,106	29,634	37,811	43,248	0.64	14.38
Brazil	21,225	26,106	29,634	37,811	43,248	0.64	14.38
Other Americas	31,521	39,256	34,717	38,285	44,359	0.66	15.87
Other countries of the Americas	31,521	39,256	34,717	38,285	44,359	0.66	15.87
EAST ASIA AND THE PACIFIC	503,899	501,793	484,815	586,903	673,850	10.03	14.81
North-East Asia	254,583	244,861	232,015	289,925	326,897	4.87	12.75
China	38,421	53,108	61,798	79,186	108,629	1.62	37.18
Japan	136,587	123,275	114,777	133,052	121,663	1.81	-8.56
Korea, Republic of	79,575	68,478	55,440	77,687	96,605	1.44	24.35
Australasia	57,450	61,772	55,669	67,676	74,787	1.11	10.51
Australia	49,768	54,361	48,715	60,240	66,783	0.99	10.86
New Zealand	7,682	7,411	6,954	7,436	8,004	0.12	7.64
Other East Asia and the Pacific	191,866	195,160	197,131	229,302	272,166	4.05	18.69
Other countries of Asia	188,615	189,037	192,021	223,236	266,790	3.97	19.51
Other countries of Oceania	3,251	6,123	5,110	6,066	5,376	0.08	-11.37
EUROPE	5,714,792	5,690,622	5,129,778	5,260,853	5,530,790	82.36	5.13
Central/Eastern Europe	1,244,462	1,451,205	1,258,082	1,417,334	1,646,597	24.52	16.18
Bulgaria	18,491	21,394	18,713	20,970	22,613	0.34	7.84
Estonia	18,393	20,689	13,480	12,505	16,288	0.24	30.25
Hungary	99,154	103,826	90,096	103,485	107,689	1.60	4.06
Latvia	20,949	20,501	9,998	8,502	10,098	0.15	18.77
Lithuania	61,453	66,180	45,168	44,550	48,737	0.73	9.40
Poland	298,621	376,592	341,136	350,637	371,127	5.53	5.84
Romania	35,118	48,435	48,367	50,762	57,484	0.86	13.24
Russian Federation	321,520	418,184	326,895	414,671	559,021	8.32	34.81
Slovakia	309,255	299,278	287,810	307,192	344,101	5.12	12.01
Ukraine	61,508	76,126	76,419	104,060	109,439	1.63	5.17
Northern Europe	932,468	864,446	716,102	712,788	646,218	9.62	-9.34
Denmark	109,935	108,552	99,563	109,292	96,311	1.43	-11.88
Finland	47,105	48,270	42,537	40,690	44,599	0.66	9.61
Iceland	4,119	4,940	3,535	3,509	3,518	0.05	0.26
Ireland	48,615	54,447	33,159	28,152	22,366	0.33	-20.55
Norway	81,445	79,773	85,001	77,343	70,948	1.06	-8.27
Sweden	75,779	84,185	80,961	85,159	80,525	1.20	-5.44
United Kingdom	565,470	484,279	371,346	368,643	327,951	4.88	-11.04
Southern Europe	837,415	806,322	726,129	693,609	736,824	10.97	6.23
Croatia	40,448	41,219	38,268	40,889	48,192	0.72	17.86
Greece	61,982	74,737	66,648	51,002	44,054	0.66	-13.62
Italy	413,085	374,632	357,492	332,551	337,645	5.03	1.53
Malta	3,283	2,172	1,803	1,916	2,407	0.04	25.63
Portugal	25,790	26,896	27,482	27,088	24,416	0.36	-9.86
Slovenia	22,836	25,723	26,009	24,480	26,045	0.39	6.39

CZECH REPUBLIC

4. Arrivals of non-resident tourists in all types of accommodation establishments, by nationality

	2007	2008	2009	2010	2011	Market share 11	% Change 11-10
Spain	256,722	247,240	194,406	196,011	225,778	3.36	15.19
Serbia and Montenegro	13,269	13,703	14,021	19,672	28,287	0.42	43.79
Western Europe	**2,376,428**	**2,277,650**	**2,160,024**	**2,148,046**	**2,220,718**	**33.07**	**3.38**
Austria	177,170	170,663	177,715	189,886	185,719	2.77	-2.19
Belgium	80,360	87,240	87,851	83,404	85,316	1.27	2.29
France	236,790	235,654	223,901	251,468	283,480	4.22	12.73
Germany	1,549,441	1,475,858	1,393,112	1,348,482	1,386,976	20.65	2.85
Liechtenstein	907	777	911	915	924	0.01	0.98
Luxembourg	3,421	3,697	5,415	5,323	5,054	0.08	-5.05
Netherlands	247,861	236,193	203,764	194,138	197,975	2.95	1.98
Switzerland	80,478	67,568	67,355	74,430	75,274	1.12	1.13
East Mediterranean Europe	**97,539**	**103,394**	**122,784**	**138,512**	**139,223**	**2.07**	**0.51**
Cyprus	8,722	8,249	7,987	8,278	7,643	0.11	-7.67
Israel	54,579	59,102	80,634	83,997	82,346	1.23	-1.97
Turkey	34,238	36,043	34,163	46,237	49,234	0.73	6.48
Other Europe	**226,480**	**187,605**	**146,657**	**150,564**	**141,210**	**2.10**	**-6.21**
Other countries of Europe	226,480	187,605	146,657	150,564	141,210	2.10	-6.21

CZECH REPUBLIC

5. Overnight stays of non-resident tourists in hotels and similar establishments, by nationality

	2007	2008	2009	2010	2011	Market share 11	% Change 11-10
TOTAL	17,837,519	17,740,781	16,013,046	16,880,869	18,027,007	100.00	6.79
AFRICA	61,493	70,029	56,814	71,152	78,046	0.43	9.69
Southern Africa	10,799	13,983	11,496	13,241	15,061	0.08	13.75
South Africa	10,799	13,983	11,496	13,241	15,061	0.08	13.75
Other Africa	50,694	56,046	45,318	57,911	62,985	0.35	8.76
Other countries of Africa	50,694	56,046	45,318	57,911	62,985	0.35	8.76
AMERICAS	1,175,346	1,115,514	1,010,235	1,155,862	1,216,515	6.75	5.25
North America	1,042,620	951,647	846,664	964,078	992,152	5.50	2.91
Canada	126,544	125,195	120,114	143,566	149,447	0.83	4.10
Mexico	40,190	37,196	30,065	39,002	50,339	0.28	29.07
United States of America	875,886	789,256	696,485	781,510	792,366	4.40	1.39
South America	52,030	67,613	74,753	98,668	115,350	0.64	16.91
Brazil	52,030	67,613	74,753	98,668	115,350	0.64	16.91
Other Americas	80,696	96,254	88,818	93,116	109,013	0.60	17.07
Other countries of the Americas	80,696	96,254	88,818	93,116	109,013	0.60	17.07
EAST ASIA AND THE PACIFIC	1,020,975	1,015,958	966,083	1,161,176	1,316,457	7.30	13.37
North-East Asia	479,110	440,710	407,374	494,443	555,377	3.08	12.32
China	72,181	96,850	106,193	132,195	182,071	1.01	37.73
Japan	288,416	244,465	219,406	247,050	230,877	1.28	-6.55
Korea, Republic of	118,513	99,395	81,775	115,198	142,429	0.79	23.64
Australasia	126,249	142,470	124,008	155,166	172,989	0.96	11.49
Australia	108,884	126,479	109,769	138,896	154,612	0.86	11.31
New Zealand	17,365	15,991	14,239	16,270	18,377	0.10	12.95
Other East Asia and the Pacific	415,616	432,778	434,701	511,567	588,091	3.26	14.96
Other countries of Asia	407,485	420,073	422,923	499,778	576,267	3.20	15.30
Other countries of Oceania	8,131	12,705	11,778	11,789	11,824	0.07	0.30
EUROPE	15,579,705	15,539,280	13,979,914	14,492,679	15,415,989	85.52	6.37
Central/Eastern Europe	3,320,341	3,910,107	3,313,849	3,879,450	4,806,764	26.66	23.90
Bulgaria	43,294	45,019	39,862	43,634	49,264	0.27	12.90
Estonia	35,045	40,000	29,788	22,053	31,360	0.17	42.20
Hungary	203,826	204,991	174,756	213,690	223,134	1.24	4.42
Latvia	34,002	33,319	18,286	15,558	19,164	0.11	23.18
Lithuania	85,581	88,613	65,956	64,702	71,018	0.39	9.76
Poland	514,796	662,994	618,352	649,343	693,354	3.85	6.78
Romania	80,786	109,503	115,283	127,306	143,815	0.80	12.97
Russian Federation	1,465,021	1,951,831	1,542,449	1,948,142	2,667,596	14.80	36.93
Slovakia	628,900	514,475	473,299	517,688	586,675	3.25	13.33
Ukraine	229,090	259,362	235,818	277,334	321,384	1.78	15.88
Northern Europe	2,508,688	2,263,129	1,896,006	1,868,866	1,662,426	9.22	-11.05
Denmark	311,926	311,428	284,961	333,323	278,625	1.55	-16.41
Finland	138,371	137,808	120,218	112,361	125,401	0.70	11.61
Iceland	11,940	11,275	8,694	9,062	10,354	0.06	14.26
Ireland	133,398	148,038	88,341	71,965	55,391	0.31	-23.03
Norway	236,687	220,894	250,016	222,229	201,504	1.12	-9.33
Sweden	193,763	211,566	207,307	213,811	203,369	1.13	-4.88
United Kingdom	1,482,603	1,222,120	936,469	906,115	787,782	4.37	-13.06
Southern Europe	2,432,125	2,288,439	2,026,641	1,935,317	2,034,797	11.29	5.14
Croatia	112,316	115,550	104,003	111,694	131,050	0.73	17.33
Greece	188,021	224,435	199,346	152,926	125,987	0.70	-17.62
Italy	1,166,334	1,041,743	983,227	926,051	922,535	5.12	-0.38
Malta	8,738	6,394	5,219	5,971	8,123	0.05	36.04
Portugal	75,884	75,564	75,679	74,952	70,418	0.39	-6.05
Slovenia	39,709	46,424	44,993	42,515	48,739	0.27	14.64

CZECH REPUBLIC

5. Overnight stays of non-resident tourists in hotels and similar establishments, by nationality

	2007	2008	2009	2010	2011	Market share 11	% Change 11-10
Spain	804,945	738,747	575,220	566,193	649,549	3.60	14.72
Serbia and Montenegro	36,178	39,582	38,954	55,015	78,396	0.43	42.50
Western Europe	**6,398,071**	**6,220,823**	**5,928,794**	**5,944,796**	**6,074,507**	**33.70**	**2.18**
Austria	336,152	336,649	345,584	373,309	361,679	2.01	-3.12
Belgium	195,850	216,547	220,146	210,497	210,354	1.17	-0.07
France	570,273	559,642	538,260	624,549	709,314	3.93	13.57
Germany	4,548,154	4,408,594	4,194,151	4,090,860	4,134,975	22.94	1.08
Liechtenstein	1,881	1,531	1,537	1,881	1,857	0.01	-1.28
Luxembourg	8,484	9,010	13,853	12,654	12,941	0.07	2.27
Netherlands	537,349	529,213	454,876	452,529	467,587	2.59	3.33
Switzerland	199,928	159,637	160,387	178,517	175,800	0.98	-1.52
East Mediterranean Europe	**307,946**	**326,382**	**399,090**	**452,152**	**457,672**	**2.54**	**1.22**
Cyprus	27,456	23,443	22,980	23,028	22,644	0.13	-1.67
Israel	188,955	211,673	288,901	308,411	306,303	1.70	-0.68
Turkey	91,535	91,266	87,209	120,713	128,725	0.71	6.64
Other Europe	**612,534**	**530,400**	**415,534**	**412,098**	**379,823**	**2.11**	**-7.83**
Other countries of Europe	612,534	530,400	415,534	412,098	379,823	2.11	-7.83

CZECH REPUBLIC

6. Overnight stays of non-resident tourists in all types of accommodation establishments, by nationality

	2007	2008	2009	2010	2011	Market share 11	% Change 11-10
TOTAL	20,610,186	19,987,022	17,746,893	18,365,947	19,424,839	100.00	5.77
AFRICA	68,669	76,738	64,047	77,616	87,561	0.45	12.81
Southern Africa	12,491	15,013	13,570	13,880	15,564	0.08	12.13
South Africa	12,491	15,013	13,570	13,880	15,564	0.08	12.13
Other Africa	56,178	61,725	50,477	63,736	71,997	0.37	12.96
Other countries of Africa	56,178	61,725	50,477	63,736	71,997	0.37	12.96
AMERICAS	1,267,673	1,191,156	1,071,563	1,218,499	1,268,806	6.53	4.13
North America	1,123,892	1,020,494	901,250	1,019,997	1,037,527	5.34	1.72
Canada	141,748	135,953	127,476	151,646	156,000	0.80	2.87
Mexico	43,698	39,510	31,460	41,762	52,131	0.27	24.83
United States of America	938,446	845,031	742,314	826,589	829,396	4.27	0.34
South America	57,594	70,744	77,968	101,183	117,483	0.60	16.11
Brazil	57,594	70,744	77,968	101,183	117,483	0.60	16.11
Other Americas	86,187	99,918	92,345	97,319	113,796	0.59	16.93
Other countries of the Americas	86,187	99,918	92,345	97,319	113,796	0.59	16.93
EAST ASIA AND THE PACIFIC	1,145,637	1,119,539	1,057,706	1,240,989	1,387,785	7.14	11.83
North-East Asia	496,344	455,652	423,022	507,766	568,386	2.93	11.94
China	76,763	101,712	111,120	136,742	187,380	0.96	37.03
Japan	294,528	249,603	225,308	251,422	234,651	1.21	-6.67
Korea, Republic of	125,053	104,337	86,594	119,602	146,355	0.75	22.37
Australasia	151,657	160,029	137,152	166,472	181,900	0.94	9.27
Australia	129,931	141,590	120,030	147,661	161,942	0.83	9.67
New Zealand	21,726	18,439	17,122	18,811	19,958	0.10	6.10
Other East Asia and the Pacific	497,636	503,858	497,532	566,751	637,499	3.28	12.48
Other countries of Asia	489,170	490,598	485,242	553,635	625,233	3.22	12.93
Other countries of Oceania	8,466	13,260	12,290	13,116	12,266	0.06	-6.48
EUROPE	18,128,207	17,599,589	15,553,577	15,828,843	16,680,687	85.87	5.38
Central/Eastern Europe	4,043,522	4,430,966	3,697,146	4,274,339	5,236,276	26.96	22.50
Bulgaria	55,467	53,069	42,744	46,409	52,372	0.27	12.85
Estonia	39,274	45,983	31,590	24,903	32,956	0.17	32.34
Hungary	232,216	230,114	192,150	229,777	237,938	1.22	3.55
Latvia	36,666	35,818	20,483	17,381	21,128	0.11	21.56
Lithuania	96,418	99,430	73,039	76,616	78,413	0.40	2.35
Poland	651,238	786,381	718,423	739,425	777,019	4.00	5.08
Romania	89,805	119,011	120,276	131,105	147,744	0.76	12.69
Russian Federation	1,706,744	2,111,252	1,662,497	2,092,320	2,864,815	14.75	36.92
Slovakia	871,302	655,858	582,305	620,723	683,159	3.52	10.06
Ukraine	264,392	294,050	253,639	295,680	340,732	1.75	15.24
Northern Europe	2,619,985	2,365,404	1,971,360	1,939,815	1,719,639	8.85	-11.35
Denmark	355,374	350,938	316,392	361,741	301,254	1.55	-16.72
Finland	145,187	143,654	125,916	116,376	129,864	0.67	11.59
Iceland	12,438	13,023	8,906	9,339	10,475	0.05	12.16
Ireland	140,074	152,875	91,087	75,449	58,009	0.30	-23.11
Norway	241,036	231,944	253,652	225,457	204,004	1.05	-9.52
Sweden	205,519	221,040	215,927	220,996	208,897	1.08	-5.47
United Kingdom	1,520,357	1,251,930	959,480	930,457	807,136	4.16	-13.25
Southern Europe	2,510,765	2,354,663	2,087,408	1,986,789	2,087,523	10.75	5.07
Croatia	117,207	119,485	109,733	116,052	134,320	0.69	15.74
Greece	192,051	228,943	202,184	156,070	128,466	0.66	-17.69
Italy	1,202,820	1,073,038	1,013,057	947,233	946,206	4.87	-0.11
Malta	9,096	6,777	5,360	6,094	8,298	0.04	36.17
Portugal	80,903	79,193	79,484	78,510	73,830	0.38	-5.96
Slovenia	45,832	50,651	49,304	45,675	52,767	0.27	15.53

CZECH REPUBLIC

6. Overnight stays of non-resident tourists in all types of accommodation establishments, by nationality

	2007	2008	2009	2010	2011	Market share 11	% Change 11-10
Spain	822,399	754,290	587,193	579,671	662,989	3.41	14.37
Serbia and Montenegro	40,457	42,286	41,093	57,484	80,647	0.42	40.29
Western Europe	**7,962,365**	**7,536,214**	**6,945,606**	**6,729,373**	**6,768,995**	**34.85**	**0.59**
Austria	358,963	357,826	364,287	391,722	380,184	1.96	-2.95
Belgium	220,671	243,160	241,499	226,078	228,509	1.18	1.08
France	610,394	593,443	568,151	649,458	739,150	3.81	13.81
Germany	5,634,733	5,291,228	4,851,927	4,609,595	4,578,249	23.57	-0.68
Liechtenstein	2,013	1,636	1,656	1,927	1,907	0.01	-1.04
Luxembourg	9,050	9,671	14,152	13,356	13,351	0.07	-0.04
Netherlands	914,484	869,668	736,412	652,844	644,627	3.32	-1.26
Switzerland	212,057	169,582	167,522	184,393	183,018	0.94	-0.75
East Mediterranean Europe	**336,824**	**357,445**	**428,188**	**479,140**	**481,548**	**2.48**	**0.50**
Cyprus	28,207	24,222	23,486	23,752	23,171	0.12	-2.45
Israel	213,519	239,193	314,341	332,110	325,646	1.68	-1.95
Turkey	95,098	94,030	90,361	123,278	132,731	0.68	7.67
Other Europe	**654,746**	**554,897**	**423,869**	**419,387**	**386,706**	**1.99**	**-7.79**
Other countries of Europe	654,746	554,897	423,869	419,387	386,706	1.99	-7.79

DEMOCRATIC REPUBLIC OF THE CONGO

1. Arrivals of non-resident tourists at national borders, by nationality

		2007	2008	2009	2010	2011	Market share 11	% Change 11-10
TOTAL	(*)	47,492	49,971	53,402	81,117	186,000	100.00	129.30
AFRICA		27,767	27,969	31,328	20,301	43,765	23.53	115.58
East Africa						11,926	6.41	
Burundi						2,107	1.13	
Kenya						2,668	1.43	
Rwanda						2,665	1.43	
United Republic of Tanzania						2,593	1.39	
Zambia						1,893	1.02	
Central Africa		1,667		1,916	10,219	10,955	5.89	7.20
Angola						5,529	2.97	
Congo		666		805	3,995	5,426	2.92	35.82
Other countries of Central Africa		1,001		1,111	6,224			
North Africa						6,906	3.71	
Morocco						1,698	0.91	
Tunisia						1,850	0.99	
Other countries of North Africa						3,358	1.81	
Southern Africa						4,962	2.67	
South Africa						4,962	2.67	
Other Africa		26,100	27,969	29,412	10,082	9,016	4.85	-10.57
Other countries of Africa		26,100		29,412	10,082	9,016	4.85	-10.57
All countries of Africa			27,969					
AMERICAS		2,933	3,665	3,433	7,184	20,507	11.03	185.45
Central America						2,585	1.39	
Panama						89	0.05	
Other countries of Central America						2,496	1.34	
North America						12,386	6.66	
Canada						6,694	3.60	
Mexico						1,540	0.83	
Other countries of North America						4,152	2.23	
South America						5,536	2.98	
Brazil						1,708	0.92	
Paraguay						1,131	0.61	
Other countries of South America						2,697	1.45	
Other Americas		2,933	3,665	3,433	7,184			
All countries of the Americas		2,933	3,665	3,433	7,184			
EAST ASIA AND THE PACIFIC		5,478	5,233	5,540	3,884	14,272	7.67	267.46
South-East Asia					85	1,670	0.90	1864.71
Thailand					85	1,670	0.90	1864.71
Australasia					178	2,489	1.34	1298.31
Australia, New Zealand					178	2,489	1.34	1298.31
Other East Asia and the Pacific		5,478	5,233	5,540	3,621	10,113	5.44	179.29
Other countries of Asia					3,621	10,113	5.44	179.29
All countries of Asia		5,117	4,969	5,244				
All countries of Oceania		361	264	296				
EUROPE		11,314	13,104	13,101	35,012	67,895	36.50	93.92
Central/Eastern Europe						7,322	3.94	
Russian Federation						1,980	1.06	
Ukraine						1,872	1.01	
Other countries Central/East Europe						3,470	1.87	
Northern Europe						10,925	5.87	
Norway						1,826	0.98	
United Kingdom						5,997	3.22	

DEMOCRATIC REPUBLIC OF THE CONGO

1. Arrivals of non-resident tourists at national borders, by nationality

	2007	2008	2009	2010	2011	Market share 11	% Change 11-10
Other countries of Northern Europe					3,102	1.67	
Southern Europe	**609**	**1,102**	**1,182**	**4,153**	**10,975**	**5.90**	**164.27**
Italy	609	1,102	1,182	2,012	4,053	2.18	101.44
Portugal					2,244	1.21	
Spain					2,657	1.43	
Other countries of Southern Europe				2,141	2,021	1.09	-5.60
Western Europe	**6,868**	**8,218**	**8,165**	**25,036**	**36,068**	**19.39**	**44.06**
Belgium	3,033	4,159	4,087	12,047	15,631	8.40	29.75
France	2,992	2,793	2,654	10,038	14,734	7.92	46.78
Germany	843	1,266	1,424	1,595	3,081	1.66	93.17
Other countries of Western Europe				1,356	2,622	1.41	93.36
East Mediterranean Europe				**353**	**2,605**	**1.40**	**637.96**
Israel				353	2,605	1.40	637.96
Other Europe	**3,837**	**3,784**	**3,754**	**5,470**			
Other countries of Europe	3,837	3,784	3,754	5,470			
MIDDLE EAST				**1,650**	**6,060**	**3.26**	**267.27**
Lebanon				1,243	3,560	1.91	186.40
Other countries of Middle East				407	2,500	1.34	514.25
SOUTH ASIA				**2,767**	**5,668**	**3.05**	**104.84**
India				2,767	5,668	3.05	104.84
NOT SPECIFIED				**10,319**	**27,833**	**14.96**	**169.73**
Other countries of the World					27,833	14.96	
Nationals Residing Abroad				10,319			

DENMARK

3. Arrivals of non-resident tourists in hotels and similar establishments, by country of residence

		2007	2008	2009	2010	2011	Market share 11	% Change 11-10
TOTAL	(*)	2,100,235	2,056,812	1,892,468	2,157,344	1,427,554	100.00	-33.83
AMERICAS		134,560	136,899	142,854	154,726	122,796	8.60	-20.64
North America		123,401	122,035	127,827	136,337	104,894	7.35	-23.06
Canada		10,292	12,629	13,665	14,561	11,422	0.80	-21.56
United States of America		113,109	109,406	114,162	121,776	93,472	6.55	-23.24
Other Americas		11,159	14,864	15,027	18,389	17,902	1.25	-2.65
Other countries of the Americas		11,159	14,864	15,027	18,389	17,902	1.25	-2.65
EAST ASIA AND THE PACIFIC		73,426	65,946	66,150	73,319	50,562	3.54	-31.04
North-East Asia		29,435	27,922	29,584	32,625	19,778	1.39	-39.38
Japan		29,435	27,922	29,584	32,625	19,778	1.39	-39.38
South-East Asia		43,991	38,024	36,566	40,694	30,784	2.16	-24.35
All countries of South-East Asia		43,991	38,024	36,566	40,694	30,784	2.16	-24.35
EUROPE		1,842,875	1,804,329	1,631,994	1,866,553	1,201,413	84.16	-35.63
Central/Eastern Europe		16,185	17,324	16,418	17,858	16,315	1.14	-8.64
Poland		16,185	17,324	16,418	17,858	16,315	1.14	-8.64
Northern Europe		1,211,874	1,157,557	1,010,917	1,153,621	764,675	53.57	-33.72
Finland		44,984	45,469	45,284	52,872	49,862	3.49	-5.69
Norway		393,647	379,738	361,167	394,494	253,406	17.75	-35.76
Sweden		551,803	532,363	425,779	509,385	337,321	23.63	-33.78
United Kingdom		221,440	199,987	178,687	196,870	124,086	8.69	-36.97
Southern Europe		95,361	94,999	103,179	113,243	74,683	5.23	-34.05
Italy		44,765	45,044	49,141	53,314	47,678	3.34	-10.57
Spain		50,596	49,955	54,038	59,929	27,005	1.89	-54.94
Western Europe		379,929	378,915	377,299	431,231	284,271	19.91	-34.08
Austria		7,187	7,276	7,960	13,054	8,864	0.62	-32.10
France		41,107	39,896	45,773	51,792	43,833	3.07	-15.37
Germany		216,552	214,855	204,221	232,219	131,274	9.20	-43.47
Netherlands		70,501	71,601	69,469	78,183	55,327	3.88	-29.23
Switzerland		24,495	23,632	27,255	29,948	31,580	2.21	5.45
Belgium / Luxembourg		20,087	21,655	22,621	26,035	13,393	0.94	-48.56
Other Europe		139,526	155,534	124,181	150,600	61,469	4.31	-59.18
Other countries of Europe		139,526	155,534	124,181	150,600	61,469	4.31	-59.18
NOT SPECIFIED		49,374	49,638	51,470	62,746	52,783	3.70	-15.88
Other countries of the World		49,374	49,638	51,470	62,746	52,783	3.70	-15.88

DENMARK

4. Arrivals of non-resident tourists in all types of accommodation establishments, by country of residence

		2007	2008	2009	2010	2011	Market share 11	% Change 11-10
TOTAL	(*)	9,832,042	9,563,857	9,264,870	9,425,096	7,969,792	100.00	-15.44
AMERICAS		624,992	627,050	647,752	645,508	686,294	8.61	6.32
North America		558,966	557,398	589,593	583,730	618,901	7.77	6.03
Canada		80,704	83,025	77,559	77,925	87,705	1.10	12.55
United States of America		478,262	474,373	512,034	505,805	531,196	6.67	5.02
Other Americas		66,026	69,652	58,159	61,778	67,393	0.85	9.09
Other countries of the Americas		66,026	69,652	58,159	61,778	67,393	0.85	9.09
EAST ASIA AND THE PACIFIC		197,862	190,727	182,297	190,452	166,178	2.09	-12.75
North-East Asia		34,574	33,233	30,726	33,837	20,687	0.26	-38.86
Japan		34,574	33,233	30,726	33,837	20,687	0.26	-38.86
South-East Asia		163,288	157,494	151,571	156,615	145,491	1.83	-7.10
All countries of South-East Asia		163,288	157,494	151,571	156,615	145,491	1.83	-7.10
EUROPE		8,557,664	8,330,154	7,988,695	8,128,384	6,631,674	83.21	-18.41
Central/Eastern Europe		98,578	98,640	91,520	92,107	87,570	1.10	-4.93
Poland		98,578	98,640	91,520	92,107	87,570	1.10	-4.93
Northern Europe		4,039,894	3,925,567	3,639,024	3,789,674	3,374,228	42.34	-10.96
Finland		59,252	57,493	57,483	65,521	62,434	0.78	-4.71
Norway		1,728,419	1,693,932	1,628,381	1,665,429	1,481,569	18.59	-11.04
Sweden		1,489,141	1,433,781	1,241,798	1,336,600	1,176,246	14.76	-12.00
United Kingdom		763,082	740,361	711,362	722,124	653,979	8.21	-9.44
Southern Europe		410,286	409,408	316,881	327,122	279,475	3.51	-14.57
Italy		223,627	223,456	169,588	173,964	132,174	1.66	-24.02
Spain		186,659	185,952	147,293	153,158	147,301	1.85	-3.82
Western Europe		3,575,729	3,449,058	3,337,909	3,349,660	2,817,746	35.36	-15.88
Austria		53,446	53,532	42,971	48,442	48,859	0.61	0.86
France		243,857	243,178	234,620	241,755	243,695	3.06	0.80
Germany		2,723,110	2,593,135	2,538,209	2,526,299	2,055,025	25.79	-18.65
Netherlands		341,116	344,607	319,267	323,513	267,568	3.36	-17.29
Switzerland		103,344	102,646	92,594	95,897	102,160	1.28	6.53
Belgium / Luxembourg		110,856	111,960	110,248	113,754	100,439	1.26	-11.71
Other Europe		433,177	447,481	603,361	569,821	72,655	0.91	-87.25
Other countries of Europe		433,177	447,481	603,361	569,821	72,655	0.91	-87.25
NOT SPECIFIED		451,524	415,926	446,126	460,752	485,646	6.09	5.40
Other countries of the World		451,524	415,926	446,126	460,752	485,646	6.09	5.40

DENMARK

5. Overnight stays of non-resident tourists in hotels and similar establishments, by country of residence

		2007	2008	2009	2010	2011	Market share 11	% Change 11-10
TOTAL	(*)	4,845,926	4,751,680	4,434,605	5,074,913	5,591,303	100.00	10.18
AMERICAS		408,480	413,163	431,758	467,686	518,723	9.28	10.91
North America		378,800	373,600	391,009	416,958	450,409	8.06	8.02
Canada		27,480	33,785	37,152	40,126	52,991	0.95	32.06
United States of America		351,320	339,815	353,857	376,832	397,418	7.11	5.46
Other Americas		29,680	39,563	40,749	50,728	68,314	1.22	34.67
Other countries of the Americas		29,680	39,563	40,749	50,728	68,314	1.22	34.67
EAST ASIA AND THE PACIFIC		215,240	192,926	193,646	214,596	228,467	4.09	6.46
North-East Asia		81,391	77,185	81,651	89,357	89,669	1.60	0.35
Japan		81,391	77,185	81,651	89,357	89,669	1.60	0.35
South-East Asia		133,849	115,741	111,995	125,239	138,798	2.48	10.83
All countries of South-East Asia		133,849	115,741	111,995	125,239	138,798	2.48	10.83
EUROPE		4,068,682	3,991,500	3,649,142	4,197,280	4,644,165	83.06	10.65
Central/Eastern Europe		45,766	48,989	46,443	50,516	63,763	1.14	26.22
Poland		45,766	48,989	46,443	50,516	63,763	1.14	26.22
Northern Europe		2,479,704	2,358,611	2,080,994	2,384,952	2,657,092	47.52	11.41
Finland		107,300	108,359	105,718	122,099	151,241	2.70	23.87
Norway		871,491	835,757	795,048	879,665	962,984	17.22	9.47
Sweden		975,223	939,857	751,752	907,694	1,011,348	18.09	11.42
United Kingdom		525,690	474,638	428,476	475,494	531,519	9.51	11.78
Southern Europe		268,717	267,201	293,227	327,276	321,779	5.75	-1.68
Italy		150,804	150,933	166,386	184,397	180,266	3.22	-2.24
Spain		117,913	116,268	126,841	142,879	141,513	2.53	-0.96
Western Europe		878,087	875,022	875,918	1,006,870	1,112,555	19.90	10.50
Austria		20,463	20,714	22,658	37,151	38,504	0.69	3.64
France		100,970	98,017	113,184	129,445	148,639	2.66	14.83
Germany		467,722	463,858	439,583	501,766	533,889	9.55	6.40
Netherlands		176,031	178,769	173,471	195,282	198,797	3.56	1.80
Switzerland		69,729	67,273	77,577	85,226	122,573	2.19	43.82
Belgium / Luxembourg		43,172	46,391	49,445	58,000	70,153	1.25	20.95
Other Europe		396,408	441,677	352,560	427,666	488,976	8.75	14.34
Other countries of Europe		396,408	441,677	352,560	427,666	488,976	8.75	14.34
NOT SPECIFIED		153,524	154,091	160,059	195,351	199,948	3.58	2.35
Other countries of the World		153,524	154,091	160,059	195,351	199,948	3.58	2.35

DENMARK

6. Overnight stays of non-resident tourists in all types of accommodation establishments, by country of residence

		2007	2008	2009	2010	2011	Market share 11	% Change 11-10
TOTAL	(*)	47,331,619	45,852,357	43,984,095	44,361,815	45,923,275	100.00	3.52
AMERICAS		2,697,740	2,701,036	2,673,126	2,696,883	2,828,852	6.16	4.89
North America		2,269,485	2,263,189	2,245,932	2,258,517	2,366,382	5.15	4.78
Canada		432,864	439,161	376,110	379,119	405,774	0.88	7.03
United States of America		1,836,621	1,824,028	1,869,822	1,879,398	1,960,608	4.27	4.32
Other Americas		428,255	437,847	427,194	438,366	462,470	1.01	5.50
Other countries of the Americas		428,255	437,847	427,194	438,366	462,470	1.01	5.50
EAST ASIA AND THE PACIFIC		742,739	721,115	712,777	738,729	752,366	1.64	1.85
North-East Asia		90,387	86,850	86,256	94,329	94,676	0.21	0.37
Japan		90,387	86,850	86,256	94,329	94,676	0.21	0.37
South-East Asia		652,352	634,265	626,521	644,400	657,690	1.43	2.06
All countries of South-East Asia		652,352	634,265	626,521	644,400	657,690	1.43	2.06
EUROPE		41,311,533	39,947,835	38,086,453	38,346,505	39,642,554	86.32	3.38
Central/Eastern Europe		1,044,765	1,047,295	1,020,454	1,016,069	1,015,017	2.21	-0.10
Poland		1,044,765	1,047,295	1,020,454	1,016,069	1,015,017	2.21	-0.10
Northern Europe		14,018,320	13,622,331	12,559,044	12,927,175	13,417,556	29.22	3.79
Finland		194,964	175,960	176,606	197,533	227,271	0.49	15.05
Norway		6,662,272	6,497,089	6,193,991	6,306,417	6,505,947	14.17	3.16
Sweden		4,448,634	4,289,861	3,734,035	3,925,394	4,117,932	8.97	4.90
United Kingdom		2,712,450	2,659,421	2,454,412	2,497,831	2,566,406	5.59	2.75
Southern Europe		1,630,934	1,621,764	1,543,969	1,577,749	1,626,688	3.54	3.10
Italy		944,519	938,103	897,200	914,919	938,297	2.04	2.56
Spain		686,415	683,661	646,769	662,830	688,391	1.50	3.86
Western Europe		21,867,994	20,864,248	20,152,466	19,940,571	20,824,930	45.35	4.43
Austria		211,859	211,597	203,081	219,006	227,447	0.50	3.85
France		1,306,449	1,303,955	1,306,349	1,329,176	1,365,065	2.97	2.70
Germany		17,794,137	16,788,074	16,237,180	15,976,463	16,798,913	36.58	5.15
Netherlands		1,805,617	1,811,010	1,676,310	1,664,214	1,614,719	3.52	-2.97
Switzerland		372,136	369,511	344,740	356,263	404,515	0.88	13.54
Belgium / Luxembourg		377,796	380,101	384,806	395,449	414,271	0.90	4.76
Other Europe		2,749,520	2,792,197	2,810,520	2,884,941	2,758,363	6.01	-4.39
Other countries of Europe		2,749,520	2,792,197	2,810,520	2,884,941	2,758,363	6.01	-4.39
NOT SPECIFIED		2,579,607	2,482,371	2,511,739	2,579,698	2,699,503	5.88	4.64
Other countries of the World		2,579,607	2,482,371	2,511,739	2,579,698	2,699,503	5.88	4.64

DOMINICA

1. Arrivals of non-resident tourists at national borders, by country of residence

	2007	2008	2009	2010	2011	Market share 11	% Change 11-10
TOTAL	81,086	81,112	74,924	76,518	75,546	100.00	-1.27
AMERICAS	69,429	66,645	62,894	64,789	62,901	83.26	-2.91
Caribbean	45,906	40,965	40,540	41,536	40,820	54.03	-1.72
Antigua and Barbuda	5,380	4,068	3,763	3,670	3,479	4.61	-5.20
Bahamas	100	94	106	126	134	0.18	6.35
Barbados	2,631	1,956	1,935	1,961	1,897	2.51	-3.26
Bermuda	51	85	58	48	60	0.08	25.00
British Virgin Islands	1,483	979	1,085	1,089	1,079	1.43	-0.92
Cayman Islands	16	48	19	10	22	0.03	120.00
Cuba	232	105	76	88	73	0.10	-17.05
Dominican Republic	613	154	183	300	224	0.30	-25.33
Grenada	515	312	397	325	419	0.55	28.92
Guadeloupe	12,660	14,029	15,053	15,707	15,089	19.97	-3.93
Haiti	2,556	745	974	831	705	0.93	-15.16
Jamaica	557	550	592	526	555	0.73	5.51
Martinique	6,337	6,180	5,409	6,096	6,428	8.51	5.45
Montserrat	211	112	114	98	131	0.17	33.67
Aruba	56	61	34	73	42	0.06	-42.47
Bonaire	2	8	12	9	3	0.00	-66.67
Curaçao	89	109	102	117	107	0.14	-8.55
Puerto Rico	245	187	360	296	246	0.33	-16.89
Saint Kitts and Nevis	664	525	478	579	494	0.65	-14.68
Anguilla	125	545	443	418	334	0.44	-20.10
Saint Lucia	2,632	2,081	1,952	1,914	2,080	2.75	8.67
Sint Maarten	2,342	2,272	1,993	2,089	1,898	2.51	-9.14
Saint Vincent and the Grenadines	758	501	536	469	548	0.73	16.84
Trinidad and Tobago	1,876	1,325	1,335	1,356	1,621	2.15	19.54
Turks and Caicos Islands	9	18	37	26	24	0.03	-7.69
United States Virgin Islands	3,751	3,830	3,426	3,230	3,103	4.11	-3.93
Other countries of the Caribbean	15	86	68	85	25	0.03	-70.59
Central America	82	106	92	99	200	0.26	102.02
Belize	23	25	38	38	45	0.06	18.42
Other countries of Central America	59	81	54	61	155	0.21	154.10
North America	22,550	23,906	20,847	22,150	20,855	27.61	-5.85
Canada	2,265	3,346	2,618	2,859	2,986	3.95	4.44
Mexico	33	42	36	25	49	0.06	96.00
United States of America	20,252	20,518	18,193	19,266	17,820	23.59	-7.51
South America	891	1,668	1,415	1,004	1,026	1.36	2.19
Argentina	24	15	21	24	16	0.02	-33.33
Brazil	35	12	17	27	48	0.06	77.78
Colombia	42	26	40	36	48	0.06	33.33
French Guiana	6	78	81	53	136	0.18	156.60
Guyana	320	250	279	293	295	0.39	0.68
Suriname	32	38	30	32	50	0.07	56.25
Venezuela	391	1,212	909	501	410	0.54	-18.16
Other countries of South America	41	37	38	38	23	0.03	-39.47
EAST ASIA AND THE PACIFIC	514	359	360	475	557	0.74	17.26
North-East Asia	442	279	309	368	462	0.61	25.54
China	287	147	178	227	341	0.45	50.22
Taiwan, Province of China	24	38	20	26	30	0.04	15.38
Japan	131	94	111	115	91	0.12	-20.87
Australasia	72	80	51	107	95	0.13	-11.21
Australia	72	80	51	107	95	0.13	-11.21
EUROPE	10,784	13,787	11,590	10,725	11,538	15.27	7.58
Northern Europe	6,703	7,748	4,851	5,080	5,138	6.80	1.14

DOMINICA

1. Arrivals of non-resident tourists at national borders, by country of residence

	2007	2008	2009	2010	2011	Market share 11	% Change 11-10
Denmark	88	124	106	81	78	0.10	-3.70
Ireland	78	67	61	58	63	0.08	8.62
Norway	28	42	39	44	55	0.07	25.00
Sweden	199	304	291	296	320	0.42	8.11
United Kingdom	6,310	7,211	4,354	4,601	4,622	6.12	0.46
Southern Europe	**201**	**234**	**269**	**241**	**259**	**0.34**	**7.47**
Greece	5	6	20	10	11	0.01	10.00
Italy	123	104	124	107	135	0.18	26.17
Portugal	9	21	28	12	9	0.01	-25.00
Spain	64	103	97	112	104	0.14	-7.14
Western Europe	**3,625**	**5,485**	**6,172**	**5,092**	**5,699**	**7.54**	**11.92**
Austria	91	137	127	129	147	0.19	13.95
Belgium	180	173	165	163	187	0.25	14.72
France	2,046	3,783	4,469	3,323	3,680	4.87	10.74
Germany	751	879	966	898	1,011	1.34	12.58
Luxembourg		9	3	8	11	0.01	37.50
Netherlands	300	220	172	182	185	0.24	1.65
Switzerland	257	284	270	389	478	0.63	22.88
Other Europe	**255**	**320**	**298**	**312**	**442**	**0.59**	**41.67**
Other countries of Europe	255	320	298	312	442	0.59	41.67
NOT SPECIFIED	**359**	**321**	**80**	**529**	**550**	**0.73**	**3.97**
Other countries of the World	359	321	80	529	550	0.73	3.97

DOMINICAN REPUBLIC

1. Arrivals of non-resident tourists at national borders, by country of residence

		2007	2008	2009	2010	2011	Market share 11	% Change 11-10
TOTAL	(*)	3,979,582	3,979,672	3,992,303	4,124,543	4,306,431	100.00	4.41
AMERICAS		2,046,288	2,127,963	2,202,697	2,367,965	2,559,180	59.43	8.08
Caribbean		139,426	133,470	138,236	154,201	143,254	3.33	-7.10
Cuba		3,921	3,876	3,295	3,818	3,838	0.09	0.52
Guadeloupe		4,470	5,157	5,334	5,188	3,436	0.08	-33.77
Haiti		7,762	7,120	5,456	9,518	9,717	0.23	2.09
Jamaica		1,832	1,292	882	1,124	1,027	0.02	-8.63
Martinique		2,492	4,639	3,386	4,252	3,833	0.09	-9.85
Aruba		2,354	2,420	1,910	1,873	1,888	0.04	0.80
Curaçao		4,697	4,183	4,366	4,407	4,382	0.10	-0.57
Puerto Rico		104,277	97,592	107,610	118,201	109,505	2.54	-7.36
Sint Maarten		2,699	3,012	2,944	2,520	2,654	0.06	5.32
Trinidad and Tobago		1,857	1,467	943	1,438	1,207	0.03	-16.06
Turks and Caicos Islands		1,454	1,220	1,041	1,036	918	0.02	-11.39
United States Virgin Islands		1,611	1,492	1,069	826	849	0.02	2.78
Central America		26,886	28,512	30,083	29,124	35,033	0.81	20.29
Costa Rica		9,559	8,717	8,110	8,411	9,618	0.22	14.35
El Salvador		3,273	3,760	3,462	3,710	3,870	0.09	4.31
Guatemala		4,789	5,149	5,783	5,420	6,708	0.16	23.76
Honduras		1,839	2,230	1,759	2,177	2,458	0.06	12.91
Panama		7,426	8,656	10,969	9,406	12,379	0.29	31.61
North America		1,713,621	1,771,326	1,819,294	1,902,316	1,988,935	46.19	4.55
Canada		591,871	639,796	650,111	662,058	668,290	15.52	0.94
Mexico		21,844	23,632	18,308	20,695	23,467	0.54	13.39
United States of America		1,099,906	1,107,898	1,150,875	1,219,563	1,297,178	30.12	6.36
South America		160,787	188,621	208,580	276,016	383,450	8.90	38.92
Argentina		27,632	35,476	43,130	69,182	97,462	2.26	40.88
Bolivia		1,071	1,137	3,053	5,106	7,621	0.18	49.26
Brazil		10,940	13,513	19,570	37,153	76,625	1.78	106.24
Chile		21,128	28,541	29,495	40,729	49,862	1.16	22.42
Colombia		26,069	31,137	29,156	31,263	40,982	0.95	31.09
Ecuador		12,690	16,686	15,797	16,597	18,786	0.44	13.19
Peru		11,181	16,049	19,825	24,636	30,646	0.71	24.40
Uruguay		2,098	2,567	3,865	4,454	5,626	0.13	26.31
Venezuela		46,878	42,384	42,635	45,196	53,079	1.23	17.44
Other countries of South America		1,100	1,131	2,054	1,700	2,761	0.06	62.41
Other Americas		5,568	6,034	6,504	6,308	8,508	0.20	34.88
Other countries of the Americas		5,568	6,034	6,504	6,308	8,508	0.20	34.88
EAST ASIA AND THE PACIFIC		7,672	7,624	6,753	8,345	9,773	0.23	17.11
North-East Asia		4,965	4,350	3,831	4,738	4,989	0.12	5.30
China		534	491	381	646	901	0.02	39.47
Taiwan, Province of China		593	564	477	455	518	0.01	13.85
Japan		2,576	2,281	2,036	2,231	2,270	0.05	1.75
Korea, Republic of		1,262	1,014	937	1,406	1,300	0.03	-7.54
Australasia		1,519	1,874	1,397	1,676	1,361	0.03	-18.79
Australia		1,519	1,874	1,397	1,676	1,361	0.03	-18.79
Other East Asia and the Pacific		1,188	1,400	1,525	1,931	3,423	0.08	77.27
Other countries of Asia		1,188	1,400	1,525	1,931	3,423	0.08	77.27
EUROPE		1,343,209	1,310,611	1,204,701	1,142,666	1,132,009	26.29	-0.93
Central/Eastern Europe		31,449	54,010	63,195	92,670	139,462	3.24	50.49
Bulgaria		482	536	499	582	555	0.01	-4.64
Czech Republic		3,465	4,726	5,526	6,112	5,996	0.14	-1.90
Hungary		710	768	704	803	780	0.02	-2.86
Poland		2,944	5,436	3,795	4,934	6,906	0.16	39.97

DOMINICAN REPUBLIC

1. Arrivals of non-resident tourists at national borders, by country of residence

	2007	2008	2009	2010	2011	Market share 11	% Change 11-10
Romania	469	565	592	748	971	0.02	29.81
Russian Federation	21,440	39,734	49,752	76,059	120,752	2.80	58.76
Ukraine	1,939	2,245	2,327	3,432	3,502	0.08	2.04
Northern Europe	**233,144**	**228,822**	**198,892**	**185,826**	**149,997**	**3.48**	**-19.28**
Denmark	2,683	2,298	2,061	2,145	1,709	0.04	-20.33
Finland	2,191	2,768	4,445	4,245	2,383	0.06	-43.86
Ireland	998	2,893	1,767	1,564	1,096	0.03	-29.92
Norway	1,860	2,207	2,575	1,891	1,527	0.04	-19.25
Sweden	4,549	5,702	6,153	7,760	5,339	0.12	-31.20
United Kingdom	220,863	212,954	181,891	168,221	137,943	3.20	-18.00
Southern Europe	**442,365**	**400,067**	**390,347**	**321,994**	**299,872**	**6.96**	**-6.87**
Greece	683	868	567	495	454	0.01	-8.28
Italy	140,423	127,383	115,775	94,952	99,822	2.32	5.13
Portugal	33,894	32,178	42,730	36,941	29,403	0.68	-20.41
Spain	267,365	239,638	231,275	189,606	170,193	3.95	-10.24
Western Europe	**631,953**	**623,377**	**545,410**	**530,292**	**540,275**	**12.55**	**1.88**
Austria	11,233	9,642	10,049	9,640	8,239	0.19	-14.53
Belgium	42,096	43,176	38,129	38,187	36,955	0.86	-3.23
France	278,147	279,408	247,038	230,975	246,416	5.72	6.69
Germany	214,942	206,940	178,533	181,318	183,847	4.27	1.39
Luxembourg	430	391	473	495	435	0.01	-12.12
Netherlands	55,857	49,960	41,605	40,100	37,861	0.88	-5.58
Switzerland	29,248	33,860	29,583	29,577	26,522	0.62	-10.33
East Mediterranean Europe	**2,302**	**1,710**	**1,445**	**1,476**	**1,204**	**0.03**	**-18.43**
Israel	2,302	1,710	1,445	1,476	1,204	0.03	-18.43
Other Europe	**1,996**	**2,625**	**5,412**	**10,408**	**1,199**	**0.03**	**-88.48**
Other countries of Europe	1,996	2,625	5,412	10,408	1,199	0.03	-88.48
SOUTH ASIA	**663**	**754**	**806**	**848**	**964**	**0.02**	**13.68**
India	663	754	806	848	964	0.02	13.68
NOT SPECIFIED	**581,750**	**532,720**	**577,346**	**604,719**	**604,505**	**14.04**	**-0.04**
Other countries of the World	542	778	659	1,286	1,071	0.02	-16.72
Nationals Residing Abroad	581,208	531,942	576,687	603,433	603,434	14.01	0.00

ECUADOR

2. Arrivals of non-resident visitors at national borders, by nationality

		2007	2008	2009	2010	2011	Market share 11	% Change 11-10
TOTAL	(*)	937,487	1,005,297	968,499	1,047,098	1,140,978	100.00	8.97
AFRICA		1,360	1,560	3,254	3,227	3,292	0.29	2.01
East Africa		130	163	546	461	177	0.02	-61.61
Burundi		2	3	2	3	1	0.00	-66.67
Comoros		3	4	1	5	6	0.00	20.00
Ethiopia		23	44	175	188	14	0.00	-92.55
Djibouti		2	1	4	3	2	0.00	-33.33
Kenya		49	52	267	164	58	0.01	-64.63
Madagascar		7	8	10	17	12	0.00	-29.41
Malawi		5	3	2	1	2	0.00	100.00
Mauritius		2	3	1	7	9	0.00	28.57
Mozambique		12	8	13	18	16	0.00	-11.11
Rwanda		4	2	1	5			
Seychelles			2	1		1	0.00	
Zimbabwe		9	10	12	20	14	0.00	-30.00
Uganda		6	8	16	14	23	0.00	64.29
United Republic of Tanzania		3	9	29	13	17	0.00	30.77
Zambia		3	6	12	3	2	0.00	-33.33
Central Africa		97	86	180	174	143	0.01	-17.82
Angola		14	14	30	27	9	0.00	-66.67
Cameroon		53	41	85	73	70	0.01	-4.11
Central African Republic		3	2	15	15	10	0.00	-33.33
Chad		4	6	6	13	19	0.00	46.15
Congo		15	15	32	38	27	0.00	-28.95
Equatorial Guinea			1	2	2	4	0.00	100.00
Gabon		5	5	4	2	4	0.00	100.00
Sao Tome and Principe		3	2	6	4			
North Africa		103	260	534	513	499	0.04	-2.73
Algeria		30	65	173	129	183	0.02	41.86
Morocco		33	47	90	82	93	0.01	13.41
Western Sahara		24	128	233	240	160	0.01	-33.33
Sudan		1	2	10	33	33	0.00	
Tunisia		15	18	28	29	30	0.00	3.45
Southern Africa		660	630	606	627	986	0.09	57.26
Botswana		2	2	15	13	1	0.00	-92.31
Lesotho		2	2	4	3	5	0.00	66.67
Namibia		2	2	25	13	5	0.00	-61.54
South Africa		654	621	556	594	972	0.09	63.64
Swaziland			3	6	4	3	0.00	-25.00
West Africa		164	199	847	675	372	0.03	-44.89
Cape Verde		11	12	15	37	36	0.00	-2.70
Benin		7	13	27	30	24	0.00	-20.00
Gambia			1	9	7	2	0.00	-71.43
Ghana		17	19	66	49	70	0.01	42.86
Guinea		16	29	79	67	44	0.00	-34.33
Liberia		6	6	9	7	9	0.00	28.57
Mali		13		3	8	11	0.00	37.50
Mauritania			7	31	24	26	0.00	8.33
Nigeria		66	94	545	359	80	0.01	-77.72
Senegal		19	16	30	32	22	0.00	-31.25
Sierra Leone			2	29	48	40	0.00	-16.67
Burkina Faso		9		4	7	8	0.00	14.29
Other Africa		206	222	541	777	1,115	0.10	43.50
Other countries of Africa		206	222	541	777	1,115	0.10	43.50
AMERICAS		729,610	753,266	734,524	810,281	884,434	77.52	9.15
Caribbean		7,372	14,424	31,209	31,707	29,931	2.62	-5.60

ECUADOR

2. Arrivals of non-resident visitors at national borders, by nationality

	2007	2008	2009	2010	2011	Market share 11	% Change 11-10
Antigua and Barbuda	11	3	6	7	5	0.00	-28.57
Bahamas	57	29	47	61	60	0.01	-1.64
Barbados	21	50	55	33	43	0.00	30.30
Bermuda	23		24	10	10	0.00	
Cuba	4,763	10,904	27,065	27,001	24,061	2.11	-10.89
Dominica	25	41	44	64	38	0.00	-40.63
Dominican Republic	2,153	2,408	2,480	2,619	2,447	0.21	-6.57
Grenada	7	13	16	20	11	0.00	-45.00
Guadeloupe	17		12	15	14	0.00	-6.67
Haiti	134	270	1,257	1,681	2,545	0.22	51.40
Jamaica	96	118	137	119	161	0.01	35.29
Curaçao	3	3	13	8	8	0.00	
Puerto Rico	39	21	26	31	39	0.00	25.81
Saint Lucia	20	19	15	8	28	0.00	250.00
Saint Vincent and the Grenadines	3	2		4	7	0.00	75.00
Trinidad and Tobago		182			398	0.03	
Other countries of the Caribbean		361	12	26	56	0.00	115.38
Central America	**11,422**	**13,649**	**13,652**	**15,772**	**20,947**	**1.84**	**32.81**
Belize	30	64	57	41	37	0.00	-9.76
Costa Rica	3,078	4,045	3,921	4,560	4,833	0.42	5.99
El Salvador	1,238	1,310	1,419	1,994	2,655	0.23	33.15
Guatemala	1,659	1,780	2,048	2,296	2,230	0.20	-2.87
Honduras	1,022	1,115	1,072	1,256	1,391	0.12	10.75
Nicaragua	804	831	856	985	912	0.08	-7.41
Panama	3,582	4,504	4,279	4,640	8,889	0.78	91.57
Other countries of Central America	9						
North America	**273,552**	**280,934**	**278,280**	**288,705**	**284,700**	**24.95**	**-1.39**
Canada	21,571	22,839	22,489	23,867	24,832	2.18	4.04
Mexico	10,963	13,689	13,695	15,757	18,278	1.60	16.00
United States of America	241,018	244,406	242,096	249,081	241,590	21.17	-3.01
South America	**437,264**	**444,251**	**411,381**	**474,097**	**548,856**	**48.10**	**15.77**
Argentina	19,226	21,718	22,675	30,653	37,456	3.28	22.19
Bolivia	4,444	4,797	4,487	5,522	4,962	0.43	-10.14
Brazil	13,400	15,052	14,395	15,083	17,539	1.54	16.28
Chile	21,674	24,212	25,195	28,478	34,854	3.05	22.39
Colombia	203,326	200,487	160,116	203,916	265,563	23.28	30.23
Guyana	18	36	51	54	45	0.00	-16.67
Paraguay	836	884	1,233	1,115	1,374	0.12	23.23
Peru	150,439	147,420	150,548	154,216	144,968	12.71	-6.00
Suriname	23	54	74	87	80	0.01	-8.05
Uruguay	2,663	2,758	2,967	3,152	3,460	0.30	9.77
Venezuela	21,110	26,771	29,416	31,558	38,246	3.35	21.19
Other countries of South America	105	62	224	263	309	0.03	17.49
Other Americas		**8**	**2**				
Other countries of the Americas		8	2				
EAST ASIA AND THE PACIFIC	**23,828**	**34,134**	**30,247**	**31,859**	**40,275**	**3.53**	**26.42**
North-East Asia	**12,557**	**21,230**	**14,888**	**14,674**	**15,870**	**1.39**	**8.15**
China	4,855	14,287	7,844	6,879	9,295	0.81	35.12
Taiwan, Province of China	284	588	654	718	777	0.07	8.22
Hong Kong, China	140	152	143	158	217	0.02	37.34
Japan	4,760	5,533	4,951	5,106	5,113	0.45	0.14
Korea, Republic of	2,513	663	1,294	1,810	443	0.04	-75.52
Mongolia	5	7	2	3	25	0.00	733.33
South-East Asia	**2,112**	**3,190**	**2,939**	**3,499**	**9,637**	**0.84**	**175.42**
Brunei Darussalam	1	1	2	1			
Myanmar	4	42	130	158	351	0.03	122.15
Cambodia	12	7	4	2	3	0.00	50.00

ECUADOR

2. Arrivals of non-resident visitors at national borders, by nationality

	2007	2008	2009	2010	2011	Market share 11	% Change 11-10
Indonesia	111	325	194	262	382	0.03	45.80
Malaysia	87	187	192	251	257	0.02	2.39
Philippines	1,598	2,202	2,060	2,330	8,001	0.70	243.39
Singapore	165	199	201	292	368	0.03	26.03
Viet Nam	46	166	84	55	82	0.01	49.09
Thailand	88	61	72	148	193	0.02	30.41
Australasia	**7,988**	**9,696**	**9,876**	**10,820**	**11,879**	**1.04**	**9.79**
Australia	6,423	7,902	8,241	9,167	10,237	0.90	11.67
New Zealand	1,565	1,794	1,635	1,653	1,642	0.14	-0.67
Melanesia	**13**	**3**	**49**	**65**	**33**	**0.00**	**-49.23**
Fiji		2	4	3	5	0.00	66.67
New Caledonia	13		45	62	26	0.00	-58.06
Papua New Guinea		1			2	0.00	
Micronesia		**7**	**5**	**38**	**86**	**0.01**	**126.32**
Kiribati		2	4	34	30	0.00	-11.76
Micronesia, Federated States of		3	1	2	39	0.00	1850.00
Marshall Islands		2		2	17	0.00	750.00
Polynesia	**11**	**8**	**9**	**17**	**18**	**0.00**	**5.88**
French Polynesia	11	8	9	17	18	0.00	5.88
Other East Asia and the Pacific	**1,147**		**2,481**	**2,746**	**2,752**	**0.24**	**0.22**
Other countries of Asia	1,106		2,481	2,613	2,752	0.24	5.32
Other countries of Oceania	41			133			
EUROPE	**179,700**	**198,177**	**197,062**	**197,527**	**202,202**	**17.72**	**2.37**
Central/Eastern Europe	**7,738**	**5,949**	**9,156**	**9,288**	**8,665**	**0.76**	**-6.71**
Azerbaijan	13	30	32		37	0.00	
Armenia	15	22	11		18	0.00	
Bulgaria	219	221	225	268	278	0.02	3.73
Belarus	43	82	113	113	170	0.01	50.44
Czech Republic	725	892	919	846	900	0.08	6.38
Estonia	133	150	109	103	107	0.01	3.88
Georgia	5	14	23		103	0.01	
Hungary	403	467	398	360	363	0.03	0.83
Kazakhstan	61	48	60		119	0.01	
Kyrgyzstan	2	1	6		8	0.00	
Latvia	258	122	186	132	137	0.01	3.79
Lithuania	238	287	284	185	324	0.03	75.14
Republic of Moldova		20		32	32	0.00	
Poland	1,328	1,783	2,144	1,903	2,458	0.22	29.16
Romania	400	643	567	617	939	0.08	52.19
Russian Federation	2,782	141	2,768	3,350	226	0.02	-93.25
Slovakia	213	41	461	381	83	0.01	-78.22
Tajikistan		1	1		5	0.00	
Turkmenistan		1	1		2	0.00	
Ukraine	900	977	840	998	2,347	0.21	135.17
Uzbekistan		6	8		9	0.00	
Northern Europe	**39,918**	**38,504**	**37,536**	**34,880**	**35,027**	**3.07**	**0.42**
Denmark	2,987	3,148	2,867	2,867	2,793	0.24	-2.58
Finland	980	1,038	1,047	1,116	1,233	0.11	10.48
Iceland	196	110	104	99	163	0.01	64.65
Ireland	2,667	2,916	2,871	2,398	2,388	0.21	-0.42
Norway	2,160	2,201	1,993	2,026	1,934	0.17	-4.54
Sweden	3,914	3,868	3,624	3,777	3,645	0.32	-3.49
United Kingdom	27,014	25,223	25,030	22,597	22,871	2.00	1.21
Southern Europe	**61,943**	**66,476**	**73,869**	**76,727**	**78,460**	**6.88**	**2.26**
Albania	26	33	56	71	100	0.01	40.85
Andorra	29	23	15	23	36	0.00	56.52
Bosnia and Herzegovina	8	24	9	9	11	0.00	22.22

ECUADOR

2. Arrivals of non-resident visitors at national borders, by nationality

	2007	2008	2009	2010	2011	Market share 11	% Change 11-10
Croatia	266	246	218	248	421	0.04	69.76
Greece	529	535	544	562	491	0.04	-12.63
Holy See	5	4	2	4	1	0.00	-75.00
Italy	13,071	13,799	14,759	15,076	14,640	1.28	-2.89
Malta	34	39	49	51	23	0.00	-54.90
Portugal	1,400	1,405	1,520	1,404	1,781	0.16	26.85
San Marino	3	1	3	4	8	0.00	100.00
Slovenia	214	269	294	245	284	0.02	15.92
Spain	46,358	49,937	56,400	59,030	60,664	5.32	2.77
Serbia and Montenegro		161					
Western Europe	**66,341**	**70,347**	**71,823**	**72,156**	**75,102**	**6.58**	**4.08**
Austria	2,599	2,571	2,456	2,522	2,787	0.24	10.51
Belgium	4,653	4,851	5,021	4,945	5,129	0.45	3.72
France	16,856	18,876	19,810	20,272	20,426	1.79	0.76
Germany	23,302	24,227	24,841	25,011	26,662	2.34	6.60
Liechtenstein	16	18	18	23	22	0.00	-4.35
Luxembourg	102	136	197	137	154	0.01	12.41
Monaco	3	5	4	8	4	0.00	-50.00
Netherlands	10,085	11,123	10,690	10,354	10,466	0.92	1.08
Switzerland	8,725	8,540	8,786	8,884	9,452	0.83	6.39
East Mediterranean Europe	**3,713**	**4,592**	**4,678**	**4,319**	**4,948**	**0.43**	**14.56**
Cyprus	26	28	22	19	28	0.00	47.37
Israel	3,687	4,262	4,335	4,300	4,246	0.37	-1.26
Turkey		302	321		674	0.06	
Other Europe	**47**	**12,309**		**157**			
Other countries of Europe	47	12,309		157			
MIDDLE EAST	**302**	**443**	**532**	**551**	**540**	**0.05**	**-2.00**
Bahrain		14	4	6	3	0.00	-50.00
Palestine		2					
Iraq	24	7	13	8	12	0.00	50.00
Jordan	41	83	67	66	70	0.01	6.06
Kuwait	5	6	13	30	21	0.00	-30.00
Lebanon	130	133	222	228	201	0.02	-11.84
Libya		6			13	0.00	
Oman	4	2	5	4			
Qatar		1	10	11	2	0.00	-81.82
Saudi Arabia	11	25	27	52	49	0.00	-5.77
Syrian Arab Republic		26			8	0.00	
United Arab Emirates		2	11	13	15	0.00	15.38
Egypt	68	56	115	133	122	0.01	-8.27
Yemen	19	78	45		24	0.00	
Other countries of Middle East		2					
SOUTH ASIA	**1,093**	**1,666**	**2,880**	**3,653**	**3,719**	**0.33**	**1.81**
Afghanistan	11	28	70	62	13	0.00	-79.03
Bangladesh	11	107	321	362	115	0.01	-68.23
Bhutan		2	2				
Sri Lanka	22	35	178	255	344	0.03	34.90
India	795	1,212	1,570	2,060	3,073	0.27	49.17
Iran, Islamic Republic of	128	13		232	17	0.00	-92.67
Maldives		8	8	5	6	0.00	20.00
Nepal	12	82	234	159	23	0.00	-85.53
Pakistan	114	179	497	518	128	0.01	-75.29
NOT SPECIFIED	**1,594**	**16,051**			**6,516**	**0.57**	
Other countries of the World	1,594	16,051			6,516	0.57	

EGYPT

2. Arrivals of non-resident visitors at national borders, by nationality

		2007	2008	2009	2010	2011	Market share 11	% Change 11-10
TOTAL	(*)	11,090,863	12,835,351	12,535,885	14,730,813	9,845,066	100.00	-33.17
AFRICA		387,221	400,979	455,262	491,416	434,867	4.42	-11.51
East Africa		28,804	29,624	42,019	48,167	34,970	0.36	-27.40
Burundi		639	503	574	467	304	0.00	-34.90
Comoros		2,090	1,955	850	877	447	0.00	-49.03
Ethiopia		5,129	4,911	6,409	6,668	4,879	0.05	-26.83
Eritrea		4,827	2,986	5,323	6,661	4,743	0.05	-28.79
Djibouti		1,352	1,653	2,131	2,545	1,781	0.02	-30.02
Kenya		6,623	7,080	8,233	9,613	8,301	0.08	-13.65
Malawi		260	447	429	445	258	0.00	-42.02
Mauritius		591	671	1,004	999	529	0.01	-47.05
Mozambique		292	408	343	405	235	0.00	-41.98
Rwanda		549	426	510	419	385	0.00	-8.11
Seychelles		92	92	85	126	110	0.00	-12.70
Somalia		1,395	2,805	6,781	6,350	4,414	0.04	-30.49
Zimbabwe		1,108	1,401	1,046	1,372	627	0.01	-54.30
Uganda		1,875	1,822	2,495	2,533	3,138	0.03	23.88
United Republic of Tanzania		1,530	1,719	4,709	7,567	4,310	0.04	-43.04
Zambia		452	745	1,097	1,120	509	0.01	-54.55
Central Africa		5,201	5,808	5,940	6,030	23,187	0.24	284.53
Angola		560	576	678	547	303	0.00	-44.61
Cameroon		1,123	997	1,264	1,185	936	0.01	-21.01
Central African Republic		164	255	116	188	67	0.00	-64.36
Chad		2,161	2,199	2,292	2,620	20,758	0.21	692.29
Congo		827	928	1,035	686	443	0.00	-35.42
Democratic Republic of the Congo		67	561	242	532	464	0.00	-12.78
Gabon		285	290	301	262	216	0.00	-17.56
Sao Tome and Principe		14	2	12	10			
North Africa		266,963	271,482	296,555	319,137	282,187	2.87	-11.58
Algeria		28,153	37,958	44,585	22,782	20,982	0.21	-7.90
Morocco		29,313	39,495	53,663	57,591	37,274	0.38	-35.28
Sudan		169,143	159,124	159,588	189,731	200,376	2.04	5.61
Tunisia		40,354	34,905	38,719	49,033	23,555	0.24	-51.96
Southern Africa		37,954	36,142	32,981	38,260	19,604	0.20	-48.76
Botswana			152	166		103	0.00	
Lesotho		128	151	147	107	79	0.00	-26.17
Namibia		264	288	416	389	181	0.00	-53.47
South Africa		37,394	35,414	31,930	37,635	19,164	0.19	-49.08
Swaziland		168	137	322	129	77	0.00	-40.31
West Africa		47,004	56,789	76,006	77,846	74,271	0.75	-4.59
Benin		541	464	543	387	253	0.00	-34.63
Gambia		213	314	308	348	155	0.00	-55.46
Ghana		5,237	6,161	8,291	10,018	8,366	0.08	-16.49
Guinea		1,311	1,447	1,679	1,491	1,520	0.02	1.95
Côte d'Ivoire		1,120	1,185	1,056	1,262	702	0.01	-44.37
Liberia		301	224	185	276	178	0.00	-35.51
Mali		719	653	729	739	1,612	0.02	118.13
Mauritania		1,165	1,247	1,781	2,008	1,396	0.01	-30.48
Niger		477	2,170	1,156	1,343	10,670	0.11	694.49
Nigeria		34,057	40,636	57,967	57,731	47,889	0.49	-17.05
Guinea-Bissau		107	222	62	36	73	0.00	102.78
Senegal		1,127	1,384	1,425	1,432	999	0.01	-30.24
Sierra Leone		252	263	297	248	149	0.00	-39.92
Togo		377	419	527	527	309	0.00	-41.37
Other Africa		1,295	1,134	1,761	1,976	648	0.01	-67.21
Other countries of Africa		1,295	1,134	1,761	1,976	648	0.01	-67.21

EGYPT

2. Arrivals of non-resident visitors at national borders, by nationality

	2007	2008	2009	2010	2011	Market share 11	% Change 11-10
AMERICAS	429,863	486,099	488,785	563,365	287,187	2.92	-49.02
Caribbean	2,512	2,622	3,259	3,393	1,715	0.02	-49.45
Bahamas	64	51	83	63	22	0.00	-65.08
Barbados	266	82	58	60	32	0.00	-46.67
Cuba	629	760	823	742	437	0.00	-41.11
Dominica	797	681	801	941	382	0.00	-59.40
Haiti	77	70	104	125	67	0.00	-46.40
Jamaica	311	394	742	645	192	0.00	-70.23
Trinidad and Tobago	368	584	648	817	583	0.01	-28.64
Central America	4,433	4,837	7,497	9,082	4,083	0.04	-55.04
Costa Rica	938	1,279	1,360	2,333	663	0.01	-71.58
El Salvador	911	1,535	1,425	1,125	788	0.01	-29.96
Guatemala	844	660	1,326	1,796	494	0.01	-72.49
Honduras	1,449	1,018	2,577	2,907	387	0.00	-86.69
Nicaragua	74	98	448	387	191	0.00	-50.65
Panama	217	247	361	534	1,560	0.02	192.13
North America	366,678	420,463	421,593	476,314	240,990	2.45	-49.41
Canada	76,921	85,052	88,591	96,418	50,687	0.51	-47.43
Mexico	17,234	16,299	11,720	18,373	5,695	0.06	-69.00
United States of America	272,523	319,112	321,282	361,523	184,608	1.88	-48.94
South America	55,747	57,699	55,869	74,027	40,184	0.41	-45.72
Argentina	9,704	10,449	9,949	14,341	6,397	0.06	-55.39
Bolivia	553	453	536	770	422	0.00	-45.19
Brazil	19,445	22,075	19,695	30,384	17,249	0.18	-43.23
Chile	4,727	4,519	4,263	4,847	2,370	0.02	-51.10
Colombia	10,250	9,521	9,731	11,073	7,218	0.07	-34.81
Ecuador	2,652	2,653	2,618	3,529	2,124	0.02	-39.81
Guyana	56	33	33	39	17	0.00	-56.41
Paraguay	200	173	226	260	122	0.00	-53.08
Peru	2,560	2,413	3,362	3,691	1,806	0.02	-51.07
Suriname	230	252	70	85	47	0.00	-44.71
Uruguay	1,379	1,228	1,295	1,549	930	0.01	-39.96
Venezuela	3,991	3,930	4,091	3,459	1,482	0.02	-57.16
Other Americas	493	478	567	549	215	0.00	-60.84
Other countries of the Americas	493	478	567	549	215	0.00	-60.84
EAST ASIA AND THE PACIFIC	526,196	494,891	448,416	559,018	277,866	2.82	-50.29
North-East Asia	293,453	252,452	208,812	288,997	109,687	1.11	-62.05
China	80,447	67,714	80,933	106,227	48,620	0.49	-54.23
Taiwan, Province of China	14,952	18,331	7,414	11,042	6,743	0.07	-38.93
Japan	129,590	108,225	92,409	126,393	27,635	0.28	-78.14
Korea, Republic of	68,230	57,857	27,585	45,024	26,437	0.27	-41.28
Mongolia	234	325	471	311	252	0.00	-18.97
South-East Asia	145,882	152,011	154,479	176,156	121,454	1.23	-31.05
Cambodia	64	70	107	77	77	0.00	
Indonesia	37,383	33,303	35,377	44,841	31,236	0.32	-30.34
Malaysia	25,699	26,727	29,592	32,564	25,681	0.26	-21.14
Philippines	55,057	64,191	62,358	67,477	44,332	0.45	-34.30
Singapore	7,931	7,224	6,707	8,889	4,189	0.04	-52.87
Viet Nam	1,763	2,002	1,760	2,233	1,942	0.02	-13.03
Thailand	17,985	18,494	18,578	20,075	13,997	0.14	-30.28
Australasia	70,291	78,667	74,772	84,007	43,573	0.44	-48.13
Australia	58,842	66,653	63,029	71,723	36,676	0.37	-48.86
New Zealand	11,449	12,014	11,743	12,284	6,897	0.07	-43.85
Polynesia	35	19	51	54	5	0.00	-90.74
Samoa	35	19	51	54	5	0.00	-90.74

EGYPT

2. Arrivals of non-resident visitors at national borders, by nationality

	2007	2008	2009	2010	2011	Market share 11	% Change 11-10
Other East Asia and the Pacific	**16,535**	**11,742**	**10,302**	**9,804**	**3,147**	**0.03**	**-67.90**
Other countries of Asia	16,535	11,742	10,302	9,804	3,147	0.03	-67.90
EUROPE	**7,936,508**	**9,621,738**	**9,416,206**	**11,176,923**	**7,211,060**	**73.25**	**-35.48**
Central/Eastern Europe	**2,221,251**	**2,913,014**	**2,879,908**	**3,943,193**	**2,480,873**	**25.20**	**-37.08**
Azerbaijan	2,248	2,480	2,870	2,927	1,146	0.01	-60.85
Armenia	3,795	7,247	5,834	8,725	3,381	0.03	-61.25
Bulgaria	16,336	18,457	15,562	15,513	5,896	0.06	-61.99
Czech Republic/Slovakia	206,729	268,189	216,798	287,617	158,674	1.61	-44.83
Estonia	40,300	50,112	35,353	29,405	18,638	0.19	-36.62
Georgia	2,390	3,005	3,049	5,726	3,883	0.04	-32.19
Hungary	49,821	65,598	58,528	68,428	48,381	0.49	-29.30
Kazakhstan	10,908	21,867	13,114	17,950	5,512	0.06	-69.29
Poland	335,016	598,928	454,567	593,596	378,134	3.84	-36.30
Romania	35,529	50,459	38,903	55,649	23,864	0.24	-57.12
Russian Federation	1,516,561	1,825,312	2,035,330	2,855,723	1,832,388	18.61	-35.83
Uzbekistan	1,618	1,360		1,934	976	0.01	-49.53
Northern Europe	**1,339,235**	**1,607,857**	**1,801,029**	**2,023,857**	**1,371,079**	**13.93**	**-32.25**
Denmark	61,828	84,744	100,349	135,051	93,347	0.95	-30.88
Finland	37,050	63,763	65,227	93,865	42,191	0.43	-55.05
Iceland	731	743	624	879	614	0.01	-30.15
Ireland	31,836	36,744	62,458	30,733	18,976	0.19	-38.26
Norway	48,000	66,577	66,948	97,431	64,716	0.66	-33.58
Sweden	104,778	153,427	158,699	209,992	116,822	1.19	-44.37
United Kingdom	1,055,012	1,201,859	1,346,724	1,455,906	1,034,413	10.51	-28.95
Southern Europe	**1,279,305**	**1,375,935**	**1,309,096**	**1,450,553**	**671,699**	**6.82**	**-53.69**
Albania	3,902	5,686	5,127	4,034	3,115	0.03	-22.78
Croatia	8,376	10,018	9,407	11,891	5,248	0.05	-55.87
Greece	55,198	62,291	45,849	53,236	18,678	0.19	-64.91
Italy	983,293	1,073,159	1,047,997	1,144,384	555,246	5.64	-51.48
Malta	1,599	1,689	2,081	2,821	4,524	0.05	60.37
Portugal	14,726	15,878	17,182	20,451	8,607	0.09	-57.91
Slovenia	17,387	25,358	22,979	26,930	14,272	0.14	-47.00
Spain	171,084	156,236	136,227	149,402	34,909	0.35	-76.63
Serbia and Montenegro	23,740	25,620	22,247	37,404	27,100	0.28	-27.55
Western Europe	**2,284,711**	**2,669,047**	**2,603,121**	**2,860,729**	**1,985,465**	**20.17**	**-30.60**
Austria	179,500	208,547	214,298	240,516	168,298	1.71	-30.03
Belgium	175,199	209,007	189,475	195,919	155,793	1.58	-20.48
France	464,239	586,861	551,694	599,363	344,949	3.50	-42.45
Germany	1,085,930	1,202,509	1,202,339	1,328,960	964,599	9.80	-27.42
Luxembourg	4,640	7,166	9,056	7,920	4,933	0.05	-37.71
Monaco	174	102	182	183	61	0.00	-66.67
Netherlands	232,343	279,765	249,017	291,154	206,684	2.10	-29.01
Switzerland	142,686	175,090	187,060	196,714	140,148	1.42	-28.76
East Mediterranean Europe	**294,691**	**276,494**	**258,767**	**299,024**	**215,329**	**2.19**	**-27.99**
Cyprus	10,829	11,215	9,411	9,195	3,566	0.04	-61.22
Israel	234,494	213,125	203,275	226,456	177,808	1.81	-21.48
Turkey	49,368	52,154	46,081	63,373	33,955	0.34	-46.42
Other Europe	**517,315**	**779,391**	**564,285**	**599,567**	**486,615**	**4.94**	**-18.84**
Other countries of Europe	517,315	779,391	564,285	599,567	486,615	4.94	-18.84
MIDDLE EAST	**1,686,953**	**1,675,960**	**1,571,212**	**1,761,245**	**1,511,401**	**15.35**	**-14.19**
Bahrain	19,419	21,035	19,098	20,290	12,587	0.13	-37.96
Palestine	118,370	68,353	104,712	177,333	229,844	2.33	29.61
Iraq	24,888	26,170	32,437	38,432	35,137	0.36	-8.57
Jordan	182,050	173,913	164,247	171,217	151,835	1.54	-11.32
Kuwait	128,575	133,758	138,376	145,402	76,512	0.78	-47.38
Lebanon	67,002	68,959	74,822	75,475	52,340	0.53	-30.65

EGYPT

2. Arrivals of non-resident visitors at national borders, by nationality

	2007	2008	2009	2010	2011	Market share 11	% Change 11-10
Libya	439,469	481,548	410,222	451,068	524,544	5.33	16.29
Oman	20,396	23,318	19,037	20,435	12,391	0.13	-39.36
Qatar	25,658	24,451	21,123	24,787	16,129	0.16	-34.93
Saudi Arabia	412,466	402,287	347,971	374,946	198,320	2.01	-47.11
Syrian Arab Republic	114,922	112,450	106,864	115,657	102,367	1.04	-11.49
United Arab Emirates	52,426	53,552	49,578	53,815	24,661	0.25	-54.17
Yemen	81,312	86,166	82,725	92,388	74,734	0.76	-19.11
SOUTH ASIA	**105,874**	**116,199**	**118,004**	**144,192**	**101,718**	**1.03**	**-29.46**
Afghanistan	576	720	894	1,126	732	0.01	-34.99
Bangladesh	3,395	3,844	6,965	6,252	12,023	0.12	92.31
Sri Lanka	5,494	5,243	5,414	5,667	2,457	0.02	-56.64
India	82,481	88,811	86,698	114,248	73,443	0.75	-35.72
Iran, Islamic Republic of	988	943	3,503	849	542	0.01	-36.16
Maldives	229	279	230	258	218	0.00	-15.50
Nepal	977	1,191	1,413	1,589	1,558	0.02	-1.95
Pakistan	11,734	15,168	12,887	14,203	10,745	0.11	-24.35
NOT SPECIFIED	**18,248**	**39,485**	**38,000**	**34,654**	**20,967**	**0.21**	**-39.50**
Other countries of the World	18,248	39,485	38,000	34,654	20,967	0.21	-39.50

EGYPT

5. Overnight stays of non-resident tourists in hotels and similar establishments, by nationality

	2007	2008	2009	2010	2011	Market share 11	% Change 11-10
TOTAL	111,465,764	129,233,930	126,533,535	147,385,089	114,213,521	100.00	-22.51
AFRICA	5,088,137	5,112,829	5,357,057	5,956,672	6,100,700	5.34	2.42
East Africa	310,913	329,869	450,945	468,586	377,237	0.33	-19.49
Burundi	6,151	4,027	7,443	6,302	3,824	0.00	-39.32
Comoros	23,813	36,174	22,437	11,993	9,950	0.01	-17.03
Ethiopia	73,912	90,499	144,588	154,521	114,463	0.10	-25.92
Eritrea	54,527	32,524	37,741	35,698	38,814	0.03	8.73
Djibouti	21,401	20,493	31,778	34,214	26,808	0.02	-21.65
Kenya	46,778	62,707	78,238	93,421	90,525	0.08	-3.10
Malawi	2,893	3,913	4,468	6,326	3,131	0.00	-50.51
Mauritius	5,990	4,848	6,812	9,787	6,227	0.01	-36.37
Mozambique	3,186	4,033	4,703	4,090	2,943	0.00	-28.04
Rwanda	4,739	5,124	6,977	6,641	4,256	0.00	-35.91
Seychelles	1,172	509	628	1,560	873	0.00	-44.04
Somalia	24,259	21,502	45,404	41,305	19,461	0.02	-52.88
Zimbabwe	7,803	7,933	7,110	7,775	4,692	0.00	-39.65
Uganda	14,309	14,606	20,981	16,995	21,878	0.02	28.73
United Republic of Tanzania	15,503	15,033	23,913	27,674	23,436	0.02	-15.31
Zambia	4,477	5,944	7,724	10,284	5,956	0.01	-42.08
Central Africa	95,190	93,325	108,539	110,183	416,279	0.36	277.81
Angola	7,782	8,208	9,769	7,539	5,174	0.00	-31.37
Cameroon	15,999	11,308	18,014	14,996	11,708	0.01	-21.93
Chad	56,821	57,429	60,846	65,681	391,786	0.34	496.50
Congo	10,516	12,338	15,847	18,236	4,510	0.00	-75.27
Gabon	4,072	4,042	4,063	3,731	3,101	0.00	-16.89
North Africa	4,148,100	3,918,583	4,094,967	4,706,765	4,607,119	4.03	-2.12
Algeria	299,302	363,696	447,637	198,863	140,645	0.12	-29.28
Morocco	349,523	361,179	419,087	459,692	385,108	0.34	-16.22
Sudan	3,113,277	2,885,978	2,939,349	3,676,806	3,909,918	3.42	6.34
Tunisia	385,998	307,730	288,894	371,404	171,448	0.15	-53.84
Southern Africa	242,249	251,161	205,790	227,142	159,839	0.14	-29.63
Lesotho	2,516	1,204	1,174	1,311	669	0.00	-48.97
Namibia	2,954	2,831	5,617	4,016	2,198	0.00	-45.27
South Africa	235,621	245,160	196,939	220,803	156,679	0.14	-29.04
Swaziland	1,158	1,966	2,060	1,012	293	0.00	-71.05
West Africa	271,162	497,436	467,852	428,039	516,223	0.45	20.60
Ghana	20,432	24,188	29,868	34,278	44,467	0.04	29.72
Guinea	11,821	13,020	19,692	14,898	13,074	0.01	-12.24
Côte d'Ivoire	11,868	10,995	12,313	13,540	9,018	0.01	-33.40
Liberia	2,801	2,828	2,022	2,756	1,664	0.00	-39.62
Mali	6,770	7,271	10,482	5,916	14,381	0.01	143.09
Mauritania	16,066	12,489	17,655	14,735	15,121	0.01	2.62
Niger	4,922	56,911	15,221	7,269	58,604	0.05	706.22
Nigeria	175,879	347,168	337,594	316,364	344,069	0.30	8.76
Senegal	14,509	15,901	16,001	12,304	12,439	0.01	1.10
Sierra Leone	2,240	2,558	3,604	2,487	1,832	0.00	-26.34
Togo	3,854	4,107	3,400	3,492	1,554	0.00	-55.50
Other Africa	20,523	22,455	28,964	15,957	24,003	0.02	50.42
Other countries of Africa	20,523	22,455	28,964	15,957	24,003	0.02	50.42
AMERICAS	5,510,136	5,988,387	5,813,541	6,621,105	4,351,353	3.81	-34.28
Caribbean	20,776	24,758	26,897	23,784	17,809	0.02	-25.12
Bahamas	462	348	742	203	165	0.00	-18.72
Barbados	669	853	534	381	53	0.00	-86.09
Cuba	5,406	7,849	9,139	5,738	4,702	0.00	-18.06
Dominica	3,874	5,128	4,597	4,016	4,197	0.00	4.51

EGYPT

5. Overnight stays of non-resident tourists in hotels and similar establishments, by nationality

	2007	2008	2009	2010	2011	Market share 11	% Change 11-10
Haiti	669	557	1,267	471	171	0.00	-63.69
Jamaica	1,992	1,971	2,272	2,773	2,203	0.00	-20.56
Trinidad and Tobago	7,704	8,052	8,346	10,202	6,318	0.01	-38.07
Central America	**36,966**	**52,640**	**49,037**	**53,795**	**26,650**	**0.02**	**-50.46**
Costa Rica	10,721	12,538	11,457	13,939	7,405	0.01	-46.88
El Salvador	12,546	27,099	16,800	10,811	5,281	0.00	-51.15
Guatemala	6,696	5,948	10,198	17,022	6,145	0.01	-63.90
Honduras	4,256	3,536	5,644	5,642	5,218	0.00	-7.52
Nicaragua	874	1,446	1,574	1,789	726	0.00	-59.42
Panama	1,873	2,073	3,364	4,592	1,875	0.00	-59.17
North America	**4,917,659**	**5,303,908**	**5,201,244**	**5,869,144**	**3,824,276**	**3.35**	**-34.84**
Canada	1,157,194	1,101,333	1,133,889	1,255,121	858,008	0.75	-31.64
Mexico	147,037	146,115	110,542	144,387	63,865	0.06	-55.77
United States of America	3,613,428	4,056,460	3,956,813	4,469,636	2,902,403	2.54	-35.06
South America	**529,850**	**603,993**	**533,105**	**670,634**	**480,695**	**0.42**	**-28.32**
Argentina	88,207	99,677	102,793	134,008	76,337	0.07	-43.04
Bolivia	6,020	6,629	5,222	6,350	5,692	0.00	-10.36
Brazil	194,485	212,873	175,243	257,884	186,480	0.16	-27.69
Chile	41,708	43,420	42,883	49,486	29,718	0.03	-39.95
Colombia	96,540	99,998	99,401	105,020	89,722	0.08	-14.57
Ecuador	25,466	26,534	23,561	36,417	26,976	0.02	-25.92
Paraguay	2,300	1,487	3,500	2,869	1,744	0.00	-39.21
Peru	21,755	21,557	22,449	25,477	19,147	0.02	-24.85
Suriname	546	918	871	249	81	0.00	-67.47
Uruguay	15,894	16,345	16,524	15,206	14,008	0.01	-7.88
Venezuela	36,929	74,555	40,658	37,668	30,790	0.03	-18.26
Other Americas	**4,885**	**3,088**	**3,258**	**3,748**	**1,923**	**0.00**	**-48.69**
Other countries of the Americas	4,885	3,088	3,258	3,748	1,923	0.00	-48.69
EAST ASIA AND THE PACIFIC	**4,334,587**	**4,084,051**	**3,818,962**	**5,861,271**	**2,921,263**	**2.56**	**-50.16**
North-East Asia	**1,870,182**	**1,737,958**	**1,652,441**	**2,288,906**	**1,228,574**	**1.08**	**-46.32**
China	595,128	540,852	642,331	880,756	555,323	0.49	-36.95
Taiwan, Province of China	112,007	86,844	66,174	179,137	66,242	0.06	-63.02
Japan	841,987	745,838	707,721	877,508	332,490	0.29	-62.11
Korea, Republic of	316,687	361,697	227,518	347,497	270,570	0.24	-22.14
Mongolia	4,373	2,727	8,697	4,008	3,949	0.00	-1.47
South-East Asia	**1,243,414**	**1,158,156**	**1,025,127**	**1,161,642**	**946,086**	**0.83**	**-18.56**
Cambodia	716	310	530	646	204	0.00	-68.42
Indonesia	405,714	423,877	331,638	327,675	259,983	0.23	-20.66
Malaysia	201,989	197,960	206,536	245,785	223,029	0.20	-9.26
Philippines	470,135	380,850	324,148	410,095	296,380	0.26	-27.73
Singapore	86,717	77,338	86,415	97,862	69,880	0.06	-28.59
Thailand	78,143	77,821	75,860	79,579	96,610	0.08	21.40
Australasia	**1,090,246**	**1,082,839**	**1,056,791**	**1,122,553**	**702,092**	**0.61**	**-37.46**
Australia	951,422	935,995	919,436	977,937	604,408	0.53	-38.20
New Zealand	138,824	146,844	137,355	144,616	97,684	0.09	-32.45
Polynesia	**38**	**18**	**45**	**56**	**4**	**0.00**	**-92.86**
Samoa	38	18	45	56	4	0.00	-92.86
Other East Asia and the Pacific	**130,707**	**105,080**	**84,558**	**1,288,114**	**44,507**	**0.04**	**-96.54**
Other countries of Asia	130,707	105,080	84,558	1,288,114	44,507	0.04	-96.54
EUROPE	**73,373,241**	**90,870,680**	**89,331,393**	**102,969,099**	**73,976,481**	**64.77**	**-28.16**
Central/Eastern Europe	**20,254,589**	**22,120,075**	**24,974,882**	**33,738,278**	**20,299,965**	**17.77**	**-39.83**
Azerbaijan	16,472	22,522	27,527	25,061	21,582	0.02	-13.88
Armenia	34,761	65,054	64,241	71,008	27,741	0.02	-60.93
Bulgaria	119,514	173,243	138,967	129,931	70,745	0.06	-45.55
Czech Republic/Slovakia	1,705,717	2,119,978	1,843,756	2,441,086	1,435,309	1.26	-41.20

EGYPT

5. Overnight stays of non-resident tourists in hotels and similar establishments, by nationality

	2007	2008	2009	2010	2011	Market share 11	% Change 11-10
Estonia	332,870	391,799	263,617	223,861	157,134	0.14	-29.81
Georgia	22,446	24,411	27,762	58,858	35,334	0.03	-39.97
Hungary	435,822	589,160	523,747	557,788	477,576	0.42	-14.38
Kazakhstan	119,498	260,121	125,919	169,429	65,082	0.06	-61.59
Poland	2,872,202	4,529,071	3,721,789	4,546,312	3,248,698	2.84	-28.54
Romania	270,427	561,880	319,827	477,899	327,330	0.29	-31.51
Russian Federation	14,324,860	13,382,836	17,917,730	25,037,045	14,433,434	12.64	-42.35
Northern Europe	**12,718,713**	**17,427,199**	**18,306,200**	**21,001,596**	**16,302,687**	**14.27**	**-22.37**
Denmark	692,745	1,119,794	1,129,413	1,469,239	1,266,824	1.11	-13.78
Finland	415,699	704,038	558,535	914,589	564,362	0.49	-38.29
Iceland	7,076	9,299	6,781	9,396	6,719	0.01	-28.49
Ireland	323,169	413,763	337,774	332,812	258,976	0.23	-22.19
Norway	518,012	778,045	733,639	1,062,004	939,160	0.82	-11.57
Sweden	1,195,424	1,948,731	1,746,785	2,315,656	1,809,540	1.58	-21.86
United Kingdom	9,566,588	12,453,529	13,793,273	14,897,900	11,457,106	10.03	-23.10
Southern Europe	**11,202,228**	**13,467,392**	**11,778,286**	**12,945,224**	**7,393,784**	**6.47**	**-42.88**
Albania	33,842	87,621	58,796	49,028	43,332	0.04	-11.62
Croatia	120,731	178,623	127,828	117,065	83,720	0.07	-28.48
Greece	444,613	455,660	345,479	400,846	228,658	0.20	-42.96
Italy	8,003,500	10,310,777	9,307,804	9,972,492	6,007,113	5.26	-39.76
Malta	18,957	15,739	21,774	31,145	16,257	0.01	-47.80
Portugal	174,195	153,118	172,143	196,867	112,236	0.10	-42.99
Slovenia	161,361	239,567	202,543	229,338	118,547	0.10	-48.31
Spain	2,021,977	1,670,138	1,329,254	1,546,783	473,383	0.41	-69.40
Serbia and Montenegro	223,052	356,149	212,665	401,660	310,538	0.27	-22.69
Western Europe	**23,496,056**	**30,584,190**	**28,474,255**	**30,490,671**	**24,299,933**	**21.28**	**-20.30**
Austria	1,962,159	2,720,936	2,451,865	2,778,529	2,545,486	2.23	-8.39
Belgium	1,847,485	2,114,218	1,951,145	2,005,681	1,665,382	1.46	-16.97
France	4,183,457	6,117,383	5,603,877	5,253,060	3,484,272	3.05	-33.67
Germany	11,444,786	14,389,205	13,578,690	14,920,653	11,982,252	10.49	-19.69
Luxembourg	50,327	75,516	90,078	88,874	44,246	0.04	-50.21
Monaco	2,965	1,109	963	1,486	322	0.00	-78.33
Netherlands	2,588,963	3,214,069	2,930,926	3,471,090	2,921,817	2.56	-15.82
Switzerland	1,415,914	1,951,754	1,866,711	1,971,298	1,656,156	1.45	-15.99
East Mediterranean Europe	**1,686,522**	**2,335,736**	**1,564,214**	**1,862,701**	**1,554,914**	**1.36**	**-16.52**
Cyprus	76,277	72,285	72,403	77,869	55,205	0.05	-29.11
Israel	1,191,528	1,820,323	1,068,808	1,168,750	1,069,937	0.94	-8.45
Turkey	418,717	443,128	423,003	616,082	429,772	0.38	-30.24
Other Europe	**4,015,133**	**4,936,088**	**4,233,556**	**2,930,629**	**4,125,198**	**3.61**	**40.76**
Other countries of Europe	4,015,133	4,936,088	4,233,556	2,930,629	4,125,198	3.61	40.76
MIDDLE EAST	**21,907,966**	**21,391,309**	**20,833,755**	**24,313,983**	**25,593,272**	**22.41**	**5.26**
Bahrain	369,353	338,794	308,319	310,250	191,067	0.17	-38.42
Palestine	1,779,441	953,861	1,254,741	2,555,718	3,685,800	3.23	44.22
Iraq	487,582	468,652	490,934	538,607	750,661	0.66	39.37
Jordan	1,705,084	1,705,117	1,669,592	1,936,773	2,535,977	2.22	30.94
Kuwait	2,038,704	2,109,507	2,158,996	2,126,279	1,111,225	0.97	-47.74
Lebanon	709,870	673,407	685,059	722,037	735,614	0.64	1.88
Libya	4,910,713	5,397,908	5,194,416	6,151,782	8,351,661	7.31	35.76
Oman	410,425	385,979	306,367	320,584	251,165	0.22	-21.65
Qatar	426,944	346,585	329,682	369,349	270,589	0.24	-26.74
Saudi Arabia	5,505,863	5,459,214	4,846,004	5,236,041	3,901,955	3.42	-25.48
Syrian Arab Republic	1,212,892	1,191,379	1,180,034	1,384,272	1,602,653	1.40	15.78
United Arab Emirates	727,553	664,207	751,068	778,397	321,717	0.28	-58.67
Yemen	1,623,542	1,696,699	1,658,543	1,883,894	1,883,188	1.65	-0.04
SOUTH ASIA	**984,065**	**1,101,577**	**1,006,483**	**1,248,102**	**1,056,534**	**0.93**	**-15.35**
Afghanistan	6,774	7,598	12,784	14,414	7,718	0.01	-46.45

EGYPT

5. Overnight stays of non-resident tourists in hotels and similar establishments, by nationality

	2007	2008	2009	2010	2011	Market share 11	% Change 11-10
Bangladesh	26,691	29,756	53,998	41,861	128,775	0.11	207.63
Sri Lanka	89,128	70,656	63,998	71,920	44,048	0.04	-38.75
India	690,396	794,752	698,893	929,390	711,653	0.62	-23.43
Iran, Islamic Republic of	15,983	10,674	12,631	14,620	5,672	0.00	-61.20
Maldives	5,425	2,122	1,864	1,885	2,033	0.00	7.85
Nepal	18,004	16,542	16,489	21,112	17,423	0.02	-17.47
Pakistan	131,664	169,477	145,826	152,900	139,212	0.12	-8.95
NOT SPECIFIED	**267,632**	**685,097**	**372,344**	**414,857**	**213,918**	**0.19**	**-48.44**
Other countries of the World	267,632	685,097	372,344	414,857	213,918	0.19	-48.44

EL SALVADOR

1. Arrivals of non-resident tourists at national borders, by nationality

	2007	2008	2009	2010	2011	Market share 11	% Change 11-10
TOTAL	1,338,543	1,384,773	1,090,926	1,149,562	1,184,497	100.00	3.04
AFRICA	569	172	91	172	1,042	0.09	505.81
Southern Africa	294	46	11	156	120	0.01	-23.08
South Africa	294	46	11	156	120	0.01	-23.08
Other Africa	275	126	80	16	922	0.08	5662.50
Other countries of Africa	275	126	80	16	922	0.08	5662.50
AMERICAS	1,285,051	1,342,824	1,066,917	1,122,757	1,139,773	96.22	1.52
Caribbean	4,804	3,249	2,452	2,602	3,086	0.26	18.60
Cuba	642	519	596	861	580	0.05	-32.64
Dominican Republic	2,285	2,009	1,321	1,292	1,847	0.16	42.96
Haiti	109	120	95	95	110	0.01	15.79
Jamaica	398	198	162	119	154	0.01	29.41
Trinidad and Tobago	384	222	66	156	152	0.01	-2.56
Other countries of the Caribbean	986	181	212	79	243	0.02	207.59
Central America	852,660	889,531	673,324	739,843	734,798	62.03	-0.68
Belize	2,770	2,342	1,611	2,508	1,317	0.11	-47.49
Costa Rica	44,782	27,668	17,714	18,443	20,300	1.71	10.07
Guatemala	488,453	537,578	462,944	518,957	535,246	45.19	3.14
Honduras	189,453	213,075	138,104	145,868	126,446	10.68	-13.31
Nicaragua	113,883	96,956	42,844	43,488	40,756	3.44	-6.28
Panama	13,319	11,912	10,107	10,579	10,733	0.91	1.46
North America	386,543	422,907	371,280	356,608	368,640	31.12	3.37
Canada	33,827	32,050	26,333	20,432	28,205	2.38	38.04
Mexico	32,418	28,999	17,633	17,607	19,699	1.66	11.88
United States of America	320,298	361,858	327,314	318,569	320,736	27.08	0.68
South America	41,044	27,137	19,861	23,704	33,249	2.81	40.27
Argentina	5,807	4,291	2,673	2,501	3,727	0.31	49.02
Bolivia	798	607	409	401	562	0.05	40.15
Brazil	5,849	4,337	3,613	4,180	4,816	0.41	15.22
Chile	3,766	2,872	1,511	2,090	2,194	0.19	4.98
Colombia	9,103	6,661	5,957	7,698	12,062	1.02	56.69
Ecuador	1,858	1,503	1,016	1,108	1,706	0.14	53.97
Paraguay	380	229	243	322	458	0.04	42.24
Peru	7,731	3,292	1,914	2,269	4,334	0.37	91.01
Uruguay	964	838	69	1,183	680	0.06	-42.52
Venezuela	4,432	2,497	501	1,871	2,656	0.22	41.96
Other countries of South America	356	10	1,955	81	54	0.00	-33.33
EAST ASIA AND THE PACIFIC	11,699	8,556	5,068	6,750	9,838	0.83	45.75
North-East Asia	7,140	4,676	1,845	4,011	5,453	0.46	35.95
China	338	1,714	704	2,276	1,527	0.13	-32.91
Taiwan, Province of China	1,605	309					
Japan	3,615	1,882	863	839	3,184	0.27	279.50
Korea, Republic of	1,582	771	278	896	742	0.06	-17.19
Australasia	2,911	1,707	1,803	1,784	2,764	0.23	54.93
Australia	2,728	1,584	1,706	1,745	2,508	0.21	43.72
New Zealand	183	123	97	39	256	0.02	556.41
Other East Asia and the Pacific	1,648	2,173	1,420	955	1,621	0.14	69.74
Other countries of Asia	1,600	2,150	1,323	916	1,590	0.13	73.58
Other countries of Oceania	48	23	97	39	31	0.00	-20.51
EUROPE	41,190	33,198	18,842	19,879	33,811	2.85	70.08
Central/Eastern Europe	798	3,566	900	1,004	347	0.03	-65.44
Czech Republic/Slovakia	555	2,994	677	877	250	0.02	-71.49
Poland	243	572	223	127	97	0.01	-23.62

EL SALVADOR

1. Arrivals of non-resident tourists at national borders, by nationality

	2007	2008	2009	2010	2011	Market share 11	% Change 11-10
Northern Europe	**7,554**	**6,215**	**3,145**	**2,238**	**3,921**	**0.33**	**75.20**
Denmark	559	1,311	286	284	275	0.02	-3.17
Finland	326	176	105	68	145	0.01	113.24
Iceland	105	12	539	22	91	0.01	313.64
Ireland	986	891	421	407	341	0.03	-16.22
Norway	401	270	135	161	197	0.02	22.36
Sweden	1,928	1,379	632	537	953	0.08	77.47
United Kingdom	3,249	2,176	1,027	759	1,919	0.16	152.83
Southern Europe	**17,005**	**12,037**	**8,575**	**8,462**	**16,174**	**1.37**	**91.14**
Greece	188	172	109	46	61	0.01	32.61
Italy	4,448	3,054	2,843	2,475	5,228	0.44	111.23
Portugal	325	232	85	86	265	0.02	208.14
Spain	12,003	8,543	5,496	5,843	10,620	0.90	81.76
Yugoslavia, SFR (former)	41	36	42	12			
Western Europe	**12,536**	**9,630**	**5,401**	**5,233**	**11,129**	**0.94**	**112.67**
Austria	429	199	185	146	365	0.03	150.00
Belgium	915	822	260	365	471	0.04	29.04
France	2,302	2,063	1,780	1,332	3,023	0.26	126.95
Germany	5,671	4,128	1,968	2,020	4,993	0.42	147.18
Netherlands	1,954	1,273	419	589	1,368	0.12	132.26
Switzerland	1,265	1,145	789	781	909	0.08	16.39
East Mediterranean Europe	**1,170**	**542**	**376**	**477**	**460**	**0.04**	**-3.56**
Israel	1,170	542	376	477	460	0.04	-3.56
Other Europe	**2,127**	**1,208**	**445**	**2,465**	**1,780**	**0.15**	**-27.79**
Other countries of Europe	2,127	1,208	445	2,465	1,780	0.15	-27.79
MIDDLE EAST	**34**	**23**	**8**	**4**	**33**	**0.00**	**725.00**
Egypt	34	23	8	4	33	0.00	725.00

EL SALVADOR

3. Arrivals of non-resident tourists in hotels and similar establishments, by nationality

	2007	2008	2009	2010	2011	Market share 11	% Change 11-10
TOTAL	374,983	376,170	461,436	595,281	642,280	100.00	7.90
AFRICA	5	2	48	70	202	0.03	188.57
Southern Africa	3		48	70	47	0.01	-32.86
South Africa	3		48	70	47	0.01	-32.86
Other Africa	2	2			155	0.02	
Other countries of Africa	2				155	0.02	
All countries of Africa		2					
AMERICAS	354,840	361,976	451,021	586,178	624,801	97.28	6.59
Caribbean	2,191	1,413	1,299	1,057	1,691	0.26	59.98
Cuba	6	5	316	350	318	0.05	-9.14
Dominican Republic	1,232	1,083	700	525	1,013	0.16	92.95
Jamaica	215	107	50	39	84	0.01	115.38
Trinidad and Tobago	207	120	86	48	83	0.01	72.92
Other countries of the Caribbean	531	98	147	95	193	0.03	103.16
Central America	278,509	288,159	316,414	457,164	504,219	78.50	10.29
Belize	936	792	596	676	722	0.11	6.80
Costa Rica	15,136	9,352	6,554	4,970	11,132	1.73	123.98
Guatemala	160,701	176,863	241,194	372,871	416,082	64.78	11.59
Honduras	52,478	59,022	44,193	48,064	41,991	6.54	-12.64
Nicaragua	44,756	38,104	20,137	27,732	28,406	4.42	2.43
Panama	4,502	4,026	3,740	2,851	5,886	0.92	106.45
North America	59,602	63,414	119,173	115,975	99,466	15.49	-14.23
Canada	12,854	12,179	8,690	6,835	11,022	1.72	61.26
Mexico	6,711	6,003	2,469	2,579	11,403	1.78	342.15
United States of America	40,037	45,232	108,014	106,561	77,041	11.99	-27.70
South America	14,538	8,990	7,861	7,248	13,308	2.07	83.61
Argentina	3,118	2,304	1,902	1,264	2,177	0.34	72.23
Colombia	4,888	3,577	4,240	3,891	7,047	1.10	81.11
Peru	4,152	1,768	1,362	1,147	2,532	0.39	120.75
Venezuela	2,380	1,341	357	946	1,552	0.24	64.06
Other Americas			6,274	4,734	6,117	0.95	29.21
Other countries of the Americas			6,274	4,734	6,117	0.95	29.21
EAST ASIA AND THE PACIFIC	77	66	2,537	2,379	3,852	0.60	61.92
North-East Asia	36	32	830	1,266	1,841	0.29	45.42
China	3	15	373	925	597	0.09	-35.46
Japan	33	17	457	341	1,244	0.19	264.81
Australasia	27	15	955	725	1,080	0.17	48.97
Australia	25	14	904	709	980	0.15	38.22
New Zealand	2	1	51	16	100	0.02	525.00
Other East Asia and the Pacific	14	19	752	388	931	0.14	139.95
Other countries of Asia	14	19	701	372	911	0.14	144.89
Other countries of Oceania			51	16	20	0.00	25.00
EUROPE	20,041	14,112	7,830	6,652	13,423	2.09	101.79
Northern Europe	2,503	1,813	767	474	883	0.14	86.29
Ireland	583	527	223	165	133	0.02	-19.39
United Kingdom	1,920	1,286	544	309	750	0.12	142.72
Southern Europe	9,723	6,854	4,420	3,381	6,193	0.96	83.17
Italy	2,629	1,805	1,507	1,006	2,043	0.32	103.08
Spain	7,094	5,049	2,913	2,375	4,150	0.65	74.74
Western Europe	5,867	4,411	2,208	1,601	3,667	0.57	129.04
France	1,360	1,219	943	541	1,181	0.18	118.30
Germany	3,352	2,440	1,043	821	1,951	0.30	137.64

EL SALVADOR

3. Arrivals of non-resident tourists in hotels and similar establishments, by nationality

	2007	2008	2009	2010	2011	Market share 11	% Change 11-10
Netherlands	1,155	752	222	239	535	0.08	123.85
East Mediterranean Europe	**691**	**320**	**199**	**194**	**180**	**0.03**	**-7.22**
Israel	691	320	199	194	180	0.03	-7.22
Other Europe	**1,257**	**714**	**236**	**1,002**	**2,500**	**0.39**	**149.50**
Other countries of Europe	1,257	714	236	1,002	2,500	0.39	149.50
MIDDLE EAST	**20**	**14**		**2**	**2**	**0.00**	
Egypt	20	14		2	2	0.00	

EL SALVADOR

5. Overnight stays of non-resident tourists in hotels and similar establishments, by nationality

	2007	2008	2009	2010	2011	Market share 11	% Change 11-10
TOTAL			2,741,223	2,815,521	2,694,470	100.00	-4.30
AFRICA					1,803	0.07	
Other Africa					1,803	0.07	
All countries of Africa					1,803	0.07	
AMERICAS			2,667,294	2,767,057	2,538,226	94.20	-8.27
Caribbean			6,130	6,505	14,046	0.52	115.93
All countries of the Caribbean			6,130	6,505	14,046	0.52	115.93
Central America			1,683,310	1,809,771	1,390,387	51.60	-23.17
Belize			4,029	6,270	5,994	0.22	-4.40
Costa Rica			44,285	26,448	92,393	3.43	249.34
Guatemala			1,157,361	1,297,393	954,245	35.41	-26.45
Honduras			345,260	364,670	152,449	5.66	-58.20
Nicaragua			107,110	108,720	136,456	5.06	25.51
Panama			25,265	6,270	48,850	1.81	679.11
North America			928,202	891,521	932,237	34.60	4.57
Canada			65,834	51,080	98,532	3.66	92.90
Mexico			44,084	44,018	98,421	3.65	123.59
United States of America			818,284	796,423	735,284	27.29	-7.68
South America			49,652	59,260	201,556	7.48	240.12
All countries of South America			49,652	59,260	201,556	7.48	240.12
EAST ASIA AND THE PACIFIC			8,163	10,579	36,045	1.34	240.72
Other East Asia and the Pacific			8,163	10,579	36,045	1.34	240.72
All countries East Asia/Pacific			8,163	10,579	36,045	1.34	240.72
EUROPE			65,766	37,885	118,396	4.39	212.51
Southern Europe			13,740	26,294	37,100	1.38	41.10
Spain			13,740	26,294	37,100	1.38	41.10
Western Europe			4,921	9,090	17,443	0.65	91.89
Germany			4,921	9,090	17,443	0.65	91.89
Other Europe			47,105	2,501	63,853	2.37	2453.10
Other countries of Europe			47,105	2,501	63,853	2.37	2453.10

EL SALVADOR

6. Overnight stays of non-resident tourists in all types of accommodation establishments, by nationality

	2007	2008	2009	2010	2011	Market share 11	% Change 11-10
TOTAL	9,383,397	9,642,351	5,844,349	6,045,433	6,404,634	100.00	5.94
AFRICA	5,349	1,617	683	1,118	4,613	0.07	312.61
Other Africa	5,349	1,617	683	1,118	4,613	0.07	312.61
All countries of Africa	5,349	1,617	683	1,118	4,613	0.07	312.61
AMERICAS	9,107,689	9,447,888	5,712,853	5,932,413	6,004,796	93.76	1.22
Caribbean	45,158	30,541	18,390	16,913	25,614	0.40	51.45
All countries of the Caribbean	45,158	30,541	18,390	16,913	25,614	0.40	51.45
Central America	3,432,000	3,397,116	2,760,903	3,443,471	2,150,875	33.58	-37.54
Belize	31,578	26,699	12,086	16,302	10,931	0.17	-32.95
Costa Rica	510,515	315,415	132,856	119,880	168,490	2.63	40.55
Guatemala	1,611,895	1,774,007	1,481,422	2,335,307	1,227,534	19.17	-47.44
Honduras	682,031	767,070	925,889	656,406	459,061	7.17	-30.06
Nicaragua	444,144	378,128	132,856	195,696	195,775	3.06	0.04
Panama	151,837	135,797	75,794	119,880	89,084	1.39	-25.69
North America	5,220,091	5,748,861	2,784,604	2,317,953	3,483,323	54.39	50.28
Canada	321,357	304,475	197,501	132,808	252,150	3.94	89.86
Mexico	382,532	342,188	132,251	114,446	170,025	2.65	48.56
United States of America	4,516,202	5,102,198	2,454,852	2,070,699	3,061,148	47.80	47.83
South America	410,440	271,370	148,956	154,076	344,984	5.39	123.91
All countries of South America	410,440	271,370	148,956	154,076	344,984	5.39	123.91
EAST ASIA AND THE PACIFIC	109,971	80,426	62,038	32,026	92,242	1.44	188.02
Other East Asia and the Pacific	109,971	80,426	62,038	32,026	92,242	1.44	188.02
All countries East Asia/Pacific	109,971	80,426	62,038	32,026	92,242	1.44	188.02
EUROPE	160,388	112,420	68,775	79,876	302,983	4.73	279.32
Southern Europe	97,224	69,198	41,219	37,980	94,942	1.48	149.98
Spain	97,224	69,198	41,219	37,980	94,942	1.48	149.98
Western Europe	45,935	33,437	14,763	30,300	44,637	0.70	47.32
Germany	45,935	33,437	14,763	30,300	44,637	0.70	47.32
Other Europe	17,229	9,785	12,793	11,596	163,404	2.55	1309.14
Other countries of Europe	17,229	9,785	12,793	11,596	163,404	2.55	1309.14

ERITREA

2. Arrivals of non-resident visitors at national borders, by nationality

	2007	2008	2009	2010	2011	Market share 11	% Change 11-10
TOTAL	80,503	69,897	79,334	83,947	107,090	100.00	27.57
AFRICA	5,051	4,929	6,825	7,854	21,319	19.91	171.44
East Africa	1,467	677	466	804	662	0.62	-17.66
Ethiopia	56	38	32	68	49	0.05	-27.94
Kenya	610	312	234	247	343	0.32	38.87
Madagascar	3	1					
Malawi	18	14	11	15	7	0.01	-53.33
Mauritius	1						
Mozambique	16	10	3	3	8	0.01	166.67
Somalia	460	152	44	75	30	0.03	-60.00
Zimbabwe	70	50	38	101	73	0.07	-27.72
Uganda	137	29	22	67	35	0.03	-47.76
United Republic of Tanzania	51	19	14	14	15	0.01	7.14
Zambia	45	52	68	214	102	0.10	-52.34
North Africa	2,413	3,570	5,866	6,220	19,653	18.35	215.96
Sudan	2,413	3,570	5,866	6,220	19,653	18.35	215.96
Southern Africa	193	168	157	460	471	0.44	2.39
Botswana	9	2	2	6	3	0.00	-50.00
Namibia	12	7	2	4	16	0.01	300.00
South Africa	172	159	153	450	452	0.42	0.44
Other Africa	978	514	336	370	533	0.50	44.05
Other countries of Africa	978	514	336	370	533	0.50	44.05
AMERICAS	983	858	775	1,149	1,314	1.23	14.36
North America	775	728	710	1,085	1,269	1.18	16.96
Canada	269	229	199	347	438	0.41	26.22
United States of America	506	499	511	738	831	0.78	12.60
Other Americas	208	130	65	64	45	0.04	-29.69
Other countries of the Americas	208	130	65	64	45	0.04	-29.69
EAST ASIA AND THE PACIFIC	1,935	1,824	1,403	1,436	1,698	1.59	18.25
North-East Asia	1,161	1,322	858	659	1,010	0.94	53.26
China	374	468	671	594	871	0.81	46.63
Japan	743	773	151	60	78	0.07	30.00
Korea, Republic of	44	81	36	5	61	0.06	1120.00
South-East Asia	167	95	211	272	179	0.17	-34.19
Indonesia	30	12	27	34	48	0.04	41.18
Malaysia	43	35	2	5	12	0.01	140.00
Philippines	93	47	182	233	117	0.11	-49.79
Singapore	1	1			2	0.00	
Australasia	249	191	196	215	322	0.30	49.77
Australia	204	165	183	186	291	0.27	56.45
New Zealand	45	26	13	29	31	0.03	6.90
Other East Asia and the Pacific	358	216	138	290	187	0.17	-35.52
Other countries of Asia	358	216	138	290	187	0.17	-35.52
EUROPE	5,408	5,182	5,064	4,869	5,169	4.83	6.16
Northern Europe	1,105	1,040	1,249	1,143	1,324	1.24	15.84
United Kingdom	731	680	843	703	968	0.90	37.70
Scandinavia	374	360	406	440	356	0.33	-19.09
Southern Europe	2,023	2,108	1,944	1,754	1,694	1.58	-3.42
Italy	2,023	2,108	1,944	1,754	1,694	1.58	-3.42
Western Europe	1,609	1,499	1,373	1,609	1,610	1.50	0.06
France	406	270	372	381	260	0.24	-31.76
Germany	825	742	775	880	1,004	0.94	14.09

ERITREA

2. Arrivals of non-resident visitors at national borders, by nationality

	2007	2008	2009	2010	2011	Market share 11	% Change 11-10
Netherlands	162	267	78	151	159	0.15	5.30
Switzerland	157	156	75	104	138	0.13	32.69
Benelux	53	58	49	41	47	0.04	14.63
Other countries of Western Europe	6	6	24	52	2	0.00	-96.15
East Mediterranean Europe	**48**	**52**	**25**	**19**	**35**	**0.03**	**84.21**
Israel	48	52	25	19	35	0.03	84.21
Other Europe	**623**	**483**	**473**	**344**	**506**	**0.47**	**47.09**
Other countries of Europe	623	483	473	344	506	0.47	47.09
MIDDLE EAST	**2,249**	**1,494**	**1,343**	**1,326**	**1,224**	**1.14**	**-7.69**
Saudi Arabia	413	553	423	261	392	0.37	50.19
Egypt	175	347	262	282	304	0.28	7.80
Yemen	290	161	275	473	299	0.28	-36.79
Other countries of Middle East	1,371	433	383	310	229	0.21	-26.13
SOUTH ASIA	**2,973**	**395**	**718**	**730**	**577**	**0.54**	**-20.96**
India	2,973	395	718	730	577	0.54	-20.96
NOT SPECIFIED	**61,904**	**55,215**	**63,206**	**66,583**	**75,789**	**70.77**	**13.83**
Other countries of the World		44	41				
Nationals Residing Abroad	61,904	55,171	63,165	66,583	75,789	70.77	13.83

ESTONIA

3. Arrivals of non-resident tourists in hotels and similar establishments, by country of residence

	2007	2008	2009	2010	2011	Market share 11	% Change 11-10
TOTAL	1,286,423	1,353,034	1,307,548	1,487,497	1,702,592	100.00	14.46
AFRICA	888	1,087	880	1,155	1,946	0.11	68.48
Southern Africa	249	258	219	230	404	0.02	75.65
South Africa	249	258	219	230	404	0.02	75.65
Other Africa	639	829	661	925	1,542	0.09	66.70
Other countries of Africa	639	829	661	925	1,542	0.09	66.70
AMERICAS	24,393	22,477	20,387	24,996	29,728	1.75	18.93
North America	22,740	20,259	18,509	21,748	25,918	1.52	19.17
Canada	2,978	2,861	3,876	2,807	3,725	0.22	32.70
United States of America	19,762	17,398	14,633	18,941	22,193	1.30	17.17
South America	691	777	1,034	1,833	1,700	0.10	-7.26
Brazil	691	777	1,034	1,833	1,700	0.10	-7.26
Other Americas	962	1,441	844	1,415	2,110	0.12	49.12
Other countries of the Americas	962	1,441	844	1,415	2,110	0.12	49.12
EAST ASIA AND THE PACIFIC	14,359	16,087	18,164	19,943	26,416	1.55	32.46
North-East Asia	7,737	8,843	10,016	11,464	15,534	0.91	35.50
China	797	1,701	1,888	2,642	5,185	0.30	96.25
Japan	6,341	6,578	6,973	6,988	8,263	0.49	18.25
Korea, Republic of	599	564	1,155	1,834	2,086	0.12	13.74
Australasia	3,364	3,295	3,046	3,127	4,383	0.26	40.17
Australia	3,364	3,295	3,046	3,127	4,383	0.26	40.17
Other East Asia and the Pacific	3,258	3,949	5,102	5,352	6,499	0.38	21.43
Other countries of Asia	2,601	3,110	4,487	4,708	5,696	0.33	20.99
Other countries of Oceania	657	839	615	644	803	0.05	24.69
EUROPE	1,245,200	1,312,582	1,264,256	1,429,858	1,632,102	95.86	14.14
Central/Eastern Europe	177,612	215,800	206,269	261,785	353,824	20.78	35.16
Bulgaria	782	925	916	1,501	1,559	0.09	3.86
Czech Republic	4,852	4,299	4,385	3,855	4,588	0.27	19.01
Hungary	3,132	3,062	2,015	2,447	3,318	0.19	35.59
Latvia	62,299	67,755	59,849	63,625	74,751	4.39	17.49
Lithuania	31,528	36,285	29,077	29,848	41,543	2.44	39.18
Poland	16,445	18,253	15,001	17,491	24,807	1.46	41.83
Romania	923	1,028	1,128	1,257	2,213	0.13	76.05
Russian Federation	53,624	78,494	89,429	135,665	192,456	11.30	41.86
Slovakia	779	1,154	860	1,393	1,469	0.09	5.46
Ukraine	3,248	4,545	3,609	4,703	7,120	0.42	51.39
Northern Europe	889,292	897,890	889,818	975,315	1,030,368	60.52	5.64
Denmark	13,152	13,652	11,354	10,341	12,821	0.75	23.98
Finland	678,657	707,477	730,011	810,711	812,998	47.75	0.28
Iceland	1,978	1,019	546	717	947	0.06	32.08
Ireland	3,110	2,810	2,297	1,986	7,185	0.42	261.78
Norway	53,875	45,838	39,318	39,258	49,984	2.94	27.32
Sweden	86,680	83,484	74,833	78,696	82,839	4.87	5.26
United Kingdom	51,840	43,610	31,459	33,606	63,594	3.74	89.23
Southern Europe	42,710	45,756	37,391	42,780	61,287	3.60	43.26
Greece	2,589	2,404	2,240	3,319	2,613	0.15	-21.27
Italy	21,559	23,542	17,673	20,851	30,262	1.78	45.13
Malta	103	216	212	258	247	0.01	-4.26
Portugal	2,542	2,376	2,358	2,100	2,703	0.16	28.71
Slovenia	974	1,064	787	1,149	1,126	0.07	-2.00
Spain	14,943	16,154	14,121	15,103	24,336	1.43	61.13
Western Europe	118,637	130,692	110,386	122,082	152,872	8.98	25.22
Austria	5,181	7,646	6,078	4,819	7,131	0.42	47.98

ESTONIA

3. Arrivals of non-resident tourists in hotels and similar establishments, by country of residence

	2007	2008	2009	2010	2011	Market share 11	% Change 11-10
Belgium	5,410	6,130	5,460	5,760	8,502	0.50	47.60
France	14,676	16,163	14,776	16,694	19,008	1.12	13.86
Germany	77,718	83,034	68,236	77,447	94,082	5.53	21.48
Luxembourg	493	722	814	878	964	0.06	9.79
Netherlands	10,413	10,931	9,863	10,100	15,063	0.88	49.14
Switzerland	4,746	6,066	5,159	6,384	8,122	0.48	27.22
East Mediterranean Europe	**1,400**	**3,286**	**2,834**	**3,567**	**4,861**	**0.29**	**36.28**
Cyprus	528	569	286	380	470	0.03	23.68
Turkey	872	2,717	2,548	3,187	4,391	0.26	37.78
Other Europe	**15,549**	**19,158**	**17,558**	**24,329**	**28,890**	**1.70**	**18.75**
Other countries of Europe	15,549	19,158	17,558	24,329	28,890	1.70	18.75
NOT SPECIFIED	**1,583**	**801**	**3,861**	**11,545**	**12,400**	**0.73**	**7.41**
Other countries of the World	1,583	801	3,861	11,545	12,400	0.73	7.41

ESTONIA

4. Arrivals of non-resident tourists in all types of accommodation establishments, by country of residence

	2007	2008	2009	2010	2011	Market share 11	% Change 11-10
TOTAL	1,380,323	1,433,346	1,380,540	1,563,952	1,807,919	100.00	15.60
AFRICA	1,013	1,152	1,031	1,221	2,057	0.11	68.47
Southern Africa	266	268	258	259	433	0.02	67.18
South Africa	266	268	258	259	433	0.02	67.18
Other Africa	747	884	773	962	1,624	0.09	68.81
Other countries of Africa	747	884	773	962	1,624	0.09	68.81
AMERICAS	27,787	24,990	23,023	27,213	32,454	1.80	19.26
North America	25,846	22,532	20,864	23,742	28,095	1.55	18.33
Canada	3,677	3,347	4,580	3,239	4,271	0.24	31.86
United States of America	22,169	19,185	16,284	20,503	23,824	1.32	16.20
South America	842	878	1,162	1,899	1,985	0.11	4.53
Brazil	842	878	1,162	1,899	1,985	0.11	4.53
Other Americas	1,099	1,580	997	1,572	2,374	0.13	51.02
Other countries of the Americas	1,099	1,580	997	1,572	2,374	0.13	51.02
EAST ASIA AND THE PACIFIC	17,101	18,164	20,210	21,687	29,348	1.62	35.33
North-East Asia	8,581	9,474	10,663	12,063	16,692	0.92	38.37
China	1,020	1,895	2,058	2,823	5,549	0.31	96.56
Japan	6,799	6,862	7,253	7,235	8,732	0.48	20.69
Korea, Republic of	762	717	1,352	2,005	2,411	0.13	20.25
Australasia	4,799	4,171	3,849	3,695	5,472	0.30	48.09
Australia	4,799	4,171	3,849	3,695	5,472	0.30	48.09
Other East Asia and the Pacific	3,721	4,519	5,698	5,929	7,184	0.40	21.17
Other countries of Asia	2,754	3,336	4,753	5,063	6,216	0.34	22.77
Other countries of Oceania	967	1,183	945	866	968	0.05	11.78
EUROPE	1,332,798	1,388,201	1,332,335	1,502,008	1,731,493	95.77	15.28
Central/Eastern Europe	200,730	241,233	227,474	285,508	385,521	21.32	35.03
Bulgaria	847	993	1,005	1,625	1,668	0.09	2.65
Czech Republic	5,465	5,113	5,232	4,550	5,669	0.31	24.59
Hungary	3,638	3,648	2,306	2,800	3,694	0.20	31.93
Latvia	74,667	79,527	68,320	72,684	85,229	4.71	17.26
Lithuania	35,561	41,396	33,441	34,107	47,003	2.60	37.81
Poland	18,555	20,859	17,062	19,522	27,093	1.50	38.78
Romania	1,033	1,136	1,167	1,343	2,295	0.13	70.89
Russian Federation	56,407	82,280	93,947	141,964	203,204	11.24	43.14
Slovakia	909	1,362	978	1,643	1,860	0.10	13.21
Ukraine	3,648	4,919	4,016	5,270	7,806	0.43	48.12
Northern Europe	929,368	926,796	917,900	1,004,269	1,071,562	59.27	6.70
Denmark	14,053	14,281	12,036	11,140	13,902	0.77	24.79
Finland	707,124	728,181	750,984	832,874	840,714	46.50	0.94
Iceland	2,159	1,082	588	761	994	0.05	30.62
Ireland	3,699	3,129	2,512	2,192	8,243	0.46	276.05
Norway	55,999	47,240	40,915	40,414	51,510	2.85	27.46
Sweden	90,221	86,308	77,470	81,196	86,287	4.77	6.27
United Kingdom	56,113	46,575	33,395	35,692	69,912	3.87	95.88
Southern Europe	50,176	51,655	42,462	48,332	69,540	3.85	43.88
Albania	113	159	94	173	198	0.01	14.45
Croatia	944	660	526	719	1,232	0.07	71.35
Greece	2,712	2,535	2,337	3,447	2,711	0.15	-21.35
Italy	24,901	26,280	19,959	23,017	33,618	1.86	46.06
Malta	118	271	248	315	314	0.02	-0.32
Portugal	2,763	2,644	2,617	2,471	3,026	0.17	22.46
Slovenia	1,171	1,262	974	1,330	1,335	0.07	0.38
Spain	17,454	17,844	15,707	16,860	27,106	1.50	60.77

ESTONIA

4. Arrivals of non-resident tourists in all types of accommodation establishments, by country of residence

	2007	2008	2009	2010	2011	Market share 11	% Change 11-10
Western Europe	**135,284**	**145,850**	**124,060**	**135,403**	**170,941**	**9.46**	**26.25**
Austria	6,085	8,561	6,859	5,473	7,841	0.43	43.27
Belgium	6,094	6,860	6,077	6,418	9,197	0.51	43.30
France	17,813	18,522	16,864	19,319	22,301	1.23	15.44
Germany	87,109	91,915	75,966	84,454	103,559	5.73	22.62
Luxembourg	590	779	890	902	992	0.05	9.98
Netherlands	12,229	12,533	11,595	11,713	17,968	0.99	53.40
Switzerland	5,364	6,680	5,809	7,124	9,083	0.50	27.50
East Mediterranean Europe	**1,529**	**3,441**	**3,071**	**3,974**	**5,208**	**0.29**	**31.05**
Cyprus	549	580	326	414	479	0.03	15.70
Turkey	980	2,861	2,745	3,560	4,729	0.26	32.84
Other Europe	**15,711**	**19,226**	**17,368**	**24,522**	**28,721**	**1.59**	**17.12**
Other countries of Europe	15,711	19,226	17,368	24,522	28,721	1.59	17.12
NOT SPECIFIED	**1,624**	**839**	**3,941**	**11,823**	**12,567**	**0.70**	**6.29**
Other countries of the World	1,624	839	3,941	11,823	12,567	0.70	6.29

ESTONIA

5. Overnight stays of non-resident tourists in hotels and similar establishments, by country of residence

	2007	2008	2009	2010	2011	Market share 11	% Change 11-10
TOTAL	2,668,077	2,727,007	2,555,011	3,002,781	3,478,042	100.00	15.83
AFRICA	2,260	2,524	1,944	2,787	3,816	0.11	36.92
Southern Africa	777	475	455	539	657	0.02	21.89
South Africa	777	475	455	539	657	0.02	21.89
Other Africa	1,483	2,049	1,489	2,248	3,159	0.09	40.52
Other countries of Africa	1,483	2,049	1,489	2,248	3,159	0.09	40.52
AMERICAS	56,594	51,585	46,958	53,996	64,839	1.86	20.08
North America	53,191	46,640	43,039	46,752	56,528	1.63	20.91
Canada	7,032	6,575	9,409	6,110	8,747	0.25	43.16
United States of America	46,159	40,065	33,630	40,642	47,781	1.37	17.57
South America	1,430	1,830	2,148	3,996	3,797	0.11	-4.98
Brazil	1,430	1,830	2,148	3,996	3,797	0.11	-4.98
Other Americas	1,973	3,115	1,771	3,248	4,514	0.13	38.98
Other countries of the Americas	1,973	3,115	1,771	3,248	4,514	0.13	38.98
EAST ASIA AND THE PACIFIC	28,419	30,248	33,695	38,152	48,752	1.40	27.78
North-East Asia	15,024	15,657	17,464	20,238	26,527	0.76	31.08
China	2,637	3,204	3,548	4,665	8,469	0.24	81.54
Japan	11,139	11,495	12,363	12,677	14,855	0.43	17.18
Korea, Republic of	1,248	958	1,553	2,896	3,203	0.09	10.60
Australasia	7,094	6,963	6,310	6,962	9,277	0.27	33.25
Australia	7,094	6,963	6,310	6,962	9,277	0.27	33.25
Other East Asia and the Pacific	6,301	7,628	9,921	10,952	12,948	0.37	18.22
Other countries of Asia	4,841	6,048	8,682	9,276	11,136	0.32	20.05
Other countries of Oceania	1,460	1,580	1,239	1,676	1,812	0.05	8.11
EUROPE	2,577,033	2,640,897	2,464,562	2,888,022	3,335,568	95.90	15.50
Central/Eastern Europe	349,512	419,591	394,986	522,252	715,840	20.58	37.07
Bulgaria	1,971	2,126	3,658	5,449	4,710	0.14	-13.56
Czech Republic	8,247	8,596	7,774	7,610	9,696	0.28	27.41
Hungary	13,061	7,535	4,605	6,864	8,762	0.25	27.65
Latvia	93,116	102,682	88,626	97,436	111,767	3.21	14.71
Lithuania	50,755	58,425	45,612	45,987	65,522	1.88	42.48
Poland	29,630	39,395	26,625	30,640	43,913	1.26	43.32
Romania	2,344	2,380	2,496	3,484	4,934	0.14	41.62
Russian Federation	140,093	182,900	205,037	310,840	446,742	12.84	43.72
Slovakia	2,038	3,520	2,014	3,089	3,277	0.09	6.09
Ukraine	8,257	12,032	8,539	10,853	16,517	0.47	52.19
Northern Europe	1,861,580	1,809,929	1,727,616	1,978,864	2,107,122	60.58	6.48
Denmark	28,208	29,749	23,626	21,523	25,159	0.72	16.89
Finland	1,361,074	1,367,177	1,367,795	1,612,483	1,617,598	46.51	0.32
Iceland	5,858	2,428	1,355	1,985	2,357	0.07	18.74
Ireland	8,898	7,339	5,565	5,332	17,440	0.50	227.08
Norway	142,402	121,855	104,416	99,161	118,550	3.41	19.55
Sweden	186,649	177,469	152,235	162,442	171,475	4.93	5.56
United Kingdom	128,491	103,912	72,624	75,938	154,543	4.44	103.51
Southern Europe	92,041	100,649	80,023	95,793	134,896	3.88	40.82
Greece	5,980	5,606	4,955	7,424	5,511	0.16	-25.77
Italy	48,978	52,514	39,458	47,414	68,573	1.97	44.63
Malta	284	794	570	491	591	0.02	20.37
Portugal	5,355	5,311	5,269	5,809	5,631	0.16	-3.06
Slovenia	2,149	2,344	2,137	2,277	2,473	0.07	8.61
Spain	29,295	34,080	27,634	32,378	52,117	1.50	60.96
Western Europe	237,198	265,008	221,861	240,615	313,537	9.01	30.31
Austria	10,743	16,468	12,980	9,954	14,880	0.43	49.49

ESTONIA

5. Overnight stays of non-resident tourists in hotels and similar establishments, by country of residence

	2007	2008	2009	2010	2011	Market share 11	% Change 11-10
Belgium	10,252	12,513	12,224	12,619	18,650	0.54	47.79
France	29,852	32,721	30,104	34,230	37,789	1.09	10.40
Germany	153,442	166,278	133,783	148,813	191,846	5.52	28.92
Luxembourg	1,083	1,571	1,533	1,703	1,868	0.05	9.69
Netherlands	22,186	24,038	21,130	21,167	32,482	0.93	53.46
Switzerland	9,640	11,419	10,107	12,129	16,022	0.46	32.10
East Mediterranean Europe	**3,507**	**6,777**	**5,834**	**8,294**	**10,154**	**0.29**	**22.43**
Cyprus	1,377	1,453	602	1,064	1,338	0.04	25.75
Turkey	2,130	5,324	5,232	7,230	8,816	0.25	21.94
Other Europe	**33,195**	**38,943**	**34,242**	**42,204**	**54,019**	**1.55**	**27.99**
Other countries of Europe	33,195	38,943	34,242	42,204	54,019	1.55	27.99
NOT SPECIFIED	**3,771**	**1,753**	**7,852**	**19,824**	**25,067**	**0.72**	**26.45**
Other countries of the World	3,771	1,753	7,852	19,824	25,067	0.72	26.45

ESTONIA

6. Overnight stays of non-resident tourists in all types of accommodation establishments, by country of residence

	2007	2008	2009	2010	2011	Market share 11	% Change 11-10
TOTAL	2,915,456	2,932,662	2,740,696	3,203,721	3,748,865	100.00	17.02
AFRICA	2,736	2,761	2,309	2,910	4,214	0.11	44.81
Southern Africa	832	498	544	596	761	0.02	27.68
South Africa	832	498	544	596	761	0.02	27.68
Other Africa	1,904	2,263	1,765	2,314	3,453	0.09	49.22
Other countries of Africa	1,904	2,263	1,765	2,314	3,453	0.09	49.22
AMERICAS	66,656	59,445	55,624	61,255	72,277	1.93	17.99
North America	62,581	53,863	51,103	53,582	62,703	1.67	17.02
Canada	8,982	7,849	11,493	7,277	10,316	0.28	41.76
United States of America	53,599	46,014	39,610	46,305	52,387	1.40	13.13
South America	1,713	2,168	2,495	4,122	4,326	0.12	4.95
Brazil	1,713	2,168	2,495	4,122	4,326	0.12	4.95
Other Americas	2,362	3,414	2,026	3,551	5,248	0.14	47.79
Other countries of the Americas	2,362	3,414	2,026	3,551	5,248	0.14	47.79
EAST ASIA AND THE PACIFIC	36,075	36,629	39,571	43,893	57,269	1.53	30.47
North-East Asia	17,579	17,726	19,174	21,520	29,129	0.78	35.36
China	3,776	4,344	4,268	5,057	9,429	0.25	86.45
Japan	12,246	12,143	12,998	13,303	15,967	0.43	20.03
Korea, Republic of	1,557	1,239	1,908	3,160	3,733	0.10	18.13
Australasia	10,713	9,495	8,643	8,390	11,982	0.32	42.81
Australia	10,713	9,495	8,643	8,390	11,982	0.32	42.81
Other East Asia and the Pacific	7,783	9,408	11,754	13,983	16,158	0.43	15.55
Other countries of Asia	5,434	7,184	9,620	11,886	13,969	0.37	17.52
Other countries of Oceania	2,349	2,224	2,134	2,097	2,189	0.06	4.39
EUROPE	2,806,128	2,831,975	2,634,927	3,074,832	3,589,403	95.75	16.73
Central/Eastern Europe	412,641	482,436	446,534	578,495	793,482	21.17	37.16
Bulgaria	2,272	2,399	4,578	5,856	5,470	0.15	-6.59
Czech Republic	10,859	11,223	10,008	9,768	12,488	0.33	27.85
Hungary	15,442	9,205	5,426	8,079	10,136	0.27	25.46
Latvia	119,429	123,299	103,091	112,122	130,154	3.47	16.08
Lithuania	61,207	69,555	55,465	55,535	77,428	2.07	39.42
Poland	38,274	48,254	31,878	36,442	52,153	1.39	43.11
Romania	2,955	2,801	2,700	3,719	5,304	0.14	42.62
Russian Federation	149,663	198,319	220,945	330,276	475,905	12.69	44.09
Slovakia	2,461	4,020	2,499	4,143	5,172	0.14	24.84
Ukraine	10,079	13,361	9,944	12,555	19,272	0.51	53.50
Northern Europe	1,957,790	1,882,155	1,794,481	2,047,552	2,201,059	58.71	7.50
Denmark	30,946	31,684	25,725	23,489	27,928	0.74	18.90
Finland	1,425,926	1,415,884	1,416,113	1,664,139	1,677,119	44.74	0.78
Iceland	6,347	2,547	1,452	2,056	2,478	0.07	20.53
Ireland	10,339	8,342	6,170	5,893	19,820	0.53	236.33
Norway	148,254	125,683	108,207	102,019	122,443	3.27	20.02
Sweden	195,748	185,592	158,492	168,165	179,523	4.79	6.75
United Kingdom	140,230	112,423	78,322	81,791	171,748	4.58	109.98
Southern Europe	113,815	117,321	94,629	112,817	159,106	4.24	41.03
Albania	315	413	299	370	666	0.02	80.00
Croatia	2,067	1,500	1,420	1,667	2,346	0.06	40.73
Greece	6,451	6,027	5,293	7,876	5,761	0.15	-26.85
Italy	60,393	60,692	46,856	54,451	79,455	2.12	45.92
Malta	312	948	637	621	710	0.02	14.33
Portugal	6,201	6,487	6,549	7,610	7,408	0.20	-2.65
Slovenia	2,634	2,744	2,486	2,853	3,233	0.09	13.32
Spain	35,442	38,510	31,089	37,369	59,527	1.59	59.30

ESTONIA

6. Overnight stays of non-resident tourists in all types of accommodation establishments, by country of residence

	2007	2008	2009	2010	2011	Market share 11	% Change 11-10
Western Europe	**280,168**	**301,476**	**257,020**	**278,869**	**366,843**	**9.79**	**31.55**
Austria	14,034	19,219	14,684	12,862	17,612	0.47	36.93
Belgium	11,839	14,237	14,258	14,678	20,445	0.55	39.29
France	37,791	38,416	35,908	44,236	51,223	1.37	15.79
Germany	177,355	187,665	154,260	167,508	218,698	5.83	30.56
Luxembourg	1,257	1,670	1,680	1,758	1,923	0.05	9.39
Netherlands	26,873	27,662	24,876	24,227	38,930	1.04	60.69
Switzerland	11,019	12,607	11,354	13,600	18,012	0.48	32.44
East Mediterranean Europe	**4,227**	**7,427**	**7,233**	**11,599**	**11,986**	**0.32**	**3.34**
Cyprus	1,448	1,550	901	1,331	1,384	0.04	3.98
Turkey	2,779	5,877	6,332	10,268	10,602	0.28	3.25
Other Europe	**37,487**	**41,160**	**35,030**	**45,500**	**56,927**	**1.52**	**25.11**
Other countries of Europe	37,487	41,160	35,030	45,500	56,927	1.52	25.11
NOT SPECIFIED	**3,861**	**1,852**	**8,265**	**20,831**	**25,702**	**0.69**	**23.38**
Other countries of the World	3,861	1,852	8,265	20,831	25,702	0.69	23.38

ETHIOPIA

1. Arrivals of non-resident tourists at national borders, by country of residence

		2007	2008	2009	2010	2011	Market share 11	% Change 11-10
TOTAL	(*)	311,947	330,157	427,286	468,305	523,438	100.00	11.77
AFRICA		91,674	115,999	150,102	140,076	160,311	30.63	14.45
East Africa		41,266	39,137	49,143	53,291	52,087	9.95	-2.26
Eritrea		299	362	628	686	340	0.06	-50.44
Djibouti		4,562	5,038	7,276	8,140	5,962	1.14	-26.76
Kenya		10,172	10,417	15,532	15,322	19,904	3.80	29.90
Malawi		4,194	1,926	2,657	3,878	3,625	0.69	-6.52
Rwanda		3,694	2,994	3,306	4,123	2,542	0.49	-38.35
Somalia		5,218	6,275	4,020	4,543	1,842	0.35	-59.45
Zimbabwe		2,385	3,211	3,597	3,692	5,260	1.00	42.47
Uganda		5,214	4,527	6,330	7,151	7,148	1.37	-0.04
United Republic of Tanzania		5,528	4,387	5,797	5,756	5,464	1.04	-5.07
Central Africa		5,322	4,794	5,423	5,190	3,966	0.76	-23.58
Chad		5,322	4,794	5,423	5,190	3,966	0.76	-23.58
North Africa		8,430	9,792	12,515	12,979	17,922	3.42	38.08
Sudan		8,430	9,792	12,515	12,979	17,922	3.42	38.08
Southern Africa		7,678	6,402	8,427	10,541	13,433	2.57	27.44
South Africa		7,678	6,402	8,427	10,541	13,433	2.57	27.44
West Africa		14,693	17,036	18,811	17,938	23,034	4.40	28.41
Ghana		4,508	3,728	3,255	4,407	4,764	0.91	8.10
Mali		3,161	3,564	3,651	3,097	1,833	0.35	-40.81
Nigeria		7,024	9,744	11,905	10,434	16,437	3.14	57.53
Other Africa		14,285	38,838	55,783	40,137	49,869	9.53	24.25
Other countries of Africa		14,285	38,838	55,783	40,137	49,869	9.53	24.25
AMERICAS		68,289	59,240	77,826	95,203	96,246	18.39	1.10
North America		53,108	58,252	76,647	88,601	93,933	17.95	6.02
Canada		8,391	8,574	9,490	11,871	12,889	2.46	8.58
United States of America		44,717	49,678	67,157	76,730	81,044	15.48	5.62
Other Americas		15,181	988	1,179	6,602	2,313	0.44	-64.97
Other countries of the Americas		15,181	988	1,179	6,602	2,313	0.44	-64.97
EAST ASIA AND THE PACIFIC		26,341	23,141	30,837	38,669	35,768	6.83	-7.50
North-East Asia		15,211	16,986	23,210	27,892	26,424	5.05	-5.26
China		12,325	13,791	18,968	22,722	20,197	3.86	-11.11
Japan		1,905	2,012	2,770	3,377	3,283	0.63	-2.78
Korea, Republic of		981	1,183	1,472	1,793	2,944	0.56	64.19
South-East Asia		1,129	835	1,213	2,045	1,406	0.27	-31.25
Philippines		1,129	835	1,213	2,045	1,406	0.27	-31.25
Australasia		3,800	3,664	4,340	5,221	5,874	1.12	12.51
Australia		3,304	3,120	3,835	4,655	4,914	0.94	5.56
New Zealand		496	544	505	566	960	0.18	69.61
Other East Asia and the Pacific		6,201	1,656	2,074	3,511	2,064	0.39	-41.21
Other countries of Asia		6,199	1,656	2,065	3,456	1,054	0.20	-69.50
Other countries of Oceania		2		9	55	1,010	0.19	1736.36
EUROPE		88,666	95,354	118,689	136,690	162,784	31.10	19.09
Central/Eastern Europe		1,126	933	1,296	1,269	1,740	0.33	37.12
Russian Federation		1,126	933	1,296	1,269	1,740	0.33	37.12
Northern Europe		27,844	29,400	37,504	43,295	49,252	9.41	13.76
Denmark		1,353	1,470	2,121	2,313	2,622	0.50	13.36
Finland		908	1,062	1,346	2,028	2,213	0.42	9.12
Norway		2,611	2,824	3,307	4,521	5,068	0.97	12.10
Sweden		5,878	5,761	7,576	9,343	10,404	1.99	11.36
United Kingdom		17,094	18,283	23,154	25,090	28,945	5.53	15.36

ETHIOPIA

1. Arrivals of non-resident tourists at national borders, by country of residence

	2007	2008	2009	2010	2011	Market share 11	% Change 11-10
Southern Europe	10,675	12,225	15,393	17,641	20,129	3.85	14.10
Greece	793	990	925	1,113	965	0.18	-13.30
Italy	9,882	11,235	14,468	16,528	19,164	3.66	15.95
Western Europe	30,868	35,153	46,580	51,377	69,490	13.28	35.26
Austria	1,825	1,473	2,194	2,172	3,772	0.72	73.66
Belgium	2,273	2,805	4,073	4,506	6,998	1.34	55.30
France	7,338	8,965	12,000	12,635	16,517	3.16	30.72
Germany	11,691	12,643	16,695	18,777	24,780	4.73	31.97
Netherlands	4,769	6,372	7,864	8,863	9,052	1.73	2.13
Switzerland	2,972	2,895	3,754	4,424	8,371	1.60	89.22
East Mediterranean Europe	7,616	8,755	8,885	10,448	9,165	1.75	-12.28
Israel	6,539	7,249	6,608	7,484	6,369	1.22	-14.90
Turkey	1,077	1,506	2,277	2,964	2,796	0.53	-5.67
Other Europe	10,537	8,888	9,031	12,660	13,008	2.49	2.75
Other countries of Europe	10,537	8,888	9,031	12,660	13,008	2.49	2.75
MIDDLE EAST	27,537	25,228	37,428	42,301	47,583	9.09	12.49
Kuwait	399	1,101	1,854	1,194	2,158	0.41	80.74
Saudi Arabia	8,330	7,160	10,456	14,019	18,891	3.61	34.75
United Arab Emirates	5,646	6,650	9,271	11,077	8,255	1.58	-25.48
Egypt	2,739	2,422	4,123	3,671	2,956	0.56	-19.48
Yemen	4,269	5,641	6,918	6,847	5,340	1.02	-22.01
Other countries of Middle East	6,154	2,254	4,806	5,493	9,983	1.91	81.74
SOUTH ASIA	9,440	11,195	12,404	15,366	20,746	3.96	35.01
India	8,895	10,560	11,525	14,607	19,667	3.76	34.64
Pakistan	545	635	879	759	1,079	0.21	42.16

FIJI

1. Arrivals of non-resident tourists at national borders, by country of residence

		2007	2008	2009	2010	2011	Market share 11	% Change 11-10
TOTAL	(*)	539,881	585,031	542,186	631,868	675,050	100.00	6.83
AMERICAS		81,679	81,538	65,044	66,092	69,188	10.25	4.68
North America		81,679	81,538	65,044	66,092	69,188	10.25	4.68
Canada		16,992	17,871	13,452	12,970	14,099	2.09	8.70
United States of America		64,687	63,667	51,592	53,122	55,089	8.16	3.70
EAST ASIA AND THE PACIFIC		387,941	430,808	415,414	503,660	542,354	80.34	7.68
North-East Asia		33,742	30,316	25,052	39,943	40,812	6.05	2.18
China				4,087	18,147	24,389	3.61	34.40
Taiwan, Province of China		958	977	1,086	1,710			
Hong Kong, China					1,748	1,706	0.25	-2.40
Japan		22,800	21,918	14,975	12,011	9,616	1.42	-19.94
Korea, Republic of		9,984	7,421	4,904	6,327	5,101	0.76	-19.38
South-East Asia		419	566					
Malaysia		419	566					
Australasia		306,745	347,626	339,487	416,042	448,010	66.37	7.68
Australia		207,001	247,608	248,589	318,185	344,829	51.08	8.37
New Zealand		99,744	100,018	90,898	97,857	103,181	15.28	5.44
Other East Asia and the Pacific		47,035	52,300	50,875	47,675	53,532	7.93	12.29
Other countries of Asia		12,814	16,364	15,797	8,477	14,709	2.18	73.52
Other countries East Asia/Pacific		34,221	35,936	35,078	39,198	38,823	5.75	-0.96
EUROPE		61,096	63,447	55,139	53,901	56,408	8.36	4.65
Northern Europe		40,534	39,515	31,055	27,995	29,333	4.35	4.78
Denmark		1,519	1,351	1,345	1,025	1,139	0.17	11.12
Finland		435	570	523	498	629	0.09	26.31
Norway		1,489	1,626	1,509	1,126	1,599	0.24	42.01
Sweden		2,306	2,033	1,465	1,533	1,912	0.28	24.72
United Kingdom		34,785	33,935	26,213	23,813	24,054	3.56	1.01
Southern Europe		3,278	3,950	4,374	4,834	4,600	0.68	-4.84
Italy		2,381	2,879	3,255	3,582	3,252	0.48	-9.21
Spain		897	1,071	1,119	1,252	1,348	0.20	7.67
Western Europe		14,885	16,904	17,188	18,014	18,736	2.78	4.01
Austria		1,292	1,065	1,012	1,102	1,065	0.16	-3.36
Belgium		365	348	343	403			
France		3,466	4,507	4,683	4,603	4,995	0.74	8.52
Germany		6,190	6,983	7,223	7,710	8,319	1.23	7.90
Netherlands		1,936	2,230	2,077	2,010	2,017	0.30	0.35
Switzerland		1,636	1,771	1,850	2,186	2,340	0.35	7.04
Other Europe		2,399	3,078	2,522	3,058	3,739	0.55	22.27
Other countries of Europe		2,399	3,078	2,522	3,058	3,739	0.55	22.27
SOUTH ASIA					1,836	2,188	0.32	19.17
India					1,836	2,188	0.32	19.17
NOT SPECIFIED		9,165	9,238	6,589	6,379	4,912	0.73	-23.00
Other countries of the World		9,165	9,238	6,589	6,379	4,912	0.73	-23.00

FIJI

5. Overnight stays of non-resident tourists in hotels and similar establishments, by country of residence

	2007	2008	2009	2010	2011	Market share 11	% Change 11-10
TOTAL	2,390,354	2,489,146	2,356,903	2,889,509	3,102,536	100.00	7.37
AMERICAS	299,260	288,707	240,957	264,710	271,405	8.75	2.53
North America	299,260	288,707	240,957	264,710	271,405	8.75	2.53
Canada	36,974	42,722	34,132	37,961	39,296	1.27	3.52
United States of America	262,286	245,985	206,825	226,749	232,109	7.48	2.36
EAST ASIA AND THE PACIFIC	1,726,208	1,852,541	1,732,209	2,171,475	2,324,761	74.93	7.06
North-East Asia	83,910	77,042	65,078	50,842	40,851	1.32	-19.65
Japan	83,910	77,042	65,078	50,842	40,851	1.32	-19.65
Australasia	1,549,351	1,709,860	1,604,548	2,050,037	2,198,908	70.87	7.26
Australia	1,115,053	1,300,673	1,264,015	1,698,625	1,835,563	59.16	8.06
New Zealand	434,298	409,187	340,533	351,412	363,345	11.71	3.40
Other East Asia and the Pacific	92,947	65,639	62,583	70,596	85,002	2.74	20.41
Other countries of Oceania	92,947	65,639	62,583	70,596	85,002	2.74	20.41
EUROPE	242,140	221,948	237,444	253,374	258,621	8.34	2.07
Northern Europe	144,409	132,717	143,592	134,985	124,693	4.02	-7.62
United Kingdom	144,409	132,717	143,592	134,985	124,693	4.02	-7.62
Other Europe	97,731	89,231	93,852	118,389	133,928	4.32	13.13
Other countries of Europe	97,731	89,231	93,852	118,389	133,928	4.32	13.13
NOT SPECIFIED	122,746	125,950	146,293	199,950	247,749	7.99	23.91
Other countries of the World	122,746	125,950	146,293	199,950	247,749	7.99	23.91

FINLAND

2. Arrivals of non-resident visitors at national borders, by country of residence

		2007	2008	2009	2010	2011	Market share 11	% Change 11-10
TOTAL	(*)	5,736,000	6,072,000	5,695,000	6,182,000	7,260,000	100.00	17.44
AFRICA		11,000	11,000	7,000	14,000	11,000	0.15	-21.43
Other Africa		11,000	11,000	7,000	14,000	11,000	0.15	-21.43
All countries of Africa		11,000	11,000	7,000	14,000	11,000	0.15	-21.43
AMERICAS		174,000	163,000	151,000	150,000	181,000	2.49	20.67
North America		143,000	137,000	127,000	121,000	145,000	2.00	19.83
Canada		21,000	21,000	23,000	32,000	24,000	0.33	-25.00
Mexico		2,000	2,000					
United States of America		120,000	114,000	104,000	89,000	121,000	1.67	35.96
South America		31,000	26,000	24,000	29,000	35,000	0.48	20.69
Brazil		13,000						
All countries of South America		18,000	26,000	24,000	29,000	35,000	0.48	20.69
Other Americas						1,000	0.01	
Other countries of the Americas						1,000	0.01	
EAST ASIA AND THE PACIFIC		312,000	314,000	310,000	347,000	427,000	5.88	23.05
North-East Asia		230,000	202,000	203,000	220,000	270,000	3.72	22.73
China		78,000	66,000	61,000	73,000	74,000	1.02	1.37
Taiwan, Province of China		8,000	6,000					
Hong Kong, China		10,000	3,000					
Japan		103,000	105,000	142,000	109,000	150,000	2.07	37.61
Korea, Republic of		31,000	22,000		38,000	46,000	0.63	21.05
South-East Asia		9,000	9,000					
Singapore		4,000	3,000					
Thailand		5,000	6,000					
Australasia		44,000	53,000		43,000	23,000	0.32	-46.51
Australia		41,000	51,000		43,000	23,000	0.32	-46.51
New Zealand		3,000	2,000					
Other East Asia and the Pacific		29,000	50,000	107,000	84,000	134,000	1.85	59.52
Other countries of Asia		29,000	50,000	107,000	84,000	132,000	1.82	57.14
Other countries of Oceania						2,000	0.03	
EUROPE		5,205,000	5,540,000	5,182,000	5,646,000	6,641,000	91.47	17.62
Central/Eastern Europe		2,825,000	3,061,000	2,889,000	3,302,000	4,134,000	56.94	25.20
Czech Republic		19,000	21,000		22,000	26,000	0.36	18.18
Estonia		561,000	522,000	583,000	561,000	708,000	9.75	26.20
Hungary		21,000	25,000		20,000			
Latvia		41,000	59,000	54,000	37,000	39,000	0.54	5.41
Lithuania		28,000	33,000	16,000	29,000	38,000	0.52	31.03
Poland		53,000	40,000	44,000	55,000	62,000	0.85	12.73
Romania		10,000	6,000					
Russian Federation		2,070,000	2,331,000	2,192,000	2,561,000	3,261,000	44.92	27.33
Slovakia		3,000	3,000					
Ukraine		19,000	21,000		17,000			
Northern Europe		1,406,000	1,397,000	1,278,000	1,272,000	1,291,000	17.78	1.49
Denmark		106,000	89,000	98,000	102,000	116,000	1.60	13.73
Iceland		5,000	4,000					
Ireland		21,000	36,000					
Norway		194,000	187,000	160,000	195,000	216,000	2.98	10.77
Sweden		768,000	765,000	753,000	712,000	681,000	9.38	-4.35
United Kingdom		312,000	316,000	267,000	263,000	278,000	3.83	5.70
Southern Europe		205,000	262,000	202,000	213,000	228,000	3.14	7.04
Greece		17,000	21,000					
Italy		91,000	102,000	79,000	85,000	108,000	1.49	27.06
Portugal		10,000	20,000		18,000			

FINLAND

2. Arrivals of non-resident visitors at national borders, by country of residence

	2007	2008	2009	2010	2011	Market share 11	% Change 11-10
Slovenia	4,000	3,000					
Spain	83,000	116,000	123,000	110,000	120,000	1.65	9.09
Western Europe	**735,000**	**769,000**	**667,000**	**747,000**	**821,000**	**11.31**	**9.91**
Austria	38,000	50,000	44,000	47,000	35,000	0.48	-25.53
Belgium	57,000	57,000	64,000	57,000	48,000	0.66	-15.79
France	131,000	120,000	94,000	132,000	145,000	2.00	9.85
Germany	350,000	376,000	332,000	363,000	399,000	5.50	9.92
Luxembourg	4,000	2,000					
Netherlands	90,000	93,000	80,000	86,000	101,000	1.39	17.44
Switzerland	65,000	71,000	53,000	62,000	93,000	1.28	50.00
East Mediterranean Europe	**12,000**	**17,000**					
Cyprus	1,000	1,000					
Israel	6,000	10,000					
Turkey	5,000	6,000					
Other Europe	**22,000**	**34,000**	**146,000**	**112,000**	**167,000**	**2.30**	**49.11**
Other countries of Europe	22,000	34,000	146,000	112,000	167,000	2.30	49.11
MIDDLE EAST	**12,000**	**12,000**	**9,000**				
All countries of Middle East	12,000	12,000	9,000				
SOUTH ASIA	**22,000**	**32,000**	**23,000**	**25,000**			
India	18,000	32,000	23,000	25,000			
Other countries of South Asia	4,000						
NOT SPECIFIED			**13,000**				
Other countries of the World			13,000				

FINLAND

4. Arrivals of non-resident tourists in all types of accommodation establishments, by country of residence

	2007	2008	2009	2010	2011	Market share 11	% Change 11-10
TOTAL	2,472,449	2,494,334	2,220,267	2,318,712	2,622,586	100.00	13.11
AFRICA	5,340	4,988	5,904	6,666	7,233	0.28	8.51
East Africa	941	826	1,002	1,446	1,506	0.06	4.15
British Indian Ocean Territory		4		5	2	0.00	-60.00
Burundi	5			13	7	0.00	-46.15
Ethiopia	112	94	125	190	209	0.01	10.00
Eritrea		5	10	23	31	0.00	34.78
Djibouti				9	27	0.00	200.00
Kenya	258	194	276	435	388	0.01	-10.80
Madagascar			4	9	2	0.00	-77.78
Malawi	14	9	8	33	16	0.00	-51.52
Mauritius	37	38	15	39	25	0.00	-35.90
Mozambique	33	36	46	26	90	0.00	246.15
Reunion			3	16	34	0.00	112.50
Rwanda	6	14	11	26	32	0.00	23.08
Seychelles	19	9	43	18	29	0.00	61.11
Somalia	80	73	54	72	84	0.00	16.67
Zimbabwe	31	54	28	54	55	0.00	1.85
Uganda	57	22	51	49	102	0.00	108.16
United Republic of Tanzania	245	200	252	330	296	0.01	-10.30
Zambia	44	74	76	99	77	0.00	-22.22
Central Africa	288	224	221	597	458	0.02	-23.28
Angola	9	22	27	430	159	0.01	-63.02
Cameroon	36	34	56	72	62	0.00	-13.89
Central African Republic	21	17	22	7	18	0.00	157.14
Chad				5	4	0.00	-20.00
Congo	24	48	45	33	116	0.00	251.52
Democratic Republic of the Congo	187	97	59	24	67	0.00	179.17
Gabon	11	6	12	23	32	0.00	39.13
Sao Tome and Principe				3			
North Africa	964	1,000	994	796	785	0.03	-1.38
Algeria	561	499	362	259	200	0.01	-22.78
Morocco	197	274	310	259	334	0.01	28.96
Sudan	75	46	90	94	65	0.00	-30.85
Tunisia	131	181	232	184	186	0.01	1.09
Southern Africa	2,411	2,358	2,198	2,264	2,686	0.10	18.64
Botswana	35	13	10	102	43	0.00	-57.84
Namibia	138	62	112	77	119	0.00	54.55
South Africa	2,201	2,231	2,022	1,975	2,389	0.09	20.96
Swaziland	37	52	54	110	135	0.01	22.73
West Africa	736	580	1,489	1,563	1,798	0.07	15.04
Benin	24	16	25	26	22	0.00	-15.38
Gambia	24	16	43	30	43	0.00	43.33
Ghana	48	54	139	115	256	0.01	122.61
Guinea	11			30	30	0.00	
Côte d'Ivoire	60	30	8	24	47	0.00	95.83
Liberia	9	5	17	22	8	0.00	-63.64
Mali	7	8	42	42	89	0.00	111.90
Mauritania	6		9	12	14	0.00	16.67
Niger	55	114	151	206	184	0.01	-10.68
Nigeria	215	186	470	505	651	0.02	28.91
Guinea-Bissau					7	0.00	
Saint Helena			47	42	3	0.00	-92.86
Senegal	42	29	111	150	94	0.00	-37.33
Sierra Leone	224	117	417	346	326	0.01	-5.78
Togo	11	5	5	9	20	0.00	122.22

FINLAND

4. Arrivals of non-resident tourists in all types of accommodation establishments, by country of residence

	2007	2008	2009	2010	2011	Market share 11	% Change 11-10
Burkina Faso			5	4	4	0.00	
AMERICAS	**117,098**	**107,107**	**90,882**	**97,324**	**119,984**	**4.58**	**23.28**
Caribbean	**493**	**466**	**841**	**531**	**730**	**0.03**	**37.48**
Antigua and Barbuda	49	13	8	12	13	0.00	8.33
Bahamas	185	124	243	16	14	0.00	-12.50
Barbados	7		10	5	22	0.00	340.00
Bermuda		6	122	11	16	0.00	45.45
Cayman Islands		7	28	6	7	0.00	16.67
Cuba	122	125	145	99	261	0.01	163.64
Dominica			7	31	20	0.00	-35.48
Dominican Republic	13	24	22	30	43	0.00	43.33
Grenada			9	30	9	0.00	-70.00
Guadeloupe			4	16	30	0.00	87.50
Haiti	5	4	10	44	27	0.00	-38.64
Jamaica		39	63	86	103	0.00	19.77
Netherlands Antilles	53	29	38	30	26	0.00	-13.33
Puerto Rico	16	31	71	57	50	0.00	-12.28
Saint Kitts and Nevis	5			10	1	0.00	-90.00
Anguilla			10	17	11	0.00	-35.29
Saint Vincent and the Grenadines			8	6	2	0.00	-66.67
Trinidad and Tobago	27	51	19	18	21	0.00	16.67
Turks and Caicos Islands		5	14		11	0.00	
United States Virgin Islands	11	8	10	7	43	0.00	514.29
Central America	**326**	**236**	**422**	**658**	**737**	**0.03**	**12.01**
Belize	22	29	30	24	27	0.00	12.50
Costa Rica	102	63	177	185	271	0.01	46.49
El Salvador	47	57	31	206	239	0.01	16.02
Guatemala	30	22	59	99	27	0.00	-72.73
Honduras	37	11	18	37	44	0.00	18.92
Nicaragua	58	30	55	40	60	0.00	50.00
Panama	30	24	52	67	69	0.00	2.99
North America	**108,058**	**99,112**	**82,478**	**87,500**	**106,724**	**4.07**	**21.97**
Canada	12,424	12,832	11,805	11,308	14,291	0.54	26.38
Greenland	37	25	55	39	71	0.00	82.05
Mexico	1,849	1,948	1,765	1,983	2,634	0.10	32.83
United States of America	93,748	84,307	68,853	74,170	89,728	3.42	20.98
South America	**8,221**	**7,293**	**7,141**	**8,635**	**11,793**	**0.45**	**36.57**
Argentina	1,464	826	820	1,061	1,514	0.06	42.70
Bolivia	46	73	34	60	85	0.00	41.67
Brazil	4,031	4,213	4,239	5,277	6,563	0.25	24.37
Chile	864	636	540	834	1,002	0.04	20.14
Colombia	291	265	495	485	566	0.02	16.70
Ecuador	69	57	71	132	147	0.01	11.36
Falkland Islands, Malvinas			8	14	17	0.00	21.43
French Guiana				7			
Guyana				16	11	0.00	-31.25
Paraguay	17	13	12	11	24	0.00	118.18
Peru	186	210	211	195	307	0.01	57.44
Suriname			24	26	29	0.00	11.54
Uruguay	998	344	398	272	1,140	0.04	319.12
Venezuela	255	656	289	245	388	0.01	58.37
EAST ASIA AND THE PACIFIC	**193,835**	**177,552**	**144,300**	**159,050**	**192,810**	**7.35**	**21.23**
North-East Asia	**159,614**	**140,801**	**114,836**	**126,618**	**152,385**	**5.81**	**20.35**
China	53,299	39,866	32,603	39,217	50,280	1.92	28.21
Taiwan, Province of China	7,941	5,913	4,021	4,236	6,863	0.26	62.02
Hong Kong, China	2,876	3,149	3,610	3,285	6,107	0.23	85.91

FINLAND

4. Arrivals of non-resident tourists in all types of accommodation establishments, by country of residence

	2007	2008	2009	2010	2011	Market share 11	% Change 11-10
Japan	82,473	80,180	65,949	68,747	75,680	2.89	10.08
Korea, Dem. People's Republic of	795	1,039	1,123	1,358	850	0.03	-37.41
Korea, Republic of	12,159	10,602	7,450	9,578	12,446	0.47	29.94
Macao, China	45	8	22	60	63	0.00	5.00
Mongolia	26	44	58	137	96	0.00	-29.93
South-East Asia	**11,860**	**11,149**	**10,186**	**13,184**	**19,016**	**0.73**	**44.24**
Brunei Darussalam			13	2	8	0.00	300.00
Myanmar	132	48	34	87	43	0.00	-50.57
Cambodia	7	6	14	8	14	0.00	75.00
Indonesia	725	990	869	1,293	2,276	0.09	76.02
Lao People's Democratic Republic	51	59	75	62	69	0.00	11.29
Malaysia	1,174	1,287	1,143	1,168	1,420	0.05	21.58
Philippines	665	722	967	1,221	1,327	0.05	8.68
Singapore	3,779	3,079	2,427	2,356	5,244	0.20	122.58
Viet Nam	275	338	505	501	520	0.02	3.79
Thailand	5,052	4,620	4,139	6,486	8,095	0.31	24.81
Australasia	**22,130**	**25,404**	**19,135**	**18,988**	**20,984**	**0.80**	**10.51**
Australia	20,075	23,159	17,684	17,547	19,337	0.74	10.20
New Zealand	2,055	2,245	1,451	1,441	1,647	0.06	14.30
Melanesia	**45**	**58**	**56**	**143**	**134**	**0.01**	**-6.29**
Solomon Islands	10	9	15	20	10	0.00	-50.00
Fiji	10	21		92	64	0.00	-30.43
New Caledonia	20	15	31	23	34	0.00	47.83
Papua New Guinea	5	13	10	8	26	0.00	225.00
Micronesia	**103**	**20**	**14**	**36**	**33**	**0.00**	**-8.33**
Kiribati	28			19	17	0.00	-10.53
Guam	75	20	14	17	14	0.00	-17.65
Nauru					2	0.00	
Polynesia	**83**	**120**	**73**	**81**	**258**	**0.01**	**218.52**
American Samoa	69	97	55	27	207	0.01	666.67
Cook Islands					11	0.00	
French Polynesia				7	20	0.00	185.71
Tokelau	14	10	18	42	13	0.00	-69.05
Tonga		13		5	5	0.00	
Tuvalu					2	0.00	
EUROPE	**2,017,072**	**2,056,016**	**1,846,249**	**1,921,558**	**2,150,835**	**82.01**	**11.93**
Central/Eastern Europe	**578,998**	**670,201**	**623,189**	**691,669**	**831,157**	**31.69**	**20.17**
Azerbaijan	59	90	218	153	234	0.01	52.94
Armenia	157	189	203	143	203	0.01	41.96
Bulgaria	2,023	2,191	2,586	2,099	2,633	0.10	25.44
Belarus	1,214	1,080	1,280	2,097	2,040	0.08	-2.72
Czech Republic	12,505	12,316	11,748	11,999	13,924	0.53	16.04
Estonia	94,561	92,182	73,071	82,448	91,814	3.50	11.36
Georgia	1,336	1,117	976	924	1,176	0.04	27.27
Hungary	9,717	8,684	9,731	9,408	10,612	0.40	12.80
Kazakhstan	546	658	775	776	704	0.03	-9.28
Kyrgyzstan	17	37	34	48	36	0.00	-25.00
Latvia	19,551	21,060	17,227	20,163	21,189	0.81	5.09
Lithuania	11,666	13,377	10,931	11,337	12,091	0.46	6.65
Republic of Moldova	164	109	114	94	204	0.01	117.02
Poland	26,472	26,817	24,418	26,331	28,395	1.08	7.84
Romania	6,330	5,700	6,306	5,983	6,042	0.23	0.99
Russian Federation	385,928	476,635	456,388	509,237	630,064	24.02	23.73
Slovakia	3,231	3,123	2,914	3,707	3,768	0.14	1.65
Tajikistan		41		28	22	0.00	-21.43
Turkmenistan	19	21	7	6	17	0.00	183.33
Ukraine	3,442	4,700	4,179	4,606	5,895	0.22	27.99

FINLAND

4. Arrivals of non-resident tourists in all types of accommodation establishments, by country of residence

	2007	2008	2009	2010	2011	Market share 11	% Change 11-10
Uzbekistan	60	74	83	82	94	0.00	14.63
Northern Europe	**695,152**	**668,832**	**574,800**	**584,252**	**617,437**	**23.54**	**5.68**
Denmark	60,142	59,140	48,591	48,569	55,968	2.13	15.23
Faeroe Islands	128	99	378	139	195	0.01	40.29
Iceland	4,771	4,048	3,266	3,384	4,332	0.17	28.01
Ireland	12,060	10,887	7,754	6,894	7,235	0.28	4.95
Norway	96,911	90,223	74,967	80,403	87,851	3.35	9.26
Sweden	326,930	312,858	278,169	290,922	307,045	11.71	5.54
United Kingdom	194,210	191,577	161,675	153,941	154,811	5.90	0.57
Southern Europe	**170,466**	**158,965**	**137,558**	**133,855**	**153,120**	**5.84**	**14.39**
Albania	544	540	505	360	268	0.01	-25.56
Andorra	85	123	116	157	82	0.00	-47.77
Bosnia and Herzegovina	148	245	227	210	287	0.01	36.67
Croatia	1,298	1,803	1,418	1,450	2,001	0.08	38.00
Gibraltar		8		50	40	0.00	-20.00
Greece	11,299	10,777	9,088	7,588	7,825	0.30	3.12
Holy See				5	1	0.00	-80.00
Italy	77,810	75,325	65,270	61,656	72,412	2.76	17.45
Malta	362	283	380	377	413	0.02	9.55
Montenegro			9	50	7	0.00	-86.00
Portugal	6,710	7,213	7,365	8,212	7,330	0.28	-10.74
San Marino	19	15	64	39	58	0.00	48.72
Serbia			369	623	759	0.03	21.83
Slovenia	3,722	3,293	2,511	3,055	3,071	0.12	0.52
Spain	66,775	59,200	50,077	50,023	58,320	2.22	16.59
TFYR of Macedonia	170	140	159		246	0.01	
Serbia and Montenegro	1,524						
Western Europe	**561,416**	**545,935**	**498,518**	**495,406**	**534,613**	**20.38**	**7.91**
Austria	22,369	22,705	23,572	24,892	29,413	1.12	18.16
Belgium	24,947	23,115	21,181	21,713	23,112	0.88	6.44
France	90,670	87,881	79,877	82,813	83,460	3.18	0.78
Germany	282,612	283,051	249,277	246,137	270,897	10.33	10.06
Liechtenstein	428	553	605	195	273	0.01	40.00
Luxembourg	1,547	1,792	1,721	1,675	1,892	0.07	12.96
Monaco	139	181	226	178	199	0.01	11.80
Netherlands	84,055	77,449	74,867	68,907	71,922	2.74	4.38
Switzerland	54,649	49,208	47,192	48,896	53,445	2.04	9.30
East Mediterranean Europe	**11,040**	**12,083**	**12,184**	**16,376**	**14,508**	**0.55**	**-11.41**
Cyprus	523	657	754	687	619	0.02	-9.90
Israel	5,947	5,862	5,364	8,023	6,294	0.24	-21.55
Turkey	4,570	5,564	6,066	7,666	7,595	0.29	-0.93
MIDDLE EAST	**3,316**	**3,866**	**4,008**	**3,793**	**4,278**	**0.16**	**12.79**
Bahrain	361	605	230	99	107	0.00	8.08
Iraq	118	148	164	167	161	0.01	-3.59
Jordan	111	149	121	128	167	0.01	30.47
Kuwait	170	244	178	168	226	0.01	34.52
Lebanon	139	176	296	214	168	0.01	-21.50
Libya	46	60	64	68	25	0.00	-63.24
Oman	37	21	101	232	119	0.00	-48.71
Qatar	45	83	119	157	136	0.01	-13.38
Saudi Arabia	1,092	1,160	1,184	811	761	0.03	-6.17
Syrian Arab Republic	109	65	81	85	112	0.00	31.76
United Arab Emirates	529	490	726	912	1,260	0.05	38.16
Egypt	559	646	690	720	1,016	0.04	41.11
Yemen		19	54	32	20	0.00	-37.50
SOUTH ASIA	**15,651**	**18,910**	**15,625**	**16,849**	**18,604**	**0.71**	**10.42**

FINLAND

4. Arrivals of non-resident tourists in all types of accommodation establishments, by country of residence

	2007	2008	2009	2010	2011	Market share 11	% Change 11-10
Afghanistan	938	946	948	781	538	0.02	-31.11
Bangladesh	68	54	132	97	125	0.00	28.87
Bhutan	7		6		7	0.00	
Sri Lanka	98	57	89	54	124	0.00	129.63
India	13,097	16,079	12,941	14,100	15,827	0.60	12.25
Iran, Islamic Republic of	853	1,201	913	1,165	1,249	0.05	7.21
Maldives			5	9	7	0.00	-22.22
Nepal	37	83	155	170	185	0.01	8.82
Pakistan	553	490	436	473	542	0.02	14.59
NOT SPECIFIED	**120,137**	**125,895**	**113,299**	**113,472**	**128,842**	**4.91**	**13.55**
Other countries of the World	120,137	125,895	113,299	113,472	128,842	4.91	13.55

FINLAND

5. Overnight stays of non-resident tourists in hotels and similar establishments, by country of residence

	2007	2008	2009	2010	2011	Market share 11	% Change 11-10
TOTAL	4,634,829	4,767,662	4,197,575	4,296,915	4,711,041	100.00	9.64
AFRICA	19,519	17,178	19,267	18,612	18,790	0.40	0.96
East Africa	4,138	2,251	3,479	3,639	4,115	0.09	13.08
British Indian Ocean Territory		5		8	4	0.00	-50.00
Burundi	11			26	18	0.00	-30.77
Ethiopia	248	221	439	547	487	0.01	-10.97
Eritrea		6	15	41	43	0.00	4.88
Djibouti				28	33	0.00	17.86
Kenya	1,075	629	1,243	1,087	1,070	0.02	-1.56
Madagascar		9	17	21	3	0.00	-85.71
Malawi	71	13	40	113	39	0.00	-65.49
Mauritius	80	69	54	54	82	0.00	51.85
Mozambique	97	117	184	76	211	0.00	177.63
Reunion			9	40	31	0.00	-22.50
Rwanda	8	30	33	47	42	0.00	-10.64
Seychelles	48	19	90	58	68	0.00	17.24
Somalia	356	156	69	108	82	0.00	-24.07
Zimbabwe	47	110	57	66	136	0.00	106.06
Uganda	225	79	220	126	346	0.01	174.60
United Republic of Tanzania	1,696	505	710	802	1,038	0.02	29.43
Zambia	176	283	299	391	382	0.01	-2.30
Central Africa	740	385	410	1,448	839	0.02	-42.06
Angola	9	44	41	1,090	259	0.01	-76.24
Cameroon	66	65	110	189	121	0.00	-35.98
Central African Republic	72	26	51	18	23	0.00	27.78
Chad	15			12	6	0.00	-50.00
Congo	35	43	67	47	188	0.00	300.00
Democratic Republic of the Congo	535	191	104	26	149	0.00	473.08
Gabon	8	16	37	60	86	0.00	43.33
Sao Tome and Principe				6	7	0.00	16.67
North Africa	2,904	2,616	2,672	2,449	1,764	0.04	-27.97
Algeria	1,708	1,426	842	901	424	0.01	-52.94
Morocco	429	575	731	593	735	0.02	23.95
Sudan	246	124	358	369	153	0.00	-58.54
Tunisia	521	491	741	586	452	0.01	-22.87
Southern Africa	7,699	7,791	6,270	6,624	8,114	0.17	22.49
Botswana	174	21	40	128	107	0.00	-16.41
Namibia	463	316	325	271	328	0.01	21.03
South Africa	6,966	7,331	5,756	5,983	7,357	0.16	22.97
Swaziland	96	123	149	242	322	0.01	33.06
West Africa	2,087	1,532	4,003	4,447	3,958	0.08	-11.00
Benin	62	49	85	86	36	0.00	-58.14
Gambia	39	30	55	82	53	0.00	-35.37
Ghana	493	429	725	564	1,128	0.02	100.00
Guinea	85			84	52	0.00	-38.10
Côte d'Ivoire	151	59	22	88	101	0.00	14.77
Liberia	8	16	43	42	13	0.00	-69.05
Mali	17		78	100	131	0.00	31.00
Mauritania	32	10	56	54	51	0.00	-5.56
Niger	140	255	295	483	357	0.01	-26.09
Nigeria	607	353	1,256	1,339	1,104	0.02	-17.55
Guinea-Bissau					24	0.00	
Saint Helena	23		198	207	5	0.00	-97.58
Senegal	97	45	281	357	207	0.00	-42.02
Sierra Leone	311	274	857	901	654	0.01	-27.41
Togo	9	12	12	36	34	0.00	-5.56

FINLAND

5. Overnight stays of non-resident tourists in hotels and similar establishments, by country of residence

	2007	2008	2009	2010	2011	Market share 11	% Change 11-10
Burkina Faso	13		40	24	8	0.00	-66.67
Other Africa	**1,951**	**2,603**	**2,433**	**5**			
Other countries of Africa	1,951	2,603	2,433	5			
AMERICAS	**269,916**	**256,922**	**220,461**	**231,342**	**263,612**	**5.60**	**13.95**
Caribbean	**1,157**	**1,248**	**3,124**	**1,382**	**1,576**	**0.03**	**14.04**
Antigua and Barbuda		32	17	23	21	0.00	-8.70
Bahamas	350	230	371	24	39	0.00	62.50
Barbados	22	5	22	22	66	0.00	200.00
Bermuda	15	24	903	39	23	0.00	-41.03
Cayman Islands		21	267	7	28	0.00	300.00
Cuba	350	275	312	165	472	0.01	186.06
Dominica			11	92	34	0.00	-63.04
Dominican Republic	37	49	34	68	156	0.00	129.41
Grenada			11	72	12	0.00	-83.33
Guadeloupe			9	53	74	0.00	39.62
Haiti	25	15	34	83	50	0.00	-39.76
Jamaica	34	67	187	243	161	0.00	-33.74
Netherlands Antilles	125	62	105	69	46	0.00	-33.33
Aruba					41	0.00	
Puerto Rico	24	63	444	148	86	0.00	-41.89
Saint Kitts and Nevis	30			38	1	0.00	-97.37
Anguilla			86	57	27	0.00	-52.63
Saint Vincent and the Grenadines			88	76	3	0.00	-96.05
Trinidad and Tobago	116	386	153	78	60	0.00	-23.08
Turks and Caicos Islands	8	11	47	8	18	0.00	125.00
United States Virgin Islands	21	8	23	17	158	0.00	829.41
Central America	**781**	**687**	**1,343**	**1,433**	**1,354**	**0.03**	**-5.51**
Belize	77	137	95	71	48	0.00	-32.39
Costa Rica	283	144	530	514	538	0.01	4.67
El Salvador	88	81	63	292	358	0.01	22.60
Guatemala	56	42	153	192	47	0.00	-75.52
Honduras	70	18	48	63	47	0.00	-25.40
Nicaragua	162	209	246	141	145	0.00	2.84
Panama	45	56	208	160	171	0.00	6.88
North America	**247,534**	**235,587**	**198,154**	**207,918**	**234,361**	**4.97**	**12.72**
Canada	31,197	31,747	30,326	29,277	32,595	0.69	11.33
Greenland	63	51	307	95	169	0.00	77.89
Mexico	4,234	4,579	4,603	4,959	5,118	0.11	3.21
United States of America	212,040	199,210	162,918	173,587	196,479	4.17	13.19
South America	**19,663**	**19,371**	**17,812**	**20,601**	**26,321**	**0.56**	**27.77**
Argentina	2,709	1,928	2,265	2,405	3,433	0.07	42.74
Bolivia	66	104	70	83	165	0.00	98.80
Brazil	10,824	11,308	11,365	13,039	15,605	0.33	19.68
Chile	2,945	1,815	1,237	1,791	2,002	0.04	11.78
Colombia	1,060	595	1,236	1,263	1,183	0.03	-6.33
Ecuador	127	94	146	262	302	0.01	15.27
Falkland Islands, Malvinas				56	20	29	0.00	45.00
Guyana	13		10	44	16	0.00	-63.64
Paraguay	19	89	19	16	113	0.00	606.25
Peru	569	722	479	377	758	0.02	101.06
Suriname	20		75	58	135	0.00	132.76
Uruguay	667	412	205	598	1,773	0.04	196.49
Venezuela	644	2,304	649	645	807	0.02	25.12
Other Americas	**781**	**29**	**28**	**8**			
Other countries of the Americas	781	29	28	8			
EAST ASIA AND THE PACIFIC	**348,403**	**345,776**	**290,970**	**310,617**	**352,656**	**7.49**	**13.53**

FINLAND

5. Overnight stays of non-resident tourists in hotels and similar establishments, by country of residence

	2007	2008	2009	2010	2011	Market share 11	% Change 11-10
North-East Asia	282,129	272,532	228,043	243,179	274,949	5.84	13.06
China	91,935	84,891	65,950	75,332	89,244	1.89	18.47
Taiwan, Province of China	10,921	9,416	6,779	7,876	10,569	0.22	34.19
Hong Kong, China	4,365	4,531	6,015	5,303	9,385	0.20	76.98
Japan	151,200	149,294	130,171	132,540	141,527	3.00	6.78
Korea, Dem. People's Republic of	1,650	2,124	2,827	2,722	1,531	0.03	-43.75
Korea, Republic of	21,885	22,041	16,074	18,931	22,236	0.47	17.46
Macao, China	109	13	78	141	123	0.00	-12.77
Mongolia	64	222	149	334	334	0.01	
South-East Asia	24,784	24,871	23,211	27,736	32,118	0.68	15.80
Brunei Darussalam	24		31	10	16	0.00	60.00
Myanmar	202	128	36	175	82	0.00	-53.14
Cambodia	26	7	106	14	29	0.00	107.14
Indonesia	1,623	1,987	1,814	2,374	3,588	0.08	51.14
Lao People's Democratic Republic	131	92	123	109	156	0.00	43.12
Malaysia	2,761	2,814	3,083	3,235	3,079	0.07	-4.82
Philippines	1,396	1,565	3,356	3,364	2,237	0.05	-33.50
Singapore	8,338	7,239	6,496	5,763	12,310	0.26	113.60
Viet Nam	654	987	1,112	1,084	1,121	0.02	3.41
Thailand	9,629	10,052	7,054	11,608	9,500	0.20	-18.16
Australasia	40,988	48,002	39,448	39,147	44,828	0.95	14.51
Australia	37,107	43,738	36,309	36,410	41,371	0.88	13.63
New Zealand	3,881	4,264	3,139	2,737	3,457	0.07	26.31
Melanesia	97	126	195	279	279	0.01	
Solomon Islands	25	26	71	46	34	0.00	-26.09
Fiji	16	25		156	114	0.00	-26.92
New Caledonia	32	46	57	40	70	0.00	75.00
Vanuatu			31	21			
Papua New Guinea	24	29	36	16	61	0.00	281.25
Micronesia	204	31	33	87	70	0.00	-19.54
Kiribati	36			48	32	0.00	-33.33
Guam	168	31	33	32	35	0.00	9.38
Nauru					3	0.00	
Micronesia, Federated States of				7			
Polynesia	201	214	40	189	412	0.01	117.99
American Samoa	157	161		34	286	0.01	741.18
French Polynesia			8	15	72	0.00	380.00
Tokelau	34	26	32	124	43	0.00	-65.32
Tonga		27		16	6	0.00	-62.50
Wallis and Futuna Islands	10				5	0.00	
EUROPE	3,714,900	3,838,340	3,415,728	3,484,840	3,810,834	80.89	9.35
Central/Eastern Europe	1,145,890	1,279,908	1,160,003	1,268,560	1,502,726	31.90	18.46
Azerbaijan	114	242	517	372	606	0.01	62.90
Armenia	608	678	699	577	406	0.01	-29.64
Bulgaria	5,160	5,835	6,449	5,931	5,914	0.13	-0.29
Belarus	3,395	3,188	3,502	8,040	6,484	0.14	-19.35
Czech Republic	24,422	23,819	23,304	23,373	26,909	0.57	15.13
Estonia	164,992	154,392	125,169	152,605	171,737	3.65	12.54
Georgia	2,635	2,091	2,015	1,793	2,319	0.05	29.34
Hungary	24,215	20,609	20,572	19,432	22,448	0.48	15.52
Kazakhstan	1,900	2,635	3,634	3,142	2,338	0.05	-25.59
Kyrgyzstan	96	124	95	187	123	0.00	-34.22
Latvia	28,341	30,222	25,131	30,237	28,712	0.61	-5.04
Lithuania	19,487	20,539	16,588	17,526	19,427	0.41	10.85
Republic of Moldova	514	293	371	276	412	0.01	49.28
Poland	58,753	58,836	52,615	56,075	61,322	1.30	9.36

FINLAND

5. Overnight stays of non-resident tourists in hotels and similar establishments, by country of residence

	2007	2008	2009	2010	2011	Market share 11	% Change 11-10
Romania	12,658	14,185	14,082	14,553	15,573	0.33	7.01
Russian Federation	776,451	919,045	843,842	909,186	1,110,551	23.57	22.15
Slovakia	11,277	8,518	6,750	10,190	9,417	0.20	-7.59
Tajikistan	11	59	11	52	46	0.00	-11.54
Turkmenistan	18	62		10	52	0.00	420.00
Ukraine	10,694	14,308	14,422	14,786	17,748	0.38	20.03
Uzbekistan	149	228	235	217	182	0.00	-16.13
Northern Europe	**1,190,179**	**1,192,942**	**1,008,357**	**988,580**	**1,014,509**	**21.53**	**2.62**
Denmark	98,013	101,702	79,848	79,708	88,542	1.88	11.08
Faeroe Islands	362	272	1,758	454	309	0.01	-31.94
Iceland	10,939	9,237	7,387	7,984	10,129	0.22	26.87
Ireland	25,366	26,978	16,974	15,567	14,145	0.30	-9.13
Norway	153,194	137,522	112,556	119,062	130,089	2.76	9.26
Sweden	443,040	436,835	384,158	404,164	427,838	9.08	5.86
United Kingdom	459,265	480,396	405,676	361,641	343,457	7.29	-5.03
Southern Europe	**331,431**	**316,375**	**291,042**	**281,281**	**304,738**	**6.47**	**8.34**
Albania	1,480	1,276	1,364	912	647	0.01	-29.06
Andorra	239	232	214	295	145	0.00	-50.85
Bosnia and Herzegovina	634	489	623	664	776	0.02	16.87
Croatia	3,770	5,686	3,774	3,609	4,950	0.11	37.16
Gibraltar	9	19	1,379	105	89	0.00	-15.24
Greece	26,671	23,619	23,054	18,015	17,077	0.36	-5.21
Holy See				10	2	0.00	-80.00
Italy	146,947	148,868	137,134	127,207	138,225	2.93	8.66
Malta	1,214	819	1,086	946	1,033	0.02	9.20
Montenegro	7		25	107	16	0.00	-85.05
Portugal	14,893	15,270	18,148	19,129	16,711	0.35	-12.64
San Marino	46	38	122	89	161	0.00	80.90
Serbia	3,095		844	1,908	1,870	0.04	-1.99
Slovenia	7,283	7,020	5,524	6,167	5,821	0.12	-5.61
Spain	124,254	113,039	97,363	101,576	116,727	2.48	14.92
TFYR of Macedonia	889		388	542	488	0.01	-9.96
Western Europe	**1,017,315**	**1,017,122**	**925,766**	**910,614**	**955,502**	**20.28**	**4.93**
Austria	39,162	41,215	41,249	42,519	49,857	1.06	17.26
Belgium	48,467	46,096	41,836	42,319	44,824	0.95	5.92
France	208,254	203,978	184,659	185,221	186,464	3.96	0.67
Germany	475,020	490,084	437,459	424,910	450,681	9.57	6.07
Liechtenstein	843	1,156	1,378	497	407	0.01	-18.11
Luxembourg	3,244	3,622	3,801	3,662	3,517	0.07	-3.96
Monaco	237	343	441	355	323	0.01	-9.01
Netherlands	155,030	146,405	132,727	129,637	130,465	2.77	0.64
Switzerland	87,058	84,223	82,216	81,494	88,964	1.89	9.17
East Mediterranean Europe	**30,085**	**31,993**	**30,560**	**35,805**	**33,359**	**0.71**	**-6.83**
Cyprus	1,609	1,778	1,843	1,841	1,952	0.04	6.03
Israel	15,752	15,917	14,210	17,345	15,321	0.33	-11.67
Turkey	12,724	14,298	14,507	16,619	16,086	0.34	-3.21
MIDDLE EAST	**10,553**	**14,330**	**13,008**	**11,266**	**11,410**	**0.24**	**1.28**
Bahrain	670	1,149	623	220	227	0.00	3.18
Iraq	251	374	326	425	722	0.02	69.88
Jordan	346	440	427	131	419	0.01	219.85
Kuwait	576	1,043	510	653	568	0.01	-13.02
Lebanon	519	751	726	729	429	0.01	-41.15
Libya	108	396	143	195	65	0.00	-66.67
Oman	68	72	312	400	301	0.01	-24.75
Qatar	165	507	603	569	273	0.01	-52.02
Saudi Arabia	4,213	5,814	4,704	3,038	2,344	0.05	-22.84
Syrian Arab Republic	290	93	201	323	285	0.01	-11.76

FINLAND

5. Overnight stays of non-resident tourists in hotels and similar establishments, by country of residence

	2007	2008	2009	2010	2011	Market share 11	% Change 11-10
United Arab Emirates	1,506	1,368	1,807	2,283	3,103	0.07	35.92
Egypt	1,835	2,196	2,238	2,169	2,603	0.06	20.01
Yemen	6	127	388	131	71	0.00	-45.80
SOUTH ASIA	**55,759**	**73,093**	**60,290**	**66,698**	**58,961**	**1.25**	**-11.60**
Afghanistan	2,385	2,183	2,393	2,242	1,576	0.03	-29.71
Bangladesh	172	100	294	222	351	0.01	58.11
Bhutan			20		10	0.00	
Sri Lanka	371	274	295	147	250	0.01	70.07
India	48,691	63,393	51,406	57,589	52,196	1.11	-9.36
Iran, Islamic Republic of	2,669	3,610	2,418	2,767	2,866	0.06	3.58
Maldives	13	19	26	33	35	0.00	6.06
Nepal	91	136	546	474	410	0.01	-13.50
Pakistan	1,367	3,378	2,892	3,224	1,267	0.03	-60.70
NOT SPECIFIED	**215,779**	**222,023**	**177,851**	**173,540**	**194,778**	**4.13**	**12.24**
Other countries of the World	215,779	222,023	177,851	173,540	194,778	4.13	12.24

FINLAND

6. Overnight stays of non-resident tourists in all types of accommodation establishments, by country of residence

	2007	2008	2009	2010	2011	Market share 11	% Change 11-10
TOTAL	5,328,215	5,502,542	4,890,006	5,005,068	5,507,468	100.00	10.04
AFRICA	18,343	15,620	17,475	19,572	20,115	0.37	2.77
East Africa	4,310	2,397	3,569	3,900	4,435	0.08	13.72
British Indian Ocean Territory		5		8	4	0.00	-50.00
Burundi	11			27	18	0.00	-33.33
Ethiopia	260	258	445	565	509	0.01	-9.91
Eritrea	5	8	19	41	51	0.00	24.39
Djibouti		4		28	33	0.00	17.86
Kenya	1,093	656	1,266	1,131	1,092	0.02	-3.45
Madagascar	6	10	18	25	3	0.00	-88.00
Malawi	74	13	40	125	39	0.00	-68.80
Mauritius	82	86	54	132	82	0.00	-37.88
Mozambique	103	118	188	76	211	0.00	177.63
Reunion			9	40	49	0.00	22.50
Rwanda	6	30	33	52	46	0.00	-11.54
Seychelles	60	19	90	62	70	0.00	12.90
Somalia	377	175	87	128	251	0.00	96.09
Zimbabwe	93	119	65	92	141	0.00	53.26
Uganda	227	81	220	135	371	0.01	174.81
United Republic of Tanzania	1,732	524	733	842	1,083	0.02	28.62
Zambia	181	291	302	391	382	0.01	-2.30
Central Africa	825	468	384	1,525	869	0.02	-43.02
Angola	11	47	41	1,091	259	0.00	-76.26
Cameroon	84	72		236	134	0.00	-43.22
Central African Republic	72	26	69	18	33	0.00	83.33
Chad	15			16	6	0.00	-62.50
Congo	40	92	91	47	191	0.00	306.38
Democratic Republic of the Congo	535	215	140	51	153	0.00	200.00
Gabon	68	12	43	60	86	0.00	43.33
Sao Tome and Principe		4		6	7	0.00	16.67
North Africa	3,076	2,813	2,872	2,568	1,939	0.04	-24.49
Algeria	1,732	1,472	909	922	465	0.01	-49.57
Morocco	493	676	832	667	841	0.02	26.09
Sudan	303	166	363	370	158	0.00	-57.30
Tunisia	548	499	768	609	475	0.01	-22.00
Southern Africa	7,956	8,160	6,379	6,861	8,498	0.15	23.86
Botswana	174	21	44	128	107	0.00	-16.41
Lesotho				9	22	0.00	144.44
Namibia	469	320	327	273	367	0.01	34.43
South Africa	7,217	7,696	6,008	6,209	7,644	0.14	23.11
Swaziland	96	123		242	358	0.01	47.93
West Africa	2,176	1,782	4,271	4,718	4,374	0.08	-7.29
Benin	62	49	103	39	40	0.00	2.56
Gambia	39	36	77	82	79	0.00	-3.66
Ghana	504	457	781	582	1,179	0.02	102.58
Guinea	85	14		110	59	0.00	-46.36
Côte d'Ivoire	154	57	24	109	105	0.00	-3.67
Liberia	8	20	56	45	13	0.00	-71.11
Mali	17	13	79	102	131	0.00	28.43
Mauritania	32	6	57	56	51	0.00	-8.93
Niger	142	255	305	556	374	0.01	-32.73
Nigeria	639	522	1,349	1,500	1,353	0.02	-9.80
Guinea-Bissau					24	0.00	
Saint Helena	23		207	207	5	0.00	-97.58
Senegal	117	57	315	360	257	0.00	-28.61
Sierra Leone	330	284	860	910	658	0.01	-27.69

FINLAND

6. Overnight stays of non-resident tourists in all types of accommodation establishments, by country of residence

	2007	2008	2009	2010	2011	Market share 11	% Change 11-10
Togo	11	12	15	36	37	0.00	2.78
Burkina Faso	13		43	24	9	0.00	-62.50
AMERICAS	**277,809**	**265,941**	**228,274**	**239,089**	**276,012**	**5.01**	**15.44**
Caribbean	**1,232**	**1,339**	**3,170**	**1,335**	**1,590**	**0.03**	**19.10**
Antigua and Barbuda	57	32	17	23	21	0.00	-8.70
Bahamas	350	230	371	30	39	0.00	30.00
Barbados	22		22	22	66	0.00	200.00
Bermuda	15	29	991	39	23	0.00	-41.03
Cayman Islands		21	267	7	28	0.00	300.00
Cuba	365	330	334	175	509	0.01	190.86
Dominica			11	92	34	0.00	-63.04
Dominican Republic	37	73	38	68	156	0.00	129.41
Grenada			11	72	13	0.00	-81.94
Guadeloupe			9	53	74	0.00	39.62
Haiti	21	16	34	85	50	0.00	-41.18
Jamaica	36	74	199	243	161	0.00	-33.74
Netherlands Antilles	125	62	105	69	46	0.00	-33.33
Puerto Rico	24	63	442	149	86	0.00	-42.28
Saint Kitts and Nevis	30			38	1	0.00	-97.37
Anguilla			86	57	27	0.00	-52.63
Saint Lucia	5			10	20	0.00	100.00
Trinidad and Tobago	119	390	163	78	60	0.00	-23.08
Turks and Caicos Islands	5	11	47	8	18	0.00	125.00
United States Virgin Islands	21	8	23	17	158	0.00	829.41
Central America	**842**	**722**	**1,374**	**1,524**	**1,444**	**0.03**	**-5.25**
Belize	77	137	95	71	48	0.00	-32.39
Costa Rica	289	159	533	546	576	0.01	5.49
El Salvador	89	83	63	304	358	0.01	17.76
Guatemala	69	45	165	200	47	0.00	-76.50
Honduras	72	24	49	63	63	0.00	
Nicaragua	192	217	254	151	178	0.00	17.88
Panama	54	57	215	189	174	0.00	-7.94
North America	**253,879**	**243,122**	**204,630**	**214,566**	**242,508**	**4.40**	**13.02**
Canada	32,812	33,680	32,295	30,455	34,754	0.63	14.12
Greenland	78	55	307	95	169	0.00	77.89
Mexico	4,577	5,000	5,134	5,534	5,731	0.10	3.56
United States of America	216,412	204,387	166,894	178,482	201,854	3.67	13.09
South America	**21,856**	**20,758**	**19,100**	**21,664**	**30,470**	**0.55**	**40.65**
Argentina	2,841	2,041	2,368	2,538	3,660	0.07	44.21
Bolivia	71	138	79	104	175	0.00	68.27
Brazil	11,173	11,875	11,877	13,489	16,339	0.30	21.13
Chile	3,124	1,939	1,326	1,925	2,180	0.04	13.25
Colombia	1,110	636	1,257	1,324	1,618	0.03	22.21
Ecuador	153	106	151	267	341	0.01	27.72
Falkland Islands, Malvinas			56	21	29	0.00	38.10
French Guiana	12			16			
Guyana	13		10	44	16	0.00	-63.64
Paraguay	19	97	20	16	116	0.00	625.00
Peru	616	802	519	446	851	0.02	90.81
Suriname	20	5	75	58	135	0.00	132.76
Uruguay	2,033	790	612	672	4,129	0.07	514.43
Venezuela	671	2,329	750	744	881	0.02	18.41
EAST ASIA AND THE PACIFIC	**361,859**	**363,579**	**306,455**	**327,557**	**396,783**	**7.20**	**21.13**
North-East Asia	**290,017**	**281,330**	**235,910**	**252,112**	**285,874**	**5.19**	**13.39**
China	93,579	87,074	67,542	77,540	92,099	1.67	18.78
Taiwan, Province of China	11,194	9,875	7,268	8,272	11,136	0.20	34.62

FINLAND

6. Overnight stays of non-resident tourists in all types of accommodation establishments, by country of residence

	2007	2008	2009	2010	2011	Market share 11	% Change 11-10
Hong Kong, China	4,567	4,819	6,159	5,497	9,792	0.18	78.13
Japan	156,047	154,020	134,363	136,804	146,433	2.66	7.04
Korea, Dem. People's Republic of	1,655	2,147	2,921	2,777	1,541	0.03	-44.51
Korea, Republic of	22,798	23,149	17,419	20,730	24,385	0.44	17.63
Macao, China	113	22	78	141	123	0.00	-12.77
Mongolia	64	224	160	351	365	0.01	3.99
South-East Asia	**25,647**	**28,646**	**26,904**	**31,932**	**61,397**	**1.11**	**92.27**
Brunei Darussalam	24		31	10	18	0.00	80.00
Myanmar	306	130	49	176	84	0.00	-52.27
Cambodia	26	11	106	14	30	0.00	114.29
Indonesia	1,654	2,021	1,837	2,421	3,668	0.07	51.51
Lao People's Democratic Republic	131	101	123	113	156	0.00	38.05
Malaysia	2,884	2,957	3,151	3,470	3,214	0.06	-7.38
Philippines	1,440	1,605	3,357	3,453	2,289	0.04	-33.71
Singapore	8,509	7,350	6,652	6,028	12,757	0.23	111.63
Viet Nam	758	1,023	1,436	1,127	1,259	0.02	11.71
Thailand	9,915	13,448	10,162	15,120	37,922	0.69	150.81
Australasia	**45,701**	**53,212**	**43,265**	**42,957**	**48,752**	**0.89**	**13.49**
Australia	41,204	48,237	39,767	39,677	44,875	0.81	13.10
New Zealand	4,497	4,975	3,498	3,280	3,877	0.07	18.20
Melanesia	**103**	**148**	**172**	**280**	**279**	**0.01**	**-0.36**
Solomon Islands	25	26	71	46	34	0.00	-26.09
Fiji	16	46		157	114	0.00	-27.39
New Caledonia	38	47	62	40	70	0.00	75.00
Papua New Guinea	24	29	39	16	61	0.00	281.25
All countries of Melanesia				21			
Micronesia	**219**	**31**	**33**	**87**	**71**	**0.00**	**-18.39**
Kiribati	51			48	33	0.00	-31.25
Guam	168	31	33	32	35	0.00	9.38
Nauru					3	0.00	
Micronesia, Federated States of				7			
Polynesia	**172**	**212**	**171**	**189**	**410**	**0.01**	**116.93**
American Samoa	160	162	129	34	286	0.01	741.18
French Polynesia			12	15	72	0.00	380.00
Tokelau	12	23	30	124	43	0.00	-65.32
Tonga		27		16	6	0.00	-62.50
Tuvalu					3	0.00	
EUROPE	**4,380,364**	**4,540,859**	**4,074,071**	**4,157,709**	**4,543,390**	**82.50**	**9.28**
Central/Eastern Europe	**1,320,232**	**1,494,168**	**1,380,370**	**1,512,867**	**1,782,115**	**32.36**	**17.80**
Azerbaijan	128	250	527	439	642	0.01	46.24
Armenia	688	733	709	587	432	0.01	-26.41
Bulgaria	5,628	6,292	6,836	6,400	6,207	0.11	-3.02
Belarus	7,195	6,616	6,753	10,683	9,621	0.17	-9.94
Czech Republic	28,769	30,380	28,175	27,936	32,474	0.59	16.24
Estonia	211,924	205,627	167,816	205,429	228,187	4.14	11.08
Georgia	2,687	2,167	2,090	1,856	2,369	0.04	27.64
Hungary	26,836	22,478	22,719	22,214	25,388	0.46	14.29
Kazakhstan	1,928	2,841	3,760	3,295	2,391	0.04	-27.44
Kyrgyzstan	96	124	99	191	134	0.00	-29.84
Latvia	42,240	45,428	33,446	39,002	38,528	0.70	-1.22
Lithuania	24,390	27,444	21,747	24,037	25,277	0.46	5.16
Republic of Moldova	537	304	432	293	434	0.01	48.12
Poland	69,475	68,915	63,935	67,902	74,860	1.36	10.25
Romania	16,020	18,609	16,758	18,204	17,360	0.32	-4.64
Russian Federation	856,178	1,030,345	979,526	1,056,424	1,286,598	23.36	21.79
Slovakia	12,736	9,717	8,866	11,424	10,934	0.20	-4.29
Tajikistan	18	66	9	56	47	0.00	-16.07

FINLAND

6. Overnight stays of non-resident tourists in all types of accommodation establishments, by country of residence

	2007	2008	2009	2010	2011	Market share 11	% Change 11-10
Turkmenistan	19	62	6	17	53	0.00	211.76
Ukraine	12,587	15,532	15,903	16,255	19,893	0.36	22.38
Uzbekistan	153	238	258	223	286	0.01	28.25
Northern Europe	**1,437,309**	**1,451,556**	**1,223,492**	**1,194,777**	**1,236,933**	**22.46**	**3.53**
Denmark	104,271	110,173	87,449	85,609	94,823	1.72	10.76
Faeroe Islands	379	283	1,841	483	346	0.01	-28.36
Iceland	11,227	9,728	7,707	8,360	10,572	0.19	26.46
Ireland	28,013	29,218	18,922	16,827	16,772	0.30	-0.33
Norway	201,447	182,531	149,279	159,377	173,254	3.15	8.71
Sweden	576,038	571,904	494,002	517,849	552,129	10.03	6.62
United Kingdom	515,934	547,719	464,292	406,272	389,037	7.06	-4.24
Southern Europe	**367,179**	**353,806**	**320,967**	**311,941**	**340,072**	**6.17**	**9.02**
Albania	1,492	1,300	1,409	952	748	0.01	-21.43
Andorra	281	256	221	295	153	0.00	-48.14
Bosnia and Herzegovina	747	553	634	671	798	0.01	18.93
Croatia	4,255	6,127	3,911	3,838	5,152	0.09	34.24
Gibraltar	9	19	1,379	105	89	0.00	-15.24
Greece	27,559	24,703	24,277	18,924	17,810	0.32	-5.89
Holy See			5	10	2	0.00	-80.00
Italy	164,533	167,418	151,658	142,389	156,509	2.84	9.92
Malta	1,249	859	1,172	989	1,118	0.02	13.04
Montenegro			26	107	16	0.00	-85.05
Portugal	15,653	17,193	18,912	19,875	17,606	0.32	-11.42
San Marino	46	38	122	109	173	0.00	58.72
Serbia			971	2,063	2,131	0.04	3.30
Slovenia	8,711	8,247	6,590	7,248	7,191	0.13	-0.79
Spain	138,532	126,508	109,240	113,804	130,046	2.36	14.27
TFYR of Macedonia	913	585	440	562	530	0.01	-5.69
Serbia and Montenegro	3,199						
Western Europe	**1,224,100**	**1,207,465**	**1,116,337**	**1,099,502**	**1,148,255**	**20.85**	**4.43**
Austria	48,237	49,899	48,921	50,836	57,325	1.04	12.76
Belgium	53,079	50,419	45,909	46,521	49,021	0.89	5.37
France	238,408	230,448	212,887	213,414	213,588	3.88	0.08
Germany	572,147	579,970	525,880	510,280	541,031	9.82	6.03
Liechtenstein	867	1,156	1,410	524	471	0.01	-10.11
Luxembourg	3,551	3,906	4,046	3,934	3,891	0.07	-1.09
Monaco	237	343	450	355	326	0.01	-8.17
Netherlands	191,221	182,077	169,213	165,779	164,593	2.99	-0.72
Switzerland	116,353	109,247	107,621	107,859	118,009	2.14	9.41
East Mediterranean Europe	**31,544**	**33,864**	**32,905**	**38,622**	**36,015**	**0.65**	**-6.75**
Cyprus	1,648	1,831	1,889	1,875	1,992	0.04	6.24
Israel	16,768	17,203	15,701	19,370	17,320	0.31	-10.58
Turkey	13,128	14,830	15,315	17,377	16,703	0.30	-3.88
MIDDLE EAST	**10,804**	**14,573**	**13,231**	**11,749**	**11,647**	**0.21**	**-0.87**
Bahrain	670	1,149	629	220	227	0.00	3.18
Iraq	352	383	376	444	752	0.01	69.37
Jordan	350	451	434	345	435	0.01	26.09
Kuwait	585	1,085	511	664	571	0.01	-14.01
Lebanon	540	759	767	745	462	0.01	-37.99
Libya	115	398	146	215	69	0.00	-67.91
Oman	68	72	313	400	301	0.01	-24.75
Qatar	165	509	607	581	273	0.00	-53.01
Saudi Arabia	4,213	5,840	4,714	3,064	2,376	0.04	-22.45
Syrian Arab Republic	296	110	204	325	306	0.01	-5.85
United Arab Emirates	1,516	1,386	1,830	2,304	3,105	0.06	34.77
Egypt	1,922	2,304	2,312	2,297	2,687	0.05	16.98
Yemen	12	127	388	145	83	0.00	-42.76

FINLAND

6. Overnight stays of non-resident tourists in all types of accommodation establishments, by country of residence

	2007	2008	2009	2010	2011	Market share 11	% Change 11-10
SOUTH ASIA	**56,801**	**73,977**	**61,207**	**68,094**	**60,849**	**1.10**	**-10.64**
Afghanistan	2,411	2,189	2,404	2,266	1,616	0.03	-28.68
Bangladesh	187	122	328	259	364	0.01	40.54
Bhutan	10		20		10	0.00	
Sri Lanka	375	299	324	147	264	0.00	79.59
India	49,589	63,997	52,138	58,657	53,672	0.97	-8.50
Iran, Islamic Republic of	2,725	3,736	2,484	2,924	3,032	0.06	3.69
Maldives	9	19	26	33	35	0.00	6.06
Nepal	97	163	556	523	470	0.01	-10.13
Pakistan	1,398	3,452	2,927	3,285	1,386	0.03	-57.81
NOT SPECIFIED	**222,235**	**227,993**	**189,293**	**181,298**	**198,672**	**3.61**	**9.58**
Other countries of the World	222,235	227,993	189,293	181,298	198,672	3.61	9.58

FRANCE

1. Arrivals of non-resident tourists at national borders, by country of residence

		2007	2008	2009	2010	2011	Market share 11	% Change 11-10
TOTAL	(*)	80,852,000	79,219,000	76,766,000	77,648,325	81,411,043	100.00	4.85
AFRICA		1,576,000	1,765,000	1,823,000	1,721,397	2,069,018	2.54	20.19
North Africa		942,000	1,125,000	1,268,000	1,191,148	1,344,353	1.65	12.86
All countries of North Africa	(*)	942,000	1,125,000	1,268,000	1,191,148	1,344,353	1.65	12.86
Other Africa		634,000	640,000	555,000	530,249	724,665	0.89	36.67
Other countries of Africa		634,000	640,000	555,000	530,249	724,665	0.89	36.67
AMERICAS		6,023,000	5,963,000	5,491,000	5,679,079	6,607,872	8.12	16.35
North America		4,761,000	4,609,000	4,288,000	4,192,314	4,760,629	5.85	13.56
Canada		922,000	896,000	873,000	961,804	925,477	1.14	-3.78
Mexico		440,000	385,000	354,000	321,363	509,828	0.63	58.65
United States of America		3,399,000	3,328,000	3,061,000	2,909,147	3,325,324	4.08	14.31
Other Americas		1,262,000	1,354,000	1,203,000	1,486,765	1,847,243	2.27	24.25
Other countries of the Americas		1,262,000	1,354,000	1,203,000	1,486,765	1,847,243	2.27	24.25
EAST ASIA AND THE PACIFIC		3,206,000	3,484,000	3,371,000	3,648,810	4,222,449	5.19	15.72
North-East Asia		1,530,000	1,452,000	1,437,000	1,505,608	1,748,678	2.15	16.14
China	(*)	832,000	778,000	740,000	909,631	1,127,137	1.38	23.91
Japan		698,000	674,000	697,000	595,977	621,541	0.76	4.29
Other East Asia and the Pacific		1,676,000	2,032,000	1,934,000	2,143,202	2,473,771	3.04	15.42
Other countries of Asia		773,000	948,000	842,000	932,244	1,094,053	1.34	17.36
All countries of Oceania		903,000	1,084,000	1,092,000	1,210,958	1,379,718	1.69	13.94
EUROPE		69,272,000	67,304,000	65,246,000	65,709,669	67,731,803	83.20	3.08
Central/Eastern Europe		1,547,000	1,811,000	1,278,000	1,187,584	1,571,185	1.93	32.30
Poland		390,000	481,000	365,000	370,308	436,164	0.54	17.78
Other countries Central/East Europe		1,157,000	1,330,000	913,000	817,276	1,135,021	1.39	38.88
Northern Europe		16,521,000	16,043,000	14,362,000	14,411,002	14,435,116	17.73	0.17
Denmark		698,000	658,000	696,000	614,136	654,937	0.80	6.64
Finland		165,000	278,000	182,000	285,953	267,255	0.33	-6.54
Sweden		649,000	732,000	603,000	614,269	689,534	0.85	12.25
United Kingdom/Ireland		15,009,000	14,375,000	12,881,000	12,896,644	12,823,390	15.75	-0.57
Southern Europe		14,773,000	15,026,000	13,447,000	13,359,596	14,612,796	17.95	9.38
Greece		307,000	270,000	357,000	244,151	171,327	0.21	-29.83
Italy		8,141,000	8,233,000	7,250,000	7,178,166	7,986,946	9.81	11.27
Portugal		726,000	883,000	966,000	998,223	987,153	1.21	-1.11
Spain		5,599,000	5,640,000	4,874,000	4,939,056	5,467,370	6.72	10.70
Western Europe		35,087,000	33,109,000	34,900,000	35,368,819	35,549,830	43.67	0.51
Austria		564,000	747,000	646,000	765,220	1,004,026	1.23	31.21
Germany		13,041,000	11,645,000	10,692,000	11,409,526	11,648,128	14.31	2.09
Netherlands		6,824,000	6,244,000	7,224,000	7,002,184	6,496,711	7.98	-7.22
Switzerland	(*)	5,303,000	5,065,000	5,438,000	5,450,197	5,666,834	6.96	3.97
Belgium / Luxembourg		9,355,000	9,408,000	10,900,000	10,741,692	10,734,131	13.19	-0.07
Other Europe		1,344,000	1,315,000	1,259,000	1,382,668	1,562,876	1.92	13.03
Other countries of Europe		1,344,000	1,315,000	1,259,000	1,382,668	1,562,876	1.92	13.03
MIDDLE EAST		775,000	703,000	835,000	889,370	779,901	0.96	-12.31
All countries of Middle East		775,000	703,000	835,000	889,370	779,901	0.96	-12.31

FRANCE

3. Arrivals of non-resident tourists in hotels and similar establishments, by country of residence

		2007	2008	2009	2010	2011	Market share 11	% Change 11-10
TOTAL	(*)	33,254,493	32,137,170	28,765,875	29,500,638	30,262,220	100.00	2.58
AFRICA		412,959	416,939	416,147	433,959	454,676	1.50	4.77
North Africa		165,941	179,030	182,986	206,040	202,725	0.67	-1.61
All countries of North Africa		165,941	179,030	182,986	206,040	202,725	0.67	-1.61
Other Africa		247,018	237,909	233,161	227,919	251,951	0.83	10.54
Other countries of Africa		247,018	237,909	233,161	227,919	251,951	0.83	10.54
AMERICAS		4,018,547	3,605,956	3,297,733	3,573,000	3,807,590	12.58	6.57
North America		3,363,913	2,912,108	2,644,740	2,750,429	2,865,287	9.47	4.18
Canada		425,598	423,298	371,351	403,184	428,512	1.42	6.28
United States of America		2,938,315	2,488,810	2,273,389	2,347,245	2,436,775	8.05	3.81
Other Americas		654,634	693,848	652,993	822,571	942,303	3.11	14.56
Other countries of the Americas		654,634	693,848	652,993	822,571	942,303	3.11	14.56
EAST ASIA AND THE PACIFIC		2,857,431	2,528,215	2,459,439	2,802,070	3,150,363	10.41	12.43
North-East Asia		1,825,206	1,556,281	1,507,798	1,696,261	1,838,287	6.07	8.37
China		530,488	416,525	395,210	567,294	728,996	2.41	28.50
Japan		1,294,718	1,139,756	1,112,588	1,128,967	1,109,291	3.67	-1.74
Australasia		279,113	285,173	253,192	319,151	369,033	1.22	15.63
Australia		279,113	285,173	253,192	319,151	369,033	1.22	15.63
Other East Asia and the Pacific		753,112	686,761	698,449	786,658	943,043	3.12	19.88
Other countries East Asia/Pacific		753,112	686,761	698,449	786,658	943,043	3.12	19.88
EUROPE		25,565,986	25,180,344	22,203,552	22,203,237	22,318,562	73.75	0.52
Central/Eastern Europe		946,213	1,152,584	932,590	1,125,930	1,330,744	4.40	18.19
Bulgaria		24,965	32,168	23,876	25,763	26,264	0.09	1.94
Czech Republic		63,536	82,827	66,121	91,993	110,075	0.36	19.66
Estonia		6,240	7,902	5,709	6,623	10,078	0.03	52.17
Hungary		53,067	54,986	56,438	56,670	68,135	0.23	20.23
Latvia		7,462	5,989	5,643	8,098	9,966	0.03	23.07
Lithuania		17,526	16,710	12,407	18,058	20,535	0.07	13.72
Poland		167,409	216,715	194,398	206,571	233,215	0.77	12.90
Romania		78,293	110,182	88,998	103,163	126,943	0.42	23.05
Russian Federation		498,778	593,695	452,463	581,221	695,762	2.30	19.71
Slovakia		28,937	31,410	26,537	27,770	29,771	0.10	7.21
Northern Europe		8,567,516	7,958,339	6,423,132	6,220,033	6,042,173	19.97	-2.86
Denmark		239,742	218,432	202,401	214,811	216,016	0.71	0.56
Finland		84,415	94,610	95,532	102,261	116,116	0.38	13.55
Iceland		21,279	18,144	14,393	14,407	21,337	0.07	48.10
Ireland		270,075	267,763	230,997	218,994	212,715	0.70	-2.87
Norway		148,087	150,442	136,376	153,949	166,002	0.55	7.83
Sweden		249,115	247,177	200,340	225,477	260,138	0.86	15.37
United Kingdom		7,554,803	6,961,771	5,543,093	5,290,134	5,049,849	16.69	-4.54
Southern Europe		6,202,060	6,034,807	5,338,970	5,402,525	5,150,548	17.02	-4.66
Croatia		18,162	26,765	18,274	16,019	19,308	0.06	20.53
Greece		140,180	152,550	146,790	128,429	109,358	0.36	-14.85
Italy		3,080,536	3,108,112	2,790,805	2,753,302	2,547,150	8.42	-7.49
Malta		9,395	13,967	7,584	12,465	11,733	0.04	-5.87
Portugal		273,792	279,888	258,253	285,639	269,944	0.89	-5.49
Slovenia		18,340	19,199	18,267	17,689	18,084	0.06	2.23
Spain		2,661,655	2,434,326	2,098,997	2,188,982	2,174,971	7.19	-0.64
Western Europe		9,266,504	9,386,149	8,989,714	8,832,428	9,186,330	30.36	4.01
Austria		183,882	188,392	168,817	176,899	180,566	0.60	2.07
Belgium		2,621,774	2,732,157	2,780,830	2,703,367	2,776,012	9.17	2.69
Germany		3,305,270	3,230,890	2,915,293	2,961,428	3,044,555	10.06	2.81
Luxembourg		99,327	105,667	109,364	120,975	132,090	0.44	9.19

FRANCE

3. Arrivals of non-resident tourists in hotels and similar establishments, by country of residence

	2007	2008	2009	2010	2011	Market share 11	% Change 11-10
Netherlands	1,868,196	1,947,591	1,845,505	1,708,485	1,740,397	5.75	1.87
Switzerland	1,188,055	1,181,452	1,169,905	1,161,274	1,312,710	4.34	13.04
East Mediterranean Europe	**80,707**	**94,899**	**78,054**	**110,862**	**127,120**	**0.42**	**14.67**
Cyprus	9,584	12,747	9,822	14,050	14,201	0.05	1.07
Turkey	71,123	82,152	68,232	96,812	112,919	0.37	16.64
Other Europe	**502,986**	**553,566**	**441,092**	**511,459**	**481,647**	**1.59**	**-5.83**
Other countries of Europe	502,986	553,566	441,092	511,459	481,647	1.59	-5.83
MIDDLE EAST	**399,570**	**405,716**	**389,004**	**488,372**	**531,029**	**1.75**	**8.73**
All countries of Middle East	399,570	405,716	389,004	488,372	531,029	1.75	8.73

FRANCE

5. Overnight stays of non-resident tourists in hotels and similar establishments, by country of residence

		2007	2008	2009	2010	2011	Market share 11	% Change 11-10
TOTAL	(*)	72,393,344	71,064,602	63,203,046	64,920,009	66,531,774	100.00	2.48
AFRICA		971,324	1,003,129	1,014,682	1,084,530	1,125,192	1.69	3.75
North Africa		378,261	422,420	433,374	492,705	490,290	0.74	-0.49
All countries of North Africa		378,261	422,420	433,374	492,705	490,290	0.74	-0.49
Other Africa		593,063	580,709	581,308	591,825	634,902	0.95	7.28
Other countries of Africa		593,063	580,709	581,308	591,825	634,902	0.95	7.28
AMERICAS		9,611,815	8,673,036	8,177,377	8,927,903	9,554,010	14.36	7.01
North America		7,959,719	6,873,893	6,428,335	6,670,289	6,970,489	10.48	4.50
Canada		976,993	996,645	912,536	972,684	1,040,536	1.56	6.98
United States of America		6,982,726	5,877,248	5,515,799	5,697,605	5,929,953	8.91	4.08
Other Americas		1,652,096	1,799,143	1,749,042	2,257,614	2,583,521	3.88	14.44
Other countries of the Americas		1,652,096	1,799,143	1,749,042	2,257,614	2,583,521	3.88	14.44
EAST ASIA AND THE PACIFIC		6,071,506	5,480,219	5,311,596	6,054,390	6,709,726	10.08	10.82
North-East Asia		3,838,850	3,308,083	3,185,836	3,601,998	3,825,222	5.75	6.20
China		1,037,312	827,163	787,259	1,135,802	1,425,143	2.14	25.47
Japan		2,801,538	2,480,920	2,398,577	2,466,196	2,400,079	3.61	-2.68
Australasia		642,309	675,563	620,935	773,935	905,152	1.36	16.95
Australia		642,309	675,563	620,935	773,935	905,152	1.36	16.95
Other East Asia and the Pacific		1,590,347	1,496,573	1,504,825	1,678,457	1,979,352	2.98	17.93
Other countries East Asia/Pacific		1,590,347	1,496,573	1,504,825	1,678,457	1,979,352	2.98	17.93
EUROPE		54,671,166	54,757,802	47,584,765	47,487,562	47,703,196	71.70	0.45
Central/Eastern Europe		2,319,118	2,879,278	2,306,107	2,811,538	3,360,381	5.05	19.52
Bulgaria		59,611	78,875	56,735	61,434	63,159	0.09	2.81
Czech Republic		131,610	172,060	137,018	184,850	228,132	0.34	23.41
Estonia		13,784	18,312	14,096	16,278	25,037	0.04	53.81
Hungary		117,590	120,345	122,960	123,711	149,052	0.22	20.48
Latvia		16,794	15,746	13,357	20,150	23,810	0.04	18.16
Lithuania		37,146	35,577	27,637	38,988	44,207	0.07	13.39
Poland		362,800	461,908	394,792	437,865	507,607	0.76	15.93
Romania		179,277	258,848	215,504	250,006	302,306	0.45	20.92
Russian Federation		1,336,943	1,646,336	1,264,371	1,618,949	1,947,541	2.93	20.30
Slovakia		63,563	71,271	59,637	59,307	69,530	0.10	17.24
Northern Europe		18,066,392	17,210,125	13,784,180	13,114,328	12,940,552	19.45	-1.33
Denmark		545,134	500,678	480,447	507,530	513,918	0.77	1.26
Finland		195,703	224,072	237,551	254,255	290,536	0.44	14.27
Iceland		51,695	44,778	37,553	32,195	45,955	0.07	42.74
Ireland		740,559	779,330	640,646	594,492	556,262	0.84	-6.43
Norway		351,208	370,605	334,715	389,393	417,336	0.63	7.18
Sweden		577,048	582,414	491,988	550,374	647,723	0.97	17.69
United Kingdom		15,605,045	14,708,248	11,561,280	10,786,089	10,468,822	15.74	-2.94
Southern Europe		14,234,024	14,174,075	12,510,498	12,553,739	11,807,781	17.75	-5.94
Croatia		44,962	62,393	43,236	36,735	44,517	0.07	21.18
Greece		386,281	426,942	422,277	359,587	294,792	0.44	-18.02
Italy		6,931,459	7,227,364	6,479,711	6,358,381	5,823,314	8.75	-8.42
Malta		31,501	48,033	25,150	41,378	35,601	0.05	-13.96
Portugal		604,672	620,543	582,836	640,313	587,338	0.88	-8.27
Slovenia		41,557	43,120	36,386	39,107	40,102	0.06	2.54
Spain		6,193,592	5,745,680	4,920,902	5,078,238	4,982,117	7.49	-1.89
Western Europe		18,688,302	18,989,572	17,767,289	17,552,574	18,155,607	27.29	3.44
Austria		409,040	428,958	386,168	409,640	412,709	0.62	0.75
Belgium		5,300,267	5,460,783	5,347,716	5,253,448	5,327,365	8.01	1.41
Germany		6,720,795	6,652,298	5,914,513	6,023,998	6,187,813	9.30	2.72
Luxembourg		209,683	217,081	222,704	248,607	264,340	0.40	6.33

FRANCE

5. Overnight stays of non-resident tourists in hotels and similar establishments, by country of residence

	2007	2008	2009	2010	2011	Market share 11	% Change 11-10
Netherlands	3,574,561	3,749,982	3,483,710	3,235,647	3,289,240	4.94	1.66
Switzerland	2,473,956	2,480,470	2,412,478	2,381,234	2,674,140	4.02	12.30
East Mediterranean Europe	**212,514**	**246,380**	**209,409**	**300,426**	**331,430**	**0.50**	**10.32**
Cyprus	28,254	37,971	28,988	42,144	40,481	0.06	-3.95
Turkey	184,260	208,409	180,421	258,282	290,949	0.44	12.65
Other Europe	**1,150,816**	**1,258,372**	**1,007,282**	**1,154,957**	**1,107,445**	**1.66**	**-4.11**
Other countries of Europe	1,150,816	1,258,372	1,007,282	1,154,957	1,107,445	1.66	-4.11
MIDDLE EAST	**1,067,533**	**1,150,416**	**1,114,626**	**1,365,624**	**1,439,650**	**2.16**	**5.42**
All countries of Middle East	1,067,533	1,150,416	1,114,626	1,365,624	1,439,650	2.16	5.42

FRANCE

6. Overnight stays of non-resident tourists in all types of accommodation establishments, by country of residence

		2007	2008	2009	2010	2011	Market share 11	% Change 11-10
TOTAL	(*)	**536,346,000**	**526,159,000**	**512,189,000**	**525,290,807**	**581,314,319**	**100.00**	**10.67**
AFRICA		**21,074,000**	**23,532,000**	**25,232,000**	**25,287,693**	**30,759,519**	**5.29**	**21.64**
North Africa		**12,876,000**	**15,296,000**	**17,852,000**	**18,129,051**	**20,580,301**	**3.54**	**13.52**
All countries of North Africa	(*)	12,876,000	15,296,000	17,852,000	18,129,051	20,580,301	3.54	13.52
Other Africa		**8,198,000**	**8,236,000**	**7,380,000**	**7,158,642**	**10,179,218**	**1.75**	**42.19**
Other countries of Africa		8,198,000	8,236,000	7,380,000	7,158,642	10,179,218	1.75	42.19
AMERICAS		**50,068,000**	**52,017,000**	**48,277,000**	**50,257,940**	**60,440,716**	**10.40**	**20.26**
North America		**39,145,000**	**40,758,000**	**37,506,000**	**38,059,369**	**44,904,727**	**7.72**	**17.99**
Canada		8,584,000	8,732,000	8,676,000	9,877,596	10,140,460	1.74	2.66
Mexico		3,489,000	3,638,000	2,929,000	2,582,545	3,688,016	0.63	42.81
United States of America		27,072,000	28,388,000	25,901,000	25,599,228	31,076,251	5.35	21.40
Other Americas		**10,923,000**	**11,259,000**	**10,771,000**	**12,198,571**	**15,535,989**	**2.67**	**27.36**
Other countries of the Americas		10,923,000	11,259,000	10,771,000	12,198,571	15,535,989	2.67	27.36
EAST ASIA AND THE PACIFIC		**22,153,000**	**25,390,000**	**25,746,000**	**28,131,807**	**33,359,545**	**5.74**	**18.58**
North-East Asia		**9,396,000**	**9,132,000**	**9,555,000**	**10,171,243**	**12,068,681**	**2.08**	**18.65**
China	(*)	5,150,000	5,021,000	5,383,000	6,567,036	7,964,491	1.37	21.28
Japan		4,246,000	4,111,000	4,172,000	3,604,207	4,104,190	0.71	13.87
Other East Asia and the Pacific		**12,757,000**	**16,258,000**	**16,191,000**	**17,960,564**	**21,290,864**	**3.66**	**18.54**
Other countries of Asia		5,740,000	7,381,000	7,233,000	8,161,291	9,964,620	1.71	22.10
All countries of Oceania		7,017,000	8,877,000	8,958,000	9,799,273	11,326,244	1.95	15.58
EUROPE		**435,599,000**	**418,746,000**	**405,119,000**	**412,801,195**	**448,696,129**	**77.19**	**8.70**
Central/Eastern Europe		**13,487,000**	**15,258,000**	**10,774,000**	**10,668,886**	**15,561,930**	**2.68**	**45.86**
Poland		3,994,000	4,218,000	3,059,000	3,289,252	3,881,131	0.67	17.99
Other countries Central/East Europe		9,493,000	11,040,000	7,715,000	7,379,634	11,680,799	2.01	58.28
Northern Europe		**101,366,000**	**100,209,000**	**91,146,000**	**93,648,852**	**101,089,550**	**17.39**	**7.95**
Denmark		4,797,000	4,290,000	4,652,000	4,080,089	4,889,548	0.84	19.84
Finland		1,053,000	1,965,000	1,269,000	1,706,775	1,865,910	0.32	9.32
Sweden		4,640,000	4,882,000	3,469,000	3,623,595	4,693,684	0.81	29.53
United Kingdom/Ireland		90,876,000	89,072,000	81,756,000	84,238,393	89,640,408	15.42	6.41
Southern Europe		**82,854,000**	**82,355,000**	**74,855,000**	**72,619,935**	**83,901,992**	**14.43**	**15.54**
Greece		2,768,000	2,264,000	2,512,000	1,736,860	1,267,832	0.22	-27.00
Italy		43,137,000	44,674,000	40,657,000	40,487,586	46,565,363	8.01	15.01
Portugal		6,932,000	7,481,000	6,948,000	6,716,569	7,141,683	1.23	6.33
Spain		30,017,000	27,936,000	24,738,000	23,678,920	28,927,114	4.98	22.16
Western Europe		**227,039,000**	**210,598,000**	**218,447,000**	**224,807,827**	**234,161,090**	**40.28**	**4.16**
Austria		4,581,000	6,579,000	5,471,000	7,044,550	10,022,988	1.72	42.28
Germany		87,499,000	78,482,000	70,768,000	76,798,195	82,089,380	14.12	6.89
Netherlands		52,435,000	46,981,000	54,196,000	54,288,511	51,057,299	8.78	-5.95
Switzerland	(*)	30,375,000	26,934,000	28,506,000	28,078,131	30,043,024	5.17	7.00
Belgium / Luxembourg		52,149,000	51,622,000	59,506,000	58,598,440	60,948,399	10.48	4.01
Other Europe		**10,853,000**	**10,326,000**	**9,897,000**	**11,055,695**	**13,981,567**	**2.41**	**26.46**
Other countries of Europe		10,853,000	10,326,000	9,897,000	11,055,695	13,981,567	2.41	26.46
MIDDLE EAST		**7,452,000**	**6,474,000**	**7,815,000**	**8,812,172**	**8,058,410**	**1.39**	**-8.55**
All countries of Middle East		7,452,000	6,474,000	7,815,000	8,812,172	8,058,410	1.39	-8.55

FRENCH POLYNESIA

1. Arrivals of non-resident tourists at national borders, by country of residence

		2007	2008	2009	2010	2011	Market share 11	% Change 11-10
TOTAL	(*)	218,241	196,496	160,447	153,919	162,776	100.00	5.75
AFRICA		764	338	278	275	272	0.17	-1.09
Other Africa		764	338	278	275	272	0.17	-1.09
All countries of Africa		764	338	278	275	272	0.17	-1.09
AMERICAS		81,445	70,506	51,716	53,338	63,547	39.04	19.14
Central America		229	108	135	134	137	0.08	2.24
All countries of Central America		229	108	135	134	137	0.08	2.24
North America		74,223	63,833	45,790	47,302	57,876	35.56	22.35
Canada		7,301	7,271	4,265	5,468	7,458	4.58	36.39
Mexico		1,373	1,200	745	814	1,033	0.63	26.90
United States of America		64,910	54,995	40,403	40,735	49,097	30.16	20.53
Hawaii, USA		639	367	377	285	288	0.18	1.05
South America		6,993	6,565	5,791	5,902	5,534	3.40	-6.24
Argentina		1,797	1,951	1,433	1,253	1,098	0.67	-12.37
Brazil		2,654	2,455	2,047	2,360	2,530	1.55	7.20
Chile		1,864	1,585	1,706	1,849	1,328	0.82	-28.18
Other countries of South America		678	574	605	440	578	0.36	31.36
EAST ASIA AND THE PACIFIC		50,260	42,386	35,106	33,196	34,052	20.92	2.58
North-East Asia		24,482	20,261	17,948	15,682	14,846	9.12	-5.33
China		440	388	543	1,143	978	0.60	-14.44
Taiwan, Province of China		91	195	188	91	158	0.10	73.63
Hong Kong, China		140	259	99	1	214	0.13	21300.00
Japan		23,240	18,769	16,353	13,761	12,990	7.98	-5.60
Korea, Republic of		571	650	765	686	506	0.31	-26.24
South-East Asia		728	668	674	659	616	0.38	-6.53
Indonesia		96	83	128	98	86	0.05	-12.24
Malaysia		88	70	62	104	72	0.04	-30.77
Philippines		238	202	187	176	121	0.07	-31.25
Singapore		227	202	191	200	200	0.12	
Thailand		79	111	106	81	137	0.08	69.14
Australasia		19,944	16,773	11,471	12,073	13,720	8.43	13.64
Australia		11,746	10,228	6,557	6,945	8,236	5.06	18.59
New Zealand		8,198	6,545	4,914	5,128	5,484	3.37	6.94
Melanesia		3,942	3,911	4,006	4,048	4,085	2.51	0.91
Fiji		181	96	131	108	139	0.09	28.70
New Caledonia		3,761	3,815	3,875	3,940	3,946	2.42	0.15
Polynesia		616	373	379	342	361	0.22	5.56
Cook Islands		464	309	268	265	284	0.17	7.17
Tonga		66	18	36	5	23	0.01	360.00
Samoa	(*)	86	46	75	72	54	0.03	-25.00
Other East Asia and the Pacific		548	400	628	392	424	0.26	8.16
Other countries of Asia		163	51	79	56	77	0.05	37.50
Other countries of Oceania		385	349	549	336	347	0.21	3.27
EUROPE		85,205	82,838	72,857	66,561	64,272	39.48	-3.44
Central/Eastern Europe		744	805	601	519	699	0.43	34.68
Russian Federation		744	805	601	519	699	0.43	34.68
Northern Europe		7,922	6,337	4,523	3,790	3,522	2.16	-7.07
Denmark		225	259	228	236	162	0.10	-31.36
Finland		577	301	234	232	205	0.13	-11.64
Norway		329	272	168	158	201	0.12	27.22
Sweden		558	528	411	324	283	0.17	-12.65
United Kingdom		6,233	4,977	3,482	2,840	2,671	1.64	-5.95

FRENCH POLYNESIA

1. Arrivals of non-resident tourists at national borders, by country of residence

	2007	2008	2009	2010	2011	Market share 11	% Change 11-10
Southern Europe	**21,176**	**20,232**	**16,835**	**15,623**	**14,320**	**8.80**	**-8.34**
Italy	14,385	13,802	11,944	11,208	10,471	6.43	-6.58
Portugal	499	470	337	311	374	0.23	20.26
Spain	6,292	5,960	4,554	4,104	3,475	2.13	-15.33
Western Europe	**52,760**	**53,042**	**48,551**	**44,976**	**43,817**	**26.92**	**-2.58**
Austria	963	998	999	757	688	0.42	-9.11
Belgium	1,007	2,025	995	796	852	0.52	7.04
France	43,161	42,374	39,256	36,544	35,835	22.01	-1.94
Germany	4,426	4,511	4,346	4,256	3,604	2.21	-15.32
Luxembourg	140	168	143	198	109	0.07	-44.95
Netherlands	566	726	676	565	487	0.30	-13.81
Switzerland	2,497	2,240	2,136	1,860	2,242	1.38	20.54
Other Europe	**2,603**	**2,422**	**2,347**	**1,653**	**1,914**	**1.18**	**15.79**
Other countries of Europe	2,603	2,422	2,347	1,653	1,914	1.18	15.79
MIDDLE EAST	**343**	**182**	**201**	**231**	**201**	**0.12**	**-12.99**
All countries of Middle East	343	182	201	231	201	0.12	-12.99
SOUTH ASIA	**224**	**246**	**289**	**318**	**432**	**0.27**	**35.85**
India	224	246	289	318	432	0.27	35.85

FRENCH POLYNESIA

3. Arrivals of non-resident tourists in hotels and similar establishments, by country of residence

	2007	2008	2009	2010	2011	Market share 11	% Change 11-10
TOTAL	190,102	172,827	138,151	133,032	142,056	100.00	6.78
AFRICA	593	271	213	219	206	0.15	-5.94
Other Africa	593	271	213	219	206	0.15	-5.94
All countries of Africa	593	271	213	219	206	0.15	-5.94
AMERICAS	77,703	67,364	48,539	50,606	60,773	42.78	20.09
Central America	219	92	128	129	126	0.09	-2.33
All countries of Central America	219	92	128	129	126	0.09	-2.33
North America	70,970	61,108	43,089	45,015	55,422	39.01	23.12
Canada	6,993	7,047	4,067	5,303	7,241	5.10	36.55
Mexico	1,348	1,166	710	783	1,005	0.71	28.35
United States of America	62,285	52,762	38,175	38,807	47,049	33.12	21.24
Hawaii, USA	344	133	137	122	127	0.09	4.10
South America	6,514	6,164	5,322	5,462	5,225	3.68	-4.34
Argentina	1,760	1,939	1,402	1,213	1,088	0.77	-10.31
Brazil	2,552	2,360	1,966	2,252	2,469	1.74	9.64
Chile	1,581	1,314	1,387	1,581	1,111	0.78	-29.73
Other countries of South America	621	551	567	416	557	0.39	33.89
EAST ASIA AND THE PACIFIC	45,278	37,931	31,156	29,146	29,949	21.08	2.76
North-East Asia	24,067	19,864	17,740	15,496	14,610	10.28	-5.72
China	373	334	503	1,081	923	0.65	-14.62
Taiwan, Province of China	83	166	175	85	140	0.10	64.71
Hong Kong, China	123	235	97	1	197	0.14	19600.00
Japan	22,929	18,494	16,209	13,657	12,859	9.05	-5.84
Korea, Republic of	559	635	756	672	491	0.35	-26.93
South-East Asia	617	576	584	566	544	0.38	-3.89
Indonesia	61	72	108	71	71	0.05	
Malaysia	77	57	50	88	64	0.05	-27.27
Philippines	215	180	168	165	114	0.08	-30.91
Singapore	207	187	174	176	185	0.13	5.11
Thailand	57	80	84	66	110	0.08	66.67
Australasia	18,208	15,311	10,113	10,832	12,489	8.79	15.30
Australia	11,024	9,668	6,055	6,483	7,680	5.41	18.46
New Zealand	7,184	5,643	4,058	4,349	4,809	3.39	10.58
Melanesia	1,758	1,832	2,117	1,913	1,949	1.37	1.88
Fiji	137	57	123	75	100	0.07	33.33
New Caledonia	1,621	1,775	1,994	1,838	1,849	1.30	0.60
Polynesia	278	129	185	133	130	0.09	-2.26
Cook Islands	194	88	81	99	70	0.05	-29.29
Tonga	35	12	34	3	18	0.01	500.00
Samoa	49	29	70	31	42	0.03	35.48
Other East Asia and the Pacific	350	219	417	206	227	0.16	10.19
Other countries of Asia	146	40	63	45	64	0.05	42.22
Other countries of Oceania	204	179	354	161	163	0.11	1.24
EUROPE	66,019	66,862	57,781	52,551	50,518	35.56	-3.87
Central/Eastern Europe	728	795	581	515	689	0.49	33.79
Russian Federation	728	795	581	515	689	0.49	33.79
Northern Europe	7,610	6,148	4,344	3,641	3,388	2.38	-6.95
Denmark	204	240	217	221	155	0.11	-29.86
Finland	551	289	230	225	198	0.14	-12.00
Norway	312	257	154	144	192	0.14	33.33
Sweden	528	518	388	310	269	0.19	-13.23
United Kingdom	6,015	4,844	3,355	2,741	2,574	1.81	-6.09

FRENCH POLYNESIA

3. Arrivals of non-resident tourists in hotels and similar establishments, by country of residence

	2007	2008	2009	2010	2011	Market share 11	% Change 11-10
Southern Europe	**20,745**	**19,978**	**16,543**	**15,409**	**14,062**	**9.90**	**-8.74**
Italy	14,159	13,676	11,828	11,083	10,332	7.27	-6.78
Portugal	482	464	328	307	361	0.25	17.59
Spain	6,104	5,838	4,387	4,019	3,369	2.37	-16.17
Western Europe	**34,444**	**37,602**	**34,033**	**31,398**	**30,552**	**21.51**	**-2.69**
Austria	937	986	982	740	683	0.48	-7.70
Belgium	876	1,888	873	693	725	0.51	4.62
France	25,384	27,379	25,187	23,364	22,958	16.16	-1.74
Germany	4,260	4,406	4,230	4,148	3,514	2.47	-15.28
Luxembourg	124	155	130	191	101	0.07	-47.12
Netherlands	538	713	655	540	475	0.33	-12.04
Switzerland	2,325	2,075	1,976	1,722	2,096	1.48	21.72
Other Europe	**2,492**	**2,339**	**2,280**	**1,588**	**1,827**	**1.29**	**15.05**
Other countries of Europe	2,492	2,339	2,280	1,588	1,827	1.29	15.05
MIDDLE EAST	**293**	**159**	**185**	**202**	**180**	**0.13**	**-10.89**
All countries of Middle East	293	159	185	202	180	0.13	-10.89
SOUTH ASIA	**216**	**240**	**277**	**308**	**430**	**0.30**	**39.61**
India	216	240	277	308	430	0.30	39.61

FRENCH POLYNESIA

5. Overnight stays of non-resident tourists in hotels and similar establishments, by country of residence

	2007	2008	2009	2010	2011	Market share 11	% Change 11-10
TOTAL	2,133,274	1,967,581	1,601,188	1,569,826	1,657,407	100.00	5.58
AFRICA	8,843	3,794	2,911	2,833	2,833	0.17	
Other Africa	8,843	3,794	2,911	2,833	2,833	0.17	
All countries of Africa	8,843	3,794	2,911	2,833	2,833	0.17	
AMERICAS	787,755	688,873	482,246	506,164	590,195	35.61	16.60
Central America	2,087	933	1,364	1,498	1,122	0.07	-25.10
All countries of Central America	2,087	933	1,364	1,498	1,122	0.07	-25.10
North America	712,271	621,563	425,814	445,653	534,201	32.23	19.87
Canada	82,897	82,885	48,205	62,979	82,105	4.95	30.37
Mexico	15,120	11,401	6,711	7,383	8,459	0.51	14.57
United States of America	610,443	525,842	369,538	373,683	442,229	26.68	18.34
Hawaii, USA	3,811	1,435	1,360	1,608	1,408	0.08	-12.44
South America	73,397	66,377	55,068	59,013	54,872	3.31	-7.02
Argentina	21,750	21,684	16,434	14,010	13,529	0.82	-3.43
Brazil	29,693	26,744	21,016	24,908	24,896	1.50	-0.05
Chile	14,892	12,227	12,101	15,410	10,828	0.65	-29.73
Other countries of South America	7,062	5,722	5,517	4,685	5,619	0.34	19.94
EAST ASIA AND THE PACIFIC	353,263	281,295	238,941	231,803	251,157	15.15	8.35
North-East Asia	167,712	123,804	111,427	98,496	98,263	5.93	-0.24
China	3,168	2,999	4,356	9,465	8,052	0.49	-14.93
Taiwan, Province of China	1,085	1,432	1,419	704	1,322	0.08	87.78
Hong Kong, China	1,170	2,180	865	1	1,891	0.11	189000.00
Japan	158,458	112,938	100,200	84,081	83,243	5.02	-1.00
Korea, Republic of	3,831	4,255	4,587	4,245	3,755	0.23	-11.54
South-East Asia	8,062	5,800	6,923	5,561	5,234	0.32	-5.88
Indonesia	1,586	874	1,315	853	721	0.04	-15.47
Malaysia	675	610	605	937	821	0.05	-12.38
Philippines	2,973	1,775	1,709	1,227	984	0.06	-19.80
Singapore	1,978	1,652	1,765	1,839	1,491	0.09	-18.92
Thailand	850	889	1,529	705	1,217	0.07	72.62
Australasia	154,244	129,723	90,083	102,763	119,934	7.24	16.71
Australia	96,577	85,543	56,383	65,594	77,965	4.70	18.86
New Zealand	57,667	44,180	33,700	37,169	41,969	2.53	12.91
Melanesia	17,218	18,853	24,425	21,392	24,071	1.45	12.52
Fiji	1,240	390	1,138	709	1,010	0.06	42.45
New Caledonia	15,978	18,463	23,287	20,683	23,061	1.39	11.50
Polynesia	2,032	946	1,629	1,242	1,377	0.08	10.87
Cook Islands	1,182	593	659	913	601	0.04	-34.17
Tonga	504	269	682	22	131	0.01	495.45
Samoa	346	84	288	307	645	0.04	110.10
Other East Asia and the Pacific	3,995	2,169	4,454	2,349	2,278	0.14	-3.02
Other countries of Asia	1,821	406	736	764	626	0.04	-18.06
Other countries of Oceania	2,174	1,763	3,718	1,585	1,652	0.10	4.23
EUROPE	977,665	989,760	873,019	824,401	808,104	48.76	-1.98
Central/Eastern Europe	9,646	10,103	7,250	6,008	8,607	0.52	43.26
Russian Federation	9,646	10,103	7,250	6,008	8,607	0.52	43.26
Northern Europe	73,702	65,264	45,831	40,233	35,964	2.17	-10.61
Denmark	2,689	3,718	3,338	3,416	2,215	0.13	-35.16
Finland	5,441	3,395	2,201	2,684	2,167	0.13	-19.26
Norway	3,369	3,154	1,895	1,976	2,319	0.14	17.36
Sweden	6,186	6,310	4,262	3,885	3,513	0.21	-9.58
United Kingdom	56,017	48,687	34,135	28,272	25,750	1.55	-8.92

FRENCH POLYNESIA

5. Overnight stays of non-resident tourists in hotels and similar establishments, by country of residence

	2007	2008	2009	2010	2011	Market share 11	% Change 11-10
Southern Europe	**240,855**	**213,802**	**178,393**	**162,466**	**148,594**	**8.97**	**-8.54**
Italy	175,945	156,028	135,168	123,124	113,602	6.85	-7.73
Portugal	6,010	5,443	3,171	3,053	3,797	0.23	24.37
Spain	58,900	52,331	40,054	36,289	31,195	1.88	-14.04
Western Europe	**614,880**	**674,044**	**615,218**	**596,736**	**593,303**	**35.80**	**-0.58**
Austria	14,315	12,778	12,471	10,600	9,440	0.57	-10.94
Belgium	14,904	23,953	14,739	11,837	12,265	0.74	3.62
France	481,283	533,401	488,396	481,901	482,488	29.11	0.12
Germany	56,045	58,785	57,548	53,935	46,516	2.81	-13.76
Luxembourg	2,450	2,300	1,835	2,915	1,718	0.10	-41.06
Netherlands	6,365	8,715	7,704	6,964	6,060	0.37	-12.98
Switzerland	39,518	34,112	32,525	28,584	34,816	2.10	21.80
Other Europe	**38,582**	**26,547**	**26,327**	**18,958**	**21,636**	**1.31**	**14.13**
Other countries of Europe	38,582	26,547	26,327	18,958	21,636	1.31	14.13
MIDDLE EAST	**3,147**	**1,761**	**1,978**	**2,347**	**2,037**	**0.12**	**-13.21**
All countries of Middle East	3,147	1,761	1,978	2,347	2,037	0.12	-13.21
SOUTH ASIA	**2,601**	**2,098**	**2,093**	**2,278**	**3,081**	**0.19**	**35.25**
India	2,601	2,098	2,093	2,278	3,081	0.19	35.25

FRENCH POLYNESIA

6. Overnight stays of non-resident tourists in all types of accommodation establishments, by country of residence

	2007	2008	2009	2010	2011	Market share 11	% Change 11-10
TOTAL	2,897,204	2,602,805	2,204,955	2,166,994	2,281,874	100.00	5.30
AFRICA	14,219	5,424	4,321	5,868	5,171	0.23	-11.88
Other Africa	14,219	5,424	4,321	5,868	5,171	0.23	-11.88
All countries of Africa	14,219	5,424	4,321	5,868	5,171	0.23	-11.88
AMERICAS	852,304	748,884	539,282	559,071	640,922	28.09	14.64
Central America	2,238	1,487	1,650	1,582	1,385	0.06	-12.45
All countries of Central America	2,238	1,487	1,650	1,582	1,385	0.06	-12.45
North America	767,930	673,094	474,378	491,536	578,347	25.35	17.66
Canada	90,131	88,554	52,840	67,846	88,141	3.86	29.91
Mexico	15,639	12,164	7,439	8,992	9,206	0.40	2.38
United States of America	654,033	567,018	409,241	410,715	476,477	20.88	16.01
Hawaii, USA	8,127	5,358	4,858	3,983	4,523	0.20	13.56
South America	82,136	74,303	63,254	65,953	61,190	2.68	-7.22
Argentina	22,419	22,090	16,997	14,430	13,683	0.60	-5.18
Brazil	31,749	29,420	23,186	27,606	26,337	1.15	-4.60
Chile	19,202	16,435	16,704	18,556	14,967	0.66	-19.34
Other countries of South America	8,766	6,358	6,367	5,361	6,203	0.27	15.71
EAST ASIA AND THE PACIFIC	440,543	357,036	311,768	306,380	330,019	14.46	7.72
North-East Asia	175,370	129,712	114,526	102,025	103,762	4.55	1.70
China	4,311	3,792	5,021	10,923	9,164	0.40	-16.10
Taiwan, Province of China	1,282	1,895	1,598	824	1,943	0.09	135.80
Hong Kong, China	1,502	2,795	881	1	2,451	0.11	245000.00
Japan	164,295	116,798	102,346	85,818	85,537	3.75	-0.33
Korea, Republic of	3,980	4,432	4,680	4,459	4,667	0.20	4.66
South-East Asia	10,667	8,530	11,067	7,879	7,662	0.34	-2.75
Indonesia	2,195	1,489	2,450	1,696	1,171	0.05	-30.96
Malaysia	1,088	1,045	1,005	1,180	1,083	0.05	-8.22
Philippines	3,276	2,145	2,029	1,414	1,206	0.05	-14.71
Singapore	2,463	1,894	2,121	2,320	1,898	0.08	-18.19
Thailand	1,645	1,957	3,462	1,269	2,304	0.10	81.56
Australasia	181,146	153,218	113,636	123,910	142,081	6.23	14.66
Australia	108,572	95,417	66,511	74,142	88,400	3.87	19.23
New Zealand	72,574	57,801	47,125	49,768	53,681	2.35	7.86
Melanesia	58,070	55,869	58,579	61,370	64,715	2.84	5.45
Fiji	1,887	1,124	1,220	1,312	1,777	0.08	35.44
New Caledonia	56,183	54,745	57,359	60,058	62,938	2.76	4.80
Polynesia	6,729	4,107	3,891	4,555	4,402	0.19	-3.36
Cook Islands	3,788	2,761	2,741	2,999	3,183	0.14	6.14
Tonga	743	344	348	53	190	0.01	258.49
Samoa	2,198	1,002	802	1,503	1,029	0.05	-31.54
Other East Asia and the Pacific	8,561	5,600	10,069	6,641	7,397	0.32	11.38
Other countries of Asia	2,290	635	1,200	1,169	2,019	0.09	72.71
Other countries of Oceania	6,271	4,965	8,869	5,472	5,378	0.24	-1.72
EUROPE	1,582,819	1,487,016	1,344,929	1,289,821	1,299,966	56.97	0.79
Central/Eastern Europe	10,339	10,545	7,811	6,133	8,762	0.38	42.87
Russian Federation	10,339	10,545	7,811	6,133	8,762	0.38	42.87
Northern Europe	80,764	69,349	49,853	44,092	39,706	1.74	-9.95
Denmark	3,154	4,222	3,955	3,748	2,314	0.10	-38.26
Finland	5,923	3,809	2,245	2,807	2,341	0.10	-16.60
Norway	3,773	3,521	2,159	2,308	2,779	0.12	20.41
Sweden	6,881	6,425	4,863	4,195	3,854	0.17	-8.13
United Kingdom	61,033	51,372	36,631	31,034	28,418	1.25	-8.43

FRENCH POLYNESIA

6. Overnight stays of non-resident tourists in all types of accommodation establishments, by country of residence

	2007	2008	2009	2010	2011	Market share 11	% Change 11-10
Southern Europe	251,291	220,274	185,035	169,435	156,422	6.85	-7.68
Italy	181,539	159,250	137,994	126,849	117,760	5.16	-7.17
Portugal	6,629	5,551	3,292	3,139	4,164	0.18	32.65
Spain	63,123	55,473	43,749	39,447	34,498	1.51	-12.55
Western Europe	1,199,161	1,158,114	1,074,293	1,048,989	1,070,680	46.92	2.07
Austria	15,044	13,032	12,730	10,872	9,604	0.42	-11.66
Belgium	19,089	27,862	17,870	15,682	15,898	0.70	1.38
France	1,050,728	1,005,332	936,340	921,390	948,470	41.57	2.94
Germany	59,542	60,993	60,118	57,119	49,204	2.16	-13.86
Luxembourg	2,787	2,610	2,065	3,071	1,958	0.09	-36.24
Netherlands	6,881	9,083	8,127	7,656	6,340	0.28	-17.19
Switzerland	45,090	39,202	37,043	33,199	39,206	1.72	18.09
Other Europe	41,264	28,734	27,937	21,172	24,396	1.07	15.23
Other countries of Europe	41,264	28,734	27,937	21,172	24,396	1.07	15.23
MIDDLE EAST	4,308	2,260	2,364	3,353	2,691	0.12	-19.74
All countries of Middle East	4,308	2,260	2,364	3,353	2,691	0.12	-19.74
SOUTH ASIA	3,011	2,185	2,291	2,501	3,105	0.14	24.15
India	3,011	2,185	2,291	2,501	3,105	0.14	24.15

GAMBIA

1. Arrivals of non-resident tourists at national borders, by nationality

		2007	2008	2009	2010	2011	Market share 11	% Change 11-10
TOTAL	(*)	142,626	146,759	141,569	91,099	106,393	100.00	16.79
AFRICA		3,247	2,568	3,111	2,274	15,306	14.39	573.09
Other Africa		3,247	2,568	3,111	2,274	15,306	14.39	573.09
All countries of Africa		3,247	2,568	3,111	2,274	15,306	14.39	573.09
AMERICAS		1,639	1,786	2,342	1,504	2,236	2.10	48.67
North America		1,639	1,786	2,342	1,504	2,236	2.10	48.67
Canada		342	392	412	241	200	0.19	-17.01
United States of America		1,297	1,394	1,930	1,263	2,036	1.91	61.20
EAST ASIA AND THE PACIFIC		147	74	151	77	66	0.06	-14.29
North-East Asia		147	74	151	77	66	0.06	-14.29
Taiwan, Province of China		147	74	151	77	66	0.06	-14.29
EUROPE		121,038	123,313	115,260	72,984	86,692	81.48	18.78
Central/Eastern Europe		440	406	425	489	261	0.25	-46.63
Czech Republic		91	106	71	219	27	0.03	-87.67
Estonia		114	90	56	43	11	0.01	-74.42
Poland		235	210	298	227	223	0.21	-1.76
Northern Europe		88,361	87,117	85,814	53,891	61,571	57.87	14.25
Denmark		4,372	4,540	4,547	2,627	1,316	1.24	-49.90
Finland		6,342	5,844	3,586	1,598	2,904	2.73	81.73
Iceland		47	38	42	23	67	0.06	191.30
Ireland		887	893	1,277	1,530	2,662	2.50	73.99
Norway		3,212	5,324	4,123	1,370	1,253	1.18	-8.54
Sweden		7,458	8,370	8,302	6,493	6,387	6.00	-1.63
United Kingdom		66,043	62,108	63,937	40,250	46,982	44.16	16.73
Southern Europe		5,656	6,630	6,211	4,147	5,206	4.89	25.54
Greece		34	8	43	24	9	0.01	-62.50
Italy		482	941	1,200	245	234	0.22	-4.49
Spain		5,140	5,681	4,968	3,878	4,963	4.66	27.98
Western Europe		26,581	29,160	22,810	14,457	19,654	18.47	35.95
Austria		375	409	351	254	489	0.46	92.52
Belgium		2,746	3,192	3,118	1,983	2,234	2.10	12.66
France		717	833	1,130	834	812	0.76	-2.64
Germany		6,418	5,289	3,539	2,290	3,020	2.84	31.88
Netherlands		15,921	18,920	14,246	8,870	12,906	12.13	45.50
Switzerland		404	517	426	226	193	0.18	-14.60
NOT SPECIFIED		16,555	19,018	20,705	14,260	2,093	1.97	-85.32
Other countries of the World		2,261	2,933	3,757	3,079	2,093	1.97	-32.02
Nationals Residing Abroad		14,294	16,085	16,948	11,181			

GEORGIA

2. Arrivals of non-resident visitors at national borders, by country of residence

	2007	2008	2009	2010	2011	Market share 11	% Change 11-10
TOTAL	1,051,747	1,290,110	1,500,049	2,031,717	2,822,363	100.00	38.92
AFRICA	872	642	1,041	2,868	3,798	0.13	32.43
East Africa	116	91	172	1,713	1,448	0.05	-15.47
Ethiopia	4	11	17	32	17	0.00	-46.88
Kenya	14	23	16	26	18	0.00	-30.77
Madagascar	10	15	16	41	18	0.00	-56.10
Malawi	2	1	2		6	0.00	
Mozambique	25	7	4	1			
Rwanda	6	5	14	9	9	0.00	
Somalia	28	10	15	56	47	0.00	-16.07
Zimbabwe	5	6	61	1,263	1,122	0.04	-11.16
Uganda	9	6	12	21	25	0.00	19.05
United Republic of Tanzania	8	5	7	12	13	0.00	8.33
Zambia	5	2	8	252	173	0.01	-31.35
Central Africa	79	91	164	70	89	0.00	27.14
Angola		1	2	4	1	0.00	-75.00
Cameroon	33	34	130	38	63	0.00	65.79
Central African Republic	5	10	1	4	2	0.00	-50.00
Chad	3			1	1	0.00	
Congo	14	14	12	7	9	0.00	28.57
Democratic Republic of the Congo				1	4	0.00	300.00
Gabon	24	32	19	15	9	0.00	-40.00
North Africa	94	81	114	213	358	0.01	68.08
Algeria	39	26	13	44	34	0.00	-22.73
Morocco	17	16	46	96	262	0.01	172.92
Sudan	27	14	28	37	28	0.00	-24.32
Tunisia	11	25	27	36	34	0.00	-5.56
Southern Africa	246	130	197	248	536	0.02	116.13
Botswana			6	4			
Lesotho	1				1	0.00	
Namibia			1	16	7	0.00	-56.25
South Africa	244	130	179	228	525	0.02	130.26
Swaziland	1		11		3	0.00	
West Africa	337	249	394	624	1,367	0.05	119.07
Cape Verde	6	18	7	80	23	0.00	-71.25
Benin	2	2		4	2	0.00	-50.00
Gambia	6	3	7	1			
Ghana	16	27	68	17	62	0.00	264.71
Guinea	7	10	16	1	11	0.00	1000.00
Côte d'Ivoire	16	55	200	87	49	0.00	-43.68
Liberia	1	48	9	295	822	0.03	178.64
Mali		5	9	1	10	0.00	900.00
Mauritania	3	3			4	0.00	
Niger	268			2	5	0.00	150.00
Nigeria	6	71	60	67	325	0.01	385.07
Senegal	4	7	4	59	43	0.00	-27.12
Sierra Leone			4	3	7	0.00	133.33
Togo			2	6	2	0.00	-66.67
Burkina Faso	2		8	1	2	0.00	100.00
AMERICAS	16,881	17,553	19,654	24,427	29,289	1.04	19.90
Caribbean	87	140	172	1,217	1,031	0.04	-15.28
Antigua and Barbuda	15	63	67	1,046	682	0.02	-34.80
Bahamas	1		31	44	147	0.01	234.09
Barbados		2	2	1	1	0.00	
Cuba	9	26	15	30	37	0.00	23.33

261

GEORGIA

2. Arrivals of non-resident visitors at national borders, by country of residence

	2007	2008	2009	2010	2011	Market share 11	% Change 11-10
Dominica	5	1	9	3	11	0.00	266.67
Grenada	4		1		86	0.00	
Haiti		1	1	11	3	0.00	-72.73
Jamaica	7	7	7	26	6	0.00	-76.92
Trinidad and Tobago	46	40	39	56	58	0.00	3.57
Central America	**104**	**123**	**48**	**284**	**321**	**0.01**	**13.03**
Belize	2	2	2	5	4	0.00	-20.00
Costa Rica	18	11	5	8	21	0.00	162.50
El Salvador	56	48	7	26	9	0.00	-65.38
Guatemala	9	3	6	2	22	0.00	1000.00
Honduras	11	21	15	34	27	0.00	-20.59
Nicaragua	4	1	1	2	3	0.00	50.00
Panama	4	37	12	207	235	0.01	13.53
North America	**16,294**	**16,982**	**18,924**	**22,232**	**26,716**	**0.95**	**20.17**
Canada	1,376	1,276	1,913	2,052	2,345	0.08	14.28
Mexico	100	54	77	99	135	0.00	36.36
United States of America	14,818	15,652	16,934	20,081	24,236	0.86	20.69
South America	**396**	**308**	**510**	**694**	**1,221**	**0.04**	**75.94**
Argentina	65	79	158	97	164	0.01	69.07
Bolivia	32	11	9	15	10	0.00	-33.33
Brazil	114	102	169	257	411	0.01	59.92
Chile	24	10	13	31	148	0.01	377.42
Colombia	62	21	37	72	70	0.00	-2.78
Ecuador	9	20	50	33	135	0.00	309.09
Guyana		2	2		3	0.00	
Paraguay			1	13	12	0.00	-7.69
Peru	39	20	29	72	165	0.01	129.17
Suriname	1			2	32	0.00	1500.00
Uruguay	26	34	7	9	40	0.00	344.44
Venezuela	24	9	35	93	31	0.00	-66.67
EAST ASIA AND THE PACIFIC	**9,670**	**9,737**	**11,354**	**14,384**	**19,610**	**0.69**	**36.33**
North-East Asia	**3,856**	**3,620**	**4,152**	**5,800**	**10,962**	**0.39**	**89.00**
China	1,693	1,771	2,013	2,725	6,522	0.23	139.34
Taiwan, Province of China	33	55	447	234	359	0.01	53.42
Hong Kong, China		3	5	21	14	0.00	-33.33
Japan	1,457	1,209	919	1,798	2,469	0.09	37.32
Korea, Dem. People's Republic of				1	1	0.00	
Korea, Republic of	651	536	662	935	1,469	0.05	57.11
Mongolia	22	46	106	86	128	0.00	48.84
South-East Asia	**4,752**	**5,241**	**6,020**	**7,326**	**6,937**	**0.25**	**-5.31**
Myanmar	102	398	202	92	84	0.00	-8.70
Cambodia	19	25	6	7	11	0.00	57.14
Indonesia	94	152	188	600	311	0.01	-48.17
Malaysia	58	81	58	67	112	0.00	67.16
Philippines	4,363	4,465	5,386	6,342	6,164	0.22	-2.81
Singapore	54	68	53	115	84	0.00	-26.96
Viet Nam	4	7	35	58	61	0.00	5.17
Thailand	58	45	92	45	110	0.00	144.44
Australasia	**1,039**	**843**	**1,150**	**1,188**	**1,618**	**0.06**	**36.20**
Australia	825	641	946	951	1,319	0.05	38.70
New Zealand	214	202	204	237	299	0.01	26.16
Melanesia	**8**	**3**	**5**	**52**	**50**	**0.00**	**-3.85**
Fiji	1	2	3	2	39	0.00	1850.00
Vanuatu	7	1	2	50	11	0.00	-78.00
Micronesia	**9**	**5**		**1**			
Kiribati	9	5		1			

GEORGIA

2. Arrivals of non-resident visitors at national borders, by country of residence

	2007	2008	2009	2010	2011	Market share 11	% Change 11-10
Polynesia	**6**	**25**	**27**	**17**	**43**	**0.00**	**152.94**
Tonga			5	1	2	0.00	100.00
Tuvalu	3	24	21	2	10	0.00	400.00
Samoa	3	1	1	14	31	0.00	121.43
EUROPE	**1,009,248**	**1,243,407**	**1,447,496**	**1,956,545**	**2,695,250**	**95.50**	**37.76**
Central/Eastern Europe	**681,301**	**811,766**	**974,871**	**1,317,444**	**1,830,148**	**64.84**	**38.92**
Azerbaijan	281,629	344,936	418,992	497,969	714,418	25.31	43.47
Armenia	243,133	281,463	351,049	547,510	699,382	24.78	27.74
Bulgaria	9,104	8,547	7,123	8,738	10,309	0.37	17.98
Belarus	1,601	1,981	2,503	5,016	5,344	0.19	6.54
Czech Republic	1,648	1,947	2,290	3,060	3,897	0.14	27.35
Estonia	2,102	2,482	1,754	2,207	2,749	0.10	24.56
Hungary	693	826	808	836	1,130	0.04	35.17
Kazakhstan	5,098	4,523	5,531	8,411	18,565	0.66	120.72
Kyrgyzstan	736	787	1,107	2,222	3,183	0.11	43.25
Latvia	3,454	3,643	2,588	3,525	4,802	0.17	36.23
Lithuania	2,183	3,029	2,448	2,916	4,081	0.14	39.95
Republic of Moldova	1,185	1,261	1,880	2,390	2,737	0.10	14.52
Poland	4,491	4,479	4,634	7,105	12,082	0.43	70.05
Romania	1,340	1,782	1,614	1,933	2,347	0.08	21.42
Russian Federation	91,361	114,459	127,937	170,584	278,458	9.87	63.24
Slovakia	544	520	861	976	1,085	0.04	11.17
Tajikistan	150	194	237	333	540	0.02	62.16
Turkmenistan	451	468	375	1,287	1,126	0.04	-12.51
Ukraine	28,932	32,988	39,339	47,596	58,966	2.09	23.89
Uzbekistan	1,466	1,451	1,801	2,830	4,947	0.18	74.81
Northern Europe	**14,536**	**13,947**	**16,515**	**18,164**	**21,145**	**0.75**	**16.41**
Denmark	934	856	1,033	1,341	1,452	0.05	8.28
Faeroe Islands	3	3	3	29	15	0.00	-48.28
Finland	678	774	936	1,223	1,460	0.05	19.38
Iceland	57	37	45	47	161	0.01	242.55
Ireland	759	663	804	884	970	0.03	9.73
Norway	888	942	894	1,184	1,483	0.05	25.25
Sweden	1,442	1,721	2,167	2,471	2,991	0.11	21.04
United Kingdom	9,775	8,951	10,633	10,985	12,613	0.45	14.82
Southern Europe	**19,081**	**19,543**	**23,178**	**27,707**	**32,188**	**1.14**	**16.17**
Albania	142	113	161	329	258	0.01	-21.58
Andorra	2	2	2	6	9	0.00	50.00
Bosnia and Herzegovina	128	151	203	206	340	0.01	65.05
Croatia	418	408	533	623	1,307	0.05	109.79
Greece	12,380	12,914	14,300	16,424	17,664	0.63	7.55
Holy See	40	36	35	36	35	0.00	-2.78
Italy	4,113	3,920	4,994	5,886	6,873	0.24	16.77
Malta	53	61	86	167	91	0.00	-45.51
Montenegro	8	5	53	51	194	0.01	280.39
Portugal	199	210	283	448	559	0.02	24.78
San Marino	10	5	15	74	35	0.00	-52.70
Serbia	47	47	353	523	593	0.02	13.38
Slovenia	244	284	410	528	833	0.03	57.77
Spain	1,167	1,322	1,585	2,229	3,156	0.11	41.59
TFYR of Macedonia	130	65	165	177	241	0.01	36.16
Western Europe	**29,630**	**29,061**	**31,491**	**37,878**	**47,839**	**1.69**	**26.30**
Austria	2,376	2,614	1,794	2,488	3,144	0.11	26.37
Belgium	1,287	1,309	1,622	1,991	2,391	0.08	20.09
France	5,958	6,186	6,941	8,486	10,695	0.38	26.03
Germany	14,081	13,267	15,351	17,619	22,204	0.79	26.02
Liechtenstein	11	19	9	7	11	0.00	57.14

GEORGIA

2. Arrivals of non-resident visitors at national borders, by country of residence

	2007	2008	2009	2010	2011	Market share 11	% Change 11-10
Luxembourg	26	72	65	111	126	0.00	13.51
Monaco	1	5	6	2	7	0.00	250.00
Netherlands	4,143	4,054	4,145	5,198	6,883	0.24	32.42
Switzerland	1,747	1,535	1,558	1,976	2,378	0.08	20.34
East Mediterranean Europe	**264,700**	**369,090**	**401,441**	**555,352**	**763,930**	**27.07**	**37.56**
Cyprus	222	267	202	312	407	0.01	30.45
Israel	16,450	17,413	16,757	19,447	25,438	0.90	30.81
Turkey	248,028	351,410	384,482	535,593	738,085	26.15	37.81
MIDDLE EAST	**2,490**	**3,245**	**3,298**	**3,413**	**5,663**	**0.20**	**65.92**
Bahrain	5	3	8	5	19	0.00	280.00
Iraq	41	76	157	126	599	0.02	375.40
Jordan	131	208	155	172	216	0.01	25.58
Kuwait	24	66	46	59	110	0.00	86.44
Lebanon	195	175	249	272	481	0.02	76.84
Libya		21	13	24	26	0.00	8.33
Oman	4	4	13	21	14	0.00	-33.33
Qatar	16	2	4	22	21	0.00	-4.55
Saudi Arabia	20	39	19	189	166	0.01	-12.17
Syrian Arab Republic	1,476	1,970	2,135	2,021	3,115	0.11	54.13
United Arab Emirates	77	58	72	60	147	0.01	145.00
Egypt	494	602	391	431	740	0.03	71.69
Yemen	7	21	36	11	9	0.00	-18.18
SOUTH ASIA	**10,873**	**13,457**	**14,572**	**27,810**	**66,073**	**2.34**	**137.59**
Afghanistan	66	34	55	45	63	0.00	40.00
Bangladesh	78	140	130	77	495	0.02	542.86
Sri Lanka	76	70	282	209	280	0.01	33.97
India	2,355	2,712	3,674	5,653	4,578	0.16	-19.02
Iran, Islamic Republic of	7,986	10,038	9,848	21,313	60,191	2.13	182.41
Maldives	4	11	10	9	5	0.00	-44.44
Nepal	25	38	244	284	145	0.01	-48.94
Pakistan	283	414	329	220	316	0.01	43.64
NOT SPECIFIED	**1,713**	**2,069**	**2,634**	**2,270**	**2,680**	**0.09**	**18.06**
Other countries of the World	1,713	2,069	2,634	2,270	2,680	0.09	18.06

GEORGIA

3. Arrivals of non-resident tourists in hotels and similar establishments, by country of residence

	2007	2008	2009	2010	2011	Market share 11	% Change 11-10
TOTAL	103,521	103,698	150,898	306,547	438,477	100.00	43.04
AFRICA	219	112	434	337	1,436	0.33	326.11
Other Africa	219	112	434	337	1,436	0.33	326.11
All countries of Africa	219	112	434	337	1,436	0.33	326.11
AMERICAS	13,314	13,696	21,500	29,338	27,340	6.24	-6.81
North America	12,912	13,158	21,049	28,942	26,444	6.03	-8.63
Canada	272	193	504	3,414	543	0.12	-84.09
Mexico	12	15	14	6	6	0.00	
United States of America	12,628	12,950	20,531	25,522	25,895	5.91	1.46
South America	331	449	431	366	495	0.11	35.25
Argentina	19	15	80	138	340	0.08	146.38
Brazil	2	21	63	227	125	0.03	-44.93
Chile	33	136	131	1	12	0.00	1100.00
Uruguay	277	277	157		18	0.00	
Other Americas	71	89	20	30	401	0.09	1236.67
Other countries of the Americas	71	89	20	30	401	0.09	1236.67
EAST ASIA AND THE PACIFIC	2,423	2,077	2,881	4,787	9,627	2.20	101.11
North-East Asia	1,664	1,444	1,598	2,309	5,398	1.23	133.78
China	924	542	920	582	4,099	0.93	604.30
Japan	740	902	678	1,727	1,299	0.30	-24.78
Australasia	316	299	301	954	356	0.08	-62.68
Australia	316	299	301	954	356	0.08	-62.68
Other East Asia and the Pacific	443	334	982	1,524	3,873	0.88	154.13
Other countries of Asia	443	334	982	1,524	3,873	0.88	154.13
EUROPE	86,228	86,664	124,849	250,977	347,543	79.26	38.48
Central/Eastern Europe	30,867	36,572	63,079	124,288	171,029	39.01	37.61
Azerbaijan	6,889	7,575	14,465	30,501	48,124	10.98	57.78
Armenia	5,195	5,938	16,239	27,715	32,947	7.51	18.88
Bulgaria	695	482	1,581	1,269	1,254	0.29	-1.18
Belarus	455	392	445	1,374	1,528	0.35	11.21
Czech Republic	929	975	856	1,619	3,926	0.90	142.50
Hungary	592	265	339	1,002	692	0.16	-30.94
Kazakhstan	2,223	1,600	1,496	3,481	6,383	1.46	83.37
Kyrgyzstan	469	1,069	1,203	602	787	0.18	30.73
Republic of Moldova	180	502	264	740	1,035	0.24	39.86
Poland	1,183	1,562	3,026	4,671	6,549	1.49	40.21
Romania	500	752	550	1,568	1,133	0.26	-27.74
Russian Federation	5,066	4,679	7,479	11,436	17,379	3.96	51.97
Slovakia	252	181	370	560	528	0.12	-5.71
Tajikistan	601	384	285	735	668	0.15	-9.12
Turkmenistan	546	347	970	8,336	10,191	2.32	22.25
Ukraine	4,656	6,114	9,096	18,537	25,542	5.83	37.79
Uzbekistan	436	903	453	1,046	1,489	0.34	42.35
Other countries Central/East Europe		2,852	3,962	9,096	10,874	2.48	19.55
Northern Europe	9,110	9,495	10,625	16,342	25,409	5.79	55.48
Denmark	352	362	561	1,084	1,720	0.39	58.67
Finland	286	343	488	762	1,006	0.23	32.02
Iceland	35	136	50	81	516	0.12	537.04
Ireland	242	172	87	662	834	0.19	25.98
Norway	148	248	390	329	520	0.12	58.05
Sweden	882	1,632	939	1,835	2,349	0.54	28.01
United Kingdom	7,165	6,602	8,110	11,589	18,464	4.21	59.32
Southern Europe	4,731	4,191	6,090	9,424	17,149	3.91	81.97

GEORGIA

3. Arrivals of non-resident tourists in hotels and similar establishments, by country of residence

	2007	2008	2009	2010	2011	Market share 11	% Change 11-10
Greece	1,303	1,335	1,324	2,598	5,164	1.18	98.77
Italy	2,865	1,857	3,145	4,167	6,519	1.49	56.44
Portugal	80	173	125	280	818	0.19	192.14
Spain	480	802	1,412	2,146	4,598	1.05	114.26
Serbia and Montenegro	3	24	84	233	50	0.01	-78.54
Western Europe	**16,803**	**14,409**	**16,055**	**27,823**	**38,079**	**8.68**	**36.86**
Austria	3,561	2,919	1,159	2,438	3,081	0.70	26.37
Belgium	313	730	819	1,115	1,643	0.37	47.35
France	2,617	2,169	3,537	6,520	8,275	1.89	26.92
Germany	6,848	5,997	8,348	11,837	18,571	4.24	56.89
Luxembourg	23	168	157	1,113	229	0.05	-79.42
Netherlands	3,134	2,090	1,920	4,327	5,400	1.23	24.80
Switzerland	307	336	115	473	880	0.20	86.05
East Mediterranean Europe	**21,314**	**21,814**	**28,599**	**72,087**	**95,419**	**21.76**	**32.37**
Israel	6,773	6,854	10,667	26,367	27,359	6.24	3.76
Turkey	14,541	14,960	17,932	45,720	68,060	15.52	48.86
Other Europe	**3,403**	**183**	**401**	**1,013**	**458**	**0.10**	**-54.79**
Other countries of Europe	3,403	183	401	1,013	458	0.10	-54.79
SOUTH ASIA	**501**	**503**	**1,234**	**17,413**	**23,990**	**5.47**	**37.77**
India	188	282	688	1,355	1,415	0.32	4.43
Iran, Islamic Republic of	313	221	546	16,058	22,575	5.15	40.58
NOT SPECIFIED	**836**	**646**		**3,695**	**28,541**	**6.51**	**672.42**
Other countries of the World	836	646		3,695	28,541	6.51	672.42

GERMANY

3. Arrivals of non-resident tourists in hotels and similar establishments, by country of residence

	2007	2008	2009	2010	2011	Market share 11	% Change 11-10
TOTAL	21,869,940	22,131,203	21,467,043	23,896,638	25,310,793	100.00	5.92
AFRICA	146,966	144,895	144,609	180,743	181,422	0.72	0.38
Southern Africa	49,824	48,409	46,865	61,996	64,399	0.25	3.88
South Africa	49,824	48,409	46,865	61,996	64,399	0.25	3.88
Other Africa	97,142	96,486	97,744	118,747	117,023	0.46	-1.45
Other countries of Africa	97,142	96,486	97,744	118,747	117,023	0.46	-1.45
AMERICAS	2,545,576	2,418,916	2,322,295	2,720,333	2,754,473	10.88	1.25
North America	2,297,008	2,166,892	2,098,850	2,421,642	2,400,339	9.48	-0.88
Canada	222,912	232,011	208,940	251,173	259,836	1.03	3.45
Mexico	51,893	53,678	43,720	59,394	64,206	0.25	8.10
United States of America	2,022,203	1,881,203	1,846,190	2,111,075	2,076,297	8.20	-1.65
South America	142,784	145,834	121,725	176,576	216,933	0.86	22.86
Brazil	142,784	145,834	121,725	176,576	216,933	0.86	22.86
Other Americas	105,784	106,190	101,720	122,115	137,201	0.54	12.35
Other countries of the Americas	105,784	106,190	101,720	122,115	137,201	0.54	12.35
EAST ASIA AND THE PACIFIC	1,961,050	1,847,568	1,656,636	2,037,023	2,312,695	9.14	13.53
North-East Asia	1,304,113	1,177,131	1,059,437	1,278,733	1,493,324	5.90	16.78
China (*)	443,726	402,972	367,819	491,112	615,346	2.43	25.30
Taiwan, Province of China	82,099	74,269	62,582	71,019	94,160	0.37	32.58
Japan	636,015	573,974	517,842	586,012	624,970	2.47	6.65
Korea, Republic of	142,273	125,916	111,194	130,590	158,848	0.63	21.64
Australasia	214,589	217,490	197,796	252,881	267,027	1.05	5.59
Australia, New Zealand	214,589	217,490	197,796	252,881	267,027	1.05	5.59
Other East Asia and the Pacific	442,348	452,947	399,403	505,409	552,344	2.18	9.29
Other countries East Asia/Pacific (*)	442,348	452,947	399,403	505,409	552,344	2.18	9.29
EUROPE	16,234,869	16,698,473	16,363,802	17,995,732	19,163,324	75.71	6.49
Central/Eastern Europe	1,397,661	1,573,727	1,412,665	1,697,777	1,978,456	7.82	16.53
Czech Republic	236,524	273,907	246,627	283,448	320,627	1.27	13.12
Hungary	176,772	188,306	163,796	187,158	206,567	0.82	10.37
Poland	456,894	504,073	453,899	536,123	602,766	2.38	12.43
Russian Federation	388,347	471,230	434,314	558,700	698,679	2.76	25.05
Baltic countries	139,124	136,211	114,029	132,348	149,817	0.59	13.20
Northern Europe	4,276,111	4,188,625	3,895,275	4,347,998	4,447,148	17.57	2.28
Denmark	876,191	932,048	955,600	1,021,525	1,048,335	4.14	2.62
Finland	235,738	229,930	220,830	250,488	265,213	1.05	5.88
Iceland	38,193	37,131	33,278	30,926	33,560	0.13	8.52
Ireland	127,515	127,465	120,070	123,081	119,797	0.47	-2.67
Norway	304,148	309,952	296,674	349,394	349,537	1.38	0.04
Sweden	801,853	781,316	696,742	784,273	775,409	3.06	-1.13
United Kingdom	1,892,473	1,770,783	1,572,081	1,788,311	1,855,297	7.33	3.75
Southern Europe	2,348,216	2,324,051	2,284,089	2,429,673	2,493,084	9.85	2.61
Greece	169,732	174,927	179,664	157,339	152,300	0.60	-3.20
Italy	1,323,027	1,297,414	1,311,616	1,392,917	1,411,844	5.58	1.36
Portugal	115,608	117,938	102,422	111,561	113,138	0.45	1.41
Spain	739,849	733,772	690,387	767,856	815,802	3.22	6.24
Western Europe	7,327,579	7,613,710	7,862,667	8,472,059	9,069,147	35.83	7.05
Austria	1,067,946	1,112,266	1,156,134	1,284,219	1,393,422	5.51	8.50
Belgium	900,597	922,531	956,360	1,006,397	1,057,611	4.18	5.09
France	1,059,763	1,086,649	1,107,476	1,207,179	1,299,743	5.14	7.67
Luxembourg	163,102	172,587	186,184	198,047	202,295	0.80	2.14
Netherlands	2,561,832	2,720,042	2,793,164	2,960,893	3,055,443	12.07	3.19
Switzerland	1,574,339	1,599,635	1,663,349	1,815,324	2,060,633	8.14	13.51

GERMANY

3. Arrivals of non-resident tourists in hotels and similar establishments, by country of residence

	2007	2008	2009	2010	2011	Market share 11	% Change 11-10
East Mediterranean Europe	**291,225**	**300,620**	**298,532**	**357,075**	**400,916**	**1.58**	**12.28**
Israel	127,569	130,529	142,953	171,942	185,951	0.73	8.15
Turkey	163,656	170,091	155,579	185,133	214,965	0.85	16.11
Other Europe	**594,077**	**697,740**	**610,574**	**691,150**	**774,573**	**3.06**	**12.07**
Other countries of Europe	594,077	697,740	610,574	691,150	774,573	3.06	12.07
MIDDLE EAST	**215,601**	**234,951**	**254,820**	**331,426**	**337,139**	**1.33**	**1.72**
All countries of Middle East	215,601	234,951	254,820	331,426	337,139	1.33	1.72
NOT SPECIFIED	**765,878**	**786,400**	**724,881**	**631,381**	**561,740**	**2.22**	**-11.03**
Other countries of the World	765,878	786,400	724,881	631,381	561,740	2.22	-11.03

GERMANY

4. Arrivals of non-resident tourists in all types of accommodation establishments, by country of residence

		2007	2008	2009	2010	2011	Market share 11	% Change 11-10
TOTAL		24,420,672	24,884,017	24,219,634	26,875,288	28,374,101	100.00	5.58
AFRICA		163,564	159,670	158,458	192,895	193,193	0.68	0.15
Southern Africa		54,790	53,077	50,675	66,512	68,100	0.24	2.39
South Africa		54,790	53,077	50,675	66,512	68,100	0.24	2.39
Other Africa		108,774	106,593	107,783	126,383	125,093	0.44	-1.02
Other countries of Africa		108,774	106,593	107,783	126,383	125,093	0.44	-1.02
AMERICAS		2,705,989	2,572,554	2,475,506	2,882,982	2,914,184	10.27	1.08
North America		2,428,346	2,290,649	2,221,644	2,547,859	2,517,136	8.87	-1.21
Canada		246,126	256,243	233,526	275,413	281,876	0.99	2.35
Mexico		58,965	60,720	49,280	66,107	71,501	0.25	8.16
United States of America		2,123,255	1,973,686	1,938,838	2,206,339	2,163,759	7.63	-1.93
South America		156,272	160,284	136,274	194,960	237,125	0.84	21.63
Brazil		156,272	160,284	136,274	194,960	237,125	0.84	21.63
Other Americas		121,371	121,621	117,588	140,163	159,923	0.56	14.10
Other countries of the Americas		121,371	121,621	117,588	140,163	159,923	0.56	14.10
EAST ASIA AND THE PACIFIC		2,104,663	1,990,945	1,790,469	2,046,055	2,296,515	8.09	12.24
North-East Asia		1,373,349	1,242,796	1,113,479	1,336,237	1,552,033	5.47	16.15
China	(*)	462,293	421,452	384,576	510,611	637,362	2.25	24.82
Taiwan, Province of China		88,771	79,596	66,982	76,089	99,290	0.35	30.49
Japan		661,792	597,655	537,984	605,231	642,542	2.26	6.16
Korea, Republic of		160,493	144,093	123,937	144,306	172,839	0.61	19.77
Australasia		266,405	270,660	255,069	276,097	282,278	0.99	2.24
Australia					276,097	282,278	0.99	2.24
Australia, New Zealand		266,405	270,660	255,069				
Other East Asia and the Pacific		464,909	477,489	421,921	433,721	462,204	1.63	6.57
Other countries of Asia					389,075	420,164	1.48	7.99
Other countries East Asia/Pacific	(*)	464,909	477,489	421,921				
Other countries of Oceania					44,646	42,040	0.15	-5.84
EUROPE		18,423,468	19,095,571	18,781,861	20,609,923	21,860,790	77.04	6.07
Central/Eastern Europe		1,536,966	1,746,202	1,565,423	2,229,922	2,589,652	9.13	16.13
Bulgaria					56,077	68,444	0.24	22.05
Czech Republic		264,209	308,982	281,313	320,868	358,908	1.26	11.86
Estonia					37,503	42,326	0.15	12.86
Hungary		195,314	207,056	180,562	203,445	224,933	0.79	10.56
Latvia					42,191	50,044	0.18	18.61
Lithuania					68,474	73,470	0.26	7.30
Poland		511,179	575,228	514,561	604,274	684,193	2.41	13.23
Romania					153,693	170,581	0.60	10.99
Russian Federation		411,409	498,422	459,849	590,092	737,105	2.60	24.91
Slovakia					78,113	86,773	0.31	11.09
Ukraine					75,192	92,875	0.33	23.52
Baltic countries		154,855	156,514	129,138				
Northern Europe		4,764,741	4,724,999	4,403,474	4,906,426	4,999,834	17.62	1.90
Denmark		1,039,359	1,110,376	1,138,910	1,214,319	1,242,806	4.38	2.35
Finland		265,286	257,951	249,252	281,263	293,948	1.04	4.51
Iceland		42,379	41,422	36,862	36,488	37,910	0.13	3.90
Ireland		142,186	143,606	137,629	140,736	134,820	0.48	-4.20
Norway		337,997	349,331	328,479	387,468	388,896	1.37	0.37
Sweden		870,727	853,836	762,679	859,261	846,615	2.98	-1.47
United Kingdom		2,066,807	1,968,477	1,749,663	1,986,891	2,054,839	7.24	3.42
Southern Europe		2,553,445	2,540,423	2,502,734	2,735,986	2,796,957	9.86	2.23
Greece		177,396	183,522	188,030	166,319	160,856	0.57	-3.28
Italy		1,439,585	1,421,505	1,444,144	1,524,134	1,538,369	5.42	0.93

GERMANY

4. Arrivals of non-resident tourists in all types of accommodation establishments, by country of residence

	2007	2008	2009	2010	2011	Market share 11	% Change 11-10
Malta				11,697	11,871	0.04	1.49
Portugal	124,428	125,988	109,462	120,824	120,859	0.43	0.03
Slovenia				70,227	75,496	0.27	7.50
Spain	812,036	809,408	761,098	842,785	889,506	3.13	5.54
Western Europe	**8,613,956**	**8,996,810**	**9,321,918**	**10,047,229**	**10,706,647**	**37.73**	**6.56**
Austria	1,154,899	1,204,752	1,252,439	1,387,683	1,494,688	5.27	7.71
Belgium	1,000,907	1,026,367	1,070,316	1,131,887	1,192,592	4.20	5.36
France	1,183,532	1,220,138	1,249,522	1,366,153	1,462,096	5.15	7.02
Luxembourg	176,275	186,893	200,690	215,443	220,006	0.78	2.12
Netherlands	3,366,567	3,584,865	3,692,084	3,917,640	4,035,783	14.22	3.02
Switzerland	1,731,776	1,773,795	1,856,867	2,028,423	2,301,482	8.11	13.46
East Mediterranean Europe	**307,496**	**319,713**	**317,864**	**395,106**	**442,339**	**1.56**	**11.95**
Cyprus				13,891	14,434	0.05	3.91
Israel	136,893	141,914	155,231	187,818	203,595	0.72	8.40
Turkey	170,603	177,799	162,633	193,397	224,310	0.79	15.98
Other Europe	**646,864**	**767,424**	**670,448**	**295,254**	**325,361**	**1.15**	**10.20**
Other countries of Europe	646,864	767,424	670,448	295,254	325,361	1.15	10.20
MIDDLE EAST	**222,556**	**241,786**	**258,883**	**336,193**	**343,263**	**1.21**	**2.10**
All countries of Middle East	222,556	241,786	258,883	336,193	343,263	1.21	2.10
SOUTH ASIA				**141,524**	**160,599**	**0.57**	**13.48**
India				141,524	160,599	0.57	13.48
NOT SPECIFIED	**800,432**	**823,491**	**754,457**	**665,716**	**605,557**	**2.13**	**-9.04**
Other countries of the World	800,432	823,491	754,457	665,716	605,557	2.13	-9.04

GERMANY

5. Overnight stays of non-resident tourists in hotels and similar establishments, by country of residence

		2007	2008	2009	2010	2011	Market share 11	% Change 11-10
TOTAL		46,508,203	47,561,639	45,843,407	50,772,948	53,792,524	100.00	5.95
AFRICA		391,594	393,134	376,662	453,711	443,677	0.82	-2.21
Southern Africa		120,043	123,825	108,501	134,544	144,314	0.27	7.26
South Africa		120,043	123,825	108,501	134,544	144,314	0.27	7.26
Other Africa		271,551	269,309	268,161	319,167	299,363	0.56	-6.20
Other countries of Africa		271,551	269,309	268,161	319,167	299,363	0.56	-6.20
AMERICAS		5,556,137	5,395,749	5,090,630	5,863,967	5,923,716	11.01	1.02
North America		4,943,302	4,766,670	4,548,764	5,142,578	5,067,656	9.42	-1.46
Canada		466,954	488,265	432,096	512,524	530,166	0.99	3.44
Mexico		133,556	133,646	107,071	141,119	153,911	0.29	9.06
United States of America		4,342,792	4,144,759	4,009,597	4,488,935	4,383,579	8.15	-2.35
South America		349,708	362,163	296,142	429,256	525,484	0.98	22.42
Brazil		349,708	362,163	296,142	429,256	525,484	0.98	22.42
Other Americas		263,127	266,916	245,724	292,133	330,576	0.61	13.16
Other countries of the Americas		263,127	266,916	245,724	292,133	330,576	0.61	13.16
EAST ASIA AND THE PACIFIC		4,041,761	3,980,855	3,462,566	4,310,627	4,878,163	9.07	13.17
North-East Asia		2,484,478	2,364,904	2,030,661	2,481,330	2,870,391	5.34	15.68
China	(*)	888,320	876,020	766,508	1,032,983	1,241,960	2.31	20.23
Taiwan, Province of China		157,153	154,908	124,078	149,375	174,392	0.32	16.75
Japan		1,128,284	1,060,190	906,759	1,036,699	1,138,115	2.12	9.78
Korea, Republic of		310,721	273,786	233,316	262,273	315,924	0.59	20.46
Australasia		447,336	463,236	423,949	546,152	577,128	1.07	5.67
Australia, New Zealand		447,336	463,236	423,949	546,152	577,128	1.07	5.67
Other East Asia and the Pacific		1,109,947	1,152,715	1,007,956	1,283,145	1,430,644	2.66	11.50
Other countries East Asia/Pacific	(*)	1,109,947	1,152,715	1,007,956	1,283,145	1,430,644	2.66	11.50
EUROPE		34,368,133	35,554,880	34,783,705	38,033,826	40,519,845	75.33	6.54
Central/Eastern Europe		3,111,641	3,472,457	3,110,431	3,707,247	4,457,679	8.29	20.24
Czech Republic		496,692	547,995	499,256	565,906	651,421	1.21	15.11
Hungary		395,870	417,541	377,999	440,823	535,195	0.99	21.41
Poland		987,287	1,081,222	956,111	1,118,897	1,356,513	2.52	21.24
Russian Federation		981,685	1,175,464	1,072,476	1,343,599	1,639,107	3.05	21.99
Baltic countries		250,107	250,235	204,589	238,022	275,443	0.51	15.72
Northern Europe		8,374,218	8,221,560	7,650,809	8,503,790	8,698,831	16.17	2.29
Denmark		1,733,169	1,847,358	1,895,593	2,027,862	2,062,665	3.83	1.72
Finland		456,734	444,312	438,008	499,570	533,981	0.99	6.89
Iceland		86,868	81,681	74,762	73,615	76,905	0.14	4.47
Ireland		287,631	293,949	270,026	276,716	266,560	0.50	-3.67
Norway		552,573	562,358	551,187	645,967	656,572	1.22	1.64
Sweden		1,360,184	1,342,166	1,216,781	1,357,009	1,367,349	2.54	0.76
United Kingdom		3,897,059	3,649,736	3,204,452	3,623,051	3,734,799	6.94	3.08
Southern Europe		5,055,547	5,078,958	4,975,509	5,309,414	5,386,074	10.01	1.44
Greece		433,613	452,341	459,479	402,810	380,303	0.71	-5.59
Italy		2,740,612	2,743,350	2,747,124	2,947,684	2,931,157	5.45	-0.56
Portugal		264,155	274,457	233,117	256,445	262,877	0.49	2.51
Spain		1,617,167	1,608,810	1,535,789	1,702,475	1,811,737	3.37	6.42
Western Europe		15,752,102	16,445,603	16,920,139	18,027,338	19,152,028	35.60	6.24
Austria		2,122,235	2,195,499	2,277,439	2,527,378	2,732,558	5.08	8.12
Belgium		2,094,581	2,128,818	2,174,456	2,251,265	2,341,702	4.35	4.02
France		1,989,802	2,046,944	2,094,192	2,295,164	2,475,242	4.60	7.85
Luxembourg		365,892	382,314	411,155	430,286	435,570	0.81	1.23
Netherlands		6,071,447	6,552,553	6,701,012	6,977,366	7,122,264	13.24	2.08
Switzerland		3,108,145	3,139,475	3,261,885	3,545,879	4,044,692	7.52	14.07

GERMANY

5. Overnight stays of non-resident tourists in hotels and similar establishments, by country of residence

	2007	2008	2009	2010	2011	Market share 11	% Change 11-10
East Mediterranean Europe	**712,120**	**743,205**	**709,786**	**872,018**	**970,018**	**1.80**	**11.24**
Israel	329,317	335,658	368,306	444,757	485,488	0.90	9.16
Turkey	382,803	407,547	341,480	427,261	484,530	0.90	13.40
Other Europe	**1,362,505**	**1,593,097**	**1,417,031**	**1,614,019**	**1,855,215**	**3.45**	**14.94**
Other countries of Europe	1,362,505	1,593,097	1,417,031	1,614,019	1,855,215	3.45	14.94
MIDDLE EAST	**672,498**	**726,775**	**734,450**	**926,413**	**960,767**	**1.79**	**3.71**
All countries of Middle East	672,498	726,775	734,450	926,413	960,767	1.79	3.71
NOT SPECIFIED	**1,478,080**	**1,510,246**	**1,395,394**	**1,184,404**	**1,066,356**	**1.98**	**-9.97**
Other countries of the World	1,478,080	1,510,246	1,395,394	1,184,404	1,066,356	1.98	-9.97

GERMANY

6. Overnight stays of non-resident tourists in all types of accommodation establishments, by country of residence

		2007	2008	2009	2010	2011	Market share 11	% Change 11-10
TOTAL		54,779,477	56,536,906	54,823,716	60,310,448	63,746,372	100.00	5.70
AFRICA		476,152	463,399	448,260	513,985	504,517	0.79	-1.84
Southern Africa		136,533	141,343	123,220	149,026	156,752	0.25	5.18
South Africa		136,533	141,343	123,220	149,026	156,752	0.25	5.18
Other Africa		339,619	322,056	325,040	364,959	347,765	0.55	-4.71
Other countries of Africa		339,619	322,056	325,040	364,959	347,765	0.55	-4.71
AMERICAS		6,047,354	5,880,884	5,562,598	6,350,191	6,429,114	10.09	1.24
North America		5,349,049	5,157,891	4,918,084	5,515,227	5,439,369	8.53	-1.38
Canada		531,179	556,503	499,531	579,401	597,579	0.94	3.14
Mexico		156,327	155,948	127,248	166,453	180,193	0.28	8.25
United States of America		4,661,543	4,445,440	4,291,305	4,769,373	4,661,597	7.31	-2.26
South America		386,622	404,608	339,588	482,310	586,590	0.92	21.62
Brazil		386,622	404,608	339,588	482,310	586,590	0.92	21.62
Other Americas		311,683	318,385	304,926	352,654	403,155	0.63	14.32
Other countries of the Americas		311,683	318,385	304,926	352,654	403,155	0.63	14.32
EAST ASIA AND THE PACIFIC		4,440,947	4,417,449	3,851,425	4,267,183	4,770,515	7.48	11.80
North-East Asia		2,662,172	2,559,379	2,182,324	2,632,462	3,041,171	4.77	15.53
China	(*)	950,759	942,988	820,187	1,092,470	1,322,564	2.07	21.06
Taiwan, Province of China		170,503	167,733	134,740	160,878	186,472	0.29	15.91
Japan		1,193,745	1,130,328	959,969	1,084,285	1,185,279	1.86	9.31
Korea, Republic of		347,165	318,330	267,428	294,829	346,856	0.54	17.65
Australasia		574,860	596,610	562,589	613,212	637,644	1.00	3.98
Australia					613,212	637,644	1.00	3.98
Australia, New Zealand		574,860	596,610	562,589				
Other East Asia and the Pacific		1,203,915	1,261,460	1,106,512	1,021,509	1,091,700	1.71	6.87
Other countries of Asia					923,769	997,508	1.56	7.98
Other countries East Asia/Pacific	(*)	1,203,915	1,261,460	1,106,512				
Other countries of Oceania					97,740	94,192	0.15	-3.63
EUROPE		41,441,039	43,328,769	42,624,382	46,456,990	49,268,358	77.29	6.05
Central/Eastern Europe		3,661,460	4,102,134	3,683,872	5,269,138	6,320,231	9.91	19.95
Bulgaria					142,014	173,845	0.27	22.41
Czech Republic		585,149	656,259	606,507	672,257	765,879	1.20	13.93
Estonia					68,751	80,347	0.13	16.87
Hungary		463,331	495,179	445,567	510,219	618,408	0.97	21.20
Latvia					84,129	99,889	0.16	18.73
Lithuania					125,968	139,190	0.22	10.50
Poland		1,228,823	1,346,876	1,192,951	1,380,549	1,716,479	2.69	24.33
Romania					401,726	465,393	0.73	15.85
Russian Federation		1,095,723	1,308,499	1,199,072	1,486,471	1,786,603	2.80	20.19
Slovakia					220,444	267,996	0.42	21.57
Ukraine					176,610	206,202	0.32	16.76
Baltic countries		288,434	295,321	239,775				
Northern Europe		9,621,987	9,614,770	8,963,273	9,952,349	10,155,974	15.93	2.05
Denmark		2,131,938	2,296,078	2,360,550	2,528,220	2,583,749	4.05	2.20
Finland		518,678	509,257	502,844	574,818	600,392	0.94	4.45
Iceland		101,359	94,171	87,199	89,025	88,452	0.14	-0.64
Ireland		330,095	345,736	329,938	331,405	312,169	0.49	-5.80
Norway		627,073	652,915	623,853	733,407	749,284	1.18	2.16
Sweden		1,500,265	1,494,198	1,359,645	1,514,850	1,525,431	2.39	0.70
United Kingdom		4,412,579	4,222,415	3,699,244	4,180,624	4,296,497	6.74	2.77
Southern Europe		5,630,683	5,712,163	5,607,912	6,145,142	6,226,372	9.77	1.32
Greece		465,609	491,863	499,064	438,501	414,230	0.65	-5.53
Italy		3,036,460	3,070,813	3,101,720	3,295,849	3,262,617	5.12	-1.01

GERMANY

6. Overnight stays of non-resident tourists in all types of accommodation establishments, by country of residence

	2007	2008	2009	2010	2011	Market share 11	% Change 11-10
Malta				29,642	30,830	0.05	4.01
Portugal	295,611	306,961	256,603	292,773	290,202	0.46	-0.88
Slovenia				158,871	183,319	0.29	15.39
Spain	1,833,003	1,842,526	1,750,525	1,929,506	2,045,174	3.21	5.99
Western Europe	**20,194,008**	**21,212,870**	**21,927,960**	**23,391,115**	**24,655,304**	**38.68**	**5.40**
Austria	2,386,205	2,482,052	2,573,826	2,838,779	3,030,904	4.75	6.77
Belgium	2,421,613	2,473,257	2,540,634	2,639,425	2,755,820	4.32	4.41
France	2,351,218	2,431,320	2,509,231	2,735,869	2,933,315	4.60	7.22
Luxembourg	435,396	455,023	486,020	507,506	517,564	0.81	1.98
Netherlands	8,996,531	9,689,240	9,962,061	10,483,114	10,653,148	16.71	1.62
Switzerland	3,603,045	3,681,978	3,856,188	4,186,422	4,764,553	7.47	13.81
East Mediterranean Europe	**780,825**	**822,049**	**786,909**	**998,998**	**1,111,834**	**1.74**	**11.29**
Cyprus				35,692	36,982	0.06	3.61
Israel	369,871	382,439	416,107	505,206	554,795	0.87	9.82
Turkey	410,954	439,610	370,802	458,100	520,057	0.82	13.52
Other Europe	**1,552,076**	**1,864,783**	**1,654,456**	**700,248**	**798,643**	**1.25**	**14.05**
Other countries of Europe	1,552,076	1,864,783	1,654,456	700,248	798,643	1.25	14.05
MIDDLE EAST	**724,721**	**776,550**	**770,980**	**968,336**	**1,006,856**	**1.58**	**3.98**
All countries of Middle East	724,721	776,550	770,980	968,336	1,006,856	1.58	3.98
SOUTH ASIA				**455,655**	**547,480**	**0.86**	**20.15**
India				455,655	547,480	0.86	20.15
NOT SPECIFIED	**1,649,264**	**1,669,855**	**1,566,071**	**1,298,108**	**1,219,532**	**1.91**	**-6.05**
Other countries of the World	1,649,264	1,669,855	1,566,071	1,298,108	1,219,532	1.91	-6.05

GREECE

1. Arrivals of non-resident tourists at national borders, by country of residence

		2007	2008	2009	2010	2011	Market share 11	% Change 11-10
TOTAL	(*)	16,165,265	15,938,806	14,914,534	15,007,490	16,427,248	100.00	9.46
AFRICA		46,325	44,569	25,576	28,314	33,775	0.21	19.29
Southern Africa		34,242	35,689	20,539	19,985	21,981	0.13	9.99
South Africa		34,242	35,689	20,539	19,985	21,981	0.13	9.99
Other Africa		12,083	8,880	5,037	8,329	11,794	0.07	41.60
Other countries of Africa		12,083	8,880	5,037	8,329	11,794	0.07	41.60
AMERICAS		842,815	849,014	729,446	691,379	719,661	4.38	4.09
North America		788,282	780,149	675,168	622,129	632,527	3.85	1.67
Canada		158,796	158,447	134,983	113,358	142,287	0.87	25.52
Mexico		12,008	8,877	8,909	10,470	5,532	0.03	-47.16
United States of America		617,478	612,825	531,276	498,301	484,708	2.95	-2.73
South America		32,921	41,783	38,418	51,787	65,952	0.40	27.35
Argentina		9,389	14,298	13,878	17,772	13,834	0.08	-22.16
Brazil		23,532	27,485	24,540	34,015	52,118	0.32	53.22
Other Americas		21,612	27,082	15,860	17,463	21,182	0.13	21.30
Other countries of the Americas		21,612	27,082	15,860	17,463	21,182	0.13	21.30
EAST ASIA AND THE PACIFIC		230,309	217,999	206,209	199,452	207,360	1.26	3.96
North-East Asia		28,779	21,258	19,681	31,264	27,809	0.17	-11.05
China			5,941	7,793	13,620	15,838	0.10	16.28
Japan		28,779	10,926	6,765	10,021	10,125	0.06	1.04
Korea, Republic of			4,391	5,123	7,623	1,846	0.01	-75.78
Australasia		125,636	136,086	133,869	108,088	115,902	0.71	7.23
Australia		125,636	136,086	133,869	108,088	115,902	0.71	7.23
Other East Asia and the Pacific		75,894	60,655	52,659	60,100	63,649	0.39	5.91
Other countries of Asia		58,069	36,819	25,016	42,015	44,572	0.27	6.09
Other countries of Oceania		17,825	23,836	27,643	18,085	19,077	0.12	5.49
EUROPE		14,987,571	14,766,811	13,884,208	14,034,319	15,429,714	93.93	9.94
Central/Eastern Europe		2,076,455	2,133,018	1,902,280	2,281,324	2,551,433	15.53	11.84
Bulgaria		701,666	623,476	657,130	664,389	686,209	4.18	3.28
Czech Republic		269,774	267,596	267,833	294,936	309,062	1.88	4.79
Estonia		28,732	26,018	21,242	13,842	9,862	0.06	-28.75
Hungary		201,703	180,914	70,894	109,160	69,756	0.42	-36.10
Latvia		11,861	31,010	12,027	21,948	7,846	0.05	-64.25
Lithuania		16,399	34,537	37,501	16,295	13,666	0.08	-16.13
Poland		227,363	270,039	203,487	402,170	450,618	2.74	12.05
Romania		350,723	327,261	307,596	257,939	223,699	1.36	-13.27
Russian Federation		199,591	309,071	276,021	451,239	738,927	4.50	63.76
Slovakia		68,643	63,096	48,549	49,406	41,788	0.25	-15.42
Northern Europe		3,552,657	3,429,941	3,294,786	2,782,059	2,790,183	16.99	0.29
Denmark		267,648	245,946	264,040	240,563	244,986	1.49	1.84
Finland		174,201	147,746	170,341	205,282	167,632	1.02	-18.34
Iceland			4,476	3,340				
Ireland		77,450	93,534	73,167	65,623	58,939	0.36	-10.19
Norway		213,349	277,303	315,595	187,319	226,627	1.38	20.98
Sweden		311,358	382,922	356,154	281,069	333,906	2.03	18.80
United Kingdom		2,508,651	2,278,014	2,112,149	1,802,203	1,758,093	10.70	-2.45
Southern Europe		2,274,376	2,361,460	1,895,695	2,016,863	2,263,450	13.78	12.23
Albania		213,725	242,999	234,276	242,083	411,245	2.50	69.88
Italy		1,251,779	1,099,983	935,011	843,613	938,232	5.71	11.22
Malta		21,744	11,702	4,367	9,651	1,368	0.01	-85.83
Portugal		17,948	24,678	13,300	19,497	34,642	0.21	77.68
Slovenia		33,037	75,185	45,924	40,082	31,130	0.19	-22.33
Spain		182,644	219,917	164,461	155,302	154,774	0.94	-0.34

GREECE

1. Arrivals of non-resident tourists at national borders, by country of residence

		2007	2008	2009	2010	2011	Market share 11	% Change 11-10
Serbia and Montenegro		553,499	686,996	498,356	706,635	692,059	4.21	-2.06
Western Europe		**5,556,983**	**5,276,551**	**5,040,130**	**4,406,588**	**5,083,455**	**30.95**	**15.36**
Austria		377,341	354,748	352,223	338,367	310,358	1.89	-8.28
Belgium		408,654	420,748	334,240	339,836	432,625	2.63	27.30
France		991,117	910,021	962,435	868,346	1,149,388	7.00	32.37
Germany		2,711,662	2,469,151	2,364,486	2,038,871	2,240,481	13.64	9.89
Luxembourg		20,145	25,135	22,792	18,593	28,475	0.17	53.15
Netherlands		737,771	756,940	651,440	528,157	560,723	3.41	6.17
Switzerland		310,293	339,808	352,514	274,418	361,405	2.20	31.70
East Mediterranean Europe		**748,248**	**766,771**	**717,537**	**1,333,121**	**1,217,957**	**7.41**	**-8.64**
Cyprus		492,475	474,941	434,746	574,764	439,757	2.68	-23.49
Israel		73,283	84,221	82,443	197,159	226,110	1.38	14.68
Turkey		182,490	207,609	200,348	561,198	552,090	3.36	-1.62
Other Europe		**778,852**	**799,070**	**1,033,780**	**1,214,364**	**1,523,236**	**9.27**	**25.43**
Other countries of Europe		778,852	799,070	1,033,780	1,214,364	1,523,236	9.27	25.43
MIDDLE EAST		**46,276**	**47,702**	**55,844**	**44,837**	**27,990**	**0.17**	**-37.57**
Lebanon	(*)	14,009	11,457	14,753	4,639	4,916	0.03	5.97
Egypt	(*)	14,644	13,556	12,610	15,925	4,675	0.03	-70.64
Other countries of Middle East		17,623	22,689	28,481	24,273	18,399	0.11	-24.20
SOUTH ASIA		**641**	**847**	**1,647**	**9,189**	**8,748**	**0.05**	**-4.80**
Iran, Islamic Republic of		641	847	1,647	9,189	8,748	0.05	-4.80
NOT SPECIFIED		**11,328**	**11,864**	**11,604**				
Other countries of the World		11,328	11,864	11,604				

GREECE

3. Arrivals of non-resident tourists in hotels and similar establishments, by country of residence

	2007	2008	2009	2010	2011	Market share 11	% Change 11-10
TOTAL	8,745,901	8,657,775	8,542,307	8,964,224			
AFRICA	38,267	38,640	37,283	45,813			
Southern Africa	2,749	1,437	1,516	1,615			
South Africa	2,749	1,437	1,516	1,615			
Other Africa	35,518	37,203	35,767	44,198			
Other countries of Africa	35,518	37,203	35,767	44,198			
AMERICAS	936,530	835,832	784,527	811,559			
North America	854,028	751,449	698,606	713,437			
Canada	124,503	118,213	110,149	110,993			
United States of America	729,525	633,236	588,457	602,444			
South America	32,087	37,533	34,549	41,974			
Brazil	32,087	37,533	34,549	41,974			
Other Americas	50,415	46,850	51,372	56,148			
Other countries of the Americas	50,415	46,850	51,372	56,148			
EAST ASIA AND THE PACIFIC	519,955	505,147	496,523	622,797			
North-East Asia	169,129	145,312	144,108	138,496			
China	51,245	49,883	48,033	59,268			
Japan	117,884	95,429	96,075	79,228			
Australasia	129,504	133,547	114,951	149,887			
Australia	129,504	133,547	114,951	149,887			
Other East Asia and the Pacific	221,322	226,288	237,464	334,414			
Other countries of Asia	213,483	217,169	229,923	325,352			
Other countries of Oceania	7,839	9,119	7,541	9,062			
EUROPE	7,250,134	7,277,317	7,219,060	7,476,544			
Central/Eastern Europe	815,390	977,290	930,426	1,042,816			
Czech Republic	124,595	149,116	164,347	151,759			
Estonia	15,037	16,805	14,294	15,353			
Hungary	63,117	61,060	47,746	43,399			
Latvia	14,538	14,497	11,208	9,080			
Lithuania	23,355	24,189	17,461	15,703			
Poland	172,075	210,658	231,087	234,075			
Russian Federation	336,349	426,843	376,138	494,020			
Slovakia	44,232	43,760	39,336	35,849			
Ukraine	22,092	30,362	28,809	43,578			
Northern Europe	1,826,780	1,789,628	1,822,281	1,938,724			
Denmark	147,036	158,872	158,482	164,095			
Finland	118,992	112,433	126,025	129,759			
Iceland	6,507	6,097	3,970	3,082			
Ireland	45,028	44,893	42,870	40,344			
Norway	161,618	173,053	181,891	207,069			
Sweden	230,714	234,614	242,262	284,355			
United Kingdom	1,116,885	1,059,666	1,066,781	1,110,020			
Southern Europe	933,116	857,197	844,945	867,639			
Italy	684,357	624,161	600,955	656,834			
Malta	2,624	3,682	5,131	4,017			
Portugal	22,646	21,220	21,765	20,153			
Slovenia	33,392	39,350	35,465	30,576			
Spain	190,097	168,784	181,629	156,059			
Western Europe	2,918,753	2,813,695	2,822,129	2,824,398			
Austria	229,718	192,185	191,743	175,593			
Belgium	239,014	233,136	225,718	232,627			
France	665,361	678,145	749,442	737,178			
Germany	1,223,988	1,162,613	1,136,774	1,163,238			

GREECE

3. Arrivals of non-resident tourists in hotels and similar establishments, by country of residence

		2007	2008	2009	2010	2011	Market share 11	% Change 11-10
Luxembourg		13,541	15,550	12,814	11,229			
Netherlands		386,866	386,567	360,959	360,747			
Switzerland	(*)	160,265	145,499	144,679	143,786			
East Mediterranean Europe		**243,480**	**247,310**	**230,711**	**253,482**			
Cyprus		184,002	185,930	169,978	177,129			
Turkey		59,478	61,380	60,733	76,353			
Other Europe		**512,615**	**592,197**	**568,568**	**549,485**			
Other countries of Europe		512,615	592,197	568,568	549,485			
NOT SPECIFIED		**1,015**	**839**	**4,914**	**7,511**			
Other countries of the World		1,015	839	4,914	7,511			

GREECE

4. Arrivals of non-resident tourists in all types of accommodation establishments, by country of residence

	2007	2008	2009	2010	2011	Market share 11	% Change 11-10
TOTAL	8,953,757	8,886,342	8,781,095	9,196,924			
AFRICA	38,417	38,810	37,504	46,093			
Southern Africa	2,760	1,485	1,550	1,663			
South Africa	2,760	1,485	1,550	1,663			
Other Africa	35,657	37,325	35,954	44,430			
Other countries of Africa	35,657	37,325	35,954	44,430			
AMERICAS	938,376	843,700	787,843	815,038			
North America	855,618	758,699	701,449	716,216			
Canada	125,033	120,997	111,296	112,313			
United States of America	730,585	637,702	590,153	603,903			
South America	32,194	37,679	34,749	42,140			
Brazil	32,194	37,679	34,749	42,140			
Other Americas	50,564	47,322	51,645	56,682			
Other countries of the Americas	50,564	47,322	51,645	56,682			
EAST ASIA AND THE PACIFIC	523,446	514,340	503,190	630,840			
North-East Asia	169,219	145,464	144,202	138,612			
China	51,269	49,944	48,096	59,342			
Japan	117,950	95,520	96,106	79,270			
Australasia	131,623	140,035	120,243	155,742			
Australia	131,623	140,035	120,243	155,742			
Other East Asia and the Pacific	222,604	228,841	238,745	336,486			
Other countries of Asia	214,076	217,679	230,419	326,126			
Other countries of Oceania	8,528	11,162	8,326	10,360			
EUROPE	7,452,471	7,488,603	7,447,642	7,697,419			
Central/Eastern Europe	827,999	989,397	943,611	1,054,705			
Czech Republic	127,579	152,101	167,117	154,061			
Estonia	15,167	17,023	14,491	15,540			
Hungary	66,280	63,770	50,562	45,989			
Latvia	14,746	14,647	11,310	9,183			
Lithuania	23,504	24,336	17,653	15,813			
Poland	177,314	215,763	237,055	239,536			
Russian Federation	336,559	427,171	376,589	494,555			
Slovakia	44,566	44,133	39,898	36,317			
Ukraine	22,284	30,453	28,936	43,711			
Northern Europe	1,834,003	1,800,865	1,832,848	1,948,282			
Denmark	148,820	161,027	160,463	166,271			
Finland	119,245	112,737	126,309	129,971			
Iceland	6,522	6,109	3,984	3,096			
Ireland	45,353	45,814	43,501	40,842			
Norway	161,714	173,359	182,179	207,416			
Sweden	231,238	235,321	242,848	284,998			
United Kingdom	1,121,111	1,066,498	1,073,564	1,115,688			
Southern Europe	974,263	898,783	889,395	909,213			
Italy	719,328	660,103	639,105	692,595			
Malta	2,632	3,734	5,451	4,049			
Portugal	22,943	21,421	22,170	20,444			
Slovenia	36,161	41,627	38,150	33,079			
Spain	193,199	171,898	184,519	159,046			
Western Europe	3,051,955	2,951,000	2,970,561	2,968,753			
Austria	241,079	202,789	203,996	187,287			
Belgium	242,805	236,879	230,155	236,960			
France	703,083	717,225	790,787	777,158			
Germany	1,273,912	1,215,964	1,195,325	1,217,220			

GREECE

4. Arrivals of non-resident tourists in all types of accommodation establishments, by country of residence

		2007	2008	2009	2010	2011	Market share 11	% Change 11-10
Luxembourg		13,580	15,607	12,880	11,289			
Netherlands		411,363	410,899	385,918	387,692			
Switzerland	(*)	166,133	151,637	151,500	151,147			
East Mediterranean Europe		**244,117**	**247,958**	**231,367**	**254,288**			
Cyprus		184,321	186,332	170,404	177,493			
Turkey		59,796	61,626	60,963	76,795			
Other Europe		**520,134**	**600,600**	**579,860**	**562,178**			
Other countries of Europe		520,134	600,600	579,860	562,178			
NOT SPECIFIED		**1,047**	**889**	**4,916**	**7,534**			
Other countries of the World		1,047	889	4,916	7,534			

GREECE

5. Overnight stays of non-resident tourists in hotels and similar establishments, by country of residence

	2007	2008	2009	2010	2011	Market share 11	% Change 11-10
TOTAL	47,410,260	47,233,616	45,925,585	48,243,634			
AFRICA	116,825	118,897	113,352	120,683			
Southern Africa	7,808	4,085	5,004	5,054			
South Africa	7,808	4,085	5,004	5,054			
Other Africa	109,017	114,812	108,348	115,629			
Other countries of Africa	109,017	114,812	108,348	115,629			
AMERICAS	2,024,992	1,752,995	1,664,877	1,715,269			
North America	1,822,722	1,545,520	1,460,114	1,487,159			
Canada	280,648	263,894	253,912	253,154			
United States of America	1,542,074	1,281,626	1,206,202	1,234,005			
South America	80,761	92,487	81,156	98,118			
Brazil	80,761	92,487	81,156	98,118			
Other Americas	121,509	114,988	123,607	129,992			
Other countries of the Americas	121,509	114,988	123,607	129,992			
EAST ASIA AND THE PACIFIC	1,188,212	1,163,160	1,215,251	1,580,516			
North-East Asia	311,724	261,853	247,995	240,026			
China	104,421	98,890	92,937	108,841			
Japan	207,303	162,963	155,058	131,185			
Australasia	318,925	311,999	271,811	346,096			
Australia	318,925	311,999	271,811	346,096			
Other East Asia and the Pacific	557,563	589,308	695,445	994,394			
Other countries of Asia	539,720	569,012	677,889	973,389			
Other countries of Oceania	17,843	20,296	17,556	21,005			
EUROPE	44,074,021	44,195,194	42,915,120	44,805,322			
Central/Eastern Europe	5,513,924	6,761,551	6,473,313	7,411,441			
Czech Republic	1,020,793	1,187,155	1,296,205	1,200,054			
Estonia	87,542	104,340	86,759	89,982			
Hungary	386,277	372,708	278,030	261,180			
Latvia	82,311	86,343	67,982	53,634			
Lithuania	140,857	152,967	120,061	102,320			
Poland	1,032,935	1,357,097	1,466,042	1,497,626			
Russian Federation	2,283,502	2,991,588	2,713,015	3,655,568			
Slovakia	358,287	328,504	290,110	282,382			
Ukraine	121,420	180,849	155,109	268,695			
Northern Europe	12,500,526	12,043,035	12,025,104	12,927,181			
Denmark	954,114	1,056,943	1,031,557	1,091,539			
Finland	824,745	767,725	851,657	881,678			
Iceland	35,655	37,323	19,612	13,119			
Ireland	273,721	253,048	236,494	212,770			
Norway	1,248,029	1,303,311	1,310,086	1,517,015			
Sweden	1,531,193	1,529,135	1,570,400	1,851,611			
United Kingdom	7,633,069	7,095,550	7,005,298	7,359,449			
Southern Europe	4,165,032	3,841,162	3,515,676	3,405,767			
Italy	3,452,487	3,159,042	2,806,170	2,789,213			
Malta	10,155	14,563	22,252	17,271			
Portugal	73,358	67,295	69,801	66,021			
Slovenia	185,957	219,516	208,494	177,661			
Spain	443,075	380,746	408,959	355,601			
Western Europe	19,317,847	18,531,304	17,987,125	18,014,357			
Austria	1,578,983	1,350,641	1,211,417	1,175,892			
Belgium	1,564,315	1,523,693	1,452,533	1,471,804			
France	2,971,105	3,182,160	3,480,867	3,404,558			
Germany	9,324,130	8,756,063	8,332,465	8,509,308			

GREECE

5. Overnight stays of non-resident tourists in hotels and similar establishments, by country of residence

		2007	2008	2009	2010	2011	Market share 11	% Change 11-10
Luxembourg		95,281	108,665	90,724	81,101			
Netherlands		2,795,505	2,727,542	2,552,027	2,513,056			
Switzerland	(*)	988,528	882,540	867,092	858,638			
East Mediterranean Europe		**662,911**	**675,152**	**614,701**	**677,384**			
Cyprus		533,583	548,944	495,477	525,704			
Turkey		129,328	126,208	119,224	151,680			
Other Europe		**1,913,781**	**2,342,990**	**2,299,201**	**2,369,192**			
Other countries of Europe		1,913,781	2,342,990	2,299,201	2,369,192			
NOT SPECIFIED		**6,210**	**3,370**	**16,985**	**21,844**			
Other countries of the World		6,210	3,370	16,985	21,844			

GREECE

6. Overnight stays of non-resident tourists in all types of accommodation establishments, by country of residence

	2007	2008	2009	2010	2011	Market share 11	% Change 11-10
TOTAL	48,081,473	47,973,949	46,676,987	48,986,136			
AFRICA	117,660	119,353	114,011	121,483			
Southern Africa	7,825	4,202	5,083	5,203			
South Africa	7,825	4,202	5,083	5,203			
Other Africa	109,835	115,151	108,928	116,280			
Other countries of Africa	109,835	115,151	108,928	116,280			
AMERICAS	2,030,586	1,771,301	1,672,432	1,723,589			
North America	1,827,214	1,561,762	1,466,392	1,493,714			
Canada	281,755	270,703	256,506	256,299			
United States of America	1,545,459	1,291,059	1,209,886	1,237,415			
South America	81,245	92,914	81,628	98,540			
Brazil	81,245	92,914	81,628	98,540			
Other Americas	122,127	116,625	124,412	131,335			
Other countries of the Americas	122,127	116,625	124,412	131,335			
EAST ASIA AND THE PACIFIC	1,196,086	1,185,829	1,230,135	1,600,396			
North-East Asia	312,074	262,178	248,226	240,227			
China	104,524	99,006	93,087	108,966			
Japan	207,550	163,172	155,139	131,261			
Australasia	323,537	328,405	283,840	361,433			
Australia	323,537	328,405	283,840	361,433			
Other East Asia and the Pacific	560,475	595,246	698,069	998,736			
Other countries of Asia	541,005	570,588	678,815	974,624			
Other countries of Oceania	19,470	24,658	19,254	24,112			
EUROPE	44,730,583	44,893,896	43,643,422	45,518,776			
Central/Eastern Europe	5,551,048	6,798,510	6,513,312	7,448,812			
Czech Republic	1,029,217	1,196,075	1,304,435	1,207,537			
Estonia	87,779	104,710	87,233	90,412			
Hungary	395,566	381,234	286,772	268,718			
Latvia	82,689	86,675	68,168	53,813			
Lithuania	141,160	153,257	120,520	102,656			
Poland	1,048,543	1,373,192	1,483,854	1,515,522			
Russian Federation	2,284,045	2,992,321	2,714,642	3,656,772			
Slovakia	359,099	329,942	292,305	284,424			
Ukraine	122,950	181,104	155,383	268,958			
Northern Europe	12,528,076	12,079,205	12,058,253	12,960,034			
Denmark	963,836	1,066,901	1,040,490	1,101,202			
Finland	825,501	768,473	852,338	882,435			
Iceland	35,708	37,336	19,645	13,170			
Ireland	275,250	255,863	238,108	214,181			
Norway	1,248,374	1,304,017	1,310,892	1,518,004			
Sweden	1,533,410	1,531,684	1,573,083	1,854,258			
United Kingdom	7,645,997	7,114,931	7,023,697	7,376,784			
Southern Europe	4,285,263	3,965,365	3,642,299	3,528,191			
Italy	3,558,272	3,270,159	2,918,214	2,897,992			
Malta	10,164	14,660	23,237	17,325			
Portugal	74,018	67,802	70,628	66,687			
Slovenia	192,987	225,087	215,373	184,148			
Spain	449,822	387,657	414,847	362,039			
Western Europe	19,743,819	18,984,303	18,456,065	18,460,432			
Austria	1,627,046	1,395,337	1,257,525	1,222,500			
Belgium	1,575,798	1,534,085	1,464,392	1,484,285			
France	3,056,645	3,270,879	3,574,165	3,497,512			
Germany	9,508,382	8,972,596	8,554,859	8,702,157			

GREECE

6. Overnight stays of non-resident tourists in all types of accommodation establishments, by country of residence

		2007	2008	2009	2010	2011	Market share 11	% Change 11-10
Luxembourg		95,379	108,822	90,907	81,305			
Netherlands		2,875,233	2,801,166	2,626,203	2,592,614			
Switzerland	(*)	1,005,336	901,418	888,014	880,059			
East Mediterranean Europe		**664,221**	**677,643**	**616,451**	**678,925**			
Cyprus		534,232	549,902	496,687	526,562			
Turkey		129,989	127,741	119,764	152,363			
Other Europe		**1,958,156**	**2,388,870**	**2,357,042**	**2,442,382**			
Other countries of Europe		1,958,156	2,388,870	2,357,042	2,442,382			
NOT SPECIFIED		**6,558**	**3,570**	**16,987**	**21,892**			
Other countries of the World		6,558	3,570	16,987	21,892			

GRENADA

1. Arrivals of non-resident tourists at national borders, by nationality

	2007	2008	2009	2010	2011	Market share 11	% Change 11-10
TOTAL	**130,096**	**130,363**	**113,894**	**110,419**	**118,295**	**100.00**	**7.13**
AFRICA	**965**	**644**	**725**	**667**	**617**	**0.52**	**-7.50**
East Africa	**71**	**79**	**103**	**83**	**62**	**0.05**	**-25.30**
Ethiopia	3			1			
Kenya	24	30	42	20	19	0.02	-5.00
Mauritius	3	3	7	12	5	0.00	-58.33
Zimbabwe	14	13	29	31	8	0.01	-74.19
Uganda	10	17	12	11	9	0.01	-18.18
Zambia	17	16	13	8	21	0.02	162.50
Central Africa	**4**	**3**	**6**	**6**	**4**	**0.00**	**-33.33**
Cameroon	4	1	6	6	3	0.00	-50.00
Democratic Republic of the Congo		2			1	0.00	
North Africa	**7**	**3**	**3**	**7**	**4**	**0.00**	**-42.86**
Algeria	2	3	1	2	1	0.00	-50.00
Morocco	5		2	4	3	0.00	-25.00
Sudan				1			
Southern Africa	**682**	**228**	**288**	**223**	**286**	**0.24**	**28.25**
Botswana	87	87	107	64	110	0.09	71.88
South Africa	595	141	181	159	176	0.15	10.69
West Africa	**180**	**249**	**307**	**314**	**243**	**0.21**	**-22.61**
Ghana	11	15	18	24	26	0.02	8.33
Liberia		6	2	1			
Nigeria	167	228	286	287	217	0.18	-24.39
Senegal	2		1	2			
Other Africa	**21**	**82**	**18**	**34**	**18**	**0.02**	**-47.06**
Other countries of Africa	21	82	18	34	18	0.02	-47.06
AMERICAS	**63,796**	**66,159**	**61,648**	**59,175**	**64,855**	**54.82**	**9.60**
Caribbean	**27,672**	**29,039**	**25,205**	**22,784**	**25,877**	**21.87**	**13.58**
Antigua and Barbuda	704	652	831	534	510	0.43	-4.49
Bahamas	78	119	124	109	94	0.08	-13.76
Barbados	4,596	4,791	4,027	3,579	3,526	2.98	-1.48
Cayman Islands	69	45	39	44	38	0.03	-13.64
Cuba	234	143	119	89	71	0.06	-20.22
Dominica	562	510	425	476	472	0.40	-0.84
Dominican Republic	55	30	64	35	29	0.02	-17.14
Guadeloupe	29	60	26	100	64	0.05	-36.00
Haiti	20	26	27	26	26	0.02	
Jamaica	1,315	1,724	1,212	966	987	0.83	2.17
Montserrat	60	50	52	50	35	0.03	-30.00
Saint Kitts and Nevis	267	277	333	305	300	0.25	-1.64
Anguilla	61	71	71	41	44	0.04	7.32
Saint Lucia	1,679	1,650	1,485	1,505	1,275	1.08	-15.28
Sint Maarten	154	102	103	123	95	0.08	-22.76
Saint Vincent and the Grenadines	2,214	2,146	1,930	1,712	1,922	1.62	12.27
Trinidad and Tobago	14,547	15,548	13,277	12,283	15,715	13.28	27.94
Other countries of the Caribbean	1,028	1,095	1,060	807	674	0.57	-16.48
Central America	**115**	**282**	**201**	**187**	**172**	**0.15**	**-8.02**
Belize	43	61	65	69	60	0.05	-13.04
Costa Rica	13	159	32	20	18	0.02	-10.00
Honduras	11	5	6	6	6	0.01	
Nicaragua	6	5	13	10	8	0.01	-20.00
Panama	25	25	52	48	34	0.03	-29.17
Other countries of Central America	17	27	33	34	46	0.04	35.29
North America	**33,505**	**33,715**	**33,268**	**33,446**	**36,240**	**30.64**	**8.35**
Canada	6,067	7,100	7,194	7,322	7,490	6.33	2.29

GRENADA

1. Arrivals of non-resident tourists at national borders, by nationality

	2007	2008	2009	2010	2011	Market share 11	% Change 11-10
Mexico	86	80	91	69	36	0.03	-47.83
United States of America	27,352	26,535	25,983	26,055	28,714	24.27	10.21
South America	**2,504**	**3,123**	**2,974**	**2,758**	**2,566**	**2.17**	**-6.96**
Argentina	114	127	120	120	116	0.10	-3.33
Bolivia	14	15	12	28	9	0.01	-67.86
Brazil	84	202	284	365	354	0.30	-3.01
Chile	31	31	73	39	37	0.03	-5.13
Colombia	46	70	97	64	50	0.04	-21.88
Ecuador	32	12	10	8	9	0.01	12.50
Guyana	1,276	1,205	1,122	1,113	1,073	0.91	-3.59
Paraguay	7			21	30	0.03	42.86
Peru	6	14	28	21	36	0.03	71.43
Suriname	63	72	82	114	103	0.09	-9.65
Uruguay	13	5	13	10	13	0.01	30.00
Venezuela	814	1,368	1,131	850	736	0.62	-13.41
Other countries of South America	4	2	2	5			
EAST ASIA AND THE PACIFIC	**3,382**	**1,129**	**1,442**	**1,527**	**1,432**	**1.21**	**-6.22**
North-East Asia	**96**	**77**	**81**	**94**	**101**	**0.09**	**7.45**
Japan	96	77	81	94	101	0.09	7.45
Australasia	**2,066**	**477**	**304**	**355**	**361**	**0.31**	**1.69**
Australia	1,669	411	248	313	306	0.26	-2.24
New Zealand	397	66	56	42	55	0.05	30.95
Melanesia	**2**		**4**	**3**	**2**	**0.00**	**-33.33**
Fiji	2		4	3	2	0.00	-33.33
Other East Asia and the Pacific	**1,218**	**575**	**1,053**	**1,075**	**968**	**0.82**	**-9.95**
Other countries of Asia	1,218	575	1,053	1,075	968	0.82	-9.95
EUROPE	**42,111**	**44,676**	**36,096**	**35,361**	**36,277**	**30.67**	**2.59**
Central/Eastern Europe	**395**	**549**	**384**	**547**	**490**	**0.41**	**-10.42**
Bulgaria	9	9	25	7	11	0.01	57.14
Czech Republic/Slovakia	67	115	67	144	141	0.12	-2.08
Hungary	47	43	5	38	50	0.04	31.58
Poland	80	125	87	97	115	0.10	18.56
Romania	12	26	26	16	26	0.02	62.50
Ukraine		2	4	34	2	0.00	-94.12
USSR (former)	180	227	170	211	145	0.12	-31.28
Other countries Central/East Europe		2					
Northern Europe	**35,299**	**37,103**	**29,335**	**28,073**	**29,489**	**24.93**	**5.04**
Denmark	205	327	282	231	188	0.16	-18.61
Finland	32	80	85	56	129	0.11	130.36
Ireland	493	445	502	370	367	0.31	-0.81
Norway	167	370	365	344	339	0.29	-1.45
Sweden	426	442	386	481	638	0.54	32.64
United Kingdom	33,976	35,439	27,715	26,591	27,828	23.52	4.65
Southern Europe	**975**	**897**	**825**	**986**	**754**	**0.64**	**-23.53**
Greece	21	27	28	52	44	0.04	-15.38
Italy	695	612	578	697	512	0.43	-26.54
Malta	7	15	7	3	3	0.00	
Portugal	34	42	44	38	41	0.03	7.89
Spain	214	194	165	195	154	0.13	-21.03
Serbia and Montenegro	4	7	3	1			
Western Europe	**5,348**	**6,024**	**5,457**	**5,686**	**5,429**	**4.59**	**-4.52**
Austria	529	520	545	512	500	0.42	-2.34
Belgium	118	175	134	175	171	0.14	-2.29
France	864	1,063	1,105	1,229	1,332	1.13	8.38
Germany	2,737	3,183	2,698	2,613	2,347	1.98	-10.18

GRENADA

1. Arrivals of non-resident tourists at national borders, by nationality

	2007	2008	2009	2010	2011	Market share 11	% Change 11-10
Liechtenstein				2			
Luxembourg	18	17	18	24	17	0.01	-29.17
Netherlands	502	403	340	486	357	0.30	-26.54
Switzerland	580	663	617	645	705	0.60	9.30
East Mediterranean Europe	**47**	**58**	**69**	**50**	**59**	**0.05**	**18.00**
Cyprus	5	4	1	8	5	0.00	-37.50
Israel	29	32	25	33	42	0.04	27.27
Turkey	13	22	43	9	12	0.01	33.33
Other Europe	**47**	**45**	**26**	**19**	**56**	**0.05**	**194.74**
Other countries of Europe	47	45	26	19	56	0.05	194.74
MIDDLE EAST	**87**	**97**	**64**	**59**	**52**	**0.04**	**-11.86**
Iraq		1					
Jordan	4	4	2	1	3	0.00	200.00
Lebanon	18	37	32	11	7	0.01	-36.36
Saudi Arabia	5			6	5	0.00	-16.67
Syrian Arab Republic	19	28	23	21	26	0.02	23.81
Egypt	2	4	2	4	4	0.00	
Other countries of Middle East	39	23	5	16	7	0.01	-56.25
NOT SPECIFIED	**19,755**	**17,658**	**13,919**	**13,630**	**15,062**	**12.73**	**10.51**
Other countries of the World	215	554	34	133	171	0.14	28.57
Nationals Residing Abroad	19,540	17,104	13,885	13,497	14,891	12.59	10.33

GRENADA

3. Arrivals of non-resident tourists in hotels and similar establishments, by nationality

	2007	2008	2009	2010	2011	Market share 11	% Change 11-10
TOTAL	65,993	61,882	51,098	49,530	58,077	100.00	17.26
AMERICAS	33,124	29,751	26,914	25,419	32,612	56.15	28.30
Caribbean	15,453	14,847	13,356	11,437	14,006	24.12	22.46
All countries of the Caribbean	15,453	14,847	13,356	11,437	14,006	24.12	22.46
North America	17,087	14,072	12,931	13,542	18,220	31.37	34.54
Canada	2,733	2,784	2,974	3,152	3,671	6.32	16.47
United States of America	14,354	11,288	9,957	10,390	14,549	25.05	40.03
South America	584	832	627	440	386	0.66	-12.27
Venezuela	584	832	627	440	386	0.66	-12.27
EUROPE	28,350	29,208	22,182	21,626	23,222	39.98	7.38
Northern Europe	23,490	24,374	18,352	17,518	19,158	32.99	9.36
Sweden	260	253	229	256	337	0.58	31.64
United Kingdom	23,230	24,121	18,123	17,262	18,821	32.41	9.03
Southern Europe	394	316	271	319	280	0.48	-12.23
Italy	394	316	271	319	280	0.48	-12.23
Western Europe	2,679	2,669	2,091	2,200	2,276	3.92	3.45
France	351	336	305	373	497	0.86	33.24
Germany	2,021	1,995	1,537	1,485	1,405	2.42	-5.39
Switzerland	307	338	249	342	374	0.64	9.36
Other Europe	1,787	1,849	1,468	1,589	1,508	2.60	-5.10
Other countries of Europe	1,787	1,849	1,468	1,589	1,508	2.60	-5.10
NOT SPECIFIED	4,519	2,923	2,002	2,485	2,243	3.86	-9.74
Other countries of the World	3,416	2,133	1,408	2,105	1,984	3.42	-5.75
Nationals Residing Abroad	1,103	790	594	380	259	0.45	-31.84

GRENADA

4. Arrivals of non-resident tourists in all types of accommodation establishments, by nationality

	2007	2008	2009	2010	2011	Market share 11	% Change 11-10
TOTAL	130,096	130,363	113,894	110,419	118,295	100.00	7.13
AMERICAS	63,287	64,042	60,782	57,129	64,224	54.29	12.42
Caribbean	29,054	29,039	26,474	22,902	27,284	23.06	19.13
All countries of the Caribbean	29,054	29,039	26,474	22,902	27,284	23.06	19.13
North America	33,419	33,635	33,177	33,377	36,204	30.60	8.47
Canada	6,067	7,100	7,194	7,322	7,490	6.33	2.29
United States of America	27,352	26,535	25,983	26,055	28,714	24.27	10.21
South America	814	1,368	1,131	850	736	0.62	-13.41
Venezuela	814	1,368	1,131	850	736	0.62	-13.41
EUROPE	42,082	44,676	36,086	35,350	36,235	30.63	2.50
Northern Europe	34,402	35,881	28,101	27,072	28,466	24.06	5.15
Sweden	426	442	386	481	638	0.54	32.64
United Kingdom	33,976	35,439	27,715	26,591	27,828	23.52	4.65
Southern Europe	695	612	578	697	512	0.43	-26.54
Italy	695	612	578	697	512	0.43	-26.54
Western Europe	4,181	4,909	4,420	4,487	4,384	3.71	-2.30
France	864	1,063	1,105	1,229	1,332	1.13	8.38
Germany	2,737	3,183	2,698	2,613	2,347	1.98	-10.18
Switzerland	580	663	617	645	705	0.60	9.30
Other Europe	2,804	3,274	2,987	3,094	2,873	2.43	-7.14
Other countries of Europe	2,804	3,274	2,987	3,094	2,873	2.43	-7.14
NOT SPECIFIED	24,727	21,645	17,026	17,940	17,836	15.08	-0.58
Other countries of the World	5,187	4,541	3,141	4,443	2,945	2.49	-33.72
Nationals Residing Abroad	19,540	17,104	13,885	13,497	14,891	12.59	10.33

GUADELOUPE

1. Arrivals of non-resident tourists at national borders, by country of residence

	2007	2008	2009	2010	2011	Market share 11	% Change 11-10
TOTAL (*)			346,507	392,282			
AFRICA			187				
North Africa			187				
Morocco			187				
AMERICAS			1,919	1,354			
Caribbean			1,170	709			
Dominica			94				
Haiti			140				
Martinique			936	709			
North America			281				
United States of America			281				
South America			468	645			
Guyana			468	645			
EUROPE			343,465	384,801			
Northern Europe			842				
Norway			281				
United Kingdom			561				
Southern Europe			2,666				
Italy			2,105				
Spain			561				
Western Europe			337,291	370,482			
Austria			281				
Belgium			4,631				
France			329,011	370,482			
Germany			1,403				
Luxembourg			187				
Switzerland			1,778				
Other Europe			2,666	14,319			
Other countries of Europe			2,666	14,319			
NOT SPECIFIED			936	6,127			
Other countries of the World			936	6,127			

GUAM

1. Arrivals of non-resident tourists at national borders, by country of residence

	2007	2008	2009	2010	2011	Market share 11	% Change 11-10
TOTAL	1,224,894	1,141,779	1,052,871	1,196,295	1,159,152	100.00	-3.10
AMERICAS	50,267	53,848	56,192	61,887	62,105	5.36	0.35
North America	50,267	53,848	56,192	61,887	62,105	5.36	0.35
Canada	677	773	667	661	757	0.07	14.52
United States of America	49,590	53,075	55,525	61,226	61,348	5.29	0.20
EAST ASIA AND THE PACIFIC	1,124,725	1,033,798	982,625	1,119,681	1,081,870	93.33	-3.38
North-East Asia	1,083,373	989,456	936,353	1,071,331	1,034,138	89.22	-3.47
China	1,504	1,951	3,286	4,765	7,068	0.61	48.33
Taiwan, Province of China	21,819	22,605	22,088	31,320	45,086	3.89	43.95
Hong Kong, China	6,224	4,276	2,872	6,890	8,903	0.77	29.22
Japan	931,079	850,034	825,129	893,667	824,005	71.09	-7.80
Korea, Republic of	122,747	110,590	82,978	134,689	149,076	12.86	10.68
South-East Asia	9,003	11,189	11,927	12,736	10,681	0.92	-16.14
Philippines	8,743	10,902	11,581	12,340	10,097	0.87	-18.18
Viet Nam	22	61	53	78	96	0.01	23.08
Thailand	238	226	293	318	488	0.04	53.46
Australasia	2,387	2,437	2,418	3,093	3,867	0.33	25.02
Australia	2,387	2,437	2,418	3,093	3,867	0.33	25.02
Micronesia	29,962	30,716	31,927	32,521	33,184	2.86	2.04
Nauru	23	13					
Northern Mariana Islands	17,665	17,607	17,811	18,301	18,059	1.56	-1.32
Micronesia, Federated States of	8,116	8,602	9,683	9,537	10,222	0.88	7.18
Marshall Islands	934	965	1,022	1,247	1,192	0.10	-4.41
Palau	3,224	3,529	3,411	3,436	3,711	0.32	8.00
EUROPE	1,564	1,710	2,005	1,948	2,117	0.18	8.68
Central/Eastern Europe		122	339	422	632	0.05	49.76
Russian Federation		122	339	422	632	0.05	49.76
Other Europe	1,564	1,588	1,666	1,526	1,485	0.13	-2.69
Other countries of Europe		1,588	1,666	1,526	1,485	0.13	-2.69
All countries of Europe	1,564						
NOT SPECIFIED	48,338	52,423	12,049	12,779	13,060	1.13	2.20
Other countries of the World	48,338	52,423	12,049	12,779	13,060	1.13	2.20

GUATEMALA

2. Arrivals of non-resident visitors at national borders, by nationality

		2007	2008	2009	2010	2011	Market share 11	% Change 11-10
TOTAL	(*)	1,627,551	1,715,426	1,776,868	1,875,777	1,822,663	100.00	-2.83
AMERICAS		1,443,662	1,517,540	1,563,934	1,644,754	1,599,430	87.75	-2.76
Caribbean		6,062	6,731	7,936	7,733	5,906	0.32	-23.63
Cuba		2,493	2,769	2,398	1,847	1,717	0.09	-7.04
Dominican Republic		2,694	3,021	4,612	4,688	3,038	0.17	-35.20
Other countries of the Caribbean		875	941	926	1,198	1,151	0.06	-3.92
Central America		884,293	935,604	892,696	933,817	930,258	51.04	-0.38
Belize		34,572	31,803	37,191	43,816	35,960	1.97	-17.93
Costa Rica		40,436	41,545	46,504	48,088	42,039	2.31	-12.58
El Salvador		617,798	647,568	507,802	485,888	542,316	29.75	11.61
Honduras		138,944	155,063	211,456	258,765	223,010	12.24	-13.82
Nicaragua		40,298	47,171	77,688	83,819	74,362	4.08	-11.28
Panama		12,245	12,454	12,055	13,441	12,571	0.69	-6.47
North America		496,237	515,905	604,813	645,521	604,596	33.17	-6.34
Canada		32,206	36,079	47,675	46,774	42,719	2.34	-8.67
Mexico		86,466	92,905	105,456	127,691	132,661	7.28	3.89
United States of America		377,565	386,921	451,682	471,056	429,216	23.55	-8.88
South America		57,070	59,300	58,489	57,683	58,670	3.22	1.71
Argentina		10,358	10,933	10,973	11,519	12,178	0.67	5.72
Brazil		8,883	7,689	7,444	7,640	7,313	0.40	-4.28
Chile		6,489	6,532	6,605	6,262	6,390	0.35	2.04
Colombia		15,170	16,289	16,930	15,710	15,520	0.85	-1.21
Ecuador		2,580	2,634	2,413	2,581	2,470	0.14	-4.30
Peru		4,278	4,819	4,095	3,524	3,819	0.21	8.37
Venezuela		6,028	6,681	6,267	6,759	7,425	0.41	9.85
Other countries of South America		3,284	3,723	3,762	3,688	3,555	0.20	-3.61
EAST ASIA AND THE PACIFIC		30,245	30,480	29,811	39,128	36,601	2.01	-6.46
North-East Asia		22,695	21,707	17,898	20,098	20,602	1.13	2.51
China		433	635	594	809	1,385	0.08	71.20
Taiwan, Province of China		3,415	4,114	2,817	3,382	2,351	0.13	-30.48
Japan		6,791	6,521	5,110	7,081	6,956	0.38	-1.77
Korea, Dem. People's Republic of		37	64	16	16	622	0.03	3787.50
Korea, Republic of		12,019	10,373	9,361	8,810	9,288	0.51	5.43
Australasia		5,968	7,011	9,567	12,591	10,866	0.60	-13.70
Australia		4,833	5,664	7,931	10,520	9,048	0.50	-13.99
New Zealand		1,135	1,347	1,636	2,071	1,818	0.10	-12.22
Other East Asia and the Pacific		1,582	1,762	2,346	6,439	5,133	0.28	-20.28
Other countries of Asia		1,556	1,728	2,124	6,314	5,034	0.28	-20.27
Other countries of Oceania		26	34	222	125	99	0.01	-20.80
EUROPE		151,807	165,025	180,381	189,586	184,356	10.11	-2.76
Central/Eastern Europe		5,097	6,491	12,223	10,857	10,979	0.60	1.12
Azerbaijan		137	1	1	2	5	0.00	150.00
Armenia		16	10	14	9	19	0.00	111.11
Bulgaria		182	212	234	261	235	0.01	-9.96
Belarus		30	17	30	38	18	0.00	-52.63
Czech Republic		1,047	1,047	4,475	3,160	1,551	0.09	-50.92
Estonia		159	255	275	255	245	0.01	-3.92
Georgia		8	138	17	15	184	0.01	1126.67
Hungary		385	483	531	777	482	0.03	-37.97
Kazakhstan		11	3	6	17	15	0.00	-11.76
Kyrgyzstan		1	1	4	3	6	0.00	100.00
Latvia		68	158	157	139	145	0.01	4.32
Lithuania		66	152	258	339	263	0.01	-22.42
Republic of Moldova		67	60	17	15	11	0.00	-26.67

GUATEMALA

2. Arrivals of non-resident visitors at national borders, by nationality

	2007	2008	2009	2010	2011	Market share 11	% Change 11-10
Poland	1,239	2,256	3,498	2,591	3,071	0.17	18.53
Romania	136	223	180	665	515	0.03	-22.56
Russian Federation	1,197	958	1,312	1,687	2,653	0.15	57.26
Slovakia	222	332	879	564	1,000	0.05	77.30
Tajikistan				3	3	0.00	
Turkmenistan	4	1	2	2	2	0.00	
Ukraine	116	178	314	309	548	0.03	77.35
Uzbekistan	6	6	19	6	8	0.00	33.33
Northern Europe	**32,865**	**37,502**	**42,163**	**42,900**	**39,615**	**2.17**	**-7.66**
Denmark	3,842	4,396	4,621	4,373	4,076	0.22	-6.79
Finland	1,061	1,114	1,353	1,378	1,327	0.07	-3.70
Iceland	104	125	97	173	144	0.01	-16.76
Ireland	2,096	2,168	2,776	2,904	2,835	0.16	-2.38
Norway	2,902	3,076	3,073	3,342	2,922	0.16	-12.57
Sweden	4,299	4,392	5,020	4,169	3,770	0.21	-9.57
United Kingdom	18,561	22,231	25,223	26,561	24,541	1.35	-7.61
Southern Europe	**41,484**	**41,714**	**41,037**	**44,916**	**45,706**	**2.51**	**1.76**
Albania	10	12	51	31	39	0.00	25.81
Andorra	25	30	15	31	60	0.00	93.55
Bosnia and Herzegovina	8	1	5	12	16	0.00	33.33
Croatia	89	133	113	148	151	0.01	2.03
Gibraltar	1			5	12	0.00	140.00
Greece	467	502	615	682	576	0.03	-15.54
Holy See	2	4	8	12	6	0.00	-50.00
Italy	14,932	14,746	12,630	14,582	16,819	0.92	15.34
Malta	96	73	141	58	96	0.01	65.52
Montenegro		1	9	3	13	0.00	333.33
Portugal	891	968	971	1,040	942	0.05	-9.42
San Marino	7	6	12	10	8	0.00	-20.00
Serbia		1	6	5	3	0.00	-40.00
Slovenia	299	364	540	448	518	0.03	15.63
Spain	24,581	24,806	25,863	27,788	26,426	1.45	-4.90
TFYR of Macedonia	21	31	35	34	10	0.00	-70.59
Serbia and Montenegro	55	36	23	27	11	0.00	-59.26
Western Europe	**65,409**	**70,902**	**77,235**	**80,445**	**76,160**	**4.18**	**-5.33**
Austria	2,815	2,912	3,109	3,244	3,090	0.17	-4.75
Belgium	5,042	5,476	5,866	6,868	6,127	0.34	-10.79
France	19,835	21,539	28,022	26,503	24,874	1.36	-6.15
Germany	18,587	19,630	21,334	20,979	20,516	1.13	-2.21
Liechtenstein	10	42	18	65	23	0.00	-64.62
Luxembourg	68	107	93	67	99	0.01	47.76
Monaco	18	8	5	2	6	0.00	200.00
Netherlands	13,316	15,781	12,818	16,661	15,093	0.83	-9.41
Switzerland	5,718	5,407	5,970	6,056	6,332	0.35	4.56
East Mediterranean Europe	**6,952**	**8,416**	**7,723**	**10,466**	**11,895**	**0.65**	**13.65**
Cyprus	18	18	37	31	52	0.00	67.74
Israel	6,619	8,047	7,330	9,762	11,282	0.62	15.57
Turkey	315	351	356	673	561	0.03	-16.64
Other Europe				**2**	**1**	**0.00**	**-50.00**
Other countries of Europe				2	1	0.00	-50.00
MIDDLE EAST	**454**	**281**	**467**	**431**	**537**	**0.03**	**24.59**
All countries of Middle East	454	281	467	431	537	0.03	24.59
NOT SPECIFIED	**1,383**	**2,100**	**2,275**	**1,878**	**1,739**	**0.10**	**-7.40**
Other countries of the World	1,383	2,100	2,275	1,878	1,739	0.10	-7.40

GUYANA

1. Arrivals of non-resident tourists at national borders, by country of residence

		2007	2008	2009	2010	2011	Market share 11	% Change 11-10
TOTAL	(*)	134,057	129,595	141,281	151,926	156,871	100.00	3.25
AMERICAS		117,984	118,364	130,979	141,200	107,247	68.37	-24.05
Caribbean		28,376	27,860	28,026	29,487			
All countries of the Caribbean		28,376	27,860	28,026	29,487			
North America		89,608	87,820	100,767	108,347	107,247	68.37	-1.02
Canada		19,785	21,470	23,812	25,381	23,965	15.28	-5.58
United States of America		69,823	66,350	76,955	82,966	83,282	53.09	0.38
Other Americas			2,684	2,186	3,366			
Other countries of the Americas			2,684	2,186	3,366			
EUROPE		9,978	8,937	8,277	8,357	8,284	5.28	-0.87
Other Europe		9,978	8,937	8,277	8,357	8,284	5.28	-0.87
All countries of Europe		9,978	8,937	8,277	8,357	8,284	5.28	-0.87
NOT SPECIFIED		6,095	2,294	2,025	2,369	41,340	26.35	1645.04
Other countries of the World		6,095	2,294	2,025	2,369	41,340	26.35	1645.04

HAITI

1. Arrivals of non-resident tourists at national borders, by country of residence

		2007	2008	2009	2010	2011	Market share 11	% Change 11-10
TOTAL	(*)	**386,060**	**258,070**	**387,218**	**254,732**	**348,755**	**100.00**	**36.91**
AMERICAS		**331,986**	**199,333**	**335,135**	**220,791**	**309,024**	**88.61**	**39.96**
Caribbean		**24,245**	**6,148**	**24,989**	**9,954**	**11,552**	**3.31**	**16.05**
Dominican Republic		8,819	2,638	9,910	3,168	4,487	1.29	41.64
Jamaica		5,841	451	6,050	689	819	0.23	18.87
Other countries of the Caribbean		9,585	3,059	9,029	6,097	6,246	1.79	2.44
North America		**297,882**	**186,190**	**300,288**	**204,485**	**288,014**	**82.58**	**40.85**
Canada		30,046	19,963	31,017	20,119	19,568	5.61	-2.74
Mexico		1,043	619	1,047	1,123	1,024	0.29	-8.82
United States of America		266,793	165,608	268,224	183,243	267,422	76.68	45.94
Other Americas		**9,859**	**6,995**	**9,858**	**6,352**	**9,458**	**2.71**	**48.90**
Other countries of the Americas		9,859	6,995	9,858	6,352	9,458	2.71	48.90
EUROPE		**23,372**	**21,262**	**24,573**	**26,755**	**31,437**	**9.01**	**17.50**
Western Europe		**10,246**	**14,653**	**12,508**	**14,261**	**18,432**	**5.29**	**29.25**
France		10,246	14,653	12,508	14,261	18,432	5.29	29.25
Other Europe		**13,126**	**6,609**	**12,065**	**12,494**	**13,005**	**3.73**	**4.09**
Other countries of Europe		13,126	6,609	12,065	12,494	13,005	3.73	4.09
NOT SPECIFIED		**30,702**	**37,475**	**27,510**	**7,186**	**8,294**	**2.38**	**15.42**
Other countries of the World		30,702	37,475	27,510	7,186	8,294	2.38	15.42

HONDURAS

1. Arrivals of non-resident tourists at national borders, by nationality

		2007	2008	2009	2010	2011	Market share 11	% Change 11-10
TOTAL	(*)	803,550	868,535	835,531	862,548	871,468	100.00	1.03
AFRICA		193	218	303	409	431	0.05	5.38
East Africa		21	22	36	46	49	0.01	6.52
Ethiopia		4	6	8	10	12	0.00	20.00
Kenya		13	11	20	25	26	0.00	4.00
Zimbabwe		4	5	8	11	11	0.00	
Central Africa		7	8	12	15	16	0.00	6.67
Cameroon		5	5	7	10	10	0.00	
Congo		1	1	2	2	2	0.00	
Gabon		1	2	3	3	4	0.00	33.33
North Africa		9	9	13	16	17	0.00	6.25
Algeria		1	1	1	1	2	0.00	100.00
Morocco		7	7	10	13	13	0.00	
Tunisia		1	1	2	2	2	0.00	
Southern Africa		126	142	195	266	279	0.03	4.89
South Africa		126	142	195	266	279	0.03	4.89
West Africa		20	25	30	42	46	0.01	9.52
Ghana		1	3	3	5	5	0.00	
Côte d'Ivoire		3	3	4	6	6	0.00	
Nigeria		16	19	23	31	35	0.00	12.90
Other Africa		10	12	17	24	24	0.00	
Other countries of Africa		10	12	17	24	24	0.00	
AMERICAS		731,991	789,779	744,218	753,154	758,751	87.07	0.74
Caribbean		3,668	3,203	5,226	7,060	6,479	0.74	-8.23
Antigua and Barbuda		6	5	8	10	9	0.00	-10.00
Bahamas		31	29	46	64	59	0.01	-7.81
Barbados		15	13	19	26	23	0.00	-11.54
Bermuda		1	1	1	2	1	0.00	-50.00
Cayman Islands		1,114	961	1,544	2,058	1,912	0.22	-7.09
Cuba		952	838	1,381	1,874	1,731	0.20	-7.63
Dominica		9	11	17	24	19	0.00	-20.83
Dominican Republic		929	833	1,382	1,846	1,694	0.19	-8.23
Haiti		158	140	220	321	283	0.03	-11.84
Jamaica		171	151	251	333	308	0.04	-7.51
Puerto Rico		83	73	114	155	143	0.02	-7.74
Saint Vincent and the Grenadines		8	8	12	14	12	0.00	-14.29
Trinidad and Tobago		47	45	72	97	86	0.01	-11.34
Other countries of the Caribbean		144	95	159	236	199	0.02	-15.68
Central America		408,839	453,076	394,717	434,800	409,642	47.01	-5.79
Belize		2,093	2,303	1,986	2,179	2,057	0.24	-5.60
Costa Rica		22,816	25,157	21,831	24,073	22,825	2.62	-5.18
El Salvador		151,227	167,427	145,157	159,755	150,343	17.25	-5.89
Guatemala		115,442	127,484	111,220	122,641	115,768	13.28	-5.60
Nicaragua		108,993	121,583	106,598	117,342	110,299	12.66	-6.00
Panama		8,268	9,122	7,925	8,810	8,350	0.96	-5.22
North America		306,235	320,423	325,248	285,593	316,620	36.33	10.86
Canada		17,504	18,606	19,062	16,838	18,530	2.13	10.05
Mexico		22,537	23,379	23,513	20,613	22,968	2.64	11.42
Saint Pierre and Miquelon		5	6	6	5	5	0.00	
United States of America		266,189	278,432	282,667	248,137	275,117	31.57	10.87
South America		13,249	13,077	19,027	25,701	26,010	2.98	1.20
Argentina		2,549	2,515	3,690	4,990	5,046	0.58	1.12
Bolivia		504	491	697	936	960	0.11	2.56
Brazil		1,361	1,344	1,957	2,658	2,684	0.31	0.98

HONDURAS

1. Arrivals of non-resident tourists at national borders, by nationality

	2007	2008	2009	2010	2011	Market share 11	% Change 11-10
Chile	1,652	1,634	2,381	3,209	3,257	0.37	1.50
Colombia	3,156	3,114	4,545	6,143	6,210	0.71	1.09
Ecuador	934	930	1,341	1,803	1,817	0.21	0.78
French Guiana	11	11	15	21	21	0.00	
Guyana	31	32	46	58	57	0.01	-1.72
Paraguay	159	162	229	306	307	0.04	0.33
Peru	1,139	1,118	1,625	2,190	2,220	0.25	1.37
Suriname	6	7	10	13	12	0.00	-7.69
Uruguay	426	420	605	823	829	0.10	0.73
Venezuela	1,321	1,299	1,886	2,551	2,590	0.30	1.53
EAST ASIA AND THE PACIFIC	**6,379**	**8,453**	**10,475**	**14,143**	**16,346**	**1.88**	**15.58**
North-East Asia	**4,632**	**6,146**	**7,642**	**10,337**	**11,933**	**1.37**	**15.44**
China	1,137	1,489	1,831	2,539	2,865	0.33	12.84
Taiwan, Province of China	47	62	76	87	130	0.01	49.43
Hong Kong, China	9	10	12	19	20	0.00	5.26
Japan	1,737	2,319	2,873	3,889	4,466	0.51	14.84
Korea, Dem. People's Republic of	981	1,347	1,670	2,280	2,660	0.31	16.67
Korea, Republic of	721	919	1,180	1,523	1,792	0.21	17.66
South-East Asia	**350**	**468**	**560**	**767**	**881**	**0.10**	**14.86**
Indonesia	48	63	68	90	101	0.01	12.22
Malaysia	47	63	77	104	122	0.01	17.31
Philippines	244	329	398	549	633	0.07	15.30
Thailand	11	13	17	24	25	0.00	4.17
Australasia	**1,268**	**1,661**	**2,054**	**2,740**	**3,191**	**0.37**	**16.46**
Australia	1,017	1,331	1,650	2,206	2,569	0.29	16.46
New Zealand	251	330	404	534	622	0.07	16.48
Other East Asia and the Pacific	**129**	**178**	**219**	**299**	**341**	**0.04**	**14.05**
Other countries of Asia	129	178	219	299	341	0.04	14.05
EUROPE	**64,289**	**69,160**	**79,375**	**93,268**	**94,099**	**10.80**	**0.89**
Central/Eastern Europe	**1,512**	**1,637**	**1,890**	**2,172**	**2,235**	**0.26**	**2.90**
Bulgaria	399	430	491	544	582	0.07	6.99
Czech Republic/Slovakia	245	269	316	371	373	0.04	0.54
Hungary	63	68	78	90	94	0.01	4.44
Poland	326	349	400	486	488	0.06	0.41
Romania	77	86	100	119	121	0.01	1.68
Russian Federation	306	331	382	421	433	0.05	2.85
Ukraine	96	104	123	141	144	0.02	2.13
Northern Europe	**13,914**	**14,995**	**17,289**	**20,073**	**20,255**	**2.32**	**0.91**
Denmark	1,464	1,573	1,798	2,120	2,146	0.25	1.23
Finland	525	569	651	757	763	0.09	0.79
Iceland	84	93	107	124	125	0.01	0.81
Ireland	704	756	875	1,004	1,027	0.12	2.29
Norway	1,026	1,114	1,297	1,489	1,494	0.17	0.34
Sweden	2,086	2,261	2,580	2,969	2,958	0.34	-0.37
United Kingdom	8,025	8,629	9,981	11,610	11,742	1.35	1.14
Southern Europe	**25,251**	**27,034**	**30,919**	**36,738**	**37,149**	**4.26**	**1.12**
Andorra	9	9	11	13	13	0.00	
Croatia	32	36	43	52	48	0.01	-7.69
Greece	189	206	239	286	274	0.03	-4.20
Italy	14,230	15,285	17,392	20,773	20,977	2.41	0.98
Malta	10	11	12	14	13	0.00	-7.14
Portugal	252	270	309	371	365	0.04	-1.62
Spain	10,529	11,217	12,913	15,229	15,459	1.77	1.51
Western Europe	**22,318**	**24,119**	**27,707**	**32,446**	**32,577**	**3.74**	**0.40**
Austria	676	727	829	971	981	0.11	1.03

HONDURAS

1. Arrivals of non-resident tourists at national borders, by nationality

	2007	2008	2009	2010	2011	Market share 11	% Change 11-10
Belgium	1,583	1,693	1,966	2,315	2,351	0.27	1.56
France	4,715	5,103	5,878	6,853	6,872	0.79	0.28
Germany	8,382	9,067	10,459	12,183	12,219	1.40	0.30
Luxembourg	19	19	24	26	26	0.00	
Netherlands	4,361	4,715	5,359	6,381	6,393	0.73	0.19
Switzerland	2,582	2,795	3,192	3,717	3,735	0.43	0.48
East Mediterranean Europe	**1,265**	**1,343**	**1,532**	**1,797**	**1,840**	**0.21**	**2.39**
Cyprus	6	6	8	8	8	0.00	
Israel	1,202	1,277	1,457	1,713	1,756	0.20	2.51
Turkey	57	60	67	76	76	0.01	
Other Europe	**29**	**32**	**38**	**42**	**43**	**0.00**	**2.38**
Other countries of Europe	29	32	38	42	43	0.00	2.38
MIDDLE EAST	**92**	**119**	**156**	**210**	**245**	**0.03**	**16.67**
Palestine	33	43	58	77	90	0.01	16.88
Jordan	16	21	27	36	41	0.00	13.89
Kuwait	4	6	8	9	14	0.00	55.56
Lebanon	9	12	16	21	23	0.00	9.52
Libya	1	1	2	2	3	0.00	50.00
Syrian Arab Republic	4	4	5	8	9	0.00	12.50
Egypt	25	32	40	57	65	0.01	14.04
SOUTH ASIA	**228**	**302**	**376**	**513**	**598**	**0.07**	**16.57**
Bangladesh	5	6	8	12	12	0.00	
Sri Lanka	12	15	19	25	29	0.00	16.00
India	180	242	297	408	479	0.05	17.40
Iran, Islamic Republic of	10	11	17	22	25	0.00	13.64
Pakistan	21	28	35	46	53	0.01	15.22
NOT SPECIFIED	**378**	**504**	**628**	**851**	**998**	**0.11**	**17.27**
Other countries of the World	378	504	628	851	998	0.11	17.27

HONG KONG, CHINA

1. Arrivals of non-resident tourists at national borders, by country of residence

	2007	2008	2009	2010	2011	Market share 11	% Change 11-10
TOTAL	17,153,900	17,319,400	16,926,100	20,085,155	22,316,073	100.00	11.11
AFRICA	126,500	119,000	101,700	105,322	98,132	0.44	-6.83
Southern Africa	37,800	33,900	32,100	36,993	38,550	0.17	4.21
South Africa	37,800	33,900	32,100	36,993	38,550	0.17	4.21
Other Africa	88,700	85,100	69,600	68,329	59,582	0.27	-12.80
Other countries of Africa	88,700	85,100	69,600	68,329	59,582	0.27	-12.80
AMERICAS	1,330,100	1,231,800	1,107,600	1,245,553	1,279,072	5.73	2.69
North America	1,220,400	1,119,500	1,016,500	1,129,579	1,152,460	5.16	2.03
Canada	296,300	281,900	260,700	290,827	291,454	1.31	0.22
United States of America	924,100	837,600	755,800	838,752	861,006	3.86	2.65
Other Americas	109,700	112,300	91,100	115,974	126,612	0.57	9.17
Other countries of the Americas	109,700	112,300	91,100	115,974	126,612	0.57	9.17
EAST ASIA AND THE PACIFIC	14,022,400	14,311,900	14,169,300	16,966,228	19,178,636	85.94	13.04
North-East Asia	11,467,000	11,739,900	11,708,400	14,088,673	16,118,154	72.23	14.41
China	9,092,700	9,379,700	9,663,600	11,678,055	13,599,768	60.94	16.46
Taiwan, Province of China	694,800	649,400	613,800	724,561	778,653	3.49	7.47
Japan	846,000	816,800	779,600	823,575	787,220	3.53	-4.41
Korea, Republic of	592,400	637,800	401,600	587,866	670,835	3.01	14.11
Macao, China	241,100	256,200	249,800	274,616	281,678	1.26	2.57
South-East Asia	1,922,000	1,939,100	1,890,100	2,254,040	2,438,931	10.93	8.20
Indonesia	276,900	261,900	263,900	340,147	379,915	1.70	11.69
Malaysia	370,200	372,300	326,300	424,491	452,172	2.03	6.52
Philippines	439,800	451,500	455,800	493,092	542,967	2.43	10.11
Singapore	478,900	479,500	456,700	527,560	585,727	2.62	11.03
Thailand	290,600	298,600	303,200	356,060	380,647	1.71	6.91
Other countries of South-East Asia	65,600	75,300	84,200	112,690	97,503	0.44	-13.48
Australasia	595,600	596,100	535,400	585,199	575,332	2.58	-1.69
Australia	507,100	509,900	462,600	505,907	500,225	2.24	-1.12
New Zealand	88,500	86,200	72,800	79,292	75,107	0.34	-5.28
Other East Asia and the Pacific	37,800	36,800	35,400	38,316	46,219	0.21	20.63
Other countries of Asia	33,800	33,000	31,400	32,222	39,945	0.18	23.97
Other countries of Oceania	4,000	3,800	4,000	6,094	6,274	0.03	2.95
EUROPE	1,368,600	1,325,700	1,217,500	1,317,418	1,335,876	5.99	1.40
Northern Europe	593,100	572,500	515,500	525,472	515,207	2.31	-1.95
United Kingdom	496,900	467,200	415,400	421,566	413,156	1.85	-1.99
Scandinavia	96,200	105,300	100,100	103,906	102,051	0.46	-1.79
Southern Europe	137,800	127,900	119,300	130,783	131,718	0.59	0.71
Italy	79,900	75,300	69,100	76,918	75,509	0.34	-1.83
Spain,Portugal	57,900	52,600	50,200	53,865	56,209	0.25	4.35
Western Europe	513,900	496,600	465,500	507,015	496,148	2.22	-2.14
Austria	18,400	18,600	18,400	20,310	19,156	0.09	-5.68
Belgium	24,500	23,100	23,500	24,977	24,145	0.11	-3.33
France	169,000	168,600	156,300	173,604	168,653	0.76	-2.85
Germany	177,000	170,800	156,500	170,170	163,975	0.73	-3.64
Netherlands	86,700	78,700	73,800	77,895	78,543	0.35	0.83
Switzerland	38,300	36,800	37,000	40,059	41,676	0.19	4.04
Other Europe	123,800	128,700	117,200	154,148	192,803	0.86	25.08
Other countries of Europe	123,800	128,700	117,200	154,148	192,803	0.86	25.08
MIDDLE EAST	101,600	99,500	98,600	114,601	112,259	0.50	-2.04
All countries of Middle East	101,600	99,500	98,600	114,601	112,259	0.50	-2.04
SOUTH ASIA	204,700	231,500	231,400	336,033	312,098	1.40	-7.12
India	204,700	231,500	231,400	336,033	312,098	1.40	-7.12

HONG KONG, CHINA

2. Arrivals of non-resident visitors at national borders, by country of residence

	2007	2008	2009	2010	2011	Market share 11	% Change 11-10
TOTAL	28,169,293	29,506,575	29,590,654	36,030,331	41,921,310	100.00	16.35
AFRICA	231,028	210,251	182,384	204,105	192,854	0.46	-5.51
East Africa	63,355	62,182	52,958	58,583	54,292	0.13	-7.32
Burundi	26	22	20	27	12	0.00	-55.56
Comoros	62	22	29	52	71	0.00	36.54
Ethiopia	1,041	978	905	902	637	0.00	-29.38
Eritrea	32	39	20	30	19	0.00	-36.67
Djibouti	55	50	61	42	88	0.00	109.52
Kenya	8,170	6,529	4,941	4,839	4,955	0.01	2.40
Madagascar	4,190	4,292	4,645	4,277	4,005	0.01	-6.36
Malawi	580	853	1,014	1,200	1,205	0.00	0.42
Mauritius	22,273	22,373	18,421	23,217	21,914	0.05	-5.61
Mozambique	1,039	1,238	1,558	2,100	2,344	0.01	11.62
Rwanda	268	220	352	432	298	0.00	-31.02
Seychelles	458	479	446	572	565	0.00	-1.22
Somalia	25	20	9	6	4	0.00	-33.33
Zimbabwe	1,130	1,091	1,492	2,251	2,273	0.01	0.98
Uganda	5,572	6,062	4,936	4,338	3,991	0.01	-8.00
United Republic of Tanzania	14,988	14,331	11,260	10,745	8,334	0.02	-22.44
Zambia	3,446	3,583	2,849	3,553	3,577	0.01	0.68
Central Africa	5,178	5,025	4,093	3,638	3,142	0.01	-13.63
Angola	654	688	522	538	748	0.00	39.03
Cameroon	1,519	1,635	1,228	706	597	0.00	-15.44
Central African Republic	84	58	86	96	54	0.00	-43.75
Chad	360	314	315	218	135	0.00	-38.07
Congo	568	515	372	270	209	0.00	-22.59
Democratic Republic of the Congo	1,591	1,293	1,165	1,393	1,014	0.00	-27.21
Equatorial Guinea	61	75	74	78	114	0.00	46.15
Gabon	325	422	330	331	253	0.00	-23.56
Sao Tome and Principe	16	25	1	8	18	0.00	125.00
North Africa	31,217	22,875	18,861	20,947	17,841	0.04	-14.83
Algeria	16,837	12,537	10,833	10,943	9,700	0.02	-11.36
Morocco	8,893	6,047	4,854	5,737	4,972	0.01	-13.33
Sudan	123	136	147	102	90	0.00	-11.76
Tunisia	5,364	4,155	3,027	4,165	3,079	0.01	-26.07
Southern Africa	75,176	67,748	65,484	81,785	84,364	0.20	3.15
Botswana	1,383	1,803	2,252	2,838	2,594	0.01	-8.60
Lesotho	184	198	143	274	302	0.00	10.22
Namibia	424	445	546	637	995	0.00	56.20
South Africa	72,897	65,024	62,246	77,658	79,989	0.19	3.00
Swaziland	288	278	297	378	484	0.00	28.04
West Africa	56,102	52,421	40,988	39,152	33,209	0.08	-15.18
Cape Verde	475	446	296	294	238	0.00	-19.05
Benin	2,950	3,074	2,244	2,135	2,217	0.01	3.84
Gambia	2,923	2,327	2,465	2,575	2,412	0.01	-6.33
Ghana	6,667	3,457	873	681	748	0.00	9.84
Guinea	8,228	7,094	6,143	6,056	4,896	0.01	-19.15
Côte d'Ivoire	884	759	450	390	262	0.00	-32.82
Liberia	347	362	252	286	279	0.00	-2.45
Mali	12,141	11,010	8,613	8,559	7,759	0.02	-9.35
Mauritania	595	445	417	464	368	0.00	-20.69
Niger	3,800	4,209	3,446	3,150	2,708	0.01	-14.03
Nigeria	10,501	12,535	9,870	9,189	7,584	0.02	-17.47
Guinea-Bissau	693	953	1,489	876	486	0.00	-44.52
Senegal	1,566	1,777	1,154	962	724	0.00	-24.74
Sierra Leone	325	309	195	283	256	0.00	-9.54

HONG KONG, CHINA

2. Arrivals of non-resident visitors at national borders, by country of residence

	2007	2008	2009	2010	2011	Market share 11	% Change 11-10
Togo	803	847	725	690	605	0.00	-12.32
Burkina Faso	3,204	2,817	2,356	2,562	1,667	0.00	-34.93
Other Africa					6	0.00	
Other countries of Africa					6	0.00	
AMERICAS	**1,783,609**	**1,684,734**	**1,567,807**	**1,749,558**	**1,821,096**	**4.34**	**4.09**
Caribbean	**8,236**	**7,763**	**7,941**	**8,436**	**8,872**	**0.02**	**5.17**
Antigua and Barbuda	159	100	105	156	127	0.00	-18.59
Bahamas	372	515	392	481	513	0.00	6.65
Barbados	234	250	191	215	152	0.00	-29.30
Cuba	252	329	252	349	422	0.00	20.92
Dominica	540	429	416	359	325	0.00	-9.47
Dominican Republic	2,005	1,905	1,874	2,088	2,138	0.01	2.39
Grenada	23	20	31	44	51	0.00	15.91
Haiti	91	92	98	115	126	0.00	9.57
Jamaica	2,799	2,501	2,932	2,869	3,268	0.01	13.91
Saint Kitts and Nevis	82	159	181	264	361	0.00	36.74
Saint Lucia	50	55	68	90	51	0.00	-43.33
Saint Vincent and the Grenadines	37	62	53	40	25	0.00	-37.50
Trinidad and Tobago	1,592	1,346	1,348	1,366	1,313	0.00	-3.88
Central America	**14,470**	**13,456**	**11,258**	**12,560**	**12,706**	**0.03**	**1.16**
Belize	3,708	3,036	2,631	2,529	2,638	0.01	4.31
Costa Rica	3,333	3,248	2,365	3,018	3,237	0.01	7.26
El Salvador	606	612	431	477	522	0.00	9.43
Guatemala	1,537	1,551	1,279	1,393	1,419	0.00	1.87
Honduras	1,662	1,423	944	1,113	1,147	0.00	3.05
Nicaragua	96	93	60	90	101	0.00	12.22
Panama	3,528	3,493	3,548	3,940	3,642	0.01	-7.56
North America	**1,661,800**	**1,556,843**	**1,452,058**	**1,604,013**	**1,652,971**	**3.94**	**3.05**
Canada	395,167	379,046	361,922	404,252	410,591	0.98	1.57
Mexico	35,706	31,433	20,063	28,342	30,044	0.07	6.01
United States of America (*)	1,230,927	1,146,364	1,070,073	1,171,419	1,212,336	2.89	3.49
South America	**99,103**	**106,672**	**96,547**	**124,549**	**146,547**	**0.35**	**17.66**
Argentina	10,515	10,715	9,570	13,281	13,892	0.03	4.60
Bolivia	1,777	1,804	1,750	2,063	2,670	0.01	29.42
Brazil	40,339	43,130	33,730	47,821	60,672	0.14	26.87
Chile	8,251	8,964	8,452	10,215	11,812	0.03	15.63
Colombia	13,260	15,753	15,079	19,760	20,826	0.05	5.39
Ecuador	3,040	3,190	2,742	3,237	3,992	0.01	23.32
French Guiana	5		8	2	7	0.00	250.00
Guyana	481	470	432	460	463	0.00	0.65
Paraguay	1,033	1,003	838	865	905	0.00	4.62
Peru	5,441	5,643	5,708	6,308	6,717	0.02	6.48
Suriname	2,493	2,283	2,873	2,782	3,050	0.01	9.63
Uruguay	1,572	1,527	1,685	2,273	2,402	0.01	5.68
Venezuela	10,896	12,190	13,680	15,482	19,139	0.05	23.62
Other Americas			**3**				
Other countries of the Americas			3				
EAST ASIA AND THE PACIFIC	**23,848,246**	**25,348,204**	**25,659,422**	**31,548,245**	**37,378,369**	**89.16**	**18.48**
North-East Asia	**20,564,915**	**22,043,717**	**22,474,913**	**27,852,166**	**33,418,532**	**79.72**	**19.99**
China	15,485,789	16,862,003	17,956,731	22,684,388	28,100,129	67.03	23.87
Taiwan, Province of China	2,238,731	2,240,481	2,009,644	2,164,750	2,148,733	5.13	-0.74
Japan	1,324,336	1,324,797	1,204,490	1,316,618	1,283,687	3.06	-2.50
Korea, Dem. People's Republic of	77	144	174	69	46	0.00	-33.33
Korea, Republic of	876,231	904,320	618,694	891,024	1,020,996	2.44	14.59
Macao, China	626,025	696,719	671,276	780,293	843,221	2.01	8.06
Mongolia	13,726	15,253	13,904	15,024	21,720	0.05	44.57

HONG KONG, CHINA

2. Arrivals of non-resident visitors at national borders, by country of residence

	2007	2008	2009	2010	2011	Market share 11	% Change 11-10
South-East Asia	**2,526,367**	**2,541,281**	**2,476,546**	**2,927,555**	**3,201,966**	**7.64**	**9.37**
Brunei Darussalam	7,530	9,979	11,675	11,031	10,904	0.03	-1.15
Myanmar	5,831	4,909	5,459	5,821	8,387	0.02	44.08
Cambodia	11,070	12,225	10,588	12,273	12,120	0.03	-1.25
Indonesia	366,217	348,938	353,631	453,235	520,795	1.24	14.91
Lao People's Democratic Republic	1,252	1,015	1,229	1,309	2,441	0.01	86.48
Malaysia	504,487	490,561	441,698	578,877	632,858	1.51	9.33
Philippines	552,942	568,540	563,750	603,030	659,829	1.57	9.42
Timor-Leste	295	268	243	173	135	0.00	-21.97
Singapore	631,963	632,637	623,730	709,777	793,887	1.89	11.85
Viet Nam	57,561	68,908	76,815	102,217	80,113	0.19	-21.62
Thailand	387,219	403,301	387,728	449,812	480,497	1.15	6.82
Australasia	**750,814**	**757,522**	**701,668**	**758,837**	**747,687**	**1.78**	**-1.47**
Australia	633,599	643,538	600,085	650,681	644,596	1.54	-0.94
New Zealand (*)	117,215	113,984	101,583	108,156	103,091	0.25	-4.68
Melanesia	**3,457**	**3,297**	**4,439**	**7,697**	**7,738**	**0.02**	**0.53**
Solomon Islands	86	149	129	121	200	0.00	65.29
Fiji	2,247	2,009	2,498	5,955	5,631	0.01	-5.44
Vanuatu	218	250	245	352	312	0.00	-11.36
Papua New Guinea	906	889	1,567	1,269	1,595	0.00	25.69
Micronesia	**1,737**	**1,411**	**1,070**	**1,116**	**1,396**	**0.00**	**25.09**
Kiribati	237	198	96	246	593	0.00	141.06
Nauru	934	756	624	494	340	0.00	-31.17
Micronesia, Federated States of	167	117	77	100	76	0.00	-24.00
Marshall Islands	399	340	273	276	387	0.00	40.22
Polynesia	**876**	**915**	**739**	**834**	**1,008**	**0.00**	**20.86**
Tonga	634	595	473	532	651	0.00	22.37
Tuvalu	122	178	125	103	111	0.00	7.77
Samoa	120	142	141	199	246	0.00	23.62
Other East Asia and the Pacific	**80**	**61**	**47**	**40**	**42**	**0.00**	**5.00**
Other countries of Oceania	80	61	47	40	42	0.00	5.00
EUROPE	**1,876,672**	**1,810,251**	**1,709,478**	**1,876,192**	**1,912,917**	**4.56**	**1.96**
Central/Eastern Europe	**105,716**	**114,342**	**113,476**	**171,974**	**232,052**	**0.55**	**34.93**
Azerbaijan	307	257	349	543	558	0.00	2.76
Armenia	274	143	131	213	380	0.00	78.40
Bulgaria	4,286	4,792	3,760	4,465	4,673	0.01	4.66
Belarus	645	750	722	1,115	1,354	0.00	21.43
Czech Republic	9,349	9,838	10,185	10,176	11,445	0.03	12.47
Estonia	2,869	3,537	3,619	3,993	3,766	0.01	-5.68
Georgia	224	177	271	262	444	0.00	69.47
Hungary	7,766	8,513	7,748	10,170	9,459	0.02	-6.99
Kazakhstan	2,755	1,619	2,018	2,658	3,207	0.01	20.65
Kyrgyzstan	362	276	209	317	428	0.00	35.02
Latvia	1,874	2,072	2,247	2,190	2,280	0.01	4.11
Lithuania	2,098	2,464	2,526	2,673	3,161	0.01	18.26
Republic of Moldova	164	261	176	219	322	0.00	47.03
Poland	22,852	24,590	21,477	24,641	26,889	0.06	9.12
Romania	7,714	8,372	7,102	9,363	10,162	0.02	8.53
Russian Federation	32,858	37,153	42,980	86,800	131,537	0.31	51.54
Slovakia	3,086	3,353	3,462	4,085	4,351	0.01	6.51
Tajikistan	63	51	57	105	137	0.00	30.48
Turkmenistan	53	15	16	16	124	0.00	675.00
Ukraine	5,310	5,413	3,859	7,321	16,617	0.04	126.98
Uzbekistan	801	670	533	649	758	0.00	16.80
Other countries Central/East Europe	6	26	29				

HONG KONG, CHINA

2. Arrivals of non-resident visitors at national borders, by country of residence

		2007	2008	2009	2010	2011	Market share 11	% Change 11-10
Northern Europe		758,203	730,933	672,389	682,010	673,278	1.61	-1.28
Denmark		30,013	30,618	27,688	29,156	28,781	0.07	-1.29
Finland		21,830	30,162	34,359	33,559	31,356	0.07	-6.56
Iceland		2,169	1,758	1,295	1,415	1,431	0.00	1.13
Ireland		34,589	33,178	26,876	26,657	28,169	0.07	5.67
Norway		18,624	19,673	19,377	20,940	19,870	0.05	-5.11
Sweden		49,810	51,560	48,810	54,590	57,114	0.14	4.62
United Kingdom		601,168	563,984	513,984	515,693	506,557	1.21	-1.77
Southern Europe		224,143	206,034	191,060	212,677	217,394	0.52	2.22
Albania		144	171	309	238	230	0.00	-3.36
Andorra		123	83	136	104	108	0.00	3.85
Bosnia and Herzegovina		427	619	441	498	446	0.00	-10.44
Croatia		2,953	3,423	2,610	2,824	2,962	0.01	4.89
Greece		12,219	10,380	8,397	8,784	8,346	0.02	-4.99
Holy See		10	6	11	5	5	0.00	
Italy		118,841	110,583	103,315	118,915	117,199	0.28	-1.44
Malta		941	830	707	949	798	0.00	-15.91
Portugal		18,639	16,984	15,122	13,623	19,094	0.05	40.16
San Marino		138	141	94	152	111	0.00	-26.97
Slovenia		2,254	2,464	2,253	2,327	2,544	0.01	9.33
Spain		65,131	58,149	56,108	62,350	62,787	0.15	0.70
TFYR of Macedonia		535	517	577	588	590	0.00	0.34
Serbia and Montenegro		1,788	1,684	980	1,320	2,174	0.01	64.70
Western Europe		681,852	657,985	631,970	689,383	676,699	1.61	-1.84
Austria		24,046	24,084	24,116	26,944	25,638	0.06	-4.85
Belgium		32,413	30,489	31,560	33,398	32,783	0.08	-1.84
France	(*)	231,091	229,349	217,568	239,964	233,880	0.56	-2.54
Germany		234,763	224,665	210,828	230,436	223,544	0.53	-2.99
Liechtenstein		223	183	230	282	311	0.00	10.28
Luxembourg		1,507	1,516	1,744	1,941	1,674	0.00	-13.76
Monaco		123	229	376	204	135	0.00	-33.82
Netherlands		110,816	102,310	99,450	106,544	107,564	0.26	0.96
Switzerland		46,870	45,160	46,098	49,670	51,170	0.12	3.02
East Mediterranean Europe		106,758	100,957	100,583	120,148	113,494	0.27	-5.54
Cyprus		2,312	2,140	1,626	1,777	1,920	0.00	8.05
Israel		63,435	62,106	65,266	72,914	69,525	0.17	-4.65
Turkey		41,011	36,711	33,691	45,457	42,049	0.10	-7.50
MIDDLE EAST		79,306	71,180	74,536	90,813	84,564	0.20	-6.88
Bahrain		2,500	2,250	1,664	2,466	2,094	0.00	-15.09
Iraq		121	122	117	175	183	0.00	4.57
Jordan		11,084	12,238	11,588	14,806	17,647	0.04	19.19
Kuwait		4,366	3,510	4,155	5,916	6,878	0.02	16.26
Lebanon		1,574	1,412	1,257	1,349	1,332	0.00	-1.26
Libya		44	51	64	81	11	0.00	-86.42
Oman		1,109	1,217	986	1,387	1,364	0.00	-1.66
Qatar		2,128	2,131	2,087	1,876	2,109	0.01	12.42
Saudi Arabia		19,435	15,693	19,035	28,401	21,192	0.05	-25.38
Syrian Arab Republic		822	665	596	741	651	0.00	-12.15
United Arab Emirates		11,881	12,787	16,195	13,624	14,549	0.03	6.79
Egypt		16,361	11,579	9,505	11,777	10,764	0.03	-8.60
Yemen		7,881	7,525	7,218	8,111	5,735	0.01	-29.29
Other countries of Middle East				69	103	55	0.00	-46.60

HONG KONG, CHINA

2. Arrivals of non-resident visitors at national borders, by country of residence

	2007	2008	2009	2010	2011	Market share 11	% Change 11-10
SOUTH ASIA	350,272	381,797	396,914	561,323	531,401	1.27	-5.33
Afghanistan	72	57	57	80	135	0.00	68.75
Bangladesh	7,339	6,556	6,040	4,968	4,848	0.01	-2.42
Bhutan	710	678	696	767	980	0.00	27.77
Sri Lanka	7,475	6,655	6,040	6,342	6,957	0.02	9.70
India	317,510	350,674	366,646	530,910	498,063	1.19	-6.19
Iran, Islamic Republic of	1,891	1,936	2,035	2,650	3,218	0.01	21.43
Maldives	445	332	348	439	766	0.00	74.49
Nepal	4,220	4,413	5,060	5,454	6,476	0.02	18.74
Pakistan	10,610	10,496	9,992	9,713	9,958	0.02	2.52
NOT SPECIFIED	160	158	113	95	109	0.00	14.74
Other countries of the World	160	158	113	95	109	0.00	14.74

HUNGARY

1. Arrivals of non-resident tourists at national borders, by nationality

	2007	2008	2009	2010	2011	Market share 11	% Change 11-10
TOTAL	8,637,000	8,813,000	9,058,000	9,511,000	10,250,000	100.00	7.77
AFRICA	21,000	20,000	22,000	23,000	26,000	0.25	13.04
Other Africa	21,000	20,000	22,000	23,000	26,000	0.25	13.04
All countries of Africa	21,000	20,000	22,000	23,000	26,000	0.25	13.04
AMERICAS	478,000	541,000	548,000	536,000	606,000	5.91	13.06
North America	340,000	390,000	393,000	390,000	442,000	4.31	13.33
United States of America	340,000	390,000	393,000	390,000	442,000	4.31	13.33
Other Americas	138,000	151,000	155,000	146,000	164,000	1.60	12.33
Other countries of the Americas	138,000	151,000	155,000	146,000	164,000	1.60	12.33
EAST ASIA AND THE PACIFIC	362,000	385,000	389,000	381,000	411,000	4.01	7.87
Australasia	64,000	63,000	63,000	65,000	68,000	0.66	4.62
Australia	64,000	63,000	63,000	65,000	68,000	0.66	4.62
Other East Asia and the Pacific	298,000	322,000	326,000	316,000	343,000	3.35	8.54
All countries of Asia	298,000	322,000	326,000	316,000	343,000	3.35	8.54
EUROPE	7,776,000	7,867,000	8,099,000	8,571,000	9,207,000	89.82	7.42
Central/Eastern Europe	2,383,000	2,423,000	2,421,000	2,657,000	2,806,000	27.38	5.61
Bulgaria	61,000	76,000	51,000	134,000	116,000	1.13	-13.43
Czech Republic	211,000	230,000	250,000	271,000	315,000	3.07	16.24
Poland	369,000	537,000	612,000	556,000	422,000	4.12	-24.10
Romania	1,008,000	718,000	721,000	912,000	1,153,000	11.25	26.43
Russian Federation			70,000				
Slovakia	577,000	657,000	510,000	586,000	600,000	5.85	2.39
Ukraine	157,000	205,000	207,000	198,000	200,000	1.95	1.01
Northern Europe	272,000	304,000	310,000	319,000	338,000	3.30	5.96
United Kingdom	272,000	304,000	310,000	319,000	338,000	3.30	5.96
Southern Europe	713,000	633,000	645,000	689,000	821,000	8.01	19.16
Croatia	54,000	41,000	53,000	32,000	54,000	0.53	68.75
Italy	337,000	357,000	373,000	330,000	428,000	4.18	29.70
Slovenia	14,000	16,000	8,000	14,000	6,000	0.06	-57.14
Serbia and Montenegro	308,000	219,000	211,000	313,000	333,000	3.25	6.39
Western Europe	3,575,000	3,582,000	3,714,000	3,850,000	4,016,000	39.18	4.31
Austria	979,000	918,000	922,000	935,000	965,000	9.41	3.21
France	199,000	231,000	232,000	250,000	283,000	2.76	13.20
Germany	2,038,000	2,087,000	2,182,000	2,266,000	2,287,000	22.31	0.93
Netherlands	188,000	187,000	203,000	224,000	262,000	2.56	16.96
Switzerland	171,000	159,000	175,000	175,000	219,000	2.14	25.14
Other Europe	833,000	925,000	1,009,000	1,056,000	1,226,000	11.96	16.10
Other countries of Europe	833,000	925,000	1,009,000	1,056,000	1,226,000	11.96	16.10

HUNGARY

2. Arrivals of non-resident visitors at national borders, by nationality

	2007	2008	2009	2010	2011	Market share 11	% Change 11-10
TOTAL	39,380,000	39,554,000	40,624,000	39,905,000	41,304,000	100.00	3.51
AFRICA	22,000	21,000	22,000	23,000	26,000	0.06	13.04
Other Africa	22,000	21,000	22,000	23,000	26,000	0.06	13.04
All countries of Africa	22,000	21,000	22,000	23,000	26,000	0.06	13.04
AMERICAS	533,000	548,000	557,000	547,000	615,000	1.49	12.43
North America	387,000	396,000	397,000	391,000	443,000	1.07	13.30
United States of America	387,000	396,000	397,000	391,000	443,000	1.07	13.30
Other Americas	146,000	152,000	160,000	156,000	172,000	0.42	10.26
Other countries of the Americas	146,000	152,000	160,000	156,000	172,000	0.42	10.26
EAST ASIA AND THE PACIFIC	440,000	433,000	439,000	448,000	515,000	1.25	14.96
Australasia	68,000	64,000	63,000	65,000	68,000	0.16	4.62
Australia	68,000	64,000	63,000	65,000	68,000	0.16	4.62
Other East Asia and the Pacific	372,000	369,000	376,000	383,000	447,000	1.08	16.71
All countries of Asia	372,000	369,000	376,000	383,000	447,000	1.08	16.71
EUROPE	38,385,000	38,552,000	39,606,000	38,887,000	40,148,000	97.20	3.24
Central/Eastern Europe	20,652,000	21,447,000	22,546,000	21,571,000	21,858,000	52.92	1.33
Bulgaria	1,212,000	1,243,000	1,234,000	1,191,000	1,380,000	3.34	15.87
Czech Republic	932,000	1,086,000	1,077,000	1,003,000	916,000	2.22	-8.67
Poland	1,293,000	1,526,000	1,566,000	1,540,000	1,331,000	3.22	-13.57
Romania	7,990,000	8,079,000	7,783,000	7,614,000	7,575,000	18.34	-0.51
Russian Federation			106,000				
Slovakia	7,805,000	8,142,000	9,095,000	8,404,000	8,825,000	21.37	5.01
Ukraine	1,420,000	1,371,000	1,685,000	1,819,000	1,831,000	4.43	0.66
Northern Europe	343,000	345,000	359,000	356,000	395,000	0.96	10.96
United Kingdom	343,000	345,000	359,000	356,000	395,000	0.96	10.96
Southern Europe	5,159,000	4,354,000	4,217,000	4,153,000	4,952,000	11.99	19.24
Croatia	1,119,000	990,000	971,000	868,000	934,000	2.26	7.60
Italy	617,000	616,000	625,000	581,000	663,000	1.61	14.11
Slovenia	496,000	469,000	418,000	375,000	391,000	0.95	4.27
Serbia and Montenegro	2,927,000	2,279,000	2,203,000	2,329,000	2,964,000	7.18	27.26
Western Europe	10,473,000	10,401,000	10,490,000	10,724,000	10,665,000	25.82	-0.55
Austria	6,510,000	6,397,000	6,437,000	6,696,000	6,649,000	16.10	-0.70
France	341,000	350,000	364,000	351,000	391,000	0.95	11.40
Germany	3,059,000	3,103,000	3,130,000	3,135,000	3,026,000	7.33	-3.48
Netherlands	321,000	307,000	306,000	320,000	326,000	0.79	1.88
Switzerland	242,000	244,000	253,000	222,000	273,000	0.66	22.97
Other Europe	1,758,000	2,005,000	1,994,000	2,083,000	2,278,000	5.52	9.36
Other countries of Europe	1,758,000	2,005,000	1,994,000	2,083,000	2,278,000	5.52	9.36

HUNGARY

3. Arrivals of non-resident tourists in hotels and similar establishments, by nationality

	2007	2008	2009	2010	2011	Market share 11	% Change 11-10
TOTAL	3,130,999	3,196,784	2,914,328	3,183,753	3,518,363	100.00	10.51
AFRICA	9,341	8,772	9,571	9,947	11,400	0.32	14.61
Other Africa	9,341	8,772	9,571	9,947	11,400	0.32	14.61
All countries of Africa	9,341	8,772	9,571	9,947	11,400	0.32	14.61
AMERICAS	244,563	231,431	182,413	214,547	242,138	6.88	12.86
North America	214,644	201,119	155,707	184,479	199,950	5.68	8.39
Canada	20,821	20,193	17,665	21,039	24,128	0.69	14.68
United States of America	193,823	180,926	138,042	163,440	175,822	5.00	7.58
Other Americas	29,919	30,312	26,706	30,068	42,188	1.20	40.31
Other countries of the Americas	29,919	30,312	26,706	30,068	42,188	1.20	40.31
EAST ASIA AND THE PACIFIC	112,539	99,409	89,195	98,067	96,087	2.73	-2.02
North-East Asia	93,912	74,520	70,422	76,317	69,154	1.97	-9.39
Japan	93,912	74,520	70,422	76,317	69,154	1.97	-9.39
Australasia	18,627	24,889	18,773	21,750	26,933	0.77	23.83
Australia	18,627	24,889	18,773	21,750	26,933	0.77	23.83
EUROPE	2,598,779	2,733,794	2,511,491	2,656,958	2,931,505	83.32	10.33
Central/Eastern Europe	542,820	667,003	647,068	725,302	839,953	23.87	15.81
Bulgaria	20,929	24,958	22,690	24,805	28,742	0.82	15.87
Czech Republic	69,620	94,129	115,168	127,431	154,907	4.40	21.56
Poland	83,356	111,685	103,917	115,761	133,278	3.79	15.13
Romania	188,626	231,051	191,318	195,544	201,579	5.73	3.09
Russian Federation	66,030	87,287	81,794	102,043	120,917	3.44	18.50
Slovakia	42,558	47,473	61,563	67,047	86,011	2.44	28.28
Ukraine	71,701	70,420	70,618	92,671	114,519	3.25	23.58
Northern Europe	383,965	412,275	341,800	353,109	382,369	10.87	8.29
Denmark	30,537	29,590	28,550	30,214	30,465	0.87	0.83
Finland	42,953	38,978	40,683	36,612	37,703	1.07	2.98
Norway	28,878	37,505	32,237	29,730	34,856	0.99	17.24
Sweden	59,286	59,733	55,833	56,182	65,785	1.87	17.09
United Kingdom	222,311	246,469	184,497	200,371	213,560	6.07	6.58
Southern Europe	452,329	425,258	384,787	412,039	471,352	13.40	14.39
Croatia	28,798	30,988	26,210	29,419	31,846	0.91	8.25
Greece	38,181	37,675	35,427	35,040	40,796	1.16	16.43
Italy	182,654	166,283	165,085	175,412	187,503	5.33	6.89
Serbia			28,484	43,824	54,456	1.55	24.26
Slovenia	18,344	19,449	18,629	21,286	25,083	0.71	17.84
Spain	147,735	139,234	110,952	107,058	131,668	3.74	22.99
Serbia and Montenegro	36,617	31,629					
Western Europe	1,035,600	990,537	954,389	1,044,024	1,073,518	30.51	2.83
Austria	218,953	221,061	234,358	248,742	269,049	7.65	8.16
Belgium	44,105	41,352	39,585	44,673	51,203	1.46	14.62
France	129,952	127,195	125,694	127,364	138,902	3.95	9.06
Germany	527,450	489,984	446,624	466,939	479,212	13.62	2.63
Netherlands	66,846	65,893	59,651	89,565	80,569	2.29	-10.04
Switzerland	48,294	45,052	48,477	66,741	54,583	1.55	-18.22
East Mediterranean Europe	68,261	68,517	63,489	85,204	90,116	2.56	5.76
Israel	47,691	41,525	42,027	50,956	50,970	1.45	0.03
Turkey	20,570	26,992	21,462	34,248	39,146	1.11	14.30
Other Europe	115,804	170,204	119,958	37,280	74,197	2.11	99.03
Other countries of Europe	115,804	170,204	119,958	37,280	74,197	2.11	99.03
NOT SPECIFIED	165,777	123,378	121,658	204,234	237,233	6.74	16.16
Other countries of the World	165,777	123,378	121,658	204,234	237,233	6.74	16.16

HUNGARY

4. Arrivals of non-resident tourists in all types of accommodation establishments, by nationality

		2007	2008	2009	2010	2011	Market share 11	% Change 11-10
TOTAL	(*)	3,451,186	3,516,030	3,227,942	3,462,021	3,821,751	100.00	10.39
AFRICA		9,540	9,091	9,925	10,096	11,775	0.31	16.63
Other Africa		9,540	9,091	9,925	10,096	11,775	0.31	16.63
All countries of Africa		9,540	9,091	9,925	10,096	11,775	0.31	16.63
AMERICAS		252,473	238,414	187,101	218,240	242,920	6.36	11.31
North America		220,596	206,129	158,738	187,007	202,767	5.31	8.43
Canada		22,165	21,375	18,403	21,796	24,786	0.65	13.72
United States of America		198,431	184,754	140,335	165,211	177,981	4.66	7.73
Other Americas		31,877	32,285	28,363	31,233	40,153	1.05	28.56
Other countries of the Americas		31,877	32,285	28,363	31,233	40,153	1.05	28.56
EAST ASIA AND THE PACIFIC		116,151	102,804	91,807	100,527	98,532	2.58	-1.98
North-East Asia		94,894	75,261	71,124	76,862	69,724	1.82	-9.29
Japan		94,894	75,261	71,124	76,862	69,724	1.82	-9.29
Australasia		21,257	27,543	20,683	23,665	28,808	0.75	21.73
Australia		21,257	27,543	20,683	23,665	28,808	0.75	21.73
EUROPE		3,073,022	3,040,128	2,815,773	2,927,419	3,225,209	84.39	10.17
Central/Eastern Europe		629,552	767,006	753,458	821,967	948,785	24.83	15.43
Bulgaria		22,117	25,620	23,500	25,407	29,351	0.77	15.52
Czech Republic		83,339	111,104	135,715	148,623	178,585	4.67	20.16
Poland		117,778	155,688	151,674	155,983	178,607	4.67	14.50
Romania		200,681	245,521	204,436	207,974	216,164	5.66	3.94
Russian Federation		70,660	90,816	82,982	103,766	123,394	3.23	18.92
Slovakia		58,806	64,894	82,773	85,558	105,495	2.76	23.30
Ukraine		76,171	73,363	72,378	94,656	117,189	3.07	23.81
Northern Europe		415,258	443,329	366,885	374,116	405,568	10.61	8.41
Denmark		43,827	44,151	39,001	38,473	40,233	1.05	4.57
Finland		45,143	41,269	42,827	38,747	40,320	1.06	4.06
Norway		30,025	38,815	33,018	30,560	35,523	0.93	16.24
Sweden		62,186	62,426	58,359	58,212	68,067	1.78	16.93
United Kingdom		234,077	256,668	193,680	208,124	221,425	5.79	6.39
Southern Europe		473,335	441,439	401,260	427,578	490,656	12.84	14.75
Croatia		31,428	32,946	27,714	30,615	33,190	0.87	8.41
Greece		38,637	38,290	35,849	35,422	41,901	1.10	18.29
Italy		191,381	172,959	173,161	183,259	197,495	5.17	7.77
Serbia				29,721	45,639	56,506	1.48	23.81
Slovenia		20,233	21,468	21,134	23,378	27,571	0.72	17.94
Spain		152,176	142,416	113,681	109,265	133,993	3.51	22.63
Serbia and Montenegro		39,480	33,360					
Western Europe		1,191,533	1,139,689	1,103,623	1,136,390	1,208,229	31.61	6.32
Austria		246,042	246,108	259,108	272,579	294,931	7.72	8.20
Belgium		51,360	49,525	46,522	51,199	57,920	1.52	13.13
France		141,108	137,408	138,554	139,851	150,733	3.94	7.78
Germany		608,256	564,876	520,280	528,753	542,333	14.19	2.57
Netherlands		92,339	93,084	86,927	89,565	103,947	2.72	16.06
Switzerland		52,428	48,688	52,232	54,443	58,365	1.53	7.20
East Mediterranean Europe		69,230	69,606	64,415	86,057	91,679	2.40	6.53
Israel		48,239	41,804	42,405	51,220	51,644	1.35	0.83
Turkey		20,991	27,802	22,010	34,837	40,035	1.05	14.92
Other Europe		294,114	179,059	126,132	81,311	80,292	2.10	-1.25
Other countries of Europe		294,114	179,059	126,132	81,311	80,292	2.10	-1.25
NOT SPECIFIED			125,593	123,336	205,739	243,315	6.37	18.26
Other countries of the World			125,593	123,336	205,739	243,315	6.37	18.26

HUNGARY

5. Overnight stays of non-resident tourists in hotels and similar establishments, by nationality

	2007	2008	2009	2010	2011	Market share 11	% Change 11-10
TOTAL	8,635,432	8,488,504	7,773,329	8,316,706	9,049,109	100.00	8.81
AFRICA	31,860	26,807	28,315	28,972	32,381	0.36	11.77
Other Africa	31,860	26,807	28,315	28,972	32,381	0.36	11.77
All countries of Africa	31,860	26,807	28,315	28,972	32,381	0.36	11.77
AMERICAS	668,998	604,528	485,368	550,633	606,830	6.71	10.21
North America	584,469	527,444	412,744	472,962	481,637	5.32	1.83
Canada	61,300	58,052	50,865	61,184	38,887	0.43	-36.44
United States of America	523,169	469,392	361,879	411,778	442,750	4.89	7.52
Other Americas	84,529	77,084	72,624	77,671	125,193	1.38	61.18
Other countries of the Americas	84,529	77,084	72,624	77,671	125,193	1.38	61.18
EAST ASIA AND THE PACIFIC	256,908	212,242	185,957	202,183	197,889	2.19	-2.12
North-East Asia	206,400	152,507	139,650	145,782	133,383	1.47	-8.51
Japan	206,400	152,507	139,650	145,782	133,383	1.47	-8.51
Australasia	50,508	59,735	46,307	56,401	64,506	0.71	14.37
Australia	50,508	59,735	46,307	56,401	64,506	0.71	14.37
EUROPE	6,902,003	7,399,314	6,835,685	7,069,678	7,675,611	84.82	8.57
Central/Eastern Europe	1,042,053	1,525,927	1,464,910	1,677,433	1,988,959	21.98	18.57
Bulgaria	36,228	40,884	36,692	40,363	46,792	0.52	15.93
Czech Republic	187,602	256,796	318,781	365,528	436,830	4.83	19.51
Poland	13,482	279,632	240,593	262,951	303,445	3.35	15.40
Romania	321,195	392,477	329,784	336,707	371,405	4.10	10.31
Russian Federation	233,487	301,884	273,503	366,850	451,762	4.99	23.15
Slovakia	93,805	98,318	129,017	143,945	190,760	2.11	32.52
Ukraine	156,254	155,936	136,540	161,089	187,965	2.08	16.68
Northern Europe	1,004,226	1,110,204	957,323	952,168	1,016,500	11.23	6.76
Denmark	106,340	98,742	92,387	95,861	93,296	1.03	-2.68
Finland	131,843	113,326	121,467	110,951	112,380	1.24	1.29
Norway	92,918	122,038	105,990	98,273	111,958	1.24	13.93
Sweden	80,270	173,148	162,166	162,052	185,170	2.05	14.27
United Kingdom	592,855	602,950	475,313	485,031	513,696	5.68	5.91
Southern Europe	1,251,718	1,066,075	966,244	1,019,444	1,139,061	12.59	11.73
Croatia	171,712	85,781	58,010	52,425	58,672	0.65	11.92
Greece	97,780	96,520	92,239	89,828	103,515	1.14	15.24
Italy	479,288	431,355	439,644	473,325	497,632	5.50	5.14
Serbia			57,158	85,099	104,301	1.15	22.56
Slovenia	38,358	36,179	34,888	44,575	49,089	0.54	10.13
Spain	384,310	349,267	284,305	274,192	325,852	3.60	18.84
Serbia and Montenegro	80,270	66,973					
Western Europe	3,243,555	3,086,532	2,966,372	3,057,326	3,154,810	34.86	3.19
Austria	583,148	568,410	612,313	642,781	687,892	7.60	7.02
Belgium	119,780	114,204	109,171	121,516	130,676	1.44	7.54
France	318,502	309,650	316,279	325,358	347,309	3.84	6.75
Germany	1,999,729	1,776,486	1,618,558	1,631,723	1,624,048	17.95	-0.47
Netherlands	62,047	174,605	158,134	173,896	202,135	2.23	16.24
Switzerland	160,349	143,177	151,917	162,052	162,750	1.80	0.43
East Mediterranean Europe	207,610	192,008	185,442	326,027	253,624	2.80	-22.21
Israel	152,841	127,361	135,885	164,938	165,843	1.83	0.55
Turkey	54,769	64,647	49,557	161,089	87,781	0.97	-45.51
Other Europe	152,841	418,568	295,394	37,280	122,657	1.36	229.02
Other countries of Europe	152,841	418,568	295,394	37,280	122,657	1.36	229.02
NOT SPECIFIED	775,663	245,613	238,004	465,240	536,398	5.93	15.29
Other countries of the World	775,663	245,613	238,004	465,240	536,398	5.93	15.29

HUNGARY

6. Overnight stays of non-resident tourists in all types of accommodation establishments, by nationality

	2007	2008	2009	2010	2011	Market share 11	% Change 11-10
TOTAL (*)	10,170,808	10,009,531	9,220,148	9,613,728	10,410,774	100.00	8.29
AFRICA	32,281	27,545	29,759	29,377	33,368	0.32	13.59
Other Africa	32,281	27,545	29,759	29,377	33,368	0.32	13.59
All countries of Africa	32,281	27,545	29,759	29,377	33,368	0.32	13.59
AMERICAS	686,512	621,618	496,724	562,147	619,267	5.95	10.16
North America	597,949	540,543	420,976	481,793	520,328	5.00	8.00
Canada	64,054	60,902	52,405	63,528	70,394	0.68	10.81
United States of America	533,895	479,641	368,571	418,265	449,934	4.32	7.57
Other Americas	88,563	81,075	75,748	80,354	98,939	0.95	23.13
Other countries of the Americas	88,563	81,075	75,748	80,354	98,939	0.95	23.13
EAST ASIA AND THE PACIFIC	264,279	219,363	192,130	208,421	203,628	1.96	-2.30
North-East Asia	208,630	154,248	141,170	147,423	134,717	1.29	-8.62
Japan	208,630	154,248	141,170	147,423	134,717	1.29	-8.62
Australasia	55,649	65,115	50,960	60,998	68,911	0.66	12.97
Australia	55,649	65,115	50,960	60,998	68,911	0.66	12.97
EUROPE	8,765,393	8,887,841	8,259,704	8,514,590	9,010,668	86.55	5.83
Central/Eastern Europe	1,501,566	1,827,441	1,790,603	1,969,392	2,321,340	22.30	17.87
Bulgaria	38,475	42,157	38,316	42,150	48,308	0.46	14.61
Czech Republic	229,617	311,430	385,272	436,071	514,308	4.94	17.94
Poland	312,963	422,017	393,422	393,513	448,060	4.30	13.86
Romania	352,652	430,524	369,782	370,014	415,493	3.99	12.29
Russian Federation	266,297	316,202	278,833	374,026	461,953	4.44	23.51
Slovakia	132,158	141,029	182,950	186,946	236,311	2.27	26.41
Ukraine	169,404	164,082	142,028	166,672	196,907	1.89	18.14
Northern Europe	1,243,615	1,263,418	1,076,805	1,056,682	1,131,776	10.87	7.11
Denmark	209,030	208,677	169,644	158,707	162,864	1.56	2.62
Finland	136,955	118,923	127,176	117,858	121,890	1.17	3.42
Norway	96,989	127,065	108,534	101,356	114,464	1.10	12.93
Sweden	180,423	181,660	169,936	169,013	193,588	1.86	14.54
United Kingdom	620,218	627,093	501,515	509,748	538,970	5.18	5.73
Southern Europe	1,188,843	1,107,126	1,010,473	1,064,731	1,201,761	11.54	12.87
Croatia	67,445	90,907	62,147	55,614	62,242	0.60	11.92
Greece	99,365	100,206	93,787	91,650	114,119	1.10	24.52
Italy	499,142	447,644	463,921	497,806	528,785	5.08	6.22
Serbia			59,828	90,006	109,055	1.05	21.16
Slovenia	42,649	40,763	40,408	49,267	55,451	0.53	12.55
Spain	394,247	356,592	290,382	280,388	332,109	3.19	18.45
Serbia and Montenegro	85,995	71,014					
Western Europe	4,364,890	4,056,148	3,881,897	3,863,997	3,957,699	38.02	2.43
Austria	711,413	690,111	734,195	755,553	809,500	7.78	7.14
Belgium	167,743	160,801	144,167	154,686	164,605	1.58	6.41
France	346,110	335,813	355,875	364,106	387,038	3.72	6.30
Germany	2,620,640	2,355,963	2,155,746	2,102,987	2,082,681	20.01	-0.97
Netherlands	342,713	355,593	324,521	318,099	336,532	3.23	5.79
Switzerland	176,271	157,867	167,393	168,566	177,343	1.70	5.21
East Mediterranean Europe	213,384	195,211	187,581	243,826	258,765	2.49	6.13
Israel	157,524	128,002	136,872	166,009	168,081	1.61	1.25
Turkey	55,860	67,209	50,709	77,817	90,684	0.87	16.53
Other Europe	253,095	438,497	312,345	315,962	139,327	1.34	-55.90
Other countries of Europe	253,095	438,497	312,345	315,962	139,327	1.34	-55.90
NOT SPECIFIED	422,343	253,164	241,831	299,193	543,843	5.22	81.77
Other countries of the World	422,343	253,164	241,831	299,193	543,843	5.22	81.77

ICELAND

1. Arrivals of non-resident tourists at national borders, by nationality

		2007	2008	2009	2010	2011	Market share 11	% Change 11-10
TOTAL	(*)	485,000	502,000	493,941	488,623	565,611	100.00	15.76
AMERICAS		58,252	51,101	54,998	64,652	95,547	16.89	47.79
North America		58,252	51,101	54,998	64,652	95,547	16.89	47.79
Canada		6,307	10,580	11,074	13,461	17,946	3.17	33.32
United States of America		51,945	40,521	43,924	51,191	77,601	13.72	51.59
EAST ASIA AND THE PACIFIC		15,629	12,492	12,416	10,774	15,686	2.77	45.59
North-East Asia		15,629	12,492	12,416	10,774	15,686	2.77	45.59
China		9,533	5,760	5,368	5,194	8,784	1.55	69.12
Japan		6,096	6,732	7,048	5,580	6,902	1.22	23.69
EUROPE		310,413	319,139	328,176	318,157	354,949	62.75	11.56
Northern Europe		198,882	194,378	185,460	178,132	198,470	35.09	11.42
Denmark		44,205	43,595	43,782	42,593	43,765	7.74	2.75
Finland		9,952	10,858	11,610	11,054	12,057	2.13	9.07
Norway		37,288	36,925	36,703	35,868	41,944	7.42	16.94
Sweden		33,581	32,507	31,585	28,109	32,959	5.83	17.25
United Kingdom		73,856	70,493	61,780	60,508	67,745	11.98	11.96
Southern Europe		20,846	21,384	27,105	22,378	26,824	4.74	19.87
Italy		11,162	10,842	13,224	10,068	12,792	2.26	27.06
Spain		9,684	10,542	13,881	12,310	14,032	2.48	13.99
Western Europe		90,685	103,377	115,611	117,647	129,655	22.92	10.21
France		23,738	27,313	29,786	30,204	36,747	6.50	21.66
Germany		44,358	48,976	56,467	59,453	61,372	10.85	3.23
Netherlands		15,329	19,644	20,217	18,111	20,757	3.67	14.61
Switzerland		7,260	7,444	9,141	9,879	10,779	1.91	9.11
NOT SPECIFIED		100,706	119,268	98,351	95,040	99,429	17.58	4.62
Other countries of the World		100,706	119,268	98,351	95,040	99,429	17.58	4.62

ICELAND

3. Arrivals of non-resident tourists in hotels and similar establishments, by nationality

	2007	2008	2009	2010	2011	Market share 11	% Change 11-10
TOTAL	782,465	806,163	881,354	873,706	1,016,532	100.00	16.35
AFRICA	1,195	1,895	1,852	1,936	1,949	0.19	0.67
Other Africa	1,195	1,895	1,852	1,936	1,949	0.19	0.67
All countries of Africa	1,195	1,895	1,852	1,936	1,949	0.19	0.67
AMERICAS	74,123	73,526	77,548	85,912	133,195	13.10	55.04
North America	72,635	71,567	75,686	83,866	130,162	12.80	55.20
Canada	8,803	12,561	14,068	15,825	21,999	2.16	39.01
United States of America	63,832	59,006	61,618	68,041	108,163	10.64	58.97
Other Americas	1,488	1,959	1,862	2,046	3,033	0.30	48.24
Other countries of the Americas	1,488	1,959	1,862	2,046	3,033	0.30	48.24
EAST ASIA AND THE PACIFIC	25,447	25,578	30,845	27,907	40,478	3.98	45.05
North-East Asia	17,702	14,971	16,133	12,421	17,346	1.71	39.65
China	7,933	4,678	4,922	3,773	6,082	0.60	61.20
Japan	9,769	10,293	11,211	8,648	11,264	1.11	30.25
Australasia	3,132	4,065	4,386	4,782	5,905	0.58	23.48
Australia	3,132	4,065	4,386	4,782	5,905	0.58	23.48
Other East Asia and the Pacific	4,613	6,542	10,326	10,704	17,227	1.69	60.94
Other countries of Asia	4,613	6,542	10,326	10,704	17,227	1.69	60.94
EUROPE	602,855	647,016	717,600	712,565	790,511	77.77	10.94
Northern Europe	235,194	237,244	245,847	235,889	264,669	26.04	12.20
Denmark	45,151	46,333	48,550	50,885	47,790	4.70	-6.08
Finland	10,690	10,241	12,372	11,104	12,820	1.26	15.45
Ireland	4,157	4,470	4,346	3,654	4,011	0.39	9.77
Norway	33,501	33,311	34,644	37,569	43,634	4.29	16.14
Sweden	37,563	36,087	34,967	30,515	37,806	3.72	23.89
United Kingdom	104,132	106,802	110,968	102,162	118,608	11.67	16.10
Southern Europe	70,588	74,735	92,236	66,976	90,229	8.88	34.72
Italy	40,983	39,739	50,370	35,469	47,689	4.69	34.45
Spain	29,605	34,996	41,866	31,507	42,540	4.18	35.02
Western Europe	265,686	297,403	339,647	369,404	382,637	37.64	3.58
Austria	10,171	13,294	18,658	18,387	13,262	1.30	-27.87
Belgium	8,519	10,757	13,532	17,397	16,848	1.66	-3.16
France	58,563	67,544	72,927	76,903	93,681	9.22	21.82
Germany	119,417	132,704	158,693	184,391	179,071	17.62	-2.89
Netherlands	44,808	49,381	48,602	43,336	49,729	4.89	14.75
Switzerland	24,208	23,723	27,235	28,990	30,046	2.96	3.64
Other Europe	31,387	37,634	39,870	40,296	52,976	5.21	31.47
Other countries of Europe	31,387	37,634	39,870	40,296	52,976	5.21	31.47
NOT SPECIFIED	78,845	58,148	53,509	45,386	50,399	4.96	11.05
Other countries of the World	78,845	58,148	53,509	45,386	50,399	4.96	11.05

ICELAND

4. Arrivals of non-resident tourists in all types of accommodation establishments, by nationality

	2007	2008	2009	2010	2011	Market share 11	% Change 11-10
TOTAL	1,057,601	1,106,017	1,280,105	1,223,215	1,418,343	100.00	15.95
AFRICA	1,356	2,219	1,960	2,086	2,322	0.16	11.31
Other Africa	1,356	2,219	1,960	2,086	2,322	0.16	11.31
All countries of Africa	1,356	2,219	1,960	2,086	2,322	0.16	11.31
AMERICAS	85,847	86,773	97,617	104,346	164,155	11.57	57.32
North America	83,945	84,357	95,274	101,919	160,613	11.32	57.59
Canada	11,835	17,603	21,934	22,671	32,807	2.31	44.71
United States of America	72,110	66,754	73,340	79,248	127,806	9.01	61.27
Other Americas	1,902	2,416	2,343	2,427	3,542	0.25	45.94
Other countries of the Americas	1,902	2,416	2,343	2,427	3,542	0.25	45.94
EAST ASIA AND THE PACIFIC	29,481	30,275	38,174	34,330	49,070	3.46	42.94
North-East Asia	19,334	16,557	18,909	14,782	20,519	1.45	38.81
China	8,537	5,352	6,455	4,940	7,836	0.55	58.62
Japan	10,797	11,205	12,454	9,842	12,683	0.89	28.87
Australasia	4,666	5,978	6,588	6,831	8,580	0.60	25.60
Australia	4,666	5,978	6,588	6,831	8,580	0.60	25.60
Other East Asia and the Pacific	5,481	7,740	12,677	12,717	19,971	1.41	57.04
Other countries of Asia	5,481	7,740	12,677	12,717	19,971	1.41	57.04
EUROPE	853,295	918,025	1,066,682	1,025,243	1,128,466	79.56	10.07
Northern Europe	290,347	292,510	301,702	281,319	315,965	22.28	12.32
Denmark	58,092	60,813	64,988	65,146	61,551	4.34	-5.52
Finland	13,341	12,552	15,207	13,513	15,191	1.07	12.42
Ireland	5,754	6,701	6,013	5,054	5,153	0.36	1.96
Norway	38,888	38,121	40,569	42,069	50,303	3.55	19.57
Sweden	46,031	42,551	42,928	36,488	44,124	3.11	20.93
United Kingdom	128,241	131,772	131,997	119,049	139,643	9.85	17.30
Southern Europe	101,505	106,637	134,522	99,601	131,285	9.26	31.81
Italy	56,574	55,172	69,344	50,313	65,762	4.64	30.71
Spain	44,931	51,465	65,178	49,288	65,523	4.62	32.94
Western Europe	417,133	465,943	566,679	576,691	599,260	42.25	3.91
Austria	17,524	20,614	29,275	29,036	22,190	1.56	-23.58
Belgium	15,999	19,034	26,352	31,102	30,160	2.13	-3.03
France	97,593	110,803	134,935	131,002	157,744	11.12	20.41
Germany	184,432	204,591	253,578	269,616	263,413	18.57	-2.30
Netherlands	65,718	74,832	77,165	68,458	77,072	5.43	12.58
Switzerland	35,867	36,069	45,374	47,477	48,681	3.43	2.54
Other Europe	44,310	52,935	63,779	67,632	81,956	5.78	21.18
Other countries of Europe	44,310	52,935	63,779	67,632	81,956	5.78	21.18
NOT SPECIFIED	87,622	68,725	75,672	57,210	74,330	5.24	29.92
Other countries of the World	87,622	68,725	75,672	57,210	74,330	5.24	29.92

ICELAND

5. Overnight stays of non-resident tourists in hotels and similar establishments, by nationality

	2007	2008	2009	2010	2011	Market share 11	% Change 11-10
TOTAL	1,480,025	1,517,102	1,601,754	1,627,732	1,866,432	100.00	14.66
AFRICA	2,775	4,622	4,041	3,513	4,105	0.22	16.85
Other Africa	2,775	4,622	4,041	3,513	4,105	0.22	16.85
All countries of Africa	2,775	4,622	4,041	3,513	4,105	0.22	16.85
AMERICAS	159,680	152,376	156,918	177,406	282,096	15.11	59.01
North America	156,700	148,174	152,952	173,606	276,576	14.82	59.31
Canada	20,384	23,999	25,031	30,469	44,758	2.40	46.90
United States of America	136,316	124,175	127,921	143,137	231,818	12.42	61.96
Other Americas	2,980	4,202	3,966	3,800	5,520	0.30	45.26
Other countries of the Americas	2,980	4,202	3,966	3,800	5,520	0.30	45.26
EAST ASIA AND THE PACIFIC	51,406	48,910	55,974	50,385	70,312	3.77	39.55
North-East Asia	34,618	28,787	30,093	24,672	32,458	1.74	31.56
China	15,826	9,194	9,167	7,761	11,469	0.61	47.78
Japan	18,792	19,593	20,926	16,911	20,989	1.12	24.11
Australasia	6,175	7,360	8,865	8,646	11,263	0.60	30.27
Australia	6,175	7,360	8,865	8,646	11,263	0.60	30.27
Other East Asia and the Pacific	10,613	12,763	17,016	17,067	26,591	1.42	55.80
Other countries of Asia	10,613	12,763	17,016	17,067	26,591	1.42	55.80
EUROPE	1,131,376	1,198,979	1,282,192	1,293,595	1,422,572	76.22	9.97
Northern Europe	525,425	528,210	553,612	540,167	597,417	32.01	10.60
Denmark	90,433	90,735	96,350	102,848	97,359	5.22	-5.34
Finland	26,610	26,753	30,057	29,858	33,843	1.81	13.35
Ireland	9,313	9,558	8,763	8,186	8,309	0.45	1.50
Norway	77,648	78,530	83,317	88,105	103,081	5.52	17.00
Sweden	90,473	89,793	87,597	79,018	93,209	4.99	17.96
United Kingdom	230,948	232,841	247,528	232,152	261,616	14.02	12.69
Southern Europe	97,085	105,360	122,309	93,460	126,267	6.77	35.10
Italy	54,349	54,723	65,506	47,556	65,053	3.49	36.79
Spain	42,736	50,637	56,803	45,904	61,214	3.28	33.35
Western Europe	430,974	479,644	529,840	578,500	599,464	32.12	3.62
Austria	14,983	20,860	26,562	26,894	20,911	1.12	-22.25
Belgium	13,553	17,252	19,994	26,738	25,712	1.38	-3.84
France	83,129	95,341	101,697	110,135	134,161	7.19	21.82
Germany	207,149	226,576	262,256	295,485	290,135	15.54	-1.81
Netherlands	70,924	81,546	79,459	76,657	84,204	4.51	9.85
Switzerland	41,236	38,069	39,872	42,591	44,341	2.38	4.11
Other Europe	77,892	85,765	76,431	81,468	99,424	5.33	22.04
Other countries of Europe	77,892	85,765	76,431	81,468	99,424	5.33	22.04
NOT SPECIFIED	134,788	112,215	102,629	102,833	87,347	4.68	-15.06
Other countries of the World	134,788	112,215	102,629	102,833	87,347	4.68	-15.06

ICELAND

6. Overnight stays of non-resident tourists in all types of accommodation establishments, by nationality

	2007	2008	2009	2010	2011	Market share 11	% Change 11-10
TOTAL	**1,885,138**	**1,942,698**	**2,129,575**	**2,136,308**	**2,435,561**	**100.00**	**14.01**
AFRICA	**3,119**	**4,994**	**4,159**	**3,714**	**4,734**	**0.19**	**27.46**
Other Africa	**3,119**	**4,994**	**4,159**	**3,714**	**4,734**	**0.19**	**27.46**
All countries of Africa	3,119	4,994	4,159	3,714	4,734	0.19	27.46
AMERICAS	**176,857**	**171,158**	**184,803**	**205,654**	**329,923**	**13.55**	**60.43**
North America	**173,338**	**166,352**	**180,045**	**201,158**	**323,594**	**13.29**	**60.87**
Canada	24,687	30,627	35,608	40,681	60,922	2.50	49.76
United States of America	148,651	135,725	144,437	160,477	262,672	10.78	63.68
Other Americas	**3,519**	**4,806**	**4,758**	**4,496**	**6,329**	**0.26**	**40.77**
Other countries of the Americas	3,519	4,806	4,758	4,496	6,329	0.26	40.77
EAST ASIA AND THE PACIFIC	**58,359**	**55,466**	**66,561**	**60,974**	**83,344**	**3.42**	**36.69**
North-East Asia	**37,956**	**31,029**	**34,216**	**28,781**	**37,314**	**1.53**	**29.65**
China	16,750	10,094	11,118	9,453	13,725	0.56	45.19
Japan	21,206	20,935	23,098	19,328	23,589	0.97	22.05
Australasia	**8,665**	**10,152**	**12,125**	**12,146**	**15,776**	**0.65**	**29.89**
Australia	8,665	10,152	12,125	12,146	15,776	0.65	29.89
Other East Asia and the Pacific	**11,738**	**14,285**	**20,220**	**20,047**	**30,254**	**1.24**	**50.92**
Other countries of Asia	11,738	14,285	20,220	20,047	30,254	1.24	50.92
EUROPE	**1,497,939**	**1,583,712**	**1,743,228**	**1,746,118**	**1,900,031**	**78.01**	**8.81**
Northern Europe	**613,011**	**615,857**	**637,363**	**619,523**	**685,250**	**28.14**	**10.61**
Denmark	112,146	113,930	122,266	129,359	122,978	5.05	-4.93
Finland	30,436	30,658	34,029	33,238	37,677	1.55	13.36
Ireland	11,393	12,601	11,081	10,460	10,078	0.41	-3.65
Norway	87,295	87,504	92,493	96,642	114,924	4.72	18.92
Sweden	103,274	98,815	98,890	88,720	103,014	4.23	16.11
United Kingdom	268,467	272,349	278,604	261,104	296,579	12.18	13.59
Southern Europe	**137,540**	**144,534**	**172,655**	**134,618**	**175,958**	**7.22**	**30.71**
Italy	74,401	73,835	88,020	66,523	86,562	3.55	30.12
Spain	63,139	70,699	84,635	68,095	89,396	3.67	31.28
Western Europe	**650,267**	**716,843**	**827,058**	**874,430**	**900,726**	**36.98**	**3.01**
Austria	25,289	30,615	40,115	41,156	32,151	1.32	-21.88
Belgium	23,316	27,657	35,048	44,070	42,308	1.74	-4.00
France	134,494	150,923	175,073	180,137	213,702	8.77	18.63
Germany	307,748	334,841	395,881	425,100	416,428	17.10	-2.04
Netherlands	102,125	118,054	118,597	116,548	127,252	5.22	9.18
Switzerland	57,295	54,753	62,344	67,419	68,885	2.83	2.17
Other Europe	**97,121**	**106,478**	**106,152**	**117,547**	**138,097**	**5.67**	**17.48**
Other countries of Europe	97,121	106,478	106,152	117,547	138,097	5.67	17.48
NOT SPECIFIED	**148,864**	**127,368**	**130,824**	**119,848**	**117,529**	**4.83**	**-1.93**
Other countries of the World	148,864	127,368	130,824	119,848	117,529	4.83	-1.93

INDIA

1. Arrivals of non-resident tourists at national borders, by nationality

		2007	2008	2009	2010	2011	Market share 11	% Change 11-10
TOTAL	(*)	5,081,504	5,282,603	5,167,699	5,775,692	6,309,222	100.00	9.24
AFRICA		151,355	136,424	158,605	197,090	224,292	3.55	13.80
East Africa		76,817	63,665	75,618	91,544	99,385	1.58	8.57
Burundi		203	338	559	703	857	0.01	21.91
Comoros		167	85	39	133	231	0.00	73.68
Ethiopia		3,588	3,306	3,936	3,797	6,411	0.10	68.84
Eritrea		403	369	523	638	616	0.01	-3.45
Djibouti					561	602	0.01	7.31
Kenya		25,397	14,941	22,704	29,223	30,045	0.48	2.81
Madagascar		365	686	883	2,377	1,509	0.02	-36.52
Malawi		620	731	799	1,250	1,132	0.02	-9.44
Mauritius		21,522	19,713	18,866	21,672	22,091	0.35	1.93
Mozambique		1,642	884	1,790	2,442	3,118	0.05	27.68
Reunion		161	75	59	102	29	0.00	-71.57
Rwanda		383	651	849	1,344	1,580	0.03	17.56
Seychelles		1,422	1,386	1,339	1,672	2,330	0.04	39.35
Somalia		884	637	525	555	753	0.01	35.68
Zimbabwe		1,203	711	1,053	1,798	2,052	0.03	14.13
Uganda		2,083	2,285	2,425	3,011	3,615	0.06	20.06
United Republic of Tanzania		13,960	14,872	17,020	17,645	19,470	0.31	10.34
Zambia		2,814	1,995	2,249	2,621	2,944	0.05	12.32
Central Africa		2,365	3,305	3,389	4,810	7,914	0.13	64.53
Angola		703	1,851	1,248	1,620	1,891	0.03	16.73
Cameroon		337	467	671	877	912	0.01	3.99
Central African Republic		587	59	9	15	37	0.00	146.67
Chad		95	105	154	212	1,198	0.02	465.09
Congo		498	670	1,100	1,930	3,623	0.06	87.72
Equatorial Guinea		19	15	8	11	10	0.00	-9.09
Gabon		78	120	188	134	226	0.00	68.66
Sao Tome and Principe		48	18	11	11	17	0.00	54.55
North Africa		7,967	6,843	8,768	11,766	14,529	0.23	23.48
Algeria		1,205	1,043	1,217	1,203	1,635	0.03	35.91
Morocco		1,359	1,207	1,429	1,724	2,328	0.04	35.03
Sudan		4,381	3,473	4,987	7,418	8,414	0.13	13.43
Tunisia		1,022	1,120	1,135	1,421	2,152	0.03	51.44
Southern Africa		47,679	43,795	47,179	58,271	60,815	0.96	4.37
Botswana		509	385	491	1,050	837	0.01	-20.29
Lesotho		327	282	290	523	421	0.01	-19.50
Namibia		1	477	558	613	593	0.01	-3.26
South Africa		46,042	42,337	44,308	55,688	58,430	0.93	4.92
Swaziland		800	314	1,532	397	534	0.01	34.51
West Africa		16,065	18,779	23,550	30,699	41,649	0.66	35.67
Cape Verde		28	23	22	42	21	0.00	-50.00
Benin					209	304	0.00	45.45
Gambia		103	105	161	281	380	0.01	35.23
Ghana		1,300	1,269	1,381	1,773	2,129	0.03	20.08
Guinea		198	211	280	310	341	0.01	10.00
Côte d'Ivoire		368	348	639	680	637	0.01	-6.32
Liberia		177	171	144	177	164	0.00	-7.34
Mali		238	232	273	495	815	0.01	64.65
Mauritania		600	363	190	131	559	0.01	326.72
Niger		512	338	316	475	600	0.01	26.32
Nigeria		10,863	13,997	18,338	23,893	33,537	0.53	40.36
Guinea-Bissau		87	17	12	18	34	0.00	88.89
Saint Helena					53	51	0.00	-3.77
Senegal		987	919	1,077	1,212	1,234	0.02	1.82

INDIA

1. Arrivals of non-resident tourists at national borders, by nationality

	2007	2008	2009	2010	2011	Market share 11	% Change 11-10
Sierra Leone	471	416	301	371	289	0.00	-22.10
Togo	121	171	157	297	292	0.00	-1.68
Burkina Faso	12	199	259	282	262	0.00	-7.09
Other Africa	**462**	**37**	**101**				
Other countries of Africa	462	37	101				
AMERICAS	**1,049,595**	**1,070,802**	**1,097,813**	**1,236,695**	**1,300,911**	**20.62**	**5.19**
Caribbean	**4,029**	**3,280**	**3,563**	**5,135**	**4,644**	**0.07**	**-9.56**
Antigua and Barbuda	21	31	25	65	35	0.00	-46.15
Bahamas	144	169	142	179	212	0.00	18.44
Barbados	396	290	326	451	428	0.01	-5.10
Bermuda				29	31	0.00	6.90
British Virgin Islands				15	1	0.00	-93.33
Cayman Islands				12	6	0.00	-50.00
Cuba	261	283	259	338	279	0.00	-17.46
Dominica				48	17	0.00	-64.58
Dominican Republic	188	235	255	353	459	0.01	30.03
Grenada	502	108	100	92	107	0.00	16.30
Guadeloupe	5	4	7	5	2	0.00	-60.00
Haiti	71	93	119	89	89	0.00	
Jamaica	516	463	561	892	768	0.01	-13.90
Martinique	71	28	8	12	12	0.00	
Montserrat				21	32	0.00	52.38
Netherlands Antilles		60	56	75	55	0.00	-26.67
Puerto Rico				3	7	0.00	133.33
Saint Kitts and Nevis				91	82	0.00	-9.89
Anguilla				14	8	0.00	-42.86
Saint Lucia	129	104	50	88	91	0.00	3.41
Saint Vincent and the Grenadines				47	24	0.00	-48.94
Trinidad and Tobago	1,682	1,412	1,655	2,193	1,888	0.03	-13.91
Turks and Caicos Islands				19	10	0.00	-47.37
United States Virgin Islands				4	1	0.00	-75.00
Other countries of the Caribbean	43						
Central America	**3,226**	**2,834**	**2,670**	**2,616**	**3,351**	**0.05**	**28.10**
Belize	809	349	223	356	351	0.01	-1.40
Costa Rica	586	537	561	568	1,042	0.02	83.45
El Salvador	315	309	213	204	215	0.00	5.39
Guatemala	382	515	495	411	429	0.01	4.38
Honduras	189	234	256	195	283	0.00	45.13
Nicaragua	97	97	109	92	85	0.00	-7.61
Panama	848	793	813	790	946	0.01	19.75
North America	**1,015,575**	**1,036,569**	**1,059,394**	**1,184,122**	**1,250,581**	**19.82**	**5.61**
Canada	208,214	222,364	224,069	242,372	259,017	4.11	6.87
Mexico	8,299	9,272	8,185	10,458	10,876	0.17	4.00
United States of America	799,062	804,933	827,140	931,292	980,688	15.54	5.30
South America	**26,765**	**28,119**	**32,186**	**44,822**	**42,335**	**0.67**	**-5.55**
Argentina	4,992	5,087	6,011	7,626	9,391	0.15	23.14
Bolivia	24	176	280	290	313	0.00	7.93
Brazil	10,788	11,530	13,964	15,219	17,268	0.27	13.46
Chile	2,498	2,916	2,961	11,340	3,975	0.06	-64.95
Colombia	2,891	2,762	2,945	3,663	4,085	0.06	11.52
Ecuador	553	549	606	794	1,208	0.02	52.14
Guyana	416	288	387	601	438	0.01	-27.12
Paraguay	212	242	116	228	221	0.00	-3.07
Peru	1,073	1,261	1,214	1,326	1,592	0.03	20.06
Suriname	809	512	514	493	558	0.01	13.18
Uruguay	787	917	1,068	1,387	1,199	0.02	-13.55
Venezuela	1,722	1,879	2,120	1,855	2,087	0.03	12.51

INDIA

1. Arrivals of non-resident tourists at national borders, by nationality

	2007	2008	2009	2010	2011	Market share 11	% Change 11-10
EAST ASIA AND THE PACIFIC	822,575	866,463	865,439	1,062,536	1,229,632	19.49	15.73
North-East Asia	352,037	355,230	322,797	411,947	475,951	7.54	15.54
China	88,103	98,093	100,209	119,530	142,218	2.25	18.98
Taiwan, Province of China	30,024	28,939	23,464	23,915	25,916	0.41	8.37
Hong Kong, China	914	519	1,396	1,507	1,712	0.03	13.60
Japan	145,538	145,352	124,756	168,019	193,525	3.07	15.18
Korea, Dem. People's Republic of	709	22	4	25	20	0.00	-20.00
Korea, Republic of	84,583	79,802	70,485	95,587	108,680	1.72	13.70
Macao, China	153	211	251	669	573	0.01	-14.35
Mongolia	1,929	2,292	2,232	2,695	3,307	0.05	22.71
Other countries of North-East Asia	84						
South-East Asia	303,475	332,925	360,191	439,043	520,787	8.25	18.62
Brunei Darussalam	336	5,442	303	456	556	0.01	21.93
Myanmar	7,977	12,147	12,849	14,719	25,043	0.40	70.14
Cambodia	1,433	1,596	1,133	1,715	2,076	0.03	21.05
Indonesia	17,818	19,609	20,068	26,171	32,530	0.52	24.30
Lao People's Democratic Republic	219	322	294	809			
Malaysia	112,741	115,794	135,343	179,077	208,196	3.30	16.26
Philippines	15,567	17,222	21,987	24,534	31,151	0.49	26.97
Singapore	92,908	97,851	95,328	107,487	119,022	1.89	10.73
Viet Nam	4,439	4,877	5,577	7,458	9,809	0.16	31.52
Thailand	50,037	58,065	67,309	76,617	92,404	1.46	20.61
Australasia	163,423	175,470	179,950	206,671	229,431	3.64	11.01
Australia	135,925	146,209	149,074	169,647	192,592	3.05	13.53
New Zealand	27,498	29,261	30,876	37,024	36,839	0.58	-0.50
Melanesia	2,976	2,349	2,248	2,971	2,997	0.05	0.88
Solomon Islands	48	31	40				
Fiji	2,635	2,129	2,031	2,508	2,705	0.04	7.85
New Caledonia				4	2	0.00	-50.00
Vanuatu				96	43	0.00	-55.21
Norfolk Island				7	5	0.00	-28.57
Papua New Guinea	293	189	177	356	242	0.00	-32.02
Micronesia	370	300	207	463	369	0.01	-20.30
Christmas Island, Australia				2	1	0.00	-50.00
Kiribati	77	66	30	143	83	0.00	-41.96
Guam					2	0.00	
Nauru	293	234	177	318	283	0.00	-11.01
Polynesia	265	189	46	1,441	97	0.00	-93.27
American Samoa				1,077	41	0.00	-96.19
Cook Islands				2			
French Polynesia				25	33	0.00	32.00
Niue	95	78			4	0.00	
Tonga	37			297			
Tuvalu	100	81	15	40	19	0.00	-52.50
Samoa	33	30	31				
Other East Asia and the Pacific	29						
Other countries East Asia/Pacific	29						
EUROPE	1,900,413	1,955,824	1,869,115	2,034,709	2,173,422	34.45	6.82
Central/Eastern Europe	151,821	188,178	179,088	223,327	269,414	4.27	20.64
Azerbaijan	826	8,908	859	800	1,058	0.02	32.25
Armenia	474	1,123	452	641	686	0.01	7.02
Bulgaria	2,291	2,224	2,370	2,900	2,890	0.05	-0.34
Belarus	1,708	2,155	2,536	3,493	4,567	0.07	30.75
Czech Republic	7,764	8,549	8,328	9,918	11,256	0.18	13.49
Estonia	4,828	4,205	3,496	2,594	2,754	0.04	6.17
Georgia	569	669	687	655	4,179	0.07	538.02

INDIA

1. Arrivals of non-resident tourists at national borders, by nationality

	2007	2008	2009	2010	2011	Market share 11	% Change 11-10
Hungary	5,073	5,263	4,980	6,022	6,900	0.11	14.58
Kazakhstan	5,137	7,534	6,848	8,786	9,810	0.16	11.65
Kyrgyzstan	815	1,036	1,208	1,181	1,340	0.02	13.46
Latvia	2,483	2,611	2,498	3,052	2,968	0.05	-2.75
Lithuania	1,765	3,442	2,365	2,598	3,619	0.06	39.30
Republic of Moldova	203	286	1,502	424	470	0.01	10.85
Poland	20,166	23,517	19,656	25,424	28,499	0.45	12.09
Romania	3,677	4,689	4,808	5,380	5,988	0.09	11.30
Russian Federation	75,543	91,095	94,945	122,048	144,312	2.29	18.24
Slovakia	2,046	2,833	3,092	3,571	4,061	0.06	13.72
Tajikistan	1,053	861	749	963	1,359	0.02	41.12
Turkmenistan	1,313	1,316	1,631	1,509	1,946	0.03	28.96
Ukraine	10,490	12,344	12,436	16,462	23,467	0.37	42.55
Uzbekistan	2,562	2,756	3,642	4,906	7,285	0.12	48.49
Other countries Central/East Europe	1,035	762					
Northern Europe	**945,434**	**947,202**	**915,655**	**908,900**	**954,614**	**15.13**	**5.03**
Denmark	28,347	34,253	30,857	35,541	34,683	0.55	-2.41
Faeroe Islands				7	6	0.00	-14.29
Finland	34,364	29,223	24,874	24,089	23,730	0.38	-1.49
Iceland	1,341	2,013	1,821	2,183	2,589	0.04	18.60
Ireland	18,376	18,924	19,223	20,329	22,089	0.35	8.66
Norway	19,484	22,369	22,092	22,229	24,578	0.39	10.57
Sweden	47,090	58,961	43,327	45,028	48,690	0.77	8.13
United Kingdom	796,191	776,530	769,251	759,494	798,249	12.65	5.10
Other countries of Northern Europe	241	4,929	4,210				
Southern Europe	**184,025**	**176,892**	**168,155**	**203,898**	**211,408**	**3.35**	**3.68**
Albania	286	219	279	330	394	0.01	19.39
Andorra	120	155	173	157	181	0.00	15.29
Bosnia and Herzegovina				305	329	0.01	7.87
Croatia	2,989	2,932	2,990	3,080	3,375	0.05	9.58
Gibraltar				5	10	0.00	100.00
Greece	6,455	6,672	6,664	7,441	7,253	0.11	-2.53
Italy	93,540	85,766	77,873	94,100	100,889	1.60	7.21
Malta	1,488	665	499	540	516	0.01	-4.44
Portugal	15,756	15,415	17,184	21,038	24,061	0.38	14.37
San Marino				46	57	0.00	23.91
Slovenia		1,771	2,049	3,022	2,938	0.05	-2.78
Spain	63,357	62,535	59,047	72,591	71,405	1.13	-1.63
Yugoslavia, SFR (former)		762	1,397	1,243			
Other countries of Southern Europe	34						
Western Europe	**559,613**	**589,088**	**554,595**	**638,637**	**671,642**	**10.65**	**5.17**
Austria	26,692	25,900	27,930	32,620	36,483	0.58	11.84
Belgium	34,207	36,277	34,759	37,709	40,478	0.64	7.34
France	204,827	207,802	196,462	225,232	231,423	3.67	2.75
Germany	184,195	204,344	191,616	227,720	240,235	3.81	5.50
Liechtenstein				182	174	0.00	-4.40
Luxembourg	1,091	1,053	958	1,200	1,256	0.02	4.67
Monaco				84	108	0.00	28.57
Netherlands	67,429	71,605	64,580	70,756	75,153	1.19	6.21
Switzerland	41,172	42,107	38,290	43,134	46,332	0.73	7.41
East Mediterranean Europe	**59,520**	**54,464**	**51,622**	**59,947**	**66,344**	**1.05**	**10.67**
Cyprus	755	810	759	1,008	896	0.01	-11.11
Israel	47,553	42,720	40,581	43,456	48,089	0.76	10.66
Turkey	11,212	10,934	10,282	15,483	17,359	0.28	12.12
MIDDLE EAST	**118,469**	**166,404**	**159,090**	**183,387**	**221,220**	**3.51**	**20.63**
Bahrain	6,674	7,224	7,901	7,766	9,587	0.15	23.45
Palestine	480	770	966	1,151	1,241	0.02	7.82

INDIA

1. Arrivals of non-resident tourists at national borders, by nationality

	2007	2008	2009	2010	2011	Market share 11	% Change 11-10
Iraq	4,596	7,789	16,400	28,221	30,808	0.49	9.17
Jordan	4,537	4,154	4,301	4,640	5,061	0.08	9.07
Kuwait	4,129	5,302	5,208	4,764	5,370	0.09	12.72
Lebanon	3,290	3,418	3,320	3,730	4,296	0.07	15.17
Libya	610	494	693	1,280	465	0.01	-63.67
Oman	22,284	34,042	32,971	35,485	40,577	0.64	14.35
Qatar	2,606	2,934	2,765	2,735	3,266	0.05	19.41
Saudi Arabia	16,352	16,983	15,552	21,599	26,268	0.42	21.62
Syrian Arab Republic	2,928	2,883	3,215	3,586	4,152	0.07	15.78
United Arab Emirates	32,750	63,502	47,234	45,482	66,383	1.05	45.95
Egypt	6,328	5,326	5,869	8,017	8,791	0.14	9.65
Yemen	10,898	11,583	12,695	14,931	14,955	0.24	0.16
Other countries of Middle East	7						
SOUTH ASIA	**982,468**	**1,051,846**	**1,001,401**	**1,047,444**	**1,139,659**	**18.06**	**8.80**
Afghanistan	23,045	32,438	50,446	73,389	89,605	1.42	22.10
Bangladesh	480,240	541,884	468,899	431,962	463,543	7.35	7.31
Bhutan	6,729	9,952	10,328	12,048	15,489	0.25	28.56
Sri Lanka	204,084	218,805	239,995	266,515	305,853	4.85	14.76
Iran, Islamic Republic of	33,223	30,149	34,652	49,265	43,399	0.69	-11.91
Maldives	45,787	54,956	55,159	58,152	53,999	0.86	-7.14
Nepal	83,037	78,133	88,785	104,374	119,131	1.89	14.14
Pakistan	106,283	85,529	53,137	51,739	48,640	0.77	-5.99
Other countries of South Asia	40						
NOT SPECIFIED	**56,629**	**34,840**	**16,236**	**13,831**	**20,086**	**0.32**	**45.22**
Other countries of the World	56,629	34,840	16,236	13,831	20,086	0.32	45.22

INDONESIA

1. Arrivals of non-resident tourists at national borders, by nationality

	2007	2008	2009	2010	2011	Market share 11	% Change 11-10
TOTAL	5,505,759	6,234,497	6,323,730	7,002,944	7,649,731	100.00	9.24
AFRICA	35,487	33,081	26,637	28,592	31,651	0.41	10.70
Southern Africa	13,888	14,958	12,999	14,287	16,282	0.21	13.96
South Africa	13,888	14,958	12,999	14,287	16,282	0.21	13.96
Other Africa	21,599	18,123	13,638	14,305	15,369	0.20	7.44
Other countries of Africa	21,599	18,123	13,638	14,305	15,369	0.20	7.44
AMERICAS	220,730	249,968	237,670	255,465	293,306	3.83	14.81
Central America	22,757	9,618	4,587	881	1,044	0.01	18.50
All countries of Central America	22,757	9,618	4,587	881	1,044	0.01	18.50
North America	178,732	219,955	209,046	226,026	260,334	3.40	15.18
Canada	40,466	45,408	43,948	48,349	57,129	0.75	18.16
United States of America	138,266	174,547	165,098	177,677	203,205	2.66	14.37
South America	19,241	20,395	24,037	21,364	26,193	0.34	22.60
All countries of South America	19,241	20,395	24,037	21,364	26,193	0.34	22.60
Other Americas				7,194	5,735	0.07	-20.28
Other countries of the Americas				7,194	5,735	0.07	-20.28
EAST ASIA AND THE PACIFIC	4,205,543	4,712,610	4,741,596	5,350,445	5,848,604	76.46	9.31
North-East Asia	1,405,860	1,522,344	1,461,827	1,511,249	1,652,613	21.60	9.35
China	269,216	354,641	444,598	511,188	594,997	7.78	16.39
Taiwan, Province of China	218,268	218,146	204,794	214,192	228,922	2.99	6.88
Hong Kong, China	63,774	58,260	63,801	73,658	84,985	1.11	15.38
Japan	517,356	559,888	488,320	416,151	423,113	5.53	1.67
Korea, Republic of	337,246	331,409	260,314	296,060	320,596	4.19	8.29
South-East Asia	2,357,890	2,677,990	2,637,066	2,958,976	3,131,818	40.94	5.84
Brunei Darussalam	11,594	10,536	13,668	35,874	38,679	0.51	7.82
Myanmar	14,413	17,487	18,128	15,582	22,304	0.29	43.14
Cambodia	1,987	1,959	1,975	5,265	4,628	0.06	-12.10
Lao People's Democratic Republic	956	786	969	1,932	1,914	0.03	-0.93
Malaysia	799,990	1,009,722	1,041,053	1,171,737	1,173,351	15.34	0.14
Philippines	192,868	195,675	196,429	171,181	210,029	2.75	22.69
Singapore	1,160,200	1,197,267	1,138,071	1,206,360	1,324,839	17.32	9.82
Viet Nam	16,392	19,710	20,785	24,929	31,106	0.41	24.78
Thailand	71,753	66,012	93,381	111,645	115,036	1.50	3.04
Other countries of South-East Asia	87,737	158,836	112,607	214,471	209,932	2.74	-2.12
Australasia	326,738	455,190	609,245	814,920	985,834	12.89	20.97
Australia	287,103	418,899	571,541	769,585	933,376	12.20	21.28
New Zealand	39,635	36,291	37,704	45,335	52,458	0.69	15.71
Other East Asia and the Pacific	115,055	57,086	33,458	65,300	78,339	1.02	19.97
Other countries of Asia	97,178	43,972	30,344	60,410	71,742	0.94	18.76
Other countries of Oceania	17,877	13,114	3,114	4,890	6,597	0.09	34.91
EUROPE	843,699	989,854	1,028,405	1,048,543	1,110,871	14.52	5.94
Central/Eastern Europe	114,575	146,967	144,951	145,817	164,358	2.15	12.72
USSR (former)	51,687	74,483	77,018	83,836	96,438	1.26	15.03
Other countries Central/East Europe	62,888	72,484	67,933	61,981	67,920	0.89	9.58
Northern Europe	206,802	251,131	257,342	262,295	278,615	3.64	6.22
Denmark	13,909	18,434	20,062	17,565	19,950	0.26	13.58
Finland	8,517	9,819	15,591	11,566	13,137	0.17	13.58
Norway	14,799	16,468	16,261	16,226	17,803	0.23	9.72
Sweden	20,821	21,806	22,166	24,603	26,504	0.35	7.73
United Kingdom	148,756	184,604	183,262	192,335	201,221	2.63	4.62
Southern Europe	80,095	81,652	77,559	81,414	86,574	1.13	6.34
Italy	39,135	40,006	38,028	39,211	42,256	0.55	7.77

INDONESIA

1. Arrivals of non-resident tourists at national borders, by nationality

	2007	2008	2009	2010	2011	Market share 11	% Change 11-10
Portugal	12,222	11,368	11,331	11,629	13,661	0.18	17.47
Spain	28,738	30,278	28,200	30,574	30,657	0.40	0.27
Western Europe	**404,755**	**487,148**	**536,310**	**540,997**	**564,771**	**7.38**	**4.39**
Austria	16,275	16,855	17,399	16,889	17,374	0.23	2.87
Belgium	20,567	22,854	25,781	24,493	24,579	0.32	0.35
France	114,094	129,446	165,656	160,913	171,736	2.24	6.73
Germany	111,512	142,767	133,032	144,411	149,110	1.95	3.25
Netherlands	111,882	141,202	154,932	158,957	163,268	2.13	2.71
Switzerland	30,425	34,024	39,510	35,334	38,704	0.51	9.54
Other Europe	**37,472**	**22,956**	**12,243**	**18,020**	**16,553**	**0.22**	**-8.14**
Other countries of Europe	37,472	22,956	12,243	18,020	16,553	0.22	-8.14
MIDDLE EAST	**57,032**	**73,391**	**113,935**	**143,002**	**163,497**	**2.14**	**14.33**
Bahrain	615	891	746	832	879	0.01	5.65
Kuwait	2,567	2,160	5,875	2,729	4,164	0.05	52.58
Qatar	823	1,155	6,579	5,076	4,501	0.06	-11.33
Saudi Arabia	32,164	42,647	73,000	94,440	110,908	1.45	17.44
United Arab Emirates	1,889	2,960	3,871	4,970	4,720	0.06	-5.03
Egypt	2,616	3,744	3,316	3,650	4,469	0.06	22.44
Yemen	4,324	3,831	3,522	5,597	6,729	0.09	20.23
Other countries of Middle East	12,034	16,003	17,026	25,708	27,127	0.35	5.52
SOUTH ASIA	**143,268**	**175,593**	**175,487**	**176,897**	**201,802**	**2.64**	**14.08**
Bangladesh	6,390	6,155	6,347	5,557	6,394	0.08	15.06
Sri Lanka	6,591	6,774	6,715	6,195	7,019	0.09	13.30
India	123,465	155,391	156,545	159,373	181,791	2.38	14.07
Pakistan	6,822	7,273	5,880	5,772	6,598	0.09	14.31

INDONESIA

1. Arrivals of non-resident tourists at national borders, by country of residence

	2007	2008	2009	2010	2011	Market share 11	% Change 11-10
TOTAL	5,505,759	6,234,497	6,323,730	7,002,944	7,649,731	100.00	9.24
AFRICA	27,777	29,753	28,375	27,200	31,640	0.41	16.32
Southern Africa	13,404	15,012	15,831	12,691	15,579	0.20	22.76
South Africa	13,404	15,012	15,831	12,691	15,579	0.20	22.76
Other Africa	14,373	14,741	12,544	14,509	16,061	0.21	10.70
Other countries of Africa	14,373	14,741	12,544	14,509	16,061	0.21	10.70
AMERICAS	220,202	239,678	229,824	258,584	297,061	3.88	14.88
Central America	18,077	12,116	5,923	1,491	2,315	0.03	55.26
All countries of Central America	18,077	12,116	5,923	1,491	2,315	0.03	55.26
North America	187,995	214,115	205,631	223,520	258,562	3.38	15.68
Canada	32,343	39,784	35,400	43,159	54,287	0.71	25.78
United States of America	155,652	174,331	170,231	180,361	204,275	2.67	13.26
South America	14,130	13,447	18,270	23,288	26,566	0.35	14.08
All countries of South America	14,130	13,447	18,270	23,288	26,566	0.35	14.08
Other Americas				10,285	9,618	0.13	-6.49
Other countries of the Americas				10,285	9,618	0.13	-6.49
EAST ASIA AND THE PACIFIC	4,315,873	4,848,796	4,834,790	5,375,990	5,923,760	77.44	10.19
North-East Asia	1,370,744	1,509,870	1,398,507	1,455,116	1,601,386	20.93	10.05
China	230,476	337,082	395,013	469,365	574,179	7.51	22.33
Taiwan, Province of China	227,586	224,194	203,239	213,442	221,877	2.90	3.95
Hong Kong, China	76,019	81,073	67,967	78,339	86,646	1.13	10.60
Japan	508,820	546,713	475,766	418,971	412,623	5.39	-1.52
Korea, Republic of	327,843	320,808	256,522	274,999	306,061	4.00	11.30
South-East Asia	2,490,076	2,794,607	2,772,684	3,052,285	3,284,664	42.94	7.61
Brunei Darussalam	11,209	12,134	15,709	39,063	48,193	0.63	23.37
Malaysia	891,353	1,117,454	1,179,366	1,277,476	1,302,237	17.02	1.94
Philippines	137,317	159,003	162,463	189,486	223,779	2.93	18.10
Singapore	1,352,412	1,397,056	1,272,862	1,373,126	1,505,588	19.68	9.65
Viet Nam	9,754	12,215	14,456	28,196	36,917	0.48	30.93
Thailand	68,050	76,842	109,547	123,825	141,771	1.85	14.49
Other countries of South-East Asia	19,981	19,903	18,281	21,113	26,179	0.34	23.99
Australasia	340,107	472,811	616,030	803,905	967,792	12.65	20.39
Australia	314,432	450,178	584,437	771,792	931,109	12.17	20.64
New Zealand	25,675	22,633	31,593	32,113	36,683	0.48	14.23
Other East Asia and the Pacific	114,946	71,508	47,569	64,684	69,918	0.91	8.09
Other countries of Asia	108,862	62,605	41,115	58,783	62,761	0.82	6.77
Other countries of Oceania	6,084	8,903	6,454	5,901	7,157	0.09	21.28
EUROPE	796,730	924,745	978,369	1,038,420	1,045,865	13.67	0.72
Central/Eastern Europe	100,707	126,342	129,969	139,426	152,801	2.00	9.59
USSR (former)	52,928	69,628	72,829	79,398	87,426	1.14	10.11
Other countries Central/East Europe	47,779	56,714	57,140	60,028	65,375	0.85	8.91
Northern Europe	185,684	218,955	244,143	264,815	268,722	3.51	1.48
Denmark	15,144	17,507	19,010	16,755	17,817	0.23	6.34
Finland	9,937	10,535	18,688	13,740	14,117	0.18	2.74
Norway	16,095	17,434	16,141	17,482	16,578	0.22	-5.17
Sweden	22,909	23,067	21,033	24,579	27,525	0.36	11.99
United Kingdom	121,599	150,412	169,271	192,259	192,685	2.52	0.22
Southern Europe	81,407	79,130	81,623	81,716	82,811	1.08	1.34
Italy	29,570	33,300	40,448	38,908	46,145	0.60	18.60
Portugal	37,954	33,407	29,119	13,165	11,070	0.14	-15.91
Spain	13,883	12,423	12,056	29,643	25,596	0.33	-13.65
Western Europe	392,423	475,195	508,052	533,918	525,671	6.87	-1.54

INDONESIA

1. Arrivals of non-resident tourists at national borders, by country of residence

	2007	2008	2009	2010	2011	Market share 11	% Change 11-10
Austria	16,206	17,696	16,771	16,472	15,041	0.20	-8.69
Belgium	27,245	21,996	23,836	22,328	22,551	0.29	1.00
France	104,473	125,216	159,924	163,110	148,381	1.94	-9.03
Germany	112,160	137,854	128,649	145,244	145,160	1.90	-0.06
Netherlands	106,987	140,771	143,485	151,836	159,063	2.08	4.76
Switzerland	25,352	31,662	35,387	34,928	35,475	0.46	1.57
Other Europe	**36,509**	**25,123**	**14,582**	**18,545**	**15,860**	**0.21**	**-14.48**
Other countries of Europe	36,509	25,123	14,582	18,545	15,860	0.21	-14.48
MIDDLE EAST	**55,348**	**67,271**	**122,069**	**144,661**	**175,885**	**2.30**	**21.58**
Bahrain	534	1,000	740	1,889	1,675	0.02	-11.33
Kuwait	2,227	2,083	7,606	5,819	5,014	0.07	-13.83
Saudi Arabia	39,238	47,480	92,032	105,549	128,784	1.68	22.01
Egypt	2,210	2,747	3,031	3,235	2,942	0.04	-9.06
Other countries of Middle East	11,139	13,961	18,660	28,169	37,470	0.49	33.02
SOUTH ASIA	**89,829**	**124,254**	**130,303**	**158,089**	**175,520**	**2.29**	**11.03**
Bangladesh	7,133	7,549	6,324	8,724	8,991	0.12	3.06
Sri Lanka	6,953	6,740	5,741	6,024	6,207	0.08	3.04
India	68,908	102,179	110,658	137,027	154,237	2.02	12.56
Pakistan	6,835	7,786	7,580	6,314	6,085	0.08	-3.63

INDONESIA

3. Arrivals of non-resident tourists in hotels and similar establishments, by country of residence

	2007	2008	2009	2010	2011	Market share 11	% Change 11-10
TOTAL	4,298,330	4,804,838	5,359,218	5,588,783	6,045,250	100.00	8.17
AFRICA	20,939	23,061	21,174	23,120	24,603	0.41	6.41
Other Africa	20,939	23,061	21,174	23,120	24,603	0.41	6.41
All countries of Africa	20,939	23,061	21,174	23,120	24,603	0.41	6.41
AMERICAS	169,849	183,714	185,259	210,438	170,264	2.82	-19.09
Central America	16,336	11,186	5,201	1,260	1,987	0.03	57.70
All countries of Central America	16,336	11,186	5,201	1,260	1,987	0.03	57.70
North America	141,076	160,964	163,674	181,180	139,925	2.31	-22.77
Canada	24,596	30,673	27,711	33,200	41,964	0.69	26.40
United States of America	116,480	130,291	135,963	147,980	97,961	1.62	-33.80
South America	12,437	11,564	16,384	20,416	21,223	0.35	3.95
All countries of South America	12,437	11,564	16,384	20,416	21,223	0.35	3.95
Other Americas				7,582	7,129	0.12	-5.97
Other countries of the Americas				7,582	7,129	0.12	-5.97
EAST ASIA AND THE PACIFIC	3,348,007	3,704,980	4,161,852	4,259,161	4,705,662	77.84	10.48
North-East Asia	1,194,526	1,305,950	1,239,025	1,120,241	1,248,584	20.65	11.46
China	179,754	264,960	339,804	365,297	447,912	7.41	22.62
Taiwan, Province of China	198,953	192,774	177,727	181,350	187,437	3.10	3.36
Hong Kong, China	65,264	71,190	59,967	61,860	64,945	1.07	4.99
Japan	484,055	518,876	444,071	280,671	282,152	4.67	0.53
Korea, Republic of	266,500	258,150	217,456	231,063	266,138	4.40	15.18
South-East Asia	1,780,523	2,000,520	2,463,107	2,428,002	2,612,808	43.22	7.61
Brunei Darussalam	7,645	8,381	10,904	26,856	37,230	0.62	38.63
Malaysia	696,632	861,171	1,058,092	1,075,004	1,090,476	18.04	1.44
Philippines	84,672	98,647	125,899	117,348	144,464	2.39	23.11
Singapore	915,513	952,200	1,159,110	1,077,207	1,179,577	19.51	9.50
Thailand	54,239	59,098	87,299	102,440	120,196	1.99	17.33
Other countries of South-East Asia	21,822	21,023	21,803	29,147	40,865	0.68	40.20
Australasia	285,248	347,487	431,052	666,043	791,269	13.09	18.80
Australia	266,001	329,147	405,082	639,636	766,025	12.67	19.76
New Zealand	19,247	18,340	25,970	26,407	25,244	0.42	-4.40
Other East Asia and the Pacific	87,710	51,023	28,668	44,875	53,001	0.88	18.11
Other countries of Asia	83,042	44,282	23,949	40,685	47,894	0.79	17.72
Other countries of Oceania	4,668	6,741	4,719	4,190	5,107	0.08	21.89
EUROPE	662,075	764,444	805,587	880,989	867,694	14.35	-1.51
Central/Eastern Europe	89,430	110,787	111,354	123,035	131,738	2.18	7.07
USSR (former)	49,313	64,304	63,973	71,879	77,827	1.29	8.28
Other countries Central/East Europe	40,117	46,483	47,381	51,156	53,911	0.89	5.39
Northern Europe	152,114	177,635	196,578	221,313	219,603	3.63	-0.77
Denmark	12,897	14,767	16,158	14,769	16,277	0.27	10.21
Finland	8,062	8,621	16,093	11,971	12,166	0.20	1.63
Norway	13,957	15,197	13,683	15,777	14,876	0.25	-5.71
Sweden	19,475	20,281	18,348	21,540	22,976	0.38	6.67
United Kingdom	97,723	118,769	132,296	157,256	153,308	2.54	-2.51
Southern Europe	69,639	66,325	65,710	66,474	67,842	1.12	2.06
Italy	23,770	25,778	29,551	31,208	37,494	0.62	20.14
Portugal					9,255	0.15	
Spain					21,093	0.35	
Spain,Portugal	45,869	40,547	36,159	35,266			
Western Europe	322,028	389,086	419,673	454,452	435,532	7.20	-4.16
Austria	14,119	14,272	12,646	13,850	12,245	0.20	-11.59
Belgium	22,990	18,082	19,523	19,476	18,293	0.30	-6.07

INDONESIA

3. Arrivals of non-resident tourists in hotels and similar establishments, by country of residence

	2007	2008	2009	2010	2011	Market share 11	% Change 11-10
France	87,058	105,384	135,691	141,744	123,323	2.04	-13.00
Germany	94,424	116,374	105,490	122,015	119,879	1.98	-1.75
Netherlands	81,237	107,955	116,644	126,671	132,048	2.18	4.24
Switzerland	22,200	27,019	29,679	30,696	29,744	0.49	-3.10
Other Europe	**28,864**	**20,611**	**12,272**	**15,715**	**12,979**	**0.21**	**-17.41**
Other countries of Europe	28,864	20,611	12,272	15,715	12,979	0.21	-17.41
MIDDLE EAST	**36,700**	**44,082**	**96,208**	**115,263**	**156,974**	**2.60**	**36.19**
Bahrain	376	694	525	1,379	1,490	0.02	8.05
Kuwait					3,303	0.05	
Saudi Arabia	26,548	32,231	77,738	85,665	119,521	1.98	39.52
Egypt	1,550	1,905	2,302	2,263	1,941	0.03	-14.23
Other countries of Middle East	8,226	9,252	15,643	25,956	30,719	0.51	18.35
SOUTH ASIA	**60,760**	**84,557**	**89,138**	**99,812**	**120,053**	**1.99**	**20.28**
Bangladesh	5,392	5,485	4,550	5,551	7,203	0.12	29.76
Sri Lanka	4,551	4,396	3,630	4,191	4,169	0.07	-0.52
India	46,435	69,222	75,499	85,142	104,373	1.73	22.59
Pakistan	4,382	5,454	5,459	4,928	4,308	0.07	-12.58

IRAN, ISLAMIC REPUBLIC OF

2. Arrivals of non-resident visitors at national borders, by nationality

	2007	2008	2009	2010	2011	Market share 11	% Change 11-10
TOTAL			2,116,244	2,938,054	3,353,713	100.00	14.15
AFRICA			4,079	5,568	6,831	0.20	22.68
East Africa			785	946	1,979	0.06	109.20
Ethiopia			182	349	479	0.01	37.25
Kenya			349	309	352	0.01	13.92
Somalia			41	74	204	0.01	175.68
Zimbabwe			17	123	70	0.00	-43.09
Uganda			196	91	79	0.00	-13.19
United Republic of Tanzania					795	0.02	
North Africa			1,326	1,437	1,482	0.04	3.13
Algeria			247	422	280	0.01	-33.65
Morocco			241	198	173	0.01	-12.63
Sudan			584	530	608	0.02	14.72
Tunisia			254	287	421	0.01	46.69
West Africa			813	868	349	0.01	-59.79
Gambia			33	17	6	0.00	-64.71
Ghana			86	114	86	0.00	-24.56
Guinea			67	76	67	0.00	-11.84
Mali			51	53	70	0.00	32.08
Mauritania			19	52	21	0.00	-59.62
Nigeria			365	383	38	0.00	-90.08
Senegal			192	173	61	0.00	-64.74
Other Africa			1,155	2,317	3,021	0.09	30.38
Other countries of Africa			1,155	2,317	3,021	0.09	30.38
AMERICAS			6,151	7,146	6,463	0.19	-9.56
Caribbean			141	53	94	0.00	77.36
Bahamas			1	1			
Cuba			121	26	74	0.00	184.62
Dominican Republic			19	26	20	0.00	-23.08
Central America			13	17	20	0.00	17.65
Guatemala			3	1	15	0.00	1400.00
Panama			10	16	5	0.00	-68.75
North America			3,766	4,336	4,287	0.13	-1.13
Canada			1,826	2,540	2,506	0.07	-1.34
Mexico			196	187	202	0.01	8.02
United States of America			1,744	1,609	1,579	0.05	-1.86
South America			1,323	1,686	1,538	0.05	-8.78
Argentina			188	193	214	0.01	10.88
Brazil			588	835	735	0.02	-11.98
Chile			89	67	84	0.00	25.37
Colombia			111	116	109	0.00	-6.03
Ecuador			56	92	97	0.00	5.43
Peru			42	43	41	0.00	-4.65
Uruguay			40	35	40	0.00	14.29
Venezuela			209	305	218	0.01	-28.52
Other Americas			908	1,054	524	0.02	-50.28
Other countries of the Americas			908	1,054	524	0.02	-50.28
EAST ASIA AND THE PACIFIC			27,831	33,624	52,596	1.57	56.42
North-East Asia			18,960	22,088	37,497	1.12	69.76
China			4,378	7,648	22,728	0.68	197.18
Taiwan, Province of China			1,548	1,712	1,597	0.05	-6.72
Japan			5,647	5,592	4,937	0.15	-11.71
Korea, Dem. People's Republic of			96	77	108	0.00	40.26
Korea, Republic of			7,270	7,017	8,075	0.24	15.08

IRAN, ISLAMIC REPUBLIC OF

2. Arrivals of non-resident visitors at national borders, by nationality

	2007	2008	2009	2010	2011	Market share 11	% Change 11-10
Mongolia			21	42	52	0.00	23.81
South-East Asia			**6,018**	**8,122**	**10,533**	**0.31**	**29.68**
Indonesia			1,510	1,916	2,725	0.08	42.22
Malaysia			187	1,748	3,157	0.09	80.61
Philippines			2,046	2,399	2,286	0.07	-4.71
Singapore			26	178	883	0.03	396.07
Viet Nam			155	192	134	0.00	-30.21
Thailand			2,094	1,689	1,348	0.04	-20.19
Australasia			**2,853**	**3,414**	**4,399**	**0.13**	**28.85**
Australia			2,853	3,414	3,849	0.11	12.74
New Zealand					550	0.02	
Other East Asia and the Pacific					**167**	**0.00**	
Other countries East Asia/Pacific					167	0.00	
EUROPE			**1,187,149**	**1,738,398**	**2,000,785**	**59.66**	**15.09**
Central/Eastern Europe			**813,256**	**1,379,203**	**1,434,739**	**42.78**	**4.03**
Azerbaijan			383,588	690,333	732,201	21.83	6.06
Armenia			331,868	566,932	533,820	15.92	-5.84
Bulgaria			489	1,431	1,158	0.03	-19.08
Czech Republic			554	821	845	0.03	2.92
Georgia			323	194	3,203	0.10	1551.03
Hungary			483	525	606	0.02	15.43
Kazakhstan			613	1,222	1,794	0.05	46.81
Kyrgyzstan			188	402	560	0.02	39.30
Lithuania			81	133	212	0.01	59.40
Poland			821	1,052	1,066	0.03	1.33
Romania			1,368	1,340	1,194	0.04	-10.90
Russian Federation			6,155	11,281	13,413	0.40	18.90
Tajikistan			2,327	3,222	3,754	0.11	16.51
Turkmenistan			80,533	95,000	135,683	4.05	42.82
Ukraine			2,853	3,819	2,614	0.08	-31.55
Uzbekistan			1,012	1,496	2,616	0.08	74.87
Northern Europe			**16,026**	**17,195**	**16,482**	**0.49**	**-4.15**
Denmark			2,142	2,158	2,016	0.06	-6.58
Finland			673	578	680	0.02	17.65
Iceland			100	30	71	0.00	136.67
Ireland			638	701	730	0.02	4.14
Norway			1,806	1,655	1,840	0.05	11.18
Sweden			3,941	4,257	4,594	0.14	7.92
United Kingdom			6,726	7,816	6,551	0.20	-16.18
Southern Europe			**16,073**	**14,117**	**15,149**	**0.45**	**7.31**
Albania			88	72	87	0.00	20.83
Bosnia and Herzegovina			124	189	223	0.01	17.99
Greece			945	758	702	0.02	-7.39
Italy			10,982	9,167	10,010	0.30	9.20
Montenegro				18	35	0.00	94.44
Portugal			502	505	504	0.02	-0.20
Serbia			183	341	427	0.01	25.22
Slovenia			713	544	489	0.01	-10.11
Spain			2,536	2,523	2,672	0.08	5.91
Western Europe			**38,882**	**37,790**	**35,327**	**1.05**	**-6.52**
Austria			4,200	3,480	3,292	0.10	-5.40
Belgium			489	1,431	1,444	0.04	0.91
France			8,037	6,057	5,993	0.18	-1.06
Germany			18,072	18,488	16,851	0.50	-8.85
Luxembourg			41	44	41	0.00	-6.82
Netherlands			5,739	6,240	5,466	0.16	-12.40

IRAN, ISLAMIC REPUBLIC OF

2. Arrivals of non-resident visitors at national borders, by nationality

	2007	2008	2009	2010	2011	Market share 11	% Change 11-10
Switzerland			2,304	2,050	2,240	0.07	9.27
East Mediterranean Europe			**300,015**	**288,165**	**419,973**	**12.52**	**45.74**
Cyprus			187	134	120	0.00	-10.45
Turkey			299,828	288,031	419,853	12.52	45.77
Other Europe			**2,897**	**1,928**	**79,115**	**2.36**	**4003.48**
Other countries of Europe			2,897	1,928	79,115	2.36	4003.48
MIDDLE EAST			**518,819**	**740,004**	**782,096**	**23.32**	**5.69**
Bahrain			14,689	36,837	13,362	0.40	-63.73
Palestine			167	96	197	0.01	105.21
Iraq			440,989	548,008	589,074	17.56	7.49
Jordan			850	860	786	0.02	-8.60
Kuwait			16,302	49,572	54,641	1.63	10.23
Lebanon			11,947	17,416	20,484	0.61	17.62
Libya			103	128	261	0.01	103.91
Oman			7,707	10,816	9,798	0.29	-9.41
Qatar			1,300	2,568	2,417	0.07	-5.88
Saudi Arabia			14,601	60,107	74,275	2.21	23.57
Syrian Arab Republic			4,117	2,891	8,442	0.25	192.01
United Arab Emirates			5,022	9,607	6,719	0.20	-30.06
Egypt			857	975	1,415	0.04	45.13
Yemen			168	123	225	0.01	82.93
SOUTH ASIA			**314,314**	**413,180**	**426,896**	**12.73**	**3.32**
Afghanistan			175,155	214,649	202,369	6.03	-5.72
Bangladesh			655	653	819	0.02	25.42
Sri Lanka			535	655	734	0.02	12.06
India			22,277	23,903	34,770	1.04	45.46
Maldives			46	44	49	0.00	11.36
Nepal			187	208	235	0.01	12.98
Pakistan			115,459	173,068	187,920	5.60	8.58
NOT SPECIFIED			**57,901**	**134**	**78,046**	**2.33**	**58143.28**
Other countries of the World			57,901	134	78,046	2.33	58143.28

IRAQ

2. Arrivals of non-resident visitors at national borders, by nationality

	2007	2008	2009	2010	2011	Market share 11	% Change 11-10
TOTAL		863,657	1,261,921	1,517,766			
AFRICA			24	44			
East Africa			5	44			
Madagascar			3				
Mauritius				44			
United Republic of Tanzania			2				
West Africa			19				
Nigeria			19				
AMERICAS			42	30			
North America			42	30			
Canada				6			
United States of America			42	24			
EAST ASIA AND THE PACIFIC				35			
North-East Asia				1			
Japan				1			
South-East Asia				34			
Indonesia				34			
EUROPE			776	8,564	3,483		
Central/Eastern Europe			749	7,775	2,246		
Azerbaijan			739	7,717	2,246		
Russian Federation				58			
Ukraine			10				
Northern Europe					28		
Ireland					1		
United Kingdom					27		
Western Europe				27			
France				27			
East Mediterranean Europe			27	762	1,209		
Turkey			27	762	1,209		
MIDDLE EAST			4,355	10,752	15,076		
Bahrain			2,959	6,258	7,021		
Jordan					130		
Kuwait			192	94	820		
Lebanon			129	1,916	4,466		
Saudi Arabia			1,075	2,423	2,490		
Syrian Arab Republic					104		
United Arab Emirates				35	45		
Yemen				26			
SOUTH ASIA			852,405	1,194,149	1,443,151		
Afghanistan			234	382	1,673		
Bangladesh				346	11		
Sri Lanka			7				
India			6,031	13,876	13,860		
Iran, Islamic Republic of			840,362	1,161,541	1,413,792		
Pakistan			5,771	18,004	13,815		
NOT SPECIFIED			6,121	48,390	55,947		
Other countries of the World			6,121	48,390	55,947		

IRELAND

1. Arrivals of non-resident tourists at national borders, by country of residence

	2007	2008	2009	2010	2011	Market share 11	% Change 11-10
TOTAL	8,333,000	8,026,000	7,189,000	7,134,000	7,630,000	100.00	6.95
AFRICA	39,000	54,000	43,000				
Other Africa	39,000	54,000	43,000				
All countries of Africa	39,000	54,000	43,000				
AMERICAS	1,099,000	985,000	921,000	864,000	917,000	12.02	6.13
North America	1,071,000	952,000	891,000	864,000	917,000	12.02	6.13
Canada	96,000	103,000	82,000	86,000	99,000	1.30	15.12
United States of America	975,000	849,000	809,000	778,000	818,000	10.72	5.14
Other Americas	28,000	33,000	30,000				
Other countries of the Americas	28,000	33,000	30,000				
EAST ASIA AND THE PACIFIC	249,000	256,000	233,000	135,000	141,000	1.85	4.44
North-East Asia	16,000	14,000	11,000				
Japan	16,000	14,000	11,000				
Australasia	147,000	157,000	132,000	135,000	141,000	1.85	4.44
Australia	122,000	134,000	113,000				
New Zealand	25,000	23,000	19,000				
Australia, New Zealand				135,000	141,000	1.85	4.44
Other East Asia and the Pacific	86,000	85,000	90,000				
Other countries East Asia/Pacific	86,000	85,000	90,000				
EUROPE	6,946,000	6,731,000	5,992,000	5,959,000	6,361,000	83.37	6.75
Central/Eastern Europe	351,000	332,000	258,000				
Czech Republic	43,000	45,000	35,000				
Poland	308,000	287,000	223,000				
Northern Europe	4,519,000	4,307,000	3,769,000	3,948,000	4,129,000	54.12	4.58
Denmark	54,000	57,000	45,000				
Sweden	96,000	80,000	59,000				
United Kingdom (*)	4,369,000	4,170,000	3,665,000	3,948,000	4,129,000	54.12	4.58
Southern Europe	514,000	475,000	532,000	428,000	450,000	5.90	5.14
Italy	265,000	232,000	276,000	214,000	213,000	2.79	-0.47
Spain	249,000	243,000	256,000	214,000	237,000	3.11	10.75
Western Europe	1,166,000	1,213,000	1,128,000	725,000	820,000	10.75	13.10
Austria	40,000	51,000	45,000				
Belgium	82,000	85,000	93,000				
France	394,000	412,000	390,000	344,000	400,000	5.24	16.28
Germany	436,000	456,000	408,000	381,000	420,000	5.50	10.24
Netherlands	155,000	151,000	134,000				
Switzerland	59,000	58,000	58,000				
Other Europe	396,000	404,000	305,000	858,000	962,000	12.61	12.12
Other countries of Europe	396,000	404,000	305,000	858,000	962,000	12.61	12.12
NOT SPECIFIED				176,000	211,000	2.77	19.89
Other countries of the World				176,000	211,000	2.77	19.89

IRELAND

6. Overnight stays of non-resident tourists in all types of accommodation establishments, by country of residence

		2007	2008	2009	2010	2011	Market share 11	% Change 11-10
TOTAL	(*)	56,330,000	60,057,000	52,917,000	53,045,000	55,248,000	100.00	4.15
AMERICAS		9,602,000	8,715,000	8,252,000	8,780,000	8,904,000	16.12	1.41
North America		9,602,000	8,715,000	8,252,000	8,780,000	8,904,000	16.12	1.41
Canada		1,248,000	1,016,000	1,019,000	1,064,000	1,055,000	1.91	-0.85
United States of America		8,354,000	7,699,000	7,233,000	7,716,000	7,849,000	14.21	1.72
EAST ASIA AND THE PACIFIC		1,414,000	1,685,000	1,565,000				
Australasia		1,414,000	1,685,000	1,565,000				
Australia		1,414,000	1,685,000	1,565,000				
EUROPE		43,334,000	46,167,000	39,935,000	39,662,000	41,374,000	74.89	4.32
Northern Europe		17,763,000	17,301,000	15,438,000	18,624,000	18,217,000	32.97	-2.19
United Kingdom	(*)	17,763,000	17,301,000	15,438,000	18,624,000	18,217,000	32.97	-2.19
Southern Europe		5,107,000	5,810,000	5,667,000	4,648,000	5,740,000	10.39	23.49
Italy		2,501,000	2,851,000	2,624,000	2,049,000	2,608,000	4.72	27.28
Spain		2,606,000	2,959,000	3,043,000	2,599,000	3,132,000	5.67	20.51
Western Europe		9,539,000	12,629,000	11,412,000	7,247,000	8,353,000	15.12	15.26
Belgium		444,000	653,000	754,000				
France		3,789,000	5,092,000	5,049,000	3,531,000	4,491,000	8.13	27.19
Germany		3,644,000	5,222,000	4,044,000	3,716,000	3,862,000	6.99	3.93
Netherlands		1,000,000	1,127,000	954,000				
Switzerland		662,000	535,000	611,000				
Other Europe		10,925,000	10,427,000	7,418,000	9,143,000	9,064,000	16.41	-0.86
Other countries of Europe		10,925,000	10,427,000	7,418,000	9,143,000	9,064,000	16.41	-0.86
NOT SPECIFIED		1,980,000	3,490,000	3,165,000	4,603,000	4,970,000	9.00	7.97
Other countries of the World		1,980,000	3,490,000	3,165,000	4,603,000	4,970,000	9.00	7.97

ISRAEL

1. Arrivals of non-resident tourists at national borders, by country of residence

		2007	2008	2009	2010	2011	Market share 11	% Change 11-10
TOTAL	(*)	2,066,852	2,572,317	2,321,267	2,803,125	2,820,218	100.00	0.61
AFRICA		66,023	73,866	75,615	72,080	85,389	3.03	18.46
East Africa		7,652	7,639	5,627	8,773	9,276	0.33	5.73
Burundi		29	71	57	108	53	0.00	-50.93
Comoros		2	2			5	0.00	
Ethiopia		4,399	3,128	1,852	3,191	3,445	0.12	7.96
Eritrea		67	75	59	291	319	0.01	9.62
Kenya		1,058	1,539	1,318	2,428	2,744	0.10	13.01
Madagascar		48	54	79	53	65	0.00	22.64
Malawi		60	78	83	110	107	0.00	-2.73
Mauritius		206	255	291	286	248	0.01	-13.29
Mozambique		40	81	50	55	52	0.00	-5.45
Reunion		1						
Rwanda		79	200	158	158	155	0.01	-1.90
Seychelles		46	39	13	18	22	0.00	22.22
Somalia		17				2	0.00	
Zimbabwe		374	351	357	492	518	0.02	5.28
Uganda		447	736	596	658	671	0.02	1.98
United Republic of Tanzania		682	850	584	744	705	0.02	-5.24
Zambia		97	180	130	181	165	0.01	-8.84
Central Africa		1,039	1,849	1,439	1,425	1,696	0.06	19.02
Angola		398	815	433	598	689	0.02	15.22
Cameroon		266	289	400	492	475	0.02	-3.46
Central African Republic		45	40	34	57	113	0.00	98.25
Chad		14	28	19	8	27	0.00	237.50
Congo		268	566	358	152	178	0.01	17.11
Democratic Republic of the Congo				64				
Equatorial Guinea		21	26		36	92	0.00	155.56
Gabon		27	85	131	82	122	0.00	48.78
North Africa		3,801	3,799	3,395	3,462	3,568	0.13	3.06
Algeria		9	10	15	4	12	0.00	200.00
Morocco		2,644	2,566	2,305	2,473	2,409	0.09	-2.59
Sudan		3	9	1	3	24	0.00	700.00
Tunisia		1,145	1,214	1,074	982	1,123	0.04	14.36
Southern Africa		19,248	22,825	18,210	23,694	22,320	0.79	-5.80
Botswana		65	100					
Lesotho		28	37	21	16	18	0.00	12.50
Namibia		89	62	93	2,473	90	0.00	-96.36
South Africa		18,996	22,574	18,055	21,130	22,094	0.78	4.56
Swaziland		70	52	41	75	118	0.00	57.33
West Africa		34,207	37,640	46,772	34,296	48,072	1.70	40.17
Cape Verde		29	23	59	18	14	0.00	-22.22
Benin		81	113	88	114	169	0.01	48.25
Gambia		33	23	13	55	17	0.00	-69.09
Ghana		575	810	488	708	1,146	0.04	61.86
Guinea		67	31	64	185	34	0.00	-81.62
Côte d'Ivoire		862	1,433	938	1,054	798	0.03	-24.29
Liberia		43	45	45	67	63	0.00	-5.97
Mali		25	45	32	67	26	0.00	-61.19
Mauritania				5		2	0.00	
Niger		732	357	353	29	33	0.00	13.79
Nigeria		31,161	34,300	43,866	31,616	44,972	1.59	42.24
Guinea-Bissau				8	5	1	0.00	-80.00
Senegal		429	119	486	110	510	0.02	363.64
Sierra Leone		19	56	40	58	57	0.00	-1.72
Togo		57	73	146	92	78	0.00	-15.22

ISRAEL

1. Arrivals of non-resident tourists at national borders, by country of residence

	2007	2008	2009	2010	2011	Market share 11	% Change 11-10
Burkina Faso	94	212	141	118	152	0.01	28.81
Other Africa	**76**	**114**	**172**	**430**	**457**	**0.02**	**6.28**
Other countries of Africa	76	114	172	430	457	0.02	6.28
AMERICAS	**672,870**	**783,253**	**686,651**	**809,400**	**776,156**	**27.52**	**-4.11**
Caribbean	**1,913**	**2,409**	**1,895**	**2,419**	**2,366**	**0.08**	**-2.19**
Antigua and Barbuda	15	35	9	22	12	0.00	-45.45
Bahamas	131	141	275	59	95	0.00	61.02
Barbados	66	233	65	42	129	0.00	207.14
Bermuda	14	9	4	3	17	0.00	466.67
Cayman Islands	14	4	17	30	3	0.00	-90.00
Cuba	190	177	146	145	161	0.01	11.03
Dominica	31	28	26	43	34	0.00	-20.93
Dominican Republic	778	760	646	1,020	847	0.03	-16.96
Grenada	9	17	16	24	24	0.00	
Haiti	102	148	131	118	207	0.01	75.42
Jamaica	306	284	173	237	193	0.01	-18.57
Martinique	1						
Montserrat				1			
Puerto Rico			1	1			
Saint Kitts and Nevis	6	6	15	16	16	0.00	
Saint Lucia	5	27	6	71	13	0.00	-81.69
Saint Vincent and the Grenadines	10	7	5	10	14	0.00	40.00
Trinidad and Tobago	217	525	359	575	595	0.02	3.48
Turks and Caicos Islands	18	6	1	2	5	0.00	150.00
United States Virgin Islands		2			1	0.00	
Central America	**5,488**	**6,587**	**5,293**	**7,793**	**6,665**	**0.24**	**-14.47**
Belize	16	31	18	30	34	0.00	13.33
Costa Rica	1,358	2,282	1,525	2,260	1,995	0.07	-11.73
El Salvador	810	966	672	1,123	743	0.03	-33.84
Guatemala	1,149	971	915	1,323	1,125	0.04	-14.97
Honduras	519	418	394	672	672	0.02	
Nicaragua	114	154	142	172	220	0.01	27.91
Panama	1,522	1,765	1,627	2,213	1,876	0.07	-15.23
North America	**609,774**	**696,263**	**612,419**	**697,981**	**664,145**	**23.55**	**-4.85**
Canada	58,094	68,860	59,492	70,172	64,388	2.28	-8.24
Mexico	18,117	22,260	14,952	22,694	18,711	0.66	-17.55
United States of America	533,563	605,143	537,975	605,115	581,046	20.60	-3.98
South America	**55,695**	**77,994**	**67,044**	**101,207**	**102,980**	**3.65**	**1.75**
Argentina	15,074	19,666	16,003	22,286	21,628	0.77	-2.95
Bolivia	411	559	512	607	686	0.02	13.01
Brazil	20,130	31,216	27,891	48,778	53,054	1.88	8.77
Chile	3,355	5,514	4,244	5,832	5,687	0.20	-2.49
Colombia	7,165	9,027	7,896	10,933	9,506	0.34	-13.05
Ecuador	2,550	3,069	2,701	3,495	3,352	0.12	-4.09
Guyana	29	27	28	41	67	0.00	63.41
Paraguay	272	308	332	524	481	0.02	-8.21
Peru	1,535	2,146	2,336	3,276	2,811	0.10	-14.19
Suriname	23	17	31	48	42	0.00	-12.50
Uruguay	2,107	2,564	2,275	2,615	2,556	0.09	-2.26
Venezuela	3,038	3,879	2,794	2,768	3,108	0.11	12.28
Other countries of South America	6	2	1	4	2	0.00	-50.00
EAST ASIA AND THE PACIFIC	**109,873**	**130,005**	**94,765**	**142,345**	**147,149**	**5.22**	**3.37**
North-East Asia	**53,545**	**61,458**	**39,503**	**64,219**	**66,233**	**2.35**	**3.14**
China	7,596	8,923	7,570	12,890	16,806	0.60	30.38
Taiwan, Province of China	3,444	3,657	2,514	3,893	4,478	0.16	15.03
Hong Kong, China	2,086	3,414	2,186	4,052	3,258	0.12	-19.60

ISRAEL

1. Arrivals of non-resident tourists at national borders, by country of residence

	2007	2008	2009	2010	2011	Market share 11	% Change 11-10
Japan	10,676	14,506	9,768	13,165	13,444	0.48	2.12
Korea, Dem. People's Republic of		47		16			
Korea, Republic of	29,602	30,712	17,299	29,953	28,005	0.99	-6.50
Macao, China	42	46	59	53	49	0.00	-7.55
Mongolia	99	153	107	197	193	0.01	-2.03
South-East Asia	**30,620**	**37,671**	**28,553**	**43,071**	**48,071**	**1.70**	**11.61**
Brunei Darussalam		15	1	2	12	0.00	500.00
Myanmar				372	343	0.01	-7.80
Cambodia	10	31	24	48	69	0.00	43.75
Indonesia	11,402	14,336	9,587	17,742	21,946	0.78	23.70
Lao People's Democratic Republic	3	39	67	150	240	0.01	60.00
Malaysia	1,951	2,293	634	1,583	2,943	0.10	85.91
Philippines	6,633	8,970	7,321	10,241	9,376	0.33	-8.45
Timor-Leste				1	42	0.00	4100.00
Singapore	7,358	8,574	6,468	8,659	8,270	0.29	-4.49
Viet Nam	577	657	1,054	1,315	1,603	0.06	21.90
Thailand	2,686	2,756	3,397	2,958	3,227	0.11	9.09
Australasia	**24,555**	**29,599**	**26,215**	**34,622**	**32,273**	**1.14**	**-6.78**
Australia	21,584	26,443	23,543	30,738	28,889	1.02	-6.02
New Zealand	2,971	3,156	2,672	3,884	3,384	0.12	-12.87
Melanesia	**157**	**224**	**210**	**398**	**530**	**0.02**	**33.17**
Solomon Islands	2	3	6	10	9	0.00	-10.00
Fiji	123	140	116	194	358	0.01	84.54
Vanuatu	3	18	12	16	17	0.00	6.25
Papua New Guinea	29	63	76	178	146	0.01	-17.98
Micronesia	**2**	**24**	**4**	**11**	**16**	**0.00**	**45.45**
Kiribati		17		2	3	0.00	50.00
Micronesia, Federated States of			3	8	3	0.00	-62.50
Palau	2	7	1	1	10	0.00	900.00
Polynesia	**20**	**12**	**6**	**18**	**26**	**0.00**	**44.44**
American Samoa	4	12	6	1	1	0.00	
Cook Islands	1						
Tonga	12			10	20	0.00	100.00
Samoa	3			7	5	0.00	-28.57
Other East Asia and the Pacific	**974**	**1,017**	**274**	**6**			
Other countries of Asia	971	996	259				
Other countries of Oceania	3	21	15	6			
EUROPE	**1,171,006**	**1,521,264**	**1,406,930**	**1,704,345**	**1,730,182**	**61.35**	**1.52**
Central/Eastern Europe	**329,625**	**495,470**	**435,618**	**576,584**	**652,760**	**23.15**	**13.21**
Azerbaijan	2,666	2,873	2,695	2,912	2,851	0.10	-2.09
Armenia	534	891	811	1,503	1,404	0.05	-6.59
Bulgaria	5,165	8,620	6,148	7,165	7,489	0.27	4.52
Belarus	8,945	11,838	9,655	11,420	11,800	0.42	3.33
Czech Republic	9,725	16,385	10,943	13,709	13,028	0.46	-4.97
Estonia	1,976	2,620	3,057	5,252	3,555	0.13	-32.31
Georgia	5,125	6,015	4,555	4,477	4,312	0.15	-3.69
Hungary	10,034	13,793	9,433	11,787	11,418	0.40	-3.13
Kazakhstan	4,921	6,149	4,534	6,501	9,603	0.34	47.72
Kyrgyzstan	488	465	411	496	634	0.02	27.82
Latvia	5,181	5,863	4,168	4,749	5,370	0.19	13.08
Lithuania	5,483	7,355	4,153	5,124	5,093	0.18	-0.60
Republic of Moldova	3,410	4,411	3,121	4,434	3,630	0.13	-18.13
Poland	52,092	86,900	53,840	69,435	60,410	2.14	-13.00
Romania	19,123	37,322	28,881	38,475	37,790	1.34	-1.78
Russian Federation	132,304	205,570	231,366	318,472	353,419	12.53	10.97
Slovakia	5,354	8,872	8,143	11,595	10,194	0.36	-12.08

ISRAEL

1. Arrivals of non-resident tourists at national borders, by country of residence

	2007	2008	2009	2010	2011	Market share 11	% Change 11-10
Tajikistan	115	179	181	251	319	0.01	27.09
Turkmenistan	124	122	165	122	125	0.00	2.46
Ukraine	49,909	64,298	46,455	55,296	106,807	3.79	93.16
USSR (former)		23	13	7	4	0.00	-42.86
Uzbekistan	3,442	4,906	2,890	3,402	3,505	0.12	3.03
Other countries Central/East Europe	3,509						
Northern Europe	**212,142**	**239,563**	**230,856**	**247,409**	**251,117**	**8.90**	**1.50**
Denmark	11,216	12,226	12,740	15,182	18,934	0.67	24.71
Finland	8,685	12,268	17,776	19,503	18,255	0.65	-6.40
Iceland	306	393	234	355	320	0.01	-9.86
Ireland	7,315	9,065	7,490	9,145	8,864	0.31	-3.07
Norway	9,778	13,449	12,050	14,209	15,993	0.57	12.56
Sweden	14,023	16,806	17,029	20,246	20,739	0.74	2.44
United Kingdom	160,819	175,356	163,537	168,769	168,012	5.96	-0.45
Southern Europe	**162,689**	**239,414**	**204,631**	**264,267**	**206,805**	**7.33**	**-21.74**
Albania	438	1,033	659	473	545	0.02	15.22
Andorra	87	62	50	66	54	0.00	-18.18
Bosnia and Herzegovina	409	556	345	418	643	0.02	53.83
Croatia	3,358	5,199	5,291	6,097	5,124	0.18	-15.96
Greece	20,812	28,822	18,408	24,200	18,979	0.67	-21.57
Holy See	267	240	289	270	250	0.01	-7.41
Italy	79,649	120,901	116,489	150,176	113,307	4.02	-24.55
Malta	894	1,448	1,514	2,209	1,215	0.04	-45.00
Montenegro				394	322	0.01	-18.27
Portugal	5,026	11,616	6,886	13,557	8,458	0.30	-37.61
San Marino	119	291	98	104	64	0.00	-38.46
Serbia	608	1,099	1,397	2,964	4,063	0.14	37.08
Slovenia	1,459	2,420	2,189	2,560	1,965	0.07	-23.24
Spain	45,479	61,232	48,994	59,737	51,033	1.81	-14.57
TFYR of Macedonia	603	882	580	621	563	0.02	-9.34
Yugoslavia, SFR (former)	3,481	3,613	1,344	361	107	0.00	-70.36
Serbia and Montenegro			98	60	113	0.00	88.33
Western Europe	**443,727**	**518,645**	**512,922**	**591,976**	**595,797**	**21.13**	**0.65**
Austria	17,004	23,822	23,574	28,805	27,738	0.98	-3.70
Belgium	20,928	23,419	23,732	31,192	31,769	1.13	1.85
France	242,404	257,168	253,969	274,114	269,454	9.55	-1.70
Germany	98,938	137,722	139,806	171,487	170,987	6.06	-0.29
Liechtenstein	53	86	56	76	80	0.00	5.26
Luxembourg	546	644	639	728	776	0.03	6.59
Monaco	34	15	24	87	44	0.00	-49.43
Netherlands	40,398	48,413	44,511	53,377	58,668	2.08	9.91
Switzerland	23,422	27,356	26,611	32,110	36,281	1.29	12.99
East Mediterranean Europe	**22,823**	**28,172**	**22,862**	**24,109**	**23,703**	**0.84**	**-1.68**
Cyprus	9,094	11,906	9,428	10,432	10,206	0.36	-2.17
Turkey	13,729	16,266	13,434	13,677	13,497	0.48	-1.32
Other Europe			41				
Other countries of Europe			41				
MIDDLE EAST	**13,433**	**17,912**	**18,069**	**20,928**	**23,230**	**0.82**	**11.00**
Bahrain	3	3		3	1	0.00	-66.67
Iraq	111	144	123	158	157	0.01	-0.63
Jordan	10,459	15,646	15,039	17,824	20,263	0.72	13.68
Kuwait	4	3	31	5	8	0.00	60.00
Lebanon	180	242	398	224	239	0.01	6.70
Libya			8	3	3	0.00	
Oman	2	2	1	1	4	0.00	300.00
Qatar	20	20	10	9	8	0.00	-11.11
Saudi Arabia	3	7		4			

ISRAEL

1. Arrivals of non-resident tourists at national borders, by country of residence

	2007	2008	2009	2010	2011	Market share 11	% Change 11-10
Syrian Arab Republic	79	90	125	84	67	0.00	-20.24
United Arab Emirates	32	41		15	8	0.00	-46.67
Egypt	2,495	1,688	2,263	2,586	2,449	0.09	-5.30
Yemen	45	26	71	12	23	0.00	91.67
SOUTH ASIA	**27,631**	**33,209**	**25,746**	**43,080**	**41,425**	**1.47**	**-3.84**
Afghanistan	2	6	1	6	2	0.00	-66.67
Bangladesh	30	41	10	16	9	0.00	-43.75
Bhutan	3	27		4	25	0.00	525.00
Sri Lanka	1,846	2,086	1,363	1,943	1,955	0.07	0.62
India	24,091	29,413	23,058	40,109	38,481	1.36	-4.06
Iran, Islamic Republic of	985	700	400	474	409	0.01	-13.71
Maldives	25	19	9	30	64	0.00	113.33
Nepal	638	895	894	493	471	0.02	-4.46
Pakistan	11	22	11	5	9	0.00	80.00
NOT SPECIFIED	**6,016**	**12,808**	**13,491**	**10,947**	**16,687**	**0.59**	**52.43**
Other countries of the World	6,016	12,808	13,491	10,947	16,687	0.59	52.43

ISRAEL

2. Arrivals of non-resident visitors at national borders, by country of residence

		2007	2008	2009	2010	2011	Market share 11	% Change 11-10
TOTAL	(*)	2,293,684	3,034,064	2,739,737	3,443,988	3,362,073	100.00	-2.38
AFRICA		69,741	77,039	78,496	72,692	88,429	2.63	21.65
East Africa		9,689	9,767	7,795	10,777	11,258	0.33	4.46
Burundi		29	71	57	109	53	0.00	-51.38
Comoros		2	2			5	0.00	
Ethiopia		6,387	5,224	3,965	5,118	5,341	0.16	4.36
Eritrea		67	75	59	291	324	0.01	11.34
Kenya		1,070	1,548	1,358	2,434	2,771	0.08	13.85
Madagascar		48	54	79	54	67	0.00	24.07
Malawi		60	83	86	111	107	0.00	-3.60
Mauritius		210	255	293	293	279	0.01	-4.78
Mozambique		52	89	50	57	55	0.00	-3.51
Reunion		1						
Rwanda		79	200	158	160	155	0.00	-3.13
Seychelles		46	39	13	63	22	0.00	-65.08
Somalia		17				2	0.00	
Zimbabwe		393	355	362	502	525	0.02	4.58
Uganda		448	737	598	659	680	0.02	3.19
United Republic of Tanzania		683	853	587	745	705	0.02	-5.37
Zambia		97	182	130	181	167	0.00	-7.73
Central Africa		1,052	1,867	1,453	1,455	1,703	0.05	17.04
Angola		401	818	435	608	765	0.02	25.82
Cameroon		269	298	404	494	498	0.01	0.81
Central African Republic		49	43	37	65	115	0.00	76.92
Chad		14	28	19	9	27	0.00	200.00
Congo		271	568	361	157	182	0.01	15.92
Democratic Republic of the Congo				64				
Equatorial Guinea		21	26		36	92	0.00	155.56
Gabon		27	86	133	86	24	0.00	-72.09
North Africa		3,823	3,825	3,408	3,514	3,624	0.11	3.13
Algeria		9	10	15	5	14	0.00	180.00
Morocco		2,644	2,572	2,313	2,516	2,449	0.07	-2.66
Sudan		3	9	1	3	24	0.00	700.00
Tunisia		1,167	1,234	1,079	990	1,137	0.03	14.85
Southern Africa		19,594	23,302	18,706	22,053	23,134	0.69	4.90
Botswana		65	100					
Lesotho		28	38	22	19	20	0.00	5.26
Namibia		89	62	93	105	90	0.00	-14.29
South Africa		19,341	23,047	18,550	21,826	22,886	0.68	4.86
Swaziland		71	55	41	103	138	0.00	33.98
West Africa		35,506	38,150	46,908	34,451	48,248	1.44	40.05
Cape Verde		29	24	59	19	14	0.00	-26.32
Benin		81	115	88	118	193	0.01	63.56
Gambia		33	23	13	55	17	0.00	-69.09
Ghana		605	821	516	716	1,155	0.03	61.31
Guinea		68	31	68	185	36	0.00	-80.54
Côte d'Ivoire		873	1,515	969	1,087	802	0.02	-26.22
Liberia		43	45	45	68	63	0.00	-7.35
Mali		25	45	32	67	26	0.00	-61.19
Mauritania				5		6	0.00	
Niger		732	357	353	29	38	0.00	31.03
Nigeria		32,415	34,713	43,942	31,723	45,093	1.34	42.15
Senegal		430	119	486	111	515	0.02	363.96
Sierra Leone		20	56	40	58	57	0.00	-1.72
Togo		57	73	150	97	79	0.00	-18.56
Burkina Faso		95	213	142	118	154	0.00	30.51

ISRAEL

2. Arrivals of non-resident visitors at national borders, by country of residence

	2007	2008	2009	2010	2011	Market share 11	% Change 11-10
Other Africa	77	128	226	442	462	0.01	4.52
Other countries of Africa	77	128	226	442	462	0.01	4.52
AMERICAS	687,932	814,544	734,596	879,191	855,218	25.44	-2.73
Caribbean	1,950	2,492	1,989	2,622	4,625	0.14	76.39
Antigua and Barbuda	15	37	11	25	15	0.00	-40.00
Bahamas	131	147	276	78	156	0.00	100.00
Barbados	66	236	66	55	138	0.00	150.91
Bermuda	15	9	4	4	19	0.00	375.00
Cayman Islands	14	4	17	30	3	0.00	-90.00
Cuba	192	180	148	148	172	0.01	16.22
Dominica	31	29	26	45	76	0.00	68.89
Dominican Republic	805	813	655	1,099	1,000	0.03	-9.01
Grenada	10	17	16	25	26	0.00	4.00
Haiti	102	150	131	128	209	0.01	63.28
Jamaica	309	289	179	259	2,110	0.06	714.67
Martinique	1						
Puerto Rico			1	3	2	0.00	-33.33
Saint Kitts and Nevis	6	6	15	19	16	0.00	-15.79
Saint Lucia	5	27	6	71	17	0.00	-76.06
Saint Vincent and the Grenadines	11	7	6	10	17	0.00	70.00
Trinidad and Tobago	219	531	431	621	643	0.02	3.54
Turks and Caicos Islands	18	8	1	2	5	0.00	150.00
United States Virgin Islands		2			1	0.00	
Central America	5,539	6,767	5,511	8,737	7,126	0.21	-18.44
Belize	16	31	18	30	35	0.00	16.67
Costa Rica	1,371	2,372	1,632	2,747	2,401	0.07	-12.60
El Salvador	826	982	688	1,176	768	0.02	-34.69
Guatemala	1,155	988	982	1,562	1,221	0.04	-21.83
Honduras	522	461	400	725	722	0.02	-0.41
Nicaragua	119	158	143	200			
Panama	1,530	1,775	1,648	2,297	1,979	0.06	-13.84
North America	623,850	725,122	656,313	758,790	731,744	21.76	-3.56
Canada	59,870	73,779	67,183	79,716	76,637	2.28	-3.86
Mexico	18,461	23,227	16,327	27,015	21,236	0.63	-21.39
United States of America	545,519	628,116	572,803	652,059	633,871	18.85	-2.79
South America	56,514	79,977	70,113	109,037	111,719	3.32	2.46
Argentina	15,291	20,201	16,409	23,364	23,129	0.69	-1.01
Bolivia	420	571	533	749	711	0.02	-5.07
Brazil	20,402	31,767	28,945	51,983	56,889	1.69	9.44
Chile	3,425	5,787	4,700	6,377	6,381	0.19	0.06
Colombia	7,340	9,368	8,291	12,197	11,033	0.33	-9.54
Ecuador	2,596	3,227	2,907	4,206	3,820	0.11	-9.18
Guyana	29	27	28	42	71	0.00	69.05
Paraguay	272	315	337	544	515	0.02	-5.33
Peru	1,548	2,190	2,401	3,508	2,950	0.09	-15.91
Suriname	23	17	31	50	45	0.00	-10.00
Uruguay	2,117	2,587	2,419	2,857	2,774	0.08	-2.91
Venezuela	3,051	3,920	3,112	3,160	3,401	0.10	7.63
Other Americas	79	186	670	5	4	0.00	-20.00
Other countries of the Americas	79	186	670	5	4	0.00	-20.00
EAST ASIA AND THE PACIFIC	115,412	140,446	102,996	159,938	161,588	4.81	1.03
North-East Asia	58,499	69,017	44,021	75,592	73,032	2.17	-3.39
China	7,758	9,083	7,714	13,258	17,418	0.52	31.38
Taiwan, Province of China	3,495	3,778	2,660	4,049	4,789	0.14	18.28
Hong Kong, China	2,245	3,679	2,335	4,499	3,723	0.11	-17.25
Japan	10,926	14,735	10,031	13,866	14,112	0.42	1.77

ISRAEL

2. Arrivals of non-resident visitors at national borders, by country of residence

	2007	2008	2009	2010	2011	Market share 11	% Change 11-10
Korea, Dem. People's Republic of				16	16	0.00	
Korea, Republic of	33,925	37,540	21,113	39,644	32,718	0.97	-17.47
Macao, China	42	46	59	53	52	0.00	-1.89
Mongolia	108	156	109	207	204	0.01	-1.45
South-East Asia	**30,905**	**38,205**	**29,428**	**43,953**	**49,478**	**1.47**	**12.57**
Brunei Darussalam		15	1	2	12	0.00	500.00
Myanmar				373	345	0.01	-7.51
Cambodia	10	31	24	48	70	0.00	45.83
Indonesia	11,410	14,357	9,595	17,823	22,019	0.65	23.54
Lao People's Democratic Republic	3	39	67	150	240	0.01	60.00
Malaysia	1,952	2,316	640	1,611	3,276	0.10	103.35
Philippines	6,834	9,347	8,077	10,659	9,999	0.30	-6.19
Timor-Leste				7	42	0.00	500.00
Singapore	7,385	8,637	6,520	8,901	8,487	0.25	-4.65
Viet Nam	577	663	1,054	1,328	1,610	0.05	21.23
Thailand	2,734	2,800	3,450	3,051	3,378	0.10	10.72
Australasia	**24,803**	**31,585**	**28,627**	**39,950**	**38,481**	**1.14**	**-3.68**
Australia	21,781	28,039	25,465	35,188	34,203	1.02	-2.80
New Zealand	3,022	3,546	3,162	4,762	4,278	0.13	-10.16
Melanesia	**157**	**226**	**223**	**404**	**554**	**0.02**	**37.13**
Solomon Islands	2	3	6	10	9	0.00	-10.00
Fiji	123	142	129	200	380	0.01	90.00
Vanuatu	3	18	12	16	17	0.00	6.25
Papua New Guinea	29	63	76	178	148	0.00	-16.85
Micronesia	**3**	**24**	**4**	**12**	**16**	**0.00**	**33.33**
Kiribati	1	17		2	3	0.00	50.00
Micronesia, Federated States of			3	9	3	0.00	-66.67
Palau	2	7	1	1	10	0.00	900.00
Polynesia	**17**	**22**	**6**	**21**	**27**	**0.00**	**28.57**
American Samoa	1		6	1	1	0.00	
Cook Islands	1			1			
French Polynesia	12			2			
Tonga		10		10	20	0.00	100.00
Samoa	3	12		7	6	0.00	-14.29
Other East Asia and the Pacific	**1,028**	**1,367**	**687**	**6**			
Other countries of Asia	1,023	1,356	669				
Other countries of Oceania	5	11	18	6			
EUROPE	**1,367,600**	**1,936,303**	**1,764,666**	**2,253,137**	**2,175,690**	**64.71**	**-3.44**
Central/Eastern Europe	**490,816**	**849,887**	**723,680**	**952,844**	**884,454**	**26.31**	**-7.18**
Azerbaijan	2,777	3,186	2,991	3,142	2,994	0.09	-4.71
Armenia	659	1,487	1,170	2,283	1,878	0.06	-17.74
Bulgaria	5,426	10,148	7,016	8,135	8,304	0.25	2.08
Belarus	10,765	17,934	14,442	17,760	15,187	0.45	-14.49
Czech Republic	24,076	38,328	23,540	25,184	19,037	0.57	-24.41
Estonia	2,694	3,986	4,023	7,695	4,015	0.12	-47.82
Georgia	5,244	6,351	4,675	4,546	4,345	0.13	-4.42
Hungary	10,622	18,000	11,825	15,339	13,745	0.41	-10.39
Kazakhstan	8,395	13,549	10,736	12,224	14,607	0.43	19.49
Kyrgyzstan	553	655	659	709	750	0.02	5.78
Latvia	6,680	7,693	5,094	5,722	5,910	0.18	3.29
Lithuania	9,806	13,352	7,229	9,134	6,969	0.21	-23.70
Republic of Moldova	3,753	5,509	3,823	4,619	3,867	0.12	-16.28
Poland	86,455	156,252	96,880	128,961	95,958	2.85	-25.59
Romania	19,508	38,689	30,494	41,306	40,255	1.20	-2.54
Russian Federation	204,782	367,423	408,304	554,364	491,418	14.62	-11.35
Slovakia	9,160	15,949	12,909	16,815	13,495	0.40	-19.74

ISRAEL

2. Arrivals of non-resident visitors at national borders, by country of residence

	2007	2008	2009	2010	2011	Market share 11	% Change 11-10
Tajikistan	136	313	260	283	402	0.01	42.05
Turkmenistan	128	149	236	191	171	0.01	-10.47
Ukraine	75,569	125,477	73,924	90,711	137,266	4.08	51.32
USSR (former)	71	82	13	7	4	0.00	-42.86
Uzbekistan	3,483	5,162	3,437	3,714	3,877	0.12	4.39
Other countries Central/East Europe	74	213					
Northern Europe	**227,189**	**257,954**	**251,791**	**283,555**	**311,362**	**9.26**	**9.81**
Denmark	11,377	12,540	13,150	15,949	20,688	0.62	29.71
Finland	8,791	12,447	17,952	19,783	18,640	0.55	-5.78
Iceland	316	404	238	384	389	0.01	1.30
Ireland	7,948	9,746	8,580	10,427	10,713	0.32	2.74
Norway	9,927	13,756	12,764	15,288	17,981	0.53	17.62
Sweden	14,285	17,266	17,793	21,374	21,857	0.65	2.26
United Kingdom	174,545	191,795	181,314	200,350	221,094	6.58	10.35
Southern Europe	**164,164**	**255,712**	**223,946**	**325,218**	**255,735**	**7.61**	**-21.37**
Albania	498	1,090	715	591	625	0.02	5.75
Andorra	88	64	52	87	60	0.00	-31.03
Bosnia and Herzegovina	436	625	360	511	690	0.02	35.03
Croatia	3,460	5,348	5,398	6,833	6,791	0.20	-0.61
Greece	21,357	33,056	20,642	28,957	19,791	0.59	-31.65
Holy See	268	247	292	274	256	0.01	-6.57
Italy	81,802	125,649	125,704	185,383	151,245	4.50	-18.41
Malta	899	1,455	1,517	2,342	1,437	0.04	-38.64
Montenegro				485	401	0.01	-17.32
Portugal	5,178	11,986	7,208	15,341	9,569	0.28	-37.62
San Marino	119	291	102	140	82	0.00	-41.43
Serbia			877	4,720	5,062	0.15	7.25
Slovenia	1,689	2,862	2,348	3,332	2,682	0.08	-19.51
Spain	47,098	65,504	54,144	74,967	56,210	1.67	-25.02
TFYR of Macedonia	658	1,166	694	699	596	0.02	-14.74
Yugoslavia, SFR (former)		5,251	2,337	484	125	0.00	-74.17
Serbia and Montenegro	614	1,118	1,556	72	113	0.00	56.94
Western Europe	**455,287**	**538,867**	**539,160**	**663,771**	**698,564**	**20.78**	**5.24**
Austria	18,556	24,571	24,924	32,388	35,164	1.05	8.57
Belgium	21,969	24,782	26,127	35,255	37,040	1.10	5.06
France	246,431	264,306	263,885	302,695	300,567	8.94	-0.70
Germany	101,947	143,209	148,322	199,942	220,688	6.56	10.38
Liechtenstein	53	89	59	86	97	0.00	12.79
Luxembourg	553	667	663	837	989	0.03	18.16
Monaco	34	16	26	104	60	0.00	-42.31
Netherlands	41,891	53,267	47,587	57,962	63,047	1.88	8.77
Switzerland	23,853	27,960	27,567	34,502	40,912	1.22	18.58
East Mediterranean Europe	**26,219**	**33,883**	**25,735**	**27,749**	**25,575**	**0.76**	**-7.83**
Cyprus	11,990	16,299	11,521	12,699	11,552	0.34	-9.03
Turkey	14,229	17,584	14,214	15,050	14,023	0.42	-6.82
Other Europe	**3,925**		**354**				
Other countries of Europe	3,925		354				
MIDDLE EAST	**14,750**	**19,241**	**19,085**	**21,645**	**23,891**	**0.71**	**10.38**
Bahrain	3	3		3	1	0.00	-66.67
Iraq	111	146	123	158	157	0.00	-0.63
Jordan	11,509	16,807	15,885	18,310	20,708	0.62	13.10
Kuwait	4	3	31	7	9	0.00	28.57
Lebanon	181	243	400	228	239	0.01	4.82
Libya			8	3	3	0.00	
Oman	2	2	1	1	4	0.00	300.00
Qatar	30	24	10	10	8	0.00	-20.00
Saudi Arabia	3	7		4			

ISRAEL

2. Arrivals of non-resident visitors at national borders, by country of residence

	2007	2008	2009	2010	2011	Market share 11	% Change 11-10
Syrian Arab Republic	79	90	125	84	67	0.00	-20.24
United Arab Emirates	32	44		15	9	0.00	-40.00
Egypt	2,749	1,846	2,431	2,810	2,663	0.08	-5.23
Yemen	47	26	71	12	23	0.00	91.67
SOUTH ASIA	**27,809**	**33,461**	**26,078**	**43,381**	**41,780**	**1.24**	**-3.69**
Afghanistan	2	6	1	6	2	0.00	-66.67
Bangladesh	30	41	10	17	14	0.00	-17.65
Bhutan	3	27		4	25	0.00	525.00
Sri Lanka	1,851	2,089	1,373	1,956	1,966	0.06	0.51
India	24,264	29,652	23,374	40,394	38,870	1.16	-3.77
Iran, Islamic Republic of	985	701	401	476	411	0.01	-13.66
Maldives	25	19	9	30			
Nepal	638	903	899	493	477	0.01	-3.25
Pakistan	11	23	11	5	15	0.00	200.00
NOT SPECIFIED	**10,440**	**13,030**	**13,820**	**14,004**	**15,477**	**0.46**	**10.52**
Other countries of the World	10,440	13,030	13,820	14,004	15,477	0.46	10.52

ISRAEL

3. Arrivals of non-resident tourists in hotels and similar establishments, by country of residence

		2007	2008	2009	2010	2011	Market share 11	% Change 11-10
TOTAL	(*)	**2,747,500**	**3,373,000**	**2,620,800**	**3,237,000**	**3,231,900**	**100.00**	**-0.16**
AMERICAS		**995,200**	**1,205,600**	**883,500**	**1,133,000**	**1,103,900**	**34.16**	**-2.57**
North America		**921,000**	**1,100,600**	**814,700**	**1,010,900**	**973,100**	**30.11**	**-3.74**
All countries of North America		921,000	1,100,600	814,700	1,010,900	973,100	30.11	-3.74
South America		**74,200**	**105,000**	**68,800**	**122,100**	**130,800**	**4.05**	**7.13**
All countries of South America	(*)	74,200	105,000	68,800	122,100	130,800	4.05	7.13
EUROPE		**1,197,200**	**1,565,100**	**1,255,300**	**1,547,700**	**1,522,600**	**47.11**	**-1.62**
Other Europe		**1,197,200**	**1,565,100**	**1,255,300**	**1,547,700**	**1,522,600**	**47.11**	**-1.62**
All countries of Europe		1,197,200	1,565,100	1,255,300	1,547,700	1,522,600	47.11	-1.62
NOT SPECIFIED		**555,100**	**602,300**	**482,000**	**556,300**	**605,400**	**18.73**	**8.83**
Other countries of the World		555,100	602,300	482,000	556,300	605,400	18.73	8.83

ISRAEL

5. Overnight stays of non-resident tourists in hotels and similar establishments, by country of residence

		2007	2008	2009	2010	2011	Market share 11	% Change 11-10
TOTAL	(*)	8,405,900	10,187,500	8,108,800	9,933,100	9,949,200	100.00	0.16
AMERICAS		2,993,800	3,488,000	2,628,200	3,313,900	3,212,000	32.28	-3.07
North America		2,764,700	3,181,500	2,421,800	2,958,300	2,828,700	28.43	-4.38
All countries of North America		2,764,700	3,181,500	2,421,800	2,958,300	2,828,700	28.43	-4.38
South America		229,100	306,500	206,400	355,600	383,300	3.85	7.79
All countries of South America	(*)	229,100	306,500	206,400	355,600	383,300	3.85	7.79
EUROPE		3,951,700	5,073,300	4,173,300	5,149,700	5,119,000	51.45	-0.60
Other Europe		3,951,700	5,073,300	4,173,300	5,149,700	5,119,000	51.45	-0.60
All countries of Europe		3,951,700	5,073,300	4,173,300	5,149,700	5,119,000	51.45	-0.60
NOT SPECIFIED		1,460,400	1,626,200	1,307,300	1,469,500	1,618,200	16.26	10.12
Other countries of the World		1,460,400	1,626,200	1,307,300	1,469,500	1,618,200	16.26	10.12

ITALY

1. Arrivals of non-resident tourists at national borders, by nationality

	2007	2008	2009	2010	2011	Market share 11	% Change 11-10
TOTAL (*)	43,654,122	42,733,683	43,238,919	43,626,118	46,118,848	100.00	5.71
AFRICA	264,662	300,031	248,441	318,179	280,199	0.61	-11.94
East Africa	20,771	33,021	34,856	28,227	32,911	0.07	16.59
All countries of East Africa	20,771	33,021	34,856	28,227	32,911	0.07	16.59
Central Africa	10,682	12,304	10,830	10,973	13,033	0.03	18.77
All countries of Central Africa	10,682	12,304	10,830	10,973	13,033	0.03	18.77
North Africa	114,213	127,636	105,245	189,253	124,915	0.27	-34.00
Algeria	20,191	22,992	12,664	7,560	11,303	0.02	49.51
Morocco	48,958	73,857	62,194	145,241	72,468	0.16	-50.10
Tunisia	43,263	25,934	27,363	34,166	34,921	0.08	2.21
Other countries of North Africa	1,801	4,853	3,024	2,286	6,223	0.01	172.22
Southern Africa	77,922	82,443	64,956	55,431	67,232	0.15	21.29
South Africa	77,246	80,504	64,124	55,431	66,054	0.14	19.16
Other countries of Southern Africa	676	1,939	832		1,178	0.00	
West Africa	41,074	44,627	32,554	34,295	42,108	0.09	22.78
All countries of West Africa	41,074	44,627	32,554	34,295	42,108	0.09	22.78
AMERICAS	3,440,062	3,394,811	3,390,307	3,501,730	4,067,153	8.82	16.15
Caribbean	17,264	23,934	20,044	15,363	28,884	0.06	88.01
All countries of the Caribbean	17,264	23,934	20,044	15,363	28,884	0.06	88.01
Central America	20,209	23,319	19,114	20,173	28,114	0.06	39.36
Costa Rica	7,516	7,479	7,969	8,613	14,904	0.03	73.04
Panama	928	5,020	2,336	2,149	2,663	0.01	23.92
Other countries of Central America	11,765	10,820	8,809	9,411	10,547	0.02	12.07
North America	2,916,145	2,815,658	2,862,090	2,963,977	3,400,653	7.37	14.73
Canada	397,510	425,998	512,890	561,294	574,527	1.25	2.36
Mexico	81,450	119,798	87,465	74,338	111,543	0.24	50.05
United States of America	2,436,839	2,269,448	2,261,735	2,327,342	2,714,583	5.89	16.64
Other countries of North America	346	414		1,003			
South America	486,444	531,900	489,059	502,217	609,502	1.32	21.36
Argentina	113,818	115,257	138,165	127,537	130,821	0.28	2.57
Brazil	229,384	252,193	188,892	234,199	293,309	0.64	25.24
Chile	48,130	39,219	31,657	47,787	51,437	0.11	7.64
Colombia	19,480	15,812	18,572	15,683	18,433	0.04	17.53
Peru	9,486	20,213	28,052	21,395	23,732	0.05	10.92
Suriname	367	278					
Venezuela	34,040	52,941	45,467	36,215	60,891	0.13	68.14
Other countries of South America	31,739	35,987	38,254	19,401	30,879	0.07	59.16
EAST ASIA AND THE PACIFIC	1,326,583	1,253,482	1,299,901	1,324,474	1,512,096	3.28	14.17
North-East Asia	579,166	538,025	565,451	573,999	640,954	1.39	11.66
China	160,082	158,226	138,210	136,780	209,651	0.45	53.28
Taiwan, Province of China	15,107	17,178	10,138	8,124	15,946	0.03	96.28
Hong Kong, China	21,657	19,132	26,748	26,199	40,524	0.09	54.68
Japan	320,681	283,819	320,591	340,210	314,239	0.68	-7.63
Korea, Republic of	59,020	51,645	59,972	59,996	58,490	0.13	-2.51
Other countries of North-East Asia	2,619	8,025	9,792	2,690	2,104	0.00	-21.78
South-East Asia	95,998	89,339	132,965	119,679	94,826	0.21	-20.77
Indonesia	12,883	7,121	12,474	14,938	9,573	0.02	-35.92
Malaysia	19,706	14,914	16,729	26,154	21,905	0.05	-16.25
Philippines	12,928	15,769	19,154	21,682	14,217	0.03	-34.43
Singapore	24,408	31,156	28,743	20,146	28,623	0.06	42.08
Thailand	22,843	14,189	51,196	33,206	18,444	0.04	-44.46
Other countries of South-East Asia	3,230	6,190	4,669	3,553	2,064	0.00	-41.91

ITALY

1. Arrivals of non-resident tourists at national borders, by nationality

	2007	2008	2009	2010	2011	Market share 11	% Change 11-10
Australasia	640,739	615,660	597,408	624,205	769,764	1.67	23.32
Australia	555,847	518,897	526,755	548,288	693,265	1.50	26.44
New Zealand	84,892	96,763	70,653	75,917	76,499	0.17	0.77
Melanesia	1,108	1,203		1,555	2,449	0.01	57.49
All countries of Melanesia	1,108	1,203		1,555	2,449	0.01	57.49
Micronesia	1,528	52		1,293	384	0.00	-70.30
All countries of Micronesia	1,528	52		1,293	384	0.00	-70.30
Polynesia	8,044	9,203	4,077	3,743	3,719	0.01	-0.64
American Samoa	4,978	8,285	1,668	3,743	2,945	0.01	-21.32
Samoa		593	776				
Other countries of Polynesia	3,066	325	1,633		774	0.00	
EUROPE	38,207,533	37,342,336	37,853,912	37,921,219	39,743,414	86.18	4.81
Central/Eastern Europe	4,964,554	4,584,706	4,366,233	4,894,033	5,246,233	11.38	7.20
Czech Republic	956,098	802,406	772,544	816,161	953,555	2.07	16.83
Hungary	1,033,945	919,012	620,833	525,595	504,221	1.09	-4.07
Poland	1,110,738	986,576	1,033,409	1,124,044	1,182,758	2.56	5.22
Romania	757,627	663,014	672,205	672,377	644,841	1.40	-4.10
Russian Federation	246,368	397,221	431,470	595,275	745,453	1.62	25.23
Slovakia	466,130	382,223	360,843	411,974	388,003	0.84	-5.82
Other countries Central/East Europe	393,648	434,254	474,929	748,607	827,402	1.79	10.53
Northern Europe	6,329,097	5,553,558	5,062,988	4,920,559	5,045,420	10.94	2.54
Denmark	484,447	428,867	451,417	470,812	443,135	0.96	-5.88
Finland	198,818	257,948	216,965	217,226	259,229	0.56	19.34
Ireland	564,149	300,213	336,040	348,638	279,313	0.61	-19.88
Norway	276,490	324,067	261,533	264,516	235,290	0.51	-11.05
Sweden	401,135	465,579	429,538	444,826	625,500	1.36	40.62
United Kingdom	4,390,542	3,761,619	3,361,357	3,163,036	3,195,408	6.93	1.02
Other countries of Northern Europe	13,516	15,265	6,138	11,505	7,545	0.02	-34.42
Southern Europe	3,629,591	3,527,019	4,023,658	4,621,045	4,595,039	9.96	-0.56
Albania	59,584	72,564	86,930	88,965	139,383	0.30	56.67
Bosnia and Herzegovina	15,081	23,228	107,867	265,236	257,321	0.56	-2.98
Croatia	125,133	153,794	261,155	390,919	359,940	0.78	-7.92
Greece	342,443	428,961	438,965	473,474	369,346	0.80	-21.99
Malta	80,761	77,509	40,835	58,598	72,553	0.16	23.81
Montenegro	14,553	4,982					
Portugal	206,078	210,496	223,691	284,028	273,900	0.59	-3.57
Serbia	56,724	48,842	121,695	267,995	248,613	0.54	-7.23
Slovenia	105,169	208,134	245,459	255,651	170,561	0.37	-33.28
Spain	2,612,789	2,286,773	2,463,309	2,484,724	2,610,373	5.66	5.06
Other countries of Southern Europe	11,276	11,736	33,752	51,455	93,049	0.20	80.84
Western Europe	23,039,474	23,461,407	24,135,839	23,217,166	24,602,584	53.35	5.97
Austria	2,479,120	3,098,816	3,403,807	3,361,695	3,205,214	6.95	-4.65
Belgium	1,026,186	1,104,889	1,112,551	1,104,115	1,397,291	3.03	26.55
France	4,803,694	4,820,493	4,935,031	4,843,586	4,982,877	10.80	2.88
Germany	9,895,962	9,803,190	9,546,257	8,960,697	9,874,509	21.41	10.20
Luxembourg	105,151	97,500	108,020	89,597	101,609	0.22	13.41
Netherlands	1,760,209	1,927,042	1,922,473	1,592,483	1,758,978	3.81	10.46
Switzerland	2,916,608	2,537,807	2,952,608	3,183,639	3,235,773	7.02	1.64
Other countries of Western Europe	52,544	71,670	155,092	81,354	46,333	0.10	-43.05
East Mediterranean Europe	219,317	190,389	239,402	242,408	231,327	0.50	-4.57
Israel	79,021	51,932	72,915	105,578	79,291	0.17	-24.90
Turkey	140,296	138,457	166,487	136,830	152,036	0.33	11.11
Other Europe	25,500	25,257	25,792	26,008	22,811	0.05	-12.29
Other countries of Europe	25,500	25,257	25,792	26,008	22,811	0.05	-12.29

ITALY

1. Arrivals of non-resident tourists at national borders, by nationality

	2007	2008	2009	2010	2011	Market share 11	% Change 11-10
MIDDLE EAST	**242,048**	**235,612**	**222,200**	**289,353**	**246,530**	**0.53**	**-14.80**
Jordan	11,065	16,647	15,429	16,158	27,599	0.06	70.81
Kuwait	12,095	9,278					
Lebanon	15,470	14,646	17,277	16,875	9,708	0.02	-42.47
Libya	28,118	22,924	12,695	14,841	8,687	0.02	-41.47
Saudi Arabia	29,899	26,049	15,687	47,494	40,126	0.09	-15.51
United Arab Emirates	70,267	71,516	80,049	95,716	62,256	0.13	-34.96
Egypt	43,480	54,712	46,559	47,639	42,623	0.09	-10.53
Other countries of Middle East	31,654	19,840	34,504	50,630	55,531	0.12	9.68
SOUTH ASIA	**173,234**	**207,411**	**224,158**	**270,007**	**269,061**	**0.58**	**-0.35**
India	108,941	135,517	139,094	182,552	188,408	0.41	3.21
Iran, Islamic Republic of	21,180	27,872	31,173	16,912	33,441	0.07	97.74
Pakistan	26,207	25,175	29,359	33,383	17,669	0.04	-47.07
Other countries of South Asia	16,906	18,847	24,532	37,160	29,543	0.06	-20.50
NOT SPECIFIED				**1,156**	**395**	**0.00**	**-65.83**
Other countries of the World				1,156	395	0.00	-65.83

ITALY

2. Arrivals of non-resident visitors at national borders, by nationality

	2007	2008	2009	2010	2011	Market share 11	% Change 11-10
TOTAL (*)	70,270,689	70,718,861	71,692,233	73,225,219	75,866,005	100.00	3.61
AFRICA	373,049	359,968	287,673	377,484	360,837	0.48	-4.41
East Africa	29,028	35,773	35,510	31,368	37,040	0.05	18.08
All countries of East Africa	29,028	35,773	35,510	31,368	37,040	0.05	18.08
Central Africa	12,003	14,086	11,826	11,347	14,197	0.02	25.12
Sao Tome and Principe				74			
Other countries of Central Africa				11,273			
All countries of Central Africa	12,003	14,086	11,826		14,197	0.02	
North Africa	162,332	168,115	131,023	231,918	182,336	0.24	-21.38
Algeria	34,921	36,144	19,538	17,896	25,264	0.03	41.17
Morocco	60,149	83,854	66,324	150,887	86,979	0.11	-42.35
Tunisia	65,146	43,083	41,266	60,849	63,231	0.08	3.91
Other countries of North Africa	2,116	5,034	3,895	2,286	6,862	0.01	200.17
Southern Africa	80,650	85,792	71,258	60,088	69,011	0.09	14.85
South Africa	79,974	83,853	70,426	60,088	67,833	0.09	12.89
Other countries of Southern Africa	676	1,939	832		1,178	0.00	
West Africa	89,036	56,202	38,056	42,763	58,253	0.08	36.22
All countries of West Africa	89,036	56,202	38,056	42,763	58,253	0.08	36.22
AMERICAS	4,152,001	3,922,420	3,760,644	3,968,611	4,828,460	6.36	21.67
Caribbean	19,606	27,942	20,674	16,603	36,015	0.05	116.92
All countries of the Caribbean	19,606	27,942	20,674	16,603	36,015	0.05	116.92
Central America	34,157	27,997	21,139	23,661	34,393	0.05	45.36
Costa Rica	14,118	8,990	8,053	9,827	14,904	0.02	51.66
Panama	3,269	5,020	3,055	2,619	3,170	0.00	21.04
Other countries of Central America	16,770	13,987	10,031	11,215	16,319	0.02	45.51
North America	3,464,142	3,196,349	3,143,205	3,311,017	3,957,155	5.22	19.51
Canada	524,976	510,157	547,752	604,640	636,858	0.84	5.33
Mexico	86,169	122,520	89,316	77,019	118,782	0.16	54.22
United States of America	2,852,651	2,563,258	2,506,137	2,621,863	3,201,515	4.22	22.11
Other countries of North America	346	414		7,495			
South America	634,096	670,132	575,626	617,330	800,897	1.06	29.74
Argentina	151,670	145,087	162,298	155,949	162,180	0.21	4.00
Brazil	283,756	299,295	221,802	274,543	398,721	0.53	45.23
Chile	56,180	46,769	32,032	52,491	53,247	0.07	1.44
Colombia	23,785	16,945	20,317	16,472	20,690	0.03	25.61
Peru	12,405	25,470	28,905	23,924	26,154	0.03	9.32
Suriname	367	278					
Venezuela	55,885	78,798	59,717	56,189	97,105	0.13	72.82
Other countries of South America	50,048	57,490	50,555	37,762	42,800	0.06	13.34
EAST ASIA AND THE PACIFIC	1,456,015	1,362,724	1,396,924	1,416,478	1,646,410	2.17	16.23
North-East Asia	647,661	591,953	610,831	608,046	680,841	0.90	11.97
China	167,987	163,796	145,995	145,991	223,815	0.30	53.31
Taiwan, Province of China	19,143	17,399	12,727	8,817	17,598	0.02	99.59
Hong Kong, China	21,882	19,330	27,466	29,269	50,484	0.07	72.48
Japan	373,414	318,699	349,710	359,855	326,895	0.43	-9.16
Korea, Republic of	60,201	52,915	60,222	60,955	58,836	0.08	-3.48
Other countries of North-East Asia	5,034	19,814	14,711	3,159	3,213	0.00	1.71
South-East Asia	114,651	105,746	143,730	132,132	111,828	0.15	-15.37
Indonesia	14,890	7,793	15,012	17,037	11,008	0.01	-35.39
Malaysia	21,490	16,719	17,734	27,654	22,075	0.03	-20.17
Philippines	21,189	18,785	21,933	25,757	19,567	0.03	-24.03
Singapore	30,673	40,348	31,075	21,699	34,512	0.05	59.05
Thailand	23,102	15,476	52,307	34,993	22,370	0.03	-36.07

ITALY

2. Arrivals of non-resident visitors at national borders, by nationality

	2007	2008	2009	2010	2011	Market share 11	% Change 11-10
Other countries of South-East Asia	3,307	6,625	5,669	4,992	2,296	0.00	-54.01
Australasia	**678,350**	**642,087**	**631,827**	**665,008**	**846,988**	**1.12**	**27.37**
Australia	589,681	541,146	555,249	584,401	765,527	1.01	30.99
New Zealand	88,669	100,941	76,578	80,607	81,461	0.11	1.06
Melanesia	**1,251**	**1,203**	**160**	**1,555**	**2,449**	**0.00**	**57.49**
All countries of Melanesia	1,251	1,203	160	1,555	2,449	0.00	57.49
Micronesia	**1,528**	**52**		**1,293**	**384**	**0.00**	**-70.30**
All countries of Micronesia	1,528	52		1,293	384	0.00	-70.30
Polynesia	**12,574**	**21,683**	**10,376**	**8,444**	**3,920**	**0.01**	**-53.58**
American Samoa	9,508	19,351	7,077	5,011	3,146	0.00	-37.22
Samoa		593	776				
Other countries of Polynesia	3,066	1,739	2,523	3,433	774	0.00	-77.45
EUROPE	**63,528,197**	**64,492,956**	**65,745,321**	**66,821,317**	**68,359,168**	**90.11**	**2.30**
Central/Eastern Europe	**5,725,087**	**5,307,274**	**5,143,307**	**5,749,328**	**6,211,261**	**8.19**	**8.03**
Czech Republic	1,070,894	912,557	897,923	915,028	1,101,088	1.45	20.33
Hungary	1,138,238	1,089,036	734,637	655,307	658,379	0.87	0.47
Poland	1,245,151	1,100,451	1,164,908	1,257,219	1,287,725	1.70	2.43
Romania	930,049	827,773	859,744	863,342	982,513	1.30	13.80
Russian Federation	294,366	435,814	457,208	645,416	792,560	1.04	22.80
Slovakia	518,385	413,197	410,843	475,148	431,024	0.57	-9.29
Other countries Central/East Europe	528,004	528,446	618,044	937,868	957,972	1.26	2.14
Northern Europe	**6,889,943**	**6,046,031**	**5,438,643**	**5,239,507**	**5,436,515**	**7.17**	**3.76**
Denmark	550,641	479,604	493,788	516,566	464,582	0.61	-10.06
Finland	219,814	278,651	235,631	237,220	279,397	0.37	17.78
Ireland	571,774	315,842	349,829	361,657	287,609	0.38	-20.47
Norway	295,185	344,315	281,075	282,464	248,948	0.33	-11.87
Sweden	472,510	503,434	455,663	481,502	668,911	0.88	38.92
United Kingdom	4,765,588	4,108,223	3,615,588	3,348,204	3,479,523	4.59	3.92
Other countries of Northern Europe	14,431	15,962	7,069	11,894	7,545	0.01	-36.56
Southern Europe	**7,862,976**	**8,697,206**	**9,746,658**	**10,250,804**	**10,322,189**	**13.61**	**0.70**
Albania	75,620	83,866	97,835	99,047	150,063	0.20	51.51
Bosnia and Herzegovina	40,709	24,731	152,527	293,249	260,725	0.34	-11.09
Croatia	948,150	866,387	1,133,295	1,239,545	1,146,611	1.51	-7.50
Greece	501,165	611,364	552,039	598,570	467,671	0.62	-21.87
Malta	129,796	115,980	87,304	91,671	100,367	0.13	9.49
Montenegro	18,103	7,296					
Portugal	249,259	249,007	274,309	380,725	340,350	0.45	-10.60
Serbia	102,310	76,477	159,160	303,033	284,991	0.38	-5.95
Slovenia	2,699,676	3,899,696	4,225,605	4,116,591	4,394,410	5.79	6.75
Spain	3,055,063	2,741,560	3,005,610	3,045,843	3,061,249	4.04	0.51
Other countries of Southern Europe	43,125	20,842	58,974	82,530	115,752	0.15	40.25
Western Europe	**42,726,908**	**44,172,375**	**45,105,222**	**45,248,161**	**46,052,599**	**60.70**	**1.78**
Austria	6,798,074	6,573,010	7,317,666	7,660,061	6,502,564	8.57	-15.11
Belgium	1,220,291	1,265,137	1,288,870	1,248,305	1,672,460	2.20	33.98
France	9,851,016	10,107,314	10,168,307	9,975,720	10,165,234	13.40	1.90
Germany	11,441,371	11,516,663	11,422,068	10,856,813	11,681,707	15.40	7.60
Luxembourg	160,576	120,841	129,698	114,445	119,621	0.16	4.52
Netherlands	2,003,281	2,237,507	2,148,031	1,806,616	2,079,358	2.74	15.10
Switzerland	11,000,079	12,007,628	12,234,105	13,297,391	13,565,237	17.88	2.01
Other countries of Western Europe	252,220	344,275	396,477	288,810	266,418	0.35	-7.75
East Mediterranean Europe	**288,552**	**240,027**	**283,176**	**303,813**	**310,597**	**0.41**	**2.23**
Israel	106,506	75,291	90,331	142,026	134,292	0.18	-5.45
Turkey	182,046	164,736	192,845	161,787	176,305	0.23	8.97
Other Europe	**34,731**	**30,043**	**28,315**	**29,704**	**26,007**	**0.03**	**-12.45**
Other countries of Europe	34,731	30,043	28,315	29,704	26,007	0.03	-12.45

ITALY

2. Arrivals of non-resident visitors at national borders, by nationality

	2007	2008	2009	2010	2011	Market share 11	% Change 11-10
MIDDLE EAST	**388,248**	**311,533**	**260,945**	**349,821**	**362,070**	**0.48**	**3.50**
Jordan	12,411	17,865	16,431	18,212	29,050	0.04	59.51
Kuwait	16,913	11,448					
Lebanon	51,935	28,694	20,146	26,459	36,590	0.05	38.29
Libya	50,442	34,232	18,294	26,463	22,568	0.03	-14.72
Saudi Arabia	35,186	27,487	18,841	53,503	43,982	0.06	-17.80
United Arab Emirates	91,287	81,832	86,828	112,934	80,829	0.11	-28.43
Egypt	85,286	85,022	54,427	54,849	70,402	0.09	28.36
Other countries of Middle East	44,788	24,953	45,978	57,401	78,649	0.10	37.02
SOUTH ASIA	**373,179**	**269,260**	**240,726**	**290,352**	**308,665**	**0.41**	**6.31**
India	274,773	175,576	144,105	189,629	208,132	0.27	9.76
Iran, Islamic Republic of	47,747	44,726	35,824	24,932	38,683	0.05	55.15
Pakistan	31,686	28,020	31,719	35,924	23,852	0.03	-33.60
Other countries of South Asia	18,973	20,938	29,078	39,867	37,998	0.05	-4.69
NOT SPECIFIED				**1,156**	**395**	**0.00**	**-65.83**
Other countries of the World				1,156	395	0.00	-65.83

ITALY

3. Arrivals of non-resident tourists in hotels and similar establishments, by nationality

		2007	2008	2009	2010	2011	Market share 11	% Change 11-10
TOTAL	(*)	34,768,963	33,666,586	32,632,696	35,020,415	37,983,634	100.00	8.46
AFRICA		244,646	253,731	250,004	261,939	287,903	0.76	9.91
Southern Africa		63,617	58,618	52,763	61,542	70,950	0.19	15.29
South Africa		63,617	58,618	52,763	61,542	70,950	0.19	15.29
Other Africa		181,029	195,113	197,241	200,397	216,953	0.57	8.26
Other countries of Africa		181,029	195,113	197,241	200,397	216,953	0.57	8.26
AMERICAS		6,020,648	5,339,344	4,949,563	5,503,571	6,002,579	15.80	9.07
North America		5,217,434	4,497,745	4,134,823	4,503,592	4,740,665	12.48	5.26
Canada		557,307	543,382	501,488	574,369	601,077	1.58	4.65
Mexico		176,922	163,932	135,467	165,582	187,990	0.49	13.53
United States of America		4,483,205	3,790,431	3,497,868	3,763,641	3,951,598	10.40	4.99
South America		803,214	841,599	814,740	999,979	1,261,914	3.32	26.19
Argentina		160,926	154,827	168,435	205,447	262,304	0.69	27.67
Brazil		384,488	437,967	399,018	533,471	695,086	1.83	30.29
Venezuela		49,897	52,294	52,114	49,766	59,860	0.16	20.28
Other countries of South America		207,903	196,511	195,173	211,295	244,664	0.64	15.79
EAST ASIA AND THE PACIFIC		3,487,277	3,179,241	3,006,496	3,612,759	4,218,725	11.11	16.77
North-East Asia		2,523,866	2,230,156	2,141,170	2,525,936	2,966,141	7.81	17.43
China		775,013	686,391	696,778	929,308	1,291,762	3.40	39.00
Japan		1,414,807	1,247,846	1,238,474	1,304,394	1,345,981	3.54	3.19
Korea, Republic of		334,046	295,919	205,918	292,234	328,398	0.86	12.38
Australasia		634,299	648,667	573,459	674,490	736,905	1.94	9.25
Australia		549,355	565,384	501,313	595,227	656,600	1.73	10.31
New Zealand		84,944	83,283	72,146	79,263	80,305	0.21	1.31
Other East Asia and the Pacific		329,112	300,418	291,867	412,333	515,679	1.36	25.06
Other countries of Asia		329,112	300,418	291,867	412,333	515,679	1.36	25.06
EUROPE		24,210,058	24,066,750	23,545,983	24,711,162	26,419,114	69.55	6.91
Central/Eastern Europe		2,156,246	2,433,953	2,181,461	2,524,728	2,978,424	7.84	17.97
Czech Republic		255,896	299,767	312,073	342,037	357,376	0.94	4.48
Estonia		25,684	40,125	26,268	25,906	36,008	0.09	38.99
Hungary		246,780	249,859	230,371	242,192	256,357	0.67	5.85
Latvia		24,093	34,912	25,918	27,219	35,794	0.09	31.50
Lithuania		78,894	82,375	52,508	54,384	69,716	0.18	28.19
Poland		554,724	657,423	621,581	682,019	761,582	2.01	11.67
Russian Federation		907,405	994,898	838,921	1,069,232	1,372,237	3.61	28.34
Slovakia		62,770	74,594	73,821	81,739	89,354	0.24	9.32
Northern Europe		4,541,798	4,387,004	3,902,653	3,941,823	4,032,572	10.62	2.30
Denmark		323,375	350,290	335,233	344,390	335,989	0.88	-2.44
Finland		196,101	220,552	213,831	214,958	228,490	0.60	6.30
Iceland		28,742	26,354	20,599	19,747	19,094	0.05	-3.31
Ireland		386,572	372,535	335,319	304,677	293,654	0.77	-3.62
Norway		294,782	301,872	271,662	294,226	308,167	0.81	4.74
Sweden		433,849	464,884	428,173	480,807	512,006	1.35	6.49
United Kingdom		2,878,377	2,650,517	2,297,836	2,283,018	2,335,172	6.15	2.28
Southern Europe		2,648,241	2,518,924	2,419,587	2,520,293	2,585,925	6.81	2.60
Croatia		161,623	161,178	151,649	142,111	143,113	0.38	0.71
Greece		346,434	349,115	328,778	319,467	315,987	0.83	-1.09
Malta		39,370	45,086	46,700	51,279	56,031	0.15	9.27
Portugal		188,638	194,812	197,166	214,588	217,714	0.57	1.46
Slovenia		146,818	154,382	147,442	150,015	161,765	0.43	7.83
Spain		1,765,358	1,614,351	1,547,852	1,642,833	1,691,315	4.45	2.95

ITALY

3. Arrivals of non-resident tourists in hotels and similar establishments, by nationality

	2007	2008	2009	2010	2011	Market share 11	% Change 11-10
Western Europe	**13,322,250**	**13,079,387**	**13,540,694**	**13,996,316**	**14,845,638**	**39.08**	**6.07**
Austria	1,374,233	1,341,066	1,463,284	1,524,404	1,593,639	4.20	4.54
Belgium	734,695	754,249	783,832	800,229	852,979	2.25	6.59
France	2,701,924	2,662,764	2,732,413	2,838,922	3,025,404	7.97	6.57
Germany	6,310,860	6,138,269	6,289,216	6,456,004	6,809,122	17.93	5.47
Luxembourg	49,587	51,796	54,839	54,209	56,938	0.15	5.03
Netherlands	860,585	882,252	892,568	918,543	956,303	2.52	4.11
Switzerland	1,290,366	1,248,991	1,324,542	1,404,005	1,551,253	4.08	10.49
East Mediterranean Europe	**397,270**	**424,572**	**390,511**	**468,123**	**511,461**	**1.35**	**9.26**
Cyprus	15,708	19,970	16,285	19,031	18,516	0.05	-2.71
Israel	215,980	234,508	222,325	252,876	264,895	0.70	4.75
Turkey	165,582	170,094	151,901	196,216	228,050	0.60	16.22
Other Europe	**1,144,253**	**1,222,910**	**1,111,077**	**1,259,879**	**1,465,094**	**3.86**	**16.29**
Other countries of Europe	1,144,253	1,222,910	1,111,077	1,259,879	1,465,094	3.86	16.29
MIDDLE EAST	**171,131**	**190,184**	**212,806**	**246,834**	**289,156**	**0.76**	**17.15**
Egypt	33,006	35,489	37,951	39,664	38,335	0.10	-3.35
Other countries of Middle East	138,125	154,695	174,855	207,170	250,821	0.66	21.07
SOUTH ASIA	**138,529**	**150,137**	**147,569**	**184,676**	**236,277**	**0.62**	**27.94**
India	138,529	150,137	147,569	184,676	236,277	0.62	27.94
NOT SPECIFIED	**496,674**	**487,199**	**520,275**	**499,474**	**529,880**	**1.40**	**6.09**
Other countries of the World	496,674	487,199	520,275	499,474	529,880	1.40	6.09

ITALY

4. Arrivals of non-resident tourists in all types of accommodation establishments, by nationality

	2007	2008	2009	2010	2011	Market share 11	% Change 11-10
TOTAL	42,873,122	41,796,724	41,124,722	43,794,338	47,460,809	100.00	8.37
AFRICA	270,659	281,938	277,994	289,502	323,857	0.68	11.87
Southern Africa	74,001	68,960	63,038	71,950	84,255	0.18	17.10
South Africa	74,001	68,960	63,038	71,950	84,255	0.18	17.10
Other Africa	196,658	212,978	214,956	217,552	239,602	0.50	10.14
Other countries of Africa	196,658	212,978	214,956	217,552	239,602	0.50	10.14
AMERICAS	6,738,532	5,982,827	5,571,671	6,195,100	6,785,181	14.30	9.52
North America	5,847,043	5,052,001	4,670,934	5,090,819	5,387,397	11.35	5.83
Canada	652,582	635,182	588,776	670,055	708,380	1.49	5.72
Mexico	197,924	183,172	153,481	185,244	212,345	0.45	14.63
United States of America	4,996,537	4,233,647	3,928,677	4,235,520	4,466,672	9.41	5.46
South America	891,489	930,826	900,737	1,104,281	1,397,784	2.95	26.58
Argentina	181,940	175,907	190,837	231,503	297,233	0.63	28.39
Brazil	423,599	478,562	436,377	580,610	757,691	1.60	30.50
Venezuela	54,751	57,678	57,583	55,240	66,316	0.14	20.05
Other countries of South America	231,199	218,679	215,940	236,928	276,544	0.58	16.72
EAST ASIA AND THE PACIFIC	3,758,366	3,461,486	3,278,798	3,921,679	4,574,445	9.64	16.65
North-East Asia	2,636,219	2,343,791	2,250,841	2,643,095	3,111,195	6.56	17.71
China	806,129	716,545	727,570	965,857	1,342,518	2.83	39.00
Japan	1,474,014	1,307,729	1,298,068	1,363,444	1,410,677	2.97	3.46
Korea, Republic of	356,076	319,517	225,203	313,794	358,000	0.75	14.09
Australasia	773,249	796,315	713,880	836,382	910,092	1.92	8.81
Australia	660,560	683,627	613,799	729,960	803,884	1.69	10.13
New Zealand	112,689	112,688	100,081	106,422	106,208	0.22	-0.20
Other East Asia and the Pacific	348,898	321,380	314,077	442,202	553,158	1.17	25.09
Other countries of Asia	348,898	321,380	314,077	442,202	553,158	1.17	25.09
EUROPE	31,217,217	31,167,898	31,044,562	32,383,435	34,630,439	72.97	6.94
Central/Eastern Europe	2,748,605	3,092,554	2,833,442	3,234,612	3,766,341	7.94	16.44
Czech Republic	461,284	522,719	540,417	584,478	612,930	1.29	4.87
Estonia	30,876	46,646	31,158	31,398	41,453	0.09	32.02
Hungary	371,369	375,956	335,402	350,577	367,577	0.77	4.85
Latvia	27,651	40,231	30,731	32,855	43,591	0.09	32.68
Lithuania	88,477	91,582	60,105	63,081	81,269	0.17	28.83
Poland	703,250	840,259	811,024	888,472	989,436	2.08	11.36
Russian Federation	954,345	1,046,199	894,659	1,140,432	1,474,137	3.11	29.26
Slovakia	111,353	128,962	129,946	143,319	155,948	0.33	8.81
Northern Europe	5,446,379	5,334,666	4,780,832	4,842,851	4,948,929	10.43	2.19
Denmark	555,581	606,809	582,009	601,085	579,740	1.22	-3.55
Finland	227,639	255,242	249,324	251,453	269,455	0.57	7.16
Iceland	33,582	31,506	24,337	23,868	22,552	0.05	-5.51
Ireland	457,165	443,657	402,495	365,193	351,383	0.74	-3.78
Norway	344,762	355,664	324,784	350,400	369,221	0.78	5.37
Sweden	522,082	556,467	513,491	574,731	609,826	1.28	6.11
United Kingdom	3,305,568	3,085,321	2,684,392	2,676,121	2,746,752	5.79	2.64
Southern Europe	2,985,723	2,855,207	2,769,729	2,879,943	2,967,086	6.25	3.03
Croatia	185,903	184,453	175,431	163,619	166,120	0.35	1.53
Greece	370,869	375,660	355,853	344,641	342,634	0.72	-0.58
Malta	44,728	50,580	52,995	58,543	64,817	0.14	10.72
Portugal	212,193	219,931	220,538	239,012	242,831	0.51	1.60
Slovenia	195,131	204,729	203,988	206,354	220,852	0.47	7.03
Spain	1,976,899	1,819,854	1,760,924	1,867,774	1,929,832	4.07	3.32

ITALY

4. Arrivals of non-resident tourists in all types of accommodation establishments, by nationality

	2007	2008	2009	2010	2011	Market share 11	% Change 11-10
Western Europe	18,328,971	18,063,820	18,980,303	19,502,832	20,753,343	43.73	6.41
Austria	1,833,428	1,774,887	1,948,791	2,011,317	2,115,524	4.46	5.18
Belgium	916,711	943,350	994,999	1,013,042	1,079,541	2.27	6.56
France	3,245,682	3,215,689	3,332,807	3,449,866	3,689,634	7.77	6.95
Germany	8,943,586	8,674,799	9,085,679	9,302,743	9,873,213	20.80	6.13
Luxembourg	58,295	60,985	64,037	64,329	67,008	0.14	4.16
Netherlands	1,682,377	1,792,595	1,836,907	1,851,034	1,933,447	4.07	4.45
Switzerland	1,648,892	1,601,515	1,717,083	1,810,501	1,994,976	4.20	10.19
East Mediterranean Europe	435,996	465,390	434,714	520,028	568,428	1.20	9.31
Cyprus	16,908	21,178	17,388	20,569	19,958	0.04	-2.97
Israel	241,221	261,783	252,455	289,049	302,765	0.64	4.75
Turkey	177,867	182,429	164,871	210,410	245,705	0.52	16.77
Other Europe	1,271,543	1,356,261	1,245,542	1,403,169	1,626,312	3.43	15.90
Other countries of Europe	1,271,543	1,356,261	1,245,542	1,403,169	1,626,312	3.43	15.90
MIDDLE EAST	183,412	203,093	226,341	261,281	306,390	0.65	17.26
Egypt	35,967	38,836	41,295	43,160	41,998	0.09	-2.69
Other countries of Middle East	147,445	164,257	185,046	218,121	264,392	0.56	21.21
SOUTH ASIA	147,472	160,055	157,708	197,152	251,631	0.53	27.63
India	147,472	160,055	157,708	197,152	251,631	0.53	27.63
NOT SPECIFIED	557,464	539,427	567,648	546,189	588,866	1.24	7.81
Other countries of the World	557,464	539,427	567,648	546,189	588,866	1.24	7.81

ITALY

5. Overnight stays of non-resident tourists in hotels and similar establishments, by nationality

	2007	2008	2009	2010	2011	Market share 11	% Change 11-10
TOTAL (*)	113,017,439	110,491,709	106,828,579	111,551,526	120,014,027	100.00	7.59
AFRICA	782,818	839,069	781,987	782,638	1,127,921	0.94	44.12
Southern Africa	181,196	188,665	155,501	170,553	206,296	0.17	20.96
South Africa	181,196	188,665	155,501	170,553	206,296	0.17	20.96
Other Africa	601,622	650,404	626,486	612,085	921,625	0.77	50.57
Other countries of Africa	601,622	650,404	626,486	612,085	921,625	0.77	50.57
AMERICAS	14,766,405	13,194,994	12,259,124	13,412,419	14,774,746	12.31	10.16
North America	12,730,921	11,065,913	10,195,123	10,979,562	11,795,941	9.83	7.44
Canada	1,481,584	1,415,268	1,301,640	1,459,085	1,656,449	1.38	13.53
Mexico	416,672	387,110	329,798	380,543	425,837	0.35	11.90
United States of America	10,832,665	9,263,535	8,563,685	9,139,934	9,713,655	8.09	6.28
South America	2,035,484	2,129,081	2,064,001	2,432,857	2,978,805	2.48	22.44
Argentina	436,797	422,665	433,805	516,089	641,449	0.53	24.29
Brazil	949,913	1,059,437	976,487	1,247,397	1,582,610	1.32	26.87
Venezuela	146,705	149,331	153,638	141,684	165,396	0.14	16.74
Other countries of South America	502,069	497,648	500,071	527,687	589,350	0.49	11.69
EAST ASIA AND THE PACIFIC	6,828,391	6,390,073	6,033,692	6,925,435	7,924,700	6.60	14.43
North-East Asia	4,447,965	4,020,243	3,868,385	4,323,597	4,939,757	4.12	14.25
China	1,196,057	1,101,656	1,120,082	1,404,270	1,895,228	1.58	34.96
Japan	2,699,229	2,395,971	2,341,372	2,414,679	2,471,480	2.06	2.35
Korea, Republic of	552,679	522,616	406,931	504,648	573,049	0.48	13.55
Australasia	1,594,350	1,616,225	1,434,028	1,662,709	1,838,566	1.53	10.58
Australia	1,369,281	1,399,710	1,243,145	1,451,206	1,624,804	1.35	11.96
New Zealand	225,069	216,515	190,883	211,503	213,762	0.18	1.07
Other East Asia and the Pacific	786,076	753,605	731,279	939,129	1,146,377	0.96	22.07
Other countries of Asia	786,076	753,605	731,279	939,129	1,146,377	0.96	22.07
EUROPE	88,373,136	87,809,408	85,394,447	87,994,204	93,501,667	77.91	6.26
Central/Eastern Europe	7,570,129	8,594,328	7,928,309	9,119,265	10,368,002	8.64	13.69
Czech Republic	1,092,840	1,268,887	1,375,188	1,478,895	1,542,005	1.28	4.27
Estonia	72,773	110,717	80,156	87,842	115,715	0.10	31.73
Hungary	817,621	833,480	748,646	765,236	804,953	0.67	5.19
Latvia	83,158	106,741	86,140	85,843	102,640	0.09	19.57
Lithuania	185,262	191,189	142,040	148,652	185,029	0.15	24.47
Poland	1,888,473	2,312,769	2,216,059	2,412,767	2,487,718	2.07	3.11
Russian Federation	3,154,186	3,440,569	2,965,533	3,801,556	4,752,783	3.96	25.02
Slovakia	275,816	329,976	314,547	338,474	377,159	0.31	11.43
Northern Europe	16,954,184	16,454,468	14,317,327	14,231,652	14,809,878	12.34	4.06
Denmark	1,221,320	1,321,890	1,269,074	1,287,186	1,268,999	1.06	-1.41
Finland	717,413	783,467	740,426	733,575	779,682	0.65	6.29
Iceland	108,971	103,585	80,874	71,863	70,991	0.06	-1.21
Ireland	1,550,604	1,512,182	1,300,099	1,165,921	1,119,810	0.93	-3.95
Norway	1,040,839	1,060,651	949,952	992,868	1,039,100	0.87	4.66
Sweden	1,549,417	1,682,418	1,537,476	1,703,565	1,825,339	1.52	7.15
United Kingdom	10,765,620	9,990,275	8,439,426	8,276,674	8,705,957	7.25	5.19
Southern Europe	7,114,954	6,811,042	6,556,123	6,710,662	6,885,335	5.74	2.60
Croatia	498,521	482,137	453,271	412,143	393,114	0.33	-4.62
Greece	933,672	957,336	891,998	853,639	829,791	0.69	-2.79
Malta	139,101	156,082	148,209	171,231	175,554	0.15	2.52
Portugal	565,738	582,830	560,775	568,408	581,631	0.48	2.33
Slovenia	413,973	442,693	421,663	427,894	456,855	0.38	6.77
Spain	4,563,949	4,189,964	4,080,207	4,277,347	4,448,390	3.71	4.00

ITALY

5. Overnight stays of non-resident tourists in hotels and similar establishments, by nationality

	2007	2008	2009	2010	2011	Market share 11	% Change 11-10
Western Europe	**51,784,017**	**50,812,758**	**52,011,396**	**52,891,926**	**55,747,098**	**46.45**	**5.40**
Austria	4,918,701	4,711,025	5,085,735	5,273,070	5,584,362	4.65	5.90
Belgium	2,959,939	3,008,502	3,094,207	3,088,377	3,229,371	2.69	4.57
France	7,852,762	7,663,227	7,780,100	7,956,900	8,621,882	7.18	8.36
Germany	27,885,517	27,361,414	27,768,674	28,091,376	29,306,486	24.42	4.33
Luxembourg	234,608	238,942	253,555	249,711	264,721	0.22	6.01
Netherlands	3,058,705	3,129,654	3,160,459	3,193,313	3,267,142	2.72	2.31
Switzerland	4,873,785	4,699,994	4,868,666	5,039,179	5,473,134	4.56	8.61
East Mediterranean Europe	**1,137,807**	**1,159,326**	**1,075,768**	**1,270,977**	**1,408,162**	**1.17**	**10.79**
Cyprus	51,360	61,420	52,742	61,417	58,012	0.05	-5.54
Israel	615,314	624,896	605,880	716,764	779,624	0.65	8.77
Turkey	471,133	473,010	417,146	492,796	570,526	0.48	15.77
Other Europe	**3,812,045**	**3,977,486**	**3,505,524**	**3,769,722**	**4,283,192**	**3.57**	**13.62**
Other countries of Europe	3,812,045	3,977,486	3,505,524	3,769,722	4,283,192	3.57	13.62
MIDDLE EAST	**603,363**	**664,245**	**708,535**	**773,622**	**886,737**	**0.74**	**14.62**
Egypt	123,319	132,421	135,776	140,341	146,560	0.12	4.43
Other countries of Middle East	480,044	531,824	572,759	633,281	740,177	0.62	16.88
SOUTH ASIA	**311,639**	**332,124**	**337,851**	**387,672**	**479,236**	**0.40**	**23.62**
India	311,639	332,124	337,851	387,672	479,236	0.40	23.62
NOT SPECIFIED	**1,351,687**	**1,261,796**	**1,312,943**	**1,275,536**	**1,319,020**	**1.10**	**3.41**
Other countries of the World	1,351,687	1,261,796	1,312,943	1,275,536	1,319,020	1.10	3.41

ITALY

6. Overnight stays of non-resident tourists in all types of accommodation establishments, by nationality

	2007	2008	2009	2010	2011	Market share 11	% Change 11-10
TOTAL	163,465,680	161,797,434	159,493,866	165,202,498	176,474,062	100.00	6.82
AFRICA	1,019,477	1,104,421	1,028,095	1,027,597	1,501,871	0.85	46.15
Southern Africa	220,457	229,829	191,669	210,938	255,991	0.15	21.36
South Africa	220,457	229,829	191,669	210,938	255,991	0.15	21.36
Other Africa	799,020	874,592	836,426	816,659	1,245,880	0.71	52.56
Other countries of Africa	799,020	874,592	836,426	816,659	1,245,880	0.71	52.56
AMERICAS	17,429,923	15,551,410	14,513,549	15,883,627	17,500,991	9.92	10.18
North America	15,002,011	13,056,361	12,080,237	13,046,664	14,038,324	7.95	7.60
Canada	1,839,729	1,739,697	1,612,960	1,798,679	2,024,178	1.15	12.54
Mexico	483,819	450,830	387,160	440,692	498,265	0.28	13.06
United States of America	12,678,463	10,865,834	10,080,117	10,807,293	11,515,881	6.53	6.56
South America	2,427,912	2,495,049	2,433,312	2,836,963	3,462,667	1.96	22.06
Argentina	528,951	501,713	519,315	609,771	757,589	0.43	24.24
Brazil	1,125,925	1,226,481	1,137,182	1,427,733	1,809,011	1.03	26.71
Venezuela	167,672	174,117	178,425	163,986	191,695	0.11	16.90
Other countries of South America	605,364	592,738	598,390	635,473	704,372	0.40	10.84
EAST ASIA AND THE PACIFIC	7,724,198	7,382,734	6,970,551	7,961,682	9,088,145	5.15	14.15
North-East Asia	4,804,670	4,440,341	4,287,190	4,733,489	5,416,203	3.07	14.42
China	1,314,727	1,221,174	1,254,039	1,564,035	2,089,115	1.18	33.57
Japan	2,882,194	2,595,488	2,534,836	2,593,846	2,665,424	1.51	2.76
Korea, Republic of	607,749	623,679	498,315	575,608	661,664	0.37	14.95
Australasia	2,025,063	2,086,210	1,846,456	2,147,422	2,367,349	1.34	10.24
Australia	1,718,420	1,764,169	1,572,543	1,861,752	2,081,771	1.18	11.82
New Zealand	306,643	322,041	273,913	285,670	285,578	0.16	-0.03
Other East Asia and the Pacific	894,465	856,183	836,905	1,080,771	1,304,593	0.74	20.71
Other countries of Asia	894,465	856,183	836,905	1,080,771	1,304,593	0.74	20.71
EUROPE	134,606,854	135,071,788	134,234,320	137,485,494	145,229,651	82.30	5.63
Central/Eastern Europe	11,389,353	12,814,604	11,995,567	13,662,293	15,195,030	8.61	11.22
Czech Republic	2,451,726	2,737,307	2,841,017	3,077,661	3,168,776	1.80	2.96
Estonia	89,061	132,794	100,553	108,633	134,152	0.08	23.49
Hungary	1,602,902	1,610,168	1,366,001	1,453,372	1,482,498	0.84	2.00
Latvia	100,379	130,006	109,296	111,807	135,326	0.08	21.04
Lithuania	224,297	229,048	174,487	186,380	231,275	0.13	24.09
Poland	2,884,588	3,519,711	3,400,700	3,736,189	3,883,908	2.20	3.95
Russian Federation	3,405,731	3,730,458	3,294,957	4,208,604	5,318,880	3.01	26.38
Slovakia	630,669	725,112	708,556	779,647	840,215	0.48	7.77
Northern Europe	22,512,195	22,369,491	19,652,109	19,686,308	20,103,858	11.39	2.12
Denmark	3,029,813	3,374,085	3,208,729	3,311,712	3,139,703	1.78	-5.19
Finland	871,022	948,638	901,719	903,041	958,010	0.54	6.09
Iceland	135,057	131,455	96,917	89,837	84,211	0.05	-6.26
Ireland	1,982,680	1,952,516	1,706,869	1,533,856	1,448,777	0.82	-5.55
Norway	1,349,336	1,393,464	1,255,530	1,316,970	1,366,480	0.77	3.76
Sweden	2,063,395	2,211,562	2,013,300	2,193,686	2,311,576	1.31	5.37
United Kingdom	13,080,892	12,357,771	10,469,045	10,337,206	10,795,101	6.12	4.43
Southern Europe	8,512,320	8,213,873	7,989,916	8,146,446	8,350,266	4.73	2.50
Croatia	677,213	657,415	640,887	559,823	526,812	0.30	-5.90
Greece	1,067,064	1,077,392	1,022,691	971,217	952,829	0.54	-1.89
Malta	163,386	183,753	177,540	202,203	207,217	0.12	2.48
Portugal	667,247	698,721	651,567	671,622	680,305	0.39	1.29
Slovenia	631,347	668,601	664,166	678,568	718,615	0.41	5.90
Spain	5,306,063	4,927,991	4,833,065	5,063,013	5,264,488	2.98	3.98

ITALY

6. Overnight stays of non-resident tourists in all types of accommodation establishments, by nationality

	2007	2008	2009	2010	2011	Market share 11	% Change 11-10
Western Europe	85,893,023	85,253,357	88,733,229	89,590,427	94,427,763	53.51	5.40
Austria	7,893,293	7,482,993	8,078,701	8,226,147	8,670,900	4.91	5.41
Belgium	4,129,185	4,258,189	4,434,026	4,425,339	4,614,934	2.62	4.28
France	10,267,003	10,158,629	10,447,586	10,623,637	11,432,007	6.48	7.61
Germany	46,497,062	45,401,981	47,278,488	47,801,927	50,199,797	28.45	5.02
Luxembourg	289,117	293,531	309,707	308,829	320,997	0.18	3.94
Netherlands	9,620,138	10,675,969	10,875,329	10,674,451	11,043,799	6.26	3.46
Switzerland	7,197,225	6,982,065	7,309,392	7,530,097	8,145,329	4.62	8.17
East Mediterranean Europe	1,309,770	1,340,620	1,267,778	1,491,744	1,648,181	0.93	10.49
Cyprus	57,135	66,864	57,348	67,900	63,995	0.04	-5.75
Israel	724,330	741,852	734,500	871,404	936,832	0.53	7.51
Turkey	528,305	531,904	475,930	552,440	647,354	0.37	17.18
Other Europe	4,990,193	5,079,843	4,595,721	4,908,276	5,504,553	3.12	12.15
Other countries of Europe	4,990,193	5,079,843	4,595,721	4,908,276	5,504,553	3.12	12.15
MIDDLE EAST	698,391	777,548	818,238	874,432	1,001,851	0.57	14.57
Egypt	146,410	170,608	170,842	170,056	181,312	0.10	6.62
Other countries of Middle East	551,981	606,940	647,396	704,376	820,539	0.46	16.49
SOUTH ASIA	352,697	389,659	394,709	461,311	554,886	0.31	20.28
India	352,697	389,659	394,709	461,311	554,886	0.31	20.28
NOT SPECIFIED	1,634,140	1,519,874	1,534,404	1,508,355	1,596,667	0.90	5.85
Other countries of the World	1,634,140	1,519,874	1,534,404	1,508,355	1,596,667	0.90	5.85

JAMAICA

1. Arrivals of non-resident tourists at national borders, by country of residence

	2007	2008	2009	2010	2011	Market share 11	% Change 11-10
TOTAL (*)	**1,700,785**	**1,767,271**	**1,831,097**	**1,921,678**	**1,951,752**	**100.00**	**1.56**
AFRICA	**1,449**	**1,213**	**1,237**	**1,169**	**1,200**	**0.06**	**2.65**
Other Africa	**1,449**	**1,213**	**1,237**	**1,169**	**1,200**	**0.06**	**2.65**
All countries of Africa	1,449	1,213	1,237	1,169	1,200	0.06	2.65
AMERICAS	**1,398,318**	**1,470,488**	**1,542,976**	**1,639,875**	**1,687,308**	**86.45**	**2.89**
Caribbean	**60,389**	**64,467**	**62,823**	**56,031**	**63,360**	**3.25**	**13.08**
Antigua and Barbuda	2,236	2,799	2,554	2,235	2,290	0.12	2.46
Bahamas	5,586	4,378	5,031	4,884	5,999	0.31	22.83
Barbados	5,383	6,107	5,027	4,469	5,422	0.28	21.32
Bermuda	3,208	3,393	3,369	3,112	2,710	0.14	-12.92
British Virgin Islands	939	966	1,025	1,054	1,031	0.05	-2.18
Cayman Islands	19,685	20,287	23,384	18,409	18,035	0.92	-2.03
Cuba	1,083	839	1,067	562	646	0.03	14.95
Dominica	398	584	543	387	418	0.02	8.01
Dominican Republic	1,851	1,595	1,111	1,038	1,293	0.07	24.57
Grenada	796	1,010	640	450	527	0.03	17.11
Guadeloupe	148	194	121	185	322	0.02	74.05
Haiti	264	273	288	447	392	0.02	-12.30
Montserrat	111	146	154	149	143	0.01	-4.03
Aruba	397	508	400	398	409	0.02	2.76
Bonaire	23	1					
Curaçao	902	1,910	1,279	778	893	0.05	14.78
Puerto Rico	1,454	1,693	1,346	1,447	1,486	0.08	2.70
Saint Kitts and Nevis	864	1,068	1,103	950	913	0.05	-3.89
Saint Lucia	1,492	1,712	1,308	990	1,055	0.05	6.57
Sint Maarten	804	950	789	941	1,079	0.06	14.67
Saint Vincent and the Grenadines	632	841	595	445	676	0.03	51.91
Trinidad and Tobago	9,684	10,621	9,622	10,330	15,513	0.79	50.17
Turks and Caicos Islands	1,765	1,815	1,445	1,545	1,522	0.08	-1.49
Other countries of the Caribbean	684	777	622	826	586	0.03	-29.06
Central America	**3,129**	**3,609**	**3,441**	**3,251**	**3,655**	**0.19**	**12.43**
Belize	524	582	592	481	612	0.03	27.23
Costa Rica	710	812	799	758	846	0.04	11.61
El Salvador	213	299	177	142	174	0.01	22.54
Guatemala	306	284	348	527	501	0.03	-4.93
Honduras	147	361	156	131	203	0.01	54.96
Nicaragua	69	90	85	76	102	0.01	34.21
Panama	1,160	1,181	1,284	1,136	1,217	0.06	7.13
North America	**1,325,483**	**1,390,737**	**1,465,338**	**1,570,118**	**1,606,627**	**82.32**	**2.33**
Canada	190,650	236,193	290,307	325,191	378,938	19.42	16.53
Mexico	2,301	3,602	2,187	1,984	2,124	0.11	7.06
United States of America	1,132,532	1,150,942	1,172,844	1,242,943	1,225,565	62.79	-1.40
South America	**9,317**	**11,675**	**11,374**	**10,475**	**13,666**	**0.70**	**30.46**
Argentina	1,164	1,762	1,695	1,779	2,168	0.11	21.87
Bolivia	34	52	34	51	56	0.00	9.80
Brazil	1,454	1,865	1,550	1,683	1,597	0.08	-5.11
Chile	529	812	893	741	1,023	0.05	38.06
Colombia	1,878	1,045	1,001	1,110	1,489	0.08	34.14
Ecuador	343	1,865	1,844	1,481	2,979	0.15	101.15
Guyana	2,160	2,295	2,079	1,827	2,376	0.12	30.05
Paraguay	29	17	30	22	58	0.00	163.64
Peru	341	482	465	393	485	0.02	23.41
Suriname	418	469	431	441	480	0.02	8.84
Uruguay	82	148	190	139	168	0.01	20.86
Venezuela	873	852	1,145	786	759	0.04	-3.44
Other countries of South America	12	11	17	22	28	0.00	27.27

JAMAICA

1. Arrivals of non-resident tourists at national borders, by country of residence

	2007	2008	2009	2010	2011	Market share 11	% Change 11-10
EAST ASIA AND THE PACIFIC	8,620	7,863	7,138	6,760	7,429	0.38	9.90
North-East Asia	4,418	4,110	4,013	3,703	4,281	0.22	15.61
China	1,077	935	1,142	1,302	1,703	0.09	30.80
Taiwan, Province of China	54	118	69	76	74	0.00	-2.63
Japan	3,049	2,846	2,511	1,950	2,027	0.10	3.95
Korea, Republic of	238	211	291	375	477	0.02	27.20
South-East Asia	503	559	450	587	424	0.02	-27.77
Philippines	366	441	322	479	323	0.02	-32.57
Singapore	137	118	128	108	101	0.01	-6.48
Australasia	3,179	2,783	2,218	2,121	2,269	0.12	6.98
Australia	2,729	2,439	1,903	1,869	2,040	0.10	9.15
New Zealand	450	344	315	252	229	0.01	-9.13
Other East Asia and the Pacific	520	411	457	349	455	0.02	30.37
Other countries of Asia	520	411	457	349	455	0.02	30.37
EUROPE	290,269	286,142	277,931	272,139	253,749	13.00	-6.76
Central/Eastern Europe	3,461	5,041	4,336	4,533	4,893	0.25	7.94
Czech Republic/Slovakia	653	680	578	473	772	0.04	63.21
Hungary	316	722	276	389	286	0.01	-26.48
Poland	903	1,326	1,294	1,299	1,443	0.07	11.09
Russian Federation	1,302	1,881	1,744	1,945	1,976	0.10	1.59
Ukraine	287	432	444	427	416	0.02	-2.58
Northern Europe	193,142	195,986	191,225	190,825	179,726	9.21	-5.82
Denmark	1,076	851	794	772	648	0.03	-16.06
Finland	279	404	526	427	451	0.02	5.62
Ireland	3,940	3,431	2,838	2,737	2,459	0.13	-10.16
Norway	831	1,061	958	915	1,054	0.05	15.19
Sweden	1,359	1,803	1,597	1,619	1,607	0.08	-0.74
United Kingdom	185,657	188,436	184,512	184,355	173,507	8.89	-5.88
Southern Europe	47,370	40,112	36,703	34,107	23,492	1.20	-31.12
Greece	187	390	291	249	273	0.01	9.64
Italy	17,394	14,563	14,588	13,700	11,700	0.60	-14.60
Portugal	11,907	9,649	9,056	10,076	4,686	0.24	-53.49
Spain	17,882	15,510	12,768	10,082	6,833	0.35	-32.23
Western Europe	42,572	41,168	42,848	40,233	43,079	2.21	7.07
Austria	2,551	2,252	2,623	2,641	2,545	0.13	-3.63
Belgium	6,338	6,187	6,610	5,228	5,276	0.27	0.92
France	3,587	3,916	3,779	3,762	4,748	0.24	26.21
Germany	19,895	18,962	20,220	18,857	19,939	1.02	5.74
Luxembourg	242	210	248	207	212	0.01	2.42
Netherlands	7,804	7,541	7,023	6,677	7,200	0.37	7.83
Switzerland	2,155	2,100	2,345	2,861	3,159	0.16	10.42
East Mediterranean Europe	1,375	1,442	1,132	824	704	0.04	-14.56
Israel	1,135	1,135	879	683	597	0.03	-12.59
Turkey	240	307	253	141	107	0.01	-24.11
Other Europe	2,349	2,393	1,687	1,617	1,855	0.10	14.72
Other countries of Europe	2,349	2,393	1,687	1,617	1,855	0.10	14.72
MIDDLE EAST	477	577	532	542	649	0.03	19.74
Saudi Arabia	19	28	19	16	36	0.00	125.00
Other countries of Middle East	458	549	513	526	613	0.03	16.54
SOUTH ASIA	1,604	923	1,248	1,152	1,362	0.07	18.23
India	1,525	904	1,232	1,127	1,330	0.07	18.01
Pakistan	79	19	16	25	32	0.00	28.00
NOT SPECIFIED	48	65	35	41	55	0.00	34.15
Other countries of the World	48	65	35	41	55	0.00	34.15

JAMAICA

6. Overnight stays of non-resident tourists in all types of accommodation establishments, by country of residence

		2007	2008	2009	2010	2011	Market share 11	% Change 11-10
TOTAL	(*)	**15,077,110**	**15,014,185**	**15,535,167**	**15,903,420**	**15,932,132**	**100.00**	**0.18**
AMERICAS		**10,877,006**	**11,074,891**	**11,655,659**	**12,155,998**	**12,430,885**	**78.02**	**2.26**
Caribbean		**460,495**	**435,559**	**426,111**	**395,983**	**410,946**	**2.58**	**3.78**
All countries of the Caribbean		460,495	435,559	426,111	395,983	410,946	2.58	3.78
North America		**10,308,534**	**10,510,569**	**11,110,489**	**11,641,691**	**11,885,744**	**74.60**	**2.10**
Canada, United States		10,308,534	10,510,569	11,110,489	11,641,691	11,885,744	74.60	2.10
Other Americas		**107,977**	**128,763**	**119,059**	**118,324**	**134,195**	**0.84**	**13.41**
Other countries of the Americas	(*)	107,977	128,763	119,059	118,324	134,195	0.84	13.41
EUROPE		**4,003,524**	**3,808,593**	**3,740,515**	**3,608,147**	**3,344,357**	**20.99**	**-7.31**
Other Europe		**4,003,524**	**3,808,593**	**3,740,515**	**3,608,147**	**3,344,357**	**20.99**	**-7.31**
All countries of Europe	(*)	4,003,524	3,808,593	3,740,515	3,608,147	3,344,357	20.99	-7.31
NOT SPECIFIED		**196,580**	**130,701**	**138,993**	**139,275**	**156,890**	**0.98**	**12.65**
Other countries of the World		196,580	130,701	138,993	139,275	156,890	0.98	12.65

JAPAN

2. Arrivals of non-resident visitors at national borders, by nationality

		2007	2008	2009	2010	2011	Market share 11	% Change 11-10
TOTAL	(*)	8,346,969	8,350,835	6,789,658	8,611,175	6,218,752	100.00	-27.78
AFRICA		20,114	20,542	17,219	19,076	16,777	0.27	-12.05
Southern Africa		6,020	5,610	4,290	4,635	3,942	0.06	-14.95
South Africa		6,020	5,610	4,290	4,635	3,942	0.06	-14.95
West Africa		2,127	2,272	2,090	2,333	1,834	0.03	-21.39
Ghana		915	859	792	957	799	0.01	-16.51
Nigeria		1,212	1,413	1,298	1,376	1,035	0.02	-24.78
Other Africa		11,967	12,660	10,839	12,108	11,001	0.18	-9.14
Other countries of Africa		11,967	12,660	10,839	12,108	11,001	0.18	-9.14
AMERICAS		1,054,019	1,005,692	908,098	945,377	716,808	11.53	-24.18
Central America					357	291	0.00	-18.49
El Salvador					357	291	0.00	-18.49
North America		1,010,078	960,846	869,129	899,785	680,266	10.94	-24.40
Canada		165,993	168,307	152,756	153,303	101,299	1.63	-33.92
Mexico		28,203	24,194	16,454	19,248	13,080	0.21	-32.04
United States of America		815,882	768,345	699,919	727,234	565,887	9.10	-22.19
South America		35,729	37,369	32,398	38,137	31,038	0.50	-18.61
Argentina		5,240	4,358	4,379	4,896	3,768	0.06	-23.04
Bolivia		554	459	459	518	384	0.01	-25.87
Brazil		18,853	20,981	16,899	21,393	18,470	0.30	-13.66
Chile		2,736	2,764	2,667	3,053	2,579	0.04	-15.53
Colombia		3,019	3,181	2,973	3,052	2,238	0.04	-26.67
Ecuador		707	890	683	845	480	0.01	-43.20
Peru		2,554	2,370	2,164	2,452	1,857	0.03	-24.27
Venezuela		2,066	2,366	2,174	1,928	1,262	0.02	-34.54
Other Americas		8,212	7,477	6,571	7,098	5,213	0.08	-26.56
Other countries of the Americas		8,212	7,477	6,571	7,098	5,213	0.08	-26.56
EAST ASIA AND THE PACIFIC		6,267,798	6,306,921	4,940,971	6,653,648	4,796,321	77.13	-27.91
North-East Asia		5,370,098	5,333,609	4,092,862	5,660,930	4,083,956	65.67	-27.86
China		942,439	1,000,416	1,006,085	1,412,875	1,043,246	16.78	-26.16
Taiwan, Province of China		1,385,255	1,390,228	1,024,292	1,268,278	993,974	15.98	-21.63
Hong Kong, China		432,042	550,190	449,568	508,691	364,865	5.87	-28.27
Korea, Republic of		2,600,694	2,382,397	1,586,772	2,439,816	1,658,073	26.66	-32.04
Macao, China				17,199	21,330	13,292	0.21	-37.68
Mongolia		9,668	10,378	8,946	9,940	10,506	0.17	5.69
South-East Asia		616,089	660,119	592,793	722,112	515,154	8.28	-28.66
Brunei Darussalam		1,088	1,150	1,138	1,388	971	0.02	-30.04
Myanmar		4,679	5,106	4,905	5,095	5,106	0.08	0.22
Cambodia		2,652	2,701	3,008	3,189	3,069	0.05	-3.76
Indonesia		64,178	66,593	63,617	80,632	61,911	1.00	-23.22
Lao People's Democratic Republic		1,820	2,160	2,145	2,209	2,111	0.03	-4.44
Malaysia		100,890	105,663	89,509	114,519	81,516	1.31	-28.82
Philippines		89,532	82,177	71,485	77,377	63,099	1.01	-18.45
Singapore		151,860	167,894	145,224	180,960	111,354	1.79	-38.46
Viet Nam		31,909	34,794	34,221	41,862	41,048	0.66	-1.94
Thailand		167,481	191,881	177,541	214,881	144,969	2.33	-32.54
Australasia		257,255	275,713	243,226	257,812	186,574	3.00	-27.63
Australia		222,518	242,031	211,659	225,751	162,578	2.61	-27.98
New Zealand		34,737	33,682	31,567	32,061	23,996	0.39	-25.16
Other East Asia and the Pacific		24,356	37,480	12,090	12,794	10,637	0.17	-16.86
Other countries of Asia		20,823	34,205	9,103	9,734	8,061	0.13	-17.19
Other countries of Oceania		3,533	3,275	2,987	3,060	2,576	0.04	-15.82

JAPAN

2. Arrivals of non-resident visitors at national borders, by nationality

	2007	2008	2009	2010	2011	Market share 11	% Change 11-10
EUROPE	897,944	909,626	820,128	877,284	582,787	9.37	-33.57
Central/Eastern Europe	97,570	100,186	76,200	84,204	58,191	0.94	-30.89
Bulgaria	2,485	2,742	2,434	2,238	1,783	0.03	-20.33
Czech Republic	5,943	5,792	4,943	5,319	4,525	0.07	-14.93
Hungary	5,540	4,821	4,455	4,371	3,182	0.05	-27.20
Poland	9,027	10,265	8,638	10,253	7,451	0.12	-27.33
Romania	3,823	3,698	3,550	4,664	3,227	0.05	-30.81
Russian Federation	64,244	66,270	46,952	51,457	33,793	0.54	-34.33
Slovakia	2,123	2,285	1,786	2,192	1,356	0.02	-38.14
Ukraine	4,385	4,313	3,442	3,710	2,874	0.05	-22.53
Northern Europe	309,261	294,565	259,062	266,428	200,414	3.22	-24.78
Denmark	14,305	14,486	13,116	14,606	10,821	0.17	-25.91
Finland	18,870	20,025	17,797	16,960	10,943	0.18	-35.48
Iceland				589	546	0.01	-7.30
Ireland	13,681	12,513	10,450	10,738	8,294	0.13	-22.76
Norway	10,668	10,848	9,855	10,302	7,905	0.13	-23.27
Sweden	29,792	30,129	26,384	29,188	21,806	0.35	-25.29
United Kingdom	221,945	206,564	181,460	184,045	140,099	2.25	-23.98
Southern Europe	106,762	113,569	116,229	123,728	65,312	1.05	-47.21
Croatia	1,596	1,700	1,325	1,402	918	0.01	-34.52
Greece	4,315	4,494	4,350	4,363	2,459	0.04	-43.64
Italy	54,022	56,243	59,607	62,394	34,035	0.55	-45.45
Montenegro				70	41	0.00	-41.43
Portugal	13,351	10,280	8,463	10,313	6,227	0.10	-39.62
Serbia				973	754	0.01	-22.51
Spain	33,478	40,852	42,484	44,076	20,814	0.33	-52.78
Serbia and Montenegro				137	64	0.00	-53.28
Western Europe	348,311	361,864	333,803	365,507	235,749	3.79	-35.50
Austria	13,217	13,453	13,684	14,440	8,539	0.14	-40.87
Belgium	14,828	15,773	13,899	15,981	10,708	0.17	-33.00
France	137,787	147,580	141,251	151,011	95,438	1.53	-36.80
Germany	125,193	126,207	110,692	124,360	80,772	1.30	-35.05
Luxembourg				873	432	0.01	-50.52
Netherlands	33,290	34,487	31,186	32,837	23,450	0.38	-28.59
Switzerland	23,996	24,364	23,091	26,005	16,410	0.26	-36.90
East Mediterranean Europe	20,413	22,903	20,043	24,118	13,508	0.22	-43.99
Israel	12,511	13,173	12,205	14,189	6,931	0.11	-51.15
Turkey	7,902	9,730	7,838	9,929	6,577	0.11	-33.76
Other Europe	15,627	16,539	14,791	13,299	9,613	0.15	-27.72
Other countries of Europe	15,627	16,539	14,791	13,299	9,613	0.15	-27.72
MIDDLE EAST	3,294	3,956	7,332	10,448	7,106	0.11	-31.99
Lebanon				935	611	0.01	-34.65
Saudi Arabia			2,750	3,749	2,866	0.05	-23.55
United Arab Emirates			1,180	2,175	1,045	0.02	-51.95
Egypt	3,294	3,956	3,402	3,589	2,584	0.04	-28.00
SOUTH ASIA	102,860	102,991	95,270	104,679	98,460	1.58	-5.94
Bangladesh	6,149	6,168	6,360	6,213	6,118	0.10	-1.53
Sri Lanka	10,676	9,535	8,538	9,570	10,040	0.16	4.91
India	67,583	67,323	58,918	66,819	59,354	0.95	-11.17
Iran, Islamic Republic of	4,344	4,384	4,898	4,831	3,787	0.06	-21.61
Nepal	6,478	8,253	9,221	9,484	11,041	0.18	16.42
Pakistan	7,630	7,328	7,335	7,762	8,120	0.13	4.61
NOT SPECIFIED	940	1,107	640	663	493	0.01	-25.64
Other countries of the World	940	1,107	640	663	493	0.01	-25.64

JORDAN

1. Arrivals of non-resident tourists at national borders, by nationality

	2007	2008	2009	2010	2011	Market share 11	% Change 11-10
TOTAL	3,430,954	3,728,726	3,788,890	4,207,408	3,959,654	100.00	-5.89
AFRICA	54,708	49,884	46,387	49,762	49,947	1.26	0.37
East Africa	3,650	3,019	3,587	4,666	4,342	0.11	-6.94
Ethiopia	923	1,454	2,113	3,106	2,264	0.06	-27.11
Eritrea	438	373	358	407	367	0.01	-9.83
Djibouti	48	35	49	26	25	0.00	-3.85
Kenya	518	465	486	599	1,191	0.03	98.83
Mauritius	115	160	234	296	299	0.01	1.01
Somalia	1,608	532	347	232	196	0.00	-15.52
Central Africa	146	122	92	164	363	0.01	121.34
Chad	146	122	92	164	363	0.01	121.34
North Africa	40,409	35,207	32,490	34,354	32,072	0.81	-6.64
Algeria	7,346	6,854	6,166	6,270	7,400	0.19	18.02
Morocco	6,171	4,850	4,782	4,293	3,337	0.08	-22.27
Sudan	19,699	18,330	17,589	19,511	17,843	0.45	-8.55
Tunisia	7,193	5,173	3,953	4,280	3,492	0.09	-18.41
Southern Africa	8,167	9,435	8,072	8,193	9,792	0.25	19.52
South Africa	8,167	9,435	8,072	8,193	9,792	0.25	19.52
West Africa	862	908	739	449	581	0.01	29.40
Mauritania	390	312	229	10	16	0.00	60.00
Nigeria	371	353	448	364	478	0.01	31.32
Senegal	101	243	62	75	87	0.00	16.00
Other Africa	1,474	1,193	1,407	1,936	2,797	0.07	44.47
Other countries of Africa	1,474	1,193	1,407	1,936	2,797	0.07	44.47
AMERICAS	177,782	200,371	189,776	215,121	189,283	4.78	-12.01
North America	169,018	186,163	177,563	194,439	168,862	4.26	-13.15
Canada	16,702	19,422	18,682	34,960	27,785	0.70	-20.52
Mexico	3,022	4,863	2,944	5,373	3,565	0.09	-33.65
United States of America	149,294	161,878	155,937	154,106	137,512	3.47	-10.77
South America	5,457	9,774	8,691	16,222	15,582	0.39	-3.95
Argentina	1,096	2,565	2,111	3,172	2,446	0.06	-22.89
Brazil	2,528	4,561	4,495	8,215	8,317	0.21	1.24
Chile	51	105	75	1,952	1,794	0.05	-8.09
Colombia	1,016	1,660	1,244	1,510	1,835	0.05	21.52
Venezuela	766	883	766	1,373	1,190	0.03	-13.33
Other Americas	3,307	4,434	3,522	4,460	4,839	0.12	8.50
Other countries of the Americas	3,307	4,434	3,522	4,460	4,839	0.12	8.50
EAST ASIA AND THE PACIFIC	126,069	146,029	138,404	148,981	154,149	3.89	3.47
North-East Asia	37,584	42,127	35,239	49,738	46,348	1.17	-6.82
China	11,197	13,007	12,594	13,882	12,118	0.31	-12.71
Taiwan, Province of China	2,150	2,526	1,617	2,320	2,089	0.05	-9.96
Hong Kong, China	39	82	200	436	1,931	0.05	342.89
Japan	12,291	13,233	12,506	18,779	12,480	0.32	-33.54
Korea, Dem. People's Republic of	250	58	25	14	52	0.00	271.43
Korea, Republic of	11,657	13,221	8,297	14,307	17,678	0.45	23.56
South-East Asia	67,733	77,810	76,496	64,716	78,892	1.99	21.90
Brunei Darussalam				247	312	0.01	26.32
Indonesia	38,088	41,626	39,165	32,282	39,551	1.00	22.52
Malaysia	5,551	7,207	6,922	11,890	15,585	0.39	31.08
Philippines	18,963	22,641	25,249	11,893	13,058	0.33	9.80
Singapore	3,202	3,841	2,373	4,544	5,410	0.14	19.06
Viet Nam	187	413	136				
Thailand	1,742	2,082	2,651	3,860	4,976	0.13	28.91

JORDAN

1. Arrivals of non-resident tourists at national borders, by nationality

	2007	2008	2009	2010	2011	Market share 11	% Change 11-10
Australasia	**20,229**	**25,539**	**25,952**	**33,716**	**28,120**	**0.71**	**-16.60**
Australia	16,508	21,311	21,620	28,420	23,926	0.60	-15.81
New Zealand	3,721	4,228	4,332	5,296	4,194	0.11	-20.81
Melanesia	**151**	**193**	**347**	**418**	**268**	**0.01**	**-35.89**
Fiji	151	193	347	418	268	0.01	-35.89
Other East Asia and the Pacific	**372**	**360**	**370**	**393**	**521**	**0.01**	**32.57**
Other countries of Asia	372	360	370	393	521	0.01	32.57
EUROPE	**570,859**	**657,628**	**602,394**	**744,992**	**626,886**	**15.83**	**-15.85**
Central/Eastern Europe	**42,858**	**65,433**	**48,230**	**69,403**	**64,738**	**1.63**	**-6.72**
Bulgaria	1,551	2,755	2,151	2,051	1,855	0.05	-9.56
Belarus				1,096	1,091	0.03	-0.46
Czech Republic	2,393	3,798	2,802	2,738	2,592	0.07	-5.33
Hungary	1,166	2,794	1,978	5,857	4,360	0.11	-25.56
Poland	8,814	16,288	9,073	9,944	10,513	0.27	5.72
Romania	1,744	3,732	3,428	4,437	4,536	0.11	2.23
Russian Federation	18,758	24,833	20,777	29,292	25,173	0.64	-14.06
Slovakia	1,050	2,035	1,749	1,087	1,672	0.04	53.82
Ukraine	5,999	7,878	5,302	7,608	7,780	0.20	2.26
Other countries Central/East Europe	1,383	1,320	970	5,293	5,166	0.13	-2.40
Northern Europe	**88,219**	**90,871**	**101,601**	**109,933**	**113,995**	**2.88**	**3.69**
Denmark	4,831	4,635	6,057	8,730	11,840	0.30	35.62
Finland	3,096	5,160	6,498	4,808	3,189	0.08	-33.67
Iceland	181	188	186	210	261	0.01	24.29
Ireland	3,484	3,750	3,715	4,816	3,950	0.10	-17.98
Norway	2,898	4,752	7,072	7,815	12,182	0.31	55.88
Sweden	8,763	11,062	14,902	16,373	15,066	0.38	-7.98
United Kingdom	64,966	61,324	63,171	67,181	67,507	1.70	0.49
Southern Europe	**70,058**	**99,827**	**84,909**	**115,546**	**68,713**	**1.74**	**-40.53**
Bosnia and Herzegovina	954	868	708	801	612	0.02	-23.60
Croatia	795	1,355	864	1,420	1,155	0.03	-18.66
Greece	4,931	5,970	4,768	5,222	3,351	0.08	-35.83
Holy See	107	86	136				
Italy	26,320	41,832	43,529	57,747	36,484	0.92	-36.82
Malta	216	244	229	306	264	0.01	-13.73
Portugal	1,897	4,540	3,528	5,203	2,573	0.06	-50.55
Slovenia	1,292	2,020	1,318	1,688	983	0.02	-41.77
Spain	31,911	39,762	29,256	42,657	22,944	0.58	-46.21
TFYR of Macedonia				304	201	0.01	-33.88
Serbia and Montenegro		3,150	573	86			
Other countries of Southern Europe	1,635			112	146	0.00	30.36
Western Europe	**104,413**	**129,457**	**141,501**	**196,284**	**156,370**	**3.95**	**-20.33**
Austria	6,483	5,505	6,522	9,581	8,874	0.22	-7.38
Belgium	6,619	11,078	12,296	16,983	15,942	0.40	-6.13
France	34,410	46,501	53,637	74,893	51,956	1.31	-30.63
Germany	34,115	39,555	41,622	61,080	52,245	1.32	-14.46
Luxembourg	299	319	341	490	326	0.01	-33.47
Netherlands	14,630	18,278	18,545	23,604	19,561	0.49	-17.13
Switzerland	7,857	8,221	8,538	9,653	7,466	0.19	-22.66
East Mediterranean Europe	**260,104**	**262,676**	**220,704**	**234,853**	**205,682**	**5.19**	**-12.42**
Cyprus	1,941	1,879	1,563	1,768	1,567	0.04	-11.37
Israel	226,277	228,601	185,489	197,276	172,465	4.36	-12.58
Turkey	31,886	32,196	33,652	35,809	31,650	0.80	-11.61
Other Europe	**5,207**	**9,364**	**5,449**	**18,973**	**17,388**	**0.44**	**-8.35**
Other countries of Europe	5,207	9,364	5,449	18,973	17,388	0.44	-8.35

JORDAN

1. Arrivals of non-resident tourists at national borders, by nationality

		2007	2008	2009	2010	2011	Market share 11	% Change 11-10
MIDDLE EAST		**1,689,532**	**1,777,094**	**1,867,473**	**2,054,551**	**1,892,950**	**47.81**	**-7.87**
Bahrain		49,401	48,403	44,983	28,475	19,473	0.49	-31.61
Palestine		255,606	266,845	285,610	324,116	348,257	8.80	7.45
Iraq		205,984	180,800	212,670	235,121	286,031	7.22	21.65
Kuwait		87,434	88,146	89,682	57,767	46,450	1.17	-19.59
Lebanon		105,004	104,723	96,064	104,168	69,020	1.74	-33.74
Libya		26,222	31,230	34,261	45,898	22,168	0.56	-51.70
Oman		17,381	19,722	16,192	15,633	12,154	0.31	-22.25
Qatar		14,347	13,692	13,310	9,146	7,234	0.18	-20.91
Saudi Arabia		543,715	606,711	644,360	541,401	516,608	13.05	-4.58
Syrian Arab Republic		284,093	304,707	310,471	571,824	455,595	11.51	-20.33
United Arab Emirates		23,259	29,745	27,565	22,682	15,894	0.40	-29.93
Egypt		44,892	50,791	39,885	55,978	53,673	1.36	-4.12
Yemen		32,194	31,579	52,420	42,342	40,393	1.02	-4.60
SOUTH ASIA		**64,895**	**73,571**	**71,778**	**65,243**	**77,078**	**1.95**	**18.14**
Afghanistan		535	1,064	1,786	1,133	1,056	0.03	-6.80
Bangladesh		5,672	6,118	7,239	2,948	3,224	0.08	9.36
Sri Lanka		15,933	15,325	15,360	10,152	10,426	0.26	2.70
India		30,240	36,663	29,760	40,342	51,550	1.30	27.78
Iran, Islamic Republic of		1,559	1,298	1,216	866	960	0.02	10.85
Nepal		1,546	2,335	4,021	1,159	917	0.02	-20.88
Pakistan		9,410	10,768	12,396	8,643	8,945	0.23	3.49
NOT SPECIFIED		**747,109**	**824,149**	**872,678**	**928,758**	**969,361**	**24.48**	**4.37**
Other countries of the World	(*)	2,907	5,124	11,260				
Nationals Residing Abroad		744,202	819,025	861,418	928,758	969,361	24.48	4.37

JORDAN

2. Arrivals of non-resident visitors at national borders, by nationality

	2007	2008	2009	2010	2011	Market share 11	% Change 11-10
TOTAL	6,528,555	7,100,478	7,084,552	8,078,380	6,812,470	100.00	-15.67
AFRICA	76,590	68,659	63,584	68,722	58,144	0.85	-15.39
East Africa	6,003	4,304	4,867	5,179	4,879	0.07	-5.79
Ethiopia	1,168	1,841	2,675	3,106	2,264	0.03	-27.11
Eritrea	555	472	453	407	367	0.01	-9.83
Djibouti	52	38	53	49	44	0.00	-10.20
Kenya	706	634	662	629	1,313	0.02	108.74
Mauritius	145	202	296	336	332	0.00	-1.19
Somalia	3,377	1,117	728	652	559	0.01	-14.26
Central Africa	185	154	116	164	363	0.01	121.34
Chad	185	154	116	164	363	0.01	121.34
North Africa	58,937	51,661	47,418	52,083	38,983	0.57	-25.15
Algeria	14,604	13,626	12,258	18,453	11,494	0.17	-37.71
Morocco	6,879	5,407	5,331	4,417	3,423	0.05	-22.50
Sudan	26,932	25,060	24,047	22,769	20,109	0.30	-11.68
Tunisia	10,522	7,568	5,782	6,444	3,957	0.06	-38.59
Southern Africa	8,596	9,930	8,496	8,860	10,493	0.15	18.43
South Africa	8,596	9,930	8,496	8,860	10,493	0.15	18.43
West Africa	1,017	1,090	892	455	588	0.01	29.23
Mauritania	420	336	246	10	16	0.00	60.00
Nigeria	469	447	567	370	485	0.01	31.08
Senegal	128	307	79	75	87	0.00	16.00
Other Africa	1,852	1,520	1,795	1,981	2,838	0.04	43.26
Other countries of Africa	1,852	1,520	1,795	1,981	2,838	0.04	43.26
AMERICAS	214,402	244,245	230,436	250,246	216,890	3.18	-13.33
North America	201,928	223,475	212,871	224,556	192,123	2.82	-14.44
Canada	30,343	35,284	33,939	39,048	30,970	0.45	-20.69
Mexico	4,084	6,571	3,978	6,843	4,506	0.07	-34.15
United States of America	167,501	181,620	174,954	178,665	156,647	2.30	-12.32
South America	8,366	15,262	13,191	20,279	19,253	0.28	-5.06
Argentina	1,708	3,995	3,289	4,698	3,579	0.05	-23.82
Brazil	3,198	5,770	5,686	9,939	10,110	0.15	1.72
Chile	1,092	2,250	1,607	2,338	2,167	0.03	-7.31
Colombia	1,073	1,753	1,314	1,817	2,109	0.03	16.07
Venezuela	1,295	1,494	1,295	1,487	1,288	0.02	-13.38
Other Americas	4,108	5,508	4,374	5,411	5,514	0.08	1.90
Other countries of the Americas	4,108	5,508	4,374	5,411	5,514	0.08	1.90
EAST ASIA AND THE PACIFIC	143,235	166,153	157,281	173,664	169,649	2.49	-2.31
North-East Asia	42,150	47,313	39,219	50,541	47,169	0.69	-6.67
China	12,428	14,437	13,979	13,976	12,208	0.18	-12.65
Taiwan, Province of China	2,459	2,890	1,850	2,501	2,246	0.03	-10.20
Hong Kong, China	52	110	268	439	1,975	0.03	349.89
Japan	12,827	13,810	13,052	19,052	12,829	0.19	-32.66
Korea, Dem. People's Republic of	275	64	27	14	52	0.00	271.43
Korea, Republic of	14,109	16,002	10,043	14,559	17,859	0.26	22.67
South-East Asia	76,306	87,647	86,178	84,780	90,155	1.32	6.34
Indonesia	42,986	46,979	44,202	40,729	42,792	0.63	5.07
Malaysia	6,272	8,143	7,822	12,600	15,977	0.23	26.80
Philippines	21,366	25,510	28,448	22,315	20,572	0.30	-7.81
Singapore	3,557	4,267	2,636	5,078	5,546	0.08	9.22
Viet Nam	206	455	150	198	292	0.00	47.47
Thailand	1,919	2,293	2,920	3,860	4,976	0.07	28.91

JORDAN

2. Arrivals of non-resident visitors at national borders, by nationality

	2007	2008	2009	2010	2011	Market share 11	% Change 11-10
Australasia	**24,061**	**30,375**	**30,866**	**37,095**	**31,065**	**0.46**	**-16.26**
Australia	19,635	25,347	25,714	31,025	26,175	0.38	-15.63
New Zealand	4,426	5,028	5,152	6,070	4,890	0.07	-19.44
Melanesia	**180**	**229**	**413**	**536**	**353**	**0.01**	**-34.14**
Fiji	180	229	413	536	353	0.01	-34.14
Other East Asia and the Pacific	**538**	**589**	**605**	**712**	**907**	**0.01**	**27.39**
Other countries of Asia	538	589	605	712	907	0.01	27.39
EUROPE	**889,086**	**1,020,139**	**930,747**	**1,117,010**	**897,420**	**13.17**	**-19.66**
Central/Eastern Europe	**112,095**	**174,403**	**128,805**	**156,416**	**112,894**	**1.66**	**-27.82**
Bulgaria	1,940	3,446	2,690	2,906	2,398	0.04	-17.48
Belarus	1,159		1,420	1,545	1,345	0.02	-12.94
Czech Republic	7,403	11,748	8,668	8,303	4,786	0.07	-42.36
Hungary	1,991	4,771	3,377	7,518	5,016	0.07	-33.28
Poland	19,375	35,805	19,946	24,563	15,266	0.22	-37.85
Romania	2,529	5,412	4,972	5,444	5,357	0.08	-1.60
Russian Federation	63,319	83,822	70,132	79,142	56,624	0.83	-28.45
Slovakia	1,875	3,633	3,122	3,678	2,629	0.04	-28.52
Ukraine	12,504	16,419	11,051	12,509	10,685	0.16	-14.58
Other countries Central/East Europe		9,347	3,427	10,808	8,788	0.13	-18.69
Northern Europe	**120,552**	**122,297**	**135,048**	**152,623**	**141,555**	**2.08**	**-7.25**
Denmark	5,935	5,694	7,441	9,490	13,044	0.19	37.45
Finland	3,391	5,651	7,116	7,727	6,197	0.09	-19.80
Iceland	181	188	186	210	261	0.00	24.29
Ireland	4,048	4,358	4,317	5,386	4,210	0.06	-21.83
Norway	3,391	5,560	8,275	9,327	14,293	0.21	53.24
Sweden	9,570	12,081	16,274	17,505	15,877	0.23	-9.30
United Kingdom	94,036	88,765	91,439	102,978	87,673	1.29	-14.86
Southern Europe	**76,382**	**112,652**	**97,477**	**129,596**	**75,437**	**1.11**	**-41.79**
Bosnia and Herzegovina	3,136	2,855	2,328	2,213	1,227	0.02	-44.55
Croatia	1,027	1,749	1,115	1,599	1,247	0.02	-22.01
Greece	5,325	6,447	5,138	5,458	3,505	0.05	-35.78
Holy See	125	101	160				
Italy	29,872	47,478	49,403	65,756	40,861	0.60	-37.86
Malta	254	286	269	306	264	0.00	-13.73
Portugal	2,073	4,962	3,856	5,565	2,717	0.04	-51.18
Slovenia	1,493	2,334	1,522	1,749	1,006	0.01	-42.48
Spain	33,077	41,215	30,325	44,190	23,875	0.35	-45.97
TFYR of Macedonia		1,838	2,734	2,556	555	0.01	-78.29
Serbia and Montenegro		3,387	627	96	31	0.00	-67.71
Other countries of Southern Europe				108	149	0.00	37.96
Western Europe	**129,785**	**161,674**	**176,800**	**240,861**	**179,792**	**2.64**	**-25.35**
Austria	7,296	6,195	7,340	9,881	9,103	0.13	-7.87
Belgium	9,615	16,092	17,862	21,375	18,578	0.27	-13.09
France	42,267	57,118	65,884	102,890	63,076	0.93	-38.70
Germany	45,990	53,323	56,110	69,460	59,074	0.87	-14.95
Luxembourg	299	319	341	552	364	0.01	-34.06
Netherlands	15,680	19,589	19,876	25,842	21,114	0.31	-18.30
Switzerland	8,638	9,038	9,387	10,861	8,483	0.12	-21.89
East Mediterranean Europe	**424,112**	**428,305**	**381,926**	**416,741**	**369,643**	**5.43**	**-11.30**
Cyprus	1,963	1,900	1,580	1,987	1,761	0.03	-11.37
Israel	276,622	279,463	226,759	243,975	211,889	3.11	-13.15
Turkey	145,527	146,942	153,587	170,779	155,993	2.29	-8.66
Other Europe	**26,160**	**20,808**	**10,691**	**20,773**	**18,099**	**0.27**	**-12.87**
Other countries of Europe	26,160	20,808	10,691	20,773	18,099	0.27	-12.87

JORDAN

2. Arrivals of non-resident visitors at national borders, by nationality

	2007	2008	2009	2010	2011	Market share 11	% Change 11-10
MIDDLE EAST	**4,787,072**	**5,123,967**	**5,133,608**	**5,418,565**	**4,366,252**	**64.09**	**-19.42**
Bahrain	94,547	92,636	86,092	100,221	43,645	0.64	-56.45
Palestine	345,963	361,174	386,573	408,383	441,574	6.48	8.13
Iraq	274,553	240,985	283,464	241,482	292,129	4.29	20.97
Kuwait	137,113	138,229	140,638	142,110	69,420	1.02	-51.15
Lebanon	194,413	193,893	177,860	189,612	108,638	1.59	-42.71
Libya	29,837	35,536	38,985	48,685	23,264	0.34	-52.22
Oman	19,856	22,530	18,497	21,440	13,730	0.20	-35.96
Qatar	19,173	18,297	17,787	15,725	9,127	0.13	-41.96
Saudi Arabia	1,006,803	1,123,453	1,193,168	1,332,680	1,074,190	15.77	-19.40
Syrian Arab Republic	1,981,646	2,125,439	2,165,646	2,451,995	1,903,749	27.95	-22.36
United Arab Emirates	29,687	37,965	35,182	36,932	18,045	0.26	-51.14
Egypt	616,872	697,921	548,068	383,168	326,511	4.79	-14.79
Yemen	36,609	35,909	41,648	46,132	42,230	0.62	-8.46
SOUTH ASIA	**74,147**	**84,177**	**82,169**	**101,060**	**114,361**	**1.68**	**13.16**
Afghanistan	640	1,272	2,135	2,826	2,518	0.04	-10.90
Bangladesh	6,351	6,850	8,105	5,387	5,428	0.08	0.76
Sri Lanka	17,698	17,023	17,062	13,415	12,166	0.18	-9.31
India	34,610	41,962	34,061	51,461	64,971	0.95	26.25
Iran, Islamic Republic of	1,748	1,456	1,364	1,037	1,132	0.02	9.16
Nepal	1,703	2,572	4,428	5,445	4,807	0.07	-11.72
Pakistan	11,397	13,042	15,014	21,489	23,339	0.34	8.61
NOT SPECIFIED	**344,023**	**393,138**	**486,727**	**949,113**	**989,754**	**14.53**	**4.28**
Other countries of the World	3,951	6,964	15,303				
Nationals Residing Abroad	340,072	386,174	471,424	949,113	989,754	14.53	4.28

KAZAKHSTAN

2. Arrivals of non-resident visitors at national borders, by country of residence

	2007	2008	2009	2010	2011	Market share 11	% Change 11-10
TOTAL	5,310,582	4,721,456	4,329,848	4,712,657			
AFRICA	2,272	1,805	2,818	3,577			
East Africa	138	156	277	1,900			
Ethiopia	22	14	14	20			
Kenya	41	34	52	56			
Madagascar	2	2	1	8			
Zimbabwe	51	34	21	27			
Uganda	14	61	167	1,786			
United Republic of Tanzania	6	5	16	1			
Zambia	2	6	6	2			
Central Africa	36	34	859	15			
Angola	27	17	7	5			
Chad	2	2	831	2			
Congo	7	15	21	8			
North Africa	296	233	384	425			
Algeria	85	82	150	139			
Morocco	109	64	94	142			
Sudan	27	31	41	46			
Tunisia	75	56	99	98			
Southern Africa	1,466	1,103	1,045	983			
South Africa	1,466	1,103	1,045	983			
West Africa	336	279	253	254			
Ghana	53	39	41	40			
Côte d'Ivoire	16	7	6	15			
Liberia	2	4	3	4			
Mali	4	6	2	3			
Mauritania	8	4	6	6			
Niger	10	4	11	2			
Nigeria	226	203	153	156			
Guinea-Bissau	1	1	1	1			
Senegal	12	8	27	21			
Burkina Faso	4	3	3	6			
AMERICAS	33,222	28,860	31,190	32,207			
Caribbean	245	222	281	352			
Barbados			1	3			
Cuba	183	179	208	238			
Dominica	1	3		4			
Jamaica	9	4	6	3			
Anguilla	4	3	2	2			
Saint Lucia	1		11	63			
Trinidad and Tobago	47	33	53	39			
Central America	40	37	111	142			
Costa Rica	9	8	14	17			
El Salvador	5	16	59	78			
Guatemala	3	3	4	12			
Honduras	7	4	21	15			
Panama	16	6	13	20			
North America	31,595	27,355	29,195	30,133			
Canada	5,550	5,127	5,071	5,343			
Mexico	89	72	143	187			
United States of America	25,956	22,156	23,981	24,603			
South America	1,342	1,246	1,603	1,580			
Argentina	249	251	331	277			
Brazil	496	325	582	452			
Chile	48	79	62	203			

KAZAKHSTAN

2. Arrivals of non-resident visitors at national borders, by country of residence

	2007	2008	2009	2010	2011	Market share 11	% Change 11-10
Colombia	263	271	270	255			
Ecuador	55	53	59	49			
Peru	36	38	62	83			
Uruguay	7	32	6	51			
Venezuela	188	197	231	210			
EAST ASIA AND THE PACIFIC	**219,908**	**212,003**	**206,829**	**174,842**			
North-East Asia	**209,090**	**202,578**	**195,489**	**163,287**			
China	171,753	172,083	169,866	133,861			
Taiwan, Province of China	210	319	259	223			
Hong Kong, China	4	15	13	51			
Japan	5,223	5,013	4,292	4,528			
Korea, Dem. People's Republic of	152	114	117	187			
Korea, Republic of	21,079	16,078	12,775	13,842			
Mongolia	10,669	8,956	8,167	10,595			
South-East Asia	**7,010**	**5,844**	**7,316**	**7,605**			
Myanmar	12	11	5	19			
Cambodia	18	12	20	21			
Indonesia	465	412	632	508			
Lao People's Democratic Republic	12	17	46	17			
Malaysia	1,450	1,211	1,230	1,511			
Philippines	3,240	2,541	3,375	3,721			
Singapore	715	561	495	463			
Viet Nam	122	107	383	190			
Thailand	976	972	1,130	1,155			
Australasia	**3,802**	**3,575**	**4,018**	**3,941**			
Australia	3,129	2,947	3,370	3,341			
New Zealand	673	628	648	600			
Melanesia	**6**	**6**	**6**	**4**			
Papua New Guinea	6	6	6	4			
Polynesia				**5**			
Samoa				5			
EUROPE	**5,018,562**	**4,447,837**	**4,047,626**	**4,454,928**			
Central/Eastern Europe	**4,714,209**	**4,214,502**	**3,813,169**	**4,217,829**			
Azerbaijan	46,523	42,109	55,923	73,639			
Armenia	10,760	8,754	13,037	18,597			
Bulgaria	1,715	1,486	1,596	3,652			
Belarus	20,153	16,457	24,481	29,710			
Czech Republic	2,138	1,874	2,950	2,957			
Estonia	615	511	672	618			
Georgia	10,733	7,964	7,312	7,844			
Hungary	3,668	2,547	2,979	3,024			
Kyrgyzstan	1,076,478	1,045,781	1,043,015	1,115,711			
Latvia	1,866	1,743	1,998	2,298			
Lithuania	5,349	3,837	4,747	4,566			
Republic of Moldova	9,672	7,089	8,611	9,569			
Poland	7,208	6,011	5,648	6,255			
Romania	3,983	2,483	2,094	2,190			
Russian Federation	1,339,506	1,105,981	1,122,709	1,269,697			
Slovakia	782	751	918	1,166			
Tajikistan	552,999	394,125	203,579	173,592			
Turkmenistan	30,966	18,743	31,933	30,646			
Ukraine	54,105	51,007	81,224	68,217			
Uzbekistan	1,534,990	1,495,249	1,197,743	1,393,881			
Northern Europe	**33,947**	**24,891**	**33,761**	**35,248**			
Denmark	1,362	1,012	1,001	1,115			
Finland	1,274	1,237	1,255	1,376			

KAZAKHSTAN

2. Arrivals of non-resident visitors at national borders, by country of residence

	2007	2008	2009	2010	2011	Market share 11	% Change 11-10
Iceland	62	69	130	210			
Ireland	1,269	1,142	1,082	1,287			
Norway	1,002	826	1,761	2,505			
Sweden	1,284	1,184	1,236	1,603			
United Kingdom	27,694	19,421	27,296	27,152			
Southern Europe	**18,023**	**15,449**	**20,481**	**22,478**			
Albania	78	79	87	106			
Bosnia and Herzegovina	315	216	136	179			
Croatia	969	785	1,021	1,190			
Greece	1,308	1,143	1,270	1,601			
Italy	11,939	10,237	14,178	14,514			
Malta	50	43	32	70			
Portugal	676	495	486	572			
Serbia	44		449	985			
Slovenia	571	507	496	537			
Spain	2,073	1,944	2,326	2,687			
Other countries of Southern Europe				37			
Western Europe	**124,890**	**106,582**	**107,785**	**109,686**			
Austria	3,419	3,245	3,515	4,014			
Belgium	1,891	1,653	2,323	2,927			
France	7,165	7,058	8,363	9,370			
Germany	102,210	85,364	83,869	82,670			
Liechtenstein	5	7	11	13			
Luxembourg	121	112	129	301			
Monaco	11	8	11	8			
Netherlands	7,769	7,171	7,594	8,021			
Switzerland	2,299	1,964	1,970	2,362			
East Mediterranean Europe	**127,493**	**86,413**	**72,430**	**69,687**			
Cyprus	82	54	79	122			
Israel	5,956	5,123	4,607	4,248			
Turkey	121,455	81,236	67,744	65,317			
MIDDLE EAST	**4,551**	**3,832**	**5,227**	**6,228**			
Bahrain	26	56	150	31			
Palestine	160	91	164	152			
Iraq	75	67	111	153			
Jordan	592	511	546	747			
Kuwait	101	78	130	107			
Lebanon	548	523	697	791			
Libya	120	35	81	186			
Oman	83	79	85	130			
Qatar	119	107	127	99			
Saudi Arabia	321	290	493	387			
Syrian Arab Republic	398	318	526	610			
United Arab Emirates	1,173	984	820	882			
Egypt	832	687	1,297	1,953			
Yemen	3	6					
SOUTH ASIA	**26,372**	**23,064**	**26,611**	**23,551**			
Afghanistan	3,169	2,900	4,625	2,396			
Bangladesh	233	213	511	361			
Bhutan	4	4	6	7			
Sri Lanka	140	98	116	173			
India	9,280	9,022	11,790	11,949			
Iran, Islamic Republic of	10,492	8,165	6,980	6,387			
Nepal	104	101	112	95			
Pakistan	2,950	2,561	2,471	2,183			
NOT SPECIFIED	**5,695**	**4,055**	**9,547**	**17,324**			
Other countries of the World	5,695	4,055	9,547	17,324			

KENYA

2. Arrivals of non-resident visitors at national borders, by country of residence

	2007	2008	2009	2010	2011	Market share 11	% Change 11-10
TOTAL	1,817,000	1,203,000	1,490,000	1,609,000			
AFRICA	205,000	136,000	158,000	279,000			
Other Africa	205,000	136,000	158,000	279,000			
All countries of Africa	205,000	136,000	158,000	279,000			
AMERICAS	134,000	89,000	111,000	131,000			
Other Americas	134,000	89,000	111,000	131,000			
All countries of the Americas	134,000	89,000	111,000	131,000			
EAST ASIA AND THE PACIFIC	168,000	111,000	122,000	162,000			
Other East Asia and the Pacific	168,000	111,000	122,000	162,000			
All countries of Asia	168,000	111,000	122,000	162,000			
EUROPE	1,237,000	819,000	1,040,000	932,000			
Other Europe	1,237,000	819,000	1,040,000	932,000			
All countries of Europe	1,237,000	819,000	1,040,000	932,000			
NOT SPECIFIED	73,000	48,000	59,000	105,000			
Other countries of the World	73,000	48,000	59,000	105,000			

KENYA

5. Overnight stays of non-resident tourists in hotels and similar establishments, by country of residence

	2007	2008	2009	2010	2011	Market share 11	% Change 11-10
TOTAL	5,044,400	2,080,100	4,062,400	4,260,100			
AFRICA	399,100	283,600	485,700	451,700			
East Africa	106,900	86,300	174,100	129,400			
Uganda	52,200	43,200	103,000	67,900			
United Republic of Tanzania	54,700	43,100	71,100	61,500			
North Africa	43,900	17,000	25,400	28,300			
All countries of North Africa	43,900	17,000	25,400	28,300			
Southern Africa	73,600	52,600	87,800	88,100			
All countries of Southern Africa	73,600	52,600	87,800	88,100			
West Africa	35,600	26,300	45,400	55,100			
All countries of West Africa	35,600	26,300	45,400	55,100			
Other Africa	139,100	101,400	153,000	150,800			
Other countries of Africa	139,100	101,400	153,000	150,800			
AMERICAS	369,100	197,000	325,700	347,100			
North America	334,900	180,300	292,300	314,000			
Canada	64,000	32,200	58,500	59,800			
United States of America	270,900	148,100	233,800	254,200			
Other Americas	34,200	16,700	33,400	33,100			
Other countries of the Americas	34,200	16,700	33,400	33,100			
EAST ASIA AND THE PACIFIC	187,500	107,600	166,900	194,600			
North-East Asia	88,900	38,900	71,000	91,500			
China	43,200	20,700	33,200	50,700			
Japan	45,700	18,200	37,800	40,800			
Australasia	56,900	42,300	54,900	60,200			
Australia, New Zealand	56,900	42,300	54,900	60,200			
Other East Asia and the Pacific	41,700	26,400	41,000	42,900			
Other countries of Asia	41,700	26,400	41,000	42,900			
EUROPE	3,837,700	1,323,600	2,798,100	2,933,400			
Northern Europe	1,352,900	535,300	1,007,000	1,048,800			
United Kingdom	1,223,100	486,600	909,700	964,700			
Scandinavia	129,800	48,700	97,300	84,100			
Southern Europe	536,500	158,200	383,200	651,000			
Italy	536,500	158,200	383,200	651,000			
Western Europe	1,404,600	470,100	1,044,900	869,000			
France	304,300	63,800	231,800	222,700			
Germany	926,100	339,500	685,600	563,200			
Switzerland	174,200	66,800	127,500	83,100			
Other Europe	543,700	160,000	363,000	364,600			
Other countries of Europe	543,700	160,000	363,000	364,600			
MIDDLE EAST	38,000	20,000	37,500	36,600			
All countries of Middle East	38,000	20,000	37,500	36,600			
SOUTH ASIA	60,500	51,200	83,300	91,100			
India	60,500	51,200	83,300	91,100			
NOT SPECIFIED	152,500	97,100	165,200	205,600			
Other countries of the World	152,500	97,100	165,200	205,600			

KIRIBATI

1. Arrivals of non-resident tourists at national borders, by nationality

		2007	2008	2009	2010	2011	Market share 11	% Change 11-10
TOTAL	(*)	**4,709**	**3,871**	**3,944**	**4,701**	**5,264**	**100.00**	**11.98**
AMERICAS		**1,109**	**928**	**699**	**827**	**1,063**	**20.19**	**28.54**
North America		**1,109**	**928**	**699**	**827**	**1,063**	**20.19**	**28.54**
Canada		37	41	47	51	67	1.27	31.37
United States of America		1,072	887	652	776	996	18.92	28.35
EAST ASIA AND THE PACIFIC		**3,069**	**2,481**	**2,695**	**3,240**	**2,887**	**54.84**	**-10.90**
North-East Asia		**247**	**190**	**288**	**429**	**298**	**5.66**	**-30.54**
Taiwan, Province of China				54	185	62	1.18	-66.49
Japan		247	190	234	244	236	4.48	-3.28
Australasia		**1,220**	**1,152**	**1,286**	**1,383**	**1,432**	**27.20**	**3.54**
Australia		908	868	934	913	809	15.37	-11.39
New Zealand		312	284	352	470	623	11.84	32.55
Other East Asia and the Pacific		**1,602**	**1,139**	**1,121**	**1,428**	**1,157**	**21.98**	**-18.98**
Other countries of Asia		496	370	379	387			
Other countries of Oceania		1,106	769	742	1,041	1,157	21.98	11.14
EUROPE		**297**	**304**	**382**	**368**	**412**	**7.83**	**11.96**
Northern Europe		**157**	**129**	**135**	**153**	**226**	**4.29**	**47.71**
United Kingdom		157	129	135	153	226	4.29	47.71
Southern Europe		**7**	**10**	**11**	**14**			
Italy		7	10	11	14			
Western Europe		**103**	**114**	**185**	**144**	**112**	**2.13**	**-22.22**
France		59	71	120	72	43	0.82	-40.28
Germany		33	40	50	55	69	1.31	25.45
Switzerland		11	3	15	17			
Other Europe		**30**	**51**	**51**	**57**	**74**	**1.41**	**29.82**
Other countries of Europe		30	51	51	57	74	1.41	29.82
NOT SPECIFIED		**234**	**158**	**168**	**266**	**902**	**17.14**	**239.10**
Other countries of the World		234	158	168	266	902	17.14	239.10

KOREA, REPUBLIC OF

2. Arrivals of non-resident visitors at national borders, by nationality

		2007	2008	2009	2010	2011	Market share 11	% Change 11-10
TOTAL	(*)	6,448,240	6,890,841	7,817,533	8,797,658	9,794,796	100.00	11.33
AFRICA		19,211	20,720	22,487	26,892	30,334	0.31	12.80
East Africa		2,514	3,259	4,874	5,949	7,438	0.08	25.03
Burundi		31	15	14	27	70	0.00	159.26
Comoros		2	2	6		13	0.00	
Ethiopia		482	464	439	599	915	0.01	52.75
Eritrea		4	10	11	18	29	0.00	61.11
Djibouti		1	6	12	13	14	0.00	7.69
Kenya		727	686	816	1,017	1,312	0.01	29.01
Madagascar		43	70	107	88	109	0.00	23.86
Malawi		52	26	28	94	101	0.00	7.45
Mauritius		175	264	495	567	502	0.01	-11.46
Mozambique		48	89	83	90	174	0.00	93.33
Reunion						3	0.00	
Rwanda		86	106	109	121	229	0.00	89.26
Seychelles		39	60	43	83	71	0.00	-14.46
Somalia		8	7	11	9	16	0.00	77.78
Zimbabwe		141	183	186	270	258	0.00	-4.44
Uganda		227	244	246	295	402	0.00	36.27
United Republic of Tanzania		344	930	2,175	2,534	3,060	0.03	20.76
Zambia		104	97	93	124	160	0.00	29.03
Central Africa		1,068	917	1,028	1,440	1,674	0.02	16.25
Angola		196	195	314	438	476	0.00	8.68
Cameroon		202	310	318	386	444	0.00	15.03
Central African Republic		13	10	6	25	35	0.00	40.00
Chad		15	8	4	21	36	0.00	71.43
Congo		253	100	90	63	103	0.00	63.49
Democratic Republic of the Congo		236	188	157	328	327	0.00	-0.30
Equatorial Guinea		12	14	6	34	40	0.00	17.65
Gabon		136	92	127	140	204	0.00	45.71
Sao Tome and Principe		5		6	5	9	0.00	80.00
North Africa		2,563	3,063	3,198	3,536	4,164	0.04	17.76
Algeria		515	700	667	804	1,000	0.01	24.38
Morocco		764	849	943	887	1,280	0.01	44.31
Western Sahara						1	0.00	
Sudan		781	903	965	1,085	978	0.01	-9.86
Tunisia		503	611	623	760	905	0.01	19.08
Southern Africa		6,218	7,162	7,768	9,869	10,172	0.10	3.07
Botswana		33	27	23	27	57	0.00	111.11
Lesotho		22	32	13	20	31	0.00	55.00
Namibia		73	151	163	154	183	0.00	18.83
South Africa		6,050	6,910	7,530	9,633	9,833	0.10	2.08
Swaziland		40	42	39	35	68	0.00	94.29
West Africa		6,847	6,319	5,619	6,098	6,882	0.07	12.86
Cape Verde		59	26	20	29	23	0.00	-20.69
Benin		88	64	73	52	77	0.00	48.08
Gambia		46	18	34	27	41	0.00	51.85
Ghana		2,342	1,891	1,673	2,062	2,214	0.02	7.37
Guinea		52	72	87	45	110	0.00	144.44
Côte d'Ivoire		148	253	180	206	142	0.00	-31.07
Liberia		118	107	89	105	158	0.00	50.48
Mali		64	60	75	53	96	0.00	81.13
Mauritania		19	13	8	14	43	0.00	207.14
Niger		34	27	28	38	63	0.00	65.79
Nigeria		3,549	3,471	3,024	3,032	3,390	0.03	11.81
Guinea-Bissau		15	9	3	6	14	0.00	133.33

KOREA, REPUBLIC OF

2. Arrivals of non-resident visitors at national borders, by nationality

	2007	2008	2009	2010	2011	Market share 11	% Change 11-10
Saint Helena	2	7	5	9	14	0.00	55.56
Senegal	171	181	228	274	330	0.00	20.44
Sierra Leone	21	19	29	45	35	0.00	-22.22
Togo	76	45	37	55	52	0.00	-5.45
Burkina Faso	43	56	26	46	80	0.00	73.91
Other Africa	**1**				**4**	**0.00**	
Other countries of Africa	1				4	0.00	
AMERICAS	**716,336**	**744,615**	**751,697**	**813,860**	**827,383**	**8.45**	**1.66**
Caribbean	**3,056**	**1,444**	**1,292**	**1,731**	**2,058**	**0.02**	**18.89**
Antigua and Barbuda	19	12	16	28	22	0.00	-21.43
Bahamas	21	47	33	75	83	0.00	10.67
Barbados	49	34	36	58	79	0.00	36.21
Bermuda	4	3		4	2	0.00	-50.00
British Virgin Islands	316	75	50	109	112	0.00	2.75
Cuba	1,660	227	132	85	221	0.00	160.00
Dominica	45	41	38	37	40	0.00	8.11
Dominican Republic	276	274	344	343	451	0.00	31.49
Grenada	15	17	8	12	28	0.00	133.33
Haiti	96	48	42	66	86	0.00	30.30
Jamaica	189	286	312	442	500	0.01	13.12
Montserrat	1		4	4			
Netherlands Antilles	27	10		16	10	0.00	-37.50
Puerto Rico		1	4	4	7	0.00	75.00
Saint Kitts and Nevis	10	6	19	24	54	0.00	125.00
Saint Lucia	13	26	30	11	22	0.00	100.00
Saint Vincent and the Grenadines	7	85	44	91	34	0.00	-62.64
Trinidad and Tobago	308	252	180	322	271	0.00	-15.84
Turks and Caicos Islands					36	0.00	
Central America	**3,001**	**2,429**	**2,994**	**3,873**	**3,734**	**0.04**	**-3.59**
Belize	91	80	70	53	39	0.00	-26.42
Costa Rica	537	336	548	669	757	0.01	13.15
El Salvador	897	569	639	694	685	0.01	-1.30
Guatemala	524	623	581	680	742	0.01	9.12
Honduras	470	297	620	918	762	0.01	-16.99
Nicaragua	68	135	133	316	191	0.00	-39.56
Panama	414	389	403	543	558	0.01	2.76
North America	**691,486**	**720,357**	**726,048**	**782,037**	**792,085**	**8.09**	**1.28**
Canada	98,116	104,022	109,249	121,214	122,223	1.25	0.83
Mexico	6,046	6,252	5,472	7,934	8,359	0.09	5.36
United States of America	587,324	610,083	611,327	652,889	661,503	6.75	1.32
South America	**18,785**	**20,374**	**21,356**	**26,206**	**29,503**	**0.30**	**12.58**
Argentina	2,157	2,194	2,350	3,196	2,984	0.03	-6.63
Bolivia	386	438	451	534	572	0.01	7.12
Brazil	9,181	9,844	10,145	12,747	14,639	0.15	14.84
Chile	1,857	1,842	1,735	2,109	2,828	0.03	34.09
Colombia	1,553	1,840	2,376	2,303	2,674	0.03	16.11
Ecuador	510	495	546	815	868	0.01	6.50
Guyana	35	35	77	58	50	0.00	-13.79
Paraguay	337	326	377	451	445	0.00	-1.33
Peru	1,607	1,525	1,690	2,127	2,424	0.02	13.96
Suriname	30	41	38	40	54	0.00	35.00
Uruguay	199	188	150	206	280	0.00	35.92
Venezuela	933	1,606	1,421	1,620	1,685	0.02	4.01
Other Americas	**8**	**11**	**7**	**13**	**3**	**0.00**	**-76.92**
Other countries of the Americas	8	11	7	13	3	0.00	-76.92

KOREA, REPUBLIC OF

2. Arrivals of non-resident visitors at national borders, by nationality

	2007	2008	2009	2010	2011	Market share 11	% Change 11-10
EAST ASIA AND THE PACIFIC	4,696,553	5,035,806	6,029,612	6,769,195	7,678,884	78.40	13.44
North-East Asia	3,823,515	4,073,601	5,037,628	5,583,188	6,277,955	64.09	12.44
China	1,068,925	1,167,891	1,342,317	1,875,157	2,220,196	22.67	18.40
Taiwan, Province of China	335,224	320,244	380,628	406,352	428,208	4.37	5.38
Hong Kong, China	140,138	160,325	215,769	228,582	280,849	2.87	22.87
Japan	2,235,963	2,378,102	3,053,311	3,023,009	3,289,051	33.58	8.80
Macao, China	3,781	4,462	7,157	8,130	11,647	0.12	43.26
Mongolia	39,484	42,577	38,446	41,958	48,004	0.49	14.41
South-East Asia	764,550	834,036	860,971	1,039,112	1,244,309	12.70	19.75
Brunei Darussalam	799	924	925	1,268	1,434	0.01	13.09
Myanmar	43,271	50,636	56,044	57,916	70,168	0.72	21.15
Cambodia	4,350	6,895	6,041	7,194	12,438	0.13	72.89
Indonesia	67,450	81,001	80,988	95,239	124,474	1.27	30.70
Lao People's Democratic Republic	747	930	1,104	1,999	2,477	0.03	23.91
Malaysia	83,049	83,754	80,105	113,675	156,281	1.60	37.48
Philippines	263,799	276,710	271,962	297,452	337,268	3.44	13.39
Timor-Leste	80	137	230	583	530	0.01	-9.09
Singapore	93,951	95,960	96,622	112,855	124,565	1.27	10.38
Viet Nam	60,262	76,402	75,978	90,213	105,531	1.08	16.98
Thailand	146,792	160,687	190,972	260,718	309,143	3.16	18.57
Australasia	101,611	120,573	123,106	139,382	149,102	1.52	6.97
Australia	80,528	96,138	99,153	112,409	122,494	1.25	8.97
New Zealand	21,083	24,435	23,953	26,973	26,608	0.27	-1.35
Melanesia	3,331	4,033	4,517	4,827	4,299	0.04	-10.94
Solomon Islands	103	78	109	94	130	0.00	38.30
Fiji	3,029	3,678	4,127	4,486	3,856	0.04	-14.04
New Caledonia					3	0.00	
Vanuatu	35	16	30	33	49	0.00	48.48
Papua New Guinea	164	261	251	214	261	0.00	21.96
Micronesia	1,845	2,363	2,119	1,423	1,834	0.02	28.88
Kiribati	1,696	2,170	1,909	1,254	1,605	0.02	27.99
Nauru	27	31	11	9	25	0.00	177.78
Micronesia, Federated States of	31	52	77	66	86	0.00	30.30
Marshall Islands	52	58	45	67	55	0.00	-17.91
Palau	39	52	77	27	63	0.00	133.33
Polynesia	1,003	596	700	457	419	0.00	-8.32
American Samoa	29		8	9	4	0.00	-55.56
French Polynesia	3	3	4	6	69	0.00	1050.00
Tonga	70	77	111	139	112	0.00	-19.42
Tuvalu	811	400	440	131	142	0.00	8.40
Samoa	90	116	137	172	92	0.00	-46.51
Other East Asia and the Pacific	698	604	571	806	966	0.01	19.85
Other countries of Asia	659	604	567	806	966	0.01	19.85
Other countries of Oceania	39		4				
EUROPE	605,440	645,748	645,624	708,948	752,961	7.69	6.21
Central/Eastern Europe	232,905	236,986	224,765	256,329	279,822	2.86	9.17
Azerbaijan	576	488	506	679	706	0.01	3.98
Armenia	142	188	207	195	283	0.00	45.13
Bulgaria	7,674	6,171	6,220	7,525	8,103	0.08	7.68
Belarus	690	862	813	772	859	0.01	11.27
Czech Republic	4,721	6,455	6,307	6,589	7,103	0.07	7.80
Estonia	452	740	771	759	905	0.01	19.24
Georgia	429	778	677	687	842	0.01	22.56
Hungary	2,049	1,889	2,144	2,365	2,384	0.02	0.80
Kazakhstan	5,035	5,831	5,699	7,417	8,421	0.09	13.54
Kyrgyzstan	3,086	2,632	2,652	2,424	2,109	0.02	-13.00

KOREA, REPUBLIC OF

2. Arrivals of non-resident visitors at national borders, by nationality

	2007	2008	2009	2010	2011	Market share 11	% Change 11-10
Latvia	2,552	2,159	1,958	2,559	2,111	0.02	-17.51
Lithuania	951	1,052	1,142	1,366	1,572	0.02	15.08
Republic of Moldova	148	198	178	191	218	0.00	14.14
Poland	10,297	11,054	10,598	11,555	13,451	0.14	16.41
Romania	7,843	6,618	6,601	8,699	9,780	0.10	12.43
Russian Federation	140,426	136,342	137,054	150,730	154,835	1.58	2.72
Slovakia	1,584	1,623	1,682	1,841	2,558	0.03	38.95
Tajikistan	477	564	410	696	1,171	0.01	68.25
Turkmenistan	81	262	196	196	199	0.00	1.53
Ukraine	25,785	27,326	22,597	25,373	31,162	0.32	22.82
Uzbekistan	17,907	23,754	16,353	23,711	31,050	0.32	30.95
Northern Europe	**120,864**	**137,016**	**137,223**	**147,564**	**158,582**	**1.62**	**7.47**
Denmark	8,481	8,764	7,813	7,978	8,435	0.09	5.73
Faeroe Islands	1				1	0.00	
Finland	5,414	9,625	9,131	9,339	10,320	0.11	10.50
Iceland	296	278	214	308	384	0.00	24.68
Ireland	5,903	6,589	5,991	6,257	7,199	0.07	15.06
Norway	9,952	12,323	10,968	12,821	13,371	0.14	4.29
Sweden	12,161	12,423	11,941	13,351	14,228	0.15	6.57
United Kingdom	78,656	87,014	91,165	97,510	104,644	1.07	7.32
Southern Europe	**48,172**	**52,916**	**56,433**	**61,626**	**65,085**	**0.66**	**5.61**
Albania	122	95	101	122	143	0.00	17.21
Andorra	29	13	23	26	17	0.00	-34.62
Bosnia and Herzegovina	36	34	42	75	52	0.00	-30.67
Croatia	6,240	6,455	6,001	5,755	6,117	0.06	6.29
Greece	6,949	7,080	7,885	7,975	8,802	0.09	10.37
Holy See	14	9	8	12	5	0.00	-58.33
Italy	20,343	21,156	22,894	25,686	26,442	0.27	2.94
Malta	186	164	148	212	240	0.00	13.21
Montenegro		44	347	1,287	1,522	0.02	18.26
Portugal	3,702	3,830	5,003	5,574	6,397	0.07	14.76
San Marino	11	10	30	5	27	0.00	440.00
Serbia		42	503	1,047	1,304	0.01	24.55
Slovenia	850	1,103	974	973	924	0.01	-5.04
Spain	8,754	10,623	10,691	12,590	12,884	0.13	2.34
TFYR of Macedonia	39	56	99	206	158	0.00	-23.30
Serbia and Montenegro	897	2,202	1,684	81	51	0.00	-37.04
Western Europe	**181,933**	**197,751**	**204,308**	**214,440**	**220,186**	**2.25**	**2.68**
Austria	6,835	7,621	8,017	8,956	9,227	0.09	3.03
Belgium	6,314	6,913	6,828	7,803	7,793	0.08	-0.13
France	52,842	59,789	61,426	66,192	69,459	0.71	4.94
Germany	85,330	91,555	97,691	98,119	99,468	1.02	1.37
Liechtenstein	30	25	34	26	49	0.00	88.46
Luxembourg	347	347	451	465	480	0.00	3.23
Monaco	16	12	11	12	17	0.00	41.67
Netherlands	21,345	21,875	20,358	22,669	23,279	0.24	2.69
Switzerland	8,874	9,614	9,492	10,198	10,414	0.11	2.12
East Mediterranean Europe	**19,422**	**20,402**	**22,552**	**28,751**	**28,986**	**0.30**	**0.82**
Cyprus	190	241	359	438	472	0.00	7.76
Israel	7,607	7,587	9,784	11,993	11,216	0.11	-6.48
Turkey	11,625	12,574	12,409	16,320	17,298	0.18	5.99
Other Europe	**2,144**	**677**	**343**	**238**	**300**	**0.00**	**26.05**
Other countries of Europe	2,144	677	343	238	300	0.00	26.05

KOREA, REPUBLIC OF

2. Arrivals of non-resident visitors at national borders, by nationality

	2007	2008	2009	2010	2011	Market share 11	% Change 11-10
MIDDLE EAST	**15,859**	**18,208**	**19,759**	**24,574**	**29,340**	**0.30**	**19.39**
Bahrain	177	202	296	261	328	0.00	25.67
Palestine	129	148	207	257	253	0.00	-1.56
Iraq	1,928	1,674	1,975	2,210	2,090	0.02	-5.43
Jordan	1,840	2,509	3,007	3,137	3,520	0.04	12.21
Kuwait	771	702	463	870	1,047	0.01	20.34
Lebanon	820	853	824	1,198	1,335	0.01	11.44
Libya	1,106	1,327	2,162	1,726	800	0.01	-53.65
Oman	404	435	366	721	873	0.01	21.08
Qatar	362	345	318	311	506	0.01	62.70
Saudi Arabia	2,258	2,664	3,040	3,875	6,904	0.07	78.17
Syrian Arab Republic	1,425	1,706	1,829	1,853	2,263	0.02	22.13
United Arab Emirates	884	1,010	887	2,433	2,958	0.03	21.58
Egypt	3,307	4,162	3,852	5,138	5,845	0.06	13.76
Yemen	448	471	533	584	618	0.01	5.82
SOUTH ASIA	**100,662**	**118,036**	**113,740**	**134,503**	**148,431**	**1.52**	**10.36**
Afghanistan	377	528	611	780	1,028	0.01	31.79
Bangladesh	5,875	7,202	6,718	8,899	9,302	0.09	4.53
Bhutan	153	158	180	250	278	0.00	11.20
Sri Lanka	8,364	13,959	9,406	12,517	15,674	0.16	25.22
India	68,276	73,130	72,779	86,547	92,047	0.94	6.35
Iran, Islamic Republic of	6,155	8,054	7,854	8,387	9,532	0.10	13.65
Maldives	350	208	263	279	354	0.00	26.88
Nepal	3,470	5,107	6,994	7,574	10,095	0.10	33.28
Pakistan	7,642	9,690	8,935	9,270	10,121	0.10	9.18
NOT SPECIFIED	**294,179**	**307,708**	**234,614**	**319,686**	**327,463**	**3.34**	**2.43**
Other countries of the World	118	157	194	192	203	0.00	5.73
Nationals Residing Abroad	294,061	307,551	234,420	319,494	327,260	3.34	2.43

KUWAIT

2. Arrivals of non-resident visitors at national borders, by nationality

	2007	2008	2009	2010	2011	Market share 11	% Change 11-10
TOTAL	4,481,616	4,735,910	5,087,781	5,207,785	5,574,302	100.00	7.04
AFRICA	54,708	64,768	73,260	95,080	113,314	2.03	19.18
East Africa	14,758	22,801	28,071	50,575	69,836	1.25	38.08
Burundi	16	26	14	11	22	0.00	100.00
Comoros	85	92	166	425	303	0.01	-28.71
Ethiopia	9,629	17,039	21,109	43,611	63,866	1.15	46.44
Eritrea	992	985	1,207	1,044	969	0.02	-7.18
Djibouti	68	74	95	92	82	0.00	-10.87
Kenya	787	875	1,293	1,622	1,416	0.03	-12.70
Madagascar	36	244	600	705	458	0.01	-35.04
Malawi	37	50	40	50	92	0.00	84.00
Mauritius	131	108	124	143	86	0.00	-39.86
Mozambique	14	22	31	17	32	0.00	88.24
Rwanda	8	3	1	3	15	0.00	400.00
Seychelles	17	40	35	24	34	0.00	41.67
Somalia	2,556	2,647	2,674	2,170	1,935	0.03	-10.83
Zimbabwe	132	147	271	241	187	0.00	-22.41
Uganda	80	189	203	131	117	0.00	-10.69
United Republic of Tanzania	152	202	169	211	212	0.00	0.47
Zambia	18	58	39	75	10	0.00	-86.67
Central Africa	2,334	1,727	1,465	1,219	949	0.02	-22.15
Angola	21	24	21	12	20	0.00	66.67
Cameroon	90	140	82	108	50	0.00	-53.70
Central African Republic	16	32	101	32	34	0.00	6.25
Chad	2,173	1,471	1,216	1,032	794	0.01	-23.06
Congo		1	2		7	0.00	
Democratic Republic of the Congo	30	52	35	30	36	0.00	20.00
Gabon	4	7	8	5	8	0.00	60.00
North Africa	25,421	27,428	29,498	31,462	31,973	0.57	1.62
Algeria	2,501	3,041	3,201	3,694	3,566	0.06	-3.47
Morocco	10,336	10,474	11,086	11,808	11,451	0.21	-3.02
Sudan	7,974	8,318	8,302	8,043	9,049	0.16	12.51
Tunisia	4,610	5,595	6,909	7,917	7,907	0.14	-0.13
Southern Africa	4,064	4,892	5,568	5,337	4,550	0.08	-14.75
Botswana	1		5	6	29	0.00	383.33
Lesotho	8	1	1	62	13	0.00	-79.03
Namibia	11	22	4	15	13	0.00	-13.33
South Africa	4,037	4,764	5,350	5,023	4,424	0.08	-11.93
Swaziland	7	105	208	231	71	0.00	-69.26
West Africa	8,123	7,918	8,657	6,485	5,960	0.11	-8.10
Cape Verde	1	1	4	2			
Benin	132	185	172	203	226	0.00	11.33
Gambia	49	33	37	54	66	0.00	22.22
Ghana	5,108	4,681	5,045	3,084	2,662	0.05	-13.68
Guinea	126	132	108	97	70	0.00	-27.84
Côte d'Ivoire	69	158	84	58	89	0.00	53.45
Liberia	321	293	263	288	224	0.00	-22.22
Mali	96	109	101	120	143	0.00	19.17
Mauritania	313	269	294	266	293	0.01	10.15
Niger	143	118	147	173	189	0.00	9.25
Nigeria	1,050	1,168	1,615	1,281	1,173	0.02	-8.43
Guinea-Bissau	7	3		21	6	0.00	-71.43
Saint Helena	11	10	1		1	0.00	
Senegal	292	371	410	336	385	0.01	14.58
Sierra Leone	205	123	121	133	158	0.00	18.80
Togo	138	192	195	299	174	0.00	-41.81

KUWAIT

2. Arrivals of non-resident visitors at national borders, by nationality

	2007	2008	2009	2010	2011	Market share 11	% Change 11-10
Burkina Faso	62	72	60	70	101	0.00	44.29
Other Africa	**8**	**2**	**1**	**2**	**46**	**0.00**	**2200.00**
Other countries of Africa	8	2	1	2	46	0.00	2200.00
AMERICAS	**189,775**	**219,039**	**229,288**	**226,943**	**222,973**	**4.00**	**-1.75**
Caribbean	**513**	**471**	**516**	**478**	**578**	**0.01**	**20.92**
Bahamas	4	9	4	17	15	0.00	-11.76
Barbados	15	17	21	12	11	0.00	-8.33
Bermuda			1	4	8	0.00	100.00
Cuba	28	39	44	18	33	0.00	83.33
Dominican Republic	276	205	177	165	196	0.00	18.79
Grenada	26	22	24	30	13	0.00	-56.67
Guadeloupe		3					
Haiti	26	45	41	31	72	0.00	132.26
Jamaica	42	41	59	61	88	0.00	44.26
Martinique	17	1					
Aruba		1	1	6	4	0.00	-33.33
Curaçao					1	0.00	
Saint Kitts and Nevis	1	3		4	2	0.00	-50.00
Saint Lucia	3	4	4	7	7	0.00	
Saint Vincent and the Grenadines					3	0.00	
Trinidad and Tobago	75	81	140	123	125	0.00	1.63
Central America	**246**	**300**	**423**	**399**	**290**	**0.01**	**-27.32**
Belize	164	151	162	175	153	0.00	-12.57
Costa Rica	3	10	27	21	24	0.00	14.29
El Salvador	16	41	127	159	50	0.00	-68.55
Guatemala	9	11	26	10	20	0.00	100.00
Honduras	17	27	40	4	21	0.00	425.00
Nicaragua	1	7	8	4	2	0.00	-50.00
Panama	36	53	33	26	20	0.00	-23.08
North America	**186,003**	**215,147**	**224,756**	**222,270**	**218,016**	**3.91**	**-1.91**
Canada	33,951	36,867	40,440	41,156	39,130	0.70	-4.92
Mexico	282	374	374	276	369	0.01	33.70
United States of America	151,770	177,906	183,942	180,838	178,517	3.20	-1.28
South America	**3,012**	**3,114**	**3,588**	**3,789**	**4,081**	**0.07**	**7.71**
Argentina	409	438	514	441	609	0.01	38.10
Bolivia	79	85	66	99	86	0.00	-13.13
Brazil	1,080	1,082	1,143	1,374	1,252	0.02	-8.88
Chile	115	84	103	99	72	0.00	-27.27
Colombia	403	440	542	420	410	0.01	-2.38
Ecuador	63	89	130	166	138	0.00	-16.87
French Guiana		1	6	20			
Guyana	7	9	8	20	17	0.00	-15.00
Paraguay	1	7	14	6	9	0.00	50.00
Peru	134	89	77	42	52	0.00	23.81
Suriname	7	9	19	9	12	0.00	33.33
Uruguay	29	12	33	29	51	0.00	75.86
Venezuela	685	769	933	1,064	1,373	0.02	29.04
Other Americas	**1**	**7**	**5**	**7**	**8**	**0.00**	**14.29**
Other countries of the Americas	1	7	5	7	8	0.00	14.29
EAST ASIA AND THE PACIFIC	**235,562**	**244,241**	**249,653**	**229,734**	**226,602**	**4.07**	**-1.36**
North-East Asia	**25,675**	**25,951**	**20,855**	**25,571**	**31,941**	**0.57**	**24.91**
China	7,586	9,546	8,207	10,925	14,208	0.25	30.05
Taiwan, Province of China	216	98	155	158	196	0.00	24.05
Hong Kong, China	223	273	212	244	211	0.00	-13.52
Japan	6,551	6,215	4,606	4,959	4,798	0.09	-3.25
Korea, Dem. People's Republic of	1,143	831	728		442	0.01	

KUWAIT

2. Arrivals of non-resident visitors at national borders, by nationality

	2007	2008	2009	2010	2011	Market share 11	% Change 11-10
Korea, Republic of	9,643	8,795	6,838	9,111	11,677	0.21	28.16
Macao, China	2	2	3	4	10	0.00	150.00
Mongolia	311	191	106	170	399	0.01	134.71
South-East Asia	**191,626**	**199,097**	**207,446**	**184,929**	**179,100**	**3.21**	**-3.15**
Brunei Darussalam	10	4	31	37	14	0.00	-62.16
Myanmar	126	211	332	188	376	0.01	100.00
Cambodia	19	55	100	64	70	0.00	9.38
Indonesia	58,793	65,391	63,419	35,664	25,793	0.46	-27.68
Lao People's Democratic Republic	1	4	72	20	14	0.00	-30.00
Malaysia	2,747	4,067	3,495	4,105	4,320	0.08	5.24
Philippines	118,750	117,812	130,417	135,182	139,988	2.51	3.56
Timor-Leste	3	19	7	8	6	0.00	-25.00
Singapore	1,537	1,535	1,275	1,457	1,323	0.02	-9.20
Viet Nam	452	1,147	737	573	526	0.01	-8.20
Thailand	9,188	8,852	7,561	7,631	6,670	0.12	-12.59
Australasia	**15,502**	**17,841**	**20,293**	**18,557**	**15,293**	**0.27**	**-17.59**
Australia	12,903	14,915	16,990	15,306	12,543	0.23	-18.05
New Zealand	2,599	2,926	3,303	3,251	2,750	0.05	-15.41
Melanesia	**2,626**	**1,241**	**941**	**565**	**147**	**0.00**	**-73.98**
Fiji	2,626	1,241	941	565	147	0.00	-73.98
Micronesia	**71**	**39**	**33**	**45**	**22**	**0.00**	**-51.11**
Kiribati		2					
Marshall Islands	4	4	4	7	5	0.00	-28.57
Palau	67	33	29	38	17	0.00	-55.26
Polynesia	**44**	**55**	**19**	**16**	**15**	**0.00**	**-6.25**
Cook Islands	5	7	12	8	9	0.00	12.50
Tonga	38	44	4	7	6	0.00	-14.29
Samoa	1	4	3	1			
Other East Asia and the Pacific	**18**	**17**	**66**	**51**	**84**	**0.00**	**64.71**
Other countries of Asia	18	17	66	51	84	0.00	64.71
EUROPE	**177,528**	**181,162**	**184,248**	**191,455**	**188,306**	**3.38**	**-1.64**
Central/Eastern Europe	**23,145**	**26,413**	**21,729**	**25,211**	**20,218**	**0.36**	**-19.80**
Azerbaijan	213	202	289	290	340	0.01	17.24
Armenia	496	440	464	526	586	0.01	11.41
Bulgaria	4,732	4,177	3,301	3,490	3,223	0.06	-7.65
Belarus	456	604	602	454	376	0.01	-17.18
Czech Republic/Slovakia	1	2					
Czech Republic	781	884	686	1,353	779	0.01	-42.42
Estonia	74	103	29	38	33	0.00	-13.16
Georgia	3,688	3,659	2,731	1,832	1,135	0.02	-38.05
Hungary	1,203	1,166	1,197	1,380	1,345	0.02	-2.54
Kazakhstan	266	313	197	238	277	0.00	16.39
Kyrgyzstan	79	257	512	634	696	0.01	9.78
Latvia	62	48	63	85	98	0.00	15.29
Lithuania	117	132	108	107	120	0.00	12.15
Republic of Moldova	45	65	60	54	52	0.00	-3.70
Poland	1,679	1,810	1,593	1,955	1,806	0.03	-7.62
Romania	2,563	2,392	3,688	5,609	3,499	0.06	-37.62
Russian Federation	3,914	7,466	3,969	2,579	3,190	0.06	23.69
Slovakia	628	606	576	2,772	915	0.02	-66.99
Tajikistan	88	106	69	118	129	0.00	9.32
Turkmenistan	16	18	36	48	12	0.00	-75.00
Ukraine	1,389	1,371	981	1,050	1,051	0.02	0.10
Uzbekistan	655	592	578	599	556	0.01	-7.18
Northern Europe	**82,063**	**81,349**	**83,734**	**83,947**	**87,000**	**1.56**	**3.64**
Denmark	3,647	2,990	3,367	3,206	3,063	0.05	-4.46

KUWAIT

2. Arrivals of non-resident visitors at national borders, by nationality

	2007	2008	2009	2010	2011	Market share 11	% Change 11-10
Finland	1,730	1,308	1,094	1,025	1,097	0.02	7.02
Iceland	88	91	139	81	110	0.00	35.80
Ireland	2,697	2,935	2,936	3,000	3,174	0.06	5.80
Norway	1,893	2,187	2,566	2,659	2,433	0.04	-8.50
Sweden	7,369	6,298	6,512	6,614	6,826	0.12	3.21
United Kingdom	64,639	65,540	67,120	67,362	70,297	1.26	4.36
Southern Europe	**18,054**	**19,253**	**24,125**	**25,325**	**24,199**	**0.43**	**-4.45**
Albania	206	224	98	199	205	0.00	3.02
Andorra			2	2	7	0.00	250.00
Bosnia and Herzegovina	1,610	1,575	1,509	1,124	1,327	0.02	18.06
Croatia	444	481	615	806	774	0.01	-3.97
Greece	1,729	1,869	1,887	2,416	2,759	0.05	14.20
Holy See	10	17	11				
Italy	7,708	8,806	11,222	10,925	10,021	0.18	-8.27
Malta	144	124	116	222	169	0.00	-23.87
Montenegro				11	33	0.00	200.00
Portugal	1,131	1,043	867	1,141	989	0.02	-13.32
San Marino	2	3	10	3	7	0.00	133.33
Serbia	48	25	235	628	923	0.02	46.97
Slovenia	125	173	153	286	231	0.00	-19.23
Spain	2,797	2,762	5,118	6,771	6,382	0.11	-5.75
TFYR of Macedonia	648	676	852	791	372	0.01	-52.97
Serbia and Montenegro	1,452	1,475	1,430				
Western Europe	**39,724**	**41,601**	**42,666**	**44,451**	**44,669**	**0.80**	**0.49**
Austria	1,674	1,814	1,984	1,997	1,914	0.03	-4.16
Belgium	1,697	1,745	2,374	2,755	2,407	0.04	-12.63
France	13,947	14,345	14,907	15,084	15,209	0.27	0.83
Germany	13,587	14,579	14,159	15,283	14,962	0.27	-2.10
Liechtenstein	18	22	18	13	23	0.00	76.92
Luxembourg	112	115	111	97	87	0.00	-10.31
Monaco	8	9	3	6			
Netherlands	6,524	6,589	7,070	7,101	7,869	0.14	10.82
Switzerland	2,157	2,383	2,040	2,115	2,198	0.04	3.92
East Mediterranean Europe	**14,540**	**12,534**	**11,893**	**11,764**	**11,653**	**0.21**	**-0.94**
Cyprus	472	368	323	286	380	0.01	32.87
Turkey	14,068	12,166	11,570	11,478	11,273	0.20	-1.79
Other Europe	**2**	**12**	**101**	**757**	**567**	**0.01**	**-25.10**
Other countries of Europe	2	12	101	757	567	0.01	-25.10
MIDDLE EAST	**2,618,506**	**2,778,066**	**2,996,469**	**3,103,394**	**3,434,185**	**61.61**	**10.66**
Bahrain	108,216	112,910	125,962	122,192	121,482	2.18	-0.58
Palestine	7,682	7,170	7,480	7,622	6,640	0.12	-12.88
Iraq	81,640	100,872	89,908	69,080	70,058	1.26	1.42
Jordan	79,973	85,356	90,023	94,480	97,267	1.74	2.95
Lebanon	110,289	117,055	119,998	117,686	104,739	1.88	-11.00
Libya	473	551	535	677	455	0.01	-32.79
Oman	15,969	16,645	16,711	18,035	17,865	0.32	-0.94
Qatar	31,399	29,236	32,170	30,873	33,023	0.59	6.96
Saudi Arabia	1,349,441	1,425,049	1,613,460	1,708,661	2,063,815	37.02	20.79
Syrian Arab Republic	289,848	304,605	306,561	307,949	269,013	4.83	-12.64
United Arab Emirates	26,871	36,355	41,763	45,957	45,659	0.82	-0.65
Egypt	508,434	532,753	540,708	569,452	594,099	10.66	4.33
Yemen	8,271	9,509	11,190	10,730	10,070	0.18	-6.15
SOUTH ASIA	**1,191,690**	**1,224,937**	**1,316,151**	**1,327,607**	**1,351,987**	**24.25**	**1.84**
Afghanistan	19,515	23,534	20,045	12,607	12,457	0.22	-1.19
Bangladesh	99,183	93,585	104,757	102,390	107,817	1.93	5.30
Bhutan	27	24	36	72	123	0.00	70.83

KUWAIT

2. Arrivals of non-resident visitors at national borders, by nationality

	2007	2008	2009	2010	2011	Market share 11	% Change 11-10
Sri Lanka	83,457	90,896	95,250	99,330	100,782	1.81	1.46
India	653,392	673,671	733,117	751,059	789,694	14.17	5.14
Iran, Islamic Republic of	93,248	90,839	89,219	81,136	72,067	1.29	-11.18
Maldives	46	22	16	14	41	0.00	192.86
Nepal	46,191	37,939	54,209	52,971	53,812	0.97	1.59
Pakistan	196,631	214,427	219,502	228,028	215,194	3.86	-5.63
NOT SPECIFIED	**13,847**	**23,697**	**38,712**	**33,572**	**36,935**	**0.66**	**10.02**
Other countries of the World	13,847	23,697	38,712	33,572	36,935	0.66	10.02

KYRGYZSTAN

1. Arrivals of non-resident tourists at national borders, by country of residence

	2007	2008	2009	2010	2011	Market share 11	% Change 11-10
TOTAL	1,655,833	2,435,386	2,146,740	1,316,207	3,114,372	100.00	136.62
AMERICAS	15,407	9,580	11,323	9,142	14,782	0.47	61.69
North America	15,407	9,580	11,323	9,142	14,782	0.47	61.69
Canada	1,632	1,597	1,859	1,669	1,904	0.06	14.08
United States of America	13,775	7,983	9,464	7,473	12,878	0.41	72.33
EAST ASIA AND THE PACIFIC	30,813	30,152	30,913	24,957	32,909	1.06	31.86
North-East Asia	29,168	28,393	28,696	23,499	31,175	1.00	32.67
China	20,201	21,921	21,879	18,167	25,059	0.80	37.94
Japan	2,550	1,946	2,027	1,125	2,435	0.08	116.44
Korea, Republic of	6,417	4,526	4,790	4,207	3,681	0.12	-12.50
South-East Asia				85	127	0.00	49.41
Malaysia				85	127	0.00	49.41
Australasia	1,645	1,759	2,217	1,373	1,607	0.05	17.04
Australia	1,292	1,504	1,883	1,189	1,375	0.04	15.64
New Zealand	353	255	334	184	232	0.01	26.09
EUROPE	1,595,211	2,383,543	2,089,309	1,271,252	3,049,493	97.92	139.88
Central/Eastern Europe	1,549,558	2,341,668	2,050,089	1,242,151	3,010,896	96.68	142.39
Azerbaijan	1,566	1,237	1,158	984	3,983	0.13	304.78
Armenia	580	508	407	293	982	0.03	235.15
Belarus	1,192	938	937	517	1,685	0.05	225.92
Czech Republic	471	734	497	143	499	0.02	248.95
Georgia	729	698	865	610	898	0.03	47.21
Hungary	220	238	428	214	359	0.01	67.76
Kazakhstan	1,125,214	1,078,945	1,036,322	837,609	1,437,739	46.16	71.65
Lithuania	345	463	286	167	418	0.01	150.30
Republic of Moldova	1,081	896	852	468	1,223	0.04	161.32
Poland	861	1,014	786	524	713	0.02	36.07
Russian Federation	118,604	193,998	157,008	132,493	1,020,102	32.75	669.93
Tajikistan	10,228	296,761	366,304	121,058	99,552	3.20	-17.77
Turkmenistan	1,885	3,789	5,313	4,902	306	0.01	-93.76
Ukraine	3,186	3,026	4,175	1,525	9,074	0.29	495.02
Uzbekistan	283,396	758,423	474,751	140,644	433,363	13.91	208.13
Northern Europe	6,584	5,311	6,501	4,595	5,098	0.16	10.95
Denmark	313	339	411	406	253	0.01	-37.68
Finland	240	245	291	230	126	0.00	-45.22
Ireland	369	254	618	345	271	0.01	-21.45
Norway	422	380	523	371	513	0.02	38.27
Sweden	721	832	831	527	808	0.03	53.32
United Kingdom	4,519	3,261	3,827	2,716	3,127	0.10	15.13
Southern Europe	3,174	2,692	2,430	1,361	2,058	0.07	51.21
Italy	1,044	1,112	1,278	902	1,427	0.05	58.20
Spain	2,130	1,580	1,152	459	631	0.02	37.47
Western Europe	17,602	17,279	17,051	11,461	15,460	0.50	34.89
Austria	675	765	1,046	536	510	0.02	-4.85
Belgium	864	775	956	426	592	0.02	38.97
France	3,917	3,308	2,981	2,105	3,633	0.12	72.59
Germany	9,794	10,010	9,374	6,980	8,432	0.27	20.80
Netherlands	787	684	788	385	146	0.00	-62.08
Switzerland	1,565	1,737	1,906	1,029	2,147	0.07	108.65
East Mediterranean Europe	18,293	16,593	13,238	11,684	15,981	0.51	36.78
Israel	1,183	982	973	586	744	0.02	26.96
Turkey	17,110	15,611	12,265	11,098	15,237	0.49	37.30

KYRGYZSTAN

1. Arrivals of non-resident tourists at national borders, by country of residence

	2007	2008	2009	2010	2011	Market share 11	% Change 11-10
MIDDLE EAST	**168**	**194**	**197**	**127**	**122**	**0.00**	**-3.94**
Saudi Arabia	168	194	197	127	122	0.00	-3.94
SOUTH ASIA	**7,262**	**6,838**	**7,283**	**5,785**	**7,173**	**0.23**	**23.99**
Afghanistan	634	525	461	404	493	0.02	22.03
India	1,277	1,038	1,669	1,725	1,990	0.06	15.36
Iran, Islamic Republic of	3,620	3,576	3,201	1,574	2,646	0.08	68.11
Pakistan	1,731	1,699	1,952	2,082	2,044	0.07	-1.83
NOT SPECIFIED	**6,972**	**5,079**	**7,715**	**4,944**	**9,893**	**0.32**	**100.10**
Other countries of the World	6,972	5,079	7,715	4,944	9,893	0.32	100.10

LAO PEOPLE´S DEMOCRATIC REPUBLIC

2. Arrivals of non-resident visitors at national borders, by nationality

	2007	2008	2009	2010	2011	Market share 11	% Change 11-10
TOTAL	1,623,943	1,736,787	2,008,363	2,513,028	2,723,564	100.00	8.38
AMERICAS	61,463	75,266	53,348	67,291	69,990	2.57	4.01
North America	58,741	69,412	50,294	63,419	64,514	2.37	1.73
Canada	13,050	14,695	10,955	13,637	14,422	0.53	5.76
United States of America	45,691	54,717	39,339	49,782	50,092	1.84	0.62
Other Americas	2,722	5,854	3,054	3,872	5,476	0.20	41.43
Other countries of the Americas	2,722	5,854	3,054	3,872	5,476	0.20	41.43
EAST ASIA AND THE PACIFIC	1,404,095	1,479,847	1,818,291	2,256,705	2,461,424	90.38	9.07
North-East Asia	100,481	158,151	176,702	226,588	228,410	8.39	0.80
China	54,920	105,852	128,226	161,854	150,791	5.54	-6.84
Taiwan, Province of China	2,731	2,665	2,519	3,346	5,029	0.18	50.30
Japan	29,770	31,569	28,081	34,076	37,883	1.39	11.17
Korea, Republic of	13,060	18,065	17,876	27,312	34,707	1.27	27.08
South-East Asia	1,272,724	1,285,531	1,611,009	1,990,932	2,191,224	80.45	10.06
Brunei Darussalam	234	338	267	197	354	0.01	79.70
Myanmar	1,247	1,698	1,794	1,652	1,765	0.06	6.84
Cambodia	4,351	5,482	7,530	6,908	7,561	0.28	9.45
Indonesia	2,032	2,043	3,158	2,245	3,338	0.12	48.69
Malaysia	7,937	15,625	13,816	15,427	17,702	0.65	14.75
Philippines	11,401	12,647	8,331	10,341	11,847	0.43	14.56
Singapore	5,486	4,866	5,286	6,087	7,130	0.26	17.13
Viet Nam	290,584	351,384	296,763	431,011	561,586	20.62	30.30
Thailand	949,452	891,448	1,274,064	1,517,064	1,579,941	58.01	4.14
Australasia	28,251	32,544	27,688	34,931	36,759	1.35	5.23
Australia	24,492	28,180	24,209	30,538	31,874	1.17	4.37
New Zealand	3,759	4,364	3,479	4,393	4,885	0.18	11.20
Other East Asia and the Pacific	2,639	3,621	2,892	4,254	5,031	0.18	18.27
Other countries East Asia/Pacific	2,639	3,621	2,892	4,254	5,031	0.18	18.27
EUROPE	152,023	172,846	132,412	181,840	185,771	6.82	2.16
Central/Eastern Europe	2,270	3,206	2,861	4,835	7,019	0.26	45.17
Russian Federation	2,270	3,206	2,861	4,835	7,019	0.26	45.17
Northern Europe	47,118	52,160	38,377	54,207	52,237	1.92	-3.63
Denmark	3,648	3,657	2,977	5,359	4,769	0.18	-11.01
Finland	2,335	2,729	1,985	2,470	2,742	0.10	11.01
Norway	2,748	2,909	2,221	2,845	3,178	0.12	11.70
Sweden	7,035	6,827	4,150	6,261	5,926	0.22	-5.35
United Kingdom	31,352	36,038	27,044	37,272	35,622	1.31	-4.43
Southern Europe	10,507	10,153	8,980	11,848	12,080	0.44	1.96
Greece	510	569	537	578	451	0.02	-21.97
Italy	6,605	6,467	5,481	7,075	6,977	0.26	-1.39
Spain	3,392	3,117	2,962	4,195	4,652	0.17	10.89
Western Europe	76,466	89,860	70,134	93,658	93,595	3.44	-0.07
Austria	2,231	2,843	2,450	2,565	3,801	0.14	48.19
Belgium	4,553	4,908	3,868	5,012	5,241	0.19	4.57
France	34,584	39,077	31,775	44,844	44,399	1.63	-0.99
Germany	19,299	25,191	17,710	22,583	21,280	0.78	-5.77
Netherlands	10,017	11,315	8,504	10,032	9,164	0.34	-8.65
Switzerland	5,782	6,526	5,827	8,622	9,710	0.36	12.62
East Mediterranean Europe	4,356	4,090	2,236	3,700	4,232	0.16	14.38
Israel	4,356	4,090	2,236	3,700	4,232	0.16	14.38
Other Europe	11,306	13,377	9,824	13,592	16,608	0.61	22.19
Other countries of Europe	11,306	13,377	9,824	13,592	16,608	0.61	22.19

LAO PEOPLE´S DEMOCRATIC REPUBLIC

2. Arrivals of non-resident visitors at national borders, by nationality

	2007	2008	2009	2010	2011	Market share 11	% Change 11-10
SOUTH ASIA	**2,361**	**2,652**	**2,280**	**3,321**	**3,227**	**0.12**	**-2.83**
India	2,361	2,652	2,280	3,321	3,227	0.12	-2.83
NOT SPECIFIED	**4,001**	**6,176**	**2,032**	**3,871**	**3,152**	**0.12**	**-18.57**
Other countries of the World	4,001	6,176	2,032	3,871	3,152	0.12	-18.57

LATVIA

2. Arrivals of non-resident visitors at national borders, by country of residence

		2007	2008	2009	2010	2011	Market share 11	% Change 11-10
TOTAL	(*)	5,209,622	5,496,205	4,726,585	5,042,260	5,538,393	100.00	9.84
AFRICA		2,958		5,059	7,422	4,345	0.08	-41.46
East Africa				317	144	656	0.01	355.56
United Republic of Tanzania				317	144	656	0.01	355.56
Central Africa		273				143	0.00	
Congo		273				143	0.00	
North Africa		1,232		3,671	5,190	1,135	0.02	-78.13
Algeria		509		660	583	188	0.00	-67.75
Morocco				1,877	3,509	947	0.02	-73.01
Tunisia		723		1,134	1,098			
Southern Africa		1,180		460	146	1,081	0.02	640.41
South Africa		1,180		460	146	1,081	0.02	640.41
West Africa		273		611	1,942	1,330	0.02	-31.51
Gambia						286	0.01	
Ghana					343			
Liberia					175			
Niger				611		279	0.01	
Nigeria		273			1,424	765	0.01	-46.28
AMERICAS		32,351	37,615	60,256	62,408	76,550	1.38	22.66
Caribbean				472	808	383	0.01	-52.60
Cuba				292	808	383	0.01	-52.60
Jamaica				180				
North America		29,126	37,615	55,904	54,772	70,354	1.27	28.45
Canada		3,591	6,064	9,099	10,417	9,074	0.16	-12.89
Mexico		1,894		1,273	2,553	1,704	0.03	-33.25
United States of America		23,641	31,551	45,532	41,802	59,576	1.08	42.52
South America		3,225		3,880	6,828	5,813	0.10	-14.87
Argentina		397		460	1,291	764	0.01	-40.82
Brazil		1,139		1,438	3,148	1,970	0.04	-37.42
Chile		546		493	1,729	1,756	0.03	1.56
Colombia		255						
Peru					197	143	0.00	-27.41
Suriname					144			
Uruguay				1,163	319	711	0.01	122.88
Venezuela		888		326		469	0.01	
EAST ASIA AND THE PACIFIC		17,502	21,911	35,405	47,040	49,521	0.89	5.27
North-East Asia		7,512	13,881	17,030	27,595	26,769	0.48	-2.99
China		2,682	5,973	5,042	13,131	13,500	0.24	2.81
Taiwan, Province of China					288			
Hong Kong, China		246		652		596	0.01	
Japan		3,101	6,347	7,937	10,483	10,072	0.18	-3.92
Korea, Republic of		933	1,561	1,973	2,402	1,323	0.02	-44.92
Mongolia		550		1,426	1,291	1,278	0.02	-1.01
South-East Asia		3,364	1,343	9,513	8,786	9,142	0.17	4.05
Indonesia		978		4,166	3,170	2,120	0.04	-33.12
Malaysia		428		1,134	2,336	711	0.01	-69.56
Philippines		1,703	1,343	1,736	2,233	2,093	0.04	-6.27
Singapore				360				
Viet Nam		255			321	1,137	0.02	254.21
Thailand				2,117	726	3,081	0.06	324.38
Australasia		6,626	6,687	8,862	10,659	13,610	0.25	27.69
Australia		4,457	4,719	5,040	5,738	9,340	0.17	62.77
New Zealand		2,169	1,968	3,822	4,921	4,270	0.08	-13.23

LATVIA

2. Arrivals of non-resident visitors at national borders, by country of residence

	2007	2008	2009	2010	2011	Market share 11	% Change 11-10
EUROPE	5,150,359	5,410,212	4,611,254	4,901,853	5,386,291	97.25	9.88
Central/Eastern Europe	3,985,171	4,169,827	3,450,735	3,537,615	3,879,175	70.04	9.66
Azerbaijan	295		4,305	4,376	3,115	0.06	-28.82
Armenia	295	2,497	2,029	9,441	8,045	0.15	-14.79
Bulgaria	5,190	3,233	5,708	10,733	11,860	0.21	10.50
Belarus	92,113	111,528	113,276	101,469	125,854	2.27	24.03
Czech Republic	38,244	32,056	28,881	31,279	42,145	0.76	34.74
Estonia	1,159,980	1,384,561	946,292	957,038	1,040,672	18.79	8.74
Georgia	3,988	5,241	17,266	23,885	16,882	0.30	-29.32
Hungary	19,915	8,810	10,517	15,821	14,339	0.26	-9.37
Kazakhstan	47,524	30,712	19,380	19,036	23,005	0.42	20.85
Kyrgyzstan	1,353		1,991	1,127	3,854	0.07	241.97
Lithuania	1,891,935	1,958,709	1,731,017	1,707,920	1,788,940	32.30	4.74
Republic of Moldova	2,095	6,548	9,467	10,239	8,548	0.15	-16.52
Poland	317,900	207,524	201,811	210,457	234,118	4.23	11.24
Romania	6,346	3,451	3,827	8,713	7,070	0.13	-18.86
Russian Federation	343,009	356,888	297,328	348,070	449,797	8.12	29.23
Slovakia	13,280	8,454	8,267	11,759	12,381	0.22	5.29
Tajikistan			1,798	4,063	3,879	0.07	-4.53
Turkmenistan			116	736	188	0.00	-74.46
Ukraine	37,582	40,196	37,462	46,528	62,322	1.13	33.95
Uzbekistan	4,127	9,419	9,997	14,925	22,161	0.40	48.48
Northern Europe	672,848	763,417	704,111	857,075	908,149	16.40	5.96
Denmark	53,128	42,515	51,798	65,418	63,997	1.16	-2.17
Finland	144,954	198,102	172,919	202,644	188,915	3.41	-6.77
Iceland	4,085	3,604	4,986	6,130	16,418	0.30	167.83
Ireland	15,294	22,249	21,539	22,282	25,593	0.46	14.86
Norway	88,803	80,309	87,446	121,438	150,077	2.71	23.58
Sweden	281,360	323,456	271,840	352,486	351,185	6.34	-0.37
United Kingdom	85,224	93,182	93,583	86,677	111,964	2.02	29.17
Southern Europe	81,057	94,040	85,709	113,331	138,023	2.49	21.79
Albania			180	146			
Andorra					379	0.01	
Bosnia and Herzegovina			163	144			
Croatia	1,854	3,713	3,544	4,007	8,692	0.16	116.92
Greece	2,754	5,241	4,065	6,666	6,581	0.12	-1.28
Italy	46,682	55,357	41,392	53,482	71,540	1.29	33.76
Malta	2,911	1,683	3,814	4,285	3,964	0.07	-7.49
Montenegro				197			
Portugal	3,326	7,067	9,164	12,927	13,956	0.25	7.96
Serbia				2,355	523	0.01	-77.79
Slovenia	1,758	2,480	2,728	4,709	4,818	0.09	2.31
Spain	21,226	18,499	18,145	22,108	26,100	0.47	18.06
TFYR of Macedonia	546		2,514	2,305	1,470	0.03	-36.23
Western Europe	398,680	373,334	348,770	360,688	431,176	7.79	19.54
Austria	20,358	15,695	9,918	16,045	21,419	0.39	33.49
Belgium	13,845	21,548	23,802	41,150	48,766	0.88	18.51
France	38,098	40,312	35,513	35,490	49,204	0.89	38.64
Germany	264,837	261,778	226,461	218,449	249,112	4.50	14.04
Liechtenstein			681	806	1,422	0.03	76.43
Luxembourg	2,464	2,231	2,699	5,837	7,129	0.13	22.13
Monaco			940	351	848	0.02	141.60
Netherlands	42,463	19,903	31,053	28,833	32,048	0.58	11.15
Switzerland	16,615	11,867	17,703	13,727	21,228	0.38	54.64
East Mediterranean Europe	12,603	9,594	21,929	33,144	29,768	0.54	-10.19
Cyprus	509		2,711	5,511	3,015	0.05	-45.29
Israel	6,318	4,228	9,601	15,699	18,464	0.33	17.61

LATVIA

2. Arrivals of non-resident visitors at national borders, by country of residence

	2007	2008	2009	2010	2011	Market share 11	% Change 11-10
Turkey	5,776	5,366	9,617	11,934	8,289	0.15	-30.54
MIDDLE EAST	**2,173**		**1,924**	**7,514**	**1,858**	**0.03**	**-75.27**
Bahrain				175	191	0.00	9.14
Iraq	151			146	383	0.01	162.33
Jordan	158		158	197	188	0.00	-4.57
Kuwait				1,303	765	0.01	-41.29
Lebanon			455	2,949			
Qatar	255			1,055			
Saudi Arabia			180	144			
Syrian Arab Republic				518			
United Arab Emirates	255		496		191	0.00	
Egypt	1,354		635	1,027	140	0.00	-86.37
SOUTH ASIA	**2,016**	**4,329**	**7,790**	**11,283**	**11,063**	**0.20**	**-1.95**
Afghanistan				526			
Bangladesh	235		180	197			
Sri Lanka	469				188	0.00	
India	1,017	4,329	3,737	7,147	7,790	0.14	9.00
Iran, Islamic Republic of	295		2,305	1,467	188	0.00	-87.18
Nepal					564	0.01	
Pakistan			1,568	1,946	2,333	0.04	19.89
NOT SPECIFIED	**2,263**	**22,138**	**4,897**	**4,740**	**8,765**	**0.16**	**84.92**
Other countries of the World	2,263	22,138	4,897	4,740	8,765	0.16	84.92

LATVIA

4. Arrivals of non-resident tourists in all types of accommodation establishments, by country of residence

	2007	2008	2009	2010	2011	Market share 11	% Change 11-10
TOTAL	844,828	944,690	753,875	877,774	1,063,294	100.00	21.14
AFRICA	132	389	347	428	786	0.07	83.64
East Africa	56	7	15	19	59	0.01	210.53
Kenya	15	4	7	12	44	0.00	266.67
Zimbabwe	6	1	1	2	3	0.00	50.00
Uganda	31		3		10	0.00	
United Republic of Tanzania	4	2	4	5	2	0.00	-60.00
Central Africa	10	25	28	32	54	0.01	68.75
Angola		8	2	2	11	0.00	450.00
Cameroon	4	11	15	11	21	0.00	90.91
Central African Republic	2	6	6	15	21	0.00	40.00
Congo	4			3	1	0.00	-66.67
Democratic Republic of the Congo			5	1			
North Africa	7	65	56	97	167	0.02	72.16
Algeria	1	12	16	18	15	0.00	-16.67
Morocco	2	28	26	64	54	0.01	-15.63
Tunisia	4	25	14	15	98	0.01	553.33
Southern Africa	49	229	165	182	353	0.03	93.96
Namibia	8	2		11	6	0.00	-45.45
South Africa	37	116	126	132	151	0.01	14.39
Swaziland	4	111	39	39	196	0.02	402.56
West Africa	10	63	83	98	153	0.01	56.12
Benin		2					
Gambia		1			1	0.00	
Ghana		2	7	1	14	0.00	1300.00
Liberia				2	2	0.00	
Mauritania			2	2	9	0.00	350.00
Niger	1	4	3	15	18	0.00	20.00
Nigeria	2	27	30	29	46	0.00	58.62
Senegal	4		1	11	2	0.00	-81.82
Sierra Leone	3	27	40	38	61	0.01	60.53
AMERICAS	20,849	24,690	19,027	22,589	24,820	2.33	9.88
Caribbean	3	8	26	29	25	0.00	-13.79
Antigua and Barbuda			1	1	5	0.00	400.00
Barbados			9				
Cuba		7	7	13	19	0.00	46.15
Dominican Republic		1	7				
Jamaica	3		2	15	1	0.00	-93.33
Central America	10	40	53	70	94	0.01	34.29
Belize	6	1	2	1			
Costa Rica	4	19	43	33	57	0.01	72.73
Guatemala		9		21	17	0.00	-19.05
Panama		11	8	15	20	0.00	33.33
North America	20,283	23,583	17,737	21,001	22,212	2.09	5.77
Canada	2,964	2,889	2,418	2,703	3,587	0.34	32.70
Greenland	3	20	4	11	3	0.00	-72.73
Mexico	261	334	486	424	507	0.05	19.58
United States of America	17,055	20,340	14,829	17,863	18,115	1.70	1.41
South America	553	1,059	1,211	1,489	2,489	0.23	67.16
Argentina	131	345	165	320	362	0.03	13.13
Bolivia	19	42	10	11	1	0.00	-90.91
Brazil	289	523	801	848	1,647	0.15	94.22
Chile	73	34	86	85	173	0.02	103.53
Colombia	10	18	73	68	87	0.01	27.94
Ecuador	2	16	6	8	13	0.00	62.50

LATVIA

4. Arrivals of non-resident tourists in all types of accommodation establishments, by country of residence

	2007	2008	2009	2010	2011	Market share 11	% Change 11-10
Peru	21	48	15	40	54	0.01	35.00
Suriname					22	0.00	
Uruguay		7	8	66	38	0.00	-42.42
Venezuela	8	26	47	43	92	0.01	113.95
EAST ASIA AND THE PACIFIC	**11,387**	**13,464**	**14,389**	**15,482**	**18,426**	**1.73**	**19.02**
North-East Asia	**6,836**	**8,668**	**9,684**	**9,991**	**11,802**	**1.11**	**18.13**
China	382	936	1,593	1,963	2,893	0.27	47.38
Taiwan, Province of China	181	356	495	478	753	0.07	57.53
Hong Kong, China	16	55	97	144	435	0.04	202.08
Japan	6,065	6,043	6,690	5,428	5,843	0.55	7.65
Korea, Dem. People's Republic of	47	51	447	397	383	0.04	-3.53
Korea, Republic of	133	1,212	332	1,562	1,475	0.14	-5.57
Mongolia	12	15	30	19	20	0.00	5.26
South-East Asia	**573**	**541**	**979**	**1,395**	**1,421**	**0.13**	**1.86**
Indonesia	40	44	159	123	104	0.01	-15.45
Lao People's Democratic Republic	284	1	2	116	19	0.00	-83.62
Malaysia	39	82	137	51	117	0.01	129.41
Philippines	109	92	108	125	277	0.03	121.60
Singapore	30	83	103	171	328	0.03	91.81
Viet Nam	6	83	22	32	89	0.01	178.13
Thailand	65	156	448	777	487	0.05	-37.32
Australasia	**3,978**	**4,255**	**3,726**	**4,096**	**5,203**	**0.49**	**27.03**
Australia	3,556	3,934	3,395	3,636	4,616	0.43	26.95
New Zealand	422	321	331	460	587	0.06	27.61
EUROPE	**794,241**	**897,356**	**713,375**	**827,934**	**1,007,215**	**94.73**	**21.65**
Central/Eastern Europe	**286,225**	**339,513**	**265,867**	**338,473**	**447,263**	**42.06**	**32.14**
Azerbaijan	205	430	487	738	1,434	0.13	94.31
Armenia	70	131	171	290	669	0.06	130.69
Bulgaria	1,916	1,844	1,318	1,467	1,785	0.17	21.68
Belarus	12,660	14,992	14,901	15,247	16,682	1.57	9.41
Czech Republic	7,804	8,861	5,948	5,226	5,600	0.53	7.16
Estonia	76,410	82,296	58,762	62,906	81,979	7.71	30.32
Georgia	523	909	1,169	1,172	1,491	0.14	27.22
Hungary	2,898	2,731	2,122	2,873	4,375	0.41	52.28
Kazakhstan		830	484	1,157	1,665	0.16	43.91
Kyrgyzstan	17	42	51	151	184	0.02	21.85
Lithuania	82,703	107,173	71,811	84,509	100,561	9.46	18.99
Republic of Moldova	299	452	338	425	560	0.05	31.76
Poland	26,353	30,701	24,038	27,447	35,309	3.32	28.64
Romania	1,464	3,391	1,982	2,699	2,771	0.26	2.67
Russian Federation	60,055	70,778	72,227	119,007	174,343	16.40	46.50
Slovakia	1,736	2,007	1,332	1,602	2,587	0.24	61.49
Tajikistan	5	55	94	132	100	0.01	-24.24
Turkmenistan	2	17	40	22	52	0.00	136.36
Ukraine	10,707	11,314	7,667	9,479	12,746	1.20	34.47
Uzbekistan	398	559	925	1,924	2,370	0.22	23.18
Northern Europe	**283,946**	**304,402**	**231,602**	**262,686**	**290,767**	**27.35**	**10.69**
Denmark	15,986	17,100	12,686	12,859	15,075	1.42	17.23
Finland	75,286	93,025	72,024	79,655	90,991	8.56	14.23
Iceland	783	688	485	840	1,108	0.10	31.90
Ireland	11,352	12,120	6,012	4,380	4,190	0.39	-4.34
Norway	59,017	61,261	49,190	64,273	72,309	6.80	12.50
Sweden	58,823	62,830	55,609	61,155	63,135	5.94	3.24
United Kingdom	62,699	57,378	35,596	39,524	43,959	4.13	11.22
Southern Europe	**49,372**	**54,175**	**47,724**	**52,053**	**68,429**	**6.44**	**31.46**
Albania	26	60	76	118	286	0.03	142.37

LATVIA

4. Arrivals of non-resident tourists in all types of accommodation establishments, by country of residence

	2007	2008	2009	2010	2011	Market share 11	% Change 11-10
Andorra	11	14	32	31	69	0.01	122.58
Bosnia and Herzegovina	35	22	99	87	134	0.01	54.02
Croatia	293	556	626	815	529	0.05	-35.09
Gibraltar	2	4		2	13	0.00	550.00
Greece	2,765	3,357	2,836	3,216	3,431	0.32	6.69
Italy	27,551	31,372	27,303	27,510	37,963	3.57	38.00
Malta	100	101	184	160	251	0.02	56.88
Montenegro			14	10	37	0.00	270.00
Portugal	1,977	2,440	2,638	2,958	3,212	0.30	8.59
San Marino	15	4	13	3	32	0.00	966.67
Serbia	2	51	221	236	515	0.05	118.22
Slovenia	1,126	1,273	1,048	1,144	1,222	0.11	6.82
Spain	15,349	14,837	12,551	15,706	20,680	1.94	31.67
TFYR of Macedonia	11	84	83	57	55	0.01	-3.51
Serbia and Montenegro	109						
Western Europe	**168,068**	**191,083**	**159,010**	**162,488**	**184,053**	**17.31**	**13.27**
Austria	8,454	11,364	8,543	6,554	8,515	0.80	29.92
Belgium	6,057	7,562	8,811	11,005	13,092	1.23	18.96
France	17,562	20,123	18,296	19,032	19,635	1.85	3.17
Germany	111,439	122,682	93,739	98,305	113,064	10.63	15.01
Liechtenstein	13	17	18	14	107	0.01	664.29
Luxembourg	770	909	925	826	857	0.08	3.75
Monaco	20	31	77	118	127	0.01	7.63
Netherlands	16,672	19,060	18,893	18,113	18,358	1.73	1.35
Switzerland	7,081	9,335	9,708	8,521	10,298	0.97	20.85
East Mediterranean Europe	**6,630**	**8,183**	**9,172**	**12,234**	**16,703**	**1.57**	**36.53**
Cyprus	790	670	780	408	632	0.06	54.90
Israel	3,703	4,351	3,586	4,328	6,216	0.58	43.62
Turkey	2,137	3,162	4,806	7,498	9,855	0.93	31.44
MIDDLE EAST	**390**	**368**	**478**	**648**	**972**	**0.09**	**50.00**
Bahrain		6	12	16	10	0.00	-37.50
Iraq	5	19	67	91	62	0.01	-31.87
Jordan		1	11	22	17	0.00	-22.73
Kuwait	1	17	41	30	85	0.01	183.33
Lebanon	4	21	22	87	80	0.01	-8.05
Libya	50	14	8	57	55	0.01	-3.51
Qatar				4	8	0.00	100.00
Saudi Arabia	1	13	24	27	130	0.01	381.48
Syrian Arab Republic	1	12	20	29	49	0.00	68.97
United Arab Emirates	9	24	77	75	192	0.02	156.00
Egypt	319	241	196	208	282	0.03	35.58
Yemen				2	2	0.00	
SOUTH ASIA	**626**	**969**	**1,081**	**1,418**	**2,029**	**0.19**	**43.09**
Afghanistan	211	63	19	87	109	0.01	25.29
Bangladesh	10	17	28	22	11	0.00	-50.00
Sri Lanka		7	21	44	41	0.00	-6.82
India	369	719	867	913	1,411	0.13	54.55
Iran, Islamic Republic of	21	97	94	159	210	0.02	32.08
Nepal	1	2	1	19	57	0.01	200.00
Pakistan	14	64	51	174	190	0.02	9.20
NOT SPECIFIED	**17,203**	**7,454**	**5,178**	**9,275**	**9,046**	**0.85**	**-2.47**
Other countries of the World	17,203	7,454	5,178	9,275	9,046	0.85	-2.47

LATVIA

6. Overnight stays of non-resident tourists in all types of accommodation establishments, by country of residence

	2007	2008	2009	2010	2011	Market share 11	% Change 11-10
TOTAL	1,935,984	2,115,618	1,699,562	1,912,336	2,257,021	100.00	18.02
AFRICA	325	767	555	1,019	1,762	0.08	72.91
East Africa	92	23	35	105	278	0.01	164.76
Kenya	66	17	13	53	262	0.01	394.34
Zimbabwe	18	4	4	18	3	0.00	-83.33
Uganda			14		11	0.00	
United Republic of Tanzania	8	2	4	34	2	0.00	-94.12
Central Africa	19	86	43	126	135	0.01	7.14
Angola		37	2	4	14	0.00	250.00
Cameroon	8	25	19	56	46	0.00	-17.86
Central African Republic	7	24	15	60	74	0.00	23.33
Congo	4		7	5	1	0.00	-80.00
Democratic Republic of the Congo				1			
North Africa	14	151	104	187	348	0.02	86.10
Algeria	1	28	20	51	43	0.00	-15.69
Morocco	4	44	42	91	100	0.00	9.89
Tunisia	9	79	42	45	205	0.01	355.56
Southern Africa	180	406	235	378	758	0.03	100.53
Namibia	24	4		27	8	0.00	-70.37
South Africa	144	224	235	293	352	0.02	20.14
Swaziland	12	178		58	398	0.02	586.21
West Africa	20	101	138	223	243	0.01	8.97
Benin		6					
Gambia		2			1	0.00	
Ghana		6	12	5	24	0.00	380.00
Liberia				8	2	0.00	-75.00
Mauritania			12	28	15	0.00	-46.43
Niger	1	4	8	15	31	0.00	106.67
Nigeria	4	55	58	60	86	0.00	43.33
Senegal	8		1	21	4	0.00	-80.95
Sierra Leone	7	28	47	86	80	0.00	-6.98
AMERICAS	50,929	56,356	47,030	58,740	60,081	2.66	2.28
Caribbean	6	17	68	64	47	0.00	-26.56
Antigua and Barbuda			1	1	5	0.00	400.00
Barbados			28				
Cuba		13	20	32	40	0.00	25.00
Dominican Republic		4	12				
Jamaica	6		7	31	2	0.00	-93.55
Central America	19	62	79	90	180	0.01	100.00
Belize	13	1	5	2			
Costa Rica	6	29	61	41	74	0.00	80.49
Guatemala		19		24	43	0.00	79.17
Panama		13	13	23	63	0.00	173.91
North America	49,500	54,069	44,268	55,451	54,514	2.42	-1.69
Canada	6,771	7,159	5,212	6,306	8,575	0.38	35.98
Greenland	4	31	12	28	9	0.00	-67.86
Mexico	1,313	574	764	886	1,065	0.05	20.20
United States of America	41,412	46,305	38,280	48,231	44,865	1.99	-6.98
South America	1,404	2,208	2,615	3,135	5,340	0.24	70.33
Argentina	318	653	405	683	912	0.04	33.53
Bolivia	61	56	60	23	4	0.00	-82.61
Brazil	738	1,175	1,650	1,841	3,495	0.15	89.84
Chile	190	93	163	156	402	0.02	157.69
Colombia	26	24	139	151	163	0.01	7.95
Ecuador	4	37	11	10	19	0.00	90.00

LATVIA

6. Overnight stays of non-resident tourists in all types of accommodation establishments, by country of residence

	2007	2008	2009	2010	2011	Market share 11	% Change 11-10
Peru	49	82	38	83	84	0.00	1.20
Suriname					25	0.00	
Uruguay		17	43	123	69	0.00	-43.90
Venezuela	18	71	106	65	167	0.01	156.92
EAST ASIA AND THE PACIFIC	**22,116**	**24,776**	**27,824**	**29,406**	**36,012**	**1.60**	**22.46**
North-East Asia	**11,731**	**14,809**	**17,912**	**17,792**	**21,506**	**0.95**	**20.87**
China	1,165	2,150	3,231	3,804	5,521	0.24	45.14
Taiwan, Province of China	284	633	788	721	1,372	0.06	90.29
Hong Kong, China	40	122	174	306	764	0.03	149.67
Japan	9,571	10,521	11,967	9,680	9,924	0.44	2.52
Korea, Dem. People's Republic of	89	92	607	691	995	0.04	43.99
Korea, Republic of	426	1,267	1,026	2,555	2,903	0.13	13.62
Mongolia	156	24	119	35	27	0.00	-22.86
South-East Asia	**1,390**	**1,017**	**2,221**	**2,602**	**2,748**	**0.12**	**5.61**
Indonesia	323	82	380	231	189	0.01	-18.18
Lao People's Democratic Republic	403	1	3	124	19	0.00	-84.68
Malaysia	97	120	267	114	189	0.01	65.79
Philippines	264	167	360	257	561	0.02	118.29
Singapore	61	178	290	448	856	0.04	91.07
Viet Nam	21	158	58	83	172	0.01	107.23
Thailand	221	311	863	1,345	762	0.03	-43.35
Australasia	**8,995**	**8,950**	**7,691**	**9,012**	**11,758**	**0.52**	**30.47**
Australia	8,088	8,367	7,004	8,063	10,581	0.47	31.23
New Zealand	907	583	687	949	1,177	0.05	24.03
EUROPE	**1,822,835**	**1,989,715**	**1,609,225**	**1,785,749**	**2,132,688**	**94.49**	**19.43**
Central/Eastern Europe	**744,702**	**785,869**	**649,913**	**740,745**	**973,489**	**43.13**	**31.42**
Azerbaijan	618	1,331	1,242	1,956	3,790	0.17	93.76
Armenia	182	453	480	724	1,225	0.05	69.20
Bulgaria	8,423	5,331	2,542	3,757	3,492	0.15	-7.05
Belarus	93,918	102,435	131,484	82,616	83,329	3.69	0.86
Czech Republic	14,257	17,268	10,749	10,946	11,265	0.50	2.91
Estonia	126,722	129,936	90,246	95,985	127,749	5.66	33.09
Georgia	1,886	2,432	2,808	2,403	5,385	0.24	124.09
Hungary	5,591	5,346	4,443	5,051	7,877	0.35	55.95
Kazakhstan	641	2,229	1,314	2,692	4,139	0.18	53.75
Kyrgyzstan	57	265	247	607	1,273	0.06	109.72
Lithuania	170,121	196,461	120,457	128,760	180,541	8.00	40.22
Republic of Moldova	1,484	985	1,061	1,437	1,069	0.05	-25.61
Poland	68,874	64,194	42,185	45,193	57,819	2.56	27.94
Romania	3,285	8,585	4,417	6,220	6,445	0.29	3.62
Russian Federation	187,679	194,999	196,582	320,130	433,560	19.21	35.43
Slovakia	6,012	4,971	2,893	3,685	5,554	0.25	50.72
Tajikistan	14	234	535	729	589	0.03	-19.20
Turkmenistan	28	32	75	44	174	0.01	295.45
Ukraine	50,682	46,422	33,855	22,303	29,562	1.31	32.55
Uzbekistan	4,228	1,960	2,298	5,507	8,652	0.38	57.11
Northern Europe	**614,836**	**649,407**	**493,328**	**556,115**	**603,010**	**26.72**	**8.43**
Denmark	33,570	34,299	25,518	26,245	31,180	1.38	18.80
Finland	153,581	184,841	153,309	160,956	181,742	8.05	12.91
Iceland	1,803	1,479	992	2,341	2,720	0.12	16.19
Ireland	24,603	28,701	13,878	10,192	9,291	0.41	-8.84
Norway	138,320	139,703	118,591	159,181	172,330	7.64	8.26
Sweden	118,847	120,101	102,788	105,615	111,434	4.94	5.51
United Kingdom	144,112	140,283	78,252	91,585	94,313	4.18	2.98
Southern Europe	**103,511**	**128,198**	**106,701**	**110,926**	**141,046**	**6.25**	**27.15**
Albania	68	121	196	203	357	0.02	75.86

LATVIA

6. Overnight stays of non-resident tourists in all types of accommodation establishments, by country of residence

	2007	2008	2009	2010	2011	Market share 11	% Change 11-10
Andorra	16	27	106	64	146	0.01	128.13
Bosnia and Herzegovina	59	59	169	146	324	0.01	121.92
Croatia	669	1,673	1,310	2,193	1,202	0.05	-45.19
Gibraltar	4	7		5	41	0.00	720.00
Greece	6,306	8,504	6,696	7,019	8,080	0.36	15.12
Italy	56,757	71,373	60,433	59,453	78,070	3.46	31.31
Malta	252	238	358	312	461	0.02	47.76
Montenegro			15	12	141	0.01	1075.00
Portugal	5,468	7,453	5,945	6,747	7,180	0.32	6.42
San Marino	15	17	25	10	156	0.01	1460.00
Serbia	19	174	522	569	1,141	0.05	100.53
Slovenia	2,741	2,435	2,166	2,590	2,397	0.11	-7.45
Spain	30,712	35,973	28,518	31,442	41,256	1.83	31.21
TFYR of Macedonia	21	144	242	161	94	0.00	-41.61
Serbia and Montenegro	404						
Western Europe	**340,881**	**402,997**	**334,139**	**346,917**	**377,006**	**16.70**	**8.67**
Austria	18,002	23,491	17,078	13,441	16,638	0.74	23.79
Belgium	12,727	15,120	19,468	25,151	28,577	1.27	13.62
France	35,808	42,626	39,470	38,734	40,432	1.79	4.38
Germany	223,537	264,728	197,465	209,921	225,812	10.00	7.57
Liechtenstein	23	26	36	23	178	0.01	673.91
Luxembourg	1,379	2,242	2,052	1,794	1,867	0.08	4.07
Monaco	83	60	121	152	208	0.01	36.84
Netherlands	32,109	35,800	38,297	39,743	42,179	1.87	6.13
Switzerland	17,213	18,904	20,152	17,958	21,115	0.94	17.58
East Mediterranean Europe	**18,905**	**23,244**	**25,144**	**31,046**	**38,137**	**1.69**	**22.84**
Cyprus	1,664	1,700	1,722	1,191	1,927	0.09	61.80
Israel	11,453	12,642	10,417	13,519	15,036	0.67	11.22
Turkey	5,788	8,902	13,005	16,336	21,174	0.94	29.62
MIDDLE EAST	**843**	**947**	**1,389**	**1,817**	**2,096**	**0.09**	**15.35**
Bahrain		21	24	51	18	0.00	-64.71
Iraq	9	54	386	156	118	0.01	-24.36
Jordan		2	64	90	46	0.00	-48.89
Kuwait	1	43	73	37	123	0.01	232.43
Lebanon	5	37	73	228	177	0.01	-22.37
Libya	115	41	13	160	99	0.00	-38.13
Qatar				4	12	0.00	200.00
Saudi Arabia	1	21	73	80	278	0.01	247.50
Syrian Arab Republic	2	21	38	122	104	0.00	-14.75
United Arab Emirates	18	43	146	195	341	0.02	74.87
Egypt	692	664	499	692	776	0.03	12.14
Yemen				2	4	0.00	100.00
SOUTH ASIA	**2,006**	**2,375**	**2,360**	**5,410**	**4,457**	**0.20**	**-17.62**
Afghanistan	989	157	34	191	229	0.01	19.90
Bangladesh	34	42	46	49	28	0.00	-42.86
Sri Lanka		7	60	57	49	0.00	-14.04
India	889	1,735	1,941	4,521	3,302	0.15	-26.96
Iran, Islamic Republic of	48	174	203	282	344	0.02	21.99
Nepal	4	3	1	48	97	0.00	102.08
Pakistan	42	257	75	262	408	0.02	55.73
NOT SPECIFIED	**36,930**	**40,682**	**11,179**	**30,195**	**19,925**	**0.88**	**-34.01**
Other countries of the World	36,930	40,682	11,179	30,195	19,925	0.88	-34.01

LEBANON

1. Arrivals of non-resident tourists at national borders, by nationality

		2007	2008	2009	2010	2011	Market share 11	% Change 11-10
TOTAL	(*)	1,017,072	1,332,533	1,844,106	2,167,989	1,655,051	100.00	-23.66
AFRICA		59,861	50,732	66,140	66,225	82,643	4.99	24.79
East Africa		36,726	19,010	24,536	21,616	43,095	2.60	99.37
Burundi		3	13	26	2	18	0.00	800.00
Comoros		6	15	60	95	186	0.01	95.79
Ethiopia		34,312	15,198	18,031	18,676	39,158	2.37	109.67
Eritrea		369	578	709	616	468	0.03	-24.03
Djibouti		11	35	64	54	42	0.00	-22.22
Kenya		251	320	431	635	1,687	0.10	165.67
Madagascar		891	1,818	4,085	375	280	0.02	-25.33
Malawi		75	86	87	93	93	0.01	
Mauritius		63	51	133	87	128	0.01	47.13
Mozambique		109	54	39	61	97	0.01	59.02
Rwanda		21	22	87	31	35	0.00	12.90
Seychelles		17	28	62	48	35	0.00	-27.08
Somalia		152	245	223	402	308	0.02	-23.38
Zimbabwe		129	128	92	80	74	0.00	-7.50
Uganda		45	95	89	106	106	0.01	
United Republic of Tanzania		209	248	245	179	289	0.02	61.45
Zambia		63	76	73	76	91	0.01	19.74
Central Africa		1,444	1,613	1,997	1,583	1,848	0.11	16.74
Angola		89	91	78	75	96	0.01	28.00
Cameroon		180	276	450	402	560	0.03	39.30
Central African Republic		94	96	102	81	66	0.00	-18.52
Chad		24	40	107	59	58	0.00	-1.69
Congo		168	280	500	319	415	0.03	30.09
Equatorial Guinea		2	15	21	22	16	0.00	-27.27
Gabon		887	815	737	625	633	0.04	1.28
Sao Tome and Principe				2		4	0.00	
North Africa		11,130	15,538	22,904	25,572	20,327	1.23	-20.51
Algeria		2,281	3,203	4,648	5,377	4,223	0.26	-21.46
Morocco		3,642	5,281	7,503	7,830	6,318	0.38	-19.31
Sudan		2,373	3,163	4,377	4,723	3,813	0.23	-19.27
Tunisia		2,834	3,891	6,376	7,642	5,973	0.36	-21.84
Southern Africa		1,244	1,794	2,382	2,451	2,026	0.12	-17.34
Botswana				5	2	1	0.00	-50.00
Lesotho				7	4	3	0.00	-25.00
Namibia		8	20	44	22	22	0.00	
South Africa		1,236	1,774	2,326	2,418	2,000	0.12	-17.29
Swaziland					5			
West Africa		9,317	12,777	14,321	15,003	15,347	0.93	2.29
Cape Verde		1	1	13	7	7	0.00	
Benin		320	357	406	412	515	0.03	25.00
Gambia		193	225	231	293	317	0.02	8.19
Ghana		2,519	2,910	3,187	3,435	4,115	0.25	19.80
Guinea		543	663	529	574	627	0.04	9.23
Côte d'Ivoire		1,195	2,358	2,618	2,851	2,055	0.12	-27.92
Liberia		158	194	258	225	213	0.01	-5.33
Mali		95	224	184	247	255	0.02	3.24
Mauritania		128	196	233	182	179	0.01	-1.65
Niger		62	126	183	140	122	0.01	-12.86
Nigeria		1,617	2,037	2,475	2,828	2,703	0.16	-4.42
Guinea-Bissau		69	112	89	62	67	0.00	8.06
Senegal		1,101	1,695	1,997	1,796	1,809	0.11	0.72
Sierra Leone		844	1,033	1,073	1,071	1,163	0.07	8.59
Togo		204	274	351	389	587	0.04	50.90

LEBANON

1. Arrivals of non-resident tourists at national borders, by nationality

	2007	2008	2009	2010	2011	Market share 11	% Change 11-10
Burkina Faso	268	372	494	491	613	0.04	24.85
AMERICAS	**121,596**	**176,647**	**232,694**	**248,725**	**222,671**	**13.45**	**-10.48**
Caribbean	**518**	**647**	**815**	**895**	**842**	**0.05**	**-5.92**
Antigua and Barbuda	20	15	61	60	41	0.00	-31.67
Bahamas	1		3	3	6	0.00	100.00
Barbados	11	14	10	10	4	0.00	-60.00
Cuba	194	204	209	167	133	0.01	-20.36
Dominican Republic	75	151	236	335	414	0.03	23.58
Grenada	14	2	27	18	14	0.00	-22.22
Haiti	36	50	63	55	31	0.00	-43.64
Jamaica	64	53	69	57	37	0.00	-35.09
Puerto Rico	1	1		1			
Saint Kitts and Nevis	5	7	9	22	58	0.00	163.64
Saint Lucia		3	4	7	1	0.00	-85.71
Saint Vincent and the Grenadines	15	34	34	37	29	0.00	-21.62
Trinidad and Tobago	82	113	90	123	74	0.00	-39.84
Central America	**482**	**822**	**1,286**	**1,400**	**1,095**	**0.07**	**-21.79**
Belize	164	176	218	261	219	0.01	-16.09
Costa Rica	44	76	119	247	93	0.01	-62.35
El Salvador	21	31	132	109	62	0.00	-43.12
Guatemala	59	69	129	150	72	0.00	-52.00
Honduras	19	38	31	59	42	0.00	-28.81
Nicaragua	20	21	32	21	25	0.00	19.05
Panama	155	411	625	553	582	0.04	5.24
North America	**105,128**	**152,419**	**201,377**	**214,607**	**192,243**	**11.62**	**-10.42**
Canada	47,166	66,780	87,144	88,002	79,978	4.83	-9.12
Mexico	989	1,796	2,332	3,303	2,100	0.13	-36.42
United States of America	56,973	83,843	111,901	123,302	110,165	6.66	-10.65
South America	**15,468**	**22,759**	**29,216**	**31,823**	**28,491**	**1.72**	**-10.47**
Argentina	703	916	1,542	2,114	1,397	0.08	-33.92
Bolivia	46	73	82	105	94	0.01	-10.48
Brazil	6,583	9,932	13,332	15,371	13,431	0.81	-12.62
Chile	301	695	642	822	740	0.04	-9.98
Colombia	957	1,155	1,440	1,370	1,202	0.07	-12.26
Ecuador	174	300	290	399	355	0.02	-11.03
Paraguay	407	473	574	584	556	0.03	-4.79
Peru	127	176	178	287	233	0.01	-18.82
Suriname	53	49	71	93	38	0.00	-59.14
Uruguay	71	92	143	143	135	0.01	-5.59
Venezuela	6,046	8,898	10,922	10,535	10,310	0.62	-2.14
EAST ASIA AND THE PACIFIC	**63,579**	**89,452**	**128,919**	**133,451**	**112,163**	**6.78**	**-15.95**
North-East Asia	**6,806**	**7,928**	**10,088**	**14,782**	**11,164**	**0.67**	**-24.48**
China	2,028	2,472	3,895	5,938	4,862	0.29	-18.12
Taiwan, Province of China	256	427	274	414	290	0.02	-29.95
Hong Kong, China	45	65	136	215	126	0.01	-41.40
Japan	1,486	1,934	2,562	3,906	2,186	0.13	-44.03
Korea, Dem. People's Republic of	141	38	35	84	63	0.00	-25.00
Korea, Republic of	2,845	2,987	3,168	4,200	3,606	0.22	-14.14
Mongolia	5	5	18	25	31	0.00	24.00
South-East Asia	**25,761**	**39,233**	**54,772**	**58,236**	**44,615**	**2.70**	**-23.39**
Brunei Darussalam	1	2	40	24	83	0.01	245.83
Myanmar	50	78	48	47	65	0.00	38.30
Cambodia	6	6	11	229	240	0.01	4.80
Indonesia	5,593	7,451	10,567	10,525	8,446	0.51	-19.75
Lao People's Democratic Republic			3	1	14	0.00	1300.00
Malaysia	2,338	2,875	3,587	4,901	4,580	0.28	-6.55

LEBANON

1. Arrivals of non-resident tourists at national borders, by nationality

	2007	2008	2009	2010	2011	Market share 11	% Change 11-10
Philippines	17,388	28,042	39,384	41,174	30,172	1.82	-26.72
Singapore	166	392	626	828	517	0.03	-37.56
Viet Nam	68	203	218	199	143	0.01	-28.14
Thailand	151	184	288	308	355	0.02	15.26
Australasia	**30,915**	**42,193**	**63,899**	**60,302**	**56,249**	**3.40**	**-6.72**
Australia	29,937	40,884	62,140	58,150	54,522	3.29	-6.24
New Zealand	978	1,309	1,759	2,152	1,727	0.10	-19.75
Melanesia	**97**	**98**	**160**	**130**	**134**	**0.01**	**3.08**
Fiji	97	98	158	129	133	0.01	3.10
Vanuatu			1				
Papua New Guinea			1	1	1	0.00	
Polynesia				**1**	**1**	**0.00**	
Tonga				1	1	0.00	
EUROPE	**277,873**	**348,262**	**454,742**	**550,866**	**487,150**	**29.43**	**-11.57**
Central/Eastern Europe	**25,712**	**32,371**	**39,616**	**47,248**	**43,164**	**2.61**	**-8.64**
Azerbaijan	78	114	222	255	261	0.02	2.35
Armenia	991	1,511	1,810	2,123	1,889	0.11	-11.02
Bulgaria	1,082	1,537	1,842	2,591	2,167	0.13	-16.36
Belarus	1,337	1,572	1,972	2,379	2,279	0.14	-4.20
Czech Republic	1,570	1,724	2,140	2,780	1,838	0.11	-33.88
Estonia	113	162	186	380	416	0.03	9.47
Georgia	232	147	223	344	393	0.02	14.24
Hungary	921	1,433	1,657	1,886	1,411	0.09	-25.19
Kazakhstan	201	289	497	555	567	0.03	2.16
Kyrgyzstan	75	79	143	161	225	0.01	39.75
Latvia	208	391	400	614	597	0.04	-2.77
Lithuania	210	358	453	725	709	0.04	-2.21
Republic of Moldova	931	1,082	1,275	1,439	1,461	0.09	1.53
Poland	2,726	3,694	4,397	4,906	3,837	0.23	-21.79
Romania	2,222	3,157	3,933	4,639	4,190	0.25	-9.68
Russian Federation	6,856	8,333	9,838	12,175	11,121	0.67	-8.66
Slovakia	592	841	1,024	1,143	1,014	0.06	-11.29
Tajikistan	62	63	66	92	80	0.00	-13.04
Turkmenistan	47	46	54	57	72	0.00	26.32
Ukraine	5,107	5,546	7,024	7,484	8,140	0.49	8.77
Uzbekistan	151	292	460	520	497	0.03	-4.42
Northern Europe	**62,492**	**81,478**	**104,587**	**121,219**	**108,408**	**6.55**	**-10.57**
Denmark	10,321	14,510	18,078	19,332	16,830	1.02	-12.94
Finland	2,610	1,352	1,661	2,391	1,810	0.11	-24.30
Iceland	99	126	153	211	143	0.01	-32.23
Ireland	2,635	2,283	3,222	4,050	4,953	0.30	22.30
Norway	2,703	3,498	4,552	5,484	4,697	0.28	-14.35
Sweden	14,497	21,624	26,894	29,512	26,752	1.62	-9.35
United Kingdom	29,627	38,085	50,027	60,239	53,223	3.22	-11.65
Southern Europe	**38,368**	**42,726**	**58,699**	**66,961**	**52,268**	**3.16**	**-21.94**
Albania	56	49	95	98	87	0.01	-11.22
Andorra	1		9	14	3	0.00	-78.57
Bosnia and Herzegovina	190	235	306	361	251	0.02	-30.47
Croatia	429	517	679	779	641	0.04	-17.72
Greece	4,556	6,071	8,041	9,328	7,695	0.46	-17.51
Holy See	51	65	68	79	109	0.01	37.97
Italy	21,563	23,085	32,619	36,625	28,808	1.74	-21.34
Malta	125	141	252	300	258	0.02	-14.00
Portugal	1,071	1,309	1,707	2,091	1,701	0.10	-18.65
San Marino	3	20	13	17	10	0.00	-41.18
Serbia	218	312	678	1,212	1,091	0.07	-9.98
Slovenia	123	197	314	385	292	0.02	-24.16

LEBANON

1. Arrivals of non-resident tourists at national borders, by nationality

	2007	2008	2009	2010	2011	Market share 11	% Change 11-10
Spain	9,183	9,987	13,343	15,417	11,301	0.68	-26.70
TFYR of Macedonia	121	112	185	185	21	0.00	-88.65
Serbia and Montenegro	678	626	390	70			
Western Europe	**138,249**	**175,177**	**230,620**	**263,433**	**239,734**	**14.48**	**-9.00**
Austria	2,373	3,235	4,252	5,823	5,002	0.30	-14.10
Belgium	8,548	10,924	13,661	15,379	13,497	0.82	-12.24
France	72,359	91,071	120,408	139,534	128,999	7.79	-7.55
Germany	42,083	53,851	69,847	76,854	68,401	4.13	-11.00
Liechtenstein	4	13	17	13	20	0.00	53.85
Luxembourg	159	227	378	406	357	0.02	-12.07
Monaco	15	31	55	60	85	0.01	41.67
Netherlands	6,152	7,357	10,268	11,824	10,281	0.62	-13.05
Switzerland	6,556	8,468	11,734	13,540	12,935	0.78	-4.47
Other countries of Western Europe					157	0.01	
East Mediterranean Europe	**13,052**	**16,510**	**21,220**	**52,005**	**43,576**	**2.63**	**-16.21**
Cyprus	5,092	7,181	8,241	9,325	7,932	0.48	-14.94
Turkey	7,960	9,329	12,979	42,680	35,644	2.15	-16.49
MIDDLE EAST	**388,292**	**532,871**	**761,852**	**867,898**	**560,273**	**33.85**	**-35.44**
Bahrain	12,021	17,424	25,218	25,096	9,493	0.57	-62.17
Iraq	83,159	72,805	101,561	129,847	129,294	7.81	-0.43
Jordan	127,042	180,887	223,793	274,615	129,640	7.83	-52.79
Kuwait	44,534	68,936	102,537	95,824	61,756	3.73	-35.55
Libya	2,758	2,964	3,913	4,570	2,484	0.15	-45.65
Oman	2,435	4,012	5,717	6,639	4,494	0.27	-32.31
Qatar	8,380	14,093	19,358	18,436	11,171	0.67	-39.41
Saudi Arabia	63,918	101,749	173,294	191,066	111,701	6.75	-41.54
United Arab Emirates	12,273	24,673	42,974	46,923	32,058	1.94	-31.68
Egypt	29,585	41,657	57,379	67,773	62,825	3.80	-7.30
Yemen	2,187	3,671	6,108	7,109	5,357	0.32	-24.64
SOUTH ASIA	**104,729**	**133,067**	**197,941**	**299,087**	**188,242**	**11.37**	**-37.06**
Afghanistan	184	306	450	420	383	0.02	-8.81
Bangladesh	4,982	9,430	16,047	19,980	23,730	1.43	18.77
Bhutan	8	13	19	7	4	0.00	-42.86
Sri Lanka	9,945	8,903	9,997	10,338	8,864	0.54	-14.26
India	8,242	10,668	13,946	16,117	15,378	0.93	-4.59
Iran, Islamic Republic of	75,526	92,547	145,706	241,514	131,870	7.97	-45.40
Maldives	1	4	5	7	5	0.00	-28.57
Nepal	3,799	8,705	8,435	6,975	4,560	0.28	-34.62
Pakistan	2,042	2,491	3,336	3,729	3,448	0.21	-7.54
NOT SPECIFIED	**1,142**	**1,502**	**1,818**	**1,737**	**1,909**	**0.12**	**9.90**
Other countries of the World	1,142	1,502	1,818	1,737	1,909	0.12	9.90

LESOTHO

2. Arrivals of non-resident visitors at national borders, by country of residence

	2007	2008	2009	2010	2011	Market share 11	% Change 11-10
TOTAL	300,350	293,073	343,743	425,870	398,149	100.00	-6.51
AFRICA	271,475	259,407	314,218	400,823	379,507	95.32	-5.32
East Africa	5,829	8,145	6,905	6,135	4,550	1.14	-25.84
Kenya	287	253	301	386	261	0.07	-32.38
Malawi	468	404	430	333	295	0.07	-11.41
Mauritius	114	198	136	112	97	0.02	-13.39
Mozambique	225	140	210	302	359	0.09	18.87
Zimbabwe	3,457	4,149	4,513	3,819	2,619	0.66	-31.42
Uganda	242	1,294	269	268	205	0.05	-23.51
United Republic of Tanzania	286	1,038	240	208	144	0.04	-30.77
Zambia	750	669	806	707	570	0.14	-19.38
Southern Africa	264,024	249,043	306,121	393,645	374,161	93.98	-4.95
Botswana	1,679	1,796	2,060	1,922	1,419	0.36	-26.17
South Africa	261,099	246,014	302,655	390,849	371,867	93.40	-4.86
Swaziland	1,246	1,233	1,406	874	875	0.22	0.11
West Africa	335	209	206	233	154	0.04	-33.91
Ghana	107	103	84	61	59	0.01	-3.28
Nigeria	228	106	122	172	95	0.02	-44.77
Other Africa	1,287	2,010	986	810	642	0.16	-20.74
Other countries of Africa	1,287	2,010	986	810	642	0.16	-20.74
AMERICAS	3,385	4,556	4,122	3,907	3,180	0.80	-18.61
North America	3,248	3,078	4,017	3,739	3,080	0.77	-17.63
Canada	2,627	1,767	805	662	502	0.13	-24.17
United States of America	621	1,311	3,212	3,077	2,578	0.65	-16.22
Other Americas	137	1,478	105	168	100	0.03	-40.48
Other countries of the Americas	137	1,478	105	168	100	0.03	-40.48
EAST ASIA AND THE PACIFIC	4,816	5,566	5,150	3,938	2,407	0.60	-38.88
North-East Asia	2,058	2,446	2,378	1,728	860	0.22	-50.23
China	1,894	1,136	2,233	1,596	724	0.18	-54.64
Taiwan, Province of China	164	1,310	145	132	136	0.03	3.03
Australasia	766	1,813	770	871	621	0.16	-28.70
Australia	766	1,813	770	871	621	0.16	-28.70
Other East Asia and the Pacific	1,992	1,307	2,002	1,339	926	0.23	-30.84
Other countries of Asia	1,992	1,307	2,002	1,339	926	0.23	-30.84
EUROPE	19,772	22,717	19,726	16,719	12,751	3.20	-23.73
Northern Europe	5,134	6,444	5,552	4,723	3,201	0.80	-32.23
Denmark	375	1,711	248	232	117	0.03	-49.57
Ireland	331	2,106	397	349	189	0.05	-45.85
Sweden	260	382	288	316	310	0.08	-1.90
United Kingdom	4,168	2,245	4,619	3,826	2,585	0.65	-32.44
Southern Europe	343	371	422	213	291	0.07	36.62
Italy	343	371	422	213	291	0.07	36.62
Western Europe	11,578	6,933	10,862	9,653	7,485	1.88	-22.46
France	1,241	659	1,592	1,342	668	0.17	-50.22
Germany	5,778	3,349	5,015	4,425	3,927	0.99	-11.25
Netherlands	4,559	2,925	4,255	3,886	2,890	0.73	-25.63
Other Europe	2,717	8,969	2,890	2,130	1,774	0.45	-16.71
Other countries of Europe	2,717	8,969	2,890	2,130	1,774	0.45	-16.71

LESOTHO

2. Arrivals of non-resident visitors at national borders, by country of residence

	2007	2008	2009	2010	2011	Market share 11	% Change 11-10
MIDDLE EAST	**400**	**385**	**177**	**70**	**13**	**0.00**	**-81.43**
All countries of Middle East	400	385	177	70	13	0.00	-81.43
SOUTH ASIA	**304**	**404**	**256**	**285**	**261**	**0.07**	**-8.42**
India	304	404	256	285	261	0.07	-8.42
NOT SPECIFIED	**198**	**38**	**94**	**128**	**30**	**0.01**	**-76.56**
Other countries of the World	198	38	94	128	30	0.01	-76.56

LIECHTENSTEIN

3. Arrivals of non-resident tourists in hotels and similar establishments, by country of residence

	2007	2008	2009	2010	2011	Market share 11	% Change 11-10
TOTAL	58,258	58,454	52,285	49,804	53,326	100.00	7.07
AFRICA	216	177	171	132	138	0.26	4.55
Southern Africa	93	57	75	57	73	0.14	28.07
South Africa	93	57	75	57	73	0.14	28.07
Other Africa	123	120	96	75	65	0.12	-13.33
Other countries of Africa	123	120	96	75	65	0.12	-13.33
AMERICAS	3,156	2,439	2,260	2,397	2,714	5.09	13.22
North America	2,705	1,971	1,941	2,088	2,323	4.36	11.25
Canada	288	248	222	255	343	0.64	34.51
Mexico	54	52	28	23	47	0.09	104.35
United States of America	2,363	1,671	1,691	1,810	1,933	3.62	6.80
South America	168	173	154	176	230	0.43	30.68
Brazil	168	173	154	176	230	0.43	30.68
Other Americas	283	295	165	133	161	0.30	21.05
Other countries of the Americas	283	295	165	133	161	0.30	21.05
EAST ASIA AND THE PACIFIC	1,892	1,679	1,330	1,656	1,858	3.48	12.20
North-East Asia	944	806	637	752	994	1.86	32.18
China	252	171	147	272	399	0.75	46.69
Taiwan, Province of China	94	66	49	50	63	0.12	26.00
Hong Kong, China	37	39	31	43	45	0.08	4.65
Japan	461	435	361	316	400	0.75	26.58
Korea, Republic of	100	95	49	71	87	0.16	22.54
Australasia	336	303	219	289	280	0.53	-3.11
Australia	336	303	219	289	280	0.53	-3.11
Other East Asia and the Pacific	612	570	474	615	584	1.10	-5.04
Other countries of Asia	612	570	474	615	584	1.10	-5.04
EUROPE	52,885	54,067	48,210	45,393	48,252	90.48	6.30
Central/Eastern Europe	2,428	2,673	2,531	2,453	3,016	5.66	22.95
Bulgaria	114	135	93	93	95	0.18	2.15
Czech Republic	446	493	511	550	650	1.22	18.18
Estonia	27	57	63	15	32	0.06	113.33
Hungary	625	772	624	521	548	1.03	5.18
Latvia	34	36	44	51	37	0.07	-27.45
Lithuania	43	51	38	49	85	0.16	73.47
Poland	276	345	282	323	352	0.66	8.98
Romania	148	190	122	119	163	0.31	36.97
Russian Federation	613	460	593	572	911	1.71	59.27
Slovakia	102	134	161	160	143	0.27	-10.63
Northern Europe	4,752	4,174	3,808	3,404	4,143	7.77	21.71
Denmark	606	545	428	504	508	0.95	0.79
Finland	176	299	278	173	287	0.54	65.90
Iceland	110	41	45	39	67	0.13	71.79
Ireland	199	167	117	128	133	0.25	3.91
Norway	315	281	282	357	424	0.80	18.77
Sweden	702	389	444	362	457	0.86	26.24
United Kingdom	2,644	2,452	2,214	1,841	2,267	4.25	23.14
Southern Europe	3,515	3,376	2,879	2,912	2,970	5.57	1.99
Croatia	97	102	83	60	56	0.11	-6.67
Greece	259	195	235	231	192	0.36	-16.88
Italy	2,143	2,231	1,775	1,844	1,973	3.70	7.00
Malta	18	9	20	17	38	0.07	123.53
Portugal	151	165	180	153	164	0.31	7.19
Slovenia	228	135	125	86	78	0.15	-9.30

LIECHTENSTEIN

3. Arrivals of non-resident tourists in hotels and similar establishments, by country of residence

	2007	2008	2009	2010	2011	Market share 11	% Change 11-10
Spain	619	539	461	521	469	0.88	-9.98
Western Europe	**41,907**	**43,490**	**38,656**	**36,177**	**37,451**	**70.23**	**3.52**
Austria	3,047	2,964	2,525	2,355	2,447	4.59	3.91
Belgium	845	1,108	1,063	811	1,071	2.01	32.06
France	1,316	1,302	1,121	1,163	1,270	2.38	9.20
Germany	18,819	19,510	16,697	15,518	14,341	26.89	-7.58
Luxembourg	607	636	630	605	564	1.06	-6.78
Netherlands	1,326	1,175	1,086	1,112	1,167	2.19	4.95
Switzerland	15,947	16,795	15,534	14,613	16,591	31.11	13.54
East Mediterranean Europe	**53**	**107**	**68**	**131**	**129**	**0.24**	**-1.53**
Cyprus	2	10	3	16	15	0.03	-6.25
Turkey	51	97	65	115	114	0.21	-0.87
Other Europe	**230**	**247**	**268**	**316**	**543**	**1.02**	**71.84**
Other countries of Europe	230	247	268	316	543	1.02	71.84
SOUTH ASIA	**62**	**73**	**84**	**70**	**96**	**0.18**	**37.14**
India	62	73	84	70	96	0.18	37.14
NOT SPECIFIED	**47**	**19**	**230**	**156**	**268**	**0.50**	**71.79**
Other countries of the World	47	19	230	156	268	0.50	71.79

LIECHTENSTEIN

5. Overnight stays of non-resident tourists in hotels and similar establishments, by country of residence

	2007	2008	2009	2010	2011	Market share 11	% Change 11-10
TOTAL	126,111	131,095	117,806	111,458	112,459	100.00	0.90
AFRICA	686	592	556	326	357	0.32	9.51
Southern Africa	175	121	135	115	185	0.16	60.87
South Africa	175	121	135	115	185	0.16	60.87
Other Africa	511	471	421	211	172	0.15	-18.48
Other countries of Africa	511	471	421	211	172	0.15	-18.48
AMERICAS	6,890	5,498	4,452	4,679	5,463	4.86	16.76
North America	5,895	4,453	3,934	4,117	4,729	4.21	14.87
Canada	541	504	519	524	503	0.45	-4.01
Mexico	139	97	102	62	109	0.10	75.81
United States of America	5,215	3,852	3,313	3,531	4,117	3.66	16.60
South America	393	395	213	226	360	0.32	59.29
Brazil	393	395	213	226	360	0.32	59.29
Other Americas	602	650	305	336	374	0.33	11.31
Other countries of the Americas	602	650	305	336	374	0.33	11.31
EAST ASIA AND THE PACIFIC	4,838	4,396	3,155	3,682	3,837	3.41	4...
North-East Asia	2,899	2,491	1,575	1,829	2,161	1.92	18.15
China	1,004	780	383	593	864	0.77	45.70
Taiwan, Province of China	298	173	133	198	206	0.18	4.04
Hong Kong, China	66	176	54	58	96	0.09	65.52
Japan	1,152	1,071	836	719	764	0.68	6.26
Korea, Republic of	379	291	169	261	231	0.21	-11.49
Australasia	601	529	333	432	420	0.37	-2.78
Australia	601	529	333	432	420	0.37	-2.78
Other East Asia and the Pacific	1,338	1,376	1,247	1,421	1,256	1.12	-11.61
Other countries of Asia	1,338	1,376	1,247	1,421	1,256	1.12	-11.61
EUROPE	113,370	120,354	109,141	102,267	101,780	90.50	-0.48
Central/Eastern Europe	4,622	5,290	4,295	4,219	5,029	4.47	19.20
Bulgaria	252	302	194	174	151	0.13	-13.22
Czech Republic	689	807	801	757	940	0.84	24.17
Estonia	55	110	131	21	62	0.06	195.24
Hungary	1,054	1,094	877	970	851	0.76	-12.27
Latvia	54	59	112	284	49	0.04	-82.75
Lithuania	59	130	55	78	98	0.09	25.64
Poland	467	629	502	557	675	0.60	21.18
Romania	278	501	220	220	280	0.25	27.27
Russian Federation	1,545	1,366	1,025	846	1,587	1.41	87.59
Slovakia	169	292	378	312	336	0.30	7.69
Northern Europe	9,110	7,799	8,263	6,678	7,302	6.49	9.34
Denmark	945	880	822	856	967	0.86	12.97
Finland	281	477	493	294	395	0.35	34.35
Iceland	295	87	151	70	217	0.19	210.00
Ireland	423	475	243	342	280	0.25	-18.13
Norway	501	353	381	490	629	0.56	28.37
Sweden	1,271	672	1,046	673	771	0.69	14.56
United Kingdom	5,394	4,855	5,127	3,953	4,043	3.60	2.28
Southern Europe	6,272	6,657	5,076	6,147	5,439	4.84	-11.52
Croatia	211	250	129	135	100	0.09	-25.93
Greece	653	599	532	854	434	0.39	-49.18
Italy	3,628	3,825	3,146	3,216	3,644	3.24	13.31
Malta	40	24	29	46	124	0.11	169.57
Portugal	402	424	288	438	239	0.21	-45.43
Slovenia	326	216	149	139	141	0.13	1.44

LIECHTENSTEIN

5. Overnight stays of non-resident tourists in hotels and similar establishments, by country of residence

	2007	2008	2009	2010	2011	Market share 11	% Change 11-10
Spain	1,012	1,319	803	1,319	757	0.67	-42.61
Western Europe	**92,482**	**99,611**	**90,965**	**84,219**	**81,884**	**72.81**	**-2.77**
Austria	5,371	5,476	4,705	4,217	4,273	3.80	1.33
Belgium	3,190	4,474	4,174	3,176	3,890	3.46	22.48
France	2,430	2,444	2,002	2,119	2,238	1.99	5.62
Germany	42,491	45,786	39,996	37,337	32,454	28.86	-13.08
Luxembourg	2,423	2,727	2,591	2,833	2,178	1.94	-23.12
Netherlands	2,961	2,339	2,404	2,090	2,130	1.89	1.91
Switzerland	33,616	36,365	35,093	32,447	34,721	30.87	7.01
East Mediterranean Europe	**124**	**407**	**144**	**449**	**290**	**0.26**	**-35.41**
Cyprus	6	19	6	26	31	0.03	19.23
Turkey	118	388	138	423	259	0.23	-38.77
Other Europe	**760**	**590**	**398**	**555**	**1,836**	**1.63**	**230.81**
Other countries of Europe	760	590	398	555	1,836	1.63	230.81
SOUTH ASIA	**231**	**230**	**148**	**166**	**205**	**0.18**	**23.49**
India	231	230	148	166	205	0.18	23.49
NOT SPECIFIED	**96**	**25**	**354**	**338**	**817**	**0.73**	**141.72**
Other countries of the World	96	25	354	338	817	0.73	141.72

LITHUANIA

3. Arrivals of non-resident tourists in hotels and similar establishments, by country of residence

	2007	2008	2009	2010	2011	Market share 11	% Change 11-10
TOTAL	730,586	824,860	684,471	760,885	909,274	100.00	19.50
AFRICA	950	1,222	1,151	1,493	3,009	0.33	101.54
Other Africa	950	1,222	1,151	1,493	3,009	0.33	101.54
All countries of Africa	950	1,222	1,151	1,493	3,009	0.33	101.54
AMERICAS	24,638	23,968	18,760	24,209	30,879	3.40	27.55
North America	22,461	21,677	17,066	21,713	27,445	3.02	26.40
Canada	1,872	2,700	1,698	2,858	3,705	0.41	29.64
United States of America	20,589	18,977	15,368	18,855	23,740	2.61	25.91
Other Americas	2,177	2,291	1,694	2,496	3,434	0.38	37.58
Other countries of the Americas	2,177	2,291	1,694	2,496	3,434	0.38	37.58
EAST ASIA AND THE PACIFIC	15,250	18,534	17,873	20,555	29,574	3.25	43.88
North-East Asia	9,872	11,007	9,779	10,779	13,613	1.50	26.29
China	892	1,785	2,298	3,236	5,278	0.58	63.10
Japan	8,980	9,222	7,481	7,543	8,335	0.92	10.50
Other East Asia and the Pacific	5,378	7,527	8,094	9,776	15,961	1.76	63.27
Other countries of Asia	3,045	4,364	4,603	6,523	12,087	1.33	85.30
All countries of Oceania	2,333	3,163	3,491	3,253	3,874	0.43	19.09
EUROPE	689,748	781,136	646,687	714,628	845,812	93.02	18.36
Central/Eastern Europe	323,351	395,846	336,708	391,181	464,477	51.08	18.74
Bulgaria	1,275	1,386	1,409	1,131	1,694	0.19	49.78
Belarus	33,387	32,901	39,861	56,786	77,431	8.52	36.36
Czech Republic	8,429	8,624	9,270	6,564	6,779	0.75	3.28
Estonia	34,114	37,164	27,348	29,986	35,188	3.87	17.35
Hungary	2,686	2,648	2,073	2,941	3,462	0.38	17.72
Latvia	59,693	75,537	55,832	60,460	59,764	6.57	-1.15
Poland	112,152	139,471	115,661	125,988	130,426	14.34	3.52
Romania	1,821	2,102	2,377	2,074	3,892	0.43	87.66
Russian Federation	56,589	81,112	70,707	93,907	128,874	14.17	37.24
Slovakia	2,056	1,875	1,635	1,732	2,557	0.28	47.63
Ukraine	6,977	10,037	7,055	8,413	12,270	1.35	45.85
Other countries Central/East Europe	4,172	2,989	3,480	1,199	2,140	0.24	78.48
Northern Europe	138,253	147,383	105,808	122,044	131,045	14.41	7.38
Denmark	14,717	15,652	12,007	15,026	16,581	1.82	10.35
Finland	35,088	39,730	29,055	33,093	34,502	3.79	4.26
Iceland	1,922	1,707	1,718	823	907	0.10	10.21
Ireland	4,564	7,342	4,481	3,513	4,075	0.45	16.00
Norway	22,534	22,195	15,342	16,141	19,177	2.11	18.81
Sweden	22,515	21,719	18,463	19,265	24,472	2.69	27.03
United Kingdom	36,913	39,038	24,742	34,183	31,331	3.45	-8.34
Southern Europe	44,430	45,404	37,093	39,664	56,579	6.22	42.65
Greece	2,136	2,550	2,942	2,646	3,254	0.36	22.98
Italy	26,456	26,435	19,926	21,180	29,151	3.21	37.63
Portugal	2,524	2,445	2,065	2,030	2,660	0.29	31.03
Spain	13,314	13,974	12,160	13,808	21,514	2.37	55.81
Western Europe	160,164	168,728	144,525	137,348	163,603	17.99	19.12
Austria	6,449	7,795	6,478	5,902	6,484	0.71	9.86
Belgium	6,798	7,099	6,889	7,066	7,088	0.78	0.31
France	20,707	23,172	20,287	21,367	23,223	2.55	8.69
Germany	111,572	115,200	97,486	90,207	109,439	12.04	21.32
Luxembourg	758	785	816	523	694	0.08	32.70
Netherlands	9,190	10,357	8,255	8,573	11,773	1.29	37.33
Switzerland	4,690	4,320	4,314	3,710	4,902	0.54	32.13

LITHUANIA

3. Arrivals of non-resident tourists in hotels and similar establishments, by country of residence

	2007	2008	2009	2010	2011	Market share 11	% Change 11-10
East Mediterranean Europe	**7,849**	**7,849**	**7,346**	**8,028**	**12,140**	**1.34**	**51.22**
Israel	6,103	5,179	4,521	5,045	6,679	0.73	32.39
Turkey	1,746	2,670	2,825	2,983	5,461	0.60	83.07
Other Europe	**15,701**	**15,926**	**15,207**	**16,363**	**17,968**	**1.98**	**9.81**
Other countries of Europe	15,701	15,926	15,207	16,363	17,968	1.98	9.81

LITHUANIA

4. Arrivals of non-resident tourists in all types of accommodation establishments, by country of residence

	2007	2008	2009	2010	2011	Market share 11	% Change 11-10
TOTAL	849,006	909,983	752,389	840,368	1,003,843	100.00	19.45
AFRICA	961	1,253	1,177	1,523	3,034	0.30	99.21
Other Africa	961	1,253	1,177	1,523	3,034	0.30	99.21
All countries of Africa	961	1,253	1,177	1,523	3,034	0.30	99.21
AMERICAS	27,188	26,402	20,489	25,247	32,302	3.22	27.94
North America	24,617	23,565	18,756	22,665	28,727	2.86	26.75
Canada	2,019	2,890	1,795	2,999	3,877	0.39	29.28
United States of America	22,598	20,675	16,961	19,666	24,850	2.48	26.36
South America	832	1,150	1,020	1,282	1,543	0.15	20.36
Brazil	832	1,150	1,020	1,282	1,543	0.15	20.36
Other Americas	1,739	1,687	713	1,300	2,032	0.20	56.31
Other countries of the Americas	1,739	1,687	713	1,300	2,032	0.20	56.31
EAST ASIA AND THE PACIFIC	16,140	19,215	18,470	21,283	30,829	3.07	44.85
North-East Asia	10,400	11,884	11,015	12,283	16,547	1.65	34.71
China	955	1,898	2,515	3,309	5,522	0.55	66.88
Japan	9,105	9,349	7,599	7,654	8,528	0.85	11.42
Korea, Republic of	340	637	901	1,320	2,497	0.25	89.17
Australasia	2,749	3,501	3,686	3,702	4,130	0.41	11.56
Australia	2,749	3,501	3,686	3,702	4,130	0.41	11.56
Other East Asia and the Pacific	2,991	3,830	3,769	5,298	10,152	1.01	91.62
Other countries of Asia	2,991	3,830	3,769	5,298	10,152	1.01	91.62
EUROPE	804,717	863,113	712,253	792,315	937,678	93.41	18.35
Central/Eastern Europe	402,768	449,754	376,163	438,864	517,221	51.52	17.85
Bulgaria	1,386	1,452	1,522	1,189	1,764	0.18	48.36
Belarus	57,241	45,694	52,193	71,436	92,248	9.19	29.13
Czech Republic	10,245	9,348	10,066	8,618	7,852	0.78	-8.89
Estonia	39,946	41,058	30,340	32,527	37,409	3.73	15.01
Hungary	2,959	2,851	2,159	3,587	3,670	0.37	2.31
Latvia	69,965	84,722	62,815	66,519	66,145	6.59	-0.56
Poland	128,087	156,283	125,662	135,856	139,632	13.91	2.78
Romania	2,059	2,434	2,554	2,275	4,192	0.42	84.26
Russian Federation	78,586	91,992	78,690	105,869	148,267	14.77	40.05
Slovakia	2,457	1,987	1,753	1,888	2,768	0.28	46.61
Ukraine	9,837	11,933	8,409	9,100	13,274	1.32	45.87
Northern Europe	142,517	150,699	109,537	127,264	136,906	13.64	7.58
Denmark	15,137	16,042	12,338	15,416	16,925	1.69	9.79
Finland	36,613	40,639	30,211	35,137	36,483	3.63	3.83
Iceland	1,970	1,715	1,742	845	929	0.09	9.94
Ireland	4,729	7,701	4,577	3,875	4,317	0.43	11.41
Norway	22,950	22,569	15,657	16,846	20,092	2.00	19.27
Sweden	23,387	22,158	19,101	19,747	25,303	2.52	28.14
United Kingdom	37,731	39,875	25,911	35,398	32,857	3.27	-7.18
Southern Europe	48,190	48,192	39,869	43,487	63,057	6.28	45.00
Greece	2,167	2,620	2,964	2,680	3,326	0.33	24.10
Italy	27,772	27,081	20,689	22,547	31,490	3.14	39.66
Malta	141	323	205	217	293	0.03	35.02
Portugal	2,602	2,537	2,175	2,238	2,809	0.28	25.51
Slovenia	1,720	1,358	1,124	1,254	2,404	0.24	91.71
Spain	13,788	14,273	12,712	14,551	22,735	2.26	56.24

LITHUANIA

4. Arrivals of non-resident tourists in all types of accommodation establishments, by country of residence

	2007	2008	2009	2010	2011	Market share 11	% Change 11-10
Western Europe	**183,162**	**187,943**	**161,068**	**157,463**	**189,695**	**18.90**	**20.47**
Austria	6,882	8,086	6,833	6,249	6,948	0.69	11.19
Belgium	7,124	7,351	7,104	7,585	7,852	0.78	3.52
France	22,321	24,456	21,641	23,248	25,684	2.56	10.48
Germany	129,828	130,327	110,163	105,832	128,930	12.84	21.83
Luxembourg	769	803	816	544	724	0.07	33.09
Netherlands	11,327	12,437	9,876	9,997	14,137	1.41	41.41
Switzerland	4,911	4,483	4,635	4,008	5,420	0.54	35.23
East Mediterranean Europe	**9,426**	**9,118**	**8,142**	**9,015**	**13,180**	**1.31**	**46.20**
Cyprus	766	681	401	500	374	0.04	-25.20
Israel	6,769	5,655	4,830	5,413	7,151	0.71	32.11
Turkey	1,891	2,782	2,911	3,102	5,655	0.56	82.30
Other Europe	**18,654**	**17,407**	**17,474**	**16,222**	**17,619**	**1.76**	**8.61**
Other countries of Europe	18,654	17,407	17,474	16,222	17,619	1.76	8.61

LITHUANIA

5. Overnight stays of non-resident tourists in hotels and similar establishments, by country of residence

	2007	2008	2009	2010	2011	Market share 11	% Change 11-10
TOTAL	1,451,175	1,544,487	1,322,983	1,509,883	1,818,031	100.00	20.41
AFRICA	2,471	2,327	2,715	3,157	6,812	0.37	115.77
Other Africa	2,471	2,327	2,715	3,157	6,812	0.37	115.77
All countries of Africa	2,471	2,327	2,715	3,157	6,812	0.37	115.77
AMERICAS	52,722	58,037	40,088	59,025	61,071	3.36	3.47
North America	48,316	53,128	36,248	54,101	54,552	3.00	0.83
Canada	4,013	4,611	3,745	5,732	6,829	0.38	19.14
United States of America	44,303	48,517	32,503	48,369	47,723	2.62	-1.34
Other Americas	4,406	4,909	3,840	4,924	6,519	0.36	32.39
Other countries of the Americas	4,406	4,909	3,840	4,924	6,519	0.36	32.39
EAST ASIA AND THE PACIFIC	27,609	36,872	35,196	37,487	56,241	3.09	50.03
North-East Asia	16,879	20,394	16,887	17,161	20,261	1.11	18.06
China	2,511	4,835	4,418	5,238	8,497	0.47	62.22
Japan	14,368	15,559	12,469	11,923	11,764	0.65	-1.33
Other East Asia and the Pacific	10,730	16,478	18,309	20,326	35,980	1.98	77.01
Other countries of Asia	5,954	9,755	10,847	13,905	28,007	1.54	101.42
All countries of Oceania	4,776	6,723	7,462	6,421	7,973	0.44	24.17
EUROPE	1,368,373	1,447,251	1,244,984	1,410,214	1,693,907	93.17	20.12
Central/Eastern Europe	655,126	718,303	624,685	753,271	881,220	48.47	16.99
Bulgaria	3,088	2,835	2,854	2,420	3,528	0.19	45.79
Belarus	58,611	55,346	73,816	108,583	129,163	7.10	18.95
Czech Republic	14,144	13,663	24,506	11,032	13,326	0.73	20.79
Estonia	56,045	59,328	44,169	46,544	54,845	3.02	17.83
Hungary	5,082	5,652	5,159	6,435	7,348	0.40	14.19
Latvia	92,367	114,677	84,599	92,477	93,217	5.13	0.80
Poland	242,438	251,433	204,378	246,085	249,892	13.75	1.55
Romania	8,410	4,481	5,462	4,652	8,091	0.45	73.93
Russian Federation	137,927	170,122	146,956	203,133	285,646	15.71	40.62
Slovakia	7,295	3,478	3,085	3,451	5,063	0.28	46.71
Ukraine	18,051	31,074	21,360	16,152	25,799	1.42	59.73
Other countries Central/East Europe	11,668	6,214	8,341	12,307	5,302	0.29	-56.92
Northern Europe	262,147	281,598	207,753	231,042	263,691	14.50	14.13
Denmark	25,854	27,382	26,270	27,659	34,651	1.91	25.28
Finland	63,596	74,050	53,112	63,220	68,419	3.76	8.22
Iceland	4,572	4,028	2,801	1,662	1,945	0.11	17.03
Ireland	9,724	13,856	9,414	6,973	8,300	0.46	19.03
Norway	44,739	51,468	34,846	34,285	44,958	2.47	31.13
Sweden	39,719	39,076	32,824	33,684	44,739	2.46	32.82
United Kingdom	73,943	71,738	48,486	63,559	60,679	3.34	-4.53
Southern Europe	91,610	89,737	78,652	94,657	135,791	7.47	43.46
Greece	4,674	5,797	6,330	6,983	7,987	0.44	14.38
Italy	53,136	52,263	41,795	46,442	62,312	3.43	34.17
Portugal	8,253	5,038	5,670	6,366	8,207	0.45	28.92
Spain	25,547	26,639	24,857	34,866	57,285	3.15	64.30
Western Europe	310,995	310,217	282,261	283,045	339,932	18.70	20.10
Austria	13,176	13,670	12,625	10,587	12,548	0.69	18.52
Belgium	18,636	13,620	15,180	14,489	15,229	0.84	5.11
France	52,840	39,166	39,308	55,419	58,285	3.21	5.17
Germany	197,472	214,697	189,777	178,337	218,073	12.00	22.28
Luxembourg	1,343	1,282	1,355	914	1,171	0.06	28.12
Netherlands	18,374	20,101	15,792	16,313	25,667	1.41	57.34
Switzerland	9,154	7,681	8,224	6,986	8,959	0.49	28.24

LITHUANIA

5. Overnight stays of non-resident tourists in hotels and similar establishments, by country of residence

	2007	2008	2009	2010	2011	Market share 11	% Change 11-10
East Mediterranean Europe	**18,886**	**18,414**	**21,266**	**24,039**	**34,704**	**1.91**	**44.37**
Israel	15,136	12,773	12,060	14,643	19,530	1.07	33.37
Turkey	3,750	5,641	9,206	9,396	15,174	0.83	61.49
Other Europe	**29,609**	**28,982**	**30,367**	**24,160**	**38,569**	**2.12**	**59.64**
Other countries of Europe	29,609	28,982	30,367	24,160	38,569	2.12	59.64

LITHUANIA

6. Overnight stays of non-resident tourists in all types of accommodation establishments, by country of residence

	2007	2008	2009	2010	2011	Market share 11	% Change 11-10
TOTAL	**2,049,020**	**2,055,953**	**1,758,447**	**1,999,251**	**2,377,346**	**100.00**	**18.91**
AFRICA	**2,501**	**2,398**	**2,827**	**3,224**	**6,866**	**0.29**	**112.97**
Other Africa	**2,501**	**2,398**	**2,827**	**3,224**	**6,866**	**0.29**	**112.97**
All countries of Africa	2,501	2,398	2,827	3,224	6,866	0.29	112.97
AMERICAS	**57,682**	**63,488**	**46,043**	**61,964**	**65,530**	**2.76**	**5.75**
North America	**52,747**	**57,958**	**42,022**	**56,913**	**58,767**	**2.47**	**3.26**
Canada	4,443	5,030	4,103	6,027	7,507	0.32	24.56
United States of America	48,304	52,928	37,919	50,886	51,260	2.16	0.73
South America	**1,912**	**2,443**	**2,508**	**2,486**	**3,068**	**0.13**	**23.41**
Brazil	1,912	2,443	2,508	2,486	3,068	0.13	23.41
Other Americas	**3,023**	**3,087**	**1,513**	**2,565**	**3,695**	**0.16**	**44.05**
Other countries of the Americas	3,023	3,087	1,513	2,565	3,695	0.16	44.05
EAST ASIA AND THE PACIFIC	**30,144**	**39,213**	**41,574**	**39,360**	**59,084**	**2.49**	**50.11**
North-East Asia	**18,448**	**23,426**	**24,785**	**20,276**	**25,505**	**1.07**	**25.79**
China	3,034	6,028	9,896	5,350	8,920	0.38	66.73
Japan	14,623	15,790	12,686	12,140	12,101	0.51	-0.32
Korea, Republic of	791	1,608	2,203	2,786	4,484	0.19	60.95
Australasia	**5,590**	**7,391**	**7,837**	**7,416**	**8,507**	**0.36**	**14.71**
Australia	5,590	7,391	7,837	7,416	8,507	0.36	14.71
Other East Asia and the Pacific	**6,106**	**8,396**	**8,952**	**11,668**	**25,072**	**1.05**	**114.88**
Other countries of Asia	6,106	8,396	8,952	11,668	25,072	1.05	114.88
EUROPE	**1,958,693**	**1,950,854**	**1,668,003**	**1,894,703**	**2,245,866**	**94.47**	**18.53**
Central/Eastern Europe	**1,029,701**	**1,055,553**	**912,678**	**1,076,511**	**1,244,497**	**52.35**	**15.60**
Bulgaria	3,308	3,033	3,021	2,535	3,769	0.16	48.68
Belarus	239,991	229,790	250,314	293,417	312,565	13.15	6.53
Czech Republic	19,031	14,933	25,897	13,466	14,892	0.63	10.59
Estonia	66,104	67,566	49,918	51,342	60,523	2.55	17.88
Hungary	5,500	6,057	5,527	12,226	7,682	0.32	-37.17
Latvia	116,221	140,435	100,225	109,891	112,104	4.72	2.01
Poland	314,878	312,498	239,067	281,286	277,979	11.69	-1.18
Romania	11,953	10,259	7,995	5,119	8,885	0.37	73.57
Russian Federation	208,595	224,966	195,401	282,318	412,645	17.36	46.16
Slovakia	8,159	3,696	3,342	3,769	5,446	0.23	44.49
Ukraine	35,961	42,320	31,971	21,142	28,007	1.18	32.47
Northern Europe	**272,569**	**291,018**	**217,638**	**242,990**	**278,985**	**11.74**	**14.81**
Denmark	26,820	28,300	27,026	28,433	35,615	1.50	25.26
Finland	66,391	75,964	55,508	67,439	73,608	3.10	9.15
Iceland	4,650	4,037	2,878	1,699	1,980	0.08	16.54
Ireland	10,153	14,657	9,640	7,900	8,848	0.37	12.00
Norway	46,620	53,053	36,123	36,180	47,301	1.99	30.74
Sweden	41,697	40,488	34,507	34,916	46,967	1.98	34.51
United Kingdom	76,238	74,519	51,956	66,423	64,666	2.72	-2.65
Southern Europe	**100,006**	**95,432**	**84,565**	**102,852**	**151,723**	**6.38**	**47.52**
Greece	4,742	5,979	6,377	7,109	8,224	0.35	15.68
Italy	56,641	53,597	43,550	49,094	67,187	2.83	36.85
Malta	306	578	508	609	990	0.04	62.56
Portugal	8,537	5,360	6,002	6,780	8,544	0.36	26.02
Slovenia	2,701	2,501	2,129	2,541	5,802	0.24	128.34
Spain	27,079	27,417	25,999	36,719	60,976	2.56	66.06

LITHUANIA

6. Overnight stays of non-resident tourists in all types of accommodation establishments, by country of residence

	2007	2008	2009	2010	2011	Market share 11	% Change 11-10
Western Europe	**473,381**	**449,211**	**389,675**	**407,441**	**491,336**	**20.67**	**20.59**
Austria	13,924	14,233	13,225	11,104	13,435	0.57	20.99
Belgium	19,328	14,110	15,675	15,546	16,494	0.69	6.10
France	56,799	43,129	42,650	59,466	62,955	2.65	5.87
Germany	348,976	343,494	288,365	293,747	356,978	15.02	21.53
Luxembourg	1,354	1,304	1,355	958	1,224	0.05	27.77
Netherlands	23,437	24,973	19,214	19,133	30,454	1.28	59.17
Switzerland	9,563	7,968	9,191	7,487	9,796	0.41	30.84
East Mediterranean Europe	**30,645**	**25,462**	**26,648**	**30,720**	**41,852**	**1.76**	**36.24**
Cyprus	1,704	1,301	868	1,041	800	0.03	-23.15
Israel	23,813	17,687	16,133	19,988	25,394	1.07	27.05
Turkey	5,128	6,474	9,647	9,691	15,658	0.66	61.57
Other Europe	**52,391**	**34,178**	**36,799**	**34,189**	**37,473**	**1.58**	**9.61**
Other countries of Europe	52,391	34,178	36,799	34,189	37,473	1.58	9.61

LUXEMBOURG

3. Arrivals of non-resident tourists in hotels and similar establishments, by country of residence

		2007	2008	2009	2010	2011	Market share 11	% Change 11-10
TOTAL	(*)	**706,452**	**674,604**	**650,365**	**639,613**	**679,629**	**100.00**	**6.26**
AFRICA						**9,786**	**1.44**	
Southern Africa						**924**	**0.14**	
South Africa						924	0.14	
Other Africa						**8,862**	**1.30**	
Other countries of Africa						8,862	1.30	
AMERICAS		**29,883**	**29,198**	**25,783**	**27,134**	**34,868**	**5.13**	**28.50**
North America		**20,699**	**19,073**	**17,545**	**17,848**	**24,163**	**3.56**	**35.38**
Canada						3,265	0.48	
United States of America		20,699	19,073	17,545	17,848	20,898	3.07	17.09
South America						**2,254**	**0.33**	
Brazil						2,254	0.33	
Other Americas		**9,184**	**10,125**	**8,238**	**9,286**	**8,451**	**1.24**	**-8.99**
Other countries of the Americas		9,184	10,125	8,238	9,286	8,451	1.24	-8.99
EAST ASIA AND THE PACIFIC						**50,728**	**7.46**	
North-East Asia						**32,502**	**4.78**	
China						26,116	3.84	
Japan						5,219	0.77	
Korea, Republic of						1,167	0.17	
Australasia						**2,126**	**0.31**	
Australia						2,126	0.31	
Other East Asia and the Pacific						**16,100**	**2.37**	
Other countries of Asia						16,100	2.37	
EUROPE		**638,436**	**611,289**	**590,401**	**575,362**	**583,787**	**85.90**	**1.46**
Central/Eastern Europe		**14,712**	**15,039**	**13,852**	**15,349**	**24,334**	**3.58**	**58.54**
Bulgaria		1,253	1,300	1,204	978	1,175	0.17	20.14
Czech Republic		2,217	2,414	2,371	2,646	1,900	0.28	-28.19
Estonia		595	599	454	510	520	0.08	1.96
Hungary		1,687	1,746	1,719	1,553	1,636	0.24	5.34
Latvia		549	377	458	508	482	0.07	-5.12
Lithuania		891	1,114	787	661	718	0.11	8.62
Poland		4,045	4,502	3,973	5,090	4,921	0.72	-3.32
Romania		2,590	2,434	2,226	2,575	2,623	0.39	1.86
Russian Federation						8,902	1.31	
Slovakia		885	553	660	828	801	0.12	-3.26
Ukraine						656	0.10	
Northern Europe		**73,703**	**70,889**	**62,699**	**60,871**	**59,671**	**8.78**	**-1.97**
Denmark		7,547	9,212	7,554	6,613	3,977	0.59	-39.86
Finland		2,599	2,396	2,361	2,324	5,557	0.82	139.11
Iceland						760	0.11	
Ireland		2,968	2,973	2,410	2,436	2,361	0.35	-3.08
Norway						2,050	0.30	
Sweden		6,719	6,041	5,395	5,648	4,697	0.69	-16.84
United Kingdom		53,870	50,267	44,979	43,850	40,269	5.93	-8.17
Southern Europe		**45,955**	**47,259**	**42,436**	**42,045**	**40,982**	**6.03**	**-2.53**
Greece		2,193	2,803	2,204	2,233	1,906	0.28	-14.64
Italy		21,608	20,804	18,650	17,459	17,545	2.58	0.49
Malta		499	574	572	469	450	0.07	-4.05
Portugal		6,585	7,341	7,084	7,597	8,134	1.20	7.07
Slovenia		857	1,397	901	1,018	735	0.11	-27.80
Spain		14,213	14,340	13,025	13,269	12,212	1.80	-7.97
Western Europe		**478,964**	**452,493**	**450,967**	**436,139**	**446,114**	**65.64**	**2.29**
Austria		5,102	4,835	4,934	5,350	5,528	0.81	3.33

LUXEMBOURG

3. Arrivals of non-resident tourists in hotels and similar establishments, by country of residence

	2007	2008	2009	2010	2011	Market share 11	% Change 11-10
Belgium	160,799	149,481	146,932	145,823	150,393	22.13	3.13
France	98,062	99,980	104,600	108,609	115,802	17.04	6.62
Germany	108,700	99,568	95,339	89,834	96,463	14.19	7.38
Netherlands	89,432	81,334	80,221	69,600	61,535	9.05	-11.59
Switzerland	16,869	17,295	18,941	16,923	16,393	2.41	-3.13
East Mediterranean Europe	**416**	**372**	**421**	**405**	**3,894**	**0.57**	**861.48**
Cyprus	416	372	421	405	336	0.05	-17.04
Turkey					3,558	0.52	
Other Europe	**24,686**	**25,237**	**20,026**	**20,553**	**8,792**	**1.29**	**-57.22**
Other countries of Europe	24,686	25,237	20,026	20,553	8,792	1.29	-57.22
NOT SPECIFIED	**38,133**	**34,117**	**34,181**	**37,117**	**460**	**0.07**	**-98.76**
Other countries of the World	38,133	34,117	34,181	37,117	460	0.07	-98.76

LUXEMBOURG

4. Arrivals of non-resident tourists in all types of accommodation establishments, by country of residence

		2007	2008	2009	2010	2011	Market share 11	% Change 11-10
TOTAL	(*)	917,334	878,900	848,528	793,410	871,348	100.00	9.82
AFRICA						10,109	1.16	
Southern Africa						1,005	0.12	
South Africa						1,005	0.12	
Other Africa						9,104	1.04	
Other countries of Africa						9,104	1.04	
AMERICAS		33,255	32,482	28,762	25,073	37,441	4.30	49.33
North America		22,522	20,715	19,103	17,676	25,835	2.96	46.16
Canada						3,756	0.43	
United States of America		22,522	20,715	19,103	17,676	22,079	2.53	24.91
South America						2,536	0.29	
Brazil						2,536	0.29	
Other Americas		10,733	11,767	9,659	7,397	9,070	1.04	22.62
Other countries of the Americas		10,733	11,767	9,659	7,397	9,070	1.04	22.62
EAST ASIA AND THE PACIFIC						53,983	6.20	
North-East Asia						34,546	3.96	
China						27,009	3.10	
Japan						5,572	0.64	
Korea, Republic of						1,965	0.23	
Australasia						2,764	0.32	
Australia						2,764	0.32	
Other East Asia and the Pacific						16,673	1.91	
Other countries of Asia						16,673	1.91	
EUROPE		841,388	807,742	780,885	726,902	769,202	88.28	5.82
Central/Eastern Europe		17,820	18,396	16,438	16,795	27,581	3.17	64.22
Bulgaria		1,336	1,394	1,370	1,050	1,304	0.15	24.19
Czech Republic		2,667	2,903	2,989	3,017	2,416	0.28	-19.92
Estonia		675	620	507	523	597	0.07	14.15
Hungary		1,984	2,131	2,100	1,760	1,866	0.21	6.02
Latvia		562	392	473	547	999	0.11	82.63
Lithuania		977	1,164	828	713	765	0.09	7.29
Poland		5,710	6,298	5,037	5,633	5,927	0.68	5.22
Romania		2,900	2,842	2,352	2,688	2,831	0.32	5.32
Russian Federation						9,266	1.06	
Slovakia		1,009	652	782	864	932	0.11	7.87
Ukraine						678	0.08	
Northern Europe		86,194	84,462	74,086	70,942	70,797	8.12	-0.20
Denmark		9,797	11,386	9,455	7,798	5,563	0.64	-28.66
Finland		3,486	3,210	3,132	2,699	6,180	0.71	128.97
Iceland						824	0.09	
Ireland		3,474	3,406	2,862	2,924	2,780	0.32	-4.92
Norway						2,321	0.27	
Sweden		7,543	6,845	6,095	6,092	5,338	0.61	-12.38
United Kingdom		61,894	59,615	52,542	51,429	47,791	5.48	-7.07
Southern Europe		51,019	51,973	47,089	44,673	44,979	5.16	0.68
Greece		2,438	2,905	2,314	2,339	1,991	0.23	-14.88
Italy		23,490	22,563	20,381	18,412	18,984	2.18	3.11
Malta		510	579	576	471	454	0.05	-3.61
Portugal		7,243	7,900	7,682	7,918	8,765	1.01	10.70
Slovenia		1,093	1,625	1,217	1,280	959	0.11	-25.08
Spain		16,245	16,401	14,919	14,253	13,826	1.59	-3.00
Western Europe		659,386	625,832	621,390	571,275	610,770	70.09	6.91
Austria		5,688	5,458	5,570	5,833	6,072	0.70	4.10

LUXEMBOURG

4. Arrivals of non-resident tourists in all types of accommodation establishments, by country of residence

	2007	2008	2009	2010	2011	Market share 11	% Change 11-10
Belgium	190,819	177,313	172,829	165,333	175,805	20.18	6.33
France	107,157	110,003	114,271	114,710	124,687	14.31	8.70
Germany	134,655	124,256	118,559	106,524	118,933	13.65	11.65
Netherlands	202,639	189,998	189,497	160,659	167,011	19.17	3.95
Switzerland	18,428	18,804	20,664	18,216	18,262	2.10	0.25
East Mediterranean Europe	**440**	**384**	**450**	**407**	**3,969**	**0.46**	**875.18**
Cyprus	440	384	450	407	339	0.04	-16.71
Turkey					3,630	0.42	
Other Europe	**26,529**	**26,695**	**21,432**	**22,810**	**11,106**	**1.27**	**-51.31**
Other countries of Europe	26,529	26,695	21,432	22,810	11,106	1.27	-51.31
NOT SPECIFIED	**42,691**	**38,676**	**38,881**	**41,435**	**613**	**0.07**	**-98.52**
Other countries of the World	42,691	38,676	38,881	41,435	613	0.07	-98.52

LUXEMBOURG

5. Overnight stays of non-resident tourists in hotels and similar establishments, by country of residence

		2007	2008	2009	2010	2011	Market share 11	% Change 11-10
TOTAL	(*)	1,359,505	1,296,575	1,184,612	1,141,047	1,279,061	100.00	12.10
AFRICA						22,211	1.74	
Southern Africa						3,112	0.24	
South Africa						3,112	0.24	
Other Africa						19,099	1.49	
Other countries of Africa						19,099	1.49	
AMERICAS		70,266	73,022	57,489	63,103	74,515	5.83	18.08
North America		46,694	45,949	38,818	42,137	55,008	4.30	30.55
Canada						8,057	0.63	
United States of America		46,694	45,949	38,818	42,137	46,951	3.67	11.42
South America						5,079	0.40	
Brazil						5,079	0.40	
Other Americas		23,572	27,073	18,671	20,966	14,428	1.13	-31.18
Other countries of the Americas		23,572	27,073	18,671	20,966	14,428	1.13	-31.18
EAST ASIA AND THE PACIFIC						90,060	7.04	
North-East Asia						44,820	3.50	
China						35,111	2.75	
Japan						7,796	0.61	
Korea, Republic of						1,913	0.15	
Australasia						4,200	0.33	
Australia						4,200	0.33	
Other East Asia and the Pacific						41,040	3.21	
Other countries of Asia						41,040	3.21	
EUROPE		1,213,389	1,150,884	1,059,374	1,005,288	1,090,750	85.28	8.50
Central/Eastern Europe		45,212	45,585	36,856	39,093	52,972	4.14	35.50
Bulgaria		4,917	4,072	3,133	2,897	2,752	0.22	-5.01
Czech Republic		6,533	7,203	7,434	6,432	4,580	0.36	-28.79
Estonia		1,651	1,708	1,040	1,075	1,162	0.09	8.09
Hungary		4,589	4,580	5,115	4,732	4,341	0.34	-8.26
Latvia		1,670	1,008	1,166	1,093	962	0.08	-11.99
Lithuania		2,226	2,550	1,438	1,488	1,449	0.11	-2.62
Poland		13,456	16,564	10,139	11,933	13,069	1.02	9.52
Romania		7,379	6,428	5,661	6,670	7,068	0.55	5.97
Russian Federation						14,408	1.13	
Slovakia		2,791	1,472	1,730	2,773	1,878	0.15	-32.28
Ukraine						1,303	0.10	
Northern Europe		140,936	134,902	120,078	112,057	122,131	9.55	8.99
Denmark		13,167	15,935	13,253	11,521	7,240	0.57	-37.16
Finland		5,220	4,799	4,844	4,303	11,144	0.87	158.98
Iceland						2,131	0.17	
Ireland		8,036	7,822	5,826	6,310	7,139	0.56	13.14
Norway						4,495	0.35	
Sweden		12,897	11,708	9,646	10,225	8,598	0.67	-15.91
United Kingdom		101,616	94,638	86,509	79,698	81,384	6.36	2.12
Southern Europe		97,086	97,956	83,345	80,954	86,862	6.79	7.30
Greece		5,617	6,957	5,639	4,849	4,746	0.37	-2.12
Italy		45,917	44,971	36,097	34,292	36,740	2.87	7.14
Malta		2,598	2,637	2,072	1,905	1,941	0.15	1.89
Portugal		14,774	14,435	13,934	14,165	16,798	1.31	18.59
Slovenia		2,112	2,886	2,520	2,626	1,750	0.14	-33.36
Spain		26,068	26,070	23,083	23,117	24,887	1.95	7.66
Western Europe		877,585	819,824	777,148	731,644	802,778	62.76	9.72
Austria		10,936	10,483	11,472	11,364	12,038	0.94	5.93

LUXEMBOURG

5. Overnight stays of non-resident tourists in hotels and similar establishments, by country of residence

	2007	2008	2009	2010	2011	Market share 11	% Change 11-10
Belgium	292,561	268,416	248,321	238,745	273,963	21.42	14.75
France	165,968	168,627	168,284	174,419	196,435	15.36	12.62
Germany	197,564	182,714	170,455	157,734	177,354	13.87	12.44
Netherlands	177,149	156,215	145,158	119,511	112,232	8.77	-6.09
Switzerland	33,407	33,369	33,458	29,871	30,756	2.40	2.96
East Mediterranean Europe	**1,173**	**974**	**1,146**	**975**	**7,712**	**0.60**	**690.97**
Cyprus	1,173	974	1,146	975	1,375	0.11	41.03
Turkey					6,337	0.50	
Other Europe	**51,397**	**51,643**	**40,801**	**40,565**	**18,295**	**1.43**	**-54.90**
Other countries of Europe	51,397	51,643	40,801	40,565	18,295	1.43	-54.90
NOT SPECIFIED	**75,850**	**72,669**	**67,749**	**72,656**	**1,525**	**0.12**	**-97.90**
Other countries of the World	75,850	72,669	67,749	72,656	1,525	0.12	-97.90

LUXEMBOURG

6. Overnight stays of non-resident tourists in all types of accommodation establishments, by country of residence

	2007	2008	2009	2010	2011	Market share 11	% Change 11-10
TOTAL	2,341,318	2,259,116	2,075,831	1,694,085	2,054,467	100.00	21.27
AFRICA					23,010	1.12	
Southern Africa					3,367	0.16	
South Africa					3,367	0.16	
Other Africa					19,643	0.96	
Other countries of Africa					19,643	0.96	
AMERICAS	76,773	79,588	64,021	60,496	78,883	3.84	30.39
North America	50,779	49,892	42,766	44,147	57,962	2.82	31.29
Canada					8,857	0.43	
United States of America	50,779	49,892	42,766	44,147	49,105	2.39	11.23
South America					5,488	0.27	
Brazil					5,488	0.27	
Other Americas	25,994	29,696	21,255	16,349	15,433	0.75	-5.60
Other countries of the Americas	25,994	29,696	21,255	16,349	15,433	0.75	-5.60
EAST ASIA AND THE PACIFIC					95,116	4.63	
North-East Asia					47,599	2.32	
China					36,311	1.77	
Japan					8,349	0.41	
Korea, Republic of					2,939	0.14	
Australasia					5,382	0.26	
Australia					5,382	0.26	
Other East Asia and the Pacific					42,135	2.05	
Other countries of Asia					42,135	2.05	
EUROPE	2,179,422	2,098,668	1,935,468	1,553,958	1,855,614	90.32	19.41
Central/Eastern Europe	53,788	55,009	44,861	42,662	61,160	2.98	43.36
Bulgaria	5,182	4,372	3,671	3,001	3,017	0.15	0.53
Czech Republic	7,488	8,228	8,569	7,146	5,631	0.27	-21.20
Estonia	1,811	1,843	1,140	1,086	1,307	0.06	20.35
Hungary	5,154	5,355	5,962	5,210	5,210	0.25	
Latvia	1,751	1,037	1,215	1,271	1,760	0.09	38.47
Lithuania	2,424	2,683	1,590	1,682	1,771	0.09	5.29
Poland	18,323	22,257	13,426	13,236	16,217	0.79	22.52
Romania	8,453	7,537	6,928	7,089	7,621	0.37	7.50
Russian Federation					14,943	0.73	
Slovakia	3,202	1,697	2,360	2,941	2,315	0.11	-21.29
Ukraine					1,368	0.07	
Northern Europe	175,479	172,628	150,937	134,978	150,890	7.34	11.79
Denmark	20,202	23,124	18,834	14,241	11,679	0.57	-17.99
Finland	7,270	6,736	6,135	4,852	12,275	0.60	152.99
Iceland					2,314	0.11	
Ireland	9,715	9,168	7,196	7,587	8,169	0.40	7.67
Norway					4,992	0.24	
Sweden	14,859	13,545	11,174	10,893	9,938	0.48	-8.77
United Kingdom	123,433	120,055	107,598	97,405	101,523	4.94	4.23
Southern Europe	107,696	108,480	93,780	86,335	96,400	4.69	11.66
Greece	6,055	7,246	5,856	5,058	4,969	0.24	-1.76
Italy	49,778	49,092	39,779	36,249	40,375	1.97	11.38
Malta	2,647	2,650	2,081	1,912	1,947	0.09	1.83
Portugal	16,662	16,462	16,602	15,313	19,121	0.93	24.87
Slovenia	2,574	3,380	3,138	3,129	2,091	0.10	-33.17
Spain	29,980	29,650	26,324	24,674	27,897	1.36	13.06
Western Europe	1,784,999	1,706,489	1,600,591	1,245,091	1,515,492	73.77	21.72
Austria	12,456	12,089	12,824	12,430	13,028	0.63	4.81

LUXEMBOURG

6. Overnight stays of non-resident tourists in all types of accommodation establishments, by country of residence

	2007	2008	2009	2010	2011	Market share 11	% Change 11-10
Belgium	448,182	432,700	378,054	327,845	391,251	19.04	19.34
France	198,919	203,170	197,683	195,994	221,542	10.78	13.04
Germany	275,936	256,004	238,972	203,969	239,673	11.67	17.50
Netherlands	812,495	766,206	736,471	472,864	615,762	29.97	30.22
Switzerland	37,011	36,320	36,587	31,989	34,236	1.67	7.02
East Mediterranean Europe	**1,280**	**1,002**	**1,284**	**981**	**7,841**	**0.38**	**699.29**
Cyprus	1,280	1,002	1,284	981	1,380	0.07	40.67
Turkey					6,461	0.31	
Other Europe	**56,180**	**55,060**	**44,015**	**43,911**	**23,831**	**1.16**	**-45.73**
Other countries of Europe	56,180	55,060	44,015	43,911	23,831	1.16	-45.73
NOT SPECIFIED	**85,123**	**80,860**	**76,342**	**79,631**	**1,844**	**0.09**	**-97.68**
Other countries of the World	85,123	80,860	76,342	79,631	1,844	0.09	-97.68

MACAO, CHINA

2. Arrivals of non-resident visitors at national borders, by nationality

		2007	2008	2009	2010	2011	Market share 11	% Change 11-10
TOTAL	(*)	27,003,370	22,933,185	21,752,751	24,965,411	28,002,279	100.00	12.16
AFRICA		30,407	22,095	16,702	21,736	25,161	0.09	15.76
East Africa		2,542	2,753	2,015	2,932	3,950	0.01	34.72
Burundi		55	53	33	31	39	0.00	25.81
Ethiopia		61	81	61	99	101	0.00	2.02
Kenya		221	232	181	263	423	0.00	60.84
Madagascar		204	240	219	339	342	0.00	0.88
Malawi		18	9	4	12	32	0.00	166.67
Mauritius		490	751	549	705	672	0.00	-4.68
Mozambique		424	254	364	435	321	0.00	-26.21
Rwanda		18	18	31	36	97	0.00	169.44
Seychelles		237	206	126	163	164	0.00	0.61
Somalia		29	38	19	17	31	0.00	82.35
Zimbabwe		103	78	61	90	79	0.00	-12.22
Uganda		90	125	84	369	1,156	0.00	213.28
United Republic of Tanzania		540	630	247	320	439	0.00	37.19
Zambia		52	38	36	53	54	0.00	1.89
Central Africa		4,536	3,303	2,517	3,138	4,236	0.02	34.99
Angola		1,126	854	1,029	1,329	1,673	0.01	25.88
Cameroon		921	672	611	411	330	0.00	-19.71
Congo		694	398	189	223	355	0.00	59.19
Democratic Republic of the Congo		1,730	1,315	636	1,099	1,808	0.01	64.51
Equatorial Guinea		22	12	6	11	22	0.00	100.00
Gabon		16	28	30	35	19	0.00	-45.71
Sao Tome and Principe		27	24	16	30	29	0.00	-3.33
North Africa		1,343	1,135	1,177	1,300	1,310	0.00	0.77
Algeria		165	180	235	235	203	0.00	-13.62
Morocco		366	410	421	482	527	0.00	9.34
Sudan		602	299	136	151	281	0.00	86.09
Tunisia		210	246	385	432	299	0.00	-30.79
Southern Africa		4,565	4,629	4,287	4,675	5,301	0.02	13.39
Botswana		47	32	17	12	39	0.00	225.00
Lesotho		16	3	7	3	5	0.00	66.67
Namibia		48	34	28	32	60	0.00	87.50
South Africa		4,454	4,551	4,231	4,624	5,186	0.02	12.15
Swaziland			9	4	4	11	0.00	175.00
West Africa		17,049	9,998	6,366	7,544	7,891	0.03	4.60
Cape Verde		222	177	167	221	198	0.00	-10.41
Benin		43	45	47	92	183	0.00	98.91
Gambia		160	188	136	125	159	0.00	27.20
Ghana		962	674	309	453	396	0.00	-12.58
Guinea		1,405	594	385	607	915	0.00	50.74
Côte d'Ivoire		826	458	159	156	146	0.00	-6.41
Liberia		338	139	58	64	205	0.00	220.31
Mali		9,204	4,678	1,969	3,310	3,969	0.01	19.91
Mauritania		58	45	40	38	68	0.00	78.95
Niger		511	230	212	226	392	0.00	73.45
Nigeria		1,562	1,514	2,061	1,371	201	0.00	-85.34
Guinea-Bissau		208	316	265	170	191	0.00	12.35
Senegal		805	467	200	276	374	0.00	35.51
Sierra Leone		92	101	72	49	91	0.00	85.71
Togo		596	250	238	314	323	0.00	2.87
Burkina Faso		57	122	48	72	80	0.00	11.11
Other Africa		372	277	340	2,147	2,473	0.01	15.18
Other countries of Africa		372	277	340	2,147	2,473	0.01	15.18

MACAO, CHINA

2. Arrivals of non-resident visitors at national borders, by nationality

	2007	2008	2009	2010	2011	Market share 11	% Change 11-10
AMERICAS	306,802	312,920	278,788	297,154	310,564	1.11	4.51
Caribbean	857	872	658	855	844	0.00	-1.29
Antigua and Barbuda	4	3	6	17	8	0.00	-52.94
Bahamas	46	71	24	15	34	0.00	126.67
Barbados	26	20	20	20	11	0.00	-45.00
Cuba	127	89	58	80	51	0.00	-36.25
Dominican Republic	292	344	249	321	349	0.00	8.72
Haiti	7	14	12	15	16	0.00	6.67
Jamaica	161	165	165	189	209	0.00	10.58
Saint Lucia	2		3	5	9	0.00	80.00
Saint Vincent and the Grenadines	2	7	7	9	1	0.00	-88.89
Trinidad and Tobago	190	159	114	184	156	0.00	-15.22
Central America	2,315	2,585	2,409	2,676	2,755	0.01	2.95
Belize	506	468	427	497	543	0.00	9.26
Costa Rica	743	963	786	842	869	0.00	3.21
El Salvador	33	61	56	64	82	0.00	28.13
Guatemala	200	175	218	197	181	0.00	-8.12
Honduras	170	186	150	150	174	0.00	16.00
Nicaragua	31	14	15	28	22	0.00	-21.43
Panama	632	718	757	898	884	0.00	-1.56
North America	286,612	291,350	258,064	272,567	281,199	1.00	3.17
Canada	79,006	82,261	74,791	79,152	79,816	0.29	0.84
Mexico	5,120	5,649	3,679	5,145	5,368	0.02	4.33
United States of America	202,486	203,440	179,594	188,270	196,015	0.70	4.11
South America	16,947	18,088	17,562	20,908	25,594	0.09	22.41
Argentina	1,104	1,292	1,335	1,675	1,544	0.01	-7.82
Bolivia	225	236	205	186	204	0.00	9.68
Brazil	9,298	8,976	7,525	8,347	10,501	0.04	25.81
Chile	1,010	1,065	939	1,142	1,329	0.00	16.37
Colombia	1,367	1,742	1,939	2,309	3,567	0.01	54.48
Ecuador	458	479	445	605	682	0.00	12.73
Guyana	82	68	103	95	98	0.00	3.16
Paraguay	51	65	65	81	86	0.00	6.17
Peru	1,103	1,201	1,383	1,340	1,379	0.00	2.91
Suriname	141	185	152	177	199	0.00	12.43
Uruguay	124	171	153	217	167	0.00	-23.04
Venezuela	1,984	2,608	3,318	4,734	5,838	0.02	23.32
Other Americas	71	25	95	148	172	0.00	16.22
Other countries of the Americas	71	25	95	148	172	0.00	16.22
EAST ASIA AND THE PACIFIC	26,335,797	22,223,240	21,077,816	24,223,099	27,237,661	97.27	12.44
North-East Asia	25,020,641	20,594,852	19,598,355	22,740,428	25,762,927	92.00	13.29
China	14,873,576	11,613,064	10,988,796	13,228,418	16,161,927	57.72	22.18
Taiwan, Province of China	1,444,501	1,316,046	1,293,068	1,294,390	1,215,503	4.34	-6.09
Hong Kong, China	8,172,364	7,013,797	6,727,020	7,465,961	7,582,998	27.08	1.57
Japan	299,811	367,146	379,346	413,529	396,050	1.41	-4.23
Korea, Dem. People's Republic of	1,452	1,161	1,038	1,161	1,167	0.00	0.52
Korea, Republic of	225,589	279,883	204,832	331,786	398,832	1.42	20.21
Mongolia	3,348	3,755	4,255	5,183	6,450	0.02	24.45
South-East Asia	1,180,701	1,471,002	1,344,190	1,324,534	1,314,196	4.69	-0.78
Brunei Darussalam	1,322	1,711	1,940	1,829	1,816	0.01	-0.71
Myanmar	4,595	3,475	4,081	4,920	4,500	0.02	-8.54
Cambodia	3,924	4,574	3,854	4,359	4,467	0.02	2.48
Indonesia	133,662	180,510	191,494	208,468	220,454	0.79	5.75
Lao People's Democratic Republic	727	685	977	843	1,196	0.00	41.87
Malaysia	402,286	428,680	332,551	338,042	324,503	1.16	-4.01
Philippines	256,689	283,259	247,573	247,803	268,713	0.96	8.44

MACAO, CHINA

2. Arrivals of non-resident visitors at national borders, by nationality

	2007	2008	2009	2010	2011	Market share 11	% Change 11-10
Timor-Leste	134	136	144	151	174	0.00	15.23
Singapore	189,772	263,717	256,556	257,213	280,588	1.00	9.09
Viet Nam	46,655	52,029	62,428	48,465	11,423	0.04	-76.43
Thailand	140,935	252,226	242,592	212,441	196,362	0.70	-7.57
Australasia	**133,655**	**156,576**	**134,337**	**126,360**	**126,717**	**0.45**	**0.28**
Australia	118,256	139,806	120,449	111,777	111,823	0.40	0.04
New Zealand	15,399	16,770	13,888	14,583	14,894	0.05	2.13
Melanesia	**403**	**413**	**576**	**839**	**809**	**0.00**	**-3.58**
Solomon Islands	80	85	126	186	251	0.00	34.95
Fiji	238	203	306	465	366	0.00	-21.29
Vanuatu	38	45	53	108	91	0.00	-15.74
Papua New Guinea	47	80	91	80	101	0.00	26.25
Micronesia	**235**	**226**	**199**	**149**	**201**	**0.00**	**34.90**
Nauru	172	164	152	75	74	0.00	-1.33
Micronesia, Federated States of	2	13	1	28	7	0.00	-75.00
Marshall Islands	61	49	46	46	112	0.00	143.48
Palau					8	0.00	
Polynesia	**139**	**157**	**146**	**182**	**228**	**0.00**	**25.27**
Tonga	133	146	137	163	219	0.00	34.36
Samoa	6	11	9	19	9	0.00	-52.63
Other East Asia and the Pacific	**23**	**14**	**13**	**30,607**	**32,583**	**0.12**	**6.46**
Other countries of Asia	23	14	13	30,607	32,583	0.12	6.46
EUROPE	**258,245**	**272,613**	**254,112**	**244,445**	**251,672**	**0.90**	**2.96**
Central/Eastern Europe	**16,957**	**17,792**	**17,877**	**23,171**	**28,045**	**0.10**	**21.03**
Bulgaria	719	841	779	800	888	0.00	11.00
Czech Republic/Slovakia	1,614	1,625	1,895	1,552	1,946	0.01	25.39
Hungary	1,525	1,594	1,544	2,141	1,686	0.01	-21.25
Poland	4,450	4,570	3,872	4,515	4,847	0.02	7.35
Romania	2,550	2,028	1,978	2,465	2,167	0.01	-12.09
USSR (former)	6,099	7,134	7,809	11,698	16,511	0.06	41.14
Northern Europe	**99,239**	**100,028**	**84,226**	**80,142**	**81,305**	**0.29**	**1.45**
Denmark	3,751	4,248	3,556	3,434	3,599	0.01	4.80
Finland	3,824	4,256	4,474	3,807	3,316	0.01	-12.90
Iceland	250	159	166	167	109	0.00	-34.73
Ireland	4,130	4,407	3,550	3,257	3,359	0.01	3.13
Norway	2,035	2,613	2,285	2,449	2,442	0.01	-0.29
Sweden	6,719	7,168	6,698	6,569	6,825	0.02	3.90
United Kingdom	78,530	77,177	63,497	60,459	61,655	0.22	1.98
Southern Europe	**35,377**	**35,457**	**33,837**	**36,756**	**36,286**	**0.13**	**-1.28**
Albania	66	111	87	122	90	0.00	-26.23
Andorra	16	17	19	37	34	0.00	-8.11
Greece	1,090	1,727	1,048	1,028	908	0.00	-11.67
Holy See	11		9	4	1	0.00	-75.00
Italy	11,798	12,535	12,223	13,459	13,119	0.05	-2.53
Malta	97	99	78	64	98	0.00	53.13
Portugal	14,715	13,100	12,437	13,577	13,339	0.05	-1.75
San Marino	22	12	10	16	7	0.00	-56.25
Spain	7,139	7,510	7,919	8,449	8,690	0.03	2.85
Yugoslavia, SFR (former)	423	346	7				
Western Europe	**89,873**	**99,319**	**95,369**	**99,079**	**100,433**	**0.36**	**1.37**
Austria	3,991	4,310	4,233	4,482	4,095	0.01	-8.63
Belgium	4,344	4,620	4,497	4,793	4,681	0.02	-2.34
France	36,408	40,502	39,158	41,420	42,662	0.15	3.00
Germany	26,338	29,088	28,176	28,820	28,800	0.10	-0.07
Liechtenstein	32	38	40	41	57	0.00	39.02
Luxembourg	192	210	203	277	254	0.00	-8.30

MACAO, CHINA

2. Arrivals of non-resident visitors at national borders, by nationality

	2007	2008	2009	2010	2011	Market share 11	% Change 11-10
Monaco	23	17	19	24	17	0.00	-29.17
Netherlands	12,822	14,246	12,897	12,667	12,776	0.05	0.86
Switzerland	5,723	6,288	6,146	6,555	7,091	0.03	8.18
East Mediterranean Europe	**10,924**	**13,359**	**16,638**				
Cyprus	129	258	219				
Israel	8,173	10,102	14,021				
Turkey	2,622	2,999	2,398				
Other Europe	**5,875**	**6,658**	**6,165**	**5,297**	**5,603**	**0.02**	**5.78**
Other countries of Europe	5,875	6,658	6,165	5,297	5,603	0.02	5.78
MIDDLE EAST	**7,514**	**7,537**	**7,364**				
Bahrain	138	147	123				
Iraq	201	238	136				
Jordan	496	372	453				
Kuwait	486	660	654				
Lebanon	1,888	1,517	1,501				
Libya	445	517	410				
Oman	91	89	104				
Qatar	211	138	149				
Saudi Arabia	1,041	1,418	1,405				
Syrian Arab Republic	985	743	699				
Egypt	1,008	913	927				
Yemen	286	257	243				
Other countries of Middle East	238	528	560				
SOUTH ASIA	**64,532**	**94,723**	**117,933**	**178,977**	**177,221**	**0.63**	**-0.98**
Afghanistan	82	121	277	162	157	0.00	-3.09
Bangladesh	3,383	2,652	1,673	1,023	272	0.00	-73.41
Bhutan	79	113	126	116	205	0.00	76.72
Sri Lanka	913	985	805	579	568	0.00	-1.90
India	45,661	82,492	107,575	169,116	169,682	0.61	0.33
Iran, Islamic Republic of	1,106	925	1,333	3,673	3,208	0.01	-12.66
Maldives	225	133	130	157	135	0.00	-14.01
Nepal	9,933	3,979	2,885	2,109	2,019	0.01	-4.27
Pakistan	3,150	3,323	3,129	2,042	975	0.00	-52.25
NOT SPECIFIED	**73**	**57**	**36**				
Other countries of the World	73	57	36				

MACAO, CHINA

2. Arrivals of non-resident visitors at national borders, by country of residence

		2007	2008	2009	2010	2011	Market share 11	% Change 11-10
TOTAL	(*)	27,003,370	22,933,185	21,752,751	24,965,411	28,002,279	100.00	12.16
AFRICA		30,129	21,894	16,803	22,845	24,864	0.09	8.84
Southern Africa		4,446	4,543	4,228	4,624	5,185	0.02	12.13
South Africa		4,446	4,543	4,228	4,624	5,185	0.02	12.13
Other Africa		25,683	17,351	12,575	18,221	19,679	0.07	8.00
Other countries of Africa		25,683	17,351	12,575	18,221	19,679	0.07	8.00
AMERICAS		306,324	312,611	278,661	297,137	310,608	1.11	4.53
North America		286,073	290,985	257,920	272,547	281,247	1.00	3.19
Canada		78,797	82,136	74,744	79,148	79,818	0.29	0.85
Mexico		5,111	5,651	3,676	5,145	5,364	0.02	4.26
United States of America		202,165	203,198	179,500	188,254	196,065	0.70	4.15
South America		9,290	8,967	7,521	8,346	10,505	0.04	25.87
Brazil		9,290	8,967	7,521	8,346	10,505	0.04	25.87
Other Americas		10,961	12,659	13,220	16,244	18,856	0.07	16.08
Other countries of the Americas		10,961	12,659	13,220	16,244	18,856	0.07	16.08
EAST ASIA AND THE PACIFIC		26,337,971	22,224,494	21,078,253	24,226,821	27,242,195	97.29	12.45
North-East Asia		25,024,422	20,597,144	19,599,207	22,734,366	25,756,829	91.98	13.29
China		14,873,490	11,613,171	10,989,533	13,229,058	16,162,747	57.72	22.18
Taiwan, Province of China		1,444,342	1,315,865	1,292,551	1,292,734	1,215,162	4.34	-6.00
Hong Kong, China		8,176,964	7,016,479	6,727,822	7,466,139	7,582,923	27.08	1.56
Japan		299,406	366,920	379,241	413,507	396,023	1.41	-4.23
Korea, Dem. People's Republic of		1,454	1,162	1,038	1,160	1,167	0.00	0.60
Korea, Republic of		225,417	279,794	204,767	331,768	398,807	1.42	20.21
Other countries of North-East Asia		3,349	3,753	4,255				
South-East Asia		1,179,431	1,470,175	1,343,831	1,263,906	1,290,619	4.61	2.11
Indonesia		133,432	180,320	191,425	208,440	220,423	0.79	5.75
Malaysia		402,121	428,608	332,529	338,058	324,509	1.16	-4.01
Philippines		256,192	282,951	247,459	247,770	268,710	0.96	8.45
Singapore		189,666	263,631	256,520	257,196	280,602	1.00	9.10
Thailand		140,749	252,124	242,514	212,442	196,375	0.70	-7.56
All countries of South-East Asia		57,271	62,541	73,384				
Australasia		133,312	156,363	134,275	126,353	126,724	0.45	0.29
Australia		117,959	139,628	120,395	111,771	111,827	0.40	0.05
New Zealand		15,353	16,735	13,880	14,582	14,897	0.05	2.16
Other East Asia and the Pacific		806	812	940	102,196	68,023	0.24	-33.44
Other countries of Asia					100,992	66,764	0.24	-33.89
Other countries of Oceania		806	812	940	1,204	1,259	0.00	4.57
EUROPE		257,335	272,188	254,002	244,463	251,748	0.90	2.98
Central/Eastern Europe		6,085	7,123	7,806	11,702	16,512	0.06	41.10
Russian Federation		6,085	7,123	7,806	11,702	16,512	0.06	41.10
Northern Europe		88,793	88,463	73,633	70,270	71,835	0.26	2.23
Ireland		4,113	4,391	3,551	3,257	3,360	0.01	3.16
Sweden		6,704	7,163	6,698	6,574	6,838	0.02	4.02
United Kingdom		77,976	76,909	63,384	60,439	61,637	0.22	1.98
Southern Europe		33,574	33,103	32,572	35,492	35,151	0.13	-0.96
Italy		11,787	12,524	12,229	13,461	13,121	0.05	-2.53
Portugal		14,659	13,081	12,429	13,583	13,339	0.05	-1.80
Spain		7,128	7,498	7,914	8,448	8,691	0.03	2.88
Western Europe		85,147	94,354	90,601	93,925	95,473	0.34	1.65
Austria		3,989	4,304	4,234	4,474	4,096	0.01	-8.45
France		36,364	40,499	39,165	41,417	42,710	0.15	3.12
Germany		26,291	29,067	28,172	28,820	28,811	0.10	-0.03

MACAO, CHINA

2. Arrivals of non-resident visitors at national borders, by country of residence

	2007	2008	2009	2010	2011	Market share 11	% Change 11-10
Netherlands	12,800	14,218	12,888	12,664	12,769	0.05	0.83
Switzerland	5,703	6,266	6,142	6,550	7,087	0.03	8.20
Other Europe	**43,736**	**49,145**	**49,390**	**33,074**	**32,777**	**0.12**	**-0.90**
Other countries of Europe	43,736	49,145	49,390	33,074	32,777	0.12	-0.90
MIDDLE EAST	**7,517**	**7,536**	**7,334**				
All countries of Middle East	7,517	7,536	7,334				
SOUTH ASIA	**64,028**	**94,428**	**117,677**	**174,145**	**172,864**	**0.62**	**-0.74**
Bangladesh	3,338	2,606	1,566	905	209	0.00	-76.91
India	45,473	82,369	107,513	169,096	169,660	0.61	0.33
Nepal	9,744	3,891	2,827	2,102	2,019	0.01	-3.95
Pakistan	3,084	3,290	3,103	2,042	976	0.00	-52.20
Other countries of South Asia	2,389	2,272	2,668				
NOT SPECIFIED	**66**	**34**	**21**				
Other countries of the World	66	34	21				

MACAO, CHINA

3. Arrivals of non-resident tourists in hotels and similar establishments, by country of residence

		2007	2008	2009	2010	2011	Market share 11	% Change 11-10
TOTAL	(*)	5,441,536	6,193,569	6,398,389	7,288,172	8,051,777	100.00	10.48
AMERICAS		82,840	98,387	82,845	88,035	84,947	1.06	-3.51
North America		82,840	98,387	82,845	88,035	84,947	1.06	-3.51
Canada		22,346	28,403	27,450	29,782	26,726	0.33	-10.26
United States of America		60,494	69,984	55,395	58,253	58,221	0.72	-0.05
EAST ASIA AND THE PACIFIC		5,180,420	5,798,660	5,984,731	6,872,539	7,641,077	94.90	11.18
North-East Asia		4,871,368	5,212,948	5,431,239	6,278,219	7,055,066	87.62	12.37
China		2,806,714	3,057,142	3,282,433	4,012,193	4,703,663	58.42	17.23
Taiwan, Province of China		171,544	235,561	258,240	289,834	334,010	4.15	15.24
Hong Kong, China		1,667,638	1,588,549	1,600,074	1,620,471	1,632,010	20.27	0.71
Japan		147,557	221,044	210,856	228,266	233,069	2.89	2.10
Korea, Republic of		77,915	110,652	79,636	127,455	152,314	1.89	19.50
South-East Asia		268,372	531,416	506,663	495,914	499,169	6.20	0.66
Indonesia		30,266	69,851	77,325	82,884	84,971	1.06	2.52
Malaysia		84,254	129,999	114,284	120,180	120,932	1.50	0.63
Philippines		38,210	78,007	65,964	69,675	72,284	0.90	3.74
Singapore		71,299	129,613	126,732	115,951	117,212	1.46	1.09
Thailand		44,343	123,946	122,358	107,224	103,770	1.29	-3.22
Australasia		40,680	54,296	46,829	48,207	49,672	0.62	3.04
Australia		36,694	48,194	41,512	42,472	43,167	0.54	1.64
New Zealand		3,986	6,102	5,317	5,735	6,505	0.08	13.43
Other East Asia and the Pacific					50,199	37,170	0.46	-25.95
Other countries of Asia					50,199	37,170	0.46	-25.95
EUROPE		67,514	91,676	79,823	81,524	93,773	1.16	15.03
Northern Europe		18,033	22,055	19,782	18,633	20,170	0.25	8.25
United Kingdom		18,033	22,055	19,782	18,633	20,170	0.25	8.25
Southern Europe		10,426	15,505	11,563	13,213	15,254	0.19	15.45
Italy		3,619	5,773	4,842	5,681	6,625	0.08	16.62
Portugal		6,807	9,732	6,721	7,532	8,629	0.11	14.56
Western Europe		14,692	20,887	22,312	22,033	24,022	0.30	9.03
France		8,060	11,697	13,572	12,070	13,897	0.17	15.14
Germany		6,632	9,190	8,740	9,963	10,125	0.13	1.63
Other Europe		24,363	33,229	26,166	27,645	34,327	0.43	24.17
Other countries of Europe		24,363	33,229	26,166	27,645	34,327	0.43	24.17
SOUTH ASIA		21,622	51,752	78,458	120,737	123,902	1.54	2.62
India		21,622	51,752	78,458	120,737	123,902	1.54	2.62
NOT SPECIFIED		89,140	153,094	172,532	125,337	108,078	1.34	-13.77
Other countries of the World		89,140	153,094	172,532	125,337	108,078	1.34	-13.77

MACAO, CHINA

5. Overnight stays of non-resident tourists in hotels and similar establishments, by country of residence

		2007	2008	2009	2010	2011	Market share 11	% Change 11-10
TOTAL	(*)	6,941,551	8,604,636	9,133,979	10,663,207	11,684,464	100.00	9.58
AMERICAS		159,995	239,511	213,020	240,415	241,506	2.07	0.45
North America		159,995	239,511	213,020	240,415	241,506	2.07	0.45
Canada		40,979	54,487	47,649	57,705	54,858	0.47	-4.93
United States of America		119,016	185,024	165,371	182,710	186,648	1.60	2.16
EAST ASIA AND THE PACIFIC		6,485,059	7,726,246	8,003,440	9,352,712	10,361,698	88.68	10.79
North-East Asia		6,014,365	6,767,229	7,037,836	8,344,807	9,365,089	80.15	12.23
China		3,234,381	3,891,829	4,062,398	5,083,252	5,989,362	51.26	17.83
Taiwan, Province of China		232,819	383,502	439,007	505,292	583,609	4.99	15.50
Hong Kong, China		2,224,429	1,937,352	2,023,718	2,132,874	2,145,908	18.37	0.61
Japan		214,877	379,034	378,152	398,449	415,574	3.56	4.30
Korea, Republic of		107,859	175,512	134,561	224,940	230,636	1.97	2.53
South-East Asia		394,660	838,633	851,843	874,810	866,073	7.41	-1.00
Indonesia		44,477	128,671	148,912	165,835	167,433	1.43	0.96
Malaysia		112,060	184,209	183,356	194,114	181,783	1.56	-6.35
Philippines		58,967	130,188	120,162	132,299	131,776	1.13	-0.40
Singapore		111,589	201,240	204,341	199,476	207,728	1.78	4.14
Thailand		67,567	194,325	195,072	183,086	177,353	1.52	-3.13
Australasia		76,034	120,384	113,761	133,095	130,536	1.12	-1.92
Australia		66,342	107,986	99,876	115,017	110,536	0.95	-3.90
New Zealand		9,692	12,398	13,885	18,078	20,000	0.17	10.63
EUROPE		123,808	208,426	205,509	254,450	244,901	2.10	-3.75
Northern Europe		32,546	46,426	49,530	67,347	60,256	0.52	-10.53
United Kingdom		32,546	46,426	49,530	67,347	60,256	0.52	-10.53
Southern Europe		20,722	30,611	28,959	36,835	32,257	0.28	-12.43
Italy		6,586	12,631	12,654	17,130	15,321	0.13	-10.56
Portugal		14,136	17,980	16,305	19,705	16,936	0.14	-14.05
Western Europe		28,902	44,414	47,680	57,986	58,020	0.50	0.06
France		14,000	26,336	29,061	33,194	34,682	0.30	4.48
Germany		14,902	18,078	18,619	24,792	23,338	0.20	-5.86
Other Europe		41,638	86,975	79,340	92,282	94,368	0.81	2.26
Other countries of Europe		41,638	86,975	79,340	92,282	94,368	0.81	2.26
SOUTH ASIA		35,420	95,473	142,338	208,342	223,133	1.91	7.10
India		35,420	95,473	142,338	208,342	223,133	1.91	7.10
NOT SPECIFIED		137,269	334,980	569,672	607,288	613,226	5.25	0.98
Other countries of the World		137,269	334,980	569,672	607,288	613,226	5.25	0.98

MADAGASCAR

1. Arrivals of non-resident tourists at national borders, by nationality

	2007	2008	2009	2010	2011	Market share 11	% Change 11-10
TOTAL	344,348	375,010	162,687	196,052	225,055	100.00	14.79
AFRICA	64,013	83,802	36,732	40,083	39,176	17.41	-2.26
East Africa	50,838	68,622	28,304	29,927	27,847	12.37	-6.95
Comoros	542	803	348	517	4,468	1.99	764.22
Kenya	42	318	103		363	0.16	
Mauritius	12,309	15,000	6,507	7,845	7,261	3.23	-7.44
Reunion	37,878	52,501	21,149	21,565	15,360	6.82	-28.77
Seychelles	67		197		395	0.18	
Southern Africa	7,041	10,750	6,507	7,842	7,121	3.16	-9.19
South Africa	7,041	10,750	6,507	7,842	7,121	3.16	-9.19
Other Africa	6,134	4,430	1,921	2,314	4,208	1.87	81.85
Other countries of Africa	6,134	4,430	1,921	2,314	4,208	1.87	81.85
AMERICAS	13,671	11,250	4,881	5,882	9,870	4.39	67.80
North America	13,671	11,250	4,881	5,882	9,193	4.08	56.29
Canada, United States	13,671	11,250	4,881	5,882	9,193	4.08	56.29
Other Americas					677	0.30	
Other countries of the Americas					677	0.30	
EAST ASIA AND THE PACIFIC	14,084	16,500	5,694	6,861	22,955	10.20	234.57
North-East Asia	7,397	7,500	1,627	1,960	2,925	1.30	49.23
Japan	7,397	7,500	1,627	1,960	2,925	1.30	49.23
Other East Asia and the Pacific	6,687	9,000	4,067	4,901	20,030	8.90	308.69
Other countries of Asia	6,687	9,000	4,067	4,901	20,030	8.90	308.69
EUROPE	246,837	261,936	110,869	143,226	153,054	68.01	6.86
Northern Europe	10,687	15,000	3,253	3,920	10,730	4.77	173.72
United Kingdom	10,687	15,000	3,253	3,920	9,213	4.09	135.03
Scandinavia					1,517	0.67	
Southern Europe	28,819	15,375	4,881	17,645	9,182	4.08	-47.96
Italy	28,692	15,000	4,881	17,645	7,162	3.18	-59.41
Spain	127	375			2,020	0.90	
Western Europe	206,164	228,750	101,516	121,153	130,081	57.80	7.37
France	181,130	210,000	95,985	111,750	114,471	50.86	2.43
Germany	10,330	11,250	3,253	5,882	6,504	2.89	10.57
Switzerland	6,887	7,500	2,278	3,521	3,902	1.73	10.82
Benelux	7,817				5,204	2.31	
Other Europe	1,167	2,811	1,219	508	3,061	1.36	502.56
Other countries of Europe	1,167	2,811	1,219	508	3,061	1.36	502.56
NOT SPECIFIED	5,743	1,522	4,511				
Other countries of the World	5,743	1,522	4,511				

MADAGASCAR

5. Overnight stays of non-resident tourists in hotels and similar establishments, by nationality

		2007	2008	2009	2010	2011	Market share 11	% Change 11-10
TOTAL	(*)	5,607,642	5,815,169	2,413,073	3,298,025	3,763,549	100.00	14.12
AFRICA		512,104	682,645	326,804	624,549	615,279	16.35	-1.48
East Africa		311,050	424,585	183,528	420,529	401,949	10.68	-4.42
Comoros		9,214	12,848	5,916	8,789	76,519	2.03	770.62
Kenya		714	1,213	927		4,051	0.11	
Mauritius		73,854	92,500	45,549	109,830	100,825	2.68	-8.20
Reunion		227,268	313,621	126,336	301,910	214,252	5.69	-29.03
Seychelles			4,403	4,800		6,302	0.17	
Southern Africa		63,369	182,750	110,619	164,682	141,785	3.77	-13.90
South Africa		63,369	182,750	110,619	164,682	141,785	3.77	-13.90
Other Africa		137,685	75,310	32,657	39,338	71,545	1.90	81.87
Other countries of Africa		137,685	75,310	32,657	39,338	71,545	1.90	81.87
AMERICAS		232,407	191,250	82,977	99,994	167,576	4.45	67.59
North America		232,407	191,250	82,977	99,994	156,098	4.15	56.11
Canada, United States		232,407	191,250	82,977	99,994	156,098	4.15	56.11
Other Americas						11,478	0.30	
Other countries of the Americas						11,478	0.30	
EAST ASIA AND THE PACIFIC		239,428	280,500	96,798	116,637	390,245	10.37	234.58
North-East Asia		125,749	127,500	27,659	33,320	49,737	1.32	49.27
Japan		125,749	127,500	27,659	33,320	49,737	1.32	49.27
Other East Asia and the Pacific		113,679	153,000	69,139	83,317	340,508	9.05	308.69
Other countries of Asia		113,679	153,000	69,139	83,317	340,508	9.05	308.69
EUROPE		4,600,731	4,634,903	1,888,450	2,456,845	2,590,449	68.83	5.44
Northern Europe		181,679	255,000	55,301	66,640	191,296	5.08	187.06
United Kingdom		181,679	255,000	55,301	66,640	153,037	4.07	129.65
Scandinavia						38,259	1.02	
Southern Europe		260,387	276,375	102,501	317,610	163,254	4.34	-48.60
Italy		258,228	270,000	102,501	317,610	128,821	3.42	-59.44
Spain		2,159	6,375			34,433	0.91	
Western Europe		4,153,997	4,098,750	1,725,772	2,065,483	2,193,049	58.27	6.18
France		3,767,504	3,780,000	1,631,745	1,899,750	1,947,401	51.74	2.51
Germany		175,610	191,250	55,301	105,876	117,074	3.11	10.58
Switzerland		117,079	127,500	38,726	59,857	66,189	1.76	10.58
Benelux		93,804				62,385	1.66	
Other Europe		4,668	4,778	4,876	7,112	42,850	1.14	502.50
Other countries of Europe		4,668	4,778	4,876	7,112	42,850	1.14	502.50
NOT SPECIFIED		22,972	25,871	18,044				
Other countries of the World		22,972	25,871	18,044				

MALAWI

1. Arrivals of non-resident tourists at national borders, by country of residence

		2007	2008	2009	2010	2011	Market share 11	% Change 11-10
TOTAL	(*)	734,598	742,457	755,031	746,129	767,000	100.00	2.80
AFRICA		559,149	574,544	574,172	562,379	588,306	76.70	4.61
East Africa		447,036	458,711	462,612	439,600	449,237	58.57	2.19
Mozambique		111,924	139,296	188,694	159,580	196,629	25.64	23.22
Zimbabwe		171,684	143,363	77,281	128,387	131,756	17.18	2.62
Zambia		63,581	76,408	102,956	80,428	95,766	12.49	19.07
Other countries of East Africa		99,847	99,644	93,681	71,205	25,086	3.27	-64.77
Southern Africa		104,226	106,724	100,958	102,342	115,051	15.00	12.42
All countries of Southern Africa		104,226	106,724	100,958	102,342	115,051	15.00	12.42
Other Africa		7,887	9,109	10,602	20,437	24,018	3.13	17.52
Other countries of Africa		7,887	9,109	10,602	20,437	24,018	3.13	17.52
AMERICAS		47,225	44,561	46,120	45,893	44,735	5.83	-2.52
North America		45,630	43,085	43,766	44,572	43,778	5.71	-1.78
Canada, United States		45,630	43,085	43,766	44,572	43,778	5.71	-1.78
Other Americas		1,595	1,476	2,354	1,321	957	0.12	-27.55
Other countries of the Americas		1,595	1,476	2,354	1,321	957	0.12	-27.55
EAST ASIA AND THE PACIFIC		12,835	11,588	12,142	20,456	10,247	1.34	-49.91
Other East Asia and the Pacific		12,835	11,588	12,142	20,456	10,247	1.34	-49.91
All countries of Asia		12,835	11,588	12,142	20,456	10,247	1.34	-49.91
EUROPE		99,226	98,330	105,054	104,779	102,389	13.35	-2.28
Northern Europe		48,627	50,786	54,476	53,897	51,936	6.77	-3.64
United Kingdom/Ireland		48,627	50,786	54,476	53,897	51,936	6.77	-3.64
Other Europe		50,599	47,544	50,578	50,882	50,453	6.58	-0.84
Other countries of Europe		50,599	47,544	50,578	50,882	50,453	6.58	-0.84
MIDDLE EAST		1,613	1,581	1,691	2,310	3,400	0.44	47.19
All countries of Middle East		1,613	1,581	1,691	2,310	3,400	0.44	47.19
SOUTH ASIA		13,366	10,194	14,299	8,338	15,894	2.07	90.62
All countries of South Asia		13,366	10,194	14,299	8,338	15,894	2.07	90.62
NOT SPECIFIED		1,184	1,659	1,553	1,974	2,029	0.26	2.79
Other countries of the World		1,184	1,659	1,553	1,974	2,029	0.26	2.79

MALAWI

6. Overnight stays of non-resident tourists in all types of accommodation establishments, by country of residence

	2007	2008	2009	2010	2011	Market share 11	% Change 11-10
TOTAL	5,460,060	5,864,441	5,167,246	6,056,990	5,820,695	100.00	-3.90
AFRICA	3,553,567	3,806,008	3,252,681	3,818,821	3,566,241	61.27	-6.61
East Africa	2,627,887	2,728,432	2,347,201	2,689,880	2,508,426	43.09	-6.75
Mozambique	313,387	473,606	622,690	622,362	668,539	11.49	7.42
Zimbabwe	875,588	903,187	587,336	893,709	1,040,872	17.88	16.47
Zambia	368,770	443,166	391,233	450,396	497,983	8.56	10.57
Other countries of East Africa	1,070,142	908,473	745,942	723,413	301,032	5.17	-58.39
Southern Africa	858,661	955,471	798,276	1,012,063	908,903	15.62	-10.19
All countries of Southern Africa	858,661	955,471	798,276	1,012,063	908,903	15.62	-10.19
Other Africa	67,019	122,105	107,204	116,878	148,912	2.56	27.41
Other countries of Africa	67,019	122,105	107,204	116,878	148,912	2.56	27.41
AMERICAS	510,279	557,512	496,825	559,693	549,546	9.44	-1.81
North America	495,772	540,908	477,993	545,796	542,847	9.33	-0.54
Canada, United States	495,772	540,908	477,993	545,796	542,847	9.33	-0.54
Other Americas	14,507	16,604	18,832	13,897	6,699	0.12	-51.80
Other countries of the Americas	14,507	16,604	18,832	13,897	6,699	0.12	-51.80
EAST ASIA AND THE PACIFIC		137,845	194,272	157,350	336,767	5.79	114.02
Other East Asia and the Pacific		137,845	194,272	157,350	336,767	5.79	114.02
All countries of Asia		137,845	194,272	157,350	336,767	5.79	114.02
EUROPE	1,330,761	1,351,707	1,198,620	1,489,710	1,352,721	23.24	-9.20
Northern Europe	699,831	755,530	629,257	805,066	727,104	12.49	-9.68
United Kingdom/Ireland	699,831	755,530	629,257	805,066	727,104	12.49	-9.68
Other Europe	630,930	596,177	569,363	684,644	625,617	10.75	-8.62
Other countries of Europe	630,930	596,177	569,363	684,644	625,617	10.75	-8.62
NOT SPECIFIED	65,453	11,369	24,848	31,416	15,420	0.26	-50.92
Other countries of the World	65,453	11,369	24,848	31,416	15,420	0.26	-50.92

MALAYSIA

1. Arrivals of non-resident tourists at national borders, by country of residence

		2007	2008	2009	2010	2011	Market share 11	% Change 11-10
TOTAL	(*)	20,972,822	22,052,488	23,646,191	24,577,196	24,714,324	100.00	0.56
AFRICA		307,797	127,361	84,549	41,615	111,182	0.45	167.17
East Africa		149,063	46,176	24,322		26,754	0.11	
British Indian Ocean Territory			27	19		2	0.00	
Burundi			1,246	28		42	0.00	
Comoros			1,792	48		229	0.00	
Ethiopia			1,231	411		371	0.00	
Djibouti			285	187		213	0.00	
Kenya			3,485	3,296		3,523	0.01	
Madagascar			11,604	212		297	0.00	
Malawi			952	177		326	0.00	
Mauritius		10,653	10,494	11,523		10,850	0.04	
Mozambique			272	180		264	0.00	
Reunion			277	1		3	0.00	
Rwanda			847	53		129	0.00	
Seychelles			1,428	899		926	0.00	
Somalia			1,782	1,514		2,381	0.01	
Zimbabwe			2,264	1,545		2,059	0.01	
Uganda			2,076	1,253		1,998	0.01	
United Republic of Tanzania			5,069	2,545		2,254	0.01	
Zambia			1,045	431		887	0.00	
Other countries of East Africa		138,410						
Central Africa		27,752	7,889	791		1,126	0.00	
Angola			268	75		217	0.00	
Cameroon			523	409		469	0.00	
Central African Republic			20	3		5	0.00	
Chad			2,946	140		223	0.00	
Congo			294	76		75	0.00	
Democratic Republic of the Congo			3,356			1	0.00	
Equatorial Guinea			24	28		56	0.00	
Gabon			401	27		77	0.00	
Sao Tome and Principe			57	33		3	0.00	
All countries of Central Africa		27,752						
North Africa		36,414	19,689	18,586	15,220	25,422	0.10	67.03
Algeria			1,955	2,424		2,718	0.01	
Morocco			3,254	2,864	2,043	2,881	0.01	41.02
Western Sahara						3,228	0.01	
Sudan			10,693	10,993	10,914	13,703	0.06	25.55
Tunisia			3,787	2,305	2,263	2,892	0.01	27.79
All countries of North Africa		36,414						
Southern Africa		63,128	32,116	25,275	26,395	34,584	0.14	31.02
Botswana			1,635	1,288		1,424	0.01	
Lesotho			266	118		134	0.00	
Namibia			3,663	197		326	0.00	
South Africa		21,233	25,437	23,556	26,395	31,441	0.13	19.12
Swaziland			1,115	116		185	0.00	
Other countries of Southern Africa		41,895				1,074	0.00	
West Africa		31,440	21,491	15,575		23,296	0.09	
Cape Verde			103	20		17	0.00	
Benin			171	60		179	0.00	
Gambia			204	180		198	0.00	
Ghana			1,031	831		1,197	0.00	
Guinea			1,117	706		888	0.00	
Côte d'Ivoire			147	109		179	0.00	
Liberia			540	162		108	0.00	
Mali			207	213		138	0.00	

MALAYSIA

1. Arrivals of non-resident tourists at national borders, by country of residence

	2007	2008	2009	2010	2011	Market share 11	% Change 11-10
Mauritania		321	163		152	0.00	
Niger		156	22		59	0.00	
Nigeria		12,720	12,421		18,916	0.08	
Guinea-Bissau		34	30		135	0.00	
Saint Helena		360	15		11	0.00	
Senegal		3,438	386		676	0.00	
Sierra Leone		235	135		279	0.00	
Togo		537	61		93	0.00	
Burkina Faso		170	61		71	0.00	
All countries of West Africa	31,440						
AMERICAS	**472,164**	**345,217**	**345,768**	**342,521**	**339,645**	**1.37**	**-0.84**
Caribbean	**78,716**	**7,484**	**1,306**		**2,159**	**0.01**	
Antigua and Barbuda		32	9		14	0.00	
Bahamas		1,027	70		49	0.00	
Barbados		580	73		450	0.00	
Bermuda		83	1				
British Virgin Islands		47			2	0.00	
Cayman Islands		96			1	0.00	
Cuba		602	161		174	0.00	
Dominica		542	15		38	0.00	
Dominican Republic		341	107		134	0.00	
Grenada		52	7		9	0.00	
Guadeloupe		54	1		1	0.00	
Haiti		160	17		27	0.00	
Jamaica		220	168		236	0.00	
Martinique		42					
Montserrat		27			3	0.00	
Netherlands Antilles		442	60		73	0.00	
Aruba		89	3		56	0.00	
Puerto Rico		120	17		2	0.00	
Saint Kitts and Nevis		74	19		138	0.00	
Anguilla		25			5	0.00	
Saint Lucia		220	13		10	0.00	
Saint Vincent and the Grenadines		1,245	10		9	0.00	
Trinidad and Tobago		1,278	545		723	0.00	
Turks and Caicos Islands		54	10		5	0.00	
United States Virgin Islands		32					
All countries of the Caribbean	78,716						
Central America	**25,927**	**3,904**	**1,370**		**6,825**	**0.03**	
Belize		287	156		134	0.00	
Costa Rica		715	536		641	0.00	
El Salvador		373	96		203	0.00	
Guatemala		443	210		362	0.00	
Honduras		140	142		179	0.00	
Nicaragua		1,155	47		5,251	0.02	
Panama		791	183		55	0.00	
All countries of Central America	25,927						
North America	**257,727**	**306,597**	**321,468**	**328,680**	**302,773**	**1.23**	**-7.88**
Canada	46,903	77,664	88,080	91,701	86,015	0.35	-6.20
Greenland		240	1		1	0.00	
Mexico	3,726	5,441	4,816	4,014	2	0.00	-99.95
Saint Pierre and Miquelon		3					
United States of America	204,844	223,249	228,571	232,965	216,755	0.88	-6.96
Other countries of North America	2,254						
South America	**109,794**	**27,232**	**21,624**	**13,841**	**27,888**	**0.11**	**101.49**
Argentina	5,275	5,640	6,098	6,014	8,929	0.04	48.47
Bolivia		680	201		198	0.00	

MALAYSIA

1. Arrivals of non-resident tourists at national borders, by country of residence

	2007	2008	2009	2010	2011	Market share 11	% Change 11-10
Brazil	4,750	6,222	7,529	6,072	9,254	0.04	52.40
Chile		2,216	2,286		3,403	0.01	
Colombia		1,482	1,401		1,721	0.01	
Ecuador		167	5		536	0.00	
Falkland Islands, Malvinas		159					
French Guiana		5	2		1	0.00	
Guyana		72	46		54	0.00	
Paraguay		3,362	99	121	125	0.00	3.31
Peru		1,736	1,105		1,075	0.00	
Suriname		779	152		110	0.00	
Uruguay		355	364		470	0.00	
Venezuela	24,827	4,357	2,336	1,634	2,012	0.01	23.13
Other countries of South America	74,942						
EAST ASIA AND THE PACIFIC	**17,656,571**	**18,972,997**	**20,830,330**	**21,605,363**	**21,667,502**	**87.67**	**0.29**
North-East Asia	**1,595,247**	**1,849,245**	**1,844,375**	**2,021,337**	**2,138,812**	**8.65**	**5.81**
China	689,293	943,787	1,015,550	1,130,261	1,245,475	5.04	10.19
Taiwan, Province of China	201,311	190,979	197,869	211,143	233,783	0.95	10.72
Hong Kong, China	94,495	6,067	4,199		4,716	0.02	
Japan	367,567	433,462	395,746	415,881	386,974	1.57	-6.95
Korea, Dem. People's Republic of	8,830	3,091	693		1,013	0.00	
Korea, Republic of	224,867	267,461	227,312	264,052	263,428	1.07	-0.24
Macao, China	5,995	10	7		345	0.00	
Mongolia		4,388	2,999		3,078	0.01	
Other countries of North-East Asia	2,889						
South-East Asia	**15,620,290**	**16,636,977**	**18,386,363**	**18,937,179**	**18,885,302**	**76.41**	**-0.27**
Brunei Darussalam	1,172,154	1,085,115	1,061,357	1,124,406	1,239,404	5.01	10.23
Myanmar	43,674	43,131	60,338	72,792	81,946	0.33	12.58
Cambodia	23,193	35,464	43,146	48,618	49,472	0.20	1.76
Indonesia	1,804,535	2,428,605	2,405,360	2,506,509	2,134,381	8.64	-14.85
Lao People's Democratic Republic	11,231	26,564	36,663	38,111	29,520	0.12	-22.54
Philippines	327,140	397,884	447,470	486,790	362,101	1.47	-25.61
Singapore	10,492,692	11,003,492	12,733,082	13,042,004	13,372,647	54.11	2.54
Viet Nam	119,973	122,933	149,685	159,271	173,783	0.70	9.11
Thailand	1,625,698	1,493,789	1,449,262	1,458,678	1,442,048	5.83	-1.14
Australasia	**361,732**	**483,193**	**596,386**	**646,847**	**639,798**	**2.59**	**-1.09**
Australia	320,363	427,076	533,382	580,695	558,411	2.26	-3.84
New Zealand	41,369	56,117	63,004	66,152	81,387	0.33	23.03
Melanesia		**3,098**	**2,797**		**3,043**	**0.01**	
Solomon Islands		186	157		244	0.00	
Fiji		1,627	1,130		1,391	0.01	
New Caledonia		1	2		1	0.00	
Vanuatu		81	42		82	0.00	
Papua New Guinea		1,203	1,466		1,325	0.01	
Micronesia		**196**	**138**		**90**	**0.00**	
Christmas Island, Australia		1					
Cocos (Keeling) Islands		4					
Kiribati		55	45		29	0.00	
Guam		1					
Nauru		73	47		25	0.00	
Micronesia, Federated States of		6	20		12	0.00	
Marshall Islands		25	12		7	0.00	
Palau		30	11		17	0.00	
Other countries of Micronesia		1	3				
Polynesia		**288**	**271**		**254**	**0.00**	
American Samoa		15	1		20	0.00	
French Polynesia		8	1		1	0.00	
Tonga		134	160		120	0.00	

MALAYSIA

1. Arrivals of non-resident tourists at national borders, by country of residence

	2007	2008	2009	2010	2011	Market share 11	% Change 11-10
Tuvalu		44	50		26	0.00	
Samoa		87	59		87	0.00	
Other East Asia and the Pacific	79,302				203	0.00	
Other countries of Oceania	79,302				203	0.00	
EUROPE	**829,653**	**1,026,032**	**1,165,807**	**1,133,235**	**1,136,443**	**4.60**	**0.28**
Central/Eastern Europe	**64,509**	**77,404**	**80,115**	**68,670**	**112,303**	**0.45**	**63.54**
Azerbaijan		641	544		913	0.00	
Armenia		162	152		235	0.00	
Bulgaria		1,919	1,614		2,585	0.01	
Belarus		690	854		1,295	0.01	
Czech Republic	3,396	6,314	6,774	6,753	6,818	0.03	0.96
Hungary		4,927	4,242		4,385	0.02	
Kazakhstan		5,337	5,493	10,527	17,462	0.07	65.88
Kyrgyzstan		925	844		1,677	0.01	
Lithuania		909	1,100		1,720	0.01	
Poland	34,344	11,745	12,544	12,358	13,055	0.05	5.64
Romania		3,002	2,844		3,398	0.01	
Russian Federation		26,308	29,202	32,075	38,918	0.16	21.33
Slovakia		2,660	2,472		3,112	0.01	
Tajikistan		321	491		499	0.00	
Turkmenistan		436	626		750	0.00	
Ukraine		3,772	3,125		6,229	0.03	
Uzbekistan		7,336	7,194	6,957	9,252	0.04	32.99
Other countries Central/East Europe	9,901						
Commonwealth Independent States	16,868						
Northern Europe	**409,629**	**513,292**	**579,898**	**571,079**	**533,492**	**2.16**	**-6.58**
Denmark	19,773	23,817	25,916	24,869	22,269	0.09	-10.45
Faeroe Islands		32	2				
Finland	34,144	23,112	20,912	21,355	19,969	0.08	-6.49
Iceland		1,672	633		690	0.00	
Ireland	14,464	23,720	25,347	23,146	22,593	0.09	-2.39
Norway	14,954	21,516	22,487	22,773	19,891	0.08	-12.66
Svalbard and Jan Mayen Islands		179			2	0.00	
Sweden	44,746	48,649	49,509	48,971	44,138	0.18	-9.87
United Kingdom	276,213	370,591	435,091	429,965	403,940	1.63	-6.05
Isle of Man		1					
Other countries of Northern Europe	5,335	3	1				
Southern Europe	**105,430**	**80,363**	**86,932**	**72,770**	**82,101**	**0.33**	**12.82**
Albania		373	292		298	0.00	
Andorra		753	36		18	0.00	
Bosnia and Herzegovina		585	482		540	0.00	
Croatia		1,957	1,334		1,728	0.01	
Greece		3,396	3,105		2,624	0.01	
Holy See		95	8		12	0.00	
Italy	31,576	38,945	46,352	47,068	43,864	0.18	-6.81
Malta		531	410		654	0.00	
Portugal	27,981	14,482	11,685	6,264	9,842	0.04	57.12
San Marino		187	43		43	0.00	
Spain	19,256	17,365	22,771	19,438	22,104	0.09	13.72
Yugoslavia, SFR (former)		461	155		11	0.00	
Serbia and Montenegro		88	259		363	0.00	
Other countries of Southern Europe	26,617	1,145					
Western Europe	**240,505**	**346,004**	**410,032**	**411,567**	**399,340**	**1.62**	**-2.97**
Austria	12,052	14,231	14,491	10,891	13,082	0.05	20.12
Belgium	9,513	15,618	16,721	15,275	16,436	0.07	7.60
France	59,456	86,030	110,054	111,175	127,980	0.52	15.12
Germany	78,598	111,525	128,288	130,896	124,670	0.50	-4.76

MALAYSIA

1. Arrivals of non-resident tourists at national borders, by country of residence

	2007	2008	2009	2010	2011	Market share 11	% Change 11-10
Liechtenstein		339	54		85	0.00	
Luxembourg	811	638	732	549	666	0.00	21.31
Monaco		332	30		29	0.00	
Netherlands	55,604	90,802	111,139	114,887	90,590	0.37	-21.15
Switzerland	20,662	26,489	28,523	27,894	25,802	0.10	-7.50
Other countries of Western Europe	3,809						
East Mediterranean Europe	**9,580**	**8,969**	**8,830**	**9,149**	**9,207**	**0.04**	**0.63**
Cyprus		794	558		617	0.00	
Israel		23	7		13	0.00	
Turkey	9,580	8,152	8,265	9,149	8,577	0.03	-6.25
MIDDLE EAST	**225,153**	**216,351**	**196,854**	**166,636**	**236,987**	**0.96**	**42.22**
Bahrain	6,874	7,822	6,114		7,128	0.03	
Iraq		10,032	8,680		13,568	0.05	
Jordan		7,087	7,713		9,012	0.04	
Kuwait	17,650	18,853	20,170	17,632	22,833	0.09	29.50
Lebanon	8,523	5,532	5,187		4,887	0.02	
Libya		4,069	3,187		2,881	0.01	
Oman	19,525	17,472	15,280	16,377	22,062	0.09	34.71
Qatar	11,782	7,808	4,257	3,965	5,727	0.02	44.44
Saudi Arabia	78,298	74,632	77,082	86,771	87,693	0.35	1.06
Syrian Arab Republic	7,481	4,838	5,909	4,537	7,241	0.03	59.60
United Arab Emirates	38,170	34,994	22,108	25,645	24,212	0.10	-5.59
Egypt	7,066	11,926	11,006	11,709	15,359	0.06	31.17
Yemen		11,286	10,161		14,384	0.06	
Other countries of Middle East	29,784						
SOUTH ASIA	**686,614**	**826,028**	**929,954**	**997,156**	**1,124,647**	**4.55**	**12.79**
Afghanistan		1,210	1,026		757	0.00	
Bangladesh	111,467	49,184	87,443	63,886	65,603	0.27	2.69
Bhutan		451	417		503	0.00	
Sri Lanka	31,733	42,774	50,086	58,085	58,572	0.24	0.84
India	422,452	550,738	589,838	690,849	693,056	2.80	0.32
Iran, Islamic Republic of	27,215	63,165	101,664	116,252	139,617	0.56	20.10
Maldives		13,396	11,001		11,702	0.05	
Nepal	38,022	36,572	18,898	2,983	81,791	0.33	2641.90
Pakistan	44,916	68,538	69,581	65,101	73,046	0.30	12.20
Other countries of South Asia	10,809						
NOT SPECIFIED	**794,870**	**538,502**	**92,929**	**290,670**	**97,918**	**0.40**	**-66.31**
Other countries of the World	794,870	538,502	92,929	290,670	97,918	0.40	-66.31

MALAYSIA

3. Arrivals of non-resident tourists in hotels and similar establishments, by country of residence

	2007	2008	2009	2010	2011	Market share 11	% Change 11-10
TOTAL	25,394,611	28,275,844	28,443,149				
AFRICA	177,235	205,638	207,584				
Southern Africa	97,583	115,400	107,138				
South Africa	97,583	115,400	107,138				
Other Africa	79,652	90,238	100,446				
Other countries of Africa	79,652	90,238	100,446				
AMERICAS	786,493	1,147,871	1,109,637				
North America	704,427	1,055,479	1,020,688				
Canada	134,446	221,809	255,763				
United States of America	569,981	833,670	764,925				
Other Americas	82,066	92,392	88,949				
Other countries of the Americas	82,066	92,392	88,949				
EAST ASIA AND THE PACIFIC	16,007,699	18,075,992	17,545,262				
North-East Asia	6,187,892	7,872,938	6,579,715				
China	2,311,462	3,345,852	2,963,138				
Taiwan, Province of China	801,519	912,103	682,333				
Hong Kong, China	913,424	899,048	802,272				
Japan	1,499,752	2,018,867	1,684,071				
Korea, Republic of	661,735	697,068	447,901				
South-East Asia	7,996,061	8,089,013	8,893,668				
Brunei Darussalam	320,530	399,466	419,553				
Indonesia	1,422,238	1,467,821	1,574,724				
Philippines	345,954	425,615	509,661				
Singapore	5,047,062	4,814,346	5,006,188				
Viet Nam	340,310	242,121	406,483				
Thailand	519,967	739,644	977,059				
Australasia	1,697,712	1,987,757	1,959,949				
Australia	1,529,519	1,840,067	1,787,700				
New Zealand	168,193	147,690	172,249				
Other East Asia and the Pacific	126,034	126,284	111,930				
Other countries of Asia	126,034	126,284	111,930				
EUROPE	4,130,681	4,983,367	4,620,205				
Northern Europe	1,863,362	2,357,316	2,083,745				
Denmark	92,382	98,946	118,785				
Finland	42,599	63,632	91,338				
Ireland	57,935	84,467	116,944				
Norway	76,531	110,520	126,051				
Sweden	148,775	226,497	204,267				
United Kingdom	1,445,140	1,773,254	1,426,360				
Southern Europe	259,223	205,867	270,145				
Italy	221,589	177,859	203,001				
Spain	37,634	28,008	67,144				
Western Europe	1,590,107	2,036,953	1,854,752				
Austria	72,698	75,177	70,085				
Belgium	50,301	48,424	56,704				
France	278,128	296,695	314,727				
Germany	409,802	574,105	454,647				
Luxembourg	13,822	4,652	33,354				
Netherlands	494,354	651,145	527,750				
Switzerland	147,453	192,899	229,518				
Other countries of Western Europe	123,549	193,856	167,967				
Other Europe	417,989	383,231	411,563				
Other countries of Europe	417,989	383,231	411,563				

MALAYSIA

3. Arrivals of non-resident tourists in hotels and similar establishments, by country of residence

	2007	2008	2009	2010	2011	Market share 11	% Change 11-10
MIDDLE EAST	**2,164,390**	**1,387,816**	**2,582,309**				
All countries of Middle East	2,164,390	1,387,816	2,582,309				
SOUTH ASIA	**1,573,837**	**1,756,179**	**1,659,451**				
Bangladesh	86,009	96,837	142,660				
Sri Lanka	180,312	57,931	73,272				
India	1,256,477	1,434,549	1,200,295				
Pakistan	51,039	166,862	243,224				
NOT SPECIFIED	**554,276**	**718,981**	**718,701**				
Other countries of the World	554,276	718,981	718,701				

MALDIVES

1. Arrivals of non-resident tourists at national borders, by nationality

		2007	2008	2009	2010	2011	Market share 11	% Change 11-10
TOTAL	(*)	675,889	683,012	655,852	791,917	931,333	100.00	17.60
AFRICA		4,846	5,694	5,034	5,628	6,452	0.69	14.64
East Africa		362	401	596	643	776	0.08	20.68
Comoros		1	3	1	5	12	0.00	140.00
Ethiopia		35	39	34	57	35	0.00	-38.60
Eritrea		15	10	22	11	19	0.00	72.73
Djibouti		1	2	2	5			
Kenya		101	114	143	168	155	0.02	-7.74
Madagascar		17	4	5	5	7	0.00	40.00
Malawi		1	7	6	10	10	0.00	
Mauritius		22	59	218	185	229	0.02	23.78
Mozambique		15	15	15	24	62	0.01	158.33
Seychelles		41	48	47	50	81	0.01	62.00
Somalia		4	1	3		7	0.00	
Zimbabwe		36	39	30	38	63	0.01	65.79
Uganda		16	16	10	14	30	0.00	114.29
United Republic of Tanzania		39	35	43	50	45	0.00	-10.00
Zambia		18	9	17	21	21	0.00	
Central Africa		33	44	43	61	61	0.01	
Angola		8	24	21	35	29	0.00	-17.14
Cameroon		14	12	15	19	16	0.00	-15.79
Chad			1			3	0.00	
Congo		11	7	7	7	13	0.00	85.71
North Africa		770	936	1,205	1,341	1,579	0.17	17.75
Algeria		181	222	252	264	326	0.04	23.48
Morocco		312	381	476	464	552	0.06	18.97
Sudan		93	78	112	139	137	0.01	-1.44
Tunisia		184	255	365	474	564	0.06	18.99
Southern Africa		3,312	3,767	3,014	3,195	3,740	0.40	17.06
Botswana						12	0.00	
Lesotho		1		1	1			
Namibia		14	30	34	32	40	0.00	25.00
South Africa		3,293	3,732	2,975	3,157	3,684	0.40	16.69
Swaziland		4	5	4	5	4	0.00	-20.00
West Africa		338	500	159	356	149	0.02	-58.15
Cape Verde		1	2	5	6	6	0.00	
Gambia		2	1	2	4	5	0.00	25.00
Ghana		45	17	18	25	21	0.00	-16.00
Guinea		2	5	5	12	8	0.00	-33.33
Côte d'Ivoire		20	8	13	17	34	0.00	100.00
Liberia		8	1	3	4	9	0.00	125.00
Mali		36		4	2	5	0.00	150.00
Mauritania		177	373	3	81	8	0.00	-90.12
Nigeria		22	77	91	186	13	0.00	-93.01
Senegal		15	12	11	12	33	0.00	175.00
Sierra Leone		2	1	4	4	7	0.00	75.00
Togo		2	2		3			
Burkina Faso		6	1					
Other Africa		31	46	17	32	147	0.02	359.38
Other countries of Africa		31	46	17	32	147	0.02	359.38
AMERICAS		14,198	14,485	15,159	18,601	23,654	2.54	27.17
Caribbean		179	78	69	102	110	0.01	7.84
Antigua and Barbuda		1			3	2	0.00	-33.33
Bahamas		6		4		7	0.00	
Barbados		5	8	2	7	7	0.00	

MALDIVES

1. Arrivals of non-resident tourists at national borders, by nationality

	2007	2008	2009	2010	2011	Market share 11	% Change 11-10
Cuba	38	25	33	21	24	0.00	14.29
Dominica	12	12	8	26	24	0.00	-7.69
Grenada	1		2		1	0.00	
Haiti	1	1		1	3	0.00	200.00
Jamaica	70	6	4	10	10	0.00	
Saint Lucia	5	2		6	6	0.00	
Trinidad and Tobago	40	24	16	28	26	0.00	-7.14
Central America	**90**	**77**	**80**	**88**	**98**	**0.01**	**11.36**
Belize	3	7	5	10	4	0.00	-60.00
Costa Rica	14	6	16	12	26	0.00	116.67
El Salvador	7	14	7	14	11	0.00	-21.43
Guatemala	28	13	9	11	17	0.00	54.55
Honduras	29	1	1	6	5	0.00	-16.67
Nicaragua	1	2	3	5	2	0.00	-60.00
Panama	8	34	39	30	33	0.00	10.00
North America	**12,667**	**12,344**	**12,986**	**15,850**	**19,925**	**2.14**	**25.71**
Canada	2,851	2,966	3,043	3,815	4,690	0.50	22.94
Mexico	468	525	505	553	745	0.08	34.72
United States of America	9,348	8,853	9,438	11,482	14,490	1.56	26.20
South America	**1,232**	**1,981**	**2,018**	**2,554**	**3,474**	**0.37**	**36.02**
Argentina	191	245	274	288	457	0.05	58.68
Bolivia	9	8	9	19	20	0.00	5.26
Brazil	708	1,327	1,304	1,761	2,342	0.25	32.99
Chile	46	60	57	72	105	0.01	45.83
Colombia	86	95	110	151	178	0.02	17.88
Ecuador	26	45	25	34	36	0.00	5.88
Paraguay	10	12	17	18	30	0.00	66.67
Peru	57	64	55	48	89	0.01	85.42
Suriname	1	1	1		1	0.00	
Uruguay	16	12	31	18	37	0.00	105.56
Venezuela	82	112	135	145	179	0.02	23.45
Other Americas	**30**	**5**	**6**	**7**	**47**	**0.01**	**571.43**
Other countries of the Americas	30	5	6	7	47	0.01	571.43
EAST ASIA AND THE PACIFIC	**124,674**	**127,151**	**137,946**	**214,026**	**303,018**	**32.54**	**41.58**
North-East Asia	**100,668**	**102,886**	**115,434**	**186,414**	**265,096**	**28.46**	**42.21**
China	35,976	41,511	60,666	118,961	198,655	21.33	66.99
Taiwan, Province of China	2,018	2,233	1,975	3,831	5,305	0.57	38.48
Hong Kong, China	571						
Japan	41,121	38,193	36,641	38,791	35,782	3.84	-7.76
Korea, Republic of	20,976	20,934	16,135	24,808	25,285	2.71	1.92
Mongolia	6	15	17	23	29	0.00	26.09
Other countries of North-East Asia					40	0.00	
South-East Asia	**13,338**	**13,672**	**14,095**	**16,807**	**23,726**	**2.55**	**41.17**
Brunei Darussalam	15	29	16	34	46	0.00	35.29
Myanmar	110	36	60	76	139	0.01	82.89
Cambodia	27	7	15	14	54	0.01	285.71
Indonesia	943	581	677	818	1,283	0.14	56.85
Lao People's Democratic Republic	7	13	24	30	58	0.01	93.33
Malaysia	2,999	3,137	3,139	3,894	6,055	0.65	55.50
Philippines	982	871	979	1,066	1,652	0.18	54.97
Singapore	4,456	4,956	5,214	5,332	7,990	0.86	49.85
Viet Nam	136	90	158	146	234	0.03	60.27
Thailand	3,663	3,952	3,813	5,397	6,214	0.67	15.14
Other countries of South-East Asia					1	0.00	
Australasia	**10,548**	**10,552**	**8,383**	**10,725**	**14,168**	**1.52**	**32.10**
Australia	9,406	9,368	7,392	9,622	12,778	1.37	32.80

MALDIVES

1. Arrivals of non-resident tourists at national borders, by nationality

	2007	2008	2009	2010	2011	Market share 11	% Change 11-10
New Zealand	1,142	1,184	991	1,103	1,390	0.15	26.02
Melanesia	**30**	**16**	**11**	**18**	**19**	**0.00**	**5.56**
Fiji	20	16	11	17	19	0.00	11.76
Vanuatu	5			1			
Norfolk Island	5						
Micronesia	**5**		**5**	**3**			
Kiribati	2		5	2			
Micronesia, Federated States of	1						
Marshall Islands	2			1			
Polynesia	**1**			**2**	**1**	**0.00**	**-50.00**
Tonga	1			2	1	0.00	-50.00
Other East Asia and the Pacific	**84**	**25**	**18**	**57**	**8**	**0.00**	**-85.96**
Other countries of Asia	7	19	13	49			
Other countries of Oceania	77	6	5	8	8	0.00	
EUROPE	**495,371**	**497,560**	**462,192**	**505,421**	**537,769**	**57.74**	**6.40**
Central/Eastern Europe	**50,071**	**71,400**	**62,374**	**75,378**	**95,247**	**10.23**	**26.36**
Azerbaijan	187	169	244	275	288	0.03	4.73
Armenia	38	74	79	134	162	0.02	20.90
Bulgaria	784	965	902	1,051	1,368	0.15	30.16
Belarus			812	898	1,161	0.12	29.29
Czech Republic	2,766	3,811	3,851	5,137	6,471	0.69	25.97
Estonia	286	287	262	205	230	0.02	12.20
Georgia	51	57	60	77	74	0.01	-3.90
Hungary	2,568	2,052	1,848	2,434	2,596	0.28	6.66
Kazakhstan	1,294	1,656	1,756	1,572	1,731	0.19	10.11
Kyrgyzstan	27	47	66	59	83	0.01	40.68
Latvia	553	498	383	406	485	0.05	19.46
Lithuania	541	551	446	623	638	0.07	2.41
Republic of Moldova	177	187	219	266	321	0.03	20.68
Poland	2,659	3,325	3,357	3,795	4,158	0.45	9.57
Romania	1,128	1,225	1,247	1,290	1,656	0.18	28.37
Russian Federation	31,845	48,978	40,014	49,111	63,936	6.86	30.19
Slovakia	1,469	1,916	1,970	2,348	2,822	0.30	20.19
Tajikistan	7	14	21	22	43	0.00	95.45
Turkmenistan	10	17	39	42	28	0.00	-33.33
Ukraine	3,545	5,399	4,643	5,445	6,729	0.72	23.58
Uzbekistan	136	172	155	188	233	0.03	23.94
Other countries Central/East Europe					34	0.00	
Northern Europe	**134,927**	**128,591**	**116,491**	**126,222**	**119,388**	**12.82**	**-5.41**
Denmark	1,819	1,834	1,722	2,422	3,173	0.34	31.01
Finland	789	865	1,088	1,281	1,535	0.16	19.83
Iceland	56	49	26	56	57	0.01	1.79
Ireland	3,148	2,884	2,420	2,514	2,444	0.26	-2.78
Norway	1,808	2,596	2,120	2,153	2,775	0.30	28.89
Sweden	2,149	3,542	3,165	3,638	4,896	0.53	34.58
United Kingdom	125,158	116,821	105,950	114,158	104,508	11.22	-8.45
Southern Europe	**137,227**	**123,487**	**109,297**	**111,109**	**104,072**	**11.17**	**-6.33**
Albania	94	105	127	119	144	0.02	21.01
Andorra	32	35	10	31	24	0.00	-22.58
Bosnia and Herzegovina	111	120	101	109	170	0.02	55.96
Croatia	542	641	548	551	626	0.07	13.61
Greece	4,850	4,926	5,406	4,630	3,009	0.32	-35.01
Italy	117,246	103,673	89,292	89,621	83,328	8.95	-7.02
Malta	74	181	130	221	214	0.02	-3.17
Montenegro			12	24	30	0.00	25.00
Portugal	4,188	4,150	4,822	4,555	4,325	0.46	-5.05

MALDIVES

1. Arrivals of non-resident tourists at national borders, by nationality

	2007	2008	2009	2010	2011	Market share 11	% Change 11-10
Serbia	10		127	575	723	0.08	25.74
Slovenia	1,204	1,372	1,324	1,647	2,342	0.25	42.20
Spain	8,798	8,217	7,279	8,912	8,861	0.95	-0.57
TFYR of Macedonia	78	67	119	114	194	0.02	70.18
Other countries of Southern Europe					82	0.01	
Western Europe	**168,061**	**167,424**	**169,027**	**185,433**	**211,755**	**22.74**	**14.19**
Austria	13,673	13,462	13,274	14,944	16,655	1.79	11.45
Belgium	3,552	3,368	3,437	4,386	5,738	0.62	30.83
France	45,301	48,100	50,373	54,789	59,694	6.41	8.95
Germany	72,269	69,240	69,085	77,108	90,517	9.72	17.39
Liechtenstein	122	174	148	148	177	0.02	19.59
Luxembourg	423	464	519	575	725	0.08	26.09
Monaco	59	38	53	35	52	0.01	48.57
Netherlands	6,479	5,595	5,355	5,682	5,693	0.61	0.19
Switzerland	26,183	26,983	26,783	27,766	32,504	3.49	17.06
East Mediterranean Europe	**4,054**	**5,182**	**4,517**	**7,166**	**7,307**	**0.78**	**1.97**
Cyprus	304	359	379	416	332	0.04	-20.19
Israel	1,308	1,588	1,380	2,113	2,433	0.26	15.14
Turkey	2,442	3,235	2,758	4,637	4,542	0.49	-2.05
Other Europe	**1,031**	**1,476**	**486**	**113**			
Other countries of Europe	1,031	1,476	486	113			
MIDDLE EAST	**6,450**	**9,205**	**9,525**	**11,629**	**14,570**	**1.56**	**25.29**
Bahrain	296	435	438	629	612	0.07	-2.70
Palestine	51	74	84	77	121	0.01	57.14
Iraq	76	156	53	72	113	0.01	56.94
Jordan	432	551	538	577	607	0.07	5.20
Kuwait	1,004	1,340	1,181	1,409	1,797	0.19	27.54
Lebanon	660	1,139	984	1,145	1,346	0.14	17.55
Libya	78	113	82	131	32	0.00	-75.57
Oman	122	158	321	272	418	0.04	53.68
Qatar	260	313	418	595	872	0.09	46.55
Saudi Arabia	1,940	2,747	3,036	4,040	5,005	0.54	23.89
Syrian Arab Republic	128	189	191	234	398	0.04	70.09
United Arab Emirates	807	1,394	1,580	1,699	2,292	0.25	34.90
Egypt	511	548	559	689	864	0.09	25.40
Yemen	85	48	60	60	93	0.01	55.00
SOUTH ASIA	**30,350**	**28,917**	**25,996**	**36,612**	**45,870**	**4.93**	**25.29**
Afghanistan	25	23	30	155	134	0.01	-13.55
Bangladesh	1,284	455	388	525	1,496	0.16	184.95
Bhutan	31	57	45	47	93	0.01	97.87
Sri Lanka	9,654	9,752	7,833	7,872	9,670	1.04	22.84
India	17,327	16,663	15,850	25,756	30,978	3.33	20.27
Iran, Islamic Republic of	683	522	637	779	1,321	0.14	69.58
Nepal	333	254	167	222	336	0.04	51.35
Pakistan	1,013	1,191	1,046	1,256	1,842	0.20	46.66

MALI

3. Arrivals of non-resident tourists in hotels and similar establishments, by nationality

	2007	2008	2009	2010	2011	Market share 11	% Change 11-10
TOTAL	164,124	189,511	160,012	169,305	159,782	100.00	-5.62
AFRICA	29,378	47,418	44,589	47,175	52,467	32.84	11.22
West Africa	18,914	15,276	27,408	29,872	33,983	21.27	13.76
All countries of West Africa	18,914	15,276	27,408	29,872	33,983	21.27	13.76
Other Africa	10,464	32,142	17,181	17,303	18,484	11.57	6.83
Other countries of Africa	10,464	32,142	17,181	17,303	18,484	11.57	6.83
AMERICAS	17,564	19,519	26,992	23,692	20,826	13.03	-12.10
North America	17,564	19,519	26,992	23,692	20,826	13.03	-12.10
Canada	5,076	6,940	10,091	6,147	5,644	3.53	-8.18
United States of America	12,488	12,579	16,901	17,545	15,182	9.50	-13.47
EAST ASIA AND THE PACIFIC	1,416	4,672	1,307	2,668	3,148	1.97	17.99
North-East Asia	1,416	4,672	1,307	2,668	3,148	1.97	17.99
Japan	1,416	4,672	1,307	2,668	3,148	1.97	17.99
EUROPE	104,308	100,819	72,872	82,837	68,752	43.03	-17.00
Central/Eastern Europe	2,192	6,494	3,547	5,596	5,580	3.49	-0.29
Russian Federation	664	2,376	737	1,541	1,355	0.85	-12.07
Other countries Central/East Europe	1,528	4,118	2,810	4,055	4,225	2.64	4.19
Northern Europe	6,660	9,240	5,964	6,297	5,911	3.70	-6.13
United Kingdom	5,224	5,357	4,173	4,422	3,595	2.25	-18.70
Scandinavia	1,436	3,883	1,791	1,875	2,316	1.45	23.52
Southern Europe	17,064	18,433	9,695	12,392	10,766	6.74	-13.12
Italy	9,272	8,269	5,307	6,878	5,955	3.73	-13.42
Spain	7,792	10,164	4,388	5,514	4,811	3.01	-12.75
Western Europe	78,392	66,652	53,666	58,552	46,495	29.10	-20.59
Austria	988	2,638	660	1,906	1,648	1.03	-13.54
France	57,682	41,778	38,261	42,883	30,207	18.91	-29.56
Germany	6,962	9,033	5,380	4,937	5,428	3.40	9.95
Switzerland	2,480	5,037	2,723	2,520	2,815	1.76	11.71
Benelux	10,280	8,166	6,642	6,306	6,397	4.00	1.44
MIDDLE EAST	1,190	4,176	2,946	2,948	3,910	2.45	32.63
All countries of Middle East	1,190	4,176	2,946	2,948	3,910	2.45	32.63
NOT SPECIFIED	10,268	12,907	11,306	9,985	10,679	6.68	6.95
Other countries of the World	10,268	12,907	11,306	9,985	10,679	6.68	6.95

MALI

5. Overnight stays of non-resident tourists in hotels and similar establishments, by nationality

	2007	2008	2009	2010	2011	Market share 11	% Change 11-10
TOTAL	384,285	464,975	352,801	290,936	283,729	100.00	-2.48
AFRICA	87,171	114,776	107,972	97,038	93,136	32.83	-4.02
West Africa	61,329	72,956	66,435	64,929	59,451	20.95	-8.44
All countries of West Africa	61,329	72,956	66,435	64,929	59,451	20.95	-8.44
Other Africa	25,842	41,820	41,537	32,109	33,685	11.87	4.91
Other countries of Africa	25,842	41,820	41,537	32,109	33,685	11.87	4.91
AMERICAS	47,673	46,770	57,747	41,200	30,877	10.88	-25.06
North America	47,673	46,770	57,747	41,200	30,877	10.88	-25.06
Canada	12,348	15,872	20,859	10,326	9,534	3.36	-7.67
United States of America	35,325	30,898	36,888	30,874	21,343	7.52	-30.87
EAST ASIA AND THE PACIFIC	3,447	9,234	1,307	4,448	5,358	1.89	20.46
North-East Asia	3,447	9,234	1,307	4,448	5,358	1.89	20.46
Japan	3,447	9,234	1,307	4,448	5,358	1.89	20.46
EUROPE	223,020	237,700	157,888	123,796	94,768	33.40	-23.45
Central/Eastern Europe	5,760	11,244	8,007	7,380	9,299	3.28	26.00
Russian Federation	1,923	3,904	1,947	2,005	3,760	1.33	87.53
Other countries Central/East Europe	3,837	7,340	6,060	5,375	5,539	1.95	3.05
Northern Europe	15,699	21,173	13,956	9,167	8,078	2.85	-11.88
United Kingdom	11,826	14,846	9,986	6,712	5,028	1.77	-25.09
Scandinavia	3,873	6,327	3,970	2,455	3,050	1.07	24.24
Southern Europe	36,507	34,223	20,471	17,563	15,348	5.41	-12.61
Italy	19,119	15,517	11,081	9,720	7,970	2.81	-18.00
Spain	17,388	18,706	9,390	7,843	7,378	2.60	-5.93
Western Europe	165,054	171,060	115,454	89,686	62,043	21.87	-30.82
Austria	2,070	4,469	1,355	2,898	2,077	0.73	-28.33
France	118,449	122,486	81,028	65,721	37,776	13.31	-42.52
Germany	15,831	17,390	12,824	8,094	8,234	2.90	1.73
Switzerland	6,135	9,075	6,155	3,716	3,972	1.40	6.89
Benelux	22,569	17,640	14,092	9,257	9,984	3.52	7.85
MIDDLE EAST	2,976	8,606	6,101	4,409	4,969	1.75	12.70
All countries of Middle East	2,976	8,606	6,101	4,409	4,969	1.75	12.70
NOT SPECIFIED	19,998	47,889	21,786	20,045	54,621	19.25	172.49
Other countries of the World	19,998	47,889	21,786	20,045	54,621	19.25	172.49

MALTA

1. Arrivals of non-resident tourists at national borders, by nationality

		2007	2008	2009	2010	2011	Market share 11	% Change 11-10
TOTAL	(*)	1,243,510	1,290,856	1,182,489	1,336,391	1,411,748	100.00	5.64
AMERICAS		20,423	18,021	13,943	16,297	16,229	1.15	-0.42
North America		20,423	18,021	13,943	16,297	16,229	1.15	-0.42
United States of America		20,423	18,021	13,943	16,297	16,229	1.15	-0.42
EUROPE		1,142,754	1,195,405	1,088,750	1,219,453	1,298,178	91.96	6.46
Central/Eastern Europe		62,063	65,690	56,944	64,251	69,870	4.95	8.75
Bulgaria		5,127	4,495	4,960	3,189	3,175	0.22	-0.44
Czech Republic		5,675	7,381	6,796	5,923	7,624	0.54	28.72
Estonia		1,114	1,010	749	1,511	1,299	0.09	-14.03
Hungary		9,420	8,327	7,848	7,764	7,565	0.54	-2.56
Latvia		1,215	896	908	1,171	1,369	0.10	16.91
Lithuania		1,626	3,206	2,168	1,672	2,156	0.15	28.95
Poland		5,965	7,079	7,139	12,071	12,923	0.92	7.06
Romania		6,633	7,721	5,557	4,280	6,024	0.43	40.75
Russian Federation		22,909	23,412	17,239	22,727	23,811	1.69	4.77
Slovakia		2,379	2,163	3,580	3,943	3,924	0.28	-0.48
Northern Europe		597,816	570,360	489,582	533,183	559,737	39.65	4.98
Denmark		27,986	23,985	21,268	28,807	33,270	2.36	15.49
Finland		12,438	12,632	9,697	11,925	7,045	0.50	-40.92
Ireland		28,130	30,489	24,328	25,167	26,992	1.91	7.25
Norway		15,313	16,489	6,470	14,973	12,694	0.90	-15.22
Sweden		31,545	32,409	29,347	37,121	40,019	2.83	7.81
United Kingdom		482,404	454,356	398,472	415,190	439,717	31.15	5.91
Southern Europe		167,275	211,436	223,151	298,713	274,461	19.44	-8.12
Greece		7,886	8,496	7,641	5,881	4,200	0.30	-28.58
Italy		113,651	144,456	161,736	217,727	199,830	14.15	-8.22
Portugal		5,187	6,680	4,347	4,320	3,852	0.27	-10.83
Slovenia		3,123	2,307	4,129	2,977	3,467	0.25	16.46
Spain		37,428	49,497	45,298	67,808	63,112	4.47	-6.93
Western Europe		310,809	343,215	300,777	313,862	356,011	25.22	13.43
Austria		20,384	19,825	21,217	19,900	19,638	1.39	-1.32
Belgium		26,456	29,619	23,746	24,296	31,713	2.25	30.53
France		75,149	81,152	71,931	86,532	103,688	7.34	19.83
Germany		130,049	150,793	127,374	126,190	134,585	9.53	6.65
Luxembourg		1,965	2,912	2,052	1,998	2,133	0.15	6.76
Netherlands		34,783	36,920	33,418	33,426	39,074	2.77	16.90
Switzerland		22,023	21,994	21,039	21,520	25,180	1.78	17.01
East Mediterranean Europe		4,791	4,704	18,296	9,444	7,135	0.51	-24.45
Cyprus		4,791	4,704	18,296	9,444	7,135	0.51	-24.45
Other Europe						30,964	2.19	
Other countries of Europe						30,964	2.19	
MIDDLE EAST		9,259	9,403	14,282	15,864	6,208	0.44	-60.87
Libya		9,259	9,403	14,282	15,864	6,208	0.44	-60.87
NOT SPECIFIED		71,074	68,027	65,514	84,777	91,133	6.46	7.50
Other countries of the World		71,074	68,027	65,514	84,777	91,133	6.46	7.50

MALTA

4. Arrivals of non-resident tourists in all types of accommodation establishments, by country of residence

		2007	2008	2009	2010	2011	Market share 11	% Change 11-10
TOTAL	(*)	**1,243,510**	**1,290,856**	**1,182,490**	**1,336,391**	**1,411,748**	**100.00**	**5.64**
AMERICAS		**20,423**	**18,021**	**13,943**	**16,296**	**16,228**	**1.15**	**-0.42**
North America		**20,423**	**18,021**	**13,943**	**16,296**	**16,228**	**1.15**	**-0.42**
United States of America		20,423	18,021	13,943	16,296	16,228	1.15	-0.42
EUROPE		**1,002,653**	**1,035,419**	**1,012,578**	**1,153,310**	**1,286,347**	**91.12**	**11.54**
Central/Eastern Europe		**22,909**	**23,412**	**17,240**	**22,726**	**23,811**	**1.69**	**4.77**
Russian Federation		22,909	23,412	17,240	22,726	23,811	1.69	4.77
Northern Europe		**557,247**	**527,248**	**489,579**	**533,184**	**645,718**	**45.74**	**21.11**
Denmark		27,986	23,985			33,270	2.36	
Ireland				24,328	25,167	26,991	1.91	7.25
Norway		15,313	16,498			12,694	0.90	
Sweden		31,545	32,409			40,019	2.83	
United Kingdom		482,403	454,356	398,472	415,191	439,717	31.15	5.91
Scandinavia				66,779	92,826	93,027	6.59	0.22
Southern Europe		**113,653**	**144,456**	**207,035**	**285,535**	**262,942**	**18.63**	**-7.91**
Italy		113,653	144,456	161,737	217,726	199,830	14.15	-8.22
Spain				45,298	67,809	63,112	4.47	-6.93
Western Europe		**308,844**	**340,303**	**298,724**	**311,865**	**353,876**	**25.07**	**13.47**
Austria		20,384	19,825	21,218	19,899	19,638	1.39	-1.31
Belgium		26,456	29,619	23,746	24,296	31,713	2.25	30.53
France		75,149	81,152	71,930	86,533	103,688	7.34	19.82
Germany		130,049	150,793	127,373	126,190	134,584	9.53	6.65
Netherlands		34,783	36,920	33,419	33,425	39,073	2.77	16.90
Switzerland		22,023	21,994	21,038	21,522	25,180	1.78	17.00
MIDDLE EAST		**9,259**	**9,403**	**14,281**	**15,864**	**6,208**	**0.44**	**-60.87**
Libya		9,259	9,403	14,281	15,864	6,208	0.44	-60.87
NOT SPECIFIED		**211,175**	**228,013**	**141,688**	**150,921**	**102,965**	**7.29**	**-31.78**
Other countries of the World		211,175	228,013	141,688	150,921	102,965	7.29	-31.78

MALTA

6. Overnight stays of non-resident tourists in all types of accommodation establishments, by country of residence

		2007	2008	2009	2010	2011	Market share 11	% Change 11-10
TOTAL	(*)	11,016,993	10,962,465	9,949,381	11,139,981	11,680,167	100.00	4.85
AMERICAS		172,207	146,031	114,542	139,272	123,204	1.05	-11.54
North America		172,207	146,031	114,542	139,272	123,204	1.05	-11.54
United States of America		172,207	146,031	114,542	139,272	123,204	1.05	-11.54
EUROPE		8,812,800	8,734,789	8,439,908	9,426,037	10,463,437	89.58	11.01
Central/Eastern Europe		274,953	272,596	232,976	299,510	309,346	2.65	3.28
Russian Federation		274,953	272,596	232,976	299,510	309,346	2.65	3.28
Northern Europe		5,133,308	4,752,199	4,325,799	4,730,636	5,597,662	47.92	18.33
Denmark		230,887	191,083			270,706	2.32	
Ireland				185,293	197,696	217,167	1.86	9.85
Norway		124,544	123,871			111,748	0.96	
Sweden		258,834	246,857			284,697	2.44	
United Kingdom		4,519,043	4,190,388	3,632,460	3,815,300	3,985,245	34.12	4.45
Scandinavia				508,046	717,640	728,099	6.23	1.46
Southern Europe		814,807	985,622	1,410,486	1,836,319	1,696,643	14.53	-7.61
Italy		814,807	985,622	993,825	1,270,553	1,178,197	10.09	-7.27
Spain				416,661	565,766	518,446	4.44	-8.36
Western Europe		2,589,732	2,724,372	2,470,647	2,559,572	2,859,786	24.48	11.73
Austria		166,358	146,381	165,497	150,003	145,883	1.25	-2.75
Belgium		201,128	211,820	190,778	181,393	219,556	1.88	21.04
France		609,258	608,425	586,107	669,355	779,743	6.68	16.49
Germany		1,099,252	1,268,844	1,072,508	1,093,698	1,150,938	9.85	5.23
Netherlands		285,628	292,170	272,853	277,998	331,827	2.84	19.36
Switzerland		228,108	196,732	182,904	187,125	231,839	1.98	23.90
MIDDLE EAST		76,581	73,809	103,103	131,773	56,155	0.48	-57.39
Libya		76,581	73,809	103,103	131,773	56,155	0.48	-57.39
NOT SPECIFIED		1,955,405	2,007,836	1,291,828	1,442,899	1,037,371	8.88	-28.11
Other countries of the World		1,955,405	2,007,836	1,291,828	1,442,899	1,037,371	8.88	-28.11

MARSHALL ISLANDS

1. Arrivals of non-resident tourists at national borders, by nationality

		2007	2008	2009	2010	2011	Market share 11	% Change 11-10
TOTAL	(*)	**7,200**	**6,022**	**5,372**	**4,563**	**4,555**	**100.00**	**-0.18**
AMERICAS		**1,843**	**1,725**	**1,614**	**1,712**	**1,619**	**35.54**	**-5.43**
North America		**1,744**	**1,627**	**1,519**	**1,700**	**1,594**	**34.99**	**-6.24**
Canada		60	64	44	46	45	0.99	-2.17
United States of America		1,684	1,563	1,475	1,654	1,549	34.01	-6.35
Other Americas		**99**	**98**	**95**	**12**	**25**	**0.55**	**108.33**
Other countries of the Americas		99	98	95	12	25	0.55	108.33
EAST ASIA AND THE PACIFIC		**4,925**	**4,036**	**3,501**	**2,622**	**2,681**	**58.86**	**2.25**
North-East Asia		**2,426**	**2,105**	**1,909**	**1,164**	**1,030**	**22.61**	**-11.51**
China		181	93	129	105	126	2.77	20.00
Taiwan, Province of China		352	423	300	422	383	8.41	-9.24
Japan		1,798	1,501	1,431	585	464	10.19	-20.68
Korea, Republic of		95	88	49	52	57	1.25	9.62
South-East Asia		**298**	**285**	**240**	**274**	**232**	**5.09**	**-15.33**
Philippines		298	285	240	274	232	5.09	-15.33
Australasia		**550**	**308**	**307**	**321**	**357**	**7.84**	**11.21**
Australia		365	203	216	202	245	5.38	21.29
New Zealand		185	105	91	119	112	2.46	-5.88
Melanesia		**96**	**91**	**95**	**116**	**120**	**2.63**	**3.45**
Fiji		96	91	95	116	120	2.63	3.45
Micronesia		**960**	**757**	**505**	**508**	**752**	**16.51**	**48.03**
Kiribati		263	73	97	69	54	1.19	-21.74
Guam		9	26	16	14	56	1.23	300.00
Nauru		197	11	6	24	8	0.18	-66.67
Micronesia, Federated States of		430	589	327	338	539	11.83	59.47
Palau		61	58	59	63	95	2.09	50.79
Polynesia		**21**	**5**	**16**	**14**	**11**	**0.24**	**-21.43**
Tuvalu		21	5	16	14	11	0.24	-21.43
Other East Asia and the Pacific		**574**	**485**	**429**	**225**	**179**	**3.93**	**-20.44**
Other countries of Asia		421	417	369	74	63	1.38	-14.86
Other countries of Oceania		153	68	60	151	116	2.55	-23.18
EUROPE		**322**	**218**	**207**	**211**	**209**	**4.59**	**-0.95**
Northern Europe		**41**	**28**	**20**	**53**	**63**	**1.38**	**18.87**
United Kingdom		41	28	20	53	63	1.38	18.87
Western Europe		**38**	**35**	**31**	**39**	**18**	**0.40**	**-53.85**
Germany		38	35	31	39	18	0.40	-53.85
Other Europe		**243**	**155**	**156**	**119**	**128**	**2.81**	**7.56**
Other countries of Europe		243	155	156	119	128	2.81	7.56
NOT SPECIFIED		**110**	**43**	**50**	**18**	**46**	**1.01**	**155.56**
Other countries of the World		110	43	50	18	46	1.01	155.56

MARSHALL ISLANDS

1. Arrivals of non-resident tourists at national borders, by country of residence

		2007	2008	2009	2010	2011	Market share 11	% Change 11-10
TOTAL	(*)	7,200	6,022	5,372	4,563	4,559	100.00	-0.09
AMERICAS		1,703	1,480	1,354	1,332	1,322	29.00	-0.75
North America		1,612	1,408	1,297	1,323	1,297	28.45	-1.97
Canada		60	57	41	26	26	0.57	
United States of America		1,552	1,351	1,256	1,297	1,271	27.88	-2.00
Other Americas		91	72	57	9	25	0.55	177.78
Other countries of the Americas		91	72	57	9	25	0.55	177.78
EAST ASIA AND THE PACIFIC		4,382	3,663	3,263	2,934	2,877	63.11	-1.94
North-East Asia		2,300	1,933	1,731	1,080	946	20.75	-12.41
China		157	61	89	79	83	1.82	5.06
Taiwan, Province of China		313	375	255	404	378	8.29	-6.44
Japan		1,755	1,427	1,349	557	435	9.54	-21.90
Korea, Republic of		75	70	38	40	50	1.10	25.00
South-East Asia		257	236	196	216	194	4.26	-10.19
Philippines		257	236	196	216	194	4.26	-10.19
Australasia		501	275	271	274	313	6.87	14.23
Australia		332	165	177	164	204	4.47	24.39
New Zealand		169	110	94	110	109	2.39	-0.91
Melanesia		92	123	119	138	152	3.33	10.14
Fiji		92	123	119	138	152	3.33	10.14
Micronesia		833	757	654	861	982	21.54	14.05
Kiribati		215	56	76	59	48	1.05	-18.64
Guam		27	164	193	325	293	6.43	-9.85
Nauru		193	9	5	24	10	0.22	-58.33
Micronesia, Federated States of		339	474	319	383	536	11.76	39.95
Palau		59	54	61	70	95	2.08	35.71
Polynesia		15	2	8	14	10	0.22	-28.57
Tuvalu		15	2	8	14	10	0.22	-28.57
Other East Asia and the Pacific		384	337	284	351	280	6.14	-20.23
Other countries of Asia		249	254	207	85	70	1.54	-17.65
Other countries of Oceania		135	83	77	266	210	4.61	-21.05
EUROPE		278	177	153	144	137	3.01	-4.86
Northern Europe		33	13	14	26	37	0.81	42.31
United Kingdom		33	13	14	26	37	0.81	42.31
Western Europe		34	36	24	28	10	0.22	-64.29
Germany		34	36	24	28	10	0.22	-64.29
Other Europe		211	128	115	90	90	1.97	
Other countries of Europe		211	128	115	90	90	1.97	
NOT SPECIFIED		837	702	602	153	223	4.89	45.75
Other countries of the World		837	702	602	153	223	4.89	45.75

MARSHALL ISLANDS

6. Overnight stays of non-resident tourists in all types of accommodation establishments, by country of residence

	2007	2008	2009	2010	2011	Market share 11	% Change 11-10
TOTAL	33,527	24,136	27,648	33,705	34,521	100.00	2.42
AMERICAS	10,542	8,176	11,408	12,390	13,183	38.19	6.40
North America	9,996	7,844	10,950	12,301	11,010	31.89	-10.50
Canada	424	610	485	452	276	0.80	-38.94
United States of America	9,572	7,234	10,465	11,849	10,734	31.09	-9.41
Other Americas	546	332	458	89	2,173	6.29	2341.57
Other countries of the Americas	546	332	458	89	2,173	6.29	2341.57
EAST ASIA AND THE PACIFIC	18,650	13,675	12,847	19,563	19,660	56.95	0.50
North-East Asia	8,807	6,617	5,150	7,079	5,842	16.92	-17.47
China	576	297	351	326	473	1.37	45.09
Taiwan, Province of China	790	965	1,065	2,688	2,086	6.04	-22.40
Japan	7,139	5,141	3,616	3,882	2,860	8.28	-26.33
Korea, Republic of	302	214	118	183	423	1.23	131.15
South-East Asia	1,311	977	1,190	1,054	1,199	3.47	13.76
Philippines	1,311	977	1,190	1,054	1,199	3.47	13.76
Australasia	3,681	1,901	1,787	2,115	2,755	7.98	30.26
Australia	2,752	1,240	1,167	1,497	1,839	5.33	22.85
New Zealand	929	661	620	618	916	2.65	48.22
Melanesia	593	717	790	983	1,715	4.97	74.47
Fiji	593	717	790	983	1,715	4.97	74.47
Micronesia	2,854	2,502	2,708	4,686	5,864	16.99	25.14
Kiribati	658	434	458	762	833	2.41	9.32
Guam	88	656	770	1,614	1,181	3.42	-26.83
Nauru	1,027	74	43	158	67	0.19	-57.59
Micronesia, Federated States of	818	1,165	1,110	1,738	2,972	8.61	71.00
Palau	263	173	327	414	811	2.35	95.89
Polynesia	61	9		52	56	0.16	7.69
Tuvalu	61	9		52	56	0.16	7.69
Other East Asia and the Pacific	1,343	952	1,222	3,594	2,229	6.46	-37.98
Other countries of Asia	575	445	885	560	386	1.12	-31.07
Other countries of Oceania	768	507	337	3,034	1,843	5.34	-39.26
EUROPE	2,024	1,070	1,850	836	939	2.72	12.32
Northern Europe	218	166	998	227	296	0.86	30.40
United Kingdom	218	166	998	227	296	0.86	30.40
Western Europe	241	219	116	169	37	0.11	-78.11
Germany	241	219	116	169	37	0.11	-78.11
Other Europe	1,565	685	736	440	606	1.76	37.73
Other countries of Europe	1,565	685	736	440	606	1.76	37.73
NOT SPECIFIED	2,311	1,215	1,543	916	739	2.14	-19.32
Other countries of the World	2,311	1,215	1,543	916	739	2.14	-19.32

MARTINIQUE

1. Arrivals of non-resident tourists at national borders, by country of residence

		2007	2008	2009	2010	2011	Market share 11	% Change 11-10
TOTAL	(*)	**501,491**	**481,224**	**441,648**	**478,060**	**496,538**	**100.00**	**3.87**
AMERICAS		**92,980**	**85,831**	**63,145**	**85,239**	**86,363**	**17.39**	**1.32**
Caribbean		**64,242**	**64,250**	**46,624**	**56,961**	**57,761**	**11.63**	**1.40**
Barbados		2,302	1,337	1,164	2,871	2,842	0.57	-1.01
Dominica		2,738	1,383	1,166	3,648	2,841	0.57	-22.12
Guadeloupe		47,239	54,372	38,094	39,863	42,844	8.63	7.48
Saint Lucia		9,932	6,338	5,601	8,201	3,997	0.80	-51.26
Other countries of the Caribbean		2,031	820	599	2,378	5,237	1.05	120.23
North America		**17,722**	**10,397**	**7,582**	**15,998**	**15,389**	**3.10**	**-3.81**
Canada		5,356	3,349	1,292	9,535	9,570	1.93	0.37
United States of America		12,366	7,048	6,290	6,463	5,819	1.17	-9.96
South America		**11,016**	**11,184**	**8,939**	**12,280**	**13,213**	**2.66**	**7.60**
French Guiana		7,232	8,572	7,141	9,878	10,368	2.09	4.96
Venezuela		3,784	2,612	1,798	2,402	2,845	0.57	18.44
EUROPE		**405,231**	**390,644**	**367,030**	**389,306**	**404,670**	**81.50**	**3.95**
Northern Europe		**2,553**	**2,807**	**1,606**	**2,595**	**2,775**	**0.56**	**6.94**
United Kingdom/Ireland		1,761	1,786	938	1,610	1,427	0.29	-11.37
Scandinavia		792	1,021	668	985	1,348	0.27	36.85
Southern Europe		**5,627**	**1,998**	**2,029**	**2,349**	**2,497**	**0.50**	**6.30**
Italy		5,627	1,998	2,029	2,349	2,497	0.50	6.30
Western Europe		**395,007**	**385,099**	**362,994**	**383,570**	**397,285**	**80.01**	**3.58**
France		379,928	371,073	354,846	372,426	385,358	77.61	3.47
Germany		3,597	2,515	1,011	2,480	2,567	0.52	3.51
Switzerland		3,753	2,963	2,314	2,706	2,138	0.43	-20.99
Benelux		7,729	8,548	4,823	5,958	7,222	1.45	21.22
Other Europe		**2,044**	**740**	**401**	**792**	**2,113**	**0.43**	**166.79**
Other countries of Europe		2,044	740	401	792	2,113	0.43	166.79
NOT SPECIFIED		**3,280**	**4,749**	**11,473**	**3,515**	**5,505**	**1.11**	**56.61**
Other countries of the World		3,280	4,749	11,473	3,515	5,505	1.11	56.61

MARTINIQUE

3. Arrivals of non-resident tourists in hotels and similar establishments, by nationality

	2007	2008	2009	2010	2011	Market share 11	% Change 11-10
TOTAL	208,793	166,065	174,400	177,826	192,816	100.00	8.43
AMERICAS	29,124	25,815	17,003	27,085	17,954	9.31	-33.71
Caribbean	19,893	20,390	12,393	17,774	12,230	6.34	-31.19
All countries of the Caribbean	19,893	20,390	12,393	17,774	12,230	6.34	-31.19
North America	9,231	5,425	4,610	9,311	5,724	2.97	-38.52
Canada	2,415	1,419	463	4,771	3,326	1.72	-30.29
United States of America	6,816	4,006	4,147	4,540	2,398	1.24	-47.18
EUROPE	178,141	137,759	153,504	149,458	172,978	89.71	15.74
Western Europe	164,688	129,578	147,766	141,923	163,720	84.91	15.36
France	164,688	129,578	147,766	141,923	163,720	84.91	15.36
Other Europe	13,453	8,181	5,738	7,535	9,258	4.80	22.87
Other countries of Europe	13,453	8,181	5,738	7,535	9,258	4.80	22.87
NOT SPECIFIED	1,528	2,491	3,893	1,283	1,884	0.98	46.84
Other countries of the World	1,528	2,491	3,893	1,283	1,884	0.98	46.84

MARTINIQUE

4. Arrivals of non-resident tourists in all types of accommodation establishments, by nationality

	2007	2008	2009	2010	2011	Market share 11	% Change 11-10
TOTAL	501,493	481,225	441,648	478,059	496,538	100.00	3.87
AMERICAS	92,980	85,830	63,146	85,238	86,363	17.39	1.32
Caribbean	75,258	75,433	55,564	69,240	70,974	14.29	2.50
All countries of the Caribbean	75,258	75,433	55,564	69,240	70,974	14.29	2.50
North America	17,722	10,397	7,582	15,998	15,389	3.10	-3.81
Canada	5,356	3,349	1,292	9,535	9,570	1.93	0.37
United States of America	12,366	7,048	6,290	6,463	5,819	1.17	-9.96
EUROPE	405,232	390,646	367,029	389,306	404,669	81.50	3.95
Western Europe	379,928	371,073	354,846	372,426	385,358	77.61	3.47
France	379,928	371,073	354,846	372,426	385,358	77.61	3.47
Other Europe	25,304	19,573	12,183	16,880	19,311	3.89	14.40
Other countries of Europe	25,304	19,573	12,183	16,880	19,311	3.89	14.40
NOT SPECIFIED	3,281	4,749	11,473	3,515	5,506	1.11	56.64
Other countries of the World	3,281	4,749	11,473	3,515	5,506	1.11	56.64

MARTINIQUE

5. Overnight stays of non-resident tourists in hotels and similar establishments, by country of residence

	2007	2008	2009	2010	2011	Market share 11	% Change 11-10
TOTAL	1,761,161	1,340,701	1,388,809	1,401,434	1,652,360	100.00	17.90
AMERICAS	244,634	144,525	136,376	150,450	209,708	12.69	39.39
Caribbean	194,324	123,061	120,020	86,951	168,141	10.18	93.37
All countries of the Caribbean	194,324	123,061	120,020	86,951	168,141	10.18	93.37
North America	50,310	21,464	16,356	63,499	41,567	2.52	-34.54
Canada	18,221	9,242	3,720	39,177	23,881	1.45	-39.04
United States of America	32,089	12,222	12,636	24,322	17,686	1.07	-27.28
EUROPE	1,505,338	1,184,787	1,222,866	1,243,668	1,421,020	86.00	14.26
Western Europe	1,426,180	1,146,547	1,189,611	1,198,467	1,367,728	82.77	14.12
France	1,426,180	1,146,547	1,189,611	1,198,467	1,367,728	82.77	14.12
Other Europe	79,158	38,240	33,255	45,201	53,292	3.23	17.90
Other countries of Europe	79,158	38,240	33,255	45,201	53,292	3.23	17.90
NOT SPECIFIED	11,189	11,389	29,567	7,316	21,632	1.31	195.68
Other countries of the World	11,189	11,389	29,567	7,316	21,632	1.31	195.68

MARTINIQUE

6. Overnight stays of non-resident tourists in all types of accommodation establishments, by nationality

	2007	2008	2009	2010	2011	Market share 11	% Change 11-10
TOTAL	6,475,396	6,312,307	5,793,364	6,368,874	6,196,064	100.00	-2.71
AMERICAS	899,463	680,450	576,397	773,454	786,369	12.69	1.67
Caribbean	714,484	579,396	508,269	579,527	630,498	10.18	8.80
All countries of the Caribbean	714,484	579,396	508,269	579,527	630,498	10.18	8.80
North America	184,979	101,054	68,128	193,927	155,871	2.52	-19.62
Canada	66,995	43,511	15,495	134,233	89,551	1.45	-33.29
United States of America	117,984	57,543	52,633	59,694	66,320	1.07	11.10
EUROPE	5,534,792	5,578,233	5,093,806	5,561,063	5,328,580	86.00	-4.18
Western Europe	5,243,744	5,398,191	4,955,283	5,387,193	5,128,744	82.77	-4.80
France	5,243,744	5,398,191	4,955,283	5,387,193	5,128,744	82.77	-4.80
Other Europe	291,048	180,042	138,523	173,870	199,836	3.23	14.93
Other countries of Europe	291,048	180,042	138,523	173,870	199,836	3.23	14.93
NOT SPECIFIED	41,141	53,624	123,161	34,357	81,115	1.31	136.09
Other countries of the World	41,141	53,624	123,161	34,357	81,115	1.31	136.09

MAURITIUS

1. Arrivals of non-resident tourists at national borders, by country of residence

	2007	2008	2009	2010	2011	Market share 11	% Change 11-10
TOTAL	906,971	930,456	871,356	934,827	964,642	100.00	3.19
AFRICA	210,553	213,383	203,846	225,754	230,673	23.91	2.18
East Africa	124,925	124,461	125,773	140,190	139,415	14.45	-0.55
Burundi	71	43	63	76	80	0.01	5.26
Comoros	675	655	606	746	969	0.10	29.89
Ethiopia	120	121	128	88	155	0.02	76.14
Eritrea	11	5	7	11	17	0.00	54.55
Djibouti	43	23	20	26	25	0.00	-3.85
Kenya	1,790	1,997	1,386	1,548	1,914	0.20	23.64
Madagascar	8,842	10,905	8,333	9,833	11,449	1.19	16.43
Malawi	160	245	150	185	197	0.02	6.49
Mozambique	346	403	377	396	414	0.04	4.55
Reunion	95,823	96,174	104,946	114,914	113,000	11.71	-1.67
Rwanda	85	68	62	86	75	0.01	-12.79
Seychelles	14,275	10,604	7,532	10,160	8,485	0.88	-16.49
Somalia	1	8	3	1	7	0.00	600.00
Zimbabwe	1,669	1,809	1,326	1,204	1,495	0.15	24.17
Uganda	182	238	174	164	264	0.03	60.98
United Republic of Tanzania	405	541	325	321	481	0.05	49.84
Zambia	427	622	335	431	388	0.04	-9.98
Central Africa	358	566	466	519	621	0.06	19.65
Angola	90	185	123	155	208	0.02	34.19
Cameroon	87	148	147	160	183	0.02	14.38
Central African Republic	9	3	5	10	12	0.00	20.00
Chad	9	3	4	8	13	0.00	62.50
Congo	118	150	144	147	155	0.02	5.44
Democratic Republic of the Congo	10	13	3	2			
Equatorial Guinea		2		4	8	0.00	100.00
Gabon	34	62	38	30	39	0.00	30.00
Sao Tome and Principe	1	2	3		3	0.00	
North Africa	668	1,026	1,024	913	1,091	0.11	19.50
Algeria	121	242	242	223	289	0.03	29.60
Morocco	218	323	389	328	348	0.04	6.10
Sudan	89	52	55	64	64	0.01	
Tunisia	240	409	338	298	390	0.04	30.87
Southern Africa	82,859	85,783	75,446	82,944	87,856	9.11	5.92
Botswana	330	459	450	487	435	0.05	-10.68
Lesotho	72	92	86	107	125	0.01	16.82
Namibia	614	598	615	761	856	0.09	12.48
South Africa	81,733	84,448	74,176	81,458	86,232	8.94	5.86
Swaziland	110	186	119	131	208	0.02	58.78
West Africa	923	1,013	1,065	1,186	1,683	0.17	41.91
Cape Verde	24	48	31	53	33	0.00	-37.74
Benin	34	35	42	44	72	0.01	63.64
Gambia	31	22	16	26	37	0.00	42.31
Ghana	186	218	254	263	299	0.03	13.69
Guinea	80	75	18	16	68	0.01	325.00
Côte d'Ivoire	113	168	152	157	211	0.02	34.39
Liberia	2	7	5	16	13	0.00	-18.75
Mali	35	40	34	29	57	0.01	96.55
Mauritania	11	15	32	16	11	0.00	-31.25
Niger	2	2	13	8	19	0.00	137.50
Nigeria	190	203	272	318	481	0.05	51.26
Guinea-Bissau		1	5	2	2	0.00	
Senegal	125	120	129	152	222	0.02	46.05
Sierra Leone	20	17	8	18	42	0.00	133.33

MAURITIUS

1. Arrivals of non-resident tourists at national borders, by country of residence

	2007	2008	2009	2010	2011	Market share 11	% Change 11-10
Togo	35	21	18	26	70	0.01	169.23
Burkina Faso	35	21	36	42	46	0.00	9.52
Other Africa	**820**	**534**	**72**	**2**	**7**	**0.00**	**250.00**
Other countries of Africa	820	534	72	2	7	0.00	250.00
AMERICAS	**10,462**	**13,709**	**13,071**	**13,724**	**14,424**	**1.50**	**5.10**
Caribbean	**141**	**176**	**100**	**119**	**159**	**0.02**	**33.61**
Antigua and Barbuda		1		2			
Bahamas	8	1	1	7	6	0.00	-14.29
Barbados	20	10	7	6	4	0.00	-33.33
Bermuda	7	7	3				
Cuba	15	25	17	22	27	0.00	22.73
Dominica	1	3	5	3	2	0.00	-33.33
Dominican Republic	7	6	3	11	17	0.00	54.55
Grenada	1	5	4	5	2	0.00	-60.00
Guadeloupe	10	11					
Haiti	2	9	9	13	15	0.00	15.38
Jamaica	30	46	19	23	31	0.00	34.78
Martinique	11	5	1				
Anguilla	6	16	1				
Trinidad and Tobago	23	31	30	27	55	0.01	103.70
Central America	**41**	**48**	**39**	**50**	**38**	**0.00**	**-24.00**
Belize	1	2	8	1	4	0.00	300.00
Costa Rica	17	10	8	9	15	0.00	66.67
El Salvador	11	12	4	5	4	0.00	-20.00
Guatemala	3	8	6	12	6	0.00	-50.00
Honduras	5	11	9	19	9	0.00	-52.63
Nicaragua	4	5	4	4			
North America	**8,116**	**10,391**	**10,600**	**11,054**	**10,870**	**1.13**	**-1.66**
Canada	2,590	3,188	3,532	3,619	3,887	0.40	7.41
Greenland	1						
Mexico	74	114	117	119	113	0.01	-5.04
United States of America	5,451	7,089	6,951	7,316	6,870	0.71	-6.10
South America	**2,150**	**3,074**	**2,208**	**2,469**	**3,330**	**0.35**	**34.87**
Argentina	417	592	498	627	657	0.07	4.78
Bolivia	7	7	10	12	7	0.00	-41.67
Brazil	1,323	2,015	1,331	1,459	2,235	0.23	53.19
Chile	128	153	124	137	153	0.02	11.68
Colombia	43	64	64	57	79	0.01	38.60
Ecuador	11	13	15	28	27	0.00	-3.57
Guyana	14	14	7	5	13	0.00	160.00
Paraguay	11	11	17	14	21	0.00	50.00
Peru	122	124	73	68	67	0.01	-1.47
Suriname	32	9	17	8	21	0.00	162.50
Uruguay	13	27	25	15	18	0.00	20.00
Venezuela	29	45	27	39	32	0.00	-17.95
Other Americas	**14**	**20**	**124**	**32**	**27**	**0.00**	**-15.63**
Other countries of the Americas	14	20	124	32	27	0.00	-15.63
EAST ASIA AND THE PACIFIC	**39,681**	**39,843**	**26,534**	**30,911**	**45,590**	**4.73**	**47.49**
North-East Asia	**11,964**	**12,901**	**10,109**	**11,486**	**20,197**	**2.09**	**75.84**
China	7,739	8,425	6,925	7,609	15,133	1.57	98.88
Taiwan, Province of China	1,129	823	730	897	987	0.10	10.03
Hong Kong, China	649	641	382	415	593	0.06	42.89
Japan	1,730	1,751	1,351	1,485	1,545	0.16	4.04
Korea, Republic of	710	1,253	704	1,067	1,935	0.20	81.35
Macao, China	4		1		1	0.00	
Mongolia	3	8	16	13	3	0.00	-76.92

MAURITIUS

1. Arrivals of non-resident tourists at national borders, by country of residence

	2007	2008	2009	2010	2011	Market share 11	% Change 11-10
South-East Asia	**7,050**	**6,771**	**5,227**	**7,138**	**8,605**	**0.89**	**20.55**
Brunei Darussalam	9	6	18	5	10	0.00	100.00
Myanmar	9	18	21	14	71	0.01	407.14
Cambodia	4	11	11	66	69	0.01	4.55
Indonesia	1,157	1,297	853	1,275	1,615	0.17	26.67
Lao People's Democratic Republic	4	1	1	2	2	0.00	
Malaysia	1,865	1,509	1,164	1,438	1,989	0.21	38.32
Philippines	1,339	1,437	1,022	1,773	1,850	0.19	4.34
Singapore	2,020	1,758	1,657	1,909	2,461	0.26	28.92
Viet Nam	435	497	293	426	348	0.04	-18.31
Thailand	208	237	187	230	190	0.02	-17.39
Australasia	**20,552**	**20,092**	**11,113**	**12,219**	**16,725**	**1.73**	**36.88**
Australia	19,635	18,852	10,363	11,493	15,726	1.63	36.83
New Zealand	917	1,240	750	726	999	0.10	37.60
Melanesia	**93**	**60**	**21**	**22**	**30**	**0.00**	**36.36**
Solomon Islands	1				4	0.00	
Fiji	29	28	13	17	19	0.00	11.76
New Caledonia	56	31					
Vanuatu	1		6	3	3	0.00	
Papua New Guinea	6	1	2	2	4	0.00	100.00
Micronesia	**1**	**1**	**1**				
Kiribati	1						
Nauru		1	1				
Polynesia	**10**	**6**	**2**				
American Samoa	2		1				
Cook Islands			1				
French Polynesia	8	6					
Other East Asia and the Pacific	**11**	**12**	**61**	**46**	**33**	**0.00**	**-28.26**
Other countries of Asia		2	54	40	27	0.00	-32.50
Other countries of Oceania	11	10	7	6	6	0.00	
EUROPE	**596,132**	**608,929**	**579,897**	**605,790**	**610,181**	**63.25**	**0.72**
Central/Eastern Europe	**20,358**	**23,758**	**19,445**	**19,944**	**26,692**	**2.77**	**33.83**
Azerbaijan	17	66	47	73	78	0.01	6.85
Armenia	34	24	24	32	48	0.00	50.00
Bulgaria	346	629	511	498	639	0.07	28.31
Belarus	117	138	169	149	223	0.02	49.66
Czech Republic	3,044	4,166	3,487	3,477	4,081	0.42	17.37
Estonia	453	561	989	549	288	0.03	-47.54
Georgia	24	13	18	34	8	0.00	-76.47
Hungary	3,360	3,045	1,382	1,376	1,231	0.13	-10.54
Kazakhstan	277	298	276	282	204	0.02	-27.66
Latvia	317	313	268	219	250	0.03	14.16
Lithuania	343	322	309	343	372	0.04	8.45
Republic of Moldova	34	12	68	59	79	0.01	33.90
Poland	2,413	3,278	2,880	2,560	2,995	0.31	16.99
Romania	809	996	814	960	1,055	0.11	9.90
Russian Federation	5,968	6,763	5,626	6,615	12,224	1.27	84.79
Slovakia	1,230	1,308	1,172	1,366	1,263	0.13	-7.54
Tajikistan	4	1	1	4	3	0.00	-25.00
Turkmenistan		1	5	3	1	0.00	-66.67
Ukraine	1,334	1,615	1,178	1,206	1,485	0.15	23.13
USSR (former)	155	181	19		2	0.00	
Uzbekistan	21	28	37	50	24	0.00	-52.00
Other countries Central/East Europe	58		165	89	139	0.01	56.18
Northern Europe	**135,326**	**133,209**	**120,206**	**114,926**	**104,004**	**10.78**	**-9.50**
Denmark	4,062	3,350	2,770	2,678	2,549	0.26	-4.82

MAURITIUS

1. Arrivals of non-resident tourists at national borders, by country of residence

	2007	2008	2009	2010	2011	Market share 11	% Change 11-10
Faeroe Islands	1	2	1				
Finland	4,283	4,792	3,600	4,026	3,133	0.32	-22.18
Iceland	44	75	55	44	38	0.00	-13.64
Ireland	5,851	5,002	4,249	3,460	2,717	0.28	-21.47
Norway	3,897	3,764	2,475	2,674	3,060	0.32	14.44
Sweden	9,891	8,305	5,060	4,496	4,325	0.45	-3.80
United Kingdom	107,297	107,919	101,996	97,548	88,182	9.14	-9.60
Southern Europe	**86,849**	**84,844**	**72,015**	**70,548**	**68,109**	**7.06**	**-3.46**
Albania	37	45	71	49	73	0.01	48.98
Andorra	22	28	30	17	20	0.00	17.65
Bosnia and Herzegovina	40	50	37	44	36	0.00	-18.18
Croatia	271	267	244	272	368	0.04	35.29
Gibraltar		3					
Greece	2,159	2,343	1,766	1,447	1,342	0.14	-7.26
Italy	69,510	66,432	56,736	56,540	52,747	5.47	-6.71
Malta	145	182	206	247	365	0.04	47.77
Portugal	1,892	1,863	2,098	2,680	2,426	0.25	-9.48
San Marino	22	20	52	115	59	0.01	-48.70
Slovenia	1,402	1,337	1,106	991	841	0.09	-15.14
Spain	11,092	12,001	9,549	8,096	9,801	1.02	21.06
TFYR of Macedonia	14	36	29	30	21	0.00	-30.00
Serbia and Montenegro	243	237	91	20	10	0.00	-50.00
Western Europe	**351,925**	**365,358**	**366,947**	**398,851**	**409,702**	**42.47**	**2.72**
Austria	10,969	8,974	8,106	9,255	8,822	0.91	-4.68
Belgium	10,945	11,796	10,254	10,214	12,029	1.25	17.77
France	240,028	260,054	275,599	302,185	302,004	31.31	-0.06
Germany	65,165	61,484	51,279	52,886	56,331	5.84	6.51
Liechtenstein	45	31	61	80	98	0.01	22.50
Luxembourg	753	819	591	615	710	0.07	15.45
Monaco	143	112	181	174	167	0.02	-4.02
Netherlands	6,331	6,051	5,527	4,865	5,179	0.54	6.45
Switzerland	17,546	16,037	15,349	18,577	24,362	2.53	31.14
East Mediterranean Europe	**1,663**	**1,659**	**1,263**	**1,496**	**1,674**	**0.17**	**11.90**
Cyprus	579	436	278	314	291	0.03	-7.32
Israel	479	566	391	425	574	0.06	35.06
Turkey	605	657	594	757	809	0.08	6.87
Other Europe	**11**	**101**	**21**	**25**			
Other countries of Europe	11	101	21	25			
MIDDLE EAST	**4,591**	**7,158**	**5,702**	**6,012**	**6,448**	**0.67**	**7.25**
Bahrain	106	102	72	69	52	0.01	-24.64
Palestine	5	2	9	22	7	0.00	-68.18
Iraq	10	13	11	26	29	0.00	11.54
Jordan	99	138	178	156	153	0.02	-1.92
Kuwait	288	239	112	101	199	0.02	97.03
Lebanon	383	546	326	323	360	0.04	11.46
Libya	32	46	69	53	20	0.00	-62.26
Oman	99	112	52	57	78	0.01	36.84
Qatar	50	52	59	49	58	0.01	18.37
Saudi Arabia	1,094	1,283	1,161	1,197	1,188	0.12	-0.75
Syrian Arab Republic	75	70	101	64	41	0.00	-35.94
United Arab Emirates	1,971	4,109	3,141	3,470	3,780	0.39	8.93
Egypt	367	436	395	402	468	0.05	16.42
Yemen	12	10	16	23	15	0.00	-34.78
SOUTH ASIA	**44,762**	**45,848**	**41,014**	**51,348**	**55,743**	**5.78**	**8.56**
Bangladesh	276	286	496	207	226	0.02	9.18
Bhutan		1	1	3	1	0.00	-66.67

MAURITIUS

1. Arrivals of non-resident tourists at national borders, by country of residence

	2007	2008	2009	2010	2011	Market share 11	% Change 11-10
Sri Lanka	400	401	413	287	243	0.03	-15.33
India	42,974	43,911	39,252	49,779	53,955	5.59	8.39
Iran, Islamic Republic of	128	137	133	149	308	0.03	106.71
Maldives	46	51	18	28	48	0.00	71.43
Nepal	84	188	80	124	264	0.03	112.90
Pakistan	854	873	621	771	698	0.07	-9.47
NOT SPECIFIED	**790**	**1,586**	**1,292**	**1,288**	**1,583**	**0.16**	**22.90**
Other countries of the World	790	1,586	1,292	1,288	1,583	0.16	22.90

MAURITIUS

6. Overnight stays of non-resident tourists in all types of accommodation establishments, by country of residence

	2007	2008	2009	2010	2011	Market share 11	% Change 11-10
TOTAL	8,986,934	9,089,972	8,639,304	9,554,437	9,608,171	100.00	0.56
AFRICA	1,929,749	1,804,791	1,826,343	2,092,001	2,140,195	22.27	2.30
East Africa	1,195,065	1,038,194	1,167,314	1,347,076	1,370,859	14.27	1.77
Comoros	10,218	9,503	8,503	11,941	16,132	0.17	35.10
Kenya	12,642	14,309	11,767	11,715	17,507	0.18	49.44
Madagascar	98,034	106,400	96,282	110,826	104,122	1.08	-6.05
Reunion	917,369	789,617	969,927	1,110,573	1,139,460	11.86	2.60
Seychelles	133,595	93,713	67,976	90,752	79,250	0.82	-12.67
Zimbabwe	23,207	24,652	12,859	11,269	14,388	0.15	27.68
Southern Africa	676,795	699,641	602,983	680,880	700,185	7.29	2.84
South Africa	676,795	699,641	602,983	680,880	700,185	7.29	2.84
Other Africa	57,889	66,956	56,046	64,045	69,151	0.72	7.97
Other countries of Africa	57,889	66,956	56,046	64,045	69,151	0.72	7.97
AMERICAS	100,630	133,303	131,044	126,661	142,593	1.48	12.58
North America	82,724	108,452	112,498	104,772	118,711	1.24	13.30
Canada	33,058	43,175	58,423	52,631	60,443	0.63	14.84
United States of America	49,666	65,277	54,075	52,141	58,268	0.61	11.75
Other Americas	17,906	24,851	18,546	21,889	23,882	0.25	9.11
Other countries of the Americas	17,906	24,851	18,546	21,889	23,882	0.25	9.11
EAST ASIA AND THE PACIFIC	393,277	460,181	373,044	479,656	485,264	5.05	1.17
North-East Asia	104,456	120,901	84,888	99,347	133,306	1.39	34.18
China	88,967	105,809	69,196	83,408	118,558	1.23	42.14
Hong Kong, China	4,788	4,469	4,211	4,696	5,270	0.05	12.22
Japan	10,701	10,623	11,481	11,243	9,478	0.10	-15.70
South-East Asia	24,417	22,027	21,884	24,205	26,237	0.27	8.39
Malaysia	12,217	10,108	10,554	11,575	11,990	0.12	3.59
Singapore	12,200	11,919	11,330	12,630	14,247	0.15	12.80
Australasia	143,482	150,220	138,665	169,162	176,348	1.84	4.25
Australia	143,482	150,220	138,665	169,162	176,348	1.84	4.25
Other East Asia and the Pacific	120,922	167,033	127,607	186,942	149,373	1.55	-20.10
Other countries of Asia	112,793	155,903	117,511	174,229	140,317	1.46	-19.46
Other countries of Oceania	8,129	11,130	10,096	12,713	9,056	0.09	-28.77
EUROPE	6,142,439	6,283,489	5,917,949	6,431,755	6,380,803	66.41	-0.79
Northern Europe	1,244,868	1,276,932	1,344,549	1,270,462	1,121,616	11.67	-11.72
Sweden	102,886	93,180	62,581	54,857	49,536	0.52	-9.70
United Kingdom	1,141,982	1,183,752	1,281,968	1,215,605	1,072,080	11.16	-11.81
Southern Europe	671,231	669,436	597,089	603,905	559,629	5.82	-7.33
Italy	600,236	582,196	512,033	532,786	484,300	5.04	-9.10
Spain	70,995	87,240	85,056	71,119	75,329	0.78	5.92
Western Europe	3,793,364	3,859,076	3,566,833	4,105,440	4,228,967	44.01	3.01
Austria	116,972	99,371	92,209	113,700	103,742	1.08	-8.76
Belgium	132,145	148,043	138,764	139,271	142,611	1.48	2.40
France	2,542,172	2,629,452	2,498,920	2,861,874	2,939,859	30.60	2.72
Germany	735,938	731,803	579,531	685,258	694,892	7.23	1.41
Netherlands	59,007	58,561	59,667	54,328	54,217	0.56	-0.20
Switzerland	207,130	191,846	197,742	251,009	293,646	3.06	16.99
Other Europe	432,976	478,045	409,478	451,948	470,591	4.90	4.13
Other countries of Europe	432,976	478,045	409,478	451,948	470,591	4.90	4.13
SOUTH ASIA	408,128	398,835	376,783	409,138	443,743	4.62	8.46
India	408,128	398,835	376,783	409,138	443,743	4.62	8.46
NOT SPECIFIED	12,711	9,373	14,141	15,226	15,573	0.16	2.28
Other countries of the World	12,711	9,373	14,141	15,226	15,573	0.16	2.28

MEXICO

1. Arrivals of non-resident tourists at national borders, by nationality

		2007	2008	2009	2010	2011	Market share 11	% Change 11-10
TOTAL		21,605,754	22,930,584	22,346,260	23,289,749	23,403,263	100.00	0.49
AFRICA		10,328	13,340	9,884	15,005	14,701	0.06	-2.03
Other Africa		10,328	13,340	9,884	15,005	14,701	0.06	-2.03
All countries of Africa		10,328	13,340	9,884	15,005	14,701	0.06	-2.03
AMERICAS		18,698,935	19,818,344	20,178,443	20,867,904	21,152,561	90.38	1.36
Caribbean		40,454	47,825	40,965	39,249	40,873	0.17	4.14
Cuba		40,454	47,825	40,965	39,249	40,873	0.17	4.14
Central America		74,681	88,461	94,843	103,426	88,837	0.38	-14.11
Costa Rica		37,726	44,580	42,107	53,152	44,415	0.19	-16.44
Guatemala		36,955	43,881	52,736	50,274	44,422	0.19	-11.64
North America		18,100,338	19,116,815	19,484,056	19,987,581	20,117,762	85.96	0.65
Canada		945,620	1,135,001	1,222,410	1,460,418	1,563,146	6.68	7.03
United States of America	(*)	17,154,718	17,981,814	18,261,646	18,527,163	18,554,616	79.28	0.15
South America		350,491	412,086	401,457	542,831	688,018	2.94	26.75
Argentina		111,422	126,130	127,107	170,467	200,687	0.86	17.73
Brazil		60,019	76,491	68,211	117,658	196,266	0.84	66.81
Chile		53,879	59,634	54,179	67,661	76,379	0.33	12.88
Colombia		61,107	67,378	68,493	102,177	125,882	0.54	23.20
Venezuela		64,064	82,453	83,467	84,868	88,804	0.38	4.64
Other Americas		132,971	153,157	157,122	194,817	217,071	0.93	11.42
Other countries of the Americas		132,971	153,157	157,122	194,817	217,071	0.93	11.42
EAST ASIA AND THE PACIFIC		108,727	105,412	78,407	101,129	112,642	0.48	11.38
North-East Asia		108,727	105,412	78,407	101,129	112,642	0.48	11.38
Japan		71,292	69,716	52,229	66,164	72,339	0.31	9.33
Korea, Republic of		37,435	35,696	26,178	34,965	40,303	0.17	15.27
EUROPE		1,407,731	1,501,742	1,188,286	1,417,935	1,509,736	6.45	6.47
Northern Europe		283,025	311,113	257,367	295,831	330,071	1.41	11.57
United Kingdom		283,025	311,113	257,367	295,831	330,071	1.41	11.57
Southern Europe		480,852	489,678	350,528	469,085	473,679	2.02	0.98
Italy		165,453	167,415	108,547	133,292	150,690	0.64	13.05
Portugal		38,144	37,751	26,312	48,630	43,459	0.19	-10.63
Spain		277,255	284,512	215,669	287,163	279,530	1.19	-2.66
Western Europe		475,156	508,734	418,570	462,343	479,626	2.05	3.74
Belgium		31,246	36,202	30,173	31,188	30,344	0.13	-2.71
France		190,118	208,284	164,236	170,250	186,778	0.80	9.71
Germany		151,021	158,050	140,754	163,266	165,133	0.71	1.14
Netherlands		72,213	75,864	58,317	68,964	67,821	0.29	-1.66
Switzerland		30,558	30,334	25,090	28,675	29,550	0.13	3.05
Other Europe		168,698	192,217	161,821	190,676	226,360	0.97	18.71
Other countries of Europe		168,698	192,217	161,821	190,676	226,360	0.97	18.71
NOT SPECIFIED		1,380,033	1,491,746	891,241	887,776	613,623	2.62	-30.88
Other countries of the World	(*)	1,380,033	1,491,746	891,241	887,776	613,623	2.62	-30.88

MEXICO

1. Arrivals of non-resident tourists at national borders, by country of residence

		2007	2008	2009	2010	2011	Market share 11	% Change 11-10
TOTAL	(*)	21,605,754	22,930,584	22,346,261	23,289,749	23,403,274	100.00	0.49
AMERICAS		17,746,787	18,800,933	18,874,985	19,128,045	19,314,307	82.53	0.97
North America		17,746,787	18,800,933	18,874,985	19,128,045	19,314,307	82.53	0.97
Canada		592,069	819,119	613,339	600,882	759,691	3.25	26.43
United States of America		17,154,718	17,981,814	18,261,646	18,527,163	18,554,616	79.28	0.15
NOT SPECIFIED		3,858,967	4,129,651	3,471,276	4,161,704	4,088,967	17.47	-1.75
Other countries of the World		3,858,967	4,129,651	3,471,276	4,161,704	4,088,967	17.47	-1.75

MONACO

3. Arrivals of non-resident tourists in hotels and similar establishments, by nationality

	2007	2008	2009	2010	2011	Market share 11	% Change 11-10
TOTAL	327,985	323,705	264,540	279,166	294,901	100.00	5.64
AFRICA	3,293	2,832	2,342	2,881	2,836	0.96	-1.56
Other Africa	3,293	2,832	2,342	2,881	2,836	0.96	-1.56
All countries of Africa	3,293	2,832	2,342	2,881	2,836	0.96	-1.56
AMERICAS	40,910	35,368	27,456	30,863	33,143	11.24	7.39
North America	37,905	30,805	22,919	25,373	27,887	9.46	9.91
Canada	6,078	4,438	3,330	3,938	4,652	1.58	18.13
Mexico	820	795	602	738	904	0.31	22.49
United States of America	31,007	25,572	18,987	20,697	22,331	7.57	7.89
South America	2,291	2,989	3,221	3,814	3,558	1.21	-6.71
Argentina	730	698	686	659	611	0.21	-7.28
Brazil	1,561	2,291	2,535	3,155	2,947	1.00	-6.59
Other Americas	714	1,574	1,316	1,676	1,698	0.58	1.31
Other countries of the Americas	714	1,574	1,316	1,676	1,698	0.58	1.31
EAST ASIA AND THE PACIFIC	12,382	12,535	10,222	11,783	14,650	4.97	24.33
North-East Asia	8,901	8,271	6,920	7,414	9,308	3.16	25.55
China	2,457	2,254	1,796	2,888	4,311	1.46	49.27
Japan	6,444	6,017	5,124	4,526	4,997	1.69	10.41
Australasia	3,481	4,264	3,302	4,369	5,342	1.81	22.27
Australia	3,481	4,264	3,302	4,369	5,342	1.81	22.27
EUROPE	244,497	260,856	216,280	223,207	232,827	78.95	4.31
Central/Eastern Europe	10,523	16,762	13,795	14,899	17,229	5.84	15.64
Russian Federation	10,523	16,762	13,795	14,899	17,229	5.84	15.64
Northern Europe	56,169	53,939	36,575	37,524	38,124	12.93	1.60
Denmark	2,806	1,852	1,602	1,710	1,562	0.53	-8.65
Norway	1,860	1,679	1,549	1,639	2,319	0.79	41.49
Sweden	3,171	2,727	2,357	2,526	2,892	0.98	14.49
United Kingdom	48,332	47,681	31,067	31,649	31,351	10.63	-0.94
Southern Europe	71,760	72,437	60,052	61,870	60,116	20.39	-2.83
Italy	62,975	65,414	52,951	55,129	53,081	18.00	-3.71
Portugal	1,330	1,151	1,111	1,069	1,232	0.42	15.25
Spain	7,455	5,872	5,990	5,672	5,803	1.97	2.31
Western Europe	94,347	98,014	87,640	91,800	99,470	33.73	8.36
Austria	2,586	2,575	2,125	2,485	2,539	0.86	2.17
Belgium	5,847	5,665	4,632	4,509	4,821	1.63	6.92
France	57,976	62,043	56,685	61,234	65,659	22.26	7.23
Germany	12,807	13,230	11,587	11,070	13,002	4.41	17.45
Netherlands	6,313	5,109	4,741	4,342	4,608	1.56	6.13
Switzerland	8,818	9,392	7,870	8,160	8,841	3.00	8.35
East Mediterranean Europe	1,419	1,341	1,468	1,269	1,397	0.47	10.09
Israel	1,419	1,341	1,468	1,269	1,397	0.47	10.09
Other Europe	10,279	18,363	16,750	15,845	16,491	5.59	4.08
Other countries of Europe	10,279	18,363	16,750	15,845	16,491	5.59	4.08
MIDDLE EAST	4,318	7,045	4,333	5,039	5,386	1.83	6.89
All countries of Middle East	4,318	7,045	4,333	5,039	5,386	1.83	6.89
NOT SPECIFIED	22,585	5,069	3,907	5,393	6,059	2.05	12.35
Other countries of the World	22,585	5,069	3,907	5,393	6,059	2.05	12.35

MONACO

5. Overnight stays of non-resident tourists in hotels and similar establishments, by nationality

	2007	2008	2009	2010	2011	Market share 11	% Change 11-10
TOTAL	943,921	943,509	778,451	817,011	852,578	100.00	4.35
AFRICA	14,248	9,037	7,351	8,773	8,775	1.03	0.02
Other Africa	14,248	9,037	7,351	8,773	8,775	1.03	0.02
All countries of Africa	14,248	9,037	7,351	8,773	8,775	1.03	0.02
AMERICAS	137,983	120,106	92,791	103,292	106,963	12.55	3.55
North America	128,082	104,475	79,625	86,965	91,537	10.74	5.26
Canada	25,253	16,057	10,798	12,561	14,932	1.75	18.88
Mexico	3,052	2,450	1,638	2,095	2,472	0.29	18.00
United States of America	99,777	85,968	67,189	72,309	74,133	8.70	2.52
South America	7,326	10,490	9,062	10,863	9,962	1.17	-8.29
Argentina	2,782	2,781	2,567	2,464	2,089	0.25	-15.22
Brazil	4,544	7,709	6,495	8,399	7,873	0.92	-6.26
Other Americas	2,575	5,141	4,104	5,464	5,464	0.64	
Other countries of the Americas	2,575	5,141	4,104	5,464	5,464	0.64	
EAST ASIA AND THE PACIFIC	36,536	38,296	29,885	32,747	38,571	4.52	17.78
North-East Asia	24,872	24,519	19,513	19,485	23,415	2.75	20.17
China	7,022	5,771	4,118	6,361	9,484	1.11	49.10
Japan	17,850	18,748	15,395	13,124	13,931	1.63	6.15
Australasia	11,664	13,777	10,372	13,262	15,156	1.78	14.28
Australia	11,664	13,777	10,372	13,262	15,156	1.78	14.28
EUROPE	655,078	726,854	619,478	636,189	661,030	77.53	3.90
Central/Eastern Europe	41,081	77,566	65,409	70,750	78,084	9.16	10.37
Russian Federation	41,081	77,566	65,409	70,750	78,084	9.16	10.37
Northern Europe	145,548	155,514	111,182	113,894	114,311	13.41	0.37
Denmark	9,993	5,764	4,348	4,846	4,394	0.52	-9.33
Norway	7,357	4,781	4,365	4,528	6,397	0.75	41.28
Sweden	9,373	8,095	8,186	8,395	8,479	0.99	1.00
United Kingdom	118,825	136,874	94,283	96,125	95,041	11.15	-1.13
Southern Europe	170,402	175,960	151,080	155,649	153,932	18.05	-1.10
Italy	144,124	155,856	131,312	136,767	134,476	15.77	-1.68
Portugal	5,574	3,418	3,486	3,345	3,602	0.42	7.68
Spain	20,704	16,686	16,282	15,537	15,854	1.86	2.04
Western Europe	248,772	255,593	234,101	241,745	259,067	30.39	7.17
Austria	9,654	9,277	8,214	8,926	8,377	0.98	-6.15
Belgium	18,419	18,492	17,023	16,352	16,280	1.91	-0.44
France	137,226	142,395	132,822	143,867	153,985	18.06	7.03
Germany	35,717	40,176	38,001	35,831	41,176	4.83	14.92
Netherlands	19,498	14,978	13,919	12,229	13,002	1.53	6.32
Switzerland	28,258	30,275	24,122	24,540	26,247	3.08	6.96
East Mediterranean Europe	6,442	5,790	5,451	4,642	5,090	0.60	9.65
Israel	6,442	5,790	5,451	4,642	5,090	0.60	9.65
Other Europe	42,833	56,431	52,255	49,509	50,546	5.93	2.09
Other countries of Europe	42,833	56,431	52,255	49,509	50,546	5.93	2.09
MIDDLE EAST	20,757	33,272	17,550	20,968	21,529	2.53	2.68
All countries of Middle East	20,757	33,272	17,550	20,968	21,529	2.53	2.68
NOT SPECIFIED	79,319	15,944	11,396	15,042	15,710	1.84	4.44
Other countries of the World	79,319	15,944	11,396	15,042	15,710	1.84	4.44

MONGOLIA

1. Arrivals of non-resident tourists at national borders, by nationality

	2007	2008	2009	2010	2011	Market share 11	% Change 11-10
TOTAL	451,788	446,317	411,497	456,963			
AFRICA	691	592	434	595			
East Africa	125	82	85	145			
Burundi				58			
Ethiopia	17	6	16	16			
Eritrea			1				
Kenya	18	21	15	13			
Madagascar	7	1	2	2			
Malawi	2		3				
Mauritius	7	7	7	16			
Mozambique	4	2	3	11			
Reunion	16	4	3	1			
Rwanda	5	10	4	1			
Zimbabwe	6	3	8	10			
Uganda	26	18	12	8			
United Republic of Tanzania	5	6	4	6			
Zambia	12	4	7	3			
Central Africa	85	48	30	21			
Angola	5	3	1				
Cameroon	60	20	16	12			
Central African Republic	9	8	4	1			
Chad				8			
Congo	11	15	9				
Equatorial Guinea		2					
North Africa	29	39	42	73			
Algeria	12	14	11	17			
Morocco	9	10	14	35			
Sudan	3	11	12				
Tunisia	5	4	5	21			
Southern Africa	271	286	216	271			
Botswana	2	2					
Lesotho	4	1		1			
Namibia		4	1	4			
South Africa	265	257	197	258			
Swaziland		22	18	8			
West Africa	147	97	61	85			
Benin	2	5	1	8			
Gambia			1	1			
Ghana	31	40	27	24			
Guinea	19						
Côte d'Ivoire		2					
Liberia			4	6			
Mali			1	3			
Mauritania				1			
Niger		7	13	12			
Nigeria	42	24	9	21			
Guinea-Bissau				1			
Senegal	2	4	3	1			
Sierra Leone	51	15		2			
Togo			1	1			
Burkina Faso			1	4			
Other Africa	34	40					
Other countries of Africa	34	40					
AMERICAS	15,401	15,805	14,161	16,486			
Caribbean	54	38	43	42			

MONGOLIA

1. Arrivals of non-resident tourists at national borders, by nationality

	2007	2008	2009	2010	2011	Market share 11	% Change 11-10
Antigua and Barbuda	1						
Barbados	2			1			
Bermuda	5		2				
Cuba	25	24	25	26			
Dominica		1	2	2			
Dominican Republic	8	3					
Haiti			4	4			
Jamaica	8	7	1	3			
Aruba	3						
Trinidad and Tobago	2	3	9	6			
Central America	**62**	**70**	**30**	**39**			
Belize				3			
Costa Rica	11	7	5	6			
El Salvador	2	2	4	6			
Guatemala	4	1	6	5			
Honduras	44	55	9	11			
Nicaragua				1			
Panama	1	5	6	7			
North America	**14,704**	**15,188**	**13,663**	**15,799**			
Canada	2,422	2,645	2,255	2,864			
Mexico	59	69	73	127			
United States of America	12,223	12,474	11,335	12,808			
South America	**581**	**509**	**425**	**606**			
Argentina	82	74	68	179			
Bolivia	13	15	2	11			
Brazil	243	220	159	225			
Chile	105	105	84	59			
Colombia	44	28	32	32			
Ecuador	9	8	11	7			
French Guiana		1					
Guyana			1				
Paraguay	4	3	4	4			
Peru	50	18	41	51			
Uruguay	13	8	10	24			
Venezuela	18	29	13	14			
EAST ASIA AND THE PACIFIC	**283,267**	**266,582**	**241,097**	**264,401**			
North-East Asia	**274,267**	**257,365**	**233,067**	**253,808**			
China	211,007	196,832	181,523	194,333			
Taiwan, Province of China	1,280	1,404	1,086	1,235			
Hong Kong, China	434	369	434	791			
Japan	17,238	14,939	11,399	14,140			
Korea, Dem. People's Republic of	378	402	342	1,068			
Korea, Republic of	43,930	43,396	38,272	42,231			
Macao, China		23	11	10			
South-East Asia	**3,456**	**3,780**	**3,586**	**4,229**			
Brunei Darussalam	7	8	7	3			
Myanmar	7	5	7	8			
Cambodia	76	45	85	34			
Indonesia	319	226	203	246			
Lao People's Democratic Republic	59	90	92	58			
Malaysia	843	881	846	926			
Philippines	479	510	600	823			
Singapore	995	932	922	1,170			
Viet Nam	379	665	381	415			
Thailand	292	418	443	546			
Australasia	**5,463**	**5,394**	**4,431**	**6,325**			
Australia	4,502	4,466	3,721	5,443			

MONGOLIA

1. Arrivals of non-resident tourists at national borders, by nationality

	2007	2008	2009	2010	2011	Market share 11	% Change 11-10
New Zealand	961	928	710	882			
Melanesia	**22**	**29**	**7**	**29**			
Solomon Islands	2	1	6	1			
Fiji	18	18		15			
Vanuatu				1			
Papua New Guinea	2	10	1	12			
Micronesia	**3**	**3**					
Kiribati	1	2					
Micronesia, Federated States of	2	1					
Polynesia	**56**	**11**	**6**	**10**			
American Samoa	5	7		2			
Tonga	46	3	4	3			
Samoa	5	1	2	5			
EUROPE	**149,077**	**159,884**	**153,785**	**173,381**			
Central/Eastern Europe	**109,175**	**120,776**	**117,535**	**132,127**			
Azerbaijan	152	147	75	76			
Armenia	140	177	120	75			
Bulgaria	163	103	89	123			
Belarus	177	237	188	177			
Czech Republic	888	932	815	841			
Estonia	64	42	35	91			
Georgia	80	65	50	69			
Hungary	286	289	281	330			
Kazakhstan	4,882	5,473	5,053	5,757			
Kyrgyzstan	416	342	205	238			
Latvia	38	31	28	45			
Lithuania	87	71	53	79			
Republic of Moldova	77	58	40	40			
Poland	1,180	1,338	1,048	1,163			
Romania	53	62	84	106			
Russian Federation	98,759	109,975	107,911	121,705			
Slovakia	151	202	196	184			
Tajikistan	131	114	112	30			
Turkmenistan	9	5	2	4			
Ukraine	1,205	960	967	818			
Uzbekistan	237	153	183	176			
Northern Europe	**12,201**	**11,925**	**10,254**	**11,179**			
Denmark	1,053	917	660	676			
Finland	802	832	843	945			
Iceland	51	32	25	18			
Ireland	748	682	508	490			
Norway	718	787	737	816			
Sweden	2,112	1,894	1,634	1,625			
United Kingdom	6,717	6,781	5,847	6,609			
Southern Europe	**3,450**	**3,192**	**4,393**	**4,730**			
Albania	4	10	4	15			
Andorra	5	2	3	2			
Bosnia and Herzegovina	20	57	17	27			
Croatia	57	73	41	37			
Greece	188	93	92	126			
Italy	2,744	2,454	2,415	2,750			
Malta	6	2	4	9			
Portugal	202	260	278	192			
Slovenia	136	167	154	154			
Spain			1,315	1,340			
TFYR of Macedonia	17	35	13	18			
Serbia and Montenegro	71	39	57	60			

MONGOLIA

1. Arrivals of non-resident tourists at national borders, by nationality

	2007	2008	2009	2010	2011	Market share 11	% Change 11-10
Western Europe	23,178	22,660	20,457	23,420			
Austria	1,484	1,219	1,105	1,118			
Belgium	1,089	1,005	807	964			
France	6,341	6,688	6,702	7,527			
Germany	8,250	8,027	6,858	8,095			
Liechtenstein	6	6	10				
Luxembourg	48	83	37	78			
Netherlands	3,380	3,255	2,775	3,244			
Switzerland	2,580	2,377	2,163	2,394			
East Mediterranean Europe	1,073	1,235	1,146	1,925			
Cyprus	9	15	6	11			
Israel	628	642	619	757			
Turkey	436	578	521	1,157			
Other Europe		96					
Other countries of Europe		96					
MIDDLE EAST	480	610	645	616			
Bahrain	4	2	3	9			
Palestine		3	2				
Iraq	3	13	10	18			
Jordan	6	13	18	81			
Kuwait	259	203	107	233			
Lebanon	22	21	7	3			
Libya	2	2	20	26			
Oman	1	5	28	8			
Qatar	65	134	223	39			
Saudi Arabia		63	49	34			
Syrian Arab Republic	75	82	104	102			
United Arab Emirates	7	10	19	11			
Egypt	26	43	37	34			
Yemen	10	16	18	18			
SOUTH ASIA	1,202	1,407	1,327	1,473			
Afghanistan	31	16	31	17			
Bangladesh	87	65	91	82			
Bhutan	9	18	9	31			
Sri Lanka	112	81	70	69			
India	777	881	941	940			
Iran, Islamic Republic of		56	63	219			
Maldives	4	58	7	5			
Nepal	71	125					
Pakistan	111	107	115	110			
NOT SPECIFIED	1,670	1,437	48	11			
Other countries of the World	1,670	1,437	48	11			

MONGOLIA

2. Arrivals of non-resident visitors at national borders, by nationality

	2007	2008	2009	2010	2011	Market share 11	% Change 11-10
TOTAL	456,347	468,765	467,989	557,452			
AFRICA	709	567	418	597			
East Africa	128	85	87	148			
Burundi				58			
Ethiopia	18	6	16	16			
Eritrea			1				
Kenya	18	21	15	13			
Madagascar	8	1	2	2			
Malawi	2	1	3	3			
Mauritius	7	7	9	16			
Mozambique	4	2	3	11			
Reunion	16	4	3	1			
Rwanda	5	10	4	1			
Zimbabwe	6	3	8	10			
Uganda	26	18	12	8			
United Republic of Tanzania	5	6	4	6			
Zambia	13	6	7	3			
Central Africa	91	51	33	25			
Angola	6	3	1				
Cameroon	60	20	17	12			
Central African Republic	11	9	4	1			
Chad	2	1					
Congo	12	16	11	8			
Equatorial Guinea		2		4			
North Africa	36	39	43	73			
Algeria	19	14	11	17			
Morocco	9	10	15	35			
Sudan	3	11	12				
Tunisia	5	4	5	21			
Southern Africa	270	291	187	271			
Botswana	2	2					
Lesotho				1			
Namibia		5	1	4			
South Africa	268	261	168	258			
Swaziland		23	18	8			
West Africa	148	101	68	80			
Benin	2	5	1	8			
Gambia			2	1			
Ghana	31	41	31	24			
Guinea	20	3	1	1			
Liberia		2	4	6			
Mali			1				
Mauritania				1			
Niger		7	14	13			
Nigeria	42	24	9	22			
Senegal	2	4	3	1			
Sierra Leone	51	15		2			
Togo			1	1			
Burkina Faso			1				
Other Africa	36						
Other countries of Africa	36						
AMERICAS	15,550	16,037	14,202	16,686			
Caribbean	51	38	44	43			
Antigua and Barbuda	1						
Barbados	2			1			

MONGOLIA

2. Arrivals of non-resident visitors at national borders, by nationality

	2007	2008	2009	2010	2011	Market share 11	% Change 11-10
Bermuda	1		2				
Cuba	26	24	26	27			
Dominica		1		2			
Dominican Republic	8	3	2				
Haiti			4	4			
Jamaica	8	7	1	3			
Aruba	3						
Trinidad and Tobago	2	3	9	6			
Central America	**68**	**70**	**30**	**38**			
Belize				3			
Costa Rica	11	7	5	6			
El Salvador	2	2	4	6			
Guatemala	4	1	6	5			
Honduras	50	55	9	11			
Panama	1	5	6	7			
North America	**14,844**	**15,414**	**13,854**	**15,996**			
Canada	2,443	2,681	2,273	2,887			
Mexico	59	70	73	127			
United States of America	12,342	12,663	11,508	12,982			
South America	**587**	**515**	**274**	**609**			
Argentina	83	75	68	179			
Bolivia	13	16	2	11			
Brazil	247	223		227			
Chile	105	105	84	59			
Colombia	44	28	31	32			
Ecuador	9	8	11	7			
Falkland Islands, Malvinas			9	1			
French Guiana		1					
Paraguay	4	3	4	4			
Peru	51	19	42	51			
Uruguay	13	8	10	24			
Venezuela	18	29	13	14			
EAST ASIA AND THE PACIFIC	**284,632**	**287,400**	**292,096**	**360,681**			
North-East Asia	**275,774**	**278,125**	**283,964**	**350,016**			
China	212,158	217,127	232,038	290,061			
Taiwan, Province of China	1,258	1,412	1,090	1,242			
Hong Kong, China	436	370	435	793			
Japan	17,307	15,036	11,496	14,279			
Korea, Dem. People's Republic of	411	407	343	1,080			
Korea, Republic of	44,204	43,750	38,551	42,551			
Macao, China		23	11	10			
South-East Asia	**3,301**	**3,799**	**3,629**	**4,273**			
Brunei Darussalam			7	2			
Myanmar	7	5	7	8			
Cambodia	76	46	85	34			
Indonesia	347	226	204	198			
Lao People's Democratic Republic	59	93	93	66			
Malaysia	644	882	853	927			
Philippines	483	514	607	828			
Singapore	1,000	935	931	1,173			
Viet Nam	390	676	395	434			
Thailand	295	422	447	603			
Australasia	**5,478**	**5,432**	**4,457**	**6,353**			
Australia	4,514	4,491	3,741	5,471			
New Zealand	964	941	716	882			
Melanesia	**22**	**30**	**40**	**29**			

MONGOLIA

2. Arrivals of non-resident visitors at national borders, by nationality

	2007	2008	2009	2010	2011	Market share 11	% Change 11-10
Solomon Islands	2	2	6	1			
Fiji	18	18	23	15			
Vanuatu				1			
Papua New Guinea	2	10	11	12			
Micronesia	**3**	**3**					
Kiribati	1	2					
Micronesia, Federated States of	2	1					
Polynesia	**54**	**11**	**6**	**10**			
American Samoa	3	7		2			
Tonga	46	3	4	3			
Samoa	5	1	2	5			
EUROPE	**150,165**	**161,031**	**154,374**	**177,256**			
Central/Eastern Europe	**110,171**	**121,809**	**119,072**	**136,065**			
Azerbaijan	156	147	77	78			
Armenia	140	178	120	75			
Bulgaria	163	103	90	124			
Belarus	180	237	191	182			
Czech Republic	894	942	826	860			
Estonia	64	42	36	91			
Georgia	81	65	50	75			
Hungary	296	292	289	337			
Kazakhstan	4,922	5,493	5,094	5,792			
Kyrgyzstan	422	345	209	242			
Latvia	38	32	28	45			
Lithuania	87	71	10	79			
Republic of Moldova	79	58	42	40			
Poland	1,188	1,343	1,058	1,170			
Romania	54	63	85	110			
Russian Federation	99,662	110,955	109,391	125,543			
Slovakia	152	202	199	186			
Tajikistan	131	114	112	30			
Turkmenistan	9	5	2	4			
Ukraine	1,216	967	978	824			
Uzbekistan	237	155	185	178			
Northern Europe	**12,206**	**11,961**	**10,365**	**10,818**			
Denmark	1,055	918	662	676			
Finland	802	827	862	949			
Iceland	52	32	25	18			
Ireland	718	685	510	492			
Norway	719	791	744	823			
Sweden	2,117	1,900	1,667	1,632			
United Kingdom	6,743	6,808	5,895	6,228			
Southern Europe	**3,455**	**3,215**	**3,097**	**4,833**			
Albania	4	10	4	15			
Andorra	5	2	3	2			
Bosnia and Herzegovina	20	57	18	28			
Croatia	57	73	50	69			
Greece	188	94	95	126			
Italy	2,748	2,468	2,417	2,819			
Malta	6	8	4	9			
Portugal	203	261	278	192			
Slovenia	136	167	154	154			
Spain				1,340			
TFYR of Macedonia	17	36	14	19			
Serbia and Montenegro	71	39	60	60			
Western Europe	**23,235**	**22,781**	**20,693**	**23,576**			
Austria	1,488	1,226	1,113	1,122			

MONGOLIA

2. Arrivals of non-resident visitors at national borders, by nationality

	2007	2008	2009	2010	2011	Market share 11	% Change 11-10
Belgium	1,019	1,007	826	966			
France	6,357	6,714	6,737	7,543			
Germany	8,332	8,085	6,995	8,220			
Liechtenstein	6	6	10				
Luxembourg	50	83	37	78			
Netherlands	3,392	3,267	2,791	3,248			
Switzerland	2,591	2,393	2,184	2,399			
East Mediterranean Europe	**1,098**	**1,265**	**1,147**	**1,964**			
Cyprus	9	15	6	11			
Israel	630	645	604	759			
Turkey	459	605	537	1,194			
MIDDLE EAST	**486**	**584**	**612**	**619**			
Bahrain	4	2	3	9			
Palestine		3	2	2			
Iraq	3	13	10	18			
Jordan	7	13	20	81			
Kuwait	259	203	107	233			
Lebanon	23		20	26			
Libya				3			
Oman				8			
Qatar	66	134	223	39			
Saudi Arabia		63	49	34			
Syrian Arab Republic	76	82	104	102			
United Arab Emirates	7	10	19	11			
Egypt	31	43	37	34			
Yemen	10	18	18	19			
SOUTH ASIA	**1,269**	**1,370**	**1,447**	**1,597**			
Afghanistan	33	18	38	26			
Bangladesh	89	66	91	84			
Bhutan	10	18	11	31			
Sri Lanka	113	81	70	69			
India	784	893	952	949			
Iran, Islamic Republic of	50	57	63	219			
Maldives	4	2	7	5			
Nepal	73	126	98	98			
Pakistan	113	109	117	116			
NOT SPECIFIED	**3,536**	**1,776**	**4,840**	**16**			
Other countries of the World	3,536	1,776	4,840	16			

MONTENEGRO

3. Arrivals of non-resident tourists in hotels and similar establishments, by nationality

	2007	2008	2009	2010	2011	Market share 11	% Change 11-10
TOTAL	545,351	566,454	467,650	485,780	523,631	100.00	7.79
AMERICAS	8,279	8,525	7,694	8,655	8,158	1.56	-5.74
North America	8,279	8,525	7,694	8,655	8,158	1.56	-5.74
Canada	1,147	1,317	1,310	1,500	1,709	0.33	13.93
United States of America	7,132	7,208	6,384	7,155	6,449	1.23	-9.87
EAST ASIA AND THE PACIFIC	2,106	2,669	2,222	3,946	3,980	0.76	0.86
North-East Asia	756	665	510	790	1,200	0.23	51.90
Japan	756	665	510	790	1,200	0.23	51.90
Australasia	1,350	2,004	1,712	3,156	2,780	0.53	-11.91
Australia	1,140	1,639	1,411	1,626	2,392	0.46	47.11
New Zealand	210	365	301	1,530	388	0.07	-74.64
EUROPE	530,913	550,983	452,663	466,751	502,089	95.89	7.57
Central/Eastern Europe	134,339	140,127	108,438	136,046	156,128	29.82	14.76
Bulgaria	3,525	4,185	4,787	4,337	4,489	0.86	3.50
Belarus	2,305	811	766	889	1,121	0.21	26.10
Czech Republic	23,165	18,529	11,309	11,735	14,321	2.73	22.04
Estonia	323	413	217	928	204	0.04	-78.02
Hungary	7,613	8,684	7,417	8,548	8,336	1.59	-2.48
Latvia	320	536	171	551	217	0.04	-60.62
Lithuania	1,971	930	927	1,027	1,080	0.21	5.16
Poland	7,211	7,554	11,003	13,568	18,737	3.58	38.10
Romania	1,315	2,499	5,632	7,722	9,321	1.78	20.71
Russian Federation	71,677	79,137	56,226	73,981	83,055	15.86	12.27
Slovakia	7,679	5,888	4,212	5,049	5,644	1.08	11.78
Ukraine	7,235	10,961	5,771	7,711	9,603	1.83	24.54
Northern Europe	31,326	27,522	26,800	27,746	27,815	5.31	0.25
Denmark	1,288	1,058	943	1,150	1,076	0.21	-6.43
Finland	3,047	1,916	1,632	1,469	1,591	0.30	8.30
Iceland	307	260	179	397	188	0.04	-52.64
Ireland	3,205	3,240	1,404	1,474	1,333	0.25	-9.57
Norway	3,223	3,396	3,390	3,462	3,638	0.69	5.08
Sweden	5,418	5,232	7,128	7,077	6,927	1.32	-2.12
United Kingdom	14,838	12,420	12,124	12,717	13,062	2.49	2.71
Southern Europe	295,400	315,239	245,089	229,371	226,106	43.18	-1.42
Albania	18,915	17,003	16,377	17,205	17,536	3.35	1.92
Bosnia and Herzegovina	29,698	26,772	24,060	22,885	22,504	4.30	-1.66
Croatia	9,312	11,684	12,103	12,808	12,058	2.30	-5.86
Greece	2,023	3,088	2,937	3,346	3,975	0.76	18.80
Italy	17,794	16,804	18,136	19,695	25,064	4.79	27.26
Portugal	608	512	460	571	883	0.17	54.64
Serbia	187,046	208,259	143,198	128,160	121,344	23.17	-5.32
Slovenia	18,981	16,935	16,683	15,578	14,048	2.68	-9.82
Spain	1,480	1,733	1,497	2,336	2,060	0.39	-11.82
TFYR of Macedonia	9,543	12,449	9,638	6,787	6,634	1.27	-2.25
Western Europe	59,205	59,242	51,040	55,249	60,481	11.55	9.47
Austria	12,639	14,678	6,835	7,125	8,264	1.58	15.99
Belgium	6,174	6,730	5,359	5,584	5,571	1.06	-0.23
France	19,430	17,651	19,060	21,091	23,546	4.50	11.64
Germany	14,686	14,997	14,177	13,853	16,507	3.15	19.16
Luxembourg	318	209	708	240	279	0.05	16.25
Netherlands	1,850	2,221	2,356	2,281	2,521	0.48	10.52
Switzerland	4,108	2,756	2,545	5,075	3,793	0.72	-25.26

MONTENEGRO

3. Arrivals of non-resident tourists in hotels and similar establishments, by nationality

	2007	2008	2009	2010	2011	Market share 11	% Change 11-10
East Mediterranean Europe	**5,573**	**6,571**	**13,819**	**15,979**	**18,752**	**3.58**	**17.35**
Israel	4,624	4,448	11,003	9,875	11,013	2.10	11.52
Turkey	949	2,123	2,816	6,104	7,739	1.48	26.79
Other Europe	**5,070**	**2,282**	**7,477**	**2,360**	**12,807**	**2.45**	**442.67**
Other countries of Europe	5,070	2,282	7,477	2,360	12,807	2.45	442.67
NOT SPECIFIED	**4,053**	**4,277**	**5,071**	**6,428**	**9,404**	**1.80**	**46.30**
Other countries of the World	4,053	4,277	5,071	6,428	9,404	1.80	46.30

MONTENEGRO

4. Arrivals of non-resident tourists in all types of accommodation establishments, by nationality

	2007	2008	2009	2010	2011	Market share 11	% Change 11-10
TOTAL	984,138	1,030,825	1,043,933	1,087,794	1,201,099	100.00	10.42
AMERICAS	8,894	9,084	8,255	10,622	12,661	1.05	19.20
North America	8,894	9,084	8,255	10,622	12,661	1.05	19.20
Canada	1,468	1,597	1,557	1,853	2,087	0.17	12.63
United States of America	7,426	7,487	6,698	8,769	10,574	0.88	20.58
EAST ASIA AND THE PACIFIC	2,293	2,839	2,426	3,241	4,918	0.41	51.74
North-East Asia	763	700	515	863	1,431	0.12	65.82
Japan	763	700	515	863	1,431	0.12	65.82
Australasia	1,530	2,139	1,911	2,378	3,487	0.29	46.64
Australia	1,312	1,765	1,597	1,909	2,962	0.25	55.16
New Zealand	218	374	314	469	525	0.04	11.94
EUROPE	968,475	1,013,406	1,028,084	1,066,715	1,171,855	97.57	9.86
Central/Eastern Europe	211,989	244,677	260,417	293,303	415,839	34.62	41.78
Bulgaria	4,707	4,541	6,163	5,604	5,237	0.44	-6.55
Belarus	3,803	3,448	1,480	6,400	7,706	0.64	20.41
Czech Republic	33,100	29,837	25,928	24,085	24,702	2.06	2.56
Estonia	381	1,963	276	1,162	414	0.03	-64.37
Hungary	29,215	29,559	32,631	28,838	17,264	1.44	-40.13
Latvia	501	2,667	1,662	741	500	0.04	-32.52
Lithuania	4,989	3,505	2,583	4,261	5,046	0.42	18.42
Poland	11,979	13,054	15,039	25,381	39,544	3.29	55.80
Romania	1,931	3,133	7,895	14,471	22,923	1.91	58.41
Russian Federation	102,350	117,680	145,557	150,194	244,924	20.39	63.07
Slovakia	10,258	10,117	8,908	7,699	10,729	0.89	39.36
Ukraine	8,775	25,173	12,295	24,467	36,850	3.07	50.61
Northern Europe	37,010	34,207	31,626	42,617	49,570	4.13	16.32
Denmark	1,515	1,387	1,191	1,549	1,531	0.13	-1.16
Finland	3,093	2,058	1,710	1,579	2,211	0.18	40.03
Iceland	372	290	192	425	634	0.05	49.18
Ireland	3,509	3,262	1,493	3,424	4,204	0.35	22.78
Norway	6,008	6,347	5,156	6,754	8,657	0.72	28.18
Sweden	7,189	7,928	7,776	8,390	8,429	0.70	0.46
United Kingdom	15,324	12,935	14,108	20,496	23,904	1.99	16.63
Southern Europe	626,094	645,213	590,011	567,447	533,952	44.46	-5.90
Albania	37,801	30,540	39,252	37,601	27,388	2.28	-27.16
Bosnia and Herzegovina	101,394	98,822	101,874	103,025	97,497	8.12	-5.37
Croatia	12,809	18,624	15,677	17,497	20,195	1.68	15.42
Greece	2,112	3,380	2,970	3,487	4,373	0.36	25.41
Italy	37,211	31,341	42,549	39,987	34,403	2.86	-13.96
Portugal	619	518	8,466	808	5,504	0.46	581.19
Serbia	389,428	412,886	338,893	314,836	299,617	24.95	-4.83
Slovenia	20,663	17,890	18,891	22,472	20,027	1.67	-10.88
Spain	1,514	1,776	1,528	3,317	2,343	0.20	-29.36
TFYR of Macedonia	22,543	29,436	19,911	24,417	22,605	1.88	-7.42
Western Europe	81,789	79,767	79,661	100,388	96,925	8.07	-3.45
Austria	16,425	17,864	12,204	12,454	12,994	1.08	4.34
Belgium	6,708	7,172	7,473	8,146	7,201	0.60	-11.60
France	30,279	24,474	33,080	42,099	28,336	2.36	-32.69
Germany	17,891	22,297	18,329	25,381	33,427	2.78	31.70
Luxembourg	347	241	1,386	2,469	862	0.07	-65.09
Netherlands	5,510	4,629	4,225	3,468	6,647	0.55	91.67
Switzerland	4,629	3,090	2,964	6,371	7,458	0.62	17.06

MONTENEGRO

4. Arrivals of non-resident tourists in all types of accommodation establishments, by nationality

	2007	2008	2009	2010	2011	Market share 11	% Change 11-10
East Mediterranean Europe	**6,279**	**6,937**	**14,054**	**16,841**	**30,671**	**2.55**	**82.12**
Israel	5,261	4,599	11,142	10,595	11,799	0.98	11.36
Turkey	1,018	2,338	2,912	6,246	18,872	1.57	202.15
Other Europe	**5,314**	**2,605**	**52,315**	**46,119**	**44,898**	**3.74**	**-2.65**
Other countries of Europe	5,314	2,605	52,315	46,119	44,898	3.74	-2.65
NOT SPECIFIED	**4,476**	**5,496**	**5,168**	**7,216**	**11,665**	**0.97**	**61.65**
Other countries of the World	4,476	5,496	5,168	7,216	11,665	0.97	61.65

MONTENEGRO

5. Overnight stays of non-resident tourists in hotels and similar establishments, by nationality

	2007	2008	2009	2010	2011	Market share 11	% Change 11-10
TOTAL	3,061,652	3,234,096	2,388,133	2,478,239	2,647,592	100.00	6.83
AMERICAS	23,293	22,988	23,107	26,188	22,764	0.86	-13.07
North America	23,293	22,988	23,107	26,188	22,764	0.86	-13.07
Canada	3,505	4,217	3,904	4,474	5,410	0.20	20.92
United States of America	19,788	18,771	19,203	21,714	17,354	0.66	-20.08
EAST ASIA AND THE PACIFIC	5,382	6,786	5,650	6,789	8,448	0.32	24.44
North-East Asia	1,955	1,879	1,274	1,570	1,863	0.07	18.66
Japan	1,955	1,879	1,274	1,570	1,863	0.07	18.66
Australasia	3,427	4,907	4,376	5,219	6,585	0.25	26.17
Australia	2,983	4,163	3,688	4,402	5,718	0.22	29.90
New Zealand	444	744	688	817	867	0.03	6.12
EUROPE	3,016,238	3,192,988	2,344,820	2,426,615	2,591,984	97.90	6.81
Central/Eastern Europe	960,969	1,016,697	691,409	873,732	1,031,655	38.97	18.07
Bulgaria	9,727	13,782	13,126	10,393	14,252	0.54	37.13
Belarus	20,660	7,482	5,772	5,850	7,975	0.30	36.32
Czech Republic	191,376	165,094	74,237	73,549	93,548	3.53	27.19
Estonia	751	1,921	786	6,330	595	0.02	-90.60
Hungary	36,019	40,405	31,177	36,354	38,862	1.47	6.90
Latvia	1,039	2,039	447	1,994	674	0.03	-66.20
Lithuania	5,313	2,660	2,852	2,894	3,146	0.12	8.71
Poland	39,041	47,539	42,923	46,968	81,995	3.10	74.58
Romania	4,483	10,506	23,243	39,380	46,193	1.74	17.30
Russian Federation	542,375	601,557	428,511	571,981	644,972	24.36	12.76
Slovakia	58,843	44,383	27,401	28,877	36,013	1.36	24.71
Ukraine	51,342	79,329	40,934	49,162	63,430	2.40	29.02
Northern Europe	171,896	148,401	135,368	134,194	130,969	4.95	-2.40
Denmark	4,178	3,294	3,011	4,279	3,093	0.12	-27.72
Finland	17,967	10,924	7,023	5,410	6,818	0.26	26.03
Iceland	978	877	371	1,599	576	0.02	-63.98
Ireland	15,607	12,138	5,237	5,073	5,483	0.21	8.08
Norway	14,738	15,817	14,585	15,277	17,258	0.65	12.97
Sweden	32,647	34,222	39,607	38,576	36,036	1.36	-6.58
United Kingdom	85,781	71,129	65,534	63,980	61,705	2.33	-3.56
Southern Europe	1,538,623	1,680,297	1,221,678	1,097,605	1,057,412	39.94	-3.66
Albania	48,958	48,040	37,464	43,006	42,293	1.60	-1.66
Bosnia and Herzegovina	144,653	133,537	122,548	106,738	100,511	3.80	-5.83
Croatia	21,454	31,887	29,637	31,594	27,673	1.05	-12.41
Greece	4,781	9,866	5,258	5,981	6,485	0.24	8.43
Italy	58,010	53,432	59,227	62,686	78,588	2.97	25.37
Portugal	2,464	1,726	1,329	1,877	3,821	0.14	103.57
Serbia	1,144,416	1,279,062	854,589	760,121	722,192	27.28	-4.99
Slovenia	75,220	67,970	68,335	58,540	50,581	1.91	-13.60
Spain	3,405	4,831	4,393	5,906	4,887	0.18	-17.25
TFYR of Macedonia	35,262	49,946	38,898	21,156	20,381	0.77	-3.66
Western Europe	317,439	324,339	241,266	226,532	290,992	10.99	28.46
Austria	68,024	79,072	19,655	22,242	27,062	1.02	21.67
Belgium	40,594	45,007	32,337	32,645	33,272	1.26	1.92
France	96,241	96,379	91,804	100,579	121,896	4.60	21.19
Germany	84,097	85,446	76,936	42,145	87,427	3.30	107.44
Luxembourg	863	876	3,732	749	1,037	0.04	38.45
Netherlands	5,473	7,439	7,871	6,028	7,010	0.26	16.29
Switzerland	22,147	10,120	8,931	22,144	13,288	0.50	-39.99

MONTENEGRO

5. Overnight stays of non-resident tourists in hotels and similar establishments, by nationality

	2007	2008	2009	2010	2011	Market share 11	% Change 11-10
East Mediterranean Europe	**9,551**	**13,803**	**25,003**	**26,419**	**31,428**	**1.19**	**18.96**
Israel	7,671	8,505	19,311	16,509	18,862	0.71	14.25
Turkey	1,880	5,298	5,692	9,910	12,566	0.47	26.80
Other Europe	**17,760**	**9,451**	**30,096**	**68,133**	**49,528**	**1.87**	**-27.31**
Other countries of Europe	17,760	9,451	30,096	68,133	49,528	1.87	-27.31
NOT SPECIFIED	**16,739**	**11,334**	**14,556**	**18,647**	**24,396**	**0.92**	**30.83**
Other countries of the World	16,739	11,334	14,556	18,647	24,396	0.92	30.83

MONTENEGRO

6. Overnight stays of non-resident tourists in all types of accommodation establishments, by nationality

	2007	2008	2009	2010	2011	Market share 11	% Change 11-10
TOTAL	6,443,485	6,964,755	6,694,514	6,977,860	7,818,803	100.00	12.05
AMERICAS	27,899	28,072	28,765	41,051	54,025	0.69	31.60
North America	27,899	28,072	28,765	41,051	54,025	0.69	31.60
Canada	5,894	6,668	6,120	7,231	8,739	0.11	20.85
United States of America	22,005	21,404	22,645	33,820	45,286	0.58	33.90
EAST ASIA AND THE PACIFIC	6,718	8,135	7,259	10,266	16,248	0.21	58.27
North-East Asia	2,030	2,149	1,288	2,050	3,025	0.04	47.56
Japan	2,030	2,149	1,288	2,050	3,025	0.04	47.56
Australasia	4,688	5,986	5,971	8,216	13,223	0.17	60.94
Australia	4,218	5,189	5,113	6,675	11,141	0.14	66.91
New Zealand	470	797	858	1,541	2,082	0.03	35.11
EUROPE	6,389,237	6,909,950	6,642,906	6,901,660	7,706,203	98.56	11.66
Central/Eastern Europe	1,567,530	1,777,405	1,818,803	2,059,195	2,870,291	36.71	39.39
Bulgaria	18,912	16,533	23,307	18,967	18,849	0.24	-0.62
Belarus	33,280	27,683	14,187	45,636	52,935	0.68	15.99
Czech Republic	266,598	242,167	171,643	165,050	171,107	2.19	3.67
Estonia	1,272	10,382	1,350	8,857	2,641	0.03	-70.18
Hungary	200,675	187,694	205,259	183,031	98,577	1.26	-46.14
Latvia	1,641	14,722	11,371	2,966	2,683	0.03	-9.54
Lithuania	24,204	21,800	18,088	27,592	32,329	0.41	17.17
Poland	73,332	85,450	123,557	84,053	214,927	2.75	155.70
Romania	8,236	15,778	38,061	84,838	142,281	1.82	67.71
Russian Federation	789,497	897,921	1,060,458	1,217,978	1,791,616	22.91	47.10
Slovakia	83,939	76,253	61,841	52,353	71,168	0.91	35.94
Ukraine	65,944	181,022	89,681	167,874	271,178	3.47	61.54
Northern Europe	236,386	223,660	190,487	255,749	302,763	3.87	18.38
Denmark	6,964	6,986	5,371	7,606	6,717	0.09	-11.69
Finland	18,259	12,165	7,777	6,370	10,771	0.14	69.09
Iceland	1,178	1,150	454	1,795	3,303	0.04	84.01
Ireland	18,074	12,340	6,150	18,458	26,199	0.34	41.94
Norway	53,121	60,257	43,620	55,550	66,008	0.84	18.83
Sweden	48,247	55,418	47,696	50,542	50,219	0.64	-0.64
United Kingdom	90,543	75,344	79,419	115,428	139,546	1.78	20.89
Southern Europe	4,045,482	4,400,675	3,846,545	3,575,364	3,582,990	45.83	0.21
Albania	188,572	154,229	191,826	189,074	162,323	2.08	-14.15
Bosnia and Herzegovina	703,472	805,919	778,439	731,633	750,341	9.60	2.56
Croatia	44,717	82,365	59,767	66,161	89,876	1.15	35.84
Greece	5,993	12,073	5,498	6,794	9,106	0.12	34.03
Italy	205,937	151,376	225,976	199,617	143,938	1.84	-27.89
Portugal	2,550	1,747	42,710	3,381	31,572	0.40	833.81
Serbia	2,644,312	2,878,395	2,298,717	2,097,051	2,109,159	26.98	0.58
Slovenia	90,023	79,073	84,578	106,016	136,108	1.74	28.38
Spain	3,535	5,158	4,504	11,676	6,483	0.08	-44.48
TFYR of Macedonia	156,371	230,340	154,530	163,961	144,084	1.84	-12.12
Western Europe	508,827	478,548	458,024	601,875	507,588	6.49	-15.67
Austria	97,273	102,300	57,588	58,785	59,475	0.76	1.17
Belgium	44,139	48,274	46,834	48,063	43,677	0.56	-9.13
France	181,384	143,125	193,983	233,959	152,395	1.95	-34.86
Germany	116,807	137,146	109,893	151,843	182,724	2.34	20.34
Luxembourg	1,205	1,128	10,192	13,947	4,180	0.05	-70.03
Netherlands	41,826	33,658	27,647	66,161	31,472	0.40	-52.43
Switzerland	26,193	12,917	11,887	29,117	33,665	0.43	15.62

MONTENEGRO

6. Overnight stays of non-resident tourists in all types of accommodation establishments, by nationality

	2007	2008	2009	2010	2011	Market share 11	% Change 11-10
East Mediterranean Europe	**10,989**	**17,155**	**26,407**	**30,739**	**53,884**	**0.69**	**75.30**
Israel	8,823	9,313	20,163	19,729	22,815	0.29	15.64
Turkey	2,166	7,842	6,244	11,010	31,069	0.40	182.19
Other Europe	**20,023**	**12,507**	**302,640**	**378,738**	**388,687**	**4.97**	**2.63**
Other countries of Europe	20,023	12,507	302,640	378,738	388,687	4.97	2.63
NOT SPECIFIED	**19,631**	**18,598**	**15,584**	**24,883**	**42,327**	**0.54**	**70.10**
Other countries of the World	19,631	18,598	15,584	24,883	42,327	0.54	70.10

MONTSERRAT

1. Arrivals of non-resident tourists at national borders, by country of residence

	2007	2008	2009	2010	2011	Market share 11	% Change 11-10
TOTAL	7,746	7,360	6,324	5,981	5,395	100.00	-9.80
AMERICAS	5,311	4,989	4,252	4,353	3,749	69.49	-13.88
Caribbean	2,796	2,658	2,267	2,259	1,881	34.87	-16.73
All countries of the Caribbean	2,796	2,658	2,267	2,259	1,881	34.87	-16.73
North America	2,497	2,317	1,973	2,069	1,846	34.22	-10.78
Canada	388	395	367	404	320	5.93	-20.79
United States of America	2,109	1,922	1,606	1,665	1,526	28.29	-8.35
Other Americas	18	14	12	25	22	0.41	-12.00
Other countries of the Americas	18	14	12	25	22	0.41	-12.00
EAST ASIA AND THE PACIFIC	5		3	1	14	0.26	1300.00
North-East Asia	5		3	1	14	0.26	1300.00
Japan	5		3	1	14	0.26	1300.00
EUROPE	2,366	2,333	2,044	1,573	1,535	28.45	-2.42
Northern Europe	2,195	2,163	1,870	1,385	1,333	24.71	-3.75
Sweden	5	11	6	5	4	0.07	-20.00
United Kingdom	2,190	2,152	1,864	1,380	1,329	24.63	-3.70
Southern Europe	15	21	31	21	27	0.50	28.57
Italy	10	17	18	11	19	0.35	72.73
Spain	5	4	13	10	8	0.15	-20.00
Western Europe	126	116	94	114	117	2.17	2.63
Belgium	19	10	12	13	6	0.11	-53.85
France	49	48	47	51	60	1.11	17.65
Germany	39	32	18	30	31	0.57	3.33
Netherlands	13	8	5	1	7	0.13	600.00
Switzerland	6	18	12	19	13	0.24	-31.58
Other Europe	30	33	49	53	58	1.08	9.43
Other countries of Europe	30	33	49	53	58	1.08	9.43
NOT SPECIFIED	64	38	25	54	97	1.80	79.63
Other countries of the World	64	38	25	54	97	1.80	79.63

MONTSERRAT

2. Arrivals of non-resident visitors at national borders, by country of residence

	2007	2008	2009	2010	2011	Market share 11	% Change 11-10
TOTAL	8,714	8,319	7,335	7,707	7,392	100.00	-4.09
AMERICAS	6,008	5,724	5,081	5,540	5,078	68.70	-8.34
Caribbean	3,294	3,239	2,950	3,119	2,778	37.58	-10.93
All countries of the Caribbean	3,294	3,239	2,950	3,119	2,778	37.58	-10.93
North America	2,693	2,470	2,112	2,384	2,270	30.71	-4.78
Canada	435	428	378	471	396	5.36	-15.92
United States of America	2,258	2,042	1,734	1,913	1,874	25.35	-2.04
Other Americas	21	15	19	37	30	0.41	-18.92
Other countries of the Americas	21	15	19	37	30	0.41	-18.92
EUROPE	2,620	2,547	2,221	2,102	2,102	28.44	
Northern Europe	2,407	2,304	1,991	1,848	1,851	25.04	0.16
United Kingdom	2,407	2,304	1,991	1,848	1,851	25.04	0.16
Other Europe	213	243	230	254	251	3.40	-1.18
Other countries of Europe	213	243	230	254	251	3.40	-1.18
NOT SPECIFIED	86	48	33	65	212	2.87	226.15
Other countries of the World	86	48	33	65	212	2.87	226.15

MOROCCO

1. Arrivals of non-resident tourists at national borders, by nationality

	2007	2008	2009	2010	2011	Market share 11	% Change 11-10
TOTAL	7,407,617	7,878,639	8,341,237	9,288,338	9,342,133	100.00	0.58
AFRICA	192,668	213,611	222,879	255,564	298,622	3.20	16.85
East Africa	3,091	4,725	4,046	4,478	6,785	0.07	51.52
Burundi	164	286	137	193	189	0.00	-2.07
Comoros	280	242	324	470	411	0.00	-12.55
Ethiopia	323	370	479	502	549	0.01	9.36
Eritrea	78	101	90	83	116	0.00	39.76
Djibouti	305	839	381	435	361	0.00	-17.01
Kenya	547	714	883	874	870	0.01	-0.46
Madagascar	243	350	348	359	406	0.00	13.09
Malawi	62	66	122	75	27	0.00	-64.00
Mauritius	349	518	540	667	2,527	0.03	278.86
Mozambique	63	39	47	53	101	0.00	90.57
Rwanda	134	155	99	110	250	0.00	127.27
Seychelles	33	130	34	57	60	0.00	5.26
Somalia	90	128	100	77	235	0.00	205.19
Zimbabwe	92	148	135	164	140	0.00	-14.63
Uganda	138	413	138	153	173	0.00	13.07
United Republic of Tanzania	106	122	131	118	178	0.00	50.85
Zambia	84	104	58	88	192	0.00	118.18
Central Africa	12,275	17,017	19,587	21,994	34,109	0.37	55.08
Angola	506	834	1,426	2,926	4,231	0.05	44.60
Cameroon	2,382	3,591	3,703	3,869	3,443	0.04	-11.01
Central African Republic	299	393	375	855	937	0.01	9.59
Chad	342	329	268	413	430	0.00	4.12
Congo	4,339	5,799	6,905	7,906	10,228	0.11	29.37
Democratic Republic of the Congo	541	1,099	990	592	1,043	0.01	76.18
Equatorial Guinea	422	1,321	1,993	1,937	10,005	0.11	416.52
Gabon	3,444	3,651	3,927	3,496	3,792	0.04	8.47
North Africa	84,984	92,349	95,241	106,537	124,339	1.33	16.71
Algeria	53,827	58,650	59,512	68,183	80,741	0.86	18.42
Sudan	1,671	1,631	1,916	2,019	2,487	0.03	23.18
Tunisia	29,486	32,068	33,813	36,335	41,111	0.44	13.14
Southern Africa	3,979	4,231	3,765	4,739	4,117	0.04	-13.13
Botswana	42	107	76	56	95	0.00	69.64
Lesotho	14	57		1	27	0.00	2600.00
Namibia	82	95	90	53	69	0.00	30.19
South Africa	3,819	3,701	3,585	4,547	3,887	0.04	-14.52
Swaziland	22	271	14	82	39	0.00	-52.44
West Africa	88,339	95,289	100,240	117,816	129,272	1.38	9.72
Cape Verde	297	374	456	139	279	0.00	100.72
Benin	1,074	1,302	1,237	1,369	1,234	0.01	-9.86
Gambia	389	898	649	708	959	0.01	35.45
Ghana	946	784	894	781	871	0.01	11.52
Guinea	10,387	9,796	7,756	14,297	10,005	0.11	-30.02
Côte d'Ivoire	8,757	9,158	9,795	12,315	14,666	0.16	19.09
Liberia	285	383	370	398	347	0.00	-12.81
Mali	9,435	9,343	10,483	12,441	15,225	0.16	22.38
Mauritania	25,477	29,076	25,267	30,576	34,528	0.37	12.93
Niger	3,970	4,025	4,854	4,933	5,713	0.06	15.81
Nigeria	1,049	873	1,685	1,592	2,025	0.02	27.20
Guinea-Bissau	318	2,624	4,176	1,085	3,667	0.04	237.97
Senegal	22,801	23,581	28,878	32,969	36,067	0.39	9.40
Sierra Leone	377	350	364	439	323	0.00	-26.42
Togo	798	786	942	1,032	774	0.01	-25.00
Burkina Faso	1,979	1,936	2,434	2,742	2,589	0.03	-5.58

MOROCCO

1. Arrivals of non-resident tourists at national borders, by nationality

	2007	2008	2009	2010	2011	Market share 11	% Change 11-10
AMERICAS	**196,037**	**201,867**	**214,563**	**250,874**	**239,497**	**2.56**	**-4.53**
Caribbean	**1,057**	**1,183**	**1,673**	**1,464**	**2,092**	**0.02**	**42.90**
Bahamas	31	23	47	45	86	0.00	91.11
Barbados	117	14	101	163	793	0.01	386.50
Bermuda	35	31	142	10	13	0.00	30.00
Cuba	244	263	410	252	176	0.00	-30.16
Dominica	96	104	199	260	207	0.00	-20.38
Haiti	111	87	51	296	283	0.00	-4.39
Jamaica	186	421	401	129	124	0.00	-3.88
Puerto Rico	123	188	97	231	193	0.00	-16.45
Trinidad and Tobago	114	52	225	78	217	0.00	178.21
Central America	**694**	**860**	**1,376**	**3,620**	**1,301**	**0.01**	**-64.06**
Belize	43	2	194	38	9	0.00	-76.32
Costa Rica	162	236	271	315	307	0.00	-2.54
El Salvador	178	175	231	189	187	0.00	-1.06
Guatemala	92	188	330	278	421	0.00	51.44
Honduras	120	139	147	2,558	162	0.00	-93.67
Nicaragua	43	39	76	72	66	0.00	-8.33
Panama	56	81	127	170	149	0.00	-12.35
North America	**166,431**	**173,371**	**181,410**	**210,948**	**200,420**	**2.15**	**-4.99**
Canada	50,802	56,231	54,789	67,925	63,237	0.68	-6.90
Mexico	6,550	6,362	5,477	7,647	6,756	0.07	-11.65
United States of America	109,079	110,778	121,144	135,376	130,427	1.40	-3.66
South America	**27,855**	**26,453**	**30,104**	**34,842**	**35,684**	**0.38**	**2.42**
Argentina	8,189	7,219	8,077	9,615	8,447	0.09	-12.15
Bolivia	136	202	252	263	287	0.00	9.13
Brazil	10,252	10,146	10,978	13,049	14,552	0.16	11.52
Chile	3,502	2,846	2,788	3,516	3,611	0.04	2.70
Colombia	1,055	1,506	2,032	2,473	2,386	0.03	-3.52
Ecuador	613	460	622	555	630	0.01	13.51
Guyana					3	0.00	
Paraguay	57	97	155	197	163	0.00	-17.26
Peru	841	1,105	1,724	2,164	1,960	0.02	-9.43
Suriname	99	77	48	59	250	0.00	323.73
Uruguay	1,610	1,081	1,383	1,082	1,323	0.01	22.27
Venezuela	1,501	1,714	2,045	1,869	2,072	0.02	10.86
EAST ASIA AND THE PACIFIC	**73,910**	**76,127**	**77,415**	**98,995**	**87,370**	**0.94**	**-11.74**
North-East Asia	**35,548**	**34,497**	**35,762**	**48,235**	**37,552**	**0.40**	**-22.15**
China	4,374	4,665	4,129	5,769	5,882	0.06	1.96
Taiwan, Province of China	594	456	709	964	949	0.01	-1.56
Hong Kong, China	885	1,794	1,154	1,340	1,066	0.01	-20.45
Japan	16,902	15,607	19,149	24,366	22,861	0.24	-6.18
Korea, Dem. People's Republic of	110	3	620	1	912	0.01	91100.00
Korea, Republic of	12,683	11,972	10,001	15,795	5,882	0.06	-62.76
South-East Asia	**12,994**	**16,202**	**16,452**	**20,873**	**21,260**	**0.23**	**1.85**
Brunei Darussalam	34	37	64	50	76	0.00	52.00
Myanmar	84	152	109	107	82	0.00	-23.36
Cambodia	19	12	25	76	202	0.00	165.79
Indonesia	2,083	2,440	2,572	3,606	3,974	0.04	10.21
Malaysia	2,219	2,417	2,101	2,801	2,302	0.02	-17.82
Philippines	5,198	6,317	7,989	10,170	10,697	0.11	5.18
Singapore	1,076	1,299	1,412	1,832	1,662	0.02	-9.28
Viet Nam	849	1,561	342	245	314	0.00	28.16
Thailand	1,432	1,967	1,838	1,986	1,951	0.02	-1.76
Australasia	**25,319**	**25,427**	**25,201**	**29,879**	**28,541**	**0.31**	**-4.48**
Australia	22,064	21,467	20,531	24,690	23,502	0.25	-4.81

MOROCCO

1. Arrivals of non-resident tourists at national borders, by nationality

	2007	2008	2009	2010	2011	Market share 11	% Change 11-10
New Zealand	3,255	3,960	4,670	5,189	5,039	0.05	-2.89
Micronesia	**49**	**1**		**8**	**17**	**0.00**	**112.50**
Kiribati	49	1		8	17	0.00	112.50
EUROPE	**3,406,184**	**3,563,990**	**3,623,479**	**4,143,648**	**4,137,156**	**44.28**	**-0.16**
Central/Eastern Europe	**78,708**	**87,214**	**91,795**	**117,094**	**123,972**	**1.33**	**5.87**
Azerbaijan	130	201	384	334	237	0.00	-29.04
Armenia	62	87	244	96	279	0.00	190.63
Bulgaria	2,474	2,684	4,013	4,419	3,990	0.04	-9.71
Belarus	260	1,226	264	360	446	0.00	23.89
Czech Republic	5,232	4,708	5,685	5,647	10,435	0.11	84.79
Estonia	1,437	802	1,096	1,970	2,629	0.03	33.45
Hungary	5,335	4,766	5,175	5,171	4,657	0.05	-9.94
Kazakhstan	150	175	218	225	225	0.00	
Lithuania	2,870	1,926	2,093	2,753	3,644	0.04	32.36
Poland	31,142	36,596	34,686	42,040	49,933	0.53	18.77
Romania	8,744	9,372	10,974	11,834	13,172	0.14	11.31
Russian Federation	12,724	16,220	19,114	32,460	22,620	0.24	-30.31
Slovakia	2,648	2,869	3,387	5,026	7,013	0.08	39.53
Ukraine	5,410	5,186	4,368	4,509	4,562	0.05	1.18
Uzbekistan	90	396	94	250	130	0.00	-48.00
Northern Europe	**416,774**	**352,400**	**327,176**	**423,567**	**452,337**	**4.84**	**6.79**
Denmark	12,585	12,281	10,512	14,863	22,153	0.24	49.05
Finland	10,760	10,727	8,874	6,045	5,263	0.06	-12.94
Iceland	1,206	882	1,402	844	981	0.01	16.23
Ireland	14,041	15,562	17,974	20,341	15,446	0.17	-24.06
Norway	10,324	11,399	10,934	15,255	21,847	0.23	43.21
Sweden	29,554	26,787	24,535	28,159	34,506	0.37	22.54
United Kingdom	338,304	274,762	252,945	338,060	352,141	3.77	4.17
Southern Europe	**763,718**	**820,182**	**889,934**	**1,039,311**	**991,457**	**10.61**	**-4.60**
Albania	314	136	584	213	283	0.00	32.86
Andorra	712	647	872	563	676	0.01	20.07
Bosnia and Herzegovina	353	278	329	358	267	0.00	-25.42
Croatia	1,388	1,299	1,598	2,141	1,922	0.02	-10.23
Greece	7,277	7,473	7,875	7,844	5,340	0.06	-31.92
Italy	160,047	163,315	177,915	233,224	211,405	2.26	-9.36
Malta	639	620	812	792	768	0.01	-3.03
Portugal	48,641	47,055	53,079	63,077	72,995	0.78	15.72
San Marino	109	73	40	59	43	0.00	-27.12
Serbia	773	726	824	1,111	997	0.01	-10.26
Slovenia	2,724	2,762	2,897	3,274	3,429	0.04	4.73
Spain	540,186	595,279	642,817	726,540	693,255	7.42	-4.58
TFYR of Macedonia	555	519	292	115	77	0.00	-33.04
Western Europe	**2,114,023**	**2,268,543**	**2,283,962**	**2,523,278**	**2,537,790**	**27.16**	**0.58**
Austria	17,536	15,901	13,581	17,731	13,956	0.15	-21.29
Belgium	164,723	173,004	188,108	221,371	258,620	2.77	16.83
France	1,605,503	1,707,055	1,699,201	1,827,453	1,775,961	19.01	-2.82
Germany	159,844	179,037	174,384	205,417	219,576	2.35	6.89
Liechtenstein	235	202	210	103	112	0.00	8.74
Luxembourg	1,930	2,786	3,509	4,141	3,991	0.04	-3.62
Monaco	126	175	294	344	317	0.00	-7.85
Netherlands	107,257	128,093	139,611	175,078	197,642	2.12	12.89
Switzerland	56,869	62,290	65,064	71,640	67,615	0.72	-5.62
East Mediterranean Europe	**32,961**	**35,651**	**30,612**	**40,398**	**31,600**	**0.34**	**-21.78**
Cyprus	354	348	438	481	450	0.00	-6.44
Israel	16,974	19,186	13,466	19,190	8,985	0.10	-53.18
Turkey	15,633	16,117	16,708	20,727	22,165	0.24	6.94

MOROCCO

1. Arrivals of non-resident tourists at national borders, by nationality

	2007	2008	2009	2010	2011	Market share 11	% Change 11-10
MIDDLE EAST	**115,832**	**127,486**	**134,659**	**142,091**	**152,326**	**1.63**	**7.20**
Bahrain	2,473	2,781	2,956	3,028	2,870	0.03	-5.22
Palestine	1,060	1,090	1,321	1,337	1,304	0.01	-2.47
Iraq	1,542	1,537	1,486	1,688	2,085	0.02	23.52
Jordan	4,227	4,614	4,907	4,945	4,877	0.05	-1.38
Kuwait	6,640	7,562	9,131	9,111	12,649	0.14	38.83
Lebanon	8,604	7,510	6,835	7,332	6,337	0.07	-13.57
Libya	13,960	16,026	17,174	20,456	18,037	0.19	-11.83
Oman	3,278	4,409	4,076	4,305	3,777	0.04	-12.26
Qatar	3,055	2,882	2,732	2,976	3,183	0.03	6.96
Saudi Arabia	39,815	42,924	48,780	51,219	62,887	0.67	22.78
Syrian Arab Republic	5,193	5,309	4,505	4,782	4,342	0.05	-9.20
United Arab Emirates	10,301	12,384	12,496	12,659	14,552	0.16	14.95
Egypt	14,441	16,977	16,614	16,543	13,689	0.15	-17.25
Yemen	1,243	1,481	1,646	1,710	1,737	0.02	1.58
SOUTH ASIA	**11,592**	**11,901**	**11,753**	**12,242**	**12,486**	**0.13**	**1.99**
Afghanistan	283	150	123	143	330	0.00	130.77
Bangladesh	293	384	547	546	942	0.01	72.53
Sri Lanka	383	967	510	611	544	0.01	-10.97
India	6,306	6,363	6,995	7,936	7,640	0.08	-3.73
Iran, Islamic Republic of	1,847	1,689	959	519	519	0.01	
Maldives	70	85	64	58	50	0.00	-13.79
Nepal	223	195	212	272	289	0.00	6.25
Pakistan	2,187	2,068	2,343	2,157	2,172	0.02	0.70
NOT SPECIFIED	**3,411,394**	**3,683,657**	**4,056,489**	**4,384,924**	**4,414,676**	**47.26**	**0.68**
Other countries of the World	34,675	16,873	8,210	7,021	6,426	0.07	-8.47
Nationals Residing Abroad	3,376,719	3,666,784	4,048,279	4,377,903	4,408,250	47.19	0.69

MOROCCO

3. Arrivals of non-resident tourists in hotels and similar establishments, by nationality

	2007	2008	2009	2010	2011	Market share 11	% Change 11-10
TOTAL (*)	3,910,235	3,824,214	3,669,087	4,077,535	3,455,696	100.00	-15.25
AFRICA	86,440	99,724	101,948	117,966	133,845	3.87	13.46
North Africa	45,308	52,963	52,294	62,050	71,389	2.07	15.05
Algeria	30,314	36,482	35,543	42,718	50,217	1.45	17.55
Tunisia	14,994	16,481	16,751	19,332	21,172	0.61	9.52
West Africa	6,725	6,929	5,139	6,445	7,308	0.21	13.39
Mauritania	6,725	6,929	5,139	6,445	7,308	0.21	13.39
Other Africa	34,407	39,832	44,515	49,471	55,148	1.60	11.48
Other countries of Africa	34,407	39,832	44,515	49,471	55,148	1.60	11.48
AMERICAS	128,988	132,633	129,806	152,223	127,013	3.68	-16.56
North America	128,988	132,633	129,806	152,223	127,013	3.68	-16.56
Canada	27,238	28,182	28,094	32,546	28,629	0.83	-12.04
United States of America	101,750	104,451	101,712	119,677	98,384	2.85	-17.79
EAST ASIA AND THE PACIFIC	54,831	47,030	44,999	60,862	54,835	1.59	-9.90
North-East Asia	54,831	47,030	44,999	60,862	54,835	1.59	-9.90
Japan	54,831	47,030	44,999	60,862	54,835	1.59	-9.90
EUROPE	3,167,589	3,038,577	2,913,714	3,164,721	2,634,037	76.22	-16.77
Central/Eastern Europe	60,429	60,619	71,921	90,785	90,224	2.61	-0.62
Commonwealth Independent States	60,429	60,619	71,921	90,785	90,224	2.61	-0.62
Northern Europe	354,581	296,156	255,464	333,058	327,033	9.46	-1.81
Denmark	8,454	5,873	5,235	7,225	10,321	0.30	42.85
Finland	7,142	7,006	5,920	2,368	2,487	0.07	5.03
Norway	6,059	6,932	4,570	6,892	10,833	0.31	57.18
Sweden	20,775	17,941	15,173	17,089	18,237	0.53	6.72
United Kingdom	312,151	258,404	224,566	299,484	285,155	8.25	-4.78
Southern Europe	612,246	622,782	655,169	692,452	489,534	14.17	-29.30
Italy	216,014	204,417	208,211	241,119	156,827	4.54	-34.96
Portugal	39,657	40,158	41,877	50,817	44,636	1.29	-12.16
Spain	356,575	378,207	405,081	400,516	288,071	8.34	-28.08
Western Europe	2,140,333	2,059,020	1,931,160	2,048,426	1,727,246	49.98	-15.68
Austria	18,844	13,234	12,688	15,824	11,588	0.34	-26.77
Belgium	127,229	113,867	111,039	111,056	117,688	3.41	5.97
France	1,621,611	1,537,273	1,422,823	1,474,509	1,206,521	34.91	-18.17
Germany	232,175	230,740	227,808	270,965	251,097	7.27	-7.33
Netherlands	93,953	115,031	112,334	127,023	102,250	2.96	-19.50
Switzerland	46,521	48,875	44,468	49,049	38,102	1.10	-22.32
MIDDLE EAST	106,045	121,941	128,002	131,274	133,680	3.87	1.83
Libya	7,715	8,678	10,209	12,517	11,283	0.33	-9.86
Saudi Arabia	33,315	38,057	44,932	46,315	52,454	1.52	13.25
Syrian Arab Republic	2,628	2,143	2,023	2,302	2,111	0.06	-8.30
United Arab Emirates	13,136	15,804	12,153	11,527	10,259	0.30	-11.00
Egypt	9,909	11,548	12,114	12,217	11,531	0.33	-5.62
Other countries of Middle East	39,342	45,711	46,571	46,396	46,042	1.33	-0.76
NOT SPECIFIED	366,342	384,309	350,618	450,489	372,286	10.77	-17.36
Other countries of the World	348,213	363,187	332,366	434,523	353,721	10.24	-18.60
Nationals Residing Abroad	18,129	21,122	18,252	15,966	18,565	0.54	16.28

MOROCCO

5. Overnight stays of non-resident tourists in hotels and similar establishments, by nationality

	2007	2008	2009	2010	2011	Market share 11	% Change 11-10
TOTAL (*)	13,703,222	13,067,592	12,520,803	13,954,610	12,418,682	100.00	-11.01
AFRICA	263,260	300,093	291,101	330,275	366,492	2.95	10.97
North Africa	143,686	159,631	155,336	184,025	211,251	1.70	14.79
Algeria	100,261	113,135	106,274	129,270	150,366	1.21	16.32
Tunisia	43,425	46,496	49,062	54,755	60,885	0.49	11.20
West Africa	16,054	20,965	10,940	17,320	17,595	0.14	1.59
Mauritania	16,054	20,965	10,940	17,320	17,595	0.14	1.59
Other Africa	103,520	119,497	124,825	128,930	137,646	1.11	6.76
Other countries of Africa	103,520	119,497	124,825	128,930	137,646	1.11	6.76
AMERICAS	299,457	318,955	319,839	363,015	311,801	2.51	-14.11
North America	299,457	318,955	319,839	363,015	311,801	2.51	-14.11
Canada	65,589	69,041	73,286	76,900	72,380	0.58	-5.88
United States of America	233,868	249,914	246,553	286,115	239,421	1.93	-16.32
EAST ASIA AND THE PACIFIC	84,045	75,639	78,306	102,374	89,612	0.72	-12.47
North-East Asia	84,045	75,639	78,306	102,374	89,612	0.72	-12.47
Japan	84,045	75,639	78,306	102,374	89,612	0.72	-12.47
EUROPE	11,798,920	11,021,660	10,485,295	11,548,134	10,147,295	81.71	-12.13
Central/Eastern Europe	211,663	278,658	321,288	438,862	367,048	2.96	-16.36
Commonwealth Independent States	211,663	278,658	321,288	438,862	367,048	2.96	-16.36
Northern Europe	1,608,863	1,278,187	1,077,219	1,487,413	1,523,310	12.27	2.41
Denmark	40,514	21,501	14,677	22,978	41,141	0.33	79.05
Finland	48,326	52,178	35,196	7,021	8,067	0.06	14.90
Norway	29,080	31,766	15,077	25,524	42,984	0.35	68.41
Sweden	123,801	98,069	82,299	86,339	91,511	0.74	5.99
United Kingdom	1,367,142	1,074,673	929,970	1,345,551	1,339,607	10.79	-0.44
Southern Europe	1,467,732	1,484,168	1,592,660	1,734,905	1,318,904	10.62	-23.98
Italy	604,219	570,730	571,376	657,142	460,409	3.71	-29.94
Portugal	96,960	96,453	99,294	132,303	152,048	1.22	14.92
Spain	766,553	816,985	921,990	945,460	706,447	5.69	-25.28
Western Europe	8,510,662	7,980,647	7,494,128	7,886,954	6,938,033	55.87	-12.03
Austria	54,171	32,530	32,857	39,869	29,947	0.24	-24.89
Belgium	667,906	590,868	582,277	589,418	641,405	5.16	8.82
France	6,419,752	5,936,414	5,550,236	5,814,996	4,906,723	39.51	-15.62
Germany	988,958	959,079	895,617	946,323	944,226	7.60	-0.22
Netherlands	240,126	309,259	292,937	340,763	290,086	2.34	-14.87
Switzerland	139,749	152,497	140,204	155,585	125,646	1.01	-19.24
MIDDLE EAST	362,851	421,778	472,371	436,613	469,267	3.78	7.48
Libya	20,049	22,987	23,995	30,617	28,560	0.23	-6.72
Saudi Arabia	141,703	172,676	220,651	183,672	209,654	1.69	14.15
Syrian Arab Republic	8,481	5,793	7,677	7,995	12,888	0.10	61.20
United Arab Emirates	31,484	39,581	27,607	27,864	26,388	0.21	-5.30
Egypt	31,791	32,259	33,508	35,422	38,504	0.31	8.70
Other countries of Middle East	129,343	148,482	158,933	151,043	153,273	1.23	1.48
NOT SPECIFIED	894,689	929,467	873,891	1,174,199	1,034,215	8.33	-11.92
Other countries of the World	863,876	893,555	843,189	1,145,382	996,625	8.03	-12.99
Nationals Residing Abroad	30,813	35,912	30,702	28,817	37,590	0.30	30.44

MOZAMBIQUE

2. Arrivals of non-resident visitors at national borders, by country of residence

		2007	2008	2009	2010	2011	Market share 11	% Change 11-10
TOTAL	(*)	1,259,000	1,438,684	1,711,147	1,836,143			
AFRICA		1,043,310	1,213,201	1,442,962	1,465,793			
East Africa		222,913	343,821	408,964	377,152			
Malawi		118,820	96,562	114,849	228,092			
Zimbabwe		101,895	238,825	284,084	149,060			
Zambia		2,198	8,434	10,031				
Southern Africa		427,761	833,448	991,290	985,599			
South Africa		398,668	675,745	803,720	946,583			
Swaziland		29,093	157,703	187,570	39,016			
Other Africa		392,636	35,932	42,708	103,042			
Other countries of Africa		392,636	35,932	42,708	103,042			
AMERICAS		18,799	38,981	46,363	102,041			
North America		12,319	21,682	25,788	21,292			
United States of America		12,319	21,682	25,788	21,292			
Other Americas		6,480	17,299	20,575	80,749			
Other countries of the Americas		6,480	17,299	20,575	80,749			
EAST ASIA AND THE PACIFIC		12,680	18,699	22,240	28,211			
Other East Asia and the Pacific		12,680	18,699	22,240	28,211			
All countries of Asia		12,680	18,699	22,240	28,211			
EUROPE		66,233	161,850	192,502	219,089			
Northern Europe		13,537	27,900	33,184	50,420			
United Kingdom		13,537	27,900	33,184	50,420			
Southern Europe		24,585	31,406	37,353	25,810			
Portugal		24,585	31,406	37,353	25,810			
Other Europe		28,111	102,544	121,965	142,859			
Other countries of Europe		28,111	102,544	121,965	142,859			
NOT SPECIFIED		117,978	5,953	7,080	21,009			
Other countries of the World		117,978	5,953	7,080	21,009			

MYANMAR

1. Arrivals of non-resident tourists at national borders, by nationality

		2007	2008	2009	2010	2011	Market share 11	% Change 11-10
TOTAL	(*)	248,076	193,319	243,278	310,688	391,176	100.00	25.91
AFRICA		432	539	764	816	993	0.25	21.69
Other Africa		432	539	764	816	993	0.25	21.69
All countries of Africa		432	539	764	816	993	0.25	21.69
AMERICAS		19,331	16,158	18,662	20,580	27,745	7.09	34.82
North America		17,854	15,229	17,440	18,911	25,365	6.48	34.13
Canada		2,992	2,034	2,387	2,407	3,685	0.94	53.10
United States of America		14,862	13,195	15,053	16,504	21,680	5.54	31.36
Other Americas		1,477	929	1,222	1,669	2,380	0.61	42.60
Other countries of the Americas		1,477	929	1,222	1,669	2,380	0.61	42.60
EAST ASIA AND THE PACIFIC		142,904	124,242	157,092	207,450	257,008	65.70	23.89
North-East Asia		76,469	68,598	78,670	99,624	125,225	32.01	25.70
China		29,551	30,792	36,341	46,141	62,018	15.85	34.41
Taiwan, Province of China		13,707	11,472	12,276	14,170	15,542	3.97	9.68
Hong Kong, China		3,048	2,410	2,747	3,081	3,820	0.98	23.99
Japan		15,623	10,881	13,809	16,186	21,321	5.45	31.72
Korea, Republic of		13,821	12,369	12,508	18,930	22,524	5.76	18.99
Other countries of North-East Asia		719	674	989	1,116			
South-East Asia		58,663	49,496	70,333	98,992	100,374	25.66	1.40
Indonesia		1,905	1,904	2,072	2,398			
Malaysia		8,693	8,268	9,668	16,186	23,287	5.95	43.87
Philippines		1,653	1,595	1,888	2,169			
Singapore		9,310	8,599	10,712	12,114	15,391	3.93	27.05
Viet Nam		1,267	1,084	1,864	5,609			
Thailand		35,002	27,311	43,254	59,692	61,696	15.77	3.36
Other countries of South-East Asia		833	735	875	824			
Australasia		7,665	6,065	7,993	8,686	11,603	2.97	33.58
Australia		6,761	5,374	7,163	7,693	10,415	2.66	35.38
New Zealand		904	691	830	993	1,188	0.30	19.64
Other East Asia and the Pacific		107	83	96	148	19,806	5.06	13282.43
Other countries of Asia		79	69	84	139	19,787	5.06	14135.25
Other countries of Oceania		28	14	12	9	19	0.00	111.11
EUROPE		72,827	40,885	53,150	65,935	88,517	22.63	34.25
Central/Eastern Europe		1,976	1,726	4,623	6,117	7,622	1.95	24.60
Russian Federation		1,976	1,726	2,070	2,757	3,496	0.89	26.80
Other countries Central/East Europe				2,553	3,360	4,126	1.05	22.80
Northern Europe		7,724	6,419	7,770	9,504	11,056	2.83	16.33
Denmark		760	461	882	1,247			
Sweden		608	561	717	917			
United Kingdom		6,356	5,397	6,171	7,340	11,056	2.83	50.63
Southern Europe		16,858	5,618	10,456	12,981	16,369	4.18	26.10
Italy		10,130	3,030	5,975	7,169	9,710	2.48	35.44
Spain		6,728	2,588	4,481	5,812	6,659	1.70	14.57
Western Europe		42,201	23,792	28,477	35,084	44,305	11.33	26.28
Austria		2,542	1,212	1,447	1,896	1,964	0.50	3.59
Belgium		2,307	1,386	1,848	2,411	3,376	0.86	40.02
France		15,521	8,217	10,458	13,143	19,414	4.96	47.71
Germany		15,432	8,947	9,608	11,082	14,006	3.58	26.39
Netherlands		2,105	1,548	1,887	2,384			
Switzerland		4,294	2,482	3,229	4,168	5,545	1.42	33.04
Other Europe		4,068	3,330	1,824	2,249	9,165	2.34	307.51
Other countries of Europe		4,068	3,330	1,824	2,249	9,165	2.34	307.51

MYANMAR

1. Arrivals of non-resident tourists at national borders, by nationality

	2007	2008	2009	2010	2011	Market share 11	% Change 11-10
MIDDLE EAST	**2,281**	**1,379**	**1,564**	**2,208**	**2,607**	**0.67**	**18.07**
All countries of Middle East	2,281	1,379	1,564	2,208	2,607	0.67	18.07
SOUTH ASIA	**10,301**	**10,116**	**12,046**	**13,699**	**14,306**	**3.66**	**4.43**
Bangladesh	1,046	1,001	1,212	1,441	1,988	0.51	37.96
India	7,675	7,173	8,609	9,849	12,318	3.15	25.07
Pakistan			733	794			
Other countries of South Asia	1,580	1,942	1,492	1,615			

MYANMAR

5. Overnight stays of non-resident tourists in hotels and similar establishments, by nationality

	2007	2008	2009	2010	2011	Market share 11	% Change 11-10
TOTAL	1,641,142	1,739,871	2,067,863	2,485,504			
AFRICA	3,106	4,851	6,494	6,536			
Other Africa	3,106	4,851	6,494	6,536			
All countries of Africa	3,106	4,851	6,494	6,536			
AMERICAS	140,801	145,422	158,628	164,632			
North America	132,814	137,061	148,241	151,288			
Canada	20,223	18,306	20,290	19,256			
United States of America	112,591	118,755	127,951	132,032			
Other Americas	7,987	8,361	10,387	13,344			
Other countries of the Americas	7,987	8,361	10,387	13,344			
EAST ASIA AND THE PACIFIC	940,746	1,118,178	1,335,282	1,659,600			
North-East Asia	503,134	617,382	668,696	796,992			
China	136,400	277,128	308,899	369,128			
Taiwan, Province of China	128,618	103,248	104,346	113,360			
Hong Kong, China	18,268	21,690	23,350	24,648			
Japan	135,842	97,929	117,377	129,488			
Korea, Republic of	84,006	111,321	106,318	151,440			
Other countries of North-East Asia		6,066	8,406	8,928			
South-East Asia	344,340	445,464	597,830	791,936			
Indonesia		17,136	17,613	19,184			
Malaysia	73,372	74,412	82,178	129,488			
Philippines		14,355	16,048	17,352			
Singapore	74,009	77,391	91,053	96,912			
Viet Nam		9,756	15,844	44,872			
Thailand	196,959	245,799	367,660	477,536			
Other countries of South-East Asia		6,615	7,434	6,592			
Australasia	48,252	54,585	67,940	69,488			
Australia	41,902	48,366	60,885	61,544			
New Zealand	6,350	6,219	7,055	7,944			
Other East Asia and the Pacific	45,020	747	816	1,184			
Other countries of Asia	45,020	621	714	1,112			
Other countries of Oceania		126	102	72			
EUROPE	480,373	367,965	451,774	527,480			
Central/Eastern Europe	21,243	15,534	39,295	48,936			
Russian Federation	6,606	15,534	17,595	22,056			
Other countries Central/East Europe	14,637		21,700	26,880			
Northern Europe	54,528	57,771	66,045	76,032			
Denmark		4,149	7,497	9,976			
Sweden		5,049	6,095	7,336			
United Kingdom	54,528	48,573	52,453	58,720			
Southern Europe	89,129	50,562	88,876	103,848			
Italy	55,842	27,270	50,788	57,352			
Spain	33,287	23,292	38,088	46,496			
Western Europe	278,618	214,128	242,054	280,672			
Austria	27,505	10,908	12,300	15,168			
Belgium	17,759	12,474	15,708	19,288			
France	100,258	73,953	88,893	105,144			
Germany	103,504	80,523	81,668	88,656			
Netherlands		13,932	16,039	19,072			
Switzerland	29,592	22,338	27,446	33,344			
Other Europe	36,855	29,970	15,504	17,992			
Other countries of Europe	36,855	29,970	15,504	17,992			

MYANMAR

5. Overnight stays of non-resident tourists in hotels and similar establishments, by nationality

	2007	2008	2009	2010	2011	Market share 11	% Change 11-10
MIDDLE EAST	**12,383**	**12,411**	**13,294**	**17,664**			
All countries of Middle East	12,383	12,411	13,294	17,664			
SOUTH ASIA	**63,733**	**91,044**	**102,391**	**109,592**			
Bangladesh	11,466	9,009	10,302	11,528			
India	52,267	64,557	73,177	78,792			
Pakistan			6,230	6,352			
Other countries of South Asia		17,478	12,682	12,920			

NAMIBIA

1. Arrivals of non-resident tourists at national borders, by nationality

	2007	2008	2009	2010	2011	Market share 11	% Change 11-10
TOTAL	928,914	931,110	980,178	984,098			
AFRICA	690,148	676,444	723,762	714,287			
East Africa	67,473	79,529	86,175	91,896			
Zimbabwe	26,764	29,281	31,842	37,667			
Zambia	40,709	50,248	54,333	54,229			
Central Africa	336,045	310,395	309,127	296,825			
Angola	336,045	310,395	309,127	296,825			
Southern Africa	275,687	269,416	312,697	309,158			
Botswana	25,649	26,378	26,918	31,503			
South Africa	250,038	243,038	285,779	277,655			
Other Africa	10,943	17,104	15,763	16,408			
Other countries of Africa	10,943	17,104	15,763	16,408			
AMERICAS	19,342	29,201	26,657	26,175			
North America	19,342	26,346	24,940	22,793			
Canada		5,490	4,860	4,967			
United States of America	19,342	20,856	20,080	17,826			
South America		2,855	1,717	3,382			
Brazil		2,855	1,717	3,382			
EAST ASIA AND THE PACIFIC	5,783	9,778	11,484	11,294			
North-East Asia		3,661	5,119	4,228			
China		3,661	5,119	4,228			
Australasia	5,783	6,117	6,365	7,066			
Australia	5,783	6,117	6,365	7,066			
EUROPE	194,605	204,115	206,496	219,070			
Central/Eastern Europe		1,935	1,806	1,762			
Russian Federation		1,935	1,806	1,762			
Northern Europe	36,660	37,617	36,720	36,308			
United Kingdom	28,214	28,111	28,039	25,717			
Scandinavia	8,446	9,506	8,681	10,591			
Southern Europe	20,097	23,960	26,176	27,962			
Italy	10,102	11,836	12,095	10,767			
Portugal	5,027	5,965	8,653	9,124			
Spain	4,968	6,159	5,428	8,071			
Western Europe	131,427	132,947	135,460	147,015			
Austria	6,198	6,664	7,201	7,197			
Belgium	6,400	4,909	5,647	7,024			
France	15,019	14,604	15,044	17,039			
Germany	80,418	81,543	81,974	87,072			
Netherlands	13,282	14,382	14,503	16,078			
Switzerland	10,110	10,845	11,091	12,605			
Other Europe	6,421	7,656	6,334	6,023			
Other countries of Europe	6,421	7,656	6,334	6,023			
NOT SPECIFIED	19,036	11,572	11,779	13,272			
Other countries of the World	19,036	11,572	11,779	13,272			

NAMIBIA

2. Arrivals of non-resident visitors at national borders, by nationality

	2007	2008	2009	2010	2011	Market share 11	% Change 11-10
TOTAL	1,048,359			1,114,423			
AFRICA	798,458			833,316			
East Africa	129,143			160,981			
Zimbabwe	27,497			38,598			
Zambia	101,646			122,383			
Central Africa	350,202			319,987			
Angola	350,202			319,987			
Southern Africa	307,968			335,507			
Botswana	32,321			36,032			
South Africa	275,647			299,475			
Other Africa	11,145			16,841			
Other countries of Africa	11,145			16,841			
AMERICAS	20,662			28,470			
North America	20,662			24,811			
Canada				5,233			
United States of America	20,662			19,578			
South America				3,659			
Brazil				3,659			
EAST ASIA AND THE PACIFIC	6,099			11,581			
North-East Asia				4,300			
China				4,300			
Australasia	6,099			7,281			
Australia	6,099			7,281			
EUROPE	203,029			227,519			
Central/Eastern Europe				1,762			
Russian Federation				1,762			
Northern Europe	39,886			38,417			
United Kingdom	31,182			27,460			
Scandinavia	8,704			10,957			
Southern Europe	20,981			30,707			
Italy	10,556			10,866			
Portugal	5,198			11,576			
Spain	5,227			8,265			
Western Europe	135,345			150,422			
Austria	6,338			7,360			
Belgium	6,652			7,176			
France	15,562			17,187			
Germany	82,285			88,950			
Netherlands	14,140			16,954			
Switzerland	10,368			12,795			
Other Europe	6,817			6,211			
Other countries of Europe	6,817			6,211			
NOT SPECIFIED	20,111			13,537			
Other countries of the World	20,111			13,537			

NEPAL

1. Arrivals of non-resident tourists at national borders, by nationality

	2007	2008	2009	2010	2011	Market share 11	% Change 11-10
TOTAL	526,633	500,277	509,956	602,867	736,215	100.00	22.12
AFRICA	1,350	810	435	461	2,239	0.30	385.68
East Africa		204	141	219	349	0.05	59.36
Kenya		204	141	219	223	0.03	1.83
Mauritius					126	0.02	
North Africa		493	252	173	231	0.03	33.53
Algeria		416	196	53	131	0.02	147.17
Morocco		34	42	92	76	0.01	-17.39
Tunisia		43	14	28	24	0.00	-14.29
Southern Africa					1,243	0.17	
South Africa					1,243	0.17	
West Africa		113	42	69	416	0.06	502.90
Benin					321	0.04	
Nigeria		113	42	69	95	0.01	37.68
Other Africa	1,350						
All countries of Africa	1,350						
AMERICAS	43,668	44,953	45,528	51,508	62,505	8.49	21.35
Caribbean		159	294	9	53	0.01	488.89
Bahamas		159	294	9	53	0.01	488.89
Central America		541	297	30	33	0.00	10.00
Costa Rica		541	297	30	33	0.00	10.00
North America	38,738	39,388	41,695	47,437	55,735	7.57	17.49
Canada	7,399	8,132	8,965	9,322	11,404	1.55	22.33
Mexico	1,556	1,180	687	1,690	1,456	0.20	-13.85
United States of America	29,783	30,076	32,043	36,425	42,875	5.82	17.71
South America	2,918	4,865	3,242	4,032	6,684	0.91	65.77
Argentina	1,197	2,204	923	1,102	2,226	0.30	102.00
Bolivia		262	201	55	29	0.00	-47.27
Brazil	1,721	1,539	1,167	1,794	1,859	0.25	3.62
Chile		276	270	606	493	0.07	-18.65
Colombia		501	459	392	402	0.05	2.55
Peru					129	0.02	
Suriname					115	0.02	
Uruguay					1,226	0.17	
Venezuela		83	222	83	205	0.03	146.99
Other Americas	2,012						
Other countries of the Americas	2,012						
EAST ASIA AND THE PACIFIC	135,472	129,829	133,009	152,420	195,914	26.61	28.54
North-East Asia	74,872	77,531	70,912	90,129	120,214	16.33	33.38
China	27,339	35,166	32,272	46,360	61,917	8.41	33.56
Taiwan, Province of China					6,968	0.95	
Japan	27,058	23,383	22,445	23,332	26,283	3.57	12.65
Korea, Dem. People's Republic of					196	0.03	
Korea, Republic of	20,475	18,883	16,145	20,320	24,488	3.33	20.51
Mongolia		99	50	117	362	0.05	209.40
South-East Asia	30,945	36,103	44,163	43,460	52,642	7.15	21.13
Brunei Darussalam		348	401	37	18	0.00	-51.35
Myanmar		3,634	2,600	1,633	328	0.04	-79.91
Cambodia		535	319	227	141	0.02	-37.89
Indonesia	954	1,120	729	1,075	1,027	0.14	-4.47
Malaysia	5,237	5,173	5,527	6,752	7,381	1.00	9.32
Philippines	934	1,749	1,247	2,362	2,399	0.33	1.57
Timor-Leste					112	0.02	

NEPAL

1. Arrivals of non-resident tourists at national borders, by nationality

	2007	2008	2009	2010	2011	Market share 11	% Change 11-10
Singapore	3,802	4,120	5,344	8,937	6,985	0.95	-21.84
Viet Nam		735	599	909	710	0.10	-21.89
Thailand	20,018	18,689	27,397	21,528	33,541	4.56	55.80
Australasia	**14,469**	**16,121**	**17,900**	**18,767**	**22,923**	**3.11**	**22.15**
Australia	12,369	13,846	15,461	16,243	19,824	2.69	22.05
New Zealand	2,100	2,275	2,439	2,524	3,099	0.42	22.78
Melanesia		**74**	**34**	**64**	**135**	**0.02**	**110.94**
Fiji		74	34	64	26	0.00	-59.38
Vanuatu					109	0.01	
Other East Asia and the Pacific	**15,186**						
Other countries of Asia	15,149						
Other countries of Oceania	37						
EUROPE	**165,081**	**154,959**	**151,792**	**181,836**	**207,447**	**28.18**	**14.08**
Central/Eastern Europe	**16,634**	**11,198**	**8,553**	**18,875**	**15,426**	**2.10**	**-18.27**
Azerbaijan					147	0.02	
Armenia					113	0.02	
Bulgaria		328	326	327	302	0.04	-7.65
Belarus					249	0.03	
Czech Republic	2,026	1,738	1,307	2,831	2,121	0.29	-25.08
Estonia		82	90	225	87	0.01	-61.33
Hungary	1,071	918	514	1,895	726	0.10	-61.69
Kazakhstan		110	148	170	211	0.03	24.12
Latvia					224	0.03	
Lithuania					282	0.04	
Poland	3,941	2,722	1,784	3,842	3,152	0.43	-17.96
Romania					501	0.07	
Russian Federation	5,574	3,968	3,262	6,846	5,554	0.75	-18.87
Slovakia		519	426	436	564	0.08	29.36
Ukraine		813	696	2,303	1,193	0.16	-48.20
Other countries Central/East Europe	4,022						
Northern Europe	**43,022**	**47,366**	**47,728**	**51,706**	**57,166**	**7.76**	**10.56**
Denmark	3,157	3,847	4,464	4,359	6,138	0.83	40.81
Finland	1,511	1,567	1,408	3,284	2,276	0.31	-30.69
Iceland		292	179	76	171	0.02	125.00
Ireland	2,123	1,736	1,643	3,249	2,168	0.29	-33.27
Norway	2,056	3,960	2,329	2,647	3,240	0.44	22.40
Sweden	1,808	2,306	2,323	3,000	4,082	0.55	36.07
United Kingdom	32,367	33,658	35,382	35,091	39,091	5.31	11.40
Southern Europe	**28,094**	**24,303**	**23,209**	**29,262**	**33,614**	**4.57**	**14.87**
Andorra					305	0.04	
Croatia		374	585	130	198	0.03	52.31
Greece (*)	1,179	1,346	979	2,763	1,068	0.15	-61.35
Italy	11,243	7,914	7,982	10,226	12,621	1.71	23.42
Portugal		818	657	2,431	1,281	0.17	-47.31
Serbia					167	0.02	
Slovenia					201	0.03	
Spain	15,672	13,851	13,006	13,712	16,037	2.18	16.96
TFYR of Macedonia					1,736	0.24	
Western Europe	**66,742**	**65,228**	**65,905**	**74,588**	**92,602**	**12.58**	**24.15**
Austria	4,473	3,540	3,245	3,389	3,998	0.54	17.97
Belgium	4,869	4,648	4,832	5,275	6,368	0.86	20.72
France	20,250	22,402	22,154	24,550	26,720	3.63	8.84
Germany	21,323	18,552	19,246	22,583	27,472	3.73	21.65
Luxembourg					188	0.03	
Netherlands	10,589	10,900	11,147	13,471	16,836	2.29	24.98
Switzerland	5,238	5,186	5,281	5,320	11,020	1.50	107.14

NEPAL

1. Arrivals of non-resident tourists at national borders, by nationality

	2007	2008	2009	2010	2011	Market share 11	% Change 11-10
East Mediterranean Europe	7,817	6,864	6,397	7,405	8,639	1.17	16.66
Israel	7,817	5,926	5,879	4,594	6,519	0.89	41.90
Turkey		938	518	2,811	2,120	0.29	-24.58
Other Europe	2,772						
Other countries of Europe	2,772						
MIDDLE EAST		954	922	1,580	4,130	0.56	161.39
Bahrain		232	262	224	325	0.04	45.09
Jordan					200	0.03	
Kuwait					139	0.02	
Lebanon					793	0.11	
Oman					389	0.05	
Qatar					259	0.04	
Saudi Arabia		356	279	536	743	0.10	38.62
Syrian Arab Republic					165	0.02	
United Arab Emirates		231	199	583	830	0.11	42.37
Egypt		135	182	237	287	0.04	21.10
SOUTH ASIA	175,370	157,976	152,785	193,510	235,983	32.05	21.95
Afghanistan		1,371	512	442	508	0.07	14.93
Bangladesh	24,012	20,067	15,385	16,470	17,563	2.39	6.64
Bhutan	2,419	2,662	1,849	4,742	3,301	0.45	-30.39
Sri Lanka	49,947	37,817	36,362	45,531	59,884	8.13	31.52
India	96,010	91,177	93,884	120,898	149,504	20.31	23.66
Iran, Islamic Republic of	514	1,143	570	809	522	0.07	-35.48
Maldives	257	491	257	245	318	0.04	29.80
Pakistan	2,211	3,248	3,966	4,373	4,383	0.60	0.23
NOT SPECIFIED	5,692	10,796	25,485	21,552	27,997	3.80	29.90
Other countries of the World	5,692	10,796	25,485	21,552	27,997	3.80	29.90

NEPAL

1. Arrivals of non-resident tourists at national borders, by country of residence

	2007	2008	2009	2010	2011	Market share 11	% Change 11-10
TOTAL	526,705	500,277	509,956	602,867	736,215	100.00	22.12
AFRICA	1,309	493	481	437	3,017	0.41	590.39
East Africa		173	183	191	494	0.07	158.64
Kenya		173	183	191	494	0.07	158.64
Central Africa					966	0.13	
Angola					966	0.13	
North Africa		257	280	185			
Algeria		201	246	112			
Morocco		16	34	73			
Tunisia		40					
Southern Africa					1,244	0.17	
South Africa					1,244	0.17	
West Africa		63	18	61	313	0.04	413.11
Benin					313	0.04	
Nigeria		63	18	61			
Other Africa	1,309						
All countries of Africa	1,309						
AMERICAS	41,348	42,080	42,567	49,637	62,430	8.48	25.77
Caribbean		167	311	28			
Bahamas		167	311	28			
Central America		550	300	27			
Costa Rica		550	300	27			
North America	36,564	36,745	38,772	45,763	54,321	7.38	18.70
Canada	6,752	7,603	7,827	9,024	10,705	1.45	18.63
Mexico	1,501	1,151	657	1,779	1,645	0.22	-7.53
United States of America	28,311	27,991	30,288	34,960	41,971	5.70	20.05
South America	2,880	4,618	3,184	3,819	8,109	1.10	112.33
Argentina	1,216	1,930	913	1,060	2,898	0.39	173.40
Bolivia		277	192	32			
Brazil	1,664	1,572	1,150	1,682	2,363	0.32	40.49
Chile		269	271	580	638	0.09	10.00
Colombia		489	433	367	490	0.07	33.51
Uruguay					1,720	0.23	
Venezuela		81	225	98			
Other Americas	1,904						
Other countries of the Americas	1,904						
EAST ASIA AND THE PACIFIC	139,615	129,469	135,232	148,074	201,134	27.32	35.83
North-East Asia	74,848	76,588	70,360	85,621	121,506	16.50	41.91
China	25,762	36,172	33,487	44,694	64,115	8.71	43.45
Taiwan, Province of China					7,026	0.95	
Hong Kong, China	2,836						
Japan	26,321	22,065	21,066	21,594	25,856	3.51	19.74
Korea, Republic of	19,929	18,249	15,757	19,247	24,202	3.29	25.74
Mongolia		102	50	86	307	0.04	256.98
South-East Asia	32,674	38,033	47,791	44,706	56,903	7.73	27.28
Brunei Darussalam		481	439	73			
Myanmar		3,631	2,601	1,538	1,678	0.23	9.10
Cambodia		616	411	251	270	0.04	7.57
Indonesia	1,131	1,089	754	891	1,167	0.16	30.98
Malaysia	5,054	4,941	5,157	6,376	7,126	0.97	11.76
Philippines	909	1,688	1,351	2,361	2,384	0.32	0.97
Singapore	4,594	5,031	6,976	10,345	8,648	1.17	-16.40
Viet Nam		811	714	553	1,043	0.14	88.61

NEPAL

1. Arrivals of non-resident tourists at national borders, by country of residence

	2007	2008	2009	2010	2011	Market share 11	% Change 11-10
Thailand	20,986	19,745	29,388	22,318	34,587	4.70	54.97
Australasia	**14,126**	**14,784**	**17,042**	**17,687**	**22,725**	**3.09**	**28.48**
Australia	12,284	12,978	14,897	15,636	19,949	2.71	27.58
New Zealand	1,842	1,806	2,145	2,051	2,776	0.38	35.35
Melanesia		**64**	**39**	**60**			
Fiji		64	39	60			
Other East Asia and the Pacific	**17,967**						
Other countries of Asia	17,943						
Other countries of Oceania	24						
EUROPE	**157,505**	**146,590**	**143,814**	**169,694**	**212,729**	**28.89**	**25.36**
Central/Eastern Europe	**15,611**	**10,900**	**8,290**	**17,687**	**22,935**	**3.12**	**29.67**
Bulgaria		319	308	457	1,204	0.16	163.46
Belarus					268	0.04	
Czech Republic	1,976	1,721	1,284	2,540	4,170	0.57	64.17
Estonia		82	93	202			
Hungary	942	884	496	1,775	736	0.10	-58.54
Kazakhstan		126	152	159	259	0.04	62.89
Latvia					273	0.04	
Lithuania					271	0.04	
Poland	3,775	2,593	1,654	3,502	4,196	0.57	19.82
Romania					939	0.13	
Russian Federation	5,381	3,871	3,204	6,472	7,881	1.07	21.77
Slovakia		502	412	366	1,028	0.14	180.87
Ukraine		802	687	2,214	1,710	0.23	-22.76
Other countries Central/East Europe	3,537						
Northern Europe	**39,591**	**42,607**	**44,076**	**46,803**	**55,321**	**7.51**	**18.20**
Denmark	2,851	3,526	4,198	4,295	5,955	0.81	38.65
Finland	1,307	1,408	1,297	2,890	2,380	0.32	-17.65
Iceland		281	180	102	399	0.05	291.18
Ireland	1,846	1,508	1,524	2,806	2,333	0.32	-16.86
Norway	1,882	3,766	2,190	2,492	3,268	0.44	31.14
Sweden	1,646	1,993	2,096	2,758	4,005	0.54	45.21
United Kingdom	30,059	30,125	32,591	31,460	36,981	5.02	17.55
Southern Europe	**27,554**	**23,560**	**22,668**	**27,685**	**33,823**	**4.59**	**22.17**
Andorra					296	0.04	
Croatia		377	623	120	229	0.03	90.83
Greece (*)	1,160	1,348	938	2,593	1,114	0.15	-57.04
Italy	10,776	7,447	7,632	9,594	12,257	1.66	27.76
Portugal		784	600	2,168	1,346	0.18	-37.92
Slovenia					224	0.03	
Spain	15,618	13,604	12,875	13,210	15,593	2.12	18.04
TFYR of Macedonia					2,764	0.38	
Western Europe	**64,318**	**62,831**	**62,414**	**70,505**	**91,842**	**12.47**	**30.26**
Austria	4,417	3,436	3,139	3,146	3,885	0.53	23.49
Belgium	4,724	4,510	4,653	5,036	6,347	0.86	26.03
France	19,548	21,587	20,907	23,032	26,131	3.55	13.46
Germany	20,370	17,739	17,927	21,146	26,866	3.65	27.05
Liechtenstein					261	0.04	
Luxembourg					237	0.03	
Netherlands	9,899	10,136	10,377	12,659	16,343	2.22	29.10
Switzerland	5,360	5,423	5,411	5,486	11,772	1.60	114.58
East Mediterranean Europe	**7,696**	**6,692**	**6,366**	**7,014**	**8,808**	**1.20**	**25.58**
Israel	7,696	5,792	5,863	4,314	6,593	0.90	52.83
Turkey		900	503	2,700	2,215	0.30	-17.96
Other Europe	**2,735**						
Other countries of Europe	2,735						

NEPAL

1. Arrivals of non-resident tourists at national borders, by country of residence

	2007	2008	2009	2010	2011	Market share 11	% Change 11-10
MIDDLE EAST		**5,647**	**4,891**	**7,524**	**12,857**	**1.75**	**70.88**
Bahrain		365	518	481	578	0.08	20.17
Kuwait					294	0.04	
Lebanon					892	0.12	
Oman					733	0.10	
Qatar					1,692	0.23	
Saudi Arabia		527	494	755	1,231	0.17	63.05
United Arab Emirates		4,679	3,739	6,151	7,437	1.01	20.91
Egypt		76	140	137			
SOUTH ASIA	**168,041**	**149,959**	**150,951**	**177,704**	**234,599**	**31.87**	**32.02**
Afghanistan		1,191	594	483	561	0.08	16.15
Bangladesh	24,645	20,247	15,746	14,681	18,133	2.46	23.51
Bhutan	2,392	2,578	1,866	4,413	4,291	0.58	-2.76
Sri Lanka	49,955	37,640	36,319	45,392	59,785	8.12	31.71
India	88,284	84,073	91,994	108,077	147,037	19.97	36.05
Iran, Islamic Republic of	463	1,086	536	689	467	0.06	-32.22
Maldives	255	488	259	227	310	0.04	36.56
Pakistan	2,047	2,656	3,637	3,742	4,015	0.55	7.30
NOT SPECIFIED	**18,887**	**26,039**	**32,020**	**49,797**	**9,449**	**1.28**	**-81.02**
Other countries of the World	18,887	26,039	32,020	49,797	9,449	1.28	-81.02

NETHERLANDS

3. Arrivals of non-resident tourists in hotels and similar establishments, by country of residence

		2007	2008	2009	2010	2011	Market share 11	% Change 11-10
TOTAL	(*)	8,713,000	8,035,200	7,754,300	8,726,800	9,026,500	100.00	3.43
AFRICA		90,100	80,800	81,700	100,300	112,100	1.24	11.76
Other Africa		90,100	80,800	81,700	100,300	112,100	1.24	11.76
All countries of Africa		90,100	80,800	81,700	100,300	112,100	1.24	11.76
AMERICAS		1,261,700	1,059,400	1,010,100	1,215,400	1,311,300	14.53	7.89
North America		1,107,200	908,900	864,800	1,021,400	1,077,500	11.94	5.49
Canada		125,100	115,400	103,300	127,200	131,500	1.46	3.38
United States of America		982,100	793,500	761,500	894,200	946,000	10.48	5.79
Other Americas		154,500	150,500	145,300	194,000	233,800	2.59	20.52
Other countries of the Americas		154,500	150,500	145,300	194,000	233,800	2.59	20.52
EAST ASIA AND THE PACIFIC		630,000	551,200	554,800	627,000	684,800	7.59	9.22
North-East Asia		281,200	265,500	258,400	281,000	316,100	3.50	12.49
China		108,100	112,800	122,500	124,300	155,700	1.72	25.26
Taiwan, Province of China		16,600	15,900	13,700	14,500	24,600	0.27	69.66
Japan		128,800	114,400	99,300	119,000	110,500	1.22	-7.14
Korea, Republic of		27,700	22,400	22,900	23,200	25,300	0.28	9.05
South-East Asia		11,200	11,400	13,800	21,200	23,600	0.26	11.32
Indonesia		11,200	11,400	13,800	21,200	23,600	0.26	11.32
Australasia		102,500	98,300	96,700	129,700	142,700	1.58	10.02
Australia		87,600	84,800	84,700	115,600	127,100	1.41	9.95
New Zealand		14,900	13,500	12,000	14,100	15,600	0.17	10.64
Other East Asia and the Pacific		235,100	176,000	185,900	195,100	202,400	2.24	3.74
Other countries of Asia		222,100	166,500	176,100	181,100	190,600	2.11	5.25
Other countries of Oceania		13,000	9,500	9,800	14,000	11,800	0.13	-15.71
EUROPE		6,689,700	6,293,900	6,058,300	6,720,500	6,850,500	75.89	1.93
Central/Eastern Europe		239,800	251,300	223,100	264,700	304,300	3.37	14.96
Czech Republic		32,100	34,200	28,200	32,600	36,100	0.40	10.74
Hungary		30,300	27,900	22,800	26,600	30,300	0.34	13.91
Poland		77,600	77,600	68,200	80,600	88,300	0.98	9.55
Russian Federation		88,800	101,300	95,100	114,800	139,000	1.54	21.08
Slovakia		11,000	10,300	8,800	10,100	10,600	0.12	4.95
Northern Europe		2,290,600	2,033,600	1,781,000	1,983,000	1,937,700	21.47	-2.28
Denmark		143,800	130,100	117,500	135,500	122,600	1.36	-9.52
Finland		50,300	51,300	42,900	49,200	62,800	0.70	27.64
Iceland		9,300	8,200	5,400	7,100	8,000	0.09	12.68
Ireland		108,600	109,500	105,400	109,300	87,300	0.97	-20.13
Norway		86,200	88,400	85,900	96,100	104,000	1.15	8.22
Sweden		108,900	104,900	93,700	108,400	119,600	1.32	10.33
United Kingdom		1,783,500	1,541,200	1,330,200	1,477,400	1,433,400	15.88	-2.98
Southern Europe		841,200	781,500	776,400	934,500	919,300	10.18	-1.63
Greece		41,800	40,700	45,900	44,800	41,500	0.46	-7.37
Italy		352,100	341,000	343,800	411,600	407,600	4.52	-0.97
Portugal		46,000	47,600	50,900	53,200	60,000	0.66	12.78
Spain		401,300	352,200	335,800	424,900	410,200	4.54	-3.46
Western Europe		2,858,800	2,787,400	2,807,500	3,132,100	3,254,400	36.05	3.90
Austria		73,800	73,800	63,600	69,000	78,100	0.87	13.19
Belgium		675,600	692,800	712,500	796,500	808,100	8.95	1.46
France		503,600	498,900	497,900	577,900	584,100	6.47	1.07
Germany		1,415,500	1,353,500	1,357,000	1,485,100	1,562,100	17.31	5.18
Luxembourg		35,800	32,100	31,400	40,000	38,300	0.42	-4.25
Switzerland		154,500	136,300	145,100	163,600	183,700	2.04	12.29

NETHERLANDS

3. Arrivals of non-resident tourists in hotels and similar establishments, by country of residence

	2007	2008	2009	2010	2011	Market share 11	% Change 11-10
East Mediterranean Europe	**91,700**	**95,600**	**104,200**	**121,800**	**144,700**	**1.60**	**18.80**
Israel	54,100	55,300	60,600	69,600	86,200	0.95	23.85
Turkey	37,600	40,300	43,600	52,200	58,500	0.65	12.07
Other Europe	**367,600**	**344,500**	**366,100**	**284,400**	**290,100**	**3.21**	**2.00**
Other countries of Europe	367,600	344,500	366,100	284,400	290,100	3.21	2.00
SOUTH ASIA	**41,500**	**49,900**	**49,400**	**63,600**	**67,800**	**0.75**	**6.60**
India	41,500	49,900	49,400	63,600	67,800	0.75	6.60

NETHERLANDS

4. Arrivals of non-resident tourists in all types of accommodation establishments, by country of residence

	2007	2008	2009	2010	2011	Market share 11	% Change 11-10
TOTAL	11,008,000	10,104,300	9,920,600	10,883,200	11,299,500	100.00	3.83
AFRICA	91,900	83,800	83,600	103,300	114,400	1.01	10.75
Other Africa	91,900	83,800	83,600	103,300	114,400	1.01	10.75
All countries of Africa	91,900	83,800	83,600	103,300	114,400	1.01	10.75
AMERICAS	1,273,600	1,068,000	1,017,700	1,223,000	1,319,800	11.68	7.91
Other Americas	1,273,600	1,068,000	1,017,700	1,223,000	1,319,800	11.68	7.91
All countries of the Americas	1,273,600	1,068,000	1,017,700	1,223,000	1,319,800	11.68	7.91
EAST ASIA AND THE PACIFIC	738,500	667,700	673,400	770,100	849,700	7.52	10.34
Other East Asia and the Pacific	738,500	667,700	673,400	770,100	849,700	7.52	10.34
All countries of Asia	617,200	556,000	563,900	622,800	690,800	6.11	10.92
All countries of Oceania	121,300	111,700	109,500	147,300	158,900	1.41	7.88
EUROPE	8,904,000	8,284,800	8,145,900	8,786,800	9,015,600	79.79	2.60
Northern Europe	2,181,800	1,899,400	1,644,500	1,819,100	1,770,100	15.67	-2.69
Denmark	163,000	148,200	135,200	150,200	136,900	1.21	-8.85
Sweden	116,300	112,300	100,600	113,400	124,900	1.11	10.14
United Kingdom	1,902,500	1,638,900	1,408,700	1,555,500	1,508,300	13.35	-3.03
Southern Europe	833,600	738,400	719,600	882,700	863,000	7.64	-2.23
Italy	398,100	370,400	368,400	443,000	437,700	3.87	-1.20
Spain	435,500	368,000	351,200	439,700	425,300	3.76	-3.27
Western Europe	4,722,800	4,503,900	4,654,200	4,954,300	5,191,200	45.94	4.78
Belgium	1,100,700	1,108,500	1,171,800	1,256,800	1,345,000	11.90	7.02
France	612,700	574,800	574,300	668,500	666,400	5.90	-0.31
Germany	2,832,900	2,669,000	2,744,000	2,847,700	2,978,000	26.36	4.58
Switzerland	176,500	151,600	164,100	181,300	201,800	1.79	11.31
Other Europe	1,165,800	1,143,100	1,127,600	1,130,700	1,191,300	10.54	5.36
Other countries of Europe	1,165,800	1,143,100	1,127,600	1,130,700	1,191,300	10.54	5.36

NETHERLANDS

5. Overnight stays of non-resident tourists in hotels and similar establishments, by country of residence

		2007	2008	2009	2010	2011	Market share 11	% Change 11-10
TOTAL	(*)	16,327,900	14,961,300	14,428,600	16,175,000	16,684,900	100.00	3.15
AFRICA		174,700	146,900	160,500	194,400	211,600	1.27	8.85
Other Africa		174,700	146,900	160,500	194,400	211,600	1.27	8.85
All countries of Africa		174,700	146,900	160,500	194,400	211,600	1.27	8.85
AMERICAS		2,246,500	1,910,000	1,825,900	2,185,800	2,282,400	13.68	4.42
North America		1,943,700	1,626,100	1,539,500	1,812,800	1,835,700	11.00	1.26
Canada		235,100	222,100	192,800	240,500	244,900	1.47	1.83
United States of America		1,708,600	1,404,000	1,346,700	1,572,300	1,590,800	9.53	1.18
Other Americas		302,800	283,900	286,400	373,000	446,700	2.68	19.76
Other countries of the Americas		302,800	283,900	286,400	373,000	446,700	2.68	19.76
EAST ASIA AND THE PACIFIC		1,111,000	971,600	977,200	1,102,100	1,240,600	7.44	12.57
North-East Asia		477,100	439,900	426,200	465,400	541,600	3.25	16.37
China		178,700	175,400	200,500	202,700	253,200	1.52	24.91
Taiwan, Province of China		30,000	26,900	25,400	27,000	46,000	0.28	70.37
Japan		220,200	196,200	162,300	196,800	196,700	1.18	-0.05
Korea, Republic of		48,200	41,400	38,000	38,900	45,700	0.27	17.48
South-East Asia		24,000	23,000	28,300	39,000	44,200	0.26	13.33
Indonesia		24,000	23,000	28,300	39,000	44,200	0.26	13.33
Australasia		203,000	190,600	188,200	248,600	281,900	1.69	13.40
Australia		172,800	164,300	164,800	222,800	251,700	1.51	12.97
New Zealand		30,200	26,300	23,400	25,800	30,200	0.18	17.05
Other East Asia and the Pacific		406,900	318,100	334,500	349,100	372,900	2.23	6.82
Other countries of Asia		384,700	300,800	318,600	325,500	349,900	2.10	7.50
Other countries of Oceania		22,200	17,300	15,900	23,600	23,000	0.14	-2.54
EUROPE		12,702,000	11,834,100	11,368,600	12,563,900	12,813,400	76.80	1.99
Central/Eastern Europe		463,600	486,500	427,000	497,100	590,600	3.54	18.81
Czech Republic		62,600	63,200	52,400	61,600	66,400	0.40	7.79
Hungary		59,300	52,400	41,700	49,400	59,000	0.35	19.43
Poland		149,800	152,800	130,400	146,600	169,500	1.02	15.62
Russian Federation		167,400	198,400	185,200	220,700	275,300	1.65	24.74
Slovakia		24,500	19,700	17,300	18,800	20,400	0.12	8.51
Northern Europe		4,151,800	3,737,900	3,226,600	3,570,700	3,495,900	20.95	-2.09
Denmark		262,200	240,900	215,000	256,700	237,600	1.42	-7.44
Finland		90,600	91,100	79,300	90,800	118,500	0.71	30.51
Iceland		17,900	15,500	9,900	12,300	15,000	0.09	21.95
Ireland		208,100	209,000	197,000	189,000	156,700	0.94	-17.09
Norway		163,200	162,800	162,200	176,900	188,600	1.13	6.61
Sweden		199,000	180,200	163,300	189,600	208,500	1.25	9.97
United Kingdom		3,210,800	2,838,400	2,399,900	2,655,400	2,571,000	15.41	-3.18
Southern Europe		1,706,500	1,572,500	1,544,300	1,846,800	1,827,900	10.96	-1.02
Greece		82,300	84,000	91,700	87,300	81,600	0.49	-6.53
Italy		707,200	683,000	678,500	822,300	822,100	4.93	-0.02
Portugal		90,000	87,900	95,600	103,300	113,500	0.68	9.87
Spain		827,000	717,600	678,500	833,900	810,700	4.86	-2.78
Western Europe		5,486,900	5,187,000	5,259,600	5,862,400	6,066,800	36.36	3.49
Austria		152,400	159,500	129,000	130,800	157,600	0.94	20.49
Belgium		1,125,200	1,123,600	1,176,500	1,301,100	1,312,700	7.87	0.89
France		869,700	851,200	875,400	1,020,300	1,022,500	6.13	0.22
Germany		2,976,600	2,738,600	2,752,100	3,029,200	3,149,600	18.88	3.97
Luxembourg		76,400	61,600	60,200	81,000	79,200	0.47	-2.22
Switzerland		286,600	252,500	266,400	300,000	345,200	2.07	15.07

NETHERLANDS

5. Overnight stays of non-resident tourists in hotels and similar establishments, by country of residence

	2007	2008	2009	2010	2011	Market share 11	% Change 11-10
East Mediterranean Europe	**170,000**	**185,200**	**200,000**	**244,000**	**281,000**	**1.68**	**15.16**
Israel	102,600	110,500	121,200	149,900	172,000	1.03	14.74
Turkey	67,400	74,700	78,800	94,100	109,000	0.65	15.83
Other Europe	**723,200**	**665,000**	**711,100**	**542,900**	**551,200**	**3.30**	**1.53**
Other countries of Europe	723,200	665,000	711,100	542,900	551,200	3.30	1.53
SOUTH ASIA	**93,700**	**98,700**	**96,400**	**128,800**	**136,900**	**0.82**	**6.29**
India	93,700	98,700	96,400	128,800	136,900	0.82	6.29

NETHERLANDS

6. Overnight stays of non-resident tourists in all types of accommodation establishments, by country of residence

		2007	2008	2009	2010	2011	Market share 11	% Change 11-10
TOTAL	(*)	**27,952,100**	**25,267,300**	**25,013,600**	**26,799,600**	**27,738,900**	**100.00**	**3.50**
AFRICA		**181,400**	**162,600**	**171,200**	**209,100**	**224,200**	**0.81**	**7.22**
Other Africa		**181,400**	**162,600**	**171,200**	**209,100**	**224,200**	**0.81**	**7.22**
All countries of Africa		181,400	162,600	171,200	209,100	224,200	0.81	7.22
AMERICAS		**2,299,900**	**1,950,200**	**1,861,200**	**2,222,400**	**2,319,900**	**8.36**	**4.39**
Other Americas		**2,299,900**	**1,950,200**	**1,861,200**	**2,222,400**	**2,319,900**	**8.36**	**4.39**
All countries of the Americas		2,299,900	1,950,200	1,861,200	2,222,400	2,319,900	8.36	4.39
EAST ASIA AND THE PACIFIC		**1,363,700**	**1,233,100**	**1,237,300**	**1,434,100**	**1,602,600**	**5.78**	**11.75**
Other East Asia and the Pacific		**1,363,700**	**1,233,100**	**1,237,300**	**1,434,100**	**1,602,600**	**5.78**	**11.75**
All countries of Asia		1,118,900	1,011,600	1,022,800	1,148,800	1,281,800	4.62	11.58
All countries of Oceania		244,800	221,500	214,500	285,300	320,800	1.16	12.44
EUROPE		**24,107,100**	**21,921,400**	**21,743,900**	**22,934,000**	**23,592,200**	**85.05**	**2.87**
Northern Europe		**4,365,400**	**3,836,000**	**3,242,200**	**3,542,800**	**3,433,900**	**12.38**	**-3.07**
Denmark		340,400	313,900	289,400	315,000	298,500	1.08	-5.24
Sweden		223,000	204,800	181,500	204,700	226,700	0.82	10.75
United Kingdom		3,802,000	3,317,300	2,771,300	3,023,100	2,908,700	10.49	-3.78
Southern Europe		**1,811,400**	**1,542,700**	**1,467,500**	**1,787,400**	**1,770,200**	**6.38**	**-0.96**
Italy		845,500	767,300	741,200	901,600	905,400	3.26	0.42
Spain		965,900	775,400	726,300	885,800	864,800	3.12	-2.37
Western Europe		**15,475,000**	**14,183,700**	**14,689,900**	**15,315,100**	**15,946,200**	**57.49**	**4.12**
Belgium		2,863,700	2,816,800	3,039,200	3,196,000	3,460,700	12.48	8.28
France		1,248,500	1,130,200	1,137,200	1,345,800	1,301,400	4.69	-3.30
Germany		10,980,900	9,922,700	10,172,700	10,403,700	10,759,300	38.79	3.42
Switzerland		381,900	314,000	340,800	369,600	424,800	1.53	14.94
Other Europe		**2,455,300**	**2,359,000**	**2,344,300**	**2,288,700**	**2,441,900**	**8.80**	**6.69**
Other countries of Europe		2,455,300	2,359,000	2,344,300	2,288,700	2,441,900	8.80	6.69

NEW CALEDONIA

1. Arrivals of non-resident tourists at national borders, by nationality

	2007	2008	2009	2010	2011	Market share 11	% Change 11-10
TOTAL	103,399	103,672	99,379	98,562	111,875	100.00	13.51
AFRICA	190	281	251	234	278	0.25	18.80
Other Africa	190	281	251	234	278	0.25	18.80
All countries of Africa	190	281	251	234	278	0.25	18.80
AMERICAS	2,054	2,769	2,485	2,830	3,106	2.78	9.75
North America	1,857	2,533	2,218	2,432	2,745	2.45	12.87
Canada	1,076	1,592	1,307	1,276	1,266	1.13	-0.78
United States of America	781	941	911	1,156	1,479	1.32	27.94
South America	23	26	27	23	21	0.02	-8.70
Argentina	23	26	27	23	21	0.02	-8.70
Other Americas	174	210	240	375	340	0.30	-9.33
Other countries of the Americas	174	210	240	375	340	0.30	-9.33
EAST ASIA AND THE PACIFIC	53,892	48,805	47,310	47,146	48,193	43.08	2.22
North-East Asia	27,192	21,457	21,288	21,049	21,085	18.85	0.17
China	171	143	141	447	600	0.54	34.23
Hong Kong, China		7	6	7	10	0.01	42.86
Japan	26,634	20,062	18,878	18,498	18,089	16.17	-2.21
Korea, Republic of	387	1,245	2,263	2,097	2,386	2.13	13.78
Australasia	22,869	23,214	21,376	20,454	19,574	17.50	-4.30
Australia	14,119	15,487	15,073	14,292	13,625	12.18	-4.67
New Zealand	8,750	7,727	6,303	6,162	5,949	5.32	-3.46
Melanesia	1,887	2,131	1,957	2,473	2,416	2.16	-2.30
Vanuatu	1,887	2,131	1,957	2,473	2,416	2.16	-2.30
Other East Asia and the Pacific	1,944	2,003	2,689	3,170	5,118	4.57	61.45
Other countries of Asia	1,290	1,146	1,996	1,821	2,402	2.15	31.91
Other countries of Oceania	654	857	693	1,349	2,716	2.43	101.33
EUROPE	47,261	51,814	49,320	48,352	60,272	53.87	24.65
Northern Europe	1,615	1,960	1,787	1,726	1,764	1.58	2.20
United Kingdom	1,615	1,960	1,787	1,726	1,764	1.58	2.20
Southern Europe	467	750	755	835	669	0.60	-19.88
Italy	467	750	755	835	669	0.60	-19.88
Western Europe	43,463	46,966	44,564	43,845	55,651	49.74	26.93
France	42,564	45,890	43,251	42,737	54,334	48.57	27.14
Germany	562	717	905	728	898	0.80	23.35
Switzerland	337	359	408	380	419	0.37	10.26
Other Europe	1,716	2,138	2,214	1,946	2,188	1.96	12.44
Other countries of Europe	1,716	2,138	2,214	1,946	2,188	1.96	12.44
NOT SPECIFIED	2	3	13		26	0.02	
Other countries of the World	2	3	13		26	0.02	

NEW CALEDONIA

1. Arrivals of non-resident tourists at national borders, by country of residence

		2007	2008	2009	2010	2011	Market share 11	% Change 11-10
TOTAL	(*)	**103,363**	**103,672**	**99,379**	**98,562**	**111,875**	**100.00**	**13.51**
AFRICA		**628**	**713**	**1,980**	**2,238**	**1,904**	**1.70**	**-14.92**
East Africa		**437**	**450**	**1,653**	**1,946**	**1,566**	**1.40**	**-19.53**
Reunion		437	450	1,653	1,946	1,566	1.40	-19.53
Other Africa		**191**	**263**	**327**	**292**	**338**	**0.30**	**15.75**
Other countries of Africa		191	263	327	292	338	0.30	15.75
AMERICAS		**1,918**	**2,707**	**2,518**	**2,891**	**2,889**	**2.58**	**-0.07**
Caribbean		**90**	**136**	**229**	**289**	**275**	**0.25**	**-4.84**
All countries of the Caribbean	(*)	90	136	229	289	275	0.25	-4.84
North America		**1,650**	**2,390**	**2,045**	**2,255**	**2,289**	**2.05**	**1.51**
Canada		917	1,475	1,150	1,182	1,192	1.07	0.85
United States of America		733	915	895	1,073	1,097	0.98	2.24
South America		**21**	**16**	**22**	**27**	**18**	**0.02**	**-33.33**
Argentina		21	16	22	27	18	0.02	-33.33
Other Americas		**157**	**165**	**222**	**320**	**307**	**0.27**	**-4.06**
Other countries of the Americas		157	165	222	320	307	0.27	-4.06
EAST ASIA AND THE PACIFIC		**68,449**	**64,578**	**63,213**	**64,573**	**68,172**	**60.94**	**5.57**
North-East Asia		**27,376**	**21,755**	**21,415**	**21,165**	**21,546**	**19.26**	**1.80**
China		177	206	166	499	649	0.58	30.06
Hong Kong, China		101	138	111	89	98	0.09	10.11
Japan		26,755	20,225	18,926	18,534	18,455	16.50	-0.43
Korea, Republic of		343	1,186	2,212	2,043	2,344	2.10	14.73
Australasia		**25,827**	**26,609**	**25,218**	**23,957**	**23,507**	**21.01**	**-1.88**
Australia		16,352	18,185	18,567	17,551	17,040	15.23	-2.91
New Zealand		9,475	8,424	6,651	6,406	6,467	5.78	0.95
Melanesia		**2,684**	**3,136**	**2,869**	**3,652**	**4,061**	**3.63**	**11.20**
Vanuatu		2,684	3,136	2,869	3,652	4,061	3.63	11.20
Polynesia		**10,332**	**10,682**	**10,550**	**11,999**	**12,998**	**11.62**	**8.33**
French Polynesia		4,220	4,455	4,096	4,940	4,935	4.41	-0.10
Wallis and Futuna Islands		6,112	6,227	6,454	7,059	8,063	7.21	14.22
Other East Asia and the Pacific		**2,230**	**2,396**	**3,161**	**3,800**	**6,060**	**5.42**	**59.47**
Other countries of Asia		1,412	1,341	2,274	2,122	2,744	2.45	29.31
Other countries of Oceania		818	1,055	887	1,678	3,316	2.96	97.62
EUROPE		**32,252**	**35,636**	**31,652**	**28,859**	**38,886**	**34.76**	**34.74**
Northern Europe		**576**	**713**	**495**	**474**	**598**	**0.53**	**26.16**
United Kingdom		576	713	495	474	598	0.53	26.16
Southern Europe		**410**	**672**	**650**	**736**	**571**	**0.51**	**-22.42**
Italy		410	672	650	736	571	0.51	-22.42
Western Europe		**29,874**	**32,476**	**28,606**	**26,021**	**35,852**	**32.05**	**37.78**
France		29,104	31,474	27,335	24,960	34,647	30.97	38.81
Germany		403	604	765	584	691	0.62	18.32
Switzerland		367	398	506	477	514	0.46	7.76
Other Europe		**1,392**	**1,775**	**1,901**	**1,628**	**1,865**	**1.67**	**14.56**
Other countries of Europe		1,392	1,775	1,901	1,628	1,865	1.67	14.56
NOT SPECIFIED		**116**	**38**	**16**	**1**	**24**	**0.02**	**2300.00**
Other countries of the World		116	38	16	1	24	0.02	2300.00

NEW CALEDONIA

3. Arrivals of non-resident tourists in hotels and similar establishments, by country of residence

		2007	2008	2009	2010	2011	Market share 11	% Change 11-10
TOTAL	(*)	**128,677**	**102,394**	**114,842**	**133,385**	**142,437**	**100.00**	**6.79**
EAST ASIA AND THE PACIFIC		**87,312**	**65,582**	**63,428**	**73,683**	**65,362**	**45.89**	**-11.29**
North-East Asia		**49,908**	**31,371**	**28,776**	**31,173**	**27,573**	**19.36**	**-11.55**
Japan		49,908	31,371	28,776	31,173	27,573	19.36	-11.55
Australasia		**37,404**	**34,211**	**34,652**	**42,510**	**37,789**	**26.53**	**-11.11**
Australia		23,984	24,358	24,115	25,789	26,406	18.54	2.39
New Zealand		13,420	9,853	10,537	16,721	11,383	7.99	-31.92
EUROPE		**28,477**	**24,531**	**33,673**	**38,286**	**50,674**	**35.58**	**32.36**
Western Europe		**28,477**	**24,531**	**33,673**	**38,286**	**50,674**	**35.58**	**32.36**
France		28,477	24,531	33,673	38,286	50,674	35.58	32.36
NOT SPECIFIED		**12,888**	**12,281**	**17,741**	**21,416**	**26,401**	**18.54**	**23.28**
Other countries of the World		12,888	12,281	17,741	21,416	26,401	18.54	23.28

NEW CALEDONIA

5. Overnight stays of non-resident tourists in hotels and similar establishments, by country of residence

		2007	2008	2009	2010	2011	Market share 11	% Change 11-10
TOTAL	(*)	347,317	360,233	304,274	279,406	316,228	100.00	13.18
EAST ASIA AND THE PACIFIC		208,330	194,425	139,827	131,591	137,817	43.58	4.73
North-East Asia		111,440	80,825	62,322	57,168	59,367	18.77	3.85
Japan		111,440	80,825	62,322	57,168	59,367	18.77	3.85
Australasia		96,890	113,600	77,505	74,423	78,450	24.81	5.41
Australia		62,622	78,008	52,926	48,810	53,296	16.85	9.19
New Zealand		34,268	35,592	24,579	25,613	25,154	7.95	-1.79
EUROPE		95,933	114,097	113,793	97,060	122,168	38.63	25.87
Western Europe		95,933	114,097	113,793	97,060	122,168	38.63	25.87
France		95,933	114,097	113,793	97,060	122,168	38.63	25.87
NOT SPECIFIED		43,054	51,711	50,654	50,755	56,243	17.79	10.81
Other countries of the World		43,054	51,711	50,654	50,755	56,243	17.79	10.81

NEW ZEALAND

2. Arrivals of non-resident visitors at national borders, by country of residence

		2007	2008	2009	2010	2011	Market share 11	% Change 11-10
TOTAL	(*)	2,455,308	2,447,257	2,447,532	2,510,759	2,594,198	100.00	3.32
AFRICA		24,954	28,507	22,155	20,425	30,199	1.16	47.85
East Africa		2,143	1,941	1,776	2,015	2,322	0.09	15.24
Comoros		24			29	41	0.00	41.38
Ethiopia		106	23	68	46	128	0.00	178.26
Eritrea			75	18				
Kenya		263	330	385	325	374	0.01	15.08
Madagascar		22	19	70		16	0.00	
Malawi		69	49	21	130	56	0.00	-56.92
Mauritius		253	174	204	199	309	0.01	55.28
Mozambique			24		29	62	0.00	113.79
Reunion		165	199	151	341	354	0.01	3.81
Rwanda			20	27				
Seychelles		51	68	23	100	48	0.00	-52.00
Zimbabwe		613	429	439	322	333	0.01	3.42
Uganda		166	137	116	98	149	0.01	52.04
United Republic of Tanzania		248	186	182	237	239	0.01	0.84
Zambia		163	208	72	159	213	0.01	33.96
Central Africa		179	137	155	144	194	0.01	34.72
Angola		139	73	64	74	66	0.00	-10.81
Cameroon		22	42		24			
Chad				41		25	0.00	
Congo				23		16	0.00	
Democratic Republic of the Congo						25	0.00	
Equatorial Guinea		18	22	27		46	0.00	
Gabon					46	16	0.00	-65.22
North Africa		248	149	220	162	360	0.01	122.22
Algeria		19		23	22	96	0.00	336.36
Morocco		46	25	72		48	0.00	
Western Sahara			22					
Sudan		137	102	80	120	125	0.00	4.17
Tunisia		46		45	20	91	0.00	355.00
Southern Africa		21,955	25,720	19,535	17,719	26,700	1.03	50.69
Botswana		167	201	93	174	105	0.00	-39.66
Lesotho				23				
Namibia		110	126	155	144	261	0.01	81.25
South Africa		21,628	25,346	19,214	17,401	26,286	1.01	51.06
Swaziland		50	47	50		48	0.00	
West Africa		429	560	469	385	623	0.02	61.82
Gambia					24	16	0.00	-33.33
Ghana		110	163	165	168	196	0.01	16.67
Guinea			52					
Côte d'Ivoire						16	0.00	
Liberia		23	24	28				
Mali						40	0.00	
Mauritania			27		29	57	0.00	96.55
Niger		19		27				
Nigeria		230	206	249	164	208	0.01	26.83
Saint Helena			19					
Senegal			25					
Sierra Leone		24	19			20	0.00	
Togo			25			24	0.00	
Burkina Faso		23				46	0.00	
AMERICAS		290,455	295,937	275,849	268,358	268,501	10.35	0.05
Caribbean		1,576	1,740	1,509	1,272	1,513	0.06	18.95

NEW ZEALAND

2. Arrivals of non-resident visitors at national borders, by country of residence

	2007	2008	2009	2010	2011	Market share 11	% Change 11-10
Antigua and Barbuda		22	93		32	0.00	
Bahamas	134	91	119	29	78	0.00	168.97
Barbados	119	102	123	55	86	0.00	56.36
Bermuda	263	343	343	282	293	0.01	3.90
British Virgin Islands	50	66	44	47	46	0.00	-2.13
Cayman Islands	303	225	227	202	255	0.01	26.24
Cuba	47	25	18	53	16	0.00	-69.81
Dominica		50	47	25			
Dominican Republic	51	25	45		40	0.00	
Grenada	27			29			
Guadeloupe		49	21		16	0.00	
Haiti				20			
Jamaica	161	170	89	176	149	0.01	-15.34
Martinique	23		23				
Netherlands Antilles	69	52	18	24	66	0.00	175.00
Aruba					30	0.00	
Puerto Rico	118	264	89	178	138	0.01	-22.47
Saint Kitts and Nevis					16	0.00	
Saint Lucia	24				32	0.00	
Saint Vincent and the Grenadines					16	0.00	
Trinidad and Tobago	144	172	112	128	163	0.01	27.34
Turks and Caicos Islands	43	62	98		16	0.00	
United States Virgin Islands		22		24	25	0.00	4.17
Central America	**501**	**532**	**397**	**588**	**404**	**0.02**	**-31.29**
Belize				25			
Costa Rica	216	199	114	217	165	0.01	-23.96
El Salvador	24	52	23	51	16	0.00	-68.63
Guatemala	140	66	95	79	52	0.00	-34.18
Honduras	27	47		67			
Nicaragua		27	28		16	0.00	
Panama	94	141	137	149	155	0.01	4.03
North America	**267,061**	**268,957**	**249,531**	**241,574**	**236,947**	**9.13**	**-1.92**
Canada	47,792	53,267	48,656	48,942	49,154	1.89	0.43
Greenland		22	23		36	0.00	
Mexico	3,242	3,258	3,060	2,923	3,043	0.12	4.11
United States of America	216,027	212,410	197,792	189,709	184,714	7.12	-2.63
South America	**21,265**	**24,686**	**24,412**	**24,924**	**29,637**	**1.14**	**18.91**
Argentina	4,600	5,479	6,237	5,654	9,695	0.37	71.47
Bolivia	51	64	73	105	32	0.00	-69.52
Brazil	10,446	11,413	11,355	11,796	11,587	0.45	-1.77
Chile	4,062	4,839	4,369	4,938	5,382	0.21	8.99
Colombia	537	843	776	765	1,026	0.04	34.12
Ecuador	177	190	162	99	181	0.01	82.83
Falkland Islands, Malvinas	45	76	21	20	68	0.00	240.00
French Guiana			28	22			
Guyana		22					
Paraguay	94	76	75	95	120	0.00	26.32
Peru	421	397	325	419	366	0.01	-12.65
Suriname	24		23	55			
Uruguay	636	1,001	716	776	902	0.03	16.24
Venezuela	172	286	252	180	278	0.01	54.44
Other Americas	**52**	**22**					
Other countries of the Americas	52	22					
EAST ASIA AND THE PACIFIC	**1,529,711**	**1,508,819**	**1,561,724**	**1,649,581**	**1,695,011**	**65.34**	**2.75**
North-East Asia	**390,762**	**335,389**	**274,383**	**323,835**	**311,337**	**12.00**	**-3.86**
China	120,804	112,398	102,259	122,712	145,524	5.61	18.59
Taiwan, Province of China	25,695	19,249	16,584	21,192	17,975	0.69	-15.18

NEW ZEALAND

2. Arrivals of non-resident visitors at national borders, by country of residence

	2007	2008	2009	2010	2011	Market share 11	% Change 11-10
Hong Kong, China	22,687	21,776	23,572	24,287	25,397	0.98	4.57
Japan	121,652	102,482	78,426	87,735	68,963	2.66	-21.40
Korea, Dem. People's Republic of			23	29			
Korea, Republic of	99,453	79,061	52,921	67,309	52,787	2.03	-21.58
Macao, China	315	326	458	450	504	0.02	12.00
Mongolia	156	97	140	121	187	0.01	54.55
South-East Asia	**86,946**	**87,641**	**90,894**	**96,989**	**116,580**	**4.49**	**20.20**
Brunei Darussalam	916	1,157	1,340	1,369	1,192	0.05	-12.93
Myanmar	207	29	114	144	178	0.01	23.61
Cambodia	504	483	646	586	609	0.02	3.92
Indonesia	7,758	7,569	9,506	9,787	11,450	0.44	16.99
Lao People's Democratic Republic	115	173	248	226	222	0.01	-1.77
Malaysia	19,716	19,608	19,702	21,843	35,011	1.35	60.28
Philippines	8,308	9,230	7,572	8,240	8,563	0.33	3.92
Timor-Leste	144	166	89	292	238	0.01	-18.49
Singapore	26,836	28,836	29,582	30,300	38,680	1.49	27.66
Viet Nam	2,093	2,034	2,367	2,768	2,914	0.11	5.27
Thailand	20,349	18,356	19,728	21,434	17,523	0.68	-18.25
Australasia	**950,206**	**976,200**	**1,082,680**	**1,119,879**	**1,156,426**	**44.58**	**3.26**
Australia	950,206	976,200	1,082,680	1,119,879	1,156,426	44.58	3.26
Melanesia	**37,764**	**43,423**	**46,642**	**45,885**	**47,946**	**1.85**	**4.49**
Solomon Islands	815	1,030	1,027	1,130	1,341	0.05	18.67
Fiji	20,442	22,512	23,608	20,853	21,619	0.83	3.67
New Caledonia	11,772	12,888	15,217	16,148	16,597	0.64	2.78
Vanuatu	2,249	4,301	4,228	4,530	4,644	0.18	2.52
Norfolk Island	798	1,039	798	931	961	0.04	3.22
Papua New Guinea	1,688	1,653	1,764	2,293	2,784	0.11	21.41
Micronesia	**905**	**963**	**1,040**	**874**	**1,024**	**0.04**	**17.16**
Kiribati	526	638	549	577	670	0.03	16.12
Guam	97	119	210	154	162	0.01	5.19
Nauru	180	44	66	47	48	0.00	2.13
Northern Mariana Islands					32	0.00	
Micronesia, Federated States of	41	29	94		16	0.00	
Marshall Islands	19	114	121	47	48	0.00	2.13
Palau	42	19		49	48	0.00	-2.04
Polynesia	**63,105**	**65,203**	**66,085**	**62,094**	**61,698**	**2.38**	**-0.64**
American Samoa	1,663	1,667	1,174	1,228	1,109	0.04	-9.69
Cook Islands	10,782	11,346	11,042	10,577	11,309	0.44	6.92
French Polynesia	16,830	16,868	19,632	19,090	16,785	0.65	-12.07
Niue	1,794	1,960	2,151	1,889	1,959	0.08	3.71
Pitcairn		23	44		16	0.00	
Tokelau	258	373	232	291	227	0.01	-21.99
Tonga	13,314	13,513	13,469	12,167	12,914	0.50	6.14
Tuvalu	249	410	381	316	390	0.02	23.42
Wallis and Futuna Islands	315	239	282	286	202	0.01	-29.37
Samoa	17,900	18,804	17,678	16,250	16,787	0.65	3.30
Other East Asia and the Pacific	**23**			**25**			
Other countries of Oceania	23			25			
EUROPE	**517,125**	**518,767**	**491,498**	**465,308**	**475,957**	**18.35**	**2.29**
Central/Eastern Europe	**14,737**	**17,147**	**16,987**	**16,451**	**17,719**	**0.68**	**7.71**
Azerbaijan	92	116	119	29	48	0.00	65.52
Armenia			73	42			
Bulgaria	272	418	450	303	394	0.02	30.03
Belarus	46	22	75	123	98	0.00	-20.33
Czech Republic	3,162	3,386	3,811	3,605	3,877	0.15	7.55
Estonia	500	567	421	330	306	0.01	-7.27

NEW ZEALAND

2. Arrivals of non-resident visitors at national borders, by country of residence

	2007	2008	2009	2010	2011	Market share 11	% Change 11-10
Georgia	18	24		26	155	0.01	496.15
Hungary	1,306	1,302	1,157	1,191	1,145	0.04	-3.86
Kazakhstan	119	189	203	144	157	0.01	9.03
Kyrgyzstan		43		53			
Latvia	298	265	417	306	189	0.01	-38.24
Lithuania	292	306	258	204	143	0.01	-29.90
Republic of Moldova	42		69	47	16	0.00	-65.96
Poland	2,367	2,693	2,433	2,546	2,759	0.11	8.37
Romania	622	1,082	862	863	921	0.04	6.72
Russian Federation	3,132	4,009	3,952	4,135	5,112	0.20	23.63
Slovakia	659	792	778	789	644	0.02	-18.38
Tajikistan			27		16	0.00	
Turkmenistan			24				
Ukraine	1,765	1,859	1,817	1,715	1,677	0.06	-2.22
Uzbekistan	45	74	41		62	0.00	
Northern Europe	**344,096**	**337,494**	**304,697**	**277,185**	**275,942**	**10.64**	**-0.45**
Denmark	10,832	10,956	10,172	9,854	9,194	0.35	-6.70
Faeroe Islands	46	43	52	121	102	0.00	-15.70
Finland	3,486	3,700	3,951	3,942	3,817	0.15	-3.17
Iceland	309	310	301	225	414	0.02	84.00
Ireland	20,792	21,153	17,055	13,290	16,302	0.63	22.66
Norway	3,839	3,908	3,861	4,325	4,359	0.17	0.79
Sweden	12,075	12,330	10,867	11,114	11,438	0.44	2.92
United Kingdom	291,008	283,428	256,737	234,314	229,021	8.83	-2.26
Channel Islands	1,191	1,225	1,226		931	0.04	
Isle of Man	518	441	475		364	0.01	
Southern Europe	**20,589**	**21,034**	**22,536**	**22,749**	**22,396**	**0.86**	**-1.55**
Albania	51				16	0.00	
Andorra	66	47	18	25	48	0.00	92.00
Bosnia and Herzegovina					16	0.00	
Croatia	171	283	211	311	247	0.01	-20.58
Gibraltar	23	49	41		66	0.00	
Greece	857	721	941	723	787	0.03	8.85
Italy	8,217	8,151	8,460	8,617	8,952	0.35	3.89
Malta	343	373	311	352	344	0.01	-2.27
Montenegro			24		36	0.00	
Portugal	1,153	1,084	1,077	1,072	1,036	0.04	-3.36
San Marino	28		27		16	0.00	
Serbia		27	162	134	140	0.01	4.48
Slovenia	611	603	670	748	698	0.03	-6.68
Spain	8,867	9,502	10,539	10,747	9,946	0.38	-7.45
TFYR of Macedonia	42	93	55	20	48	0.00	140.00
Serbia and Montenegro	160	101					
Western Europe	**130,668**	**135,828**	**139,345**	**140,657**	**153,003**	**5.90**	**8.78**
Austria	6,549	6,747	6,819	6,930	6,909	0.27	-0.30
Belgium	4,784	4,935	4,962	5,051	5,198	0.20	2.91
France	18,673	21,125	23,227	24,579	36,607	1.41	48.94
Germany	59,765	62,300	64,564	64,648	63,719	2.46	-1.44
Liechtenstein	50	27	27	54	121	0.00	124.07
Luxembourg	427	523	353	476	504	0.02	5.88
Monaco	144	102	96	173	161	0.01	-6.94
Netherlands	25,889	25,536	24,300	23,378	23,608	0.91	0.98
Switzerland	14,387	14,533	14,997	15,368	16,176	0.62	5.26
East Mediterranean Europe	**7,035**	**7,264**	**7,933**	**8,266**	**6,897**	**0.27**	**-16.56**
Cyprus	359	369	371	277	284	0.01	2.53
Israel	5,920	5,926	6,768	6,993	5,594	0.22	-20.01
Turkey	756	969	794	996	1,019	0.04	2.31

NEW ZEALAND

2. Arrivals of non-resident visitors at national borders, by country of residence

	2007	2008	2009	2010	2011	Market share 11	% Change 11-10
MIDDLE EAST	**11,085**	**13,268**	**15,234**	**16,097**	**16,246**	**0.63**	**0.93**
Bahrain	398	546	756	668	712	0.03	6.59
Palestine		23		29	16	0.00	-44.83
Iraq	280	193	220	213	339	0.01	59.15
Jordan	135	80	152	111	93	0.00	-16.22
Kuwait	300	418	504	444	576	0.02	29.73
Lebanon	106	46	109	146	89	0.00	-39.04
Libya	47	19	73	53	16	0.00	-69.81
Oman	646	698	718	778	623	0.02	-19.92
Qatar	807	957	867	1,130	1,138	0.04	0.71
Saudi Arabia	2,981	3,923	4,292	4,418	4,189	0.16	-5.18
Syrian Arab Republic	125	51	88	26	16	0.00	-38.46
United Arab Emirates	4,903	5,960	7,088	7,699	7,977	0.31	3.61
Egypt	310	332	344	382	446	0.02	16.75
Yemen	47	22	23		16	0.00	
SOUTH ASIA	**24,692**	**26,927**	**28,461**	**32,948**	**31,927**	**1.23**	**-3.10**
Afghanistan	179	237	166	252	277	0.01	9.92
Bangladesh	284	236	380	493	377	0.01	-23.53
Bhutan		22	23		46	0.00	
Sri Lanka	1,304	1,367	1,123	1,256	1,487	0.06	18.39
India	21,853	23,860	25,336	29,486	28,262	1.09	-4.15
Iran, Islamic Republic of	252	354	341	420	505	0.02	20.24
Maldives	114	86	198	125	140	0.01	12.00
Nepal	183	189	220	289	227	0.01	-21.45
Pakistan	523	576	674	627	606	0.02	-3.35
NOT SPECIFIED	**57,286**	**55,032**	**52,611**	**58,042**	**76,357**	**2.94**	**31.55**
Other countries of the World	36,071	31,236	30,077	37,064	46,619	1.80	25.78
Nationals Residing Abroad	21,215	23,796	22,534	20,978	29,738	1.15	41.76

NICARAGUA

1. Arrivals of non-resident tourists at national borders, by nationality

	2007	2008	2009	2010	2011	Market share 11	% Change 11-10
TOTAL	799,996	857,901	931,904	1,011,251	1,060,031	100.00	4.82
AFRICA	471	706	563	605	487	0.05	-19.50
East Africa	50	99	89	88	87	0.01	-1.14
Burundi	1				1	0.00	
Ethiopia	3	11	10	22	6	0.00	-72.73
Djibouti			9	1	1	0.00	
Kenya	14	22	12	10	18	0.00	80.00
Madagascar		2	1	2	1	0.00	-50.00
Malawi		3	2	1	5	0.00	400.00
Mauritius	2	16	8	10			
Mozambique	5	4	5	6	8	0.00	33.33
Rwanda	1	2	2	1	6	0.00	500.00
Seychelles			6	7			
Somalia			3	4	8	0.00	100.00
Zimbabwe	8	13	7	4	3	0.00	-25.00
Uganda	5	8	11	8	13	0.00	62.50
United Republic of Tanzania	6	14	11	12	14	0.00	16.67
Zambia	5	4	2		3	0.00	
Central Africa	25	17	29	22	18	0.00	-18.18
Angola	9	9	7	5	5	0.00	
Cameroon	4	6	10	7	3	0.00	-57.14
Central African Republic	4		4	7	5	0.00	-28.57
Congo	8	2			3	0.00	
Equatorial Guinea			6				
Gabon			2	3	2	0.00	-33.33
North Africa	57	35	38	45	42	0.00	-6.67
Algeria	21	8	16	13	11	0.00	-15.38
Morocco	32	20	19	23	25	0.00	8.70
Sudan		1	1	1			
Tunisia	4	6	2	8	6	0.00	-25.00
Southern Africa	229	251	255	282	237	0.02	-15.96
Botswana			2	3	8	0.00	166.67
Lesotho	1			6			
Namibia			5		1	0.00	
South Africa	228	251	244	271	223	0.02	-17.71
Swaziland			4	2	5	0.00	150.00
West Africa	35	58	74	55	49	0.00	-10.91
Cape Verde			9	8			
Benin		1					
Gambia	1	7		2	1	0.00	-50.00
Ghana	7	13	9	14	22	0.00	57.14
Guinea	4	9	8	1	1	0.00	
Côte d'Ivoire			23				
Mali	1	2	2	3	1	0.00	-66.67
Mauritania		1		1			
Niger			1				
Nigeria	17	9	11	18	18	0.00	
Guinea-Bissau		3		1			
Senegal	4	7	9	4	4	0.00	
Sierra Leone		1	1	3			
Togo			1				
Burkina Faso	1	5			2	0.00	
Other Africa	75	246	78	113	54	0.01	-52.21
Other countries of Africa	75	246	78	113	54	0.01	-52.21

NICARAGUA

1. Arrivals of non-resident tourists at national borders, by nationality

	2007	2008	2009	2010	2011	Market share 11	% Change 11-10
AMERICAS	671,603	714,212	769,799	846,897	893,498	84.29	5.50
Caribbean	3,739	4,127	5,032	4,530	4,770	0.45	5.30
Antigua and Barbuda	7	6	3	4	2	0.00	-50.00
Bahamas	36	32	29	37	59	0.01	59.46
Barbados	31	24	33	27	34	0.00	25.93
Bermuda	18	14	6	8	11	0.00	37.50
Cayman Islands	76	114	154	121	88	0.01	-27.27
Cuba	1,928	2,091	2,487	2,383	2,238	0.21	-6.08
Dominica	126	69	24	11	33	0.00	200.00
Dominican Republic	1,163	1,425	1,882	1,618	1,794	0.17	10.88
Grenada	19	16	20	3	16	0.00	433.33
Guadeloupe	1		2	4	1	0.00	-75.00
Haiti	74	70	81	51	114	0.01	123.53
Jamaica	88	104	131	132	122	0.01	-7.58
Martinique					1	0.00	
Montserrat			1				
Netherlands Antilles		1		4	1	0.00	-75.00
Aruba	2	3	2	1			
Bonaire			2	2	1	0.00	-50.00
Puerto Rico	14	20	15	4	5	0.00	25.00
Saint Lucia	7	10	8	9	12	0.00	33.33
Saint Vincent and the Grenadines	33	61	57	23	41	0.00	78.26
Trinidad and Tobago	116	67	87	78	180	0.02	130.77
United States Virgin Islands			8	10	17	0.00	70.00
Central America	448,966	460,990	494,107	573,489	611,947	57.73	6.71
Belize	420	502	593	578	537	0.05	-7.09
Costa Rica	71,370	70,733	111,861	125,811	136,466	12.87	8.47
El Salvador	118,252	123,501	121,069	135,455	138,120	13.03	1.97
Guatemala	69,629	68,819	67,317	76,695	83,408	7.87	8.75
Honduras	173,816	182,511	176,120	214,776	230,965	21.79	7.54
Panama	15,479	14,924	17,147	20,174	22,451	2.12	11.29
North America	200,790	231,271	250,232	247,857	253,431	23.91	2.25
Canada	16,800	20,233	24,161	23,597	25,676	2.42	8.81
Mexico	13,328	14,436	13,423	13,781	13,769	1.30	-0.09
United States of America	170,662	196,602	212,648	210,479	213,986	20.19	1.67
South America	18,108	17,824	20,428	21,021	23,350	2.20	11.08
Argentina	2,880	2,842	3,638	3,779	3,771	0.36	-0.21
Bolivia	650	606	740	752	883	0.08	17.42
Brazil	2,327	2,451	2,667	3,226	3,659	0.35	13.42
Chile	1,566	1,578	1,685	1,585	1,920	0.18	21.14
Colombia	3,434	3,227	4,001	4,204	4,869	0.46	15.82
Ecuador	1,072	1,164	1,263	1,282	1,509	0.14	17.71
Guyana	29	51	53	32	22	0.00	-31.25
Paraguay	154	164	142	152	209	0.02	37.50
Peru	1,946	1,960	2,386	2,347	2,233	0.21	-4.86
Suriname	6	9	30	11	13	0.00	18.18
Uruguay	484	486	615	596	730	0.07	22.48
Venezuela	3,560	3,286	3,208	3,055	3,532	0.33	15.61
EAST ASIA AND THE PACIFIC	9,096	9,360	11,982	10,620	10,252	0.97	-3.47
North-East Asia	5,007	4,454	5,357	5,093	5,255	0.50	3.18
China	392	220	641	404	303	0.03	-25.00
Taiwan, Province of China	1,264	867	1,165	894	870	0.08	-2.68
Hong Kong, China	7	12	17	31	18	0.00	-41.94
Japan	1,533	1,527	1,542	1,669	1,747	0.16	4.67
Korea, Republic of	1,811	1,827	1,992	2,095	2,316	0.22	10.55
Mongolia		1			1	0.00	

NICARAGUA

1. Arrivals of non-resident tourists at national borders, by nationality

	2007	2008	2009	2010	2011	Market share 11	% Change 11-10
South-East Asia	**1,856**	**2,479**	**3,194**	**1,864**	**1,087**	**0.10**	**-41.68**
Myanmar	50	89	140	81	47	0.00	-41.98
Indonesia	513	95	782	86	124	0.01	44.19
Lao People's Democratic Republic	11	1		2			
Malaysia	32	38	50	50	50	0.00	
Philippines	1,189	2,075	2,056	1,533	741	0.07	-51.66
Singapore	28	26	43	41	52	0.00	26.83
Viet Nam	7	17	33	25	14	0.00	-44.00
Thailand	26	138	90	46	59	0.01	28.26
Australasia	**2,230**	**2,422**	**3,412**	**3,645**	**3,901**	**0.37**	**7.02**
Australia	1,819	1,944	2,787	3,017	3,255	0.31	7.89
New Zealand	411	478	625	628	646	0.06	2.87
Melanesia	**1**	**3**	**3**	**7**	**3**	**0.00**	**-57.14**
Fiji	1	2	1	4	2	0.00	-50.00
Papua New Guinea		1	2	3	1	0.00	-66.67
Micronesia		**1**	**11**	**11**	**6**	**0.00**	**-45.45**
Kiribati		1					
Micronesia, Federated States of			11	11	6	0.00	-45.45
Polynesia	**2**	**1**	**5**				
French Polynesia			5				
Tonga	2	1					
EUROPE	**52,525**	**57,649**	**71,540**	**73,644**	**75,948**	**7.16**	**3.13**
Central/Eastern Europe	**1,772**	**2,141**	**2,788**	**3,112**	**2,934**	**0.28**	**-5.72**
Azerbaijan			2	2	2	0.00	
Armenia		2		3	3	0.00	
Bulgaria	74	121	97	106	88	0.01	-16.98
Belarus					2	0.00	
Czech Republic/Slovakia	384	435	87	120	131	0.01	9.17
Czech Republic			453	587	470	0.04	-19.93
Estonia	30	72	51	57	64	0.01	12.28
Georgia	44	55	55	65	35	0.00	-46.15
Hungary	152	125	245	205	157	0.01	-23.41
Kazakhstan			6	8	8	0.00	
Kyrgyzstan				5	1	0.00	-80.00
Latvia	22	18	50	18	4	0.00	-77.78
Lithuania	25	30	39	35	92	0.01	162.86
Republic of Moldova			7	4	4	0.00	
Poland	277	356	489	550	595	0.06	8.18
Romania	149	227	221	172	208	0.02	20.93
Russian Federation	475	516	770	1,003	893	0.08	-10.97
Tajikistan			3		2	0.00	
Turkmenistan			4	4			
Ukraine	115	175	206	163	171	0.02	4.91
USSR (former)	25	9					
Uzbekistan			3	5	4	0.00	-20.00
Northern Europe	**12,962**	**17,044**	**19,119**	**17,729**	**18,071**	**1.70**	**1.93**
Denmark	1,770	1,922	2,230	2,117	2,101	0.20	-0.76
Finland	505	587	784	766	617	0.06	-19.45
Iceland	70	90	115	81	101	0.01	24.69
Ireland	807	937	1,047	1,101	992	0.09	-9.90
Norway	1,286	1,375	1,610	1,822	1,757	0.17	-3.57
Sweden	2,038	2,122	2,572	2,318	2,396	0.23	3.36
United Kingdom	6,486	10,011	10,761	9,524	10,107	0.95	6.12
Southern Europe	**15,162**	**14,941**	**16,559**	**17,823**	**17,680**	**1.67**	**-0.80**
Albania	9	11	8	5	3	0.00	-40.00
Andorra	7	9	9	13	13	0.00	

NICARAGUA

1. Arrivals of non-resident tourists at national borders, by nationality

	2007	2008	2009	2010	2011	Market share 11	% Change 11-10
Bosnia and Herzegovina			2	2	7	0.00	250.00
Croatia	64	82	64	65	50	0.00	-23.08
Greece	182	151	215	196	195	0.02	-0.51
Holy See			2	1	3	0.00	200.00
Italy	4,208	4,355	5,118	5,613	5,541	0.52	-1.28
Malta	8	7	9	8	10	0.00	25.00
Portugal	232	321	349	361	349	0.03	-3.32
San Marino		1					
Serbia			1	22	26	0.00	18.18
Slovenia	105	117	125	164	164	0.02	
Spain	10,315	9,830	10,616	11,338	11,305	1.07	-0.29
TFYR of Macedonia			6	7	9	0.00	28.57
Yugoslavia, SFR (former)	32	57		28	5	0.00	-82.14
Serbia and Montenegro			35				
Western Europe	**21,427**	**22,292**	**31,236**	**33,161**	**35,141**	**3.32**	**5.97**
Austria	1,016	1,086	1,388	1,399	1,576	0.15	12.65
Belgium	1,354	1,519	2,542	3,538	3,266	0.31	-7.69
France	4,839	5,009	6,496	7,065	7,131	0.67	0.93
Germany	7,649	7,489	10,834	11,048	12,118	1.14	9.69
Liechtenstein	2	2	5	14	6	0.00	-57.14
Luxembourg	38	43	74	75	67	0.01	-10.67
Monaco			2				
Netherlands	4,096	4,633	6,418	6,468	7,178	0.68	10.98
Switzerland	2,433	2,511	3,477	3,554	3,799	0.36	6.89
East Mediterranean Europe	**1,202**	**1,231**	**1,838**	**1,819**	**2,122**	**0.20**	**16.66**
Cyprus	12	9	15	22	14	0.00	-36.36
Israel	1,077	1,064	1,618	1,595	1,895	0.18	18.81
Turkey	113	158	205	202	213	0.02	5.45
MIDDLE EAST	**157**	**127**	**164**	**133**	**143**	**0.01**	**7.52**
Bahrain	1	1	1	4			
Palestine	29	8	13	8	19	0.00	137.50
Iraq	7	1	1				
Jordan	11	14	15	24	27	0.00	12.50
Kuwait	1	4	4	2	6	0.00	200.00
Lebanon	32	23	22	18	10	0.00	-44.44
Libya	58	60	61	49	35	0.00	-28.57
Qatar	1			1	8	0.00	700.00
Saudi Arabia	4	3	4	6	3	0.00	-50.00
Syrian Arab Republic			4	1	1	0.00	
United Arab Emirates			28	4	7	0.00	75.00
Egypt	13	13	11	14	27	0.00	92.86
Yemen				2			
SOUTH ASIA	**444**	**1,775**	**733**	**2,089**	**1,573**	**0.15**	**-24.70**
Afghanistan	1	3	2		3	0.00	
Bangladesh	3	12	35	17	14	0.00	-17.65
Sri Lanka	25	26	33	12	33	0.00	175.00
India	245	1,552	513	1,935	1,410	0.13	-27.13
Iran, Islamic Republic of	152	74	105	105	95	0.01	-9.52
Maldives					1	0.00	
Nepal	5	22	11	7	7	0.00	
Pakistan	13	86	34	13	10	0.00	-23.08
NOT SPECIFIED	**65,700**	**74,072**	**77,123**	**77,263**	**78,130**	**7.37**	**1.12**
Other countries of the World	257	54	2	53	50	0.00	-5.66
Nationals Residing Abroad	65,443	74,018	77,121	77,210	78,080	7.37	1.13

NIGER

1. Arrivals of non-resident tourists at national borders, by nationality

	2007	2008	2009	2010	2011	Market share 11	% Change 11-10
TOTAL	47,539	73,154	65,883	74,278	82,370	100.00	10.89
AFRICA	23,770	46,981	42,312	47,702	52,881	64.20	10.86
Other Africa	23,770	46,981	42,312	47,702	52,881	64.20	10.86
All countries of Africa	23,770	46,981	42,312	47,702	52,881	64.20	10.86
AMERICAS	3,898	4,528	4,078	4,598	5,107	6.20	11.07
North America	2,798	3,600	3,947	4,450	4,942	6.00	11.06
Canada	998	1,252	1,373	1,548	1,719	2.09	11.05
United States of America	1,800	2,348	2,574	2,902	3,223	3.91	11.06
Other Americas	1,100	928	131	148	165	0.20	11.49
Other countries of the Americas	1,100	928	131	148	165	0.20	11.49
EAST ASIA AND THE PACIFIC	1,778	3,063	3,158	3,560	3,954	4.80	11.07
North-East Asia	920	1,900	2,259	2,547	2,829	3.43	11.07
Japan	920	1,900	2,259	2,547	2,829	3.43	11.07
Other East Asia and the Pacific	858	1,163	899	1,013	1,125	1.37	11.06
Other countries of Asia	858	1,163	899	1,013	1,125	1.37	11.06
EUROPE	17,589	18,138	16,335	18,418	20,428	24.80	10.91
Southern Europe	1,020	775	961	1,085	1,109	1.35	2.21
Italy	1,020	775	961	1,085	1,109	1.35	2.21
Western Europe	13,972	16,317	15,255	17,331	19,237	23.35	11.00
France	12,084	14,667	13,209	14,892	16,519	20.05	10.93
Germany	880	769	953	1,207	1,345	1.63	11.43
Benelux	1,008	881	1,093	1,232	1,373	1.67	11.44
Other Europe	2,597	1,046	119	2	82	0.10	4000.00
Other countries of Europe	2,597	1,046	119	2	82	0.10	4000.00
MIDDLE EAST	504	444					
All countries of Middle East	504	444					

NIGERIA

2. Arrivals of non-resident visitors at national borders, by nationality

	2007	2008	2009	2010	2011	Market share 11	% Change 11-10
TOTAL　(*)	5,238,545	5,820,497	6,053,318	6,113,384	3,765,400	100.00	-38.41
AFRICA	3,613,664	4,014,981	4,175,489	4,185,492	872,285	23.17	-79.16
East Africa	166,220	184,689	192,077	192,803	35,887	0.95	-81.39
Ethiopia	70,045	77,827	80,941	81,053	6,307	0.17	-92.22
Kenya	36,235	40,262	41,872	41,981	22,720	0.60	-45.88
Mozambique	18,752	20,836	21,669	21,757			
Rwanda	249	277	288	379	1,520	0.04	301.06
Somalia	498	554	576	677			
Zimbabwe	19,780	21,977	22,857	22,921			
Uganda	3,341	3,712	3,860	3,886	2,720	0.07	-30.01
United Republic of Tanzania	15,209	16,899	17,575	17,666	1,900	0.05	-89.24
Zambia	2,111	2,345	2,439	2,483	720	0.02	-71.00
Central Africa	441,206	490,230	510,574	511,231	270,151	7.17	-47.16
Angola	11,515	12,795	13,385	13,496			
Cameroon	201,586	223,984	233,274	233,370	205,920	5.47	-11.76
Central African Republic	13,809	15,349	15,984	16,035	2,731	0.07	-82.97
Chad	160,290	178,100	185,527	185,633	48,400	1.29	-73.93
Congo	14,603	16,226	16,803	16,852	3,560	0.09	-78.87
Democratic Republic of the Congo	14,515	16,128	16,801	16,908	4,720	0.13	-72.08
Equatorial Guinea	970	1,078	1,123	1,195	2,900	0.08	142.68
Gabon	23,389	25,982	27,065	27,114	1,920	0.05	-92.92
Sao Tome and Principe	529	588	612	628			
North Africa	345,336	383,431	397,936	398,485	17,030	0.45	-95.73
Algeria	68,982	76,647	79,547	79,658			
Morocco	108,885	120,706	125,272	125,421			
Sudan	118,916	132,130	137,128	137,288	15,480	0.41	-88.72
Tunisia	48,553	53,948	55,989	56,118	1,550	0.04	-97.24
Southern Africa	72,985	81,102	84,346	90,682	42,440	1.13	-53.20
Botswana	12,240	13,600	14,129	14,220			
Lesotho	11,841	13,165	13,706	13,812			
Namibia	31,569	35,076	36,479	36,556			
South Africa	17,335	19,261	20,032	26,094	42,440	1.13	62.64
West Africa	2,587,917	2,875,529	2,990,556	2,992,291	506,777	13.46	-83.06
Cape Verde	517	575	598	624	4,280	0.11	585.90
Benin	740,367	822,695	855,605	855,712	65,760	1.75	-92.32
Gambia	34,161	37,956	39,475	39,587			
Ghana	39,078	43,420	45,157	45,406	177,640	4.72	291.23
Guinea	37,008	41,120	42,764	42,836	38,800	1.03	-9.42
Côte d'Ivoire	95,755	106,394	110,650	110,839	17,720	0.47	-84.01
Liberia	202,638	225,153	234,160	234,254	26,000	0.69	-88.90
Mali	69,875	77,639	80,745	80,793	29,200	0.78	-63.86
Mauritania	1,811	2,012	2,093	2,284	5,017	0.13	119.66
Niger	1,101,959	1,224,399	1,273,378	1,273,550	64,400	1.71	-94.94
Senegal	109,212	121,347	126,201	126,464	30,920	0.82	-75.55
Sierra Leone	31,314	34,793	36,185	36,257	12,960	0.34	-64.26
Togo	64,181	71,313	74,165	74,226	24,080	0.64	-67.56
Burkina Faso	60,041	66,713	69,380	69,459	10,000	0.27	-85.60
AMERICAS	221,586	244,455	256,055	257,581	176,880	4.70	-31.33
Caribbean	27,212	30,043	31,469	31,841	37,760	1.00	18.59
Barbados	3,447	3,806	3,987	4,064			
Cuba	3,915	4,323	4,527	4,609	9,960	0.26	116.10
Dominican Republic	1,102	1,216	1,274	1,342	800	0.02	-40.39
Haiti	481	531	557	574			
Jamaica	8,702	9,607	10,063	10,139	16,720	0.44	64.91
Trinidad and Tobago	9,565	10,560	11,061	11,113	10,280	0.27	-7.50

NIGERIA

2. Arrivals of non-resident visitors at national borders, by nationality

	2007	2008	2009	2010	2011	Market share 11	% Change 11-10
Central America	1,085	1,198	1,231	1,292			
Costa Rica	614	678	697	726			
Nicaragua	471	520	534	566			
North America	132,619	146,306	153,248	153,707	109,800	2.92	-28.57
Canada	19,534	21,550	22,573	22,678	13,320	0.35	-41.26
Mexico	44,429	49,014	51,339	51,454			
United States of America	68,656	75,742	79,336	79,575	96,480	2.56	21.24
South America	60,670	66,908	70,107	70,741	29,320	0.78	-58.55
Argentina	12,024	13,261	13,895	14,105			
Bolivia	1,146	1,264	1,325	1,396			
Brazil	22,896	25,251	26,458	26,547	10,080	0.27	-62.03
Chile	11,017	12,150	12,731	12,777	19,240	0.51	50.58
Colombia	9,142	10,083	10,565	10,603			
Guyana	582	638	669	718			
Paraguay	1,559	1,719	1,801	1,852			
Peru	1,443	1,592	1,668	1,697			
Venezuela	861	950	995	1,046			
EAST ASIA AND THE PACIFIC	302,260	337,587	351,092	352,351	339,879	9.03	-3.54
North-East Asia	166,024	184,491	191,873	192,579	270,940	7.20	40.69
China	65,679	72,984	75,904	76,143	241,280	6.41	216.88
Taiwan, Province of China	42,687	47,434	49,333	49,527			
Hong Kong, China	31,610	35,127	36,532	36,710			
Japan	23,475	26,087	27,130	27,340	26,300	0.70	-3.80
Korea, Republic of	2,573	2,859	2,974	2,859	3,360	0.09	17.52
South-East Asia	130,869	145,433	151,250	151,690	45,659	1.21	-69.90
Myanmar	157	174	181	230			
Indonesia	32,167	35,747	37,177	37,199	6,440	0.17	-82.69
Malaysia	35,021	36,750	38,220	38,291	17,499	0.46	-54.30
Philippines	27,220	30,250	31,460	31,569	11,120	0.30	-64.78
Singapore	20,064	24,520	25,500	25,611	10,600	0.28	-58.61
Thailand	16,240	17,992	18,712	18,790			
Australasia	5,367	7,663	7,969	8,082	23,280	0.62	188.05
Australia	3,591	5,127	5,332	5,404	10,880	0.29	101.33
New Zealand	1,776	2,536	2,637	2,678	12,400	0.33	363.03
EUROPE	867,461	963,874	1,000,609	1,002,737	448,853	11.92	-55.24
Central/Eastern Europe	168,333	187,087	194,019	194,379	56,973	1.51	-70.69
Bulgaria	26,647	29,615	30,713	30,752	7,920	0.21	-74.25
Czech Republic/Slovakia	21,563	23,965	24,853	24,905	7,293	0.19	-70.72
Hungary	32,151	35,733	37,057	37,096			
Poland	24,138	26,828	27,822	27,893	18,120	0.48	-35.04
Romania	41,207	45,798	47,457	47,546	5,080	0.13	-89.32
Russian Federation	22,627	25,148	26,117	26,187	12,560	0.33	-52.04
Ukraine					6,000	0.16	
Northern Europe	203,121	225,549	234,341	234,791	233,301	6.20	-0.63
Denmark	30,757	34,150	35,481	35,550	21,141	0.56	-40.53
Finland	34,408	38,208	39,697	39,775	14,240	0.38	-64.20
Ireland	19,357	21,494	22,332	22,371	2,240	0.06	-89.99
Norway	23,887	26,524	27,558	27,589	5,920	0.16	-78.54
Sweden	21,855	24,269	25,215	25,277	480	0.01	-98.10
United Kingdom	72,857	80,904	84,058	84,229	189,280	5.03	124.72
Southern Europe	184,210	204,726	212,533	213,016	48,558	1.29	-77.20
Croatia					530	0.01	
Greece	3,831	4,258	4,420	4,468	5,559	0.15	24.42
Italy	123,697	137,473	142,712	142,813	26,480	0.70	-81.46
Portugal	15,013	16,685	17,321	17,392	9,120	0.24	-47.56

NIGERIA

2. Arrivals of non-resident visitors at national borders, by nationality

	2007	2008	2009	2010	2011	Market share 11	% Change 11-10
Spain	39,211	43,668	45,332	45,514	6,869	0.18	-84.91
Yugoslavia, SFR (former)	2,458	2,642	2,748	2,829			
Western Europe	**264,936**	**294,367**	**305,584**	**306,161**	**94,541**	**2.51**	**-69.12**
Austria	7,952	8,836	9,171	9,250	880	0.02	-90.49
Belgium	12,902	14,335	14,881	14,982	6,320	0.17	-57.82
France	116,704	129,668	134,609	134,718	19,200	0.51	-85.75
Germany	113,842	126,488	131,309	131,418	47,360	1.26	-63.96
Luxembourg	2,092	2,325	2,414	2,485			
Netherlands	10,120	11,244	11,673	11,781	16,880	0.45	43.28
Switzerland	1,324	1,471	1,527	1,527	3,901	0.10	155.47
East Mediterranean Europe	**46,861**	**52,145**	**54,132**	**54,390**	**15,480**	**0.41**	**-71.54**
Cyprus	5,330	5,956	6,183	6,254			
Israel	28,488	31,683	32,890	33,029	13,680	0.36	-58.58
Turkey	13,043	14,506	15,059	15,107	1,800	0.05	-88.08
MIDDLE EAST	**94,756**	**105,357**	**109,559**	**110,692**	**38,423**	**1.02**	**-65.29**
Iraq	7,152	7,947	8,265	8,301			
Jordan	3,640	4,045	4,201	4,253			
Kuwait	1,384	1,538	1,599	1,648			
Lebanon	36,001	40,004	41,601	41,683	24,840	0.66	-40.41
Libya	9,064	10,072	10,474	10,518	1,840	0.05	-82.51
Saudi Arabia	3,603	4,003	4,163	4,224	1,120	0.03	-73.48
Syrian Arab Republic	1,716	1,906	1,983	2,661			
United Arab Emirates					1,400	0.04	
Egypt	30,812	34,304	35,674	35,779	9,223	0.24	-74.22
Yemen	1,384	1,538	1,599	1,625			
SOUTH ASIA	**123,627**	**137,364**	**142,858**	**143,412**	**212,920**	**5.65**	**48.47**
Afghanistan	754	837	871	883			
Bangladesh	823	920	957	1,006			
Sri Lanka	2,076	2,307	2,400	2,524			
India	49,351	54,835	57,028	57,229	202,200	5.37	253.32
Iran, Islamic Republic of	18,568	20,632	20,871	20,913			
Nepal	98	109	114	158			
Pakistan	51,957	57,724	60,617	60,699	10,720	0.28	-82.34
NOT SPECIFIED	**15,191**	**16,879**	**17,656**	**61,119**	**1,676,160**	**44.51**	**2642.45**
Other countries of the World	15,191	16,879	17,656	61,119			
Nationals Residing Abroad					1,676,160	44.51	

NIUE

1. Arrivals of non-resident tourists at national borders, by country of residence

		2007	2008	2009	2010	2011	Market share 11	% Change 11-10
TOTAL	(*)	**3,463**	**4,748**	**4,662**	**6,214**	**6,094**	**100.00**	**-1.93**
AMERICAS		**208**	**315**	**203**	**298**	**1,176**	**19.30**	**294.63**
North America		**208**	**315**	**189**	**290**	**1,165**	**19.12**	**301.72**
Canada		31	59	32	60	239	3.92	298.33
United States of America		177	256	157	230	926	15.20	302.61
Other Americas				**14**	**8**	**11**	**0.18**	**37.50**
Other countries of the Americas				14	8	11	0.18	37.50
EAST ASIA AND THE PACIFIC		**3,026**	**3,913**	**3,550**	**4,156**	**4,432**	**72.73**	**6.64**
North-East Asia		**21**	**59**	**20**	**35**	**30**	**0.49**	**-14.29**
China		11	32	6	22	6	0.10	-72.73
Japan		10	27	14	13	24	0.39	84.62
Australasia		**2,888**	**3,324**	**3,151**	**3,474**	**4,166**	**68.36**	**19.92**
Australia		371	546	461	539	611	10.03	13.36
New Zealand		2,517	2,778	2,690	2,935	3,555	58.34	21.12
Other East Asia and the Pacific		**117**	**530**	**379**	**647**	**236**	**3.87**	**-63.52**
Other countries of Asia		12	93	146	445	20	0.33	-95.51
Other countries of Oceania		105	437	233	202	216	3.54	6.93
EUROPE		**206**	**492**	**889**	**1,602**	**402**	**6.60**	**-74.91**
Northern Europe		**82**	**113**	**71**	**138**	**108**	**1.77**	**-21.74**
Denmark				24	35			
United Kingdom		82	113	47	103	108	1.77	4.85
Southern Europe				**17**	**13**			
Italy				17	13			
Western Europe		**42**	**154**	**682**	**1,255**	**99**	**1.62**	**-92.11**
Austria				38	60			
France		18	82	101	45	48	0.79	6.67
Germany		24	72	475	1,043	51	0.84	-95.11
Netherlands				17	27			
Switzerland				51	80			
Other Europe		**82**	**225**	**119**	**196**	**195**	**3.20**	**-0.51**
Other countries of Europe		82	225	119	196	195	3.20	-0.51
NOT SPECIFIED		**23**	**28**	**20**	**158**	**84**	**1.38**	**-46.84**
Other countries of the World		23	28	20	158	84	1.38	-46.84

NORTHERN MARIANA ISLANDS

2. Arrivals of non-resident visitors at national borders, by nationality

	2007	2008	2009	2010	2011	Market share 11	% Change 11-10
TOTAL	389,345	397,274	353,956	379,091	340,957	100.00	-10.06
AMERICAS	28,082	31,361	29,555	27,319	24,155	7.08	-11.58
North America	28,082	31,361	29,555	27,319	24,155	7.08	-11.58
Canada	209	295	296	193	175	0.05	-9.33
United States of America	27,873	31,066	29,259	27,126	23,980	7.03	-11.60
EAST ASIA AND THE PACIFIC	355,921	356,997	316,064	345,874	310,394	91.04	-10.26
North-East Asia	349,265	351,577	310,475	343,043	306,862	90.00	-10.55
China	39,447	26,407	29,528	41,623	54,186	15.89	30.18
Taiwan, Province of China	445	284	418	208	222	0.07	6.73
Hong Kong, China	884	471	286	369	2,005	0.59	443.36
Japan	200,168	213,299	191,111	185,032	142,946	41.92	-22.75
Korea, Republic of	108,321	111,116	89,132	115,811	107,503	31.53	-7.17
South-East Asia	5,099	1,862	1,660	772	565	0.17	-26.81
Philippines	5,025	1,780	1,591	703	544	0.16	-22.62
Thailand	74	82	69	69	21	0.01	-69.57
Australasia	312	2,125	2,584	977	2,037	0.60	108.50
Australia	312	2,125	2,584	977	2,037	0.60	108.50
Micronesia	1,245	1,433	1,345	1,082	930	0.27	-14.05
Micronesia, Federated States of	850	861	911	813	665	0.20	-18.20
Palau	395	572	434	269	265	0.08	-1.49
EUROPE	4,676	7,742	7,309	4,961	5,646	1.66	13.81
Central/Eastern Europe	3,672	6,814	6,222	4,391	5,276	1.55	20.15
Russian Federation	3,672	6,814	6,222	4,391	5,276	1.55	20.15
Other Europe	1,004	928	1,087	570	370	0.11	-35.09
Other countries of Europe	1,004	928	1,087	570	370	0.11	-35.09
NOT SPECIFIED	666	1,174	1,028	937	762	0.22	-18.68
Other countries of the World	666	1,174	1,028	937	762	0.22	-18.68

NORWAY

1. Arrivals of non-resident tourists at national borders, by nationality

		2007	2008	2009	2010	2011	Market share 11	% Change 11-10
TOTAL	(*)	4,377,000	4,347,000	4,346,000	4,767,000	4,963,000	100.00	4.11
AMERICAS		177,000	136,000	132,000	160,000	164,000	3.30	2.50
North America		177,000	136,000	132,000	160,000	164,000	3.30	2.50
United States of America		177,000	136,000	132,000	160,000	164,000	3.30	2.50
EAST ASIA AND THE PACIFIC		32,000	29,000	25,000	28,000	27,000	0.54	-3.57
North-East Asia		32,000	29,000	25,000	28,000	27,000	0.54	-3.57
Japan		32,000	29,000	25,000	28,000	27,000	0.54	-3.57
EUROPE		3,939,000	3,967,000	3,943,000	4,313,000	4,471,000	90.09	3.66
Central/Eastern Europe		201,000	266,000	257,000	288,000	303,000	6.11	5.21
Poland		156,000	202,000	188,000	206,000	195,000	3.93	-5.34
Russian Federation		45,000	64,000	69,000	82,000	108,000	2.18	31.71
Northern Europe		2,293,000	2,302,000	2,319,000	2,438,000	2,490,000	50.17	2.13
Denmark		576,000	571,000	539,000	545,000	538,000	10.84	-1.28
Finland		254,000	260,000	239,000	250,000	294,000	5.92	17.60
Sweden		1,087,000	1,130,000	1,239,000	1,336,000	1,339,000	26.98	0.22
United Kingdom		376,000	341,000	302,000	307,000	319,000	6.43	3.91
Southern Europe		144,000	137,000	130,000	143,000	156,000	3.14	9.09
Italy		65,000	60,000	62,000	69,000	85,000	1.71	23.19
Spain		79,000	77,000	68,000	74,000	71,000	1.43	-4.05
Western Europe		1,095,000	1,031,000	1,039,000	1,188,000	1,200,000	24.18	1.01
Austria		27,000	27,000	28,000	31,000	36,000	0.73	16.13
Belgium		42,000	40,000	37,000	51,000	47,000	0.95	-7.84
France		133,000	127,000	128,000	133,000	134,000	2.70	0.75
Germany		650,000	603,000	617,000	730,000	719,000	14.49	-1.51
Netherlands		197,000	195,000	188,000	194,000	203,000	4.09	4.64
Switzerland		46,000	39,000	41,000	49,000	61,000	1.23	24.49
Other Europe		206,000	231,000	198,000	256,000	322,000	6.49	25.78
Other countries of Europe		206,000	231,000	198,000	256,000	322,000	6.49	25.78
NOT SPECIFIED		229,000	215,000	246,000	266,000	301,000	6.06	13.16
Other countries of the World		229,000	215,000	246,000	266,000	301,000	6.06	13.16

NORWAY

5. Overnight stays of non-resident tourists in hotels and similar establishments, by nationality

		2007	2008	2009	2010	2011	Market share 11	% Change 11-10
TOTAL	(*)	5,067,552	4,893,806	4,426,610	4,798,028	4,898,885	100.00	2.10
AFRICA		29,608	33,165	28,469	28,419	40,329	0.82	41.91
Southern Africa		6,703	7,132	5,031	5,353	6,345	0.13	18.53
South Africa		6,703	7,132	5,031	5,353	6,345	0.13	18.53
Other Africa		22,905	26,033	23,438	23,066	33,984	0.69	47.33
Other countries of Africa		22,905	26,033	23,438	23,066	33,984	0.69	47.33
AMERICAS		368,610	347,866	302,991	366,634	375,674	7.67	2.47
North America		337,946	315,065	274,233	328,883	327,916	6.69	-0.29
Canada		19,753	20,002	18,180	20,205	21,913	0.45	8.45
Mexico		5,338	5,119	5,367	6,532	7,249	0.15	10.98
United States of America		312,855	289,944	250,686	302,146	298,754	6.10	-1.12
South America		30,664	32,801	28,758	37,751	47,758	0.97	26.51
Brazil		12,515	16,914	15,079	21,025	28,757	0.59	36.78
Other countries of South America		18,149	15,887	13,679	16,726	19,001	0.39	13.60
EAST ASIA AND THE PACIFIC		412,180	379,148	330,286	401,483	462,263	9.44	15.14
North-East Asia		218,281	185,381	159,991	199,541	225,682	4.61	13.10
China		68,743	43,606	41,562	63,617	86,179	1.76	35.47
Japan		110,908	103,796	95,316	100,836	97,875	2.00	-2.94
Korea, Republic of		38,630	37,979	23,113	35,088	41,628	0.85	18.64
Australasia		34,675	37,246	28,252	36,583	41,247	0.84	12.75
Australia		34,675	37,246	28,252	36,583	41,247	0.84	12.75
Other East Asia and the Pacific		159,224	156,521	142,043	165,359	195,334	3.99	18.13
Other countries of Asia		145,052	140,697	132,018	154,496	182,245	3.72	17.96
Other countries of Oceania		14,172	15,824	10,025	10,863	13,089	0.27	20.49
EUROPE		4,257,154	4,133,627	3,764,864	4,001,492	4,020,619	82.07	0.48
Central/Eastern Europe		299,249	363,668	301,251	359,614	368,179	7.52	2.38
Czech Republic		17,655	20,965	20,231	22,819	30,770	0.63	34.84
Estonia		11,022	20,519	11,150	8,710	8,073	0.16	-7.31
Hungary		10,588	13,687	9,051	10,338	9,645	0.20	-6.70
Latvia		9,928	12,677	9,421	12,242	13,958	0.28	14.02
Lithuania		9,941	12,739	11,439	18,004	17,536	0.36	-2.60
Poland		110,217	139,970	111,350	132,445	122,886	2.51	-7.22
Russian Federation		113,026	127,708	111,524	135,869	143,854	2.94	5.88
Slovakia		9,084	4,835	5,796	8,244	7,806	0.16	-5.31
Ukraine		7,788	10,568	11,289	10,943	13,651	0.28	24.75
Northern Europe		1,881,348	1,783,495	1,620,761	1,670,595	1,673,142	34.15	0.15
Denmark		565,643	540,630	512,279	519,076	491,279	10.03	-5.36
Finland		73,120	67,649	66,825	75,487	76,315	1.56	1.10
Iceland		19,129	13,233	11,722	15,746	16,981	0.35	7.84
Ireland		17,358	20,442	16,587	19,045	23,816	0.49	25.05
Sweden		560,289	579,329	568,062	601,797	610,446	12.46	1.44
United Kingdom		645,809	562,212	445,286	439,444	454,305	9.27	3.38
Southern Europe		468,259	389,687	375,647	403,304	393,948	8.04	-2.32
Greece		17,547	17,546	15,564	14,048	11,979	0.24	-14.73
Italy		164,578	139,001	157,245	168,845	152,965	3.12	-9.41
Malta		1,037	876	836	1,193	1,415	0.03	18.61
Portugal		14,069	15,176	17,567	17,124	16,730	0.34	-2.30
Slovenia		2,920	3,752	2,904	4,758	4,298	0.09	-9.67
Spain		268,108	213,336	181,531	197,336	206,561	4.22	4.67
Western Europe		1,374,720	1,378,069	1,301,354	1,378,192	1,357,629	27.71	-1.49
Austria		26,981	30,808	30,850	37,485	37,609	0.77	0.33
Belgium		36,047	39,736	38,672	49,761	47,412	0.97	-4.72
France		202,870	201,231	209,560	219,043	211,972	4.33	-3.23

NORWAY

5. Overnight stays of non-resident tourists in hotels and similar establishments, by nationality

	2007	2008	2009	2010	2011	Market share 11	% Change 11-10
Germany	720,138	729,381	664,459	708,652	699,776	14.28	-1.25
Liechtenstein	1,605	2,280	1,122	1,595	1,445	0.03	-9.40
Luxembourg	1,945	2,370	3,140	2,665	3,156	0.06	18.42
Netherlands	320,576	309,379	291,484	285,860	278,474	5.68	-2.58
Switzerland	64,558	62,884	62,067	73,131	77,785	1.59	6.36
East Mediterranean Europe	**8,387**	**11,583**	**9,171**	**12,135**	**10,801**	**0.22**	**-10.99**
Cyprus	1,237	1,902	1,372	1,729	1,334	0.03	-22.85
Turkey	7,150	9,681	7,799	10,406	9,467	0.19	-9.02
Other Europe	**225,191**	**207,125**	**156,680**	**177,652**	**216,920**	**4.43**	**22.10**
Other countries of Europe	225,191	207,125	156,680	177,652	216,920	4.43	22.10

NORWAY

6. Overnight stays of non-resident tourists in all types of accommodation establishments, by nationality

	2007	2008	2009	2010	2011	Market share 11	% Change 11-10
TOTAL	8,325,773	8,146,872	7,525,174	7,903,186	7,844,241	100.00	-0.75
AFRICA	32,455	36,260	42,319	34,507	44,678	0.57	29.48
Southern Africa	7,500	8,284	6,012	5,831	6,979	0.09	19.69
South Africa	7,500	8,284	6,012	5,831	6,979	0.09	19.69
Other Africa	24,955	27,976	36,307	28,676	37,699	0.48	31.47
Other countries of Africa	24,955	27,976	36,307	28,676	37,699	0.48	31.47
AMERICAS	395,319	370,217	324,554	388,266	400,579	5.11	3.17
North America	360,991	334,615	292,442	346,739	349,229	4.45	0.72
Canada	23,548	23,678	21,873	24,328	25,876	0.33	6.36
Mexico	6,716	5,753	6,230	6,975	7,977	0.10	14.37
United States of America	330,727	305,184	264,339	315,436	315,376	4.02	-0.02
South America	34,328	35,602	32,112	41,527	51,350	0.65	23.65
Brazil	13,847	18,339	16,827	22,882	30,862	0.39	34.87
Other countries of South America	20,481	17,263	15,285	18,645	20,488	0.26	9.88
EAST ASIA AND THE PACIFIC	438,976	409,676	365,700	431,898	495,132	6.31	14.64
North-East Asia	227,265	195,502	175,722	210,155	238,111	3.04	13.30
China	70,694	45,861	51,795	68,133	91,715	1.17	34.61
Japan	115,962	107,661	98,607	104,014	101,124	1.29	-2.78
Korea, Republic of	40,609	41,980	25,320	38,008	45,272	0.58	19.11
Australasia	41,620	45,119	34,724	43,917	48,411	0.62	10.23
Australia	41,620	45,119	34,724	43,917	48,411	0.62	10.23
Other East Asia and the Pacific	170,091	169,055	155,254	177,826	208,610	2.66	17.31
Other countries of Asia	154,269	151,451	143,214	165,176	194,103	2.47	17.51
Other countries of Oceania	15,822	17,604	12,040	12,650	14,507	0.18	14.68
EUROPE	7,459,023	7,330,719	6,792,601	7,048,515	6,903,852	88.01	-2.05
Central/Eastern Europe	602,954	696,035	571,836	668,528	701,684	8.95	4.96
Czech Republic	71,121	83,027	79,855	91,349	95,136	1.21	4.15
Estonia	34,946	45,821	30,536	25,314	26,867	0.34	6.13
Hungary	16,768	20,259	13,048	14,941	15,276	0.19	2.24
Latvia	33,381	39,371	28,430	34,933	37,113	0.47	6.24
Lithuania	41,407	53,294	45,764	59,391	71,296	0.91	20.05
Poland	250,224	274,029	203,962	235,939	233,399	2.98	-1.08
Russian Federation	130,434	154,739	141,166	172,811	186,401	2.38	7.86
Slovakia	15,841	13,767	15,685	20,566	19,456	0.25	-5.40
Ukraine	8,832	11,728	13,390	13,284	16,740	0.21	26.02
Northern Europe	2,877,861	2,795,579	2,563,567	2,587,196	2,493,677	31.79	-3.61
Denmark	1,006,816	1,001,359	949,997	914,053	841,484	10.73	-7.94
Finland	154,164	150,672	146,013	148,685	147,471	1.88	-0.82
Iceland	25,606	18,261	16,519	20,834	25,025	0.32	20.12
Ireland	23,188	24,323	20,807	24,358	27,303	0.35	12.09
Sweden	912,915	945,097	905,649	958,838	932,923	11.89	-2.70
United Kingdom	755,172	655,867	524,582	520,428	519,471	6.62	-0.18
Southern Europe	585,792	500,720	481,830	515,286	497,120	6.34	-3.53
Greece	18,716	18,574	17,006	15,604	13,367	0.17	-14.34
Italy	228,275	194,704	211,861	222,540	200,287	2.55	-10.00
Malta	1,169	1,090	1,075	1,289	1,506	0.02	16.83
Portugal	18,209	20,199	21,252	21,368	20,994	0.27	-1.75
Slovenia	5,657	7,608	8,446	8,847	7,359	0.09	-16.82
Spain	313,766	258,545	222,190	245,638	253,607	3.23	3.24
Western Europe	3,127,761	3,090,586	2,980,764	3,061,582	2,954,387	37.66	-3.50
Austria	64,536	69,401	66,930	76,045	75,953	0.97	-0.12
Belgium	65,857	71,943	72,873	88,866	84,820	1.08	-4.55
France	291,826	288,340	298,526	318,280	309,784	3.95	-2.67

NORWAY

6. Overnight stays of non-resident tourists in all types of accommodation establishments, by nationality

	2007	2008	2009	2010	2011	Market share 11	% Change 11-10
Germany	1,703,050	1,688,603	1,590,305	1,637,206	1,594,621	20.33	-2.60
Liechtenstein	2,036	3,050	1,614	2,084	1,942	0.02	-6.81
Luxembourg	5,144	3,835	7,602	6,427	4,573	0.06	-28.85
Netherlands	873,342	845,503	825,603	799,515	742,328	9.46	-7.15
Switzerland	121,970	119,911	117,311	133,159	140,366	1.79	5.41
East Mediterranean Europe	**9,605**	**12,783**	**10,262**	**13,559**	**11,755**	**0.15**	**-13.30**
Cyprus	1,318	2,019	1,473	1,789	1,378	0.02	-22.97
Turkey	8,287	10,764	8,789	11,770	10,377	0.13	-11.84
Other Europe	**255,050**	**235,016**	**184,342**	**202,364**	**245,229**	**3.13**	**21.18**
Other countries of Europe	255,050	235,016	184,342	202,364	245,229	3.13	21.18

OMAN

3. Arrivals of non-resident tourists in hotels and similar establishments, by nationality

	2007	2008	2009	2010	2011	Market share 11	% Change 11-10
TOTAL	1,182,407	1,378,078	1,279,678	1,048,052			
AFRICA	16,296	19,355	30,486	21,755			
East Africa	495	864	1,323	996			
United Republic of Tanzania	495	864	1,323	996			
North Africa	7,705	9,525	7,860	7,435			
Morocco	2,357	2,987	1,960	2,049			
Sudan	2,658	3,231	3,118	2,639			
Tunisia	2,690	3,307	2,782	2,747			
Southern Africa	4,541	4,973	11,571	7,119			
South Africa	4,541	4,973	11,571	7,119			
Other Africa	3,555	3,993	9,732	6,205			
Other countries of Africa	3,555	3,993	9,732	6,205			
AMERICAS	46,367	57,110	156,958	95,350			
North America	41,076	50,668	141,449	84,135			
Canada	10,867	12,038	30,145	17,374			
United States of America	30,209	38,630	111,304	66,761			
South America	1,076	2,410	5,384	4,763			
Brazil	1,076	2,410	5,384	4,763			
Other Americas	4,215	4,032	10,125	6,452			
Other countries of the Americas	4,215	4,032	10,125	6,452			
EAST ASIA AND THE PACIFIC	82,929	104,046	144,500	107,747			
North-East Asia	13,173	16,718	19,753	14,404			
China	5,454	6,443	6,800	5,422			
Japan	7,719	10,275	12,953	8,982			
South-East Asia	13,862	24,238	31,309	21,967			
Indonesia			2,184	2,578			
Philippines	13,862	24,238	16,419	13,492			
Thailand			12,706	5,897			
Australasia	14,943	20,351	43,319	26,877			
Australia	12,075	17,288	33,770	22,169			
New Zealand	2,868	3,063	9,549	4,708			
Other East Asia and the Pacific	40,951	42,739	50,119	44,499			
Other countries of Asia	32,121	39,390	28,445	26,647			
Other countries of Oceania	8,830	3,349	21,674	17,852			
EUROPE	382,305	437,137	387,059	339,011			
Central/Eastern Europe	5,573	5,474	5,578	4,518			
Czech Republic	1,384	591	636	807			
Russian Federation	4,189	4,883	4,942	3,711			
Northern Europe	140,904	165,885	131,537	99,843			
Denmark	5,220	5,743	3,877	3,005			
Finland	775	1,003	985	1,017			
Ireland	1,987	4,287	4,115	4,313			
Norway	1,926	1,878	2,657	1,579			
Sweden	26,672	30,251	19,232	8,252			
United Kingdom	104,324	122,723	100,671	81,677			
Southern Europe	21,054	30,888	27,301	25,751			
Italy	17,990	23,544	21,849	20,909			
Portugal	824	3,320	1,112	1,093			
Spain	2,240	4,024	4,340	3,749			
Western Europe	186,220	202,060	182,543	174,922			
Austria	8,002	8,775	7,309	6,726			
Belgium	4,614	6,806	5,945	6,071			

OMAN

3. Arrivals of non-resident tourists in hotels and similar establishments, by nationality

	2007	2008	2009	2010	2011	Market share 11	% Change 11-10
France	38,062	39,704	35,828	38,217			
Germany	100,531	101,737	85,768	81,372			
Netherlands	14,225	20,615	22,327	18,638			
Switzerland	20,786	24,423	25,366	23,898			
East Mediterranean Europe			4,709	5,659			
Cyprus			604	852			
Turkey			4,105	4,807			
Other Europe	28,554	32,830	35,391	28,318			
Other countries of Europe	28,554	32,830	35,391	28,318			
MIDDLE EAST	202,988	242,661	288,840	219,698			
Bahrain	26,735	13,363	15,759	9,567			
Jordan	7,758	10,068	13,129	13,633			
Kuwait	13,190	16,102	20,728	13,487			
Lebanon	10,617	12,841	14,313	14,946			
Libya			1,224	605			
Qatar	9,503	10,281	14,836	9,074			
Saudi Arabia	21,192	24,177	25,312	17,550			
Syrian Arab Republic	4,231	6,311	6,452	6,931			
United Arab Emirates	83,279	112,785	130,487	93,585			
Egypt	16,430	22,648	26,853	26,807			
Other countries of Middle East	10,053	14,085	19,747	13,513			
SOUTH ASIA	186,584	189,469	193,521	192,508			
Sri Lanka	4,409	5,879	6,789	7,120			
India	153,041	156,723	162,832	158,739			
Iran, Islamic Republic of	2,966	5,000	5,751	5,771			
Pakistan	26,168	21,867	18,149	20,878			
NOT SPECIFIED	264,938	328,300	78,314	71,983			
Other countries of the World	264,938	328,300	78,314	71,983			

OMAN

5. Overnight stays of non-resident tourists in hotels and similar establishments, by nationality

	2007	2008	2009	2010	2011	Market share 11	% Change 11-10
TOTAL	1,685,656	1,661,164	1,452,207	1,365,296			
AFRICA	23,005	24,144	35,759	27,320			
East Africa	723	808	1,614	1,218			
United Republic of Tanzania	723	808	1,614	1,218			
North Africa	11,055	12,175	9,175	8,828			
Morocco	4,238	4,163	2,287	2,579			
Sudan	3,490	3,906	3,855	3,007			
Tunisia	3,327	4,106	3,033	3,242			
Southern Africa	5,777	6,145	13,365	9,672			
South Africa	5,777	6,145	13,365	9,672			
Other Africa	5,450	5,016	11,605	7,602			
Other countries of Africa	5,450	5,016	11,605	7,602			
AMERICAS	76,702	78,561	210,061	166,856			
North America	69,373	70,698	191,547	149,280			
Canada	15,985	14,588	36,574	22,519			
United States of America	53,388	56,110	154,973	126,761			
South America	1,676	2,861	7,309	10,222			
Brazil	1,676	2,861	7,309	10,222			
Other Americas	5,653	5,002	11,205	7,354			
Other countries of the Americas	5,653	5,002	11,205	7,354			
EAST ASIA AND THE PACIFIC	119,621	118,799	168,576	149,787			
North-East Asia	23,643	18,773	23,066	20,175			
China	8,615	7,742	9,174	8,598			
Japan	15,028	11,031	13,892	11,577			
South-East Asia	16,992	25,570	18,450	13,195			
Philippines	16,992	25,570	18,450	13,195			
Australasia	21,982	23,967	52,156	32,741			
Australia	17,920	20,414	41,055	27,498			
New Zealand	4,062	3,553	11,101	5,243			
Other East Asia and the Pacific	57,004	50,489	74,904	83,676			
Other countries of Asia	44,978	42,932	53,843	62,162			
Other countries of Oceania	12,026	7,557	21,061	21,514			
EUROPE	614,859	580,375	441,632	456,149			
Central/Eastern Europe	8,652	8,957	5,954	5,343			
Russian Federation	8,652	8,957	5,954	5,343			
Northern Europe	254,311	232,848	162,485	155,892			
Denmark	7,112	7,462	4,193	4,469			
Sweden	48,400	46,492	25,841	24,451			
United Kingdom	198,799	178,894	132,451	126,972			
Southern Europe	29,194	35,314	29,417	30,618			
Italy	25,445	30,035	24,364	24,498			
Spain	3,749	5,279	5,053	6,120			
Western Europe	273,353	249,713	199,378	220,270			
Austria	14,147	12,146	8,558	8,848			
Belgium	7,750	8,842	7,559	8,053			
France	57,296	51,611	39,935	47,585			
Germany	135,687	118,351	89,782	100,722			
Netherlands	20,438	26,742	24,355	24,194			
Switzerland	38,035	32,021	29,189	30,868			
Other Europe	49,349	53,543	44,398	44,026			
Other countries of Europe	49,349	53,543	44,398	44,026			

OMAN

5. Overnight stays of non-resident tourists in hotels and similar establishments, by nationality

	2007	2008	2009	2010	2011	Market share 11	% Change 11-10
MIDDLE EAST	**275,709**	**290,847**	**322,397**	**281,526**			
Bahrain	31,305	17,143	20,507	15,243			
Jordan	12,292	14,765	15,592	20,430			
Kuwait	21,206	23,100	27,118	21,150			
Lebanon	16,401	17,342	17,003	18,984			
Qatar	13,449	13,030	18,835	13,689			
Saudi Arabia	30,100	30,713	33,905	27,334			
Syrian Arab Republic	9,847	9,077	9,535	10,751			
United Arab Emirates	102,744	119,940	126,356	99,708			
Egypt	23,714	27,578	31,798	35,111			
Other countries of Middle East	14,651	18,159	21,748	19,126			
SOUTH ASIA	**227,953**	**204,428**	**206,567**	**216,706**			
Sri Lanka	5,763	6,157	6,677	7,313			
India	187,139	168,636	172,793	177,241			
Iran, Islamic Republic of	4,167	6,506	6,531	7,617			
Pakistan	30,884	23,129	20,566	24,535			
NOT SPECIFIED	**347,807**	**364,010**	**67,215**	**66,952**			
Other countries of the World	347,807	364,010	67,215	66,952			

PAKISTAN

1. Arrivals of non-resident tourists at national borders, by nationality

	2007	2008	2009	2010	2011	Market share 11	% Change 11-10
TOTAL	839,500	822,828	854,905				
AFRICA	15,840	15,767	14,659				
East Africa	5,856	5,294	5,428				
Burundi	16	10	3				
Comoros	9	11	8				
Ethiopia	287	330	544				
Eritrea	41	31	15				
Djibouti	112	90	85				
Kenya	1,741	1,565	1,489				
Madagascar	83	92	69				
Malawi	283	267	234				
Mauritius	861	664	554				
Mozambique	498	563	567				
Reunion	16						
Rwanda	16	90	308				
Seychelles		24	9				
Somalia	742	470	347				
Zimbabwe	175	191	141				
Uganda	142	104	67				
United Republic of Tanzania	672	640	772				
Zambia	162	152	216				
Central Africa	138	130	109				
Angola	17	25	26				
Cameroon	54	47	38				
Chad	30	34	31				
Congo	31	24	14				
Gabon	6						
North Africa	2,078	2,313	2,109				
Algeria	161	170	203				
Morocco	484	291	495				
Sudan	1,206	1,684	1,242				
Tunisia	227	168	169				
Southern Africa	5,830	6,243	6,136				
Botswana	51	45	36				
Lesotho	93	77	80				
Namibia	51	7	123				
South Africa	5,608	6,020	5,846				
Swaziland	27	94	51				
West Africa	1,895	1,787	877				
Benin	13	16	5				
Gambia	25	25	11				
Ghana	120	94	118				
Guinea	23	15	14				
Liberia	20	50	50				
Mali	19	5	14				
Mauritania	12	6	19				
Niger	27	27	41				
Nigeria	1,471	1,462	499				
Guinea-Bissau		2	1				
Senegal	102	39	63				
Sierra Leone	48	35	25				
Togo	6	6	13				
Burkina Faso	9	5	4				
Other Africa	43						
Other countries of Africa	43						

PAKISTAN

1. Arrivals of non-resident tourists at national borders, by nationality

	2007	2008	2009	2010	2011	Market share 11	% Change 11-10
AMERICAS	160,615	155,870	162,451				
Caribbean	220	229	287				
Antigua and Barbuda		7	9				
Cuba	38	23	16				
Dominica	32	32	23				
Grenada		30	27				
Haiti	1	3	2				
Jamaica	15	10	4				
Netherlands Antilles		20	56				
Puerto Rico		3	54				
Anguilla	5	3	2				
Trinidad and Tobago	129	98	94				
Central America	520	350	348				
Belize		18	27				
Costa Rica		15	11				
El Salvador	16	8	15				
Guatemala		27	20				
Honduras	32	30	61				
Nicaragua		10	23				
Panama	472	242	191				
North America	158,681	154,162	160,614				
Canada	36,524	39,875	42,954				
Mexico	215	193	195				
United States of America	121,942	114,094	117,465				
South America	1,194	1,129	1,202				
Argentina	229	212	177				
Bolivia	22	25	42				
Brazil	390	362	271				
Chile	203	203	206				
Colombia	119	110	117				
Ecuador	42	24	125				
Guyana	20	15	13				
Paraguay	5	8	9				
Peru	78	86	163				
Suriname	13	25	3				
Uruguay	19	20	25				
Venezuela	54	39	51				
EAST ASIA AND THE PACIFIC	87,092	75,967	88,984				
North-East Asia	47,927	43,862	42,813				
China	30,406	30,078	29,996				
Taiwan, Province of China	1,005	790	927				
Hong Kong, China	30	10	7				
Japan	11,025	8,294	6,705				
Korea, Dem. People's Republic of	199	130	218				
Korea, Republic of	5,162	4,495	4,926				
Macao, China	28		1				
Mongolia	72	65	33				
South-East Asia	25,481	18,181	31,443				
Brunei Darussalam	159	111	67				
Myanmar	543	811	2,213				
Cambodia	112	80	81				
Indonesia	2,607	1,778	3,099				
Lao People's Democratic Republic	38	28	22				
Malaysia	8,903	5,758	5,027				
Philippines	4,420	3,575	15,603				
Timor-Leste	4		1				

PAKISTAN

1. Arrivals of non-resident tourists at national borders, by nationality

	2007	2008	2009	2010	2011	Market share 11	% Change 11-10
Singapore	5,208	3,243	2,585				
Viet Nam	263	179	575				
Thailand	3,224	2,618	2,170				
Australasia	**13,623**	**13,842**	**14,597**				
Australia	12,039	12,227	13,223				
New Zealand	1,584	1,615	1,374				
Melanesia	**61**	**82**	**131**				
Fiji	59	63	128				
Papua New Guinea	2	19	3				
EUROPE	**386,751**	**389,207**	**378,643**				
Central/Eastern Europe	**9,988**	**8,231**	**12,145**				
Azerbaijan	432	475	354				
Armenia	14	16	12				
Bulgaria	251	252	660				
Belarus	122	116	140				
Czech Republic/Slovakia		10					
Czech Republic	870	751	1,639				
Estonia	72	47	70				
Georgia	111	72	152				
Hungary	436	443	323				
Kazakhstan	734	625	396				
Kyrgyzstan	164	148	129				
Latvia	63	70	182				
Lithuania	85	87	174				
Republic of Moldova		5	11				
Poland	1,042	1,035	974				
Romania	487	550	624				
Russian Federation	2,649	1,581	2,488				
Slovakia	172	197	198				
Tajikistan	153	105	133				
Turkmenistan	192	149	85				
Ukraine	1,466	987	3,048				
Uzbekistan	473	510	353				
Northern Europe	**304,863**	**314,389**	**301,404**				
Denmark	7,478	7,203	5,747				
Finland	799	718	525				
Iceland	55	34	1,075				
Ireland	2,905	2,919	2,882				
Norway	14,178	13,954	12,441				
Sweden	3,904	3,841	3,383				
United Kingdom	275,544	285,720	275,351				
Southern Europe	**10,001**	**9,257**	**9,287**				
Albania	58	54	32				
Andorra	4	3	2				
Bosnia and Herzegovina	151	123	87				
Croatia	172	153	311				
Greece	761	703	808				
Italy	4,881	4,678	4,385				
Malta	61	48	38				
Portugal	775	622	687				
Slovenia	143	121	90				
Spain	2,794	2,576	2,736				
TFYR of Macedonia		39	22				
Serbia and Montenegro	201	137	89				
Western Europe	**54,537**	**52,157**	**50,840**				
Austria	2,515	2,383	2,301				
Belgium	3,462	3,648	4,109				

PAKISTAN

1. Arrivals of non-resident tourists at national borders, by nationality

	2007	2008	2009	2010	2011	Market share 11	% Change 11-10
France	11,145	10,944	10,685				
Germany	23,941	22,414	21,493				
Liechtenstein		8	9				
Luxembourg	67	48	83				
Monaco	24	19	13				
Netherlands	10,475	10,287	9,976				
Switzerland	2,908	2,406	2,171				
East Mediterranean Europe	**7,283**	**5,173**	**4,967**				
Cyprus	186	132	120				
Turkey	7,097	5,041	4,847				
Other Europe	**79**						
Other countries of Europe	79						
MIDDLE EAST	**35,887**	**28,966**	**27,951**				
Bahrain	3,699	3,579	3,774				
Palestine	285	367	259				
Iraq	293	388	487				
Jordan	2,298	1,817	1,493				
Kuwait	578	459	477				
Lebanon	1,165	924	736				
Libya	399	426	279				
Oman	7,891	7,555	7,311				
Qatar	683	523	436				
Saudi Arabia	8,520	4,550	4,482				
Syrian Arab Republic	1,922	570	1,160				
United Arab Emirates	4,721	4,621	3,997				
Egypt	2,659	2,499	2,305				
Yemen	774	688	755				
SOUTH ASIA	**148,856**	**153,117**	**178,242**				
Afghanistan	80,459	66,353	96,617				
Bangladesh	6,352	12,230	6,941				
Bhutan	90	48	38				
Sri Lanka	4,312	3,943	3,639				
India	48,242	54,101	42,694				
Iran, Islamic Republic of	7,405	14,178	26,557				
Maldives	341	224	187				
Nepal	1,655	2,040	1,569				
NOT SPECIFIED	**4,459**	**3,934**	**3,975**				
Other countries of the World	4,459	3,934	3,975				

PALAU

1. Arrivals of non-resident tourists at national borders, by country of residence

		2007	2008	2009	2010	2011	Market share 11	% Change 11-10
TOTAL	(*)	88,175	79,259	71,887	85,593	109,057	100.00	27.41
AMERICAS		5,956	5,235	5,193	5,809	5,890	5.40	1.39
North America		5,956	5,235	5,193	5,809	5,890	5.40	1.39
United States of America		5,956	5,235	5,193	5,809	5,890	5.40	1.39
EAST ASIA AND THE PACIFIC		78,738	69,927	62,970	75,701	98,658	90.46	30.33
North-East Asia		73,474	64,968	56,843	67,841	93,513	85.75	37.84
China		464	439	534	725	1,699	1.56	134.34
Taiwan, Province of China		29,005	19,981	16,278	22,161	37,632	34.51	69.81
Hong Kong, China		465	344	334	493	701	0.64	42.19
Japan		29,198	30,018	26,688	29,318	37,800	34.66	28.93
Korea, Republic of		14,342	14,186	13,009	15,144	15,681	14.38	3.55
South-East Asia		1,719	949	998	1,139	1,123	1.03	-1.40
Philippines		1,719	949	998	913	913	0.84	
Singapore					226	210	0.19	-7.08
Australasia		733	711	700	1,241	1,134	1.04	-8.62
Australia		733	711	700	1,241	1,134	1.04	-8.62
Micronesia		2,812	3,299	4,429	5,480	2,888	2.65	-47.30
Guam		1,848	2,258	3,374	3,336	1,932	1.77	-42.09
Northern Mariana Islands					657	319	0.29	-51.45
Micronesia, Federated States of		964	1,041	1,055	1,487	637	0.58	-57.16
EUROPE		2,517	3,151	2,923	3,402	3,535	3.24	3.91
Central/Eastern Europe		302	637	295	562	577	0.53	2.67
Russian Federation		302	637	295	562	577	0.53	2.67
Northern Europe		389	335	373	311	260	0.24	-16.40
United Kingdom		389	335	373	311	260	0.24	-16.40
Southern Europe		328	344	327	384	273	0.25	-28.91
Italy		328	344	327	384	273	0.25	-28.91
Western Europe		616	808	854	1,123	1,317	1.21	17.28
France					245	279	0.26	13.88
Germany		476	621	629	662	749	0.69	13.14
Switzerland		140	187	225	216	289	0.26	33.80
Other Europe		882	1,027	1,074	1,022	1,108	1.02	8.41
Other countries of Europe		882	1,027	1,074	1,022	1,108	1.02	8.41
NOT SPECIFIED		964	946	801	681	974	0.89	43.02
Other countries of the World		964	946	801	681	974	0.89	43.02

PALESTINE

3. Arrivals of non-resident tourists in hotels and similar establishments, by nationality

	2007	2008	2009	2010	2011	Market share 11	% Change 11-10
TOTAL	**264,168**	**387,143**	**395,622**	**521,927**	**448,500**	**100.00**	**-14.07**
AFRICA	**4,951**	**9,679**	**11,736**	**14,126**	**27,837**	**6.21**	**97.06**
Other Africa	**4,951**	**9,679**	**11,736**	**14,126**	**27,837**	**6.21**	**97.06**
All countries of Africa	4,951	9,679	11,736	14,126	27,837	6.21	97.06
AMERICAS	**32,440**	**39,453**	**62,958**	**87,721**	**56,701**	**12.64**	**-35.36**
North America	**23,118**	**31,685**	**49,890**	**72,354**	**42,813**	**9.55**	**-40.83**
Canada, United States	23,118	31,685	49,890	72,354	42,813	9.55	-40.83
Other Americas	**9,322**	**7,768**	**13,068**	**15,367**	**13,888**	**3.10**	**-9.62**
Other countries of the Americas	9,322	7,768	13,068	15,367	13,888	3.10	-9.62
EAST ASIA AND THE PACIFIC	**20,424**	**41,344**	**41,157**	**67,218**	**58,394**	**13.02**	**-13.13**
Australasia	**3,542**	**3,455**	**1,580**	**4,553**	**4,944**	**1.10**	**8.59**
Australia, New Zealand	3,542	3,455	1,580	4,553	4,944	1.10	8.59
Other East Asia and the Pacific	**16,882**	**37,889**	**39,577**	**62,665**	**53,450**	**11.92**	**-14.71**
All countries of Asia	16,882	37,889	39,577	62,665	53,450	11.92	-14.71
EUROPE	**203,468**	**293,659**	**275,694**	**350,543**	**300,768**	**67.06**	**-14.20**
East Mediterranean Europe	**47,846**	**25,577**	**44,195**	**44,003**	**44,065**	**9.82**	**0.14**
Israel	47,846	25,577	44,195	44,003	44,065	9.82	0.14
Other Europe	**155,622**	**268,082**	**231,499**	**306,540**	**256,703**	**57.24**	**-16.26**
Other countries of Europe	155,622	268,082	231,499	306,540	256,703	57.24	-16.26
MIDDLE EAST	**2,885**	**3,008**	**4,077**	**2,319**	**4,800**	**1.07**	**106.99**
All countries of Middle East	2,885	3,008	4,077	2,319	4,800	1.07	106.99

PALESTINE

5. Overnight stays of non-resident tourists in hotels and similar establishments, by nationality

	2007	2008	2009	2010	2011	Market share 11	% Change 11-10
TOTAL	596,564	1,012,870	926,312	1,165,519	1,112,523	100.00	-4.55
AFRICA	8,842	17,170	19,442	27,088	50,363	4.53	85.92
Other Africa	8,842	17,170	19,442	27,088	50,363	4.53	85.92
All countries of Africa	8,842	17,170	19,442	27,088	50,363	4.53	85.92
AMERICAS	84,183	113,427	149,612	190,830	149,938	13.48	-21.43
North America	61,148	89,031	120,508	157,176	110,217	9.91	-29.88
Canada, United States	61,148	89,031	120,508	157,176	110,217	9.91	-29.88
Other Americas	23,035	24,396	29,104	33,654	39,721	3.57	18.03
Other countries of the Americas	23,035	24,396	29,104	33,654	39,721	3.57	18.03
EAST ASIA AND THE PACIFIC	58,151	110,181	89,195	150,976	140,001	12.58	-7.27
Australasia	5,448	7,115	3,633	8,705	10,273	0.92	18.01
Australia, New Zealand	5,448	7,115	3,633	8,705	10,273	0.92	18.01
Other East Asia and the Pacific	52,703	103,066	85,562	142,271	129,728	11.66	-8.82
All countries of Asia	52,703	103,066	85,562	142,271	129,728	11.66	-8.82
EUROPE	440,855	766,756	660,388	787,729	752,319	67.62	-4.50
East Mediterranean Europe	67,193	47,581	80,312	77,191	73,538	6.61	-4.73
Israel	67,193	47,581	80,312	77,191	73,538	6.61	-4.73
Other Europe	373,662	719,175	580,076	710,538	678,781	61.01	-4.47
Other countries of Europe	373,662	719,175	580,076	710,538	678,781	61.01	-4.47
MIDDLE EAST	4,533	5,336	7,675	8,896	19,902	1.79	123.72
All countries of Middle East	4,533	5,336	7,675	8,896	19,902	1.79	123.72

PANAMA

2. Arrivals of non-resident visitors at national borders, by country of residence

		2007	2008	2009	2010	2011	Market share 11	% Change 11-10
TOTAL	(*)	948,946	1,136,079	1,054,663	1,162,713	1,310,292	100.00	12.69
AFRICA		646	1,071	851	1,000	1,920	0.15	92.00
Southern Africa		288	340	279	319	668	0.05	109.40
South Africa		288	340	279	319	668	0.05	109.40
Other Africa		358	731	572	681	1,252	0.10	83.85
Other countries of Africa		358	731	572	681	1,252	0.10	83.85
AMERICAS		835,948	983,844	916,458	1,006,007	1,134,147	86.56	12.74
Caribbean		56,138	78,389	28,787	30,546	32,677	2.49	6.98
Bahamas		851	991	393	373	626	0.05	67.83
Barbados		663	826	421	451	485	0.04	7.54
Bermuda		138	174	194	142	186	0.01	30.99
Cuba		4,538	4,877	5,032	5,025	5,461	0.42	8.68
Dominican Republic		11,917	19,222	9,649	11,704	13,412	1.02	14.59
Haiti		7,748	11,166	5,759	4,462	4,081	0.31	-8.54
Jamaica		9,636	13,682	3,345	2,763	2,857	0.22	3.40
Curaçao		1,747	1,976	40	106	86	0.01	-18.87
Puerto Rico		14,920	20,372	664	1,069	750	0.06	-29.84
Other countries of the Caribbean		3,980	5,103	3,290	4,451	4,733	0.36	6.34
Central America		103,351	145,418	100,477	114,080	111,545	8.51	-2.22
Belize		1,279	1,454	736	1,070	967	0.07	-9.63
Costa Rica		42,158	65,438	37,759	39,524	40,524	3.09	2.53
El Salvador		15,567	20,359	15,569	16,547	16,696	1.27	0.90
Guatemala		23,494	27,629	26,064	32,780	27,107	2.07	-17.31
Honduras		10,950	14,542	10,383	12,270	13,921	1.06	13.46
Nicaragua		9,903	15,996	9,966	11,889	12,330	0.94	3.71
North America		344,133	368,090	316,945	348,999	383,896	29.30	10.00
Canada		39,097	44,171	37,849	48,029	52,731	4.02	9.79
Mexico		46,787	51,533	44,904	48,132	51,422	3.92	6.84
United States of America		258,249	272,386	234,190	252,837	279,742	21.35	10.64
Other countries of North America				2	1	1	0.00	
South America		332,326	391,947	470,249	512,382	606,029	46.25	18.28
Argentina		19,093	23,598	41,989	47,216	62,357	4.76	32.07
Bolivia		5,009	6,647	4,942	6,744	9,544	0.73	41.52
Brazil		15,932	18,603	24,338	31,520	47,890	3.65	51.94
Chile		13,478	15,880	13,035	16,232	19,020	1.45	17.18
Colombia		174,476	213,776	177,224	219,250	218,962	16.71	-0.13
Ecuador		47,387	50,129	22,172	30,861	43,975	3.36	42.49
Paraguay		1,358	1,662	821	1,078	1,319	0.10	22.36
Peru		20,761	23,251	11,853	15,431	22,382	1.71	45.05
Uruguay		2,714	2,991	10,556	11,400	11,163	0.85	-2.08
Venezuela		31,157	34,403	162,581	131,608	168,184	12.84	27.79
Other countries of South America		961	1,007	738	1,042	1,233	0.09	18.33
EAST ASIA AND THE PACIFIC		27,001	33,286	22,550	27,020	33,140	2.53	22.65
North-East Asia		7,651	8,762	4,715	5,485	6,002	0.46	9.43
Taiwan, Province of China		1,962	2,287	1,582	1,497	1,477	0.11	-1.34
Japan		5,689	6,475	3,133	3,988	4,525	0.35	13.47
Australasia		2,185	4,451	2,925	3,243	3,790	0.29	16.87
Australia		1,768	3,471	2,352	2,439	3,138	0.24	28.66
New Zealand		417	980	573	804	652	0.05	-18.91
Other East Asia and the Pacific		17,165	20,073	14,910	18,292	23,348	1.78	27.64
Other countries of Asia		17,105	19,980	14,823	18,214	23,227	1.77	27.52
Other countries of Oceania		60	93	87	78	121	0.01	55.13

PANAMA

2. Arrivals of non-resident visitors at national borders, by country of residence

	2007	2008	2009	2010	2011	Market share 11	% Change 11-10
EUROPE	85,283	117,812	114,729	128,595	140,994	10.76	9.64
Northern Europe	9,404	12,682	10,818	11,181	11,556	0.88	3.35
United Kingdom	9,404	12,682	10,818	11,181	11,556	0.88	3.35
Southern Europe	32,538	43,489	39,633	47,660	49,917	3.81	4.74
Greece	1,031	1,463	1,034	1,001	1,062	0.08	6.09
Italy	14,952	19,784	13,399	15,814	16,295	1.24	3.04
Spain	16,555	22,242	25,200	30,845	32,560	2.48	5.56
Western Europe	27,368	37,622	33,567	36,345	41,294	3.15	13.62
France	11,752	15,775	11,166	11,665	12,361	0.94	5.97
Germany	8,517	12,024	9,087	9,742	12,847	0.98	31.87
Netherlands	3,273	4,537	9,610	10,732	11,110	0.85	3.52
Switzerland	3,826	5,286	3,704	4,206	4,976	0.38	18.31
East Mediterranean Europe	3,762	6,476	6,800	7,826	8,312	0.63	6.21
Israel	3,762	6,476	6,800	7,826	8,312	0.63	6.21
Other Europe	12,211	17,543	23,911	25,583	29,915	2.28	16.93
Other countries of Europe	12,211	17,543	23,911	25,583	29,915	2.28	16.93
MIDDLE EAST	68	66	75	91	91	0.01	
Egypt	68	66	75	91	91	0.01	

PAPUA NEW GUINEA

1. Arrivals of non-resident tourists at national borders, by country of residence

	2007	2008	2009	2010	2011	Market share 11	% Change 11-10
TOTAL	104,122	114,207	125,891	146,350	165,059	100.00	12.78
AFRICA	725	947	877	1,056	1,671	1.01	58.24
Other Africa	725	947	877	1,056	1,671	1.01	58.24
All countries of Africa	725	947	877	1,056	1,671	1.01	58.24
AMERICAS	7,868	8,197	9,029	10,869	11,715	7.10	7.78
North America	7,544	7,854	8,567	10,362	11,024	6.68	6.39
Canada	1,385	1,745	1,937	1,927	2,067	1.25	7.27
United States of America	6,159	6,109	6,630	8,435	8,957	5.43	6.19
South America	32	46	21	14	8	0.00	-42.86
Chile	32	46	21	14	8	0.00	-42.86
Other Americas	292	297	441	493	683	0.41	38.54
Other countries of the Americas	292	297	441	493	683	0.41	38.54
EAST ASIA AND THE PACIFIC	85,026	93,542	102,717	119,610	131,593	79.72	10.02
North-East Asia	7,054	10,078	10,064	12,220	12,098	7.33	-1.00
China	3,707	5,424	6,492	7,435	7,063	4.28	-5.00
Japan	3,347	3,865	2,767	3,804	3,500	2.12	-7.99
Korea, Republic of		789	805	981	1,535	0.93	56.47
South-East Asia	12,870	15,273	15,092	19,072	24,869	15.07	30.40
Indonesia	1,902	2,007	1,831	2,249	2,377	1.44	5.69
Malaysia	4,490	4,772	5,017	5,915	6,563	3.98	10.96
Philippines	6,478	7,661	7,333	9,551	14,292	8.66	49.64
Singapore		833	911	1,357	1,637	0.99	20.63
Australasia	58,741	64,123	72,527	82,398	86,451	52.38	4.92
Australia	54,098	58,724	66,842	75,355	77,396	46.89	2.71
New Zealand	4,643	5,399	5,685	7,043	9,055	5.49	28.57
Other East Asia and the Pacific	6,361	4,068	5,034	5,920	8,175	4.95	38.09
Other countries of Asia	3,244	1,197	1,270	2,064	3,418	2.07	65.60
Other countries of Oceania	3,117	2,871	3,764	3,856	4,757	2.88	23.37
EUROPE	8,563	9,237	9,022	12,065	15,130	9.17	25.40
Central/Eastern Europe	372	514	411	559	575	0.35	2.86
Russian Federation	372	514	411	559	575	0.35	2.86
Northern Europe	3,910	4,257	4,067	5,445	6,315	3.83	15.98
United Kingdom	3,515	3,800	3,669	5,102	5,753	3.49	12.76
Scandinavia	395	457	398	343	562	0.34	63.85
Southern Europe	285	331	293	270	453	0.27	67.78
Italy	285	331	293	270	453	0.27	67.78
Western Europe	1,951	1,923	2,318	3,141	4,495	2.72	43.11
France	459	515	584	830	1,271	0.77	53.13
Germany	1,492	1,408	1,219	1,680	2,480	1.50	47.62
Netherlands			515	631	744	0.45	17.91
East Mediterranean Europe	70	100	144	55	132	0.08	140.00
Israel	70	100	144	55	132	0.08	140.00
Other Europe	1,975	2,112	1,789	2,595	3,160	1.91	21.77
Other countries of Europe	1,975	2,112	1,789	2,595	3,160	1.91	21.77
SOUTH ASIA	1,940	2,284	2,382	2,750	4,950	3.00	80.00
India	1,940	2,284	2,382	2,750	4,950	3.00	80.00
NOT SPECIFIED			1,864				
Other countries of the World			1,864				

PARAGUAY

1. Arrivals of non-resident tourists at national borders, by nationality

		2007	2008	2009	2010	2011	Market share 11	% Change 11-10
TOTAL	(*)	415,702	428,215	439,246	465,264	523,740	100.00	12.57
AFRICA		484	301	401	386	354	0.07	-8.29
East Africa		31	15	103	91	34	0.01	-62.64
Burundi		1	1	2	1			
Ethiopia		1		10	9	3	0.00	-66.67
Eritrea		1						
Kenya		12	4	15	18	13	0.00	-27.78
Madagascar			2	6	3	5	0.00	66.67
Malawi				5	4			
Mauritius		1				1	0.00	
Mozambique		7	6	6	7	4	0.00	-42.86
Rwanda		1	1			2	0.00	
Somalia				1				
Zimbabwe		2	1	32	28	1	0.00	-96.43
Uganda				4	1	3	0.00	200.00
United Republic of Tanzania		5		14	14	1	0.00	-92.86
Zambia				8	6	1	0.00	-83.33
Central Africa		41	25	39	62	58	0.01	-6.45
Angola		16	7	28	40	40	0.01	
Cameroon		18	11	3	13	5	0.00	-61.54
Central African Republic			1			3	0.00	
Congo		6	6	5	6	4	0.00	-33.33
Equatorial Guinea				3	3	6	0.00	100.00
Sao Tome and Principe		1						
North Africa		20	39	12	8	6	0.00	-25.00
Algeria		8	9	6	4	1	0.00	-75.00
Morocco		10	26	4	1	4	0.00	300.00
Sudan			2					
Tunisia		2	2	2	3	1	0.00	-66.67
Southern Africa		331	179	185	192	220	0.04	14.58
Botswana		2	2	3	2			
Lesotho				1				
Namibia		2	2	3	9	3	0.00	-66.67
South Africa		326	175	176	181	216	0.04	19.34
Swaziland		1		2		1	0.00	
West Africa		61	43	62	33	33	0.01	
Cape Verde		6	5	8	2	8	0.00	300.00
Benin		1	1	3				
Gambia				3	1			
Ghana		6	5	9	9	1	0.00	-88.89
Guinea		12	1	3	1			
Côte d'Ivoire		2	3	3	4	1	0.00	-75.00
Liberia			1	2				
Mauritania		6	2	2				
Nigeria		15	11	17	9	15	0.00	66.67
Guinea-Bissau		6				4	0.00	
Senegal		3	11	3	3	2	0.00	-33.33
Sierra Leone		1	1	1				
Togo			1					
Burkina Faso		3	1	8	4	2	0.00	-50.00
Other Africa						3	0.00	
Other countries of Africa						3	0.00	
AMERICAS		369,993	384,216	394,649	432,963	480,529	91.75	10.99
Caribbean		706	633	612	316	683	0.13	116.14
Antigua and Barbuda		1		2	1	1	0.00	

PARAGUAY

1. Arrivals of non-resident tourists at national borders, by nationality

	2007	2008	2009	2010	2011	Market share 11	% Change 11-10
Bahamas	2	24	4		5	0.00	
Barbados	4	7	6	2	9	0.00	350.00
Cuba	459	396	337	190	381	0.07	100.53
Dominican Republic	154	140	113	96	219	0.04	128.13
Haiti	47	22	33	13	29	0.01	123.08
Jamaica	22	27	15	9	14	0.00	55.56
Martinique	1						
Puerto Rico	5	2	1	1	3	0.00	200.00
Saint Kitts and Nevis		1					
Anguilla				1	3	0.00	200.00
Saint Lucia		3	2		1	0.00	
Saint Vincent and the Grenadines	5		89		1	0.00	
Trinidad and Tobago	6	11	10	3	12	0.00	300.00
Other countries of the Caribbean					5	0.00	
Central America	**1,251**	**1,537**	**1,546**	**868**	**1,901**	**0.36**	**119.01**
Belize	5	15	9	1	103	0.02	10200.00
Costa Rica	343	305	346	253	526	0.10	107.91
El Salvador	187	258	250	166	239	0.05	43.98
Guatemala	216	220	361	202	298	0.06	47.52
Honduras	125	204	120	45	134	0.03	197.78
Nicaragua	96	183	144	64	163	0.03	154.69
Panama	279	352	316	137	438	0.08	219.71
North America	**18,348**	**17,293**	**18,858**	**13,290**	**15,454**	**2.95**	**16.28**
Canada	2,132	2,239	2,669	1,647	1,606	0.31	-2.49
Mexico	1,676	1,813	2,177	1,501	2,563	0.49	70.75
United States of America	14,540	13,241	14,012	10,142	11,285	2.15	11.27
South America	**349,688**	**364,753**	**373,633**	**418,489**	**462,491**	**88.31**	**10.51**
Argentina	184,745	195,948	196,149	218,418	222,901	42.56	2.05
Bolivia	6,122	6,905	13,203	11,646	23,256	4.44	99.69
Brazil	126,592	134,985	131,429	159,280	176,440	33.69	10.77
Chile	12,707	9,517	11,115	9,829	11,706	2.24	19.10
Colombia	2,696	2,348	3,017	2,482	4,177	0.80	68.29
Ecuador	1,142	856	1,266	779	1,815	0.35	132.99
Guyana	5	4	3	4	15	0.00	275.00
Peru	3,808	3,577	5,044	4,141	6,219	1.19	50.18
Suriname	11	60	2		23	0.00	
Uruguay	10,623	9,327	11,130	11,216	14,154	2.70	26.19
Venezuela	1,237	1,226	1,275	694	1,784	0.34	157.06
Other countries of South America					1	0.00	
EAST ASIA AND THE PACIFIC	**9,174**	**8,390**	**8,478**	**7,177**	**8,037**	**1.53**	**11.98**
North-East Asia	**8,445**	**7,750**	**7,743**	**6,574**	**7,408**	**1.41**	**12.69**
China	172	146	218	193	363	0.07	88.08
Taiwan, Province of China	558	461	531	327	455	0.09	39.14
Hong Kong, China			1	2	1	0.00	-50.00
Japan	3,685	3,816	3,319	3,134	2,666	0.51	-14.93
Korea, Republic of	4,030	3,321	3,672	2,917	3,923	0.75	34.49
Mongolia		6	2	1			
South-East Asia	**183**	**169**	**189**	**152**	**138**	**0.03**	**-9.21**
Brunei Darussalam	2						
Myanmar			1				
Cambodia		1	2				
Indonesia	96	74	96	56	29	0.01	-48.21
Lao People's Democratic Republic				3	11	0.00	266.67
Malaysia	23	23	26	40	16	0.00	-60.00
Philippines	21	34	43	32	62	0.01	93.75
Singapore	12	8	2	5	7	0.00	40.00
Viet Nam	10	10	11	5	9	0.00	80.00

PARAGUAY

1. Arrivals of non-resident tourists at national borders, by nationality

	2007	2008	2009	2010	2011	Market share 11	% Change 11-10
Thailand	19	19	8	11	4	0.00	-63.64
Australasia	**539**	**466**	**543**	**447**	**472**	**0.09**	**5.59**
Australia	406	353	391	319	341	0.07	6.90
New Zealand	133	113	152	128	131	0.03	2.34
Melanesia	**7**	**5**	**3**	**3**	**1**	**0.00**	**-66.67**
Solomon Islands		2			1	0.00	
Fiji	5	1	3	2			
Vanuatu		2					
Papua New Guinea	2			1			
Micronesia					**1**		
Guam					1		
Other East Asia and the Pacific					**18**	**0.00**	
Other countries of Asia					16	0.00	
Other countries of Oceania					2	0.00	
EUROPE	**35,133**	**34,259**	**34,716**	**24,181**	**34,014**	**6.49**	**40.66**
Central/Eastern Europe	**933**	**1,075**	**1,040**	**652**	**1,035**	**0.20**	**58.74**
Azerbaijan	12	3	5		4	0.00	
Armenia	1	2	3	3	7	0.00	133.33
Bulgaria	29	18	22	20	51	0.01	155.00
Belarus	8	3	14	3			
Czech Republic	112	156	142	83	160	0.03	92.77
Estonia	6	4	51	48	24	0.00	-50.00
Georgia		1	1				
Hungary	111	173	102	18	81	0.02	350.00
Kazakhstan	1	5	2				
Latvia	9	14	25	11	26	0.00	136.36
Lithuania	13	13	24	11	19	0.00	72.73
Republic of Moldova		1	1		7	0.00	
Poland	251	223	353	195	292	0.06	49.74
Romania	34	50	1	2	2	0.00	
Russian Federation	257	311	202	196	265	0.05	35.20
Slovakia	50	46	51	22	35	0.01	59.09
Ukraine	38	49	41	40	57	0.01	42.50
Uzbekistan	1	3			5	0.00	
Northern Europe	**4,445**	**3,747**	**3,666**	**2,456**	**3,668**	**0.70**	**49.35**
Denmark	624	293	323	213	431	0.08	102.35
Finland	226	123	132	103	137	0.03	33.01
Iceland	15	23	15	15	20	0.00	33.33
Ireland	342	308	307	229	230	0.04	0.44
Norway	366	350	321	218	342	0.07	56.88
Sweden	618	575	518	296	531	0.10	79.39
United Kingdom	2,254	2,075	2,050	1,382	1,977	0.38	43.05
Southern Europe	**11,210**	**11,571**	**11,416**	**7,772**	**12,138**	**2.32**	**56.18**
Albania		2	1	3	6	0.00	100.00
Andorra	2	3	1	1	11	0.00	1000.00
Bosnia and Herzegovina	2	2	4				
Croatia	16	21	55	10	24	0.00	140.00
Greece	527	351	116	176	101	0.02	-42.61
Holy See	1	5	29	4	7	0.00	75.00
Italy	3,302	3,055	3,270	2,376	3,008	0.57	26.60
Malta	1	3	3	3	7	0.00	133.33
Portugal	359	344	336	238	557	0.11	134.03
San Marino	4						
Serbia	1						
Slovenia	54	26	32	29	50	0.01	72.41
Spain	6,936	7,751	7,557	4,929	8,364	1.60	69.69

PARAGUAY

1. Arrivals of non-resident tourists at national borders, by nationality

	2007	2008	2009	2010	2011	Market share 11	% Change 11-10
TFYR of Macedonia		1	4		3	0.00	
Serbia and Montenegro	5	7	8	3			
Western Europe	**17,971**	**17,255**	**18,053**	**12,969**	**16,551**	**3.16**	**27.62**
Austria	713	591	706	610	702	0.13	15.08
Belgium	644	613	701	436	521	0.10	19.50
France	3,293	3,038	3,414	2,568	3,632	0.69	41.43
Germany	10,362	10,467	10,289	7,173	9,057	1.73	26.27
Liechtenstein	2	7	5	5	5	0.00	
Luxembourg	39	20	23	19	51	0.01	168.42
Monaco	2		3				
Netherlands	873	822	1,065	701	859	0.16	22.54
Switzerland	2,043	1,697	1,847	1,457	1,724	0.33	18.33
East Mediterranean Europe	**574**	**611**	**541**	**332**	**618**	**0.12**	**86.14**
Cyprus	11	15	22	2	8	0.00	300.00
Israel	546	523	462	298	508	0.10	70.47
Turkey	17	73	57	32	102	0.02	218.75
Other Europe					**4**	**0.00**	
Other countries of Europe					4	0.00	
MIDDLE EAST	**377**	**642**	**654**	**348**	**468**	**0.09**	**34.48**
Palestine	3	3	4	3	7	0.00	133.33
Iraq	1		8	4	10	0.00	150.00
Jordan	5	3	6	10	8	0.00	-20.00
Kuwait		3	1		1	0.00	
Lebanon	313	589	583	316	399	0.08	26.27
Libya					1	0.00	
Qatar	1		4	1			
Saudi Arabia	6	5	11	1	2	0.00	100.00
Syrian Arab Republic	7	8	10	4	7	0.00	75.00
United Arab Emirates	11	6	5	1	11	0.00	1000.00
Egypt	30	25	22	8	22	0.00	175.00
SOUTH ASIA	**427**	**393**	**348**	**209**	**338**	**0.06**	**61.72**
Afghanistan			3	2			
Bangladesh	17	44	24	16	28	0.01	75.00
Sri Lanka	13	10	3		1	0.00	
India	345	300	258	177	281	0.05	58.76
Iran, Islamic Republic of		6	26	8	9	0.00	12.50
Maldives	1		1				
Nepal	6	6	5	1	1	0.00	
Pakistan	45	27	28	5	18	0.00	260.00
NOT SPECIFIED	**114**	**14**					
Other countries of the World	114	14					

PERU

1. Arrivals of non-resident tourists at national borders, by country of residence

		2007	2008	2009	2010	2011	Market share 11	% Change 11-10
TOTAL	(*)	1,916,400	2,057,620	2,139,961	2,299,187	2,597,803	100.00	12.99
AFRICA		3,819	3,511	3,478	3,714	4,247	0.16	14.35
North Africa		261	101	136	130	229	0.01	76.15
Morocco		261	101	136	130	229	0.01	76.15
Southern Africa		2,766	2,666	2,444	2,689	2,994	0.12	11.34
South Africa		2,766	2,666	2,444	2,689	2,994	0.12	11.34
Other Africa		792	744	898	895	1,024	0.04	14.41
Other countries of Africa		792	744	898	895	1,024	0.04	14.41
AMERICAS		1,399,083	1,485,900	1,581,215	1,746,961	1,996,759	76.86	14.30
Caribbean		4,904	6,407	9,815	8,574	7,406	0.29	-13.62
Cuba		2,480	3,285	5,139	4,855	4,172	0.16	-14.07
Dominican Republic		2,424	3,122	4,676	3,719	3,234	0.12	-13.04
Central America		24,010	25,564	27,578	31,321	40,229	1.55	28.44
Costa Rica		6,896	7,630	7,842	8,765	9,302	0.36	6.13
El Salvador		2,737	2,822	2,938	2,663	4,948	0.19	85.81
Guatemala		2,468	3,033	2,971	2,797	3,451	0.13	23.38
Panama		6,510	7,344	8,956	10,718	10,960	0.42	2.26
Other countries of Central America		5,399	4,735	4,871	6,378	11,568	0.45	81.37
North America		457,459	503,172	509,543	508,284	515,394	19.84	1.40
Canada		43,992	51,975	54,595	52,955	57,454	2.21	8.50
Mexico		31,639	30,589	28,623	38,097	46,005	1.77	20.76
United States of America		381,828	420,608	426,325	417,232	411,935	15.86	-1.27
South America		912,710	950,757	1,034,279	1,198,782	1,433,730	55.19	19.60
Argentina		82,722	97,478	121,172	127,062	147,403	5.67	16.01
Bolivia		87,399	86,619	93,408	86,181	88,042	3.39	2.16
Brazil		53,558	64,573	82,764	87,674	117,537	4.52	34.06
Chile		470,457	452,705	464,153	595,944	741,717	28.55	24.46
Colombia		62,811	76,559	87,225	98,642	112,816	4.34	14.37
Ecuador		119,471	128,063	136,054	152,445	160,841	6.19	5.51
Paraguay		2,396	2,775	3,914	3,914	4,631	0.18	18.32
Uruguay		6,121	7,962	8,648	8,219	10,303	0.40	25.36
Venezuela		27,633	33,871	36,789	38,469	50,185	1.93	30.46
Other countries of South America		142	152	152	232	255	0.01	9.91
EAST ASIA AND THE PACIFIC		94,495	109,250	103,333	95,966	116,608	4.49	21.51
North-East Asia		58,513	66,727	59,525	53,129	71,190	2.74	33.99
China		7,465	8,043	9,257	9,484	11,896	0.46	25.43
Taiwan, Province of China		1,793	2,406	2,057	2,269	2,489	0.10	9.70
Hong Kong, China		513	379	369	615	952	0.04	54.80
Japan		39,864	46,059	40,018	30,604	43,794	1.69	43.10
Korea, Republic of		8,878	9,840	7,824	10,157	12,059	0.46	18.73
South-East Asia		4,025	6,491	5,618	6,131	7,554	0.29	23.21
Indonesia		775	1,143	1,114	1,432	1,533	0.06	7.05
Malaysia		526	869	748	916	1,246	0.05	36.03
Philippines		1,783	2,528	2,492	2,268	2,628	0.10	15.87
Singapore		565	1,014	661	868	1,348	0.05	55.30
Thailand		376	937	603	647	799	0.03	23.49
Australasia		30,458	33,844	36,210	35,022	35,570	1.37	1.56
Australia		25,617	28,542	30,947	29,659	30,436	1.17	2.62
New Zealand		4,841	5,302	5,263	5,363	5,134	0.20	-4.27
Other East Asia and the Pacific		1,499	2,188	1,980	1,684	2,294	0.09	36.22
Other countries of Asia		1,423	2,095	1,909	1,619	2,240	0.09	38.36
Other countries of Oceania		76	93	71	65	54	0.00	-16.92

PERU

1. Arrivals of non-resident tourists at national borders, by country of residence

	2007	2008	2009	2010	2011	Market share 11	% Change 11-10
EUROPE	**414,588**	**454,214**	**446,431**	**447,061**	**474,961**	**18.28**	**6.24**
Central/Eastern Europe	**17,326**	**24,394**	**24,277**	**23,384**	**26,850**	**1.03**	**14.82**
Belarus	3,545	5,297	6,340	7,316	8,216	0.32	12.30
Czech Republic	3,386	3,624	3,569	3,052	3,211	0.12	5.21
Poland	5,256	8,169	7,510	6,140	6,268	0.24	2.08
Russian Federation	4,100	5,560	5,373	5,487	7,429	0.29	35.39
Ukraine	1,039	1,744	1,485	1,389	1,726	0.07	24.26
Northern Europe	**97,436**	**100,960**	**89,125**	**83,751**	**85,130**	**3.28**	**1.65**
Denmark	5,031	5,854	5,903	5,760	6,023	0.23	4.57
Finland	2,233	2,510	2,334	2,451	2,445	0.09	-0.24
Ireland	8,776	10,022	7,587	6,346	5,525	0.21	-12.94
Norway	5,144	6,188	5,701	5,675	5,827	0.22	2.68
Sweden	9,185	9,931	8,971	9,337	9,895	0.38	5.98
United Kingdom	67,067	66,455	58,629	54,182	55,415	2.13	2.28
Southern Europe	**109,361**	**127,995**	**134,484**	**142,003**	**154,450**	**5.95**	**8.77**
Italy	34,622	39,825	40,426	41,831	45,192	1.74	8.03
Portugal	2,559	3,264	3,344	3,506	4,027	0.16	14.86
Spain	72,180	84,906	90,714	96,666	105,231	4.05	8.86
Western Europe	**168,261**	**174,676**	**173,585**	**174,407**	**183,740**	**7.07**	**5.35**
Austria	6,693	6,025	6,087	6,454	6,791	0.26	5.22
Belgium	8,924	7,775	5,864	4,755	4,534	0.17	-4.65
France	59,781	63,920	66,071	66,985	72,900	2.81	8.83
Germany	50,445	52,173	51,864	53,201	56,197	2.16	5.63
Netherlands	24,262	27,031	25,530	24,795	24,486	0.94	-1.25
Switzerland	18,156	17,752	18,169	18,217	18,832	0.72	3.38
East Mediterranean Europe	**12,462**	**13,511**	**14,477**	**13,928**	**14,356**	**0.55**	**3.07**
Israel	11,740	12,569	13,657	12,978	12,809	0.49	-1.30
Turkey	722	942	820	950	1,547	0.06	62.84
Other Europe	**9,742**	**12,678**	**10,483**	**9,588**	**10,435**	**0.40**	**8.83**
Other countries of Europe	9,742	12,678	10,483	9,588	10,435	0.40	8.83
MIDDLE EAST	**98**	**88**	**131**	**141**	**222**	**0.01**	**57.45**
Egypt	98	88	131	141	222	0.01	57.45
SOUTH ASIA	**2,682**	**3,714**	**4,305**	**4,411**	**4,177**	**0.16**	**-5.30**
India	2,069	3,046	3,406	3,526	3,471	0.13	-1.56
Pakistan	613	668	899	885	706	0.03	-20.23
NOT SPECIFIED	**1,635**	**943**	**1,068**	**933**	**829**	**0.03**	**-11.15**
Other countries of the World	1,635	943	1,068	933	829	0.03	-11.15

PERU

3. Arrivals of non-resident tourists in hotels and similar establishments, by nationality

	2007	2008	2009	2010	2011	Market share 11	% Change 11-10
TOTAL	3,386,003	4,467,113	4,059,169	4,251,391	5,588,809	100.00	31.46
AMERICAS	1,619,471	2,181,705	2,022,093	2,165,492	2,912,547	52.11	34.50
North America	956,560	1,295,952	1,109,647	1,154,883	1,425,012	25.50	23.39
Canada	125,697	170,362	165,732	172,370	215,767	3.86	25.18
Mexico	59,185	84,043	69,139	90,940	131,395	2.35	44.49
United States of America	771,678	1,041,547	874,776	891,573	1,077,850	19.29	20.89
South America	662,911	885,753	912,446	1,010,609	1,487,535	26.62	47.19
Argentina	140,308	196,295	204,249	222,241	334,018	5.98	50.30
Bolivia	34,573	39,357	41,813	45,300	53,902	0.96	18.99
Brazil	115,402	149,889	199,831	198,902	326,174	5.84	63.99
Chile	171,846	218,859	192,057	237,145	350,517	6.27	47.81
Colombia	100,582	145,382	131,737	157,716	223,966	4.01	42.01
Ecuador	66,128	88,623	95,312	101,072	123,533	2.21	22.22
Venezuela	34,072	47,348	47,447	48,233	75,425	1.35	56.38
EAST ASIA AND THE PACIFIC	133,584	164,744	158,392	108,777	206,148	3.69	89.51
North-East Asia	133,584	164,744	158,392	108,777	206,148	3.69	89.51
Japan	133,584	164,744	158,392	108,777	206,148	3.69	89.51
EUROPE	699,734	915,855	841,356	854,745	1,049,158	18.77	22.75
Southern Europe	302,977	400,339	336,763	349,372	435,316	7.79	24.60
Italy	112,297	145,276	107,791	111,734	143,469	2.57	28.40
Spain	190,680	255,063	228,972	237,638	291,847	5.22	22.81
Western Europe	396,757	515,516	504,593	505,373	613,842	10.98	21.46
France	228,720	306,956	326,148	316,715	369,601	6.61	16.70
Germany	168,037	208,560	178,445	188,658	244,241	4.37	29.46
NOT SPECIFIED	933,214	1,204,809	1,037,328	1,122,377	1,420,956	25.43	26.60
Other countries of the World	933,214	1,204,809	1,037,328	1,122,377	1,420,956	25.43	26.60

PERU

5. Overnight stays of non-resident tourists in hotels and similar establishments, by nationality

	2007	2008	2009	2010	2011	Market share 11	% Change 11-10
TOTAL	6,654,290	8,328,056	7,604,279	7,949,126	9,908,724	100.00	24.65
AMERICAS	3,492,509	4,393,186	4,058,005	4,288,946	5,420,366	54.70	26.38
North America	1,935,087	2,472,559	2,124,252	2,161,854	2,519,168	25.42	16.53
Canada	251,859	317,768	320,226	320,784	385,454	3.89	20.16
Mexico	141,080	193,549	156,512	210,692	267,154	2.70	26.80
United States of America	1,542,148	1,961,242	1,647,514	1,630,378	1,866,560	18.84	14.49
South America	1,557,422	1,920,627	1,933,753	2,127,092	2,901,198	29.28	36.39
Argentina	322,523	434,245	422,672	449,343	623,137	6.29	38.68
Bolivia	78,254	80,319	77,705	85,129	98,748	1.00	16.00
Brazil	280,710	319,715	423,346	424,202	636,938	6.43	50.15
Chile	391,908	448,991	391,576	480,123	696,246	7.03	45.01
Colombia	255,910	334,571	307,325	359,916	430,651	4.35	19.65
Ecuador	137,908	182,491	193,726	206,109	241,507	2.44	17.17
Venezuela	90,209	120,295	117,403	122,270	173,971	1.76	42.28
EAST ASIA AND THE PACIFIC	204,561	241,529	231,365	167,612	337,533	3.41	101.38
North-East Asia	204,561	241,529	231,365	167,612	337,533	3.41	101.38
Japan	204,561	241,529	231,365	167,612	337,533	3.41	101.38
EUROPE	1,236,755	1,539,599	1,451,178	1,461,215	1,757,462	17.74	20.27
Southern Europe	568,382	711,726	600,781	625,504	775,289	7.82	23.95
Italy	210,932	263,726	200,741	195,593	260,676	2.63	33.27
Spain	357,450	448,000	400,040	429,911	514,613	5.19	19.70
Western Europe	668,373	827,873	850,397	835,711	982,173	9.91	17.53
France	367,206	469,312	510,419	487,926	557,739	5.63	14.31
Germany	301,167	358,561	339,978	347,785	424,434	4.28	22.04
NOT SPECIFIED	1,720,465	2,153,742	1,863,731	2,031,353	2,393,363	24.15	17.82
Other countries of the World	1,720,465	2,153,742	1,863,731	2,031,353	2,393,363	24.15	17.82

PHILIPPINES

1. Arrivals of non-resident tourists at national borders, by country of residence

	2007	2008	2009	2010	2011	Market share 11	% Change 11-10
TOTAL	3,091,993	3,139,422	3,017,099	3,520,472	3,917,454	100.00	11.28
AFRICA	3,090	3,317	3,082	3,584	4,193	0.11	16.99
Southern Africa	2,387	2,540	2,311	2,774	3,221	0.08	16.11
South Africa	2,387	2,540	2,311	2,774	3,221	0.08	16.11
West Africa	703	777	771	810	972	0.02	20.00
Nigeria	703	777	771	810	972	0.02	20.00
AMERICAS	674,921	685,427	686,293	711,356	747,656	19.09	5.10
North America	671,744	681,922	682,696	707,706	743,448	18.98	5.05
Canada	91,308	102,381	99,012	106,345	117,423	3.00	10.42
Mexico	1,453	1,295	1,147	1,195	1,498	0.04	25.36
United States of America	578,983	578,246	582,537	600,166	624,527	15.94	4.06
South America	3,177	3,505	3,597	3,650	4,208	0.11	15.29
Argentina	524	594	687	684	786	0.02	14.91
Brazil	1,634	1,594	1,595	1,652	2,078	0.05	25.79
Colombia	415	511	573	581	689	0.02	18.59
Peru	376	446	422	403	391	0.01	-2.98
Venezuela	228	360	320	330	264	0.01	-20.00
EAST ASIA AND THE PACIFIC	1,829,095	1,798,719	1,643,595	2,064,400	2,397,497	61.20	16.14
North-East Asia	1,430,077	1,370,059	1,202,995	1,563,013	1,837,681	46.91	17.57
China	157,601	163,689	155,019	187,446	243,137	6.21	29.71
Taiwan, Province of China	112,206	118,782	102,274	142,455	181,738	4.64	27.58
Hong Kong, China	111,948	116,653	122,786	133,746	112,106	2.86	-16.18
Japan	395,012	359,306	324,980	358,744	375,496	9.59	4.67
Korea, Republic of	653,310	611,629	497,936	740,622	925,204	23.62	24.92
South-East Asia	235,615	254,077	255,586	298,176	331,672	8.47	11.23
Brunei Darussalam	3,040	3,456	3,592	4,072	5,247	0.13	28.86
Myanmar	4,559	5,116	5,445	3,983	3,246	0.08	-18.50
Cambodia	1,665	1,834	1,942	2,244	2,469	0.06	10.03
Indonesia	25,535	27,830	29,188	31,997	34,542	0.88	7.95
Lao People's Democratic Republic	782	814	831	1,079	971	0.02	-10.01
Malaysia	65,695	69,676	68,679	79,694	91,752	2.34	15.13
Singapore	94,008	100,177	98,305	121,083	137,802	3.52	13.81
Viet Nam	10,676	13,675	13,392	17,311	17,781	0.45	2.72
Thailand	29,655	31,499	34,212	36,713	37,862	0.97	3.13
Australasia	122,720	132,186	142,852	158,792	183,518	4.68	15.57
Australia	112,466	121,514	132,330	147,469	170,736	4.36	15.78
New Zealand	10,254	10,672	10,522	11,323	12,782	0.33	12.89
Melanesia	1,263	2,020	2,835	3,475	3,594	0.09	3.42
Papua New Guinea	1,263	2,020	2,835	3,475	3,594	0.09	3.42
Micronesia	39,420	40,377	39,327	40,944	41,032	1.05	0.21
Guam	39,409	40,364	39,323	40,928	41,013	1.05	0.21
Nauru	11	13	4	16	19	0.00	18.75
EUROPE	300,372	322,864	329,840	360,991	389,823	9.95	7.99
Central/Eastern Europe	14,599	16,819	16,522	21,821	27,171	0.69	24.52
Poland	1,746	2,249	2,372	2,917	3,263	0.08	11.86
Russian Federation	8,163	10,959	10,674	14,642	20,185	0.52	37.86
Other countries Central/East Europe	4,690	3,611	3,476	4,262	3,723	0.10	-12.65
Northern Europe	124,684	136,260	138,950	150,178	164,205	4.19	9.34
Denmark	11,882	11,890	10,971	11,609	13,004	0.33	12.02
Finland	2,477	2,954	3,331	4,024	4,780	0.12	18.79
Ireland	4,681	5,176	5,475	5,368	6,023	0.15	12.20
Norway	12,925	14,963	14,781	16,742	17,959	0.46	7.27
Sweden	13,049	13,855	13,383	15,510	17,973	0.46	15.88

PHILIPPINES

1. Arrivals of non-resident tourists at national borders, by country of residence

	2007	2008	2009	2010	2011	Market share 11	% Change 11-10
United Kingdom	79,670	87,422	91,009	96,925	104,466	2.67	7.78
Southern Europe	**28,961**	**31,229**	**29,281**	**32,388**	**33,531**	**0.86**	**3.53**
Greece	1,722	1,914	1,666	2,104	1,855	0.05	-11.83
Italy	14,382	15,136	15,047	16,350	15,798	0.40	-3.38
Montenegro		26					
Portugal	998	990	865	1,175	1,230	0.03	4.68
Serbia		157					
Spain	11,666	12,946	11,703	12,759	14,648	0.37	14.81
Serbia and Montenegro	193	60					
Western Europe	**128,199**	**134,663**	**138,946**	**149,193**	**157,265**	**4.01**	**5.41**
Austria	9,682	10,120	10,974	11,537	11,603	0.30	0.57
Belgium	8,090	9,143	9,729	10,512	10,959	0.28	4.25
France	19,273	22,891	24,572	27,302	29,591	0.76	8.38
Germany	55,894	55,303	55,912	58,725	61,193	1.56	4.20
Luxembourg	405	494	462	666	555	0.01	-16.67
Netherlands	17,705	18,527	18,586	19,227	21,029	0.54	9.37
Switzerland	17,150	18,185	18,711	21,224	22,335	0.57	5.23
East Mediterranean Europe	**3,929**	**3,893**	**6,141**	**7,411**	**7,651**	**0.20**	**3.24**
Israel	3,929	3,893	4,061	4,525	4,990	0.13	10.28
Turkey			2,080	2,886	2,661	0.07	-7.80
MIDDLE EAST	**31,759**	**36,615**	**46,811**	**48,716**	**55,829**	**1.43**	**14.60**
Bahrain	2,699	2,928	3,014	3,334	3,304	0.08	-0.90
Jordan	502	538	635	691	755	0.02	9.26
Kuwait	2,995	3,952	9,605	5,230	5,430	0.14	3.82
Qatar			2,932	3,378	3,602	0.09	6.63
Saudi Arabia	16,358	17,515	19,101	22,214	27,945	0.71	25.80
United Arab Emirates	8,490	10,931	10,488	12,734	13,404	0.34	5.26
Egypt	715	751	1,036	1,135	1,389	0.04	22.38
SOUTH ASIA	**37,596**	**43,662**	**46,960**	**50,914**	**61,259**	**1.56**	**20.32**
Bangladesh	1,785	1,924	2,107	2,569	2,862	0.07	11.41
Sri Lanka	3,472	3,756	3,664	3,732	4,077	0.10	9.24
India	27,341	31,135	32,817	34,581	42,844	1.09	23.89
Iran, Islamic Republic of	2,166	3,196	4,256	5,516	6,258	0.16	13.45
Nepal	1,075	1,246	1,411	1,794	1,874	0.05	4.46
Pakistan	1,757	2,405	2,705	2,722	3,344	0.09	22.85
NOT SPECIFIED	**215,160**	**248,818**	**260,518**	**280,511**	**261,197**	**6.67**	**-6.89**
Other countries of the World	34,421	53,531	62,597	52,066	54,045	1.38	3.80
Nationals Residing Abroad (*)	180,739	195,287	197,921	228,445	207,152	5.29	-9.32

PHILIPPINES

3. Arrivals of non-resident tourists in hotels and similar establishments, by country of residence

		2007	2008	2009	2010	2011	Market share 11	% Change 11-10
TOTAL	(*)	1,027,365	979,739	669,891				
AFRICA		1,018	1,048	632				
Southern Africa		813	789	475				
South Africa		813	789	475				
West Africa		205	259	157				
Nigeria		205	259	157				
AMERICAS		167,042	159,663	112,604				
North America		166,067	158,571	111,900				
Canada		29,440	30,279	20,601				
Mexico		655	529	328				
United States of America		135,972	127,763	90,971				
South America		975	1,092	704				
Argentina		170	162	145				
Brazil		492	515	363				
Colombia		128	180	80				
Peru		108	86	51				
Venezuela		77	149	65				
EAST ASIA AND THE PACIFIC		709,465	658,990	438,607				
North-East Asia		554,549	498,602	326,465				
China		53,014	53,322	36,537				
Taiwan, Province of China		36,528	31,838	21,658				
Hong Kong, China		48,200	47,643	38,274				
Japan		155,579	135,349	94,260				
Korea, Republic of		261,228	230,450	135,736				
South-East Asia		91,997	97,414	68,709				
Brunei Darussalam		1,242	1,429	1,018				
Myanmar		345	369	326				
Cambodia		561	655	516				
Indonesia		7,704	8,174	5,740				
Lao People's Democratic Republic		263	259	159				
Malaysia		21,320	22,284	15,709				
Singapore		46,109	48,797	34,725				
Viet Nam		2,419	2,903	2,106				
Thailand		12,034	12,544	8,410				
Australasia		48,762	49,292	34,038				
Australia		44,490	45,309	31,350				
New Zealand		4,272	3,983	2,688				
Melanesia		338	612	595				
Papua New Guinea		338	612	595				
Micronesia		13,819	13,070	8,800				
Guam		13,813	13,063	8,800				
Nauru		6	7					
EUROPE		89,280	91,279	66,530				
Central/Eastern Europe		2,878	3,620	2,894				
Poland		360	463	294				
USSR (former)		2,075	2,782	2,312				
Commonwealth Independent States		443	375	288				
Northern Europe		38,286	39,172	27,699				
Denmark		2,704	2,698	1,962				
Finland		708	746	607				
Ireland		1,386	1,441	1,089				
Norway		3,938	4,552	3,083				
Sweden		3,651	3,712	2,676				

PHILIPPINES

3. Arrivals of non-resident tourists in hotels and similar establishments, by country of residence

	2007	2008	2009	2010	2011	Market share 11	% Change 11-10
United Kingdom	25,899	26,023	18,282				
Southern Europe	**8,419**	**8,455**	**5,899**				
Greece	617	612	435				
Italy	3,841	3,696	2,670				
Portugal	235	305	180				
Spain	3,676	3,771	2,614				
Serbia and Montenegro	50	71					
Western Europe	**38,333**	**38,595**	**28,560**				
Austria	2,824	2,830	2,014				
Belgium	2,613	2,892	2,051				
France	5,536	6,117	4,901				
Germany	16,145	15,458	11,339				
Luxembourg	133	175	103				
Netherlands	6,059	5,942	4,194				
Switzerland	5,023	5,181	3,958				
East Mediterranean Europe	**1,364**	**1,437**	**1,478**				
Israel	1,364	1,437	1,153				
Turkey			325				
MIDDLE EAST	**12,523**	**14,983**	**11,892**				
Bahrain	1,328	1,352	994				
Jordan	214	230	189				
Kuwait	1,068	1,360	1,825				
Qatar			755				
Saudi Arabia	6,067	7,018	4,901				
United Arab Emirates	3,631	4,773	2,958				
Egypt	215	250	270				
SOUTH ASIA	**8,826**	**10,854**	**8,813**				
Bangladesh	423	498	394				
Sri Lanka	602	696	386				
India	6,160	7,229	5,990				
Iran, Islamic Republic of	921	1,356	1,193				
Nepal	271	308	281				
Pakistan	449	767	569				
NOT SPECIFIED	**39,211**	**42,922**	**30,813**				
Other countries of the World	9,617	13,899	11,294				
Nationals Residing Abroad (*)	29,594	29,023	19,519				

PHILIPPINES

4. Arrivals of non-resident tourists in all types of accommodation establishments, by country of residence

	2007	2008	2009	2010	2011	Market share 11	% Change 11-10
TOTAL (*)	3,041,872	3,084,753	2,960,282	3,461,007	3,884,055	100.00	12.22
AFRICA	3,008	3,238	2,950	3,466	4,152	0.11	19.79
Southern Africa	2,310	2,462	2,180	2,657	3,181	0.08	19.72
South Africa	2,310	2,462	2,180	2,657	3,181	0.08	19.72
West Africa	698	776	770	809	971	0.02	20.02
Nigeria	698	776	770	809	971	0.02	20.02
AMERICAS	673,751	683,151	684,028	709,423	745,291	19.19	5.06
North America	670,774	680,000	680,833	706,129	741,124	19.08	4.96
Canada	91,193	102,067	98,563	106,062	117,055	3.01	10.36
Mexico	1,429	1,259	1,095	1,124	1,475	0.04	31.23
United States of America	578,152	576,674	581,175	598,943	622,594	16.03	3.95
South America	2,977	3,151	3,195	3,294	4,167	0.11	26.50
Argentina	512	548	665	644	781	0.02	21.27
Brazil	1,598	1,510	1,492	1,565	2,060	0.05	31.63
Colombia	352	438	437	505	681	0.02	34.85
Peru	293	303	282	254	383	0.01	50.79
Venezuela	222	352	319	326	262	0.01	-19.63
EAST ASIA AND THE PACIFIC	1,802,189	1,769,713	1,612,169	2,034,014	2,377,612	61.21	16.89
North-East Asia	1,417,431	1,357,735	1,189,983	1,551,201	1,828,624	47.08	17.88
China	148,448	154,840	146,566	180,346	238,126	6.13	32.04
Taiwan, Province of China	111,933	118,306	101,033	141,216	180,603	4.65	27.89
Hong Kong, China	111,826	116,620	122,715	133,721	112,076	2.89	-16.19
Japan	394,628	358,743	323,638	357,660	374,128	9.63	4.60
Korea, Republic of	650,596	609,226	496,031	738,258	923,691	23.78	25.12
South-East Asia	222,535	238,526	240,037	282,845	321,147	8.27	13.54
Brunei Darussalam	3,022	3,422	3,576	4,052	5,210	0.13	28.58
Myanmar	1,436	1,404	1,763	1,693	1,652	0.04	-2.42
Cambodia	1,665	1,833	1,940	2,242	2,440	0.06	8.83
Indonesia	21,313	23,106	24,030	27,207	31,640	0.81	16.29
Lao People's Democratic Republic	778	814	831	1,078	942	0.02	-12.62
Malaysia	64,790	68,621	67,616	78,116	90,133	2.32	15.38
Singapore	93,741	100,113	98,113	120,961	137,741	3.55	13.87
Viet Nam	6,926	9,393	9,574	12,137	14,419	0.37	18.80
Thailand	28,864	29,820	32,594	35,359	36,970	0.95	4.56
Australasia	121,568	131,068	140,000	155,560	183,221	4.72	17.78
Australia	111,390	120,512	129,608	144,432	170,480	4.39	18.03
New Zealand	10,178	10,556	10,392	11,128	12,741	0.33	14.49
Melanesia	1,235	2,007	2,822	3,464	3,588	0.09	3.58
Papua New Guinea	1,235	2,007	2,822	3,464	3,588	0.09	3.58
Micronesia	39,420	40,377	39,327	40,944	41,032	1.06	0.21
Guam	39,409	40,364	39,323	40,928	41,013	1.06	0.21
Nauru	11	13	4	16	19	0.00	18.75
EUROPE	278,546	297,226	314,335	341,812	384,006	9.89	12.34
Central/Eastern Europe	3,251	3,734	12,593	17,427	25,178	0.65	44.48
Poland	1,407	1,967	1,958	2,403	3,035	0.08	26.30
Russian Federation			8,843	12,643	19,388	0.50	53.35
Commonwealth Independent States	1,844	1,767	1,792	2,381	2,755	0.07	15.71
Northern Europe	121,358	131,621	134,152	144,198	162,000	4.17	12.35
Denmark	11,681	11,801	10,915	11,541	12,952	0.33	12.23
Finland	2,459	2,943	3,310	4,013	4,780	0.12	19.11
Ireland	4,637	5,127	5,398	5,260	5,997	0.15	14.01
Norway	12,894	14,942	14,758	16,692	17,930	0.46	7.42
Sweden	13,008	13,819	13,345	15,404	17,949	0.46	16.52

PHILIPPINES

4. Arrivals of non-resident tourists in all types of accommodation establishments, by country of residence

		2007	2008	2009	2010	2011	Market share 11	% Change 11-10
United Kingdom		76,679	82,989	86,426	91,288	102,392	2.64	12.16
Southern Europe		**25,644**	**27,176**	**26,726**	**29,662**	**33,283**	**0.86**	**12.21**
Greece		1,606	1,792	1,583	1,977	1,751	0.05	-11.43
Italy		12,491	12,783	13,165	14,118	15,711	0.40	11.28
Portugal		911	930	814	1,123	1,217	0.03	8.37
Spain		10,466	11,487	11,164	12,444	14,604	0.38	17.36
Serbia and Montenegro		170	184					
Western Europe		**124,366**	**130,805**	**135,031**	**143,440**	**156,012**	**4.02**	**8.76**
Austria		9,446	9,926	10,728	11,056	11,550	0.30	4.47
Belgium		8,027	8,773	9,547	10,392	10,917	0.28	5.05
France		17,968	21,185	23,584	26,360	29,540	0.76	12.06
Germany		54,179	54,243	54,007	55,904	60,355	1.55	7.96
Luxembourg		402	481	449	655	550	0.01	-16.03
Netherlands		17,376	18,315	18,322	18,858	20,861	0.54	10.62
Switzerland		16,968	17,882	18,394	20,215	22,239	0.57	10.01
East Mediterranean Europe		**3,927**	**3,890**	**5,833**	**7,085**	**7,533**	**0.19**	**6.32**
Israel		3,927	3,890	4,057	4,521	4,990	0.13	10.37
Turkey				1,776	2,564	2,543	0.07	-0.82
MIDDLE EAST		**31,740**	**36,595**	**46,775**	**48,641**	**55,782**	**1.44**	**14.68**
Bahrain		2,699	2,928	3,014	3,334	3,304	0.09	-0.90
Jordan		502	538	635	691	755	0.02	9.26
Kuwait		2,995	3,952	9,605	5,230	5,430	0.14	3.82
Qatar				2,932	3,378	3,602	0.09	6.63
Saudi Arabia		16,357	17,515	19,100	22,214	27,945	0.72	25.80
United Arab Emirates		8,490	10,931	10,488	12,731	13,404	0.35	5.29
Egypt		697	731	1,001	1,063	1,342	0.03	26.25
SOUTH ASIA		**34,041**	**39,721**	**41,634**	**45,410**	**57,366**	**1.48**	**26.33**
Bangladesh		1,498	1,699	1,923	2,333	2,680	0.07	14.87
Sri Lanka		2,203	2,461	2,123	2,464	3,129	0.08	26.99
India		25,434	28,871	29,293	30,691	40,195	1.03	30.97
Iran, Islamic Republic of		2,142	3,115	4,232	5,513	6,237	0.16	13.13
Nepal		1,058	1,221	1,389	1,762	1,853	0.05	5.16
Pakistan		1,706	2,354	2,674	2,647	3,272	0.08	23.61
NOT SPECIFIED		**218,597**	**255,109**	**258,391**	**278,241**	**259,846**	**6.69**	**-6.61**
Other countries of the World		37,858	59,822	60,470	49,796	52,694	1.36	5.82
Nationals Residing Abroad	(*)	180,739	195,287	197,921	228,445	207,152	5.33	-9.32

POLAND

2. Arrivals of non-resident visitors at national borders, by nationality

		2007	2008	2009	2010	2011	Market share 11	% Change 11-10
TOTAL	(*)	66,207,767	59,935,000	53,840,000	58,340,000	60,745,000	100.00	4.12
AFRICA		16,861	15,000	20,000	20,000	15,000	0.02	-25.00
East Africa		1,868						
Burundi		10						
Comoros		6						
Ethiopia		119						
Eritrea		19						
Djibouti		1						
Kenya		472						
Madagascar		94						
Malawi		20						
Mauritius		350						
Mozambique		91						
Reunion		3						
Rwanda		40						
Seychelles		21						
Somalia		18						
Zimbabwe		231						
Uganda		111						
United Republic of Tanzania		153						
Zambia		109						
Central Africa		1,161						
Angola		225						
Cameroon		465						
Central African Republic		16						
Chad		6						
Congo		405						
Equatorial Guinea		6						
Gabon		32						
Sao Tome and Principe		6						
North Africa		5,211						
Algeria		1,468						
Morocco		1,532						
Sudan		113						
Tunisia		2,098						
Southern Africa		4,755						
Botswana		21						
Lesotho		2						
Namibia		48						
South Africa		4,671						
Swaziland		13						
West Africa		3,866						
Cape Verde		116						
Benin		52						
Gambia		57						
Ghana		378						
Guinea		159						
Côte d'Ivoire		142						
Liberia		15						
Mali		98						
Mauritania		20						
Niger		21						
Nigeria		2,391						
Guinea-Bissau		23						
Saint Helena		1						
Senegal		199						

POLAND

2. Arrivals of non-resident visitors at national borders, by nationality

	2007	2008	2009	2010	2011	Market share 11	% Change 11-10
Sierra Leone	50						
Togo	101						
Burkina Faso	43						
Other Africa		15,000	20,000	20,000	15,000	0.02	-25.00
All countries of Africa		15,000	20,000	20,000	15,000	0.02	-25.00
AMERICAS	452,903	380,000	338,000	395,000	400,000	0.66	1.27
Caribbean	1,614						
Antigua and Barbuda	9						
Bahamas	8						
Barbados	54						
Bermuda	6						
Cuba	889						
Dominica	19						
Dominican Republic	159						
Grenada	8						
Guadeloupe	1						
Haiti	70						
Jamaica	241						
Netherlands Antilles	1						
Puerto Rico	2						
Saint Kitts and Nevis	6						
Saint Lucia	10						
Saint Vincent and the Grenadines	11						
Trinidad and Tobago	119						
United States Virgin Islands	1						
Central America	1,656						
Belize	19						
Costa Rica	568						
El Salvador	129						
Guatemala	288						
Honduras	153						
Nicaragua	185						
Panama	314						
North America	420,931	350,000	298,000	340,000	365,000	0.60	7.35
Canada	77,994	80,000	68,000	75,000	80,000	0.13	6.67
Greenland	1						
Mexico	11,957				15,000	0.02	
United States of America	330,979	270,000	230,000	265,000	270,000	0.44	1.89
South America	28,702	20,000	10,000	15,000	25,000	0.04	66.67
Argentina	4,381				10,000	0.02	
Bolivia	428						
Brazil	15,387	20,000	10,000	15,000	15,000	0.02	
Chile	2,527						
Colombia	1,667						
Ecuador	586						
Falkland Islands, Malvinas	1						
French Guiana	5						
Guyana	23						
Paraguay	221						
Peru	1,207						
Suriname	15						
Uruguay	657						
Venezuela	1,597						
Other Americas		10,000	30,000	40,000	10,000	0.02	-75.00
Other countries of the Americas		10,000	30,000	40,000	10,000	0.02	-75.00

POLAND

2. Arrivals of non-resident visitors at national borders, by nationality

	2007	2008	2009	2010	2011	Market share 11	% Change 11-10
EAST ASIA AND THE PACIFIC	228,844	220,000	207,000	280,000	300,000	0.49	7.14
North-East Asia	146,571	128,000	100,000	135,000	135,000	0.22	
China	18,313	20,000	25,000	35,000	40,000	0.07	14.29
Taiwan, Province of China	5,214				10,000	0.02	
Hong Kong, China	4,038	3,000	5,000	5,000	5,000	0.01	
Japan	47,532	42,000	35,000	60,000	45,000	0.07	-25.00
Korea, Dem. People's Republic of	494						
Korea, Republic of	63,810	63,000	35,000	35,000	35,000	0.06	
Macao, China	21						
Mongolia	7,149						
South-East Asia	27,313				30,000	0.05	
Brunei Darussalam	15						
Myanmar	128						
Cambodia	56						
Indonesia	1,475				5,000	0.01	
Lao People's Democratic Republic	42						
Malaysia	4,902				5,000	0.01	
Philippines	3,313				5,000	0.01	
Singapore	4,072				10,000	0.02	
Viet Nam	10,885						
Thailand	2,425				5,000	0.01	
Australasia	54,886	45,000	37,000	55,000	65,000	0.11	18.18
Australia	47,153	45,000	37,000	55,000	55,000	0.09	
New Zealand	7,733				10,000	0.02	
Melanesia	28						
Fiji	17						
New Caledonia	1						
Vanuatu	6						
Papua New Guinea	4						
Micronesia	9						
Kiribati	8						
Nauru	1						
Polynesia	37						
American Samoa	2						
Tokelau	8						
Tonga	4						
Tuvalu	19						
Samoa	4						
Other East Asia and the Pacific		47,000	70,000	90,000	70,000	0.12	-22.22
Other countries East Asia/Pacific		47,000	70,000	90,000	70,000	0.12	-22.22
EUROPE	65,373,132	59,290,000	53,221,000	57,540,000	59,950,000	98.69	4.19
Central/Eastern Europe	24,118,947	21,515,000	24,170,000	28,475,000	31,030,000	51.08	8.97
Azerbaijan	4,093						
Armenia	5,910				20,000	0.03	
Bulgaria	73,055	95,000	85,000	80,000	85,000	0.14	6.25
Belarus	3,861,442	2,130,000	2,360,000	3,090,000	3,450,000	5.68	11.65
Czech Republic	7,292,127	7,820,000	8,180,000	9,240,000	10,840,000	17.85	17.32
Estonia	236,071	185,000	130,000	115,000	120,000	0.20	4.35
Georgia	4,322				5,000	0.01	
Hungary	272,959	255,000	225,000	220,000	230,000	0.38	4.55
Kazakhstan	42,831	35,000			40,000	0.07	
Kyrgyzstan	5,667						
Latvia	484,639	540,000	390,000	350,000	360,000	0.59	2.86
Lithuania	1,391,659	1,930,000	2,640,000	2,690,000	2,420,000	3.98	-10.04
Republic of Moldova	61,205	55,000			40,000	0.07	
Romania	98,942	120,000	90,000	120,000	120,000	0.20	

POLAND

2. Arrivals of non-resident visitors at national borders, by nationality

	2007	2008	2009	2010	2011	Market share 11	% Change 11-10
Russian Federation	1,626,424	1,290,000	1,210,000	1,530,000	1,850,000	3.05	20.92
Slovakia	3,209,857	3,740,000	5,040,000	6,010,000	5,620,000	9.25	-6.49
Tajikistan	581						
Turkmenistan	216						
Ukraine	5,443,755	3,320,000	3,820,000	5,030,000	5,830,000	9.60	15.90
Uzbekistan	3,192						
Northern Europe	**1,270,505**	**1,212,000**	**1,085,000**	**1,150,000**	**1,100,000**	**1.81**	**-4.35**
Denmark	149,897	130,000	120,000	125,000	110,000	0.18	-12.00
Finland	81,750	80,000	75,000	90,000	95,000	0.16	5.56
Iceland	7,568	2,000			5,000	0.01	
Ireland	118,847	90,000	80,000	80,000	85,000	0.14	6.25
Norway	142,375	145,000	120,000	120,000	120,000	0.20	
Sweden	221,963	210,000	190,000	195,000	185,000	0.30	-5.13
United Kingdom	548,105	555,000	500,000	540,000	500,000	0.82	-7.41
Southern Europe	**633,583**	**540,000**	**551,000**	**580,000**	**630,000**	**1.04**	**8.62**
Albania	1,884						
Andorra	36						
Bosnia and Herzegovina	3,470						
Croatia	37,670	35,000	30,000	20,000	20,000	0.03	
Greece	25,377	30,000	45,000	35,000	40,000	0.07	14.29
Holy See	42						
Italy	326,749	275,000	255,000	285,000	315,000	0.52	10.53
Malta	904		1,000				
Portugal	70,925	70,000	70,000	75,000	70,000	0.12	-6.67
San Marino	109						
Serbia					10,000	0.02	
Slovenia	24,775	20,000	20,000	20,000	20,000	0.03	
Spain	118,549	110,000	130,000	145,000	155,000	0.26	6.90
TFYR of Macedonia	5,112						
Serbia and Montenegro	17,981						
Western Europe	**39,219,920**	**35,720,000**	**27,145,000**	**27,030,000**	**26,975,000**	**44.41**	**-0.20**
Austria	317,817	320,000	325,000	345,000	355,000	0.58	2.90
Belgium	115,245	110,000	110,000	125,000	130,000	0.21	4.00
France	257,958	240,000	240,000	260,000	280,000	0.46	7.69
Germany	38,102,725	34,630,000	26,070,000	25,860,000	25,740,000	42.37	-0.46
Liechtenstein	93						
Luxembourg	4,515		5,000	10,000	20,000	0.03	100.00
Monaco	40						
Netherlands	362,850	355,000	335,000	370,000	390,000	0.64	5.41
Switzerland	58,677	65,000	60,000	60,000	60,000	0.10	
East Mediterranean Europe	**130,177**	**120,000**	**120,000**	**145,000**	**175,000**	**0.29**	**20.69**
Cyprus	1,441		5,000	5,000			
Israel	78,184	65,000	60,000	70,000	90,000	0.15	28.57
Turkey	50,552	55,000	55,000	70,000	85,000	0.14	21.43
Other Europe		**183,000**	**150,000**	**160,000**	**40,000**	**0.07**	**-75.00**
Other countries of Europe		183,000	150,000	160,000	40,000	0.07	-75.00
MIDDLE EAST	**9,507**	**10,000**	**15,000**	**15,000**	**15,000**	**0.02**	
Bahrain	53						
Iraq	780						
Jordan	867						
Kuwait	535						
Lebanon	1,513						
Libya	681						
Oman	53						
Qatar	94						
Saudi Arabia	1,019						
Syrian Arab Republic	1,207						

POLAND

2. Arrivals of non-resident visitors at national borders, by nationality

	2007	2008	2009	2010	2011	Market share 11	% Change 11-10
United Arab Emirates	225						
Egypt	2,331						
Yemen	149						
All countries of Middle East		10,000	15,000	15,000	15,000	0.02	
SOUTH ASIA	**19,721**	**20,000**	**20,000**	**30,000**	**20,000**	**0.03**	**-33.33**
Afghanistan	549						
Bangladesh	661						
Bhutan	11						
Sri Lanka	652						
India	13,449	15,000	10,000	15,000	15,000	0.02	
Iran, Islamic Republic of	1,766						
Maldives	6						
Nepal	423						
Pakistan	2,204						
Other countries of South Asia		5,000	10,000	15,000	5,000	0.01	-66.67
NOT SPECIFIED	**106,799**		**19,000**	**60,000**	**45,000**	**0.07**	**-25.00**
Other countries of the World	106,799		19,000	60,000	45,000	0.07	-25.00

POLAND

3. Arrivals of non-resident tourists in hotels and similar establishments, by country of residence

		2007	2008	2009	2010	2011	Market share 11	% Change 11-10
TOTAL	(*)	3,833,228	3,565,828	3,394,053	3,667,358	3,907,422	100.00	6.55
AFRICA		5,863	5,866	8,089	8,370	7,530	0.19	-10.04
East Africa		734	740	615	1,065	618	0.02	-41.97
British Indian Ocean Territory		6	7					
Burundi		59	59	39	33	42	0.00	27.27
Comoros				4	2			
Ethiopia		27	60	112	205	54	0.00	-73.66
Eritrea		15	2					
Djibouti		4	2	23	4	8	0.00	100.00
Kenya		105	192	153	173	167	0.00	-3.47
Madagascar		33	23	5	36	17	0.00	-52.78
Malawi		14	2	10	12	4	0.00	-66.67
Mauritius		47	35	23	57	33	0.00	-42.11
Mozambique		55	12	5	13	21	0.00	61.54
Reunion		22	31	1				
Rwanda		78	101	14	138	25	0.00	-81.88
Seychelles		14	47	18	17	20	0.00	17.65
Somalia		57	15	23	45	52	0.00	15.56
Zimbabwe		64	24	62	29	56	0.00	93.10
Uganda		47	37	60	98	68	0.00	-30.61
United Republic of Tanzania		29	34	34	171	37	0.00	-78.36
Zambia		58	57	29	32	14	0.00	-56.25
Central Africa		469	332	656	822	655	0.02	-20.32
Angola		253	116	292	581	402	0.01	-30.81
Cameroon		83	55	95	86	80	0.00	-6.98
Central African Republic		3	15	36	37	80	0.00	116.22
Chad		8	3	25	3	4	0.00	33.33
Congo		84	94	147	88	71	0.00	-19.32
Democratic Republic of the Congo		18	23	43	23	15	0.00	-34.78
Equatorial Guinea		1			4	3	0.00	-25.00
Gabon		11	21	18				
Sao Tome and Principe		8	5					
North Africa		1,496	1,311	2,402	3,005	2,841	0.07	-5.46
Algeria		675	434	962	1,556	1,632	0.04	4.88
Morocco		397	490	533	826	500	0.01	-39.47
Western Sahara		154	4	355	69	19	0.00	-72.46
Sudan		15	26	71	56	116	0.00	107.14
Tunisia		255	357	481	498	574	0.01	15.26
Southern Africa		1,498	1,689	2,207	1,755	2,090	0.05	19.09
Botswana		2	41	125	60	5	0.00	-91.67
Lesotho		31		1	5	5	0.00	
Namibia		13	75	124	26	48	0.00	84.62
South Africa		1,340	1,413	1,765	1,664	2,032	0.05	22.12
Swaziland		112	160	192				
West Africa		1,666	1,794	2,209	1,723	1,326	0.03	-23.04
Cape Verde		16	22	8	7	14	0.00	100.00
Benin		5	39	37	26	15	0.00	-42.31
Gambia		282	82	17	33	4	0.00	-87.88
Ghana		59	35	31	78	65	0.00	-16.67
Guinea		76	51	27	5	10	0.00	100.00
Côte d'Ivoire		42	55	14	138	36	0.00	-73.91
Liberia		8	15	7	20	12	0.00	-40.00
Mali		28	20	19	28	27	0.00	-3.57
Mauritania		12	298	46	15	23	0.00	53.33
Niger		69	144	364	382	164	0.00	-57.07
Nigeria		751	707	945	609	571	0.01	-6.24

POLAND

3. Arrivals of non-resident tourists in hotels and similar establishments, by country of residence

	2007	2008	2009	2010	2011	Market share 11	% Change 11-10
Guinea-Bissau	99	4	2		14	0.00	
Saint Helena	13	4	22	24	7	0.00	-70.83
Senegal	61	76	409	145	91	0.00	-37.24
Sierra Leone	131	218	243	195	232	0.01	18.97
Togo	7	14	14	3	18	0.00	500.00
Burkina Faso	7	10	4	15	23	0.00	53.33
AMERICAS	**219,957**	**186,723**	**171,859**	**203,579**	**208,953**	**5.35**	**2.64**
Caribbean	**739**	**1,124**	**735**	**673**	**1,662**	**0.04**	**146.95**
Antigua and Barbuda	143	10	9				
Bahamas	19	89	28	100	599	0.02	499.00
Barbados	35	267	120	59	26	0.00	-55.93
Bermuda	14	27	23	13	28	0.00	115.38
British Virgin Islands	18	154	1				
Cayman Islands		1	20	20	13	0.00	-35.00
Cuba	212	226	224	232	255	0.01	9.91
Dominica	11	11	8	18	31	0.00	72.22
Dominican Republic	26	26	28	54	122	0.00	125.93
Grenada	5	25	2				
Guadeloupe	3	3	11		1	0.00	
Haiti	8	33	12	16	40	0.00	150.00
Jamaica	66	91	124	48	73	0.00	52.08
Martinique		5	2		3	0.00	
Netherlands Antilles	6	6	1				
Aruba	16	10	16	11	3	0.00	-72.73
Puerto Rico	73	61	80	86	451	0.01	424.42
Saint Kitts and Nevis	1	1	3				
Anguilla	1	2	12				
Saint Lucia	2	10					
Trinidad and Tobago	10	64	10	16	17	0.00	6.25
Turks and Caicos Islands	5	1	1				
United States Virgin Islands	65	1					
Central America	**801**	**845**	**580**	**665**	**680**	**0.02**	**2.26**
Belize	229	70	90	36	65	0.00	80.56
Costa Rica	233	230	192	150	195	0.00	30.00
El Salvador	63	67	57	54	106	0.00	96.30
Guatemala	29	68	49	64	56	0.00	-12.50
Honduras	192	57	88	167	173	0.00	3.59
Nicaragua	17	229	33	135	31	0.00	-77.04
Panama	38	124	71	59	54	0.00	-8.47
North America	**208,309**	**171,535**	**158,082**	**186,488**	**190,195**	**4.87**	**1.99**
Canada	19,414	19,641	21,468	25,478	26,549	0.68	4.20
Greenland		1	5	1			
Mexico	4,477	3,851	3,355	3,598	5,051	0.13	40.38
Saint Pierre and Miquelon	1	2					
United States of America	184,417	148,040	133,254	157,411	158,595	4.06	0.75
South America	**10,108**	**13,219**	**12,462**	**15,753**	**16,416**	**0.42**	**4.21**
Argentina	1,654	2,141	2,063	2,046	2,967	0.08	45.01
Bolivia	132	53	605	1,041	1,036	0.03	-0.48
Brazil	5,624	7,865	6,955	9,488	9,310	0.24	-1.88
Chile	1,563	828	748	887	1,007	0.03	13.53
Colombia	275	506	437	571	719	0.02	25.92
Ecuador	66	116	253	176	125	0.00	-28.98
Falkland Islands, Malvinas	3		84	1	7	0.00	600.00
French Guiana	8	15	2	1	4	0.00	300.00
Guyana	19	14	1	3	85	0.00	2733.33
Paraguay	12	4	14	61	74	0.00	21.31
Peru	231	273	450	280	270	0.01	-3.57

POLAND

3. Arrivals of non-resident tourists in hotels and similar establishments, by country of residence

	2007	2008	2009	2010	2011	Market share 11	% Change 11-10
Suriname	122	136	65	33			
Uruguay	126	177	278	464	463	0.01	-0.22
Venezuela	273	1,091	507	701	349	0.01	-50.21
EAST ASIA AND THE PACIFIC	**112,225**	**112,338**	**111,645**	**141,195**	**145,032**	**3.71**	**2.72**
North-East Asia	**90,800**	**88,597**	**86,574**	**109,545**	**103,918**	**2.66**	**-5.14**
China	15,649	19,100	18,990	25,421	32,000	0.82	25.88
Taiwan, Province of China	931	1,036	1,382	1,295	1,920	0.05	48.26
Hong Kong, China	1,255	1,713	3,403	3,912	4,566	0.12	16.72
Japan	41,141	35,781	32,860	48,772	37,353	0.96	-23.41
Korea, Dem. People's Republic of	4,757	5,018	11,709	15,859	14,364	0.37	-9.43
Korea, Republic of	26,824	25,678	17,786	13,734	13,291	0.34	-3.23
Macao, China	5	17	55	62	48	0.00	-22.58
Mongolia	238	254	389	490	376	0.01	-23.27
South-East Asia	**6,075**	**6,487**	**8,568**	**10,647**	**17,916**	**0.46**	**68.27**
Brunei Darussalam	59	6	5	54	12	0.00	-77.78
Myanmar	16	7	10	2	3	0.00	50.00
Cambodia	8	36	7	38	11	0.00	-71.05
Indonesia	664	1,008	1,013	885	2,522	0.06	184.97
Lao People's Democratic Republic	15	17	17	16	43	0.00	168.75
Malaysia	1,317	983	952	1,170	2,041	0.05	74.44
Philippines	541	820	991	824	2,317	0.06	181.19
Timor-Leste	7	11		1	3	0.00	200.00
Singapore	1,136	1,462	2,052	4,004	5,738	0.15	43.31
Viet Nam	1,340	905	1,870	1,666	1,681	0.04	0.90
Thailand	972	1,232	1,651	1,987	3,545	0.09	78.41
Australasia	**14,907**	**16,426**	**16,363**	**20,883**	**23,091**	**0.59**	**10.57**
Australia	13,455	14,893	14,713	18,647	20,988	0.54	12.55
New Zealand	1,452	1,533	1,650	2,236	2,103	0.05	-5.95
Melanesia	**70**	**92**	**94**	**35**	**65**	**0.00**	**85.71**
Solomon Islands	1	9					
Fiji	12	26	46	8	14	0.00	75.00
New Caledonia	10	18	13	8	35	0.00	337.50
Norfolk Island	45	8	27				
Papua New Guinea	2	31	8	19	16	0.00	-15.79
Micronesia	**62**	**55**	**3**	**2**	**14**	**0.00**	**600.00**
Kiribati		19					
Guam		2	3	2	8	0.00	300.00
Nauru	11	33					
Micronesia, Federated States of					6	0.00	
Marshall Islands	2						
Palau	49	1					
Polynesia	**311**	**681**	**43**	**83**	**28**	**0.00**	**-66.27**
American Samoa	167	262	28				
French Polynesia	3	23	9	36	24	0.00	-33.33
Niue	6	52					
Tokelau	17	6					
Tonga		8	1	47	4	0.00	-91.49
Tuvalu	28	9					
Wallis and Futuna Islands	16	299					
Samoa	74	22	5				
EUROPE	**3,436,630**	**3,202,245**	**3,063,367**	**3,260,437**	**3,494,942**	**89.44**	**7.19**
Central/Eastern Europe	**774,464**	**705,566**	**639,280**	**727,434**	**870,726**	**22.28**	**19.70**
Azerbaijan	992	662	915	720	793	0.02	10.14
Armenia	832	459	2,376	3,119	3,521	0.09	12.89
Bulgaria	7,185	8,339	8,450	9,297	9,488	0.24	2.05
Belarus	84,662	59,060	63,213	72,545	93,956	2.40	29.51

POLAND

3. Arrivals of non-resident tourists in hotels and similar establishments, by country of residence

	2007	2008	2009	2010	2011	Market share 11	% Change 11-10
Czech Republic	64,422	68,895	66,975	68,726	77,388	1.98	12.60
Estonia	50,610	38,522	31,558	30,510	34,057	0.87	11.63
Georgia	960	1,412	1,780	1,979	1,663	0.04	-15.97
Hungary	41,192	41,627	40,192	41,239	44,522	1.14	7.96
Kazakhstan	3,572	2,267	2,369	2,494	3,650	0.09	46.35
Kyrgyzstan	238	169	95	184	288	0.01	56.52
Latvia	50,452	48,251	34,689	40,106	46,530	1.19	16.02
Lithuania	92,060	94,548	88,702	87,690	91,868	2.35	4.76
Republic of Moldova	3,141	2,579	2,077	2,099	2,349	0.06	11.91
Romania	16,429	19,491	17,785	23,302	24,693	0.63	5.97
Russian Federation	196,483	184,442	149,529	198,801	255,376	6.54	28.46
Slovakia	25,788	28,446	33,244	36,316	42,123	1.08	15.99
Tajikistan	98	85	47	164	60	0.00	-63.41
Turkmenistan	37	13	31	26	56	0.00	115.38
Ukraine	134,662	105,954	94,935	107,365	137,399	3.52	27.97
Uzbekistan	649	345	318	752	946	0.02	25.80
Northern Europe	**759,512**	**741,392**	**671,581**	**692,474**	**698,763**	**17.88**	**0.91**
Denmark	96,802	84,511	81,265	74,855	78,987	2.02	5.52
Faeroe Islands	28	72	4				
Finland	38,446	40,794	42,831	52,596	59,813	1.53	13.72
Iceland	2,539	1,993	1,662	2,531	1,750	0.04	-30.86
Ireland	57,066	45,932	37,327	38,081	37,775	0.97	-0.80
Norway	91,735	94,679	86,554	96,225	98,166	2.51	2.02
Svalbard and Jan Mayen Islands		10	11	2			
Sweden	109,360	103,159	97,659	93,584	97,968	2.51	4.68
United Kingdom	363,536	370,242	324,268	334,600	324,304	8.30	-3.08
Southern Europe	**352,169**	**318,625**	**323,206**	**349,942**	**400,845**	**10.26**	**14.55**
Albania	955	325	1,384	1,313	1,631	0.04	24.22
Andorra	407	94	122	372	276	0.01	-25.81
Bosnia and Herzegovina	743	743	1,167	774	1,131	0.03	46.12
Croatia	6,235	6,736	6,067	6,570	7,757	0.20	18.07
Gibraltar	9	9	26	38	46	0.00	21.05
Greece	10,389	11,338	15,014	12,218	14,071	0.36	15.17
Holy See	10	10	161	138	108	0.00	-21.74
Italy	197,148	172,632	168,068	181,952	195,474	5.00	7.43
Malta	633	787	515	714	1,285	0.03	79.97
Montenegro	285	158	126	153	372	0.01	143.14
Portugal	14,183	13,924	16,659	18,212	19,771	0.51	8.56
San Marino	62	22	116	26	179	0.00	588.46
Serbia	1,429	1,543	1,793	4,014	3,537	0.09	-11.88
Slovenia	8,181	7,205	8,176	7,869	9,005	0.23	14.44
Spain	110,970	102,595	103,125	114,920	145,465	3.72	26.58
TFYR of Macedonia	530	504	687	659	737	0.02	11.84
Western Europe	**1,401,562**	**1,320,710**	**1,286,299**	**1,335,250**	**1,360,478**	**34.82**	**1.89**
Austria	50,888	50,489	50,882	54,543	57,533	1.47	5.48
Belgium	53,349	51,755	50,908	57,511	60,923	1.56	5.93
France	169,171	164,111	156,874	166,367	177,404	4.54	6.63
Germany	1,002,835	925,394	903,444	928,727	928,048	23.75	-0.07
Liechtenstein	211	283	1,122	246	337	0.01	36.99
Luxembourg	2,504	2,449	2,732	3,271	3,363	0.09	2.81
Monaco	246	231	398	278	207	0.01	-25.54
Netherlands	95,688	94,449	89,011	92,260	98,327	2.52	6.58
Switzerland	26,670	31,549	30,928	32,047	34,336	0.88	7.14
East Mediterranean Europe	**148,923**	**115,952**	**143,001**	**155,337**	**164,130**	**4.20**	**5.66**
Cyprus	2,613	2,465	2,413	2,194	1,976	0.05	-9.94
Israel	135,860	101,527	126,974	138,007	143,915	3.68	4.28
Turkey	10,450	11,960	13,614	15,136	18,239	0.47	20.50

POLAND

3. Arrivals of non-resident tourists in hotels and similar establishments, by country of residence

	2007	2008	2009	2010	2011	Market share 11	% Change 11-10
MIDDLE EAST	**4,836**	**4,585**	**6,591**	**6,658**	**8,620**	**0.22**	**29.47**
Bahrain	335	112	157	213	159	0.00	-25.35
Iraq	401	350	554	421	657	0.02	56.06
Jordan	165	225	274	201	408	0.01	102.99
Kuwait	308	462	519	484	676	0.02	39.67
Lebanon	272	395	836	461	610	0.02	32.32
Libya	163	227	207	281	308	0.01	9.61
Oman	20	24	40	96	26	0.00	-72.92
Qatar	139	46	297	285	237	0.01	-16.84
Saudi Arabia	991	659	1,022	1,476	2,216	0.06	50.14
Syrian Arab Republic	204	158	290	299	467	0.01	56.19
United Arab Emirates	534	748	1,080	989	1,271	0.03	28.51
Egypt	1,207	1,153	1,277	1,422	1,546	0.04	8.72
Yemen	97	26	38	30	39	0.00	30.00
SOUTH ASIA	**9,829**	**12,005**	**12,962**	**14,644**	**16,266**	**0.42**	**11.08**
Afghanistan	436	223	1,224	1,219	1,440	0.04	18.13
Bangladesh	255	353	765	784	918	0.02	17.09
Bhutan	343	1,074	262	394	107	0.00	-72.84
Sri Lanka	115	83	92	135	177	0.00	31.11
India	5,869	7,260	8,231	9,226	10,826	0.28	17.34
Iran, Islamic Republic of	1,938	2,272	1,567	2,147	1,892	0.05	-11.88
Maldives	4	8	8	46	15	0.00	-67.39
Nepal	120	199	169	110	85	0.00	-22.73
Pakistan	749	533	644	583	806	0.02	38.25
NOT SPECIFIED	**43,888**	**42,066**	**19,540**	**32,475**	**26,079**	**0.67**	**-19.70**
Other countries of the World	43,888	42,066	19,540	32,475	26,079	0.67	-19.70

POLAND

4. Arrivals of non-resident tourists in all types of accommodation establishments, by country of residence

	2007	2008	2009	2010	2011	Market share 11	% Change 11-10
TOTAL	4,387,404	4,046,312	3,861,942	4,134,970	4,409,550	100.00	6.64
AFRICA	6,657	6,538	8,783	9,318	9,209	0.21	-1.17
East Africa	813	824	689	1,231	788	0.02	-35.99
British Indian Ocean Territory	6	7					
Burundi	59	60	45	33	42	0.00	27.27
Comoros			4	2			
Ethiopia	35	72	135	228	78	0.00	-65.79
Eritrea	15	3					
Djibouti	4	5	23	4	9	0.00	125.00
Kenya	135	220	161	218	203	0.00	-6.88
Madagascar	33	24	6	38	19	0.00	-50.00
Malawi	14	3	10	15	7	0.00	-53.33
Mauritius	49	44	24	61	36	0.00	-40.98
Mozambique	58	12	5	13	24	0.00	84.62
Reunion	22	31	1				
Rwanda	81	101	14	147	28	0.00	-80.95
Seychelles	18	47	18	17	20	0.00	17.65
Somalia	57	31	24	84	52	0.00	-38.10
Zimbabwe	70	30	70	36	62	0.00	72.22
Uganda	53	41	75	110	102	0.00	-7.27
United Republic of Tanzania	44	35	42	178	45	0.00	-74.72
Zambia	60	58	32	47	61	0.00	29.79
Central Africa	532	435	740	930	711	0.02	-23.55
Angola	282	155	295	619	419	0.01	-32.31
Cameroon	94	80	114	115	102	0.00	-11.30
Central African Republic	4	16	38	46	81	0.00	76.09
Chad	9	3	31	8	4	0.00	-50.00
Congo	105	122	167	114	87	0.00	-23.68
Democratic Republic of the Congo	18	33	51	24	15	0.00	-37.50
Equatorial Guinea	1			4	3	0.00	-25.00
Gabon	11	21	44				
Sao Tome and Principe	8	5					
North Africa	1,790	1,495	2,537	3,294	3,162	0.07	-4.01
Algeria	897	482	1,022	1,644	1,778	0.04	8.15
Morocco	428	560	560	950	581	0.01	-38.84
Western Sahara	154	4	355	69	19	0.00	-72.46
Sudan	22	29	76	64	137	0.00	114.06
Tunisia	289	420	524	567	647	0.01	14.11
Southern Africa	1,686	1,798	2,314	1,892	2,457	0.06	29.86
Botswana	4	42	125	60	5	0.00	-91.67
Lesotho	32	4	2	11	5	0.00	-54.55
Namibia	15	78	130	26	281	0.01	980.77
South Africa	1,499	1,500	1,865	1,795	2,166	0.05	20.67
Swaziland	136	174	192				
West Africa	1,836	1,986	2,503	1,971	2,091	0.05	6.09
Cape Verde	16	22	8	7	14	0.00	100.00
Benin	9	46	38	26	16	0.00	-38.46
Gambia	351	131	23	35	7	0.00	-80.00
Ghana	68	45	36	91	89	0.00	-2.20
Guinea	77	53	43	17	11	0.00	-35.29
Côte d'Ivoire	42	57	34	142	36	0.00	-74.65
Liberia	8	15	7	20	13	0.00	-35.00
Mali	29	20	20	30	27	0.00	-10.00
Mauritania	12	299	48	15	24	0.00	60.00
Niger	70	145	377	455	213	0.00	-53.19
Nigeria	815	802	1,059	720	1,224	0.03	70.00

POLAND

4. Arrivals of non-resident tourists in all types of accommodation establishments, by country of residence

	2007	2008	2009	2010	2011	Market share 11	% Change 11-10
Guinea-Bissau	104	4	2		14	0.00	
Saint Helena	13	4	51	24	7	0.00	-70.83
Senegal	72	89	471	175	119	0.00	-32.00
Sierra Leone	131	221	243	195	233	0.01	19.49
Togo	12	16	18	4	18	0.00	350.00
Burkina Faso	7	17	25	15	26	0.00	73.33
AMERICAS	**234,350**	**198,941**	**184,464**	**217,610**	**225,130**	**5.11**	**3.46**
Caribbean	**832**	**1,418**	**773**	**751**	**1,719**	**0.04**	**128.89**
Antigua and Barbuda	143	10	9				
Bahamas	19	232	33	108	600	0.01	455.56
Barbados	86	271	132	65	26	0.00	-60.00
Bermuda	14	47	25	13	28	0.00	115.38
British Virgin Islands	18	176	1				
Cayman Islands		1	20	20	13	0.00	-35.00
Cuba	223	237	231	279	277	0.01	-0.72
Dominica	11	14	8	18	31	0.00	72.22
Dominican Republic	30	32	30	56	126	0.00	125.00
Grenada	6	25	2				
Guadeloupe	3	3	12	3	1	0.00	-66.67
Haiti	8	34	13	17	48	0.00	182.35
Jamaica	83	98	126	48	75	0.00	56.25
Martinique		5	2		3	0.00	
Netherlands Antilles	6	6	1				
Aruba	16	11	17	11	3	0.00	-72.73
Puerto Rico	80	115	85	93	457	0.01	391.40
Saint Kitts and Nevis	1	1	3				
Anguilla	3	4	12				
Saint Lucia	2	10					
Trinidad and Tobago	10	64	10	20	31	0.00	55.00
Turks and Caicos Islands	5	21	1				
United States Virgin Islands	65	1					
Central America	**907**	**868**	**1,516**	**1,437**	**1,294**	**0.03**	**-9.95**
Belize	229	70	90	41	68	0.00	65.85
Costa Rica	277	243	198	249	220	0.00	-11.65
El Salvador	63	70	59	56	111	0.00	98.21
Guatemala	39	72	55	74	65	0.00	-12.16
Honduras	214	57	930	777	722	0.02	-7.08
Nicaragua	45	229	113	143	45	0.00	-68.53
Panama	40	127	71	97	63	0.00	-35.05
North America	**220,565**	**181,896**	**168,322**	**197,815**	**203,052**	**4.60**	**2.65**
Canada	22,189	22,313	24,197	28,135	29,289	0.66	4.10
Greenland		1	5	2			
Mexico	4,979	4,404	3,697	4,082	5,765	0.13	41.23
Saint Pierre and Miquelon	2	3					
United States of America	193,395	155,175	140,423	165,596	167,998	3.81	1.45
South America	**12,046**	**14,759**	**13,853**	**17,607**	**19,065**	**0.43**	**8.28**
Argentina	1,879	2,292	2,265	2,339	3,230	0.07	38.09
Bolivia	155	63	620	1,046	1,047	0.02	0.10
Brazil	6,615	8,817	7,689	10,467	10,890	0.25	4.04
Chile	1,669	961	882	1,019	1,229	0.03	20.61
Colombia	372	603	498	643	941	0.02	46.35
Ecuador	94	148	306	254	180	0.00	-29.13
Falkland Islands, Malvinas	3		84	1	7	0.00	600.00
French Guiana	8	15	2	1	4	0.00	300.00
Guyana	29	14	1	3	89	0.00	2866.67
Paraguay	14	9	17	89	77	0.00	-13.48
Peru	599	310	509	386	370	0.01	-4.15

POLAND

4. Arrivals of non-resident tourists in all types of accommodation establishments, by country of residence

	2007	2008	2009	2010	2011	Market share 11	% Change 11-10
Suriname	128	137	69	33			
Uruguay	137	227	326	517	547	0.01	5.80
Venezuela	344	1,163	585	809	454	0.01	-43.88
EAST ASIA AND THE PACIFIC	**121,185**	**121,129**	**120,014**	**151,559**	**156,583**	**3.55**	**3.31**
North-East Asia	**94,347**	**92,364**	**90,107**	**113,881**	**108,818**	**2.47**	**-4.45**
China	16,514	20,189	20,033	26,578	33,182	0.75	24.85
Taiwan, Province of China	1,054	1,293	1,575	1,510	2,125	0.05	40.73
Hong Kong, China	1,373	1,808	3,566	4,231	4,958	0.11	17.18
Japan	42,722	37,175	34,386	50,499	39,202	0.89	-22.37
Korea, Dem. People's Republic of	5,020	5,237	12,022	16,413	15,006	0.34	-8.57
Korea, Republic of	27,314	26,301	17,901	13,943	13,702	0.31	-1.73
Macao, China	5	17	65	63	52	0.00	-17.46
Mongolia	345	344	559	644	591	0.01	-8.23
South-East Asia	**6,704**	**7,204**	**9,230**	**11,838**	**18,986**	**0.43**	**60.38**
Brunei Darussalam	60	6	5	54	16	0.00	-70.37
Myanmar	17	7	10	2	6	0.00	200.00
Cambodia	8	37	7	41	13	0.00	-68.29
Indonesia	683	1,124	1,169	980	2,578	0.06	163.06
Lao People's Democratic Republic	17	18	18	17	47	0.00	176.47
Malaysia	1,500	1,196	1,138	1,403	2,242	0.05	59.80
Philippines	625	861	1,015	1,025	2,489	0.06	142.83
Timor-Leste	8	11		1	3	0.00	200.00
Singapore	1,271	1,628	2,146	4,243	6,025	0.14	42.00
Viet Nam	1,483	1,041	2,010	1,956	1,837	0.04	-6.08
Thailand	1,032	1,275	1,712	2,116	3,730	0.08	76.28
Australasia	**19,678**	**20,671**	**20,527**	**25,700**	**28,662**	**0.65**	**11.53**
Australia	17,469	18,377	18,216	22,902	25,959	0.59	13.35
New Zealand	2,209	2,294	2,311	2,798	2,703	0.06	-3.40
Melanesia	**76**	**107**	**96**	**53**	**71**	**0.00**	**33.96**
Solomon Islands	3	11					
Fiji	13	39	48	8	19	0.00	137.50
New Caledonia	13	18	13	26	36	0.00	38.46
Norfolk Island	45	8	27				
Papua New Guinea	2	31	8	19	16	0.00	-15.79
Micronesia	**62**	**62**	**5**	**2**	**14**	**0.00**	**600.00**
Kiribati		25					
Guam		2	3	2	8	0.00	300.00
Nauru	11	34	2				
Micronesia, Federated States of					6	0.00	
Marshall Islands	2						
Palau	49	1					
Polynesia	**318**	**721**	**49**	**85**	**32**	**0.00**	**-62.35**
American Samoa	169	262	28				
French Polynesia	8	25	15	38	28	0.00	-26.32
Niue	6	52					
Tokelau	17	6					
Tonga		8	1	47	4	0.00	-91.49
Tuvalu	28	9					
Wallis and Futuna Islands	16	337					
Samoa	74	22	5				
EUROPE	**3,964,327**	**3,659,440**	**3,507,918**	**3,696,478**	**3,966,041**	**89.94**	**7.29**
Central/Eastern Europe	**919,071**	**820,306**	**743,407**	**830,132**	**993,938**	**22.54**	**19.73**
Azerbaijan	1,039	723	998	830	903	0.02	8.80
Armenia	937	579	2,485	3,203	3,651	0.08	13.99
Bulgaria	8,774	9,673	9,539	10,203	10,584	0.24	3.73
Belarus	99,173	66,319	71,485	81,928	107,304	2.43	30.97

POLAND

4. Arrivals of non-resident tourists in all types of accommodation establishments, by country of residence

	2007	2008	2009	2010	2011	Market share 11	% Change 11-10
Czech Republic	78,217	81,213	78,708	79,603	89,567	2.03	12.52
Estonia	54,413	41,789	34,592	32,486	36,152	0.82	11.28
Georgia	1,179	1,662	2,364	2,174	2,032	0.05	-6.53
Hungary	52,679	51,534	48,063	48,153	52,708	1.20	9.46
Kazakhstan	3,949	2,629	2,638	2,815	4,013	0.09	42.56
Kyrgyzstan	264	203	125	237	378	0.01	59.49
Latvia	59,175	55,895	38,112	43,265	50,691	1.15	17.16
Lithuania	108,189	111,383	101,950	100,255	103,789	2.35	3.53
Republic of Moldova	3,624	3,043	2,625	3,210	2,931	0.07	-8.69
Romania	19,049	22,291	20,552	25,836	27,371	0.62	5.94
Russian Federation	216,834	196,005	161,353	214,544	280,975	6.37	30.96
Slovakia	33,136	36,391	41,627	45,401	50,928	1.15	12.17
Tajikistan	102	93	49	196	109	0.00	-44.39
Turkmenistan	41	14	37	27	59	0.00	118.52
Ukraine	177,578	138,433	125,707	134,930	168,738	3.83	25.06
Uzbekistan	719	434	398	836	1,055	0.02	26.20
Northern Europe	**811,529**	**792,417**	**717,561**	**744,176**	**747,170**	**16.94**	**0.40**
Denmark	103,228	91,126	87,299	79,932	84,630	1.92	5.88
Faeroe Islands	28	73	8				
Finland	42,949	46,101	47,492	58,511	64,834	1.47	10.81
Iceland	2,700	2,106	1,785	2,722	1,905	0.04	-30.01
Ireland	61,488	49,003	40,525	42,122	41,243	0.94	-2.09
Norway	97,251	101,355	91,042	102,124	104,421	2.37	2.25
Svalbard and Jan Mayen Islands		10	11	2			
Sweden	123,013	114,343	108,850	102,784	106,586	2.42	3.70
United Kingdom	380,872	388,300	340,549	355,979	343,551	7.79	-3.49
Southern Europe	**381,042**	**343,408**	**350,611**	**381,226**	**435,968**	**9.89**	**14.36**
Albania	1,013	381	1,477	1,418	1,702	0.04	20.03
Andorra	416	98	130	373	290	0.01	-22.25
Bosnia and Herzegovina	828	860	1,239	852	1,276	0.03	49.77
Croatia	7,135	7,635	7,090	7,564	8,852	0.20	17.03
Gibraltar	9	16	26	38	46	0.00	21.05
Greece	11,225	11,863	15,601	12,805	14,702	0.33	14.81
Holy See	10	10	204	141	155	0.00	9.93
Italy	212,402	185,010	180,442	194,892	208,737	4.73	7.10
Malta	689	902	584	775	1,373	0.03	77.16
Montenegro	319	175	170	188	383	0.01	103.72
Portugal	15,737	15,553	18,285	20,299	22,181	0.50	9.27
San Marino	66	22	118	32	197	0.00	515.63
Serbia	1,780	2,125	2,374	4,855	4,726	0.11	-2.66
Slovenia	9,512	8,029	9,251	8,866	10,014	0.23	12.95
Spain	119,214	110,094	112,831	126,883	160,397	3.64	26.41
TFYR of Macedonia	687	635	789	1,245	937	0.02	-24.74
Western Europe	**1,701,108**	**1,583,611**	**1,550,661**	**1,582,580**	**1,621,143**	**36.76**	**2.44**
Austria	56,107	54,601	54,810	59,050	62,469	1.42	5.79
Belgium	60,487	57,647	56,663	63,964	66,987	1.52	4.73
France	193,128	182,607	174,044	187,267	198,572	4.50	6.04
Germany	1,246,132	1,142,337	1,126,573	1,128,378	1,141,632	25.89	1.17
Liechtenstein	222	310	1,149	267	351	0.01	31.46
Luxembourg	2,693	2,621	2,838	3,593	3,565	0.08	-0.78
Monaco	248	251	415	300	219	0.00	-27.00
Netherlands	113,205	109,721	101,006	105,631	110,934	2.52	5.02
Switzerland	28,886	33,516	33,163	34,130	36,414	0.83	6.69
East Mediterranean Europe	**151,577**	**119,698**	**145,678**	**158,364**	**167,822**	**3.81**	**5.97**
Cyprus	2,678	2,496	2,532	2,255	2,048	0.05	-9.18
Israel	137,448	104,120	128,419	139,567	145,572	3.30	4.30
Turkey	11,451	13,082	14,727	16,542	20,202	0.46	22.13

POLAND

4. Arrivals of non-resident tourists in all types of accommodation establishments, by country of residence

	2007	2008	2009	2010	2011	Market share 11	% Change 11-10
MIDDLE EAST	5,288	5,024	7,061	7,198	9,264	0.21	28.70
Bahrain	338	112	165	229	159	0.00	-30.57
Iraq	426	384	614	520	767	0.02	47.50
Jordan	219	249	313	228	433	0.01	89.91
Kuwait	335	476	543	498	680	0.02	36.55
Lebanon	347	429	866	500	632	0.01	26.40
Libya	186	245	229	303	347	0.01	14.52
Oman	22	28	42	99	27	0.00	-72.73
Qatar	140	49	325	288	265	0.01	-7.99
Saudi Arabia	1,045	677	1,085	1,535	2,304	0.05	50.10
Syrian Arab Republic	235	215	338	328	489	0.01	49.09
United Arab Emirates	555	754	1,105	1,074	1,361	0.03	26.72
Egypt	1,342	1,364	1,398	1,565	1,756	0.04	12.20
Yemen	98	42	38	31	44	0.00	41.94
SOUTH ASIA	10,504	12,564	14,134	18,472	17,072	0.39	-7.58
Afghanistan	449	233	1,248	3,757	1,458	0.03	-61.19
Bangladesh	282	365	791	859	928	0.02	8.03
Bhutan	347	1,075	263	398	109	0.00	-72.61
Sri Lanka	142	112	118	153	190	0.00	24.18
India	6,275	7,561	8,943	9,952	11,324	0.26	13.79
Iran, Islamic Republic of	2,039	2,391	1,648	2,255	2,048	0.05	-9.18
Maldives	4	8	9	46	16	0.00	-65.22
Nepal	145	234	419	325	121	0.00	-62.77
Pakistan	821	585	695	727	878	0.02	20.77
NOT SPECIFIED	45,093	42,676	19,568	34,335	26,251	0.60	-23.54
Other countries of the World	45,093	42,676	19,568	34,335	26,251	0.60	-23.54

POLAND

5. Overnight stays of non-resident tourists in hotels and similar establishments, by country of residence

		2007	2008	2009	2010	2011	Market share 11	% Change 11-10
TOTAL	(*)	8,408,772	7,939,328	7,478,048	8,029,202	8,397,392	100.00	4.59
AFRICA		16,055	17,672	20,722	20,737	20,073	0.24	-3.20
East Africa		2,311	2,103	1,466	2,180	1,583	0.02	-27.39
British Indian Ocean Territory		14	17					
Burundi		106	84	74	46	74	0.00	60.87
Comoros				4	4			
Ethiopia		105	195	156	365	151	0.00	-58.63
Eritrea		162	10					
Djibouti		6	2	52	4	16	0.00	300.00
Kenya		587	615	517	409	382	0.00	-6.60
Madagascar		67	76	7	100	66	0.00	-34.00
Malawi		100	2	27	29	21	0.00	-27.59
Mauritius		105	90	32	136	83	0.00	-38.97
Mozambique		74	17	9	48	58	0.00	20.83
Reunion		46	147	2				
Rwanda		113	112	30	224	196	0.00	-12.50
Seychelles		21	108	33	47	31	0.00	-34.04
Somalia		146	21	49	107	93	0.00	-13.08
Zimbabwe		311	94	179	92	103	0.00	11.96
Uganda		94	88	188	298	192	0.00	-35.57
United Republic of Tanzania		49	62	39	212	74	0.00	-65.09
Zambia		205	363	68	59	43	0.00	-27.12
Central Africa		926	910	1,421	1,604	1,908	0.02	18.95
Angola		517	274	595	1,212	954	0.01	-21.29
Cameroon		136	115	163	124	159	0.00	28.23
Central African Republic		9	23	175	65	553	0.01	750.77
Chad		22	5	93	4	16	0.00	300.00
Congo		151	234	263	165	182	0.00	10.30
Democratic Republic of the Congo		40	178	105	28	37	0.00	32.14
Equatorial Guinea		1			6	7	0.00	16.67
Gabon		36	60	27				
Sao Tome and Principe		14	21					
North Africa		3,653	3,982	5,582	8,007	7,787	0.09	-2.75
Algeria		1,791	1,713	2,144	4,051	4,081	0.05	0.74
Morocco		812	1,281	1,273	2,597	1,644	0.02	-36.70
Western Sahara		403	4	602	130	45	0.00	-65.38
Sudan		30	61	167	144	234	0.00	62.50
Tunisia		617	923	1,396	1,085	1,783	0.02	64.33
Southern Africa		3,732	4,382	5,288	4,490	5,498	0.07	22.45
Botswana		7	54	132	79	25	0.00	-68.35
Lesotho		82		7	13	19	0.00	46.15
Namibia		24	87	233	60	130	0.00	116.67
South Africa		3,491	4,015	4,628	4,338	5,324	0.06	22.73
Swaziland		128	226	288				
West Africa		5,433	6,295	6,965	4,456	3,297	0.04	-26.01
Cape Verde		32	44	16	14	42	0.00	200.00
Benin		8	100	116	94	51	0.00	-45.74
Gambia		615	238	34	83	5	0.00	-93.98
Ghana		184	89	62	183	335	0.00	83.06
Guinea		407	349	118	17	24	0.00	41.18
Côte d'Ivoire		106	138	38	168	68	0.00	-59.52
Liberia		33	105	11	56	38	0.00	-32.14
Mali		104	66	35	57	92	0.00	61.40
Mauritania		24	364	86	28	28	0.00	
Niger		113	282	651	1,017	365	0.00	-64.11
Nigeria		3,000	3,751	3,737	1,664	1,443	0.02	-13.28

POLAND

5. Overnight stays of non-resident tourists in hotels and similar establishments, by country of residence

	2007	2008	2009	2010	2011	Market share 11	% Change 11-10
Guinea-Bissau	113	8	3		14	0.00	
Saint Helena	18	8	61	31	8	0.00	-74.19
Senegal	308	299	1,376	651	338	0.00	-48.08
Sierra Leone	218	371	587	365	350	0.00	-4.11
Togo	21	44	30	3	20	0.00	566.67
Burkina Faso	129	39	4	25	76	0.00	204.00
AMERICAS	**499,613**	**431,228**	**388,543**	**450,356**	**463,590**	**5.52**	**2.94**
Caribbean	**2,083**	**3,742**	**1,732**	**1,558**	**4,019**	**0.05**	**157.96**
Antigua and Barbuda	264	22	18				
Bahamas	168	436	59	195	1,539	0.02	689.23
Barbados	64	622	173	110	73	0.00	-33.64
Bermuda	45	38	35	14	116	0.00	728.57
British Virgin Islands	37	353	1				
Cayman Islands		4	50	56	27	0.00	-51.79
Cuba	724	787	639	541	669	0.01	23.66
Dominica	51	36	21	59	79	0.00	33.90
Dominican Republic	202	79	235	189	336	0.00	77.78
Grenada	7	93	2				
Guadeloupe	6	5	17		5	0.00	
Haiti	10	66	19	56	159	0.00	183.93
Jamaica	114	692	248	136	156	0.00	14.71
Martinique		15	2		34	0.00	
Netherlands Antilles	10	12	1				
Aruba	22	15	26	15	16	0.00	6.67
Puerto Rico	103	116	145	143	738	0.01	416.08
Saint Kitts and Nevis	1	4	6				
Anguilla	2	4	14				
Saint Lucia	2	24					
Trinidad and Tobago	16	312	19	44	72	0.00	63.64
Turks and Caicos Islands	11	1	2				
United States Virgin Islands	224	6					
Central America	**1,794**	**1,556**	**1,300**	**1,266**	**1,432**	**0.02**	**13.11**
Belize	474	98	131	77	105	0.00	36.36
Costa Rica	409	544	350	273	417	0.00	52.75
El Salvador	103	114	112	88	184	0.00	109.09
Guatemala	60	110	150	119	176	0.00	47.90
Honduras	605	156	334	317	309	0.00	-2.52
Nicaragua	24	371	74	257	96	0.00	-62.65
Panama	119	163	149	135	145	0.00	7.41
North America	**471,529**	**395,657**	**357,942**	**413,234**	**415,694**	**4.95**	**0.60**
Canada	42,473	43,760	46,492	55,395	56,280	0.67	1.60
Greenland		2	19	2			
Mexico	14,796	10,951	7,397	8,960	12,902	0.15	44.00
Saint Pierre and Miquelon	1	2					
United States of America	414,259	340,942	304,034	348,877	346,512	4.13	-0.68
South America	**24,207**	**30,273**	**27,569**	**34,298**	**42,445**	**0.51**	**23.75**
Argentina	3,782	4,796	4,465	4,458	7,237	0.09	62.34
Bolivia	710	118	1,699	2,309	2,513	0.03	8.83
Brazil	14,747	18,276	15,431	21,052	25,389	0.30	20.60
Chile	2,536	1,818	1,469	1,807	2,274	0.03	25.84
Colombia	679	1,205	1,359	1,407	1,868	0.02	32.76
Ecuador	149	303	528	400	266	0.00	-33.50
Falkland Islands, Malvinas	3		86	2	8	0.00	300.00
French Guiana	8	32	7	1	39	0.00	3800.00
Guyana	29	25	3	3	143	0.00	4666.67
Paraguay	25	22	30	168	225	0.00	33.93
Peru	463	660	783	607	610	0.01	0.49

POLAND

5. Overnight stays of non-resident tourists in hotels and similar establishments, by country of residence

	2007	2008	2009	2010	2011	Market share 11	% Change 11-10
Suriname	241	212	93	66			
Uruguay	247	312	461	802	1,148	0.01	43.14
Venezuela	588	2,494	1,155	1,216	725	0.01	-40.38
EAST ASIA AND THE PACIFIC	**287,931**	**255,718**	**221,960**	**292,648**	**280,049**	**3.33**	**-4.31**
North-East Asia	**235,884**	**196,557**	**164,718**	**224,414**	**197,875**	**2.36**	**-11.83**
China	35,980	45,553	35,840	54,866	62,809	0.75	14.48
Taiwan, Province of China	2,117	2,225	2,680	2,531	4,284	0.05	69.26
Hong Kong, China	2,037	3,009	6,777	7,856	8,510	0.10	8.32
Japan	114,326	92,059	70,599	101,297	72,520	0.86	-28.41
Korea, Dem. People's Republic of	7,860	11,233	22,619	30,110	23,309	0.28	-22.59
Korea, Republic of	73,098	41,905	25,273	26,802	25,621	0.31	-4.41
Macao, China	6	23	195	102	91	0.00	-10.78
Mongolia	460	550	735	850	731	0.01	-14.00
South-East Asia	**18,824**	**21,096**	**20,774**	**22,646**	**32,559**	**0.39**	**43.77**
Brunei Darussalam	285	46	13	80	18	0.00	-77.50
Myanmar	26	14	17	5	7	0.00	40.00
Cambodia	12	54	26	70	67	0.00	-4.29
Indonesia	2,440	3,506	1,971	2,038	4,304	0.05	111.19
Lao People's Democratic Republic	19	44	37	33	51	0.00	54.55
Malaysia	6,171	6,907	4,976	5,137	4,677	0.06	-8.95
Philippines	2,138	2,651	2,512	1,724	4,362	0.05	153.02
Timor-Leste	7	15		1	6	0.00	500.00
Singapore	2,541	3,498	4,244	6,770	9,276	0.11	37.02
Viet Nam	2,904	1,667	3,558	3,094	3,206	0.04	3.62
Thailand	2,281	2,694	3,420	3,694	6,585	0.08	78.26
Australasia	**32,074**	**36,290**	**36,154**	**45,265**	**49,371**	**0.59**	**9.07**
Australia	28,928	32,619	31,439	40,306	44,741	0.53	11.00
New Zealand	3,146	3,671	4,715	4,959	4,630	0.06	-6.63
Melanesia	**256**	**300**	**215**	**109**	**183**	**0.00**	**67.89**
Solomon Islands	3	21					
Fiji	31	61	93	20	53	0.00	165.00
New Caledonia	40	77	26	13	61	0.00	369.23
Norfolk Island	180	24	84				
Papua New Guinea	2	117	12	76	69	0.00	-9.21
Micronesia	**165**	**151**	**13**	**2**	**22**	**0.00**	**1000.00**
Kiribati		28					
Guam		20	13	2	16	0.00	700.00
Nauru	16	93					
Micronesia, Federated States of					6	0.00	
Marshall Islands	2						
Palau	147	10					
Polynesia	**728**	**1,324**	**86**	**212**	**39**	**0.00**	**-81.60**
American Samoa	265	519	46				
French Polynesia	6	46	27	150	25	0.00	-83.33
Niue	13	113					
Tokelau	59	7					
Tonga		21	2	62	14	0.00	-77.42
Tuvalu	81	38					
Wallis and Futuna Islands	48	529					
Samoa	256	51	11				
EUROPE	**7,474,634**	**7,107,836**	**6,757,450**	**7,147,489**	**7,514,760**	**89.49**	**5.14**
Central/Eastern Europe	**1,264,378**	**1,230,703**	**1,133,044**	**1,245,609**	**1,422,092**	**16.93**	**14.17**
Azerbaijan	2,519	1,882	2,364	2,039	2,513	0.03	23.25
Armenia	1,720	966	6,664	7,830	9,317	0.11	18.99
Bulgaria	17,179	24,087	19,447	17,852	21,385	0.25	19.79
Belarus	127,740	85,000	84,504	100,399	126,589	1.51	26.09

POLAND

5. Overnight stays of non-resident tourists in hotels and similar establishments, by country of residence

	2007	2008	2009	2010	2011	Market share 11	% Change 11-10
Czech Republic	114,240	129,379	145,521	150,899	153,983	1.83	2.04
Estonia	60,981	45,956	38,970	36,553	42,981	0.51	17.59
Georgia	2,495	4,484	15,936	15,851	4,661	0.06	-70.59
Hungary	81,782	85,278	80,692	84,227	90,651	1.08	7.63
Kazakhstan	9,313	5,105	4,897	5,254	7,445	0.09	41.70
Kyrgyzstan	362	294	232	582	899	0.01	54.47
Latvia	59,357	58,094	42,741	48,878	57,067	0.68	16.75
Lithuania	118,556	126,848	118,738	116,183	119,978	1.43	3.27
Republic of Moldova	16,492	16,228	10,731	5,771	5,537	0.07	-4.05
Romania	36,979	48,119	43,429	50,647	56,908	0.68	12.36
Russian Federation	302,477	325,423	277,456	313,057	383,731	4.57	22.58
Slovakia	50,554	55,449	64,611	88,294	94,274	1.12	6.77
Tajikistan	484	244	216	440	109	0.00	-75.23
Turkmenistan	98	59	67	63	212	0.00	236.51
Ukraine	258,564	215,390	175,161	199,268	241,771	2.88	21.33
Uzbekistan	2,486	2,418	667	1,522	2,081	0.02	36.73
Northern Europe	**1,739,316**	**1,669,463**	**1,513,900**	**1,537,774**	**1,559,441**	**18.57**	**1.41**
Denmark	236,691	203,893	195,061	172,905	178,090	2.12	3.00
Faeroe Islands	148	142	4				
Finland	79,761	81,920	89,536	106,234	121,936	1.45	14.78
Iceland	5,752	5,150	3,475	5,545	3,949	0.05	-28.78
Ireland	136,042	110,836	91,898	94,366	94,655	1.13	0.31
Norway	225,399	215,500	211,537	240,910	245,009	2.92	1.70
Svalbard and Jan Mayen Islands		16	23	15			
Sweden	220,542	210,072	206,559	195,175	203,457	2.42	4.24
United Kingdom	834,981	841,934	715,807	722,624	712,345	8.48	-1.42
Southern Europe	**766,739**	**711,397**	**703,608**	**739,941**	**837,877**	**9.98**	**13.24**
Albania	2,676	635	3,213	3,178	3,982	0.05	25.30
Andorra	992	164	193	930	548	0.01	-41.08
Bosnia and Herzegovina	1,411	1,393	2,502	4,599	3,211	0.04	-30.18
Croatia	14,482	16,415	13,765	16,812	17,822	0.21	6.01
Gibraltar	20	16	37	144	103	0.00	-28.47
Greece	25,118	28,109	36,397	26,242	28,691	0.34	9.33
Holy See	25	12	374	246	174	0.00	-29.27
Italy	443,766	398,082	374,970	397,485	420,638	5.01	5.82
Malta	2,133	2,641	1,398	2,439	4,021	0.05	64.86
Montenegro	595	430	347	336	1,063	0.01	216.37
Portugal	32,222	33,956	35,512	36,687	44,338	0.53	20.85
San Marino	97	38	257	58	305	0.00	425.86
Serbia	3,622	4,189	4,962	8,466	9,486	0.11	12.05
Slovenia	15,043	13,960	17,139	15,482	16,692	0.20	7.82
Spain	223,020	210,241	210,777	225,405	285,020	3.39	26.45
TFYR of Macedonia	1,517	1,116	1,765	1,432	1,783	0.02	24.51
Western Europe	**3,426,418**	**3,271,411**	**3,127,648**	**3,327,263**	**3,370,504**	**40.14**	**1.30**
Austria	103,104	96,668	100,498	100,215	107,819	1.28	7.59
Belgium	108,539	101,772	99,348	113,774	118,769	1.41	4.39
France	339,126	334,525	312,494	324,221	350,702	4.18	8.17
Germany	2,629,480	2,489,128	2,377,950	2,540,966	2,533,533	30.17	-0.29
Liechtenstein	469	475	1,497	486	605	0.01	24.49
Luxembourg	4,506	4,548	4,937	6,836	6,533	0.08	-4.43
Monaco	390	412	601	386	337	0.00	-12.69
Netherlands	186,036	182,438	170,440	179,677	187,680	2.23	4.45
Switzerland	54,768	61,445	59,883	60,702	64,526	0.77	6.30
East Mediterranean Europe	**277,783**	**224,862**	**279,250**	**296,902**	**324,846**	**3.87**	**9.41**
Cyprus	5,598	6,686	6,334	5,928	4,180	0.05	-29.49
Israel	247,601	188,868	242,475	258,838	281,377	3.35	8.71
Turkey	24,584	29,308	30,441	32,136	39,289	0.47	22.26

POLAND

5. Overnight stays of non-resident tourists in hotels and similar establishments, by country of residence

	2007	2008	2009	2010	2011	Market share 11	% Change 11-10
MIDDLE EAST	**14,164**	**11,330**	**17,626**	**20,015**	**25,821**	**0.31**	**29.01**
Bahrain	819	254	763	883	865	0.01	-2.04
Iraq	1,006	847	941	750	2,043	0.02	172.40
Jordan	459	501	530	457	977	0.01	113.79
Kuwait	766	1,104	1,195	1,332	1,898	0.02	42.49
Lebanon	693	807	1,505	1,036	1,233	0.01	19.02
Libya	340	595	397	862	586	0.01	-32.02
Oman	51	48	163	635	269	0.00	-57.64
Qatar	1,279	231	1,522	2,765	1,384	0.02	-49.95
Saudi Arabia	2,481	1,742	2,568	3,508	7,264	0.09	107.07
Syrian Arab Republic	382	310	522	520	959	0.01	84.42
United Arab Emirates	1,895	1,682	3,700	2,730	3,245	0.04	18.86
Egypt	3,725	3,161	3,743	4,493	4,955	0.06	10.28
Yemen	268	48	77	44	143	0.00	225.00
SOUTH ASIA	**29,941**	**33,906**	**33,415**	**39,877**	**46,033**	**0.55**	**15.44**
Afghanistan	1,073	447	2,928	4,590	6,255	0.07	36.27
Bangladesh	865	826	1,959	1,628	2,899	0.03	78.07
Bhutan	458	1,074	278	399	212	0.00	-46.87
Sri Lanka	240	229	190	333	514	0.01	54.35
India	20,395	23,717	22,201	26,395	29,273	0.35	10.90
Iran, Islamic Republic of	4,468	5,669	4,014	4,990	4,948	0.06	-0.84
Maldives	8	27	11	126	34	0.00	-73.02
Nepal	196	632	466	204	187	0.00	-8.33
Pakistan	2,238	1,285	1,368	1,212	1,711	0.02	41.17
NOT SPECIFIED	**86,434**	**81,638**	**38,332**	**58,080**	**47,066**	**0.56**	**-18.96**
Other countries of the World	86,434	81,638	38,332	58,080	47,066	0.56	-18.96

POLAND

6. Overnight stays of non-resident tourists in all types of accommodation establishments, by country of residence

	2007	2008	2009	2010	2011	Market share 11	% Change 11-10
TOTAL	10,918,100	10,173,237	9,609,447	10,064,628	10,620,264	100.00	5.52
AFRICA	18,976	19,849	23,095	25,862	26,068	0.25	0.80
East Africa	2,669	2,477	1,803	2,958	2,152	0.02	-27.25
British Indian Ocean Territory	14	17					
Burundi	106	93	83	46	74	0.00	60.87
Comoros			4	4			
Ethiopia	118	235	229	527	244	0.00	-53.70
Eritrea	162	16					
Djibouti	6	8	52	4	17	0.00	325.00
Kenya	701	783	538	629	528	0.00	-16.06
Madagascar	67	80	15	106	78	0.00	-26.42
Malawi	100	5	27	34	24	0.00	-29.41
Mauritius	108	107	33	152	89	0.00	-41.45
Mozambique	77	17	9	48	61	0.00	27.08
Reunion	46	147	2				
Rwanda	118	112	30	235	200	0.00	-14.89
Seychelles	37	108	33	47	31	0.00	-34.04
Somalia	146	40	51	222	93	0.00	-58.11
Zimbabwe	327	189	315	192	170	0.00	-11.46
Uganda	109	92	238	343	262	0.00	-23.62
United Republic of Tanzania	220	63	65	261	137	0.00	-47.51
Zambia	207	365	79	108	144	0.00	33.33
Central Africa	1,410	1,312	1,744	1,957	2,367	0.02	20.95
Angola	595	416	654	1,365	1,074	0.01	-21.32
Cameroon	176	220	254	212	467	0.00	120.28
Central African Republic	11	28	187	95	555	0.01	484.21
Chad	23	5	101	9	16	0.00	77.78
Congo	514	295	350	232	211	0.00	-9.05
Democratic Republic of the Congo	40	267	118	38	37	0.00	-2.63
Equatorial Guinea	1			6	7	0.00	16.67
Gabon	36	60	80				
Sao Tome and Principe	14	21					
North Africa	4,190	4,490	6,064	10,117	9,495	0.09	-6.15
Algeria	2,066	1,840	2,435	4,270	4,726	0.04	10.68
Morocco	979	1,470	1,331	4,174	2,530	0.02	-39.39
Western Sahara	403	4	602	130	45	0.00	-65.38
Sudan	40	65	176	154	277	0.00	79.87
Tunisia	702	1,111	1,520	1,389	1,917	0.02	38.01
Southern Africa	4,454	4,658	5,747	4,871	6,472	0.06	32.87
Botswana	9	57	132	79	25	0.00	-68.35
Lesotho	83	4	23	19	19	0.00	
Namibia	34	94	240	60	803	0.01	1238.33
South Africa	4,138	4,232	5,064	4,713	5,625	0.05	19.35
Swaziland	190	271	288				
West Africa	6,253	6,912	7,737	5,959	5,582	0.05	-6.33
Cape Verde	32	44	16	14	42	0.00	200.00
Benin	21	110	117	94	52	0.00	-44.68
Gambia	1,167	522	70	85	10	0.00	-88.24
Ghana	219	109	91	215	436	0.00	102.79
Guinea	408	351	140	36	25	0.00	-30.56
Côte d'Ivoire	106	140	130	176	68	0.00	-61.36
Liberia	33	105	11	56	40	0.00	-28.57
Mali	106	66	38	59	92	0.00	55.93
Mauritania	24	365	88	28	33	0.00	17.86
Niger	114	285	674	2,057	477	0.00	-76.81
Nigeria	3,175	3,995	4,129	1,939	3,183	0.03	64.16

POLAND

6. Overnight stays of non-resident tourists in all types of accommodation establishments, by country of residence

	2007	2008	2009	2010	2011	Market share 11	% Change 11-10
Guinea-Bissau	124	8	3		14	0.00	
Saint Helena	18	8	90	31	8	0.00	-74.19
Senegal	328	335	1,444	774	649	0.01	-16.15
Sierra Leone	218	376	587	365	351	0.00	-3.84
Togo	31	47	34	5	20	0.00	300.00
Burkina Faso	129	46	75	25	82	0.00	228.00
AMERICAS	**546,739**	**471,598**	**427,512**	**493,842**	**510,862**	**4.81**	**3.45**
Caribbean	**2,295**	**4,948**	**1,883**	**1,761**	**4,232**	**0.04**	**140.32**
Antigua and Barbuda	264	22	18				
Bahamas	168	834	69	212	1,540	0.01	626.42
Barbados	164	631	239	123	73	0.00	-40.65
Bermuda	45	158	41	14	116	0.00	728.57
British Virgin Islands	37	431	1				
Cayman Islands		4	50	56	27	0.00	-51.79
Cuba	788	807	685	672	723	0.01	7.59
Dominica	51	61	21	59	79	0.00	33.90
Dominican Republic	206	97	245	191	343	0.00	79.58
Grenada	8	93	2				
Guadeloupe	6	5	19	4	5	0.00	25.00
Haiti	10	68	20	57	167	0.00	192.98
Jamaica	141	706	252	136	177	0.00	30.15
Martinique		15	2		34	0.00	
Netherlands Antilles	10	12	1				
Aruba	22	17	27	15	16	0.00	6.67
Puerto Rico	117	454	150	171	843	0.01	392.98
Saint Kitts and Nevis	1	4	6				
Anguilla	4	6	14				
Saint Lucia	2	24					
Trinidad and Tobago	16	312	19	51	89	0.00	74.51
Turks and Caicos Islands	11	181	2				
United States Virgin Islands	224	6					
Central America	**2,111**	**1,598**	**3,628**	**3,300**	**2,758**	**0.03**	**-16.42**
Belize	474	98	131	82	114	0.00	39.02
Costa Rica	607	570	374	639	481	0.00	-24.73
El Salvador	103	118	114	102	192	0.00	88.24
Guatemala	92	114	156	137	192	0.00	40.15
Honduras	631	156	2,438	1,510	1,489	0.01	-1.39
Nicaragua	83	371	266	271	132	0.00	-51.29
Panama	121	171	149	559	158	0.00	-71.74
North America	**513,490**	**429,124**	**390,051**	**448,751**	**454,374**	**4.28**	**1.25**
Canada	51,316	52,717	54,822	64,142	64,778	0.61	0.99
Greenland		2	19	3			
Mexico	16,116	13,255	8,251	10,631	15,572	0.15	46.48
Saint Pierre and Miquelon	3	3					
United States of America	446,055	363,147	326,959	373,975	374,024	3.52	0.01
South America	**28,843**	**35,928**	**31,950**	**40,030**	**49,498**	**0.47**	**23.65**
Argentina	4,878	5,421	5,121	5,381	7,838	0.07	45.66
Bolivia	758	135	1,729	2,318	2,535	0.02	9.36
Brazil	17,114	22,312	17,624	23,497	29,395	0.28	25.10
Chile	2,710	2,094	1,759	2,195	2,742	0.03	24.92
Colombia	886	1,388	1,522	1,662	2,584	0.02	55.48
Ecuador	213	485	839	841	383	0.00	-54.46
Falkland Islands, Malvinas	3		86	2	8	0.00	300.00
French Guiana	8	32	7	1	39	0.00	3800.00
Guyana	58	25	3	3	151	0.00	4933.33
Paraguay	31	32	37	280	234	0.00	-16.43
Peru	923	735	918	851	812	0.01	-4.58

POLAND

6. Overnight stays of non-resident tourists in all types of accommodation establishments, by country of residence

	2007	2008	2009	2010	2011	Market share 11	% Change 11-10
Suriname	251	215	97	66			
Uruguay	285	388	571	959	1,282	0.01	33.68
Venezuela	725	2,666	1,637	1,974	1,495	0.01	-24.27
EAST ASIA AND THE PACIFIC	**309,266**	**286,891**	**243,534**	**317,019**	**311,619**	**2.93**	**-1.70**
North-East Asia	**244,160**	**215,066**	**174,133**	**234,855**	**212,601**	**2.00**	**-9.48**
China	38,314	57,754	39,383	58,167	66,542	0.63	14.40
Taiwan, Province of China	2,379	2,707	3,242	3,065	4,781	0.05	55.99
Hong Kong, China	2,261	3,245	7,054	8,553	9,866	0.09	15.35
Japan	118,107	95,559	74,193	105,300	76,584	0.72	-27.27
Korea, Dem. People's Republic of	8,373	11,977	23,418	31,279	25,940	0.24	-17.07
Korea, Republic of	74,114	43,057	25,589	27,208	26,483	0.25	-2.66
Macao, China	6	23	220	117	96	0.00	-17.95
Mongolia	606	744	1,034	1,166	2,309	0.02	98.03
South-East Asia	**20,868**	**24,283**	**23,467**	**25,495**	**36,413**	**0.34**	**42.82**
Brunei Darussalam	286	46	13	80	25	0.00	-68.75
Myanmar	29	14	17	5	16	0.00	220.00
Cambodia	12	55	26	75	73	0.00	-2.67
Indonesia	2,480	4,431	3,305	2,279	4,514	0.04	98.07
Lao People's Democratic Republic	21	45	47	34	57	0.00	67.65
Malaysia	6,495	8,072	5,315	5,601	5,163	0.05	-7.82
Philippines	2,722	2,783	2,613	2,241	5,331	0.05	137.88
Timor-Leste	9	15		1	6	0.00	500.00
Singapore	2,816	3,824	4,429	7,457	9,858	0.09	32.20
Viet Nam	3,596	2,233	4,131	3,718	4,235	0.04	13.91
Thailand	2,402	2,765	3,571	4,004	7,135	0.07	78.20
Australasia	**43,070**	**45,599**	**45,594**	**56,287**	**62,351**	**0.59**	**10.77**
Australia	38,436	40,311	39,392	50,090	56,364	0.53	12.53
New Zealand	4,634	5,288	6,202	6,197	5,987	0.06	-3.39
Melanesia	**268**	**346**	**217**	**166**	**189**	**0.00**	**13.86**
Solomon Islands	11	23					
Fiji	32	105	95	20	58	0.00	190.00
New Caledonia	43	77	26	70	62	0.00	-11.43
Norfolk Island	180	24	84				
Papua New Guinea	2	117	12	76	69	0.00	-9.21
Micronesia	**165**	**194**	**26**	**2**	**22**	**0.00**	**1000.00**
Kiribati		70					
Guam		20	13	2	16	0.00	700.00
Nauru	16	94	13				
Micronesia, Federated States of					6	0.00	
Marshall Islands	2						
Palau	147	10					
Polynesia	**735**	**1,403**	**97**	**214**	**43**	**0.00**	**-79.91**
American Samoa	267	519	46				
French Polynesia	11	50	38	152	29	0.00	-80.92
Niue	13	113					
Tokelau	59	7					
Tonga		21	2	62	14	0.00	-77.42
Tuvalu	81	38					
Wallis and Futuna Islands	48	604					
Samoa	256	51	11				
EUROPE	**9,900,334**	**9,260,421**	**8,802,443**	**9,083,870**	**9,644,744**	**90.81**	**6.17**
Central/Eastern Europe	**1,644,262**	**1,571,415**	**1,428,204**	**1,525,689**	**1,734,920**	**16.34**	**13.71**
Azerbaijan	2,622	2,121	2,932	2,514	2,902	0.03	15.43
Armenia	2,142	1,384	6,982	8,089	9,618	0.09	18.90
Bulgaria	21,830	28,851	24,208	20,935	26,336	0.25	25.80
Belarus	167,787	111,505	110,874	128,721	166,008	1.56	28.97

POLAND

6. Overnight stays of non-resident tourists in all types of accommodation establishments, by country of residence

	2007	2008	2009	2010	2011	Market share 11	% Change 11-10
Czech Republic	149,142	170,684	185,282	182,037	182,488	1.72	0.25
Estonia	66,474	51,125	45,398	39,420	46,080	0.43	16.89
Georgia	4,026	6,337	19,092	16,480	6,384	0.06	-61.26
Hungary	108,738	110,708	98,695	102,314	109,595	1.03	7.12
Kazakhstan	10,923	7,817	6,461	6,955	8,796	0.08	26.47
Kyrgyzstan	426	435	330	696	1,185	0.01	70.26
Latvia	70,926	67,875	48,525	54,450	64,043	0.60	17.62
Lithuania	150,728	158,702	146,607	139,407	141,070	1.33	1.19
Republic of Moldova	17,640	17,804	12,394	8,453	6,669	0.06	-21.10
Romania	48,826	60,572	55,041	69,533	74,049	0.70	6.49
Russian Federation	354,618	364,182	314,452	356,019	439,405	4.14	23.42
Slovakia	67,557	74,516	87,764	110,548	116,362	1.10	5.26
Tajikistan	493	349	222	1,032	1,023	0.01	-0.87
Turkmenistan	106	60	95	64	221	0.00	245.31
Ukraine	396,613	333,110	261,125	275,695	330,374	3.11	19.83
Uzbekistan	2,645	3,278	1,725	2,327	2,312	0.02	-0.64
Northern Europe	**1,888,327**	**1,811,326**	**1,646,811**	**1,678,802**	**1,690,748**	**15.92**	**0.71**
Denmark	257,298	225,635	215,086	189,395	195,853	1.84	3.41
Faeroe Islands	148	148	50				
Finland	89,374	93,995	98,262	117,164	132,129	1.24	12.77
Iceland	6,174	5,428	4,085	5,935	4,246	0.04	-28.46
Ireland	148,150	119,170	100,562	106,780	103,997	0.98	-2.61
Norway	238,224	230,785	224,005	256,073	261,127	2.46	1.97
Svalbard and Jan Mayen Islands		16	23	15			
Sweden	265,420	245,986	242,071	226,951	233,081	2.19	2.70
United Kingdom	883,539	890,163	762,667	776,489	760,315	7.16	-2.08
Southern Europe	**844,082**	**773,145**	**777,522**	**826,288**	**923,809**	**8.70**	**11.80**
Albania	2,809	792	3,620	3,433	4,200	0.04	22.34
Andorra	1,052	177	209	938	569	0.01	-39.34
Bosnia and Herzegovina	1,760	2,062	2,852	4,942	3,769	0.04	-23.74
Croatia	16,838	18,668	16,447	19,381	20,682	0.19	6.71
Gibraltar	20	25	37	144	103	0.00	-28.47
Greece	28,453	30,165	38,505	28,300	30,780	0.29	8.76
Holy See	25	12	497	252	234	0.00	-7.14
Italy	486,825	427,114	408,730	430,151	454,508	4.28	5.66
Malta	2,269	2,913	1,578	2,756	4,229	0.04	53.45
Montenegro	678	473	558	456	1,091	0.01	139.25
Portugal	36,396	38,471	39,842	41,738	50,117	0.47	20.08
San Marino	101	38	271	84	419	0.00	398.81
Serbia	5,153	6,421	7,610	11,012	12,420	0.12	12.79
Slovenia	17,794	15,890	20,070	17,862	18,644	0.18	4.38
Spain	241,625	228,102	234,380	252,341	318,698	3.00	26.30
TFYR of Macedonia	2,284	1,822	2,316	12,498	3,346	0.03	-73.23
Western Europe	**5,230,908**	**4,866,456**	**4,656,940**	**4,742,259**	**4,953,847**	**46.65**	**4.46**
Austria	123,331	107,889	111,382	112,274	119,380	1.12	6.33
Belgium	129,143	117,435	114,459	131,160	133,359	1.26	1.68
France	405,653	385,550	359,408	380,666	403,854	3.80	6.09
Germany	4,276,320	3,960,270	3,797,376	3,828,542	4,002,950	37.69	4.56
Liechtenstein	537	511	1,528	513	633	0.01	23.39
Luxembourg	5,124	5,040	5,348	7,763	7,066	0.07	-8.98
Monaco	397	499	710	500	378	0.00	-24.40
Netherlands	230,541	222,707	201,404	214,978	216,947	2.04	0.92
Switzerland	59,862	66,555	65,325	65,863	69,280	0.65	5.19
East Mediterranean Europe	**292,755**	**238,079**	**292,966**	**310,832**	**341,420**	**3.21**	**9.84**
Cyprus	5,757	6,832	6,839	6,165	4,617	0.04	-25.11
Israel	254,405	196,656	252,245	267,809	288,906	2.72	7.88
Turkey	32,593	34,591	33,882	36,858	47,897	0.45	29.95

POLAND

6. Overnight stays of non-resident tourists in all types of accommodation establishments, by country of residence

	2007	2008	2009	2010	2011	Market share 11	% Change 11-10
MIDDLE EAST	**16,505**	**14,129**	**20,722**	**23,400**	**29,779**	**0.28**	**27.26**
Bahrain	824	254	782	899	865	0.01	-3.78
Iraq	1,137	1,086	1,178	1,359	2,533	0.02	86.39
Jordan	723	612	739	579	1,184	0.01	104.49
Kuwait	915	1,236	1,349	1,399	1,919	0.02	37.17
Lebanon	970	887	1,641	1,156	1,275	0.01	10.29
Libya	495	669	582	1,004	786	0.01	-21.71
Oman	53	61	169	640	270	0.00	-57.81
Qatar	1,283	236	1,710	2,795	1,719	0.02	-38.50
Saudi Arabia	2,602	1,793	2,798	3,712	7,519	0.07	102.56
Syrian Arab Republic	488	417	720	869	1,192	0.01	37.17
United Arab Emirates	1,984	1,729	4,170	3,897	4,174	0.04	7.11
Egypt	4,762	5,068	4,807	5,022	6,191	0.06	23.28
Yemen	269	81	77	69	152	0.00	120.29
SOUTH ASIA	**36,993**	**37,029**	**53,656**	**58,210**	**49,475**	**0.47**	**-15.01**
Afghanistan	1,101	476	2,966	8,622	6,285	0.06	-27.11
Bangladesh	965	851	2,495	1,827	2,916	0.03	59.61
Bhutan	462	1,075	280	403	214	0.00	-46.90
Sri Lanka	287	273	343	393	535	0.01	36.13
India	26,765	25,969	34,300	34,791	31,282	0.29	-10.09
Iran, Islamic Republic of	4,796	6,199	4,397	5,342	5,604	0.05	4.90
Maldives	8	27	13	126	35	0.00	-72.22
Nepal	237	724	7,272	4,466	384	0.00	-91.40
Pakistan	2,372	1,435	1,590	2,240	2,220	0.02	-0.89
NOT SPECIFIED	**89,287**	**83,320**	**38,485**	**62,425**	**47,717**	**0.45**	**-23.56**
Other countries of the World	89,287	83,320	38,485	62,425	47,717	0.45	-23.56

PORTUGAL

3. Arrivals of non-resident tourists in hotels and similar establishments, by country of residence

	2007	2008	2009	2010	2011	Market share 11	% Change 11-10
TOTAL	6,290,607	6,421,762	5,911,079	6,256,808	6,792,220	100.00	8.56
AFRICA	67,143	66,113	72,785	73,519	82,981	1.22	12.87
Southern Africa	10,562	9,484	6,941	8,497	10,208	0.15	20.14
South Africa	10,562	9,484	6,941	8,497	10,208	0.15	20.14
Other Africa	56,581	56,629	65,844	65,022	72,773	1.07	11.92
Other countries of Africa	56,581	56,629	65,844	65,022	72,773	1.07	11.92
AMERICAS	623,765	657,972	607,432	743,093	860,255	12.67	15.77
North America	333,651	303,147	285,548	322,548	351,429	5.17	8.95
Canada	77,995	78,859	59,676	69,459	86,492	1.27	24.52
United States of America	255,656	224,288	225,872	253,089	264,937	3.90	4.68
South America	236,828	295,971	260,801	355,226	433,344	6.38	21.99
Brazil	236,828	295,971	260,801	355,226	433,344	6.38	21.99
Other Americas	53,286	58,854	61,083	65,319	75,482	1.11	15.56
Other countries of the Americas	53,286	58,854	61,083	65,319	75,482	1.11	15.56
EAST ASIA AND THE PACIFIC	203,496	190,427	181,740	221,740	253,807	3.74	14.46
North-East Asia	103,132	98,414	88,383	114,810	125,097	1.84	8.96
China	23,117	22,665	21,647	29,089	37,258	0.55	28.08
Japan	65,286	62,471	56,727	60,942	57,857	0.85	-5.06
Korea, Republic of	14,729	13,278	10,009	24,779	29,982	0.44	21.00
Australasia	28,556	29,281	25,334	29,481	34,051	0.50	15.50
Australia	28,556	29,281	25,334	29,481	34,051	0.50	15.50
Other East Asia and the Pacific	71,808	62,732	68,023	77,449	94,659	1.39	22.22
Other countries of Asia	48,994	54,283	62,224	71,211	88,336	1.30	24.05
Other countries of Oceania	22,814	8,449	5,799	6,238	6,323	0.09	1.36
EUROPE	5,396,203	5,507,250	5,049,122	5,218,456	5,595,177	82.38	7.22
Central/Eastern Europe	160,690	192,934	171,187	203,747	258,004	3.80	26.63
Bulgaria	6,083	6,018	6,584	7,043	6,842	0.10	-2.85
Hungary	22,643	22,485	16,646	16,422	18,165	0.27	10.61
Poland	66,128	76,422	72,596	82,609	102,417	1.51	23.98
Romania	19,249	25,245	19,942	21,101	22,591	0.33	7.06
USSR (former)	46,587	62,764	55,419	76,572	107,989	1.59	41.03
Northern Europe	1,698,601	1,732,964	1,386,825	1,431,672	1,535,947	22.61	7.28
Denmark	84,994	91,836	76,368	86,693	74,899	1.10	-13.60
Finland	65,061	79,068	74,647	75,031	70,353	1.04	-6.23
Iceland	4,053	4,478	2,213	4,135	2,546	0.04	-38.43
Ireland	162,434	164,739	146,703	148,647	154,546	2.28	3.97
Norway	76,899	70,756	55,776	58,085	64,889	0.96	11.71
Sweden	96,771	102,277	79,878	86,906	84,460	1.24	-2.81
United Kingdom	1,208,389	1,219,810	951,240	972,175	1,084,254	15.96	11.53
Southern Europe	1,701,317	1,608,775	1,615,501	1,666,233	1,696,479	24.98	1.82
Greece	19,879	17,932	17,570	14,417	18,221	0.27	26.39
Italy	378,641	355,061	309,075	344,508	363,427	5.35	5.49
Spain	1,302,797	1,235,782	1,288,856	1,307,308	1,314,831	19.36	0.58
Western Europe	1,744,294	1,844,259	1,723,294	1,798,845	1,950,529	28.72	8.43
Austria	77,391	67,336	68,680	63,340	67,583	1.00	6.70
Belgium	140,502	147,859	136,618	135,527	146,513	2.16	8.11
France	472,937	532,754	527,501	542,195	619,753	9.12	14.30
Germany	665,585	678,918	636,281	643,359	650,096	9.57	1.05
Luxembourg	10,819	9,604	11,103	10,597	12,887	0.19	21.61
Netherlands	283,525	311,933	287,335	304,404	338,848	4.99	11.32
Switzerland	93,535	95,855	55,776	99,423	114,849	1.69	15.52

PORTUGAL

3. Arrivals of non-resident tourists in hotels and similar establishments, by country of residence

	2007	2008	2009	2010	2011	Market share 11	% Change 11-10
East Mediterranean Europe	**6,907**	**7,639**	**6,618**	**8,740**	**11,083**	**0.16**	**26.81**
Turkey	6,907	7,639	6,618	8,740	11,083	0.16	26.81
Other Europe	**84,394**	**120,679**	**145,697**	**109,219**	**143,135**	**2.11**	**31.05**
Other countries of Europe	84,394	120,679	145,697	109,219	143,135	2.11	31.05

PORTUGAL

4. Arrivals of non-resident tourists in all types of accommodation establishments, by country of residence

	2007	2008	2009	2010	2011	Market share 11	% Change 11-10
TOTAL	6,787,797	6,961,707	6,439,022	6,756,354	7,263,644	100.00	7.51
AFRICA	70,030	67,619	73,882	75,446	84,319	1.16	11.76
Southern Africa	11,849	9,794	7,163	8,944	10,464	0.14	16.99
South Africa	11,849	9,794	7,163	8,944	10,464	0.14	16.99
Other Africa	58,181	57,825	66,719	66,502	73,855	1.02	11.06
Other countries of Africa	58,181	57,825	66,719	66,502	73,855	1.02	11.06
AMERICAS	642,586	676,186	622,683	759,506	874,361	12.04	15.12
North America	341,118	308,875	290,834	328,002	356,165	4.90	8.59
Canada	81,269	81,807	62,058	71,851	88,732	1.22	23.49
United States of America	259,849	227,068	228,776	256,151	267,433	3.68	4.40
South America	246,190	306,228	268,913	363,871	440,787	6.07	21.14
Brazil	246,190	306,228	268,913	363,871	440,787	6.07	21.14
Other Americas	55,278	61,083	62,936	67,633	77,409	1.07	14.45
Other countries of the Americas	55,278	61,083	62,936	67,633	77,409	1.07	14.45
EAST ASIA AND THE PACIFIC	212,794	201,612	190,419	229,173	261,440	3.60	14.08
North-East Asia	105,294	100,573	89,799	116,108	126,292	1.74	8.77
China	23,529	23,152	21,929	29,424	37,587	0.52	27.74
Japan	66,446	63,486	57,641	61,690	58,492	0.81	-5.18
Korea, Republic of	15,319	13,935	10,229	24,994	30,213	0.42	20.88
Australasia	32,737	34,783	30,308	33,143	38,225	0.53	15.33
Australia	32,737	34,783	30,308	33,143	38,225	0.53	15.33
Other East Asia and the Pacific	74,763	66,256	70,312	79,922	96,923	1.33	21.27
Other countries of Asia	49,800	55,185	62,887	72,417	89,359	1.23	23.40
Other countries of Oceania	24,963	11,071	7,425	7,505	7,564	0.10	0.79
EUROPE	5,862,387	6,016,290	5,552,038	5,692,229	6,043,524	83.20	6.17
Central/Eastern Europe	168,557	204,304	181,256	212,829	266,584	3.67	25.26
Bulgaria	6,338	6,320	6,941	7,358	7,178	0.10	-2.45
Hungary	23,769	23,919	17,694	17,271	18,933	0.26	9.62
Poland	71,185	83,918	79,323	89,095	108,350	1.49	21.61
Romania	20,017	26,182	20,622	21,885	23,395	0.32	6.90
USSR (former)	47,248	63,965	56,676	77,220	108,728	1.50	40.80
Northern Europe	1,749,484	1,789,132	1,436,703	1,478,999	1,576,701	21.71	6.61
Denmark	89,076	95,927	79,924	89,879	78,116	1.08	-13.09
Finland	66,568	80,951	76,455	76,757	72,518	1.00	-5.52
Iceland	4,074	4,516	2,231	4,192	2,566	0.04	-38.79
Ireland	166,453	168,705	149,809	151,786	156,990	2.16	3.43
Norway	78,263	72,292	57,199	59,380	66,291	0.91	11.64
Sweden	99,136	104,870	81,962	88,864	86,822	1.20	-2.30
United Kingdom	1,245,914	1,261,871	989,123	1,008,141	1,113,398	15.33	10.44
Southern Europe	1,845,490	1,764,218	1,767,778	1,818,614	1,836,104	25.28	0.96
Greece	20,462	18,620	18,319	14,722	18,657	0.26	26.73
Italy	401,994	380,226	330,105	364,908	382,711	5.27	4.88
Spain	1,423,034	1,365,372	1,419,354	1,438,984	1,434,736	19.75	-0.30
Western Europe	1,999,621	2,121,535	2,006,249	2,057,084	2,203,102	30.33	7.10
Austria	81,672	71,867	72,873	67,169	71,523	0.98	6.48
Belgium	158,292	169,913	154,990	152,851	162,325	2.23	6.20
France	594,259	665,737	663,022	666,958	747,153	10.29	12.02
Germany	722,084	736,200	702,542	695,247	701,458	9.66	0.89
Luxembourg	11,165	10,072	11,745	11,078	13,487	0.19	21.75
Netherlands	331,005	363,215	337,349	356,749	384,694	5.30	7.83
Switzerland	101,144	104,531	63,728	107,032	122,462	1.69	14.42

PORTUGAL

4. Arrivals of non-resident tourists in all types of accommodation establishments, by country of residence

	2007	2008	2009	2010	2011	Market share 11	% Change 11-10
East Mediterranean Europe	**7,050**	**7,830**	**6,737**	**8,873**	**11,347**	**0.16**	**27.88**
Turkey	7,050	7,830	6,737	8,873	11,347	0.16	27.88
Other Europe	**92,185**	**129,271**	**153,315**	**115,830**	**149,686**	**2.06**	**29.23**
Other countries of Europe	92,185	129,271	153,315	115,830	149,686	2.06	29.23

PORTUGAL

5. Overnight stays of non-resident tourists in hotels and similar establishments, by country of residence

	2007	2008	2009	2010	2011	Market share 11	% Change 11-10
TOTAL	26,768,530	26,204,245	23,214,377	23,608,207	26,003,760	100.00	10.15
AFRICA	240,911	235,565	266,501	268,870	292,404	1.12	8.75
Southern Africa	12,277	31,657	23,388	26,925	33,413	0.13	24.10
South Africa	12,277	31,657	23,388	26,925	33,413	0.13	24.10
Other Africa	228,634	203,908	243,113	241,945	258,991	1.00	7.05
Other countries of Africa	228,634	203,908	243,113	241,945	258,991	1.00	7.05
AMERICAS	1,632,371	1,674,192	1,482,342	1,785,586	2,064,495	7.94	15.62
North America	943,486	860,174	738,068	800,925	864,745	3.33	7.97
Canada	290,807	292,121	207,890	224,106	252,847	0.97	12.82
United States of America	652,679	568,053	530,178	576,819	611,898	2.35	6.08
South America	558,749	672,970	595,511	828,510	1,015,458	3.91	22.56
Brazil	558,749	672,970	595,511	828,510	1,015,458	3.91	22.56
Other Americas	130,136	141,048	148,763	156,151	184,292	0.71	18.02
Other countries of the Americas	130,136	141,048	148,763	156,151	184,292	0.71	18.02
EAST ASIA AND THE PACIFIC	475,615	438,573	433,282	484,508	556,593	2.14	14.88
North-East Asia	171,197	190,592	172,618	214,763	231,637	0.89	7.86
China	25,222	48,980	47,124	59,812	74,861	0.29	25.16
Japan	130,585	120,214	108,278	117,721	113,267	0.44	-3.78
Korea, Republic of	15,390	21,398	17,216	37,230	43,509	0.17	16.87
Australasia	78,601	76,307	67,630	74,038	87,805	0.34	18.59
Australia	78,601	76,307	67,630	74,038	87,805	0.34	18.59
Other East Asia and the Pacific	225,817	171,674	193,034	195,707	237,151	0.91	21.18
Other countries of Asia	172,042	146,545	172,936	180,177	220,043	0.85	22.13
Other countries of Oceania	53,775	25,129	20,098	15,530	17,108	0.07	10.16
EUROPE	24,419,633	23,855,915	21,032,252	21,069,243	23,090,268	88.80	9.59
Central/Eastern Europe	644,173	807,577	652,778	754,449	994,900	3.83	31.87
Bulgaria	18,795	17,652	18,382	19,896	21,726	0.08	9.20
Hungary	78,371	76,216	55,551	57,445	62,971	0.24	9.62
Poland	259,061	353,851	301,687	338,544	429,573	1.65	26.89
Romania	87,708	104,582	69,866	66,225	84,854	0.33	28.13
USSR (former)	200,238	255,276	207,292	272,339	395,776	1.52	45.32
Northern Europe	10,535,205	10,099,163	7,989,061	7,857,143	8,574,675	32.97	9.13
Denmark	475,345	482,287	388,854	434,122	362,288	1.39	-16.55
Finland	369,622	408,340	401,017	393,782	380,438	1.46	-3.39
Iceland	5,264	32,129	16,250	28,494	9,334	0.04	-67.24
Ireland	1,047,347	1,023,505	872,146	826,785	865,949	3.33	4.74
Norway	414,110	335,154	263,453	273,625	290,201	1.12	6.06
Sweden	518,373	515,670	377,660	405,382	407,902	1.57	0.62
United Kingdom	7,705,144	7,302,078	5,669,681	5,494,953	6,258,563	24.07	13.90
Southern Europe	4,453,787	4,058,436	4,065,206	4,190,547	4,419,837	17.00	5.47
Greece	62,371	59,872	58,225	43,452	56,515	0.22	30.06
Italy	1,010,500	929,096	803,211	869,313	918,210	3.53	5.62
Spain	3,380,916	3,069,468	3,203,770	3,277,782	3,445,112	13.25	5.10
Western Europe	8,450,057	8,479,346	7,896,037	7,895,256	8,611,941	33.12	9.08
Austria	349,077	294,959	307,855	266,003	289,739	1.11	8.92
Belgium	602,140	585,559	552,940	510,108	567,767	2.18	11.30
France	1,442,344	1,590,488	1,595,447	1,619,416	1,931,067	7.43	19.24
Germany	3,851,143	3,657,516	3,341,911	3,279,012	3,392,161	13.04	3.45
Luxembourg	45,700	43,878	45,284	42,866	48,786	0.19	13.81
Netherlands	1,825,862	1,974,157	1,789,147	1,843,369	1,992,895	7.66	8.11
Switzerland	333,791	332,789	263,453	334,482	389,526	1.50	16.46

PORTUGAL

5. Overnight stays of non-resident tourists in hotels and similar establishments, by country of residence

	2007	2008	2009	2010	2011	Market share 11	% Change 11-10
East Mediterranean Europe	**7,867**	**20,975**	**18,114**	**22,902**	**29,759**	**0.11**	**29.94**
Turkey	7,867	20,975	18,114	22,902	29,759	0.11	29.94
Other Europe	**328,544**	**390,418**	**411,056**	**348,946**	**459,156**	**1.77**	**31.58**
Other countries of Europe	328,544	390,418	411,056	348,946	459,156	1.77	31.58

PORTUGAL

6. Overnight stays of non-resident tourists in all types of accommodation establishments, by country of residence

	2007	2008	2009	2010	2011	Market share 11	% Change 11-10
TOTAL	28,669,799	28,126,581	25,024,678	25,386,084	27,860,103	100.00	9.75
AFRICA	250,477	240,313	269,905	277,411	296,810	1.07	6.99
Southern Africa	15,894	32,651	23,973	27,914	34,176	0.12	22.43
South Africa	15,894	32,651	23,973	27,914	34,176	0.12	22.43
Other Africa	234,583	207,662	245,932	249,497	262,634	0.94	5.27
Other countries of Africa	234,583	207,662	245,932	249,497	262,634	0.94	5.27
AMERICAS	1,682,254	1,720,215	1,518,453	1,829,088	2,106,853	7.56	15.19
North America	963,404	874,578	749,296	813,649	876,451	3.15	7.72
Canada	299,331	299,398	212,555	229,296	258,611	0.93	12.78
United States of America	664,073	575,180	536,741	584,353	617,840	2.22	5.73
South America	584,002	699,127	616,386	854,456	1,041,180	3.74	21.85
Brazil	584,002	699,127	616,386	854,456	1,041,180	3.74	21.85
Other Americas	134,848	146,510	152,771	160,983	189,222	0.68	17.54
Other countries of the Americas	134,848	146,510	152,771	160,983	189,222	0.68	17.54
EAST ASIA AND THE PACIFIC	502,731	465,042	453,336	502,231	597,457	2.14	18.96
North-East Asia	177,186	194,904	175,146	217,356	233,912	0.84	7.62
China	27,195	49,781	47,693	60,429	75,579	0.27	25.07
Japan	133,399	122,358	109,890	119,251	114,441	0.41	-4.03
Korea, Republic of	16,592	22,765	17,563	37,676	43,892	0.16	16.50
Australasia	90,768	90,001	78,953	83,014	111,130	0.40	33.87
Australia	90,768	90,001	78,953	83,014	111,130	0.40	33.87
Other East Asia and the Pacific	234,777	180,137	199,237	201,861	252,415	0.91	25.04
Other countries of Asia	174,169	148,643	174,717	183,800	225,945	0.81	22.93
Other countries of Oceania	60,608	31,494	24,520	18,061	26,470	0.10	46.56
EUROPE	26,234,337	25,701,011	22,782,984	22,777,354	24,858,983	89.23	9.14
Central/Eastern Europe	669,035	835,114	677,274	779,780	1,025,421	3.68	31.50
Bulgaria	19,719	18,372	19,181	20,720	22,734	0.08	9.72
Hungary	81,707	79,247	57,811	59,376	66,734	0.24	12.39
Poland	273,825	371,085	317,452	354,935	450,480	1.62	26.92
Romania	89,742	107,311	72,354	70,499	87,232	0.31	23.74
USSR (former)	204,042	259,099	210,476	274,250	398,241	1.43	45.21
Northern Europe	10,896,271	10,464,028	8,299,604	8,145,104	8,863,685	31.81	8.82
Denmark	494,484	499,017	403,189	448,050	376,360	1.35	-16.00
Finland	377,308	416,088	409,470	401,517	392,306	1.41	-2.29
Iceland	5,335	32,281	16,275	28,633	9,404	0.03	-67.16
Ireland	1,073,777	1,042,689	889,769	844,271	880,667	3.16	4.31
Norway	428,218	348,766	277,630	288,228	303,621	1.09	5.34
Sweden	533,077	530,434	391,407	419,147	424,754	1.52	1.34
United Kingdom	7,984,072	7,594,753	5,911,864	5,715,258	6,476,573	23.25	13.32
Southern Europe	4,879,303	4,487,148	4,475,777	4,616,274	4,853,777	17.42	5.14
Greece	64,081	61,849	63,374	44,081	57,720	0.21	30.94
Italy	1,067,519	990,475	852,761	913,932	970,194	3.48	6.16
Spain	3,747,703	3,434,824	3,559,642	3,658,261	3,825,863	13.73	4.58
Western Europe	9,435,935	9,481,647	8,885,462	8,846,151	9,604,981	34.48	8.58
Austria	361,301	306,287	319,275	276,170	301,794	1.08	9.28
Belgium	669,998	657,587	618,754	574,808	632,650	2.27	10.06
France	1,827,715	1,982,158	1,980,920	1,989,283	2,325,934	8.35	16.92
Germany	4,082,701	3,883,691	3,567,813	3,479,508	3,615,029	12.98	3.89
Luxembourg	46,993	45,727	47,388	44,751	52,382	0.19	17.05
Netherlands	2,090,204	2,250,176	2,066,269	2,125,748	2,261,326	8.12	6.38
Switzerland	357,023	356,021	285,043	355,883	415,866	1.49	16.85

PORTUGAL

6. Overnight stays of non-resident tourists in all types of accommodation establishments, by country of residence

	2007	2008	2009	2010	2011	Market share 11	% Change 11-10
East Mediterranean Europe	**8,291**	**21,323**	**18,360**	**23,207**	**30,301**	**0.11**	**30.57**
Turkey	8,291	21,323	18,360	23,207	30,301	0.11	30.57
Other Europe	**345,502**	**411,751**	**426,507**	**366,838**	**480,818**	**1.73**	**31.07**
Other countries of Europe	345,502	411,751	426,507	366,838	480,818	1.73	31.07

PUERTO RICO

1. Arrivals of non-resident tourists at national borders, by country of residence

		2007	2008	2009	2010	2011	Market share 11	% Change 11-10
TOTAL	(*)	**3,687,000**	**3,716,300**	**3,183,300**	**3,185,600**	**3,047,900**	**100.00**	**-4.32**
AMERICAS		**2,886,700**	**2,912,000**	**2,704,100**	**2,639,700**	**2,593,800**	**85.10**	**-1.74**
Caribbean		**19,400**	**17,200**	**13,000**	**8,800**	**7,200**	**0.24**	**-18.18**
United States Virgin Islands		19,400	17,200	13,000	8,800	7,200	0.24	-18.18
North America		**2,867,300**	**2,894,800**	**2,691,100**	**2,630,900**	**2,586,600**	**84.86**	**-1.68**
United States of America		2,867,300	2,894,800	2,691,100	2,630,900	2,586,600	84.86	-1.68
NOT SPECIFIED		**800,300**	**804,300**	**479,200**	**545,900**	**454,100**	**14.90**	**-16.82**
Other countries of the World		800,300	804,300	479,200	545,900	454,100	14.90	-16.82

PUERTO RICO

3. Arrivals of non-resident tourists in hotels and similar establishments, by country of residence

		2007	2008	2009	2010	2011	Market share 11	% Change 11-10
TOTAL	(*)	1,387,697	1,335,322	1,280,937	1,349,449	1,414,082	100.00	4.79
AFRICA		1,108	1,484	1,456	1,327	1,361	0.10	2.56
Other Africa		1,108	1,484	1,456	1,327	1,361	0.10	2.56
All countries of Africa		1,108	1,484	1,456	1,327	1,361	0.10	2.56
AMERICAS		1,315,662	1,272,899	1,218,956	1,289,492	1,355,330	95.85	5.11
Caribbean		42,148	36,531	30,714	30,275	30,905	2.19	2.08
Cuba		191	42	25	30	49	0.00	63.33
Dominican Republic		6,952	6,129	5,948	6,056	6,123	0.43	1.11
United States Virgin Islands		4,114	2,575			1,804	0.13	
Other countries of the Caribbean	(*)	30,891	27,785	24,741	24,189	22,929	1.62	-5.21
Central America		3,756	3,935	3,243	3,272	3,615	0.26	10.48
Belize		101	23	19	38	50	0.00	31.58
Costa Rica		1,232	1,142	690	785	795	0.06	1.27
El Salvador		164	125	98	113	175	0.01	54.87
Guatemala		393	374	422	443	550	0.04	24.15
Honduras		104	94	91	142	159	0.01	11.97
Nicaragua		114	91	49	45	75	0.01	66.67
Panama		930	853	788	766	888	0.06	15.93
Other countries of Central America		718	1,233	1,086	940	923	0.07	-1.81
North America		1,257,484	1,219,787	1,173,826	1,244,696	1,308,692	92.55	5.14
Canada		15,664	16,690	15,012	19,632	23,290	1.65	18.63
Mexico		11,243	10,856	8,388	8,195	8,057	0.57	-1.68
United States of America		1,230,577	1,192,241	1,150,426	1,216,869	1,277,345	90.33	4.97
South America		12,274	12,646	11,173	11,249	12,118	0.86	7.73
Argentina		1,742	1,870	1,961	2,230	2,035	0.14	-8.74
Bolivia		241	396	450	463	453	0.03	-2.16
Brazil		1,572	2,024	1,882	1,916	2,300	0.16	20.04
Chile		720	846	650	637	649	0.05	1.88
Colombia		2,815	1,996	2,023	2,123	2,501	0.18	17.80
Ecuador		225	199	186	159	175	0.01	10.06
French Guiana		18	15	5	3	18	0.00	500.00
Guyana		15	9	15	17	27	0.00	58.82
Paraguay		34	41	27	64	41	0.00	-35.94
Peru		517	451	335	380	418	0.03	10.00
Suriname		23	14	20	30	19	0.00	-36.67
Uruguay		177	218	142	193	169	0.01	-12.44
Venezuela		2,962	3,083	2,465	2,403	2,909	0.21	21.06
Other countries of South America		1,213	1,484	1,012	631	404	0.03	-35.97
EAST ASIA AND THE PACIFIC		3,912	3,472	2,997	3,342	3,926	0.28	17.47
North-East Asia		1,212	1,231	1,194	1,240	1,584	0.11	27.74
China		133	429	448	514	636	0.04	23.74
Taiwan, Province of China		22	25	18	20	52	0.00	160.00
Hong Kong, China		300	139	86	81	91	0.01	12.35
Japan		757	638	642	625	805	0.06	28.80
South-East Asia		359	332	199	162	209	0.01	29.01
Philippines		333	256	113	153	186	0.01	21.57
Thailand		26	76	86	9	23	0.00	155.56
Australasia		1,285	1,108	861	891	1,261	0.09	41.53
Australia		1,224	1,018	781	813	1,175	0.08	44.53
New Zealand		61	90	80	78	86	0.01	10.26
Other East Asia and the Pacific		1,056	801	743	1,049	872	0.06	-16.87
Other countries of Asia		1,056	801	743	1,049	872	0.06	-16.87

PUERTO RICO

3. Arrivals of non-resident tourists in hotels and similar establishments, by country of residence

	2007	2008	2009	2010	2011	Market share 11	% Change 11-10
EUROPE	37,881	29,903	29,951	24,315	26,231	1.85	7.88
Central/Eastern Europe	704	1,074	1,431	1,101	1,334	0.09	21.16
Bulgaria	24	27	16	28	64	0.00	128.57
Czech Republic	22	61	82	78	113	0.01	44.87
Hungary	71	84	46	48	110	0.01	129.17
Poland	27	60	161	82	142	0.01	73.17
Romania	35	43	40	33	44	0.00	33.33
Russian Federation	525	799	879	746	771	0.05	3.35
Slovakia				27	10	0.00	-62.96
Baltic countries			207	59	80	0.01	35.59
Northern Europe	8,507	6,614	5,087	6,015	6,216	0.44	3.34
Denmark	598	547	656	612	670	0.05	9.48
Finland	387	207	241	369	354	0.03	-4.07
Iceland	7	25	11	33	34	0.00	3.03
Ireland	268	382	313	346	487	0.03	40.75
Norway	390	406	301	358	348	0.02	-2.79
Sweden	650	789	677	762	852	0.06	11.81
United Kingdom	6,207	4,258	2,888	3,535	3,471	0.25	-1.81
Southern Europe	11,002	9,044	9,081	6,972	6,873	0.49	-1.42
Albania			38	53	62	0.00	16.98
Gibraltar	25	6	33	3	4	0.00	33.33
Greece	138	156	437	442	407	0.03	-7.92
Italy	1,530	1,371	1,413	1,306	1,404	0.10	7.50
Malta	29	22	16	14	7	0.00	-50.00
Portugal	220	146	296	146	210	0.01	43.84
San Marino	3	4	12	6	3	0.00	-50.00
Spain	8,992	7,267	6,754	4,739	4,666	0.33	-1.54
Yugoslavia, SFR (former)	65	72	82	263	110	0.01	-58.17
Western Europe	6,828	6,275	6,253	6,738	7,999	0.57	18.71
Austria	301	328	215	265	351	0.02	32.45
Belgium	590	585	479	636	566	0.04	-11.01
France	1,424	1,243	1,499	1,521	1,933	0.14	27.09
Germany	2,758	2,582	2,676	2,932	3,586	0.25	22.31
Luxembourg	15	22	25	29	45	0.00	55.17
Netherlands	837	808	784	808	823	0.06	1.86
Switzerland	903	707	575	547	695	0.05	27.06
East Mediterranean Europe	389	395	414	431	561	0.04	30.16
Israel	301	332	310	355	480	0.03	35.21
Turkey	88	63	104	76	81	0.01	6.58
Other Europe	10,451	6,501	7,685	3,058	3,248	0.23	6.21
Other countries of Europe	10,451	6,501	7,685	3,058	3,248	0.23	6.21
MIDDLE EAST	79	82	111	135	38	0.00	-71.85
Iraq	8						
Saudi Arabia	63	59	102	50	35	0.00	-30.00
Egypt	8	23	9	85	3	0.00	-96.47
SOUTH ASIA		57	210	167	338	0.02	102.40
India		57	210	167	338	0.02	102.40
NOT SPECIFIED	29,055	27,425	27,256	30,671	26,858	1.90	-12.43
Other countries of the World (*)	29,055	27,425	27,256	30,671	26,858	1.90	-12.43

QATAR

3. Arrivals of non-resident tourists in hotels and similar establishments, by country of residence

		2007	2008	2009	2010	2011	Market share 11	% Change 11-10
TOTAL	(*)	963,573	1,404,850	1,658,569	1,518,953	2,527,285	100.00	66.38
AFRICA					86,118	52,353	2.07	-39.21
Other Africa					86,118	52,353	2.07	-39.21
All countries of Africa					86,118	52,353	2.07	-39.21
EAST ASIA AND THE PACIFIC		203,465	216,742	264,550	298,395	567,543	22.46	90.20
Other East Asia and the Pacific		203,465	216,742	264,550	298,395	567,543	22.46	90.20
All countries of Asia		203,465	216,742	264,550	298,395	567,543	22.46	90.20
EUROPE		265,965	329,059	406,725	730,034	1,079,523	42.71	47.87
Other Europe		265,965	329,059	406,725	730,034	1,079,523	42.71	47.87
All countries of Europe	(*)	265,965	329,059	406,725	730,034	1,079,523	42.71	47.87
MIDDLE EAST		361,139	628,440	679,859	404,406	827,866	32.76	104.71
Bahrain					23,028	38,500	1.52	67.19
Kuwait					29,031	46,307	1.83	59.51
Oman					12,573	18,637	0.74	48.23
Saudi Arabia					100,453	203,871	8.07	102.95
United Arab Emirates					62,619	86,380	3.42	37.95
Other countries of Middle East					176,702	434,171	17.18	145.71
All countries of Middle East		361,139	628,440	679,859				
NOT SPECIFIED		133,004	230,609	307,435				
Other countries of the World		133,004	230,609	307,435				

QATAR

5. Overnight stays of non-resident tourists in hotels and similar establishments, by country of residence

		2007	2008	2009	2010	2011	Market share 11	% Change 11-10
TOTAL	(*)	1,245,191	1,992,786	1,535,145	1,467,034	2,358,575	100.00	60.77
AFRICA					81,175	48,245	2.05	-40.57
Other Africa					81,175	48,245	2.05	-40.57
All countries of Africa					81,175	48,245	2.05	-40.57
EAST ASIA AND THE PACIFIC		257,246	299,177	283,557	324,222	541,929	22.98	67.15
Other East Asia and the Pacific		257,246	299,177	283,557	324,222	541,929	22.98	67.15
All countries of Asia		257,246	299,177	283,557	324,222	541,929	22.98	67.15
EUROPE		325,137	503,902	377,394	679,776	1,023,782	43.41	50.61
Other Europe		325,137	503,902	377,394	679,776	1,023,782	43.41	50.61
All countries of Europe	(*)	325,137	503,902	377,394	679,776	1,023,782	43.41	50.61
MIDDLE EAST		489,580	809,993	606,729	381,861	744,619	31.57	95.00
Bahrain					20,658	34,770	1.47	68.31
Kuwait					24,335	37,683	1.60	54.85
Oman					12,887	17,905	0.76	38.94
Saudi Arabia					75,589	157,165	6.66	107.92
United Arab Emirates					53,757	71,164	3.02	32.38
Other countries of Middle East					194,635	425,932	18.06	118.84
All countries of Middle East		489,580	809,993	606,729				
NOT SPECIFIED		173,228	379,714	267,465				
Other countries of the World		173,228	379,714	267,465				

REPUBLIC OF MOLDOVA

2. Arrivals of non-resident visitors at national borders, by nationality

		2007	2008	2009	2010	2011	Market share 11	% Change 11-10
TOTAL	(*)	14,722	8,710	9,189	8,956	10,788	100.00	20.46
AFRICA		7		2	2	14	0.13	600.00
Central Africa						1	0.01	
Congo						1	0.01	
North Africa		1			1	2	0.02	100.00
Algeria					1	2	0.02	100.00
Sudan		1						
Southern Africa		1			1	5	0.05	400.00
South Africa		1			1	3	0.03	200.00
Swaziland						2	0.02	
West Africa		5		2		6	0.06	
Benin				2				
Ghana						5	0.05	
Mauritania		2				1	0.01	
Senegal		3						
AMERICAS		580	305	232	524	651	6.03	24.24
Caribbean						23	0.21	
British Virgin Islands						23	0.21	
North America		546	272	227	490	611	5.66	24.69
Canada		30	33	33	38	53	0.49	39.47
Mexico		1			1			
United States of America		515	239	194	451	558	5.17	23.73
South America		34	33	5	34	17	0.16	-50.00
Argentina		2		2	1	2	0.02	100.00
Bolivia		2		1				
Brazil		27	33		29	11	0.10	-62.07
Colombia		1		1				
Ecuador				1				
Peru		2			3	4	0.04	33.33
Venezuela					1			
EAST ASIA AND THE PACIFIC		293	188	107	162	545	5.05	236.42
North-East Asia		264	169	106	133	487	4.51	266.17
China		20	19	8	27	166	1.54	514.81
Taiwan, Province of China		22	14	22		40	0.37	
Japan		168	119	76	93	258	2.39	177.42
Korea, Dem. People's Republic of		9	17					
Korea, Republic of		42			12	23	0.21	91.67
Mongolia		3			1			
South-East Asia		19	11	1	3	34	0.32	1033.33
Indonesia		10	11					
Malaysia		9						
Philippines					1	1	0.01	
Singapore				1		2	0.02	
Viet Nam						29	0.27	
Thailand					2	2	0.02	
Australasia		10	8		26	24	0.22	-7.69
Australia		9	6		25	16	0.15	-36.00
New Zealand		1	2		1	8	0.07	700.00
EUROPE		13,794	8,209	8,837	8,229	9,559	88.61	16.16
Central/Eastern Europe		7,763	5,280	4,744	4,685	5,459	50.60	16.52
Azerbaijan		56	37	76	29	13	0.12	-55.17
Armenia		27	23	49	23	39	0.36	69.57
Bulgaria		359	46	380	324	289	2.68	-10.80

REPUBLIC OF MOLDOVA

2. Arrivals of non-resident visitors at national borders, by nationality

	2007	2008	2009	2010	2011	Market share 11	% Change 11-10
Belarus	290	145	176	105	44	0.41	-58.10
Czech Republic	157	140	40	24	57	0.53	137.50
Estonia	85	40	42	70	76	0.70	8.57
Georgia	67	21	53	7	85	0.79	1114.29
Hungary	146	36	31	18	84	0.78	366.67
Kazakhstan	48	23	56	23	16	0.15	-30.43
Kyrgyzstan	5	9	15	5	11	0.10	120.00
Latvia	30	95	14	80	40	0.37	-50.00
Lithuania	79	57	34	12	69	0.64	475.00
Poland	188	140	291	204	371	3.44	81.86
Romania	3,034	1,070	765	1,698	1,600	14.83	-5.77
Russian Federation	1,767	1,793	1,713	1,327	1,404	13.01	5.80
Slovakia	85	54	11	6	52	0.48	766.67
Tajikistan	2	4	4		3	0.03	
Turkmenistan	1		2		12	0.11	
Ukraine	1,335	1,542	979	730	1,189	11.02	62.88
Uzbekistan	2	5	13		5	0.05	
Northern Europe	**1,301**	**652**	**1,032**	**625**	**965**	**8.95**	**54.40**
Denmark	266	20	100	15	54	0.50	260.00
Finland	35	56	84	66	128	1.19	93.94
Ireland	39	35	10	7	12	0.11	71.43
Norway	180	46	35	33	87	0.81	163.64
Sweden	140	65	59	99	334	3.10	237.37
United Kingdom	641	430	744	405	350	3.24	-13.58
Southern Europe	**1,121**	**700**	**612**	**764**	**789**	**7.31**	**3.27**
Albania	24	3	3		3	0.03	
Bosnia and Herzegovina	6	6	2	2	52	0.48	2500.00
Croatia	51	47	85	37	12	0.11	-67.57
Greece	83	86	118	91	86	0.80	-5.49
Italy	755	440	258	474	445	4.12	-6.12
Malta	25						
Montenegro					3	0.03	
Portugal	7	32	44	5	14	0.13	180.00
San Marino		1			50	0.46	
Serbia				19	16	0.15	-15.79
Slovenia	58	20	8	53	31	0.29	-41.51
Spain	92	45	60	79	69	0.64	-12.66
TFYR of Macedonia	4	8	8	4	8	0.07	100.00
Serbia and Montenegro	16	12	26				
Western Europe	**1,961**	**954**	**1,265**	**1,392**	**1,689**	**15.66**	**21.34**
Austria	206	115	147	103	95	0.88	-7.77
Belgium	63	16	17	103	46	0.43	-55.34
France	436	174	196	283	248	2.30	-12.37
Germany	892	502	460	482	1,001	9.28	107.68
Luxembourg	3			2	2	0.02	
Netherlands	262	125	154	311	219	2.03	-29.58
Switzerland	99	22	291	108	78	0.72	-27.78
East Mediterranean Europe	**1,648**	**623**	**1,184**	**763**	**657**	**6.09**	**-13.89**
Cyprus	74	13	26	12	42	0.39	250.00
Israel	174	149	156	225	138	1.28	-38.67
Turkey	1,400	461	1,002	526	477	4.42	-9.32
MIDDLE EAST	**27**	**4**	**5**	**24**	**10**	**0.09**	**-58.33**
Iraq		1	1	1			
Jordan		1		1			
Kuwait	2				1	0.01	
Lebanon	9		1	1			
Syrian Arab Republic	4		3		3	0.03	

REPUBLIC OF MOLDOVA

2. Arrivals of non-resident visitors at national borders, by nationality

	2007	2008	2009	2010	2011	Market share 11	% Change 11-10
United Arab Emirates	5	2		2	6	0.06	200.00
Egypt	7			19			
SOUTH ASIA	**21**	**4**	**6**	**15**	**9**	**0.08**	**-40.00**
Afghanistan				12			
Bangladesh					1	0.01	
India	21	4	5	2	6	0.06	200.00
Iran, Islamic Republic of			1	1	1	0.01	
Pakistan					1	0.01	

REPUBLIC OF MOLDOVA

4. Arrivals of non-resident tourists in all types of accommodation establishments, by nationality

		2007	2008	2009	2010	2011	Market share 11	% Change 11-10
TOTAL	(*)	70,302	73,288	59,563	63,593	75,000	100.00	17.94
AFRICA		89	54	127	127	300	0.40	136.22
Other Africa		89	54	127	127	300	0.40	136.22
All countries of Africa		89	54	127	127	300	0.40	136.22
AMERICAS		4,085	3,559	3,703	3,666	5,245	6.99	43.07
North America		4,021	3,452	3,636	3,524	4,960	6.61	40.75
Canada		259	393	274	388	495	0.66	27.58
United States of America		3,740	3,040	3,328	3,132	4,419	5.89	41.09
Other countries of North America		22	19	34	4	46	0.06	1050.00
South America		47	100	60	108	201	0.27	86.11
All countries of South America		47	100	60	108	201	0.27	86.11
Other Americas		17	7	7	34	84	0.11	147.06
Other countries of the Americas		17	7	7	34	84	0.11	147.06
EAST ASIA AND THE PACIFIC		972	829	806	1,006	1,968	2.62	95.63
North-East Asia		576	473	453	525	985	1.31	87.62
China		211	143	144	188	518	0.69	175.53
Japan		365	330	309	337	467	0.62	38.58
Other East Asia and the Pacific		396	356	353	481	983	1.31	104.37
Other countries of Asia		288	248	220	426	837	1.12	96.48
All countries of Oceania		108	108	133	55	146	0.19	165.45
EUROPE		65,156	68,846	54,927	58,794	67,487	89.98	14.79
Central/Eastern Europe		37,954	42,743	31,669	36,332	40,749	54.33	12.16
Azerbaijan		447	397	451	332	471	0.63	41.87
Armenia		209	321	252	167	324	0.43	94.01
Bulgaria		1,285	1,431	1,458	1,384	1,163	1.55	-15.97
Belarus		1,324	1,455	1,379	932	923	1.23	-0.97
Czech Republic		614	923	684	438	1,145	1.53	161.42
Estonia		291	333	241	504	456	0.61	-9.52
Georgia		306	435	259	433	616	0.82	42.26
Hungary		701	715	450	480	755	1.01	57.29
Kazakhstan		426	496	362	247	247	0.33	
Kyrgyzstan		130	129	124	510	112	0.15	-78.04
Latvia		250	400	178	273	332	0.44	21.61
Lithuania		507	710	440	400	506	0.67	26.50
Poland		1,389	2,145	1,639	1,390	1,872	2.50	34.68
Romania		14,855	15,858	8,796	15,403	16,097	21.46	4.51
Russian Federation		6,798	8,428	7,314	6,484	7,840	10.45	20.91
Slovakia		330	322	240	198	292	0.39	47.47
Tajikistan		99	131	117	60	186	0.25	210.00
Turkmenistan		30	45	39	268	30	0.04	-88.81
Ukraine		7,855	7,944	7,115	6,083	7,194	9.59	18.26
Uzbekistan		108	125	131	346	188	0.25	-45.66
Northern Europe		4,271	3,913	4,112	4,062	5,215	6.95	28.39
Denmark		331	245	367	302	311	0.41	2.98
Finland		306	354	360	764	510	0.68	-33.25
Ireland		330	367	385	172	466	0.62	170.93
Norway		475	296	377	342	598	0.80	74.85
Sweden		772	800	781	889	1,432	1.91	61.08
United Kingdom		2,057	1,851	1,842	1,593	1,898	2.53	19.15
Southern Europe		7,279	7,151	6,157	6,118	7,272	9.70	18.86
Albania		81	79	37	139	104	0.14	-25.18
Bosnia and Herzegovina		65	80	36	106	162	0.22	52.83
Croatia		195	158	233	221	247	0.33	11.76

REPUBLIC OF MOLDOVA

4. Arrivals of non-resident tourists in all types of accommodation establishments, by nationality

	2007	2008	2009	2010	2011	Market share 11	% Change 11-10
Greece	1,082	864	923	598	648	0.86	8.36
Italy	4,775	4,766	3,777	3,942	4,447	5.93	12.81
Montenegro					49	0.07	
Portugal	93	146	138	148	347	0.46	134.46
Serbia				148	201	0.27	35.81
Slovenia	235	287	283	345	388	0.52	12.46
Spain	608	535	573	471	679	0.91	44.16
Serbia and Montenegro	145	236	157				
Western Europe	**8,268**	**8,875**	**8,390**	**7,966**	**9,011**	**12.01**	**13.12**
Austria	975	1,059	927	820	1,003	1.34	22.32
Belgium	511	505	388	405	577	0.77	42.47
France	1,862	1,878	1,805	1,479	2,130	2.84	44.02
Germany	3,471	4,018	2,959	3,468	3,863	5.15	11.39
Luxembourg	41	50	77	22	31	0.04	40.91
Netherlands	1,016	973	979	1,283	1,036	1.38	-19.25
Switzerland	392	392	1,255	489	371	0.49	-24.13
East Mediterranean Europe	**6,613**	**5,455**	**3,969**	**3,837**	**4,306**	**5.74**	**12.22**
Cyprus					204	0.27	
Israel	1,101	1,217	878	1,299	1,321	1.76	1.69
Turkey	5,512	4,238	3,091	2,538	2,781	3.71	9.57
Other Europe	**771**	**709**	**630**	**479**	**934**	**1.25**	**94.99**
Other countries of Europe	771	709	630	479	934	1.25	94.99

REPUBLIC OF MOLDOVA

6. Overnight stays of non-resident tourists in all types of accommodation establishments, by nationality

		2007	2008	2009	2010	2011	Market share 11	% Change 11-10
TOTAL	(*)	201,006	201,624	147,762	162,755	173,893	100.00	6.84
AFRICA		310	145	293	401	687	0.40	71.32
Other Africa		310	145	293	401	687	0.40	71.32
All countries of Africa		310	145	293	401	687	0.40	71.32
AMERICAS		13,159	11,939	11,410	12,780	12,646	7.27	-1.05
North America		12,979	11,574	11,185	12,097	10,963	6.30	-9.37
Canada		737	1,195	1,079	1,500	1,208	0.69	-19.47
United States of America		12,175	10,335	10,032	10,593	9,565	5.50	-9.70
Other countries of North America		67	44	74	4	190	0.11	4650.00
South America		122	347	207	560	918	0.53	63.93
All countries of South America		122	347	207	560	918	0.53	63.93
Other Americas		58	18	18	123	765	0.44	521.95
Other countries of the Americas		58	18	18	123	765	0.44	521.95
EAST ASIA AND THE PACIFIC		2,715	2,168	2,268	2,817	5,481	3.15	94.57
North-East Asia		1,595	1,329	1,374	1,429	2,978	1.71	108.40
China		673	581	514	569	1,771	1.02	211.25
Japan		922	748	860	860	1,207	0.69	40.35
Other East Asia and the Pacific		1,120	839	894	1,388	2,503	1.44	80.33
Other countries of Asia		788	600	639	1,188	2,181	1.25	83.59
All countries of Oceania		332	239	255	200	322	0.19	61.00
EUROPE		184,822	187,372	133,791	146,757	155,079	89.18	5.67
Central/Eastern Europe		93,929	106,433	75,438	86,134	93,390	53.71	8.42
Azerbaijan		1,519	1,273	1,260	1,074	1,237	0.71	15.18
Armenia		821	1,220	897	641	948	0.55	47.89
Bulgaria		3,884	3,866	2,867	2,512	2,815	1.62	12.06
Belarus		3,976	4,440	6,151	3,092	3,188	1.83	3.10
Czech Republic		1,622	2,127	1,297	918	2,288	1.32	149.24
Estonia		712	931	604	1,099	1,140	0.66	3.73
Georgia		839	1,209	821	1,169	1,449	0.83	23.95
Hungary		1,660	1,867	1,028	1,146	1,497	0.86	30.63
Kazakhstan		1,216	1,124	962	724	653	0.38	-9.81
Kyrgyzstan		525	409	431	1,377	346	0.20	-74.87
Latvia		674	1,106	455	799	741	0.43	-7.26
Lithuania		1,345	1,658	1,089	1,006	1,103	0.63	9.64
Poland		3,349	4,783	3,964	3,084	4,211	2.42	36.54
Romania		34,526	38,226	19,144	37,728	36,487	20.98	-3.29
Russian Federation		20,302	23,956	20,114	17,043	20,117	11.57	18.04
Slovakia		720	752	491	511	573	0.33	12.13
Tajikistan		316	487	328	199	458	0.26	130.15
Turkmenistan		84	135	324	538	121	0.07	-77.51
Ukraine		15,571	16,457	12,834	10,811	13,596	7.82	25.76
Uzbekistan		268	407	377	663	422	0.24	-36.35
Northern Europe		11,735	10,765	10,776	11,016	12,803	7.36	16.22
Denmark		1,106	725	1,191	712	803	0.46	12.78
Finland		562	747	941	2,102	1,251	0.72	-40.49
Ireland		889	969	945	528	1,345	0.77	154.73
Norway		1,246	818	1,103	1,045	1,437	0.83	37.51
Sweden		2,027	2,210	1,941	2,195	3,177	1.83	44.74
United Kingdom		5,905	5,296	4,655	4,434	4,790	2.75	8.03
Southern Europe		17,856	17,271	14,161	15,658	17,816	10.25	13.78
Albania		286	240	92	309	254	0.15	-17.80
Bosnia and Herzegovina		184	224	126	289	340	0.20	17.65
Croatia		619	436	538	628	611	0.35	-2.71

REPUBLIC OF MOLDOVA

6. Overnight stays of non-resident tourists in all types of accommodation establishments, by nationality

	2007	2008	2009	2010	2011	Market share 11	% Change 11-10
Greece	2,993	1,894	2,053	1,556	1,300	0.75	-16.45
Italy	11,057	11,628	9,044	10,287	11,274	6.48	9.59
Montenegro					110	0.06	
Portugal	201	422	284	335	1,004	0.58	199.70
Serbia				374	456	0.26	21.93
Slovenia	511	619	495	750	859	0.49	14.53
Spain	1,580	1,322	1,173	1,130	1,608	0.92	42.30
Serbia and Montenegro	425	486	356				
Western Europe	**21,022**	**22,139**	**19,535**	**19,495**	**20,502**	**11.79**	**5.17**
Austria	2,502	2,295	1,827	1,819	2,086	1.20	14.68
Belgium	1,309	1,154	949	880	1,140	0.66	29.55
France	4,713	4,365	4,296	3,653	4,675	2.69	27.98
Germany	8,980	10,847	7,305	8,790	9,112	5.24	3.66
Luxembourg	86	97	154	46	43	0.02	-6.52
Netherlands	2,526	2,476	2,381	3,100	2,490	1.43	-19.68
Switzerland	906	905	2,623	1,207	956	0.55	-20.80
East Mediterranean Europe	**38,092**	**28,859**	**12,341**	**13,151**	**9,212**	**5.30**	**-29.95**
Cyprus					554	0.32	
Israel	3,094	3,671	2,470	4,472	3,631	2.09	-18.81
Turkey	34,998	25,188	9,871	8,679	5,027	2.89	-42.08
Other Europe	**2,188**	**1,905**	**1,540**	**1,303**	**1,356**	**0.78**	**4.07**
Other countries of Europe	2,188	1,905	1,540	1,303	1,356	0.78	4.07

REUNION

1. Arrivals of non-resident tourists at national borders, by country of residence

		2007	2008	2009	2010	2011	Market share 11	% Change 11-10
TOTAL	(*)	381,547	396,400	421,900	420,300	471,300	100.00	12.13
AFRICA		33,245	20,800	20,300	18,400	18,200	3.86	-1.09
East Africa		30,155	20,800	20,300	18,400	18,200	3.86	-1.09
Comoros		610						
Madagascar		5,475						
Mauritius		23,715	20,800	20,300	18,400	18,200	3.86	-1.09
Seychelles		355						
Southern Africa		1,847						
South Africa		1,847						
Other Africa		1,243						
Other countries of Africa		1,243						
AMERICAS		1,721						
North America		1,440						
Canada		956						
United States of America		484						
Other Americas		281						
Other countries of the Americas		281						
EAST ASIA AND THE PACIFIC		2,491						
North-East Asia		250						
China		250						
South-East Asia		99						
Singapore		99						
Australasia		1,569						
Australia		1,569						
Other East Asia and the Pacific		573						
Other countries of Asia		469						
Other countries of Oceania		104						
EUROPE		304,307	328,200	359,700	363,400	401,200	85.13	10.40
Northern Europe		1,888						
Denmark		59						
United Kingdom		1,829						
Southern Europe		3,939						
Greece		58						
Italy		935						
Portugal		1,480						
Spain		1,466						
Western Europe		295,681	311,000	344,300	346,200	381,600	80.97	10.23
Belgium		3,779						
France		280,708	311,000	344,300	346,200	381,600	80.97	10.23
Germany		6,795						
Luxembourg		376						
Netherlands		527						
Switzerland		3,496						
Other Europe		2,799	17,200	15,400	17,200	19,600	4.16	13.95
Other countries of Europe		2,799	17,200	15,400	17,200	19,600	4.16	13.95
SOUTH ASIA		418						
India		418						
NOT SPECIFIED		39,365	47,400	41,900	38,500	51,900	11.01	34.81
Other countries of the World		39,365	47,400	41,900	38,500	51,900	11.01	34.81

ROMANIA

2. Arrivals of non-resident visitors at national borders, by country of residence

	2007	2008	2009	2010	2011	Market share 11	% Change 11-10
TOTAL	7,721,741	8,862,119	7,575,298	7,498,307	7,611,124	100.00	1.50
AFRICA	10,701	12,638	12,803	14,464	15,568	0.20	7.63
East Africa	708	827	968	1,293	1,469	0.02	13.61
Burundi	4	11	6	8	10	0.00	25.00
Comoros	1	3	3	7	1	0.00	-85.71
Ethiopia	3	45	36	44	69	0.00	56.82
Eritrea	32	47	6	6	11	0.00	83.33
Djibouti			1		1	0.00	
Kenya	92	98	100	118	153	0.00	29.66
Madagascar	20	53	84	102	76	0.00	-25.49
Mauritius	381	445	532	695	712	0.01	2.45
Mozambique	17	4	21	21	14	0.00	-33.33
Rwanda	4	8	13	14	14	0.00	
Somalia	10	7	3	8	9	0.00	12.50
Zimbabwe	68	35	47	46	71	0.00	54.35
Uganda	18	12	23	31	30	0.00	-3.23
United Republic of Tanzania	40	43	75	176	273	0.00	55.11
Zambia	18	16	18	17	25	0.00	47.06
Central Africa	533	690	645	653	789	0.01	20.83
Angola	104	102	126	97	149	0.00	53.61
Cameroon	165	279	269	316	359	0.00	13.61
Central African Republic	50	31	26	13	14	0.00	7.69
Chad	2	4	5	8	8	0.00	
Congo	173	228	183	119	130	0.00	9.24
Democratic Republic of the Congo		4	15	43	79	0.00	83.72
Equatorial Guinea	5	2	1	11	7	0.00	-36.36
Gabon	34	36	18	45	42	0.00	-6.67
Sao Tome and Principe		4	2	1	1	0.00	
North Africa	6,212	7,319	8,029	9,165	9,492	0.12	3.57
Algeria	887	666	761	748	896	0.01	19.79
Morocco	1,534	2,100	2,197	2,472	2,887	0.04	16.79
Sudan	221	416	334	356	296	0.00	-16.85
Tunisia	3,570	4,137	4,737	5,589	5,413	0.07	-3.15
Southern Africa	1,809	1,761	1,249	1,465	1,834	0.02	25.19
Botswana	9	8	8	10	10	0.00	
Lesotho	3	2	1	2	1	0.00	-50.00
Namibia	67	11	15	59	51	0.00	-13.56
South Africa	1,730	1,740	1,225	1,394	1,772	0.02	27.12
West Africa	1,439	2,041	1,912	1,860	1,963	0.03	5.54
Cape Verde	42	117	63	84	69	0.00	-17.86
Benin	56	87	47	34	53	0.00	55.88
Gambia	9	17	11	15	6	0.00	-60.00
Ghana	120	124	149	143	177	0.00	23.78
Guinea	138	187	144	69	66	0.00	-4.35
Côte d'Ivoire	57	140	150	160	192	0.00	20.00
Liberia	37	41	15	11	17	0.00	54.55
Mali	26	34	20	21	19	0.00	-9.52
Mauritania	21	38	49	35	23	0.00	-34.29
Niger	10	24	24	39	28	0.00	-28.21
Nigeria	710	918	911	948	1,023	0.01	7.91
Guinea-Bissau	7	23	3	5	9	0.00	80.00
Senegal	117	175	249	218	198	0.00	-9.17
Sierra Leone	18	32	15	37	30	0.00	-18.92
Togo	32	42	24	20	22	0.00	10.00
Burkina Faso	39	42	38	21	31	0.00	47.62

ROMANIA

2. Arrivals of non-resident visitors at national borders, by country of residence

	2007	2008	2009	2010	2011	Market share 11	% Change 11-10
Other Africa				28	21	0.00	-25.00
Other countries of Africa				28	21	0.00	-25.00
AMERICAS	188,807	191,709	168,744	170,757	182,169	2.39	6.68
Caribbean	507	601	545	542	505	0.01	-6.83
Cuba	355	396	390	311	245	0.00	-21.22
Dominican Republic	75	136	102	160	186	0.00	16.25
Haiti	12	21	16	21	13	0.00	-38.10
Jamaica	65	48	37	50	61	0.00	22.00
Central America	565	744	695	834	918	0.01	10.07
Belize	5	10	1	4	11	0.00	175.00
Costa Rica	173	224	237	301	272	0.00	-9.63
El Salvador	52	70	55	69	70	0.00	1.45
Guatemala	86	158	142	172	151	0.00	-12.21
Honduras	156	148	132	168	268	0.00	59.52
Nicaragua	37	45	49	45	75	0.00	66.67
Panama	56	89	79	75	71	0.00	-5.33
North America	179,111	180,257	158,019	158,688	168,589	2.22	6.24
Canada	37,240	39,989	36,592	38,740	41,595	0.55	7.37
Mexico	2,431	2,958	2,293	2,999	3,659	0.05	22.01
United States of America	139,440	137,310	119,134	116,949	123,335	1.62	5.46
South America	8,624	10,107	9,485	10,427	11,949	0.16	14.60
Argentina	1,754	2,093	1,961	1,841	2,193	0.03	19.12
Bolivia	150	137	194	181	204	0.00	12.71
Brazil	3,446	4,169	3,741	4,331	5,216	0.07	20.43
Chile	660	784	681	768	885	0.01	15.23
Colombia	656	687	680	787	744	0.01	-5.46
Ecuador	561	543	532	538	543	0.01	0.93
Guyana	4	9	6	5	9	0.00	80.00
Paraguay	60	101	89	112	120	0.00	7.14
Peru	531	644	630	792	900	0.01	13.64
Suriname	5	9	5	13	17	0.00	30.77
Uruguay	121	198	205	270	251	0.00	-7.04
Venezuela	676	733	761	789	867	0.01	9.89
Other Americas				266	208	0.00	-21.80
Other countries of the Americas				266	208	0.00	-21.80
EAST ASIA AND THE PACIFIC	79,998	97,417	70,145	79,098	92,027	1.21	16.35
North-East Asia	43,221	52,733	41,899	44,748	51,524	0.68	15.14
China	16,822	26,182	19,681	17,796	18,570	0.24	4.35
Taiwan, Province of China	923	927	647	903	1,813	0.02	100.78
Hong Kong, China	891	977	788	824	1,225	0.02	48.67
Japan	15,512	13,095	10,345	12,333	13,544	0.18	9.82
Korea, Dem. People's Republic of	103	174	96	114	114	0.00	
Korea, Republic of	8,676	11,129	10,109	12,628	16,077	0.21	27.31
Mongolia	294	249	233	150	181	0.00	20.67
South-East Asia	22,924	28,883	14,662	20,829	25,072	0.33	20.37
Myanmar	1,274	1,191	850	664	1,324	0.02	99.40
Cambodia	11	9	25	27	38	0.00	40.74
Indonesia	2,165	3,288	1,279	2,001	2,405	0.03	20.19
Lao People's Democratic Republic	5		6	5			
Malaysia	1,315	1,702	1,293	2,078	1,764	0.02	-15.11
Philippines	15,879	18,130	7,824	13,372	16,668	0.22	24.65
Singapore	631	683	548	593	735	0.01	23.95
Viet Nam	936	1,572	1,678	1,062	1,154	0.02	8.66
Thailand	708	2,308	1,159	1,027	984	0.01	-4.19

ROMANIA

2. Arrivals of non-resident visitors at national borders, by country of residence

	2007	2008	2009	2010	2011	Market share 11	% Change 11-10
Australasia	**13,830**	**15,761**	**13,502**	**13,323**	**15,263**	**0.20**	**14.56**
Australia	11,515	12,927	11,218	11,117	12,976	0.17	16.72
New Zealand	2,315	2,834	2,284	2,206	2,287	0.03	3.67
Melanesia	**3**	**5**	**41**	**23**	**16**	**0.00**	**-30.43**
Fiji	3	5	41	23	16	0.00	-30.43
Other East Asia and the Pacific	**20**	**35**	**41**	**175**	**152**	**0.00**	**-13.14**
Other countries East Asia/Pacific	20	35	41	175	152	0.00	-13.14
EUROPE	**7,394,449**	**8,506,343**	**7,278,936**	**7,179,264**	**7,266,677**	**95.47**	**1.22**
Central/Eastern Europe	**4,935,465**	**5,913,628**	**5,065,085**	**5,008,381**	**4,955,252**	**65.11**	**-1.06**
Azerbaijan	2,538	2,682	2,499	3,191	4,024	0.05	26.10
Armenia	740	1,260	1,511	1,836	2,067	0.03	12.58
Bulgaria	818,018	1,114,082	877,287	786,452	797,382	10.48	1.39
Belarus	47,463	37,190	42,933	56,757	56,871	0.75	0.20
Czech Republic	109,962	135,368	100,656	79,709	80,145	1.05	0.55
Estonia	4,023	6,179	3,913	4,471	3,981	0.05	-10.96
Georgia	3,224	4,520	7,573	9,900	16,617	0.22	67.85
Hungary	1,743,093	1,950,383	1,836,334	1,734,844	1,545,502	20.31	-10.91
Kazakhstan	621	1,053	1,266	1,948	2,226	0.03	14.27
Kyrgyzstan	93	208	114	183	288	0.00	57.38
Latvia	3,219	4,153	3,760	3,669	4,425	0.06	20.61
Lithuania	7,412	10,156	10,155	9,153	8,771	0.12	-4.17
Republic of Moldova	1,109,933	1,428,559	1,042,871	1,216,140	1,330,322	17.48	9.39
Poland	191,022	276,525	222,783	237,922	249,731	3.28	4.96
Russian Federation	53,868	62,648	73,203	91,907	119,502	1.57	30.02
Slovakia	119,763	148,444	113,990	97,676	84,310	1.11	-13.68
Tajikistan	22	21	48	84	94	0.00	11.90
Turkmenistan	39	148	129	207	348	0.00	68.12
Ukraine	720,216	729,758	723,813	672,065	648,394	8.52	-3.52
Uzbekistan	188	291	242	219	252	0.00	15.07
Other countries Central/East Europe	8		5	48			
Northern Europe	**197,916**	**206,636**	**165,980**	**154,462**	**184,131**	**2.42**	**19.21**
Denmark	18,108	16,522	13,168	10,827	13,652	0.18	26.09
Finland	9,636	10,110	8,975	8,266	10,549	0.14	27.62
Iceland	735	916	1,075	2,122	1,767	0.02	-16.73
Ireland	14,269	14,579	11,071	10,046	13,054	0.17	29.94
Norway	12,048	11,978	8,714	7,608	10,446	0.14	37.30
Sweden	24,625	24,381	19,363	23,964	25,559	0.34	6.66
United Kingdom	118,495	128,150	103,614	91,629	109,104	1.43	19.07
Southern Europe	**832,183**	**909,609**	**804,001**	**827,506**	**879,960**	**11.56**	**6.34**
Albania	3,779	4,549	4,919	4,720	6,757	0.09	43.16
Bosnia and Herzegovina	5,015	5,006	3,971	3,603	5,952	0.08	65.20
Croatia	26,531	27,398	25,192	20,326	19,362	0.25	-4.74
Greece	104,507	117,901	89,747	70,593	83,083	1.09	17.69
Holy See	15	5	8	9	7	0.00	-22.22
Italy	397,592	433,167	374,702	330,909	352,310	4.63	6.47
Malta	882	902	1,083	1,465	1,603	0.02	9.42
Portugal	15,520	15,671	20,209	47,460	47,234	0.62	-0.48
San Marino	190	252	156	217	231	0.00	6.45
Slovenia	28,695	36,612	34,563	23,224	16,774	0.22	-27.77
Spain	69,523	70,969	66,952	63,306	77,101	1.01	21.79
TFYR of Macedonia	8,698	13,365	12,474	17,899	19,015	0.25	6.23
Serbia and Montenegro	171,236	183,812	170,025	243,775	250,531	3.29	2.77
Western Europe	**1,026,850**	**1,066,725**	**901,923**	**834,887**	**882,888**	**11.60**	**5.75**
Austria	217,965	210,143	180,579	177,544	192,814	2.53	8.60
Belgium	42,708	43,878	36,772	42,407	49,856	0.66	17.57
France	184,515	183,361	150,052	131,050	153,118	2.01	16.84

ROMANIA

2. Arrivals of non-resident visitors at national borders, by country of residence

	2007	2008	2009	2010	2011	Market share 11	% Change 11-10
Germany	473,431	521,675	442,805	394,387	381,336	5.01	-3.31
Liechtenstein	99	222	151	214	479	0.01	123.83
Luxembourg	2,072	1,372	980	854	1,329	0.02	55.62
Monaco	29	20	17	27	25	0.00	-7.41
Netherlands	79,334	79,951	66,947	66,157	78,315	1.03	18.38
Switzerland	26,697	26,103	23,620	22,247	25,616	0.34	15.14
East Mediterranean Europe	**402,035**	**409,745**	**341,947**	**354,028**	**364,446**	**4.79**	**2.94**
Cyprus	12,702	11,463	8,492	7,955	10,408	0.14	30.84
Israel	105,130	95,758	75,918	81,179	83,376	1.10	2.71
Turkey	284,203	302,524	257,537	264,894	270,662	3.56	2.18
MIDDLE EAST	**29,195**	**31,793**	**26,520**	**33,482**	**33,500**	**0.44**	**0.05**
Bahrain	61	60	67	90	101	0.00	12.22
Palestine	459	503	554	587	573	0.01	-2.39
Iraq	2,036	1,979	2,300	2,470	2,634	0.03	6.64
Jordan	2,285	2,396	2,385	2,532	2,520	0.03	-0.47
Kuwait	515	468	427	421	532	0.01	26.37
Lebanon	4,834	5,334	5,051	5,267	4,884	0.06	-7.27
Libya	267	289	220	326	184	0.00	-43.56
Oman	40	65	103	121	204	0.00	68.60
Qatar	140	199	89	77	133	0.00	72.73
Saudi Arabia	597	565	583	563	853	0.01	51.51
Syrian Arab Republic	12,403	13,858	9,846	14,193	13,839	0.18	-2.49
United Arab Emirates	501	444	395	480	473	0.01	-1.46
Egypt	4,947	5,517	4,405	6,191	6,397	0.08	3.33
Yemen	110	116	95	164	173	0.00	5.49
SOUTH ASIA	**17,106**	**20,500**	**17,083**	**20,825**	**20,710**	**0.27**	**-0.55**
Afghanistan	58	227	185	218	203	0.00	-6.88
Bangladesh	133	998	456	274	202	0.00	-26.28
Sri Lanka	661	451	557	477	569	0.01	19.29
India	8,088	9,364	6,662	8,861	9,040	0.12	2.02
Iran, Islamic Republic of	6,429	7,368	7,416	8,873	8,626	0.11	-2.78
Maldives	82	68	53	129	36	0.00	-72.09
Nepal	66	149	65	223	186	0.00	-16.59
Pakistan	1,589	1,875	1,689	1,770	1,848	0.02	4.41
NOT SPECIFIED	**1,485**	**1,719**	**1,067**	**417**	**473**	**0.01**	**13.43**
Other countries of the World	1,485	1,719	1,067	417	473	0.01	13.43

ROMANIA

3. Arrivals of non-resident tourists in hotels and similar establishments, by country of residence

	2007	2008	2009	2010	2011	Market share 11	% Change 11-10
TOTAL	1,531,019	1,439,231	1,255,703	1,323,585	1,494,024	100.00	12.88
AFRICA	6,970	7,730	7,435	8,854	10,279	0.69	16.09
Other Africa	6,970	7,730	7,435	8,854	10,279	0.69	16.09
All countries of Africa (*)	6,970	7,730	7,435	8,854	10,279	0.69	16.09
AMERICAS	119,774	97,239	93,504	105,060	107,766	7.21	2.58
North America	112,956	90,236	88,063	98,014	100,209	6.71	2.24
Canada	13,760	12,984	10,732	12,174	11,991	0.80	-1.50
Mexico	1,053	1,459	1,411	1,535	2,429	0.16	58.24
United States of America	98,143	75,793	75,920	84,305	85,789	5.74	1.76
Other Americas	6,818	7,003	5,441	7,046	7,557	0.51	7.25
Other countries of the Americas	6,818	7,003	5,441	7,046	7,557	0.51	7.25
EAST ASIA AND THE PACIFIC	54,977	54,619	47,908	53,586	66,003	4.42	23.17
North-East Asia	24,491	22,865	18,681	19,188	25,447	1.70	32.62
China	6,211	7,622	6,929	5,936	9,046	0.61	52.39
Japan	18,280	15,243	11,752	13,252	16,401	1.10	23.76
Other East Asia and the Pacific	30,486	31,754	29,227	34,398	40,556	2.71	17.90
Other countries of Asia	22,299	23,314	21,944	26,107	30,045	2.01	15.08
All countries of Oceania	8,187	8,440	7,283	8,291	10,511	0.70	26.78
EUROPE	1,341,720	1,264,622	1,085,493	1,132,656	1,288,795	86.26	13.79
Central/Eastern Europe	217,942	232,238	198,652	191,838	250,097	16.74	30.37
Bulgaria	19,949	26,227	23,764	24,538	31,276	2.09	27.46
Czech Republic	17,811	19,652	18,530	17,070	19,705	1.32	15.44
Hungary	94,512	89,818	75,569	75,056	85,544	5.73	13.97
Republic of Moldova	17,531	22,246	19,893	7,455	25,757	1.72	245.50
Poland	32,690	31,497	29,689	35,573	45,672	3.06	28.39
Russian Federation	14,382	17,101	13,101	14,714	19,261	1.29	30.90
Slovakia	8,640	11,958	7,510	7,724	9,524	0.64	23.30
Ukraine	12,427	13,739	10,596	9,708	13,358	0.89	37.60
Northern Europe	142,872	129,988	115,105	114,469	130,023	8.70	13.59
Denmark	13,453	12,129	11,104	11,091	13,868	0.93	25.04
Finland	7,711	8,020	7,366	6,332	6,046	0.40	-4.52
Ireland	7,780	7,849	6,957	7,684	7,922	0.53	3.10
Norway	11,717	8,928	8,004	7,455	8,628	0.58	15.73
Sweden	12,692	11,513	10,893	10,512	12,811	0.86	21.87
United Kingdom	89,519	81,549	70,781	71,395	80,748	5.40	13.10
Southern Europe	316,664	296,935	252,047	262,369	300,468	20.11	14.52
Greece	36,533	37,530	36,706	35,824	36,773	2.46	2.65
Italy	193,775	164,017	141,131	144,496	171,537	11.48	18.71
Montenegro	385	644	543	422	550	0.04	30.33
Portugal	11,590	12,567	7,446	8,692	10,391	0.70	19.55
Serbia	6,281	8,486	7,868	6,714	9,103	0.61	35.58
Slovenia	6,510	6,715	5,362	5,640	5,268	0.35	-6.60
Spain	61,590	66,976	52,991	60,581	66,846	4.47	10.34
Western Europe	507,575	458,681	404,019	411,095	448,888	30.05	9.19
Austria	77,933	70,109	57,791	61,013	61,722	4.13	1.16
Belgium	23,078	23,508	22,815	23,126	23,986	1.61	3.72
France	117,354	112,813	99,246	97,934	107,839	7.22	10.11
Germany	226,094	203,092	170,994	175,425	196,714	13.17	12.14
Luxembourg	2,234	1,138	1,143	1,047	1,413	0.09	34.96
Netherlands	44,908	42,956	36,594	36,286	40,402	2.70	11.34
Switzerland	15,974	5,065	15,436	16,264	16,812	1.13	3.37

ROMANIA

3. Arrivals of non-resident tourists in hotels and similar establishments, by country of residence

	2007	2008	2009	2010	2011	Market share 11	% Change 11-10
East Mediterranean Europe	**106,954**	**92,364**	**74,479**	**96,460**	**113,991**	**7.63**	**18.17**
Israel	80,949	65,906	53,606	71,630	86,647	5.80	20.96
Turkey	26,005	26,458	20,873	24,830	27,344	1.83	10.12
Other Europe	**49,713**	**54,416**	**41,191**	**56,425**	**45,328**	**3.03**	**-19.67**
Other countries of Europe	49,713	54,416	41,191	56,425	45,328	3.03	-19.67
NOT SPECIFIED	**7,578**	**15,021**	**21,363**	**23,429**	**21,181**	**1.42**	**-9.59**
Other countries of the World	7,578	15,021	21,363	23,429	21,181	1.42	-9.59

ROMANIA

4. Arrivals of non-resident tourists in all types of accommodation establishments, by country of residence

		2007	2008	2009	2010	2011	Market share 11	% Change 11-10
TOTAL		1,550,957	1,465,891	1,275,590	1,343,078	1,514,781	100.00	12.78
AFRICA		6,979	7,882	7,437	8,875	10,292	0.68	15.97
Other Africa		6,979	7,882	7,437	8,875	10,292	0.68	15.97
All countries of Africa	(*)	6,979	7,882	7,437	8,875	10,292	0.68	15.97
AMERICAS		119,920	97,504	93,625	105,166	107,836	7.12	2.54
North America		113,095	90,436	88,162	98,075	100,277	6.62	2.25
Canada		13,835	13,037	10,780	12,196	12,023	0.79	-1.42
Mexico		1,054	1,464	1,411	1,536	2,429	0.16	58.14
United States of America		98,206	75,935	75,971	84,343	85,825	5.67	1.76
Other Americas		6,825	7,068	5,463	7,091	7,559	0.50	6.60
Other countries of the Americas		6,825	7,068	5,463	7,091	7,559	0.50	6.60
EAST ASIA AND THE PACIFIC		55,209	54,970	47,015	53,653	66,077	4.36	23.16
North-East Asia		24,531	22,890	18,714	19,203	25,469	1.68	32.63
China		6,245	7,632	6,946	5,949	9,063	0.60	52.34
Japan		18,286	15,258	11,768	13,254	16,406	1.08	23.78
Other East Asia and the Pacific		30,678	32,080	28,301	34,450	40,608	2.68	17.88
Other countries of Asia		22,349	23,356	20,903	26,119	30,076	1.99	15.15
All countries of Oceania		8,329	8,724	7,398	8,331	10,532	0.70	26.42
EUROPE		1,361,262	1,290,414	1,106,150	1,151,955	1,309,395	86.44	13.67
Central/Eastern Europe		222,995	237,408	202,823	208,844	249,216	16.45	19.33
Bulgaria		20,052	26,368	23,820	24,605	31,352	2.07	27.42
Czech Republic		18,366	19,902	18,804	17,221	20,086	1.33	16.64
Hungary		96,290	92,178	76,906	75,904	86,489	5.71	13.95
Republic of Moldova		18,554	22,818	20,094	21,479	25,952	1.71	20.82
Poland		33,335	32,842	31,579	37,254	47,006	3.10	26.18
Russian Federation		15,143	17,400	13,402	14,900	19,503	1.29	30.89
Slovakia		8,752	12,057	7,561	7,773	5,357	0.35	-31.08
Ukraine		12,503	13,843	10,657	9,708	13,471	0.89	38.76
Northern Europe		143,520	131,774	115,898	115,041	130,403	8.61	13.35
Denmark		13,506	12,369	11,162	11,146	13,901	0.92	24.72
Finland		7,742	8,061	7,409	6,348	6,059	0.40	-4.55
Ireland		7,802	8,162	6,989	7,696	7,950	0.52	3.30
Norway		11,801	9,111	8,037	7,495	8,645	0.57	15.34
Sweden		12,782	11,610	10,944	10,566	12,854	0.85	21.65
United Kingdom		89,887	82,461	71,357	71,790	80,994	5.35	12.82
Southern Europe		317,557	298,573	252,673	263,439	301,519	19.91	14.45
Greece		36,559	37,592	36,735	35,854	36,845	2.43	2.76
Italy		194,374	165,018	141,568	145,304	172,245	11.37	18.54
Montenegro		385	644	543	422	550	0.04	30.33
Portugal		11,599	12,614	7,456	8,700	10,397	0.69	19.51
Serbia		6,290	8,577	7,881	6,721	9,118	0.60	35.66
Slovenia		6,551	6,809	5,423	5,761	5,357	0.35	-7.01
Spain		61,799	67,319	53,067	60,677	67,007	4.42	10.43
Western Europe		520,080	482,986	417,626	424,961	464,196	30.64	9.23
Austria		78,591	70,821	58,401	61,330	62,123	4.10	1.29
Belgium		23,353	24,164	23,197	23,754	24,601	1.62	3.57
France		118,505	115,192	100,330	99,225	109,346	7.22	10.20
Germany		234,854	213,005	181,084	184,626	206,932	13.66	12.08
Luxembourg		2,234	1,142	1,145	1,051	1,417	0.09	34.82
Netherlands		46,378	44,624	37,713	38,038	42,428	2.80	11.54
Switzerland		16,165	14,038	15,756	16,937	17,349	1.15	2.43

ROMANIA

4. Arrivals of non-resident tourists in all types of accommodation establishments, by country of residence

	2007	2008	2009	2010	2011	Market share 11	% Change 11-10
East Mediterranean Europe	**107,040**	**92,725**	**75,657**	**96,637**	**114,066**	**7.53**	**18.04**
Israel	80,984	66,187	53,649	71,672	86,679	5.72	20.94
Turkey	26,056	26,538	22,008	24,965	27,387	1.81	9.70
Other Europe	**50,070**	**46,948**	**41,473**	**43,033**	**49,995**	**3.30**	**16.18**
Other countries of Europe	50,070	46,948	41,473	43,033	49,995	3.30	16.18
NOT SPECIFIED	**7,587**	**15,121**	**21,363**	**23,429**	**21,181**	**1.40**	**-9.59**
Other countries of the World	7,587	15,121	21,363	23,429	21,181	1.40	-9.59

ROMANIA

5. Overnight stays of non-resident tourists in hotels and similar establishments, by country of residence

	2007	2008	2009	2010	2011	Market share 11	% Change 11-10
TOTAL	3,497,156	3,251,357	2,581,861	2,673,714	2,978,217	100.00	11.39
AFRICA	23,696	18,545	18,184	23,426	23,548	0.79	0.52
Other Africa	23,696	18,545	18,184	23,426	23,548	0.79	0.52
All countries of Africa (*)	23,696	18,545	18,184	23,426	23,548	0.79	0.52
AMERICAS	250,626	207,921	170,573	198,437	212,257	7.13	6.96
North America	233,816	191,301	159,421	182,902	194,854	6.54	6.53
Canada	28,247	27,894	21,066	25,195	23,647	0.79	-6.14
Mexico	2,451	3,587	3,315	3,351	12,705	0.43	279.14
United States of America	203,118	159,820	135,040	154,356	158,502	5.32	2.69
Other Americas	16,810	16,620	11,152	15,535	17,403	0.58	12.02
Other countries of the Americas	16,810	16,620	11,152	15,535	17,403	0.58	12.02
EAST ASIA AND THE PACIFIC	125,088	148,321	105,115	119,008	132,426	4.45	11.27
North-East Asia	53,587	73,715	41,704	40,429	49,450	1.66	22.31
China	18,590	46,733	21,192	18,050	21,362	0.72	18.35
Japan	34,997	26,982	20,512	22,379	28,088	0.94	25.51
Other East Asia and the Pacific	71,501	74,606	63,411	78,579	82,976	2.79	5.60
Other countries of Asia	56,383	58,459	27,085	62,859	64,569	2.17	2.72
All countries of Oceania	15,118	16,147	36,326	15,720	18,407	0.62	17.09
EUROPE	3,085,086	2,850,301	2,251,663	2,293,900	2,575,787	86.49	12.29
Central/Eastern Europe	519,904	537,153	438,831	417,645	506,898	17.02	21.37
Bulgaria	39,350	60,167	59,893	45,653	55,863	1.88	22.36
Czech Republic	34,417	41,348	33,645	30,738	34,851	1.17	13.38
Hungary	206,856	193,184	162,445	152,770	175,619	5.90	14.96
Republic of Moldova	48,246	54,320	54,155	53,905	64,764	2.17	20.14
Poland	78,065	75,371	53,712	66,281	90,101	3.03	35.94
Russian Federation	47,379	49,685	32,195	33,111	42,216	1.42	27.50
Slovakia	20,490	27,461	19,954	15,307	18,833	0.63	23.04
Ukraine	45,101	35,617	22,832	19,880	24,651	0.83	24.00
Northern Europe	309,694	294,533	228,647	226,188	244,210	8.20	7.97
Denmark	32,614	27,671	24,824	25,093	30,434	1.02	21.28
Finland	16,933	19,488	16,039	13,184	11,879	0.40	-9.90
Ireland	16,411	16,533	14,976	15,214	16,665	0.56	9.54
Norway	29,047	26,974	16,898	14,725	16,700	0.56	13.41
Sweden	27,428	23,934	20,102	20,162	24,074	0.81	19.40
United Kingdom	187,261	179,933	135,808	137,810	144,458	4.85	4.82
Southern Europe	683,733	644,954	506,579	521,502	611,470	20.53	17.25
Greece	81,348	85,745	70,431	72,038	96,135	3.23	33.45
Italy	424,454	368,545	295,924	296,239	339,604	11.40	14.64
Montenegro	990	1,708	804	945	976	0.03	3.28
Portugal	37,026	29,707	16,543	19,879	23,059	0.77	16.00
Serbia	12,902	21,502	16,730	12,938	18,721	0.63	44.70
Slovenia	14,340	13,164	10,267	10,471	9,214	0.31	-12.00
Spain	112,673	124,583	95,880	108,992	123,761	4.16	13.55
Western Europe	1,123,271	998,566	799,412	813,908	870,311	29.22	6.93
Austria	141,074	133,241	97,786	106,036	106,699	3.58	0.63
Belgium	46,763	48,598	43,758	44,393	44,789	1.50	0.89
France	261,358	236,269	190,815	188,030	209,080	7.02	11.20
Germany	551,068	463,073	362,888	372,799	397,893	13.36	6.73
Luxembourg	4,435	2,429	2,184	2,187	3,212	0.11	46.87
Netherlands	89,009	89,215	74,330	71,755	79,126	2.66	10.27
Switzerland	29,564	25,741	27,651	28,708	29,512	0.99	2.80

ROMANIA

5. Overnight stays of non-resident tourists in hotels and similar establishments, by country of residence

	2007	2008	2009	2010	2011	Market share 11	% Change 11-10
East Mediterranean Europe	279,717	240,783	180,799	214,179	243,754	8.18	13.81
Israel	218,934	176,003	135,782	164,384	188,320	6.32	14.56
Turkey	60,783	64,780	45,017	49,795	55,434	1.86	11.32
Other Europe	168,767	134,312	97,395	100,478	99,144	3.33	-1.33
Other countries of Europe	168,767	134,312	97,395	100,478	99,144	3.33	-1.33
NOT SPECIFIED	12,660	26,269	36,326	38,943	34,199	1.15	-12.18
Other countries of the World	12,660	26,269	36,326	38,943	34,199	1.15	-12.18

ROMANIA

6. Overnight stays of non-resident tourists in all types of accommodation establishments, by country of residence

	2007	2008	2009	2010	2011	Market share 11	% Change 11-10
TOTAL	3,586,439	3,359,244	2,667,666	2,755,083	3,062,968	100.00	11.18
AFRICA	23,710	18,848	18,189	23,488	23,593	0.77	0.45
Other Africa	23,710	18,848	18,189	23,488	23,593	0.77	0.45
All countries of Africa (*)	23,710	18,848	18,189	23,488	23,593	0.77	0.45
AMERICAS	251,011	208,647	171,091	198,780	212,720	6.94	7.01
North America	234,174	191,708	159,896	183,088	195,296	6.38	6.67
Canada	28,362	27,971	21,247	25,251	23,931	0.78	-5.23
Mexico	2,452	3,608	3,315	3,356	12,705	0.41	278.58
United States of America	203,360	160,129	135,334	154,481	158,660	5.18	2.71
Other Americas	16,837	16,939	11,195	15,692	17,424	0.57	11.04
Other countries of the Americas	16,837	16,939	11,195	15,692	17,424	0.57	11.04
EAST ASIA AND THE PACIFIC	125,469	152,773	105,688	119,133	132,788	4.34	11.46
North-East Asia	53,650	73,764	41,826	40,466	49,513	1.62	22.36
China	18,646	46,761	21,246	18,085	21,385	0.70	18.25
Japan	35,004	27,003	20,580	22,381	28,128	0.92	25.68
Other East Asia and the Pacific	71,819	79,009	63,862	78,667	83,275	2.72	5.86
Other countries of Asia	56,514	62,525	49,779	62,891	64,702	2.11	2.88
All countries of Oceania	15,305	16,484	14,083	15,776	18,573	0.61	17.73
EUROPE	3,173,566	2,952,565	2,336,372	2,374,739	2,659,668	86.83	12.00
Central/Eastern Europe	541,566	552,035	449,444	425,539	514,397	16.79	20.88
Bulgaria	39,562	60,382	60,040	45,746	56,028	1.83	22.48
Czech Republic	37,390	41,807	34,118	31,055	35,150	1.15	13.19
Hungary	212,816	200,550	165,613	155,067	177,625	5.80	14.55
Republic of Moldova	51,072	56,112	54,667	54,336	65,273	2.13	20.13
Poland	79,403	77,677	56,975	69,315	92,332	3.01	33.21
Russian Federation	54,928	51,719	34,968	34,594	44,178	1.44	27.70
Slovakia	20,866	27,769	20,060	15,365	18,892	0.62	22.95
Ukraine	45,529	36,019	23,003	20,061	24,919	0.81	24.22
Northern Europe	311,504	299,389	230,426	227,533	245,061	8.00	7.70
Denmark	32,770	29,109	25,002	25,217	30,499	1.00	20.95
Finland	17,001	19,579	16,142	13,224	11,904	0.39	-9.98
Ireland	16,452	17,325	15,043	15,243	16,770	0.55	10.02
Norway	29,401	27,409	17,060	14,968	16,790	0.55	12.17
Sweden	27,757	24,228	20,206	20,318	24,142	0.79	18.82
United Kingdom	188,123	181,739	136,973	138,563	144,956	4.73	4.61
Southern Europe	685,352	649,454	507,754	523,356	613,190	20.02	17.16
Greece	81,396	85,877	70,512	72,080	96,260	3.14	33.55
Italy	425,575	370,418	296,735	297,627	340,733	11.12	14.48
Montenegro	990	1,708	804	945	976	0.03	3.28
Portugal	37,063	29,785	16,553	19,891	23,075	0.75	16.01
Serbia	12,934	21,748	16,775	12,966	18,756	0.61	44.66
Slovenia	14,436	13,407	10,365	10,718	9,356	0.31	-12.71
Spain	112,958	126,511	96,010	109,129	124,034	4.05	13.66
Western Europe	1,184,099	1,068,081	869,499	881,446	942,590	30.77	6.94
Austria	142,769	135,314	100,275	107,540	107,817	3.52	0.26
Belgium	47,462	49,959	44,527	45,602	45,911	1.50	0.68
France	263,600	240,899	192,790	190,304	211,340	6.90	11.05
Germany	602,055	519,790	424,532	428,587	459,617	15.01	7.24
Luxembourg	4,435	2,455	2,212	2,215	3,224	0.11	45.55
Netherlands	93,520	92,808	76,684	76,464	83,841	2.74	9.65
Switzerland	30,258	26,856	28,479	30,734	30,840	1.01	0.34

ROMANIA

6. Overnight stays of non-resident tourists in all types of accommodation establishments, by country of residence

	2007	2008	2009	2010	2011	Market share 11	% Change 11-10
East Mediterranean Europe	279,926	241,423	180,973	214,719	243,914	7.96	13.60
Israel	219,009	176,397	135,837	164,601	188,409	6.15	14.46
Turkey	60,917	65,026	45,136	50,118	55,505	1.81	10.75
Other Europe	171,119	142,183	98,276	102,146	100,516	3.28	-1.60
Other countries of Europe	171,119	142,183	98,276	102,146	100,516	3.28	-1.60
NOT SPECIFIED	12,683	26,411	36,326	38,943	34,199	1.12	-12.18
Other countries of the World	12,683	26,411	36,326	38,943	34,199	1.12	-12.18

RUSSIAN FEDERATION

2. Arrivals of non-resident visitors at national borders, by nationality

	2007	2008	2009	2010	2011	Market share 11	% Change 11-10
TOTAL	22,908,625	23,676,140	21,338,650	22,281,217			
AFRICA	29,964	35,734	34,649	36,833			
East Africa	4,092	4,067	4,871	5,041			
British Indian Ocean Territory	260	4	28	182			
Burundi	94	117	120	108			
Comoros	70	30	51	63			
Ethiopia	348	395	368	420			
Eritrea	81	50	58	69			
Djibouti	21	24	24	72			
Kenya	853	968	958	1,062			
Madagascar	260	144	243	198			
Malawi	46	60	59	53			
Mauritius	407	480	79	590			
Mozambique	107	109	1,105	158			
Rwanda	41	50	34	41			
Seychelles	155	153	515	200			
Somalia	197	86	75	116			
Zimbabwe	293	290	286	360			
Uganda	194	435	195	403			
United Republic of Tanzania	377	355	378	502			
Zambia	288	317	295	444			
Central Africa	2,464	2,603	3,531	2,981			
Angola	1,024	917	1,033	1,091			
Cameroon	625	718	806	785			
Central African Republic	8	18	144	24			
Chad	136	132	123	121			
Congo	478	522	551	328			
Democratic Republic of the Congo	10	33	672	416			
Equatorial Guinea	103	138	117	132			
Gabon	79	124	75	71			
Sao Tome and Principe	1	1	10	13			
North Africa	7,445	8,392	9,786	10,090			
Algeria	2,236	2,548	3,140	2,564			
Morocco	2,710	2,955	3,679	4,146			
Western Sahara			1	1			
Sudan	804	966	1,157	1,220			
Tunisia	1,695	1,923	1,809	2,159			
Southern Africa	7,403	11,807	7,830	8,695			
Botswana	59	57	66	123			
Lesotho	19	57	16	58			
Namibia	201	219	232	416			
South Africa	7,085	11,428	7,447	8,022			
Swaziland	39	46	69	76			
West Africa	8,560	8,865	8,631	10,026			
Cape Verde	255	280	137	323			
Benin	163	122	150	215			
Gambia	30	31	21	38			
Ghana	613	744	822	890			
Guinea	222	201	209	283			
Côte d'Ivoire	273	274	446	425			
Liberia	4,397	4,332	3,768	3,746			
Mali	184	173	169	270			
Mauritania	186	98	79	131			
Niger	74	17	51	24			
Nigeria	1,532	2,027	2,244	2,552			
Guinea-Bissau	286	108	121	749			

RUSSIAN FEDERATION

2. Arrivals of non-resident visitors at national borders, by nationality

	2007	2008	2009	2010	2011	Market share 11	% Change 11-10
Senegal	149	173	148	198			
Sierra Leone	86	179	136	65			
Togo	35	76	98	61			
Burkina Faso	75	30	32	56			
AMERICAS	**466,404**	**503,456**	**469,112**	**420,512**			
Caribbean	**47,790**	**45,799**	**52,965**	**33,947**			
Antigua and Barbuda	5,483	8,269	4,860	5,673			
Bahamas	25,613	21,028	29,122	18,871			
Barbados	798	447	670	492			
Bermuda	3,014	2,827	9,254	457			
British Virgin Islands	554	268	11				
Cayman Islands	1,476	271	919	267			
Cuba	5,069	4,386	4,172	4,053			
Dominica	397	569	330	213			
Dominican Republic	792	259	667	690			
Grenada	91	36	114	45			
Haiti	56	79	68	66			
Jamaica	348	1,056	630	447			
Martinique			15				
Netherlands Antilles	104	652	256				
Puerto Rico	10	10	15	15			
Saint Kitts and Nevis	113	846	238	120			
Anguilla	1	30	7	1,183			
Saint Lucia	5	51	139	62			
Saint Vincent and the Grenadines	3,704	4,555	1,227	999			
Trinidad and Tobago	162	160	251	294			
Central America	**26,340**	**26,274**	**21,065**	**12,854**			
Belize	3,159	1,954	1,199	1,208			
Costa Rica	319	691	454	710			
El Salvador	120	120	245	198			
Guatemala	404	453	1,202	1,002			
Honduras	486	9,331	5,397	3,022			
Nicaragua	154	319	455	396			
Panama	21,698	13,406	12,113	6,318			
North America	**350,415**	**381,338**	**354,963**	**324,394**			
Canada	46,560	62,004	59,537	48,559			
Greenland	42	11	1	8			
Mexico	10,292	14,269	10,058	13,767			
United States of America	293,521	305,054	285,367	262,060			
South America	**41,859**	**50,045**	**40,119**	**49,317**			
Argentina	5,651	7,147	9,598	9,044			
Bolivia	317	597	354	365			
Brazil	24,733	23,522	15,540	21,950			
Chile	1,698	3,126	3,207	3,438			
Colombia	2,183	3,402	3,794	4,620			
Ecuador	930	1,053	1,233	1,495			
Falkland Islands, Malvinas	16	132	57	355			
French Guiana	53						
Guyana	36	781	60	66			
Paraguay	138	117	198	185			
Peru	1,233	4,908	1,601	3,351			
Suriname	2	4	8	25			
Uruguay	1,698	2,527	813	896			
Venezuela	3,171	2,729	3,656	3,527			

RUSSIAN FEDERATION

2. Arrivals of non-resident visitors at national borders, by nationality

	2007	2008	2009	2010	2011	Market share 11	% Change 11-10
EAST ASIA AND THE PACIFIC	1,381,412	1,477,644	1,294,719	1,358,186			
North-East Asia	1,147,917	1,193,738	1,068,706	1,121,871			
China	765,120	815,469	718,581	747,640			
Taiwan, Province of China	10,284	9,585	7,844	11,940			
Hong Kong, China	3,414	5,230	8,169	14,852			
Japan	83,621	86,237	74,159	78,188			
Korea, Dem. People's Republic of	15,711	20,739	18,686	21,167			
Korea, Republic of	124,785	101,304	84,166	90,622			
Macao, China	50	73	104	95			
Mongolia	144,932	155,101	156,997	157,367			
South-East Asia	180,744	232,735	185,855	196,816			
Brunei Darussalam	65	92	211	58			
Myanmar	4,764	6,297	3,467	5,424			
Cambodia	1,793	1,101	416	443			
Indonesia	22,301	30,817	24,841	14,448			
Lao People's Democratic Republic	209	146	114	252			
Malaysia	11,083	13,249	11,844	16,508			
Philippines	79,904	92,801	79,365	81,385			
Singapore	6,433	12,486	10,226	12,283			
Viet Nam	38,337	59,596	40,809	50,823			
Thailand	15,855	16,150	14,562	15,192			
Australasia	44,157	43,824	36,948	36,199			
Australia	38,246	37,574	31,931	30,584			
New Zealand	5,911	6,250	5,017	5,615			
Melanesia	353	168	492	604			
Solomon Islands	174	3	3	434			
Fiji	45	19	39	43			
New Caledonia	1	16	3	1			
Vanuatu	123	129	443	82			
Papua New Guinea	10	1	4	44			
Micronesia	8,066	7,029	2,468	2,575			
Kiribati	51	563	118	347			
Guam	27	5	1	29			
Nauru		1	6	3			
Northern Mariana Islands				4			
Micronesia, Federated States of	2	3		1			
Marshall Islands	7,983	6,455	2,342	2,189			
Palau	3	2	1	2			
Polynesia	175	150	250	121			
American Samoa	18	1	1	11			
Pitcairn	10	86		13			
Tokelau			1				
Tonga	6	29	9	12			
Tuvalu	132	29	212	85			
Samoa	9	5	27				
EUROPE	20,395,436	21,186,817	18,790,566	19,568,815			
Central/Eastern Europe	17,180,798	17,799,810	15,578,448	16,370,280			
Azerbaijan	993,889	989,529	892,435	979,778			
Armenia	418,204	458,621	379,525	459,040			
Bulgaria	40,070	41,053	37,704	38,446			
Belarus	272,780	255,143	286,495	259,191			
Czech Republic	41,518	44,720	38,356	40,565			
Estonia	390,632	662,917	920,497	474,949			
Georgia	43,802	46,362	19,846	24,568			
Hungary	23,713	24,014	19,791	20,736			
Kazakhstan	2,895,749	2,732,118	2,590,688	2,747,358			

RUSSIAN FEDERATION

2. Arrivals of non-resident visitors at national borders, by nationality

	2007	2008	2009	2010	2011	Market share 11	% Change 11-10
Kyrgyzstan	512,210	552,715	406,504	552,909			
Latvia	398,723	423,050	516,838	569,330			
Lithuania	742,500	680,461	600,785	760,728			
Republic of Moldova	1,042,842	1,167,266	884,999	988,084			
Poland	957,455	779,826	434,529	394,872			
Romania	13,168	15,593	14,072	17,884			
Slovakia	22,319	20,195	15,863	18,512			
Tajikistan	737,536	900,682	674,572	830,160			
Turkmenistan	27,120	33,947	27,704	35,017			
Ukraine	6,421,805	6,415,361	5,604,433	5,574,067			
Uzbekistan	1,184,763	1,556,237	1,212,812	1,584,086			
Northern Europe	**1,373,172**	**1,443,552**	**1,452,439**	**1,371,633**			
Denmark	35,613	35,302	30,316	33,121			
Faeroe Islands	30	14	25	24			
Finland	975,565	1,000,238	1,057,575	1,012,621			
Iceland	2,193	1,867	1,627	1,437			
Ireland	13,107	15,483	14,078	11,990			
Norway	47,084	56,878	49,488	45,340			
Svalbard and Jan Mayen Islands		6	97				
Sweden	61,036	59,629	59,438	54,253			
United Kingdom	238,544	274,135	239,795	212,847			
Southern Europe	**466,686**	**536,029**	**470,045**	**479,838**			
Albania	1,399	1,209	1,681	1,086			
Andorra	152	150	107	127			
Bosnia and Herzegovina	9,053	8,065	5,669	5,970			
Croatia	13,030	13,399	11,954	14,638			
Gibraltar	4,418	6,405	4,467	3,711			
Greece	35,706	39,704	39,130	33,296			
Italy	206,647	224,849	190,862	198,002			
Malta	20,983	22,148	21,970	27,204			
Montenegro	1,630	2,843	4,302	4,691			
Portugal	12,249	17,969	16,281	18,434			
San Marino	91	108	179	201			
Serbia	47,052	55,332	44,342	47,939			
Slovenia	12,241	13,336	10,569	11,160			
Spain	96,624	126,646	115,975	110,601			
TFYR of Macedonia	5,411	3,866	2,557	2,778			
Western Europe	**1,056,539**	**1,082,196**	**1,008,243**	**1,034,731**			
Austria	67,208	68,370	69,715	67,606			
Belgium	39,450	36,472	32,575	33,571			
France	201,441	201,205	185,082	194,218			
Germany	613,892	636,347	592,313	611,367			
Liechtenstein	363	192	244	205			
Luxembourg	3,119	3,009	1,993	1,912			
Monaco	115	144	148	168			
Netherlands	79,751	87,866	78,752	80,720			
Switzerland	51,200	48,591	47,421	44,964			
East Mediterranean Europe	**318,241**	**325,230**	**281,391**	**312,333**			
Cyprus	16,173	15,846	14,961	15,338			
Israel	64,952	70,289	89,098	100,291			
Turkey	237,116	239,095	177,332	196,704			
MIDDLE EAST	**23,998**	**38,839**	**38,009**	**41,496**			
Bahrain	163	301	222	494			
Palestine	758	822	749	1,200			
Iraq	1,701	1,746	1,549	2,760			
Jordan	2,643	2,784	2,649	3,024			
Kuwait	308	336	649	386			

RUSSIAN FEDERATION

2. Arrivals of non-resident visitors at national borders, by nationality

	2007	2008	2009	2010	2011	Market share 11	% Change 11-10
Lebanon	4,229	4,236	4,035	4,510			
Libya	839	1,259	979	1,316			
Oman	360	421	580	623			
Qatar	200	171	203	369			
Saudi Arabia	1,198	935	1,151	1,390			
Syrian Arab Republic		14,454	13,188	12,882			
United Arab Emirates	1,655	1,001	1,070	1,083			
Egypt	8,549	9,448	9,983	10,273			
Yemen	1,395	925	1,002	1,186			
SOUTH ASIA	**100,150**	**96,376**	**93,311**	**89,407**			
Afghanistan	6,194	7,244	7,258	7,336			
Bangladesh	1,275	1,395	1,464	1,580			
Bhutan	16	21	26	57			
Sri Lanka	1,710	1,602	1,518	1,873			
India	68,044	62,163	59,815	53,364			
Iran, Islamic Republic of	17,049	18,007	18,607	20,576			
Maldives	103	152	105	122			
Nepal	1,424	1,755	1,171	1,237			
Pakistan	4,335	4,037	3,347	3,262			
NOT SPECIFIED	**511,261**	**337,274**	**618,284**	**765,968**			
Other countries of the World	511,261	337,274	618,284	765,968			

RWANDA

2. Arrivals of non-resident visitors at national borders, by nationality

	2007	2008	2009	2010	2011	Market share 11	% Change 11-10
TOTAL	609,662	668,524	693,608	666,001			
AFRICA	515,543	556,943	590,720	546,904			
East Africa	284,702	261,567	274,015	287,330			
Burundi	102,134	74,686	97,154	72,316			
Comoros	26	53	42	33			
Ethiopia	705	933	697	948			
Eritrea	394	407	421	658			
Djibouti	102	72	66	255			
Kenya	18,704	25,870	30,721	37,193			
Madagascar	213	211	241	303			
Malawi	229	346	278	566			
Mauritius	107	214	101	105			
Mozambique	121	110	161	221			
Seychelles	66	28	16	37			
Somalia	149	107	263	134			
Zimbabwe	435	748	697	850			
Uganda	127,779	113,267	111,210	133,089			
United Republic of Tanzania	33,161	44,166	31,535	40,286			
Zambia	377	349	412	336			
Central Africa	222,559	282,338	304,084	245,838			
Angola	93	127	146	268			
Cameroon	717	828	1,127	1,232			
Central African Republic	72	153	131	147			
Chad	139	139	174	318			
Congo	77	132	121	134			
Democratic Republic of the Congo	221,028	280,297	301,649	242,976			
Equatorial Guinea	389	535	659	722			
Gabon	44	127	77	41			
North Africa	719	1,108	880	947			
Algeria	133	107	197	97			
Morocco	83	56	87	173			
Sudan	278	724	404	509			
Tunisia	225	221	192	168			
Southern Africa	3,319	6,277	6,216	6,097			
Botswana	93	73	89	98			
Lesotho	31	48	108	46			
Namibia	92	72	59	39			
South Africa	3,047	5,934	5,903	5,839			
Swaziland	56	150	57	75			
West Africa	4,244	5,653	5,525	6,692			
Benin	381	509	542	761			
Gambia	134	140	147	103			
Ghana	459	733	692	995			
Guinea			3	2			
Côte d'Ivoire	520	498	612	712			
Liberia		232	183	243			
Mali	389	360	366	452			
Mauritania	142	141	140	192			
Niger	96	109	85	249			
Nigeria	732	1,120	1,027	1,149			
Senegal	549	768	630	785			
Sierra Leone	157	270	327	372			
Togo	340	270	198	189			
Burkina Faso	345	503	573	488			

RWANDA

2. Arrivals of non-resident visitors at national borders, by nationality

	2007	2008	2009	2010	2011	Market share 11	% Change 11-10
AMERICAS	23,349	31,043	28,116	33,189			
Caribbean	373	361	151	150			
Barbados	3	7	14	26			
Haiti	347	320	115	96			
Jamaica	23	34	22	28			
Central America	37	57	101	42			
Costa Rica	20	27	9	6			
Guatemala	4	20	77	22			
Nicaragua	13	7	15	5			
Panama		3		9			
North America	22,040	27,843	25,437	30,700			
Canada	4,998	6,480	5,689	6,991			
Mexico	119	112	170	298			
United States of America	16,923	21,251	19,578	23,411			
South America	899	2,782	2,427	2,297			
Argentina	58	159	83	79			
Brazil	178	207	193	220			
Chile	45	36	25	67			
Colombia	46	103	61	68			
Guyana	16	15	10	8			
Peru	74	36	47	115			
Uruguay	232	1,949	1,590	1,231			
Venezuela	22	20	19	33			
Other countries of South America	228	257	399	476			
EAST ASIA AND THE PACIFIC	6,130	7,063	8,059	10,521			
North-East Asia	3,390	3,987	4,467	5,909			
China	2,161	2,507	2,965	4,062			
Taiwan, Province of China	68	13	20	30			
Japan	705	1,046	1,110	1,042			
Korea, Republic of	456	421	372	775			
South-East Asia	362	486	1,013	1,604			
Indonesia	61	64	77	64			
Malaysia	79	107	103	196			
Philippines	179	268	588	908			
Viet Nam	17	16	28	29			
Thailand	26	31	217	407			
Australasia	2,327	2,544	2,541	2,997			
Australia	1,845	2,159	2,068	2,453			
New Zealand	482	385	473	544			
Melanesia	51	46	38	11			
Fiji	51	46	38	11			
EUROPE	40,463	49,130	46,968	54,253			
Central/Eastern Europe	1,325	2,592	2,339	2,853			
Armenia		27	14	29			
Bulgaria	94	507	72	176			
Belarus	6	44	41	28			
Czech Republic	30	84	119	302			
Estonia	6	19	18	10			
Hungary	49	41	43	62			
Kazakhstan	78	93	63	68			
Republic of Moldova	13	2	2				
Poland	463	407	466	574			
Romania	119	90	170	369			
Russian Federation	297	402	534	960			
Ukraine	170	876	797	275			

RWANDA

2. Arrivals of non-resident visitors at national borders, by nationality

	2007	2008	2009	2010	2011	Market share 11	% Change 11-10
Northern Europe	**13,349**	**14,044**	**14,650**	**16,154**			
Denmark	514	648	627	745			
Finland	216	307	350	435			
Norway	670	802	839	923			
Sweden	1,584	2,049	2,092	1,903			
United Kingdom	8,714	10,238	10,295	10,824			
Other countries of Northern Europe	1,651		447	1,324			
Southern Europe	**4,700**	**5,289**	**5,201**	**5,714**			
Bosnia and Herzegovina	32	104	116	54			
Croatia	89	134	89	104			
Holy See		2		2			
Italy	2,975	3,127	3,409	3,456			
Portugal	103	135	125	298			
Serbia	87	138	67	181			
Slovenia	91	142	42	79			
Spain	1,323	1,507	1,353	1,540			
Western Europe	**20,647**	**26,571**	**23,607**	**28,138**			
Austria	381	441	395	707			
Belgium	7,591	11,161	8,166	10,100			
France	3,329	4,165	5,058	5,990			
Germany	5,124	5,944	5,652	6,157			
Luxembourg	84	114	80	136			
Netherlands	2,728	3,356	2,979	3,376			
Switzerland	1,410	1,390	1,277	1,672			
East Mediterranean Europe	**442**	**634**	**1,171**	**1,394**			
Israel	439	556	467	455			
Turkey	3	78	704	939			
MIDDLE EAST	**1,270**	**3,366**	**2,104**	**2,784**			
Jordan	87	83	66	96			
Kuwait	6	7	7	9			
Lebanon	66	710	829	925			
Libya		261	164	398			
Oman	679	488	495	521			
Saudi Arabia	78	40	42	32			
Syrian Arab Republic	2	18	13	20			
United Arab Emirates	2	1,443	26	11			
Egypt	350	316	462	772			
SOUTH ASIA	**22,746**	**19,232**	**16,931**	**17,794**			
Bangladesh	208	148	346	388			
Sri Lanka	210	326	334	510			
India	16,721	17,111	13,085	16,178			
Iran, Islamic Republic of	42	48	65	39			
Nepal	269	134	140	127			
Pakistan	5,296	1,465	2,961	552			
NOT SPECIFIED	**161**	**1,747**	**710**	**556**			
Other countries of the World	161	1,747	710	556			

SABA

1. Arrivals of non-resident tourists at national borders, by country of residence

	2007	2008	2009	2010	2011	Market share 11	% Change 11-10
TOTAL	11,658	12,043	11,957	12,327			
AMERICAS	5,672	6,388	5,856	5,990			
Caribbean	462	1,175	1,130	1,150			
Dominican Republic	66						
Other countries of the Caribbean	396						
All countries of the Caribbean		1,175	1,130	1,150			
North America	5,210	5,213	4,726	4,840			
Canada	744	757	942	1,065			
United States of America	4,466	4,456	3,784	3,775			
EUROPE	5,236	5,655	6,101	6,337			
Northern Europe	708	493	405				
United Kingdom	623	493	405				
Scandinavia	85						
Southern Europe	28						
Italy	28						
Western Europe	4,500	4,720	5,373	5,475			
France	722	708	856	860			
Germany	271						
Netherlands	3,507	4,012	4,517	4,615			
Other Europe		442	323	862			
Other countries of Europe		442	323	862			
NOT SPECIFIED	750						
Other countries of the World	750						

SAINT KITTS AND NEVIS

1. Arrivals of non-resident tourists at national borders, by country of residence

		2007	2008	2009	2010	2011	Market share 11	% Change 11-10
TOTAL	(*)	**123,062**	**127,705**	**93,081**	**91,561**			
AMERICAS		**105,832**	**113,242**	**83,233**	**80,307**			
Caribbean		**28,822**	**28,982**	**22,410**	**19,923**			
All countries of the Caribbean		28,822	28,982	22,410	19,923			
North America		**77,010**	**84,260**	**60,823**	**60,384**			
Canada		7,116	7,805	6,413	5,720			
United States of America		69,894	76,455	54,410	54,664			
EUROPE		**12,162**	**9,970**	**6,496**	**7,655**			
Northern Europe		**12,162**	**9,970**	**6,496**	**7,655**			
United Kingdom		12,162	9,970	6,496	7,655			
NOT SPECIFIED		**5,068**	**4,493**	**3,352**	**3,599**			
Other countries of the World		5,068	4,493	3,352	3,599			

SAINT LUCIA

1. Arrivals of non-resident tourists at national borders, by country of residence

		2007	2008	2009	2010	2011	Market share 11	% Change 11-10
TOTAL	(*)	287,407	295,761	278,491	305,937	312,404	100.00	2.11
AMERICAS		192,018	197,750	189,805	216,734	219,754	70.34	1.39
Caribbean		57,273	59,757	60,183	53,998	58,876	18.85	9.03
Antigua and Barbuda		1,986	2,215	2,141	2,126	1,941	0.62	-8.70
Barbados		11,443	10,935	9,269	7,201	7,016	2.25	-2.57
Dominica		3,136	3,101	2,996	3,070	3,168	1.01	3.19
Dominican Republic		117	179	133	115	109	0.03	-5.22
Grenada		2,359	2,131	1,763	1,489	1,584	0.51	6.38
Haiti		67	106	127	116	110	0.04	-5.17
Jamaica		3,830	2,682	2,123	1,756	1,804	0.58	2.73
Netherlands Antilles		533			654	576	0.18	-11.93
Puerto Rico		347	613	931	829	1,505	0.48	81.54
Saint Kitts and Nevis		661	807	915	840	677	0.22	-19.40
Saint Vincent and the Grenadines		2,547	2,400	2,657	2,509	2,438	0.78	-2.83
Trinidad and Tobago		9,091	8,827	9,139	8,788	8,259	2.64	-6.02
United States Virgin Islands		756	1,034	828	675	675	0.22	
Other countries of the Caribbean		20,400	24,727	27,161	23,830	29,014	9.29	21.75
North America		132,073	134,875	127,248	161,239	157,749	50.50	-2.16
Canada		18,640	26,279	28,563	32,154	35,393	11.33	10.07
United States of America		113,433	108,596	98,685	129,085	122,356	39.17	-5.21
South America		1,774	1,584	1,849	1,089	1,546	0.49	41.97
Guyana		1,774	1,584	1,849	1,089	1,546	0.49	41.97
Other Americas		898	1,534	525	408	1,583	0.51	287.99
Other countries of the Americas		898	1,534	525	408	1,583	0.51	287.99
EAST ASIA AND THE PACIFIC		212	152	207	183	224	0.07	22.40
North-East Asia		212	152	207	183	224	0.07	22.40
Japan		212	152	207	183	224	0.07	22.40
EUROPE		89,647	93,601	84,238	85,695	91,759	29.37	7.08
Northern Europe		79,782	84,272	72,374	68,136	73,758	23.61	8.25
Sweden		602	579	521	719	699	0.22	-2.78
United Kingdom		79,180	83,693	71,853	67,417	73,059	23.39	8.37
Southern Europe		1,285	1,495	1,229	1,465	1,605	0.51	9.56
Italy		1,020	1,132	925	1,134	1,239	0.40	9.26
Spain		265	363	304	331	366	0.12	10.57
Western Europe		6,484	6,937	8,707	11,843	12,294	3.94	3.81
Austria		289	239	308	579	399	0.13	-31.09
Belgium		179	209	241	264	255	0.08	-3.41
France		3,642	4,271	5,356	5,822	7,428	2.38	27.59
Germany		1,592	1,823	2,416	4,142	3,041	0.97	-26.58
Netherlands		459			400	320	0.10	-20.00
Switzerland		323	395	386	636	851	0.27	33.81
Other Europe		2,096	897	1,928	4,251	4,102	1.31	-3.51
Other countries of Europe		2,096	897	1,928	4,251	4,102	1.31	-3.51
NOT SPECIFIED		5,530	4,258	4,241	3,325	667	0.21	-79.94
Other countries of the World		5,530	4,258	4,241	3,325	667	0.21	-79.94

SAINT VINCENT AND THE GRENADINES

1. Arrivals of non-resident tourists at national borders, by country of residence

		2007	2008	2009	2010	2011	Market share 11	% Change 11-10
TOTAL	(*)	**89,637**	**84,101**	**75,446**	**72,478**	**73,866**	**100.00**	**1.92**
AMERICAS		**64,518**	**60,549**	**55,424**	**53,933**	**52,391**	**70.93**	**-2.86**
Caribbean		**29,959**	**28,475**	**26,835**	**23,968**	**23,272**	**31.51**	**-2.90**
Antigua and Barbuda		1,246	1,078	1,093	921	847	1.15	-8.03
Barbados		9,574	8,993	8,335	7,375	6,562	8.88	-11.02
Grenada		1,463	1,374	1,521	1,075	1,007	1.36	-6.33
Netherlands Antilles		576	443	419	294	375	0.51	27.55
Saint Lucia		2,323	2,197	2,122	1,917	1,937	2.62	1.04
Trinidad and Tobago		8,610	8,335	7,346	6,709	7,110	9.63	5.98
Other countries of the Caribbean		6,167	6,055	5,999	5,677	5,434	7.36	-4.28
North America		**33,387**	**30,924**	**26,979**	**28,759**	**27,883**	**37.75**	**-3.05**
Canada		6,745	6,882	6,820	7,208	6,719	9.10	-6.78
United States of America		26,642	24,042	20,159	21,551	21,164	28.65	-1.80
Other Americas		**1,172**	**1,150**	**1,610**	**1,206**	**1,236**	**1.67**	**2.49**
Other countries of the Americas		1,172	1,150	1,610	1,206	1,236	1.67	2.49
EUROPE		**23,454**	**22,302**	**19,097**	**17,665**	**20,549**	**27.82**	**16.33**
Northern Europe		**17,454**	**16,276**	**14,054**	**12,957**	**15,650**	**21.19**	**20.78**
Ireland		208	225	209	190	199	0.27	4.74
Norway		122	149	144	148	165	0.22	11.49
Sweden		382	460	354	483	391	0.53	-19.05
United Kingdom		16,742	15,442	13,347	12,136	14,895	20.16	22.73
Southern Europe		**1,647**	**1,895**	**1,591**	**1,265**	**1,208**	**1.64**	**-4.51**
Italy		1,491	1,650	1,429	1,105	1,037	1.40	-6.15
Spain		156	245	162	160	171	0.23	6.88
Western Europe		**3,470**	**3,096**	**2,427**	**2,468**	**2,516**	**3.41**	**1.94**
Belgium		179	222	151	141	171	0.23	21.28
France		1,973	1,505	1,113	994	1,051	1.42	5.73
Germany		736	861	731	824	744	1.01	-9.71
Netherlands		112	123	67	193	166	0.22	-13.99
Switzerland		470	385	365	316	384	0.52	21.52
Other Europe		**883**	**1,035**	**1,025**	**975**	**1,175**	**1.59**	**20.51**
Other countries of Europe		883	1,035	1,025	975	1,175	1.59	20.51
NOT SPECIFIED		**1,665**	**1,250**	**925**	**880**	**926**	**1.25**	**5.23**
Other countries of the World		1,665	1,250	925	880	926	1.25	5.23

SAINT VINCENT AND THE GRENADINES

2. Arrivals of non-resident visitors at national borders, by country of residence

		2007	2008	2009	2010	2011	Market share 11	% Change 11-10
TOTAL	(*)	**96,436**	**89,882**	**80,631**	**77,564**	**77,807**	**100.00**	**0.31**
AMERICAS		**67,706**	**62,779**	**57,967**	**56,592**	**54,516**	**70.07**	**-3.67**
Caribbean		**32,112**	**29,829**	**28,507**	**25,654**	**24,628**	**31.65**	**-4.00**
Antigua and Barbuda		1,289	1,113	1,132	971	889	1.14	-8.44
Barbados		10,334	9,560	8,926	8,014	7,507	9.65	-6.33
Grenada		1,726	1,525	1,709	1,204	1,097	1.41	-8.89
Netherlands Antilles		589	440	422	374	386	0.50	3.21
Saint Lucia		2,658	2,382	2,347	2,139	2,133	2.74	-0.28
Trinidad and Tobago		9,100	8,601	7,754	7,092	7,415	9.53	4.55
Other countries of the Caribbean		6,416	6,208	6,217	5,860	5,201	6.68	-11.25
North America		**34,352**	**31,757**	**27,812**	**29,682**	**28,601**	**36.76**	**-3.64**
Canada		6,991	7,131	7,120	7,565	6,957	8.94	-8.04
United States of America		27,361	24,626	20,692	22,117	21,644	27.82	-2.14
Other Americas		**1,242**	**1,193**	**1,648**	**1,256**	**1,287**	**1.65**	**2.47**
Other countries of the Americas		1,242	1,193	1,648	1,256	1,287	1.65	2.47
EUROPE		**26,955**	**25,799**	**21,697**	**20,041**	**22,323**	**28.69**	**11.39**
Northern Europe		**20,337**	**19,210**	**16,036**	**14,715**	**16,890**	**21.71**	**14.78**
Ireland		301	262	266	225	227	0.29	0.89
Norway		129	162	146	165	170	0.22	3.03
Sweden		426	474	381	498	408	0.52	-18.07
United Kingdom		19,481	18,312	15,243	13,827	16,085	20.67	16.33
Southern Europe		**1,796**	**1,985**	**1,699**	**1,230**	**1,261**	**1.62**	**2.52**
Italy		1,629	1,735	1,530	1,067	1,079	1.39	1.12
Spain		167	250	169	163	182	0.23	11.66
Western Europe		**3,857**	**3,494**	**2,791**	**2,832**	**2,910**	**3.74**	**2.75**
Belgium		195	237	146	146	178	0.23	21.92
France		2,118	1,660	1,213	1,086	1,228	1.58	13.08
Germany		926	1,048	969	1,058	885	1.14	-16.35
Netherlands		117	141	67	196	180	0.23	-8.16
Switzerland		501	408	396	346	439	0.56	26.88
Other Europe		**965**	**1,110**	**1,171**	**1,264**	**1,262**	**1.62**	**-0.16**
Other countries of Europe		965	1,110	1,171	1,264	1,262	1.62	-0.16
NOT SPECIFIED		**1,775**	**1,304**	**967**	**931**	**968**	**1.24**	**3.97**
Other countries of the World		1,775	1,304	967	931	968	1.24	3.97

SAMOA

2. Arrivals of non-resident visitors at national borders, by country of residence

	2007	2008	2009	2010	2011	Market share 11	% Change 11-10
TOTAL	122,356	122,163	129,305	129,500	127,603	100.00	-1.46
AMERICAS	8,492	8,893	9,794	9,238	7,875	6.17	-14.75
North America	8,492	8,893	9,794	9,238	7,875	6.17	-14.75
Canada	435	428	530	580	450	0.35	-22.41
United States of America	8,057	8,465	9,264	8,658	7,425	5.82	-14.24
EAST ASIA AND THE PACIFIC	109,132	107,580	113,425	115,163	114,798	89.96	-0.32
North-East Asia	1,406	1,450	1,794	1,866	2,044	1.60	9.54
China	822	720	1,193	1,356	1,512	1.18	11.50
Japan	584	730	601	510	532	0.42	4.31
Australasia	72,411	74,176	79,094	81,252	80,121	62.79	-1.39
Australia	22,105	22,643	24,507	23,415	25,197	19.75	7.61
New Zealand	50,306	51,533	54,587	57,837	54,924	43.04	-5.04
Melanesia	3,160	2,439	2,538	2,636	2,646	2.07	0.38
Fiji	3,160	2,439	2,538	2,636	2,646	2.07	0.38
Polynesia	24,647	23,672	24,491	23,847	24,787	19.43	3.94
American Samoa	24,139	23,351	24,298	23,737	24,582	19.26	3.56
Cook Islands	508	321	193	110	205	0.16	86.36
Other East Asia and the Pacific	7,508	5,843	5,508	5,562	5,200	4.08	-6.51
Other countries of Asia	1,502	1,551	1,627	1,927	1,500	1.18	-22.16
Other countries of Oceania	6,006	4,292	3,881	3,635	3,700	2.90	1.79
EUROPE	4,420	5,091	5,547	4,658	4,055	3.18	-12.95
Northern Europe	2,069	2,239	2,392	2,171	1,601	1.25	-26.26
United Kingdom	1,525	1,707	1,719	1,306	1,163	0.91	-10.95
Scandinavia	544	532	673	865	438	0.34	-49.36
Western Europe	1,340	1,457	1,633	1,228	1,291	1.01	5.13
Germany	1,095	1,185	1,450	1,089	1,151	0.90	5.69
Benelux	245	272	183	139	140	0.11	0.72
Other Europe	1,011	1,395	1,522	1,259	1,163	0.91	-7.63
Other countries of Europe	1,011	1,395	1,522	1,259	1,163	0.91	-7.63
NOT SPECIFIED	312	599	539	441	875	0.69	98.41
Other countries of the World	312	599	539	441	875	0.69	98.41

SAN MARINO

2. Arrivals of non-resident visitors at national borders, by nationality

	2007	2008	2009	2010	2011	Market share 11	% Change 11-10
TOTAL	2,164,419	2,111,736	2,055,705	1,976,481	2,038,359	100.00	3.13
AFRICA	193	188	130	275	206	0.01	-25.09
East Africa				97	96		
Mozambique					96		
Somalia				97			
North Africa	62	12		44			
Algeria	50			29			
Morocco		12		15			
Tunisia	12						
Southern Africa	131	176	33	135	206	0.01	52.59
South Africa	131	176	33	135	206	0.01	52.59
AMERICAS	36,690	18,669	12,063	12,142	19,225	0.94	58.33
Caribbean	94	25			71	0.00	
Cuba	32	25			54	0.00	
Puerto Rico	62				17	0.00	
Central America					52	0.00	
Costa Rica					52	0.00	
North America	32,405	15,042	10,084	8,188	13,878	0.68	69.49
Canada	4,156	4,014	3,371	3,115	3,462	0.17	11.14
Mexico	308	278	228	70	140	0.01	100.00
United States of America	27,941	10,750	6,485	5,003	10,276	0.50	105.40
South America	4,191	3,602	1,979	3,954	5,224	0.26	32.12
Argentina	1,420	1,267	665	1,514	1,639	0.08	8.26
Bolivia	45	130					
Brazil	1,987	1,824	1,033	1,904	3,394	0.17	78.26
Chile	26	113		221			
Colombia	74	100		105			
Ecuador	83		72	33	56	0.00	69.70
Peru	39						
Uruguay				40			
Venezuela	446	128	209	60	103	0.01	71.67
Other countries of South America	71	40		77	32	0.00	-58.44
EAST ASIA AND THE PACIFIC	26,475	17,411	18,790	18,386	19,930	0.98	8.40
North-East Asia	21,506	13,426	16,045	14,952	16,731	0.82	11.90
China	17,422	9,665	9,041	10,189	12,206	0.60	19.80
Taiwan, Province of China	320	181		28	149	0.01	432.14
Hong Kong, China	113	41					
Japan	3,306	3,170	4,998	4,281	3,590	0.18	-16.14
Korea, Dem. People's Republic of			41				
Korea, Republic of	345	369	1,965	454	786	0.04	73.13
South-East Asia	1,705	1,037	960	1,327	1,602	0.08	20.72
Myanmar	71						
Cambodia	68						
Indonesia	22	25	67	208	209	0.01	0.48
Malaysia	437	338	246	282	308	0.02	9.22
Philippines	672	601	610	757	699	0.03	-7.66
Singapore	81	37					
Viet Nam	354	14			23	0.00	
Thailand		22	37	80	363	0.02	353.75
Australasia	3,264	2,948	1,785	2,107	1,597	0.08	-24.21
Australia	3,214	2,884	1,657	2,004	1,483	0.07	-26.00
New Zealand	50	64	128	103	114	0.01	10.68

SAN MARINO

2. Arrivals of non-resident visitors at national borders, by nationality

	2007	2008	2009	2010	2011	Market share 11	% Change 11-10
EUROPE	2,099,431	2,074,061	2,023,438	1,944,198	1,997,416	97.99	2.74
Central/Eastern Europe	211,642	230,300	170,000	224,078	269,567	13.22	20.30
Armenia			63	79			
Bulgaria	4,739	4,792	3,810	2,560	2,991	0.15	16.84
Belarus	901	2,267	1,371	1,378	973	0.05	-29.39
Czech Republic	13,933	14,191	12,363	12,011	10,838	0.53	-9.77
Estonia	5,579	4,797	2,387	2,428	3,471	0.17	42.96
Georgia	87	71	196	119	27	0.00	-77.31
Hungary	9,356	7,996	6,604	6,784	6,542	0.32	-3.57
Kazakhstan	101	50	50	100	23	0.00	-77.00
Latvia	3,586	3,194	1,141	1,116	1,643	0.08	47.22
Lithuania	8,676	7,812	5,179	5,000	6,266	0.31	25.32
Republic of Moldova	81	505	424	200	91	0.00	-54.50
Poland	50,241	68,382	54,556	57,208	52,725	2.59	-7.84
Romania	13,191	5,839	4,490	4,599	5,004	0.25	8.81
Russian Federation	95,014	103,983	71,212	123,517	170,781	8.38	38.27
Slovakia	3,620	3,290	1,971	1,994	2,827	0.14	41.78
Ukraine	1,866	2,516	3,733	4,915	5,365	0.26	9.16
Uzbekistan	110	50	50	70			
Other countries Central/East Europe	561	565	400				
Northern Europe	26,889	20,846	17,971	13,389	14,720	0.72	9.94
Denmark	1,576	1,823	1,901	2,035	1,450	0.07	-28.75
Finland	4,531	4,472	3,993	3,852	3,780	0.19	-1.87
Iceland		200		46	276	0.01	500.00
Ireland	513	268	230	305	260	0.01	-14.75
Norway	2,204	2,080	2,837	2,019	1,702	0.08	-15.70
Sweden	5,251	4,864	2,742	2,384	3,329	0.16	39.64
United Kingdom	12,314	6,639	5,868	2,748	3,923	0.19	42.76
Other countries of Northern Europe	500	500	400				
Southern Europe	1,512,404	1,493,157	1,513,729	1,415,331	1,416,209	69.48	0.06
Albania	350	541	773	379	258	0.01	-31.93
Andorra				132			
Bosnia and Herzegovina	941	1,233	427	1,517	1,819	0.09	19.91
Croatia	5,728	5,547	4,447	4,074	4,060	0.20	-0.34
Greece	13,018	10,282	8,493	6,100	5,848	0.29	-4.13
Italy	1,468,168	1,454,094	1,483,490	1,381,570	1,385,681	67.98	0.30
Malta	286	177	16	88	311	0.02	253.41
Portugal	1,236	814	629	565	463	0.02	-18.05
Slovenia	7,835	7,649	6,271	5,616	4,693	0.23	-16.44
Spain	3,105	2,848	1,066	2,027	3,344	0.16	64.97
TFYR of Macedonia	270	291	83	238	92	0.00	-61.34
Serbia and Montenegro	10,962	9,426	7,467	12,951	9,640	0.47	-25.57
Other countries of Southern Europe	505	255	567	74			
Western Europe	346,799	328,084	320,268	289,484	295,388	14.49	2.04
Austria	25,395	23,867	23,838	21,544	23,672	1.16	9.88
Belgium	19,577	22,913	21,684	18,342	18,291	0.90	-0.28
France	74,584	73,404	69,199	62,358	61,498	3.02	-1.38
Germany	145,132	126,049	127,913	110,676	111,885	5.49	1.09
Liechtenstein	23	18					
Luxembourg	2,713	1,269	1,533	1,989	2,298	0.11	15.54
Monaco					16	0.00	
Netherlands	31,615	34,701	33,553	32,035	33,068	1.62	3.22
Switzerland	47,760	45,863	42,548	42,540	44,660	2.19	4.98
East Mediterranean Europe	1,697	1,674	1,470	1,916	1,532	0.08	-20.04
Cyprus	247	77	185	81			
Israel	1,224	780	979	977	927	0.05	-5.12
Turkey	226	817	306	858	605	0.03	-29.49

SAN MARINO

2. Arrivals of non-resident visitors at national borders, by nationality

	2007	2008	2009	2010	2011	Market share 11	% Change 11-10
MIDDLE EAST	**696**	**272**	**393**	**457**	**469**	**0.02**	**2.63**
Iraq	66			12			
Jordan	21				19	0.00	
Lebanon				59	201	0.01	240.68
Saudi Arabia	203	28	38		27	0.00	
Syrian Arab Republic	382	244	355	366	56	0.00	-84.70
Egypt	24			20	166	0.01	730.00
SOUTH ASIA	**693**	**379**	**130**	**364**	**428**	**0.02**	**17.58**
Bangladesh	331	379	130	199			
Sri Lanka					212	0.01	
India	57			105	216	0.01	105.71
Iran, Islamic Republic of	52			60			
Pakistan	253						
NOT SPECIFIED	**241**	**756**	**761**	**659**	**685**	**0.03**	**3.95**
Other countries of the World	241	756	761	659	685	0.03	3.95

SAO TOME AND PRINCIPE

1. Arrivals of non-resident tourists at national borders, by nationality

	2007	2008	2009	2010	2011	Market share 11	% Change 11-10
TOTAL	11,815	14,456		7,963			
AFRICA	2,199	2,460		2,123			
East Africa				24			
Mozambique				24			
Central Africa	517	1,454		1,484			
Angola	377	1,141		1,105			
Cameroon	49	90		71			
Chad				2			
Congo				24			
Equatorial Guinea	24	53		138			
Gabon	67	170		144			
North Africa				2			
Morocco				2			
Southern Africa				80			
South Africa				80			
West Africa	221	470		486			
Cape Verde	93	25		251			
Benin				9			
Ghana				6			
Côte d'Ivoire				4			
Mali				5			
Nigeria	128	445		198			
Guinea-Bissau				6			
Senegal				7			
Other Africa	1,461	536		47			
Other countries of Africa	1,461	536		47			
AMERICAS	293	411		489			
Caribbean				1			
Cuba				1			
North America	32	158		327			
Canada				47			
United States of America	32	158		280			
South America				139			
Brazil				139			
Other Americas	261	253		22			
Other countries of the Americas	261	253		22			
EAST ASIA AND THE PACIFIC				85			
North-East Asia				79			
China				13			
Taiwan, Province of China				43			
Japan				23			
South-East Asia				6			
Philippines				6			
EUROPE	3,974	6,348		5,090			
Northern Europe	45	138		262			
Denmark				6			
Norway				11			
Sweden				16			
United Kingdom	45	138		229			
Southern Europe	1,175	4,942		3,807			
Italy				80			
Portugal	1,128	4,835		3,578			

SAO TOME AND PRINCIPE

1. Arrivals of non-resident tourists at national borders, by nationality

	2007	2008	2009	2010	2011	Market share 11	% Change 11-10
Spain	47	107		149			
Western Europe	**324**	**593**		**942**			
Austria				23			
Belgium				52			
France	324	593		514			
Germany				193			
Netherlands				115			
Switzerland				45			
Other Europe	**2,430**	**675**		**79**			
Other countries of Europe	2,430	675		79			
MIDDLE EAST				**27**			
Lebanon				27			
SOUTH ASIA				**5**			
India				5			
NOT SPECIFIED	**5,349**	**5,237**		**144**			
Other countries of the World	5,349	5,237		144			

SAUDI ARABIA

1. Arrivals of non-resident tourists at national borders, by nationality

	2007	2008	2009	2010	2011	Market share 11	% Change 11-10
TOTAL	11,530,834	14,757,444	10,896,712	10,850,188	17,497,890	100.00	61.27
AFRICA	601,614	1,033,258	260,717	368,610	790,301	4.52	114.40
East Africa	43,133	18,701	12,142	22,313	74,904	0.43	235.70
Burundi	20	10	16		85	0.00	
Comoros	145	65	229	1,051	2,761	0.02	162.70
Ethiopia	15,815	4,158	4,086	9,628	38,080	0.22	295.51
Eritrea	14,756	5,754	1,282	2,804	14,156	0.08	404.85
Djibouti	670	557	348	429	1,220	0.01	184.38
Kenya	4,034	4,896	1,858	1,825	6,723	0.04	268.38
Madagascar	44	5	53		171	0.00	
Malawi	136	30	787		2,015	0.01	
Mauritius	1,000	828		1,677	1,414	0.01	-15.68
Mozambique	212	63	207		1,232	0.01	
Rwanda	14				59	0.00	
Seychelles	164	33					
Somalia	4,594	1,789	1,623	1,268	3,880	0.02	205.99
Zimbabwe	117	45	739		492	0.00	
Uganda	434	86	229	758	630	0.00	-16.89
United Republic of Tanzania	885	279			1,525	0.01	
Zambia	89	103	72		261	0.00	
Other countries of East Africa	4		613	2,873	200	0.00	-93.04
Central Africa	4,614	765	5,104	3,888	7,196	0.04	85.08
Angola	81		13		599	0.00	
Cameroon	861	108	2,504	1,029	1,357	0.01	31.88
Central African Republic	21	4	36		73	0.00	
Chad	3,493	612	2,465	2,686	4,832	0.03	79.90
Congo	79	28	37		221	0.00	
Equatorial Guinea	5		8		5	0.00	
Gabon	71	13	41		97	0.00	
Other countries of Central Africa	3			173	12	0.00	-93.06
North Africa	491,364	951,638	205,734	256,445	581,493	3.32	126.75
Algeria	91,898	393,609	64,015	96,097	124,163	0.71	29.21
Morocco	57,619	66,838	41,108	60,995	108,339	0.62	77.62
Sudan	311,889	398,607	88,269	65,352	298,344	1.71	356.52
Tunisia	29,958	92,584	12,342	34,001	50,647	0.29	48.96
Southern Africa	16,719	24,039	14,144	25,203	41,244	0.24	63.65
Botswana	41	42	52		67	0.00	
Lesotho	35	6	29		126	0.00	
Namibia	43	12	16		80	0.00	
South Africa	16,476	23,979	14,024	24,996	40,910	0.23	63.67
Swaziland	26		23		59	0.00	
Other countries of Southern Africa	98			207	2	0.00	-99.03
West Africa	45,784	38,115	23,593	60,761	85,464	0.49	40.66
Benin	308	53	234		693	0.00	
Gambia	219	32	91		398	0.00	
Ghana	2,565	18,870	954	1,568	3,244	0.02	106.89
Guinea	558	98	219		892	0.01	
Côte d'Ivoire	261	90	149		512	0.00	
Liberia	101	15	102		103	0.00	
Mali	2,607	319	465				
Mauritania	3,620	393	1,128	2,354	4,261	0.02	81.01
Niger	2,336	230	609	1,965	2,905	0.02	47.84
Nigeria	30,561	10,065	17,759	51,090	66,599	0.38	30.36
Guinea-Bissau	18		6		86	0.00	
Senegal	1,779	1,862	399	1,175	2,232	0.01	89.96
Sierra Leone	114	24	123		241	0.00	

SAUDI ARABIA

1. Arrivals of non-resident tourists at national borders, by nationality

	2007	2008	2009	2010	2011	Market share 11	% Change 11-10
Togo	144	6,003	120		255	0.00	
Burkina Faso	593	61	390		1,361	0.01	
Other countries of West Africa			845	2,609	1,682	0.01	-35.53
AMERICAS	**235,900**	**297,143**	**56,841**	**53,432**	**182,108**	**1.04**	**240.82**
Caribbean	**4,855**	**3,605**	**309**	**1,369**	**1,479**	**0.01**	**8.04**
Bahamas	2				26	0.00	
Barbados	25	13	12		49	0.00	
British Virgin Islands		65	7				
Cuba	27	8	4	1,092	29	0.00	-97.34
Dominica	68	11			54	0.00	
Dominican Republic			6				
Haiti	3	99	3		15	0.00	
Jamaica	3,913	3,077	17	277	82	0.00	-70.40
Puerto Rico	17						
Saint Lucia					5	0.00	
Trinidad and Tobago	800	332	260		1,219	0.01	
Central America	**321**	**118**	**320**		**814**	**0.00**	
Belize	46	16	15		75	0.00	
Costa Rica	57	21	33		178	0.00	
El Salvador	24		33		160	0.00	
Guatemala	35	27	12		41	0.00	
Honduras	79	36	22		102	0.00	
Nicaragua	13		151		24	0.00	
Panama	67	18	54		234	0.00	
North America	**224,942**	**289,948**	**53,476**	**50,043**	**166,601**	**0.95**	**232.92**
Canada	26,959	46,568	11,468	11,716	67,877	0.39	479.35
Mexico	468	266	231	550	1,432	0.01	160.36
United States of America	197,474	243,114	41,777	37,777	97,292	0.56	157.54
Other countries of North America	41						
South America	**5,782**	**3,321**	**2,736**	**2,020**	**10,810**	**0.06**	**435.15**
Argentina	730	536	1,468	351	1,294	0.01	268.66
Bolivia	78	20	17		162	0.00	
Brazil	1,445	1,500	735	935	2,154	0.01	130.37
Chile	129	57	37		229	0.00	
Colombia	1,240	163	176		2,020	0.01	
Ecuador	215	72	14		203	0.00	
Paraguay	12		7		21	0.00	
Peru	145	33	39		257	0.00	
Suriname	11	5	1		12	0.00	
Uruguay	33	13	11		97	0.00	
Venezuela	1,744	922	231	734	4,361	0.02	494.14
Other Americas		**151**			**2,404**	**0.01**	
Other countries of the Americas		151			2,404	0.01	
EAST ASIA AND THE PACIFIC	**578,805**	**940,928**	**362,500**	**485,534**	**844,723**	**4.83**	**73.98**
North-East Asia	**45,158**	**90,738**	**39,022**	**40,655**	**66,644**	**0.38**	**63.93**
China	22,991	55,352	18,298	20,416	24,409	0.14	19.56
Hong Kong, China	441	380	237		30	0.00	
Japan	12,438	14,590	6,539	9,210	16,410	0.09	78.18
Korea, Republic of	9,249	20,400	13,842	10,932	25,738	0.15	135.44
Mongolia	12	16	105		51	0.00	
Other countries of North-East Asia	27		1	97	6	0.00	-93.81
South-East Asia	**516,810**	**831,129**	**320,255**	**436,692**	**734,899**	**4.20**	**68.29**
Brunei Darussalam	2,970	1,024	5,134	4,927	2,281	0.01	-53.70
Myanmar	1,705	12,231	479	3,149	1,244	0.01	-60.50
Cambodia	67	13	48	26	146	0.00	461.54
Indonesia	296,469	501,758	205,374	235,636	404,903	2.31	71.83

SAUDI ARABIA

1. Arrivals of non-resident tourists at national borders, by nationality

	2007	2008	2009	2010	2011	Market share 11	% Change 11-10
Malaysia	61,031	141,778	62,749	152,396	110,148	0.63	-27.72
Philippines	136,432	73,981	35,213	28,053	197,463	1.13	603.89
Singapore	11,721	4,951	4,875	5,935	9,375	0.05	57.96
Viet Nam	2,001	44,548	1,166	3,145	1,231	0.01	-60.86
Thailand	4,414	50,845	5,217	3,425	8,108	0.05	136.73
Australasia	**16,802**	**19,021**	**3,192**	**8,187**	**42,988**	**0.25**	**425.08**
Australia	14,092	17,511	2,794	6,036	37,450	0.21	520.44
New Zealand	2,710	1,510	398	2,151	5,538	0.03	157.46
Melanesia	**15**	**40**	**20**		**32**	**0.00**	
Fiji	15	40	20		32	0.00	
Micronesia					**131**	**0.00**	
Kiribati					1	0.00	
Marshall Islands					130	0.00	
Polynesia	**20**		**11**		**12**	**0.00**	
American Samoa	5		11		1	0.00	
French Polynesia	10				5	0.00	
Tonga	5				6	0.00	
Other East Asia and the Pacific					**17**	**0.00**	
Other countries of Oceania					17	0.00	
EUROPE	**656,937**	**1,185,068**	**444,667**	**367,238**	**722,534**	**4.13**	**96.75**
Central/Eastern Europe	**33,422**	**151,216**	**13,633**	**24,465**	**47,048**	**0.27**	**92.31**
Azerbaijan	747	66,467	552	974	1,762	0.01	80.90
Armenia	50	211	42		45	0.00	
Bulgaria	303	223	170		756	0.00	
Belarus	142	77	116		434	0.00	
Czech Republic	720	641	2,233		2,447	0.01	
Estonia	60	13	39		116	0.00	
Georgia	101	234	33		197	0.00	
Hungary	561	385	271		987	0.01	
Kazakhstan	3,752	394	176	4,207	2,146	0.01	-48.99
Kyrgyzstan		70					
Latvia	101	35	80		221	0.00	
Lithuania	63	35	58		138	0.00	
Republic of Moldova	30	8	22		60	0.00	
Poland	1,289	6,768	476	909	2,319	0.01	155.12
Romania	1,347	882	626	1,040	3,504	0.02	236.92
Russian Federation	17,151	73,645	3,540	3,418	5,894	0.03	72.44
Slovakia	234	145	156		767	0.00	
Tajikistan	904	135	877		1,045	0.01	
Turkmenistan	123	34	174		720	0.00	
Ukraine	979	497	738	1,212	2,560	0.01	111.22
Uzbekistan	4,403	317	2,792	9,084	5,547	0.03	-38.94
Other countries Central/East Europe	362		462	3,621	15,383	0.09	324.83
Northern Europe	**294,533**	**341,403**	**182,008**	**113,147**	**283,717**	**1.62**	**150.75**
Denmark	2,188	1,280	1,906	4,823	8,446	0.05	75.12
Finland	1,440	836	669	1,100	2,774	0.02	152.18
Iceland	186	145	69	76	258	0.00	239.47
Ireland	5,210	5,804	4,853	4,155	11,757	0.07	182.96
Norway	2,080	1,037	1,918	1,742	3,564	0.02	104.59
Sweden	40,184	41,471	2,126	3,107	5,724	0.03	84.23
United Kingdom	243,245	284,685	170,467	98,144	251,194	1.44	155.94
Other countries of Northern Europe		6,145					
Southern Europe	**52,473**	**122,184**	**26,836**	**19,506**	**45,105**	**0.26**	**131.24**
Albania	266	70	129	195	332	0.00	70.26
Andorra	2		1		2	0.00	
Bosnia and Herzegovina	361	202	281	552	885	0.01	60.33

SAUDI ARABIA

1. Arrivals of non-resident tourists at national borders, by nationality

	2007	2008	2009	2010	2011	Market share 11	% Change 11-10
Croatia	573	379	910	398	1,143	0.01	187.19
Greece	3,020	13,141	1,831	1,677	7,266	0.04	333.27
Italy	42,363	48,909	11,504	9,599	23,743	0.14	147.35
Malta	107	48	61	183	497	0.00	171.58
Portugal	829	484	856	1,049	2,281	0.01	117.45
San Marino	10		3				
Serbia			12				
Slovenia	166	41,904	97	137	221	0.00	61.31
Spain	4,316	16,965	10,999	5,460	8,392	0.05	53.70
Serbia and Montenegro	262						
Other countries of Southern Europe	198	82	152	256	343	0.00	33.98
Western Europe	**91,118**	**321,180**	**66,012**	**80,667**	**148,438**	**0.85**	**84.01**
Austria	3,363	23,964	9,954	3,726	5,377	0.03	44.31
Belgium	4,255	8,414	2,797	5,383	8,240	0.05	53.07
France	28,344	107,584	20,720	28,802	68,663	0.39	138.40
Germany	39,734	80,192	22,940	28,818	39,202	0.22	36.03
Liechtenstein					4	0.00	
Luxembourg	66	1,036	64		148	0.00	
Netherlands	10,010	95,123	5,213	10,412	19,057	0.11	83.03
Switzerland	5,346	4,867	4,324	3,421	7,747	0.04	126.45
Other countries of Western Europe				105			
East Mediterranean Europe	**185,391**	**249,085**	**156,178**	**129,453**	**198,226**	**1.13**	**53.13**
Cyprus	1,258	585	2,167	526	1,147	0.01	118.06
Turkey	184,133	248,500	154,011	128,927	197,079	1.13	52.86
MIDDLE EAST	**7,443,786**	**9,333,965**	**8,677,688**	**8,244,721**	**11,098,731**	**63.43**	**34.62**
Bahrain	483,410	594,188	624,793	820,132	1,220,651	6.98	48.84
Palestine	51,609	1,997	14,487	26,084	82,814	0.47	217.49
Iraq	49,318	24,282	64,138	171,913	44,862	0.26	-73.90
Jordan	495,105	501,269	517,167	451,099	1,666,814	9.53	269.50
Kuwait	1,660,464	2,589,988	2,475,318	2,507,813	2,578,541	14.74	2.82
Lebanon	189,004	307,492	58,337	116,129	164,157	0.94	41.36
Libya	50,322	8,202	27,835	42,976	1,651	0.01	-96.16
Oman	173,193	125,552	165,875	176,687	373,421	2.13	111.35
Qatar	596,468	808,072	1,470,382	843,762	1,058,300	6.05	25.43
Syrian Arab Republic	785,759	708,034	730,306	254,140	765,908	4.38	201.37
United Arab Emirates	955,320	1,613,574	1,889,187	1,957,613	1,531,429	8.75	-21.77
Egypt	1,622,320	1,853,663	538,287	763,901	1,157,812	6.62	51.57
Yemen	331,494	197,652	101,576	112,472	452,371	2.59	302.21
SOUTH ASIA	**2,013,792**	**1,967,082**	**1,094,282**	**1,330,271**	**3,858,203**	**22.05**	**190.03**
Afghanistan	7,929	5,562	5,140	8,793	24,403	0.14	177.53
Bangladesh	177,369	34,187	23,698	188,584	407,697	2.33	116.19
Bhutan	26				1,590	0.01	
Sri Lanka	67,499	31,381	33,308	28,779	84,913	0.49	195.05
India	613,347	601,922	247,075	389,116	1,501,308	8.58	285.83
Iran, Islamic Republic of	435,977	349,848	413,656	220,051	559,690	3.20	154.35
Maldives	1,209	188	2,456	3,466	1,729	0.01	-50.12
Nepal	67,874	126,444	32,694	25,841	57,586	0.33	122.85
Pakistan	642,562	817,550	336,255	465,571	1,219,287	6.97	161.89
Other countries of South Asia				70			
NOT SPECIFIED			**17**	**382**	**1,290**	**0.01**	**237.70**
Other countries of the World			17	382	1,290	0.01	237.70

SENEGAL

1. Arrivals of non-resident tourists at national borders, by nationality

		2007	2008	2009	2010	2011	Market share 11	% Change 11-10
TOTAL	(*)	874,623	491,552	458,912	492,261	449,954	100.00	-8.59
AFRICA		437,970	121,286	111,525	114,623	107,990	24.00	-5.79
North Africa		6,307			6,217	5,701	1.27	-8.30
Morocco		4,612			4,427	3,997	0.89	-9.71
Tunisia		1,695			1,790	1,704	0.38	-4.80
West Africa		351,236	60,610	52,803	74,901	65,317	14.52	-12.80
Gambia		109,681			7,301	6,168	1.37	-15.52
Guinea		41,402	15,779	14,114	15,327	13,269	2.95	-13.43
Côte d'Ivoire			10,182	8,659	9,981	8,975	1.99	-10.08
Mali		45,889	11,746	10,885	11,919	10,746	2.39	-9.84
Mauritania		44,838	8,916	7,847	8,139	6,773	1.51	-16.78
Nigeria			13,987	11,298	12,595	10,252	2.28	-18.60
Guinea-Bissau		109,426			4,737	4,051	0.90	-14.48
Burkina Faso					4,902	5,083	1.13	3.69
Other Africa		80,427	60,676	58,722	33,505	36,972	8.22	10.35
Other countries of Africa		80,427	60,676	58,722	33,505	36,972	8.22	10.35
AMERICAS		26,004	17,783	18,942	19,958	18,366	4.08	-7.98
North America		26,004	17,783	18,942	19,958	18,366	4.08	-7.98
United States of America		26,004	17,783	18,942	19,958	18,366	4.08	-7.98
EUROPE		324,080	280,044	263,657	271,324	257,208	57.16	-5.20
Southern Europe		28,314	26,030	25,579	26,106	24,095	5.35	-7.70
Italy		14,564	11,482	11,547	11,603	10,960	2.44	-5.54
Spain		13,750	14,548	14,032	14,503	13,135	2.92	-9.43
Western Europe		272,493	229,567	213,189	229,032	218,168	48.49	-4.74
Belgium			17,271	14,211	14,400	14,343	3.19	-0.40
France		232,294	212,296	198,978	205,114	194,892	43.31	-4.98
Germany		8,993			6,091	5,683	1.26	-6.70
Luxembourg					3,427	3,250	0.72	-5.16
Benelux		31,206						
Other Europe		23,273	24,447	24,889	16,186	14,945	3.32	-7.67
Other countries of Europe		23,273	24,447	24,889	16,186	14,945	3.32	-7.67
NOT SPECIFIED		86,569	72,439	64,788	86,356	66,390	14.75	-23.12
Other countries of the World		86,569	22,115	16,879	27,477	21,427	4.76	-22.02
Nationals Residing Abroad			50,324	47,909	58,879	44,963	9.99	-23.63

SENEGAL

1. Arrivals of non-resident tourists at national borders, by country of residence

		2007	2008	2009	2010	2011	Market share 11	% Change 11-10
TOTAL	(*)	496,066	491,552	458,912	492,261	449,954	100.00	-8.59
AFRICA		119,846	126,321	113,109	123,273	113,067	25.13	-8.28
North Africa		7,151	7,395	7,026	8,133	7,491	1.66	-7.89
Morocco		5,522	5,514	4,989	5,969	5,524	1.23	-7.46
Tunisia		1,629	1,881	2,037	2,164	1,967	0.44	-9.10
West Africa		45,667	49,187	44,687	47,332	41,044	9.12	-13.28
Gambia		6,295	7,351	7,603	7,369	6,254	1.39	-15.13
Guinea		13,960	15,167	13,740	14,841	12,843	2.85	-13.46
Mali		11,859	12,300	11,275	12,494	11,336	2.52	-9.27
Mauritania		6,949	8,292	7,286	7,623	6,266	1.39	-17.80
Guinea-Bissau		6,604	6,077	4,783	5,005	4,345	0.97	-13.19
Other Africa		67,028	69,739	61,396	67,808	64,532	14.34	-4.83
Other countries of Africa		67,028	69,739	61,396	67,808	64,532	14.34	-4.83
AMERICAS		20,128	20,146	21,690	23,048	20,672	4.59	-10.31
North America		20,128	20,146	21,690	23,048	20,672	4.59	-10.31
United States of America		20,128	20,146	21,690	23,048	20,672	4.59	-10.31
EUROPE		341,423	325,135	303,445	319,882	293,812	65.30	-8.15
Southern Europe		56,979	50,277	46,215	52,207	43,556	9.68	-16.57
Italy		28,938	27,080	25,583	29,996	23,764	5.28	-20.78
Spain		28,041	23,197	20,632	22,211	19,792	4.40	-10.89
Western Europe		266,995	253,365	237,632	249,896	234,644	52.15	-6.10
Belgium			17,812	14,771	14,895	14,744	3.28	-1.01
France		237,176	229,559	216,599	225,214	210,878	46.87	-6.37
Germany		6,658	5,994	6,262	6,178	5,695	1.27	-7.82
Luxembourg					3,609	3,327	0.74	-7.81
Benelux		23,161						
Other Europe		17,449	21,493	19,598	17,779	15,612	3.47	-12.19
Other countries of Europe		17,449	21,493	19,598	17,779	15,612	3.47	-12.19
NOT SPECIFIED		14,669	19,950	20,668	26,058	22,403	4.98	-14.03
Other countries of the World		14,669	19,950	20,668	26,058	22,403	4.98	-14.03

SERBIA

3. Arrivals of non-resident tourists in hotels and similar establishments, by nationality

	2007	2008	2009	2010	2011	Market share 11	% Change 11-10
TOTAL	586,162	563,593	569,535	612,989	680,365	100.00	10.99
AMERICAS	18,342	14,209	15,064	17,459	18,005	2.65	3.13
North America	18,342	14,209	15,064	17,459	18,005	2.65	3.13
Canada	3,974	3,687	3,429	4,081	4,177	0.61	2.35
United States of America	14,368	10,522	11,635	13,378	13,828	2.03	3.36
EAST ASIA AND THE PACIFIC	6,834	7,112	6,897	8,798	10,647	1.56	21.02
North-East Asia	2,450	2,228	2,379	2,842	3,846	0.57	35.33
Japan	2,450	2,228	2,379	2,842	3,846	0.57	35.33
Australasia	4,384	4,884	4,518	5,956	6,801	1.00	14.19
Australia	3,915	4,221	4,001	5,329	6,096	0.90	14.39
New Zealand	469	663	517	627	705	0.10	12.44
EUROPE	547,805	529,384	532,804	566,315	630,597	92.69	11.35
Central/Eastern Europe	95,067	100,836	111,019	114,325	128,645	18.91	12.53
Bulgaria	20,232	19,786	22,472	22,912	25,626	3.77	11.85
Czech Republic	8,046	7,524	8,346	9,147	8,613	1.27	-5.84
Hungary	15,408	13,765	14,666	15,050	17,144	2.52	13.91
Poland	17,720	18,858	20,624	18,997	19,810	2.91	4.28
Romania	13,190	19,298	21,073	22,478	28,292	4.16	25.87
Russian Federation	14,673	15,242	15,712	19,827	22,957	3.37	15.79
Slovakia	5,798	6,363	8,126	5,914	6,203	0.91	4.89
Northern Europe	39,766	34,720	30,722	34,321	40,246	5.92	17.26
Denmark	3,659	3,093	2,996	3,378	3,634	0.53	7.58
Finland	1,965	1,622	1,533	1,831	2,523	0.37	37.79
Iceland	954	490	321	339	342	0.05	0.88
Ireland	1,708	1,555	1,452	1,583	1,849	0.27	16.80
Norway	3,946	4,373	3,948	4,881	5,126	0.75	5.02
Sweden	6,863	6,682	6,089	6,637	9,341	1.37	40.74
United Kingdom	20,671	16,905	14,383	15,672	17,431	2.56	11.22
Southern Europe	288,428	274,444	269,557	286,275	310,181	45.59	8.35
Bosnia and Herzegovina	56,754	58,545	56,705	55,805	56,639	8.32	1.49
Croatia	38,027	36,698	38,667	43,870	48,073	7.07	9.58
Greece	21,174	21,672	21,927	23,026	25,128	3.69	9.13
Italy	30,297	29,069	28,847	30,651	36,255	5.33	18.28
Montenegro	51,116	53,506	40,108	38,026	39,096	5.75	2.81
Portugal	1,670	1,525	1,239	1,414	1,666	0.24	17.82
Slovenia	57,788	42,943	50,156	61,938	68,735	10.10	10.97
Spain	4,887	4,694	5,048	5,667	6,275	0.92	10.73
TFYR of Macedonia	26,715	25,792	26,860	25,878	28,314	4.16	9.41
Western Europe	94,585	92,291	93,665	103,716	113,684	16.71	9.61
Austria	20,566	19,201	20,585	22,978	23,948	3.52	4.22
Belgium	4,632	4,454	4,288	4,929	6,530	0.96	32.48
France	16,745	15,387	15,073	16,734	16,559	2.43	-1.05
Germany	34,970	35,894	37,348	40,739	45,774	6.73	12.36
Luxembourg	1,490	412	249	393	386	0.06	-1.78
Netherlands	10,585	11,163	9,668	10,601	11,173	1.64	5.40
Switzerland	5,597	5,780	6,454	7,342	9,314	1.37	26.86
East Mediterranean Europe	14,969	14,378	16,044	16,562	21,762	3.20	31.40
Israel	3,303	3,337	2,599	3,009	3,286	0.48	9.21
Turkey	11,666	11,041	13,445	13,553	18,476	2.72	36.32
Other Europe	14,990	12,715	11,797	11,116	16,079	2.36	44.65
Other countries of Europe	14,990	12,715	11,797	11,116	16,079	2.36	44.65
NOT SPECIFIED	13,181	12,888	14,770	20,417	21,116	3.10	3.42
Other countries of the World	13,181	12,888	14,770	20,417	21,116	3.10	3.42

SERBIA

4. Arrivals of non-resident tourists in all types of accommodation establishments, by nationality

	2007	2008	2009	2010	2011	Market share 11	% Change 11-10
TOTAL	696,045	646,494	645,022	682,681	764,167	100.00	11.94
AMERICAS	19,083	15,002	16,266	18,554	19,180	2.51	3.37
North America	19,083	15,002	16,266	18,554	19,180	2.51	3.37
Canada	4,214	3,886	3,969	4,408	4,542	0.59	3.04
United States of America	14,869	11,116	12,297	14,146	14,638	1.92	3.48
EAST ASIA AND THE PACIFIC	7,433	7,826	8,160	9,903	12,193	1.60	23.12
North-East Asia	2,566	2,342	2,929	3,011	3,988	0.52	32.45
Japan	2,566	2,342	2,929	3,011	3,988	0.52	32.45
Australasia	4,867	5,484	5,231	6,892	8,205	1.07	19.05
Australia	4,312	4,711	4,613	6,137	7,283	0.95	18.67
New Zealand	555	773	618	755	922	0.12	22.12
EUROPE	655,782	610,004	602,599	632,964	710,757	93.01	12.29
Central/Eastern Europe	105,832	108,995	120,985	123,547	139,951	18.31	13.28
Bulgaria	23,624	22,727	24,476	24,582	28,054	3.67	14.12
Czech Republic	9,000	8,022	9,271	9,844	9,278	1.21	-5.75
Hungary	16,658	14,870	16,291	16,276	18,660	2.44	14.65
Poland	18,888	19,855	22,304	20,672	21,548	2.82	4.24
Romania	15,582	20,701	22,876	23,907	30,628	4.01	28.11
Russian Federation	15,863	16,092	17,312	21,636	25,236	3.30	16.64
Slovakia	6,217	6,728	8,455	6,630	6,547	0.86	-1.25
Northern Europe	42,104	36,573	33,294	38,037	44,250	5.79	16.33
Denmark	3,890	3,404	3,208	3,633	3,872	0.51	6.58
Finland	2,124	1,765	1,728	1,999	2,692	0.35	34.67
Iceland	1,017	496	337	350	361	0.05	3.14
Ireland	1,864	1,727	1,665	1,782	2,070	0.27	16.16
Norway	4,147	4,559	4,203	5,176	5,340	0.70	3.17
Sweden	7,096	6,870	6,531	7,071	9,917	1.30	40.25
United Kingdom	21,966	17,752	15,622	18,026	19,998	2.62	10.94
Southern Europe	375,114	339,499	318,803	331,827	364,725	47.73	9.91
Bosnia and Herzegovina	62,568	64,729	63,981	63,560	65,960	8.63	3.78
Croatia	39,389	38,073	40,243	46,367	50,625	6.62	9.18
Greece	23,692	23,618	24,155	24,726	26,400	3.45	6.77
Italy	36,757	39,919	37,321	34,221	38,105	4.99	11.35
Montenegro	111,817	93,220	61,752	56,888	66,636	8.72	17.14
Portugal	1,963	1,610	1,425	1,647	1,856	0.24	12.69
Slovenia	64,838	45,661	54,766	66,686	74,674	9.77	11.98
Spain	5,604	5,043	5,581	6,151	6,850	0.90	11.36
TFYR of Macedonia	28,486	27,626	29,579	31,581	33,619	4.40	6.45
Western Europe	99,706	96,156	99,672	110,777	121,992	15.96	10.12
Austria	21,342	19,820	21,464	24,075	25,245	3.30	4.86
Belgium	4,982	4,633	4,529	5,339	7,131	0.93	33.56
France	18,390	16,324	16,542	18,339	18,191	2.38	-0.81
Germany	36,356	37,194	39,497	42,672	48,159	6.30	12.86
Luxembourg	1,523	443	261	415	443	0.06	6.75
Netherlands	11,202	11,685	10,357	12,082	12,963	1.70	7.29
Switzerland	5,911	6,057	7,022	7,855	9,860	1.29	25.53
East Mediterranean Europe	15,961	15,337	16,701	16,973	22,618	2.96	33.26
Israel	3,413	3,426	2,780	3,131	3,422	0.45	9.29
Turkey	12,548	11,911	13,921	13,842	19,196	2.51	38.68
Other Europe	17,065	13,444	13,144	11,803	17,221	2.25	45.90
Other countries of Europe	17,065	13,444	13,144	11,803	17,221	2.25	45.90
NOT SPECIFIED	13,747	13,662	17,997	21,260	22,037	2.88	3.65
Other countries of the World	13,747	13,662	17,997	21,260	22,037	2.88	3.65

SERBIA

5. Overnight stays of non-resident tourists in hotels and similar establishments, by nationality

	2007	2008	2009	2010	2011	Market share 11	% Change 11-10
TOTAL	1,239,967	1,194,593	1,184,154	1,235,654	1,387,148	100.00	12.26
AMERICAS	47,250	37,056	40,704	45,661	46,997	3.39	2.93
North America	47,250	37,056	40,704	45,661	46,997	3.39	2.93
Canada	10,192	8,799	9,172	9,917	10,701	0.77	7.91
United States of America	37,058	28,257	31,532	35,744	36,296	2.62	1.54
EAST ASIA AND THE PACIFIC	16,635	16,015	15,231	19,862	23,426	1.69	17.94
North-East Asia	5,681	4,922	5,744	7,397	8,372	0.60	13.18
Japan	5,681	4,922	5,744	7,397	8,372	0.60	13.18
Australasia	10,954	11,093	9,487	12,465	15,054	1.09	20.77
Australia	9,785	9,445	8,451	11,106	13,694	0.99	23.30
New Zealand	1,169	1,648	1,036	1,359	1,360	0.10	0.07
EUROPE	1,135,229	1,096,281	1,080,313	1,111,912	1,261,918	90.97	13.49
Central/Eastern Europe	204,736	213,082	224,885	218,272	258,003	18.60	18.20
Bulgaria	38,180	40,049	42,260	39,597	48,307	3.48	22.00
Czech Republic	19,087	15,749	16,901	17,994	17,651	1.27	-1.91
Hungary	28,337	23,397	25,316	24,745	32,547	2.35	31.53
Poland	28,005	28,235	30,006	28,547	30,972	2.23	8.49
Romania	31,348	40,777	41,141	42,033	53,871	3.88	28.16
Russian Federation	45,799	48,881	46,001	53,578	62,182	4.48	16.06
Slovakia	13,980	15,994	23,260	11,778	12,473	0.90	5.90
Northern Europe	103,445	90,095	74,015	82,990	103,776	7.48	25.05
Denmark	9,565	7,655	7,018	7,591	9,700	0.70	27.78
Finland	4,761	4,435	3,703	4,294	6,456	0.47	50.35
Iceland	2,848	1,434	984	984	1,121	0.08	13.92
Ireland	4,268	4,223	3,486	4,945	5,517	0.40	11.57
Norway	9,898	11,165	9,947	12,146	14,754	1.06	21.47
Sweden	15,259	15,412	13,688	14,196	21,531	1.55	51.67
United Kingdom	56,846	45,771	35,189	38,834	44,697	3.22	15.10
Southern Europe	565,912	545,438	538,648	545,550	594,178	42.83	8.91
Bosnia and Herzegovina	115,149	116,531	120,214	105,503	113,626	8.19	7.70
Croatia	70,556	67,246	74,597	82,410	85,443	6.16	3.68
Greece	43,442	47,007	43,540	42,996	46,509	3.35	8.17
Italy	65,326	64,329	67,493	73,909	86,436	6.23	16.95
Montenegro	108,006	113,359	84,625	76,308	81,189	5.85	6.40
Portugal	4,582	4,146	3,204	3,190	4,774	0.34	49.66
Slovenia	99,093	74,563	84,333	102,904	110,715	7.98	7.59
Spain	12,229	11,859	12,199	12,982	16,002	1.15	23.26
TFYR of Macedonia	47,529	46,398	48,443	45,348	49,484	3.57	9.12
Western Europe	198,209	190,512	187,357	206,361	229,549	16.55	11.24
Austria	39,686	34,479	38,048	41,667	42,618	3.07	2.28
Belgium	9,657	9,413	9,074	9,767	14,165	1.02	45.03
France	37,811	34,138	31,762	37,555	36,865	2.66	-1.84
Germany	75,402	76,168	74,311	78,984	90,227	6.50	14.23
Luxembourg	1,850	868	552	768	922	0.07	20.05
Netherlands	21,077	22,278	18,567	21,740	24,331	1.75	11.92
Switzerland	12,726	13,168	15,043	15,880	20,421	1.47	28.60
East Mediterranean Europe	29,291	26,009	27,302	29,482	39,681	2.86	34.59
Israel	9,319	8,358	6,092	7,256	8,015	0.58	10.46
Turkey	19,972	17,651	21,210	22,226	31,666	2.28	42.47
Other Europe	33,636	31,145	28,106	29,257	36,731	2.65	25.55
Other countries of Europe	33,636	31,145	28,106	29,257	36,731	2.65	25.55
NOT SPECIFIED	40,853	45,241	47,906	58,219	54,807	3.95	-5.86
Other countries of the World	40,853	45,241	47,906	58,219	54,807	3.95	-5.86

SERBIA

6. Overnight stays of non-resident tourists in all types of accommodation establishments, by nationality

	2007	2008	2009	2010	2011	Market share 11	% Change 11-10
TOTAL	1,475,675	1,398,887	1,469,102	1,452,156	1,643,054	100.00	13.15
AMERICAS	50,300	40,324	49,939	49,310	50,817	3.09	3.06
North America	50,300	40,324	49,939	49,310	50,817	3.09	3.06
Canada	11,106	10,032	14,918	11,072	12,235	0.74	10.50
United States of America	39,194	30,292	35,021	38,238	38,582	2.35	0.90
EAST ASIA AND THE PACIFIC	20,042	19,403	26,500	23,359	27,310	1.66	16.91
North-East Asia	7,722	6,680	12,448	8,805	9,515	0.58	8.06
Japan	7,722	6,680	12,448	8,805	9,515	0.58	8.06
Australasia	12,320	12,723	14,052	14,554	17,795	1.08	22.27
Australia	10,995	10,792	12,543	13,002	16,118	0.98	23.97
New Zealand	1,325	1,931	1,509	1,552	1,677	0.10	8.05
EUROPE	1,359,267	1,287,470	1,306,508	1,312,069	1,501,808	91.40	14.46
Central/Eastern Europe	234,804	239,954	267,327	248,357	300,646	18.30	21.05
Bulgaria	43,884	44,963	46,507	44,448	55,689	3.39	25.29
Czech Republic	21,971	18,349	21,683	20,026	19,436	1.18	-2.95
Hungary	31,497	27,360	30,505	27,793	41,005	2.50	47.54
Poland	32,146	32,521	36,123	32,276	35,180	2.14	9.00
Romania	36,852	45,396	47,572	47,068	59,911	3.65	27.29
Russian Federation	52,478	54,035	59,488	62,583	75,308	4.58	20.33
Slovakia	15,976	17,330	25,449	14,163	14,117	0.86	-0.32
Northern Europe	112,645	96,285	87,239	92,626	117,722	7.16	27.09
Denmark	10,395	8,172	7,799	8,354	10,239	0.62	22.56
Finland	5,591	5,083	4,908	4,734	6,900	0.42	45.75
Iceland	3,277	1,442	1,008	1,034	1,235	0.08	19.44
Ireland	5,210	4,751	5,158	5,382	6,194	0.38	15.09
Norway	10,847	11,704	10,937	13,165	15,533	0.95	17.99
Sweden	16,472	16,380	16,133	15,729	23,388	1.42	48.69
United Kingdom	60,853	48,753	41,296	44,228	54,233	3.30	22.62
Southern Europe	717,990	682,213	671,078	679,677	744,260	45.30	9.50
Bosnia and Herzegovina	147,318	152,939	157,106	147,569	165,538	10.08	12.18
Croatia	75,591	71,787	79,955	89,693	93,339	5.68	4.06
Greece	47,398	49,961	48,503	46,284	50,318	3.06	8.72
Italy	76,196	80,092	82,382	80,980	91,039	5.54	12.42
Montenegro	182,814	174,857	127,404	120,774	129,455	7.88	7.19
Portugal	6,040	4,877	4,891	4,614	5,732	0.35	24.23
Slovenia	112,955	80,703	96,332	114,471	124,517	7.58	8.78
Spain	15,377	14,089	17,308	15,541	19,103	1.16	22.92
TFYR of Macedonia	54,301	52,908	57,197	59,751	65,219	3.97	9.15
Western Europe	217,480	205,228	211,359	226,895	255,112	15.53	12.44
Austria	43,244	37,682	42,388	45,998	48,472	2.95	5.38
Belgium	11,033	10,242	9,935	10,799	15,551	0.95	44.00
France	43,348	37,330	38,735	42,194	41,277	2.51	-2.17
Germany	80,571	80,819	81,926	84,203	96,875	5.90	15.05
Luxembourg	2,066	941	617	821	1,121	0.07	36.54
Netherlands	23,015	24,043	20,419	25,510	29,778	1.81	16.73
Switzerland	14,203	14,171	17,339	17,370	22,038	1.34	26.87
East Mediterranean Europe	32,908	28,418	31,717	31,222	42,316	2.58	35.53
Israel	10,157	8,630	7,268	7,691	8,473	0.52	10.17
Turkey	22,751	19,788	24,449	23,531	33,843	2.06	43.82
Other Europe	43,440	35,372	37,788	33,292	41,752	2.54	25.41
Other countries of Europe	43,440	35,372	37,788	33,292	41,752	2.54	25.41
NOT SPECIFIED	46,066	51,690	86,155	67,418	63,119	3.84	-6.38
Other countries of the World	46,066	51,690	86,155	67,418	63,119	3.84	-6.38

SEYCHELLES

1. Arrivals of non-resident tourists at national borders, by country of residence

	2007	2008	2009	2010	2011	Market share 11	% Change 11-10
TOTAL	161,273	158,952	157,541	174,529	194,476	100.00	11.43
AFRICA	16,847	19,117	18,499	22,163	24,422	12.56	10.19
East Africa	7,567	9,454	8,936	10,402	11,905	6.12	14.45
Burundi	14	58	25	22	18	0.01	-18.18
Comoros	41	27	28	63	264	0.14	319.05
Ethiopia	72	78	77	46	79	0.04	71.74
Djibouti	67	66	91	48	62	0.03	29.17
Kenya	1,054	940	870	1,018	1,163	0.60	14.24
Madagascar	277	687	316	349	590	0.30	69.05
Malawi	15	27	15	21	36	0.02	71.43
Mauritius	3,159	4,086	3,476	3,631	3,867	1.99	6.50
Mozambique	57	72	62	52	131	0.07	151.92
Reunion	2,347	2,834	3,389	4,483	4,789	2.46	6.83
Rwanda	17	25	59	45	20	0.01	-55.56
Somalia	3	4		6	28	0.01	366.67
Zimbabwe	94	105	144	161	253	0.13	57.14
Uganda	127	136	154	136	185	0.10	36.03
United Republic of Tanzania	139	191	136	229	274	0.14	19.65
Zambia	84	118	94	92	146	0.08	58.70
Central Africa	120	102	164	135	168	0.09	24.44
Angola	35	44	76	52	94	0.05	80.77
Cameroon	47	30	38	11	12	0.01	9.09
Democratic Republic of the Congo	33	24	39	59	56	0.03	-5.08
Gabon	5	4	11	13	6	0.00	-53.85
North Africa	421	330	291	359	522	0.27	45.40
Algeria	30	27	32	40	126	0.06	215.00
Morocco	104	100	131	101	166	0.09	64.36
Sudan	89	58	50	55	68	0.03	23.64
Tunisia	198	145	78	163	162	0.08	-0.61
Southern Africa	8,316	8,425	8,446	10,797	10,958	5.63	1.49
Botswana	63	75	86	162	185	0.10	14.20
Lesotho	17	25	13	20	14	0.01	-30.00
Namibia	101	77	116	126	127	0.07	0.79
South Africa	8,106	8,219	8,208	10,425	10,559	5.43	1.29
Swaziland	29	29	23	64	73	0.04	14.06
West Africa	317	385	468	294	366	0.19	24.49
Ghana	56	52	73	43	105	0.05	144.19
Côte d'Ivoire	18	23	22	21	24	0.01	14.29
Nigeria	213	286	346	206	206	0.11	
Senegal	30	24	27	24	31	0.02	29.17
Other Africa	106	421	194	176	503	0.26	185.80
Other countries of Africa	106	421	194	176	503	0.26	185.80
AMERICAS	3,915	4,163	4,541	3,960	4,730	2.43	19.44
North America	3,516	3,774	4,139	3,488	3,956	2.03	13.42
Canada	603	601	493	640	666	0.34	4.06
Mexico	40	57	73	59	79	0.04	33.90
United States of America	2,873	3,116	3,573	2,789	3,211	1.65	15.13
South America	242	263	254	286	556	0.29	94.41
Argentina	131	140	115	126	208	0.11	65.08
Brazil	111	123	139	160	348	0.18	117.50
Other Americas	157	126	148	186	218	0.11	17.20
Other countries of the Americas	157	126	148	186	218	0.11	17.20
EAST ASIA AND THE PACIFIC	3,793	3,486	3,523	4,179	5,664	2.91	35.53
North-East Asia	1,811	1,484	1,512	1,738	3,302	1.70	89.99

SEYCHELLES

1. Arrivals of non-resident tourists at national borders, by country of residence

	2007	2008	2009	2010	2011	Market share 11	% Change 11-10
China	1,066	843	919	1,078	2,124	1.09	97.03
Taiwan, Province of China	40	67	58	49	36	0.02	-26.53
Hong Kong, China	100	91	73	98	129	0.07	31.63
Japan	489	392	378	299	541	0.28	80.94
Korea, Republic of	116	91	84	214	472	0.24	120.56
South-East Asia	**918**	**1,154**	**1,131**	**1,324**	**1,214**	**0.62**	**-8.31**
Indonesia	81	105	96	125	174	0.09	39.20
Malaysia	139	207	159	147	175	0.09	19.05
Philippines	183	177	216	226	213	0.11	-5.75
Singapore	392	523	511	625	526	0.27	-15.84
Thailand	123	142	149	201	126	0.06	-37.31
Australasia	**982**	**809**	**796**	**1,049**	**1,091**	**0.56**	**4.00**
Australia	844	697	675	928	980	0.50	5.60
New Zealand	138	112	121	121	111	0.06	-8.26
Other East Asia and the Pacific	**82**	**39**	**84**	**68**	**57**	**0.03**	**-16.18**
Other countries East Asia/Pacific	47	10	35	24	28	0.01	16.67
Other countries of Oceania	35	29	49	44	29	0.01	-34.09
EUROPE	**130,046**	**124,828**	**122,322**	**132,254**	**144,144**	**74.12**	**8.99**
Central/Eastern Europe	**11,495**	**12,365**	**13,210**	**14,411**	**15,962**	**8.21**	**10.76**
Bulgaria	250	212	218	220	352	0.18	60.00
Belarus	89	103	56	100	128	0.07	28.00
Czech Republic	1,333	1,409	1,392	1,303	1,849	0.95	41.90
Estonia	64	63	68	66	96	0.05	45.45
Hungary	993	927	695	632	677	0.35	7.12
Kazakhstan	195	342	153	182	212	0.11	16.48
Latvia	172	172	108	119	127	0.07	6.72
Lithuania				107	70	0.04	-34.58
Poland	850	898	824	961	1,005	0.52	4.58
Romania	316	337	272	333	445	0.23	33.63
Russian Federation	5,931	6,569	8,098	8,942	8,840	4.55	-1.14
Slovakia	346	382	223	384	592	0.30	54.17
Ukraine	768	765	915	890	1,343	0.69	50.90
Other countries Central/East Europe	188	186	188	172	226	0.12	31.40
Northern Europe	**20,313**	**17,186**	**13,846**	**15,936**	**17,096**	**8.79**	**7.28**
Denmark	1,081	1,158	737	727	814	0.42	11.97
Finland	524	557	518	694	619	0.32	-10.81
Iceland	48	45	3	5	26	0.01	420.00
Ireland	580	61	58	450	362	0.19	-19.56
Norway	656	658	482	755	856	0.44	13.38
Sweden	1,052	952	756	983	1,084	0.56	10.27
United Kingdom	16,372	13,755	11,292	12,322	13,335	6.86	8.22
Southern Europe	**31,108**	**27,908**	**30,346**	**29,841**	**30,194**	**15.53**	**1.18**
Albania	7	6	3				
Bosnia and Herzegovina	21	5	12	11	7	0.00	-36.36
Croatia	117	111	93	65	119	0.06	83.08
Greece	960	679	695	598	561	0.29	-6.19
Italy	25,546	23,818	26,114	25,602	25,674	13.20	0.28
Portugal	539	356	403	552	587	0.30	6.34
Serbia	172	118	107	56	125	0.06	123.21
Slovenia	304	288	311	317	322	0.17	1.58
Spain	3,420	2,495	2,599	2,627	2,769	1.42	5.41
Yugoslavia, SFR (former)	22	32	9	13	30	0.02	130.77
Western Europe	**64,149**	**64,969**	**63,462**	**70,570**	**79,328**	**40.79**	**12.41**
Austria	3,316	3,070	2,852	3,446	3,745	1.93	8.68
Belgium	2,245	2,225	2,185	2,247	2,512	1.29	11.79
France	31,894	31,386	31,341	35,026	39,370	20.24	12.40

SEYCHELLES

1. Arrivals of non-resident tourists at national borders, by country of residence

	2007	2008	2009	2010	2011	Market share 11	% Change 11-10
Germany	19,421	21,222	19,736	21,314	23,706	12.19	11.22
Luxembourg	312	295	301	431	446	0.23	3.48
Monaco	126	126	153	148	158	0.08	6.76
Netherlands	1,368	1,377	1,297	1,435	1,747	0.90	21.74
Switzerland	5,467	5,268	5,597	6,523	7,644	3.93	17.19
East Mediterranean Europe	**2,847**	**1,845**	**899**	**1,359**	**1,374**	**0.71**	**1.10**
Cyprus	173	174	177	116	176	0.09	51.72
Israel	2,315	1,397	436	665	661	0.34	-0.60
Turkey	359	274	286	578	537	0.28	-7.09
Other Europe	**134**	**555**	**559**	**137**	**190**	**0.10**	**38.69**
Other countries of Europe	134	555	559	137	190	0.10	38.69
MIDDLE EAST	**4,930**	**5,489**	**6,422**	**8,332**	**12,176**	**6.26**	**46.14**
Bahrain	257	239	360	280	264	0.14	-5.71
Iraq	14	1	5	7	13	0.01	85.71
Jordan	37	32	40	57	51	0.03	-10.53
Kuwait	120	149	141	182	204	0.10	12.09
Lebanon	191	146	155	211	266	0.14	26.07
Libya	16	23	44	41	20	0.01	-51.22
Oman	89	86	68	60	95	0.05	58.33
Qatar	393	729	1,033	1,121	1,390	0.71	24.00
Saudi Arabia	671	410	603	785	1,212	0.62	54.39
Syrian Arab Republic	15	17	26	41	29	0.01	-29.27
United Arab Emirates	3,035	3,553	3,842	5,387	8,488	4.36	57.56
Egypt	82	88	92	149	138	0.07	-7.38
Yemen	8	14	10	5	5	0.00	
Other countries of Middle East	2	2	3	6	1	0.00	-83.33
SOUTH ASIA	**1,742**	**1,869**	**2,234**	**3,641**	**3,340**	**1.72**	**-8.27**
Bangladesh	29	24	87	340	43	0.02	-87.35
Sri Lanka	195	302	232	208	257	0.13	23.56
India	1,110	1,241	1,616	2,671	2,380	1.22	-10.89
Iran, Islamic Republic of	100	46	84	122	188	0.10	54.10
Maldives	93	96	83	68	205	0.11	201.47
Pakistan	204	120	93	117	212	0.11	81.20
Other countries of South Asia	11	40	39	115	55	0.03	-52.17

SIERRA LEONE

1. Arrivals of non-resident tourists at national borders, by country of residence

		2007	2008	2009	2010	2011	Market share 11	% Change 11-10
TOTAL	(*)	33,421	35,670	36,775	38,615	52,442	100.00	35.81
AFRICA		10,846	11,915	12,614	10,806	15,885	30.29	47.00
East Africa					663	2,553	4.87	285.07
Burundi					12	46	0.09	283.33
Comoros					24	1	0.00	-95.83
Eritrea					9	15	0.03	66.67
Kenya					251	448	0.85	78.49
Malawi					27	167	0.32	518.52
Mozambique					2	148	0.28	7300.00
Rwanda					46	145	0.28	215.22
Seychelles					21	199	0.38	847.62
Somalia					26			
Zimbabwe					106	312	0.59	194.34
Uganda					34	406	0.77	1094.12
United Republic of Tanzania					52	366	0.70	603.85
Zambia					53	300	0.57	466.04
Central Africa					198	636	1.21	221.21
Angola					14	46	0.09	228.57
Cameroon					139	193	0.37	38.85
Central African Republic					1	3	0.01	200.00
Chad					7	40	0.08	471.43
Congo					14	308	0.59	2100.00
Equatorial Guinea					7			
Gabon					4	40	0.08	900.00
Sao Tome and Principe					12	6	0.01	-50.00
North Africa					207	411	0.78	98.55
Algeria					22	52	0.10	136.36
Morocco					92	158	0.30	71.74
Sudan					49	186	0.35	279.59
Tunisia					44	15	0.03	-65.91
Southern Africa					1,018	998	1.90	-1.96
Botswana					21	47	0.09	123.81
Lesotho					13	22	0.04	69.23
Namibia					37	66	0.13	78.38
South Africa					891	852	1.62	-4.38
Swaziland					56	11	0.02	-80.36
West Africa					6,846	11,054	21.08	61.47
Cape Verde					8	17	0.03	112.50
Benin					17	123	0.23	623.53
Gambia					509	672	1.28	32.02
Ghana					1,594	3,580	6.83	124.59
Guinea					297	642	1.22	116.16
Côte d'Ivoire					162	205	0.39	26.54
Liberia					270	647	1.23	139.63
Mali					129	136	0.26	5.43
Mauritania					17	34	0.06	100.00
Niger					4	16	0.03	300.00
Nigeria					3,480	4,003	7.63	15.03
Guinea-Bissau					18	18	0.03	
Senegal					218	689	1.31	216.06
Togo					33	151	0.29	357.58
Burkina Faso					90	121	0.23	34.44
Other Africa		10,846	11,915	12,614	1,874	233	0.44	-87.57
Other countries of Africa					1,874	233	0.44	-87.57
All countries of Africa		10,846	11,915	12,614				

SIERRA LEONE

1. Arrivals of non-resident tourists at national borders, by country of residence

	2007	2008	2009	2010	2011	Market share 11	% Change 11-10
AMERICAS	6,169	6,684	7,238	7,406	10,707	20.42	44.57
Caribbean				278	347	0.66	24.82
Haiti				4	3	0.01	-25.00
Jamaica				165	227	0.43	37.58
Trinidad and Tobago				109	117	0.22	7.34
Central America				13	2	0.00	-84.62
Costa Rica				12	2	0.00	-83.33
Guatemala				1			
North America				5,023	9,911	18.90	97.31
Canada				920	3,592	6.85	290.43
Mexico				62	249	0.47	301.61
United States of America				4,041	6,070	11.57	50.21
South America				530	214	0.41	-59.62
Argentina				338	33	0.06	-90.24
Brazil				168	127	0.24	-24.40
Chile				14			
Paraguay				5	2	0.00	-60.00
Uruguay				2			
Venezuela				3	52	0.10	1633.33
Other Americas	6,169	6,684	7,238	1,562	233	0.44	-85.08
Other countries of the Americas				1,562	233	0.44	-85.08
All countries of the Americas	6,169	6,684	7,238				
EAST ASIA AND THE PACIFIC	2,916	3,142	4,068	6,261	9,024	17.21	44.13
North-East Asia				953	4,957	9.45	420.15
China				826	4,179	7.97	405.93
Japan				89	589	1.12	561.80
Korea, Dem. People's Republic of				22	87	0.17	295.45
Korea, Republic of				15	101	0.19	573.33
Mongolia				1	1	0.00	
South-East Asia				267	403	0.77	50.94
Cambodia				18	10	0.02	-44.44
Indonesia				8	37	0.07	362.50
Malaysia				16	54	0.10	237.50
Philippines				192	257	0.49	33.85
Timor-Leste				6			
Singapore				8	12	0.02	50.00
Viet Nam				14	21	0.04	50.00
Thailand				5	12	0.02	140.00
Australasia				3,030	3,664	6.99	20.92
Australia				2,653	3,364	6.41	26.80
New Zealand				377	300	0.57	-20.42
Other East Asia and the Pacific	2,916	3,142	4,068	2,011			
Other countries of Asia				1,116			
All countries of Asia	2,916	3,142	4,068				
Other countries of Oceania				895			
EUROPE	11,327	12,713	10,574	10,295	13,807	26.33	34.11
Central/Eastern Europe				499	629	1.20	26.05
Azerbaijan				7			
Bulgaria				11	18	0.03	63.64
Belarus				1	11	0.02	1000.00
Czech Republic				21	33	0.06	57.14
Hungary				38	59	0.11	55.26
Kazakhstan				24			
Kyrgyzstan				13			

SIERRA LEONE

1. Arrivals of non-resident tourists at national borders, by country of residence

	2007	2008	2009	2010	2011	Market share 11	% Change 11-10
Latvia				165	35	0.07	-78.79
Lithuania				9	23	0.04	155.56
Poland				12	82	0.16	583.33
Romania				22	154	0.29	600.00
Russian Federation				70	149	0.28	112.86
Slovakia				7	24	0.05	242.86
Tajikistan				24	2	0.00	-91.67
Ukraine				75	39	0.07	-48.00
Northern Europe				**5,478**	**8,202**	**15.64**	**49.73**
Denmark				60	233	0.44	288.33
Finland				231	94	0.18	-59.31
Ireland				1,204	773	1.47	-35.80
Norway				81	268	0.51	230.86
Sweden				51	243	0.46	376.47
United Kingdom				3,851	6,591	12.57	71.15
Southern Europe				**1,459**	**1,168**	**2.23**	**-19.95**
Albania				7			
Bosnia and Herzegovina				9			
Croatia				14	51	0.10	264.29
Greece				19	30	0.06	57.89
Italy				480	578	1.10	20.42
Montenegro				6			
Portugal				133	53	0.10	-60.15
Serbia				2	6	0.01	200.00
Spain				789	450	0.86	-42.97
Western Europe				**1,983**	**3,630**	**6.92**	**83.06**
Austria				18	54	0.10	200.00
Belgium				109	334	0.64	206.42
France				514	1,730	3.30	236.58
Germany				537	1,033	1.97	92.36
Luxembourg				5	12	0.02	140.00
Netherlands				767	387	0.74	-49.54
Switzerland				33	80	0.15	142.42
East Mediterranean Europe				**267**	**178**	**0.34**	**-33.33**
Cyprus				25	9	0.02	-64.00
Israel				211	128	0.24	-39.34
Turkey				31	41	0.08	32.26
Other Europe	**11,327**	**12,713**	**10,574**	**609**			
Other countries of Europe				609			
All countries of Europe	11,327	12,713	10,574				
MIDDLE EAST	**965**	**888**	**1,750**	**2,667**	**1,562**	**2.98**	**-41.43**
Palestine				88	12	0.02	-86.36
Iraq				61	28	0.05	-54.10
Jordan				22	8	0.02	-63.64
Kuwait				4	16	0.03	300.00
Lebanon				1,074	1,343	2.56	25.05
Libya				15	28	0.05	86.67
Saudi Arabia				138	13	0.02	-90.58
Syrian Arab Republic				51	29	0.06	-43.14
United Arab Emirates				17	16	0.03	-5.88
Egypt				24	66	0.13	175.00
Yemen				56	3	0.01	-94.64
Other countries of Middle East				1,117			
All countries of Middle East	965	888	1,750				

SIERRA LEONE

1. Arrivals of non-resident tourists at national borders, by country of residence

	2007	2008	2009	2010	2011	Market share 11	% Change 11-10
SOUTH ASIA				1,180	1,457	2.78	23.47
Afghanistan				4	7	0.01	75.00
Bangladesh				13	65	0.12	400.00
Sri Lanka				23	45	0.09	95.65
India				1,014	1,148	2.19	13.21
Iran, Islamic Republic of				49	48	0.09	-2.04
Nepal				16	22	0.04	37.50
Pakistan				61	122	0.23	100.00
NOT SPECIFIED	1,198	328	531				
Other countries of the World	1,198	328	531				

SIERRA LEONE

5. Overnight stays of non-resident tourists in hotels and similar establishments, by country of residence

	2007	2008	2009	2010	2011	Market share 11	% Change 11-10
TOTAL	225,561	249,690	257,425	270,305	367,094	100.00	35.81
AFRICA	75,922	83,108	81,459	75,142	109,564	29.85	45.81
Other Africa	75,922	83,108	81,459	75,142	109,564	29.85	45.81
All countries of Africa	75,922	83,108	81,459	75,142	109,564	29.85	45.81
AMERICAS	43,183	46,788	51,436	52,066	73,318	19.97	40.82
Other Americas	43,183	46,788	51,436	52,066	73,318	19.97	40.82
All countries of the Americas	43,183	46,788	51,436	52,066	73,318	19.97	40.82
EAST ASIA AND THE PACIFIC	20,412	26,586	28,189	52,256	63,168	17.21	20.88
Other East Asia and the Pacific	20,412	26,586	28,189	52,256	63,168	17.21	20.88
All countries of Asia	18,053	24,290	24,605	24,723	37,520	10.22	51.76
All countries of Oceania	2,359	2,296	3,584	27,533	25,648	6.99	-6.85
EUROPE	79,289	86,992	89,705	72,088	96,649	26.33	34.07
Other Europe	79,289	86,992	89,705	72,088	96,649	26.33	34.07
All countries of Europe	79,289	86,992	89,705	72,088	96,649	26.33	34.07
MIDDLE EAST	6,755	6,216	6,636	18,753	24,395	6.65	30.09
All countries of Middle East	6,755	6,216	6,636	18,753	24,395	6.65	30.09

SINGAPORE

2. Arrivals of non-resident visitors at national borders, by nationality

		2007	2008	2009	2010	2011	Market share 11	% Change 11-10
TOTAL	(*)	10,284,545	10,116,054	9,682,690	11,641,701			
AFRICA		90,461	85,142	72,110	71,190			
East Africa		9,274	9,451	9,401	10,190			
Mauritius		9,274	9,451	9,401	10,190			
Southern Africa		42,736	41,375	36,740	34,330			
South Africa		42,736	41,375	36,740	34,330			
Other Africa		38,451	34,316	25,969	26,670			
Other countries of Africa		38,451	34,316	25,969	26,670			
AMERICAS		589,749	572,115	538,229	610,959			
Caribbean		3,966	3,701	4,081	4,449			
All countries of the Caribbean		3,966	3,701	4,081	4,449			
Central America		2,455	2,270	2,122	2,793			
All countries of Central America		2,455	2,270	2,122	2,793			
North America		561,656	543,333	508,493	575,831			
Canada		118,727	111,067	101,463	112,059			
Mexico		9,774	9,095	6,904	8,641			
United States of America		433,155	423,171	400,126	455,131			
South America		21,672	22,811	23,533	27,886			
Argentina		3,022	3,286	3,420	4,557			
Brazil		9,735	10,135	9,985	12,715			
Chile		1,844	2,019	2,698	2,493			
Colombia		2,886	2,673	2,712	3,111			
Uruguay		322	250	311	311			
Venezuela		1,743	2,266	2,061	2,069			
Other countries of South America		2,120	2,182	2,346	2,630			
EAST ASIA AND THE PACIFIC		7,002,492	6,759,583	6,487,570	8,126,315			
North-East Asia		2,592,453	2,439,057	2,065,296	2,564,646			
China		1,090,287	1,053,659	913,067	1,150,027			
Taiwan, Province of China		208,231	176,743	158,655	195,174			
Hong Kong, China		167,619	152,737	177,199	252,993			
Japan		635,972	608,111	521,688	569,676			
Korea, Dem. People's Republic of		151	559	463	136			
Korea, Republic of		480,105	435,732	284,586	379,294			
Macao, China		4,310	3,794	4,172	10,915			
Mongolia		5,778	7,722	5,466	6,431			
South-East Asia		3,554,540	3,412,988	3,539,836	4,624,705			
Brunei Darussalam		37,631	39,856	41,951	46,319			
Myanmar		69,171	85,263	72,390	81,082			
Cambodia		20,969	27,491	26,771	32,759			
Indonesia		1,960,600	1,772,487	1,756,577	2,346,790			
Lao People's Democratic Republic		2,714	3,300	3,385	5,024			
Malaysia		521,593	527,416	648,597	832,685			
Philippines		434,997	435,098	449,968	570,889			
Viet Nam		191,385	222,766	253,259	310,654			
Thailand		315,480	299,311	286,938	398,503			
Australasia		847,793	899,502	874,752	929,568			
Australia		724,904	779,776	769,549	819,953			
New Zealand		122,889	119,726	105,203	109,615			
Melanesia		5,698	5,991	6,244	5,923			
Fiji		2,598	2,466	2,197	1,811			
New Caledonia		50	44	63	53			
Papua New Guinea		3,050	3,481	3,984	4,059			

SINGAPORE

2. Arrivals of non-resident visitors at national borders, by nationality

	2007	2008	2009	2010	2011	Market share 11	% Change 11-10
Micronesia	151	189	192	157			
Guam	14	19	29	31			
Nauru	137	170	163	126			
Other East Asia and the Pacific	1,857	1,856	1,250	1,316			
Other countries of Oceania	1,857	1,856	1,250	1,316			
EUROPE	1,488,333	1,544,644	1,515,203	1,609,141			
Central/Eastern Europe	81,934	97,604	93,511	101,752			
Czech Republic	5,218	5,391	6,480	6,330			
Hungary	4,653	4,478	4,351	5,373			
Poland	11,462	13,654	13,690	14,773			
Commonwealth Independent States	60,601	74,081	68,990	75,276			
Northern Europe	776,818	770,512	723,371	730,863			
Denmark	37,341	38,212	35,651	35,158			
Finland	17,939	16,361	18,959	18,659			
Ireland	38,325	37,648	31,987	30,806			
Norway	31,178	34,547	31,936	33,108			
Sweden	42,295	40,001	36,453	40,336			
United Kingdom	609,740	603,743	568,385	572,796			
Southern Europe	89,606	99,253	106,346	117,726			
Greece	10,462	9,514	9,875	8,907			
Italy	44,872	50,071	54,198	59,902			
Portugal	8,349	8,516	10,072	12,944			
Spain	23,773	29,052	30,288	34,013			
Serbia and Montenegro	2,150	2,100	1,913	1,960			
Western Europe	485,248	522,573	539,217	599,370			
Austria	19,209	19,228	19,797	22,693			
Belgium	18,735	20,522	20,722	23,787			
France	126,056	138,940	147,540	165,255			
Germany	184,726	197,412	203,858	231,070			
Luxembourg	993	1,206	1,138	1,466			
Netherlands	86,489	89,252	91,445	92,941			
Switzerland	49,040	56,013	54,717	62,158			
East Mediterranean Europe	30,668	28,548	25,184	30,943			
Israel	11,303	11,814	11,283	13,124			
Turkey	19,365	16,734	13,901	17,819			
Other Europe	24,059	26,154	27,574	28,487			
Other countries of Europe	24,059	26,154	27,574	28,487			
MIDDLE EAST	37,777	38,347	35,875	44,730			
Bahrain	2,063	2,066	1,708	1,834			
Jordan	1,391	1,170	1,057	1,292			
Kuwait	4,017	3,618	4,119	6,090			
Lebanon	1,061	1,184	1,091	1,310			
Libya	174	227	293	606			
Saudi Arabia	7,329	6,919	7,373	8,251			
United Arab Emirates	10,010	12,254	10,464	13,194			
Egypt	5,049	4,079	3,813	4,637			
Other countries of Middle East	6,683	6,830	5,957	7,516			
SOUTH ASIA	1,051,839	1,109,267	1,033,118	1,178,866			
Afghanistan	163	358	499	370			
Bangladesh	75,874	95,150	86,459	92,410			
Sri Lanka	84,628	85,223	75,610	85,241			
India	822,419	848,683	792,245	907,350			

SINGAPORE

2. Arrivals of non-resident visitors at national borders, by nationality

	2007	2008	2009	2010	2011	Market share 11	% Change 11-10
Iran, Islamic Republic of	15,517	20,600	25,756	40,385			
Nepal	18,558	23,201	18,441	18,101			
Pakistan	25,166	25,962	25,088	25,236			
Other countries of South Asia	9,514	10,090	9,020	9,773			
NOT SPECIFIED	**23,894**	**6,956**	**585**	**500**			
Other countries of the World	23,894	6,956	585	500			

SINGAPORE

2. Arrivals of non-resident visitors at national borders, by country of residence

		2007	2008	2009	2010	2011	Market share 11	% Change 11-10
TOTAL	(*)	10,284,545	10,116,054	9,682,690	11,641,701	13,171,303	100.00	13.14
AFRICA		93,600	86,023	72,348	70,436	69,561	0.53	-1.24
East Africa		11,682	11,430	11,418	11,617	10,527	0.08	-9.38
Mauritius		11,682	11,430	11,418	11,617	10,527	0.08	-9.38
Southern Africa		42,227	40,083	34,451	32,430	33,506	0.25	3.32
South Africa		42,227	40,083	34,451	32,430	33,506	0.25	3.32
Other Africa		39,691	34,510	26,479	26,389	25,528	0.19	-3.26
Other countries of Africa		39,691	34,510	26,479	26,389	25,528	0.19	-3.26
AMERICAS		524,178	505,411	467,723	524,846	563,742	4.28	7.41
Caribbean		2,777	2,809	2,747	3,082			
All countries of the Caribbean		2,777	2,809	2,747	3,082			
Central America		1,385	1,638	1,441	1,947			
All countries of Central America		1,385	1,638	1,441	1,947			
North America		503,581	484,026	445,816	498,803	523,508	3.97	4.95
Canada		86,627	80,044	70,034	75,142	82,932	0.63	10.37
Mexico		8,069	7,351	5,078	6,466			
United States of America		408,885	396,631	370,704	417,195	440,576	3.34	5.60
South America		15,914	16,445	17,258	20,190			
Argentina		2,265	2,405	2,569	3,550			
Brazil		7,634	7,843	7,713	9,802			
Chile		1,507	1,596	2,287	2,117			
Colombia		1,809	1,625	1,570	1,781			
Uruguay		351	248	295	310			
Venezuela		1,025	1,369	1,259	1,082			
Other countries of South America		1,323	1,359	1,565	1,548			
Other Americas		521	493	461	824	40,234	0.31	4782.77
Other countries of the Americas		521	493	461	824	40,234	0.31	4782.77
EAST ASIA AND THE PACIFIC		7,322,529	7,070,353	6,785,096	8,474,870	9,887,028	75.06	16.66
North-East Asia		2,699,768	2,541,938	2,163,701	2,664,002	3,379,363	25.66	26.85
China		1,113,956	1,078,742	936,747	1,171,493	1,577,522	11.98	34.66
Taiwan, Province of China		208,156	175,924	156,761	191,186	238,488	1.81	24.74
Hong Kong, China		302,110	278,115	294,420	387,579	464,375	3.53	19.81
Japan		594,514	571,040	489,987	528,951	656,417	4.98	24.10
Korea, Dem. People's Republic of		3,210	714	844	809			
Korea, Republic of		464,292	423,018	271,987	360,703	414,879	3.15	15.02
Macao, China		7,409	6,888	7,713	16,933			
Mongolia		6,121	7,497	5,242	6,348			
Other countries of North-East Asia						27,682	0.21	
South-East Asia		3,724,736	3,571,408	3,684,848	4,821,753	5,414,250	41.11	12.29
Brunei Darussalam		50,247	54,285	56,531	62,157	62,243	0.47	0.14
Myanmar		64,728	78,582	70,272	78,338	94,184	0.72	20.23
Cambodia		23,531	29,917	29,425	34,934			
Indonesia		1,962,055	1,765,429	1,745,330	2,306,243	2,592,222	19.68	12.40
Lao People's Democratic Republic		3,000	3,573	3,590	5,196			
Malaysia		645,774	647,480	764,309	1,037,489	1,140,935	8.66	9.97
Philippines		418,775	418,938	432,072	544,449	677,723	5.15	24.48
Viet Nam		203,210	239,299	265,414	322,880	332,231	2.52	2.90
Thailand		353,416	333,905	317,905	430,067	472,708	3.59	9.91
Other countries of South-East Asia						42,004	0.32	
Australasia		885,218	943,928	924,133	976,348	1,079,034	8.19	10.52
Australia		768,490	833,156	830,299	880,558	956,039	7.26	8.57
New Zealand		116,728	110,772	93,834	95,790	122,995	0.93	28.40

SINGAPORE

2. Arrivals of non-resident visitors at national borders, by country of residence

	2007	2008	2009	2010	2011	Market share 11	% Change 11-10
Melanesia	9,543	10,060	9,489	9,455			
Fiji	2,318	2,039	1,826	1,421			
New Caledonia	1,566	1,818	1,484	1,514			
Papua New Guinea	5,659	6,203	6,179	6,520			
Micronesia	960	1,090	1,163	1,279			
Guam	900	998	1,062	1,215			
Nauru	60	92	101	64			
Other East Asia and the Pacific	2,304	1,929	1,762	2,033	14,381	0.11	607.38
Other countries of Oceania	2,304	1,929	1,762	2,033	14,381	0.11	607.38
EUROPE	1,276,669	1,333,652	1,318,260	1,386,361	1,413,639	10.73	1.97
Central/Eastern Europe	78,704	93,788	88,442	95,423	127,926	0.97	34.06
Czech Republic	4,874	5,023	6,141	6,098			
Hungary	4,610	4,786	4,447	5,673			
Poland	10,232	11,499	11,200	11,594	14,095	0.11	21.57
Russian Federation					59,378	0.45	
Other countries Central/East Europe					54,453	0.41	
Commonwealth Independent States	58,988	72,480	66,654	72,058			
Northern Europe	636,994	634,644	601,360	594,301	582,100	4.42	-2.05
Denmark	31,406	32,316	30,571	29,635	27,201	0.21	-8.21
Finland	14,528	13,380	16,035	15,611	23,905	0.18	53.13
Ireland	28,571	28,036	22,720	20,437	18,565	0.14	-9.16
Norway	29,176	32,816	30,354	31,765	32,450	0.25	2.16
Sweden	37,620	35,163	31,924	35,084	37,368	0.28	6.51
United Kingdom	495,693	492,933	469,756	461,769	442,611	3.36	-4.15
Southern Europe	80,916	89,101	95,021	101,531	95,627	0.73	-5.81
Greece	10,111	9,045	9,250	8,006	7,130	0.05	-10.94
Italy	38,746	43,035	46,770	51,086	53,520	0.41	4.76
Portugal	5,163	5,273	6,600	7,115			
Spain	24,950	29,966	30,871	33,765	34,977	0.27	3.59
Serbia and Montenegro	1,946	1,782	1,530	1,559			
Western Europe	425,579	462,245	482,467	535,112	565,232	4.29	5.63
Austria	16,696	16,649	17,505	20,093	19,889	0.15	-1.02
Belgium	17,354	18,937	19,267	21,848			
France	99,269	111,198	119,728	130,461	140,299	1.07	7.54
Germany	164,900	175,280	183,681	209,263	219,952	1.67	5.11
Luxembourg	1,906	2,163	2,098	2,551			
Netherlands	70,351	73,230	76,359	76,520	81,090	0.62	5.97
Switzerland	55,103	64,788	63,829	74,376	79,023	0.60	6.25
Belgium / Luxembourg					24,979	0.19	
East Mediterranean Europe	29,639	27,212	23,684	29,237	26,868	0.20	-8.10
Israel	11,025	11,402	10,884	12,833	12,137	0.09	-5.42
Turkey	18,614	15,810	12,800	16,404	14,731	0.11	-10.20
Other Europe	24,837	26,662	27,286	30,757	15,886	0.12	-48.35
Other countries of Europe	24,837	26,662	27,286	30,757	15,886	0.12	-48.35
MIDDLE EAST	78,353	87,690	85,709	101,461	113,551	0.86	11.92
Bahrain	3,614	3,661	3,152	3,536			
Jordan	900	762	684	769			
Kuwait	5,242	4,838	5,750	8,368	8,278	0.06	-1.08
Lebanon	759	767	784	866			
Libya	134	155	184	358			
Saudi Arabia	10,555	10,096	10,815	12,633	17,041	0.13	34.89
United Arab Emirates	41,054	51,170	49,529	56,476	62,736	0.48	11.08
Egypt	5,054	4,453	3,861	4,746	3,829	0.03	-19.32
Other countries of Middle East	11,041	11,788	10,950	13,709	21,667	0.16	58.05

SINGAPORE

2. Arrivals of non-resident visitors at national borders, by country of residence

	2007	2008	2009	2010	2011	Market share 11	% Change 11-10
SOUTH ASIA	968,389	1,026,576	953,364	1,083,673	1,123,649	8.53	3.69
Afghanistan	183	370	544	434			
Bangladesh	77,050	95,818	86,637	92,312	95,531	0.73	3.49
Sri Lanka	79,405	79,818	70,010	78,973	83,991	0.64	6.35
India	748,728	778,303	725,624	828,994	868,991	6.60	4.82
Iran, Islamic Republic of	14,235	19,083	23,917	36,932	32,434	0.25	-12.18
Nepal	16,000	19,752	15,183	14,303	12,757	0.10	-10.81
Pakistan	22,871	22,998	22,280	21,927	20,928	0.16	-4.56
Other countries of South Asia	9,917	10,434	9,169	9,798	9,017	0.07	-7.97
NOT SPECIFIED	20,827	6,349	190	54	133	0.00	146.30
Other countries of the World	20,827	6,349	190	54	133	0.00	146.30

SINT EUSTATIUS

1. Arrivals of non-resident tourists at national borders, by country of residence

		2007	2008	2009	2010	2011	Market share 11	% Change 11-10
TOTAL	(*)	**11,568**	**11,758**	**12,049**	**11,393**			
AMERICAS		**3,928**	**3,762**	**3,622**	**3,484**			
Caribbean		**395**	**425**	**382**	**385**			
Dominican Republic		395	425	382	385			
North America		**2,967**	**2,766**	**2,630**	**2,580**			
Canada		229	253	236	229			
United States of America		2,738	2,513	2,394	2,351			
South America		**328**	**297**	**364**	**267**			
Guyana		328	297	364	267			
Other Americas		**238**	**274**	**246**	**252**			
Other countries of the Americas		238	274	246	252			
EUROPE		**5,893**	**6,201**	**6,652**	**6,356**			
Western Europe		**4,666**	**5,004**	**5,327**	**5,151**			
Germany		72	51	54	49			
Netherlands		4,594	4,953	5,273	5,102			
Other Europe		**1,227**	**1,197**	**1,325**	**1,205**			
Other countries of Europe		1,227	1,197	1,325	1,205			
NOT SPECIFIED		**1,747**	**1,795**	**1,775**	**1,553**			
Other countries of the World		1,747	1,795	1,775	1,553			

SINT MAARTEN

1. Arrivals of non-resident tourists at national borders, by nationality

		2007	2008	2009	2010	2011	Market share 11	% Change 11-10
TOTAL	(*)	469,407	475,410	440,185	443,136	424,340	100.00	-4.24
AMERICAS		335,410	336,013	309,659	307,871	291,734	68.75	-5.24
Caribbean		35,209	31,152	25,266	23,780	23,314	5.49	-1.96
Antigua and Barbuda		5,431						
Dominican Republic		3,114						
Haiti		3,465						
Saint Kitts and Nevis		6,978						
Trinidad and Tobago		2,949						
Other countries of the Caribbean		13,272						
All countries of the Caribbean			31,152	25,266	23,780	23,314	5.49	-1.96
North America		286,181	291,967	272,708	269,877	252,460	59.49	-6.45
Canada		32,350	34,055	32,277	33,498	33,256	7.84	-0.72
United States of America		253,831	257,912	240,431	236,379	219,204	51.66	-7.27
South America		14,020	3,394	3,194	2,853	2,836	0.67	-0.60
Argentina		1,226						
Brazil		2,711						
Chile		374						
Venezuela		3,701	3,394	3,194	2,853	2,836	0.67	-0.60
Other countries of South America		6,008						
Other Americas			9,500	8,491	11,361	13,124	3.09	15.52
Other countries of the Americas			9,500	8,491	11,361	13,124	3.09	15.52
EUROPE		96,365	102,713	98,341	101,118	101,712	23.97	0.59
Central/Eastern Europe		518						
Russian Federation		518						
Southern Europe		4,771						
Italy		4,771						
Western Europe		77,999	85,491	81,393	84,330	16,607	3.91	-80.31
France	(*)	61,110	67,209	66,177	67,833			
Netherlands		16,889	18,282	15,216	16,497	16,607	3.91	0.67
Other Europe		13,077	17,222	16,948	16,788	85,105	20.06	406.94
Other countries of Europe		13,077	17,222	16,948	16,788	85,105	20.06	406.94
NOT SPECIFIED		37,632	36,684	32,185	34,147	30,894	7.28	-9.53
Other countries of the World		22,089	36,684	32,185	34,147	30,894	7.28	-9.53
Nationals Residing Abroad		15,543						

SLOVAKIA

4. Arrivals of non-resident tourists in all types of accommodation establishments, by nationality

	2007	2008	2009	2010	2011	Market share 11	% Change 11-10
TOTAL	1,684,526	1,766,529	1,298,075	1,326,639	1,460,361	100.00	10.08
AFRICA	2,276	3,318	1,946	2,684	2,926	0.20	9.02
East Africa	31	74	51	78	73	0.00	-6.41
Kenya	31	74	51	78	73	0.00	-6.41
North Africa	164	127	92	105	99	0.01	-5.71
Tunisia	164	127	92	105	99	0.01	-5.71
Southern Africa	424	973	490	845	624	0.04	-26.15
South Africa	424	973	490	845	624	0.04	-26.15
Other Africa	1,657	2,144	1,313	1,656	2,130	0.15	28.62
Other countries of Africa	1,657	2,144	1,313	1,656	2,130	0.15	28.62
AMERICAS	43,697	41,456	30,137	36,198	43,172	2.96	19.27
Caribbean	27	20	28	45	24	0.00	-46.67
Dominican Republic	27	20	28	45	24	0.00	-46.67
North America	38,793	36,603	25,897	29,513	34,935	2.39	18.37
Canada	5,977	6,762	4,177	4,861	6,762	0.46	39.11
Mexico	839	1,102	905	2,601	1,691	0.12	-34.99
United States of America	31,977	28,739	20,815	22,051	26,482	1.81	20.09
South America	1,775	2,620	2,084	2,751	3,870	0.27	40.68
Argentina	424	497	400	592	561	0.04	-5.24
Brazil	1,351	2,123	1,684	2,159	3,309	0.23	53.27
Other Americas	3,102	2,213	2,128	3,889	4,343	0.30	11.67
Other countries of the Americas	3,102	2,213	2,128	3,889	4,343	0.30	11.67
EAST ASIA AND THE PACIFIC	73,658	70,755	53,748	65,064	72,073	4.94	10.77
North-East Asia	48,603	45,063	35,471	43,279	47,898	3.28	10.67
China	4,286	7,675	6,540	8,337	11,857	0.81	42.22
Japan	13,496	13,743	11,351	11,523	8,865	0.61	-23.07
Korea, Republic of	30,821	23,645	17,580	23,419	27,176	1.86	16.04
South-East Asia	605	1,235	1,164	954	1,160	0.08	21.59
Thailand	605	1,235	1,164	954	1,160	0.08	21.59
Australasia	7,168	6,507	4,656	5,535	5,190	0.36	-6.23
Australia	6,293	5,669	4,014	4,881	4,545	0.31	-6.88
New Zealand	875	838	642	654	645	0.04	-1.38
Other East Asia and the Pacific	17,282	17,950	12,457	15,296	17,825	1.22	16.53
Other countries of Asia	17,282	17,950	12,457	15,296	17,825	1.22	16.53
EUROPE	1,558,688	1,647,872	1,209,816	1,219,740	1,336,504	91.52	9.57
Central/Eastern Europe	952,309	1,055,794	737,179	743,991	834,124	57.12	12.11
Bulgaria	5,924	6,891	5,626	5,416	6,517	0.45	20.33
Belarus	3,610	4,099	2,967	3,506	4,319	0.30	23.19
Czech Republic	490,986	537,180	425,414	433,321	477,159	32.67	10.12
Estonia	5,863	5,242	3,250	3,209	2,952	0.20	-8.01
Hungary	93,797	90,123	56,111	51,324	59,000	4.04	14.96
Latvia	9,955	8,335	4,472	4,734	5,460	0.37	15.34
Lithuania	24,070	19,698	12,602	13,182	15,046	1.03	14.14
Republic of Moldova	673	264	512	440	381	0.03	-13.41
Poland	243,917	308,437	164,712	161,851	172,001	11.78	6.27
Romania	16,172	20,685	17,513	18,381	20,551	1.41	11.81
Russian Federation	22,730	25,982	23,382	26,968	35,122	2.41	30.24
Ukraine	34,612	28,858	20,618	21,659	35,616	2.44	64.44
Northern Europe	115,581	118,769	77,934	79,581	82,524	5.65	3.70
Denmark	14,788	10,794	7,810	7,153	7,774	0.53	8.68
Finland	10,606	10,295	7,941	7,537	11,982	0.82	58.98
Iceland	464	523	180	293	239	0.02	-18.43

SLOVAKIA

4. Arrivals of non-resident tourists in all types of accommodation establishments, by nationality

	2007	2008	2009	2010	2011	Market share 11	% Change 11-10
Ireland	10,423	9,613	4,898	6,829	6,853	0.47	0.35
Norway	5,184	5,153	4,174	5,054	6,224	0.43	23.15
Sweden	10,923	15,763	10,616	11,754	9,976	0.68	-15.13
United Kingdom	63,193	66,628	42,315	40,961	39,476	2.70	-3.63
Southern Europe	**122,807**	**121,764**	**107,455**	**110,470**	**117,591**	**8.05**	**6.45**
Albania	659	699	228	240	380	0.03	58.33
Bosnia and Herzegovina	1,657	1,404	1,281	989	1,390	0.10	40.55
Croatia	20,639	19,545	13,360	12,283	13,487	0.92	9.80
Greece	4,708	4,591	3,748	3,815	5,130	0.35	34.47
Italy	58,184	54,722	50,982	54,439	51,957	3.56	-4.56
Malta	336	569	1,227	994	231	0.02	-76.76
Montenegro		219	112	300	372	0.03	24.00
Portugal	2,932	2,814	2,243	2,732	3,323	0.23	21.63
Serbia		4,647	3,301	4,891	7,972	0.55	62.99
Slovenia	12,641	14,338	12,614	11,953	12,901	0.88	7.93
Spain	14,166	17,693	17,549	16,926	19,635	1.34	16.00
TFYR of Macedonia	301	523	810	908	813	0.06	-10.46
Serbia and Montenegro	6,584						
Western Europe	**336,590**	**322,068**	**264,350**	**260,562**	**275,390**	**18.86**	**5.69**
Austria	62,661	62,052	50,065	51,678	58,983	4.04	14.14
Belgium	16,260	16,036	14,671	14,460	15,242	1.04	5.41
France	41,301	43,958	34,045	32,967	35,931	2.46	8.99
Germany	176,059	164,694	133,989	131,674	133,431	9.14	1.33
Liechtenstein	62	106	121	148	163	0.01	10.14
Luxembourg	649	560	548	489	419	0.03	-14.31
Netherlands	27,621	24,113	20,759	18,776	18,499	1.27	-1.48
Switzerland	11,977	10,549	10,152	10,370	12,722	0.87	22.68
East Mediterranean Europe	**14,457**	**15,739**	**12,471**	**14,394**	**16,450**	**1.13**	**14.28**
Cyprus	1,073	1,395	1,371	1,358	1,686	0.12	24.15
Israel	10,502	11,171	8,232	9,690	10,281	0.70	6.10
Turkey	2,882	3,173	2,868	3,346	4,483	0.31	33.98
Other Europe	**16,944**	**13,738**	**10,427**	**10,742**	**10,425**	**0.71**	**-2.95**
Other countries of Europe	16,944	13,738	10,427	10,742	10,425	0.71	-2.95
MIDDLE EAST	**3,592**	**533**	**516**	**551**	**579**	**0.04**	**5.08**
Egypt	3,592	533	516	551	579	0.04	5.08
SOUTH ASIA	**1,229**	**1,380**	**1,290**	**1,495**	**2,537**	**0.17**	**69.70**
India	1,229	1,380	1,290	1,495	2,537	0.17	69.70
NOT SPECIFIED	**1,386**	**1,215**	**622**	**907**	**2,570**	**0.18**	**183.35**
Other countries of the World	1,386	1,215	622	907	2,570	0.18	183.35

SLOVAKIA

6. Overnight stays of non-resident tourists in all types of accommodation establishments, by nationality

	2007	2008	2009	2010	2011	Market share 11	% Change 11-10
TOTAL	5,198,696	5,261,476	3,769,136	3,806,609	4,038,635	100.00	6.10
AFRICA	8,191	13,205	8,178	9,637	8,557	0.21	-11.21
East Africa	173	239	167	162	165	0.00	1.85
Kenya	173	239	167	162	165	0.00	1.85
North Africa	262	523	204	399	323	0.01	-19.05
Tunisia	262	523	204	399	323	0.01	-19.05
Southern Africa	1,483	1,972	1,402	2,752	1,543	0.04	-43.93
South Africa	1,483	1,972	1,402	2,752	1,543	0.04	-43.93
Other Africa	6,273	10,471	6,405	6,324	6,526	0.16	3.19
Other countries of Africa	6,273	10,471	6,405	6,324	6,526	0.16	3.19
AMERICAS	105,307	95,738	72,794	86,304	101,260	2.51	17.33
Caribbean	66	58	47	140	29	0.00	-79.29
Dominican Republic	66	58	47	140	29	0.00	-79.29
North America	92,704	83,207	62,510	70,966	82,879	2.05	16.79
Canada	13,398	16,915	10,473	12,824	18,237	0.45	42.21
Mexico	1,816	2,585	2,053	4,139	4,585	0.11	10.78
United States of America	77,490	63,707	49,984	54,003	60,057	1.49	1.21
South America	5,200	6,594	5,395	6,365	9,710	0.24	52.55
Argentina	939	1,238	780	1,141	1,140	0.03	-0.09
Brazil	4,261	5,356	4,615	5,224	8,570	0.21	64.05
Other Americas	7,337	5,879	4,842	8,833	8,642	0.21	-2.16
Other countries of the Americas	7,337	5,879	4,842	8,833	8,642	0.21	-2.16
EAST ASIA AND THE PACIFIC	164,365	156,578	135,461	174,993	194,358	4.81	11.07
North-East Asia	79,744	72,431	68,548	87,571	103,510	2.56	18.20
China	7,643	12,120	10,441	16,839	19,519	0.48	15.92
Japan	21,957	26,460	18,995	20,187	16,443	0.41	-18.55
Korea, Republic of	50,144	33,851	39,112	50,545	67,548	1.67	33.64
South-East Asia	1,019	2,735	5,433	4,200	2,092	0.05	-50.19
Thailand	1,019	2,735	5,433	4,200	2,092	0.05	-50.19
Australasia	15,412	16,430	5,204	13,723	13,716	0.34	-0.05
Australia	13,908	14,614	4,014	12,383	12,517	0.31	1.08
New Zealand	1,504	1,816	1,190	1,340	1,199	0.03	-10.52
Other East Asia and the Pacific	68,190	64,982	56,276	69,499	75,040	1.86	7.97
Other countries of Asia	68,190	64,982	56,276	69,499	75,040	1.86	7.97
EUROPE	4,909,446	4,986,808	3,540,645	3,527,429	3,719,751	92.10	5.45
Central/Eastern Europe	3,063,288	3,281,910	2,201,102	2,210,346	2,399,523	59.41	8.56
Bulgaria	15,223	18,348	13,292	10,488	12,871	0.32	22.72
Belarus	19,851	17,499	10,701	10,369	12,490	0.31	20.46
Czech Republic	1,610,881	1,704,632	1,300,870	1,350,234	1,422,506	35.22	5.35
Estonia	16,140	15,664	9,243	7,744	8,026	0.20	3.64
Hungary	247,703	225,271	136,921	120,304	143,575	3.56	19.34
Latvia	23,785	21,236	10,649	11,618	11,776	0.29	1.36
Lithuania	44,192	41,007	27,824	26,889	31,117	0.77	15.72
Republic of Moldova	1,234	659	1,650	1,405	1,049	0.03	-25.34
Poland	762,890	941,975	479,774	453,067	471,178	11.67	4.00
Romania	46,231	64,441	45,619	49,722	57,218	1.42	15.08
Russian Federation	113,361	111,132	88,213	94,325	125,636	3.11	33.19
Ukraine	161,797	120,046	76,346	74,181	102,081	2.53	37.61
Northern Europe	280,438	271,605	178,415	188,546	192,381	4.76	2.03
Denmark	47,558	30,532	20,702	19,167	21,984	0.54	14.70
Finland	29,487	24,732	18,751	19,126	32,776	0.81	71.37
Iceland	900	1,205	390	932	532	0.01	-42.92

671

SLOVAKIA

6. Overnight stays of non-resident tourists in all types of accommodation establishments, by nationality

	2007	2008	2009	2010	2011	Market share 11	% Change 11-10
Ireland	22,614	20,657	10,460	15,453	15,614	0.39	1.04
Norway	13,353	11,567	10,295	11,717	14,223	0.35	21.39
Sweden	24,825	34,202	22,633	26,935	22,444	0.56	-16.67
United Kingdom	141,701	148,710	95,184	95,216	84,808	2.10	-10.93
Southern Europe	**274,729**	**258,614**	**238,003**	**238,555**	**243,681**	**6.03**	**2.15**
Albania	1,407	1,710	485	656	966	0.02	47.26
Bosnia and Herzegovina	4,992	4,266	3,713	2,774	2,773	0.07	-0.04
Croatia	46,929	40,929	29,444	26,330	26,782	0.66	1.72
Greece	11,036	10,525	8,195	8,997	11,311	0.28	25.72
Italy	120,994	115,502	110,885	118,579	110,966	2.75	-6.42
Malta	1,061	1,732	5,767	2,196	625	0.02	-71.54
Montenegro		611	408	704	641	0.02	-8.95
Portugal	6,769	6,312	5,643	6,216	7,246	0.18	16.57
Serbia		14,718	10,923	14,662	18,483	0.46	26.06
Slovenia	26,720	25,379	23,050	23,067	24,194	0.60	4.89
Spain	30,892	35,725	37,781	32,577	37,978	0.94	16.58
TFYR of Macedonia	813	1,205	1,709	1,797	1,716	0.04	-4.51
Serbia and Montenegro	23,116						
Western Europe	**1,170,578**	**1,059,508**	**837,451**	**786,851**	**774,616**	**19.18**	**-1.55**
Austria	163,149	158,594	122,449	120,900	125,499	3.11	3.80
Belgium	41,128	39,143	35,435	35,022	35,093	0.87	0.20
France	87,577	95,660	75,680	69,368	79,757	1.97	14.98
Germany	777,872	682,274	527,821	490,780	462,503	11.45	-5.76
Liechtenstein	339	670	519	399	323	0.01	-19.05
Luxembourg	1,473	1,203	1,312	1,337	902	0.02	-32.54
Netherlands	72,267	58,756	53,063	46,894	42,861	1.06	-8.60
Switzerland	26,773	23,208	21,172	22,151	27,678	0.69	24.95
East Mediterranean Europe	**76,112**	**80,890**	**65,988**	**79,283**	**87,033**	**2.16**	**9.78**
Cyprus	6,321	7,962	6,892	7,618	7,884	0.20	3.49
Israel	63,606	65,095	52,570	64,270	69,636	1.72	8.35
Turkey	6,185	7,833	6,526	7,395	9,513	0.24	28.64
Other Europe	**44,301**	**34,281**	**19,686**	**23,848**	**22,517**	**0.56**	**-5.58**
Other countries of Europe	44,301	34,281	19,686	23,848	22,517	0.56	-5.58
MIDDLE EAST	**5,218**	**2,013**	**2,051**	**2,754**	**3,127**	**0.08**	**13.54**
Egypt	5,218	2,013	2,051	2,754	3,127	0.08	13.54
SOUTH ASIA	**4,121**	**4,822**	**3,207**	**4,063**	**6,628**	**0.16**	**63.13**
India	4,121	4,822	3,207	4,063	6,628	0.16	63.13
NOT SPECIFIED	**2,048**	**2,312**	**6,800**	**1,429**	**4,954**	**0.12**	**246.68**
Other countries of the World	2,048	2,312	6,800	1,429	4,954	0.12	246.68

SLOVENIA

3. Arrivals of non-resident tourists in hotels and similar establishments, by nationality

		2007	2008	2009	2010	2011	Market share 11	% Change 11-10
TOTAL	(*)	1,353,649	1,532,418	1,411,352	1,422,382	1,528,057	100.00	7.43
AFRICA		1,824	3,411	2,518	2,779	3,642	0.24	31.05
Southern Africa		670	808	780	956	1,419	0.09	48.43
South Africa		670	808	780	956	1,419	0.09	48.43
Other Africa		1,154	2,603	1,738	1,823	2,223	0.15	21.94
Other countries of Africa		1,154	2,603	1,738	1,823	2,223	0.15	21.94
AMERICAS		58,542	59,551	49,459	52,235	56,002	3.66	7.21
North America		54,211	53,403	42,694	45,032	46,660	3.05	3.62
Canada		7,181	8,036	7,124	7,435	8,050	0.53	8.27
United States of America		43,785	42,776	33,327	35,487	38,455	2.52	8.36
Other countries of North America		3,245	2,591	2,243	2,110	155	0.01	-92.65
South America		1,624	2,360	2,776	3,057	3,772	0.25	23.39
Brazil		1,624	2,360	2,776	3,057	3,772	0.25	23.39
Other Americas		2,707	3,788	3,989	4,146	5,570	0.36	34.35
Other countries of the Americas		2,707	3,788	3,989	4,146	5,570	0.36	34.35
EAST ASIA AND THE PACIFIC		57,217	79,664	84,457	84,888	95,273	6.23	12.23
North-East Asia		33,329	49,853	57,894	53,090	55,091	3.61	3.77
China		3,207	4,625	5,319	7,613	10,078	0.66	32.38
Japan		23,397	39,078	47,641	39,502	34,187	2.24	-13.46
Korea, Republic of		6,725	6,150	4,934	5,975	10,826	0.71	81.19
Australasia		16,446	19,110	14,477	15,551	15,423	1.01	-0.82
Australia		14,232	16,687	12,325	13,035	13,604	0.89	4.37
New Zealand		2,214	2,423	2,152	2,516	1,819	0.12	-27.70
Other East Asia and the Pacific		7,442	10,701	12,086	16,247	24,759	1.62	52.39
Other countries of Asia		6,734	10,023	11,226	15,706	24,040	1.57	53.06
Other countries of Oceania		708	678	860	541	719	0.05	32.90
EUROPE		1,236,066	1,389,792	1,274,918	1,282,480	1,373,140	89.86	7.07
Central/Eastern Europe		148,365	192,227	168,285	178,106	209,763	13.73	17.77
Bulgaria		12,760	17,772	16,135	15,654	18,147	1.19	15.93
Czech Republic		22,360	27,936	25,225	24,702	27,897	1.83	12.93
Estonia		1,984	2,096	1,438	1,568	1,860	0.12	18.62
Hungary		34,001	41,195	38,814	36,844	42,088	2.75	14.23
Latvia		3,310	5,405	2,670	3,041	2,444	0.16	-19.63
Lithuania		3,081	3,685	1,979	1,787	2,127	0.14	19.03
Poland		18,347	26,159	21,556	20,924	23,729	1.55	13.41
Romania		13,278	15,233	15,453	16,204	17,944	1.17	10.74
Russian Federation		21,105	28,803	25,045	30,414	38,019	2.49	25.00
Slovakia		10,746	12,689	11,363	12,093	13,181	0.86	9.00
Ukraine		7,393	11,254	8,607	14,875	22,327	1.46	50.10
Northern Europe		119,953	131,213	103,143	91,464	95,261	6.23	4.15
Denmark		6,949	9,243	8,058	9,277	10,139	0.66	9.29
Finland		16,577	19,116	14,071	11,953	12,559	0.82	5.07
Iceland		3,541	1,583	1,179	659	1,482	0.10	124.89
Ireland		8,068	8,053	7,481	5,127	5,132	0.34	0.10
Norway		5,574	7,717	5,759	5,637	5,343	0.35	-5.22
Sweden		12,564	16,255	11,959	10,844	11,759	0.77	8.44
United Kingdom		66,680	69,246	54,636	47,967	48,847	3.20	1.83
Southern Europe		500,706	574,074	556,443	578,563	589,086	38.55	1.82
Bosnia and Herzegovina		19,714	27,578	23,432	23,899	25,224	1.65	5.54
Croatia		85,939	99,011	82,404	82,584	87,602	5.73	6.08
Greece		4,831	6,201	6,651	6,050	6,150	0.40	1.65
Italy		316,359	346,020	352,163	348,103	348,128	22.78	0.01
Malta		797	1,497	2,183	2,195	2,664	0.17	21.37

SLOVENIA

3. Arrivals of non-resident tourists in hotels and similar establishments, by nationality

	2007	2008	2009	2010	2011	Market share 11	% Change 11-10
Montenegro	2,526	3,605	3,871	6,543	6,214	0.41	-5.03
Portugal	6,106	6,963	6,091	5,763	5,821	0.38	1.01
Serbia	35,143	46,858	46,489	67,104	70,350	4.60	4.84
Spain	21,305	25,366	23,390	23,114	24,444	1.60	5.75
TFYR of Macedonia	7,986	10,975	9,769	13,208	12,489	0.82	-5.44
Western Europe	**417,019**	**445,176**	**405,634**	**391,862**	**432,070**	**28.28**	**10.26**
Austria	168,774	172,717	169,240	164,237	181,515	11.88	10.52
Belgium	22,756	28,014	22,617	22,394	28,400	1.86	26.82
France	41,040	44,457	39,921	37,258	39,326	2.57	5.55
Germany	137,669	148,042	125,269	123,041	134,573	8.81	9.37
Luxembourg	1,059	2,296	1,107	968	1,066	0.07	10.12
Netherlands	23,394	26,707	25,355	23,309	24,294	1.59	4.23
Switzerland	22,327	22,943	22,125	20,655	22,896	1.50	10.85
East Mediterranean Europe	**40,585**	**39,086**	**31,931**	**32,817**	**35,791**	**2.34**	**9.06**
Cyprus	832	1,294	587	713	570	0.04	-20.06
Israel	29,872	26,500	23,770	21,848	22,298	1.46	2.06
Turkey	9,881	11,292	7,574	10,256	12,923	0.85	26.00
Other Europe	**9,438**	**8,016**	**9,482**	**9,668**	**11,169**	**0.73**	**15.53**
Other countries of Europe	9,438	8,016	9,482	9,668	11,169	0.73	15.53

SLOVENIA

4. Arrivals of non-resident tourists in all types of accommodation establishments, by nationality

		2007	2008	2009	2010	2011	Market share 11	% Change 11-10
TOTAL	(*)	1,751,332	1,957,691	1,823,931	1,869,106	2,036,652	100.00	8.96
AFRICA		2,100	3,760	2,911	3,396	4,437	0.22	30.65
Southern Africa		797	899	898	1,132	1,773	0.09	56.63
South Africa		797	899	898	1,132	1,773	0.09	56.63
Other Africa		1,303	2,861	2,013	2,264	2,664	0.13	17.67
Other countries of Africa		1,303	2,861	2,013	2,264	2,664	0.13	17.67
AMERICAS		66,900	65,701	55,336	61,941	67,613	3.32	9.16
North America		61,740	58,866	47,777	53,368	56,627	2.78	6.11
Canada		8,791	9,372	8,410	9,598	10,583	0.52	10.26
United States of America		49,620	46,783	37,050	41,566	45,796	2.25	10.18
Other countries of North America		3,329	2,711	2,317	2,204	248	0.01	-88.75
South America		1,851	2,549	2,998	3,591	4,290	0.21	19.47
Brazil		1,851	2,549	2,998	3,591	4,290	0.21	19.47
Other Americas		3,309	4,286	4,561	4,982	6,696	0.33	34.40
Other countries of the Americas		3,309	4,286	4,561	4,982	6,696	0.33	34.40
EAST ASIA AND THE PACIFIC		65,277	85,552	90,168	94,653	106,067	5.21	12.06
North-East Asia		35,105	51,030	58,958	55,314	57,934	2.84	4.74
China		3,503	4,911	5,638	8,234	11,050	0.54	34.20
Japan		24,506	39,733	48,182	40,455	35,321	1.73	-12.69
Korea, Republic of		7,096	6,386	5,138	6,625	11,563	0.57	74.54
Australasia		22,095	23,048	18,379	21,318	21,524	1.06	0.97
Australia		18,725	19,709	15,308	17,695	18,461	0.91	4.33
New Zealand		3,370	3,339	3,071	3,623	3,063	0.15	-15.46
Other East Asia and the Pacific		8,077	11,474	12,831	18,021	26,609	1.31	47.66
Other countries of Asia		7,308	10,624	11,793	17,071	25,631	1.26	50.14
Other countries of Oceania		769	850	1,038	950	978	0.05	2.95
EUROPE		1,617,055	1,802,678	1,675,516	1,709,116	1,858,535	91.25	8.74
Central/Eastern Europe		208,335	267,746	240,190	255,552	299,936	14.73	17.37
Bulgaria		15,213	20,716	19,507	18,833	21,800	1.07	15.75
Czech Republic		43,494	54,957	52,417	53,205	58,817	2.89	10.55
Estonia		2,575	2,842	1,958	2,072	2,525	0.12	21.86
Hungary		50,148	59,606	55,370	55,325	63,096	3.10	14.05
Latvia		4,895	6,980	3,339	3,997	3,274	0.16	-18.09
Lithuania		4,231	4,938	3,045	2,821	3,386	0.17	20.03
Poland		27,258	38,539	32,607	33,320	39,626	1.95	18.93
Romania		15,662	18,274	18,660	19,462	21,799	1.07	12.01
Russian Federation		21,980	30,585	26,842	32,690	41,360	2.03	26.52
Slovakia		14,607	17,230	16,329	17,427	19,720	0.97	13.16
Ukraine		8,272	13,079	10,116	16,400	24,533	1.20	49.59
Northern Europe		156,806	164,427	132,595	128,875	134,236	6.59	4.16
Denmark		12,115	14,974	13,723	15,255	16,576	0.81	8.66
Finland		19,473	21,828	16,549	15,082	15,629	0.77	3.63
Iceland		3,733	1,758	1,436	882	1,785	0.09	102.38
Ireland		10,813	10,008	9,354	7,715	7,719	0.38	0.05
Norway		6,990	9,270	7,150	7,448	6,876	0.34	-7.68
Sweden		16,560	19,686	14,955	14,028	14,986	0.74	6.83
United Kingdom		87,122	86,903	69,428	68,465	70,665	3.47	3.21
Southern Europe		592,503	678,121	663,976	691,750	715,444	35.13	3.43
Bosnia and Herzegovina		22,221	31,058	26,881	27,299	29,356	1.44	7.54
Croatia		106,412	123,087	104,045	103,134	110,377	5.42	7.02
Greece		5,422	6,756	7,434	6,822	6,885	0.34	0.92
Italy		368,711	406,662	417,771	412,137	420,247	20.63	1.97
Malta		1,031	1,726	2,389	2,401	2,926	0.14	21.87

SLOVENIA

4. Arrivals of non-resident tourists in all types of accommodation establishments, by nationality

	2007	2008	2009	2010	2011	Market share 11	% Change 11-10
Montenegro	2,830	4,039	4,188	7,277	6,801	0.33	-6.54
Portugal	7,701	8,107	7,330	7,422	7,644	0.38	2.99
Serbia	38,722	50,560	51,388	76,156	80,995	3.98	6.35
Spain	30,659	33,568	31,409	33,670	35,687	1.75	5.99
TFYR of Macedonia	8,794	12,558	11,141	15,432	14,526	0.71	-5.87
Western Europe	**600,395**	**638,392**	**590,074**	**581,231**	**651,247**	**31.98**	**12.05**
Austria	207,248	210,229	207,366	201,756	222,192	10.91	10.13
Belgium	35,462	41,920	33,845	35,209	45,312	2.22	28.69
France	60,464	66,233	60,527	62,104	67,019	3.29	7.91
Germany	211,067	222,218	195,240	194,386	218,894	10.75	12.61
Luxembourg	1,250	2,640	1,381	1,253	1,495	0.07	19.31
Netherlands	56,845	66,556	63,803	58,941	65,548	3.22	11.21
Switzerland	28,059	28,596	27,912	27,582	30,787	1.51	11.62
East Mediterranean Europe	**48,487**	**44,645**	**37,774**	**40,442**	**44,562**	**2.19**	**10.19**
Cyprus	1,135	1,390	616	778	685	0.03	-11.95
Israel	37,087	31,625	29,110	28,713	30,153	1.48	5.02
Turkey	10,265	11,630	8,048	10,951	13,724	0.67	25.32
Other Europe	**10,529**	**9,347**	**10,907**	**11,266**	**13,110**	**0.64**	**16.37**
Other countries of Europe	10,529	9,347	10,907	11,266	13,110	0.64	16.37

SLOVENIA

5. Overnight stays of non-resident tourists in hotels and similar establishments, by nationality

		2007	2008	2009	2010	2011	Market share 11	% Change 11-10
TOTAL	(*)	**3,706,637**	**4,051,014**	**3,684,005**	**3,715,473**	**4,005,927**	**100.00**	**7.82**
AFRICA		**5,607**	**12,204**	**6,896**	**8,440**	**13,187**	**0.33**	**56.24**
Southern Africa		**1,674**	**2,223**	**2,157**	**2,662**	**3,784**	**0.09**	**42.15**
South Africa		1,674	2,223	2,157	2,662	3,784	0.09	42.15
Other Africa		**3,933**	**9,981**	**4,739**	**5,778**	**9,403**	**0.23**	**62.74**
Other countries of Africa		3,933	9,981	4,739	5,778	9,403	0.23	62.74
AMERICAS		**135,207**	**139,873**	**111,159**	**119,261**	**126,276**	**3.15**	**5.88**
North America		**124,669**	**125,127**	**96,441**	**104,688**	**106,094**	**2.65**	**1.34**
Canada		19,084	18,238	16,506	17,617	18,867	0.47	7.10
United States of America		98,312	101,538	74,623	82,616	86,927	2.17	5.22
Other countries of North America		7,273	5,351	5,312	4,455	300	0.01	-93.27
South America		**4,187**	**5,496**	**5,939**	**5,967**	**7,542**	**0.19**	**26.40**
Brazil		4,187	5,496	5,939	5,967	7,542	0.19	26.40
Other Americas		**6,351**	**9,250**	**8,779**	**8,606**	**12,640**	**0.32**	**46.87**
Other countries of the Americas		6,351	9,250	8,779	8,606	12,640	0.32	46.87
EAST ASIA AND THE PACIFIC		**104,066**	**132,767**	**136,049**	**137,284**	**162,107**	**4.05**	**18.08**
North-East Asia		**53,087**	**72,348**	**80,420**	**73,738**	**81,305**	**2.03**	**10.26**
China		7,215	9,150	10,300	14,152	19,411	0.48	37.16
Japan		36,759	55,316	63,160	51,986	48,299	1.21	-7.09
Korea, Republic of		9,113	7,882	6,960	7,600	13,595	0.34	78.88
Australasia		**32,086**	**36,508**	**28,017**	**31,344**	**32,339**	**0.81**	**3.17**
Australia		27,434	31,908	23,856	26,066	27,807	0.69	6.68
New Zealand		4,652	4,600	4,161	5,278	4,532	0.11	-14.13
Other East Asia and the Pacific		**18,893**	**23,911**	**27,612**	**32,202**	**48,463**	**1.21**	**50.50**
Other countries of Asia		17,528	22,441	25,755	31,073	46,973	1.17	51.17
Other countries of Oceania		1,365	1,470	1,857	1,129	1,490	0.04	31.98
EUROPE		**3,461,757**	**3,766,170**	**3,429,901**	**3,450,488**	**3,704,357**	**92.47**	**7.36**
Central/Eastern Europe		**453,186**	**550,356**	**496,286**	**539,062**	**638,430**	**15.94**	**18.43**
Bulgaria		23,547	32,573	27,247	26,025	29,260	0.73	12.43
Czech Republic		52,873	64,691	58,710	60,630	69,988	1.75	15.43
Estonia		4,261	5,258	4,092	3,802	4,942	0.12	29.98
Hungary		87,529	104,475	98,547	93,131	107,350	2.68	15.27
Latvia		6,252	10,462	5,345	6,042	5,633	0.14	-6.77
Lithuania		7,834	7,622	5,019	4,566	5,043	0.13	10.45
Poland		45,471	61,163	50,074	45,255	48,668	1.21	7.54
Romania		27,261	33,432	34,094	32,495	37,521	0.94	15.47
Russian Federation		131,925	157,800	156,770	198,832	243,471	6.08	22.45
Slovakia		28,984	30,865	27,064	30,401	33,652	0.84	10.69
Ukraine		37,249	42,015	29,324	37,883	52,902	1.32	39.65
Northern Europe		**394,111**	**420,308**	**321,163**	**291,261**	**294,406**	**7.35**	**1.08**
Denmark		17,604	25,460	23,222	20,128	23,411	0.58	16.31
Finland		45,100	54,235	38,173	32,708	32,683	0.82	-0.08
Iceland		10,154	4,167	2,148	2,046	3,757	0.09	83.63
Ireland		28,938	26,504	23,926	15,968	16,274	0.41	1.92
Norway		13,527	19,727	14,950	14,217	12,896	0.32	-9.29
Sweden		32,465	42,085	31,747	27,130	28,353	0.71	4.51
United Kingdom		246,323	248,130	186,997	179,064	177,032	4.42	-1.13
Southern Europe		**1,255,318**	**1,405,898**	**1,341,168**	**1,393,598**	**1,405,182**	**35.08**	**0.83**
Bosnia and Herzegovina		65,312	84,183	59,005	55,120	56,482	1.41	2.47
Croatia		228,945	260,519	215,855	209,972	216,121	5.40	2.93
Greece		11,733	13,473	14,491	12,672	13,431	0.34	5.99
Italy		781,310	830,070	839,009	828,083	825,344	20.60	-0.33
Malta		3,144	5,143	10,988	11,251	13,778	0.34	22.46

SLOVENIA

5. Overnight stays of non-resident tourists in hotels and similar establishments, by nationality

	2007	2008	2009	2010	2011	Market share 11	% Change 11-10
Montenegro	6,405	10,033	9,530	15,855	14,695	0.37	-7.32
Portugal	11,442	14,299	11,893	11,596	10,464	0.26	-9.76
Serbia	86,613	114,278	114,736	177,041	180,134	4.50	1.75
Spain	42,500	49,864	45,173	46,002	49,827	1.24	8.31
TFYR of Macedonia	17,914	24,036	20,488	26,006	24,906	0.62	-4.23
Western Europe	**1,231,705**	**1,269,039**	**1,157,061**	**1,114,777**	**1,235,962**	**30.85**	**10.87**
Austria	537,794	528,755	519,130	499,393	545,235	13.61	9.18
Belgium	78,844	92,978	75,620	79,154	102,023	2.55	28.89
France	76,291	89,420	80,481	73,371	81,216	2.03	10.69
Germany	416,873	426,318	361,572	354,612	392,345	9.79	10.64
Luxembourg	3,231	6,083	3,291	2,322	2,583	0.06	11.24
Netherlands	60,037	68,307	63,999	61,056	62,746	1.57	2.77
Switzerland	58,635	57,178	52,968	44,869	49,814	1.24	11.02
East Mediterranean Europe	**99,944**	**98,100**	**86,554**	**87,128**	**97,138**	**2.42**	**11.49**
Cyprus	2,634	3,657	1,990	2,148	1,609	0.04	-25.09
Israel	81,329	75,466	67,898	67,081	70,864	1.77	5.64
Turkey	15,981	18,977	16,666	17,899	24,665	0.62	37.80
Other Europe	**27,493**	**22,469**	**27,669**	**24,662**	**33,239**	**0.83**	**34.78**
Other countries of Europe	27,493	22,469	27,669	24,662	33,239	0.83	34.78

SLOVENIA

6. Overnight stays of non-resident tourists in all types of accommodation establishments, by nationality

		2007	2008	2009	2010	2011	Market share 11	% Change 11-10
TOTAL	(*)	4,867,900	5,351,282	4,936,293	4,997,031	5,463,931	100.00	9.34
AFRICA		6,424	13,376	8,185	11,340	15,500	0.28	36.68
Southern Africa		2,006	2,428	2,452	3,162	4,768	0.09	50.79
South Africa		2,006	2,428	2,452	3,162	4,768	0.09	50.79
Other Africa		4,418	10,948	5,733	8,178	10,732	0.20	31.23
Other countries of Africa		4,418	10,948	5,733	8,178	10,732	0.20	31.23
AMERICAS		156,078	156,707	127,357	141,414	153,840	2.82	8.79
North America		142,905	139,565	109,694	124,012	129,885	2.38	4.74
Canada		23,301	22,148	20,102	22,772	24,894	0.46	9.32
United States of America		112,112	111,717	84,076	96,648	104,503	1.91	8.13
Other countries of North America		7,492	5,700	5,516	4,592	488	0.01	-89.37
South America		4,635	6,315	6,580	6,971	8,565	0.16	22.87
Brazil		4,635	6,315	6,580	6,971	8,565	0.16	22.87
Other Americas		8,538	10,827	11,083	10,431	15,390	0.28	47.54
Other countries of the Americas		8,538	10,827	11,083	10,431	15,390	0.28	47.54
EAST ASIA AND THE PACIFIC		125,241	150,821	154,321	161,964	186,139	3.41	14.93
North-East Asia		57,263	75,625	83,401	77,954	87,599	1.60	12.37
China		8,514	10,159	11,263	15,477	21,785	0.40	40.76
Japan		38,905	57,093	64,712	53,761	50,840	0.93	-5.43
Korea, Republic of		9,844	8,373	7,426	8,716	14,974	0.27	71.80
Australasia		43,871	45,767	36,915	44,098	45,274	0.83	2.67
Australia		37,119	39,289	30,786	36,419	38,064	0.70	4.52
New Zealand		6,752	6,478	6,129	7,679	7,210	0.13	-6.11
Other East Asia and the Pacific		24,107	29,429	34,005	39,912	53,266	0.97	33.46
Other countries of Asia		22,605	27,313	31,538	36,743	51,129	0.94	39.15
Other countries of Oceania		1,502	2,116	2,467	3,169	2,137	0.04	-32.57
EUROPE		4,580,157	5,030,378	4,646,430	4,682,313	5,108,452	93.49	9.10
Central/Eastern Europe		606,634	758,278	691,285	742,046	874,432	16.00	17.84
Bulgaria		28,368	38,851	33,699	32,426	36,436	0.67	12.37
Czech Republic		97,204	127,998	124,415	127,165	141,937	2.60	11.62
Estonia		5,468	7,005	5,246	4,874	6,442	0.12	32.17
Hungary		134,255	160,308	147,338	144,215	165,059	3.02	14.45
Latvia		10,315	14,178	7,630	8,222	7,941	0.15	-3.42
Lithuania		10,295	10,573	7,550	6,706	7,964	0.15	18.76
Poland		67,735	96,042	80,495	82,639	93,128	1.70	12.69
Romania		33,208	41,777	44,590	40,959	48,216	0.88	17.72
Russian Federation		136,722	166,119	163,903	208,341	257,173	4.71	23.44
Slovakia		40,147	43,914	39,935	43,376	50,424	0.92	16.25
Ukraine		42,917	51,513	36,484	43,123	59,712	1.09	38.47
Northern Europe		498,506	518,767	409,201	396,526	409,066	7.49	3.16
Denmark		34,137	46,782	42,790	40,059	47,605	0.87	18.84
Finland		51,926	62,015	44,915	39,947	41,012	0.75	2.67
Iceland		10,680	4,650	3,139	2,531	4,804	0.09	89.81
Ireland		36,031	31,601	28,984	22,053	22,536	0.41	2.19
Norway		17,017	23,806	18,504	18,876	16,561	0.30	-12.26
Sweden		44,063	50,364	39,039	34,592	35,819	0.66	3.55
United Kingdom		304,652	299,549	231,830	238,468	240,729	4.41	0.95
Southern Europe		1,503,159	1,698,778	1,643,436	1,688,496	1,740,156	31.85	3.06
Bosnia and Herzegovina		75,598	101,078	77,281	66,611	70,478	1.29	5.81
Croatia		295,590	335,403	288,170	274,380	291,186	5.33	6.13
Greece		13,379	15,137	16,911	14,435	15,312	0.28	6.08
Italy		911,150	987,617	1,004,783	987,268	1,005,222	18.40	1.82
Malta		3,680	5,761	11,637	11,921	14,529	0.27	21.88

SLOVENIA

6. Overnight stays of non-resident tourists in all types of accommodation establishments, by nationality

	2007	2008	2009	2010	2011	Market share 11	% Change 11-10
Montenegro	7,267	11,178	10,410	17,759	16,446	0.30	-7.39
Portugal	14,852	17,038	15,055	15,071	14,146	0.26	-6.14
Serbia	97,589	125,410	131,177	201,683	209,971	3.84	4.11
Spain	63,307	70,341	62,432	67,276	71,737	1.31	6.63
TFYR of Macedonia	20,747	29,815	25,580	32,092	31,129	0.57	-3.00
Western Europe	**1,822,273**	**1,915,405**	**1,767,215**	**1,718,709**	**1,923,304**	**35.20**	**11.90**
Austria	668,907	655,565	642,242	619,259	674,194	12.34	8.87
Belgium	115,967	135,155	111,140	117,980	152,612	2.79	29.35
France	121,204	142,651	130,752	130,968	143,478	2.63	9.55
Germany	641,225	658,714	577,961	578,262	646,696	11.84	11.83
Luxembourg	3,687	6,924	4,116	2,922	3,619	0.07	23.85
Netherlands	199,183	244,645	233,539	208,654	234,390	4.29	12.33
Switzerland	72,100	71,751	67,465	60,664	68,315	1.25	12.61
East Mediterranean Europe	**119,773**	**112,723**	**102,913**	**106,872**	**122,855**	**2.25**	**14.96**
Cyprus	3,153	3,873	2,042	2,292	1,880	0.03	-17.98
Israel	99,295	88,498	82,258	84,657	93,915	1.72	10.94
Turkey	17,325	20,352	18,613	19,923	27,060	0.50	35.82
Other Europe	**29,812**	**26,427**	**32,380**	**29,664**	**38,639**	**0.71**	**30.26**
Other countries of Europe	29,812	26,427	32,380	29,664	38,639	0.71	30.26

SOLOMON ISLANDS

1. Arrivals of non-resident tourists at national borders, by country of residence

	2007	2008	2009	2010	2011	Market share 11	% Change 11-10
TOTAL	13,748	16,264	18,308	20,521	22,941	100.00	11.79
AMERICAS	1,048	1,220	1,122	975	1,232	5.37	26.36
North America	1,048	1,220	1,122	975	1,232	5.37	26.36
Canada	95	115	88	113	192	0.84	69.91
United States of America	953	1,105	1,034	862	1,040	4.53	20.65
EAST ASIA AND THE PACIFIC	11,628	13,772	15,886	18,255	20,480	89.27	12.19
North-East Asia	583	646	938	627	771	3.36	22.97
Hong Kong, China	11	57	65	38	130	0.57	242.11
Japan	572	589	873	589	641	2.79	8.83
Australasia	6,947	8,510	10,266	12,461	13,116	57.17	5.26
Australia	5,960	7,413	8,902	10,751	11,392	49.66	5.96
New Zealand	987	1,097	1,364	1,710	1,724	7.51	0.82
Melanesia	2,241	2,211	2,323	2,757	3,774	16.45	36.89
Fiji	710	787	917	991	1,204	5.25	21.49
Vanuatu	524	518	308	405	513	2.24	26.67
Papua New Guinea	1,007	906	1,098	1,361	2,057	8.97	51.14
Other East Asia and the Pacific	1,857	2,405	2,359	2,410	2,819	12.29	16.97
Other countries of Asia	1,264	1,249	1,409	1,825	2,056	8.96	12.66
Other countries of Oceania	593	1,156	950	585	763	3.33	30.43
EUROPE	925	1,132	1,091	1,014	941	4.10	-7.20
Northern Europe	318	457	419	432	380	1.66	-12.04
United Kingdom	318	457	419	432	380	1.66	-12.04
Southern Europe	63	37	66	39	80	0.35	105.13
Italy	63	37	66	39	80	0.35	105.13
Western Europe	260	252	232	236	235	1.02	-0.42
France	48	91	81	82	60	0.26	-26.83
Germany	87	124	100	101	111	0.48	9.90
Netherlands	125	37	51	53	64	0.28	20.75
Other Europe	284	386	374	307	246	1.07	-19.87
Other countries of Europe	284	386	374	307	246	1.07	-19.87
NOT SPECIFIED	147	140	209	277	288	1.26	3.97
Other countries of the World	147	140	209	277	288	1.26	3.97

SOUTH AFRICA

1. Arrivals of non-resident tourists at national borders, by country of residence

		2007	2008	2009	2010	2011	Market share 11	% Change 11-10
TOTAL	(*)	9,090,881	9,564,207	7,011,865	8,073,552	8,339,354	100.00	3.29
AFRICA		6,862,105	7,343,765	5,083,145	5,733,499	6,129,606	73.50	6.91
East Africa		2,448,216	2,884,396	2,587,771	2,950,813	3,036,469	36.41	2.90
Burundi				960	891	1,010	0.01	13.36
Comoros				155	209	198	0.00	-5.26
Ethiopia				10,651	9,397	9,125	0.11	-2.89
Eritrea				579	602	666	0.01	10.63
Djibouti				78	79	97	0.00	22.78
Kenya		25,657	26,939	25,581	29,089	30,279	0.36	4.09
Madagascar				2,623	3,075	2,962	0.04	-3.67
Malawi		147,246	163,328	139,605	126,120	135,577	1.63	7.50
Mauritius		14,663	16,214	13,625	16,329	16,545	0.20	1.32
Mozambique		1,084,157	1,226,989	983,739	1,051,502	1,076,753	12.91	2.40
Reunion		694	830	596	348	3	0.00	-99.14
Rwanda				2,841	2,931	2,838	0.03	-3.17
Seychelles		2,379	2,480	2,166	2,861	3,182	0.04	11.22
Somalia				2,863	2,706	829	0.01	-69.36
Zimbabwe		964,027	1,226,993	1,227,631	1,513,714	1,553,008	18.62	2.60
Uganda		12,049	12,900	12,257	13,627	14,450	0.17	6.04
United Republic of Tanzania		14,288	15,682	14,732	19,641	28,645	0.34	45.84
Zambia		183,056	192,041	147,089	157,692	160,302	1.92	1.66
Central Africa		60,755	67,678	85,071	87,644	87,613	1.05	-0.04
Angola		31,227	35,993	37,254	38,543	39,217	0.47	1.75
Cameroon				4,531	6,461	5,357	0.06	-17.09
Central African Republic				120	170	143	0.00	-15.88
Chad				251	252	339	0.00	34.52
Congo				6,347	4,437	3,337	0.04	-24.79
Democratic Republic of the Congo		29,528	31,685	30,982	31,285	32,582	0.39	4.15
Equatorial Guinea				343	311	319	0.00	2.57
Gabon				5,077	6,052	6,199	0.07	2.43
Sao Tome and Principe				166	133	120	0.00	-9.77
North Africa				5,270	8,479	5,745	0.07	-32.24
Algeria				1,210	3,529	1,259	0.02	-64.32
Morocco				933	1,563	1,364	0.02	-12.73
Western Sahara				13	95	10	0.00	-89.47
Sudan				2,087	2,080	1,891	0.02	-9.09
Tunisia				1,027	1,212	1,221	0.01	0.74
Southern Africa		4,248,245	4,278,101	2,338,784	2,606,273	2,902,488	34.80	11.37
Botswana		818,403	804,701	484,258	507,042	477,937	5.73	-5.74
Lesotho		2,170,074	2,163,372	1,048,550	1,275,838	1,526,597	18.31	19.65
Namibia		220,535	221,995	177,863	190,903	197,835	2.37	3.63
Swaziland		1,039,233	1,088,033	628,113	632,490	700,119	8.40	10.69
West Africa		52,515	56,721	66,220	80,226	97,291	1.17	21.27
Cape Verde				602	554	534	0.01	-3.61
Benin				1,293	1,234	1,299	0.02	5.27
Gambia				631	748	805	0.01	7.62
Ghana		12,999	13,232	11,395	18,435	18,538	0.22	0.56
Guinea				1,334	1,931	2,127	0.03	10.15
Côte d'Ivoire				2,182	2,716	1,781	0.02	-34.43
Liberia				498	545	586	0.01	7.52
Mali				792	1,190	1,192	0.01	0.17
Mauritania				118	271	269	0.00	-0.74
Niger				244	293	296	0.00	1.02
Nigeria		39,516	43,489	42,651	46,853	64,402	0.77	37.46
Guinea-Bissau				174	230	198	0.00	-13.91
Saint Helena				143	119	80	0.00	-32.77

SOUTH AFRICA

1. Arrivals of non-resident tourists at national borders, by country of residence

	2007	2008	2009	2010	2011	Market share 11	% Change 11-10
Senegal			2,333	3,005	2,965	0.04	-1.33
Sierra Leone			766	955	930	0.01	-2.62
Togo			476	519	592	0.01	14.07
Burkina Faso			588	628	697	0.01	10.99
Other Africa	**52,374**	**56,869**	**29**	**64**			
Other countries of Africa	52,374	56,869	29	64			
AMERICAS	**387,379**	**407,408**	**333,528**	**458,249**	**433,135**	**5.19**	**-5.48**
Caribbean			**2,062**	**3,479**	**3,275**	**0.04**	**-5.86**
Antigua and Barbuda			28	96	83	0.00	-13.54
Bahamas			78	142	137	0.00	-3.52
Barbados			126	207	174	0.00	-15.94
Bermuda			65	73	58	0.00	-20.55
British Virgin Islands			26	4			
Cuba			577	1,247	1,139	0.01	-8.66
Dominica			55	116	109	0.00	-6.03
Grenada			20	33	37	0.00	12.12
Haiti			179	192	98	0.00	-48.96
Jamaica			497	695	663	0.01	-4.60
Puerto Rico			6	4	3	0.00	-25.00
Saint Lucia			38	41	43	0.00	4.88
Saint Vincent and the Grenadines			18	43	36	0.00	-16.28
Trinidad and Tobago			347	585	693	0.01	18.46
Turks and Caicos Islands			1	1	2	0.00	100.00
United States Virgin Islands			1				
Central America			**966**	**3,736**	**1,262**	**0.02**	**-66.22**
Belize			66	59	57	0.00	-3.39
Costa Rica			284	921	401	0.00	-56.46
El Salvador			113	391	93	0.00	-76.21
Guatemala			182	569	181	0.00	-68.19
Honduras			102	1,330	188	0.00	-85.86
Nicaragua			57	88	80	0.00	-9.09
Panama			162	378	262	0.00	-30.69
North America	**333,379**	**348,345**	**278,360**	**353,572**	**348,627**	**4.18**	**-1.40**
Canada	52,879	56,904	45,330	55,263	57,767	0.69	4.53
Greenland	86	78	32	9			
Mexico	3,473	3,925	2,674	15,923	3,246	0.04	-79.61
United States of America	276,941	287,438	230,324	282,377	287,614	3.45	1.85
South America	**44,843**	**49,391**	**51,752**	**97,172**	**79,864**	**0.96**	**-17.81**
Argentina	7,930	8,704	9,787	21,701	13,817	0.17	-36.33
Bolivia			549	722	690	0.01	-4.43
Brazil	32,632	35,649	32,256	53,756	54,183	0.65	0.79
Chile	3,122	3,269	2,581	7,260	3,210	0.04	-55.79
Colombia			1,582	3,146	1,831	0.02	-41.80
Ecuador			418	1,004	626	0.01	-37.65
Falkland Islands, Malvinas			5	2			
French Guiana			67	38			
Guyana			293	273	246	0.00	-9.89
Paraguay			384	1,170	530	0.01	-54.70
Peru			1,577	2,731	2,185	0.03	-19.99
Suriname			64	95	91	0.00	-4.21
Uruguay			944	2,683	1,162	0.01	-56.69
Venezuela	1,159	1,769	1,245	2,591	1,293	0.02	-50.10
Other Americas	**9,157**	**9,672**	**388**	**290**	**107**	**0.00**	**-63.10**
Other countries of the Americas	9,157	9,672	388	290	107	0.00	-63.10

SOUTH AFRICA

1. Arrivals of non-resident tourists at national borders, by country of residence

	2007	2008	2009	2010	2011	Market share 11	% Change 11-10
EAST ASIA AND THE PACIFIC	281,567	243,036	216,051	293,141	304,704	3.65	3.94
North-East Asia	113,831	71,459	87,140	123,223	138,377	1.66	12.30
China	47,378	40,320	34,561	65,920	84,862	1.02	28.73
Taiwan, Province of China	14,142	10,854	9,897	9,163	8,524	0.10	-6.97
Hong Kong, China			7,522	2,389	21	0.00	-99.12
Japan	31,855		20,513	27,577	26,284	0.32	-4.69
Korea, Dem. People's Republic of			125	420	254	0.00	-39.52
Korea, Republic of	20,456	20,285	14,311	17,489	18,290	0.22	4.58
Macao, China			122	74	1	0.00	-98.65
Mongolia			89	191	141	0.00	-26.18
South-East Asia	35,374	31,606	27,405	41,759	43,542	0.52	4.27
Brunei Darussalam			59	58	26	0.00	-55.17
Myanmar			232	401	339	0.00	-15.46
Cambodia			90	173	91	0.00	-47.40
Indonesia	4,657	3,949	3,361	5,158	4,279	0.05	-17.04
Lao People's Democratic Republic			19	72	74	0.00	2.78
Malaysia	9,681	8,535	7,025	9,175	10,337	0.12	12.66
Philippines	4,725	4,510	3,359	9,553	9,203	0.11	-3.66
Timor-Leste			17	17	3	0.00	-82.35
Singapore	7,745	7,486	6,663	6,660	7,874	0.09	18.23
Viet Nam			1,280	3,318	3,848	0.05	15.97
Thailand	8,566	7,126	5,300	7,174	7,468	0.09	4.10
Australasia	114,424	120,078	100,795	127,706	122,365	1.47	-4.18
Australia	95,571	100,133	82,753	107,905	103,506	1.24	-4.08
New Zealand	18,853	19,945	18,042	19,801	18,859	0.23	-4.76
Melanesia			229	217	281	0.00	29.49
Solomon Islands			12	12	29	0.00	141.67
Fiji			157	119	151	0.00	26.89
New Caledonia			4		2	0.00	
Vanuatu			6	15	7	0.00	-53.33
Norfolk Island			4		1	0.00	
Papua New Guinea			46	71	91	0.00	28.17
Micronesia			132	75	46	0.00	-38.67
Christmas Island, Australia			18	3			
Cocos (Keeling) Islands			16	27	1	0.00	-96.30
Kiribati			4	11	12	0.00	9.09
Guam			24	6	2	0.00	-66.67
Nauru			13	2	14	0.00	600.00
Northern Mariana Islands			29	15	1	0.00	-93.33
Micronesia, Federated States of			12	8	4	0.00	-50.00
Marshall Islands			7	2	9	0.00	350.00
Palau			9	1	3	0.00	200.00
Polynesia			270	134	87	0.00	-35.07
Cook Islands			4				
French Polynesia			140	55	4	0.00	-92.73
Pitcairn			4	2			
Tokelau			6	7	2	0.00	-71.43
Tonga			18	20	24	0.00	20.00
Tuvalu			1	4	9	0.00	125.00
Samoa			97	46	48	0.00	4.35
Other East Asia and the Pacific	17,938	19,893	80	27	6	0.00	-77.78
Other countries of Asia	17,136	19,042	27	10	1	0.00	-90.00
Other countries of Oceania	802	851	53	17	5	0.00	-70.59

SOUTH AFRICA

1. Arrivals of non-resident tourists at national borders, by country of residence

	2007	2008	2009	2010	2011	Market share 11	% Change 11-10
EUROPE	**1,438,092**	**1,433,586**	**1,248,467**	**1,354,579**	**1,306,794**	**15.67**	**-3.53**
Central/Eastern Europe	**29,577**	**25,027**	**38,908**	**47,576**	**43,370**	**0.52**	**-8.84**
Azerbaijan			136	280	160	0.00	-42.86
Armenia			58	133	100	0.00	-24.81
Bulgaria			1,927	2,515	2,233	0.03	-11.21
Belarus			449	573	665	0.01	16.06
Czech Republic	5,705		5,889	6,058	6,169	0.07	1.83
Estonia			754	959	676	0.01	-29.51
Georgia			160	251	194	0.00	-22.71
Hungary	3,083	3,041	2,480	3,115	2,882	0.03	-7.48
Kazakhstan			517	743	619	0.01	-16.69
Kyrgyzstan			105	37	7	0.00	-81.08
Latvia			693	646	608	0.01	-5.88
Lithuania			859	785	773	0.01	-1.53
Republic of Moldova			114	181	149	0.00	-17.68
Poland	9,973	10,041	9,257	9,970	9,962	0.12	-0.08
Romania			2,221	2,309	2,188	0.03	-5.24
Russian Federation	10,816	11,945	8,893	11,551	10,487	0.13	-9.21
Slovakia			1,964	3,730	2,093	0.03	-43.89
Tajikistan			31	44	53	0.00	20.45
Turkmenistan			28	31	18	0.00	-41.94
Ukraine			2,233	3,469	3,142	0.04	-9.43
Uzbekistan			140	196	192	0.00	-2.04
Northern Europe	**638,524**	**628,424**	**568,656**	**579,063**	**542,563**	**6.51**	**-6.30**
Denmark	26,010	26,747	22,540	24,212	22,970	0.28	-5.13
Faeroe Islands			46	23			
Finland	9,281	9,909	9,404	10,511	10,090	0.12	-4.01
Iceland			492	694	598	0.01	-13.83
Ireland	42,179	42,015	35,166	30,518	29,098	0.35	-4.65
Norway	20,595	20,537	18,140	19,330	20,556	0.25	6.34
Sweden	42,772	44,050	36,335	40,662	38,754	0.46	-4.69
United Kingdom	497,687	485,166	446,481	453,057	420,484	5.04	-7.19
Channel Islands			7	6			
Isle of Man			45	50	13	0.00	-74.00
Southern Europe	**123,217**	**130,438**	**114,372**	**140,473**	**131,426**	**1.58**	**-6.44**
Albania			175	223	115	0.00	-48.43
Andorra			66	62	32	0.00	-48.39
Bosnia and Herzegovina			173	267	267	0.00	
Croatia			1,103	1,266	1,159	0.01	-8.45
Gibraltar			14	6			
Greece	7,706	9,248	7,296	8,172	5,822	0.07	-28.76
Holy See			13	8	10	0.00	25.00
Italy	54,807	55,545	50,305	54,645	54,628	0.66	-0.03
Malta			473	568	550	0.01	-3.17
Portugal	29,669	31,762	26,895	40,677	40,302	0.48	-0.92
San Marino			36	25	41	0.00	64.00
Slovenia			958	2,211	1,037	0.01	-53.10
Spain	31,035	33,883	25,727	31,902	27,209	0.33	-14.71
Serbia and Montenegro			1,138	441	254	0.00	-42.40
Western Europe	**602,536**	**594,146**	**502,348**	**556,227**	**559,664**	**6.71**	**0.62**
Austria	22,753	20,904	17,210	20,389	21,841	0.26	7.12
Belgium	42,643	42,276	36,720	39,304	40,478	0.49	2.99
France	115,074	127,956	103,985	115,401	105,420	1.26	-8.65
Germany	254,934	238,306	196,643	215,800	235,774	2.83	9.26
Liechtenstein			237	200	213	0.00	6.50
Luxembourg			1,309	1,259	1,271	0.02	0.95
Monaco			94	61	93	0.00	52.46

SOUTH AFRICA

1. Arrivals of non-resident tourists at national borders, by country of residence

	2007	2008	2009	2010	2011	Market share 11	% Change 11-10
Netherlands	129,022	128,097	114,431	124,088	113,846	1.37	-8.25
Switzerland	38,110	36,607	31,719	39,725	40,728	0.49	2.52
East Mediterranean Europe	**24,529**	**27,236**	**24,183**	**31,240**	**29,771**	**0.36**	**-4.70**
Cyprus			1,585	1,972	1,672	0.02	-15.21
Israel	17,803	18,291	14,950	19,353	17,751	0.21	-8.28
Turkey	6,726	8,945	7,648	9,915	10,348	0.12	4.37
Other Europe	**19,709**	**28,315**					
Other countries of Europe	19,709	28,315					
MIDDLE EAST	**20,954**	**23,412**	**19,262**	**21,151**	**20,168**	**0.24**	**-4.65**
Bahrain			174	294	177	0.00	-39.80
Palestine			147	305	245	0.00	-19.67
Iraq			310	333	285	0.00	-14.41
Jordan			1,509	1,938	1,696	0.02	-12.49
Kuwait			550	651	632	0.01	-2.92
Lebanon			1,933	3,183	2,720	0.03	-14.55
Libya			1,181	1,711	977	0.01	-42.90
Oman			298	433	349	0.00	-19.40
Qatar			399	361	231	0.00	-36.01
Saudi Arabia	4,564	5,539	5,328	3,570	4,733	0.06	32.58
Syrian Arab Republic			420	707	498	0.01	-29.56
United Arab Emirates	1,814	2,454	1,728	1,332	1,072	0.01	-19.52
Egypt	4,297	4,862	4,999	5,967	6,251	0.07	4.76
Yemen			286	366	302	0.00	-17.49
Other countries of Middle East	10,279	10,557					
SOUTH ASIA	**51,823**	**51,929**	**74,938**	**97,552**	**119,147**	**1.43**	**22.14**
Afghanistan			998	675	206	0.00	-69.48
Bangladesh			2,943	3,829	3,900	0.05	1.85
Bhutan			9	35	27	0.00	-22.86
Sri Lanka			1,805	2,872	3,127	0.04	8.88
India	51,823	51,929	55,203	71,587	90,367	1.08	26.23
Iran, Islamic Republic of			4,037	4,566	4,773	0.06	4.53
Maldives			38	86	36	0.00	-58.14
Nepal			309	543	490	0.01	-9.76
Pakistan			9,596	13,359	16,221	0.19	21.42
NOT SPECIFIED	**48,961**	**61,071**	**36,474**	**115,381**	**25,800**	**0.31**	**-77.64**
Other countries of the World	48,961	61,071	36,474	115,381	25,800	0.31	-77.64

SOUTH AFRICA

2. Arrivals of non-resident visitors at national borders, by country of residence

		2007	2008	2009	2010	2011	Market share 11	% Change 11-10
TOTAL	(*)	9,207,697	9,728,860	9,531,615	11,303,087	12,097,490	100.00	7.03
AFRICA		6,896,534	7,388,995	7,406,780	8,725,042	9,654,943	79.81	10.66
East Africa		2,488,024	2,936,250	3,259,300	3,837,056	4,115,170	34.02	7.25
Burundi		1,146	1,289	1,041	952	1,049	0.01	10.19
Comoros		276	211	164	237	228	0.00	-3.80
Ethiopia		8,736	9,953	10,971	9,857	9,618	0.08	-2.42
Eritrea		618	570	617	645	718	0.01	11.32
Djibouti		75	81	81	86	102	0.00	18.60
Kenya		27,643	29,218	27,734	32,081	33,651	0.28	4.89
Madagascar		2,912	3,777	2,756	3,208	3,099	0.03	-3.40
Malawi		148,061	164,248	149,524	137,023	146,432	1.21	6.87
Mauritius		14,934	16,550	15,525	19,743	19,893	0.16	0.76
Mozambique		1,085,556	1,228,979	1,324,445	1,328,731	1,389,253	11.48	4.55
Reunion		696	835	632	370	3	0.00	-99.19
Rwanda		3,133	3,375	3,103	3,076	3,014	0.02	-2.02
Seychelles		2,396	2,497	2,367	3,115	3,588	0.03	15.18
Somalia		2,896	3,080	2,876	2,714	836	0.01	-69.20
Zimbabwe		977,101	1,248,043	1,526,556	2,085,579	2,279,821	18.85	9.31
Uganda		12,728	13,684	13,675	15,597	17,024	0.14	9.15
United Republic of Tanzania		14,759	16,183	16,238	21,827	32,059	0.27	46.88
Zambia		184,358	193,677	160,995	172,215	174,782	1.44	1.49
Central Africa		77,999	85,467	87,973	90,143	90,087	0.74	-0.06
Angola		32,118	36,917	38,814	39,535	39,952	0.33	1.05
Cameroon		5,088	5,529	4,731	6,737	5,610	0.05	-16.73
Central African Republic		137	130	125	175	144	0.00	-17.71
Chad		290	299	260	262	355	0.00	35.50
Congo		6,511	4,939	6,654	4,623	3,393	0.03	-26.61
Democratic Republic of the Congo		30,377	32,692	31,569	32,077	33,811	0.28	5.41
Equatorial Guinea		358	364	430	347	351	0.00	1.15
Gabon		2,994	4,433	5,218	6,244	6,346	0.05	1.63
Sao Tome and Principe		126	164	172	143	125	0.00	-12.59
North Africa		5,824	6,438	5,653	8,855	6,115	0.05	-30.94
Algeria		1,885	1,868	1,359	3,586	1,346	0.01	-62.47
Morocco		1,005	1,046	963	1,642	1,444	0.01	-12.06
Western Sahara		10	11	14	95	12	0.00	-87.37
Sudan		1,937	2,131	2,198	2,216	2,043	0.02	-7.81
Tunisia		987	1,382	1,119	1,316	1,270	0.01	-3.50
Southern Africa		4,255,619	4,285,670	3,983,336	4,703,731	5,340,433	44.14	13.54
Botswana		821,070	807,292	822,305	829,518	782,223	6.47	-5.70
Lesotho		2,171,954	2,165,505	1,890,976	2,610,507	3,160,694	26.13	21.08
Namibia		221,360	222,817	212,098	226,541	235,780	1.95	4.08
Swaziland		1,041,235	1,090,056	1,057,957	1,037,165	1,161,736	9.60	12.01
West Africa		68,927	75,170	70,372	85,174	103,137	0.85	21.09
Cape Verde		621	739	679	636	603	0.00	-5.19
Benin		1,250	1,460	1,363	1,334	1,387	0.01	3.97
Gambia		603	730	722	801	845	0.01	5.49
Ghana		13,953	14,112	12,419	19,948	20,134	0.17	0.93
Guinea		1,464	1,725	1,478	2,023	2,239	0.02	10.68
Côte d'Ivoire		2,337	2,494	2,303	2,789	1,839	0.02	-34.06
Liberia		458	579	540	578	639	0.01	10.55
Mali		958	1,013	832	1,259	1,266	0.01	0.56
Mauritania		219	204	126	280	278	0.00	-0.71
Niger		238	262	273	299	307	0.00	2.68
Nigeria		41,827	46,364	44,817	49,418	67,769	0.56	37.13
Guinea-Bissau		270	231	205	260	216	0.00	-16.92
Saint Helena		115	134	182	131	81	0.00	-38.17

SOUTH AFRICA

2. Arrivals of non-resident visitors at national borders, by country of residence

	2007	2008	2009	2010	2011	Market share 11	% Change 11-10
Senegal	2,792	3,075	2,408	3,115	3,068	0.03	-1.51
Sierra Leone	790	828	884	1,126	1,115	0.01	-0.98
Togo	449	572	504	534	619	0.01	15.92
Burkina Faso	583	648	637	643	732	0.01	13.84
Other Africa	**141**		**146**	**83**	**1**	**0.00**	**-98.80**
Other countries of Africa	141		146	83	1	0.00	-98.80
AMERICAS	**395,560**	**416,581**	**376,485**	**505,235**	**488,018**	**4.03**	**-3.41**
Caribbean	**2,653**	**2,781**	**2,386**	**3,873**	**3,707**	**0.03**	**-4.29**
Antigua and Barbuda	47	39	33	112	98	0.00	-12.50
Bahamas	153	125	95	143	148	0.00	3.50
Barbados	208	164	141	221	185	0.00	-16.29
Bermuda	128	133	116	97	62	0.00	-36.08
British Virgin Islands	38	23					
Cuba	863	941	707	1,362	1,301	0.01	-4.48
Dominica		58	56	132	120	0.00	-9.09
Dominican Republic	50						
Grenada	35	33	21	34	38	0.00	11.76
Haiti		225	206	202	120	0.00	-40.59
Jamaica	594	513	578	851	785	0.01	-7.76
Puerto Rico		15	6	5	6	0.00	20.00
Saint Lucia	50	51	39	41	54	0.00	31.71
Saint Vincent and the Grenadines	59	30	20	46	40	0.00	-13.04
Trinidad and Tobago	424	429	366	623	748	0.01	20.06
Turks and Caicos Islands	3	2	2	4	2	0.00	-50.00
United States Virgin Islands	1						
Central America	**1,169**	**1,250**	**1,113**	**3,945**	**1,535**	**0.01**	**-61.09**
Belize	97	90	83	65	62	0.00	-4.62
Costa Rica	309	422	335	984	490	0.00	-50.20
El Salvador	125	154	123	406	99	0.00	-75.62
Guatemala	244	226	207	597	194	0.00	-67.50
Honduras	140	109	132	1,343	202	0.00	-84.96
Nicaragua	67	56	62	97	85	0.00	-12.37
Panama	187	193	171	453	403	0.00	-11.04
North America	**339,797**	**355,172**	**314,769**	**392,007**	**392,937**	**3.25**	**0.24**
Canada	54,117	58,195	51,233	61,522	64,857	0.54	5.42
Greenland	49	38	34	11			
Mexico	3,569	4,055	2,903	16,447	3,556	0.03	-78.38
United States of America	282,062	292,884	260,599	314,027	324,524	2.68	3.34
South America	**51,158**	**56,806**	**57,797**	**105,091**	**89,726**	**0.74**	**-14.62**
Argentina	8,094	8,873	10,656	22,715	14,622	0.12	-35.63
Bolivia	480	499	615	789	774	0.01	-1.90
Brazil	33,341	36,436	36,722	59,838	62,083	0.51	3.75
Chile	3,267	3,381	2,911	7,562	3,493	0.03	-53.81
Colombia	1,231	1,653	1,656	3,273	1,962	0.02	-40.05
Ecuador	306	352	433	1,047	673	0.01	-35.72
Falkland Islands, Malvinas	14	10	5	2			
French Guiana	70	64	73	40	1	0.00	-97.50
Guyana	17	453	12	5	295	0.00	5800.00
Paraguay	335	373	457	1,250	584	0.00	-53.28
Peru	1,524	1,615	1,852	3,030	2,452	0.02	-19.08
Suriname	99	205	67	99	91	0.00	-8.08
Uruguay	1,181	1,080	981	2,738	1,259	0.01	-54.02
Venezuela	1,199	1,812	1,357	2,703	1,437	0.01	-46.84
Other Americas	**783**	**572**	**420**	**319**	**113**	**0.00**	**-64.58**
Other countries of the Americas	783	572	420	319	113	0.00	-64.58

SOUTH AFRICA

2. Arrivals of non-resident visitors at national borders, by country of residence

	2007	2008	2009	2010	2011	Market share 11	% Change 11-10
EAST ASIA AND THE PACIFIC	287,748	274,188	238,400	322,335	337,159	2.79	4.60
North-East Asia	125,380	110,149	95,720	135,436	152,123	1.26	12.32
China	46,325	40,275	36,480	71,921	92,587	0.77	28.73
Taiwan, Province of China	16,790	12,879	10,920	10,626	9,880	0.08	-7.02
Hong Kong, China	7,234	6,623	7,821	2,523	25	0.00	-99.01
Japan	33,516	29,124	24,424	30,936	29,558	0.24	-4.45
Korea, Dem. People's Republic of	109	124	137	457	292	0.00	-36.11
Korea, Republic of	21,196	20,914	15,714	18,690	19,639	0.16	5.08
Macao, China	154	101	132	83	1	0.00	-98.80
Mongolia	56	109	92	200	141	0.00	-29.50
South-East Asia	43,209	41,649	29,776	45,485	48,418	0.40	6.45
Brunei Darussalam	73	56	65	63	26	0.00	-58.73
Myanmar	428	585	271	456	413	0.00	-9.43
Cambodia	99	134	95	185	105	0.00	-43.24
Indonesia	6,194	5,467	3,537	5,370	4,506	0.04	-16.09
Lao People's Democratic Republic	20	51	23	88	101	0.00	14.77
Malaysia	10,059	8,848	7,767	9,841	11,192	0.09	13.73
Philippines	8,804	9,287	4,103	11,406	11,925	0.10	4.55
Timor-Leste		22	18	17			
Singapore	8,057	7,737	7,079	7,175	8,504	0.07	18.52
Viet Nam		1,289	1,331	3,404	3,913	0.03	14.95
Thailand	9,475	8,173	5,487	7,480	7,733	0.06	3.38
Australasia	115,777	121,481	111,609	140,935	136,187	1.13	-3.37
Australia	96,690	101,322	91,951	119,455	115,699	0.96	-3.14
New Zealand	19,087	20,159	19,658	21,480	20,488	0.17	-4.62
Melanesia	208	265	224	219	285	0.00	30.14
Solomon Islands	12	28	12	12	29	0.00	141.67
Fiji	148	147	164	124	154	0.00	24.19
New Caledonia	9	8	6		2	0.00	
Vanuatu		4	6	15	7	0.00	-53.33
Norfolk Island	7	5	4	1	1	0.00	
Papua New Guinea	32	73	32	67	92	0.00	37.31
Micronesia	205	290	142	79	46	0.00	-41.77
Christmas Island, Australia	19	24	19	4			
Cocos (Keeling) Islands	27	41	17	28	1	0.00	-96.43
Kiribati	53	48	4	12	12	0.00	
Guam	16	50	27	6	2	0.00	-66.67
Nauru	15	15	13	3	14	0.00	366.67
Northern Mariana Islands	47	68	33	15	1	0.00	-93.33
Micronesia, Federated States of	19	29	13	8	4	0.00	-50.00
Marshall Islands	9	9	7	2	9	0.00	350.00
Palau		6	9	1	3	0.00	200.00
Polynesia	335	286	304	148	90	0.00	-39.19
Cook Islands	4	3	4	1			
French Polynesia	175	151	171	64	4	0.00	-93.75
Pitcairn	2	8	4	2			
Tokelau	16	24	6	7	2	0.00	-71.43
Tonga	11	15	18	20	24	0.00	20.00
Tuvalu	14	12	1	4	9	0.00	125.00
Samoa	113	73	100	50	51	0.00	2.00
Other East Asia and the Pacific	2,634	68	625	33	10	0.00	-69.70
Other countries of Asia	2,525	14	551	10	5	0.00	-50.00
Other countries of Oceania	109	54	74	23	5	0.00	-78.26

SOUTH AFRICA

2. Arrivals of non-resident visitors at national borders, by country of residence

	2007	2008	2009	2010	2011	Market share 11	% Change 11-10
EUROPE	1,474,607	1,469,765	1,367,291	1,473,071	1,431,337	11.83	-2.83
Central/Eastern Europe	49,263	52,295	42,380	51,606	47,630	0.39	-7.70
Azerbaijan	137	125	140	287	165	0.00	-42.51
Armenia	72	65	59	146	103	0.00	-29.45
Bulgaria	2,269	2,517	2,091	2,684	2,414	0.02	-10.06
Belarus	642	681	493	584	707	0.01	21.06
Czech Republic	5,835	6,947	6,333	6,520	6,662	0.06	2.18
Estonia	665	802	779	1,050	732	0.01	-30.29
Georgia		208	168	258	210	0.00	-18.60
Hungary	3,185	3,155	2,743	3,418	3,072	0.03	-10.12
Kazakhstan	485	535		780	670	0.01	-14.10
Kyrgyzstan	92	73	140	73	10	0.00	-86.30
Latvia	1,126	1,194	749	678	648	0.01	-4.42
Lithuania	1,210	1,480	1,094	852	829	0.01	-2.70
Republic of Moldova	130	140	124	189	158	0.00	-16.40
Poland	10,747	10,819	10,106	10,897	11,220	0.09	2.96
Romania	2,295	2,447	2,433	2,453	2,318	0.02	-5.50
Russian Federation	12,946	13,664	10,097	12,751	11,756	0.10	-7.80
Slovakia	1,913	2,264	2,101	3,971	2,319	0.02	-41.60
Tajikistan	39	61	31	45	55	0.00	22.22
Turkmenistan	17	27	30	32	19	0.00	-40.63
Ukraine	5,275	4,968	2,525	3,733	3,365	0.03	-9.86
Uzbekistan	183	123	144	205	198	0.00	-3.41
Northern Europe	651,353	640,591	614,635	626,504	589,965	4.88	-5.83
Denmark	26,506	27,367	24,535	26,093	25,016	0.21	-4.13
Faeroe Islands	27	29	50	24			
Finland	9,607	10,187	10,140	11,527	10,960	0.09	-4.92
Iceland	966	788	587	759	684	0.01	-9.88
Ireland	42,803	42,564	38,280	33,935	31,935	0.26	-5.89
Norway	21,031	21,017	19,631	20,909	22,425	0.19	7.25
Sweden	43,823	45,129	38,581	43,125	41,155	0.34	-4.57
United Kingdom	506,481	493,415	482,779	490,071	457,777	3.78	-6.59
Channel Islands	38	12	7	8			
Isle of Man	71	83	45	53	13	0.00	-75.47
Southern Europe	128,751	138,388	138,097	165,831	161,435	1.33	-2.65
Albania	210	219	198	243	128	0.00	-47.33
Andorra	59	69	79	76	46	0.00	-39.47
Bosnia and Herzegovina		172	178	274	268	0.00	-2.19
Croatia	1,518	1,678	1,177	1,326	1,213	0.01	-8.52
Gibraltar	20	10	16	6			
Greece	8,107	9,667	8,576	9,086	6,672	0.06	-26.57
Holy See		17					
Italy	55,459	56,471	59,599	63,255	63,917	0.53	1.05
Malta	485	401	506	614	593	0.00	-3.42
Portugal	30,045	32,293	35,428	51,785	54,770	0.45	5.76
San Marino	38	51	43	27	47	0.00	74.07
Slovenia	1,011	976	1,020	2,255	1,113	0.01	-50.64
Spain	31,798	34,483	31,277	36,884	32,668	0.27	-11.43
Serbia and Montenegro	1	1,881					
Western Europe	616,103	608,479	544,140	595,169	599,472	4.96	0.72
Austria	23,059	21,201	18,508	21,697	23,294	0.19	7.36
Belgium	43,610	43,208	40,555	43,000	44,432	0.37	3.33
France	118,175	131,512	117,523	127,804	116,873	0.97	-8.55
Germany	259,856	243,578	209,644	227,514	248,400	2.05	9.18
Liechtenstein	247	232	265	220	226	0.00	2.73
Luxembourg	1,566	1,429	1,465	1,333	1,343	0.01	0.75
Monaco	108	92	113	76	113	0.00	48.68

SOUTH AFRICA

2. Arrivals of non-resident visitors at national borders, by country of residence

	2007	2008	2009	2010	2011	Market share 11	% Change 11-10
Netherlands	130,878	130,083	121,274	130,668	120,523	1.00	-7.76
Switzerland	38,604	37,144	34,793	42,857	44,268	0.37	3.29
East Mediterranean Europe	**27,116**	**30,012**	**26,536**	**33,388**	**32,549**	**0.27**	**-2.51**
Cyprus	1,522	1,694	1,726	2,113	1,821	0.02	-13.82
Israel	18,369	18,872	16,368	20,594	19,489	0.16	-5.37
Turkey	7,225	9,446	8,442	10,681	11,239	0.09	5.22
Other Europe	**2,021**		**1,503**	**573**	**286**	**0.00**	**-50.09**
Other countries of Europe	2,021		1,503	573	286	0.00	-50.09
MIDDLE EAST	**18,731**	**21,662**	**20,189**	**22,401**	**21,192**	**0.18**	**-5.40**
Bahrain	181	256	180	299	178	0.00	-40.47
Palestine	169	214	165	345	282	0.00	-18.26
Iraq	173	306	332	340	288	0.00	-15.29
Jordan	1,532	1,636	1,604	2,103	1,776	0.01	-15.55
Kuwait	875	865	561	680	636	0.01	-6.47
Lebanon	2,422	2,452	2,148	3,456	2,938	0.02	-14.99
Libya	836	961	1,351	2,078	1,297	0.01	-37.58
Oman	424	382	299	444	354	0.00	-20.27
Qatar	276	317	406	362	237	0.00	-34.53
Saudi Arabia	4,648	5,617	5,415	3,621	4,761	0.04	31.48
Syrian Arab Republic	498	620	438	722	512	0.00	-29.09
United Arab Emirates	1,868	2,495	1,771	1,358	1,092	0.01	-19.59
Egypt	4,671	5,305	5,227	6,222	6,536	0.05	5.05
Yemen	158	236	292	371	305	0.00	-17.79
SOUTH ASIA	**75,841**	**80,379**	**82,043**	**109,526**	**134,941**	**1.12**	**23.20**
Afghanistan	1,025	1,272	1,238	882	220	0.00	-75.06
Bangladesh	2,463	3,293	3,463	4,821	5,096	0.04	5.70
Bhutan	17	7	9	37	27	0.00	-27.03
Sri Lanka	2,298	2,244	2,160	3,530	3,949	0.03	11.87
India	57,999	59,186	59,878	79,529	101,255	0.84	27.32
Iran, Islamic Republic of	2,542	3,486	4,111	4,637	4,856	0.04	4.72
Maldives	88	73	47	88	39	0.00	-55.68
Nepal	358	479	345	574	490	0.00	-14.63
Pakistan	9,051	10,339	10,792	15,428	19,009	0.16	23.21
NOT SPECIFIED	**58,676**	**77,290**	**40,427**	**145,477**	**29,900**	**0.25**	**-79.45**
Other countries of the World	58,676	77,290	40,427	145,477	29,900	0.25	-79.45

SPAIN

1. Arrivals of non-resident tourists at national borders, by country of residence

	2007	2008	2009	2010	2011	Market share 11	% Change 11-10
TOTAL	58,665,505	57,192,015	52,177,640	52,676,972	56,694,298	100.00	7.63
AFRICA			267,458	302,420	535,022	0.94	76.91
Other Africa			267,458	302,420	535,022	0.94	76.91
All countries of Africa			267,458	302,420	535,022	0.94	76.91
AMERICAS	2,312,521	2,397,782	2,573,760	2,617,572	2,872,302	5.07	9.73
North America	1,367,853	1,436,763	1,532,615	1,509,219	1,609,764	2.84	6.66
Canada	124,258	151,467	182,604	189,452	228,285	0.40	20.50
Mexico	196,897	160,803	216,300	185,740	233,293	0.41	25.60
United States of America	1,046,698	1,124,493	1,133,711	1,134,027	1,148,186	2.03	1.25
South America	675,801	622,077	536,466	586,557	802,651	1.42	36.84
Argentina	217,238	212,547	257,463	276,408	299,396	0.53	8.32
Brazil	252,061	226,111	227,731	241,214	360,006	0.63	49.25
Chile	59,845	69,600	24,222	17,706	37,396	0.07	111.21
Venezuela	146,657	113,819	27,050	51,229	105,853	0.19	106.63
Other Americas	268,867	338,942	504,679	521,796	459,887	0.81	-11.86
Other countries of the Americas	268,867	338,942	504,679	521,796	459,887	0.81	-11.86
EAST ASIA AND THE PACIFIC	346,047	237,493	504,634	961,998	1,076,525	1.90	11.91
North-East Asia	346,047	237,493	229,856	332,930	334,314	0.59	0.42
Japan	346,047	237,493	229,856	332,930	334,314	0.59	0.42
Other East Asia and the Pacific			274,778	629,068	742,211	1.31	17.99
Other countries East Asia/Pacific			274,778	629,068	742,211	1.31	17.99
EUROPE	54,926,634	53,512,149	48,204,400	48,290,225	51,901,874	91.55	7.48
Central/Eastern Europe	426,688	509,032	421,993	605,276	858,545	1.51	41.84
Russian Federation	426,688	509,032	421,993	605,276	858,545	1.51	41.84
Northern Europe	21,363,052	21,027,772	18,094,666	17,191,654	18,777,636	33.12	9.23
Denmark	932,132	956,546	960,009	937,726	921,048	1.62	-1.78
Finland	512,922	509,103	517,203	507,161	564,834	1.00	11.37
Ireland	1,630,335	1,658,899	1,463,913	1,177,253	1,280,465	2.26	8.77
Norway	861,474	952,720	886,830	1,016,339	1,117,375	1.97	9.94
Sweden	1,130,057	1,175,260	969,949	1,112,935	1,282,911	2.26	15.27
United Kingdom	16,296,132	15,775,244	13,296,762	12,440,240	13,611,003	24.01	9.41
Southern Europe	6,111,772	5,661,308	5,331,450	5,534,807	5,680,122	10.02	2.63
Greece	74,119	82,753	81,787	148,881	125,820	0.22	-15.49
Italy	3,623,091	3,354,251	3,188,147	3,490,352	3,766,597	6.64	7.91
Portugal	2,414,562	2,224,304	2,061,516	1,895,574	1,787,705	3.15	-5.69
Western Europe	25,293,415	24,294,507	22,326,428	22,655,560	24,164,830	42.62	6.66
Austria	489,482	546,060	506,161	561,190	586,539	1.03	4.52
Belgium	1,724,409	1,636,636	1,599,004	1,623,375	1,779,073	3.14	9.59
France	9,004,008	8,149,265	7,955,104	8,125,354	8,498,430	14.99	4.59
Germany	10,080,606	10,062,629	8,935,147	8,814,070	9,030,697	15.93	2.46
Luxembourg	114,945	133,264	113,782	97,693	120,390	0.21	23.23
Netherlands	2,503,495	2,479,928	2,089,048	2,276,393	2,776,058	4.90	21.95
Switzerland	1,376,470	1,286,725	1,128,182	1,157,485	1,373,643	2.42	18.67
Other Europe	1,731,707	2,019,530	2,029,863	2,302,928	2,420,741	4.27	5.12
Other countries of Europe	1,731,707	2,019,530	2,029,863	2,302,928	2,420,741	4.27	5.12
MIDDLE EAST				68,276	104,851	0.18	53.57
All countries of Middle East				68,276	104,851	0.18	53.57
SOUTH ASIA				29,615	74,538	0.13	151.69
All countries of South Asia				29,615	74,538	0.13	151.69
NOT SPECIFIED	1,080,303	1,044,591	627,388	406,866	129,186	0.23	-68.25
Other countries of the World	1,080,303	1,044,591	627,388	406,866	129,186	0.23	-68.25

SPAIN

3. Arrivals of non-resident tourists in hotels and similar establishments, by country of residence

	2007	2008	2009	2010	2011	Market share 11	% Change 11-10
TOTAL (*)	35,782,747	35,757,721	32,002,230	35,655,543	39,685,289	100.00	11.30
AFRICA	358,779	353,200	327,060	387,765	425,142	1.07	9.64
Southern Africa	47,277	45,326	38,478	41,754	56,318	0.14	34.88
South Africa	47,277	45,326	38,478	41,754	56,318	0.14	34.88
Other Africa	311,502	307,874	288,582	346,011	368,824	0.93	6.59
Other countries of Africa	311,502	307,874	288,582	346,011	368,824	0.93	6.59
AMERICAS	3,374,456	3,258,171	3,198,470	3,835,945	4,376,242	11.03	14.09
North America	2,223,076	2,056,972	2,061,419	2,515,894	2,823,357	7.11	12.22
Canada	222,240	246,717	259,147	396,790	478,553	1.21	20.61
United States of America	1,673,574	1,518,108	1,532,535	1,813,566	2,012,497	5.07	10.97
Other countries of North America	327,262	292,147	269,737	305,538	332,307	0.84	8.76
South America	295,389	322,800	297,077	416,112	518,358	1.31	24.57
Brazil	295,389	322,800	297,077	416,112	518,358	1.31	24.57
Other Americas	855,991	878,399	839,974	903,939	1,034,527	2.61	14.45
Other countries of the Americas	855,991	878,399	839,974	903,939	1,034,527	2.61	14.45
EAST ASIA AND THE PACIFIC	1,270,021	1,299,055	1,188,417	1,568,090	1,847,891	4.66	17.84
North-East Asia	858,295	845,791	751,444	989,141	1,091,576	2.75	10.36
China	139,251	146,517	151,439	206,930	284,149	0.72	37.32
Japan	599,461	572,147	511,770	611,531	615,745	1.55	0.69
Korea, Republic of	119,583	127,127	88,235	170,680	191,682	0.48	12.30
Australasia	146,104	169,782	153,006	198,063	247,100	0.62	24.76
Australia	146,104	169,782	153,006	198,063	247,100	0.62	24.76
Other East Asia and the Pacific	265,622	283,482	283,967	380,886	509,215	1.28	33.69
Other countries of Asia	226,377	246,049	251,016	343,701	473,357	1.19	37.72
Other countries of Oceania	39,245	37,433	32,951	37,185	35,858	0.09	-3.57
EUROPE	29,941,011	30,047,133	26,584,436	29,075,912	32,283,344	81.35	11.03
Central/Eastern Europe	1,320,833	1,521,848	1,358,788	1,744,666	2,323,421	5.85	33.17
Bulgaria	48,434	57,409	53,999	63,675	69,498	0.18	9.14
Czech Republic	172,310	176,759	165,205	163,097	193,795	0.49	18.82
Estonia	29,865	35,186	29,096	29,435	33,000	0.08	12.11
Hungary	97,652	92,973	83,954	99,470	105,691	0.27	6.25
Latvia	32,236	31,230	24,899	33,872	35,565	0.09	5.00
Lithuania	35,148	39,706	36,858	40,081	48,158	0.12	20.15
Poland	252,673	307,582	311,680	396,108	510,031	1.29	28.76
Romania	129,190	160,528	149,479	191,711	220,564	0.56	15.05
Russian Federation	446,404	546,916	430,772	630,965	978,635	2.47	55.10
Slovakia	41,680	38,515	36,015	44,422	49,902	0.13	12.34
Ukraine	35,241	35,044	36,831	51,830	78,582	0.20	51.61
Northern Europe	10,087,998	9,908,008	8,486,289	9,031,576	9,840,976	24.80	8.96
Denmark	375,305	404,835	366,740	407,404	466,794	1.18	14.58
Finland	209,247	242,647	235,041	248,601	276,094	0.70	11.06
Iceland	46,597	48,064	33,424	32,175	37,925	0.10	17.87
Ireland	604,603	621,753	550,697	522,505	543,156	1.37	3.95
Norway	325,999	375,971	319,183	388,160	449,592	1.13	15.83
Sweden	542,974	612,616	557,479	645,936	743,599	1.87	15.12
United Kingdom	7,983,273	7,602,122	6,423,725	6,786,795	7,323,816	18.45	7.91
Southern Europe	4,121,478	4,041,460	3,553,376	4,031,634	4,272,585	10.77	5.98
Greece	137,448	141,641	129,427	175,801	148,274	0.37	-15.66
Italy	2,592,206	2,528,966	2,237,467	2,543,005	2,847,186	7.17	11.96
Malta	16,910	39,112	26,942	25,416	24,415	0.06	-3.94
Portugal	1,342,226	1,297,037	1,125,591	1,250,973	1,214,497	3.06	-2.92
Slovenia	32,688	34,704	33,949	36,439	38,213	0.10	4.87

SPAIN

3. Arrivals of non-resident tourists in hotels and similar establishments, by country of residence

	2007	2008	2009	2010	2011	Market share 11	% Change 11-10
Western Europe	**13,823,043**	**13,983,529**	**12,675,716**	**13,628,825**	**15,110,662**	**38.08**	**10.87**
Austria	308,730	317,003	278,619	337,736	388,055	0.98	14.90
Belgium	975,994	983,607	950,963	949,796	1,047,113	2.64	10.25
France	3,494,981	3,579,311	3,494,385	3,864,873	4,255,566	10.72	10.11
Germany	7,158,653	7,074,680	6,089,490	6,491,508	7,148,915	18.01	10.13
Luxembourg	77,334	71,592	63,940	67,048	75,530	0.19	12.65
Netherlands	1,247,717	1,378,110	1,272,294	1,323,332	1,488,193	3.75	12.46
Switzerland	559,634	579,226	526,025	594,532	707,290	1.78	18.97
East Mediterranean Europe	**87,056**	**122,452**	**105,216**	**148,736**	**160,881**	**0.41**	**8.17**
Cyprus	24,385	19,286	15,059	22,236	24,699	0.06	11.08
Turkey	62,671	103,166	90,157	126,500	136,182	0.34	7.65
Other Europe	**500,603**	**469,836**	**405,051**	**490,475**	**574,819**	**1.45**	**17.20**
Other countries of Europe	500,603	469,836	405,051	490,475	574,819	1.45	17.20
NOT SPECIFIED	**838,480**	**800,162**	**703,847**	**787,831**	**752,670**	**1.90**	**-4.46**
Other countries of the World	838,480	800,162	703,847	787,831	752,670	1.90	-4.46

SPAIN

4. Arrivals of non-resident tourists in all types of accommodation establishments, by country of residence

		2007	2008	2009	2010	2011	Market share 11	% Change 11-10
TOTAL	(*)	44,033,883	43,727,361	39,204,144	43,182,773	47,755,584	100.00	10.59
AFRICA		378,169	370,806	347,353	410,199	452,388	0.95	10.29
Southern Africa		49,735	47,524	40,740	44,085	59,725	0.13	35.48
South Africa		49,735	47,524	40,740	44,085	59,725	0.13	35.48
Other Africa		328,434	323,282	306,613	366,114	392,663	0.82	7.25
Other countries of Africa		328,434	323,282	306,613	366,114	392,663	0.82	7.25
AMERICAS		3,502,435	3,387,390	3,320,307	3,988,405	4,541,810	9.51	13.88
North America		2,309,000	2,143,628	2,140,165	2,605,944	2,926,015	6.13	12.28
Canada		232,079	256,453	268,611	409,078	491,421	1.03	20.13
United States of America		1,741,346	1,586,628	1,593,206	1,878,192	2,089,178	4.37	11.23
Other countries of North America		335,575	300,547	278,348	318,674	345,416	0.72	8.39
South America		301,064	328,580	302,882	424,492	526,857	1.10	24.11
Brazil		301,064	328,580	302,882	424,492	526,857	1.10	24.11
Other Americas		892,371	915,182	877,260	957,969	1,088,938	2.28	13.67
Other countries of the Americas		892,371	915,182	877,260	957,969	1,088,938	2.28	13.67
EAST ASIA AND THE PACIFIC		1,332,886	1,359,418	1,261,815	1,662,979	1,954,330	4.09	17.52
North-East Asia		896,820	881,815	793,987	1,045,961	1,151,567	2.41	10.10
China		145,412	152,480	159,503	218,795	299,607	0.63	36.94
Japan		626,447	597,039	541,064	647,000	650,171	1.36	0.49
Korea, Republic of		124,961	132,296	93,420	180,166	201,789	0.42	12.00
Australasia		152,979	177,447	162,328	210,097	261,212	0.55	24.33
Australia		152,979	177,447	162,328	210,097	261,212	0.55	24.33
Other East Asia and the Pacific		283,087	300,156	305,500	406,921	541,551	1.13	33.09
Other countries of Asia		236,627	256,774	265,680	363,575	499,139	1.05	37.29
Other countries of Oceania		46,460	43,382	39,820	43,346	42,412	0.09	-2.15
EUROPE		37,948,816	37,779,376	33,534,133	36,291,222	40,017,194	83.80	10.27
Central/Eastern Europe		1,523,283	1,763,668	1,566,685	1,978,565	2,611,312	5.47	31.98
Bulgaria		57,465	68,861	64,505	73,704	79,836	0.17	8.32
Czech Republic		209,298	222,625	199,679	199,577	231,667	0.49	16.08
Estonia		35,435	42,525	34,454	34,017	37,825	0.08	11.19
Hungary		115,525	113,620	101,457	116,380	122,071	0.26	4.89
Latvia		38,231	37,689	29,976	39,416	40,838	0.09	3.61
Lithuania		41,850	47,936	44,398	46,529	55,483	0.12	19.24
Poland		299,455	358,555	360,792	451,680	575,257	1.20	27.36
Romania		153,199	196,592	180,764	224,675	254,299	0.53	13.19
Russian Federation		483,821	589,099	466,056	682,985	1,069,851	2.24	56.64
Slovakia		49,248	46,967	43,699	52,547	57,855	0.12	10.10
Ukraine		39,756	39,199	40,905	57,055	86,330	0.18	51.31
Northern Europe		14,044,549	13,722,717	11,786,510	12,380,638	13,486,650	28.24	8.93
Denmark		590,997	613,519	542,596	582,027	643,720	1.35	10.60
Finland		372,902	403,164	383,557	393,710	438,829	0.92	11.46
Iceland		52,729	53,662	37,265	35,152	41,570	0.09	18.26
Ireland		981,754	1,004,662	859,181	805,687	834,682	1.75	3.60
Norway		538,239	601,199	529,197	595,560	697,211	1.46	17.07
Sweden		854,644	936,312	855,881	940,231	1,076,814	2.25	14.53
United Kingdom		10,653,284	10,110,199	8,578,833	9,028,271	9,753,824	20.42	8.04
Southern Europe		4,570,406	4,481,980	3,929,014	4,489,711	4,736,389	9.92	5.49
Greece		149,579	156,631	138,404	187,438	157,747	0.33	-15.84
Italy		2,879,517	2,797,530	2,472,479	2,843,261	3,167,852	6.63	11.42
Malta		20,188	47,505	32,232	29,521	28,063	0.06	-4.94
Portugal		1,482,447	1,438,225	1,244,957	1,386,989	1,338,662	2.80	-3.48
Slovenia		38,675	42,089	40,942	42,502	44,065	0.09	3.68

SPAIN

4. Arrivals of non-resident tourists in all types of accommodation establishments, by country of residence

	2007	2008	2009	2010	2011	Market share 11	% Change 11-10
Western Europe	17,145,612	17,148,704	15,682,976	16,741,389	18,373,805	38.47	9.75
Austria	356,103	361,103	317,951	376,581	431,715	0.90	14.64
Belgium	1,152,891	1,153,602	1,116,593	1,122,324	1,229,383	2.57	9.54
France	4,321,877	4,415,557	4,358,571	4,754,050	5,215,916	10.92	9.72
Germany	8,568,718	8,367,405	7,242,350	7,662,337	8,345,828	17.48	8.92
Luxembourg	98,850	90,332	77,733	78,491	90,532	0.19	15.34
Netherlands	1,974,724	2,091,916	1,965,074	2,064,753	2,253,916	4.72	9.16
Switzerland	672,449	668,789	604,704	682,853	806,515	1.69	18.11
East Mediterranean Europe	99,799	138,638	117,873	164,211	177,896	0.37	8.33
Cyprus	29,039	23,529	18,136	26,143	28,500	0.06	9.02
Turkey	70,760	115,109	99,737	138,068	149,396	0.31	8.20
Other Europe	565,167	523,669	451,075	536,708	631,142	1.32	17.60
Other countries of Europe	565,167	523,669	451,075	536,708	631,142	1.32	17.60
NOT SPECIFIED	871,577	830,371	740,536	829,968	789,862	1.65	-4.83
Other countries of the World	871,577	830,371	740,536	829,968	789,862	1.65	-4.83

SPAIN

5. Overnight stays of non-resident tourists in hotels and similar establishments, by country of residence

	2007	2008	2009	2010	2011	Market share 11	% Change 11-10
TOTAL (*)	155,092,778	155,363,549	141,227,941	153,927,193	175,474,928	100.00	14.00
AFRICA	671,610	671,296	643,911	853,072	810,137	0.46	-5.03
Southern Africa	113,040	101,306	89,509	96,034	127,365	0.07	32.62
South Africa	113,040	101,306	89,509	96,034	127,365	0.07	32.62
Other Africa	671,610	671,296	643,911	853,072	810,137	0.46	-5.03
Other countries of Africa	671,610	671,296	643,911	853,072	810,137	0.46	-5.03
AMERICAS	7,121,922	7,078,229	7,146,183	8,498,825	9,771,031	5.57	14.97
North America	4,700,046	4,464,971	4,637,580	5,591,062	6,285,560	3.58	12.42
Canada	536,680	626,508	670,029	953,720	1,136,482	0.65	19.16
United States of America	3,432,062	3,183,458	3,350,590	3,947,861	4,389,446	2.50	11.19
Other countries of North America	731,304	655,005	616,961	689,481	759,632	0.43	10.17
South America	620,910	754,503	738,504	991,426	1,226,407	0.70	23.70
Brazil	620,910	754,503	738,504	991,426	1,226,407	0.70	23.70
Other Americas	1,800,966	1,858,755	1,770,099	1,916,337	2,259,064	1.29	17.88
Other countries of the Americas	1,800,966	1,858,755	1,770,099	1,916,337	2,259,064	1.29	17.88
EAST ASIA AND THE PACIFIC	2,259,587	2,362,127	2,261,203	2,917,847	3,567,489	2.03	22.26
North-East Asia	1,356,014	1,348,835	1,245,174	1,604,230	1,794,301	1.02	11.85
China	248,396	262,209	270,323	373,936	495,850	0.28	32.60
Japan	941,621	907,220	845,591	987,041	1,028,425	0.59	4.19
Korea, Republic of	165,997	179,406	129,260	243,253	270,026	0.15	11.01
Australasia	312,885	372,823	337,522	443,068	568,892	0.32	28.40
Australia	312,885	372,823	337,522	443,068	568,892	0.32	28.40
Other East Asia and the Pacific	590,688	640,469	678,507	870,549	1,204,296	0.69	38.34
Other countries of Asia	514,952	572,739	614,125	796,765	1,127,196	0.64	41.47
Other countries of Oceania	75,736	67,730	64,382	73,784	77,100	0.04	4.49
EUROPE	142,862,145	143,304,627	129,335,156	139,555,580	159,110,648	90.67	14.01
Central/Eastern Europe	6,036,954	6,947,823	6,127,120	8,149,947	11,500,594	6.55	41.11
Bulgaria	132,695	147,368	150,467	183,842	227,839	0.13	23.93
Czech Republic	861,350	904,100	852,714	833,430	997,002	0.57	19.63
Estonia	101,110	140,391	112,131	115,554	125,429	0.07	8.55
Hungary	425,517	348,847	288,085	361,184	383,794	0.22	6.26
Latvia	96,935	100,365	89,487	104,699	132,248	0.08	26.31
Lithuania	131,382	142,851	145,506	149,572	186,504	0.11	24.69
Poland	980,362	1,366,410	1,446,449	1,770,454	2,445,566	1.39	38.13
Romania	403,859	485,943	437,149	606,685	743,820	0.42	22.60
Russian Federation	2,575,654	3,043,365	2,320,571	3,584,505	5,688,474	3.24	58.70
Slovakia	208,504	147,674	158,274	208,431	237,466	0.14	13.93
Ukraine	119,586	120,509	126,287	231,591	332,452	0.19	43.55
Northern Europe	53,212,186	52,178,073	46,823,037	49,576,077	55,081,410	31.39	11.10
Denmark	1,694,720	1,830,986	1,718,683	1,941,915	2,523,338	1.44	29.94
Finland	907,119	1,007,298	1,052,385	1,138,286	1,316,424	0.75	15.65
Iceland	263,628	284,808	168,506	184,026	221,885	0.13	20.57
Ireland	2,624,485	2,691,464	2,473,845	2,235,348	2,421,197	1.38	8.31
Norway	1,495,491	1,824,763	1,738,795	2,018,901	2,356,048	1.34	16.70
Sweden	2,596,435	3,079,740	3,013,007	3,280,840	3,940,245	2.25	20.10
United Kingdom	43,630,308	41,459,014	36,657,816	38,776,761	42,302,273	24.11	9.09
Southern Europe	12,546,178	12,473,022	10,775,541	12,169,405	13,144,753	7.49	8.01
Greece	348,467	350,133	345,572	515,089	436,267	0.25	-15.30
Italy	8,428,433	8,385,107	7,216,770	8,151,620	9,375,669	5.34	15.02
Malta	64,136	129,957	93,297	79,914	73,904	0.04	-7.52
Portugal	3,588,640	3,494,131	3,015,623	3,311,143	3,112,855	1.77	-5.99
Slovenia	116,502	113,694	104,279	111,639	146,058	0.08	30.83

SPAIN

5. Overnight stays of non-resident tourists in hotels and similar establishments, by country of residence

	2007	2008	2009	2010	2011	Market share 11	% Change 11-10
Western Europe	69,272,541	70,025,850	64,157,947	67,855,105	77,208,174	44.00	13.78
Austria	1,297,802	1,387,503	1,205,537	1,462,259	1,777,009	1.01	21.52
Belgium	5,034,007	5,038,399	5,022,613	4,931,948	5,441,149	3.10	10.32
France	9,320,155	9,821,088	9,619,625	10,527,172	12,081,589	6.89	14.77
Germany	45,141,993	44,646,808	39,731,293	41,959,464	47,247,586	26.93	12.60
Luxembourg	385,621	350,666	350,637	383,246	444,527	0.25	15.99
Netherlands	5,822,757	6,310,868	5,889,819	6,029,492	7,024,975	4.00	16.51
Switzerland	2,270,206	2,470,518	2,338,423	2,561,524	3,191,339	1.82	24.59
East Mediterranean Europe	255,423	265,518	238,353	345,569	399,238	0.23	15.53
Cyprus	103,804	47,067	39,711	62,822	78,926	0.04	25.63
Turkey	151,619	218,451	198,642	282,747	320,312	0.18	13.29
Other Europe	1,538,863	1,414,341	1,213,158	1,459,477	1,776,479	1.01	21.72
Other countries of Europe	1,538,863	1,414,341	1,213,158	1,459,477	1,776,479	1.01	21.72
NOT SPECIFIED	2,064,474	1,845,964	1,751,979	2,005,835	2,088,258	1.19	4.11
Other countries of the World	2,064,474	1,845,964	1,751,979	2,005,835	2,088,258	1.19	4.11

SPAIN

6. Overnight stays of non-resident tourists in all types of accommodation establishments, by country of residence

	2007	2008	2009	2010	2011	Market share 11	% Change 11-10
TOTAL (*)	224,997,898	223,772,578	200,551,732	213,365,670	239,389,038	100.00	12.20
AFRICA	789,884	778,169	755,276	985,928	975,303	0.41	-1.08
Southern Africa	131,881	116,452	104,043	109,534	150,516	0.06	37.41
South Africa	131,881	116,452	104,043	109,534	150,516	0.06	37.41
Other Africa	789,884	778,169	755,276	985,928	975,303	0.41	-1.08
Other countries of Africa	789,884	778,169	755,276	985,928	975,303	0.41	-1.08
AMERICAS	7,906,470	7,975,641	7,868,261	9,328,295	10,686,292	4.46	14.56
North America	5,196,982	5,030,678	5,065,453	6,025,212	6,779,909	2.83	12.53
Canada	601,986	700,642	737,643	1,037,280	1,229,442	0.51	18.53
United States of America	3,822,347	3,626,403	3,667,681	4,237,949	4,728,065	1.98	11.56
Other countries of North America	772,649	703,633	660,129	749,983	822,402	0.34	9.66
South America	658,840	798,849	777,815	1,044,060	1,282,900	0.54	22.88
Brazil	658,840	798,849	777,815	1,044,060	1,282,900	0.54	22.88
Other Americas	2,050,648	2,146,114	2,024,993	2,259,023	2,623,483	1.10	16.13
Other countries of the Americas	2,050,648	2,146,114	2,024,993	2,259,023	2,623,483	1.10	16.13
EAST ASIA AND THE PACIFIC	2,517,619	2,659,559	2,568,167	3,287,927	4,001,985	1.67	21.72
North-East Asia	1,496,844	1,507,462	1,403,007	1,798,522	2,005,407	0.84	11.50
China	274,645	291,691	303,340	419,353	553,560	0.23	32.00
Japan	1,038,937	1,016,082	953,799	1,106,837	1,150,814	0.48	3.97
Korea, Republic of	183,262	199,689	145,868	272,332	301,033	0.13	10.54
Australasia	346,411	417,511	381,097	497,831	634,454	0.27	27.44
Australia	346,411	417,511	381,097	497,831	634,454	0.27	27.44
Other East Asia and the Pacific	674,364	734,586	784,063	991,574	1,362,124	0.57	37.37
Other countries of Asia	570,532	640,831	693,770	894,655	1,257,709	0.53	40.58
Other countries of Oceania	103,832	93,755	90,293	96,919	104,415	0.04	7.73
EUROPE	211,388,395	210,197,784	187,295,365	197,413,969	221,262,518	92.43	12.08
Central/Eastern Europe	7,538,829	8,780,317	7,585,061	9,677,280	13,427,463	5.61	38.75
Bulgaria	181,145	220,155	211,471	237,372	289,858	0.12	22.11
Czech Republic	1,138,191	1,215,778	1,077,379	1,049,358	1,236,449	0.52	17.83
Estonia	142,896	211,473	158,262	150,113	160,297	0.07	6.78
Hungary	567,094	528,997	405,747	470,963	486,245	0.20	3.24
Latvia	135,570	152,873	126,069	135,873	169,207	0.07	24.53
Lithuania	184,245	217,108	204,908	193,735	237,295	0.10	22.48
Poland	1,281,666	1,715,916	1,774,022	2,089,974	2,855,516	1.19	36.63
Romania	547,774	730,787	613,919	787,577	943,625	0.39	19.81
Russian Federation	2,925,595	3,408,975	2,632,296	4,014,664	6,353,602	2.65	58.26
Slovakia	278,209	221,626	222,021	271,056	299,117	0.12	10.35
Ukraine	156,444	156,629	158,967	276,595	396,252	0.17	43.26
Northern Europe	89,005,245	87,132,194	76,003,707	78,183,507	85,882,583	35.88	9.85
Denmark	3,551,472	3,653,317	3,255,430	3,406,994	4,023,968	1.68	18.11
Finland	2,316,780	2,454,111	2,371,404	2,393,517	2,701,734	1.13	12.88
Iceland	348,281	373,833	215,399	224,600	269,278	0.11	19.89
Ireland	6,106,635	6,145,024	5,068,140	4,436,198	4,714,087	1.97	6.26
Norway	3,722,513	4,130,414	3,945,740	4,119,934	4,794,033	2.00	16.36
Sweden	5,361,766	5,874,738	5,691,244	5,892,123	6,819,388	2.85	15.74
United Kingdom	67,597,798	64,500,757	55,456,350	57,710,141	62,560,095	26.13	8.40
Southern Europe	14,975,577	14,892,697	12,657,316	14,381,746	15,426,963	6.44	7.27
Greece	432,861	470,456	402,901	576,043	498,713	0.21	-13.42
Italy	10,039,915	9,845,628	8,435,329	9,667,736	11,018,200	4.60	13.97
Malta	87,969	197,558	131,634	104,342	94,291	0.04	-9.63
Portugal	4,255,926	4,205,150	3,540,535	3,889,037	3,630,333	1.52	-6.65
Slovenia	158,906	173,905	146,917	144,588	185,426	0.08	28.24

SPAIN

6. Overnight stays of non-resident tourists in all types of accommodation establishments, by country of residence

	2007	2008	2009	2010	2011	Market share 11	% Change 11-10
Western Europe	**97,508,384**	**97,203,489**	**89,180,373**	**92,992,328**	**103,886,597**	**43.40**	**11.72**
Austria	1,662,147	1,736,144	1,511,202	1,753,595	2,116,004	0.88	20.67
Belgium	6,489,138	6,405,534	6,358,928	6,328,795	6,961,552	2.91	10.00
France	13,998,433	14,707,391	14,649,330	15,660,542	17,839,296	7.45	13.91
Germany	59,308,451	57,676,108	51,053,217	52,986,209	58,629,209	24.49	10.65
Luxembourg	513,460	486,125	449,023	453,613	545,166	0.23	20.18
Netherlands	12,397,229	13,041,044	12,250,266	12,646,078	13,920,987	5.82	10.08
Switzerland	3,139,526	3,151,143	2,908,407	3,163,496	3,874,383	1.62	22.47
East Mediterranean Europe	**343,943**	**358,199**	**311,405**	**425,169**	**491,019**	**0.21**	**15.49**
Cyprus	142,871	72,476	55,704	82,365	101,184	0.04	22.85
Turkey	201,072	285,723	255,701	342,804	389,835	0.16	13.72
Other Europe	**2,016,417**	**1,830,888**	**1,557,503**	**1,753,939**	**2,147,893**	**0.90**	**22.46**
Other countries of Europe	2,016,417	1,830,888	1,557,503	1,753,939	2,147,893	0.90	22.46
NOT SPECIFIED	**2,263,649**	**2,044,973**	**1,960,620**	**2,240,017**	**2,312,424**	**0.97**	**3.23**
Other countries of the World	2,263,649	2,044,973	1,960,620	2,240,017	2,312,424	0.97	3.23

SRI LANKA

1. Arrivals of non-resident tourists at national borders, by nationality

		2007	2008	2009	2010	2011	Market share 11	% Change 11-10
TOTAL	(*)	494,008	438,475	447,890	654,476	855,975	100.00	30.79
AFRICA		2,991	2,354	1,591	2,249	6,736	0.79	199.51
Other Africa		2,991	2,354	1,591	2,249	6,736	0.79	199.51
All countries of Africa		2,991	2,354	1,591	2,249	6,736	0.79	199.51
AMERICAS		32,442	26,924	25,710	41,146	54,825	6.40	33.25
North America		28,338	23,203	25,044	40,552	53,658	6.27	32.32
Canada		11,862	9,745	10,785	21,231	26,090	3.05	22.89
United States of America		16,476	13,458	14,259	19,321	27,568	3.22	42.68
Other Americas		4,104	3,721	666	594	1,167	0.14	96.46
Other countries of the Americas		4,104	3,721	666	594	1,167	0.14	96.46
EAST ASIA AND THE PACIFIC		75,508	67,199	75,503	110,816	141,751	16.56	27.92
North-East Asia		32,301	27,104	27,136	36,569	50,996	5.96	39.45
China		10,413	10,015	8,574	10,410	16,573	1.94	59.20
Taiwan, Province of China		2,544	1,988	2,711	5,019	7,067	0.83	40.80
Hong Kong, China		210	421	1,325	1,824	440	0.05	-75.88
Japan		14,274	10,578	10,931	14,998	20,951	2.45	39.69
Korea, Republic of		4,860	4,102	3,595	4,318	5,965	0.70	38.14
South-East Asia		18,384	17,011	20,512	31,978	36,389	4.25	13.79
Indonesia		1,404	1,258	1,039	1,281	2,011	0.23	56.99
Malaysia		6,666	5,021	6,878	13,101	15,915	1.86	21.48
Philippines		2,106	1,520	1,421	1,369	2,394	0.28	74.87
Singapore		5,691	5,702	7,976	12,514	10,666	1.25	-14.77
Thailand		2,517	3,510	3,198	3,713	5,403	0.63	45.52
Australasia		22,896	21,293	25,872	36,813	48,912	5.71	32.87
Australia		20,241	19,145	23,249	33,512	43,737	5.11	30.51
New Zealand		2,655	2,148	2,623	3,301	5,175	0.60	56.77
Other East Asia and the Pacific		1,927	1,791	1,983	5,456	5,454	0.64	-0.04
Other countries of Asia		1,830	1,706	1,832	5,244	2,955	0.35	-43.65
Other countries of Oceania		97	85	151	212	2,499	0.29	1078.77
EUROPE		221,298	195,174	196,363	290,802	372,353	43.50	28.04
Central/Eastern Europe		25,485	29,352	26,177	35,630	51,922	6.07	45.73
Russian Federation		13,530	15,831	11,390	13,312	21,291	2.49	59.94
Other countries Central/East Europe		11,955	13,521	14,787	22,318	30,631	3.58	37.25
Northern Europe		103,497	87,404	88,977	123,222	134,204	15.68	8.91
Denmark		1,782	1,336	1,306	4,301	6,640	0.78	54.38
Finland		498	489	742	1,971	3,819	0.45	93.76
Norway		2,304	1,620	1,669	3,884	5,135	0.60	32.21
Sweden		4,824	3,745	3,578	7,128	11,715	1.37	64.35
United Kingdom		94,089	80,214	81,682	105,938	106,895	12.49	0.90
Southern Europe		13,932	11,388	9,597	16,001	20,061	2.34	25.37
Italy		11,451	9,137	7,214	11,512	14,182	1.66	23.19
Spain		2,481	2,251	2,383	4,489	5,879	0.69	30.96
Western Europe		75,225	64,376	68,437	113,576	161,717	18.89	42.39
Austria		3,573	2,684	2,411	3,963	6,185	0.72	56.07
Belgium		4,653	2,394	2,613	5,371	10,853	1.27	102.07
France		9,540	10,703	16,205	31,119	50,175	5.86	61.24
Germany		35,016	30,154	29,664	45,981	55,339	6.47	20.35
Netherlands		17,532	13,180	11,297	17,628	26,004	3.04	47.52
Switzerland		4,911	5,261	6,247	9,514	13,161	1.54	38.33
Other Europe		3,159	2,654	3,175	2,373	4,449	0.52	87.48
Other countries of Europe		3,159	2,654	3,175	2,373	4,449	0.52	87.48

SRI LANKA

1. Arrivals of non-resident tourists at national borders, by nationality

	2007	2008	2009	2010	2011	Market share 11	% Change 11-10
MIDDLE EAST	**13,587**	**16,701**	**23,821**	**37,501**	**36,376**	**4.25**	**-3.00**
All countries of Middle East	13,587	16,701	23,821	37,501	36,376	4.25	-3.00
SOUTH ASIA	**148,182**	**130,123**	**124,902**	**171,962**	**243,934**	**28.50**	**41.85**
Bangladesh	1,668	1,438	1,295	1,846	4,934	0.58	167.28
India	105,906	88,628	83,650	125,112	178,359	20.84	42.56
Maldives	29,550	31,458	31,890	35,401	43,926	5.13	24.08
Nepal	885	897	679	602	858	0.10	42.52
Pakistan	10,173	7,702	7,388	9,001	15,857	1.85	76.17

SRI LANKA

1. Arrivals of non-resident tourists at national borders, by country of residence

		2007	2008	2009	2010	2011	Market share 11	% Change 11-10
TOTAL	(*)	**494,008**	**438,475**	**447,820**	**654,476**	**855,975**	**100.00**	**30.79**
AFRICA		**2,712**	**2,141**	**1,479**	**2,308**	**3,614**	**0.42**	**56.59**
East Africa		**424**	**711**	**397**	**539**	**621**	**0.07**	**15.21**
Kenya		265	540	229	297	394	0.05	32.66
Mauritius		59	93	117	179	160	0.02	-10.61
Zambia		100	78	51	63	67	0.01	6.35
North Africa		**202**	**120**	**69**	**71**	**64**	**0.01**	**-9.86**
Algeria		202	120	69	71	64	0.01	-9.86
Southern Africa		**933**	**756**	**779**	**1,415**	**1,962**	**0.23**	**38.66**
South Africa		933	756	779	1,415	1,962	0.23	38.66
West Africa		**95**	**99**	**131**	**212**	**378**	**0.04**	**78.30**
Nigeria		95	99	131	212	378	0.04	78.30
Other Africa		**1,058**	**455**	**103**	**71**	**589**	**0.07**	**729.58**
Other countries of Africa		1,058	455	103	71	589	0.07	729.58
AMERICAS		**32,317**	**28,050**	**25,565**	**40,836**	**50,093**	**5.85**	**22.67**
North America		**28,355**	**24,311**	**24,948**	**40,216**	**49,057**	**5.73**	**21.98**
Canada		11,869	10,258	10,707	21,123	24,671	2.88	16.80
United States of America		16,486	14,053	14,241	19,093	24,386	2.85	27.72
South America		**1,137**	**1,649**	**500**	**512**	**541**	**0.06**	**5.66**
Argentina		233	352	75	133	148	0.02	11.28
Bolivia		215	291	39	76	23	0.00	-69.74
Brazil		289	258	157	217	362	0.04	66.82
French Guiana		400	748	229	86	8	0.00	-90.70
Other Americas		**2,825**	**2,090**	**117**	**108**	**495**	**0.06**	**358.33**
Other countries of the Americas		2,825	2,090	117	108	495	0.06	358.33
EAST ASIA AND THE PACIFIC		**75,778**	**66,783**	**74,397**	**105,720**	**142,661**	**16.67**	**34.94**
North-East Asia		**33,871**	**26,631**	**27,216**	**35,715**	**51,588**	**6.03**	**44.44**
China		11,949	9,812	8,550	10,430	16,308	1.91	56.36
Taiwan, Province of China		2,553	1,907	2,715	5,277	7,010	0.82	32.84
Hong Kong, China		225	537	1,330	1,230	2,199	0.26	78.78
Japan		14,274	10,075	10,926	14,352	20,586	2.40	43.44
Korea, Republic of		4,870	4,300	3,695	4,426	5,485	0.64	23.93
South-East Asia		**18,774**	**17,969**	**20,813**	**32,362**	**43,672**	**5.10**	**34.95**
Myanmar		261	376	262	262	914	0.11	248.85
Indonesia		1,404	1,157	1,040	1,343	2,049	0.24	52.57
Malaysia		6,704	5,188	6,850	13,367	16,094	1.88	20.40
Philippines		2,162	1,693	1,421	1,391	2,047	0.24	47.16
Singapore		5,688	5,802	7,808	11,875	15,953	1.86	34.34
Viet Nam		88	170	224	440	735	0.09	67.05
Thailand		2,467	3,583	3,208	3,684	5,880	0.69	59.61
Australasia		**22,868**	**21,776**	**25,911**	**36,943**	**45,940**	**5.37**	**24.35**
Australia		20,241	19,536	23,239	33,456	41,728	4.87	24.73
New Zealand		2,627	2,240	2,672	3,487	4,212	0.49	20.79
Other East Asia and the Pacific		**265**	**407**	**457**	**700**	**1,461**	**0.17**	**108.71**
Other countries of Asia		209	344	300	353	934	0.11	164.59
Other countries of Oceania		56	63	157	347	527	0.06	51.87
EUROPE		**222,669**	**199,601**	**198,897**	**296,961**	**371,794**	**43.44**	**25.20**
Central/Eastern Europe		**25,573**	**29,440**	**26,310**	**35,517**	**49,249**	**5.75**	**38.66**
Bulgaria		361	242	207	703	375	0.04	-46.66
Czech Republic		1,880	2,555	2,814	4,204	5,548	0.65	31.97
Hungary		584	582	418	836	911	0.11	8.97
Lithuania		160	459	546	636	673	0.08	5.82

SRI LANKA

1. Arrivals of non-resident tourists at national borders, by country of residence

	2007	2008	2009	2010	2011	Market share 11	% Change 11-10
Poland	3,761	4,960	5,138	6,613	5,817	0.68	-12.04
Romania	236	305	272	710	726	0.08	2.25
Russian Federation	13,621	15,797	11,834	13,278	21,385	2.50	61.06
Slovakia	465	704	1,164	1,716	1,314	0.15	-23.43
Ukraine	524	952	2,577	5,703	9,967	1.16	74.77
Other countries Central/East Europe	3,981	2,884	1,340	1,118	2,533	0.30	126.57
Northern Europe	**105,374**	**90,090**	**90,286**	**124,648**	**133,679**	**15.62**	**7.25**
Denmark	1,796	1,320	1,362	4,393	6,582	0.77	49.83
Finland	497	468	738	1,950	3,649	0.43	87.13
Ireland	1,866	1,647	1,366	1,758	1,452	0.17	-17.41
Norway	2,304	1,613	1,666	3,955	4,977	0.58	25.84
Sweden	4,851	3,711	3,560	7,096	10,937	1.28	54.13
United Kingdom	94,060	81,331	81,594	105,496	106,082	12.39	0.56
Southern Europe	**14,651**	**12,212**	**11,372**	**18,333**	**21,685**	**2.53**	**18.28**
Greece	382	395	906	1,599	1,240	0.14	-22.45
Italy	11,451	9,126	7,514	11,423	13,527	1.58	18.42
Portugal	334	409	565	850	1,032	0.12	21.41
Spain	2,484	2,282	2,387	4,461	5,886	0.69	31.94
Western Europe	**73,825**	**64,604**	**68,188**	**113,623**	**159,037**	**18.58**	**39.97**
Austria	3,580	2,651	2,409	3,925	6,262	0.73	59.54
Belgium	4,669	2,378	2,617	5,398	10,122	1.18	87.51
France	8,091	10,594	15,886	31,285	48,695	5.69	55.65
Germany	35,042	30,625	29,654	45,727	55,882	6.53	22.21
Netherlands	17,526	13,030	11,291	17,861	23,966	2.80	34.18
Switzerland	4,917	5,326	6,331	9,427	14,110	1.65	49.68
East Mediterranean Europe	**2,648**	**2,974**	**2,464**	**4,583**	**7,335**	**0.86**	**60.05**
Israel	2,648	2,596	1,901	3,919	6,164	0.72	57.29
Turkey		378	563	664	1,171	0.14	76.36
Other Europe	**598**	**281**	**277**	**257**	**809**	**0.09**	**214.79**
Other countries of Europe	598	281	277	257	809	0.09	214.79
MIDDLE EAST	**10,568**	**11,672**	**20,007**	**31,057**	**47,943**	**5.60**	**54.37**
Bahrain	545	805	943	1,459	1,819	0.21	24.67
Jordan	1,446	1,398	1,108	1,708	1,478	0.17	-13.47
Kuwait	831	1,011	1,123	2,303	2,812	0.33	22.10
Lebanon	464	759	940	1,816	1,960	0.23	7.93
Oman	515	499	727	1,359	2,177	0.25	60.19
Qatar	219	312	1,158	1,574	2,788	0.33	77.13
Saudi Arabia	3,861	3,456	6,685	9,301	15,081	1.76	62.14
United Arab Emirates		2,469	5,974	9,825	17,664	2.06	79.79
Egypt		417	510	849	767	0.09	-9.66
Other countries of Middle East	2,687	546	839	863	1,397	0.16	61.88
SOUTH ASIA	**149,964**	**130,228**	**127,475**	**177,594**	**239,870**	**28.02**	**35.07**
Afghanistan	62	168	200	176	363	0.04	106.25
Bangladesh	1,686	1,599	1,294	1,954	4,726	0.55	141.86
Bhutan	342	498	668	530	824	0.10	55.47
India	106,067	85,238	83,634	126,882	171,374	20.02	35.07
Iran, Islamic Republic of	338	2,130	1,270	1,900	2,223	0.26	17.00
Maldives	29,539	31,564	31,916	35,791	44,018	5.14	22.99
Nepal	904	888	676	753	826	0.10	9.69
Pakistan	10,204	7,885	7,373	9,148	14,724	1.72	60.95
Other countries of South Asia	822	258	444	460	792	0.09	72.17

SRI LANKA

6. Overnight stays of non-resident tourists in all types of accommodation establishments, by nationality

	2007	2008	2009	2010	2011	Market share 11	% Change 11-10
TOTAL	4,940,084	4,165,511	4,075,799	6,544,760	8,559,753	100.00	30.79
AFRICA	28,714	21,421	12,569	22,265	64,666	0.76	190.44
Other Africa	28,714	21,421	12,569	22,265	64,666	0.76	190.44
All countries of Africa	28,714	21,421	12,569	22,265	64,666	0.76	190.44
AMERICAS	348,304	308,219	272,480	430,627	570,943	6.67	32.58
North America	301,108	271,753	265,887	424,628	559,471	6.54	31.76
Canada	128,110	134,481	121,871	231,418	280,207	3.27	21.08
United States of America	172,998	137,272	144,016	193,210	279,264	3.26	44.54
Other Americas	47,196	36,466	6,593	5,999	11,472	0.13	91.23
Other countries of the Americas	47,196	36,466	6,593	5,999	11,472	0.13	91.23
EAST ASIA AND THE PACIFIC	697,795	662,603	692,400	1,137,681	1,497,005	17.49	31.58
North-East Asia	271,721	224,791	213,271	345,705	488,344	5.71	41.26
China	83,304	76,114	68,592	103,059	161,421	1.89	56.63
Taiwan, Province of China	21,395	27,729	21,146	47,179	67,419	0.79	42.90
Hong Kong, China	1,953	2,989	9,540	17,328	4,092	0.05	-76.39
Japan	121,329	81,451	83,076	137,982	201,130	2.35	45.77
Korea, Republic of	43,740	36,508	30,917	40,157	54,282	0.63	35.17
South-East Asia	149,643	121,421	155,091	295,878	342,837	4.01	15.87
Indonesia	12,636	9,435	7,585	11,785	18,903	0.22	60.40
Malaysia	55,994	41,172	53,648	125,770	154,853	1.81	23.12
Philippines	18,112	12,768	11,652	12,184	21,642	0.25	77.63
Singapore	43,821	43,335	59,820	110,123	95,354	1.11	-13.41
Thailand	19,080	14,711	22,386	36,016	52,085	0.61	44.62
Australasia	263,039	283,356	292,992	419,388	550,005	6.43	31.14
Australia	232,772	260,372	266,500	385,388	495,978	5.79	28.70
New Zealand	30,267	22,984	26,492	34,000	54,027	0.63	58.90
Other East Asia and the Pacific	13,392	33,035	31,046	76,710	115,819	1.35	50.98
Other countries of Asia	12,810	32,178	29,687	74,612	90,685	1.06	21.54
Other countries of Oceania	582	857	1,359	2,098	25,134	0.29	1098.00
EUROPE	2,549,219	1,972,437	1,914,137	3,049,358	3,901,289	45.58	27.94
Central/Eastern Europe	261,568	232,574	200,674	365,657	525,555	6.14	43.73
Russian Federation	162,360	129,814	96,815	135,782	218,020	2.55	60.57
Other countries Central/East Europe	99,208	102,760	103,859	229,875	307,535	3.59	33.78
Northern Europe	1,184,250	927,461	905,446	1,316,932	1,418,104	16.57	7.68
Denmark	19,958	14,162	13,321	43,010	67,861	0.79	57.78
Finland	5,329	4,694	6,826	20,104	38,343	0.45	90.72
Norway	25,805	19,440	18,025	40,782	53,404	0.62	30.95
Sweden	51,134	43,068	37,569	74,844	121,133	1.42	61.85
United Kingdom	1,082,024	846,097	829,705	1,138,192	1,137,363	13.29	-0.07
Southern Europe	145,351	112,953	95,004	159,308	199,126	2.33	24.99
Italy	122,526	89,543	70,697	113,969	138,984	1.62	21.95
Spain	22,825	23,410	24,307	45,339	60,142	0.70	32.65
Western Europe	928,987	676,226	683,803	1,184,917	1,712,260	20.00	44.50
Austria	42,876	25,766	22,422	37,649	59,623	0.70	58.37
Belgium	55,836	25,616	27,175	54,247	110,049	1.29	102.87
France	124,020	101,679	155,568	326,750	548,915	6.41	67.99
Germany	430,697	331,644	302,573	491,997	588,807	6.88	19.68
Netherlands	215,644	135,754	112,970	176,280	266,281	3.11	51.06
Switzerland	59,914	55,767	63,095	97,994	138,585	1.62	41.42
Other Europe	29,063	23,223	29,210	22,544	46,244	0.54	105.13
Other countries of Europe	29,063	23,223	29,210	22,544	46,244	0.54	105.13

SRI LANKA

6. Overnight stays of non-resident tourists in all types of accommodation establishments, by nationality

	2007	2008	2009	2010	2011	Market share 11	% Change 11-10
MIDDLE EAST	110,055	126,928	178,658	382,510	371,035	4.33	-3.00
All countries of Middle East	110,055	126,928	178,658	382,510	371,035	4.33	-3.00
SOUTH ASIA	1,205,997	1,073,903	1,005,555	1,522,319	2,154,815	25.17	41.55
India	857,839	718,122	657,835	1,105,900	1,558,858	18.21	40.96
Maldives	271,860	295,705	292,310	336,310	454,195	5.31	35.05
Pakistan	76,298	60,076	55,410	80,109	141,762	1.66	76.96

SUDAN

1. Arrivals of non-resident tourists at national borders, by nationality

		2007	2008	2009	2010	2011	Market share 11	% Change 11-10
TOTAL	(*)	436,295	439,661	420,370	495,158	536,400	100.00	8.33
AFRICA		65,444	65,949	59,802	49,516	53,640	10.00	8.33
Other Africa		65,444	65,949	59,802	49,516	53,640	10.00	8.33
All countries of Africa		65,444	65,949	59,802	49,516	53,640	10.00	8.33
AMERICAS		15,526	15,388	21,000	19,806	21,456	4.00	8.33
Other Americas		15,526	15,388	21,000	19,806	21,456	4.00	8.33
All countries of the Americas		15,526	15,388	21,000	19,806	21,456	4.00	8.33
EAST ASIA AND THE PACIFIC		296,680	298,969	239,920	29,709	32,184	6.00	8.33
Other East Asia and the Pacific		296,680	298,969	239,920	29,709	32,184	6.00	8.33
All countries of Asia		296,680	298,969	239,920	29,709	32,184	6.00	8.33
EUROPE		56,718	57,156	99,648	74,274	80,460	15.00	8.33
Other Europe		56,718	57,156	99,648	74,274	80,460	15.00	8.33
All countries of Europe		56,718	57,156	99,648	74,274	80,460	15.00	8.33
MIDDLE EAST					272,338	295,020	55.00	8.33
All countries of Middle East					272,338	295,020	55.00	8.33
SOUTH ASIA					39,612	42,912	8.00	8.33
All countries of South Asia					39,612	42,912	8.00	8.33
NOT SPECIFIED		1,927	2,199		9,903	10,728	2.00	8.33
Other countries of the World		1,927	2,199		9,903	10,728	2.00	8.33

SURINAME

1. Arrivals of non-resident tourists at national borders, by country of residence

	2007	2008	2009	2010	2011	Market share 11	% Change 11-10
TOTAL	166,685	150,711	150,628	204,519	220,475	100.00	7.80
AFRICA	225	183	171	246	290	0.13	17.89
Other Africa	225	183	171	246	290	0.13	17.89
All countries of Africa	225	183	171	246	290	0.13	17.89
AMERICAS	52,373	51,386	59,175	88,680	103,709	47.04	16.95
Caribbean	9,777	8,845	10,497	13,417	14,448	6.55	7.68
Dominican Republic	65	38	77	71	48	0.02	-32.39
Haiti	139	101	127	202	216	0.10	6.93
Trinidad and Tobago	2,527	2,374	2,567	3,972	4,862	2.21	22.41
Other countries of the Caribbean	7,046	6,332	7,726	9,172	9,322	4.23	1.64
Central America	272	489	397	504	568	0.26	12.70
All countries of Central America	272	489	397	504	568	0.26	12.70
North America	6,147	6,166	6,284	8,320	9,726	4.41	16.90
Canada	1,257	1,193	1,320	1,720	1,972	0.89	14.65
United States of America	4,890	4,973	4,964	6,600	7,754	3.52	17.48
South America	36,177	35,886	41,997	66,439	78,967	35.82	18.86
Brazil	7,627	7,488	7,840	11,158	14,427	6.54	29.30
Colombia	211	223	178	173	286	0.13	65.32
Guyana	14,298	13,445	18,753	30,446	33,010	14.97	8.42
Venezuela	322	326	287	430	474	0.21	10.23
Other countries of South America	13,719	14,404	14,939	24,232	30,770	13.96	26.98
EAST ASIA AND THE PACIFIC	2,397	2,732	1,940	3,382	4,838	2.19	43.05
North-East Asia	1,503	1,879	1,241	2,220	2,713	1.23	22.21
China	1,320	1,737	1,069	1,980	2,470	1.12	24.75
Japan	132	99	124	206	214	0.10	3.88
Korea, Republic of	51	43	48	34	29	0.01	-14.71
South-East Asia	168	198	144	252	526	0.24	108.73
Indonesia	168	198	144	252	526	0.24	108.73
Other East Asia and the Pacific	726	655	555	910	1,599	0.73	75.71
Other countries of Asia	701	647	542	824	1,441	0.65	74.88
All countries of Oceania	25	8	13	86	158	0.07	83.72
EUROPE	110,730	95,299	87,817	110,255	108,188	49.07	-1.87
Northern Europe	534	508	471	775	1,010	0.46	30.32
United Kingdom	534	508	471	775	1,010	0.46	30.32
Western Europe	109,064	93,774	86,344	108,106	105,479	47.84	-2.43
Belgium	1,254	985	1,013	1,464	1,640	0.74	12.02
France	3,516	3,976	3,794	4,455	5,222	2.37	17.22
Germany	517	433	420	609	563	0.26	-7.55
Netherlands	103,777	88,380	81,117	101,578	98,054	44.47	-3.47
Other Europe	1,132	1,017	1,002	1,374	1,699	0.77	23.65
Other countries of Europe	1,132	1,017	1,002	1,374	1,699	0.77	23.65
MIDDLE EAST	25	30	19	47	42	0.02	-10.64
All countries of Middle East	25	30	19	47	42	0.02	-10.64
SOUTH ASIA	484	551	454	556	585	0.27	5.22
India	484	551	454	556	585	0.27	5.22
NOT SPECIFIED	451	530	1,052	1,353	2,823	1.28	108.65
Other countries of the World	451	530	1,052	1,353	2,823	1.28	108.65

SWAZILAND

2. Arrivals of non-resident visitors at national borders, by country of residence

	2007	2008	2009	2010	2011	Market share 11	% Change 11-10
TOTAL	1,230,093	1,185,998	1,343,967	1,342,531	1,328,363	100.00	-1.06
AFRICA	1,075,005	1,041,211	1,191,259	1,218,054	1,225,220	92.24	0.59
East Africa	251,900	237,915	302,780	283,808	280,437	21.11	-1.19
Kenya	2,006	2,111	2,343	2,709	2,069	0.16	-23.62
Malawi	2,996	2,846	3,109	3,017	3,183	0.24	5.50
Mozambique	226,823	209,139	266,560	241,334	236,507	17.80	-2.00
Zimbabwe	9,998	14,562	19,880	24,943	26,241	1.98	5.20
United Republic of Tanzania	3,980	3,575	4,802	4,677	5,522	0.42	18.07
Zambia	6,097	5,682	6,086	7,128	6,915	0.52	-2.99
Southern Africa	810,129	790,672	875,379	920,153	931,624	70.13	1.25
Botswana	4,357	4,331	3,931	4,053	3,710	0.28	-8.46
Lesotho	5,659	5,168	4,864	4,906	3,348	0.25	-31.76
South Africa	800,113	781,173	866,584	911,194	924,566	69.60	1.47
West Africa	3,238	3,424	3,202	2,744	2,768	0.21	0.87
Nigeria	3,238	3,424	3,202	2,744	2,768	0.21	0.87
Other Africa	9,738	9,200	9,898	11,349	10,391	0.78	-8.44
Other countries of Africa	9,738	9,200	9,898	11,349	10,391	0.78	-8.44
AMERICAS	19,184	19,607	20,187	20,499	18,826	1.42	-8.16
North America	17,901	17,780	18,242	18,333	16,914	1.27	-7.74
Canada	3,393	3,359	3,317	3,192	2,696	0.20	-15.54
United States of America	14,508	14,421	14,925	15,141	14,218	1.07	-6.10
South America	628	1,065	1,234	1,085	1,041	0.08	-4.06
Brazil	628	1,065	1,234	1,085	1,041	0.08	-4.06
Other Americas	655	762	711	1,081	871	0.07	-19.43
Other countries of the Americas	655	762	711	1,081	871	0.07	-19.43
EAST ASIA AND THE PACIFIC	12,009	11,779	10,945	11,061	9,826	0.74	-11.17
North-East Asia	5,631	4,946	4,656	4,299	4,674	0.35	8.72
China	2,557	2,738	2,137	1,980	2,344	0.18	18.38
Taiwan, Province of China	1,848	1,408	1,386	1,182	1,070	0.08	-9.48
Korea, Republic of	1,226	800	1,133	1,137	1,260	0.09	10.82
South-East Asia	712	669	569	497	339	0.03	-31.79
Philippines	712	669	569	497	339	0.03	-31.79
Australasia	3,315	3,142	2,810	2,874	2,191	0.16	-23.76
Australia	3,315	3,142	2,810	2,874	2,191	0.16	-23.76
Other East Asia and the Pacific	2,351	3,022	2,910	3,391	2,622	0.20	-22.68
Other countries of Asia	2,351	3,022	2,910	3,391	2,622	0.20	-22.68
EUROPE	118,536	107,712	114,047	85,195	66,930	5.04	-21.44
Northern Europe	25,673	25,393	28,050	24,729	18,355	1.38	-25.78
Norway	1,306	894	1,056	891	725	0.05	-18.63
Sweden	2,759	2,918	2,894	2,107	1,271	0.10	-39.68
United Kingdom	21,608	21,581	24,100	21,731	16,359	1.23	-24.72
Southern Europe	10,672	10,395	11,647	11,398	9,140	0.69	-19.81
Italy	4,168	3,595	3,478	3,104	2,225	0.17	-28.32
Portugal	6,504	6,800	8,169	8,294	6,915	0.52	-16.63
Western Europe	71,085	61,375	62,334	39,797	31,494	2.37	-20.86
Belgium	5,362	5,573	7,892	3,205	3,015	0.23	-5.93
France	15,680	16,619	16,638	12,737	8,273	0.62	-35.05
Germany	24,749	19,111	15,639	11,294	10,406	0.78	-7.86
Netherlands	19,795	17,554	19,604	10,788	8,161	0.61	-24.35
Switzerland	5,499	2,518	2,561	1,773	1,639	0.12	-7.56

SWAZILAND

2. Arrivals of non-resident visitors at national borders, by country of residence

	2007	2008	2009	2010	2011	Market share 11	% Change 11-10
East Mediterranean Europe	830	705	877	713	1,058	0.08	48.39
Israel	830	705	877	713	1,058	0.08	48.39
Other Europe	10,276	9,844	11,139	8,558	6,883	0.52	-19.57
Other countries of Europe	10,276	9,844	11,139	8,558	6,883	0.52	-19.57
MIDDLE EAST			218	213	91	0.01	-57.28
Kuwait			122	63	21	0.00	-66.67
Saudi Arabia			18	4	13	0.00	225.00
United Arab Emirates			11	30	6	0.00	-80.00
Other countries of Middle East			67	116	51	0.00	-56.03
SOUTH ASIA	5,359	5,689	7,311	7,509	7,470	0.56	-0.52
India	3,449	3,252	4,339	3,970	4,103	0.31	3.35
Iran, Islamic Republic of			43	46	67	0.01	45.65
Pakistan	1,910	2,437	2,929	3,493	3,300	0.25	-5.53

SWAZILAND

3. Arrivals of non-resident tourists in hotels and similar establishments, by country of residence

	2007	2008	2009	2010	2011	Market share 11	% Change 11-10
TOTAL	**299,226**	**323,538**	**334,391**	**338,032**	**308,389**	**100.00**	**-8.77**
AFRICA	**176,417**	**186,884**	**201,585**	**257,997**	**235,377**	**76.32**	**-8.77**
East Africa	**8,413**	**12,177**	**9,613**	**15,326**	**14,000**	**4.54**	**-8.65**
Mozambique	8,413	12,177	9,613	15,326	14,000	4.54	-8.65
Southern Africa	**156,028**	**150,814**	**170,468**	**230,768**	**219,269**	**71.10**	**-4.98**
South Africa	146,605	147,639	167,520	227,986	207,981	67.44	-8.77
Other countries of Southern Africa	9,423	3,175	2,948	2,782	11,288	3.66	305.75
Other Africa	**11,976**	**23,893**	**21,504**	**11,903**	**2,108**	**0.68**	**-82.29**
Other countries of Africa	11,976	23,893	21,504	11,903	2,108	0.68	-82.29
AMERICAS	**9,832**	**21,503**	**14,105**	**19,557**	**17,114**	**5.55**	**-12.49**
Other Americas	**9,832**	**21,503**	**14,105**	**19,557**	**17,114**	**5.55**	**-12.49**
All countries of the Americas	9,832	21,503	14,105	19,557	17,114	5.55	-12.49
EAST ASIA AND THE PACIFIC	**8,044**	**12,035**	**13,196**	**6,158**	**5,618**	**1.82**	**-8.77**
Australasia	**2,120**	**2,197**	**2,423**	**1,717**	**1,566**	**0.51**	**-8.79**
Australia	2,120	2,197	2,423	1,717	1,566	0.51	-8.79
Other East Asia and the Pacific	**5,924**	**9,838**	**10,773**	**4,441**	**4,052**	**1.31**	**-8.76**
Other countries of Asia	5,924	9,838	10,773	4,441	4,052	1.31	-8.76
EUROPE	**92,332**	**103,116**	**105,505**	**54,320**	**49,553**	**16.07**	**-8.78**
Northern Europe	**11,684**	**9,300**	**13,351**	**10,780**	**9,834**	**3.19**	**-8.78**
United Kingdom	11,684	9,300	13,351	10,780	9,834	3.19	-8.78
Southern Europe	**10,674**						
Portugal	10,674						
Other Europe	**69,974**	**93,816**	**92,154**	**43,540**	**39,719**	**12.88**	**-8.78**
Other countries of Europe	69,974	93,816	92,154	43,540	39,719	12.88	-8.78
NOT SPECIFIED	**12,601**				**727**	**0.24**	
Other countries of the World	12,601				727	0.24	

SWEDEN

2. Arrivals of non-resident visitors at national borders, by country of residence

		2007	2008	2009	2010	2011	Market share 11	% Change 11-10
TOTAL	(*)					16,678,000	100.00	
AFRICA						44,000	0.26	
Other Africa						44,000	0.26	
All countries of Africa						44,000	0.26	
AMERICAS						650,000	3.90	
North America						552,000	3.31	
Canada						66,000	0.40	
United States of America						486,000	2.91	
Other Americas						98,000	0.59	
Other countries of the Americas						98,000	0.59	
EAST ASIA AND THE PACIFIC						311,000	1.86	
Other East Asia and the Pacific						311,000	1.86	
All countries of Asia						215,000	1.29	
All countries of Oceania						96,000	0.58	
EUROPE						15,582,000	93.43	
Central/Eastern Europe						2,381,000	14.28	
All countries Central/East Europe						2,381,000	14.28	
Northern Europe						10,751,000	64.46	
Denmark						3,694,000	22.15	
Finland						2,728,000	16.36	
Norway						3,743,000	22.44	
United Kingdom						586,000	3.51	
Western Europe						2,414,000	14.47	
France						254,000	1.52	
Germany						1,796,000	10.77	
Netherlands						364,000	2.18	
Other Europe						36,000	0.22	
Other countries of Europe						36,000	0.22	
MIDDLE EAST						45,000	0.27	
All countries of Middle East						45,000	0.27	
SOUTH ASIA						44,000	0.26	
All countries of South Asia						44,000	0.26	
NOT SPECIFIED						2,000	0.01	
Other countries of the World						2,000	0.01	

SWEDEN

3. Arrivals of non-resident tourists in hotels and similar establishments, by country of residence

	2007	2008	2009	2010	2011	Market share 11	% Change 11-10
TOTAL	2,993,161	2,944,161	3,044,347	3,284,613	3,370,310	100.00	2.61
AMERICAS	248,973	226,141	200,876	244,812	259,294	7.69	5.92
North America	231,604	207,880	183,915	220,526	227,311	6.74	3.08
Canada	17,247	20,716	16,853	20,347	21,399	0.63	5.17
United States of America	214,357	187,164	167,062	200,179	205,912	6.11	2.86
Other Americas	17,369	18,261	16,961	24,286	31,983	0.95	31.69
Other countries of the Americas	17,369	18,261	16,961	24,286	31,983	0.95	31.69
EAST ASIA AND THE PACIFIC	187,426	196,598	163,802	198,254	237,675	7.05	19.88
North-East Asia	112,921	102,046	93,959	109,934	126,528	3.75	15.09
China	54,573	45,343	42,739	52,201	69,226	2.05	32.61
Japan	49,692	47,731	43,039	46,286	44,416	1.32	-4.04
Korea, Republic of	8,656	8,972	8,181	11,447	12,886	0.38	12.57
Australasia	19,100	21,838	18,456	21,944	22,941	0.68	4.54
Australia	16,432	18,747	16,332	19,878	20,763	0.62	4.45
New Zealand	2,668	3,091	2,124	2,066	2,178	0.06	5.42
Other East Asia and the Pacific	55,405	72,714	51,387	66,376	88,206	2.62	32.89
Other countries of Asia	55,405	72,714	51,387	66,376	88,206	2.62	32.89
EUROPE	2,258,232	2,288,461	2,421,540	2,521,029	2,459,976	72.99	-2.42
Central/Eastern Europe	167,232	183,208	189,146	179,559	179,833	5.34	0.15
Czech Republic	11,360	10,560	9,897	11,314	11,618	0.34	2.69
Estonia	8,360	9,224	9,608	11,969	11,271	0.33	-5.83
Hungary	9,636	8,317	9,582	8,274	9,811	0.29	18.58
Latvia	5,389	6,618	10,574	6,877	7,468	0.22	8.59
Lithuania	4,995	5,804	13,456	7,677	8,140	0.24	6.03
Poland	34,885	42,881	51,701	36,894	43,873	1.30	18.92
Russian Federation	89,976	96,148	77,655	92,395	83,604	2.48	-9.51
Slovakia	2,631	3,656	6,673	4,159	4,048	0.12	-2.67
Northern Europe	1,126,858	1,165,610	1,263,558	1,308,856	1,254,600	37.23	-4.15
Denmark	189,956	214,057	285,185	273,437	247,121	7.33	-9.62
Finland	155,137	159,670	173,405	185,440	171,935	5.10	-7.28
Iceland	10,584	7,686	6,060	7,923	7,159	0.21	-9.64
Ireland	16,704	15,881	13,488	11,918	14,563	0.43	22.19
Norway	465,074	480,897	528,083	566,916	552,421	16.39	-2.56
United Kingdom	289,403	287,419	257,337	263,222	261,401	7.76	-0.69
Southern Europe	207,232	198,200	225,569	228,353	215,510	6.39	-5.62
Greece	12,684	12,121	12,230	11,389	10,352	0.31	-9.11
Italy	106,141	105,344	130,668	127,241	120,853	3.59	-5.02
Portugal	7,951	10,778	9,134	9,627	9,555	0.28	-0.75
Spain	80,456	69,957	73,537	80,096	74,750	2.22	-6.67
Western Europe	657,713	662,997	684,771	755,932	758,930	22.52	0.40
Austria	23,050	27,238	31,219	35,835	42,322	1.26	18.10
Belgium	35,115	33,274	35,719	40,554	42,877	1.27	5.73
France	85,044	94,479	97,857	107,588	104,211	3.09	-3.14
Germany	376,179	367,632	373,038	407,418	404,026	11.99	-0.83
Luxembourg	2,836	3,308	3,346	3,496	3,675	0.11	5.12
Netherlands	83,725	86,463	87,303	95,210	95,055	2.82	-0.16
Switzerland	51,764	50,603	56,289	65,831	66,764	1.98	1.42
East Mediterranean Europe	7,888	9,888	7,938	9,599	10,081	0.30	5.02
Turkey	7,888	9,888	7,938	9,599	10,081	0.30	5.02
Other Europe	91,309	68,558	50,558	38,730	41,022	1.22	5.92
Other countries of Europe	91,309	68,558	50,558	38,730	41,022	1.22	5.92
NOT SPECIFIED	298,530	232,961	258,129	320,518	413,365	12.26	28.97
Other countries of the World	298,530	232,961	258,129	320,518	413,365	12.26	28.97

SWEDEN

4. Arrivals of non-resident tourists in all types of accommodation establishments, by country of residence

	2007	2008	2009	2010	2011	Market share 11	% Change 11-10
TOTAL	5,223,655	4,554,936	4,678,402	4,951,122	5,005,825	100.00	1.10
AMERICAS	260,141	239,202	212,567	257,437	272,807	5.45	5.97
North America	240,422	218,089	193,153	230,018	236,819	4.73	2.96
Canada	19,166	23,059	18,882	22,581	23,374	0.47	3.51
United States of America	221,256	195,030	174,271	207,437	213,445	4.26	2.90
Other Americas	19,719	21,113	19,414	27,419	35,988	0.72	31.25
Other countries of the Americas	19,719	21,113	19,414	27,419	35,988	0.72	31.25
EAST ASIA AND THE PACIFIC	199,248	216,443	182,862	216,885	257,236	5.14	18.60
North-East Asia	118,126	109,151	101,555	116,496	133,713	2.67	14.78
China	56,809	49,229	47,011	55,548	73,331	1.46	32.01
Japan	51,771	50,020	45,549	48,377	46,718	0.93	-3.43
Korea, Republic of	9,546	9,902	8,995	12,571	13,664	0.27	8.69
Australasia	22,871	26,838	22,368	26,372	27,080	0.54	2.68
Australia	19,650	23,038	19,703	23,771	24,434	0.49	2.79
New Zealand	3,221	3,800	2,665	2,601	2,646	0.05	1.73
Other East Asia and the Pacific	58,251	80,454	58,939	74,017	96,443	1.93	30.30
Other countries of Asia	58,251	80,454	58,939	74,017	96,443	1.93	30.30
EUROPE	4,424,536	3,847,867	4,005,127	4,143,159	4,048,017	80.87	-2.30
Central/Eastern Europe	225,793	237,691	241,560	232,753	245,017	4.89	5.27
Czech Republic	14,829	16,260	14,404	15,711	17,056	0.34	8.56
Estonia	11,966	12,902	12,320	17,151	17,041	0.34	-0.64
Hungary	10,599	10,608	11,296	9,849	11,052	0.22	12.21
Latvia	7,781	9,716	13,359	11,791	11,947	0.24	1.32
Lithuania	8,980	8,751	16,400	12,863	14,763	0.29	14.77
Poland	75,010	72,469	80,607	59,875	76,542	1.53	27.84
Russian Federation	93,163	101,863	82,499	99,613	91,120	1.82	-8.53
Slovakia	3,465	5,122	10,675	5,900	5,496	0.11	-6.85
Northern Europe	2,078,810	2,000,824	2,161,939	2,264,641	2,174,404	43.44	-3.98
Denmark	420,183	418,369	519,792	488,207	412,303	8.24	-15.55
Finland	214,347	198,775	213,152	225,682	211,278	4.22	-6.38
Iceland	11,245	8,403	6,636	8,817	7,897	0.16	-10.43
Ireland	18,508	17,755	14,776	15,220	18,106	0.36	18.96
Norway	1,102,167	1,042,636	1,128,207	1,238,771	1,238,971	24.75	0.02
United Kingdom	312,360	314,886	279,376	287,944	285,849	5.71	-0.73
Southern Europe	246,019	232,966	254,502	256,180	242,983	4.85	-5.15
Greece	13,096	12,748	12,852	12,041	11,072	0.22	-8.05
Italy	135,185	123,977	148,798	143,673	136,170	2.72	-5.22
Portugal	8,745	15,995	11,039	11,513	11,421	0.23	-0.80
Spain	88,993	80,246	81,813	88,953	84,320	1.68	-5.21
Western Europe	1,695,300	1,261,002	1,254,487	1,325,184	1,318,307	26.34	-0.52
Austria	26,991	32,291	36,883	46,735	53,520	1.07	14.52
Belgium	38,284	36,467	39,181	50,599	52,145	1.04	3.06
France	128,448	123,584	126,640	136,683	135,116	2.70	-1.15
Germany	1,045,616	738,470	727,792	749,480	752,248	15.03	0.37
Luxembourg	3,081	3,629	3,491	3,941	4,106	0.08	4.19
Netherlands	333,933	249,630	236,199	239,601	219,626	4.39	-8.34
Switzerland	118,947	76,931	84,301	98,145	101,546	2.03	3.47
East Mediterranean Europe	8,275	10,684	8,836	10,538	10,799	0.22	2.48
Turkey	8,275	10,684	8,836	10,538	10,799	0.22	2.48
Other Europe	170,339	104,700	83,803	53,863	56,507	1.13	4.91
Other countries of Europe	170,339	104,700	83,803	53,863	56,507	1.13	4.91
NOT SPECIFIED	339,730	251,424	277,846	333,641	427,765	8.55	28.21
Other countries of the World	339,730	251,424	277,846	333,641	427,765	8.55	28.21

SWEDEN

5. Overnight stays of non-resident tourists in hotels and similar establishments, by country of residence

		2007	2008	2009	2010	2011	Market share 11	% Change 11-10
TOTAL	(*)	5,841,769	5,830,414	6,087,096	6,363,074	6,553,766	100.00	3.00
AMERICAS		485,084	447,436	401,648	474,260	511,515	7.80	7.86
North America		451,043	411,192	367,735	427,211	444,000	6.77	3.93
Canada		33,849	41,111	33,698	39,417	41,468	0.63	5.20
United States of America		417,194	370,081	334,037	387,794	402,532	6.14	3.80
South America			12,362	13,730	22,459	26,047	0.40	15.98
Brazil			12,362	13,730	22,459	26,047	0.40	15.98
Other Americas		34,041	23,882	20,183	24,590	41,468	0.63	68.64
Other countries of the Americas		34,041	23,882	20,183	24,590	35,311	0.54	43.60
EAST ASIA AND THE PACIFIC		367,524	349,226	290,423	339,085	394,162	6.01	16.24
North-East Asia		220,880	201,999	187,869	212,967	245,850	3.75	15.44
China		106,763	89,731	85,456	101,125	134,051	2.05	32.56
Japan		97,214	94,545	86,055	89,667	86,547	1.32	-3.48
Korea, Republic of		16,903	17,723	16,358	22,175	25,252	0.39	13.88
Australasia		37,276	43,219	36,902	42,512	44,311	0.68	4.23
Australia		32,067	37,064	32,656	38,509	40,121	0.61	4.19
New Zealand		5,209	6,155	4,246	4,003	4,190	0.06	4.67
Other East Asia and the Pacific		109,368	104,008	65,652	83,606	104,001	1.59	24.39
Other countries of Asia		109,368	104,008	65,652	83,606	104,001	1.59	24.39
EUROPE		4,402,298	4,531,093	4,841,808	4,883,830	4,783,843	72.99	-2.05
Central/Eastern Europe		328,467	372,865	389,877	363,460	370,455	5.65	1.92
Bulgaria			2,848	3,657	4,496	4,943	0.08	9.94
Czech Republic		22,416	20,996	19,788	21,918	22,816	0.35	4.10
Estonia		16,421	18,298	19,210	23,186	22,074	0.34	-4.80
Hungary		18,924	16,521	19,159	16,029	19,237	0.29	20.01
Latvia		10,610	13,178	21,143	13,323	14,599	0.22	9.58
Lithuania		9,837	11,503	26,905	14,872	16,020	0.24	7.72
Poland		68,569	85,165	103,375	71,472	86,063	1.31	20.41
Romania			6,251	8,029	11,116	13,414	0.20	20.67
Russian Federation		176,484	190,837	155,269	178,991	163,335	2.49	-8.75
Slovakia		5,206	7,268	13,342	8,057	7,954	0.12	-1.28
Northern Europe		2,195,120	2,308,336	2,526,451	2,535,563	2,437,570	37.19	-3.86
Denmark		371,015	424,351	570,220	529,712	477,879	7.29	-9.79
Finland		302,966	316,162	346,719	359,242	335,730	5.12	-6.54
Iceland		20,706	15,319	12,116	15,348	13,725	0.21	-10.57
Ireland		32,886	31,555	26,969	23,088	28,045	0.43	21.47
Norway		898,190	950,086	1,055,889	1,098,250	1,076,457	16.43	-1.98
United Kingdom		569,357	570,863	514,538	509,923	505,734	7.72	-0.82
Southern Europe		402,691	395,396	458,961	447,732	426,020	6.50	-4.85
Greece		24,711	24,001	24,454	22,064	19,989	0.31	-9.40
Italy		206,495	208,562	261,268	246,496	236,411	3.61	-4.09
Malta			651	1,937	1,650	2,027	0.03	22.85
Portugal		15,555	21,338	18,264	18,650	18,581	0.28	-0.37
Slovenia			2,206	6,003	3,708	3,912	0.06	5.50
Spain		155,930	138,638	147,035	155,164	145,100	2.21	-6.49
Western Europe		1,280,983	1,310,833	1,369,182	1,464,420	1,475,156	22.51	0.73
Austria		45,082	53,881	62,421	69,421	82,089	1.25	18.25
Belgium		68,958	65,974	71,419	78,563	81,674	1.25	3.96
France		167,208	187,169	195,663	208,424	202,580	3.09	-2.80
Germany		729,627	725,778	745,879	789,265	787,890	12.02	-0.17
Luxembourg		5,551	6,593	6,691	6,773	7,110	0.11	4.98
Netherlands		163,710	171,240	174,560	184,444	185,238	2.83	0.43
Switzerland		100,847	100,198	112,549	127,530	128,575	1.96	0.82

SWEDEN

5. Overnight stays of non-resident tourists in hotels and similar establishments, by country of residence

	2007	2008	2009	2010	2011	Market share 11	% Change 11-10
East Mediterranean Europe	15,565	21,071	17,829	20,051	21,626	0.33	7.85
Cyprus		1,387	1,958	1,455	2,067	0.03	42.06
Turkey	15,565	19,684	15,871	18,596	19,559	0.30	5.18
Other Europe	179,472	122,592	79,508	52,604	53,016	0.81	0.78
Other countries of Europe	179,472	122,592	79,508	52,604	53,016	0.81	0.78
SOUTH ASIA		40,376	37,095	44,981	64,639	0.99	43.70
India		40,376	37,095	44,981	64,639	0.99	43.70
NOT SPECIFIED	586,863	462,283	516,122	620,918	805,764	12.29	29.77
Other countries of the World	586,863	462,283	516,122	620,918	805,764	12.29	29.77

SWEDEN

6. Overnight stays of non-resident tourists in all types of accommodation establishments, by country of residence

		2007	2008	2009	2010	2011	Market share 11	% Change 11-10
TOTAL	(*)	11,200,371	12,495,002	12,872,513	12,802,832	12,896,004	100.00	0.73
AMERICAS		518,974	484,970	436,557	512,699	547,029	4.24	6.70
North America		477,698	440,770	395,329	456,360	473,687	3.67	3.80
Canada		39,754	47,617	39,725	46,579	47,413	0.37	1.79
United States of America		437,944	393,153	355,604	409,781	426,274	3.31	4.02
South America					27,746	33,573	0.26	21.00
Brazil					27,746	33,573	0.26	21.00
Other Americas		41,276	44,200	41,228	28,593	39,769	0.31	39.09
Other countries of the Americas		41,276	44,200	41,228	28,593	39,769	0.31	39.09
EAST ASIA AND THE PACIFIC		404,942	445,370	383,393	380,880	440,362	3.41	15.62
North-East Asia		237,594	222,226	210,077	232,317	267,679	2.08	15.22
China		113,871	100,819	97,950	111,126	146,647	1.14	31.96
Japan		103,719	100,991	93,433	95,764	93,440	0.72	-2.43
Korea, Republic of		20,004	20,416	18,694	25,427	27,592	0.21	8.51
Australasia		48,965	57,408	48,667	55,499	56,789	0.44	2.32
Australia		42,044	49,295	42,869	49,947	51,202	0.40	2.51
New Zealand		6,921	8,113	5,798	5,552	5,587	0.04	0.63
Other East Asia and the Pacific		118,383	165,736	124,649	93,064	115,894	0.90	24.53
Other countries of Asia		118,383	165,736	124,649	93,064	115,894	0.90	24.53
EUROPE		9,599,039	10,927,210	11,466,606	11,182,645	10,975,321	85.11	-1.85
Central/Eastern Europe		494,233	524,965	595,374	588,742	640,470	4.97	8.79
Bulgaria					6,482	7,510	0.06	15.86
Czech Republic		33,077	37,009	34,183	37,528	42,578	0.33	13.46
Estonia		27,648	28,661	46,760	54,609	49,946	0.39	-8.54
Hungary		21,957	22,931	24,722	20,781	23,100	0.18	11.16
Latvia		18,250	21,843	36,179	33,086	32,145	0.25	-2.84
Lithuania		21,909	19,828	34,227	31,226	37,551	0.29	20.26
Poland		176,221	176,921	202,070	151,466	207,042	1.61	36.69
Romania					15,455	19,381	0.15	25.40
Russian Federation		187,239	206,394	192,284	225,015	208,864	1.62	-7.18
Slovakia		7,932	11,378	24,949	13,094	12,353	0.10	-5.66
Northern Europe		4,887,877	5,610,662	6,119,642	5,896,321	5,645,685	43.78	-4.25
Denmark		953,890	1,348,399	1,620,559	1,538,968	1,278,234	9.91	-16.94
Finland		418,957	475,634	521,606	527,349	503,176	3.90	-4.58
Iceland		22,658	17,675	14,005	18,225	16,199	0.13	-11.12
Ireland		38,786	36,709	30,917	32,862	39,039	0.30	18.80
Norway		2,817,122	3,084,018	3,332,729	3,176,610	3,212,709	24.91	1.14
United Kingdom		636,464	648,227	599,826	602,307	596,328	4.62	-0.99
Southern Europe		491,181	491,745	537,056	533,667	514,516	3.99	-3.59
Greece		26,009	25,778	26,338	24,035	22,142	0.17	-7.88
Italy		264,361	262,240	315,110	296,578	284,754	2.21	-3.99
Malta					1,879	2,558	0.02	36.14
Portugal		18,124	36,112	23,838	24,132	24,508	0.19	1.56
Slovenia					4,915	5,842	0.05	18.86
Spain		182,687	167,615	171,770	182,128	174,712	1.35	-4.07
Western Europe		3,415,721	4,040,355	3,990,862	4,050,886	4,061,834	31.50	0.27
Austria		56,750	68,266	85,106	106,959	121,565	0.94	13.66
Belgium		78,728	74,894	84,331	113,525	115,890	0.90	2.08
France		258,632	270,828	281,848	297,748	298,242	2.31	0.17
Germany		2,108,213	2,690,148	2,619,562	2,598,505	2,650,084	20.55	1.98
Luxembourg		6,281	7,689	7,755	8,441	8,542	0.07	1.20
Netherlands		698,625	750,975	704,576	685,834	624,255	4.84	-8.98
Switzerland		208,492	177,555	207,684	239,874	243,256	1.89	1.41

SWEDEN

6. Overnight stays of non-resident tourists in all types of accommodation establishments, by country of residence

	2007	2008	2009	2010	2011	Market share 11	% Change 11-10
East Mediterranean Europe	16,822	21,790	18,447	22,923	23,872	0.19	4.14
Cyprus				1,610	2,177	0.02	35.22
Turkey	16,822	21,790	18,447	21,313	21,695	0.17	1.79
Other Europe	293,205	237,693	205,225	90,106	88,944	0.69	-1.29
Other countries of Europe	293,205	237,693	205,225	90,106	88,944	0.69	-1.29
SOUTH ASIA				57,789	77,862	0.60	34.73
India				57,789	77,862	0.60	34.73
NOT SPECIFIED	677,416	637,452	585,957	668,819	855,430	6.63	27.90
Other countries of the World	677,416	637,452	585,957	668,819	855,430	6.63	27.90

SWITZERLAND

3. Arrivals of non-resident tourists in hotels and similar establishments, by country of residence

		2007	2008	2009	2010	2011	Market share 11	% Change 11-10
TOTAL	(*)	8,447,718	8,608,337	8,293,918	8,628,284	8,534,305	100.00	-1.09
AFRICA		85,463	88,625	79,919	77,745	74,107	0.87	-4.68
North Africa		21,041	19,755	17,881	15,931	15,931	0.19	
All countries of North Africa	(*)	21,041	19,755	17,881	15,931	15,931	0.19	
Southern Africa		27,193	26,897	20,263	22,695	23,457	0.27	3.36
South Africa		27,193	26,897	20,263	22,695	23,457	0.27	3.36
Other Africa		37,229	41,973	41,775	39,119	34,719	0.41	-11.25
Other countries of Africa		37,229	41,973	41,775	39,119	34,719	0.41	-11.25
AMERICAS		954,115	878,356	820,495	916,493	924,383	10.83	0.86
North America		821,800	746,720	701,100	778,988	768,470	9.00	-1.35
Canada		94,413	94,844	91,222	98,772	99,509	1.17	0.75
United States of America		727,387	651,876	609,878	680,216	668,961	7.84	-1.65
South America		94,543	96,715	91,213	105,286	120,704	1.41	14.64
Argentina		11,546	10,962	11,359	12,957	14,634	0.17	12.94
Brazil		56,204	59,662	55,991	66,845	79,080	0.93	18.30
Chile		4,524	4,530	4,299	4,655	5,472	0.06	17.55
Other countries of South America		22,269	21,561	19,564	20,829	21,518	0.25	3.31
Other Americas		37,772	34,921	28,182	32,219	35,209	0.41	9.28
Other countries of the Americas		37,772	34,921	28,182	32,219	35,209	0.41	9.28
EAST ASIA AND THE PACIFIC		941,200	860,776	893,139	1,096,300	1,322,811	15.50	20.66
North-East Asia		651,652	558,075	600,652	761,743	951,757	11.15	24.94
China		145,921	129,176	187,138	286,420	452,724	5.30	58.06
Taiwan, Province of China		38,928	32,593	29,367	37,600	56,767	0.67	50.98
Hong Kong, China		29,301	26,676	37,125	46,051	50,610	0.59	9.90
Japan		324,554	277,657	275,505	297,562	275,923	3.23	-7.27
Korea, Republic of		112,948	91,973	71,517	94,110	115,733	1.36	22.98
South-East Asia		149,124	168,583	173,649	196,967	226,663	2.66	15.08
Indonesia		11,284	11,049	15,930	19,660	30,691	0.36	56.11
Malaysia		16,858	15,793	15,429	21,618	25,557	0.30	18.22
Philippines		3,835	3,825	4,736	6,214	7,499	0.09	20.68
Singapore		26,762	42,268	52,171	51,431	55,310	0.65	7.54
Thailand		36,225	44,879	44,680	51,907	56,919	0.67	9.66
Other countries of South-East Asia		54,160	50,769	40,703	46,137	50,687	0.59	9.86
Other East Asia and the Pacific		140,424	134,118	118,838	137,590	144,391	1.69	4.94
Other countries of Asia		26,103	19,311	19,262	22,598	22,585	0.26	-0.06
All countries of Oceania		114,321	114,807	99,576	114,992	121,806	1.43	5.93
EUROPE		6,225,587	6,520,802	6,249,760	6,237,359	5,867,915	68.76	-5.92
Central/Eastern Europe		332,439	372,432	367,959	389,001	412,380	4.83	6.01
Bulgaria		15,503	17,530	15,632	14,970	14,449	0.17	-3.48
Belarus		4,257	4,480	5,236	6,254	5,932	0.07	-5.15
Czech Republic		34,618	42,045	40,060	42,106	42,803	0.50	1.66
Hungary		31,675	32,475	34,351	35,030	33,746	0.40	-3.67
Poland		45,775	50,325	46,920	51,020	49,148	0.58	-3.67
Romania		33,108	40,596	30,153	30,561	30,523	0.36	-0.12
Russian Federation		114,765	130,853	145,751	157,085	179,168	2.10	14.06
Slovakia		12,288	12,658	12,128	11,634	12,323	0.14	5.92
Ukraine		17,019	20,100	21,125	23,338	25,305	0.30	8.43
Baltic countries		23,431	21,370	16,603	17,003	18,983	0.22	11.65
Northern Europe		1,097,062	1,105,124	950,924	997,306	942,073	11.04	-5.54
Denmark		59,356	62,708	59,504	59,916	57,611	0.68	-3.85
Finland		35,480	38,243	38,736	40,149	38,342	0.45	-4.50
Iceland		6,381	7,210	5,531	4,689	5,020	0.06	7.06
Ireland		38,554	38,772	32,018	30,499	28,805	0.34	-5.55

SWITZERLAND

3. Arrivals of non-resident tourists in hotels and similar establishments, by country of residence

	2007	2008	2009	2010	2011	Market share 11	% Change 11-10
Norway	38,458	41,250	39,427	44,873	43,975	0.52	-2.00
Sweden	84,050	91,222	84,299	85,130	86,203	1.01	1.26
United Kingdom	834,783	825,719	691,409	732,050	682,117	7.99	-6.82
Southern Europe	**881,321**	**904,821**	**885,438**	**863,876**	**837,513**	**9.81**	**-3.05**
Croatia	10,711	11,772	11,183	10,369	9,717	0.11	-6.29
Greece	50,023	49,724	51,162	44,591	41,097	0.48	-7.84
Italy	542,201	552,953	546,564	520,542	489,182	5.73	-6.02
Portugal	44,100	53,075	43,061	44,723	46,284	0.54	3.49
Serbia				10,179	11,025	0.13	8.31
Slovenia	11,222	10,926	10,902	12,161	11,105	0.13	-8.68
Spain	211,692	215,365	212,622	221,311	229,103	2.68	3.52
Serbia and Montenegro	11,372	11,006	9,944				
Western Europe	**3,700,977**	**3,917,745**	**3,861,998**	**3,815,056**	**3,515,558**	**41.19**	**-7.85**
Austria	175,683	189,159	187,528	195,190	190,153	2.23	-2.58
Belgium	227,719	246,741	241,830	240,784	215,240	2.52	-10.61
France	634,305	670,663	685,842	700,578	680,932	7.98	-2.80
Germany	2,249,431	2,344,337	2,294,411	2,237,941	2,038,680	23.89	-8.90
Liechtenstein	11,725	12,942	12,180	13,044	12,398	0.15	-4.95
Luxembourg	39,121	41,344	43,254	44,480	40,563	0.48	-8.81
Netherlands	362,993	412,559	396,953	383,039	337,592	3.96	-11.86
East Mediterranean Europe	**94,932**	**101,987**	**93,046**	**97,011**	**100,949**	**1.18**	**4.06**
Israel	64,540	64,099	61,915	61,183	64,756	0.76	5.84
Turkey	30,392	37,888	31,131	35,828	36,193	0.42	1.02
Other Europe	**118,856**	**118,693**	**90,395**	**75,109**	**59,442**	**0.70**	**-20.86**
Other countries of Europe	118,856	118,693	90,395	75,109	59,442	0.70	-20.86
MIDDLE EAST	**108,957**	**127,671**	**114,283**	**134,388**	**144,465**	**1.69**	**7.50**
Egypt	11,796	12,074	11,548	11,430	11,423	0.13	-0.06
Other countries of Middle East	97,161	115,597	102,735	122,958	133,042	1.56	8.20
SOUTH ASIA	**132,396**	**132,107**	**136,322**	**165,999**	**200,624**	**2.35**	**20.86**
India	132,396	132,107	136,322	165,999	200,624	2.35	20.86

SWITZERLAND

5. Overnight stays of non-resident tourists in hotels and similar establishments, by country of residence

		2007	2008	2009	2010	2011	Market share 11	% Change 11-10
TOTAL	(*)	20,917,735	21,508,296	20,164,425	20,442,508	19,733,889	100.00	-3.47
AFRICA		258,960	260,608	232,588	228,776	243,150	1.23	6.28
North Africa		70,438	64,927	52,474	46,627	51,124	0.26	9.64
All countries of North Africa	(*)	70,438	64,927	52,474	46,627	51,124	0.26	9.64
Southern Africa		78,020	80,286	60,549	63,678	67,438	0.34	5.90
South Africa		78,020	80,286	60,549	63,678	67,438	0.34	5.90
Other Africa		110,502	115,395	119,565	118,471	124,588	0.63	5.16
Other countries of Africa		110,502	115,395	119,565	118,471	124,588	0.63	5.16
AMERICAS		2,224,548	2,081,131	1,908,158	2,086,735	2,115,099	10.72	1.36
North America		1,879,993	1,731,779	1,590,209	1,731,575	1,720,268	8.72	-0.65
Canada		215,064	213,403	207,353	225,140	228,137	1.16	1.33
United States of America		1,664,929	1,518,376	1,382,856	1,506,435	1,492,131	7.56	-0.95
South America		245,539	259,360	240,950	269,240	305,527	1.55	13.48
Argentina		32,403	31,129	31,573	33,417	37,851	0.19	13.27
Brazil		142,821	159,058	144,977	168,771	194,492	0.99	15.24
Chile		11,746	12,333	12,063	11,737	13,898	0.07	18.41
Other countries of South America		58,569	56,840	52,337	55,315	59,286	0.30	7.18
Other Americas		99,016	89,992	76,999	85,920	89,304	0.45	3.94
Other countries of the Americas		99,016	89,992	76,999	85,920	89,304	0.45	3.94
EAST ASIA AND THE PACIFIC		1,702,909	1,612,342	1,591,816	1,890,570	2,186,602	11.08	15.66
North-East Asia		1,056,667	944,841	958,220	1,174,915	1,399,029	7.09	19.07
China		230,180	214,349	271,717	404,218	595,264	3.02	47.26
Taiwan, Province of China		55,940	48,138	43,577	54,975	74,200	0.38	34.97
Hong Kong, China		54,770	51,077	61,506	73,207	81,956	0.42	11.95
Japan		554,861	493,901	474,720	507,138	479,743	2.43	-5.40
Korea, Republic of		160,916	137,376	106,700	135,377	167,866	0.85	24.00
South-East Asia		325,647	353,537	359,533	396,998	446,297	2.26	12.42
Indonesia		26,845	25,779	32,546	38,327	55,797	0.28	45.58
Malaysia		39,719	40,708	35,348	44,590	50,573	0.26	13.42
Philippines		13,469	14,065	14,877	17,138	18,651	0.09	8.83
Singapore		62,223	88,382	106,260	104,563	109,974	0.56	5.17
Thailand		71,954	76,200	73,278	85,851	93,402	0.47	8.80
Other countries of South-East Asia		111,437	108,403	97,224	106,529	117,900	0.60	10.67
Other East Asia and the Pacific		320,595	313,964	274,063	318,657	341,276	1.73	7.10
Other countries of Asia		67,710	58,298	56,743	65,631	70,626	0.36	7.61
All countries of Oceania		252,885	255,666	217,320	253,026	270,650	1.37	6.97
EUROPE		16,004,407	16,782,796	15,694,888	15,381,336	14,272,892	72.33	-7.21
Central/Eastern Europe		961,020	1,098,062	1,046,029	1,077,998	1,148,374	5.82	6.53
Bulgaria		38,487	41,434	37,741	38,124	38,356	0.19	0.61
Belarus		11,953	12,861	14,978	17,161	15,010	0.08	-12.53
Czech Republic		85,885	102,449	101,882	104,170	105,436	0.53	1.22
Hungary		78,387	81,665	82,413	83,597	84,364	0.43	0.92
Poland		120,286	134,238	134,546	143,288	150,097	0.76	4.75
Romania		83,726	114,351	78,822	83,536	86,785	0.44	3.89
Russian Federation		399,504	456,995	454,525	467,884	513,754	2.60	9.80
Slovakia		33,465	33,634	33,433	29,822	36,284	0.18	21.67
Ukraine		56,654	67,146	64,044	65,851	72,607	0.37	10.26
Baltic countries		52,673	53,289	43,645	44,565	45,681	0.23	2.50
Northern Europe		2,908,172	2,958,265	2,480,438	2,480,756	2,313,644	11.72	-6.74
Denmark		133,465	142,897	134,697	137,162	133,762	0.68	-2.48
Finland		82,595	93,304	96,478	97,015	95,284	0.48	-1.78
Iceland		15,696	16,386	11,983	10,966	11,494	0.06	4.81
Ireland		100,635	97,271	82,296	72,489	65,265	0.33	-9.97

SWITZERLAND

5. Overnight stays of non-resident tourists in hotels and similar establishments, by country of residence

	2007	2008	2009	2010	2011	Market share 11	% Change 11-10
Norway	93,157	100,788	93,270	108,990	104,576	0.53	-4.05
Sweden	206,729	225,918	205,494	200,577	203,516	1.03	1.47
United Kingdom	2,275,895	2,281,701	1,856,220	1,853,557	1,699,747	8.61	-8.30
Southern Europe	**1,900,426**	**1,961,676**	**1,893,828**	**1,824,961**	**1,750,731**	**8.87**	**-4.07**
Croatia	30,628	31,633	29,599	26,664	26,760	0.14	0.36
Greece	128,002	128,565	125,956	115,528	101,562	0.51	-12.09
Italy	1,133,626	1,157,902	1,137,588	1,074,447	1,007,519	5.11	-6.23
Portugal	109,279	127,719	104,800	107,642	110,019	0.56	2.21
Serbia				24,706	27,696	0.14	12.10
Slovenia	23,920	25,217	24,317	26,150	25,712	0.13	-1.67
Spain	448,248	462,132	447,181	449,824	451,463	2.29	0.36
Serbia and Montenegro	26,723	28,508	24,387				
Western Europe	**9,732,670**	**10,235,755**	**9,830,381**	**9,571,896**	**8,669,586**	**43.93**	**-9.43**
Austria	386,824	412,777	403,871	413,575	400,266	2.03	-3.22
Belgium	798,808	829,194	775,090	742,277	678,517	3.44	-8.59
France	1,367,457	1,439,158	1,433,452	1,449,278	1,394,166	7.06	-3.80
Germany	6,081,920	6,313,240	6,031,325	5,816,520	5,207,892	26.39	-10.46
Liechtenstein	25,906	29,954	26,092	26,379	26,286	0.13	-0.35
Luxembourg	123,744	130,592	134,243	134,324	115,021	0.58	-14.37
Netherlands	948,011	1,080,840	1,026,308	989,543	847,438	4.29	-14.36
East Mediterranean Europe	**246,172**	**270,814**	**238,768**	**244,468**	**252,963**	**1.28**	**3.47**
Israel	167,890	170,456	161,799	155,512	163,041	0.83	4.84
Turkey	78,282	100,358	76,969	88,956	89,922	0.46	1.09
Other Europe	**255,947**	**258,224**	**205,444**	**181,257**	**137,594**	**0.70**	**-24.09**
Other countries of Europe	255,947	258,224	205,444	181,257	137,594	0.70	-24.09
MIDDLE EAST	**389,945**	**444,119**	**412,695**	**462,239**	**455,706**	**2.31**	**-1.41**
Egypt	39,860	40,529	37,958	38,801	37,097	0.19	-4.39
Other countries of Middle East	350,085	403,590	374,737	423,438	418,609	2.12	-1.14
SOUTH ASIA	**336,966**	**327,300**	**324,280**	**392,852**	**460,440**	**2.33**	**17.20**
India	336,966	327,300	324,280	392,852	460,440	2.33	17.20

SYRIAN ARAB REPUBLIC

2. Arrivals of non-resident visitors at national borders, by nationality

		2007	2008	2009	2010	2011	Market share 11	% Change 11-10
TOTAL	(*)	5,434,253	6,950,852	7,720,795	10,969,682			
AFRICA		77,526	85,242	76,245	89,670			
North Africa		77,526	85,242	76,245	89,670			
Algeria		31,615	35,231	31,238	37,664			
Morocco		10,253	9,257	8,610	10,009			
Sudan		18,781	21,989	20,378	23,636			
Tunisia		16,877	18,765	16,019	18,361			
AMERICAS		59,584	75,375	84,293	96,601			
North America		50,886	62,773	71,523	81,839			
Canada		15,347	20,236	22,869	26,068			
United States of America		35,539	42,537	48,654	55,771			
South America		8,698	12,602	12,770	14,762			
Argentina		787	1,215	1,419	2,149			
Brazil		2,132	3,368	3,518	4,979			
Venezuela		5,779	8,019	7,833	7,634			
EAST ASIA AND THE PACIFIC		43,487	52,913	60,349	78,102			
North-East Asia		11,636	14,661	17,203	25,887			
China		4,678	6,336	8,296	12,526			
Japan		6,958	8,325	8,907	13,361			
South-East Asia		20,194	22,709	24,511	29,723			
Indonesia		17,443	18,800	19,134	21,802			
Malaysia		2,751	3,909	5,377	7,921			
Australasia		11,657	15,543	18,635	22,492			
Australia		10,597	13,896	16,867	20,349			
New Zealand		1,060	1,647	1,768	2,143			
EUROPE		731,744	904,726	1,141,584	1,959,035			
Central/Eastern Europe		66,131	81,105	94,001	99,657			
Bulgaria		4,242	4,919	4,611	5,090			
Czech Republic/Slovakia		3,135	4,348	4,476	5,190			
Hungary		3,718	4,800	4,204	4,237			
Poland		3,347	3,540	8,123	8,736			
Romania		3,829	5,328	5,469	6,131			
Ukraine		3,941	4,701	4,720	6,201			
USSR (former)		43,919	53,469	62,398	64,072			
Northern Europe		47,464	70,282	86,172	105,065			
Denmark		7,559	12,289	14,489	17,899			
Norway		2,886	4,556	5,513	7,709			
Sweden		14,280	21,807	27,137	31,412			
United Kingdom		22,739	31,630	39,033	48,045			
Southern Europe		39,617	56,465	67,943	83,529			
Greece		6,065	7,195	8,091	7,415			
Italy		13,812	24,871	33,331	44,608			
Spain		15,332	18,625	21,661	25,763			
Yugoslavia, SFR (former)		4,408	5,774	4,860	5,743			
Western Europe		86,771	125,384	150,393	201,223			
Austria		4,523	6,494	7,878	10,970			
Belgium		4,669	6,818	8,440	10,621			
France		28,828	40,487	51,086	68,515			
Germany		35,123	53,301	60,146	80,804			
Netherlands		9,397	12,627	15,936	21,206			
Switzerland		4,231	5,657	6,907	9,107			

SYRIAN ARAB REPUBLIC

2. Arrivals of non-resident visitors at national borders, by nationality

	2007	2008	2009	2010	2011	Market share 11	% Change 11-10
East Mediterranean Europe	491,761	571,490	743,075	1,469,561			
Cyprus	5,808	8,658	9,943	9,981			
Turkey	485,953	562,832	733,132	1,459,580			
MIDDLE EAST	3,123,927	4,390,535	4,711,686	6,191,855			
Bahrain	64,476	65,808	75,695	80,382			
Palestine	86,359	92,751	51,687	35,520			
Iraq	(*)	889,463	894,477	1,006,434			
Jordan	914,822	1,044,564	1,062,990	1,949,551			
Kuwait	110,388	126,977	146,724	134,255			
Lebanon	1,448,809	1,587,115	1,815,003	2,291,802			
Libya	22,434	31,749	30,433	35,967			
Oman	10,231	13,650	11,592	13,822			
Qatar	17,249	18,001	19,267	17,357			
Saudi Arabia	353,103	403,140	476,346	484,087			
United Arab Emirates	33,641	45,187	52,536	57,064			
Egypt	37,675	45,060	49,092	56,771			
Yemen	18,345	22,519	21,747	24,570			
Other countries of Middle East	6,395	4,551	4,097	4,273			
SOUTH ASIA	355,530	388,819	499,183	961,342			
Afghanistan	1,010	1,090	1,432	4,229			
India	11,490	14,619	20,984	31,056			
Iran, Islamic Republic of	330,369	361,605	455,012	891,807			
Pakistan	12,661	11,505	21,755	34,250			
NOT SPECIFIED	1,042,455	1,053,242	1,147,455	1,593,077			
Other countries of the World	81,805	94,504	82,518	80,017			
Nationals Residing Abroad	960,650	958,738	1,064,937	1,513,060			

SYRIAN ARAB REPUBLIC

3. Arrivals of non-resident tourists in hotels and similar establishments, by nationality

		2007	2008	2009	2010	2011	Market share 11	% Change 11-10
TOTAL	(*)	1,406,615	1,868,654	2,068,935	2,756,635			
AFRICA		42,993	47,414	42,409	50,167			
North Africa		42,993	47,414	42,409	50,167			
Algeria		22,653	25,244	21,762	24,108			
Morocco		4,135	3,734	3,822	5,619			
Sudan		7,103	8,316	8,132	10,575			
Tunisia		9,102	10,120	8,693	9,865			
AMERICAS		25,606	33,401	38,723	50,849			
North America		18,722	23,381	28,790	41,994			
Canada		7,980	10,523	11,516	10,960			
United States of America		10,742	12,858	17,274	31,034			
South America		6,884	10,020	9,933	8,855			
Argentina		653	1,008	1,150	1,335			
Brazil		1,897	2,998	3,002	3,219			
Venezuela		4,334	6,014	5,781	4,301			
EAST ASIA AND THE PACIFIC		31,857	38,274	43,456	49,473			
North-East Asia		9,610	12,045	13,669	17,535			
China		3,465	4,693	6,243	8,521			
Japan		6,145	7,352	7,426	9,014			
South-East Asia		16,340	18,311	19,451	18,180			
Indonesia		14,303	15,416	15,451	13,182			
Malaysia		2,037	2,895	4,000	4,998			
Australasia		5,907	7,918	10,336	13,758			
Australia		5,197	6,815	9,132	12,413			
New Zealand		710	1,103	1,204	1,345			
EUROPE		251,295	330,815	397,613	538,926			
Central/Eastern Europe		42,239	51,880	66,636	68,407			
Bulgaria		3,182	3,689	3,481	3,416			
Czech Republic/Slovakia		2,822	3,913	3,870	3,613			
Hungary		2,863	3,696	3,185	2,757			
Poland		2,343	2,478	5,869	6,049			
Romania		2,297	3,197	3,509	4,393			
Ukraine		2,956	3,526	3,560	4,148			
USSR (former)		25,776	31,381	43,162	44,031			
Northern Europe		32,720	48,482	57,772	58,553			
Denmark		5,669	9,217	10,555	9,996			
Norway		2,309	3,645	4,204	4,336			
Sweden		8,854	13,520	16,884	17,155			
United Kingdom		15,888	22,100	26,129	27,066			
Southern Europe		31,200	44,676	49,893	51,478			
Greece		3,875	4,596	5,116	4,160			
Italy		11,188	20,146	24,160	27,686			
Spain		12,655	15,373	16,807	15,572			
Yugoslavia, SFR (former)		3,482	4,561	3,810	4,060			
Western Europe		57,591	83,417	95,504	105,312			
Austria		3,573	5,130	5,931	5,981			
Belgium		3,753	5,480	6,449	5,986			
France		17,431	24,481	29,605	34,637			
Germany		24,316	36,901	39,253	41,968			
Netherlands		5,345	7,182	9,318	11,516			
Switzerland		3,173	4,243	4,948	5,224			

SYRIAN ARAB REPUBLIC

3. Arrivals of non-resident tourists in hotels and similar establishments, by nationality

	2007	2008	2009	2010	2011	Market share 11	% Change 11-10
East Mediterranean Europe	87,545	102,360	127,808	255,176			
Cyprus	2,904	4,329	5,343	5,623			
Turkey	84,641	98,031	122,465	249,553			
MIDDLE EAST	754,513	1,092,522	1,101,986	1,164,219			
Bahrain	16,221	16,556	19,640	22,376			
Palestine	19,863	21,333	11,171	5,475			
Iraq	(*)	238,627	239,075	253,496			
Jordan	342,710	391,314	375,338	461,406			
Kuwait	15,932	18,326	22,378	25,827			
Lebanon	232,453	254,643	265,905	235,194			
Libya	13,250	18,752	17,106	16,734			
Oman	2,967	3,959	3,453	4,185			
Qatar	3,277	3,420	3,756	3,651			
Saudi Arabia	76,284	87,094	100,407	83,027			
United Arab Emirates	8,242	11,071	12,517	11,541			
Egypt	14,752	17,644	21,591	30,980			
Yemen	7,155	8,782	8,514	8,548			
Other countries of Middle East	1,407	1,001	1,135	1,779			
SOUTH ASIA	204,840	223,819	343,596	781,743			
Afghanistan	808	872	1,127	2,799			
India	5,052	6,428	10,018	16,326			
Iran, Islamic Republic of	192,122	210,287	321,725	748,986			
Pakistan	6,858	6,232	10,726	13,632			
NOT SPECIFIED	95,511	102,409	101,152	121,258			
Other countries of the World	45,081	52,079	45,247	41,828			
Nationals Residing Abroad	50,430	50,330	55,905	79,430			

SYRIAN ARAB REPUBLIC

4. Arrivals of non-resident tourists in all types of accommodation establishments, by nationality

		2007	2008	2009	2010	2011	Market share 11	% Change 11-10
TOTAL	(*)	4,157,814	5,430,182	6,091,889	8,545,848			
AFRICA		69,117	75,953	68,159	79,745			
North Africa		69,117	75,953	68,159	79,745			
Algeria		29,420	32,784	28,882	34,149			
Morocco		9,399	8,486	7,742	8,756			
Sudan		16,912	19,800	18,486	21,206			
Tunisia		13,386	14,883	13,049	15,634			
AMERICAS		54,738	69,575	77,621	84,195			
North America		46,040	56,973	64,851	71,382			
Canada		15,347	20,236	22,380	22,235			
United States of America		30,693	36,737	42,471	49,147			
South America		8,698	12,602	12,770	12,813			
Argentina		787	1,215	1,419	1,841			
Brazil		2,132	3,368	3,518	4,380			
Venezuela		5,779	8,019	7,833	6,592			
EAST ASIA AND THE PACIFIC		40,915	49,521	56,937	66,696			
North-East Asia		11,183	14,048	16,517	22,560			
China		4,225	5,723	7,753	10,960			
Japan		6,958	8,325	8,764	11,600			
South-East Asia		20,194	22,709	24,449	24,896			
Indonesia		17,443	18,800	19,072	18,254			
Malaysia		2,751	3,909	5,377	6,642			
Australasia		9,538	12,764	15,971	19,240			
Australia		8,478	11,117	14,203	17,357			
New Zealand		1,060	1,647	1,768	1,883			
EUROPE		486,063	618,272	772,031	1,305,301			
Central/Eastern Europe		64,667	79,323	91,604	86,936			
Bulgaria		4,242	4,919	4,611	4,437			
Czech Republic/Slovakia		3,135	4,348	4,476	4,692			
Hungary		3,718	4,800	4,204	3,789			
Poland		3,347	3,540	8,123	7,633			
Romania		3,829	5,328	5,469	5,379			
Ukraine		3,941	4,701	4,720	5,387			
USSR (former)		42,455	51,687	60,001	55,619			
Northern Europe		44,794	66,568	82,233	92,455			
Denmark		7,559	12,289	14,489	15,805			
Norway		2,886	4,556	5,513	6,855			
Sweden		14,280	21,807	27,137	27,122			
United Kingdom		20,069	27,916	35,094	42,673			
Southern Europe		39,617	56,465	65,310	74,688			
Greece		6,065	7,195	8,040	6,575			
Italy		13,812	24,871	31,115	40,302			
Spain		15,332	18,625	21,295	22,538			
Yugoslavia, SFR (former)		4,408	5,774	4,860	5,273			
Western Europe		82,234	118,931	141,264	177,343			
Austria		4,523	6,494	7,878	9,455			
Belgium		4,669	6,818	8,440	9,464			
France		26,817	37,662	46,906	60,527			
Germany		33,772	51,251	56,690	71,430			
Netherlands		8,222	11,049	14,443	18,207			
Switzerland		4,231	5,657	6,907	8,260			

SYRIAN ARAB REPUBLIC

4. Arrivals of non-resident tourists in all types of accommodation establishments, by nationality

		2007	2008	2009	2010	2011	Market share 11	% Change 11-10
East Mediterranean Europe		254,751	296,985	391,620	873,879			
Cyprus		5,808	8,658	9,943	8,891			
Turkey		248,943	288,327	381,677	864,988			
MIDDLE EAST		2,162,649	3,235,057	3,522,115	4,574,783			
Bahrain		63,980	65,302	75,059	70,169			
Palestine		79,450	85,331	47,943	32,502			
Iraq	(*)		795,424	806,118	897,975			
Jordan		761,578	869,586	882,750	1,363,644			
Kuwait		106,214	122,176	140,716	120,977			
Lebanon		664,152	727,553	921,762	1,467,701			
Libya		21,032	29,765	28,337	31,841			
Oman		10,231	13,650	11,592	12,299			
Qatar		17,249	18,001	19,053	15,173			
Saudi Arabia		346,748	395,884	467,095	435,663			
United Arab Emirates		32,968	44,283	50,794	51,521			
Egypt		34,307	41,032	45,154	50,171			
Yemen		18,345	22,519	21,747	21,585			
Other countries of Middle East		6,395	4,551	3,995	3,562			
SOUTH ASIA		325,135	355,431	467,012	853,065			
Afghanistan		1,010	1,090	1,432	3,719			
India		8,618	10,964	16,980	27,346			
Iran, Islamic Republic of		304,956	333,789	430,880	792,258			
Pakistan		10,551	9,588	17,720	29,742			
NOT SPECIFIED		1,019,197	1,026,373	1,128,014	1,582,063			
Other countries of the World		58,547	67,635	63,077	69,003			
Nationals Residing Abroad		960,650	958,738	1,064,937	1,513,060			

SYRIAN ARAB REPUBLIC

5. Overnight stays of non-resident tourists in hotels and similar establishments, by nationality

		2007	2008	2009	2010	2011	Market share 11	% Change 11-10
TOTAL	(*)	7,893,675	10,686,192	11,530,321	12,869,132			
AFRICA		326,715	359,048	315,672	346,318			
North Africa		326,715	359,048	315,672	346,318			
Algeria		140,076	156,098	135,173	151,845			
Morocco		45,489	41,070	35,182	32,670			
Sudan		83,814	98,130	88,349	90,271			
Tunisia		57,336	63,750	56,968	71,532			
AMERICAS		201,095	257,556	286,050	312,612			
North America		168,506	210,424	238,008	265,883			
Canada		71,824	94,704	92,379	43,059			
United States of America		96,682	115,720	145,629	222,824			
South America		32,589	47,132	48,042	46,729			
Argentina		5,226	8,068	8,743	7,509			
Brazil		5,692	8,993	9,923	14,486			
Venezuela		21,671	30,071	29,376	24,734			
EAST ASIA AND THE PACIFIC		192,563	239,241	282,720	354,791			
North-East Asia		63,769	81,517	95,368	120,549			
China		33,045	44,757	55,557	64,974			
Japan		30,724	36,760	39,811	55,575			
South-East Asia		73,317	84,546	96,500	129,471			
Indonesia		57,213	61,664	66,469	96,982			
Malaysia		16,104	22,882	30,031	32,489			
Australasia		55,477	73,178	90,852	104,771			
Australia		53,701	70,419	86,229	94,345			
New Zealand		1,776	2,759	4,623	10,426			
EUROPE		1,545,599	2,087,088	2,517,393	2,876,047			
Central/Eastern Europe		390,960	478,204	646,934	615,671			
Bulgaria		25,452	29,514	27,628	26,477			
Czech Republic/Slovakia		25,394	35,219	33,660	27,999			
Hungary		20,040	25,872	23,256	22,283			
Poland		39,829	42,126	83,739	40,831			
Romania		27,569	38,362	37,246	27,821			
Ukraine		20,690	24,680	25,506	32,148			
USSR (former)		231,986	282,431	415,899	438,112			
Northern Europe		315,269	464,645	511,639	380,203			
Denmark		62,362	101,384	108,567	64,977			
Norway		16,162	25,514	29,040	28,184			
Sweden		61,975	94,642	116,687	111,507			
United Kingdom		174,770	243,105	257,345	175,535			
Southern Europe		194,652	280,149	325,657	379,635			
Greece		25,418	30,154	32,048	24,257			
Italy		72,411	130,389	163,353	212,372			
Spain		75,929	92,237	105,440	111,541			
Yugoslavia, SFR (former)		20,894	27,369	24,816	31,465			
Western Europe		395,551	570,676	653,571	706,883			
Austria		21,128	30,334	35,758	38,874			
Belgium		22,517	32,881	39,312	38,908			
France		153,789	215,986	249,341	242,494			
Germany		145,896	221,404	239,813	277,798			
Netherlands		37,412	50,271	63,965	74,852			
Switzerland		14,809	19,800	25,382	33,957			

SYRIAN ARAB REPUBLIC

5. Overnight stays of non-resident tourists in hotels and similar establishments, by nationality

		2007	2008	2009	2010	2011	Market share 11	% Change 11-10
East Mediterranean Europe		249,167	293,414	379,592	793,655			
Cyprus		14,520	21,645	29,380	36,552			
Turkey		234,647	271,769	350,212	757,103			
MIDDLE EAST		3,813,419	5,778,506	5,454,032	3,593,764			
Bahrain		194,646	198,667	217,890	134,933			
Palestine		67,036	71,998	40,969	29,105			
Iraq	(*)		1,431,763	1,310,543	807,296			
Jordan		1,713,550	1,956,570	1,714,380	1,178,750			
Kuwait		95,592	109,958	129,934	128,760			
Lebanon		697,359	763,930	754,041	491,109			
Libya		101,627	143,824	130,139	123,616			
Oman		20,769	27,710	23,098	22,039			
Qatar		36,050	37,622	37,625	19,318			
Saudi Arabia		610,276	696,756	742,792	334,917			
United Arab Emirates		68,186	91,588	97,896	53,787			
Egypt		103,264	123,506	148,474	205,331			
Yemen		96,623	118,607	99,200	53,183			
Other countries of Middle East		8,441	6,007	7,051	11,620			
SOUTH ASIA		1,251,724	1,368,759	2,067,934	4,621,581			
Afghanistan		3,232	3,488	5,259	18,192			
India		45,466	57,848	83,094	114,183			
Iran, Islamic Republic of		1,152,734	1,261,723	1,903,989	4,362,885			
Pakistan		50,292	45,700	75,592	126,321			
NOT SPECIFIED		562,560	595,994	606,520	764,019			
Other countries of the World		219,774	253,891	226,522	224,119			
Nationals Residing Abroad		342,786	342,103	379,998	539,900			

SYRIAN ARAB REPUBLIC

6. Overnight stays of non-resident tourists in all types of accommodation establishments, by nationality

		2007	2008	2009	2010	2011	Market share 11	% Change 11-10
TOTAL	(*)	56,372,904	73,492,019	77,128,427	84,775,969			
AFRICA		585,878	644,317	557,453	577,805			
North Africa		585,878	644,317	557,453	577,805			
Algeria		194,994	217,297	190,135	223,172			
Morocco		91,824	82,904	66,572	61,037			
Sudan		196,807	230,424	203,132	183,835			
Tunisia		102,253	113,692	97,614	109,761			
AMERICAS		441,771	553,725	641,010	638,403			
North America		399,932	493,507	575,466	568,469			
Canada		121,855	160,674	175,687	160,662			
United States of America		278,077	332,833	399,779	407,807			
South America		41,839	60,218	65,544	69,934			
Argentina		5,545	8,561	13,800	12,210			
Brazil		6,737	10,643	12,056	20,453			
Venezuela		29,557	41,014	39,688	37,271			
EAST ASIA AND THE PACIFIC		231,451	289,479	349,445	515,698			
North-East Asia		70,037	89,557	106,821	156,687			
China		36,467	49,392	61,829	92,175			
Japan		33,570	40,165	44,992	64,512			
South-East Asia		82,090	95,276	111,654	205,733			
Indonesia		62,272	67,116	74,117	154,240			
Malaysia		19,818	28,160	37,537	51,493			
Australasia		79,324	104,646	130,970	153,278			
Australia		76,732	100,619	124,211	138,104			
New Zealand		2,592	4,027	6,759	15,174			
EUROPE		4,594,225	5,822,270	6,552,963	7,841,108			
Central/Eastern Europe		616,702	753,618	963,078	969,868			
Bulgaria		28,209	32,711	32,391	39,959			
Czech Republic/Slovakia		26,021	36,088	36,962	42,256			
Hungary		21,494	27,749	26,616	33,438			
Poland		41,057	43,424	86,897	45,414			
Romania		32,547	45,288	44,728	42,070			
Ukraine		26,208	31,262	32,901	48,518			
USSR (former)		441,166	537,096	702,583	718,213			
Northern Europe		475,177	701,100	806,310	709,244			
Denmark		65,259	106,095	120,931	110,995			
Norway		19,107	30,164	37,046	48,144			
Sweden		155,938	238,132	278,004	190,479			
United Kingdom		234,873	326,709	370,329	359,626			
Southern Europe		248,137	370,093	452,260	558,428			
Greece		30,598	36,299	45,860	46,090			
Italy		115,116	207,287	250,671	289,004			
Spain		80,489	97,776	126,951	175,846			
Yugoslavia, SFR (former)		21,934	28,731	28,778	47,488			
Western Europe		719,560	1,045,810	1,192,710	1,339,266			
Austria		25,334	36,374	46,847	66,406			
Belgium		30,065	43,903	55,571	66,464			
France		253,689	356,290	423,885	524,644			
Germany		332,532	504,634	527,104	495,880			
Netherlands		59,694	80,213	104,078	127,865			
Switzerland		18,246	24,396	35,225	58,007			

SYRIAN ARAB REPUBLIC

6. Overnight stays of non-resident tourists in all types of accommodation establishments, by nationality

		2007	2008	2009	2010	2011	Market share 11	% Change 11-10
East Mediterranean Europe		**2,534,649**	**2,951,649**	**3,138,605**	**4,264,302**			
Cyprus		48,158	71,789	79,000	62,440			
Turkey		2,486,491	2,879,860	3,059,605	4,201,862			
MIDDLE EAST		**21,261,522**	**36,780,745**	**35,915,459**	**26,497,001**			
Bahrain		825,665	842,723	938,829	636,653			
Palestine		813,588	873,807	497,498	328,655			
Iraq	(*)		12,790,415	11,669,785	7,200,257			
Jordan		5,749,913	6,565,378	6,054,940	5,873,743			
Kuwait		1,770,585	2,036,666	2,221,736	1,064,245			
Lebanon		5,965,544	6,535,025	6,935,404	6,430,478			
Libya		186,687	264,203	250,733	253,144			
Oman		101,892	135,943	111,914	77,069			
Qatar		287,541	300,077	296,611	114,806			
Saudi Arabia		3,965,438	4,527,367	5,105,003	3,485,226			
United Arab Emirates		440,067	591,103	665,615	493,833			
Egypt		696,777	833,358	763,315	343,228			
Yemen		307,957	378,026	324,652	165,983			
Other countries of Middle East		149,868	106,654	79,424	29,681			
SOUTH ASIA		**1,661,118**	**1,816,380**	**2,517,819**	**5,209,221**			
Afghanistan		3,535	3,815	6,158	27,330			
India		63,420	80,690	123,582	352,138			
Iran, Islamic Republic of		1,524,141	1,668,246	2,273,867	4,624,482			
Pakistan		70,022	63,629	114,212	205,271			
NOT SPECIFIED		**27,596,939**	**27,585,103**	**30,594,278**	**43,496,733**			
Other countries of the World		273,983	316,515	305,159	462,049			
Nationals Residing Abroad		27,322,956	27,268,588	30,289,119	43,034,684			

TAIWAN, PROVINCE OF CHINA

2. Arrivals of non-resident visitors at national borders, by country of residence

	2007	2008	2009	2010	2011	Market share 11	% Change 11-10
TOTAL	3,716,063	3,845,187	4,395,004	5,567,277	6,087,484	100.00	9.34
AFRICA	8,607	8,499	7,735	8,254	8,938	0.15	8.29
Southern Africa	5,166	4,904	4,009	4,066	4,709	0.08	15.81
South Africa	5,166	4,904	4,009	4,066	4,709	0.08	15.81
Other Africa	3,441	3,595	3,726	4,188	4,229	0.07	0.98
Other countries of Africa	3,441	3,595	3,726	4,188	4,229	0.07	0.98
AMERICAS	468,996	461,269	442,036	474,709	495,136	8.13	4.30
North America	457,617	449,656	431,183	462,610	482,172	7.92	4.23
Canada	57,179	60,236	60,138	64,739	67,545	1.11	4.33
Mexico	2,473	2,223	1,787	2,142	2,010	0.03	-6.16
United States of America	397,965	387,197	369,258	395,729	412,617	6.78	4.27
South America	4,863	5,066	4,491	5,090	5,163	0.08	1.43
Argentina	859	884	873	984	968	0.02	-1.63
Brazil	4,004	4,182	3,618	4,106	4,195	0.07	2.17
Other Americas	6,516	6,547	6,362	7,009	7,801	0.13	11.30
Other countries of the Americas	6,516	6,547	6,362	7,009	7,801	0.13	11.30
EAST ASIA AND THE PACIFIC	3,011,008	3,121,838	3,690,485	4,817,622	5,297,032	87.02	9.95
North-East Asia	1,883,631	2,286,828	2,859,231	3,722,151	4,139,789	68.00	11.22
China		329,204	972,123	1,630,735	1,784,185	29.31	9.41
Hong Kong, China	491,437	618,667	718,806	794,362	817,944	13.44	2.97
Japan	1,166,380	1,086,691	1,000,661	1,080,153	1,294,758	21.27	19.87
Korea, Republic of	225,814	252,266	167,641	216,901	242,902	3.99	11.99
South-East Asia	700,287	725,751	689,027	911,174	1,071,975	17.61	17.65
Indonesia	95,572	110,420	106,612	123,834	156,281	2.57	26.20
Malaysia	141,308	155,783	166,987	285,734	307,898	5.06	7.76
Philippines	85,030	87,936	77,206	87,944	101,539	1.67	15.46
Singapore	204,494	205,449	194,523	241,334	299,599	4.92	24.14
Thailand	90,069	84,586	78,405	92,949	102,902	1.69	10.71
Other countries of South-East Asia	83,814	81,577	65,294	79,379	103,756	1.70	30.71
Australasia	60,523	67,310	65,158	70,898	69,503	1.14	-1.97
Australia	51,762	58,199	57,147	62,254	60,067	0.99	-3.51
New Zealand	8,761	9,111	8,011	8,644	9,436	0.16	9.16
Other East Asia and the Pacific	366,567	41,949	77,069	113,399	15,765	0.26	-86.10
Other countries of Asia	365,288	40,704	76,054	112,344	14,728	0.24	-86.89
Other countries of Oceania	1,279	1,245	1,015	1,055	1,037	0.02	-1.71
EUROPE	186,483	200,914	197,070	203,301	212,148	3.48	4.35
Central/Eastern Europe				5,457	6,667	0.11	22.17
Russian Federation				5,457	6,667	0.11	22.17
Northern Europe	45,856	54,854	50,822	50,949	50,402	0.83	-1.07
Sweden	5,888	6,463	6,007	6,519	6,983	0.11	7.12
United Kingdom	39,968	48,391	44,815	44,430	43,419	0.71	-2.28
Southern Europe	17,670	19,524	19,237	19,274	19,732	0.32	2.38
Greece	1,326	1,358	1,348	1,258	1,129	0.02	-10.25
Italy	11,440	12,752	12,237	12,246	12,407	0.20	1.31
Spain	4,904	5,414	5,652	5,770	6,196	0.10	7.38
Western Europe	92,343	92,222	91,917	98,894	105,801	1.74	6.98
Austria	5,541	5,161	4,968	5,806	6,368	0.10	9.68
Belgium	4,109	4,166	4,492	4,435	4,348	0.07	-1.96
France	23,917	24,164	25,245	26,455	29,082	0.48	9.93
Germany	39,529	40,309	39,533	42,446	44,644	0.73	5.18
Netherlands	12,445	12,126	11,230	13,158	14,401	0.24	9.45
Switzerland	6,802	6,296	6,449	6,594	6,958	0.11	5.52

TAIWAN, PROVINCE OF CHINA

2. Arrivals of non-resident visitors at national borders, by country of residence

	2007	2008	2009	2010	2011	Market share 11	% Change 11-10
Other Europe	30,614	34,314	35,094	28,727	29,546	0.49	2.85
Other countries of Europe	30,614	34,314	35,094	28,727	29,546	0.49	2.85
MIDDLE EAST	13,487	12,524	12,217	13,542	13,791	0.23	1.84
All countries of Middle East	13,487	12,524	12,217	13,542	13,791	0.23	1.84
SOUTH ASIA	19,976	19,976	18,555	23,849	23,927	0.39	0.33
India	19,976	19,976	18,555	23,849	23,927	0.39	0.33
NOT SPECIFIED	7,506	20,167	26,906	26,000	36,512	0.60	40.43
Other countries of the World	7,506	20,167	26,906	26,000	36,512	0.60	40.43

TAIWAN, PROVINCE OF CHINA

4. Arrivals of non-resident tourists in all types of accommodation establishments, by country of residence

	2007	2008	2009	2010	2011	Market share 11	% Change 11-10
TOTAL	3,240,866	3,368,990	3,899,831	5,061,513	5,519,231	100.00	9.04
AFRICA	6,593	6,860	6,277	6,645	6,634	0.12	-0.17
Southern Africa	3,669	3,668	3,086	3,066	3,246	0.06	5.87
South Africa	3,669	3,668	3,086	3,066	3,246	0.06	5.87
Other Africa	2,924	3,192	3,191	3,579	3,388	0.06	-5.34
Other countries of Africa	2,924	3,192	3,191	3,579	3,388	0.06	-5.34
AMERICAS	424,349	426,806	403,374	435,573	447,827	8.11	2.81
North America	415,207	417,105	394,748	425,735	437,624	7.93	2.79
Canada	49,524	53,174	52,611	57,285	60,033	1.09	4.80
Mexico	2,117	1,899	1,291	1,816	1,716	0.03	-5.51
United States of America	363,566	362,032	340,846	366,634	375,875	6.81	2.52
South America	4,028	4,479	3,696	4,337	4,542	0.08	4.73
Argentina	677	810	728	814	836	0.02	2.70
Brazil	3,351	3,669	2,968	3,523	3,706	0.07	5.19
Other Americas	5,114	5,222	4,930	5,501	5,661	0.10	2.91
Other countries of the Americas	5,114	5,222	4,930	5,501	5,661	0.10	2.91
EAST ASIA AND THE PACIFIC	2,611,054	2,716,482	3,270,919	4,389,655	4,819,702	87.33	9.80
North-East Asia	1,822,933	1,900,934	2,684,917	3,577,379	3,929,895	71.20	9.85
China			860,075	1,548,139	1,666,562	30.20	7.65
Hong Kong, China	469,224	590,820	690,933	768,217	789,520	14.30	2.77
Japan	1,138,894	1,065,467	975,832	1,052,541	1,242,652	22.51	18.06
Korea, Republic of	214,815	244,647	158,077	208,482	231,161	4.19	10.88
South-East Asia	455,729	485,498	488,637	689,941	783,390	14.19	13.54
Indonesia	36,521	42,264	43,472	54,229	70,444	1.28	29.90
Malaysia	130,572	144,345	153,344	271,956	287,318	5.21	5.65
Philippines	31,941	35,849	36,422	42,704	47,245	0.86	10.63
Singapore	200,937	200,519	189,115	235,754	290,029	5.25	23.02
Thailand	35,325	38,670	42,156	53,751	53,794	0.97	0.08
Other countries of South-East Asia	20,433	23,851	24,128	31,547	34,560	0.63	9.55
Australasia	53,092	57,267	55,994	60,684	60,783	1.10	0.16
Australia	45,309	49,050	48,726	52,864	52,483	0.95	-0.72
New Zealand	7,783	8,217	7,268	7,820	8,300	0.15	6.14
Other East Asia and the Pacific	279,300	272,783	41,371	61,651	45,634	0.83	-25.98
Other countries of Asia	278,181	271,616	40,441	60,728	44,716	0.81	-26.37
Other countries of Oceania	1,119	1,167	930	923	918	0.02	-0.54
EUROPE	165,983	179,001	170,053	179,090	186,429	3.38	4.10
Central/Eastern Europe				4,479	5,700	0.10	27.26
Russian Federation				4,479	5,700	0.10	27.26
Northern Europe	40,380	48,217	43,004	44,231	44,541	0.81	0.70
Sweden	5,444	6,013	5,705	6,046	6,405	0.12	5.94
United Kingdom	34,936	42,204	37,299	38,185	38,136	0.69	-0.13
Southern Europe	15,995	16,864	15,884	17,500	18,043	0.33	3.10
Greece	1,121	1,156	1,056	985	886	0.02	-10.05
Italy	10,463	10,861	10,231	11,270	11,602	0.21	2.95
Spain	4,411	4,847	4,597	5,245	5,555	0.10	5.91
Western Europe	83,113	83,982	80,401	87,815	92,622	1.68	5.47
Austria	4,788	4,552	4,145	4,733	5,269	0.10	11.32
Belgium	3,755	3,684	3,870	3,850	3,916	0.07	1.71
France	21,147	22,197	22,332	23,716	25,644	0.46	8.13
Germany	35,827	36,654	34,231	38,358	39,566	0.72	3.15
Netherlands	11,321	11,133	9,966	11,044	11,853	0.21	7.33
Switzerland	6,275	5,762	5,857	6,114	6,374	0.12	4.25

TAIWAN, PROVINCE OF CHINA

4. Arrivals of non-resident tourists in all types of accommodation establishments, by country of residence

	2007	2008	2009	2010	2011	Market share 11	% Change 11-10
Other Europe	**26,495**	**29,938**	**30,764**	**25,065**	**25,523**	**0.46**	**1.83**
Other countries of Europe	26,495	29,938	30,764	25,065	25,523	0.46	1.83
MIDDLE EAST	**12,672**	**11,851**	**11,349**	**12,630**	**12,709**	**0.23**	**0.63**
All countries of Middle East	12,672	11,851	11,349	12,630	12,709	0.23	0.63
SOUTH ASIA	**16,922**	**17,233**	**15,841**	**19,702**	**20,192**	**0.37**	**2.49**
India	16,922	17,233	15,841	19,702	20,192	0.37	2.49
NOT SPECIFIED	**3,293**	**10,757**	**22,018**	**18,218**	**25,738**	**0.47**	**41.28**
Other countries of the World	3,293	10,757	22,018	18,218	25,738	0.47	41.28

TAIWAN, PROVINCE OF CHINA

6. Overnight stays of non-resident tourists in all types of accommodation establishments, by country of residence

	2007	2008	2009	2010	2011	Market share 11	% Change 11-10
TOTAL	21,123,934	24,607,223	27,948,655	35,754,330	38,934,884	100.00	8.90
AFRICA	69,382	94,415	75,930	78,195	80,527	0.21	2.98
Southern Africa	43,775	59,750	43,869	38,613	43,382	0.11	12.35
South Africa	43,775	59,750	43,869	38,613	43,382	0.11	12.35
Other Africa	25,607	34,665	32,061	39,582	37,145	0.10	-6.16
Other countries of Africa	25,607	34,665	32,061	39,582	37,145	0.10	-6.16
AMERICAS	4,192,352	4,708,755	4,434,211	4,585,544	4,751,009	12.20	3.61
North America	4,093,570	4,585,583	4,323,272	4,468,060	4,624,435	11.88	3.50
Canada	463,503	556,732	521,194	536,943	604,594	1.55	12.60
Mexico	17,736	17,536	12,617	17,031	17,611	0.05	3.41
United States of America	3,612,331	4,011,315	3,789,461	3,914,086	4,002,230	10.28	2.25
South America	39,123	53,344	43,478	47,356	51,043	0.13	7.79
Argentina	7,097	11,462	10,396	11,430	13,021	0.03	13.92
Brazil	32,026	41,882	33,082	35,926	38,022	0.10	5.83
Other Americas	59,659	69,828	67,461	70,128	75,531	0.19	7.70
Other countries of the Americas	59,659	69,828	67,461	70,128	75,531	0.19	7.70
EAST ASIA AND THE PACIFIC	15,317,941	17,910,005	21,552,207	29,053,026	31,740,080	81.52	9.25
North-East Asia	8,041,718	9,162,728	15,570,102	21,360,551	23,423,166	60.16	9.66
China			6,832,027	11,902,626	13,162,258	33.81	10.58
Hong Kong, China	2,015,014	2,638,293	2,995,864	3,305,994	3,463,681	8.90	4.77
Japan	5,112,367	5,427,141	4,925,098	5,178,283	5,751,580	14.77	11.07
Korea, Republic of	914,337	1,097,294	817,113	973,648	1,045,647	2.69	7.39
South-East Asia	3,742,178	4,720,651	4,480,228	5,703,915	6,425,003	16.50	12.64
Indonesia	479,627	666,059	640,284	691,853	823,093	2.11	18.97
Malaysia	952,427	1,145,073	1,173,741	1,896,448	2,045,601	5.25	7.86
Philippines	318,373	489,967	433,040	449,484	475,826	1.22	5.86
Singapore	1,318,513	1,384,341	1,320,923	1,592,265	1,877,456	4.82	17.91
Thailand	310,551	451,356	411,026	469,501	511,492	1.31	8.94
Other countries of South-East Asia	362,687	583,855	501,214	604,364	691,535	1.78	14.42
Australasia	367,931	439,250	442,571	490,904	540,125	1.39	10.03
Australia	302,624	359,070	365,122	402,031	433,424	1.11	7.81
New Zealand	65,307	80,180	77,449	88,873	106,701	0.27	20.06
Other East Asia and the Pacific	3,166,114	3,587,376	1,059,306	1,497,656	1,351,786	3.47	-9.74
Other countries of Asia	3,155,933	3,576,031	1,049,739	1,487,441	1,340,780	3.44	-9.86
Other countries of Oceania	10,181	11,345	9,567	10,215	11,006	0.03	7.74
EUROPE	1,269,713	1,556,794	1,548,243	1,572,059	1,773,600	4.56	12.82
Central/Eastern Europe				53,825	63,643	0.16	18.24
Russian Federation				53,825	63,643	0.16	18.24
Northern Europe	290,780	374,340	355,294	362,450	397,677	1.02	9.72
Sweden	41,379	58,801	55,755	56,026	62,597	0.16	11.73
United Kingdom	249,401	315,539	299,539	306,424	335,080	0.86	9.35
Southern Europe	106,073	125,834	124,658	140,488	149,958	0.39	6.74
Greece	6,765	7,331	7,611	5,489	5,596	0.01	1.95
Italy	68,145	76,026	75,003	85,206	90,127	0.23	5.78
Spain	31,163	42,477	42,044	49,793	54,235	0.14	8.92
Western Europe	679,362	816,867	801,080	809,994	925,038	2.38	14.20
Austria	40,973	44,248	44,478	44,963	52,033	0.13	15.72
Belgium	25,883	28,783	34,721	32,004	34,896	0.09	9.04
France	189,930	241,823	245,079	247,128	293,062	0.75	18.59
Germany	286,474	358,131	336,545	344,795	375,832	0.97	9.00
Netherlands	88,128	88,835	85,530	86,415	109,376	0.28	26.57
Switzerland	47,974	55,047	54,727	54,689	59,839	0.15	9.42

TAIWAN, PROVINCE OF CHINA

6. Overnight stays of non-resident tourists in all types of accommodation establishments, by country of residence

	2007	2008	2009	2010	2011	Market share 11	% Change 11-10
Other Europe	**193,498**	**239,753**	**267,211**	**205,302**	**237,284**	**0.61**	**15.58**
Other countries of Europe	193,498	239,753	267,211	205,302	237,284	0.61	15.58
MIDDLE EAST	**84,143**	**87,149**	**85,839**	**92,117**	**101,194**	**0.26**	**9.85**
All countries of Middle East	84,143	87,149	85,839	92,117	101,194	0.26	9.85
SOUTH ASIA	**162,836**	**189,068**	**165,749**	**189,515**	**199,597**	**0.51**	**5.32**
India	162,836	189,068	165,749	189,515	199,597	0.51	5.32
NOT SPECIFIED	**27,567**	**61,037**	**86,476**	**183,874**	**288,877**	**0.74**	**57.11**
Other countries of the World	27,567	61,037	86,476	183,874	288,877	0.74	57.11

TAJIKISTAN

2. Arrivals of non-resident visitors at national borders, by country of residence

	2007	2008	2009	2010	2011	Market share 11	% Change 11-10
TOTAL		325,420	207,439	159,680	183,154	100.00	14.70
AFRICA		27	129	188			
Central Africa		1					
Cameroon		1					
Southern Africa		26	129	188			
South Africa		26	129	188			
AMERICAS		1,265	1,334	1,465	587	0.32	-59.93
North America		1,263	1,321	1,415	573	0.31	-59.51
Canada		190	203	221	161	0.09	-27.15
Mexico		3	4	6			
United States of America		1,070	1,114	1,188	412	0.22	-65.32
South America		2	13	50	14	0.01	-72.00
Argentina			13	24	13	0.01	-45.83
Brazil					1	0.00	
Colombia		2		26			
EAST ASIA AND THE PACIFIC		2,919	3,384	3,546	4,280	2.34	20.70
North-East Asia		2,674	3,130	3,208	4,196	2.29	30.80
China		1,522	2,437	2,694	3,788	2.07	40.61
Taiwan, Province of China		2					
Japan		716	369	294	90	0.05	-69.39
Korea, Dem. People's Republic of		434	311	200	318	0.17	59.00
Mongolia			13	20			
South-East Asia		80	84	128	43	0.02	-66.41
Indonesia		14	21	36	31	0.02	-13.89
Malaysia		11	19	33	3	0.00	-90.91
Philippines		20	12	8			
Singapore			5	8	5	0.00	-37.50
Viet Nam		34					
Thailand		1	27	43	4	0.00	-90.70
Australasia		165	170	210	41	0.02	-80.48
Australia		152	136	128	36	0.02	-71.88
New Zealand		13	34	82	5	0.00	-93.90
EUROPE		309,659	188,760	139,902	167,069	91.22	19.42
Central/Eastern Europe		303,215	182,883	134,795	164,184	89.64	21.80
Azerbaijan		349	328	315	708	0.39	124.76
Armenia		213	283	328	343	0.19	4.57
Bulgaria		29	17	23	5	0.00	-78.26
Belarus		70	342	796	785	0.43	-1.38
Czech Republic		83	70	74	77	0.04	4.05
Estonia		19	30	39	58	0.03	48.72
Georgia		91	136	184	669	0.37	263.59
Hungary		15	35	46	1	0.00	-97.83
Kazakhstan		4,394	3,956	3,464	3,694	2.02	6.64
Kyrgyzstan		33,328	29,675	24,079	7,799	4.26	-67.61
Latvia		19	103	138	112	0.06	-18.84
Lithuania		161	55				
Republic of Moldova		184	176	171	971	0.53	467.84
Poland		106	137	152	154	0.08	1.32
Romania		3	14	17	22	0.01	29.41
Russian Federation		22,103	22,556	21,138	18,490	10.10	-12.53
Slovakia		46	49	52	36	0.02	-30.77
Turkmenistan		1,288	832	756	727	0.40	-3.84
Ukraine		477	607	773	3,035	1.66	292.63
Uzbekistan		240,237	123,482	82,250	126,498	69.07	53.80

TAJIKISTAN

2. Arrivals of non-resident visitors at national borders, by country of residence

	2007	2008	2009	2010	2011	Market share 11	% Change 11-10
Northern Europe		649	847	955	513	0.28	-46.28
Denmark		7	76	99	55	0.03	-44.44
Finland		35	57	65	22	0.01	-66.15
Ireland		89	70	57	22	0.01	-61.40
Norway		15	47	53	27	0.01	-49.06
Sweden		168	235	300	60	0.03	-80.00
United Kingdom		335	362	381	327	0.18	-14.17
Southern Europe		489	515	551	246	0.13	-55.35
Croatia		2		3			
Greece		22	13				
Holy See		1					
Italy		301	346	372	189	0.10	-49.19
Portugal		6	5				
Serbia		77	41	28	2	0.00	-92.86
Spain		78	95	111	43	0.02	-61.26
TFYR of Macedonia		2	15	37	12	0.01	-67.57
Western Europe		3,182	2,582	2,117	1,465	0.80	-30.80
Austria		124	103	120	135	0.07	12.50
Belgium		135	179	234	76	0.04	-67.52
France		1,674	1,067	542	448	0.24	-17.34
Germany		1,012	985	975	570	0.31	-41.54
Luxembourg		2					
Netherlands		77	107	118	95	0.05	-19.49
Switzerland		158	141	128	141	0.08	10.16
East Mediterranean Europe		2,124	1,933	1,484	661	0.36	-55.46
Israel		102	76	43	41	0.02	-4.65
Turkey		2,022	1,857	1,441	620	0.34	-56.97
MIDDLE EAST		225	202	170	56	0.03	-67.06
Iraq		90	36				
Jordan			8	19			
Lebanon		1	13	22			
Saudi Arabia		3	30	19	17	0.01	-10.53
Syrian Arab Republic		3	16	24	10	0.01	-58.33
United Arab Emirates		23	36	59	29	0.02	-50.85
Egypt		105	63	27			
SOUTH ASIA		11,325	13,630	14,409	11,162	6.09	-22.53
Afghanistan		8,010	10,536	11,456	5,790	3.16	-49.46
Bangladesh			27	48	1	0.00	-97.92
Sri Lanka					2	0.00	
India		495	227	254	121	0.07	-52.36
Iran, Islamic Republic of		2,462	2,437	2,387	5,199	2.84	117.80
Nepal		2	18	40	3	0.00	-92.50
Pakistan		356	385	224	46	0.03	-79.46

THAILAND

1. Arrivals of non-resident tourists at national borders, by nationality

	2007	2008	2009	2010	2011	Market share 11	% Change 11-10
TOTAL	14,464,228	14,584,220	14,149,841	15,936,400	19,230,470	100.00	20.67
AFRICA	116,677	119,000	112,403	127,930	137,907	0.72	7.80
Southern Africa	52,788	48,566	43,277	57,100	68,496	0.36	19.96
South Africa	52,788	48,566	43,277	57,100	68,496	0.36	19.96
Other Africa	63,889	70,434	69,126	70,830	69,411	0.36	-2.00
Other countries of Africa	63,889	70,434	69,126	70,830	69,411	0.36	-2.00
AMERICAS	920,366	909,017	853,380	844,644	952,519	4.95	12.77
North America	865,412	849,997	796,556	780,185	876,104	4.56	12.29
Canada	183,440	180,900	169,482	168,393	194,356	1.01	15.42
United States of America	681,972	669,097	627,074	611,792	681,748	3.55	11.43
South America	21,760	23,937	25,108	30,682	37,530	0.20	22.32
Argentina	6,704	7,132	7,458	10,292	12,970	0.07	26.02
Brazil	15,056	16,805	17,650	20,390	24,560	0.13	20.45
Other Americas	33,194	35,083	31,716	33,777	38,885	0.20	15.12
Other countries of the Americas	33,194	35,083	31,716	33,777	38,885	0.20	15.12
EAST ASIA AND THE PACIFIC	8,376,003	8,395,969	7,813,650	8,956,796	11,279,400	58.65	25.93
North-East Asia	4,063,743	3,600,741	3,081,733	3,607,034	4,714,867	24.52	30.71
China	907,117	826,660	777,508	1,122,219	1,721,247	8.95	53.38
Taiwan, Province of China	427,474	393,176	362,783	369,220	447,610	2.33	21.23
Hong Kong, China	367,862	337,827	318,762	316,476	411,834	2.14	30.13
Japan	1,277,638	1,153,868	1,004,453	993,674	1,127,893	5.87	13.51
Korea, Republic of	1,083,652	889,210	618,227	805,445	1,006,283	5.23	24.94
South-East Asia	3,520,051	3,971,429	3,968,579	4,534,235	5,594,577	29.09	23.39
Brunei Darussalam	8,987	9,055	8,353	7,073	7,471	0.04	5.63
Myanmar	72,205	71,902	79,279	90,179	110,671	0.58	22.72
Cambodia	99,945	85,790	96,586	146,274	265,903	1.38	81.78
Indonesia	237,592	247,930	227,205	286,072	370,795	1.93	29.62
Lao People's Democratic Republic	513,701	621,564	655,034	715,345	891,950	4.64	24.69
Malaysia	1,540,080	1,805,332	1,757,813	2,058,956	2,500,280	13.00	21.43
Philippines	205,266	221,506	217,705	246,430	268,375	1.40	8.91
Singapore	604,603	570,047	563,575	603,538	682,364	3.55	13.06
Viet Nam	237,672	338,303	363,029	380,368	496,768	2.58	30.60
Australasia	762,343	792,367	735,103	787,410	930,947	4.84	18.23
Australia	658,148	694,473	646,705	698,046	829,855	4.32	18.88
New Zealand	104,195	97,894	88,398	89,364	101,092	0.53	13.12
Other East Asia and the Pacific	29,866	31,432	28,235	28,117	39,009	0.20	38.74
Other countries of Asia	28,137	29,468	25,878	25,895	36,422	0.19	40.65
Other countries of Oceania	1,729	1,964	2,357	2,222	2,587	0.01	16.43
EUROPE	4,033,945	4,092,889	4,170,872	4,558,425	5,226,499	27.18	14.66
Central/Eastern Europe	425,805	488,149	518,212	856,350	1,295,073	6.73	51.23
Russian Federation	277,503	324,120	336,965	644,678	1,054,187	5.48	63.52
Other countries Central/East Europe	148,302	164,029	181,247	211,672	240,886	1.25	13.80
Northern Europe	1,704,448	1,721,603	1,680,183	1,654,908	1,735,846	9.03	4.89
Denmark	141,110	149,683	144,834	152,398	164,096	0.85	7.68
Finland	143,266	155,143	156,000	146,946	157,046	0.82	6.87
Ireland	73,734	73,380	65,530	57,515	58,945	0.31	2.49
Norway	108,941	124,600	121,575	132,108	136,931	0.71	3.65
Sweden	378,387	392,274	350,819	355,214	373,856	1.94	5.25
United Kingdom	859,010	826,523	841,425	810,727	844,972	4.39	4.22
Southern Europe	253,439	239,882	245,467	235,445	281,252	1.46	19.46
Italy	171,328	159,513	170,105	168,203	185,869	0.97	10.50
Spain	82,111	80,369	75,362	67,242	95,383	0.50	41.85

THAILAND

1. Arrivals of non-resident tourists at national borders, by nationality

	2007	2008	2009	2010	2011	Market share 11	% Change 11-10
Western Europe	**1,411,939**	**1,434,432**	**1,520,427**	**1,591,325**	**1,675,492**	**8.71**	**5.29**
Austria	81,391	80,561	85,786	90,026	89,242	0.46	-0.87
Belgium	72,018	76,132	80,420	80,000	82,610	0.43	3.26
France	373,090	398,407	427,067	461,670	515,572	2.68	11.68
Germany	544,495	542,726	573,473	606,874	619,133	3.22	2.02
Netherlands	194,434	193,541	205,412	196,994	198,891	1.03	0.96
Switzerland	146,511	143,065	148,269	155,761	170,044	0.88	9.17
East Mediterranean Europe	**128,674**	**108,275**	**110,884**	**116,050**	**125,093**	**0.65**	**7.79**
Israel	128,674	108,275	110,884	116,050	125,093	0.65	7.79
Other Europe	**109,640**	**100,548**	**95,699**	**104,347**	**113,743**	**0.59**	**9.00**
Other countries of Europe	109,640	100,548	95,699	104,347	113,743	0.59	9.00
MIDDLE EAST	**307,426**	**356,055**	**373,099**	**453,284**	**476,053**	**2.48**	**5.02**
Kuwait	31,910	32,130	44,500	41,224	55,788	0.29	35.33
Saudi Arabia	22,483	16,489	10,911	8,463	12,521	0.07	47.95
United Arab Emirates	74,957	95,490	83,625	105,162	108,608	0.56	3.28
Egypt	13,037	14,122	15,733	16,729	16,703	0.09	-0.16
Other countries of Middle East	165,039	197,824	218,330	281,706	282,433	1.47	0.26
SOUTH ASIA	**709,811**	**711,290**	**826,437**	**995,321**	**1,158,092**	**6.02**	**16.35**
Bangladesh	44,789	46,682	53,420	68,081	65,150	0.34	-4.31
Sri Lanka	44,327	38,993	47,138	49,738	53,636	0.28	7.84
India	536,356	536,964	614,566	760,371	914,971	4.76	20.33
Nepal	19,546	20,589	25,499	28,621	25,382	0.13	-11.32
Pakistan	46,656	49,169	63,260	65,171	73,727	0.38	13.13
Other countries of South Asia	18,137	18,893	22,554	23,339	25,226	0.13	8.09

THAILAND

1. Arrivals of non-resident tourists at national borders, by country of residence

	2007	2008	2009	2010	2011	Market share 11	% Change 11-10
TOTAL	14,464,228	14,584,220	14,149,841	15,936,400	19,230,470	100.00	20.67
AFRICA	104,935	108,890	107,837	121,816	141,255	0.73	15.96
East Africa	30,856	28,972	35,140	36,599	42,447	0.22	15.98
Burundi	120	75	152	127	142	0.00	11.81
Comoros	30	20	49	188	470	0.00	150.00
Ethiopia	3,904	4,025	5,204	5,875	6,234	0.03	6.11
Eritrea		30	47	79	124	0.00	56.96
Djibouti	81	56	151	164	192	0.00	17.07
Kenya	5,244	4,537	6,303	5,860	6,134	0.03	4.68
Madagascar	6,371	5,239	5,362	5,229	5,622	0.03	7.52
Malawi	179	213	399	284	315	0.00	10.92
Mauritius	3,238	2,889	3,689	3,938	4,752	0.02	20.67
Mozambique	503	624	824	1,018	1,182	0.01	16.11
Reunion	616	370	3,446	4,054	6,955	0.04	71.56
Rwanda	109	165	136	211	243	0.00	15.17
Seychelles	2,299	2,903	1,323	1,570	1,597	0.01	1.72
Somalia	194	295	149	223	309	0.00	38.57
Zimbabwe	631	513	504	535	747	0.00	39.63
Uganda	2,357	2,046	2,168	2,160	2,474	0.01	14.54
United Republic of Tanzania	3,171	3,294	3,623	3,460	3,434	0.02	-0.75
Zambia	1,809	1,678	1,611	1,624	1,521	0.01	-6.34
Central Africa	4,957	6,324	5,930	4,575	5,617	0.03	22.78
Angola	2,224	2,536	2,445	1,669	1,941	0.01	16.30
Cameroon	1,025	2,283	2,048	1,436	1,866	0.01	29.94
Central African Republic	175	121	73	41	31	0.00	-24.39
Chad	41	22	22	36	70	0.00	94.44
Congo	1,356	1,058	1,185	1,117	1,022	0.01	-8.50
Democratic Republic of the Congo	33	181	20		277	0.00	
Equatorial Guinea	3	13	5	33	45	0.00	36.36
Gabon	93	70	114	219	327	0.00	49.32
Sao Tome and Principe	7	40	18	24	38	0.00	58.33
North Africa	7,720	8,473	8,226	7,802	9,379	0.05	20.21
Algeria	1,197	1,574	1,592	1,383	1,433	0.01	3.62
Morocco	4,104	4,072	3,443	3,075	4,039	0.02	31.35
Western Sahara	33	186					
Sudan	1,488	1,458	1,910	2,034	2,645	0.01	30.04
Tunisia	898	1,183	1,281	1,310	1,262	0.01	-3.66
Southern Africa	47,760	47,406	41,937	56,985	68,275	0.36	19.81
Botswana	813	546	589	649	681	0.00	4.93
Lesotho	81	116	476	215	101	0.00	-53.02
Namibia	382	309	331	506	626	0.00	23.72
South Africa	46,269	46,271	40,465	55,467	66,705	0.35	20.26
Swaziland	215	164	76	148	162	0.00	9.46
West Africa	13,642	17,585	16,104	15,319	15,184	0.08	-0.88
Cape Verde	31	416	59	46	134	0.00	191.30
Benin	406	512	477	497	531	0.00	6.84
Gambia	500	466	368	366	361	0.00	-1.37
Ghana	2,761	2,672	2,303	1,877	2,378	0.01	26.69
Guinea	1,966	2,835	2,739	2,592	2,417	0.01	-6.75
Côte d'Ivoire	648	544	695	816	693	0.00	-15.07
Liberia	918	1,171	1,371	1,019	793	0.00	-22.18
Mali	1,615	2,075	2,027	1,734	1,995	0.01	15.05
Mauritania	534	429	487	275	151	0.00	-45.09
Niger	256	253	74	150	215	0.00	43.33
Nigeria	1,635	2,407	3,099	3,334	3,606	0.02	8.16
Senegal	1,525	1,585	1,486	1,648	931	0.00	-43.51

THAILAND

1. Arrivals of non-resident tourists at national borders, by country of residence

	2007	2008	2009	2010	2011	Market share 11	% Change 11-10
Sierra Leone	156	1,453	182	198	229	0.00	15.66
Togo	542	625	535	462	500	0.00	8.23
Burkina Faso	149	142	202	305	250	0.00	-18.03
Other Africa		130	500	536	353	0.00	-34.14
Other countries of Africa		130	500	536	353	0.00	-34.14
AMERICAS	817,579	853,348	795,110	792,190	885,598	4.61	11.79
Caribbean	1,951	2,370	1,645	2,160	2,392	0.01	10.74
Antigua and Barbuda	17	75	24	21	19	0.00	-9.52
Bahamas	111	733	60	115	131	0.00	13.91
Barbados	70	270	141	166	154	0.00	-7.23
Bermuda	108	57	95	164	235	0.00	43.29
Cayman Islands	4		22	67	60	0.00	-10.45
Cuba	220	269	181	222	239	0.00	7.66
Dominica		42	41	40	91	0.00	127.50
Dominican Republic	221	187	255	210	200	0.00	-4.76
Grenada	13	8	15	8	17	0.00	112.50
Guadeloupe	72	9	8	29	79	0.00	172.41
Haiti	78	75	20	52	67	0.00	28.85
Jamaica	333	196	158	229	284	0.00	24.02
Martinique	36	12	80	75	86	0.00	14.67
Curaçao		3	4	36	74	0.00	105.56
Puerto Rico	109	123	86	153	119	0.00	-22.22
Saint Kitts and Nevis	1	17	19	52	56	0.00	7.69
Saint Lucia	5	15	10	37	27	0.00	-27.03
Saint Vincent and the Grenadines	6	4	13	20	21	0.00	5.00
Trinidad and Tobago	455	272	405	448	421	0.00	-6.03
United States Virgin Islands	1	3	8	16	12	0.00	-25.00
Other countries of the Caribbean	91						
Central America	1,569	2,222	2,204	2,507	2,773	0.01	10.61
Belize	54	267	58	134	100	0.00	-25.37
Costa Rica	539	645	731	915	952	0.00	4.04
El Salvador	68	191	121	115	176	0.00	53.04
Guatemala	204	321	644	439	437	0.00	-0.46
Honduras	227	223	211	343	417	0.00	21.57
Nicaragua	48	200	85	109	117	0.00	7.34
Panama	429	375	354	452	574	0.00	26.99
North America	785,476	813,722	755,664	744,744	826,817	4.30	11.02
Canada	149,763	153,420	147,191	148,287	170,981	0.89	15.30
Greenland	39	24	66	188	274	0.00	45.74
Mexico	12,036	11,579	8,932	9,761	10,835	0.06	11.00
United States of America	623,638	648,699	599,475	586,508	644,727	3.35	9.93
South America	28,567	34,995	35,096	41,591	52,636	0.27	26.56
Argentina	5,611	6,198	6,452	9,336	12,005	0.06	28.59
Bolivia	234	335	269	254	317	0.00	24.80
Brazil	11,026	14,524	13,890	16,753	21,231	0.11	26.73
Chile	3,685	4,973	5,607	5,989	7,748	0.04	29.37
Colombia	3,364	3,784	3,922	3,838	4,601	0.02	19.88
Ecuador	577	472	550	529	966	0.01	82.61
Guyana	71	40	46	56	77	0.00	37.50
Paraguay	74	252	93	150	158	0.00	5.33
Peru	1,575	1,804	1,671	2,058	2,314	0.01	12.44
Suriname	132	168	95	137	172	0.00	25.55
Uruguay	593	676	689	1,025	1,311	0.01	27.90
Venezuela	1,625	1,769	1,812	1,466	1,736	0.01	18.42
Other Americas	16	39	501	1,188	980	0.01	-17.51
Other countries of the Americas	16	39	501	1,188	980	0.01	-17.51

THAILAND

1. Arrivals of non-resident tourists at national borders, by country of residence

	2007	2008	2009	2010	2011	Market share 11	% Change 11-10
EAST ASIA AND THE PACIFIC	8,711,866	8,626,039	7,994,238	9,091,305	11,480,750	59.70	26.28
North-East Asia	4,224,531	3,710,434	3,189,936	3,706,326	4,829,983	25.12	30.32
China	1,003,141	937,358	815,708	1,132,267	1,704,800	8.87	50.57
Taiwan, Province of China	427,033	402,797	366,717	371,285	449,346	2.34	21.02
Hong Kong, China	448,057	343,896	378,948	391,067	531,192	2.76	35.83
Japan	1,248,700	1,110,729	982,607	980,424	1,103,073	5.74	12.51
Korea, Dem. People's Republic of	63						
Korea, Republic of	1,075,453	897,918	620,700	805,179	1,001,105	5.21	24.33
Macao, China	18,930	13,843	21,077	21,457	32,889	0.17	53.28
Mongolia	3,154	3,893	4,179	4,647	6,347	0.03	36.58
Other countries of North-East Asia					1,231	0.01	
South-East Asia	3,755,557	4,125,527	4,075,459	4,596,750	5,718,982	29.74	24.41
Brunei Darussalam	12,430	12,357	10,517	8,906	10,142	0.05	13.88
Myanmar	75,183	75,667	80,068	91,111	111,545	0.58	22.43
Cambodia	108,776	93,301	103,168	150,011	271,265	1.41	80.83
Indonesia	233,919	259,284	226,506	285,666	370,681	1.93	29.76
Lao People's Democratic Republic	521,062	624,645	657,658	718,377	895,359	4.66	24.64
Malaysia	1,551,959	1,828,324	1,748,341	2,047,175	2,492,034	12.96	21.73
Philippines	198,873	223,968	215,150	242,859	262,839	1.37	8.23
Timor-Leste	3	337	791	857	977	0.01	14.00
Singapore	799,100	651,978	651,454	654,342	789,339	4.10	20.63
Viet Nam	254,252	355,666	381,806	397,446	514,801	2.68	29.53
Australasia	728,054	785,436	723,791	782,581	925,152	4.81	18.22
Australia	638,126	694,439	645,534	702,921	835,719	4.35	18.89
New Zealand	89,928	90,997	78,257	79,660	89,433	0.47	12.27
Melanesia	2,256	1,970	3,307	4,223	5,104	0.03	20.86
Solomon Islands	82	64	84	113	371	0.00	228.32
Fiji	724	514	801	794	876	0.00	10.33
New Caledonia	973	1,009	1,391	2,071	2,442	0.01	17.91
Vanuatu	105	60	117	204	388	0.00	90.20
Papua New Guinea	372	323	914	1,041	1,027	0.01	-1.34
Micronesia	557	478	688	660	672	0.00	1.82
Kiribati	12	23	40	40	38	0.00	-5.00
Guam	211	106	316	341	382	0.00	12.02
Nauru	240	200	266	174	143	0.00	-17.82
Northern Mariana Islands	29	48	23	10	4	0.00	-60.00
Micronesia, Federated States of	20	27	19	15	31	0.00	106.67
Marshall Islands		4	9	44	33	0.00	-25.00
Palau	45	70	15	36	41	0.00	13.89
Polynesia	909	343	600	740	816	0.00	10.27
Cook Islands	20	7	37	41	43	0.00	4.88
French Polynesia	227	133	202	448	557	0.00	24.33
Tonga	492	108	92	131	116	0.00	-11.45
Tuvalu	4	39	170	5	11	0.00	120.00
Samoa	166	56	99	115	89	0.00	-22.61
Other East Asia and the Pacific	2	1,851	457	25	41	0.00	64.00
Other countries of Asia	2	1,851	442				
Other countries of Oceania			15	25	41	0.00	64.00
EUROPE	3,812,711	3,963,326	4,031,256	4,445,544	5,058,583	26.31	13.79
Central/Eastern Europe	416,891	468,649	502,040	844,587	1,278,080	6.65	51.33
Azerbaijan	674	653	695	906	1,230	0.01	35.76
Armenia	445	909	551	819	933	0.00	13.92
Bulgaria	3,481	3,289	2,809	3,419	4,339	0.02	26.91
Belarus	2,366	2,230	3,447	5,177	6,037	0.03	16.61
Czech Republic	17,960	18,264	25,507	27,370	28,764	0.15	5.09
Estonia	7,327	7,893	6,811	8,357	9,448	0.05	13.05

THAILAND

1. Arrivals of non-resident tourists at national borders, by country of residence

	2007	2008	2009	2010	2011	Market share 11	% Change 11-10
Georgia	265	200	460	631	530	0.00	-16.01
Hungary	17,437	15,771	14,374	16,757	16,163	0.08	-3.54
Kazakhstan	20,909	26,966	24,994	28,922	35,345	0.18	22.21
Kyrgyzstan	442	1,009	938	1,243	1,491	0.01	19.95
Latvia	5,527	4,126	3,278	4,233	5,079	0.03	19.99
Lithuania	3,142	3,922	4,867	5,298	6,215	0.03	17.31
Republic of Moldova	348	356	425	660	799	0.00	21.06
Poland	18,353	24,409	30,074	34,832	36,546	0.19	4.92
Romania	4,231	5,012	5,624	6,670	8,400	0.04	25.94
Russian Federation	279,771	319,587	334,915	643,839	1,052,361	5.47	63.45
Slovakia	4,886	5,577	7,544	8,426	9,124	0.05	8.28
Tajikistan	149	352	175	295	299	0.00	1.36
Turkmenistan	768	777	2,207	3,811	4,808	0.03	26.16
Ukraine	24,260	22,179	28,005	36,886	41,233	0.21	11.78
Uzbekistan	4,150	3,608	3,971	5,858	8,720	0.05	48.86
Other countries Central/East Europe		1,560	369	178	216	0.00	21.35
Northern Europe	**1,574,905**	**1,663,558**	**1,603,566**	**1,595,573**	**1,649,950**	**8.58**	**3.41**
Denmark	135,006	151,903	143,326	150,300	159,620	0.83	6.20
Finland	138,332	158,480	155,574	145,510	154,002	0.80	5.84
Iceland	2,530	3,334	2,549	3,276	3,614	0.02	10.32
Ireland	68,219	73,220	63,755	54,733	55,038	0.29	0.56
Norway	110,076	128,380	120,668	132,865	137,066	0.71	3.16
Sweden	374,320	389,665	340,381	348,640	369,144	1.92	5.88
United Kingdom	746,422	758,576	777,313	760,249	771,466	4.01	1.48
Southern Europe	**288,276**	**274,107**	**287,075**	**276,659**	**320,211**	**1.67**	**15.74**
Albania	237	320	291	289	316	0.00	9.34
Andorra	245	201	200	227	231	0.00	1.76
Bosnia and Herzegovina	184	333	314	381	597	0.00	56.69
Croatia	2,138	2,747	2,807	2,828	3,437	0.02	21.53
Greece	19,408	19,218	18,483	17,529	15,231	0.08	-13.11
Italy	158,923	147,541	164,341	161,086	174,902	0.91	8.58
Malta	1,181	1,012	1,243	1,565	1,926	0.01	23.07
Montenegro			69	164	226	0.00	37.80
Portugal	13,277	16,823	13,418	14,463	16,259	0.08	12.42
San Marino	77	269	119	174	209	0.00	20.11
Serbia	2,340	554	2,441	2,628	3,224	0.02	22.68
Slovenia	5,306	4,535	5,863	5,732	6,062	0.03	5.76
Spain	84,714	80,287	77,160	69,223	97,149	0.51	40.34
TFYR of Macedonia	246	267	326	370	442	0.00	19.46
Western Europe	**1,372,289**	**1,418,077**	**1,492,771**	**1,567,854**	**1,635,111**	**8.50**	**4.29**
Austria	74,150	76,563	87,469	88,788	86,987	0.45	-2.03
Belgium	69,042	75,254	81,514	80,246	82,699	0.43	3.06
France	351,651	384,342	401,293	439,773	484,602	2.52	10.19
Germany	537,200	531,241	556,852	596,960	603,979	3.14	1.18
Liechtenstein	547	424	514	610	676	0.00	10.82
Luxembourg	3,770	3,357	4,011	4,713	4,962	0.03	5.28
Monaco	560	405	526	643	759	0.00	18.04
Netherlands	183,347	193,740	203,675	190,539	189,727	0.99	-0.43
Switzerland	152,022	152,751	156,917	165,582	180,720	0.94	9.14
East Mediterranean Europe	**160,316**	**138,899**	**145,281**	**159,373**	**173,969**	**0.90**	**9.16**
Cyprus	4,609	3,979	3,426	3,472	3,704	0.02	6.68
Israel	123,012	100,947	111,243	115,961	125,149	0.65	7.92
Turkey	32,695	33,973	30,612	39,940	45,116	0.23	12.96
Other Europe	**34**	**36**	**523**	**1,498**	**1,262**	**0.01**	**-15.75**
Other countries of Europe	34	36	523	1,498	1,262	0.01	-15.75

THAILAND

1. Arrivals of non-resident tourists at national borders, by country of residence

	2007	2008	2009	2010	2011	Market share 11	% Change 11-10
MIDDLE EAST	**265,327**	**282,878**	**298,079**	**331,253**	**379,382**	**1.97**	**14.53**
Bahrain	14,219	14,237	18,545	20,527	23,167	0.12	12.86
Palestine	439	861	718	1,037	1,427	0.01	37.61
Iraq	1,380	1,656	1,973	2,173	2,096	0.01	-3.54
Jordan	7,072	8,070	8,913	7,459	8,348	0.04	11.92
Kuwait	35,083	31,890	47,115	45,223	60,425	0.31	33.62
Lebanon	5,815	5,457	6,036	5,666	6,494	0.03	14.61
Libya	1,299	957	1,439	2,164	866	0.00	-59.98
Oman	40,427	49,328	42,451	47,787	57,876	0.30	21.11
Qatar	16,924	15,138	15,913	22,341	27,788	0.14	24.38
Saudi Arabia	24,256	18,328	14,636	13,031	17,535	0.09	34.56
Syrian Arab Republic	4,451	3,775	4,503	4,315	4,850	0.03	12.40
United Arab Emirates	98,122	116,664	119,450	140,884	149,873	0.78	6.38
Egypt	12,268	13,048	13,394	15,215	15,094	0.08	-0.80
Yemen	3,572	3,469	2,993	3,431	3,543	0.02	3.26
SOUTH ASIA	**750,658**	**749,739**	**923,321**	**1,152,890**	**1,284,902**	**6.68**	**11.45**
Afghanistan	946	855	1,533	1,511	2,127	0.01	40.77
Bangladesh	47,999	46,839	55,818	70,598	68,024	0.35	-3.65
Bhutan	10,022	10,710	12,993	13,664	15,227	0.08	11.44
Sri Lanka	44,239	39,233	45,443	49,827	53,782	0.28	7.94
India	506,237	497,022	596,529	746,214	891,748	4.64	19.50
Iran, Islamic Republic of	65,087	79,687	114,021	167,792	147,381	0.77	-12.16
Maldives	7,829	7,332	7,784	9,197	8,672	0.05	-5.71
Nepal	20,538	21,079	26,683	29,994	26,237	0.14	-12.53
Pakistan	47,761	46,978	62,517	64,091	71,704	0.37	11.88
Other countries of South Asia		4		2			
NOT SPECIFIED	**1,152**			**1,402**			
Other countries of the World	1,152			1,402			

THAILAND

3. Arrivals of non-resident tourists in hotels and similar establishments, by country of residence

	2007	2008	2009	2010	2011	Market share 11	% Change 11-10
TOTAL	13,230,686	12,814,543	11,809,657	13,394,911	16,678,985	100.00	24.52
AFRICA	98,402	99,074	94,090	107,364	125,341	0.75	16.74
Southern Africa	42,804	41,198	35,708	49,161	59,381	0.36	20.79
South Africa	42,804	41,198	35,708	49,161	59,381	0.36	20.79
Other Africa	55,598	57,876	58,382	58,203	65,960	0.40	13.33
Other countries of Africa	55,598	57,876	58,382	58,203	65,960	0.40	13.33
AMERICAS	685,978	691,712	600,320	593,219	678,010	4.07	14.29
North America	646,024	645,223	560,343	545,037	617,599	3.70	13.31
Canada	128,167	131,855	113,047	112,121	139,435	0.84	24.36
United States of America	517,857	513,368	447,296	432,916	478,164	2.87	10.45
South America	14,840	18,295	16,908	21,998	28,796	0.17	30.90
Argentina	4,903	4,836	4,989	7,727	10,203	0.06	32.04
Brazil	9,937	13,459	11,919	14,271	18,593	0.11	30.29
Other Americas	25,114	28,194	23,069	26,184	31,615	0.19	20.74
Other countries of the Americas	25,114	28,194	23,069	26,184	31,615	0.19	20.74
EAST ASIA AND THE PACIFIC	8,081,186	7,564,208	6,812,307	7,703,950	10,072,456	60.39	30.74
North-East Asia	3,975,185	3,481,648	2,811,051	3,290,272	4,359,712	26.14	32.50
China	952,539	901,524	737,552	1,034,585	1,585,394	9.51	53.24
Taiwan, Province of China	400,052	374,626	326,387	322,872	401,209	2.41	24.26
Hong Kong, China	430,502	328,299	354,285	366,216	504,231	3.02	37.69
Japan	1,151,809	1,021,194	834,661	823,694	928,510	5.57	12.73
Korea, Republic of	1,040,283	856,005	558,166	742,905	940,368	5.64	26.58
South-East Asia	3,420,177	3,393,988	3,365,480	3,741,320	4,885,978	29.29	30.60
Brunei Darussalam	11,850	11,729	9,413	7,899	9,327	0.06	18.08
Myanmar	59,333	56,902	56,665	63,434	80,684	0.48	27.19
Cambodia	95,786	75,856	82,425	114,203	213,047	1.28	86.55
Indonesia	218,809	233,530	200,466	255,480	343,688	2.06	34.53
Lao People's Democratic Republic	422,133	315,492	439,080	448,412	599,791	3.60	33.76
Malaysia	1,480,805	1,607,078	1,514,040	1,771,632	2,278,863	13.66	28.63
Philippines	169,650	179,295	165,915	180,341	206,581	1.24	14.55
Singapore	738,028	591,827	569,176	564,058	698,750	4.19	23.88
Viet Nam	223,783	322,279	328,300	335,861	455,247	2.73	35.55
Australasia	661,254	686,139	607,971	641,929	782,190	4.69	21.85
Australia	579,927	606,949	545,001	577,413	706,856	4.24	22.42
New Zealand	81,327	79,190	62,970	64,516	75,334	0.45	16.77
Other East Asia and the Pacific	24,570	2,433	27,805	30,429	44,576	0.27	46.49
Other countries of Asia	21,842		24,018	25,663	38,944	0.23	51.75
Other countries of Oceania	2,728	2,433	3,787	4,766	5,632	0.03	18.17
EUROPE	3,414,674	3,487,501	3,192,749	3,629,839	4,258,422	25.53	17.32
Central/Eastern Europe	394,604	452,143	442,463	775,368	1,191,791	7.15	53.71
Russian Federation	271,894	309,786	300,739	599,780	988,463	5.93	64.80
Other countries Central/East Europe	122,710	142,357	141,724	175,588	203,328	1.22	15.80
Northern Europe	1,315,855	1,352,024	1,185,544	1,181,229	1,230,800	7.38	4.20
Denmark	120,856	133,901	113,462	122,325	132,702	0.80	8.48
Finland	128,842	144,073	126,718	115,461	121,881	0.73	5.56
Norway	93,407	104,565	88,528	95,734	99,739	0.60	4.18
Sweden	338,278	334,820	264,074	267,304	281,746	1.69	5.40
United Kingdom	634,472	634,665	592,762	580,405	594,732	3.57	2.47
Southern Europe	223,334	206,888	198,624	192,329	235,630	1.41	22.51
Italy	144,226	131,954	134,454	133,869	150,302	0.90	12.28
Spain	79,108	74,934	64,170	58,460	85,328	0.51	45.96

THAILAND

3. Arrivals of non-resident tourists in hotels and similar establishments, by country of residence

	2007	2008	2009	2010	2011	Market share 11	% Change 11-10
Western Europe	1,212,694	1,229,012	1,148,975	1,249,964	1,344,446	8.06	7.56
Austria	67,346	68,368	70,104	73,136	74,001	0.44	1.18
Belgium	60,097	64,113	60,572	62,511	66,966	0.40	7.13
France	307,964	334,728	302,883	350,595	403,593	2.42	15.12
Germany	482,167	463,527	435,050	478,332	494,598	2.97	3.40
Netherlands	160,173	167,535	158,499	151,030	154,122	0.92	2.05
Switzerland	134,947	130,741	121,867	134,360	151,166	0.91	12.51
East Mediterranean Europe	117,569	95,489	92,728	103,208	117,430	0.70	13.78
Israel	117,569	95,489	92,728	103,208	117,430	0.70	13.78
Other Europe	150,618	151,945	124,415	127,741	138,325	0.83	8.29
Other countries of Europe	150,618	151,945	124,415	127,741	138,325	0.83	8.29
MIDDLE EAST	315,648	347,786	381,935	466,625	494,620	2.97	6.00
Kuwait	33,594	31,344	43,408	43,172	57,806	0.35	33.90
Saudi Arabia	22,900	16,972	13,139	11,297	15,914	0.10	40.87
United Arab Emirates	92,890	110,634	108,940	130,195	138,852	0.83	6.65
Egypt	11,688	12,837	12,305	14,032	14,007	0.08	-0.18
Other countries of Middle East	154,576	175,999	204,143	267,929	268,041	1.61	0.04
SOUTH ASIA	634,798	624,262	728,256	893,914	1,050,136	6.30	17.48
Bangladesh	45,006	43,117	50,269	63,891	61,921	0.37	-3.08
Sri Lanka	41,162	36,543	40,771	46,102	49,926	0.30	8.29
India	470,568	465,617	540,141	682,264	829,328	4.97	21.56
Nepal	17,883	18,778	23,021	25,049	22,324	0.13	-10.88
Pakistan	44,045	43,566	55,805	57,605	66,422	0.40	15.31
Other countries of South Asia	16,134	16,641	18,249	19,003	20,215	0.12	6.38

THE FORMER YUGOSLAV REP OF MACEDONIA

3. Arrivals of non-resident tourists in hotels and similar establishments, by nationality

	2007	2008	2009	2010	2011	Market share 11	% Change 11-10
TOTAL	210,163	213,829	219,803	231,485	301,304	100.00	30.16
AFRICA				214	390	0.13	82.24
Southern Africa				31	48	0.02	54.84
South Africa				31	48	0.02	54.84
Other Africa				183	342	0.11	86.89
Other countries of Africa				183	342	0.11	86.89
AMERICAS	8,680	8,443	8,165	9,014	10,150	3.37	12.60
North America	8,680	8,443	8,165	8,657	9,554	3.17	10.36
Canada	942	975	1,132	1,155	1,268	0.42	9.78
United States of America	7,738	7,468	7,033	7,056	7,655	2.54	8.49
Other countries of North America				446	631	0.21	41.48
South America				132	236	0.08	78.79
Brazil				132	236	0.08	78.79
Other Americas				225	360	0.12	60.00
Other countries of the Americas				225	360	0.12	60.00
EAST ASIA AND THE PACIFIC	4,495	4,121	3,755	9,612	11,637	3.86	21.07
North-East Asia	1,837	1,084	1,152	3,034	4,823	1.60	58.97
China				818	1,616	0.54	97.56
Japan	1,837	1,084	1,152	1,538	2,142	0.71	39.27
Korea, Republic of				678	1,065	0.35	57.08
Australasia	2,658	3,037	2,603	3,677	3,852	1.28	4.76
Australia	2,496	2,808	2,446	3,524	3,642	1.21	3.35
New Zealand	162	229	157	153	210	0.07	37.25
Other East Asia and the Pacific				2,901	2,962	0.98	2.10
Other countries of Asia				1,941	2,723	0.90	40.29
Other countries of Oceania				960	239	0.08	-75.10
EUROPE	193,234	197,173	202,839	212,645	279,127	92.64	31.26
Central/Eastern Europe	29,170	29,300	34,262	31,731	37,943	12.59	19.58
Bulgaria	17,284	18,036	19,479	13,109	16,163	5.36	23.30
Belarus	114	238	156	86	1,146	0.38	1232.56
Czech Republic	1,633	1,911	1,984	1,986	2,390	0.79	20.34
Estonia				144	248	0.08	72.22
Hungary	2,924	2,041	3,014	3,100	3,083	1.02	-0.55
Latvia				219	246	0.08	12.33
Lithuania				201	257	0.09	27.86
Poland	1,475	2,018	4,445	5,736	5,895	1.96	2.77
Romania	1,924	1,770	2,143	3,007	3,559	1.18	18.36
Russian Federation	1,414	1,841	1,605	2,493	3,131	1.04	25.59
Slovakia	1,377	623	867	889	887	0.29	-0.22
Ukraine	1,025	822	569	761	938	0.31	23.26
Northern Europe	11,815	14,016	11,083	12,142	15,204	5.05	25.22
Denmark	1,122	1,608	1,178	1,188	1,198	0.40	0.84
Finland	961	943	1,048	1,137	3,083	1.02	171.15
Iceland	111	200	147	154	122	0.04	-20.78
Ireland	981	714	521	694	1,424	0.47	105.19
Norway	1,229	1,751	1,473	1,423	1,127	0.37	-20.80
Sweden	1,753	2,035	2,089	2,300	2,496	0.83	8.52
United Kingdom	5,658	6,765	4,627	5,246	5,754	1.91	9.68
Southern Europe	114,534	103,735	103,318	114,626	136,034	45.15	18.68
Albania	15,183	14,223	16,232	14,226	11,022	3.66	-22.52
Bosnia and Herzegovina	4,465	3,799	3,961	4,856	4,308	1.43	-11.29
Croatia	11,239	10,821	11,285	11,715	12,724	4.22	8.61
Greece	26,822	18,551	19,379	24,109	44,007	14.61	82.53

THE FORMER YUGOSLAV REP OF MACEDONIA

3. Arrivals of non-resident tourists in hotels and similar establishments, by nationality

	2007	2008	2009	2010	2011	Market share 11	% Change 11-10
Italy	4,969	4,910	4,899	5,650	6,522	2.16	15.43
Malta				21	57	0.02	171.43
Montenegro		2,221	2,205	3,407	3,149	1.05	-7.57
Portugal	596	518	482	622	593	0.20	-4.66
Serbia		35,956	30,671	29,324	30,587	10.15	4.31
Slovenia	10,913	11,184	12,375	11,511	13,169	4.37	14.40
Spain	1,415	1,552	1,829	1,547	1,641	0.54	6.08
Serbia and Montenegro	38,932						
Other countries of Southern Europe				7,638	8,255	2.74	8.08
Western Europe	**23,727**	**24,887**	**25,873**	**28,481**	**45,457**	**15.09**	**59.60**
Austria	4,934	4,837	5,758	5,723	5,347	1.77	-6.57
Belgium	1,601	1,497	1,596	1,643	2,335	0.77	42.12
France	3,433	3,736	4,344	4,573	4,627	1.54	1.18
Germany	8,410	8,407	8,326	8,700	9,070	3.01	4.25
Luxembourg				52	74	0.02	42.31
Netherlands	3,516	4,634	4,275	5,867	21,553	7.15	267.36
Switzerland	1,833	1,776	1,574	1,923	2,451	0.81	27.46
East Mediterranean Europe	**10,239**	**20,497**	**21,796**	**21,872**	**41,867**	**13.90**	**91.42**
Cyprus				193	631	0.21	226.94
Israel	1,744	6,424	5,928	2,799	3,212	1.07	14.76
Turkey	8,495	14,073	15,868	18,880	38,024	12.62	101.40
Other Europe	**3,749**	**4,738**	**6,507**	**3,793**	**2,622**	**0.87**	**-30.87**
Other countries of Europe	3,749	4,738	6,507	3,793	2,622	0.87	-30.87
NOT SPECIFIED	**3,754**	**4,092**	**5,044**				
Other countries of the World	3,754	4,092	5,044				

THE FORMER YUGOSLAV REP OF MACEDONIA

4. Arrivals of non-resident tourists in all types of accommodation establishments, by nationality

	2007	2008	2009	2010	2011	Market share 11	% Change 11-10
TOTAL	230,080	254,957	259,204	261,696	327,471	100.00	25.13
AFRICA				228	408	0.12	78.95
Southern Africa				32	52	0.02	62.50
South Africa				32	52	0.02	62.50
Other Africa				196	356	0.11	81.63
Other countries of Africa				196	356	0.11	81.63
AMERICAS	8,947	9,632	9,083	9,724	10,744	3.28	10.49
North America	8,947	9,632	9,083	9,353	10,084	3.08	7.82
Canada	969	1,160	1,257	1,247	1,366	0.42	9.54
United States of America	7,978	8,472	7,826	7,655	8,082	2.47	5.58
Other countries of North America				451	636	0.19	41.02
South America				142	252	0.08	77.46
Brazil				142	252	0.08	77.46
Other Americas				229	408	0.12	78.17
Other countries of the Americas				229	408	0.12	78.17
EAST ASIA AND THE PACIFIC	4,799	4,674	4,255	10,331	12,153	3.71	17.64
North-East Asia	1,861	1,236	1,268	3,160	4,928	1.50	55.95
China				853	1,664	0.51	95.08
Japan	1,861	1,236	1,268	1,621	2,194	0.67	35.35
Korea, Republic of				686	1,070	0.33	55.98
Australasia	2,938	3,438	2,987	4,174	4,227	1.29	1.27
Australia	2,755	3,165	2,784	3,967	3,974	1.21	0.18
New Zealand	183	273	203	207	253	0.08	22.22
Other East Asia and the Pacific				2,997	2,998	0.92	0.03
Other countries of Asia				2,015	2,755	0.84	36.72
Other countries of Oceania				982	243	0.07	-75.25
EUROPE	212,365	236,122	240,333	241,413	304,166	92.88	25.99
Central/Eastern Europe	32,005	36,483	42,033	36,639	42,903	13.10	17.10
Bulgaria	18,901	21,922	23,619	15,513	18,541	5.66	19.52
Belarus	114	253	178	101	1,151	0.35	1039.60
Czech Republic	1,990	2,406	2,583	2,423	2,695	0.82	11.23
Estonia				176	260	0.08	47.73
Hungary	3,037	3,254	3,365	3,492	3,342	1.02	-4.30
Latvia				239	308	0.09	28.87
Lithuania				251	280	0.09	11.55
Poland	1,728	2,434	5,827	6,182	6,758	2.06	9.32
Romania	2,137	2,240	2,677	3,351	3,882	1.19	15.85
Russian Federation	1,523	2,091	1,872	2,848	3,545	1.08	24.47
Slovakia	1,496	811	1,140	1,082	1,099	0.34	1.57
Ukraine	1,079	1,072	772	981	1,042	0.32	6.22
Northern Europe	12,209	15,779	12,611	13,095	16,373	5.00	25.03
Denmark	1,168	1,748	1,338	1,273	1,251	0.38	-1.73
Finland	1,018	1,088	1,220	1,233	3,432	1.05	178.35
Iceland	115	230	161	164	137	0.04	-16.46
Ireland	1,011	792	610	745	1,500	0.46	101.34
Norway	1,263	1,920	1,618	1,503	1,212	0.37	-19.36
Sweden	1,845	2,311	2,355	2,530	2,702	0.83	6.80
United Kingdom	5,789	7,690	5,309	5,647	6,139	1.87	8.71
Southern Europe	128,309	126,109	123,310	133,039	150,726	46.03	13.29
Albania	17,573	19,314	19,757	17,110	13,614	4.16	-20.43
Bosnia and Herzegovina	4,887	4,443	4,672	5,619	4,959	1.51	-11.75
Croatia	12,326	12,302	12,519	12,791	13,885	4.24	8.55
Greece	28,618	21,060	22,253	26,843	45,509	13.90	69.54

THE FORMER YUGOSLAV REP OF MACEDONIA

4. Arrivals of non-resident tourists in all types of accommodation establishments, by nationality

	2007	2008	2009	2010	2011	Market share 11	% Change 11-10
Italy	5,123	5,674	6,050	6,181	7,140	2.18	15.52
Malta				23	60	0.02	160.87
Montenegro		2,761	2,653	4,180	3,522	1.08	-15.74
Portugal	611	552	601	655	727	0.22	10.99
Serbia		45,134	38,744	35,840	35,692	10.90	-0.41
Slovenia	13,046	13,159	13,970	12,606	14,063	4.29	11.56
Spain	1,464	1,710	2,091	1,711	1,726	0.53	0.88
Serbia and Montenegro	44,661						
Other countries of Southern Europe				9,480	9,829	3.00	3.68
Western Europe	**25,012**	**28,613**	**29,821**	**31,240**	**47,982**	**14.65**	**53.59**
Austria	5,186	5,315	6,437	6,143	5,681	1.73	-7.52
Belgium	1,748	1,711	1,839	1,848	2,519	0.77	36.31
France	3,594	4,278	4,914	4,858	4,901	1.50	0.89
Germany	8,840	9,655	9,795	9,573	9,822	3.00	2.60
Luxembourg				53	107	0.03	101.89
Netherlands	3,705	5,606	4,988	6,612	22,219	6.79	236.04
Switzerland	1,939	2,048	1,848	2,153	2,733	0.83	26.94
East Mediterranean Europe	**10,716**	**22,093**	**23,072**	**23,126**	**43,235**	**13.20**	**86.95**
Cyprus				194	675	0.21	247.94
Israel	1,809	6,532	6,110	2,885	3,309	1.01	14.70
Turkey	8,907	15,561	16,962	20,047	39,251	11.99	95.79
Other Europe	**4,114**	**7,045**	**9,486**	**4,274**	**2,947**	**0.90**	**-31.05**
Other countries of Europe	4,114	7,045	9,486	4,274	2,947	0.90	-31.05
NOT SPECIFIED	**3,969**	**4,529**	**5,533**				
Other countries of the World	3,969	4,529	5,533				

THE FORMER YUGOSLAV REP OF MACEDONIA

5. Overnight stays of non-resident tourists in hotels and similar establishments, by nationality

	2007	2008	2009	2010	2011	Market share 11	% Change 11-10
TOTAL	457,428	474,577	468,706	468,822	667,430	100.00	42.36
AFRICA				537	1,114	0.17	107.45
Southern Africa				72	238	0.04	230.56
South Africa				72	238	0.04	230.56
Other Africa				465	876	0.13	88.39
Other countries of Africa				465	876	0.13	88.39
AMERICAS	22,359	22,109	21,647	23,864	24,948	3.74	4.54
North America	22,359	22,109	21,647	23,185	23,799	3.57	2.65
Canada	2,203	2,326	2,592	2,274	3,171	0.48	39.45
United States of America	20,156	19,783	19,055	19,939	19,309	2.89	-3.16
Other countries of North America				972	1,319	0.20	35.70
South America				268	472	0.07	76.12
Brazil				268	472	0.07	76.12
Other Americas				411	677	0.10	64.72
Other countries of the Americas				411	677	0.10	64.72
EAST ASIA AND THE PACIFIC	8,437	8,345	7,036	18,719	22,222	3.33	18.71
North-East Asia	3,197	1,840	2,057	5,354	8,279	1.24	54.63
China				1,735	3,929	0.59	126.46
Japan	3,197	1,840	2,057	2,776	3,114	0.47	12.18
Korea, Republic of				843	1,236	0.19	46.62
Australasia	5,240	6,505	4,979	7,293	8,252	1.24	13.15
Australia	5,030	6,039	4,745	7,060	7,836	1.17	10.99
New Zealand	210	466	234	233	416	0.06	78.54
Other East Asia and the Pacific				6,072	5,691	0.85	-6.27
Other countries of Asia				4,117	5,031	0.75	22.20
Other countries of Oceania				1,955	660	0.10	-66.24
EUROPE	417,117	433,527	427,495	425,702	619,146	92.77	45.44
Central/Eastern Europe	59,501	62,056	71,841	65,681	78,318	11.73	19.24
Bulgaria	33,734	34,558	37,823	23,573	29,903	4.48	26.85
Belarus	239	832	379	216	2,702	0.40	1150.93
Czech Republic	3,184	3,906	4,034	3,921	5,006	0.75	27.67
Estonia				350	902	0.14	157.71
Hungary	4,485	3,924	5,227	5,333	5,694	0.85	6.77
Latvia				541	718	0.11	32.72
Lithuania				503	960	0.14	90.85
Poland	2,774	5,077	10,998	12,008	11,397	1.71	-5.09
Romania	3,964	4,405	4,780	6,888	7,622	1.14	10.66
Russian Federation	3,435	5,425	4,543	7,963	8,952	1.34	12.42
Slovakia	5,075	1,342	2,301	2,279	2,083	0.31	-8.60
Ukraine	2,611	2,587	1,756	2,106	2,379	0.36	12.96
Northern Europe	27,187	34,560	26,012	28,839	38,442	5.76	33.30
Denmark	2,628	4,054	2,638	2,412	2,766	0.41	14.68
Finland	2,020	2,009	2,093	2,398	9,731	1.46	305.80
Iceland	209	588	483	293	217	0.03	-25.94
Ireland	2,726	1,952	1,246	1,992	3,523	0.53	76.86
Norway	2,921	5,211	3,793	3,399	2,418	0.36	-28.86
Sweden	4,179	5,329	4,850	5,010	5,780	0.87	15.37
United Kingdom	12,504	15,417	10,909	13,335	14,007	2.10	5.04
Southern Europe	245,425	212,022	205,111	219,982	259,689	38.91	18.05
Albania	30,179	26,814	28,698	25,716	19,508	2.92	-24.14
Bosnia and Herzegovina	9,625	8,382	8,947	11,813	9,638	1.44	-18.41
Croatia	21,720	21,795	23,104	23,116	25,051	3.75	8.37
Greece	54,937	34,805	32,158	38,845	74,697	11.19	92.30

THE FORMER YUGOSLAV REP OF MACEDONIA

5. Overnight stays of non-resident tourists in hotels and similar establishments, by nationality

	2007	2008	2009	2010	2011	Market share 11	% Change 11-10
Italy	10,224	10,505	10,939	12,042	15,081	2.26	25.24
Malta				62	148	0.02	138.71
Montenegro		4,533	4,492	6,413	6,448	0.97	0.55
Portugal	1,465	1,146	1,233	1,332	1,770	0.27	32.88
Serbia		78,112	66,906	59,971	60,243	9.03	0.45
Slovenia	20,823	21,503	24,720	23,654	28,343	4.25	19.82
Spain	3,792	4,427	3,914	3,413	3,278	0.49	-3.96
Serbia and Montenegro	92,660						
Other countries of Southern Europe				13,605	15,484	2.32	13.81
Western Europe	**52,772**	**60,111**	**56,660**	**62,120**	**162,044**	**24.28**	**160.86**
Austria	9,592	9,673	10,945	10,196	9,959	1.49	-2.32
Belgium	3,407	3,310	3,662	3,401	6,923	1.04	103.56
France	7,835	8,027	8,346	9,183	8,849	1.33	-3.64
Germany	19,851	19,256	20,011	20,334	19,980	2.99	-1.74
Luxembourg				152	271	0.04	78.29
Netherlands	8,450	16,176	10,434	15,117	110,061	16.49	628.06
Switzerland	3,637	3,669	3,262	3,737	6,001	0.90	60.58
East Mediterranean Europe	**23,306**	**55,352**	**53,603**	**40,935**	**72,794**	**10.91**	**77.83**
Cyprus				305	1,426	0.21	367.54
Israel	4,301	26,727	22,440	7,645	10,252	1.54	34.10
Turkey	19,005	28,625	31,163	32,985	61,116	9.16	85.28
Other Europe	**8,926**	**9,426**	**14,268**	**8,145**	**7,859**	**1.18**	**-3.51**
Other countries of Europe	8,926	9,426	14,268	8,145	7,859	1.18	-3.51
NOT SPECIFIED	**9,515**	**10,596**	**12,528**				
Other countries of the World	9,515	10,596	12,528				

THE FORMER YUGOSLAV REP OF MACEDONIA

6. Overnight stays of non-resident tourists in all types of accommodation establishments, by nationality

	2007	2008	2009	2010	2011	Market share 11	% Change 11-10
TOTAL	518,088	587,447	583,796	559,032	755,166	100.00	35.08
AFRICA				589	1,219	0.16	106.96
Southern Africa				74	251	0.03	239.19
South Africa				74	251	0.03	239.19
Other Africa				515	968	0.13	87.96
Other countries of Africa				515	968	0.13	87.96
AMERICAS	23,114	25,877	24,564	25,614	27,078	3.59	5.72
North America	23,114	25,877	24,564	24,899	25,588	3.39	2.77
Canada	2,283	2,913	2,889	2,458	3,630	0.48	47.68
United States of America	20,831	22,964	21,675	21,456	20,632	2.73	-3.84
Other countries of North America				985	1,326	0.18	34.62
South America				292	520	0.07	78.08
Brazil				292	520	0.07	78.08
Other Americas				423	970	0.13	129.31
Other countries of the Americas				423	970	0.13	129.31
EAST ASIA AND THE PACIFIC	8,955	9,576	8,070	20,978	24,252	3.21	15.61
North-East Asia	3,239	2,228	2,274	5,630	8,467	1.12	50.39
China				1,842	4,027	0.53	118.62
Japan	3,239	2,228	2,274	2,905	3,196	0.42	10.02
Korea, Republic of				883	1,244	0.16	40.88
Australasia	5,716	7,348	5,796	8,835	9,908	1.31	12.14
Australia	5,485	6,793	5,488	8,523	9,397	1.24	10.25
New Zealand	231	555	308	312	511	0.07	63.78
Other East Asia and the Pacific				6,513	5,877	0.78	-9.77
Other countries of Asia				4,472	5,213	0.69	16.57
Other countries of Oceania				2,041	664	0.09	-67.47
EUROPE	475,920	539,964	536,748	511,851	702,617	93.04	37.27
Central/Eastern Europe	66,562	77,913	90,111	77,966	92,372	12.23	18.48
Bulgaria	37,246	42,246	46,656	29,098	35,152	4.65	20.81
Belarus	239	882	466	290	2,715	0.36	836.21
Czech Republic	3,964	5,111	5,074	4,978	5,807	0.77	16.65
Estonia				517	938	0.12	81.43
Hungary	4,776	5,840	6,310	6,333	6,458	0.86	1.97
Latvia				663	982	0.13	48.11
Lithuania				743	1,051	0.14	41.45
Poland	3,549	6,243	14,099	13,140	13,730	1.82	4.49
Romania	4,475	5,846	6,393	7,940	8,757	1.16	10.29
Russian Federation	4,024	6,514	6,001	9,035	11,082	1.47	22.66
Slovakia	5,336	1,769	2,836	2,794	2,783	0.37	-0.39
Ukraine	2,953	3,462	2,276	2,435	2,917	0.39	19.79
Northern Europe	28,292	38,943	29,787	31,608	41,819	5.54	32.31
Denmark	2,808	4,482	3,088	2,680	2,899	0.38	8.17
Finland	2,227	2,397	2,391	2,710	10,459	1.38	285.94
Iceland	220	714	522	321	257	0.03	-19.94
Ireland	2,780	2,148	1,488	2,109	3,771	0.50	78.81
Norway	3,005	5,729	4,056	3,596	2,717	0.36	-24.44
Sweden	4,426	5,879	5,442	5,786	6,488	0.86	12.13
United Kingdom	12,826	17,594	12,800	14,406	15,228	2.02	5.71
Southern Europe	290,434	271,971	266,210	278,647	313,521	41.52	12.52
Albania	39,831	48,086	47,711	43,269	35,916	4.76	-16.99
Bosnia and Herzegovina	11,220	10,316	10,861	13,985	14,317	1.90	2.37
Croatia	23,793	25,034	26,061	26,111	28,531	3.78	9.27
Greece	58,525	38,918	37,478	43,043	77,651	10.28	80.40

THE FORMER YUGOSLAV REP OF MACEDONIA

6. Overnight stays of non-resident tourists in all types of accommodation establishments, by nationality

	2007	2008	2009	2010	2011	Market share 11	% Change 11-10
Italy	10,624	12,493	15,233	13,381	16,509	2.19	23.38
Malta				68	156	0.02	129.41
Montenegro		5,720	5,412	7,825	7,366	0.98	-5.87
Portugal	1,484	1,273	1,619	1,385	2,038	0.27	47.15
Serbia		99,985	88,882	74,959	72,601	9.61	-3.15
Slovenia	24,098	25,274	28,048	26,200	30,681	4.06	17.10
Spain	3,950	4,872	4,905	3,905	3,490	0.46	-10.63
Serbia and Montenegro	116,909						
Other countries of Southern Europe				24,516	24,265	3.21	-1.02
Western Europe	**55,671**	**69,010**	**66,682**	**70,459**	**169,672**	**22.47**	**140.81**
Austria	10,105	10,835	12,253	11,506	10,754	1.42	-6.54
Belgium	3,793	4,000	4,353	4,097	7,418	0.98	81.06
France	8,286	9,215	9,963	9,909	9,665	1.28	-2.46
Germany	20,758	22,465	23,845	22,767	22,222	2.94	-2.39
Luxembourg				165	472	0.06	186.06
Netherlands	8,921	18,313	12,502	17,417	112,309	14.87	544.82
Switzerland	3,808	4,182	3,766	4,598	6,832	0.90	48.59
East Mediterranean Europe	**24,408**	**58,702**	**56,036**	**44,142**	**76,523**	**10.13**	**73.36**
Cyprus				306	1,597	0.21	421.90
Israel	4,382	26,996	22,823	7,821	10,459	1.38	33.73
Turkey	20,026	31,706	33,213	36,015	64,467	8.54	79.00
Other Europe	**10,553**	**23,425**	**27,922**	**9,029**	**8,710**	**1.15**	**-3.53**
Other countries of Europe	10,553	23,425	27,922	9,029	8,710	1.15	-3.53
NOT SPECIFIED	**10,099**	**12,030**	**14,414**				
Other countries of the World	10,099	12,030	14,414				

TIMOR-LESTE

1. Arrivals of non-resident tourists at national borders, by country of residence

		2007	2008	2009	2010	2011	Market share 11	% Change 11-10
TOTAL	(*)	22,254	35,999	44,131	39,825	50,590	100.00	27.03
AMERICAS		1,950	2,879	3,402	2,523	3,185	6.30	26.24
Caribbean		171	292	279				
Cuba		171	292	279				
North America		1,351	1,765	2,274	1,720	2,207	4.36	28.31
Canada		285	470	472				
United States of America		1,066	1,295	1,802	1,720	2,207	4.36	28.31
South America		428	822	849	803	978	1.93	21.79
Brazil		428	822	849	803	978	1.93	21.79
EAST ASIA AND THE PACIFIC		12,163	20,707	26,269	28,101	34,766	68.72	23.72
North-East Asia		1,674	2,806	3,739	3,867	4,696	9.28	21.44
China		669	976	1,991	2,659	3,464	6.85	30.27
Japan		701	967	1,106	1,208	1,232	2.44	1.99
Korea, Republic of		304	863	642				
South-East Asia		5,502	8,101	10,501	12,172	16,940	33.48	39.17
Indonesia		2,758	4,212	5,443	6,744	11,179	22.10	65.76
Malaysia		655	1,232	1,956	1,756	1,829	3.62	4.16
Philippines		1,254	1,566	1,709	2,177	2,413	4.77	10.84
Singapore		835	1,091	1,393	1,495	1,519	3.00	1.61
Australasia		4,987	9,800	12,029	12,062	13,130	25.95	8.85
Australia		4,434	8,948	11,207	11,262	12,419	24.55	10.27
New Zealand		553	852	822	800	711	1.41	-11.13
EUROPE		3,639	5,117	6,066	1,925	6,918	13.67	259.38
Northern Europe		428	722	806	929	1,002	1.98	7.86
United Kingdom		428	722	806	929	1,002	1.98	7.86
Southern Europe		2,818	3,929	4,795	996	5,916	11.69	493.98
Italy		187	204	294				
Portugal		2,631	3,725	4,501	996	5,916	11.69	493.98
Western Europe		393	466	465				
Germany		393	466	465				
SOUTH ASIA		530	834	2,351	2,426	1,900	3.76	-21.68
Bangladesh		328	434	459				
India		202	400	1,464	2,027	1,451	2.87	-28.42
Pakistan				428	399	449	0.89	12.53
NOT SPECIFIED		3,972	6,462	6,043	4,850	3,821	7.55	-21.22
Other countries of the World		3,972	6,462	6,043	4,850	3,821	7.55	-21.22

TOGO

3. Arrivals of non-resident tourists in hotels and similar establishments, by country of residence

		2007	2008	2009	2010	2011	Market share 11	% Change 11-10
TOTAL		86,165	73,982	149,945	202,044	300,479	100.00	48.72
AFRICA		48,516	38,792	76,496	110,821	135,683	45.16	22.43
West Africa		24,409	19,274	40,231	48,737	65,158	21.68	33.69
Benin		7,037	5,465	12,520	13,788	16,850	5.61	22.21
Ghana		2,090	1,795	3,800	4,553	7,961	2.65	74.85
Côte d'Ivoire		5,348	3,607	6,780	8,933	11,624	3.87	30.12
Nigeria		3,445	3,303	6,873	7,845	10,103	3.36	28.78
Burkina Faso	(*)	6,489	5,104	10,258	13,618	18,620	6.20	36.73
Other Africa		24,107	19,518	36,265	62,084	70,525	23.47	13.60
Other countries of Africa		24,107	19,518	36,265	62,084	70,525	23.47	13.60
AMERICAS		2,928	2,405	5,727	5,921	7,959	2.65	34.42
North America		2,636	1,904	5,448	5,571	6,764	2.25	21.41
Canada		436	424	946	1,111	1,039	0.35	-6.48
United States of America		2,200	1,480	4,502	4,460	5,725	1.91	28.36
Other Americas		292	501	279	350	1,195	0.40	241.43
Other countries of the Americas		292	501	279	350	1,195	0.40	241.43
EAST ASIA AND THE PACIFIC		2,649	3,269	6,002	9,578	11,075	3.69	15.63
North-East Asia		73	49	326	714	860	0.29	20.45
Japan		73	49	326	714	860	0.29	20.45
Other East Asia and the Pacific		2,576	3,220	5,676	8,864	10,215	3.40	15.24
Other countries of Asia		2,576	3,220	5,676	8,864	10,215	3.40	15.24
EUROPE		31,181	29,376	61,385	75,136	144,043	47.94	91.71
Central/Eastern Europe		44	3	19	458	3,562	1.19	677.73
Russian Federation		44	3	19	458	3,562	1.19	677.73
Northern Europe		1,326	761	1,145	2,528	1,138	0.38	-54.98
United Kingdom		1,030	747	1,073	1,545	1,032	0.34	-33.20
Scandinavia		296	14	72	983	106	0.04	-89.22
Southern Europe		1,167	723	2,286	2,655	2,779	0.92	4.67
Italy		1,167	723	2,286	2,655	2,779	0.92	4.67
Western Europe		20,408	15,729	33,456	44,504	50,710	16.88	13.94
France		18,114	13,480	28,229	37,911	44,552	14.83	17.52
Germany		1,115	1,305	3,034	3,029	3,009	1.00	-0.66
Switzerland		328	236	678	868	930	0.31	7.14
Benelux		851	708	1,515	2,696	2,219	0.74	-17.69
Other Europe		8,236	12,160	24,479	24,991	85,854	28.57	243.54
Other countries of Europe		8,236	12,160	24,479	24,991	85,854	28.57	243.54
MIDDLE EAST		772	66	166	374	1,224	0.41	227.27
All countries of Middle East		772	66	166	374	1,224	0.41	227.27
NOT SPECIFIED		119	74	169	214	495	0.16	131.31
Other countries of the World		119	74	169	214	495	0.16	131.31

TOGO

5. Overnight stays of non-resident tourists in hotels and similar establishments, by country of residence

		2007	2008	2009	2010	2011	Market share 11	% Change 11-10
TOTAL		191,981	208,827	317,644	420,516	673,219	100.00	60.09
AFRICA		92,698	97,331	170,482	197,335	275,346	40.90	39.53
West Africa		43,320	46,601	103,801	85,287	129,699	19.27	52.07
Benin		9,363	11,242	21,532	16,050	25,044	3.72	56.04
Ghana		4,304	5,070	6,892	6,851	12,620	1.87	84.21
Côte d'Ivoire		9,818	9,738	17,984	18,902	29,564	4.39	56.41
Nigeria		7,451	7,605	18,950	14,580	20,118	2.99	37.98
Burkina Faso	(*)	12,384	12,946	38,443	28,904	42,353	6.29	46.53
Other Africa		49,378	50,730	66,681	112,048	145,647	21.63	29.99
Other countries of Africa		49,378	50,730	66,681	112,048	145,647	21.63	29.99
AMERICAS		6,086	7,101	13,198	18,045	25,940	3.85	43.75
North America		5,771	6,848	12,852	17,424	22,425	3.33	28.70
Canada		1,604	1,140	1,562	2,322	4,085	0.61	75.93
United States of America		4,167	5,708	11,290	15,102	18,340	2.72	21.44
Other Americas		315	253	346	621	3,515	0.52	466.02
Other countries of the Americas		315	253	346	621	3,515	0.52	466.02
EAST ASIA AND THE PACIFIC		4,921	8,510	15,840	17,561	27,840	4.14	58.53
North-East Asia		116	155	481	912	2,421	0.36	165.46
Japan		116	155	481	912	2,421	0.36	165.46
Other East Asia and the Pacific		4,805	8,355	15,359	16,649	25,419	3.78	52.68
Other countries of Asia		4,805	8,355	15,359	16,649	25,419	3.78	52.68
EUROPE		85,019	95,644	117,244	186,984	340,344	50.55	82.02
Central/Eastern Europe		152	54	14	649	1,523	0.23	134.67
Russian Federation		152	54	14	649	1,523	0.23	134.67
Northern Europe		2,880	2,221	1,907	6,377	2,040	0.30	-68.01
United Kingdom		2,471	2,109	1,831	5,230	1,921	0.29	-63.27
Scandinavia		409	112	76	1,147	119	0.02	-89.63
Southern Europe		2,195	1,748	3,290	4,742	4,414	0.66	-6.92
Italy		2,195	1,748	3,290	4,742	4,414	0.66	-6.92
Western Europe		59,595	54,146	62,041	85,197	100,562	14.94	18.03
France		54,869	48,328	51,546	72,725	86,397	12.83	18.80
Germany		2,441	3,013	6,465	4,626	6,447	0.96	39.36
Switzerland		464	664	1,234	3,200	1,684	0.25	-47.38
Benelux		1,821	2,141	2,796	4,646	6,034	0.90	29.88
Other Europe		20,197	37,475	49,992	90,019	231,805	34.43	157.51
Other countries of Europe		20,197	37,475	49,992	90,019	231,805	34.43	157.51
MIDDLE EAST		3,121	86	343	350	3,130	0.46	794.29
All countries of Middle East		3,121	86	343	350	3,130	0.46	794.29
NOT SPECIFIED		136	155	537	241	619	0.09	156.85
Other countries of the World		136	155	537	241	619	0.09	156.85

TONGA

1. Arrivals of non-resident tourists at national borders, by country of residence

		2007	2008	2009	2010	2011	Market share 11	% Change 11-10
TOTAL	(*)	46,040	49,400	50,645	45,430	46,005	100.00	1.27
AFRICA						42	0.09	
Other Africa						42	0.09	
All countries of Africa						42	0.09	
AMERICAS		6,348	6,223	7,113	6,211	5,942	12.92	-4.33
North America		6,298	6,179	7,063	6,167	5,779	12.56	-6.29
Canada		276	354	404	359	271	0.59	-24.51
United States of America		6,022	5,825	6,659	5,808	5,508	11.97	-5.17
Other Americas		50	44	50	44	163	0.35	270.45
Other countries of the Americas		50	44	50	44	163	0.35	270.45
EAST ASIA AND THE PACIFIC		36,524	39,499	39,137	36,092	36,814	80.02	2.00
North-East Asia		784	909	1,307	1,152	1,380	3.00	19.79
China		321	387	643	628	671	1.46	6.85
Japan		463	522	664	524	541	1.18	3.24
Korea, Republic of						168	0.37	
Australasia		32,424	34,266	34,276	31,629	32,573	70.80	2.98
Australia		10,414	11,431	11,598	10,214	10,320	22.43	1.04
New Zealand		22,010	22,835	22,678	21,415	22,253	48.37	3.91
Melanesia		1,703	2,099	1,671	1,540	1,535	3.34	-0.32
Fiji		1,703	2,099	1,671	1,540	1,535	3.34	-0.32
Polynesia						416	0.90	
American Samoa						130	0.28	
Samoa						286	0.62	
Other East Asia and the Pacific		1,613	2,225	1,883	1,771	910	1.98	-48.62
Other countries of Asia		348	590	619	418	356	0.77	-14.83
Other countries of Oceania		1,265	1,635	1,264	1,353	554	1.20	-59.05
EUROPE		2,868	3,478	4,248	3,001	3,176	6.90	5.83
Northern Europe		867	947	1,360	674	696	1.51	3.26
United Kingdom		867	947	1,360	674	696	1.51	3.26
Southern Europe						175	0.38	
Italy						175	0.38	
Western Europe		765	771	883	719	1,085	2.36	50.90
France						305	0.66	
Germany		765	771	883	719	780	1.70	8.48
Other Europe		1,236	1,760	2,005	1,608	1,220	2.65	-24.13
Other countries of Europe		1,236	1,760	2,005	1,608	1,220	2.65	-24.13
SOUTH ASIA						31	0.07	
India						31	0.07	
NOT SPECIFIED		300	200	147	126			
Other countries of the World		300	200	147	126			

TRINIDAD AND TOBAGO

1. Arrivals of non-resident tourists at national borders, by country of residence

		2007	2008	2009	2010	2011	Market share 11	% Change 11-10
TOTAL	(*)	449,453	437,279	418,864	385,510			
AFRICA		1,509	1,349	1,823	1,159			
East Africa		237	195	415	122			
British Indian Ocean Territory		4	4	3	4			
Burundi		1	1					
Comoros					1			
Ethiopia		9	4	6	5			
Eritrea		1	1					
Djibouti		1						
Kenya		52	63	114	35			
Madagascar		4	2		1			
Malawi		5	10	28	2			
Mauritius		39	16	23	10			
Mozambique		1	2	9				
Reunion		1		3	2			
Rwanda		5	1	12	5			
Seychelles		5	7	6	5			
Zimbabwe		17	6	13	15			
Uganda		55	53	74	11			
United Republic of Tanzania		17	15	89	13			
Zambia		20	10	35	13			
Central Africa		53	50	52	52			
Angola		27	28	1	31			
Cameroon		8	4	41	6			
Central African Republic			3		4			
Chad			5		5			
Congo			1	5	3			
Democratic Republic of the Congo		1		4				
Equatorial Guinea		17	7		2			
Gabon			2	1	1			
North Africa		40	56	23	14			
Algeria		3	17	3	2			
Morocco		15	19	2	1			
Sudan		17	8	4	2			
Tunisia		5	12	14	9			
Southern Africa		738	482	555	469			
Botswana		114	79	130	89			
Lesotho			3	4				
Namibia		8	4	4	4			
South Africa		567	366	406	370			
Swaziland		49	30	11	6			
West Africa		441	566	778	502			
Cape Verde		1						
Benin		1	4	3	1			
Gambia		6	4	11	4			
Ghana		89	190	94	123			
Guinea		9	2	7	3			
Côte d'Ivoire		3	3	6				
Liberia		5	3	5	7			
Mali			1	1	1			
Mauritania		9	2	6	1			
Niger		1		3				
Nigeria		300	332	612	348			
Guinea-Bissau		1	2					
Saint Helena		1	1					
Senegal		3	5	6	5			

TRINIDAD AND TOBAGO

1. Arrivals of non-resident tourists at national borders, by country of residence

	2007	2008	2009	2010	2011	Market share 11	% Change 11-10
Sierra Leone	8	16	22	9			
Togo			1				
Burkina Faso	4	1	1				
AMERICAS	**356,180**	**364,524**	**351,216**	**325,384**			
Caribbean	**74,285**	**69,132**	**58,752**	**54,713**			
Antigua and Barbuda	3,843	3,138	2,283	2,158			
Bahamas	1,334	1,328	1,244	1,076			
Barbados	21,491	19,350	15,672	13,576			
Bermuda	1,010	708	694	556			
British Virgin Islands	1,073	806	646	579			
Cayman Islands	548	731	579	538			
Cuba	302	369	439	467			
Dominica	1,510	1,453	1,239	1,154			
Dominican Republic	779	1,134	1,115	1,196			
Grenada	10,169	9,162	7,339	7,269			
Guadeloupe	621	628	451	525			
Haiti	194	267	188	216			
Jamaica	8,099	8,658	7,776	7,548			
Martinique	1,087	1,016	912	950			
Montserrat	198	161	147	134			
Netherlands Antilles	656	586	495	522			
Aruba	467	395	355	351			
Curaçao	925	772	730	692			
Puerto Rico	1,665	1,992	1,824	1,809			
Saint Kitts and Nevis	1,340	1,255	1,132	936			
Anguilla	338	334	245	228			
Saint Lucia	6,006	5,071	4,429	4,187			
Saint Vincent and the Grenadines	8,860	8,064	7,421	6,726			
Turks and Caicos Islands	112	179	138	94			
United States Virgin Islands	1,658	1,575	1,259	1,226			
Central America	**2,222**	**3,226**	**4,034**	**3,206**			
Belize	318	408	508	442			
Costa Rica	552	820	1,091	859			
El Salvador	168	248	245	134			
Guatemala	187	356	390	400			
Honduras	189	239	521	173			
Nicaragua	70	43	65	64			
Panama	738	1,112	1,214	1,134			
North America	**233,276**	**245,240**	**246,531**	**230,910**			
Canada	51,411	54,205	49,514	46,390			
Greenland	2						
Mexico	1,306	1,480	1,573	1,347			
Saint Pierre and Miquelon		2	6	2			
United States of America	180,557	189,553	195,438	183,171			
South America	**46,397**	**46,926**	**41,899**	**36,555**			
Argentina	673	909	1,106	730			
Bolivia	55	65	117	90			
Brazil	1,333	1,761	1,481	1,524			
Chile	337	326	511	351			
Colombia	1,897	2,305	2,431	2,313			
Ecuador	211	222	220	219			
Falkland Islands, Malvinas	8	1	1	3			
French Guiana	144	176	220	289			
Guyana	25,668	25,097	20,679	18,339			
Paraguay	10	13	40	19			
Peru	279	325	349	290			
Suriname	3,349	3,370	3,085	2,791			

TRINIDAD AND TOBAGO

1. Arrivals of non-resident tourists at national borders, by country of residence

	2007	2008	2009	2010	2011	Market share 11	% Change 11-10
Uruguay	41	104	138	54			
Venezuela	12,392	12,252	11,521	9,543			
EAST ASIA AND THE PACIFIC	**5,767**	**5,190**	**5,394**	**4,582**			
North-East Asia	**2,889**	**2,895**	**3,039**	**2,452**			
China	1,824	1,936	2,057	1,548			
Taiwan, Province of China	84	64	38	60			
Hong Kong, China	109	86	109	125			
Japan	572	446	372	374			
Korea, Dem. People's Republic of	205	205	272	266			
Korea, Republic of	92	156	189	75			
Macao, China				4			
Mongolia	3	2	2				
South-East Asia	**1,288**	**1,151**	**1,140**	**1,100**			
Brunei Darussalam	3		13	4			
Myanmar	5	24	12	12			
Cambodia		3	3	1			
Indonesia	78	50	55	39			
Malaysia	433	346	338	369			
Philippines	618	586	431	474			
Singapore	92	99	209	139			
Viet Nam	5	7	9	7			
Thailand	54	36	70	55			
Australasia	**1,560**	**1,103**	**1,130**	**1,004**			
Australia	1,290	910	950	819			
New Zealand	270	193	180	185			
Melanesia	**11**	**14**	**46**	**14**			
Solomon Islands		5	6	2			
Fiji	4	6	5	9			
New Caledonia	2		1	1			
Vanuatu	2	2	8	1			
Norfolk Island	2						
Papua New Guinea	1	1	26	1			
Micronesia	**15**	**17**	**11**	**2**			
Guam	2	5					
Nauru	7	3	2				
Northern Mariana Islands	2	2	7	1			
Micronesia, Federated States of		4	1				
Marshall Islands	3	3	1				
Wake Island	1			1			
Polynesia	**4**	**10**	**28**	**10**			
American Samoa			1				
Cook Islands		1	4				
French Polynesia		2	4	3			
Niue	1	2					
Pitcairn				1			
Tonga		1	5	5			
Tuvalu	1		4				
Wallis and Futuna Islands	1		1				
Samoa	1	4	9	1			
EUROPE	**82,511**	**63,238**	**57,667**	**52,364**			
Central/Eastern Europe	**935**	**899**	**894**	**920**			
Azerbaijan	29	9	25	13			
Armenia		1					
Bulgaria	41	49	32	23			
Belarus	5	7	1	4			
Czech Republic/Slovakia	1						

TRINIDAD AND TOBAGO

1. Arrivals of non-resident tourists at national borders, by country of residence

	2007	2008	2009	2010	2011	Market share 11	% Change 11-10
Czech Republic	90	103	105	111			
Estonia	52	49	28	78			
Georgia	1	2		1			
Hungary	75	54	72	71			
Kazakhstan	15	17	13	8			
Kyrgyzstan	1			1			
Latvia	59	41	47	63			
Lithuania	13	17	35	19			
Republic of Moldova	3	1		1			
Poland	253	277	256	256			
Romania	69	91	115	88			
Russian Federation	117	81	84	79			
Slovakia	38	30	35	39			
Tajikistan	4	2	4	2			
Turkmenistan	1	1					
Ukraine	51	49	32	60			
Uzbekistan	17	18	10	3			
Northern Europe	**65,445**	**47,968**	**42,965**	**38,264**			
Denmark	1,397	1,018	1,193	963			
Faeroe Islands	2	4	1	3			
Finland	312	234	226	206			
Iceland	8	10	17	20			
Ireland	1,314	999	722	783			
Norway	1,404	1,268	1,107	993			
Sweden	2,326	1,495	1,286	1,109			
United Kingdom	58,660	42,924	38,400	34,179			
Isle of Man	22	16	13	8			
Southern Europe	**2,246**	**2,015**	**2,226**	**2,335**			
Albania	5	4	4	1			
Andorra	1	5	10	7			
Bosnia and Herzegovina	2	13	7	8			
Croatia	53	77	29	67			
Gibraltar	2	4	6	7			
Greece	96	73	108	135			
Holy See			1				
Italy	1,110	920	1,062	966			
Malta	29	24	36	28			
Montenegro	3			2			
Portugal	125	91	98	188			
San Marino		1	1				
Slovenia	45	40	48	41			
Spain	762	745	808	879			
Serbia and Montenegro	13	18	8	6			
Western Europe	**13,681**	**12,102**	**11,288**	**10,567**			
Austria	618	469	437	533			
Belgium	452	487	453	409			
France	2,323	2,277	2,177	1,829			
Germany	5,422	4,876	4,895	4,657			
Luxembourg	9	13	14	15			
Monaco	9	5	4	2			
Netherlands	3,897	3,141	2,409	2,202			
Switzerland	951	834	899	920			
East Mediterranean Europe	**204**	**254**	**294**	**278**			
Cyprus	35	14	33	20			
Israel	114	141	203	168			
Turkey	55	99	58	90			

TRINIDAD AND TOBAGO

1. Arrivals of non-resident tourists at national borders, by country of residence

	2007	2008	2009	2010	2011	Market share 11	% Change 11-10
MIDDLE EAST	**440**	**462**	**468**	**390**			
Bahrain	7	12	4	21			
Iraq	1	6	2	4			
Jordan	5		2	1			
Kuwait	15	13	14	12			
Lebanon	34	28	31	14			
Libya	2	3	2	8			
Oman	7	11	9	6			
Qatar	28	43	32	40			
Saudi Arabia	29	31	82	63			
Syrian Arab Republic	73	65	29	25			
United Arab Emirates	170	171	188	133			
Egypt	68	79	70	63			
Yemen	1		3				
SOUTH ASIA	**3,009**	**2,329**	**2,267**	**1,620**			
Afghanistan	8	47	96	40			
Bangladesh	79	70	134	72			
Sri Lanka	128	73	50	33			
India	2,656	2,017	1,894	1,344			
Iran, Islamic Republic of	8	4	7	2			
Nepal	10	8	10	14			
Pakistan	120	110	76	115			
NOT SPECIFIED	**37**	**187**	**29**	**11**			
Other countries of the World	37	187	29	11			

TUNISIA

1. Arrivals of non-resident tourists at national borders, by nationality

		2007	2008	2009	2010	2011	Market share 11	% Change 11-10
TOTAL	(*)	6,761,906	7,050,434	6,901,406	6,902,749	4,785,119	100.00	-30.68
AFRICA		1,045,637	1,043,121	1,036,070	1,136,066	829,254	17.33	-27.01
North Africa		1,010,891	1,001,987	991,827	1,090,339	746,276	15.60	-31.56
Algeria		980,587	968,499	961,343	1,060,043	693,732	14.50	-34.56
Morocco		29,189	32,430	29,458	29,104	34,748	0.73	19.39
Sudan		1,115	1,058	1,026	1,192	17,796	0.37	1392.95
West Africa		9,627	12,049	13,063	13,279	13,100	0.27	-1.35
Mauritania		9,627	12,049	13,063	13,279	13,100	0.27	-1.35
Other Africa		25,119	29,085	31,180	32,448	69,878	1.46	115.35
Other countries of Africa		25,119	29,085	31,180	32,448	69,878	1.46	115.35
AMERICAS		36,450	38,877	39,369	39,195	24,098	0.50	-38.52
North America		33,746	36,275	36,275	36,203	22,722	0.47	-37.24
Canada		15,884	17,109	16,969	16,910	8,385	0.18	-50.41
United States of America		17,862	19,166	19,306	19,293	14,337	0.30	-25.69
South America		2,704	2,602	3,094	2,992	1,376	0.03	-54.01
Brazil		2,704	2,602	3,094	2,992	1,376	0.03	-54.01
EAST ASIA AND THE PACIFIC		16,702	16,472	17,016	20,997	16,344	0.34	-22.16
North-East Asia		14,215	13,954	14,582	17,997	14,992	0.31	-16.70
China		2,801	2,748	3,509	4,612	11,872	0.25	157.42
Japan		11,414	11,206	11,073	13,385	3,120	0.07	-76.69
Australasia		2,487	2,518	2,434	3,000	1,352	0.03	-54.93
Australia		2,487	2,518	2,434	3,000	1,352	0.03	-54.93
EUROPE		4,048,429	4,106,676	3,743,509	3,814,402	2,133,916	44.59	-44.06
Central/Eastern Europe		579,799	630,144	480,784	494,435	359,697	7.52	-27.25
Bulgaria		6,284	6,965	6,125	6,720	1,334	0.03	-80.15
Czech Republic		153,356	125,573	92,713	76,678	67,362	1.41	-12.15
Hungary		53,985	54,734	30,148	30,331	17,233	0.36	-43.18
Poland		148,707	207,531	175,319	151,372	97,457	2.04	-35.62
Romania		35,110	31,490	14,256	10,494	4,893	0.10	-53.37
Russian Federation		140,728	160,518	126,516	188,261	151,911	3.17	-19.31
Slovakia		41,629	43,333	35,707	30,579	19,507	0.41	-36.21
Northern Europe		434,383	387,445	397,519	499,754	254,258	5.31	-49.12
Denmark		18,365	26,543	23,386	31,565	6,453	0.13	-79.56
Finland		19,624	21,691	15,992	15,822	2,165	0.05	-86.32
Ireland		18,193	17,564	17,250	14,821	4,479	0.09	-69.78
Norway		15,322	18,036	18,636	21,467	4,397	0.09	-79.52
Sweden		50,106	48,689	46,603	62,797	9,267	0.19	-85.24
United Kingdom		312,773	254,922	275,652	353,282	227,497	4.75	-35.60
Southern Europe		647,442	632,361	545,042	507,857	162,784	3.40	-67.95
Greece		12,641	12,085	7,887	5,436	1,966	0.04	-63.83
Italy		444,474	444,541	383,851	354,127	120,933	2.53	-65.85
Malta		4,903	5,127	2,985	2,962	1,897	0.04	-35.96
Portugal		35,630	41,697	36,567	40,097	9,786	0.20	-75.59
Serbia		22,459	24,129	23,522	21,364	9,635	0.20	-54.90
Spain		127,335	104,782	90,230	83,871	18,567	0.39	-77.86
Western Europe		2,305,690	2,366,553	2,247,450	2,238,370	1,316,123	27.50	-41.20
Austria		89,213	72,866	60,654	53,558	23,946	0.50	-55.29
Belgium		167,443	169,061	168,108	163,124	138,426	2.89	-15.14
France		1,335,409	1,395,255	1,344,697	1,385,293	808,548	16.90	-41.63
Germany		514,040	521,513	484,154	458,631	270,668	5.66	-40.98
Luxembourg		6,930	6,823	7,111	6,201	3,484	0.07	-43.82
Netherlands		86,499	95,307	82,904	75,244	28,571	0.60	-62.03
Switzerland		106,156	105,728	99,822	96,319	42,480	0.89	-55.90

TUNISIA

1. Arrivals of non-resident tourists at national borders, by nationality

	2007	2008	2009	2010	2011	Market share 11	% Change 11-10
East Mediterranean Europe	**10,373**	**13,874**	**14,438**	**18,252**	**10,716**	**0.22**	**-41.29**
Turkey	10,373	13,874	14,438	18,252	10,716	0.22	-41.29
Other Europe	**70,742**	**76,299**	**58,276**	**55,734**	**30,338**	**0.63**	**-45.57**
Other countries of Europe	70,742	76,299	58,276	55,734	30,338	0.63	-45.57
MIDDLE EAST	**1,581,512**	**1,809,090**	**2,034,494**	**1,862,630**	**1,730,832**	**36.17**	**-7.08**
Bahrain	683	944	663	823	376	0.01	-54.31
Palestine	1,634	1,922	1,624	1,691	1,591	0.03	-5.91
Iraq	765	2,765	1,180	1,598	2,022	0.04	26.53
Jordan	2,455	2,753	2,571	2,546	2,226	0.05	-12.57
Kuwait	1,400	1,859	1,689	1,825	801	0.02	-56.11
Lebanon	4,646	4,950	5,097	4,539	3,399	0.07	-25.12
Libya	1,544,839	1,766,881	1,995,236	1,825,542	1,642,620	34.33	-10.02
Oman	1,373	1,375	1,074	1,072	514	0.01	-52.05
Qatar	937	1,212	1,051	897	992	0.02	10.59
Saudi Arabia	7,495	7,193	6,633	6,550	3,068	0.06	-53.16
Syrian Arab Republic	3,237	3,960	3,819	3,597	3,448	0.07	-4.14
United Arab Emirates	1,570	1,966	1,980	1,692	2,093	0.04	23.70
Egypt	9,798	10,240	11,151	9,135	67,282	1.41	636.53
Yemen	680	1,070	726	1,123	400	0.01	-64.38
NOT SPECIFIED	**33,176**	**36,198**	**30,948**	**29,459**	**50,675**	**1.06**	**72.02**
Other countries of the World	33,176	36,198	30,948	29,459	50,675	1.06	72.02

TUNISIA

3. Arrivals of non-resident tourists in hotels and similar establishments, by nationality

	2007	2008	2009	2010	2011	Market share 11	% Change 11-10
TOTAL	5,536,267	5,602,579	5,041,840	5,149,048	2,622,578	100.00	-49.07
AFRICA	299,407	314,940	338,012	394,026	185,406	7.07	-52.95
North Africa	268,238	279,252	301,877	353,215	155,381	5.92	-56.01
Algeria	253,956	262,432	288,109	336,768	143,672	5.48	-57.34
Morocco	14,282	16,820	13,768	16,447	11,709	0.45	-28.81
Other Africa	31,169	35,688	36,135	40,811	30,025	1.14	-26.43
Other countries of Africa	31,169	35,688	36,135	40,811	30,025	1.14	-26.43
AMERICAS	66,718	74,255	80,719	80,270	26,169	1.00	-67.40
North America	65,819	72,922	79,105	78,396	23,965	0.91	-69.43
Canada	39,933	41,855	40,469	45,927	9,588	0.37	-79.12
United States of America	25,886	31,067	38,636	32,469	14,377	0.55	-55.72
South America	899	1,333	1,614	1,874	2,204	0.08	17.61
Brazil	899	1,333	1,614	1,874	2,204	0.08	17.61
EAST ASIA AND THE PACIFIC	52,378	49,397	50,943	66,817	15,593	0.59	-76.66
North-East Asia	50,903	47,001	48,187	63,181	14,055	0.54	-77.75
China	1,825	2,670	4,663	9,572	4,556	0.17	-52.40
Japan	49,078	44,331	43,524	53,609	9,499	0.36	-82.28
Australasia	1,475	2,396	2,756	3,636	1,538	0.06	-57.70
Australia	1,475	2,396	2,756	3,636	1,538	0.06	-57.70
EUROPE	4,768,019	4,781,705	4,217,298	4,191,497	1,967,865	75.04	-53.05
Central/Eastern Europe	721,718	780,813	545,389	552,134	394,668	15.05	-28.52
Bulgaria	3,845	5,228	5,729	4,562	1,197	0.05	-73.76
Czech Republic	174,642	154,085	101,953	89,086	71,565	2.73	-19.67
Hungary	57,782	58,547	36,764	33,347	18,011	0.69	-45.99
Poland	185,910	245,517	188,509	165,150	95,955	3.66	-41.90
Romania	31,224	33,823	12,916	9,723	2,089	0.08	-78.51
Russian Federation	218,798	236,167	166,387	220,557	189,567	7.23	-14.05
Slovakia	49,517	47,446	33,131	29,709	16,284	0.62	-45.19
Northern Europe	470,120	437,021	459,474	549,488	258,974	9.87	-52.87
Ireland	6,103	7,330	9,039	8,108	2,077	0.08	-74.38
United Kingdom	360,745	310,971	327,631	412,581	235,960	9.00	-42.81
Scandinavia	103,272	118,720	122,804	128,799	20,937	0.80	-83.74
Southern Europe	906,906	878,416	785,824	658,807	142,768	5.44	-78.33
Greece	29,508	27,706	17,857	12,445	2,732	0.10	-78.05
Italy	482,113	491,740	473,022	360,571	93,501	3.57	-74.07
Malta	5,507	4,633	2,741	2,782	1,625	0.06	-41.59
Portugal	28,282	30,477	23,660	28,146	5,301	0.20	-81.17
Serbia	18,881	23,389	16,082	13,856	5,604	0.21	-59.56
Spain	342,615	300,471	252,462	241,007	34,005	1.30	-85.89
Western Europe	2,597,394	2,608,635	2,357,807	2,365,398	1,136,539	43.34	-51.95
Austria	66,725	47,576	41,549	39,925	15,605	0.60	-60.91
Belgium	206,917	197,523	181,458	178,201	116,848	4.46	-34.43
France	1,495,700	1,520,655	1,374,242	1,418,234	653,082	24.90	-53.95
Germany	623,895	633,250	563,536	552,683	286,146	10.91	-48.23
Luxembourg	26,786	34,533	35,473	31,955	14,011	0.53	-56.15
Netherlands	79,084	84,841	78,014	68,384	22,361	0.85	-67.30
Switzerland	98,287	90,257	83,535	76,016	28,486	1.09	-62.53
East Mediterranean Europe	8,540	12,239	11,576	12,315	6,476	0.25	-47.41
Turkey	8,540	12,239	11,576	12,315	6,476	0.25	-47.41
Other Europe	63,341	64,581	57,228	53,355	28,440	1.08	-46.70
Other countries of Europe	63,341	64,581	57,228	53,355	28,440	1.08	-46.70

TUNISIA

3. Arrivals of non-resident tourists in hotels and similar establishments, by nationality

	2007	2008	2009	2010	2011	Market share 11	% Change 11-10
MIDDLE EAST	186,352	210,560	207,645	242,515	320,080	12.20	31.98
Libya	142,449	165,979	169,741	202,987	299,904	11.44	47.75
Other countries of Middle East	43,903	44,581	37,904	39,528	20,176	0.77	-48.96
NOT SPECIFIED	163,393	171,722	147,223	173,923	107,465	4.10	-38.21
Other countries of the World	149,011	150,644	128,640	150,146	88,536	3.38	-41.03
Nationals Residing Abroad	14,382	21,078	18,583	23,777	18,929	0.72	-20.39

TUNISIA

5. Overnight stays of non-resident tourists in hotels and similar establishments, by nationality

	2007	2008	2009	2010	2011	Market share 11	% Change 11-10
TOTAL	34,545,666	35,048,653	31,556,910	32,136,191	17,207,634	100.00	-46.45
AFRICA	913,852	929,143	997,642	1,144,741	551,477	3.20	-51.83
North Africa	798,566	805,222	868,249	996,312	437,051	2.54	-56.13
Algeria	757,745	758,517	821,824	945,553	401,765	2.33	-57.51
Morocco	40,821	46,705	46,425	50,759	35,286	0.21	-30.48
Other Africa	115,286	123,921	129,393	148,429	114,426	0.66	-22.91
Other countries of Africa	115,286	123,921	129,393	148,429	114,426	0.66	-22.91
AMERICAS	247,615	277,757	259,458	251,585	129,607	0.75	-48.48
North America	245,293	275,156	255,228	248,579	127,224	0.74	-48.82
Canada	161,458	173,274	164,801	169,754	47,236	0.27	-72.17
United States of America	83,835	101,882	90,427	78,825	79,988	0.46	1.48
South America	2,322	2,601	4,230	3,006	2,383	0.01	-20.73
Brazil	2,322	2,601	4,230	3,006	2,383	0.01	-20.73
EAST ASIA AND THE PACIFIC	78,628	77,312	84,053	115,008	35,930	0.21	-68.76
North-East Asia	75,091	71,161	76,334	103,356	32,061	0.19	-68.98
China	3,175	7,036	8,272	18,017	14,093	0.08	-21.78
Japan	71,916	64,125	68,062	85,339	17,968	0.10	-78.95
Australasia	3,537	6,151	7,719	11,652	3,869	0.02	-66.80
Australia	3,537	6,151	7,719	11,652	3,869	0.02	-66.80
EUROPE	32,191,569	32,598,397	29,157,852	29,403,758	15,125,247	87.90	-48.56
Central/Eastern Europe	5,356,276	5,713,625	4,311,470	4,493,330	3,210,712	18.66	-28.54
Bulgaria	18,629	26,039	29,170	26,384	10,880	0.06	-58.76
Czech Republic	1,421,115	1,203,841	831,093	763,478	576,037	3.35	-24.55
Hungary	365,337	391,006	218,581	199,423	118,187	0.69	-40.74
Poland	1,354,409	1,749,104	1,508,855	1,328,247	800,813	4.65	-39.71
Romania	164,003	171,743	71,180	44,902	6,324	0.04	-85.92
Russian Federation	1,674,991	1,830,231	1,407,781	1,902,077	1,582,276	9.20	-16.81
Slovakia	357,792	341,661	244,810	228,819	116,195	0.68	-49.22
Northern Europe	3,784,357	3,417,099	3,606,448	4,281,921	2,132,066	12.39	-50.21
Denmark	144,729	166,173	151,044	148,373	29,615	0.17	-80.04
Finland	187,749	174,593	154,063	160,627	21,551	0.13	-86.58
Ireland	45,766	54,597	69,280	57,959	11,708	0.07	-79.80
Norway	85,668	95,297	87,975	101,930	19,557	0.11	-80.81
Sweden	349,959	397,561	414,058	454,243	66,640	0.39	-85.33
United Kingdom	2,970,486	2,528,878	2,730,028	3,358,789	1,982,995	11.52	-40.96
Southern Europe	4,361,131	4,231,389	3,410,170	3,194,606	693,436	4.03	-78.29
Greece	71,584	65,890	43,179	27,182	11,524	0.07	-57.60
Italy	3,013,237	3,009,982	2,397,247	2,216,105	472,386	2.75	-78.68
Malta	30,513	25,185	14,314	16,759	6,832	0.04	-59.23
Portugal	131,139	141,280	113,910	155,792	31,663	0.18	-79.68
Serbia	148,532	165,057	122,718	109,028	52,534	0.31	-51.82
Spain	966,126	823,995	718,802	669,740	118,497	0.69	-82.31
Western Europe	18,284,982	18,805,249	17,435,009	17,089,975	8,914,555	51.81	-47.84
Austria	521,249	358,411	317,173	288,858	124,451	0.72	-56.92
Belgium	1,724,319	1,624,706	1,553,429	1,503,313	1,084,538	6.30	-27.86
France	8,556,597	9,158,374	8,451,002	8,700,649	4,417,827	25.67	-49.22
Germany	6,015,152	6,099,223	5,655,768	5,336,495	2,768,191	16.09	-48.13
Luxembourg	226,693	274,462	304,744	268,263	124,703	0.72	-53.51
Netherlands	572,608	646,217	541,781	491,312	192,260	1.12	-60.87
Switzerland	668,364	643,856	611,112	501,085	202,585	1.18	-59.57
East Mediterranean Europe	32,184	46,596	50,222	45,659	20,129	0.12	-55.91
Turkey	32,184	46,596	50,222	45,659	20,129	0.12	-55.91

TUNISIA

5. Overnight stays of non-resident tourists in hotels and similar establishments, by nationality

	2007	2008	2009	2010	2011	Market share 11	% Change 11-10
Other Europe	372,639	384,439	344,533	298,267	154,349	0.90	-48.25
Other countries of Europe	372,639	384,439	344,533	298,267	154,349	0.90	-48.25
MIDDLE EAST	445,652	511,706	512,952	566,020	958,383	5.57	69.32
Libya	286,013	340,058	371,985	427,399	881,939	5.13	106.35
Other countries of Middle East	159,639	171,648	140,967	138,621	76,444	0.44	-44.85
NOT SPECIFIED	668,350	654,338	544,953	655,079	406,990	2.37	-37.87
Other countries of the World	615,409	581,354	498,141	593,672	354,203	2.06	-40.34
Nationals Residing Abroad	52,941	72,984	46,812	61,407	52,787	0.31	-14.04

TURKEY

1. Arrivals of non-resident tourists at national borders, by nationality

		2007	2008	2009	2010	2011	Market share 11	% Change 11-10
TOTAL	(*)	26,122,405	29,637,309	30,434,819	31,395,548	34,038,448	100.00	8.42
AFRICA		157,637	188,601	273,242	227,603	283,069	0.83	24.37
North Africa		122,798	145,469	213,248	173,283	211,775	0.62	22.21
Algeria		41,527	57,752	84,959	58,901	78,166	0.23	32.71
Morocco		34,969	38,871	62,286	53,765	64,647	0.19	20.24
Sudan		5,621	6,466	8,648	5,872	6,631	0.02	12.93
Tunisia		40,681	42,380	57,355	54,745	62,331	0.18	13.86
Southern Africa		12,202	17,003	20,199	22,888	27,857	0.08	21.71
South Africa		12,202	17,003	20,199	22,888	27,857	0.08	21.71
Other Africa		22,637	26,129	39,795	31,432	43,437	0.13	38.19
Other countries of Africa		22,637	26,129	39,795	31,432	43,437	0.13	38.19
AMERICAS		585,269	612,166	602,791	561,823	673,738	1.98	19.92
Central America		1,645	886	814	977	1,298	0.00	32.86
All countries of Central America		1,645	886	814	977	1,298	0.00	32.86
North America		529,235	549,875	531,388	476,118	565,829	1.66	18.84
Canada		76,708	81,912	83,281	80,636	96,135	0.28	19.22
Mexico		15,329	15,576	9,846	10,964	12,506	0.04	14.06
United States of America		395,823	411,583	393,755	370,601	442,797	1.30	19.48
Other countries of North America		41,375	40,804	44,506	13,917	14,391	0.04	3.41
South America		54,389	61,405	70,589	84,728	106,611	0.31	25.83
Argentina		10,750	12,465	12,748	14,809	16,294	0.05	10.03
Brazil		22,863	28,861	38,603	50,885	64,482	0.19	26.72
Chile		4,951	5,631	4,675	4,823	6,505	0.02	34.87
Colombia		3,097	3,511	3,751	4,252	5,225	0.02	22.88
Venezuela		4,554	5,585	5,238	4,026	4,717	0.01	17.16
Other countries of South America		8,174	5,352	5,574	5,933	9,388	0.03	58.23
EAST ASIA AND THE PACIFIC		586,786	578,201	568,632	639,550	732,984	2.15	14.61
North-East Asia		352,169	314,145	292,574	376,462	411,709	1.21	9.36
China		62,114	57,472	65,819	73,615	93,225	0.27	26.64
Japan		159,531	140,211	139,393	182,765	173,140	0.51	-5.27
Korea, Republic of		130,524	116,462	87,362	120,082	145,344	0.43	21.04
South-East Asia		78,465	89,268	98,474	103,319	122,711	0.36	18.77
Indonesia		10,895	14,297	17,472	21,490	31,933	0.09	48.59
Malaysia		23,325	25,000	28,758	31,466	34,131	0.10	8.47
Philippines		19,751	21,962	23,361	24,222	27,043	0.08	11.65
Singapore		15,592	18,234	19,275	17,686	19,193	0.06	8.52
Thailand		8,902	9,775	9,608	8,455	10,411	0.03	23.13
Australasia		108,290	117,129	125,122	111,298	124,046	0.36	11.45
Australia		92,673	99,632	107,757	93,595	105,083	0.31	12.27
New Zealand		15,617	17,497	17,365	17,703	18,963	0.06	7.12
Other East Asia and the Pacific		47,862	57,659	52,462	48,471	74,518	0.22	53.74
Other countries of Asia		47,731	57,418	52,303	45,699	74,355	0.22	62.71
Other countries of Oceania		131	241	159	2,772	163	0.00	-94.12
EUROPE		18,727,704	21,420,018	21,444,637	21,604,344	23,434,797	68.85	8.47
Central/Eastern Europe		6,995,023	8,501,015	8,341,019	8,690,458	9,513,393	27.95	9.47
Azerbaijan		423,904	465,535	428,692	475,910	562,986	1.65	18.30
Armenia		53,359	64,385	64,967	68,474	71,825	0.21	4.89
Bulgaria		1,346,225	1,509,618	1,619,231	1,447,369	1,485,051	4.36	2.60
Belarus		106,416	151,063	143,329	151,419	123,057	0.36	-18.73
Czech Republic		117,130	151,312	158,192	168,516	214,718	0.63	27.42
Estonia		23,407	33,325	36,476	34,855	34,262	0.10	-1.70
Georgia		618,645	822,689	982,111	1,094,619	1,138,870	3.35	4.04
Hungary		76,839	87,896	78,841	87,698	100,528	0.30	14.63

TURKEY

1. Arrivals of non-resident tourists at national borders, by nationality

	2007	2008	2009	2010	2011	Market share 11	% Change 11-10
Kazakhstan	188,689	216,522	225,048	246,422	314,072	0.92	27.45
Kyrgyzstan	42,979	48,388	43,252	33,621	39,670	0.12	17.99
Latvia	56,429	57,511	41,310	38,084	43,592	0.13	14.46
Lithuania	69,315	92,378	76,454	71,401	73,610	0.22	3.09
Republic of Moldova	141,648	144,884	117,108	95,965	99,686	0.29	3.88
Poland	267,838	386,212	407,294	418,394	470,586	1.38	12.47
Romania	380,558	446,376	366,019	352,151	383,984	1.13	9.04
Russian Federation	2,342,773	2,850,393	2,684,383	3,072,624	3,425,608	10.06	11.49
Slovakia	49,958	66,628	79,121	89,668	119,864	0.35	33.68
Tajikistan	35,551	35,791	19,803	17,616	16,732	0.05	-5.02
Turkmenistan	53,749	87,387	126,086	108,381	128,938	0.38	18.97
Ukraine	559,917	716,501	568,962	553,546	585,387	1.72	5.75
Uzbekistan	39,694	66,221	74,340	63,725	80,367	0.24	26.12
Northern Europe	**2,736,022**	**3,139,294**	**3,431,983**	**3,714,025**	**3,858,741**	**11.34**	**3.90**
Denmark	259,613	272,388	289,519	308,850	363,834	1.07	17.80
Finland	78,643	98,478	130,722	137,731	175,522	0.52	27.44
Iceland	7,803	8,196	7,484	6,221	5,915	0.02	-4.92
Ireland	103,310	108,796	110,344	104,360	106,582	0.31	2.13
Norway	167,672	242,399	253,166	287,955	360,225	1.06	25.10
Sweden	330,077	399,990	396,017	435,429	557,107	1.64	27.94
United Kingdom	1,788,904	2,009,047	2,244,731	2,433,479	2,289,556	6.73	-5.91
Southern Europe	**1,425,355**	**1,678,145**	**1,611,273**	**1,652,733**	**1,744,402**	**5.12**	**5.55**
Albania	56,051	63,033	60,250	49,284	51,644	0.15	4.79
Bosnia and Herzegovina	50,153	59,906	53,887	46,965	55,811	0.16	18.84
Croatia	27,171	30,252	30,664	30,253	38,005	0.11	25.62
Greece	389,685	504,328	552,288	624,421	640,002	1.88	2.50
Italy	388,368	437,005	368,304	370,977	412,559	1.21	11.21
Malta	2,574	2,564	2,765	2,634	2,801	0.01	6.34
Portugal	23,218	28,165	35,601	43,455	39,719	0.12	-8.60
Serbia	130,713	171,950	105,369	111,491	135,987	0.40	21.97
Slovenia	31,826	33,167	33,735	34,305	37,771	0.11	10.10
Spain	230,217	239,520	259,635	226,360	201,100	0.59	-11.16
TFYR of Macedonia	95,379	108,255	108,775	112,588	129,003	0.38	14.58
Western Europe	**7,081,939**	**7,551,546**	**7,713,400**	**7,372,450**	**8,161,611**	**23.98**	**10.70**
Austria	463,851	491,800	520,307	477,111	504,952	1.48	5.84
Belgium	538,753	565,074	576,449	529,833	574,015	1.69	8.34
France	703,693	826,790	864,620	853,164	1,025,646	3.01	20.22
Germany	4,098,903	4,282,477	4,347,385	4,192,147	4,557,460	13.39	8.71
Luxembourg	5,415	7,410	8,585	10,328	11,546	0.03	11.79
Netherlands	1,055,596	1,132,797	1,124,313	1,057,471	1,187,411	3.49	12.29
Switzerland	215,728	245,198	271,741	252,396	300,581	0.88	19.09
East Mediterranean Europe	**487,008**	**548,013**	**304,255**	**116,332**	**84,884**	**0.25**	**-27.03**
Cyprus	5,747	9,127	9,601	10,580	9,273	0.03	-12.35
Israel	481,261	538,886	294,654	105,752	75,611	0.22	-28.50
Other Europe	**2,357**	**2,005**	**42,707**	**58,346**	**71,766**	**0.21**	**23.00**
Other countries of Europe	2,357	2,005	42,707	58,346	71,766	0.21	23.00
MIDDLE EAST	**922,867**	**1,151,388**	**1,413,299**	**1,869,231**	**2,100,995**	**6.17**	**12.40**
Bahrain	5,615	7,933	9,000	9,338	9,490	0.03	1.63
Iraq	141,073	213,371	283,931	267,925	356,128	1.05	32.92
Jordan	59,654	73,254	87,435	96,298	94,032	0.28	-2.35
Kuwait	12,215	20,833	26,085	27,258	41,305	0.12	51.53
Lebanon	43,739	51,736	71,045	129,728	135,525	0.40	4.47
Libya	32,742	42,321	65,820	60,917	48,072	0.14	-21.09
Oman	437	5,749	5,223	5,377	6,009	0.02	11.75
Qatar	3,592	4,781	4,859	6,022	7,531	0.02	25.06
Saudi Arabia	40,366	55,033	66,011	84,530	115,928	0.34	37.14
Syrian Arab Republic	320,988	397,122	499,722	889,821	962,060	2.83	8.12

TURKEY

1. Arrivals of non-resident tourists at national borders, by nationality

	2007	2008	2009	2010	2011	Market share 11	% Change 11-10
United Arab Emirates	12,274	19,449	21,581	30,318	34,446	0.10	13.62
Egypt	50,130	53,180	63,635	59,232	76,484	0.22	29.13
Yemen	3,917	4,914	6,237	6,198	7,134	0.02	15.10
Other countries of Middle East	196,125	201,712	202,715	196,269	206,851	0.61	5.39
SOUTH ASIA	**924,721**	**1,114,440**	**1,446,493**	**1,952,485**	**1,959,407**	**5.76**	**0.35**
Bangladesh	3,270	3,659	3,226	1,995	4,542	0.01	127.67
India	42,554	50,447	48,612	56,520	62,862	0.18	11.22
Iran, Islamic Republic of	854,304	1,029,577	1,369,692	1,870,753	1,863,655	5.48	-0.38
Pakistan	24,593	30,757	24,963	23,217	28,348	0.08	22.10
NOT SPECIFIED	**4,217,421**	**4,572,495**	**4,685,725**	**4,540,512**	**4,853,458**	**14.26**	**6.89**
Other countries of the World	19,514	23,640	27,553	23,421	24,658	0.07	5.28
Nationals Residing Abroad	4,197,907	4,548,855	4,658,172	4,517,091	4,828,800	14.19	6.90

TURKEY

2. Arrivals of non-resident visitors at national borders, by nationality

		2007	2008	2009	2010	2011	Market share 11	% Change 11-10
TOTAL	(*)	27,214,988	30,979,979	32,006,149	33,027,943	36,151,328	100.00	9.46
AFRICA		163,867	196,689	282,879	235,636	297,680	0.82	26.33
East Africa		3,676	3,504	4,751	4,243	4,354	0.01	2.62
Kenya		3,676	3,504	4,751	4,243	4,354	0.01	2.62
North Africa		124,855	147,675	215,428	176,520	215,479	0.60	22.07
Algeria		43,250	59,571	86,405	60,766	80,395	0.22	32.30
Morocco		35,244	39,184	62,763	54,374	65,632	0.18	20.70
Sudan		5,634	6,469	8,651	5,885	6,648	0.02	12.97
Tunisia		40,727	42,451	57,609	55,495	62,804	0.17	13.17
Southern Africa		14,464	20,925	24,619	26,968	34,400	0.10	27.56
South Africa		14,464	20,925	24,619	26,968	34,400	0.10	27.56
West Africa		7,298	8,932	11,657	12,269	18,127	0.05	47.75
Nigeria		5,242	6,607	8,294	8,157	13,631	0.04	67.11
Senegal		2,056	2,325	3,363	4,112	4,496	0.01	9.34
Other Africa		13,574	15,653	26,424	15,636	25,320	0.07	61.93
Other countries of Africa		13,574	15,653	26,424	15,636	25,320	0.07	61.93
AMERICAS		907,156	990,564	973,609	957,652	1,161,816	3.21	21.32
Caribbean		2,056	2,325	3,363	1,248	4,496	0.01	260.26
Dominican Republic		2,056	2,325	3,363	1,248	4,496	0.01	260.26
Central America		719	742	1,387	777	1,340	0.00	72.46
Panama		719	742	1,387	777	1,340	0.00	72.46
North America		829,289	894,281	863,433	839,201	995,184	2.75	18.59
Canada		133,497	151,685	156,575	153,765	193,315	0.53	25.72
Mexico		25,290	27,321	21,505	22,697	29,528	0.08	30.10
United States of America		662,048	693,199	675,566	646,859	761,549	2.11	17.73
Other countries of North America		8,454	22,076	9,787	15,880	10,792	0.03	-32.04
South America		75,092	93,216	105,426	116,426	160,796	0.44	38.11
Argentina		14,355	18,463	20,550	22,121	27,072	0.07	22.38
Brazil		32,412	43,089	52,809	64,586	89,950	0.25	39.27
Chile		6,926	8,381	7,412	8,075	11,860	0.03	46.87
Colombia		4,868	5,929	7,140	6,951	9,634	0.03	38.60
Ecuador		2,238	2,271	2,466	2,683	3,820	0.01	42.38
Paraguay		146	323	364	430	562	0.00	30.70
Peru		1,639	1,702	1,904	2,014	2,675	0.01	32.82
Uruguay		5,469	2,472	2,528	2,832	5,548	0.02	95.90
Venezuela		6,403	9,397	9,060	6,734	8,463	0.02	25.68
Other countries of South America		636	1,189	1,193		1,212	0.00	
EAST ASIA AND THE PACIFIC		610,784	610,745	614,345	702,630	834,170	2.31	18.72
North-East Asia		383,540	354,826	333,920	398,525	469,786	1.30	17.88
China		64,614	60,828	67,684	75,994	97,106	0.27	27.78
Hong Kong, China			6,139	6,657	5,991	10,156	0.03	69.52
Japan		168,690	148,077	149,191	193,759	187,780	0.52	-3.09
Korea, Republic of		132,324	119,696	89,715	122,781	149,163	0.41	21.49
Other countries of North-East Asia		17,912	20,086	20,673		25,581	0.07	
South-East Asia		92,405	105,489	123,584	115,622	185,045	0.51	60.04
Indonesia		11,411	15,384	22,068	23,435	39,016	0.11	66.49
Malaysia		23,814	25,940	29,537	32,543	35,900	0.10	10.32
Philippines		24,102	27,691	35,845	31,464	51,504	0.14	63.69
Singapore		16,482	19,143	20,070	18,921	20,748	0.06	9.66
Thailand		10,517	10,095	9,964	9,259	11,083	0.03	19.70
Other countries of South-East Asia		6,079	7,236	6,100		26,794	0.07	
Australasia		134,697	150,105	156,632	156,817	179,141	0.50	14.24
Australia		113,806	126,533	132,472	132,174	152,313	0.42	15.24

TURKEY

2. Arrivals of non-resident visitors at national borders, by nationality

	2007	2008	2009	2010	2011	Market share 11	% Change 11-10
New Zealand	20,891	23,572	24,160	24,643	26,828	0.07	8.87
Other East Asia and the Pacific	**142**	**325**	**209**	**31,666**	**198**	**0.00**	**-99.37**
Other countries of Asia				28,855			
Other countries of Oceania	142	325	209	2,811	198	0.00	-92.96
EUROPE	**19,401,929**	**22,290,322**	**22,494,148**	**22,745,584**	**24,844,852**	**68.72**	**9.23**
Central/Eastern Europe	**7,052,191**	**8,568,317**	**8,410,238**	**8,750,891**	**9,599,683**	**26.55**	**9.70**
Azerbaijan	425,026	467,547	430,241	477,441	565,484	1.56	18.44
Armenia	53,393	64,395	65,050	68,529	71,869	0.20	4.87
Bulgaria	1,347,616	1,512,243	1,623,640	1,448,923	1,488,228	4.12	2.71
Belarus	106,555	152,640	144,554	151,664	123,330	0.34	-18.68
Czech Republic	123,621	159,224	166,505	174,508	222,764	0.62	27.65
Estonia	24,100	33,686	36,845	35,136	34,671	0.10	-1.32
Georgia	619,893	824,609	984,606	1,097,198	1,142,171	3.16	4.10
Hungary	81,524	95,173	82,443	90,542	104,084	0.29	14.96
Kazakhstan	188,882	216,689	225,433	246,516	314,335	0.87	27.51
Kyrgyzstan	42,981	48,406	43,255	33,668	39,681	0.11	17.86
Latvia	56,635	57,907	41,545	39,107	44,748	0.12	14.42
Lithuania	69,963	92,912	77,166	72,138	76,017	0.21	5.38
Republic of Moldova	141,947	145,028	119,016	96,114	99,958	0.28	4.00
Poland	274,556	396,472	418,632	427,575	487,591	1.35	14.04
Romania	382,971	449,206	369,887	356,616	390,395	1.08	9.47
Russian Federation	2,353,333	2,863,857	2,696,784	3,087,737	3,446,915	9.53	11.63
Slovakia	51,850	69,363	81,699	91,401	121,923	0.34	33.39
Tajikistan	35,551	35,791	19,805	17,616	16,734	0.05	-5.01
Turkmenistan	53,749	87,405	126,088	108,383	128,942	0.36	18.97
Ukraine	578,189	729,370	582,607	566,296	599,427	1.66	5.85
Uzbekistan	39,856	66,394	74,437	63,783	80,416	0.22	26.08
Northern Europe	**2,921,236**	**3,353,395**	**3,677,178**	**4,002,608**	**4,227,490**	**11.69**	**5.62**
Denmark	266,847	277,997	296,108	314,369	372,402	1.03	18.46
Finland	83,623	102,634	138,159	143,328	187,219	0.52	30.62
Iceland	9,165	9,256	7,969	6,447	6,166	0.02	-4.36
Ireland	108,101	115,121	117,654	111,495	118,600	0.33	6.37
Norway	174,410	250,543	264,289	299,316	376,290	1.04	25.72
Sweden	338,678	407,590	407,984	447,065	573,963	1.59	28.38
United Kingdom	1,940,412	2,190,254	2,445,015	2,680,588	2,592,850	7.17	-3.27
Southern Europe	**1,652,945**	**2,007,354**	**2,074,141**	**2,099,549**	**2,275,967**	**6.30**	**8.40**
Albania	56,698	63,945	61,247	50,163	53,286	0.15	6.23
Bosnia and Herzegovina	50,215	60,032	54,137	47,219	56,265	0.16	19.16
Croatia	28,763	31,698	33,743	33,249	41,892	0.12	25.99
Greece	433,338	562,226	607,779	661,260	697,453	1.93	5.47
Italy	504,914	597,325	629,516	665,478	749,419	2.07	12.61
Malta	2,992	3,472	3,562	3,392	5,798	0.02	70.93
Montenegro			12,370		13,731	0.04	
Portugal	29,909	35,789	46,093	53,309	49,424	0.14	-7.29
Serbia	130,933	172,631	106,042	112,408	137,172	0.38	22.03
Slovenia	34,681	36,853	38,894	38,524	41,816	0.12	8.55
Spain	285,090	335,085	371,908	321,916	300,466	0.83	-6.66
TFYR of Macedonia	95,412	108,298	108,850	112,631	129,245	0.36	14.75
Western Europe	**7,265,575**	**7,791,255**	**8,002,587**	**7,707,499**	**8,645,466**	**23.91**	**12.17**
Austria	473,273	505,764	537,721	497,931	530,800	1.47	6.60
Belgium	549,890	578,680	592,651	544,728	594,679	1.64	9.17
France	739,442	877,408	935,047	923,037	1,132,458	3.13	22.69
Germany	4,192,512	4,396,948	4,481,571	4,370,248	4,815,156	13.32	10.18
Luxembourg	6,283	10,705	9,937	11,204	13,174	0.04	17.58
Netherlands	1,081,675	1,166,101	1,157,131	1,087,823	1,229,730	3.40	13.05
Switzerland	222,500	255,649	288,529	272,528	329,469	0.91	20.89

TURKEY

2. Arrivals of non-resident visitors at national borders, by nationality

	2007	2008	2009	2010	2011	Market share 11	% Change 11-10
East Mediterranean Europe	509,982	570,001	330,004	125,882	96,246	0.27	-23.54
Cyprus	6,410	10,264	13,538	15,560	16,826	0.05	8.14
Israel	503,572	559,737	316,466	110,322	79,420	0.22	-28.01
Other Europe				59,155			
Other countries of Europe				59,155			
MIDDLE EAST	961,078	1,173,637	1,483,080	1,873,353	2,169,591	6.00	15.81
Bahrain	5,657	8,016	9,056	9,419	9,631	0.03	2.25
Palestine	3,661	3,941	5,505	4,479	4,958	0.01	10.69
Iraq	141,082	213,385	283,957	267,936	356,187	0.99	32.94
Jordan	59,703	73,305	87,844	96,406	94,416	0.26	-2.06
Kuwait	12,270	20,928	26,156	27,332	41,594	0.12	52.18
Lebanon	44,300	52,123	71,977	130,557	137,027	0.38	4.96
Libya	32,792	42,321	65,839	60,942	48,074	0.13	-21.12
Oman	443	5,776	5,241	5,391	6,034	0.02	11.93
Qatar	3,593	4,788	4,916	6,041	7,592	0.02	25.67
Saudi Arabia	40,513	55,226	66,324	84,915	116,588	0.32	37.30
Syrian Arab Republic	322,487	398,331	501,016	891,192	965,967	2.67	8.39
United Arab Emirates	12,288	19,510	21,667	30,366	34,533	0.10	13.72
Egypt	51,056	53,764	64,814	60,340	78,579	0.22	30.23
Yemen	3,919	4,914	6,244	6,199	7,135	0.02	15.10
Other countries of Middle East	227,314	217,309	262,524	191,838	261,276	0.72	36.20
SOUTH ASIA	952,753	1,145,527	1,472,363	1,972,576	1,989,761	5.50	0.87
Afghanistan	23,913	25,181	19,113	14,662	15,402	0.04	5.05
Bangladesh	3,296	3,661	3,252	2,013	5,924	0.02	194.29
India	44,436	54,060	52,357	61,559	72,980	0.20	18.55
Iran, Islamic Republic of	854,488	1,029,716	1,369,896	1,870,953	1,863,926	5.16	-0.38
Pakistan	24,816	30,859	25,058	23,389	28,872	0.08	23.44
Other countries of South Asia	1,804	2,050	2,687		2,657	0.01	
NOT SPECIFIED	4,217,421	4,572,495	4,685,725	4,540,512	4,853,458	13.43	6.89
Other countries of the World	19,514	23,640	27,553	23,421	24,658	0.07	5.28
Nationals Residing Abroad	4,197,907	4,548,855	4,658,172	4,517,091	4,828,800	13.36	6.90

TURKEY

3. Arrivals of non-resident tourists in hotels and similar establishments, by nationality

	2007	2008	2009	2010	2011	Market share 11	% Change 11-10
TOTAL (*)	14,788,115	13,629,454	14,362,499	17,111,736	18,790,691	100.00	9.81
AFRICA	66,969	68,557	85,579	180,617	148,845	0.79	-17.59
North Africa	46,096	39,804	58,173	71,638	96,698	0.51	34.98
Algeria	15,336	11,086	16,313	18,905	31,313	0.17	65.63
Morocco	11,645	10,524	21,335	23,619	35,449	0.19	50.09
Sudan	2,658	1,914	3,531	3,148	5,549	0.03	76.27
Tunisia	16,457	16,280	16,994	25,966	24,387	0.13	-6.08
Southern Africa	13,727	11,405	14,036	17,922	25,245	0.13	40.86
South Africa	13,727	11,405	14,036	17,922	25,245	0.13	40.86
Other Africa	7,146	17,348	13,370	91,057	26,902	0.14	-70.46
Other countries of Africa	7,146	17,348	13,370	91,057	26,902	0.14	-70.46
AMERICAS	624,858	563,784	565,358	670,495	825,697	4.39	23.15
Central America	1,030	562	1,159	1,563	2,451	0.01	56.81
All countries of Central America	1,030	562	1,159	1,563	2,451	0.01	56.81
North America	568,525	511,953	496,372	573,532	690,084	3.67	20.32
Canada	82,447	49,807	44,492	57,509	87,039	0.46	51.35
Mexico	12,771	13,338	10,925	9,150	11,136	0.06	21.70
United States of America	468,527	435,239	402,239	470,243	572,421	3.05	21.73
Other countries of North America	4,780	13,569	38,716	36,630	19,488	0.10	-46.80
South America	55,303	51,269	67,827	95,400	133,162	0.71	39.58
Argentina	20,803	15,882	13,636	21,966	33,439	0.18	52.23
Brazil	21,749	22,051	40,846	60,742	79,711	0.42	31.23
Chile	3,263	3,050	5,261	3,357	4,680	0.02	39.41
Colombia	2,306	1,978	1,937	3,513	4,750	0.03	35.21
Venezuela	4,828	4,992	2,174	2,659	2,723	0.01	2.41
Other countries of South America	2,354	3,316	3,973	3,163	7,859	0.04	148.47
EAST ASIA AND THE PACIFIC	1,003,126	881,610	787,127	898,129	1,084,143	5.77	20.71
North-East Asia	832,998	702,956	580,125	631,461	786,304	4.18	24.52
China	67,386	52,814	47,718	63,560	113,444	0.60	78.48
Japan	515,244	466,642	430,706	413,508	412,388	2.19	-0.27
Korea, Republic of	250,368	183,500	101,701	154,393	260,472	1.39	68.71
South-East Asia	57,562	59,751	85,475	90,876	113,794	0.61	25.22
Indonesia	4,021	7,187	8,262	10,453	19,078	0.10	82.51
Malaysia	24,286	19,913	31,342	37,088	38,070	0.20	2.65
Philippines	4,865	4,461	5,178	4,902	6,977	0.04	42.33
Singapore	14,788	20,769	31,465	31,110	34,571	0.18	11.13
Thailand	9,602	7,421	9,228	7,323	15,098	0.08	106.17
Australasia	102,154	102,682	108,056	127,068	145,178	0.77	14.25
Australia	90,493	94,064	99,164	112,065	132,395	0.70	18.14
New Zealand	11,661	8,618	8,892	15,003	12,783	0.07	-14.80
Other East Asia and the Pacific	10,412	16,221	13,471	48,724	38,867	0.21	-20.23
Other countries of Asia	9,171	14,703	12,389	45,226	28,250	0.15	-37.54
All countries of Oceania	1,241	1,518	1,082	3,498	10,617	0.06	203.52
EUROPE	12,258,648	11,392,325	11,997,563	14,066,151	15,338,653	81.63	9.05
Central/Eastern Europe	3,992,496	3,440,265	3,541,263	4,006,528	4,450,274	23.68	11.08
Azerbaijan		59,824	78,758	85,532	111,442	0.59	30.29
Armenia		12,792	21,262	16,943	14,062	0.07	-17.00
Bulgaria	116,031	119,402	128,412	149,420	135,651	0.72	-9.21
Belarus		38,665	39,249	44,619	47,161	0.25	5.70
Czech Republic	119,925	87,623	114,066	122,884	174,899	0.93	42.33
Estonia		12,839	17,329	26,186	24,236	0.13	-7.45
Georgia		35,888	45,051	47,867	43,623	0.23	-8.87
Hungary	53,707	56,705	49,441	64,320	59,323	0.32	-7.77

TURKEY

3. Arrivals of non-resident tourists in hotels and similar establishments, by nationality

	2007	2008	2009	2010	2011	Market share 11	% Change 11-10
Kazakhstan		97,295	127,596	145,637	172,148	0.92	18.20
Kyrgyzstan		10,847	10,911	10,986	14,035	0.07	27.75
Latvia		17,499	12,708	18,928	20,352	0.11	7.52
Lithuania		69,628	45,666	53,493	57,214	0.30	6.96
Republic of Moldova		28,368	32,863	39,444	44,427	0.24	12.63
Poland	157,327	187,632	212,989	270,327	311,361	1.66	15.18
Romania	207,339	215,599	201,619	212,955	208,741	1.11	-1.98
Russian Federation		2,054,253	2,045,159	2,344,193	2,549,215	13.57	8.75
Slovakia		24,491	42,780	59,553	86,327	0.46	44.96
Tajikistan		7,592	4,721	3,985	13,571	0.07	240.55
Turkmenistan		13,094	15,740	21,820	22,525	0.12	3.23
Ukraine		272,630	275,305	247,723	314,751	1.68	27.06
Uzbekistan		17,599	19,638	19,713	25,210	0.13	27.89
Commonwealth Independent States	3,338,167						
Northern Europe	**1,324,846**	**1,269,528**	**1,650,996**	**2,109,166**	**2,314,032**	**12.31**	**9.71**
Denmark		85,043	82,965	94,358	135,164	0.72	43.25
Finland		43,670	61,242	71,357	82,751	0.44	15.97
Iceland	13,226	7,772	5,779	6,392	5,210	0.03	-18.49
Ireland	58,129	48,213	70,886	65,476	85,486	0.45	30.56
Norway		76,366	97,334	149,087	229,215	1.22	53.75
Sweden		141,365	153,068	234,312	348,455	1.85	48.71
United Kingdom	960,570	867,099	1,179,722	1,488,184	1,427,751	7.60	-4.06
Scandinavia	292,921						
Southern Europe	**961,646**	**1,029,591**	**1,226,172**	**1,199,618**	**1,141,344**	**6.07**	**-4.86**
Albania	30,953	26,625	30,505	28,890	23,609	0.13	-18.28
Bosnia and Herzegovina		23,868	24,575	27,783	34,192	0.18	23.07
Croatia		16,526	17,028	19,966	35,698	0.19	78.79
Greece	160,466	190,748	201,220	243,232	224,117	1.19	-7.86
Italy	275,564	307,395	428,935	349,605	411,653	2.19	17.75
Malta		1,429	1,562	1,579	1,533	0.01	-2.91
Montenegro			8	72	158	0.00	119.44
Portugal	17,512	32,962	50,946	64,667	38,971	0.21	-39.74
Serbia		43,321	46,711	57,816	59,110	0.31	2.24
Slovenia		16,599	18,365	20,687	45,273	0.24	118.85
Spain	339,534	346,081	376,837	353,195	236,552	1.26	-33.03
TFYR of Macedonia		24,037	29,488	32,126	30,478	0.16	-5.13
Yugoslavia, SFR (former)	137,617						
Western Europe	**5,305,159**	**5,263,226**	**5,265,506**	**6,642,861**	**7,265,100**	**38.66**	**9.37**
Austria	184,936	176,613	263,973	246,480	271,668	1.45	10.22
Belgium		435,457	474,758	454,774	466,602	2.48	2.60
France	513,647	518,838	627,269	762,928	935,719	4.98	22.65
Germany	3,246,047	3,413,746	3,142,293	4,328,235	4,571,741	24.33	5.63
Luxembourg		10,770	11,556	13,214	17,148	0.09	29.77
Netherlands		599,390	607,770	681,948	795,739	4.23	16.69
Switzerland	132,729	108,412	137,887	155,282	206,483	1.10	32.97
Benelux	1,227,800						
East Mediterranean Europe	**607,861**	**382,027**	**302,143**	**101,681**	**121,498**	**0.65**	**19.49**
Cyprus	92,595	85,715	76,139	13,706	71,259	0.38	419.91
Israel	515,266	296,312	226,004	87,975	50,239	0.27	-42.89
Other Europe	**66,640**	**7,688**	**11,483**	**6,297**	**46,405**	**0.25**	**636.94**
Other countries of Europe	66,640	7,688	11,483	6,297	46,405	0.25	636.94
MIDDLE EAST	**459,513**	**436,219**	**559,668**	**763,074**	**801,485**	**4.27**	**5.03**
Bahrain	5,882	6,542	7,353	7,386	9,844	0.05	33.28
Iraq	69,787	71,837	105,817	129,815	165,889	0.88	27.79
Jordan	48,121	54,343	76,663	57,835	55,580	0.30	-3.90
Kuwait	11,961	18,763	23,081	26,914	38,991	0.21	44.87
Lebanon	35,287	35,940	47,729	84,934	81,192	0.43	-4.41

TURKEY

3. Arrivals of non-resident tourists in hotels and similar establishments, by nationality

	2007	2008	2009	2010	2011	Market share 11	% Change 11-10
Libya	8,042	12,334	16,832	26,834	32,433	0.17	20.87
Oman	2,094						
Qatar	3,963	5,778	3,968	6,524	7,015	0.04	7.53
Saudi Arabia	101,142	77,807	89,463	134,463	172,789	0.92	28.50
Syrian Arab Republic	68,874	59,446	76,370	121,355	71,777	0.38	-40.85
United Arab Emirates	30,188	30,866	37,402	47,509	49,101	0.26	3.35
Egypt	52,623	37,860	43,559	51,039	63,762	0.34	24.93
Yemen	2,614	1,902	3,631	4,532	4,572	0.02	0.88
Other countries of Middle East	18,935	22,801	27,800	63,934	48,540	0.26	-24.08
SOUTH ASIA	**250,828**	**238,856**	**312,878**	**447,938**	**501,883**	**2.67**	**12.04**
Bangladesh	844	1,085	1,709	1,545	2,941	0.02	90.36
India	34,732	34,703	36,212	45,516	67,084	0.36	47.39
Iran, Islamic Republic of	202,844	188,382	259,500	383,312	410,040	2.18	6.97
Pakistan	12,408	14,686	15,457	17,565	21,818	0.12	24.21
NOT SPECIFIED	**124,173**	**48,103**	**54,318**	**85,332**	**89,985**	**0.48**	**5.45**
Other countries of the World	124,173	48,103	54,318	85,332	89,985	0.48	5.45

TURKEY

4. Arrivals of non-resident tourists in all types of accommodation establishments, by nationality

		2007	2008	2009	2010	2011	Market share 11	% Change 11-10
TOTAL	(*)	14,794,270	13,647,606	14,388,998	17,415,364	19,264,058	100.00	10.62
AFRICA		66,925	68,568	85,785	180,872	149,710	0.78	-17.23
North Africa		46,098	39,808	58,263	71,793	97,213	0.50	35.41
Algeria		15,338	11,086	16,326	18,917	31,404	0.16	66.01
Morocco		11,645	10,524	21,367	23,668	35,569	0.18	50.28
Sudan		2,658	1,914	3,534	3,166	5,750	0.03	81.62
Tunisia		16,457	16,284	17,036	26,042	24,490	0.13	-5.96
Southern Africa		13,727	11,408	14,039	17,942	25,342	0.13	41.24
South Africa		13,727	11,408	14,039	17,942	25,342	0.13	41.24
Other Africa		7,100	17,352	13,483	91,137	27,155	0.14	-70.20
Other countries of Africa		7,100	17,352	13,483	91,137	27,155	0.14	-70.20
AMERICAS		627,966	563,975	572,082	695,331	858,692	4.46	23.49
Central America		1,030	562	1,159	1,566	2,457	0.01	56.90
All countries of Central America		1,030	562	1,159	1,566	2,457	0.01	56.90
North America		571,628	512,144	503,071	595,285	719,122	3.73	20.80
Canada		82,451	49,930	44,561	58,176	88,394	0.46	51.94
Mexico		12,771	13,338	10,951	9,267	11,348	0.06	22.46
United States of America		468,543	435,307	402,709	490,639	599,740	3.11	22.24
Other countries of North America		7,863	13,569	44,850	37,203	19,640	0.10	-47.21
South America		55,308	51,269	67,852	98,480	137,113	0.71	39.23
Argentina		20,803	15,882	13,645	22,528	33,586	0.17	49.09
Brazil		21,749	22,051	40,856	62,961	83,153	0.43	32.07
Chile		3,268	3,050	5,261	3,390	4,691	0.02	38.38
Colombia		2,306	1,978	1,937	3,514	4,818	0.03	37.11
Venezuela		4,828	4,992	2,174	2,659	2,727	0.01	2.56
Other countries of South America		2,354	3,316	3,979	3,428	8,138	0.04	137.40
EAST ASIA AND THE PACIFIC		1,003,157	881,860	788,010	972,190	1,202,579	6.24	23.70
North-East Asia		833,012	702,980	580,695	735,566	897,382	4.66	22.00
China		67,386	52,820	47,945	68,569	124,986	0.65	82.28
Japan		515,246	466,658	430,985	500,873	489,160	2.54	-2.34
Korea, Republic of		250,380	183,502	101,765	166,124	283,236	1.47	70.50
South-East Asia		57,562	59,751	85,530	92,499	115,425	0.60	24.79
Indonesia		4,021	7,187	8,276	10,780	19,487	0.10	80.77
Malaysia		24,286	19,913	31,362	37,383	38,406	0.20	2.74
Philippines		4,865	4,461	5,194	4,972	7,052	0.04	41.83
Singapore		14,788	20,769	31,469	31,772	35,283	0.18	11.05
Thailand		9,602	7,421	9,229	7,592	15,197	0.08	100.17
Australasia		102,162	102,908	108,308	128,324	147,307	0.76	14.79
Australia		90,497	94,233	99,393	113,310	134,433	0.70	18.64
New Zealand		11,665	8,675	8,915	15,014	12,874	0.07	-14.25
Other East Asia and the Pacific		10,421	16,221	13,477	15,801	42,465	0.22	168.75
Other countries of Asia		9,171	14,703	12,392	12,272	31,820	0.17	159.29
All countries of Oceania		1,250	1,518	1,085	3,529	10,645	0.06	201.64
EUROPE		12,261,661	11,409,987	12,012,783	14,282,998	15,641,789	81.20	9.51
Central/Eastern Europe		4,055,253	3,444,368	3,544,735	4,021,775	4,481,312	23.26	11.43
Azerbaijan		62,859	59,842	78,953	85,829	111,835	0.58	30.30
Armenia		11,007	12,792	21,267	16,949	14,062	0.07	-17.03
Bulgaria		116,115	119,599	128,594	150,170	137,663	0.71	-8.33
Belarus		30,042	38,667	39,279	44,640	47,253	0.25	5.85
Czech Republic		98,931	89,050	114,182	124,979	190,104	0.99	52.11
Estonia		7,213	12,839	17,335	26,358	24,429	0.13	-7.32
Georgia		34,715	35,888	45,165	47,941	43,752	0.23	-8.74
Hungary		53,749	56,863	49,443	64,920	60,151	0.31	-7.35

TURKEY

4. Arrivals of non-resident tourists in all types of accommodation establishments, by nationality

	2007	2008	2009	2010	2011	Market share 11	% Change 11-10
Kazakhstan	122,921	97,295	127,748	145,863	172,460	0.90	18.23
Kyrgyzstan	13,395	10,851	11,000	10,994	14,056	0.07	27.85
Latvia	15,962	17,499	12,710	18,928	20,352	0.11	7.52
Lithuania	35,915	69,628	45,666	53,722	57,496	0.30	7.03
Republic of Moldova	41,078	28,378	33,204	39,453	44,565	0.23	12.96
Poland	157,327	188,783	213,249	270,892	312,286	1.62	15.28
Romania	207,354	215,671	201,822	213,907	209,220	1.09	-2.19
Russian Federation	2,707,854	2,055,205	2,046,457	2,352,400	2,557,505	13.28	8.72
Slovakia	21,034	24,519	42,780	60,252	87,070	0.45	44.51
Tajikistan	6,896	7,592	4,759	4,014	13,635	0.07	239.69
Turkmenistan	12,757	13,094	15,850	21,931	22,712	0.12	3.56
Ukraine	282,596	272,683	275,492	247,900	315,441	1.64	27.25
Uzbekistan	15,533	17,630	19,780	19,733	25,265	0.13	28.03
Northern Europe	**1,324,910**	**1,270,491**	**1,655,059**	**2,119,469**	**2,331,365**	**12.10**	**10.00**
Denmark	78,360	85,269	83,048	94,696	135,755	0.70	43.36
Finland	34,055	43,671	61,270	71,602	83,417	0.43	16.50
Iceland	13,226	7,781	5,886	6,457	5,260	0.03	-18.54
Ireland	58,138	48,236	70,933	65,570	86,098	0.45	31.31
Norway	65,060	76,366	99,946	151,991	234,798	1.22	54.48
Sweden	115,446	141,393	153,257	235,140	349,825	1.82	48.77
United Kingdom	960,625	867,775	1,180,719	1,494,013	1,436,212	7.46	-3.87
Southern Europe	**962,385**	**1,029,889**	**1,228,386**	**1,245,370**	**1,197,890**	**6.22**	**-3.81**
Albania	30,953	26,625	30,541	28,896	23,654	0.12	-18.14
Bosnia and Herzegovina	34,359	23,877	24,600	27,818	34,256	0.18	23.14
Croatia	17,270	16,528	17,028	19,968	35,837	0.19	79.47
Greece	160,466	190,853	202,289	245,473	230,514	1.20	-6.09
Italy	275,602	307,467	429,688	360,830	429,276	2.23	18.97
Malta	662	1,429	1,562	1,586	1,541	0.01	-2.84
Montenegro			8	72	158	0.00	119.44
Portugal	17,512	32,962	50,971	69,908	44,329	0.23	-36.59
Serbia	46,515	43,349	46,752	57,869	59,185	0.31	2.27
Slovenia	14,452	16,630	18,373	20,707	45,463	0.24	119.55
Spain	339,534	346,130	377,053	380,081	263,132	1.37	-30.77
TFYR of Macedonia	25,060	24,039	29,521	32,162	30,545	0.16	-5.03
Western Europe	**5,307,422**	**5,275,497**	**5,270,735**	**6,723,216**	**7,457,986**	**38.71**	**10.93**
Austria	184,975	176,803	264,163	248,559	274,668	1.43	10.50
Belgium	577,685	435,495	474,845	455,798	468,468	2.43	2.78
France	513,697	519,670	627,822	786,450	995,943	5.17	26.64
Germany	3,247,991	3,418,538	3,145,853	4,379,380	4,694,645	24.37	7.20
Luxembourg	7,844	10,773	11,556	13,217	17,202	0.09	30.15
Netherlands	642,487	605,597	608,528	684,089	799,403	4.15	16.86
Switzerland	132,743	108,621	137,968	155,723	207,657	1.08	33.35
East Mediterranean Europe	**607,863**	**382,052**	**302,380**	**153,144**	**126,573**	**0.66**	**-17.35**
Cyprus	92,595	85,721	76,338	65,059	76,053	0.39	16.90
Israel	515,268	296,331	226,042	88,085	50,520	0.26	-42.65
Other Europe	**3,828**	**7,690**	**11,488**	**20,024**	**46,663**	**0.24**	**133.04**
Other countries of Europe	3,828	7,690	11,488	20,024	46,663	0.24	133.04
MIDDLE EAST	**459,515**	**436,231**	**562,886**	**749,285**	**814,932**	**4.23**	**8.76**
Bahrain	5,882	6,542	7,358	8,632	9,921	0.05	14.93
Iraq	69,787	71,842	106,061	130,081	166,398	0.86	27.92
Jordan	48,121	54,344	76,667	58,040	58,109	0.30	0.12
Kuwait	11,961	18,763	23,097	27,492	39,552	0.21	43.87
Lebanon	35,289	35,941	47,736	85,888	81,600	0.42	-4.99
Libya	8,042	12,334	16,847	26,896	32,537	0.17	20.97
Oman	2,094						
Qatar	3,963	5,778	3,968	6,703	7,196	0.04	7.35
Saudi Arabia	101,142	77,807	89,621	136,810	175,356	0.91	28.17

TURKEY

4. Arrivals of non-resident tourists in all types of accommodation establishments, by nationality

	2007	2008	2009	2010	2011	Market share 11	% Change 11-10
Syrian Arab Republic	68,874	59,447	79,091	129,205	75,187	0.39	-41.81
United Arab Emirates	30,188	30,868	37,417	48,331	49,604	0.26	2.63
Egypt	52,623	37,862	43,586	51,100	64,019	0.33	25.28
Yemen	2,614	1,902	3,631	4,582	4,638	0.02	1.22
Other countries of Middle East	18,935	22,801	27,806	35,525	50,815	0.26	43.04
SOUTH ASIA	**250,855**	**238,882**	**313,101**	**448,820**	**504,456**	**2.62**	**12.40**
Bangladesh	844	1,085	1,709	1,560	2,949	0.02	89.04
India	34,747	34,707	36,221	45,942	67,901	0.35	47.80
Iran, Islamic Republic of	202,852	188,399	259,698	383,660	411,647	2.14	7.29
Pakistan	12,412	14,691	15,473	17,658	21,959	0.11	24.36
NOT SPECIFIED	**124,191**	**48,103**	**54,351**	**85,868**	**91,900**	**0.48**	**7.02**
Other countries of the World	124,191	48,103	54,351	85,868	91,900	0.48	7.02

TURKEY

5. Overnight stays of non-resident tourists in hotels and similar establishments, by nationality

		2007	2008	2009	2010	2011	Market share 11	% Change 11-10
TOTAL	(*)	56,491,464	56,872,545	59,873,585	73,924,293	78,257,238	100.00	5.86
AFRICA		163,005	206,723	239,502	760,744	442,666	0.57	-41.81
North Africa		117,521	114,879	166,387	224,150	296,287	0.38	32.18
Algeria		40,532	32,860	46,119	62,174	110,427	0.14	77.61
Morocco		26,807	28,766	62,616	73,780	103,892	0.13	40.81
Sudan		6,446	7,043	8,051	9,222	12,713	0.02	37.86
Tunisia		43,736	46,210	49,601	78,974	69,255	0.09	-12.31
Southern Africa		28,864	24,809	30,543	38,231	58,995	0.08	54.31
South Africa		28,864	24,809	30,543	38,231	58,995	0.08	54.31
Other Africa		16,620	67,035	42,572	498,363	87,384	0.11	-82.47
Other countries of Africa		16,620	67,035	42,572	498,363	87,384	0.11	-82.47
AMERICAS		1,688,787	1,226,175	1,213,247	1,475,098	2,106,718	2.69	42.82
Central America		2,247	1,340	2,592	3,455	5,262	0.01	52.30
All countries of Central America		2,247	1,340	2,592	3,455	5,262	0.01	52.30
North America		1,534,810	1,117,308	1,056,621	1,250,278	1,822,250	2.33	45.75
Canada		208,792	102,214	95,639	122,030	186,418	0.24	52.76
Mexico		24,628	25,625	21,517	19,464	26,532	0.03	36.31
United States of America		1,280,576	944,290	861,460	1,010,691	1,563,398	2.00	54.69
Other countries of North America		20,814	45,179	78,005	98,093	45,902	0.06	-53.21
South America		151,730	107,527	154,034	221,365	279,206	0.36	26.13
Argentina		77,597	33,220	27,761	60,839	75,402	0.10	23.94
Brazil		47,621	45,164	78,374	129,608	162,069	0.21	25.05
Chile		7,709	7,229	24,487	8,400	10,447	0.01	24.37
Colombia		4,684	4,366	4,612	7,585	10,440	0.01	37.64
Venezuela		9,179	9,627	4,953	6,255	6,397	0.01	2.27
Other countries of South America		4,940	7,921	13,847	8,678	14,451	0.02	66.52
EAST ASIA AND THE PACIFIC		1,523,121	1,373,295	1,299,111	1,473,576	1,800,824	2.30	22.21
North-East Asia		1,184,069	987,738	805,109	922,909	1,150,270	1.47	24.64
China		129,599	126,970	94,638	129,901	206,148	0.26	58.70
Japan		717,208	617,505	564,617	576,610	606,808	0.78	5.24
Korea, Republic of		337,262	243,263	145,854	216,398	337,314	0.43	55.88
South-East Asia		93,390	96,916	140,536	146,608	194,652	0.25	32.77
Indonesia		8,166	13,167	14,728	18,875	31,949	0.04	69.27
Malaysia		36,754	31,262	51,739	53,519	64,074	0.08	19.72
Philippines		9,198	9,677	11,796	11,190	15,257	0.02	36.34
Singapore		25,103	31,398	48,392	49,965	62,071	0.08	24.23
Thailand		14,169	11,412	13,881	13,059	21,301	0.03	63.11
Australasia		220,504	248,701	324,915	285,884	341,457	0.44	19.44
Australia		197,580	233,700	306,865	256,750	317,065	0.41	23.49
New Zealand		22,924	15,001	18,050	29,134	24,392	0.03	-16.28
Other East Asia and the Pacific		25,158	39,940	28,551	118,175	114,445	0.15	-3.16
Other countries of Asia		23,320	36,246	24,652	108,674	64,914	0.08	-40.27
All countries of Oceania		1,838	3,694	3,899	9,501	49,531	0.06	421.32
EUROPE		50,936,574	52,125,354	54,777,957	66,808,767	70,037,614	89.50	4.83
Central/Eastern Europe		16,105,010	16,721,774	17,032,704	19,153,341	20,207,385	25.82	5.50
Azerbaijan			182,512	265,305	304,033	351,877	0.45	15.74
Armenia			41,262	72,281	59,401	47,101	0.06	-20.71
Bulgaria		254,908	342,777	387,122	428,868	373,211	0.48	-12.98
Belarus			153,280	240,075	252,010	243,280	0.31	-3.46
Czech Republic		490,422	477,314	579,391	614,268	713,512	0.91	16.16
Estonia			61,849	93,731	143,767	127,224	0.16	-11.51
Georgia			79,914	131,301	119,365	105,320	0.13	-11.77
Hungary		171,098	247,120	209,527	316,227	281,164	0.36	-11.09

TURKEY

5. Overnight stays of non-resident tourists in hotels and similar establishments, by nationality

	2007	2008	2009	2010	2011	Market share 11	% Change 11-10
Kazakhstan		427,211	598,343	725,185	820,144	1.05	13.09
Kyrgyzstan		27,401	25,808	26,851	31,893	0.04	18.78
Latvia		97,151	68,539	99,093	101,856	0.13	2.79
Lithuania		306,539	205,498	275,576	268,688	0.34	-2.50
Republic of Moldova		115,346	140,742	181,778	181,468	0.23	-0.17
Poland	588,289	940,900	1,023,017	1,455,787	1,353,244	1.73	-7.04
Romania	624,683	762,459	754,973	900,166	818,250	1.05	-9.10
Russian Federation		10,854,943	10,594,606	11,540,679	12,504,898	15.98	8.35
Slovakia		144,168	239,148	390,416	373,526	0.48	-4.33
Tajikistan		16,208	11,945	11,700	53,889	0.07	360.59
Turkmenistan		32,450	35,781	44,390	56,145	0.07	26.48
Ukraine		1,368,080	1,277,169	1,176,919	1,313,844	1.68	11.63
Uzbekistan		42,890	78,402	86,862	86,851	0.11	-0.01
Commonwealth Independent States	13,975,610						
Northern Europe	**6,066,864**	**6,235,399**	**7,915,451**	**10,295,216**	**11,162,624**	**14.26**	**8.43**
Denmark		407,500	424,950	447,875	667,373	0.85	49.01
Finland		233,855	314,509	335,372	410,695	0.52	22.46
Iceland	29,438	28,489	30,956	21,417	22,497	0.03	5.04
Ireland	279,372	184,431	324,930	296,304	392,913	0.50	32.60
Norway		431,989	480,635	821,156	924,423	1.18	12.58
Sweden		682,238	712,347	1,017,083	1,516,503	1.94	49.10
United Kingdom	4,393,082	4,266,897	5,627,124	7,356,009	7,228,220	9.24	-1.74
Scandinavia	1,364,972						
Southern Europe	**2,420,317**	**2,549,004**	**2,888,676**	**3,071,508**	**2,899,345**	**3.70**	**-5.61**
Albania	109,190	107,854	126,948	118,909	73,730	0.09	-37.99
Bosnia and Herzegovina		82,282	76,943	113,457	109,308	0.14	-3.66
Croatia		52,956	45,973	55,183	96,854	0.12	75.51
Greece	338,772	416,755	434,905	549,864	479,398	0.61	-12.82
Italy	775,795	742,672	946,224	851,921	1,038,782	1.33	21.93
Malta		3,404	4,293	3,696	4,148	0.01	12.23
Montenegro			65	125	288	0.00	130.40
Portugal	43,527	65,846	111,211	155,417	113,688	0.15	-26.85
Serbia		192,139	169,436	227,249	241,089	0.31	6.09
Slovenia		67,387	77,364	87,120	122,562	0.16	40.68
Spain	716,812	742,275	800,952	809,997	532,169	0.68	-34.30
TFYR of Macedonia		75,434	94,362	98,570	87,329	0.11	-11.40
Yugoslavia, SFR (former)	436,221						
Western Europe	**24,726,835**	**25,492,247**	**26,160,413**	**33,951,969**	**35,318,089**	**45.13**	**4.02**
Austria	928,788	850,868	1,235,296	1,272,529	1,411,417	1.80	10.91
Belgium		2,252,590	2,426,030	2,458,136	2,253,374	2.88	-8.33
France	1,855,245	1,817,726	2,155,145	2,511,518	3,139,182	4.01	24.99
Germany	16,036,395	16,905,488	16,453,952	23,116,350	23,516,104	30.05	1.73
Luxembourg		59,998	60,958	76,375	92,191	0.12	20.71
Netherlands		3,107,529	3,172,840	3,721,425	3,964,994	5.07	6.55
Switzerland	557,435	498,048	656,192	795,636	940,827	1.20	18.25
Benelux	5,348,972						
East Mediterranean Europe	**1,301,139**	**1,092,348**	**732,765**	**312,128**	**292,911**	**0.37**	**-6.16**
Cyprus	173,747	165,968	147,282	59,973	145,276	0.19	142.24
Israel	1,127,392	926,380	585,483	252,155	147,635	0.19	-41.45
Other Europe	**316,409**	**34,582**	**47,948**	**24,605**	**157,260**	**0.20**	**539.14**
Other countries of Europe	316,409	34,582	47,948	24,605	157,260	0.20	539.14
MIDDLE EAST	**1,142,094**	**1,119,334**	**1,326,076**	**1,921,503**	**2,131,279**	**2.72**	**10.92**
Bahrain	13,636	18,186	17,920	20,936	28,564	0.04	36.43
Iraq	184,127	190,520	257,193	310,869	404,696	0.52	30.18
Jordan	124,842	131,721	167,641	156,654	146,505	0.19	-6.48
Kuwait	30,285	47,754	61,374	78,473	117,581	0.15	49.84
Lebanon	77,426	100,518	121,396	210,549	228,156	0.29	8.36

TURKEY

5. Overnight stays of non-resident tourists in hotels and similar establishments, by nationality

	2007	2008	2009	2010	2011	Market share 11	% Change 11-10
Libya	24,959	34,098	43,935	75,073	94,077	0.12	25.31
Oman	6,961						
Qatar	10,803	15,575	10,375	20,850	25,705	0.03	23.29
Saudi Arabia	267,865	212,345	216,813	358,747	495,531	0.63	38.13
Syrian Arab Republic	160,550	138,304	170,987	254,731	181,053	0.23	-28.92
United Arab Emirates	70,260	86,449	92,732	134,156	136,530	0.17	1.77
Egypt	133,360	92,889	111,004	139,242	183,168	0.23	31.55
Yemen	5,863	5,083	9,433	12,789	12,062	0.02	-5.68
Other countries of Middle East	31,157	45,892	45,273	148,434	77,651	0.10	-47.69
SOUTH ASIA	**697,257**	**712,863**	**912,636**	**1,311,944**	**1,544,555**	**1.97**	**17.73**
Bangladesh	1,705	2,381	3,859	3,642	6,977	0.01	91.57
India	86,073	98,248	96,602	120,979	171,817	0.22	42.02
Iran, Islamic Republic of	578,958	573,839	776,692	1,147,783	1,311,620	1.68	14.27
Pakistan	30,521	38,395	35,483	39,540	54,141	0.07	36.93
NOT SPECIFIED	**340,626**	**108,801**	**105,056**	**172,661**	**193,582**	**0.25**	**12.12**
Other countries of the World	340,626	108,801	105,056	172,661	193,582	0.25	12.12

TURKEY

6. Overnight stays of non-resident tourists in all types of accommodation establishments, by nationality

		2007	2008	2009	2010	2011	Market share 11	% Change 11-10
TOTAL	(*)	56,539,898	56,918,298	59,986,967	74,325,670	78,888,865	100.00	6.14
AFRICA		162,813	206,734	240,046	761,198	444,569	0.56	-41.60
North Africa		117,525	114,883	166,561	224,407	297,229	0.38	32.45
Algeria		40,536	32,860	46,132	62,203	110,634	0.14	77.86
Morocco		26,807	28,766	62,684	73,843	104,165	0.13	41.06
Sudan		6,446	7,043	8,057	9,259	13,017	0.02	40.59
Tunisia		43,736	46,214	49,688	79,102	69,413	0.09	-12.25
Southern Africa		28,864	24,812	30,546	38,263	59,221	0.08	54.77
South Africa		28,864	24,812	30,546	38,263	59,221	0.08	54.77
Other Africa		16,424	67,039	42,939	498,528	88,119	0.11	-82.32
Other countries of Africa		16,424	67,039	42,939	498,528	88,119	0.11	-82.32
AMERICAS		1,711,650	1,227,286	1,234,057	1,502,454	2,151,725	2.73	43.21
Central America		2,247	1,340	2,592	3,476	5,270	0.01	51.61
All countries of Central America		2,247	1,340	2,592	3,476	5,270	0.01	51.61
North America		1,557,641	1,118,419	1,077,362	1,274,380	1,861,689	2.36	46.09
Canada		208,812	103,218	95,749	122,855	189,000	0.24	53.84
Mexico		24,628	25,625	21,562	19,603	26,919	0.03	37.32
United States of America		1,280,640	944,397	862,735	1,033,107	1,599,660	2.03	54.84
Other countries of North America		43,561	45,179	97,316	98,815	46,110	0.06	-53.34
South America		151,762	107,527	154,103	224,598	284,766	0.36	26.79
Argentina		77,597	33,220	27,794	61,457	75,697	0.10	23.17
Brazil		47,621	45,164	78,404	131,872	166,922	0.21	26.58
Chile		7,741	7,229	24,487	8,478	10,464	0.01	23.43
Colombia		4,684	4,366	4,612	7,587	10,535	0.01	38.86
Venezuela		9,179	9,627	4,953	6,255	6,401	0.01	2.33
Other countries of South America		4,940	7,921	13,853	8,949	14,747	0.02	64.79
EAST ASIA AND THE PACIFIC		1,523,395	1,374,074	1,300,629	1,514,793	1,925,331	2.44	27.10
North-East Asia		1,184,139	987,793	805,979	1,027,664	1,265,824	1.60	23.17
China		129,599	126,988	94,984	135,052	218,223	0.28	61.58
Japan		717,212	617,539	565,034	664,353	687,219	0.87	3.44
Korea, Republic of		337,328	243,266	145,961	228,259	360,382	0.46	57.88
South-East Asia		93,390	96,916	140,633	148,551	196,761	0.25	32.45
Indonesia		8,166	13,167	14,742	19,254	32,410	0.04	68.33
Malaysia		36,754	31,262	51,763	53,832	64,520	0.08	19.85
Philippines		9,198	9,677	11,847	11,319	15,432	0.02	36.34
Singapore		25,103	31,398	48,399	50,776	62,867	0.08	23.81
Thailand		14,169	11,412	13,882	13,370	21,532	0.03	61.05
Australasia		220,595	249,425	325,427	287,429	344,527	0.44	19.87
Australia		197,643	234,203	307,350	258,263	319,914	0.41	23.87
New Zealand		22,952	15,222	18,077	29,166	24,613	0.03	-15.61
Other East Asia and the Pacific		25,271	39,940	28,590	51,149	118,219	0.15	131.13
Other countries of Asia		23,320	36,246	24,658	41,586	68,518	0.09	64.76
All countries of Oceania		1,951	3,694	3,932	9,563	49,701	0.06	419.72
EUROPE		50,962,043	52,169,159	54,861,766	67,185,489	70,456,510	89.31	4.87
Central/Eastern Europe		16,415,101	16,731,091	17,040,896	19,173,876	20,246,957	25.67	5.60
Azerbaijan		158,242	182,544	265,804	305,304	352,927	0.45	15.60
Armenia		32,077	41,262	72,293	59,414	47,101	0.06	-20.72
Bulgaria		255,176	343,122	387,482	430,122	377,536	0.48	-12.23
Belarus		118,055	153,282	240,163	252,067	243,420	0.31	-3.43
Czech Republic		408,269	480,893	579,646	616,487	728,868	0.92	18.23
Estonia		38,173	61,849	93,746	143,955	127,423	0.16	-11.48
Georgia		72,208	79,914	131,573	119,497	105,533	0.13	-11.69
Hungary		171,187	248,286	209,529	316,898	282,251	0.36	-10.93

TURKEY

6. Overnight stays of non-resident tourists in all types of accommodation establishments, by nationality

	2007	2008	2009	2010	2011	Market share 11	% Change 11-10
Kazakhstan	438,486	427,211	598,700	725,788	820,855	1.04	13.10
Kyrgyzstan	31,975	27,474	26,026	26,876	31,934	0.04	18.82
Latvia	65,672	97,151	68,541	99,093	101,856	0.13	2.79
Lithuania	177,394	306,539	205,498	275,826	269,068	0.34	-2.45
Republic of Moldova	155,040	115,356	141,392	181,791	181,809	0.23	0.01
Poland	588,289	942,312	1,023,361	1,456,762	1,354,592	1.72	-7.01
Romania	624,747	762,662	755,333	901,401	819,130	1.04	-9.13
Russian Federation	11,853,707	10,856,861	10,598,132	11,550,617	12,515,472	15.86	8.35
Slovakia	82,223	144,443	239,148	391,174	374,352	0.47	-4.30
Tajikistan	17,508	16,208	12,020	11,757	54,066	0.07	359.86
Turkmenistan	34,375	32,450	36,025	44,769	56,623	0.07	26.48
Ukraine	1,053,174	1,368,310	1,277,592	1,177,377	1,315,090	1.67	11.70
Uzbekistan	39,124	42,962	78,892	86,901	87,051	0.11	0.17
Northern Europe	**6,067,337**	**6,238,493**	**7,955,653**	**10,339,025**	**11,208,792**	**14.21**	**8.41**
Denmark	371,619	408,004	425,481	448,974	669,073	0.85	49.02
Finland	144,806	233,856	314,622	335,723	412,142	0.52	22.76
Iceland	29,438	28,510	31,322	21,513	22,558	0.03	4.86
Ireland	279,417	184,463	324,981	296,520	394,576	0.50	33.07
Norway	343,493	431,989	515,450	853,600	949,040	1.20	11.18
Sweden	505,054	682,291	713,702	1,019,359	1,519,418	1.93	49.06
United Kingdom	4,393,510	4,269,380	5,630,095	7,363,336	7,241,985	9.18	-1.65
Southern Europe	**2,421,946**	**2,550,310**	**2,894,934**	**3,121,575**	**2,969,147**	**3.76**	**-4.88**
Albania	109,190	107,854	127,080	118,962	73,836	0.09	-37.93
Bosnia and Herzegovina	97,962	82,293	77,093	113,581	109,389	0.14	-3.69
Croatia	46,616	52,958	45,973	55,188	97,129	0.12	76.00
Greece	338,772	417,243	437,943	554,235	491,098	0.62	-11.39
Italy	775,872	742,887	948,587	864,644	1,061,724	1.35	22.79
Malta	1,471	3,404	4,293	3,743	4,161	0.01	11.17
Montenegro			65	125	288	0.00	130.40
Portugal	43,527	65,846	111,281	160,730	119,441	0.15	-25.69
Serbia	165,387	192,277	169,505	227,354	241,192	0.31	6.09
Slovenia	58,061	67,677	77,378	87,171	123,011	0.16	41.11
Spain	716,812	742,435	801,320	837,163	560,413	0.71	-33.06
TFYR of Macedonia	68,276	75,436	94,416	98,679	87,465	0.11	-11.36
Western Europe	**24,745,382**	**25,522,290**	**26,188,754**	**34,062,125**	**35,573,689**	**45.09**	**4.44**
Austria	929,036	851,266	1,235,901	1,275,012	1,415,987	1.79	11.06
Belgium	2,275,977	2,252,679	2,426,247	2,459,627	2,256,942	2.86	-8.24
France	1,855,376	1,819,184	2,156,631	2,538,021	3,207,763	4.07	26.39
Germany	16,053,937	16,914,003	16,474,891	23,190,309	23,684,650	30.02	2.13
Luxembourg	37,176	60,001	60,958	76,382	92,348	0.12	20.90
Netherlands	3,036,324	3,126,114	3,177,548	3,725,732	3,971,501	5.03	6.60
Switzerland	557,556	499,043	656,578	797,042	944,498	1.20	18.50
East Mediterranean Europe	**1,301,145**	**1,092,391**	**733,541**	**404,224**	**300,178**	**0.38**	**-25.74**
Cyprus	173,747	165,978	147,983	151,775	152,088	0.19	0.21
Israel	1,127,398	926,413	585,558	252,449	148,090	0.19	-41.34
Other Europe	**11,132**	**34,584**	**47,988**	**84,664**	**157,747**	**0.20**	**86.32**
Other countries of Europe	11,132	34,584	47,988	84,664	157,747	0.20	86.32
MIDDLE EAST	**1,142,105**	**1,119,354**	**1,332,171**	**1,874,316**	**2,155,669**	**2.73**	**15.01**
Bahrain	13,636	18,186	17,927	24,651	28,687	0.04	16.37
Iraq	184,127	190,526	257,647	311,566	405,828	0.51	30.25
Jordan	124,842	131,722	167,654	157,164	149,990	0.19	-4.56
Kuwait	30,285	47,754	61,421	80,875	119,202	0.15	47.39
Lebanon	77,437	100,519	121,410	212,176	228,863	0.29	7.86
Libya	24,959	34,098	43,980	75,222	94,236	0.12	25.28
Oman	6,961						
Qatar	10,803	15,575	10,375	21,305	26,124	0.03	22.62
Saudi Arabia	267,865	212,345	217,118	364,700	502,198	0.64	37.70

TURKEY

6. Overnight stays of non-resident tourists in all types of accommodation establishments, by nationality

	2007	2008	2009	2010	2011	Market share 11	% Change 11-10
Syrian Arab Republic	160,550	138,305	176,097	267,585	186,472	0.24	-30.31
United Arab Emirates	70,260	86,457	92,767	136,902	137,733	0.17	0.61
Egypt	133,360	92,892	111,058	139,471	183,601	0.23	31.64
Yemen	5,863	5,083	9,433	12,890	12,219	0.02	-5.21
Other countries of Middle East	31,157	45,892	45,284	69,809	80,516	0.10	15.34
SOUTH ASIA	**697,357**	**712,890**	**913,204**	**1,313,594**	**1,550,249**	**1.97**	**18.02**
Bangladesh	1,705	2,381	3,859	3,685	7,001	0.01	89.99
India	86,110	98,252	96,618	121,560	173,954	0.22	43.10
Iran, Islamic Republic of	578,977	573,857	777,220	1,148,675	1,314,890	1.67	14.47
Pakistan	30,565	38,400	35,507	39,674	54,404	0.07	37.13
NOT SPECIFIED	**340,535**	**108,801**	**105,094**	**173,826**	**204,812**	**0.26**	**17.83**
Other countries of the World	340,535	108,801	105,094	173,826	204,812	0.26	17.83

TURKS AND CAICOS ISLANDS

1. Arrivals of non-resident tourists at national borders, by country of residence

	2007	2008	2009	2010	2011	Market share 11	% Change 11-10
TOTAL					354,223	100.00	
AMERICAS					344,337	97.21	
Caribbean					39,913	11.27	
All countries of the Caribbean					39,913	11.27	
North America					304,424	85.94	
Canada					42,282	11.94	
United States of America					262,142	74.00	
EUROPE					6,902	1.95	
Other Europe					6,902	1.95	
All countries of Europe					6,902	1.95	
NOT SPECIFIED					2,984	0.84	
Other countries of the World					2,984	0.84	

TUVALU

1. Arrivals of non-resident tourists at national borders, by nationality

	2007	2008	2009	2010	2011	Market share 11	% Change 11-10
TOTAL	1,130	1,651	1,580	1,657	1,232	100.00	-25.65
AMERICAS	65	79	83	97	94	7.63	-3.09
North America	65	79	83	97	94	7.63	-3.09
Canada	11	12	13	26	9	0.73	-65.38
United States of America	54	67	70	71	85	6.90	19.72
EAST ASIA AND THE PACIFIC	851	1,320	1,267	1,288	909	73.78	-29.43
North-East Asia	227	432	471	418	190	15.42	-54.55
China		20	74	41	9	0.73	-78.05
Taiwan, Province of China					31	2.52	
Japan	227	412	397	377	150	12.18	-60.21
Australasia	243	345	382	350	249	20.21	-28.86
Australia	138	205	194	166	116	9.42	-30.12
New Zealand	105	140	188	184	133	10.80	-27.72
Melanesia	218	324	251	285	311	25.24	9.12
Fiji	218	324	251	285	311	25.24	9.12
Micronesia	17	23	51	34	22	1.79	-35.29
Kiribati	17	23	51	34	22	1.79	-35.29
Other East Asia and the Pacific	146	196	112	201	137	11.12	-31.84
Other countries of Asia	80	124	54	133	48	3.90	-63.91
All countries of Oceania	66	72	58	68	89	7.22	30.88
EUROPE	87	136	143	134	81	6.57	-39.55
Northern Europe	35	44	54	42	22	1.79	-47.62
United Kingdom	35	44	54	42	22	1.79	-47.62
Western Europe	34	30	45	45	24	1.95	-46.67
France	16	12	15	17	8	0.65	-52.94
Germany	18	18	30	28	16	1.30	-42.86
Other Europe	18	62	44	47	35	2.84	-25.53
Other countries of Europe	18	62	44	47	35	2.84	-25.53
NOT SPECIFIED	127	116	87	138	148	12.01	7.25
Other countries of the World	127	116	87	138	148	12.01	7.25

UGANDA

1. Arrivals of non-resident tourists at national borders, by country of residence

	2007	2008	2009	2010	2011	Market share 11	% Change 11-10
TOTAL	641,743	843,864	806,655	945,899	1,151,356	100.00	21.72
AFRICA	479,802	624,352	630,014	675,931	873,348	75.85	29.21
East Africa	386,190	484,720	515,714	520,159	675,592	58.68	29.88
Ethiopia	7,895	8,319	5,907	6,657	6,148	0.53	-7.65
Kenya	199,598	249,786	261,329	294,170	344,210	29.90	17.01
Rwanda	123,262	181,339	199,530	177,043	266,221	23.12	50.37
United Republic of Tanzania	55,435	45,276	48,948	42,289	59,013	5.13	39.55
Central Africa	4,745	12,495	11,664	20,306	42,147	3.66	107.56
Democratic Republic of the Congo	4,745	12,495	11,664	20,306	42,147	3.66	107.56
North Africa	10,299	16,169	15,088	22,909	39,333	3.42	71.69
Sudan	10,299	16,169	15,088	22,909	39,333	3.42	71.69
Southern Africa	12,190	13,940					
South Africa	12,190	13,940					
Other Africa	66,378	97,028	87,548	112,557	116,276	10.10	3.30
Other countries of Africa	66,378	97,028	87,548	112,557	116,276	10.10	3.30
AMERICAS	42,388	53,950	47,065	65,175	59,477	5.17	-8.74
North America	40,652	51,604	44,970	54,209	56,419	4.90	4.08
Canada	8,308	9,186	6,999	8,353	8,550	0.74	2.36
United States of America	32,344	42,418	37,971	45,856	47,869	4.16	4.39
Other Americas	1,736	2,346	2,095	10,966	3,058	0.27	-72.11
Other countries of the Americas	1,736	2,346	2,095	10,966	3,058	0.27	-72.11
EAST ASIA AND THE PACIFIC	14,466	14,687	19,357	28,163	29,899	2.60	6.16
North-East Asia	6,093	8,037	6,814	8,002	10,633	0.92	32.88
China	4,220	6,088	4,629	5,692	6,971	0.61	22.47
Japan	1,873	1,949	2,185	2,310	3,662	0.32	58.53
Australasia	4,163	6,264	4,638	5,534	5,250	0.46	-5.13
Australia	3,566	5,342	4,087	4,870	4,827	0.42	-0.88
New Zealand	597	922	551	664	423	0.04	-36.30
Other East Asia and the Pacific	4,210	386	7,905	14,627	14,016	1.22	-4.18
Other countries of Asia	4,210	386	7,905	14,300	12,778	1.11	-10.64
Other countries of Oceania				327	1,238	0.11	278.59
EUROPE	77,391	106,020	79,710	112,870	154,542	13.42	36.92
Central/Eastern Europe	1,093	1,221	1,038	1,104	5,018	0.44	354.53
Czech Republic/Slovakia	415	505	425	371	483	0.04	30.19
Russian Federation	678	716	613	733	4,535	0.39	518.69
Northern Europe	49,250	66,504	47,827	52,374	50,222	4.36	-4.11
Denmark	2,852	3,389	3,000	3,145	4,159	0.36	32.24
Finland	450	585	730	577	513	0.04	-11.09
Ireland	1,633	2,615	1,820	2,143	1,663	0.14	-22.40
Norway	2,517	3,528	2,827	2,874	1,877	0.16	-34.69
Sweden	3,131	4,575	3,734	4,464	4,308	0.37	-3.49
United Kingdom	38,667	51,812	35,716	39,171	37,702	3.27	-3.75
Southern Europe	3,787	5,142	4,595	5,622	5,348	0.46	-4.87
Italy	3,679	5,063	4,567	5,505	5,335	0.46	-3.09
Serbia and Montenegro	108	79	28	117	13	0.00	-88.89
Western Europe	19,062	26,916	21,669	46,203	81,809	7.11	77.06
Austria	639	1,331	897	20,304	53,820	4.67	165.07
Belgium	3,301	4,422	2,787	3,629	5,156	0.45	42.08
France	2,775	3,958	3,467	3,893	4,437	0.39	13.97
Germany	5,802	8,083	6,778	8,650	8,960	0.78	3.58
Netherlands	4,790	7,136	6,017	7,651	8,380	0.73	9.53
Switzerland	1,755	1,986	1,723	2,076	1,056	0.09	-49.13

UGANDA

1. Arrivals of non-resident tourists at national borders, by country of residence

	2007	2008	2009	2010	2011	Market share 11	% Change 11-10
Other Europe	**4,199**	**6,237**	**4,581**	**7,567**	**12,145**	**1.05**	**60.50**
Other countries of Europe	4,199	6,237	4,581	7,567	12,145	1.05	60.50
MIDDLE EAST	**4,971**	**9,720**	**8,942**	**15,538**	**8,652**	**0.75**	**-44.32**
Egypt	948	1,725	1,244	1,843	1,409	0.12	-23.55
Other countries of Middle East	4,023	7,995	7,698	13,695	7,243	0.63	-47.11
SOUTH ASIA	**14,803**	**18,845**	**14,937**	**18,898**	**21,755**	**1.89**	**15.12**
India	12,408	16,236	12,946	16,747	19,419	1.69	15.96
Pakistan	2,395	2,609	1,991	2,151	2,336	0.20	8.60
NOT SPECIFIED	**7,922**	**16,290**	**6,630**	**29,324**	**3,683**	**0.32**	**-87.44**
Other countries of the World	7,922	16,290	6,630	29,324	3,683	0.32	-87.44

UKRAINE

1. Arrivals of non-resident tourists at national borders, by country of residence

	2007	2008	2009	2010	2011	Market share 11	% Change 11-10
TOTAL	23,122,157	25,449,078	20,798,342	21,203,327	21,415,296	100.00	1.00
AFRICA	10,216	9,789	10,252	12,219	14,977	0.07	22.57
East Africa	654	1,611	748	1,052	1,730	0.01	64.45
British Indian Ocean Territory					21	0.00	
Burundi				4	4	0.00	
Comoros				4	21	0.00	425.00
Ethiopia		168	128	104	207	0.00	99.04
Eritrea				19	24	0.00	26.32
Djibouti				8	3	0.00	-62.50
Kenya	159	212	244	223	320	0.00	43.50
Madagascar				20	35	0.00	75.00
Malawi				14	5	0.00	-64.29
Mauritius	150			87	90	0.00	3.45
Mozambique				21	39	0.00	85.71
Rwanda		244		48	158	0.00	229.17
Seychelles				5	9	0.00	80.00
Somalia	116	156	110	119	84	0.00	-29.41
Zimbabwe	229			81	85	0.00	4.94
Uganda		831	126	125	73	0.00	-41.60
United Republic of Tanzania			140	126	490	0.00	288.89
Zambia				44	62	0.00	40.91
Central Africa	594	445	863	1,213	1,381	0.01	13.85
Angola			151	160	293	0.00	83.13
Cameroon	311	254	417	504	457	0.00	-9.33
Central African Republic				4	36	0.00	800.00
Chad	131			22	17	0.00	-22.73
Congo	152	191	155	286	343	0.00	19.93
Democratic Republic of the Congo			140	176	170	0.00	-3.41
Equatorial Guinea				19	26	0.00	36.84
Gabon				42	30	0.00	-28.57
Sao Tome and Principe					9	0.00	
North Africa	4,583	4,199	4,720	4,771	5,269	0.02	10.44
Algeria	687	631	675	677	837	0.00	23.63
Morocco	1,554	1,592	1,956	1,925	2,297	0.01	19.32
Sudan	542	453	538	758	719	0.00	-5.15
Tunisia	1,800	1,523	1,551	1,411	1,416	0.01	0.35
Southern Africa	1,071	1,184	1,085	1,345	2,099	0.01	56.06
Botswana				13	8	0.00	-38.46
Lesotho				3	828	0.00	27500.00
Namibia				29	61	0.00	110.34
South Africa	1,071	1,184	1,085	1,297	1,196	0.01	-7.79
Swaziland				3	6	0.00	100.00
West Africa	3,314	2,350	2,836	3,838	4,498	0.02	17.20
Cape Verde	1,157			12	12	0.00	
Benin				14	54	0.00	285.71
Gambia				2	2	0.00	
Ghana	265	231	261	312	417	0.00	33.65
Guinea	195	231	160	99	97	0.00	-2.02
Côte d'Ivoire				77	82	0.00	6.49
Liberia				48	68	0.00	41.67
Mali				46	60	0.00	30.43
Mauritania				16	11	0.00	-31.25
Niger				15	20	0.00	33.33
Nigeria	1,697	1,888	2,415	2,997	3,518	0.02	17.38
Guinea-Bissau				3	11	0.00	266.67
Senegal				109	72	0.00	-33.94

UKRAINE

1. Arrivals of non-resident tourists at national borders, by country of residence

	2007	2008	2009	2010	2011	Market share 11	% Change 11-10
Sierra Leone				20	31	0.00	55.00
Togo				22	26	0.00	18.18
Burkina Faso				46	17	0.00	-63.04
AMERICAS	**167,103**	**163,371**	**161,412**	**162,853**	**165,068**	**0.77**	**1.36**
Caribbean	**880**	**829**	**786**	**842**	**745**	**0.00**	**-11.52**
Antigua and Barbuda				9			
Bahamas				11	18	0.00	63.64
Barbados				5	27	0.00	440.00
Bermuda				4			
British Virgin Islands				5	3	0.00	-40.00
Cuba	880	679	786	702	564	0.00	-19.66
Dominica				1	12	0.00	1100.00
Dominican Republic				34	43	0.00	26.47
Grenada				3	2	0.00	-33.33
Haiti				1	5	0.00	400.00
Jamaica				12	21	0.00	75.00
Montserrat				10	4	0.00	-60.00
Netherlands Antilles				2	1	0.00	-50.00
Puerto Rico				1	1	0.00	
Saint Kitts and Nevis				7	14	0.00	100.00
Anguilla				10	7	0.00	-30.00
Saint Lucia				1	1	0.00	
Saint Vincent and the Grenadines				2			
Trinidad and Tobago				20	21	0.00	5.00
United States Virgin Islands		150		2	1	0.00	-50.00
Central America			**135**	**277**	**400**	**0.00**	**44.40**
Belize				14	4	0.00	-71.43
Costa Rica				74	70	0.00	-5.41
El Salvador				11	237	0.00	2054.55
Guatemala				56	16	0.00	-71.43
Honduras			135	28	10	0.00	-64.29
Nicaragua				21	19	0.00	-9.52
Panama				73	44	0.00	-39.73
North America	**162,279**	**158,197**	**155,488**	**155,539**	**157,462**	**0.74**	**1.24**
Canada	28,485	28,855	31,372	28,349	28,409	0.13	0.21
Greenland	393				2	0.00	
Mexico	1,025	1,220	1,115	1,337	1,127	0.01	-15.71
United States of America	132,376	128,122	123,001	125,853	127,924	0.60	1.65
South America	**3,944**	**4,345**	**5,003**	**6,195**	**6,461**	**0.03**	**4.29**
Argentina	1,212	1,319	1,465	1,716	1,710	0.01	-0.35
Bolivia				173	151	0.00	-12.72
Brazil	1,666	1,845	2,290	2,427	2,740	0.01	12.90
Chile	147	264	211	382	255	0.00	-33.25
Colombia	171	151	217	278	224	0.00	-19.42
Ecuador	164	211	235	270	264	0.00	-2.22
French Guiana					20	0.00	
Guyana				3			
Paraguay				29	30	0.00	3.45
Peru	430	335	384	397	350	0.00	-11.84
Suriname				2	7	0.00	250.00
Uruguay				84	108	0.00	28.57
Venezuela	154	220	201	434	579	0.00	33.41
Other countries of South America					23	0.00	

UKRAINE

1. Arrivals of non-resident tourists at national borders, by country of residence

	2007	2008	2009	2010	2011	Market share 11	% Change 11-10
EAST ASIA AND THE PACIFIC	48,651	45,648	43,750	45,652	49,785	0.23	9.05
North-East Asia	32,519	31,114	28,839	30,111	34,830	0.16	15.67
China	17,160	16,574	16,137	16,794	19,057	0.09	13.48
Taiwan, Province of China	471	544	1,073	378	546	0.00	44.44
Hong Kong, China				134	240	0.00	79.10
Japan	6,903	6,437	5,439	6,206	7,585	0.04	22.22
Korea, Dem. People's Republic of	1,207	577	333	299	220	0.00	-26.42
Korea, Republic of	5,151	5,985	5,374	5,645	6,322	0.03	11.99
Macao, China				4	2	0.00	-50.00
Mongolia	1,627	997	483	651	858	0.00	31.80
South-East Asia	8,549	8,250	8,817	8,759	8,305	0.04	-5.18
Brunei Darussalam				24	3	0.00	-87.50
Myanmar				167	12	0.00	-92.81
Cambodia				14	48	0.00	242.86
Indonesia	367	273	612	583	569	0.00	-2.40
Lao People's Democratic Republic				22	36	0.00	63.64
Malaysia	2,522	2,166	2,452	1,651	1,106	0.01	-33.01
Philippines	749	288	1,371	1,236	480	0.00	-61.17
Singapore	361	419	208	357	1,159	0.01	224.65
Viet Nam	4,139	4,756	3,694	4,351	4,445	0.02	2.16
Thailand	411	348	480	354	447	0.00	26.27
Australasia	7,583	6,284	6,094	6,742	6,638	0.03	-1.54
Australia	6,874	5,277	5,224	5,769	5,706	0.03	-1.09
New Zealand	709	1,007	870	973	932	0.00	-4.21
Melanesia				7	8	0.00	14.29
Solomon Islands				3			
Fiji				1	4	0.00	300.00
New Caledonia				2	3	0.00	50.00
Vanuatu				1	1	0.00	
Micronesia				30			
Kiribati				12			
Marshall Islands				17			
Palau				1			
Polynesia				3	1	0.00	-66.67
American Samoa				2	1	0.00	-50.00
Tonga				1			
Other East Asia and the Pacific					3	0.00	
Other countries East Asia/Pacific					3	0.00	
EUROPE	22,825,500	25,163,875	20,514,394	20,911,215	21,117,959	98.61	0.99
Central/Eastern Europe	22,063,555	24,368,372	19,784,002	20,130,512	20,243,653	94.53	0.56
Azerbaijan	71,112	80,350	66,996	77,123	85,482	0.40	10.84
Armenia	57,995	56,050	53,373	52,492	53,627	0.25	2.16
Bulgaria	16,674	24,588	25,102	27,099	31,661	0.15	16.83
Belarus	2,918,694	3,407,064	2,984,672	3,058,023	2,643,988	12.35	-13.54
Czech Republic	50,415	43,959	46,646	46,461	51,858	0.24	11.62
Estonia	19,997	21,094	16,016	16,712	17,867	0.08	6.91
Georgia	50,472	53,544	40,544	36,039	35,861	0.17	-0.49
Hungary	1,251,724	1,033,376	814,790	944,777	862,051	4.03	-8.76
Kazakhstan	54,629	48,565	43,524	50,787	61,826	0.29	21.74
Kyrgyzstan	11,122	9,859	10,520	18,102	21,501	0.10	18.78
Latvia	39,773	44,737	35,555	36,602	36,936	0.17	0.91
Lithuania	52,645	56,991	48,314	48,907	48,677	0.23	-0.47
Republic of Moldova	3,998,674	4,418,821	4,339,138	4,063,459	4,071,785	19.01	0.20
Poland	4,430,140	5,242,980	2,546,132	2,089,647	1,720,104	8.03	-17.68
Romania	1,010,065	1,440,466	1,077,299	910,450	735,233	3.43	-19.25
Russian Federation	7,258,222	7,638,222	6,964,435	7,900,436	9,018,487	42.11	14.15

UKRAINE

1. Arrivals of non-resident tourists at national borders, by country of residence

	2007	2008	2009	2010	2011	Market share 11	% Change 11-10
Slovakia	664,605	644,918	537,511	609,994	564,337	2.64	-7.48
Tajikistan	25,149	19,875	29,463	27,851	27,149	0.13	-2.52
Turkmenistan	3,374	6,039	7,631	10,082	14,060	0.07	39.46
Uzbekistan	78,074	76,874	96,341	105,469	141,163	0.66	33.84
Northern Europe	**113,855**	**119,490**	**119,819**	**117,530**	**127,844**	**0.60**	**8.78**
Denmark	10,605	10,996	12,697	12,051	12,601	0.06	4.56
Finland	7,801	8,298	7,992	8,020	9,764	0.05	21.75
Iceland	480	512	566	532	674	0.00	26.69
Ireland	4,830	5,091	4,951	4,945	6,117	0.03	23.70
Norway	8,142	8,892	10,712	10,848	12,022	0.06	10.82
Sweden	15,865	16,992	16,050	16,544	19,491	0.09	17.81
United Kingdom	66,132	68,709	66,851	64,590	67,175	0.31	4.00
Southern Europe	**136,559**	**132,175**	**128,763**	**137,629**	**155,643**	**0.73**	**13.09**
Albania	483	468	567	427	493	0.00	15.46
Andorra				23	39	0.00	69.57
Bosnia and Herzegovina	1,469	1,924	999	997	1,014	0.00	1.71
Croatia	3,720	4,078	3,172	3,575	3,432	0.02	-4.00
Greece	16,107	18,156	16,377	16,926	17,364	0.08	2.59
Holy See				14	21	0.00	50.00
Italy	77,054	70,625	73,737	79,174	86,964	0.41	9.84
Malta	423	418	408	447	479	0.00	7.16
Montenegro	879	1,999	1,643	2,037	1,239	0.01	-39.18
Portugal	3,383	3,959	3,909	4,857	6,783	0.03	39.65
San Marino				61	64	0.00	4.92
Serbia	10,011	5,203	5,065	6,340	12,135	0.06	91.40
Slovenia	6,527	7,570	5,499	5,885	6,980	0.03	18.61
Spain	13,669	14,135	13,453	14,021	16,441	0.08	17.26
TFYR of Macedonia	2,834	3,640	3,934	2,845	2,195	0.01	-22.85
Western Europe	**369,037**	**369,986**	**349,953**	**373,552**	**389,847**	**1.82**	**4.36**
Austria	31,623	30,044	27,218	27,512	28,094	0.13	2.12
Belgium	11,741	12,913	13,455	13,796	14,998	0.07	8.71
France	48,160	50,403	49,810	56,268	62,088	0.29	10.34
Germany	235,479	231,632	213,995	227,725	231,718	1.08	1.75
Liechtenstein	107			92	91	0.00	-1.09
Luxembourg	665	811	661	865	825	0.00	-4.62
Monaco				26	15	0.00	-42.31
Netherlands	28,019	30,305	31,548	31,965	33,216	0.16	3.91
Switzerland	13,243	13,878	13,266	15,303	18,802	0.09	22.86
East Mediterranean Europe	**142,494**	**173,852**	**131,857**	**151,992**	**200,972**	**0.94**	**32.23**
Cyprus	3,706	4,061	3,476	3,913	4,428	0.02	13.16
Israel	58,932	90,353	68,303	81,969	120,181	0.56	46.62
Turkey	79,856	79,438	60,078	66,110	76,363	0.36	15.51
MIDDLE EAST	**26,308**	**23,253**	**27,856**	**29,059**	**28,572**	**0.13**	**-1.68**
Bahrain	339	353	563	425	364	0.00	-14.35
Palestine	636	574	753	668	591	0.00	-11.53
Iraq	1,660	1,596	2,633	4,337	5,201	0.02	19.92
Jordan	5,162	3,613	5,221	5,243	5,728	0.03	9.25
Kuwait	890	517	1,188	928	978	0.00	5.39
Lebanon	4,167	3,806	4,693	4,730	4,696	0.02	-0.72
Libya	2,943	2,970	3,198	2,924	998	0.00	-65.87
Oman				87	125	0.00	43.68
Qatar				171	174	0.00	1.75
Saudi Arabia	812	713	792	1,140	1,362	0.01	19.47
Syrian Arab Republic	6,653	6,084	5,290	4,919	4,333	0.02	-11.91
United Arab Emirates	405	306	573	681	1,169	0.01	71.66
Egypt	2,453	2,534	2,684	2,572	2,649	0.01	2.99
Yemen	188	187	268	234	204	0.00	-12.82

UKRAINE

1. Arrivals of non-resident tourists at national borders, by country of residence

	2007	2008	2009	2010	2011	Market share 11	% Change 11-10
SOUTH ASIA	**17,572**	**17,389**	**19,871**	**23,012**	**21,819**	**0.10**	**-5.18**
Afghanistan	918	798	943	991	1,056	0.00	6.56
Bangladesh	219	211	184	245	342	0.00	39.59
Bhutan					6	0.00	
Sri Lanka	199	196	299	431	417	0.00	-3.25
India	7,370	7,262	8,183	10,152	9,254	0.04	-8.85
Iran, Islamic Republic of	7,483	7,698	8,863	9,677	8,289	0.04	-14.34
Maldives				36	45	0.00	25.00
Nepal	116		172	183	1,180	0.01	544.81
Pakistan	1,267	1,224	1,227	1,297	1,230	0.01	-5.17
NOT SPECIFIED	**26,807**	**25,753**	**20,807**	**19,317**	**17,116**	**0.08**	**-11.39**
Other countries of the World	26,807	25,753	20,807	19,317	17,116	0.08	-11.39

UNITED KINGDOM

2. Arrivals of non-resident visitors at national borders, by country of residence

	2007	2008	2009	2010	2011	Market share 11	% Change 11-10
TOTAL	32,778,102	31,888,118	29,889,075	29,803,000	30,797,000	100.00	3.34
AFRICA	653,917	644,718	596,415	571,000	527,000	1.71	-7.71
East Africa	94,589	118,678	97,964	86,000	89,000	0.29	3.49
Zimbabwe	20,993	20,474	11,451	8,000	6,000	0.02	-25.00
Other countries of East Africa	73,596	98,204	86,513	78,000	83,000	0.27	6.41
North Africa	38,981	46,332	44,578	51,000	44,000	0.14	-13.73
All countries of North Africa	38,981	46,332	44,578	51,000	44,000	0.14	-13.73
Southern Africa	296,613	273,595	244,544	208,000	193,000	0.63	-7.21
South Africa	296,613	273,595	244,544	208,000	193,000	0.63	-7.21
West Africa	194,505	174,532	181,811	195,000	182,000	0.59	-6.67
Nigeria	153,501	150,023	145,113	168,000	142,000	0.46	-15.48
Other countries of West Africa	41,004	24,509	36,698	27,000	40,000	0.13	48.15
Other Africa	29,229	31,581	27,518	31,000	19,000	0.06	-38.71
Other countries of Africa	29,229	31,581	27,518	31,000	19,000	0.06	-38.71
AMERICAS	4,826,687	4,211,749	4,020,126	3,839,000	4,177,000	13.56	8.80
Caribbean	111,494	73,088	89,784	71,000	76,000	0.25	7.04
All countries of the Caribbean	111,494	73,088	89,784	71,000	76,000	0.25	7.04
North America	4,461,018	3,871,154	3,644,923	3,464,000	3,664,000	11.90	5.77
Canada	851,995	856,652	686,872	686,000	740,000	2.40	7.87
Mexico	58,468	64,694	80,839	67,000	78,000	0.25	16.42
United States of America	3,550,555	2,949,808	2,877,212	2,711,000	2,846,000	9.24	4.98
South America	217,727	248,295	250,724	275,000	411,000	1.33	49.45
Argentina	40,984	35,616	69,113	63,000	80,000	0.26	26.98
Brazil	131,487	178,734	151,087	177,000	276,000	0.90	55.93
Chile	21,114	19,688	13,688	13,000	23,000	0.07	76.92
Colombia	13,670	6,248	6,845	18,000	13,000	0.04	-27.78
Venezuela	10,472	8,009	9,991	4,000	19,000	0.06	375.00
Other Americas	36,448	19,212	34,695	29,000	26,000	0.08	-10.34
Other countries of the Americas	36,448	19,212	34,695	29,000	26,000	0.08	-10.34
EAST ASIA AND THE PACIFIC	2,315,607	2,146,669	2,065,639	2,202,000	2,433,000	7.90	10.49
North-East Asia	778,773	632,894	581,599	609,000	708,000	2.30	16.26
China	143,353	107,860	89,187	109,000	149,000	0.48	36.70
Taiwan, Province of China	34,262	27,821	38,834	31,000	33,000	0.11	6.45
Hong Kong, China	136,173	129,957	143,472	131,000	149,000	0.48	13.74
Japan	307,633	238,910	235,471	223,000	237,000	0.77	6.28
Korea, Republic of	157,352	128,346	74,635	115,000	140,000	0.45	21.74
South-East Asia	253,908	244,412	301,288	323,000	329,000	1.07	1.86
Malaysia	86,571	75,626	120,970	133,000	130,000	0.42	-2.26
Singapore	97,925	118,475	111,108	123,000	134,000	0.44	8.94
Thailand	69,412	50,311	69,210	67,000	65,000	0.21	-2.99
Australasia	1,168,257	1,164,306	1,099,471	1,173,000	1,281,000	4.16	9.21
Australia	940,822	955,487	912,259	986,000	1,093,000	3.55	10.85
New Zealand	227,435	208,819	187,212	187,000	188,000	0.61	0.53
Other East Asia and the Pacific	114,669	105,057	83,281	97,000	115,000	0.37	18.56
Other countries of Asia	114,669	105,057	83,281	97,000	115,000	0.37	18.56
EUROPE	24,020,354	23,826,127	22,241,150	22,203,000	22,604,000	73.40	1.81
Central/Eastern Europe	3,131,143	3,346,728	2,594,122	2,547,000	2,645,000	8.59	3.85
Czech Republic	397,538	434,929	389,074	278,000	287,000	0.93	3.24
Hungary	332,555	299,636	260,340	214,000	211,000	0.69	-1.40
Poland	1,294,070	1,491,797	1,040,553	1,101,000	1,058,000	3.44	-3.91
Russian Federation	223,891	207,740	137,287	170,000	211,000	0.69	24.12
Other countries Central/East Europe	883,089	912,626	766,868	784,000	878,000	2.85	11.99

UNITED KINGDOM

2. Arrivals of non-resident visitors at national borders, by country of residence

	2007	2008	2009	2010	2011	Market share 11	% Change 11-10
Northern Europe	**5,205,097**	**5,311,367**	**4,949,677**	**4,798,000**	**5,004,000**	**16.25**	**4.29**
Denmark	561,077	561,410	618,804	558,000	622,000	2.02	11.47
Finland	197,824	179,054	167,331	170,000	233,000	0.76	37.06
Iceland	120,024	70,241	38,500	34,000	41,000	0.13	20.59
Ireland	2,970,119	3,069,999	2,947,552	2,629,000	2,574,000	8.36	-2.09
Norway	608,518	688,161	573,163	649,000	739,000	2.40	13.87
Sweden	747,535	742,502	604,327	758,000	795,000	2.58	4.88
Southern Europe	**4,561,247**	**4,364,109**	**4,077,714**	**3,981,000**	**4,078,000**	**13.24**	**2.44**
Gibraltar	39,352	25,721	28,207	27,000	28,000	0.09	3.70
Greece	166,493	203,657	192,529	174,000	225,000	0.73	29.31
Italy	1,614,725	1,639,316	1,220,907	1,472,000	1,526,000	4.96	3.67
Malta	78,773	84,595	74,990	66,000	64,000	0.21	-3.03
Portugal	279,890	274,519	255,096	316,000	283,000	0.92	-10.44
Spain	2,227,008	1,974,004	2,163,809	1,809,000	1,836,000	5.96	1.49
Yugoslavia, SFR (former)	155,006	162,297	142,176	117,000	116,000	0.38	-0.85
Western Europe	**10,714,306**	**10,374,648**	**10,230,223**	**10,480,000**	**10,464,000**	**33.98**	**-0.15**
Austria	289,943	285,664	286,148	288,000	271,000	0.88	-5.90
Belgium	994,855	970,262	903,127	1,136,000	984,000	3.20	-13.38
France	3,403,945	3,636,332	3,784,473	3,618,000	3,633,000	11.80	0.41
Germany	3,375,730	2,899,571	2,779,754	3,004,000	2,947,000	9.57	-1.90
Luxembourg	88,217	62,149	60,171	53,000	73,000	0.24	37.74
Netherlands	1,823,421	1,818,249	1,715,460	1,758,000	1,788,000	5.81	1.71
Switzerland	738,195	702,421	701,090	623,000	768,000	2.49	23.27
East Mediterranean Europe	**408,561**	**429,275**	**389,414**	**397,000**	**413,000**	**1.34**	**4.03**
Cyprus	129,072	138,817	133,704	110,000	124,000	0.40	12.73
Israel	137,584	160,212	157,994	158,000	164,000	0.53	3.80
Turkey	141,905	130,246	97,716	129,000	125,000	0.41	-3.10
MIDDLE EAST	**489,559**	**537,585**	**596,237**	**529,000**	**589,000**	**1.91**	**11.34**
Saudi Arabia	81,657	93,914	88,605	79,000	105,000	0.34	32.91
United Arab Emirates	187,342	231,735	246,260	213,000	241,000	0.78	13.15
Egypt	38,435	41,535	47,936	42,000	41,000	0.13	-2.38
Other countries of Middle East	182,125	170,401	213,436	195,000	202,000	0.66	3.59
SOUTH ASIA	**471,978**	**521,270**	**369,508**	**456,000**	**467,000**	**1.52**	**2.41**
Bangladesh	12,704	21,550	10,365	13,000	19,000	0.06	46.15
India	335,892	359,237	272,754	371,000	356,000	1.16	-4.04
Iran, Islamic Republic of	30,316	38,006	25,958	15,000	27,000	0.09	80.00
Pakistan	93,066	102,477	60,431	57,000	65,000	0.21	14.04
NOT SPECIFIED				**3,000**			
Other countries of the World				3,000			

UNITED KINGDOM

6. Overnight stays of non-resident tourists in all types of accommodation establishments, by country of residence

	2007	2008	2009	2010	2011	Market share 11	% Change 11-10
TOTAL	251,520,106	245,774,778	229,387,112	227,846,000	235,196,000	100.00	3.23
AFRICA	10,900,654	11,674,895	10,982,197	8,343,000	8,754,000	3.72	4.93
East Africa	1,793,243	3,013,558	2,079,945	1,667,000	1,772,000	0.75	6.30
Zimbabwe	466,900	590,844	208,776	269,000	134,000	0.06	-50.19
Other countries of East Africa	1,326,343	2,422,714	1,871,169	1,398,000	1,638,000	0.70	17.17
North Africa	909,680	915,695	821,911	746,000	700,000	0.30	-6.17
All countries of North Africa	909,680	915,695	821,911	746,000	700,000	0.30	-6.17
Southern Africa	4,576,481	3,941,943	4,745,254	2,564,000	2,316,000	0.98	-9.67
South Africa	4,576,481	3,941,943	4,745,254	2,564,000	2,316,000	0.98	-9.67
West Africa	3,330,504	3,306,382	2,925,410	2,980,000	3,552,000	1.51	19.19
Nigeria	2,732,590	2,495,533	2,216,268	2,428,000	2,292,000	0.97	-5.60
Other countries of West Africa	597,914	810,849	709,142	552,000	1,260,000	0.54	128.26
Other Africa	290,746	497,317	409,677	386,000	414,000	0.18	7.25
Other countries of Africa	290,746	497,317	409,677	386,000	414,000	0.18	7.25
AMERICAS	43,064,810	38,621,607	36,647,738	35,589,000	36,452,000	15.50	2.42
Caribbean	1,340,187	1,239,674	1,533,973	1,108,000	1,022,000	0.43	-7.76
All countries of the Caribbean	1,340,187	1,239,674	1,533,973	1,108,000	1,022,000	0.43	-7.76
North America	37,522,451	33,395,225	31,362,700	30,659,000	31,088,000	13.22	1.40
Canada	8,108,842	8,114,689	6,802,042	7,413,000	7,061,000	3.00	-4.75
Mexico	557,391	538,365	789,409	507,000	694,000	0.30	36.88
United States of America	28,856,218	24,742,171	23,771,249	22,739,000	23,333,000	9.92	2.61
South America	3,759,335	3,744,915	3,300,866	3,368,000	4,033,000	1.71	19.74
Argentina	378,108	433,444	676,202	649,000	580,000	0.25	-10.63
Brazil	2,483,096	2,489,983	2,248,968	1,764,000	2,652,000	1.13	50.34
Chile	385,223	536,774	96,517	215,000	252,000	0.11	17.21
Colombia	435,009	197,587	181,067	627,000	430,000	0.18	-31.42
Venezuela	77,899	87,127	98,112	113,000	119,000	0.05	5.31
Other Americas	442,837	241,793	450,199	454,000	309,000	0.13	-31.94
Other countries of the Americas	442,837	241,793	450,199	454,000	309,000	0.13	-31.94
EAST ASIA AND THE PACIFIC	30,900,125	29,457,116	30,005,010	32,306,000	32,601,000	13.86	0.91
North-East Asia	8,635,613	7,652,950	6,817,481	8,395,000	8,137,000	3.46	-3.07
China	2,856,353	2,312,391	1,166,119	2,303,000	2,906,000	1.24	26.18
Taiwan, Province of China	383,685	639,898	382,795	837,000	261,000	0.11	-68.82
Hong Kong, China	1,157,205	1,147,778	1,648,135	1,497,000	1,759,000	0.75	17.50
Japan	2,691,317	2,175,191	2,591,520	1,905,000	1,949,000	0.83	2.31
Korea, Republic of	1,547,053	1,377,692	1,028,912	1,853,000	1,262,000	0.54	-31.89
South-East Asia	3,606,209	3,018,492	4,605,929	4,683,000	4,491,000	1.91	-4.10
Malaysia	1,352,274	1,325,864	2,415,213	1,899,000	2,073,000	0.88	9.16
Singapore	855,510	928,629	1,053,611	1,226,000	1,255,000	0.53	2.37
Thailand	1,398,425	763,999	1,137,105	1,558,000	1,163,000	0.49	-25.35
Australasia	16,409,290	16,497,552	16,534,306	16,788,000	17,132,000	7.28	2.05
Australia	12,153,565	13,198,603	13,309,858	13,929,000	13,601,000	5.78	-2.35
New Zealand	4,255,725	3,298,949	3,224,448	2,859,000	3,531,000	1.50	23.50
Other East Asia and the Pacific	2,249,013	2,288,122	2,047,294	2,440,000	2,841,000	1.21	16.43
Other countries of Asia	2,249,013	2,288,122	2,047,294	2,440,000	2,841,000	1.21	16.43
EUROPE	146,187,966	145,851,141	132,954,907	132,140,000	137,466,000	58.45	4.03
Central/Eastern Europe	34,998,732	35,025,681	26,355,757	23,997,000	26,444,000	11.24	10.20
Czech Republic	3,494,515	2,817,728	2,301,997	1,831,000	1,865,000	0.79	1.86
Hungary	2,094,930	1,799,713	1,909,268	1,536,000	1,762,000	0.75	14.71
Poland	15,868,887	17,308,004	12,028,477	10,731,000	10,141,000	4.31	-5.50
Russian Federation	2,531,732	1,671,433	1,307,573	1,683,000	2,240,000	0.95	33.10
Other countries Central/East Europe	11,008,668	11,428,803	8,808,442	8,216,000	10,436,000	4.44	27.02

UNITED KINGDOM

6. Overnight stays of non-resident tourists in all types of accommodation establishments, by country of residence

	2007	2008	2009	2010	2011	Market share 11	% Change 11-10
Northern Europe	20,767,861	21,489,366	19,615,071	19,935,000	22,383,000	9.52	12.28
Denmark	2,626,156	2,602,988	2,943,301	2,923,000	2,864,000	1.22	-2.02
Finland	1,003,928	1,267,448	775,290	805,000	1,262,000	0.54	56.77
Iceland	528,003	264,032	170,247	138,000	272,000	0.12	97.10
Ireland	10,404,127	10,394,784	9,874,615	9,519,000	10,225,000	4.35	7.42
Norway	2,588,754	3,397,167	2,573,138	2,807,000	3,442,000	1.46	22.62
Sweden	3,616,893	3,562,947	3,278,480	3,743,000	4,318,000	1.84	15.36
Southern Europe	30,425,008	30,081,349	29,826,772	29,334,000	28,838,000	12.26	-1.69
Gibraltar					150,000	0.06	
Greece	1,101,271	1,752,489	2,041,851	1,408,000	1,566,000	0.67	11.22
Italy	10,613,163	11,189,106	8,293,632	10,330,000	9,676,000	4.11	-6.33
Malta					583,000	0.25	
Portugal	1,722,038	2,126,826	1,575,699	2,353,000	1,917,000	0.82	-18.53
Spain	15,658,423	13,874,348	17,115,037	14,367,000	13,719,000	5.83	-4.51
Yugoslavia, SFR (former)	1,330,113	1,138,580	800,553	876,000	1,227,000	0.52	40.07
Western Europe	54,231,429	54,432,937	52,250,184	54,143,000	55,437,000	23.57	2.39
Austria	1,477,846	1,825,065	1,643,383	1,569,000	1,759,000	0.75	12.11
Belgium	2,833,556	2,929,099	2,925,268	4,002,000	3,101,000	1.32	-22.51
France	18,139,745	20,178,582	19,007,830	18,614,000	18,705,000	7.95	0.49
Germany	19,280,255	17,374,318	17,300,078	18,143,000	18,822,000	8.00	3.74
Luxembourg	403,578	267,530	177,002	259,000	319,000	0.14	23.17
Netherlands	8,307,750	8,482,702	7,255,632	7,870,000	8,413,000	3.58	6.90
Switzerland	3,788,699	3,375,641	3,940,991	3,686,000	4,318,000	1.84	17.15
East Mediterranean Europe	2,868,197	2,338,805	2,464,037	2,525,000	4,364,000	1.86	72.83
Cyprus					1,368,000	0.58	
Israel	954,703	996,383	1,067,238	1,155,000	1,160,000	0.49	0.43
Turkey	1,913,494	1,342,422	1,396,799	1,370,000	1,836,000	0.78	34.01
Other Europe	2,896,739	2,483,003	2,443,086	2,206,000			
Other countries of Europe	2,896,739	2,483,003	2,443,086	2,206,000			
MIDDLE EAST	6,730,283	7,243,536	8,701,807	7,217,000	8,263,000	3.51	14.49
Saudi Arabia	1,509,236	1,650,536	1,549,915	923,000	1,890,000	0.80	104.77
United Arab Emirates	2,164,813	2,400,399	2,862,588	2,872,000	2,831,000	1.20	-1.43
Egypt	529,546	450,364	734,685	559,000	472,000	0.20	-15.56
Other countries of Middle East	2,526,688	2,742,237	3,554,619	2,863,000	3,070,000	1.31	7.23
SOUTH ASIA	13,736,268	12,926,483	10,095,453	12,251,000	11,660,000	4.96	-4.82
Bangladesh	512,783	639,027	343,966	391,000	399,000	0.17	2.05
India	9,069,393	7,643,815	7,293,377	9,720,000	8,341,000	3.55	-14.19
Iran, Islamic Republic of	726,630	847,881	487,212	492,000	515,000	0.22	4.67
Pakistan	3,427,462	3,795,760	1,970,898	1,648,000	2,405,000	1.02	45.93

UNITED REPUBLIC OF TANZANIA

2. Arrivals of non-resident visitors at national borders, by country of residence

	2007	2008	2009	2010	2011	Market share 11	% Change 11-10
TOTAL	719,031	770,469	714,367	782,699	867,994	100.00	10.90
AFRICA	305,748	373,053	348,765	392,137	445,750	51.35	13.67
East Africa	258,268	321,282	304,856	334,986	354,635	40.86	5.87
Burundi	11,039	11,721	14,581	17,440	34,341	3.96	96.91
Comoros	4,316	3,864	3,206	2,657	3,835	0.44	44.34
Ethiopia	1,275	1,734	1,349	1,575	1,675	0.19	6.35
Eritrea	144	54	90	113	137	0.02	21.24
Djibouti	93	282	40	193	413	0.05	113.99
Kenya	130,823	184,269	177,929	193,474	171,473	19.76	-11.37
Madagascar	353	70	78	222	211	0.02	-4.95
Malawi	19,136	21,459	19,851	22,233	6,523	0.75	-70.66
Mauritius	295	403	366	292	475	0.05	62.67
Mozambique	3,766	3,706	6,253	6,151	11,301	1.30	83.73
Rwanda	14,699	14,394	14,331	14,754	17,676	2.04	19.80
Seychelles	164	1,234	171	180	375	0.04	108.33
Somalia	802	947	784	1,326	8,569	0.99	546.23
Zimbabwe	6,309	7,781	6,002	7,524	17,099	1.97	127.26
Uganda	30,385	31,682	32,826	31,869	32,634	3.76	2.40
Zambia	34,669	37,682	26,999	34,983	47,898	5.52	36.92
Central Africa	10,648	9,390	7,968	14,465	22,511	2.59	55.62
Angola	435	377	270	517	656	0.08	26.89
Cameroon	938	739	817	710	593	0.07	-16.48
Central African Republic	11	202	219	186	701	0.08	276.88
Chad	37	26	36	48	94	0.01	95.83
Congo	368	271	605	416	146	0.02	-64.90
Democratic Republic of the Congo	8,374	7,638	5,879	11,836	19,043	2.19	60.89
Gabon	340	112	133	664	1,149	0.13	73.04
Sao Tome and Principe	145	25	9	88	129	0.01	46.59
North Africa	831	1,133	1,907	3,899	3,886	0.45	-0.33
Algeria	68	118	86	105	249	0.03	137.14
Morocco	109	184	118	3,039	465	0.05	-84.70
Sudan	543	719	1,574	612	328	0.04	-46.41
Tunisia	111	112	129	143	2,844	0.33	1888.81
Southern Africa	30,608	30,795	27,510	32,442	39,069	4.50	20.43
Botswana	965	879	639	741	944	0.11	27.40
Lesotho	296	296	296	261	493	0.06	88.89
Namibia	582	597	663	895	1,210	0.14	35.20
South Africa	28,394	28,721	25,586	29,823	33,543	3.86	12.47
Swaziland	371	302	326	722	2,879	0.33	298.75
West Africa	5,393	10,453	6,524	6,345	25,649	2.95	304.24
Cape Verde	354	43	21	52	716	0.08	1276.92
Benin	252	164	155	143	125	0.01	-12.59
Gambia	156	317	221	222	427	0.05	92.34
Ghana	916	1,186	1,340	1,750	4,242	0.49	142.40
Guinea	142	554	586	304	110	0.01	-63.82
Côte d'Ivoire	185	4,922	189	414	9,630	1.11	2226.09
Liberia	251	109	82	165	182	0.02	10.30
Mali	130	181	148	97	2,065	0.24	2028.87
Mauritania	248	291	147	254	304	0.04	19.69
Niger	250	33	108	147	165	0.02	12.24
Nigeria	1,342	1,819	2,397	1,982	5,027	0.58	153.63
Guinea-Bissau	18	4	8	59	1,082	0.12	1733.90
Senegal	283	257	364	267	389	0.04	45.69
Sierra Leone	156	233	150	156	665	0.08	326.28
Togo	154	120	100	154	175	0.02	13.64
Burkina Faso	556	220	508	179	345	0.04	92.74

UNITED REPUBLIC OF TANZANIA

2. Arrivals of non-resident visitors at national borders, by country of residence

	2007	2008	2009	2010	2011	Market share 11	% Change 11-10
AMERICAS	80,699	87,835	68,289	70,558	95,503	11.00	35.35
Caribbean	528	1,039	1,168	1,667	2,226	0.26	33.53
Antigua and Barbuda	10	131	206	64	408	0.05	537.50
Bahamas	10	17	22	12	27	0.00	125.00
Barbados	15	102	55	21	11	0.00	-47.62
Bermuda	141	30	14	12	873	0.10	7175.00
Cuba	38	61	59	74	123	0.01	66.22
Dominica	32	109	266	713	102	0.01	-85.69
Grenada	10	2	7	15	21	0.00	40.00
Haiti	18	23	12	24	24	0.00	
Jamaica	148	146	199	155	152	0.02	-1.94
Saint Kitts and Nevis	4	9	4	4	7	0.00	75.00
Saint Lucia	18	3	8	17	5	0.00	-70.59
Saint Vincent and the Grenadines	3	4	1	104	14	0.00	-86.54
Trinidad and Tobago	58	102	55	93	196	0.02	110.75
Other countries of the Caribbean	23	300	260	359	263	0.03	-26.74
Central America	2,243	473	204	600	696	0.08	16.00
Belize	1,974	265	5	3	314	0.04	10366.67
Costa Rica	61	84	36	411	195	0.02	-52.55
El Salvador	39	27	33	20	20	0.00	
Guatemala	25	35	59	46	68	0.01	47.83
Honduras	104	5	24	46	31	0.00	-32.61
Nicaragua	16	11	17	50	21	0.00	-58.00
Panama	24	46	30	24	47	0.01	95.83
North America	74,229	84,151	63,179	64,800	65,426	7.54	0.97
Canada	15,198	16,482	14,642	14,819	16,839	1.94	13.63
Mexico	690	716	594	766	821	0.09	7.18
United States of America	58,341	66,953	47,943	49,215	47,766	5.50	-2.94
South America	3,699	2,172	3,738	3,491	27,155	3.13	677.86
Argentina	405	263	293	331	588	0.07	77.64
Bolivia	41	84	102	70	131	0.02	87.14
Brazil	711	666	1,138	1,482	1,308	0.15	-11.74
Chile	163	309	660	312	873	0.10	179.81
Colombia	306	444	411	337	376	0.04	11.57
Ecuador	51	42	44	398	1,216	0.14	205.53
Guyana	13	17	18	56	19	0.00	-66.07
Paraguay	34	45	88	36	122	0.01	238.89
Peru	136	137	148	125	1,102	0.13	781.60
Suriname	8	10	4	37	4,620	0.53	12386.49
Uruguay	1,717	36	698	189	16,609	1.91	8687.83
Venezuela	114	119	134	118	191	0.02	61.86
EAST ASIA AND THE PACIFIC	29,760	32,442	31,013	42,520	39,619	4.56	-6.82
North-East Asia	13,318	16,016	15,437	19,915	16,683	1.92	-16.23
China	6,353	8,982	7,883	10,997	9,018	1.04	-18.00
Taiwan, Province of China	152	177	370	277	135	0.02	-51.26
Hong Kong, China	66	138	92	46	233	0.03	406.52
Japan	4,021	3,890	4,168	4,130	3,984	0.46	-3.54
Korea, Dem. People's Republic of	314	425	197	115	251	0.03	118.26
Korea, Republic of	2,393	2,389	2,687	4,309	3,025	0.35	-29.80
Mongolia	19	15	40	41	37	0.00	-9.76
South-East Asia	4,567	3,099	2,982	8,601	5,548	0.64	-35.50
Brunei Darussalam	95	10	11	312	905	0.10	190.06
Myanmar	49	56	94	334	456	0.05	36.53
Cambodia	98	28	45	24	354	0.04	1375.00
Indonesia	542	405	321	614	792	0.09	28.99
Malaysia	1,909	611	540	4,531	844	0.10	-81.37

UNITED REPUBLIC OF TANZANIA

2. Arrivals of non-resident visitors at national borders, by country of residence

	2007	2008	2009	2010	2011	Market share 11	% Change 11-10
Philippines	991	965	912	1,470	1,226	0.14	-16.60
Singapore	348	347	307	441	400	0.05	-9.30
Viet Nam	149	149	80	154	138	0.02	-10.39
Thailand	386	528	672	721	433	0.05	-39.94
Australasia	**11,846**	**13,168**	**12,443**	**13,694**	**15,704**	**1.81**	**14.68**
Australia	10,033	10,941	10,389	11,644	13,394	1.54	15.03
New Zealand	1,813	2,227	2,054	2,050	2,310	0.27	12.68
Melanesia	**26**	**159**	**146**	**310**	**1,681**	**0.19**	**442.26**
Solomon Islands	1		45	53	1,519	0.18	2766.04
Fiji	25	149	83	252	157	0.02	-37.70
Papua New Guinea		10	18	5	5	0.00	
Polynesia	**3**		**5**		**3**	**0.00**	
Samoa	3		5		3	0.00	
EUROPE	**274,410**	**245,873**	**233,559**	**242,828**	**249,910**	**28.79**	**2.92**
Central/Eastern Europe	**37,301**	**10,160**	**12,819**	**17,616**	**12,881**	**1.48**	**-26.88**
Azerbaijan	8	13	173	54	249	0.03	361.11
Armenia	33	27	573	80	49	0.01	-38.75
Bulgaria	535	200	532	470	256	0.03	-45.53
Belarus	22	98	86	44	750	0.09	1604.55
Czech Republic	1,191	1,548	1,942	1,639	780	0.09	-52.41
Estonia	237	194	129	191	210	0.02	9.95
Hungary	2,562	1,685	1,262	933	605	0.07	-35.16
Kazakhstan	24,936	41	119	417	299	0.03	-28.30
Latvia	303	134	125	102	172	0.02	68.63
Lithuania	1,771	136	131	102	211	0.02	106.86
Republic of Moldova	50	39	24	47	53	0.01	12.77
Poland	1,668	2,250	2,241	2,206	2,933	0.34	32.96
Romania	375	556	1,708	1,176	2,123	0.24	80.53
Russian Federation	2,901	2,224	2,794	5,204	2,585	0.30	-50.33
Slovakia	169	263	307	251	449	0.05	78.88
Tajikistan	2	3	18	14	19	0.00	35.71
Ukraine	510	380	369	4,263	377	0.04	-91.16
Uzbekistan	19	12	13	93	533	0.06	473.12
Other countries Central/East Europe	9	357	273	330	228	0.03	-30.91
Northern Europe	**83,955**	**91,589**	**80,369**	**78,224**	**81,832**	**9.43**	**4.61**
Denmark	5,917	7,196	5,856	7,898	2,178	0.25	-72.42
Finland	3,015	3,493	2,594	2,719	2,625	0.30	-3.46
Iceland	407	157	229	410	549	0.06	33.90
Ireland	4,423	4,271	3,322	3,096	5,642	0.65	82.24
Norway	6,189	7,411	5,818	6,492	5,915	0.68	-8.89
Sweden	8,850	10,816	8,797	9,022	6,554	0.76	-27.36
United Kingdom	55,154	58,245	53,753	48,587	58,369	6.72	20.13
Southern Europe	**68,190**	**57,399**	**59,899**	**71,553**	**59,234**	**6.82**	**-17.22**
Albania	28	23	29	25	38	0.00	52.00
Andorra	32	21	19	18	54	0.01	200.00
Bosnia and Herzegovina	30	39	36	42	29	0.00	-30.95
Croatia	181	242	233	244	445	0.05	82.38
Greece	575	614	798	710	583	0.07	-17.89
Italy	54,194	45,950	47,804	59,603	45,590	5.25	-23.51
Malta	34	64	57	177	102	0.01	-42.37
Montenegro		28	1		791	0.09	
Portugal	1,097	1,259	1,201	1,239	1,022	0.12	-17.51
San Marino	109	35	67	248	2,143	0.25	764.11
Serbia		163	158	156	1,153	0.13	639.10
Slovenia	366	428	334	496	236	0.03	-52.42
Spain	11,428	8,470	9,053	8,478	6,826	0.79	-19.49
TFYR of Macedonia	49	28	69	34	222	0.03	552.94

UNITED REPUBLIC OF TANZANIA

2. Arrivals of non-resident visitors at national borders, by country of residence

	2007	2008	2009	2010	2011	Market share 11	% Change 11-10
Serbia and Montenegro	67	35	40	83			
Western Europe	**81,326**	**81,846**	**76,937**	**70,558**	**91,304**	**10.52**	**29.40**
Austria	4,006	3,445	2,735	3,809	4,126	0.48	8.32
Belgium	5,778	7,229	5,799	5,510	7,323	0.84	32.90
France	21,314	19,598	20,127	15,650	21,919	2.53	40.06
Germany	24,468	27,100	25,508	25,246	36,010	4.15	42.64
Liechtenstein	18	7	13	32	16	0.00	-50.00
Luxembourg	217	156	170	206	276	0.03	33.98
Monaco	2	8	29	59	19	0.00	-67.80
Netherlands	18,990	16,945	16,507	14,598	15,500	1.79	6.18
Switzerland	6,533	7,358	6,049	5,448	6,115	0.70	12.24
East Mediterranean Europe	**3,638**	**4,879**	**3,535**	**4,877**	**4,659**	**0.54**	**-4.47**
Cyprus	158	113	182	221	182	0.02	-17.65
Israel	2,911	3,980	2,334	2,805	3,007	0.35	7.20
Turkey	569	786	1,019	1,851	1,470	0.17	-20.58
MIDDLE EAST	**11,444**	**10,377**	**11,121**	**10,521**	**15,281**	**1.76**	**45.24**
Bahrain	47	38	43	56	64	0.01	14.29
Palestine	11	41	63	32	98	0.01	206.25
Iraq	123	34	86	61	118	0.01	93.44
Jordan	141	215	285	295	1,799	0.21	509.83
Kuwait	67	57	71	57	103	0.01	80.70
Lebanon	307	428	381	303	281	0.03	-7.26
Libya	107	289	238	220	139	0.02	-36.82
Oman	5,162	5,747	5,520	5,440	3,288	0.38	-39.56
Qatar	132	64	57	190	1,416	0.16	645.26
Saudi Arabia	150	288	356	299	284	0.03	-5.02
Syrian Arab Republic	212	123	157	189	897	0.10	374.60
United Arab Emirates	3,844	1,433	1,917	1,199	4,931	0.57	311.26
Egypt	646	889	1,170	1,186	1,138	0.13	-4.05
Yemen	495	731	777	994	725	0.08	-27.06
SOUTH ASIA	**16,970**	**20,889**	**21,620**	**24,135**	**21,931**	**2.53**	**-9.13**
Afghanistan	26	32	32	17	36	0.00	111.76
Bangladesh	169	479	661	397	725	0.08	82.62
Bhutan	6	1	6	5	4	0.00	-20.00
Sri Lanka	797	456	471	816	648	0.07	-20.59
India	14,042	17,530	17,002	19,101	17,731	2.04	-7.17
Iran, Islamic Republic of	370	475	503	636	524	0.06	-17.61
Nepal	476	184	288	504	1,792	0.21	255.56
Pakistan	1,084	1,732	2,657	2,659	471	0.05	-82.29

UNITED STATES OF AMERICA

1. Arrivals of non-resident tourists at national borders, by country of residence

	2007	2008	2009	2010	2011	Market share 11	% Change 11-10
TOTAL	55,978,277	57,942,451	54,962,184	59,795,616	62,711,157	100.00	4.88
AFRICA	276,300	311,136	290,861	311,205	325,989	0.52	4.75
East Africa	48,396	51,772	49,707	50,749	51,634	0.08	1.74
Burundi	600	501	479	671	677	0.00	0.89
Comoros	20	22	30	19	21	0.00	10.53
Ethiopia	7,782	8,713	8,629	8,630	9,979	0.02	15.63
Eritrea	320	245	248	263	231	0.00	-12.17
Djibouti	181	224	354	363	340	0.00	-6.34
Kenya	16,468	17,296	15,833	15,173	13,422	0.02	-11.54
Madagascar	718	880	780	703	729	0.00	3.70
Malawi	1,200	1,304	1,210	1,331	1,347	0.00	1.20
Mauritius	1,581	1,776	2,005	2,523	2,669	0.00	5.79
Mozambique	749	949	1,151	1,132	1,210	0.00	6.89
Reunion	249	437	513	533	566	0.00	6.19
Rwanda	1,490	1,752	1,649	1,840	2,139	0.00	16.25
Seychelles	199	213	186	217	186	0.00	-14.29
Somalia	49	55	72	98	107	0.00	9.18
Zimbabwe	4,521	4,260	3,854	4,158	4,335	0.01	4.26
Uganda	4,862	5,891	5,404	5,115	5,611	0.01	9.70
United Republic of Tanzania	4,612	4,765	5,000	4,986	5,013	0.01	0.54
Zambia	2,795	2,489	2,310	2,994	3,052	0.00	1.94
Central Africa	15,140	15,933	17,008	18,213	19,352	0.03	6.25
Angola	5,113	5,633	6,446	6,610	7,726	0.01	16.88
Cameroon	5,339	5,222	5,072	5,517	5,359	0.01	-2.86
Central African Republic	292	230	166	234	225	0.00	-3.85
Chad	458	275	424	265	245	0.00	-7.55
Congo	1,416	1,587	1,841	2,077	2,310	0.00	11.22
Democratic Republic of the Congo	788	888	1,058	1,189	920	0.00	-22.62
Equatorial Guinea	223	303	397	368	460	0.00	25.00
Gabon	1,466	1,762	1,584	1,793	1,927	0.00	7.47
Sao Tome and Principe	45	33	20	160	180	0.00	12.50
North Africa	22,534	26,545	27,770	30,428	33,578	0.05	10.35
Algeria	3,283	4,274	4,592	4,116	5,054	0.01	22.79
Morocco	13,922	16,426	16,919	18,657	20,230	0.03	8.43
Western Sahara	8	2	1	27	141	0.00	422.22
Sudan	1,311	1,395	1,547	2,006	2,499	0.00	24.58
Tunisia	4,010	4,448	4,711	5,622	5,654	0.01	0.57
Southern Africa	97,841	98,331	83,243	85,019	92,020	0.15	8.23
Botswana	2,356	2,572	2,300	2,279	2,163	0.00	-5.09
Lesotho	242	246	259	298	339	0.00	13.76
Namibia	1,208	1,246	1,251	1,430	1,732	0.00	21.12
South Africa	93,719	93,692	78,934	80,174	86,597	0.14	8.01
Swaziland	316	575	499	838	1,189	0.00	41.89
West Africa	92,389	118,555	113,133	126,796	129,405	0.21	2.06
Cape Verde	2,070	2,180	2,708	2,517	1,773	0.00	-29.56
Benin	1,389	1,715	1,582	1,876	1,804	0.00	-3.84
Gambia	1,384	1,381	1,859	2,341	2,288	0.00	-2.26
Ghana	14,625	18,507	17,069	18,554	19,127	0.03	3.09
Guinea	2,522	2,348	1,827	1,536	1,604	0.00	4.43
Côte d'Ivoire	1,944	2,583	2,892	2,422	1,584	0.00	-34.60
Liberia	1,749	1,345	1,086	1,543	1,877	0.00	21.65
Mali	2,778	3,273	3,115	3,106	2,832	0.00	-8.82
Mauritania	414	473	496	636	525	0.00	-17.45
Niger	1,084	1,084	1,039	978	894	0.00	-8.59
Nigeria	52,996	72,669	68,505	79,427	82,945	0.13	4.43
Guinea-Bissau	18	25	24	37	45	0.00	21.62

UNITED STATES OF AMERICA

1. Arrivals of non-resident tourists at national borders, by country of residence

	2007	2008	2009	2010	2011	Market share 11	% Change 11-10
Senegal	5,212	6,623	6,536	7,176	6,967	0.01	-2.91
Sierra Leone	1,367	1,517	1,474	1,734	1,929	0.00	11.25
Togo	1,136	1,181	1,039	1,142	1,277	0.00	11.82
Burkina Faso	1,701	1,651	1,882	1,771	1,934	0.00	9.20
AMERICAS	**36,462,985**	**37,133,338**	**35,911,508**	**38,644,479**	**40,423,276**	**64.46**	**4.60**
Caribbean	**1,316,902**	**1,201,149**	**1,206,068**	**1,200,740**	**1,091,419**	**1.74**	**-9.10**
Antigua and Barbuda	20,611	19,713	17,213	16,719	15,639	0.02	-6.46
Bahamas	256,433	180,914	224,812	243,204	222,741	0.36	-8.41
Barbados	55,916	54,891	52,010	54,486	51,323	0.08	-5.81
Bermuda	23,311	23,445	20,743	17,378	10,822	0.02	-37.73
British Virgin Islands	22,338	22,195	23,961	20,262	15,113	0.02	-25.41
Cayman Islands	53,530	51,078	51,085	46,558	42,402	0.07	-8.93
Cuba	17,208	22,395	32,666	37,871	36,964	0.06	-2.39
Dominica	5,352	6,635	6,857	7,379	5,911	0.01	-19.89
Dominican Republic	263,452	226,184	227,948	239,972	230,188	0.37	-4.08
Grenada	8,325	8,673	8,202	8,507	7,928	0.01	-6.81
Guadeloupe	7,613	9,750	9,964	8,205	6,221	0.01	-24.18
Haiti	83,837	91,748	80,572	87,334	79,461	0.13	-9.01
Jamaica	221,521	204,982	185,526	178,791	159,235	0.25	-10.94
Martinique	7,080	8,175	8,014	7,706	7,015	0.01	-8.97
Montserrat	761	726	593	344	191	0.00	-44.48
Netherlands Antilles	66,250	65,516	43,114	26,615	10,755	0.02	-59.59
Aruba			22,368	16,074	14,752	0.02	-8.22
Saint Kitts and Nevis	11,086	11,045	10,222	10,328	9,496	0.02	-8.06
Anguilla	6,712	6,280	5,020	3,362	2,518	0.00	-25.10
Saint Lucia	15,520	13,814	13,397	15,072	13,111	0.02	-13.01
Saint Vincent and the Grenadines	6,155	6,043	6,002	6,221	6,057	0.01	-2.64
Trinidad and Tobago	143,009	147,613	141,406	136,628	132,931	0.21	-2.71
Turks and Caicos Islands	20,882	19,334	14,373	11,724	10,645	0.02	-9.20
Central America	**786,281**	**775,590**	**757,905**	**760,441**	**747,168**	**1.19**	**-1.75**
Belize	22,184	20,757	20,227	18,641	17,319	0.03	-7.09
Costa Rica	160,444	165,257	157,471	165,594	168,722	0.27	1.89
El Salvador	159,783	136,494	123,185	112,346	97,967	0.16	-12.80
Guatemala	201,286	188,177	189,455	188,218	183,671	0.29	-2.42
Honduras	111,059	116,902	115,405	115,616	119,671	0.19	3.51
Nicaragua	44,196	45,171	42,194	41,050	40,276	0.06	-1.89
Panama	87,329	102,832	109,968	118,976	119,542	0.19	0.48
North America	**32,086,000**	**32,601,000**	**31,206,000**	**33,433,000**	**34,828,000**	**55.54**	**4.17**
Canada (*)	17,759,000	18,915,000	17,977,000	19,964,000	21,337,000	34.02	6.88
Mexico (*)	14,327,000	13,686,000	13,229,000	13,469,000	13,491,000	21.51	0.16
South America	**2,273,802**	**2,555,599**	**2,741,535**	**3,250,298**	**3,756,689**	**5.99**	**15.58**
Argentina	266,971	318,144	356,428	436,192	512,258	0.82	17.44
Bolivia	27,611	29,942	31,966	32,504	34,467	0.05	6.04
Brazil	639,431	769,232	892,611	1,197,866	1,508,279	2.41	25.91
Chile	123,152	130,813	126,609	146,736	171,459	0.27	16.85
Colombia	389,752	419,268	424,526	494,739	496,814	0.79	0.42
Ecuador	155,328	152,112	168,432	195,546	210,910	0.34	7.86
Falkland Islands, Malvinas	64	130	110	51	60	0.00	17.65
French Guiana	303	314	536	612	760	0.00	24.18
Guyana	13,760	12,974	14,774	15,601	16,427	0.03	5.29
Paraguay	10,973	12,062	12,564	14,657	16,567	0.03	13.03
Peru	148,967	162,883	160,474	173,269	171,870	0.27	-0.81
Suriname	6,008	7,022	8,630	8,941	9,043	0.01	1.14
Uruguay	32,804	33,550	36,690	41,980	46,695	0.07	11.23
Venezuela	458,678	507,153	507,185	491,604	561,080	0.89	14.13

UNITED STATES OF AMERICA

1. Arrivals of non-resident tourists at national borders, by country of residence

	2007	2008	2009	2010	2011	Market share 11	% Change 11-10
EAST ASIA AND THE PACIFIC	6,562,889	6,343,399	5,905,954	7,369,149	7,728,449	12.32	4.88
North-East Asia	5,191,791	4,939,772	4,545,697	5,721,747	5,906,523	9.42	3.23
China	397,405	492,958	524,817	801,738	1,089,405	1.74	35.88
Taiwan, Province of China	311,020	294,893	239,545	291,107	290,313	0.46	-0.27
Hong Kong, China	142,419	139,359	116,023	131,712	128,512	0.20	-2.43
Japan	3,531,489	3,249,578	2,918,268	3,386,076	3,249,569	5.18	-4.03
Korea, Dem. People's Republic of	23	17	27	127	132	0.00	3.94
Korea, Republic of	806,175	759,394	743,846	1,107,518	1,145,216	1.83	3.40
Macao, China	3,260	3,573	3,171	3,469	3,376	0.01	-2.68
South-East Asia	537,380	552,008	488,275	552,150	578,493	0.92	4.77
Brunei Darussalam	1,168	1,210	1,080	1,095	1,332	0.00	21.64
Myanmar	1,136	1,174	1,536	1,960	1,891	0.00	-3.52
Cambodia	2,568	2,664	2,314	2,611	2,380	0.00	-8.85
Indonesia	53,829	49,348	50,243	54,539	66,069	0.11	21.14
Lao People's Democratic Republic	1,976	1,503	1,103	808	685	0.00	-15.22
Malaysia	55,762	54,262	43,292	54,080	59,857	0.10	10.68
Philippines	171,829	179,820	171,680	177,525	166,829	0.27	-6.03
Timor-Leste				6	4	0.00	-33.33
Singapore	135,209	141,474	107,400	139,319	159,302	0.25	14.34
Viet Nam	36,894	43,733	40,423	45,914	46,826	0.07	1.99
Thailand	77,009	76,820	69,204	74,293	73,318	0.12	-1.31
Australasia	817,271	835,252	854,588	1,078,866	1,226,826	1.96	13.71
Australia	669,536	689,927	723,576	904,247	1,037,852	1.65	14.78
New Zealand	147,735	145,325	131,012	174,619	188,974	0.30	8.22
Melanesia	7,319	7,733	7,152	8,140	8,233	0.01	1.14
Solomon Islands	116	132	138	88	106	0.00	20.45
Fiji	5,246	5,133	4,588	6,456	6,888	0.01	6.69
New Caledonia	1,244	1,605	1,459	782	481	0.00	-38.49
Vanuatu	226	225	189	165	159	0.00	-3.64
Papua New Guinea	487	638	778	649	599	0.00	-7.70
Micronesia	231	256	308	349	393	0.00	12.61
Christmas Island, Australia	3		5	7	12	0.00	71.43
Cocos (Keeling) Islands	20	11	6	4	10	0.00	150.00
Kiribati	190	233	282	258	279	0.00	8.14
Nauru	18	12	15	80	92	0.00	15.00
Polynesia	8,897	8,378	9,934	7,897	7,981	0.01	1.06
Cook Islands	290	311	227	66	45	0.00	-31.82
French Polynesia	4,777	5,181	7,027	5,237	5,677	0.01	8.40
Niue	8	3	7	6	17	0.00	183.33
Pitcairn	4		1	2	5	0.00	150.00
Tonga	2,322	1,459	1,353	1,316	1,133	0.00	-13.91
Tuvalu	20	18	15	57	72	0.00	26.32
Wallis and Futuna Islands	43	67	40	21	12	0.00	-42.86
Samoa	1,433	1,339	1,264	1,192	1,020	0.00	-14.43
EUROPE	11,839,074	13,249,818	11,978,394	12,436,645	13,115,324	20.91	5.46
Central/Eastern Europe	521,447	594,074	581,807	620,111	689,554	1.10	11.20
Azerbaijan	2,636	3,236	3,121	3,518	3,841	0.01	9.18
Armenia	3,271	3,713	3,546	3,183	3,032	0.00	-4.74
Bulgaria	20,299	23,771	20,000	20,200	20,444	0.03	1.21
Belarus	6,192	5,762	5,764	6,693	7,710	0.01	15.19
Czech Republic/Slovakia	5,512	7,287	7,397	4,206	1,935	0.00	-53.99
Czech Republic	42,915	49,485	65,060	63,909	75,618	0.12	18.32
Estonia	10,253	11,686	15,677	10,753	11,997	0.02	11.57
Georgia	2,525	2,987	2,966	3,496	3,492	0.01	-0.11
Hungary	40,467	42,209	48,806	51,333	58,313	0.09	13.60
Kazakhstan	7,444	9,133	8,459	10,852	12,836	0.02	18.28

UNITED STATES OF AMERICA

1. Arrivals of non-resident tourists at national borders, by country of residence

	2007	2008	2009	2010	2011	Market share 11	% Change 11-10
Kyrgyzstan	1,075	1,252	1,279	1,716	1,851	0.00	7.87
Latvia	9,728	10,240	11,270	11,529	12,568	0.02	9.01
Lithuania	9,480	11,355	14,264	8,846	4,081	0.01	-53.87
Republic of Moldova	3,368	3,795	3,976	4,828	5,220	0.01	8.12
Poland	138,525	146,887	115,327	114,702	111,158	0.18	-3.09
Romania	44,466	49,968	41,411	45,444	45,776	0.07	0.73
Russian Federation	114,850	142,998	142,650	174,511	221,888	0.35	27.15
Slovakia	16,468	19,297	27,711	30,911	33,540	0.05	8.51
Tajikistan	1,166	1,440	1,010	1,047	1,246	0.00	19.01
Turkmenistan	358	300	504	596	560	0.00	-6.04
Ukraine	36,464	43,348	37,157	42,591	47,417	0.08	11.33
USSR (former)	228	261	265	289	300	0.00	3.81
Uzbekistan	3,757	3,664	4,187	4,958	4,731	0.01	-4.58
Northern Europe	**5,859,831**	**6,123,300**	**5,216,618**	**5,214,135**	**5,315,486**	**8.48**	**1.94**
Denmark	217,593	256,604	245,623	258,788	274,420	0.44	6.04
Finland	96,173	118,448	114,364	111,840	121,059	0.19	8.24
Iceland	46,796	41,155	28,526	39,153	49,689	0.08	26.91
Ireland	491,055	531,198	411,203	360,492	346,879	0.55	-3.78
Norway	172,882	213,983	193,318	221,145	249,167	0.40	12.67
Sweden	337,474	397,017	324,417	371,853	438,972	0.70	18.05
United Kingdom	4,497,858	4,564,895	3,899,167	3,850,864	3,835,300	6.12	-0.40
Southern Europe	**1,344,583**	**1,654,200**	**1,538,052**	**1,693,265**	**1,807,548**	**2.88**	**6.75**
Albania	5,178	6,317	5,230	5,480	4,775	0.01	-12.86
Andorra	1,361	1,791	1,449	1,453	1,266	0.00	-12.87
Bosnia and Herzegovina	4,939	4,370	3,897	4,233	4,386	0.01	3.61
Croatia	14,447	17,270	15,407	15,105	15,241	0.02	0.90
Gibraltar	1,659	2,058	1,656	1,304	984	0.00	-24.54
Greece	58,292	63,760	56,748	64,581	62,948	0.10	-2.53
Holy See	15	19	15	32	59	0.00	84.38
Italy	634,152	779,463	753,310	838,225	891,571	1.42	6.36
Malta	5,084	5,063	4,902	5,380	4,961	0.01	-7.79
Portugal	80,611	89,158	74,457	93,584	96,434	0.15	3.05
San Marino	524	700	694	674	767	0.00	13.80
Slovenia	16,125	20,637	19,213	18,845	19,307	0.03	2.45
Spain	516,471	658,333	596,766	639,654	700,183	1.12	9.46
TFYR of Macedonia	3,723	3,804	3,585	4,059	4,395	0.01	8.28
Yugoslavia, SFR (former)	2,002	1,457	723	656	271	0.00	-58.69
Western Europe	**3,694,425**	**4,426,898**	**4,229,228**	**4,476,847**	**4,868,536**	**7.76**	**8.75**
Austria	131,339	158,764	162,569	168,403	179,482	0.29	6.58
Belgium	216,579	265,383	245,710	254,892	259,490	0.41	1.80
France	997,506	1,243,942	1,204,490	1,342,207	1,504,182	2.40	12.07
Germany	1,524,151	1,782,299	1,686,825	1,726,193	1,823,797	2.91	5.65
Liechtenstein	1,496	1,661	1,877	1,909	2,273	0.00	19.07
Luxembourg	14,613	18,712	18,084	17,748	17,856	0.03	0.61
Monaco	5,520	6,380	6,156	4,725	3,941	0.01	-16.59
Netherlands	506,852	607,802	547,790	570,179	601,013	0.96	5.41
Switzerland	296,369	341,955	355,727	390,591	476,502	0.76	22.00
East Mediterranean Europe	**418,788**	**451,346**	**412,689**	**432,287**	**434,200**	**0.69**	**0.44**
Cyprus	10,143	11,517	10,174	10,136	9,505	0.02	-6.23
Israel	313,077	332,257	308,213	306,914	302,673	0.48	-1.38
Turkey	95,568	107,572	94,302	115,237	122,022	0.19	5.89
MIDDLE EAST	**195,986**	**227,629**	**246,018**	**296,242**	**363,024**	**0.58**	**22.54**
Bahrain	6,623	7,517	6,566	7,733	7,299	0.01	-5.61
Iraq	788	872	1,263	2,207	3,786	0.01	71.55
Jordan	15,572	15,712	15,559	16,459	17,246	0.03	4.78
Kuwait	24,864	28,258	29,888	33,296	39,420	0.06	18.39
Lebanon	19,251	18,253	17,969	18,847	20,346	0.03	7.95

UNITED STATES OF AMERICA

1. Arrivals of non-resident tourists at national borders, by country of residence

	2007	2008	2009	2010	2011	Market share 11	% Change 11-10
Libya	1,476	4,099	2,904	4,440	1,095	0.00	-75.34
Oman	4,175	4,771	4,727	4,812	5,629	0.01	16.98
Qatar	7,850	10,759	11,523	14,931	19,101	0.03	27.93
Saudi Arabia	38,938	48,590	62,030	89,409	132,920	0.21	48.67
Syrian Arab Republic	4,609	4,643	5,105	5,625	5,509	0.01	-2.06
United Arab Emirates	40,498	48,564	51,472	55,425	63,415	0.10	14.42
Egypt	30,449	34,855	36,044	41,949	46,346	0.07	10.48
Yemen	867	718	936	1,072	857	0.00	-20.06
Other countries of Middle East	26	18	32	37	55	0.00	48.65
SOUTH ASIA	**641,043**	**677,131**	**629,449**	**737,896**	**755,095**	**1.20**	**2.33**
Afghanistan	717	714	1,138	1,261	1,722	0.00	36.56
Bangladesh	8,196	8,741	10,175	11,561	12,596	0.02	8.95
Bhutan	309	368	230	210	225	0.00	7.14
Sri Lanka	12,044	11,552	9,778	10,853	12,125	0.02	11.72
India	567,045	598,971	549,474	650,935	663,465	1.06	1.92
Iran, Islamic Republic of	6,520	6,098	10,139	11,460	14,559	0.02	27.04
Maldives	249	243	181	149	158	0.00	6.04
Nepal	11,892	14,706	11,908	12,513	12,089	0.02	-3.39
Pakistan	34,071	35,738	36,426	38,954	38,156	0.06	-2.05

UNITED STATES VIRGIN ISLANDS

3. Arrivals of non-resident tourists in hotels and similar establishments, by nationality

	2007	2008	2009	2010	2011	Market share 11	% Change 11-10
TOTAL	679,578	740,020	787,153	748,996	680,704	100.00	-9.12
AFRICA	115	73	69	62	229	0.03	269.35
Other Africa	115	73	69	62	229	0.03	269.35
All countries of Africa	115	73	69	62	229	0.03	269.35
AMERICAS	651,167	720,276	766,929	731,749	653,183	95.96	-10.74
Caribbean	31,363	28,851	30,069	27,030	27,742	4.08	2.63
Bahamas	286	196	250	66	146	0.02	121.21
Barbados	546	272	222	130	203	0.03	56.15
British Virgin Islands	8,113	5,963	7,859	6,792	6,137	0.90	-9.64
Dominican Republic	63	50	41	45	82	0.01	82.22
Jamaica	489	230	503	230	258	0.04	12.17
Puerto Rico	20,682	21,319	19,776	19,019	18,856	2.77	-0.86
Trinidad and Tobago	333	108	115	68	146	0.02	114.71
Other countries of the Caribbean	851	713	1,303	680	1,914	0.28	181.47
Central America	262	338	146	169	274	0.04	62.13
Costa Rica	119	164	63	51	60	0.01	17.65
El Salvador	2	6	2	2			
Guatemala	13	5	6	1	20	0.00	1900.00
Honduras	6	13	6	35	8	0.00	-77.14
Nicaragua	1		7	3	5	0.00	66.67
Panama		18	56	75	177	0.03	136.00
Other countries of Central America	121	132	6	2	4	0.00	100.00
North America	618,519	689,939	735,717	703,643	623,451	91.59	-11.40
Canada	6,018	9,112	10,412	6,601	6,901	1.01	4.54
Mexico	222	262	395	154	306	0.04	98.70
United States of America	612,279	680,565	724,910	696,888	616,244	90.53	-11.57
South America	1,023	1,148	997	907	1,716	0.25	89.20
Argentina	347	320	219	229	493	0.07	115.28
Bolivia	33	49	22	59	55	0.01	-6.78
Brazil	346	309	257	244	338	0.05	38.52
Chile	112	153	347	216	450	0.07	108.33
Colombia	18	55	70	20	86	0.01	330.00
Ecuador	1	1	7	4	2	0.00	-50.00
Guyana			1	6			
Paraguay					1	0.00	
Peru		27	1	20	115	0.02	475.00
Uruguay	6	10	2				
Venezuela	160	197	70	89	118	0.02	32.58
Other countries of South America		27	1	20	58	0.01	190.00
EAST ASIA AND THE PACIFIC	351	377	318	367	458	0.07	24.80
North-East Asia	184	105	118	137	93	0.01	-32.12
Taiwan, Province of China		4		1	1	0.00	
Japan	184	101	118	136	92	0.01	-32.35
Australasia	167	272	200	230	365	0.05	58.70
Australia	147	251	188	213	298	0.04	39.91
New Zealand	20	21	12	17	67	0.01	294.12
EUROPE	14,837	15,798	16,434	14,393	22,566	3.32	56.78
Northern Europe	8,882	9,839	11,040	9,841	17,248	2.53	75.27
Denmark	6,474	7,077	9,012	8,191	15,393	2.26	87.93
Finland	497	145	53	41	57	0.01	39.02
Norway	193	284	405	174	341	0.05	95.98
Sweden		41	133	179	274	0.04	53.07
United Kingdom	1,718	2,292	1,437	1,256	1,183	0.17	-5.81

UNITED STATES VIRGIN ISLANDS

3. Arrivals of non-resident tourists in hotels and similar establishments, by nationality

	2007	2008	2009	2010	2011	Market share 11	% Change 11-10
Southern Europe	**3,173**	**3,484**	**3,275**	**2,569**	**2,073**	**0.30**	**-19.31**
Greece	397	112	112	89	388	0.06	335.96
Italy	2,776	3,330	2,861	1,908	1,307	0.19	-31.50
Portugal		27	1	20	13	0.00	-35.00
Spain		15	301	552	365	0.05	-33.88
Western Europe	**1,638**	**1,615**	**1,484**	**1,360**	**2,347**	**0.34**	**72.57**
Austria	110	162	119	48	120	0.02	150.00
France	366	433	317	280	309	0.05	10.36
Germany	503	567	477	724	1,135	0.17	56.77
Netherlands	458	320	241	159	329	0.05	106.92
Switzerland	201	133	330	149	454	0.07	204.70
Other Europe	**1,144**	**860**	**635**	**623**	**898**	**0.13**	**44.14**
Other countries of Europe	1,144	860	635	623	898	0.13	44.14
NOT SPECIFIED	**13,108**	**3,496**	**3,403**	**2,425**	**4,268**	**0.63**	**76.00**
Other countries of the World	13,108	3,496	3,403	2,425	4,268	0.63	76.00

URUGUAY

2. Arrivals of non-resident visitors at national borders, by nationality

	2007	2008	2009	2010	2011	Market share 11	% Change 11-10
TOTAL	**1,815,281**	**1,997,884**	**2,098,780**	**2,407,676**	**2,960,155**	**100.00**	**22.95**
AMERICAS	**1,406,790**	**1,544,086**	**1,643,319**	**1,888,374**	**2,401,187**	**81.12**	**27.16**
North America	**90,406**	**93,123**	**90,660**	**87,010**	**87,264**	**2.95**	**0.29**
Canada	8,726	9,976	10,411	10,212	10,361	0.35	1.46
Mexico	16,747	14,778	13,026	14,370	16,327	0.55	13.62
United States of America	64,933	68,369	67,223	62,428	60,576	2.05	-2.97
South America	**1,285,379**	**1,418,597**	**1,515,944**	**1,759,347**	**2,286,025**	**77.23**	**29.94**
Argentina	908,116	1,025,574	1,150,492	1,261,516	1,723,005	58.21	36.58
Bolivia	2,747	2,737	3,209	3,959	4,468	0.15	12.86
Brazil	286,319	300,791	263,414	376,894	426,315	14.40	13.11
Chile	43,219	39,236	41,106	53,194	57,283	1.94	7.69
Paraguay	23,888	27,708	34,347	36,672	42,980	1.45	17.20
Peru	13,637	12,396	11,722	13,673	15,623	0.53	14.26
Venezuela	7,453	10,155	11,654	13,439	16,351	0.55	21.67
Other Americas	**31,005**	**32,366**	**36,715**	**42,017**	**27,898**	**0.94**	**-33.60**
Other countries of the Americas	31,005	32,366	36,715	42,017	27,898	0.94	-33.60
EAST ASIA AND THE PACIFIC	**12,855**	**14,374**	**17,193**	**17,327**	**18,516**	**0.63**	**6.86**
North-East Asia	**5,156**	**5,779**	**5,359**	**6,482**	**7,100**	**0.24**	**9.53**
Japan	2,507	2,663	2,673	3,046	3,177	0.11	4.30
Other countries of North-East Asia	2,649	3,116	2,686	3,436	3,923	0.13	14.17
Australasia	**6,667**	**7,770**	**10,985**	**10,077**	**9,593**	**0.32**	**-4.80**
Australia	4,969	5,958	8,198	7,512	7,571	0.26	0.79
New Zealand	1,698	1,812	2,787	2,565	2,022	0.07	-21.17
Other East Asia and the Pacific	**1,032**	**825**	**849**	**768**	**1,823**	**0.06**	**137.37**
Other countries East Asia/Pacific	1,032	825	849	768	1,823	0.06	137.37
EUROPE	**132,636**	**139,282**	**140,398**	**146,774**	**151,049**	**5.10**	**2.91**
Northern Europe	**27,598**	**28,482**	**26,709**	**28,064**	**30,854**	**1.04**	**9.94**
Denmark	1,860	1,832	1,742	1,893	2,187	0.07	15.53
Finland	3,499	2,366	1,767	1,757	2,270	0.08	29.20
Ireland	3,015	3,320	2,489	2,374	2,136	0.07	-10.03
Norway	1,577	2,180	1,998	2,429	2,158	0.07	-11.16
Sweden	4,337	4,387	3,750	3,874	4,683	0.16	20.88
United Kingdom	13,310	14,397	14,963	15,737	17,420	0.59	10.69
Southern Europe	**53,941**	**53,966**	**50,683**	**52,529**	**53,889**	**1.82**	**2.59**
Greece	1,503	1,471	1,033	1,362	912	0.03	-33.04
Italy	16,642	17,267	16,098	16,603	17,518	0.59	5.51
Portugal	2,721	2,896	2,470	3,033	3,152	0.11	3.92
Spain	33,075	32,332	31,082	31,531	32,307	1.09	2.46
Western Europe	**41,789**	**45,569**	**51,563**	**53,632**	**56,045**	**1.89**	**4.50**
Austria	1,943	1,994	2,511	2,867	2,794	0.09	-2.55
Belgium	2,176	2,353	2,461	2,190	2,742	0.09	25.21
France	14,198	15,430	17,573	18,505	19,250	0.65	4.03
Germany	14,923	16,499	18,450	19,102	20,267	0.68	6.10
Luxembourg	93	78	56	103	78	0.00	-24.27
Netherlands	4,466	4,827	5,296	5,018	4,834	0.16	-3.67
Switzerland	3,990	4,388	5,216	5,847	6,080	0.21	3.98
East Mediterranean Europe	**3,406**	**3,438**	**3,601**	**3,680**	**3,601**	**0.12**	**-2.15**
Israel	3,406	3,438	3,601	3,680	3,601	0.12	-2.15
Other Europe	**5,902**	**7,827**	**7,842**	**8,869**	**6,660**	**0.22**	**-24.91**
Other countries of Europe	5,902	7,827	7,842	8,869	6,660	0.22	-24.91

URUGUAY

2. Arrivals of non-resident visitors at national borders, by nationality

	2007	2008	2009	2010	2011	Market share 11	% Change 11-10
MIDDLE EAST	234	261	226	567	349	0.01	-38.45
All countries of Middle East	234	261	226	567	349	0.01	-38.45
NOT SPECIFIED	262,766	299,881	297,644	354,634	389,054	13.14	9.71
Other countries of the World	2,738	26,100	769	1,656	50,705	1.71	2961.90
Nationals Residing Abroad	260,028	273,781	296,875	352,978	338,349	11.43	-4.14

UZBEKISTAN

1. Arrivals of non-resident tourists at national borders, by country of residence

	2007	2008	2009	2010	2011	Market share 11	% Change 11-10
TOTAL	903,100	1,069,300	1,214,700	974,573			
AFRICA	2,000	2,500	100	35			
Other Africa	2,000	2,500	100	35			
All countries of Africa	2,000	2,500	100	35			
AMERICAS	8,000	8,000	6,500	1,189			
Other Americas	8,000	8,000	6,500	1,189			
All countries of the Americas	8,000	8,000	6,500	1,189			
EAST ASIA AND THE PACIFIC	442,700	578,600	649,300	768,160			
Other East Asia and the Pacific	442,700	578,600	649,300	768,160			
All countries of Asia	442,700	578,600	649,300	768,160			
EUROPE	370,400	385,200	333,200	156,766			
Other Europe	370,400	385,200	333,200	156,766			
All countries of Europe	370,400	385,200	333,200	156,766			
MIDDLE EAST	50,000	55,000	66,800	36,839			
All countries of Middle East	50,000	55,000	66,800	36,839			
SOUTH ASIA	30,000	40,000	158,800	11,584			
All countries of South Asia	30,000	40,000	158,800	11,584			

VANUATU

1. Arrivals of non-resident tourists at national borders, by country of residence

	2007	2008	2009	2010	2011	Market share 11	% Change 11-10
TOTAL	81,344	90,656	98,648	97,180	93,960	100.00	-3.31
AMERICAS	2,578	2,578	2,405	2,395	1,922	2.05	-19.75
North America	2,578	2,578	2,405	2,395	1,922	2.05	-19.75
All countries of North America	2,578	2,578	2,405	2,395	1,922	2.05	-19.75
EAST ASIA AND THE PACIFIC	73,214	81,162	89,141	87,333	84,645	90.09	-3.08
North-East Asia	745	589	604	517	630	0.67	21.86
Japan	745	589	604	517	630	0.67	21.86
Australasia	61,092	67,167	75,656	70,687	69,242	73.69	-2.04
Australia	47,474	53,251	63,868	58,760	57,843	61.56	-1.56
New Zealand	13,618	13,916	11,788	11,927	11,399	12.13	-4.43
Melanesia	8,477	9,648	9,192	11,410	11,376	12.11	-0.30
New Caledonia	8,477	9,648	9,192	11,410	11,376	12.11	-0.30
Other East Asia and the Pacific	2,900	3,758	3,689	4,719	3,397	3.62	-28.01
Other countries of Oceania	2,900	3,758	3,689	4,719	3,397	3.62	-28.01
EUROPE	3,785	4,886	4,913	4,888	5,265	5.60	7.71
Other Europe	3,785	4,886	4,913	4,888	5,265	5.60	7.71
All countries of Europe	3,785	4,886	4,913	4,888	5,265	5.60	7.71
NOT SPECIFIED	1,767	2,030	2,189	2,564	2,128	2.26	-17.00
Other countries of the World	1,767	2,030	2,189	2,564	2,128	2.26	-17.00

VENEZUELA

1. Arrivals of non-resident tourists at national borders, by nationality

		2007	2008	2009	2010	2011	Market share 11	% Change 11-10
TOTAL	(*)	770,567	744,709	615,188	535,270	625,224	100.00	16.81
AFRICA		710	721	736	294	598	0.10	103.40
Southern Africa		445	452	456	204	368	0.06	80.39
South Africa		445	452	456	204	368	0.06	80.39
West Africa		265	269	280	90	230	0.04	155.56
Nigeria		265	269	280	90	230	0.04	155.56
AMERICAS		420,056	408,219	339,636	320,077	400,313	64.03	25.07
Caribbean		42,803	39,480	33,110	36,163	40,444	6.47	11.84
Barbados		661	671	488	230	431	0.07	87.39
Cuba		12,095	12,175	10,259	8,323	8,366	1.34	0.52
Dominican Republic		9,453	9,604	7,983	7,096	8,470	1.35	19.36
Grenada		645	655	498	123	308	0.05	150.41
Haiti		650	660	831	269	651	0.10	142.01
Jamaica		298	303	292	245	256	0.04	4.49
Puerto Rico		166	169	164	159	143	0.02	-10.06
Saint Lucia		367	373	372	312	505	0.08	61.86
Trinidad and Tobago		18,468	14,870	12,223	19,406	21,314	3.41	9.83
Central America		11,286	11,377	10,760	8,542	11,586	1.85	35.64
Costa Rica		3,399	3,426	2,880	2,366	3,085	0.49	30.39
El Salvador		668	678	751	283	749	0.12	164.66
Guatemala		1,203	1,221	1,515	1,269	1,415	0.23	11.51
Honduras		612	621	747	610	598	0.10	-1.97
Nicaragua		732	743	916	783	909	0.15	16.09
Panama		4,672	4,688	3,951	3,231	4,830	0.77	49.49
North America		135,890	130,257	109,848	97,667	106,970	17.11	9.53
Canada		26,670	25,870	18,165	21,196	24,748	3.96	16.76
Mexico		19,146	17,405	15,624	13,211	14,143	2.26	7.05
United States of America		90,074	86,982	76,059	63,260	68,079	10.89	7.62
South America		230,077	227,105	185,918	177,705	241,313	38.60	35.79
Argentina		26,863	26,055	24,601	25,407	37,916	6.06	49.23
Bolivia		2,484	2,522	1,844	1,566	2,137	0.34	36.46
Brazil		55,133	58,539	42,813	48,293	58,921	9.42	22.01
Chile		15,359	15,424	13,175	10,833	11,297	1.81	4.28
Colombia		79,735	77,417	61,659	57,414	94,279	15.08	64.21
Ecuador		16,563	14,661	12,636	10,451	13,090	2.09	25.25
Guyana		453	460	616	328	643	0.10	96.04
Paraguay		783	795	616	558	607	0.10	8.78
Peru		28,259	26,720	24,069	19,608	19,123	3.06	-2.47
Uruguay		4,445	4,512	3,889	3,247	3,300	0.53	1.63
EAST ASIA AND THE PACIFIC		19,163	19,451	14,897	11,151	13,389	2.14	20.07
North-East Asia		14,392	14,494	13,086	10,403	11,821	1.89	13.63
China		8,698	8,733	7,415	6,023	6,315	1.01	4.85
Taiwan, Province of China		364	370	459	155	331	0.05	113.55
Japan		4,332	4,378	3,840	3,261	4,089	0.65	25.39
Korea, Dem. People's Republic of		289	293	280	229	227	0.04	-0.87
Korea, Republic of		709	720	1,092	735	859	0.14	16.87
Australasia		4,771	4,957	1,811	748	1,568	0.25	109.63
Australia		4,366	4,546	1,419	611	1,266	0.20	107.20
New Zealand		405	411	392	137	302	0.05	120.44
EUROPE		316,041	301,579	241,431	194,567	195,850	31.32	0.66
Central/Eastern Europe		12,368	14,475	9,828	8,500	11,804	1.89	38.87
Bulgaria		438	445	375	312	313	0.05	0.32
Czech Republic		3,921	4,496	2,878	3,593	3,575	0.57	-0.50

VENEZUELA

1. Arrivals of non-resident tourists at national borders, by nationality

	2007	2008	2009	2010	2011	Market share 11	% Change 11-10
Hungary	671	681	699	253	465	0.07	83.79
Lithuania	935	949	397	223	338	0.05	51.57
Poland	3,534	4,991	2,802	2,200	4,517	0.72	105.32
Romania	915	929	846	376	682	0.11	81.38
Russian Federation	1,705	1,731	1,627	1,363	1,646	0.26	20.76
Ukraine	249	253	204	180	268	0.04	48.89
Northern Europe	**51,328**	**53,816**	**33,436**	**18,883**	**20,487**	**3.28**	**8.49**
Denmark	5,727	7,480	4,012	2,369	2,389	0.38	0.84
Finland	4,417	4,342	2,462	241	683	0.11	183.40
Ireland	819	831	636	221	476	0.08	115.38
Norway	2,933	2,977	2,080	379	1,261	0.20	232.72
Sweden	11,986	11,006	7,127	4,173	3,798	0.61	-8.99
United Kingdom	25,446	27,180	17,119	11,500	11,880	1.90	3.30
Southern Europe	**152,336**	**139,129**	**127,215**	**99,953**	**96,068**	**15.37**	**-3.89**
Croatia	264	268	231	174	185	0.03	6.32
Greece	606	615	942	325	772	0.12	137.54
Italy	56,005	52,131	45,926	37,497	36,482	5.84	-2.71
Portugal	20,160	19,466	17,268	13,972	13,355	2.14	-4.42
Spain	75,301	66,649	62,848	47,985	45,274	7.24	-5.65
Western Europe	**97,819**	**91,936**	**68,943**	**66,416**	**66,006**	**10.56**	**-0.62**
Austria	3,033	3,079	3,545	3,078	2,853	0.46	-7.31
Belgium	3,443	3,708	2,573	2,066	2,026	0.32	-1.94
France	25,036	23,026	19,739	22,766	22,858	3.66	0.40
Germany	37,686	37,719	27,040	22,067	18,545	2.97	-15.96
Netherlands	19,985	17,651	10,528	11,442	15,148	2.42	32.39
Switzerland	8,636	6,753	5,518	4,997	4,576	0.73	-8.43
East Mediterranean Europe	**2,190**	**2,223**	**2,009**	**815**	**1,485**	**0.24**	**82.21**
Israel	1,874	1,902	1,639	484	1,137	0.18	134.92
Turkey	316	321	370	331	348	0.06	5.14
MIDDLE EAST	**10,309**	**10,389**	**8,970**	**6,946**	**7,654**	**1.22**	**10.19**
Jordan	503	511	497	86	353	0.06	310.47
Lebanon	5,258	5,293	4,474	3,658	3,698	0.59	1.09
Libya	324	329	331	285	284	0.05	-0.35
Syrian Arab Republic	3,939	3,967	3,364	2,803	3,085	0.49	10.06
Egypt	285	289	304	114	234	0.04	105.26
SOUTH ASIA	**1,397**	**1,418**	**1,698**	**694**	**1,382**	**0.22**	**99.14**
India	845	858	1,131	224	875	0.14	290.63
Iran, Islamic Republic of	552	560	567	470	507	0.08	7.87
NOT SPECIFIED	**2,891**	**2,932**	**7,820**	**1,541**	**6,038**	**0.97**	**291.82**
Other countries of the World	2,891	2,932	7,820	1,541	6,038	0.97	291.82

VIET NAM

2. Arrivals of non-resident visitors at national borders, by country of residence

	2007	2008	2009	2010	2011	Market share 11	% Change 11-10
TOTAL	4,229,300	4,235,800	3,747,400	5,049,800	6,014,000	100.00	19.09
AMERICAS	497,800	501,600	487,600	533,200	546,300	9.08	2.46
North America	497,800	501,600	487,600	533,200	546,300	9.08	2.46
Canada	89,500	86,800	84,600	102,200	106,400	1.77	4.11
United States of America	408,300	414,800	403,000	431,000	439,900	7.31	2.06
EAST ASIA AND THE PACIFIC	2,728,300	2,790,800	2,422,300	3,497,700	4,383,600	72.89	25.33
North-East Asia	1,787,600	1,788,600	1,505,700	2,177,400	2,795,800	46.49	28.40
China	574,600	643,300	518,900	905,400	1,416,800	23.56	56.48
Taiwan, Province of China	319,300	303,200	270,000	334,000	361,100	6.00	8.11
Japan	418,300	393,100	356,700	442,100	481,500	8.01	8.91
Korea, Republic of	475,400	449,000	360,100	495,900	536,400	8.92	8.17
South-East Asia	696,400	746,700	681,000	1,017,500	1,271,500	21.14	24.96
Cambodia	150,200	129,700	118,300	254,600	423,400	7.04	66.30
Indonesia	23,300	24,900	27,300	51,500	55,400	0.92	7.57
Lao People's Democratic Republic	31,700	30,900	26,100	37,400	118,500	1.97	216.84
Malaysia	153,500	174,500	165,600	211,300	233,100	3.88	10.32
Philippines	32,500	45,800	45,700	69,200	86,800	1.44	25.43
Singapore	138,200	158,500	138,400	170,700	172,500	2.87	1.05
Thailand	167,000	182,400	159,600	222,800	181,800	3.02	-18.40
Australasia	244,300	255,500	235,600	302,800	316,300	5.26	4.46
Australia	224,600	234,700	217,200	278,200	289,800	4.82	4.17
New Zealand	19,700	20,800	18,400	24,600	26,500	0.44	7.72
EUROPE	619,800	623,500	617,900	757,000	811,600	13.50	7.21
Central/Eastern Europe	43,300	49,000	55,200	82,800	101,600	1.69	22.71
Russian Federation	43,300	49,000	55,200	82,800	101,600	1.69	22.71
Northern Europe	164,100	171,800	176,500	207,900	231,500	3.85	11.35
Denmark	21,300	20,400	19,600	24,400	25,700	0.43	5.33
Norway	11,800	15,200	13,300	16,800	19,500	0.32	16.07
Sweden	23,500	29,100	28,100	27,500	30,000	0.50	9.09
United Kingdom	107,500	107,100	115,500	139,200	156,300	2.60	12.28
Southern Europe	49,400	45,700	41,100	54,300	60,800	1.01	11.97
Italy	22,500	21,100	20,000	24,700	28,300	0.47	14.57
Spain	26,900	24,600	21,100	29,600	32,500	0.54	9.80
Western Europe	363,000	357,000	345,100	412,000	417,700	6.95	1.38
Belgium	19,600	17,000	16,000	20,400	21,900	0.36	7.35
France	183,800	182,100	173,000	199,400	211,400	3.52	6.02
Germany	101,800	102,800	101,800	123,200	113,900	1.89	-7.55
Netherlands	36,600	35,400	34,700	43,700	45,000	0.75	2.97
Switzerland	21,200	19,700	19,600	25,300	25,500	0.42	0.79
NOT SPECIFIED	383,400	319,900	219,600	261,900	272,500	4.53	4.05
Other countries of the World	383,400	319,900	219,600	261,900	272,500	4.53	4.05

YEMEN

1. Arrivals of non-resident tourists at national borders, by nationality

		2007	2008	2009	2010	2011	Market share 11	% Change 11-10
TOTAL	(*)	948,118	1,022,737	1,028,127	1,024,762			
AFRICA		20,181	17,715	23,587	33,387			
East Africa		14,695	13,720	18,920	26,961			
Ethiopia		4,115	4,624	6,711	9,359			
Eritrea				2,487	5,361			
Djibouti		5,613	4,242	7,169	8,636			
Kenya		1,174	996	1,382	1,998			
Somalia		2,784	3,001					
United Republic of Tanzania		1,009	857	1,171	1,607			
North Africa		3,671	3,507	3,190	4,494			
Algeria		406	458					
Morocco		426	334					
Sudan		2,451	2,275	3,190	4,494			
Tunisia		388	440					
Southern Africa		458	402	425	391			
South Africa		458	402	425	391			
West Africa		83	86					
Mauritania		83	86					
Other Africa		1,274		1,052	1,541			
Other countries of Africa		1,274		1,052	1,541			
AMERICAS		17,615	18,118	25,493	28,006			
North America		14,631	16,172	23,441	25,784			
Canada		3,618	3,301	3,914	3,321			
United States of America		11,013	12,871	19,527	22,463			
Other Americas		2,984	1,946	2,052	2,222			
Other countries of the Americas		2,984	1,946	2,052	2,222			
EAST ASIA AND THE PACIFIC		19,668	20,466	26,004	26,222			
North-East Asia		7,685	7,622	8,331	7,261			
China		4,227	4,695	5,843	5,331			
Japan		2,216	1,874	1,465	987			
Korea, Republic of		1,242	1,053	1,023	943			
South-East Asia		7,851	8,250	12,192	12,553			
Indonesia		4,521	4,647	6,799	6,832			
Malaysia		1,262	1,295	2,560	2,427			
Philippines		1,847	1,875	2,833	3,294			
Thailand		221	433					
Australasia		1,029	1,147	1,440	1,296			
Australia		1,029	1,147	1,440	1,296			
Other East Asia and the Pacific		3,103	3,447	4,041	5,112			
Other countries of Asia		3,103	3,447	4,041	5,112			
EUROPE		33,079	36,099	43,493	37,730			
Central/Eastern Europe		1,581	1,700	1,615	1,501			
Bulgaria		212	147					
Poland		247	236					
Romania		217	222					
Russian Federation		905	1,095	1,615	1,501			
Northern Europe		8,892	9,128	13,844	10,949			
United Kingdom		8,892	9,128	13,844	10,949			
Southern Europe		4,239	3,497	2,749	2,003			
Greece		249	191					
Italy		3,418	2,937	2,749	2,003			
Spain		572	369					

YEMEN

1. Arrivals of non-resident tourists at national borders, by nationality

	2007	2008	2009	2010	2011	Market share 11	% Change 11-10
Western Europe	**11,641**	**13,733**	**13,555**	**12,412**			
Austria	631	561	532	331			
Belgium	778	418					
France	5,388	5,123	6,141	5,567			
Germany	2,551	5,477	4,257	4,559			
Netherlands	1,577	1,591	2,058	1,565			
Switzerland	716	563	567	390			
East Mediterranean Europe	**3,988**	**4,160**	**4,619**	**5,673**			
Turkey	3,988	4,160	4,619	5,673			
Other Europe	**2,738**	**3,881**	**7,111**	**5,192**			
Other countries of Europe	2,738	3,881	7,111	5,192			
MIDDLE EAST	**268,540**	**293,275**	**289,737**	**376,882**			
Bahrain	2,970	2,307	4,205	4,568			
Palestine	2,210	2,609					
Iraq	2,997	2,283	3,447	3,271			
Jordan	6,158	6,604	7,880	9,069			
Kuwait	940	1,249					
Lebanon	2,334	2,221	3,142	2,795			
Libya	322	241					
Oman	41,855	50,232	46,098	49,559			
Qatar	3,840	2,899	4,964	3,643			
Saudi Arabia	162,537	176,305	163,000	235,412			
Syrian Arab Republic	9,896	8,436	10,792	14,668			
United Arab Emirates	20,244	20,942	22,438	21,681			
Egypt	11,921	10,263	14,293	18,204			
Other countries of Middle East	316	6,684	9,478	14,012			
SOUTH ASIA	**20,307**	**18,824**	**25,607**	**33,793**			
India	14,667	13,867	19,608	26,112			
Pakistan	5,640	4,957	5,999	7,681			
NOT SPECIFIED	**568,728**	**618,240**	**594,206**	**488,742**			
Nationals Residing Abroad	568,728	618,240	594,206	488,742			

YEMEN

5. Overnight stays of non-resident tourists in hotels and similar establishments, by nationality

		2007	2008	2009	2010	2011	Market share 11	% Change 11-10
TOTAL	(*)	10,997,312	11,891,336	11,790,252	16,506,710			
AFRICA		161,472	127,248	188,696	267,096			
East Africa		117,576	85,752	151,360	215,688			
Ethiopia		32,920	36,992	53,688	74,872			
Eritrea				19,896	42,888			
Djibouti		44,904	33,936	57,352	69,088			
Kenya		9,392	7,968	11,056	15,984			
Somalia		22,272						
United Republic of Tanzania		8,088	6,856	9,368	12,856			
North Africa		29,360	25,384	25,520	35,952			
Algeria		3,248	3,664					
Morocco		3,408						
Sudan		19,600	18,200	25,520	35,952			
Tunisia		3,104	3,520					
Southern Africa		3,664		3,400	3,128			
South Africa		3,664		3,400	3,128			
West Africa		664						
Mauritania		664						
Other Africa		10,208	16,112	8,416	12,328			
Other countries of Africa		10,208	16,112	8,416	12,328			
AMERICAS		140,904	144,944	203,944	224,048			
North America		126,744	129,376	187,528	206,272			
Canada		28,944	26,408	31,312	26,568			
United States of America		97,800	102,968	156,216	179,704			
Other Americas		14,160	15,568	16,416	17,776			
Other countries of the Americas		14,160	15,568	16,416	17,776			
EAST ASIA AND THE PACIFIC		157,344	150,344	208,032	208,976			
North-East Asia		61,480	60,976	66,656	57,288			
China		33,816	37,560	46,752	42,648			
Japan		17,728	14,992	11,720	7,896			
Korea, Republic of		9,936	8,424	8,184	6,744			
South-East Asia		62,808	66,000	97,536	100,424			
Indonesia		36,168	37,176	54,392	54,656			
Malaysia		10,096	10,360	20,480	19,416			
Philippines		14,776	15,000	22,664	26,352			
Thailand		1,768	3,464					
Australasia		8,232	9,176	11,520	10,368			
Australia		8,232	9,176	11,520	10,368			
Other East Asia and the Pacific		24,824	14,192	32,320	40,896			
Other countries of Asia		24,824	14,192	32,320	40,896			
EUROPE		264,632	279,928	347,944	301,840			
Central/Eastern Europe		12,648	8,760	12,920	12,008			
Bulgaria		1,696						
Poland		1,976						
Romania		1,736						
Russian Federation		7,240	8,760	12,920	12,008			
Northern Europe		71,136	73,024	110,752	87,592			
United Kingdom		71,136	73,024	110,752	87,592			
Southern Europe		33,912	26,920	21,992	16,024			
Greece		1,992						
Italy		27,344	23,496	21,992	16,024			
Spain		4,576	3,424					

YEMEN

5. Overnight stays of non-resident tourists in hotels and similar establishments, by nationality

	2007	2008	2009	2010	2011	Market share 11	% Change 11-10
Western Europe	93,128	110,008	108,440	99,296			
Austria	5,048	4,488	4,256	2,648			
Belgium	6,224	3,488					
France	43,104	40,984	49,128	44,536			
Germany	20,408	43,816	34,056	36,472			
Netherlands	12,616	12,728	16,464	12,520			
Switzerland	5,728	4,504	4,536	3,120			
East Mediterranean Europe	31,904	33,280	36,952	45,384			
Turkey	31,904	33,280	36,952	45,384			
Other Europe	21,904	27,936	56,888	41,536			
Other countries of Europe	21,904	27,936	56,888	41,536			
MIDDLE EAST	2,148,312	2,324,448	2,317,896	3,015,856			
Bahrain	23,760	18,456	33,640	36,544			
Palestine	17,680	20,872					
Iraq	23,976	18,264	27,576	26,168			
Jordan	49,264	52,832	63,040	72,552			
Kuwait	7,520	9,992					
Lebanon	18,672	17,768	25,136	22,360			
Libya	2,576						
Oman	334,840	401,856	368,784	397,272			
Qatar	30,720	23,192	39,712	29,144			
Saudi Arabia	1,300,296	1,410,440	1,304,000	1,883,296			
Syrian Arab Republic	79,168	67,488	86,336	117,344			
United Arab Emirates	161,952	167,536	179,504	173,448			
Egypt	95,368	82,104	114,344	145,632			
Other countries of Middle East	2,520	33,648	75,824	112,096			
SOUTH ASIA	162,456	150,592	204,856	270,344			
India	117,336	110,936	156,864	208,896			
Pakistan	45,120	39,656	47,992	61,448			
NOT SPECIFIED	7,962,192	8,713,832	8,318,884	12,218,550			
Other countries of the World		58,472					
Nationals Residing Abroad	7,962,192	8,655,360	8,318,884	12,218,550			

ZAMBIA

1. Arrivals of non-resident tourists at national borders, by country of residence

	2007	2008	2009	2010	2011	Market share 11	% Change 11-10
TOTAL	897,413	811,775	709,948	815,164			
AFRICA	660,551	606,641	467,045	583,377			
East Africa	405,853	362,500	276,338	316,600			
Kenya	10,541	12,331	10,378	12,785			
Zimbabwe	278,010	226,428	171,232	171,806			
United Republic of Tanzania	92,732	106,284	81,288	121,275			
Other countries of East Africa	24,570	17,457	13,440	10,734			
Central Africa	96,576	80,674	57,955	80,314			
All countries of Central Africa	96,576	80,674	57,955	80,314			
North Africa	2,289	4,859	1,397	2,671			
All countries of North Africa	2,289	4,859	1,397	2,671			
Southern Africa	151,998	154,511	125,604	178,643			
South Africa	125,231	95,415	84,413	144,980			
Other countries of Southern Africa	26,767	59,096	41,191	33,663			
West Africa	3,835	4,097	5,751	5,149			
All countries of West Africa	3,835	4,097	5,751	5,149			
AMERICAS	50,606	47,360	63,089	41,703			
North America	46,373	43,053	58,939	36,899			
Canada	7,246	9,183	9,488	7,378			
United States of America	39,127	33,870	49,451	29,521			
Other Americas	4,233	4,307	4,150	4,804			
Other countries of the Americas	4,233	4,307	4,150	4,804			
EAST ASIA AND THE PACIFIC	28,095	34,658	38,542	64,271			
North-East Asia	4,835	4,241	5,373	26,660			
China				18,319			
Japan	4,835	4,241	5,373	8,341			
Australasia	13,008	17,873	20,308	13,880			
Australia	9,389	14,517	16,316	10,430			
New Zealand	3,619	3,356	3,992	3,450			
Other East Asia and the Pacific	10,252	12,544	12,861	23,731			
Other countries of Asia	10,252	12,544	12,861	23,731			
EUROPE	145,729	109,182	128,340	104,399			
Northern Europe	79,695	60,591	72,190	65,405			
Denmark	3,625	3,982	2,665	3,752			
Sweden	3,523	3,301	3,166	3,640			
United Kingdom	66,858	46,516	53,370	50,958			
Scandinavia	5,689	6,792	12,989	7,055			
Southern Europe	10,971	5,190	8,238	5,515			
Italy	10,971	5,190	8,238	5,515			
Western Europe	19,762	21,363	19,368	16,189			
France	9,288	9,264	6,701	6,418			
Germany	10,474	12,099	12,667	9,771			
Other Europe	35,301	22,038	28,544	17,290			
Other countries of Europe	35,301	22,038	28,544	17,290			
SOUTH ASIA	12,432	13,934	12,932	21,414			
India	12,432	13,934	12,932	21,414			

ZIMBABWE

2. Arrivals of non-resident visitors at national borders, by country of residence

	2007	2008	2009	2010	2011	Market share 11	% Change 11-10
TOTAL	2,505,988	1,955,597	2,017,264	2,239,165	2,423,280	100.00	8.22
AFRICA	2,289,958	1,731,528	1,678,884	1,951,330	2,041,291	84.24	4.61
East Africa	552,767	565,295	493,791	389,022	508,728	20.99	30.77
Kenya	26,645	21,459	25,808	8,509	6,514	0.27	-23.45
Malawi	111,177	63,597	108,103	67,291	138,676	5.72	106.08
Mauritius	1,058	875	967	1,066	2,779	0.11	160.69
Mozambique	94,290	118,117	110,058	131,653	148,857	6.14	13.07
Seychelles	660	280	360	434	1,321	0.05	204.38
Uganda	4,435	4,387	6,906	2,893	11,555	0.48	299.41
United Republic of Tanzania	13,237	10,236	11,391	8,454	14,038	0.58	66.05
Zambia	301,265	346,344	230,198	168,722	184,988	7.63	9.64
Central Africa	44,014	30,476	27,580	18,036	17,137	0.71	-4.98
Angola	23,478	10,439	8,131	2,285	3,297	0.14	44.29
Democratic Republic of the Congo	20,536	20,037	19,449	15,751	13,840	0.57	-12.13
Southern Africa	1,632,047	1,115,218	1,137,761	1,522,208	1,471,791	60.74	-3.31
Botswana	227,777	147,780	183,212	114,718	119,098	4.91	3.82
Lesotho	7,804	4,551	5,367	4,957	6,655	0.27	34.25
Namibia	17,373	19,860	33,806	19,917	23,322	0.96	17.10
South Africa	1,362,982	936,727	912,244	1,368,238	1,309,463	54.04	-4.30
Swaziland	16,111	6,300	3,132	14,378	13,253	0.55	-7.82
West Africa	9,178	5,395	4,656	3,290	5,126	0.21	55.81
Ghana	1,589	1,619	1,258	1,428	3,857	0.16	170.10
Nigeria	7,589	3,776	3,398	1,862	1,269	0.05	-31.85
Other Africa	51,952	15,144	15,096	18,774	38,509	1.59	105.12
Other countries of Africa	51,952	15,144	15,096	18,774	38,509	1.59	105.12
AMERICAS	39,747	43,412	57,842	69,008	89,756	3.70	30.07
Caribbean	1,961	1,935	2,513	804	892	0.04	10.95
All countries of the Caribbean	1,961	1,935	2,513	804	892	0.04	10.95
North America	31,866	38,172	49,355	63,343	80,596	3.33	27.24
Canada	4,948	5,480	5,538	4,098	6,999	0.29	70.79
Mexico	454	418	546	2,829	992	0.04	-64.93
United States of America	26,464	32,274	43,271	56,416	72,605	3.00	28.70
South America	1,717	1,700	2,643	2,986	5,778	0.24	93.50
Argentina	685	655	1,058	1,027	1,682	0.07	63.78
Brazil	1,032	1,045	1,585	1,959	4,096	0.17	109.09
Other Americas	4,203	1,605	3,331	1,875	2,490	0.10	32.80
Other countries of the Americas	4,203	1,605	3,331	1,875	2,490	0.10	32.80
EAST ASIA AND THE PACIFIC	57,650	63,194	104,366	84,092	125,257	5.17	48.95
North-East Asia	31,895	37,181	61,534	37,385	75,591	3.12	102.20
Hong Kong, China	12,349	14,169	30,102	12,343	30,549	1.26	147.50
Japan	12,949	14,803	18,389	18,593	32,784	1.35	76.32
Korea, Republic of	6,597	8,209	13,043	6,449	12,258	0.51	90.08
South-East Asia	2,505	2,326	4,016	5,537	7,114	0.29	28.48
Malaysia	1,774	1,770	2,416	3,497	3,452	0.14	-1.29
Singapore	731	556	1,600	2,040	3,662	0.15	79.51
Australasia	18,947	20,201	33,041	37,708	38,841	1.60	3.00
Australia	12,724	13,866	22,612	25,240	26,833	1.11	6.31
New Zealand	6,223	6,335	10,429	12,468	12,008	0.50	-3.69
Other East Asia and the Pacific	4,303	3,486	5,775	3,462	3,711	0.15	7.19
Other countries of Asia	2,823	2,143	2,363	2,155	1,333	0.06	-38.14
Other countries of Oceania	1,480	1,343	3,412	1,307	2,378	0.10	81.94

ZIMBABWE

2. Arrivals of non-resident visitors at national borders, by country of residence

	2007	2008	2009	2010	2011	Market share 11	% Change 11-10
EUROPE	112,111	111,121	160,316	128,082	158,141	6.53	23.47
Northern Europe	30,813	30,558	42,165	35,169	47,627	1.97	35.42
United Kingdom	22,295	22,778	27,580	24,192	35,913	1.48	48.45
Scandinavia	8,518	7,780	14,585	10,977	11,714	0.48	6.71
Southern Europe	18,233	20,118	29,446	23,342	27,432	1.13	17.52
Italy	6,247	7,655	14,161	9,221	13,806	0.57	49.72
Portugal	7,865	8,461	9,883	4,951	5,482	0.23	10.73
Spain	4,121	4,002	5,402	9,170	8,144	0.34	-11.19
Western Europe	53,046	50,453	77,430	57,997	69,629	2.87	20.06
Austria	3,316	3,247	5,520	6,475	6,245	0.26	-3.55
France	14,446	15,134	27,193	13,687	16,232	0.67	18.59
Germany	15,459	14,929	22,936	16,910	24,300	1.00	43.70
Netherlands	17,547	14,722	16,967	14,088	15,927	0.66	13.05
Switzerland	2,278	2,421	4,814	6,837	6,925	0.29	1.29
East Mediterranean Europe	2,992	2,960	4,451	2,851	3,838	0.16	34.62
Israel	2,992	2,960	4,451	2,851	3,838	0.16	34.62
Other Europe	7,027	7,032	6,824	8,723	9,615	0.40	10.23
Other countries of Europe	7,027	7,032	6,824	8,723	9,615	0.40	10.23
MIDDLE EAST	874	928	5,456	1,758	2,863	0.12	62.86
Saudi Arabia	70	92	116	62	60	0.00	-3.23
United Arab Emirates	154	197	208	101	503	0.02	398.02
Egypt	650	639	1,198	641	728	0.03	13.57
Other countries of Middle East			3,934	954	1,572	0.06	64.78
SOUTH ASIA	5,648	5,414	10,400	4,895	5,972	0.25	22.00
India	3,990	3,911	5,446	3,571	3,499	0.14	-2.02
Iran, Islamic Republic of	625	215	1,368	758	1,228	0.05	62.01
Pakistan	1,033	1,288	3,586	566	1,245	0.05	119.96

NOTES 2007 - 2011

1. Arrivals of non-resident tourists at national borders, by nationality

Belarus	Total	Organized tourism.
Bhutan	Total	Total arrivals 2010: 40,873; 2011: 65,756. The huge margin of difference in 2010 and 2011 as compared to the previous years is because starting from 2010 the regional high end tourists are included in the total figures.
Bolivia	Total	2007-2010: preliminary data.
Brunei Darussalam	Total	Air arrivals.
Burundi	Total	Including nationals residing abroad. From 2010: break in the series due to implementation of improved methodology for distinguishing visitors (tourists) from other travellers.
Central African Republic	Total	Arrivals by air to Bangui only.
Comoros	Total	Air arrivals.
Democratic Republic of the Congo	Total	2007-2010: arrival by air only; 2011: the arrivals data relate only to three border posts (N'Djili airport in Kinshasa, the Luano airport in Lubumbashi, and the land border-crossing of Kasumbalesa in Katanga province).
Gambia	Total	Charter tourists only.
Honduras	Total	Excluding tourists arrivals by sea.
Iceland	Total	Source: Icelandic Tourist Board.
India	Total	Excluding nationals residing abroad.
Italy	Total	Seasonal and border workers are excluded.
Jordan	Other countries of the World	U.N. passport.
Kiribati	Total	Air arrivals. Tarawa and Christmas Island.
Lebanon	Total	Excluding Syrian nationals, Palestinians and students.
Maldives	Total	Arrivals by air.
Malta	Total	Data based on departures by air and by sea.
Marshall Islands	Total	Air arrivals. 2009: air and sea arrivals.
Mexico	United States of America	Includes tourists arriving by air and land, border tourists and domestic tourists residing in the United States of America.
	Other countries of the World	Includes border tourists from the southern zone.
Myanmar	Total	Including tourist arrivals through border entry points to Yangon.
Nepal	Greece	Including Cyprus.
Norway	Total	Figures are based on "The Guest Survey" carried out by "Institute of Transport Economics".
Paraguay	Total	Excluding nationals residing abroad and crew members. E/d cards in the "Silvio Petirossi" airport and passenger counts at the national border crossings - National Police and SENATUR.
Senegal	Total	2008-2011: arrivals by air at "Léopold Sédar Senghor (LSS)" only. Including the nationals residing abroad. Country estimated totals: 2008: 866,700 2009: 810,000 2010: 900,000 2011: 1,001,000
Sint Maarten	Total	Arrivals at Princess Juliana International Airport. Including visitors to St. Maarten (the French side of the island).
	France	Including residents of the French West Indies.
Sri Lanka	Total	Excluding nationals residing abroad.

NOTES 2007 - 2011

1. Arrivals of non-resident tourists at national borders, by nationality

Sudan	**Total**	Including nationals residing abroad.
Tunisia	**Total**	Excluding nationals residing abroad.
Turkey	**Total**	Turkish citizens resident abroad are included. Departing visitors survey carrying out at departure gates.
Venezuela	**Total**	2010,2011: including cruise passengers: 2010: 9,015; 2011: 30,543.

NOTES 2007 - 2011

1. Arrivals of non-resident tourists at national borders, by country of residence

Andorra	Total	Since May 2009 a new methodology has been applied and therefore, the information is not comparable to previous years.
Anguilla	Total	Excluding nationals residing abroad.
Antigua and Barbuda	Total	Air arrivals. Excluding nationals residing abroad.
Bermuda	Total	Air arrivals.
Cayman Islands	Total	Air arrivals.
Cook Islands	Total	Air and sea arrivals.
Curaçao	Total	Arrivals by air.
Dominican Republic	Total	Arrivals by air.
Ethiopia	Total	2007,2008: arrivals to Bole airport only. 2009-2011: arrivals through all ports of entry.
Fiji	Total	Excluding nationals residing abroad.
France	Total	Source: "DGCIS", "Banque de France". Non resident visitor survey ("EVE") - results 2009 revised and 2010 provisional.
	All countries of North Africa	Algeria, Egypt, Libya, Morocco and Tunisia.
	China	Including Hong Kong, China and Macao, China.
	Switzerland	Including Liechtenstein.
French Polynesia	Total	Air arrivals. Excluding nationals residing abroad.
	Samoa	Including American Samoa.
Greece	Total	From 2008, the information is based on the border survey conducted by the Bank of Greece.
	Lebanon	Including Syria.
	Egypt	Including Sudan.
Guadeloupe	Total	Arrivals by air.
Guyana	Total	Arrivals to Timehri Airport only.
Haiti	Total	Air arrivals. From 2007 including nationals residing abroad.
Ireland	United Kingdom	Including Northern Ireland resident arrivals. Change in methodology in estimating Northern Ireland tourists in 2010; as a result figures prior to 2010 not directly comparable.
Israel	Total	Excluding nationals residing abroad. From 2007 excluding day visitors.
Jamaica	Total	Air arrivals. Including nationals residing abroad.
Malawi	Total	Departures.
Malaysia	Total	Includes Singapore residents crossing the frontier by road through Johore Causeway.
Marshall Islands	Total	Air arrivals. 2009: air and sea arrivals.
Martinique	Total	Including French overseas departments and territories.
Mexico	Total	Including nationals residing abroad.
Nepal	Greece	Including Cyprus.
New Caledonia	Total	Including nationals residing abroad.
	All countries of the Caribbean	Martinique, Guadeloupe and Guyana.
Niue	Total	Including Niuans residing usually in New Zealand.
Palau	Total	Air arrivals (Palau International Airport).

NOTES 2007 - 2011

1. Arrivals of non-resident tourists at national borders, by country of residence

Peru	**Total**	Including nationals residing abroad. 2007-2011: preliminary data.
Philippines	**Nationals Residing Abroad**	Philippine passport holders permanently residing abroad; excludes overseas Filipino workers.
Puerto Rico	**Total**	Arrivals by air. Fiscal year July to June. Source: "Junta de Planificación de Puerto Rico".
Reunion	**Total**	Source: INSEE: Survey on Tourism Flows
Saint Kitts and Nevis	**Total**	Air arrivals.
Saint Lucia	**Total**	Excluding nationals residing abroad.
Saint Vincent and the Grenadines	**Total**	Arrivals by air.
Senegal	**Total**	Arrivals by air at "Léopold Sédar Senghor (LSS)" only. Including the nationals residing abroad. Total 2007: 874,623 Country estimated totals: 2008: 866,700 2009: 810,000 2010: 900,000 2011: 1,001,000
Sierra Leone	**Total**	Arrivals by air.
Sint Eustatius	**Total**	Excluding Netherlands Antillean residents.
South Africa	**Total**	2007,2008: excluding arrivals by work and contract workers. Since 2009 a new methodology has been applied and therefore, the information is not comparable to previous years.
Sri Lanka	**Total**	Excluding nationals residing abroad.
Timor-Leste	**Total**	Arrivals by air at Dili Airport.
Tonga	**Total**	Arrivals by air.
Trinidad and Tobago	**Total**	Arrivals by air.
United States of America	**Canada**	Historical data may reflect revisions made by "Statistics Canada".
	Mexico	Historical data may reflect revisions made by "Banco de México".

NOTES 2007 - 2011

2. Arrivals of non-resident visitors at national borders, by nationality

Albania	Total	Excluding nationals residing abroad.
Algeria	Total	Including nationals residing abroad.
Bahrain	Total	Excluding nationals residing abroad.
Belize	Total	Including transit passengers and border permits.
Colombia	Total	Arrivals of foreign travellers at checkpoints of the Administrative Department of Security (DAS). Excluding cruise passengers and non-resident travellers arriving through terrestrial border integration zones. Total arrivals (in thousands): 2007: 2,381 2008: 2,545 2009: 2,649 2010: 2,681 2010: data by country of residence.
Ecuador	Total	Excluding nationals residing abroad. 2011: provisional data.
Egypt	Total	Excluding nationals residing abroad.
Guatemala	Total	2009-2011: data compiled by country of residence.
Italy	Total	Border survey. Seasonal and border workers are excluded.
Japan	Total	Excluding nationals residing abroad.
Korea, Republic of	Total	Including nationals residing abroad and crew members.
Macao, China	Total	Since 2008, excluding data on non-resident workers, students, etc. Source of data: Public Security Police
Nigeria	Total	Source: Nigerian Tourism Development Corporation (NTDC)
Poland	Total	2008-2011: Since Poland joined the Schengen area, precise counting of incoming traffic is not possible. Data presented here are based on surveys by the Institute of Tourism. Only approximate results for main countries can be given.
Republic of Moldova	Total	Visitors who have benefited from tourism servies provided by the tourism agencies and tour operators (titulars of tourism licences). Excluding the left side of the river Nistru and the municipality of Bender.
Singapore	Total	Excluding Malaysian citizens arriving by land.
Syrian Arab Republic	Total	Survey of the incoming tourism in 2004, 2006 and 2007.
	Iraq	The Iraqi nationals are included from 2008 only and they have been excluded in the previous years (from the beginning of 2008, they have to require a visa to enter Syria; if they arrived previously to this date, it is considered that they staid for a period longer than a year, becoming residents).
Turkey	Total	Turkish citizens resident abroad are included. Departing visitors survey carrying out at departure gates.

NOTES 2007 - 2011

2. Arrivals of non-resident visitors at national borders, by country of residence

Australia	**Total**	Excluding nationals residing abroad and crew members. Source: Australian Bureau of Statistics
Canada	**China**	Including Mongolia and Tibet.
	Estonia	Including Latvia and Lithuania.
	Denmark	Including Faeroe Islands.
	Italy	Including San Marino, the Holy See and Malta.
	France	Including Andorra and Monaco.
	Switzerland	Including Liechtenstein.
Finland	**Total**	Border survey.
Hong Kong, China	**United States of America**	Including Guam.
	New Zealand	Including Cook Islands.
	France	Including New Caledonia and French Polynesia.
Israel	**Total**	Excluding nationals residing abroad.
Latvia	**Total**	Non-resident departures. Survey of persons crossing the state border.
Macao, China	**Total**	Since 2008, excluding data on non-resident workers, students, etc. Source of data: Public Security Police
Mozambique	**Total**	Note 2008: Change of methodology. Until 2007 the data correspond only to 12 border posts. From 2008, the data of all the border posts of the country are used.
New Zealand	**Total**	Data regarding to short term movements are compiled from a random sample of passenger declarations. Including nationals residing abroad. Source: Statistics New Zealand (International Travel and Migration).
Panama	**Total**	Total number of visitors broken down by permanent residence who arrived in Panama at Tucumen International Airport.
Saint Vincent and the Grenadines	**Total**	Arrivals by air.
Singapore	**Total**	Excluding Malaysian citizens arriving by land.
South Africa	**Total**	2007,2008: Excluding nationals residing abroad. Including arrivals by purpose of holiday, business, study, work, transit, border traffic and contract workers. Since 2009 a new methodology has been applied and therefore, the information is not comparable to previous years.
Sweden	**Total**	Data for 2011 according to new national border survey (IBIS, Incoming Visitors to Sweden). No data collected during 2004 to 2010. The new border survey (IBIS) started in 2011. Source: Swedish Agency for Economic and Regional Growth.

NOTES 2007 - 2011

3. Arrivals of non-resident tourists in hotels and similar establishments, by nationality

Bolivia	**Total**	2007-2010: preliminary data. Hotel arrivals in the regional capitals.
Chad	**Total**	2010: Partial data.
Italy	**Total**	Arrivals at hotels only.
Morocco	**Total**	Arrivals in classified hotels, holiday villages, tourist residences and Riad.
Slovenia	**Total**	2008: New methodology of accommodation statistics survey.
Syrian Arab Republic	**Total**	Survey of the incoming tourism in 2004, 2006 and 2007.
	Iraq	The Iraqi nationals are included from 2008 only and they have been excluded in the previous years (from the beginning of 2008, they have to require a visa to enter Syria; if they arrived previously to this date, it is considered that they staid for a period longer than a year, becoming residents).
Turkey	**Total**	Arrivals at licensed establishments including: hotels, motels, boarding houses, inns, apartment hotels, holiday villages and special hotels. Results of a monthly survey carried out among accommodation establishments licensed by the Ministry of Tourism.

NOTES 2007 - 2011

3. Arrivals of non-resident tourists in hotels and similar establishments, by country of residence

Austria	Total	Hotels only.
Cape Verde	Belgium	Including Netherlands.
Congo	Total	Source: "Direction Générale de l'Industrie Touristique", surveys 2007 to 2010
Croatia	Total	According to the Regulation on Classification, Minimum Standards and Categorization of Accommodation Facilities data for hotels and similar establishments do not include Inns and Bed and breakfast since 2006.
Curaçao	Total	Large and small hotels, guest houses, apartments and bungalows.
Denmark	Total	Hotels only. 2011: change of methodology.
France	Total	Source: "INSEE", "DGCIS", regional partners. Hotel occupancy survey ("EFH"). Including unclassified hotels.
Germany	China	Including Hong Kong, China.
	Other countries East Asia/Pacific	Including India.
Israel	Total	Arrivals at tourist hotels and not yet listed hotels.
	All countries of South America	Including Central America.
Luxembourg	Total	Arrivals in hotels, guest houses and inns.
Macao, China	Total	Source of data: Monthly Survey of Travel Agencies
Netherlands	Total	Hotels and boarding houses.
New Caledonia	Total	It refers to hotels in Noumea.
Philippines	Total	Air arrivals.
	Nationals Residing Abroad	Philippine passport holders permanently residing abroad; excludes overseas Filipino workers.
Poland	Total	Excluding hostels.
Puerto Rico	Total	Fiscal year July to June. Hotels registered by the "Compañía de Turismo de Puerto Rico".
	Other countries of the Caribbean	Aggregated data of tourists coming from minor Antilles who did not specify their country of origin are included.
	Other countries of the World	Including crew members.
Qatar	Total	Arrivals at hotels only. 2007-2009: including domestic tourism.
	All countries of Europe	2010-2011: Europe and Americas.
Romania	All countries of Africa	Including Egypt and Libya.
Spain	Total	Arrivals at hotels and "hostales" (accommodation establishments providing limited services).
Switzerland	Total	Including health establishments.
	All countries of North Africa	Algeria, Libya, Morocco and Tunisia.
Togo	Burkina Faso	Including Mali and Niger.

NOTES 2007 - 2011

4. Arrivals of non-resident tourists in all types of accommodation establishments, by nationality

Hungary	**Total**	Collective accommodation establishments.
Republic of Moldova	**Total**	Excluding the left side of the river Nistru and the municipality of Bender.
Slovenia	**Total**	2008: New methodology of accommodation statistics survey.
Syrian Arab Republic	**Total**	Excluding private accommodation. Survey of the incoming tourism in 2004, 2006 and 2007.
	Iraq	The Iraqi nationals are included from 2008 only and they have been excluded in the previous years (from the beginning of 2008, they have to require a visa to enter Syria; if they arrived previously to this date, it is considered that they staid for a period longer than a year, becoming residents).
Turkey	**Total**	Results of a monthly survey carried out among accommodation establishments licensed by the Ministry of Tourism.

NOTES 2007 - 2011

4. Arrivals of non-resident tourists in all types of accommodation establishments, by country of residence

Austria	**Total**	Only paid accommodation; excluding stays at friends and relatives and second homes.
Belgium	**Total**	Hotel establishments, campings, holiday centres, holiday villages and specific categories of accommodation.
Croatia	**Total**	Excluding arrivals in ports of nautical tourism.
Denmark	**Total**	Including non-commercial tourism. 2011: change of methodology.
Germany	**China**	Including Hong Kong, China.
	Other countries East Asia/Pacific	Including India.
Luxembourg	**Total**	Hotels, inns, guest houses, youth hostels, private tourist lodgings, camping sites and others.
Malta	**Total**	Data based on departures by air and by sea. Source: National Statistics Office.
Philippines	**Total**	Air arrivals.
	Nationals Residing Abroad	Philippine passport holders permanently residing abroad; excludes overseas Filipino workers.
Romania	**All countries of Africa**	Including Egypt and Libya.
Spain	**Total**	Arrivals at hotels, "hostales", camping, tourism apartments and rural dwellings.

NOTES 2007 - 2011

5. Overnight stays of non-resident tourists in hotels and similar establishments, by nationality

Bolivia	Total	2007-2010: preliminary data. Hotel nights in the regional capitals.
Chad	Total	2010: Partial data.
Italy	Total	Nights in hotels only.
Madagascar	Total	All star-establishments (registered and non-registered).
Morocco	Total	Overnight stays in classified hotels, holiday villages, tourist residences and Riad.
Norway	Total	Nights in registered establishments. Figures relate to establishments with 20 or more beds.
Slovenia	Total	2008: New methodology of accommodation statistics survey.
Syrian Arab Republic	Total	Survey of the incoming tourism in 2004, 2006 and 2007.
	Iraq	The Iraqi nationals are included from 2008 only and they have been excluded in the previous years (from the beginning of 2008, they have to require a visa to enter Syria; if they arrived previously to this date, it is considered that they staid for a period longer than a year, becoming residents).
Turkey	Total	Classified hotels, motels, boarding houses, inns, apartment hotels, holiday villages and special hotels. Results of a monthly survey carried out among accommodation establishments licensed by the Ministry of Tourism.
Yemen	Total	Including nationals residing abroad.

NOTES 2007 - 2011

5. Overnight stays of non-resident tourists in hotels and similar establishments, by country of residence

Austria	**Total**	Hotels only.
Cape Verde	**Belgium**	Including Netherlands.
Congo	**Total**	Source: "Direction Générale de l'Industrie Touristique", surveys 2007 to 2010
Croatia	**Total**	According to the Regulation on Classification, Minimum Standards and Categorization of Accommodation Facilities data for hotels and similar establishments do not include Inns and Bed and breakfast since 2006.
Denmark	**Total**	Hotels only. 2011: change of methodology.
France	**Total**	Source: "INSEE", "DGCIS", regional partners. Hotel occupancy survey ("EFH"). Including unclassified hotels.
Germany	**China**	Including Hong Kong, China.
	Other countries East Asia/Pacific	Including India.
Israel	**Total**	Nights in tourist hotels and apartment hotels.
	All countries of South America	Including Central America.
Luxembourg	**Total**	Nights in hotels, guest houses and inns.
Macao, China	**Total**	Source of data: Monthly Survey of Hotels and Similar Establishments
Netherlands	**Total**	Hotels and boarding houses.
New Caledonia	**Total**	It refers to hotels in Noumea.
Poland	**Total**	Excluding hostels.
Qatar	**Total**	Nights in hotels only. 2007-2009: including domestic tourism.
	All countries of Europe	2010-2011: Europe and Americas.
Romania	**All countries of Africa**	Including Egypt and Libya.
Spain	**Total**	Nights in hotels and "hostales" (accommodation establishments providing limited services).
Sweden	**Total**	Nights in hotels only.
Switzerland	**Total**	Including health establishments.
	All countries of North Africa	Algeria, Libya, Morocco and Tunisia.
Togo	**Burkina Faso**	Including Mali and Niger.

NOTES 2007 - 2011

6. Overnight stays of non-resident tourists in all types of accommodation establishments, by nationality

Hungary	**Total**	Collective accommodation establishments.
Republic of Moldova	**Total**	Excluding the left side of the river Nistru and the municipality of Bender.
Slovenia	**Total**	2008: New methodology of accommodation statistics survey.
Syrian Arab Republic	**Total**	Survey of the incoming tourism in 2004, 2006 and 2007.
	Iraq	The Iraqi nationals are included from 2008 only and they have been excluded in the previous years (from the beginning of 2008, they have to require a visa to enter Syria; if they arrived previously to this date, it is considered that they staid for a period longer than a year, becoming residents).
Turkey	**Total**	Results of a monthly survey carried out among accommodation establishments licensed by the Ministry of Tourism.

NOTES 2007 - 2011

6. Overnight stays of non-resident tourists in all types of accommodation establishments, by country of residence

Austria	**Total**	Only paid accommodation; excluding stays at friends and relatives and second homes.
Bahamas	**Total**	Nights in all forms of commercial accommodation.
Belgium	**Total**	Hotel establishments, campings, holiday centres, holiday villages and specific categories of accommodation.
Canada	**China**	Including Mongolia and Tibet.
	Estonia	Including Latvia and Lithuania.
	Denmark	Including Faeroe Islands.
	Italy	Including San Marino, the Holy See and Malta.
	France	Including Andorra and Monaco.
	Switzerland	Including Liechtenstein.
Croatia	**Total**	Excluding overnight stays at ports of nautical tourism.
Denmark	**Total**	Including non-commercial tourism. 2011: change of methodology.
France	**Total**	Source: "DGCIS", "Banque de France". Non resident visitor survey ("EVE") - results 2009 revised and 2010 provisional.
	All countries of North Africa	Algeria, Egypt, Libya, Morocco and Tunisia.
	China	Including Hong Kong, China and Macao, China.
	Switzerland	Including Liechtenstein.
Germany	**China**	Including Hong Kong, China.
	Other countries East Asia/Pacific	Including India.
Ireland	**Total**	Including nights spent in private homes and holiday homes where no payment is made.
	United Kingdom	Including Northern Ireland residents.
Jamaica	**Total**	Information obtained by multiplying the average length of stay by the number of stop-overs of each country origin. Excluding nationals residing abroad.
	Other countries of the Americas	Latin America.
	All countries of Europe	United Kingdom and rest of Europe.
Malta	**Total**	Data based on departures by air and by sea. Source: National Statistics Office.
Netherlands	**Total**	Excluding overnight stays at fixed pitches (hired on a yearly or seasonal basis).
Romania	**All countries of Africa**	Including Egypt and Libya.
Spain	**Total**	Nights in hotels, "hostales", camping, tourism apartments and rural dwellings.
Sweden	**Total**	2007: Nights in hotels, youth hostels, holiday villages and camping. 2008-2011: Nights in hotels, youth hostels, holiday villages, camping and commercially arranged rentals in private cottages and apartments (SoL).

NOTES 2007 - 2011

1. Arrivées de touristes non résidents aux frontières nationales, par nationalité

Bélarus	**Total**	Tourisme organisé.
Bhoutan	**Total**	Total des arrivées 2010: 40.873; 2011: 65.756. L'écart important que l'on peut observer en 2010 et 2011 par rapport aux années précédentes tient au fait que l'on a inclus les touristes régionaux haut de gamme dans les totaux à partir de 2010.
Bolivie	**Total**	2007-2010: données préliminaires.
Brunéi Darussalam	**Total**	Arrivées par voie aérienne.
Burundi	**Total**	Y compris les nationaux résidant à l'étranger. A partir de 2010: rupture de série due à la mise en œuvre d'une méthodologie améliorée qui distingue les visiteurs (touristes) des autres voyageurs.
Comores	**Total**	Arrivées par voie aérienne.
Gambie	**Total**	Arrivées en vols à la demande seulement.
Honduras	**Total**	Sont exclus les arrivées de touristes par voie maritime.
Îles Marshall	**Total**	Arrivées par voie aérienne. 2009: arrivées par voies aérienne et maritime.
	Autres pays du monde	Comprend les touristes frontaliers de la zone méridionale.
Inde	**Total**	À l'exclusion des nationaux résidant à l'étranger.
Islande	**Total**	Source: "Icelandic Tourist Board".
Italie	**Total**	À l'exclusion des travailleurs saisonniers et frontaliers.
Jordanie	**Autres pays du monde**	Passeport de l'ONU.
Kiribati	**Total**	Arrivées par voie aérienne. Tarawa et Île Christmas.
Liban	**Total**	À l'exclusion des ressortissants syriens, palestiniens et sous-études.
Maldives	**Total**	Arrivées par voie aérienne.
Malte	**Total**	Données tirées des départs par voies aérienne et maritime.
Mexique	**États-Unis d'Amérique**	Comprend les touristes d'entrée arrivant par voie aérienne et terrestre, les touristes frontaliers et les touristes nationaux résidant aux États-Unis d'Amérique.
Myanmar	**Total**	Comprenant les arrivées de touristes aux postes-frontières de Yangon.
Népal	**Grèce**	Y compris Chypre.
Norvège	**Total**	Les chiffres se fondent sur "l'Enquête auprès de la clientèle" de l'Institut d'Économie des Transports.
Paraguay	**Total**	À l'exclusion des nationaux résidant à l'étranger et des membres des équipages. Cartes d'embarquement et de débarquement à l'aéroport Silvio Petirossi et comptages des passagers lors du franchissement des frontières nationales – Police nationale et SENATUR.
République centrafricaine	**Total**	Arrivées par voie aérienne à Bangui uniquement.
République démocratique du Congo	**Total**	2007-2010 : arrivées par voie aérienne uniquement ; 2011 : les données des entrées ne concernent que 3 postes frontalières (aéroport de N'Djili à Kinshasa ; aéroport de la Luano à Lubumbashi et le poste terrestre de Kasumbalesa de la province du Katanga).
Saint-Martin	**Total**	Arrivées à l'aéroport international "Princess Juliana". Y compris les visiteurs à St. Martin (partie française de l'île).
	France	Y compris les résidents des Antilles françaises.

NOTES 2007 - 2011

1. Arrivées de touristes non résidents aux frontières nationales, par nationalité

Sénégal	**Total**	2008-2011: arrivées par voie aérienne à l'aéroport Léopold Sédar Senghor (LSS) seulement. Y compris les nationaux résidant à l'étranger. Totaux estimés par le pays: 2008: 866.700 2009: 810.000 2010: 900.000 2011: 1.001.000
Soudan	**Total**	Y compris les nationaux résidant à l'étranger.
Sri Lanka	**Total**	À l'exclusion des nationaux résidant à l'étranger.
Tunisie	**Total**	À l'exclusion des nationaux résidant à l'étranger.
Turquie	**Total**	Y compris les citoyens turcs résidant à l'étranger. Enquête faite au départ des visiteurs effectué aux portes d'embarquement.
Venezuela	**Total**	2010,2011: y compris les passagers en croisière: 2010: 9.015; 2011: 30.543.
Yémen	**Total**	Y compris les nationaux résidant à l'étranger.

1. Arrivées de touristes non résidents aux frontières nationales, par nationalité

NOTES 2007 - 2011

1. Arrivées de touristes non résidents aux frontières nationales, par pays de résidence

Afrique du Sud	Total	2007,2008: à l'exclusion des arrivées par travail et les travailleurs contractuels. À partir de 2009, une nouvelle méthodologie a été aplliquée. L'information n'est donc pas comparable à celle des années précédentes.
Andorre	Total	Depuis mai 2009, une nouvelle méthodologie a été aplliquée. L'information n'est donc pas comparable à celle des années précédentes.
Anguilla	Total	À l'exclusion des nationaux résidant à l'étranger.
Antigua-et-Barbuda	Total	Arrivées par voie aérienne. À l'exclusion des nationaux résidant à l'étranger.
Bermudes	Total	Arrivées par voie aérienne.
Curaçao	Total	Arrivées par voie aérienne.
États-Unis d'Amérique	Canada	Les données historiques peuvent refléter les révisions apportées par "Statistics Canada".
	Mexique	Les données historiques peuvent refléter les révisions apportées par "Banco de México".
Éthiopie	Total	2007,2008: arrivées à l'aéroport de Bole seulement. 2009-2011: arrivées à travers tous les ports d'entrée.
Fidji	Total	À l'exclusion des nationaux résidant à l'étranger.
France	Total	Source: DGCIS, Banque de France. Enquête auprès des visiteurs venant de l'étranger (EVE) – résultats 2009 révisés et 2010 provisoires.
	Chine	Y compris Hong-Kong (Chine) et Macao (Chine).
	Suisse	Y compris Liechtenstein.
	Toutes pays Afrique du Nord	Algérie, Égypte, Libye, Maroc et Tunisie.
Grèce	Total	A partir de 2008, l'information est basée sur l'enquête aux frontières réalisée par la Banque de Grèce.
	Égypte	Y compris le Soudan.
	Liban	Y compris la Syrie.
Guadeloupe	Total	Arrivées par voie aérienne.
Guyane	Total	Arrivées à l'aéroport de Timehri seulement.
Haïti	Total	Arrivées par voie aérienne. Depuis 2007, les nationaux résidant à l'étranger sont inclus.
Îles Caïmanes	Total	Arrivées par voie aérienne.
Îles Cook	Total	Arrivées par voies aérienne et maritime.
Îles Marshall	Total	Arrivées par voie aérienne. 2009: arrivées par voies aérienne et maritime.
Irlande	Royaume-Uni	Y compris les arrivées des résidents de l'Irlande du nord. Changement de méthodologie de l'estimation des touristes d'Irlande du Nord en 2010; par conséquent les chiffres antérieurs à 2010 ne sont pas directement comparables.
Israël	Total	À l'exclusion des nationaux résidant à l'étranger. À partir de 2007, à l'exclusion des visiteurs de la journée.
Jamaïque	Total	Arrivées par voie aérienne. À l'inclusion des nationaux résidant à l'étranger.
Malaisie	Total	Y compris les résidents de Singapour traversant la frontière par voie terrestre à travers le Johore Causeway.
Malawi	Total	Départs.
Martinique	Total	Y compris les départements et territoires français d'outremer.
Mexique	Total	Y compris les nationaux résidant à l'étranger.
Népal	Grèce	Y compris Chypre.

NOTES 2007 - 2011

1. Arrivées de touristes non résidents aux frontières nationales, par pays de résidence

Nioué	Total	Y compris les nationaux de Niue résidant habituellement en Nouvelle Zélande.
Nouvelle-Calédonie	Total	Y compris les nationaux résidant à l'étranger.
	Toutes pays Caraïbes	Martinique, Guadeloupe et Guyane.
Palaos	Total	Arrivées par voie aérienne (aéroport international de Palaos).
Pérou	Total	Y compris les nationaux résidant à l'étranger. 2007-2011: données préliminaires.
Philippines	Nationaux résidents à l'étranger	Titulaires d'un passeport philippin résidant en permanence à l'étranger; travailleurs philippins exclus.
Polynésie française	Total	Arrivées par voie aérienne. À l'exclusion des nationaux résidant à l'étranger.
	Samoa	Y compris les Samoa américaines.
Porto Rico	Total	Arrivées par voie aérienne. Année fiscale de juillet à juin. Source: "Junta de Planificación de Puerto Rico".
République dominicaine	Total	Arrivées par voie aérienne.
Réunion	Total	Source: INSEE - Enquête flux touristiques.
Sainte-Lucie	Total	À l'exclusion des nationaux résidant à l'étranger.
Saint-Eustache	Total	À l'exclusion des résidents des Antilles néerlandaises.
Saint-Kitts-et-Nevis	Total	Arrivées par voie aérienne.
Saint-Vincent-et-les Grenadines	Total	Arrivées par voie aérienne.
Sénégal	Total	Arrivées par voie aérienne à l'aéroport Léopold Sédar Senghor (LSS) seulement. Y compris les nationaux résidant à l'étranger. Total 2007: 874.623 Totaux estimés par le pays: 2008: 866.700 2009: 810.000 2010: 900.000 2011: 1.001.000
Sierra Leone	Total	Arrivées par voie aérienne.
Sri Lanka	Total	À l'exclusion des nationaux résidant à l'étranger.
Timor-Leste	Total	Arrivées par voie aérienne à l'aéroport de Dili.
Tonga	Total	Arrivées par voie aérienne.
Trinité-et-Tobago	Total	Arrivées par voie aérienne.

NOTES 2007 - 2011

2. Arrivées de visiteurs non résidents aux frontières nationales, par nationalité

Albanie	**Total**	À l'exclusion des nationaux résidant à l'étranger.
Algérie	**Total**	Y compris les nationaux résidant à l'étranger.
Bahreïn	**Total**	À l'exclusion des nationaux résidant à l'étranger.
Belize	**Total**	Y compris passagers en transit et passagers à la frontière.
Colombie	**Total**	Arrivées de voyageurs étrangers par des points de contrôle du Département administratif de sécurité (DAS). Sont exclus les passagers en croisière et les voyageurs non résidents arrivés par des zones d'intégration frontalière terrestre. Total des arrivées (en milliers) : 2007: 2.381 2008: 2.545 2009: 2.649 2010: 2.681 2010: données selon le pays de résidence.
Corée (République de)	**Total**	Y compris les nationaux résidant à l'étranger et les membres des équipages.
Égypte	**Total**	À l'exclusion des nationaux résidant à l'étranger.
Équateur	**Total**	À l'exclusion des nationaux résidant à l'étranger. 2011: données provisoires.
Guatemala	**Total**	2009-2011: données compilées par pays de résidence.
Italie	**Total**	Enquête aux frontières. À l'exclusion des travailleurs saisonniers et frontaliers.
Japon	**Total**	À l'exclusion des nationaux résidant à l'étranger.
Macao (Chine)	**Total**	Sont exclues, depuis 2008, les données sur les travailleurs non résidents, étudiants, etc. Source des données: Force de sécurité publique
Nigéria	**Total**	Source: "Nigerian Tourism Development Corporation (NTDC)"
Pologne	**Total**	2008-2011: Depuis que la Pologne est entrée dans l'espace Schengen, le comptage précis du trafic entrant n'est pas possible. Les données présentées ici sont basées sur les enquêtes de l'Institut du Tourisme. Seuls des résultats approximatifs des principaux pays peuvent être fournis.
République arabe syrienne	**Total**	Enquête du tourisme récepteur en 2004, 2006 et 2007.
	Iraq	Les citoyens de l'Iraq sont inclus uniquement à partir de 2008 et ont été exclus des années précédentes (depuis le début de l'année 2008, ils doivent demander un visa pour entrer en Syrie ; s'ils sont entrés avant 2008, il est considéré que leur séjour est maintenant supérieur à un an et qu'ils sont de ce fait devenus des résidents).
République de Moldova	**Total**	Visiteurs qui ont bénéficié des services touristiques des agences de tourisme et des voyagistes (titulaires d'une licence touristique). À l'exception de la rive gauche de la rivière Nistru et de la municipalité de Bender.
Singapour	**Total**	À l'exclusion des arrivées de Malaisiens par voie terrestre.
Turquie	**Total**	Y compris les citoyens turcs résidant à l'étranger. Enquête faite au départ des visiteurs effectué aux portes d'embarquement.

NOTES 2007 - 2011

2. Arrivées de visiteurs non résidents aux frontières nationales, par pays de résidence

Afrique du Sud	**Total**	2007,2008: À l'exclusion des nationaux résidant à l'étranger. Y compris les arrivées par motif de vacances, affaires, études, travail, transit, trafic frontalier et travailleurs contractuels. À partir de 2009, une nouvelle méthodologie a été apIIiquée. L'information n'est donc pas comparable à celle des années précédentes.
Australie	**Total**	À l'exclusion des nationaux résidant à l'étranger et les membres des équipages. Source: "Australian Bureau of Statistics"
Canada	**Chine**	Y compris la Mongolie et le Tibet.
	Danemark	Y compris les Îles Féroé.
	Estonie	Y compris la Lettonie et la Lituanie.
	France	Y compris Andorre et Monaco.
	Italie	Y compris Saint-Marin, le Saint Siège et Malte.
	Suisse	Y compris le Liechtenstein.
Finlande	**Total**	Enquête aux frontières.
Hong-Kong (Chine)	**États-Unis d'Amérique**	Y compris Guam.
	France	Y compris la Nouvelle-Calédonie et la Polynésie française.
	Nouvelle-Zélande	Y compris les Îles Cook.
Israël	**Total**	À l'exclusion des nationaux résidant à l'étranger.
Lettonie	**Total**	Départs des non-résidents. Enquête auprès des personnes qui traversent les frontières du pays.
Macao (Chine)	**Total**	Sont exclues, depuis 2008, les données sur les travailleurs non résidents, étudiants, etc. Source des données: Force de sécurité publique
Mozambique	**Total**	Note 2008: Changement de méthodologie. Jusqu'en 2007, les données correspondent seulement à 12 postes frontaliers. A partir de 2008, les données de tous les postes frontaliers du pays sont utilisées.
Nouvelle-Zélande	**Total**	Les données relatives aux mouvements de courte durée sont obtenues à partir d'un échantillon aléatoire de déclarations des passagers. Y compris les nationaux résidant à l'étranger. Source: Statistiques de la Nouvelle Zélande ("International Travel and Migration").
Panama	**Total**	Nombre total de visiteurs arrivés au Panama par l'aéroport international de Tocumen, classés selon leur résidence permanente.
Saint-Vincent-et-les Grenadines	**Total**	Arrivées par voie aérienne.
Singapour	**Total**	À l'exclusion des arrivées de Malaisiens par voie terrestre.
Suède	**Total**	Données pour 2011 d'après la nouvelle enquête aux frontières nationales (IBIS, visiteurs entrant en Suède). Pas de données recueillies entre 2004 et 2010. La nouvelle enquête à la frontière (IBIS) a commencé en 2011. Source : Agence suédoise pour la croissance économique et régionale.

NOTES 2007 - 2011

3. Arrivées de touristes non résidents dans les hôtels et établissements assimilés, par nationalité

Bolivie	Total	2007-2010: données préliminaires. Mouvement hôtelier dans les capitales de département.
Italie	Total	Arrivées dans les hôtels uniquement.
Maroc	Total	Arrivées dans les hôtels homologués, villages de vacances, résidences touristiques et Riad.
République arabe syrienne	Total	Enquête du tourisme récepteur en 2004, 2006 et 2007.
	Iraq	Les citoyens de l'Iraq sont inclus uniquement à partir de 2008 et ont été exclus des années précédentes (depuis le début de l'année 2008, ils doivent demander un visa pour entrer en Syrie ; s'ils sont entrés avant 2008, il est considéré que leur séjour est maintenant supérieur à un an et qu'ils sont de ce fait devenus des résidents).
Slovénie	Total	2008: Nouvelle méthodologie de l'enquête sur l'hébergement.
Tchad	Total	2010: Données partielles.
Turquie	Total	Arrivées dans les établissements homologues y compris: hôtels, motels, pensions, auberges, hôtels-appartements, villages de vacances et hôtels spéciaux. Résultats de l'enquête mensuelle réalisée auprès des établissements d'hébergement classés par le Ministère du Tourisme.

NOTES 2007 - 2011

3. Arrivées de touristes non résidents dans les hôtels et établissements assimilés, par pays de résidence

Allemagne	**Chine**	Y compris Hong-Kong, Chine.
Autriche	**Total**	Hôtels uniquement.
Cap-Vert	**Belgique**	Y compris les Pays-Bas.
Congo	**Total**	Source: Direction Générale de l'Industrie Touristique, enquêtes 2007 à 2010
Croatie	**Total**	Conformément au Règlement sur la classification, les normes minimales et la catégorisation des structures d'hébergement, les données relatives aux hôtels et établissements assimilés ne comprennent pas les auberges et chambres d'hôtes depuis 2006.
Curaçao	**Total**	Grands et petits hôtels, pensions de famille, appartements et bungalows.
Danemark	**Total**	Hôtels uniquement. 2011: changement de méthodologie.
Espagne	**Total**	Arrivées dans les hôtels et les "hostales" (établissements d'hébergement offrant des services limités).
France	**Total**	Source: INSEE, DGCIS, partenaires régionaux. Enquête de fréquentation hôtelière (EFH). Y compris hôtels non homologués.
	Autres pays Asie Est/Pacifique	Y compris l'Inde.
Israël	**Total**	Arrivées dans les hôtels de tourisme et les hôtels non encore enregistrés.
	Toutes pays Amérique du Sud	Y compris l'Amérique centrale.
Luxembourg	**Total**	Arrivées dans les hôtels, pensions de famille et auberges.
Macao (Chine)	**Total**	Source des données: Enquête mensuelle auprès des agences de voyage
Nouvelle-Calédonie	**Total**	Il s'agit des hôtels de Nouméa.
Pays-Bas	**Total**	Hôtels et pensions.
Philippines	**Total**	Arrivées par voie aérienne.
	Nationaux résidents à l'étranger	Titulaires d'un passeport philippin résidant en permanence à l'étranger; travailleurs philippins exclus.
Pologne	**Total**	À l'exclusion des hôtelleries.
Porto Rico	**Total**	Année fiscale de juillet à juin. Hôtels enregistrés par la "Compañía de Turismo de Puerto Rico".
	Autres pays Caraïbes	Les données agrégées des touristes en provenance des petites Antilles qui n'ont pas spécifié leur pays d'origine son inclues.
	Autres pays du monde	Y compris les membres des équipages.
Qatar	**Total**	Arrivées dans les hôtels uniquement. 2007-2009: y compris le tourisme interne.
	Toutes pays d'Europe	2010-2011: Europe et Amériques.
Roumanie	**Toutes les pays d'Afrique**	Y compris l'Égypte et la Libye.
Suisse	**Total**	Y compris les établissements de cure.
	Toutes pays Afrique du Nord	Algérie, Libye, Maroc et Tunisie.
Togo	**Burkina Faso**	Y compris le Mali et le Niger.

NOTES 2007 - 2011

4. Arrivées de touristes non résidents dans tous les types d'établissements d'hébergement, par nationalité

Hongrie	**Total**	Établissements d'hébergement collectif.
République arabe syrienne	**Total**	À l'exclusion de l'hébergement chez des particuliers. Enquête du tourisme récepteur en 2004, 2006 et 2007.
	Iraq	Les citoyens de l'Iraq sont inclus uniquement à partir de 2008 et ont été exclus des années précédentes (depuis le début de l'année 2008, ils doivent demander un visa pour entrer en Syrie ; s'ils sont entrés avant 2008, il est considéré que leur séjour est maintenant supérieur à un an et qu'ils sont de ce fait devenus des résidents).
République de Moldova	**Total**	À l'exception de la rive gauche de la rivière Nistru et de la municipalité de Bender.
Slovénie	**Total**	2008: Nouvelle méthodologie de l'enquête sur l'hébergement.
Turquie	**Total**	Résultats de l'enquête mensuelle réalisée auprès des établissements d'hébergement classés par le Ministère du Tourisme.

NOTES 2007 - 2011

4. Arrivées de touristes non résidents dans tous les types d'établissements d'hébergement, par pays de résidence

Allemagne	**Chine**	Y compris Hong-Kong, Chine.
Autriche	**Total**	Seulement logement payé; sont exclus les séjours chez des amis et membres de la famille et des résidences secondaires.
Belgique	**Total**	Établissements hôteliers, terrains de camping, centres de vacances, villages de vacances et catégories spécifiques d'hébergement.
Croatie	**Total**	À l'exclusion des arrivées dans des ports à tourisme nautique.
Danemark	**Total**	Y compris le tourisme non commercial. 2011: changement de méthodologie.
	Autres pays Asie Est/Pacifique	Y compris l'Inde.
Espagne	**Total**	Arrivées dans hôtels, "hostales", camping, appartements touristiques et logements ruraux.
Luxembourg	**Total**	Hôtels, auberges, pensions de famille, auberges de jeunesse, logements touristiques privés, terrains de camping et autres.
Malte	**Total**	Données tirées des départs par voies aérienne et maritime. Source: "National Statistics Office".
Philippines	**Total**	Arrivées par voie aérienne.
	Nationaux résidents à l'étranger	Titulaires d'un passeport philippin résidant en permanence à l'étranger; travailleurs philippins exclus.
Roumanie	**Toutes les pays d'Afrique**	Y compris l'Égypte et la Libye.

NOTES 2007 - 2011

5. Nuitées de touristes non résidents dans les hôtels et établissements assimilés, par nationalité

Bolivie	**Total**	2007-2010: données préliminaires. Nuitées dans les capitales de département.
Italie	**Total**	Nuitées dans les hôtels uniquement.
Madagascar	**Total**	Établissements de classe étoile (classés et non classés).
Maroc	**Total**	Nuitées dans les hôtels homologués, villages de vacances, résidences touristiques et Riad.
Norvège	**Total**	Nuitées dans les établissements homologués. Les données ne couvrent que les établissements avec une capacité d'au moins 20 lits.
République arabe syrienne	**Total**	Enquête du tourisme récepteur en 2004, 2006 et 2007.
	Iraq	Les citoyens de l'Iraq sont inclus uniquement à partir de 2008 et ont été exclus des années précédentes (depuis le début de l'année 2008, ils doivent demander un visa pour entrer en Syrie ; s'ils sont entrés avant 2008, il est considéré que leur séjour est maintenant supérieur à un an et qu'ils sont de ce fait devenus des résidents).
Slovénie	**Total**	2008: Nouvelle méthodologie de l'enquête sur l'hébergement.
Tchad	**Total**	2010: Données partielles.
Turquie	**Total**	Hôtels classés, motels, pensions de familles, auberges, aparthôtels, villages de vacances et hôtels spéciaux. Résultats de l'enquête mensuelle réalisée auprès des établissements d'hébergement classés par le Ministère du Tourisme.
Yémen	**Total**	Y compris les nationaux résidant à l'étranger.

NOTES 2007 - 2011

5. Nuitées de touristes non résidents dans les hôtels et établissements assimilés, par pays de résidence

Allemagne	**Chine**	Y compris Hong-Kong, Chine.
Autriche	**Total**	Hôtels uniquement.
Cap-Vert	**Belgique**	Y compris les Pays-Bas.
Congo	**Total**	Source: Direction Générale de l'Industrie Touristique, enquêtes 2007 à 2010
Croatie	**Total**	Conformément au Règlement sur la classification, les normes minimales et la catégorisation des structures d'hébergement, les données relatives aux hôtels et établissements assimilés ne comprennent pas les auberges et chambres d'hôtes depuis 2006.
Danemark	**Total**	Hôtels uniquement. 2011: changement de méthodologie.
Espagne	**Total**	Nuitées dans les hôtels et les "hostales" (établissements d'hébergement offrant des services limités).
France	**Total**	Source: INSEE, DGCIS, partenaires régionaux. Enquête de fréquentation hôtelière (EFH). Y compris hôtels non homologués.
	Autres pays Asie Est/Pacifique	Y compris l'Inde.
Israël	**Total**	Nuitées dans les hôtels de tourisme et aparthôtels.
	Toutes pays Amérique du Sud	Y compris l'Amérique centrale.
Luxembourg	**Total**	Nuitées dans les hôtels, pensions de famille et auberges.
Macao (Chine)	**Total**	Source des données: Enquête mensuelle auprès des hôtels et établissements comparables
Nouvelle-Calédonie	**Total**	Il s'agit des hôtels de Nouméa.
Pays-Bas	**Total**	Hôtels et pensions.
Pologne	**Total**	À l'exclusion des hôtelleries.
Qatar	**Total**	Nuitées dans les hôtels uniquement. 2007-2009: y compris le tourisme interne.
	Toutes pays d'Europe	2010-2011: Europe et Amériques.
Roumanie	**Toutes les pays d'Afrique**	Y compris l'Égypte et la Libye.
Suède	**Total**	Nuitées dans les hôtels uniquement.
Suisse	**Total**	Y compris les établissements de cure.
	Toutes pays Afrique du Nord	Algérie, Libye, Maroc et Tunisie.
Togo	**Burkina Faso**	Y compris le Mali et le Niger.

NOTES 2007 - 2011

6. Nuitées de touristes non résidents dans tous les types d'établissements d'hébergement, par nationalité

Hongrie	**Total**	Établissements d'hébergement collectif.
République arabe syrienne	**Total**	Enquête du tourisme récepteur en 2004, 2006 et 2007.
	Iraq	Les citoyens de l'Iraq sont inclus uniquement à partir de 2008 et ont été exclus des années précédentes (depuis le début de l'année 2008, ils doivent demander un visa pour entrer en Syrie ; s'ils sont entrés avant 2008, il est considéré que leur séjour est maintenant supérieur à un an et qu'ils sont de ce fait devenus des résidents).
République de Moldova	**Total**	À l'exception de la rive gauche de la rivière Nistru et de la municipalité de Bender.
Slovénie	**Total**	2008: Nouvelle méthodologie de l'enquête sur l'hébergement.
Turquie	**Total**	Résultats de l'enquête mensuelle réalisée auprès des établissements d'hébergement classés par le Ministère du Tourisme.

NOTES 2007 - 2011

6. Nuitées de touristes non résidents dans tous les types d'établissements d'hébergement, par pays de résidence

Allemagne	**Chine**	Y compris Hong-Kong, Chine.
Autriche	**Total**	Seulement logement payé; sont exclus les séjours chez des amis et membres de la famille et des résidences secondaires.
Bahamas	**Total**	Nuitées dans tout moyen d'hébergement commercial.
Belgique	**Total**	Établissements hôteliers, terrains de camping, centres de vacances, villages de vacances et catégories spécifiques d'hébergement.
Canada	**Chine**	Y compris la Mongolie et le Tibet.
	Danemark	Y compris les Îles Féroé.
	Estonie	Y compris la Lettonie et la Lituanie.
	France	Y compris Andorre et Monaco.
	Italie	Y compris Saint-Marin, le Saint Siège et Malte.
	Suisse	Y compris le Liechtenstein.
Croatie	**Total**	À l'exclusion des nuitées dans des ports à tourisme nautique.
Danemark	**Total**	Y compris le tourisme non commercial. 2011: changement de méthodologie.
Espagne	**Total**	Nuitées dans hôtels, "hostales", camping, appartements touristiques et logements ruraux.
France	**Total**	Source: DGCIS, Banque de France. Enquête auprès des visiteurs venant de l'étranger (EVE) – résultats 2009 révisés et 2010 provisoires.
	Chine	Y compris Hong-Kong (Chine) et Macao (Chine).
	Suisse	Y compris Liechtenstein.
	Toutes pays Afrique du Nord	Algérie, Égypte, Libye, Maroc et Tunisie.
	Autres pays Asie Est/Pacifique	Y compris l'Inde.
Irlande	**Total**	Y compris nuitées dans hébergement privé non payant (maisons privées et maisons de vacances).
	Royaume-Uni	Y compris les résidents de l'Irlande du Nord.
Jamaïque	**Total**	L'information à été obtenue en multipliant la durée moyenne de séjour par le nombre de touristes (stop-over) provenant de chaque pays d'origine. À l'exclusion des nationaux résidant à l'étranger.
	Autres pays Amériques	Amérique latine.
	Toutes pays d'Europe	Royaume-Uni et le reste de l'Europe.
Malte	**Total**	Données tirées des départs par voies aérienne et maritime. Source: "National Statistics Office".
Pays-Bas	**Total**	À l'exclusion des nuitées dans des installations fixes (louées sur une base annuelle ou saisonnière).
Roumanie	**Toutes les pays d'Afrique**	Y compris l'Égypte et la Libye.
Suède	**Total**	2007: Nuitées dans les hôtels, auberges de jeunesse, villages de vacances et camping. 2008-2011: Nuitées dans les hôtels, auberges de jeunesse, villages de vacances, camping et location de chalets et d'appartements privés par l'intermédiaire d'une agence.

NOTAS 2007 - 2011

1. Llegadas de turistas no residentes en las fronteras nacionales, por nacionalidad

Belarús	Total	Turismo organizado.
Bhután	Total	Total de llegadas 2010: 40.873; 2011: 65.756. El gran margen de diferencia en 2010 y 2011 en comparación con los años anteriores se debe a que a partir de 2010 se incluyen en las cifras totales los turistas regionales de alto nivel de renta.
Bolivia	Total	2007-2010: datos preliminares.
Brunei Darussalam	Total	Llegadas por vía aérea.
Burundi	Total	Incluidos los nacionales residentes en el extranjero. A partir de 2010: ruptura en la serie debido a la implementación de una mejora en la metodología que distingue a los visitantes (turistas) de otros viajeros.
Comoras	Total	Llegadas por vía aérea.
Gambia	Total	Llegadas en vuelos fletados únicamente.
Honduras	Total	Excluidas las llegadas de turistas por vía marítima.
India	Total	Excluidos los nacionales residentes en el extranjero.
Islandia	Total	Fuente: "Icelandic Tourist Board".
Islas Marshall	Total	Llegadas por vía aérea. 2009: llegadas por vías aérea y marítima.
	Otros países del Mundo	Incluye turistas fronterizos de la zona sur.
Italia	Total	Excluidos los trabajadores estacionales y fronterizos.
Jordania	Otros países del Mundo	Pasaporte de la ONU.
Kiribati	Total	Llegadas por vía aérea. Tarawa e Isla Christmas.
Líbano	Total	Excluidos nacionales de Siria, Palestina y estudiantes.
Maldivas	Total	Llegadas por vía aérea.
Malta	Total	Datos procedentes de las salidas por vías aérea y marítima.
México	Estados Unidos de América	Incluye turistas de internación vía aérea y terrestre, turistas fronterizos y turistas nacionales residentes en los Estados Unidos de Américas.
Myanmar	Total	Incluidas las llegadas de turistas a través de los puntos de entrada fronterizos a Yangon.
Nepal	Grecia	Incluido Chipre.
Noruega	Total	Las cifras se basan en "The Guest Survey", un estudio realizado por el "Institute of Transport Economics".
Paraguay	Total	Excluidos los nacionales residentes en el extranjero y los miembros de tripulaciones. Tarjetas E/D en el aeropuerto Silvio Petirossi y planillas de pasajeros en los puestos terrestres - Policía Nacional y SENATUR.
República Centroafricana	Total	Llegadas por vía aérea a Bangui únicamente.
República Democrática del Congo	Total	2007-2010: llegadas por vía aérea únicamente; 2011: los datos de entradas se refieren solo a 3 puestos fronterizos (aeropuerto de N'Djili, en Kinshasa; aeropuerto de Luano, en Lubumbashi, y puesto terrestre de Kasumbalesa, en la provincia de Katanga).
San Martín	Total	Llegadas al aeropuerto internacional "Princess Juliana". Incluidos los visitantes a San Martín (parte francesa de la isla).
	Francia	Incluidos los residentes de las Antillas Francesas.

NOTAS 2007 - 2011

1. Llegadas de turistas no residentes en las fronteras nacionales, por nacionalidad

Senegal	**Total**	2008-2011: llegadas por vía aérea al aeropuerto "Léopold Sédar Senghor (LSS)" únicamente. Incluidos los nacionales residentes en el extranjero. Totales estimados por el país: 2008: 866.700 2009: 810.000 2010: 900.000 2011: 1.001.000
Sri Lanka	**Total**	Excluidos los nacionales residentes en el extranjero.
Sudán	**Total**	Incluidos los nacionales residentes en el extranjero.
Túnez	**Total**	Excluidos los nacionales residentes en el extranjero.
Turquía	**Total**	Incluidos los ciudadanos turcos residentes en el extranjero. Encuesta a la salida de los visitantes que se lleva a cabo en las puertas de embarque.
Venezuela	**Total**	2010,2011: incluye pasajeros en crucero: 2010: 9.015; 2011: 30.543.
Yemen	**Total**	Incluidos los nacionales residentes en el extranjero.

NOTAS 2007 - 2011

1. Llegadas de turistas no residentes en las fronteras nacionales, por país de residencia

Andorra	**Total**	Desde mayo de 2009 se aplicó una nueva metodología y por lo tanto la información no es comparable con años anteriores.
Anguila	**Total**	Excluidos los nacionales residentes en el extranjero.
Antigua y Barbuda	**Total**	Llegadas por vía aérea. Excluidos los nacionales residentes en el extranjero.
Bermuda	**Total**	Llegadas por vía aérea.
Curaçao	**Total**	Llegadas por vía aérea.
Estados Unidos de América	**Canadá**	Los datos históricos pueden reflejar revisiones hechas por "Statistics Canada".
	México	Los datos históricos pueden reflejar revisiones hechas por "Banco de México".
Etiopía	**Total**	2007,2008: llegadas al aeropuerto de Bole únicamente. 2009-2011: llegadas a todos los puestos fronterizos.
Fiji	**Total**	Excluidos los nacionales residentes en el extranjero.
Filipinas	**Nacionales residentes en el extranjero**	Titulares de pasaportes filipino que residen permanentemente en el extranjero; están excluidos los trabajadores filipinos.
Francia	**Total**	Fuente: "DGCIS", "Banque de France". Encuesta a los visitantes que vienen del extranjero ("EVE") - resultados 2009 revisados y 2010 provisionales
	China	Incluye Hong-Kong (China) y Macao (China).
	Suiza	Incluye Liechtentein.
	Todos los países de África del Norte	Argelia, Egipto, Libia, Marruecos y Túnez.
Grecia	**Total**	A partir de 2008, la información se basa en la encuesta en fronteras realizada por el Banco de Grecia.
	Egipto	Incluido Sudán.
	Líbano	Incluido Siria.
Guadalupe	**Total**	Llegadas por vía aérea.
Guyana	**Total**	Llegadas al aeropuerto de Timehri únicamente.
Haití	**Total**	Llegadas por vía aérea. A partir de 2007 se incluye a los nacionales residentes en el extranjero.
Irlanda	**Reino Unido**	Incluidas las llegadas de los residentes de Irlanda del Norte. Cambio en la metodología de estimación de turistas del norte de Irlanda en 2010; como resultado las cifras anteriores a 2010 no son directamente comparables.
Islas Caimán	**Total**	Llegadas por vía aérea.
Islas Cook	**Total**	Llegadas por vías aérea y marítima.
Islas Marshall	**Total**	Llegadas por vía aérea. 2009: llegadas por vías aérea y marítima.
Israel	**Total**	Excluidos los nacionales residentes en el extranjero. A partir de 2007, excluidos los visitantes del día.
Jamaica	**Total**	Llegadas por vía aérea. Incluidos los nacionales residentes en el extranjero.
Malasia	**Total**	Incluidos residentes de Singapur que atraviesan la frontera por vía terrestre a través de Johore Causeway.
Malawi	**Total**	Salidas.
Martinica	**Total**	Incluidos los departamentos y territorios franceses de ultramar.
México	**Total**	Incluidos los nacionales residentes en el extranjero.
Nepal	**Grecia**	Incluido Chipre.
Niue	**Total**	Incluidos los nacionales de Niue que residen habitualmente en Nueva Zelandia.

NOTAS 2007 - 2011

1. Llegadas de turistas no residentes en las fronteras nacionales, por país de residencia

Nueva Caledonia	**Total**	Incluidos los nacionales residentes en el extranjero.
	Todos los países del Caribe	Martinica, Guadalupe y Guyana.
Palau	**Total**	Llegadas por vía aérea (aeropuerto internacional de Palau).
Perú	**Total**	Incluidos los nacionales residentes en el extranjero. 2007-2011: datos preliminares.
Polinesia Francesa	**Total**	Llegadas por vía aérea. Excluidos los nacionales residentes en el extranjero.
	Samoa	Incluida Samoa americana.
Puerto Rico	**Total**	Llegadas por vía aérea. Año fiscal de julio a junio. Fuente: Junta de Planificación de Puerto Rico.
República Dominicana	**Total**	Llegadas por vía aérea.
Reunión	**Total**	Fuente: INSEE, encuesta de flujos turísticos
San Eustaquio	**Total**	Excluidos los residentes de las Antillas neerlandesas.
Saint Kitts y Nevis	**Total**	Llegadas por vía aérea.
San Vicente y las Granadinas	**Total**	Llegadas por vía aérea.
Santa Lucía	**Total**	Excluidos los nacionales residentes en el extranjero.
Senegal	**Total**	Llegadas por vía aérea al aeropuerto "Léopold Sédar Senghor (LSS)" únicamente. Incluidos los nacionales residentes en el extranjero. Total 2007: 874.623 Totales estimados por el país: 2008: 866.700 2009: 810.000 2010: 900.000 2011: 1.001.000
Sierra Leona	**Total**	Llegadas por vía aérea.
Sri Lanka	**Total**	Excluidos los nacionales residentes en el extranjero.
Sudáfrica	**Total**	2007,2008: excluidas las llegadas por trabajo y los trabajadores con contrato. A partir de 2009 se aplicó una nueva metodología y por lo tanto la información no es comparable con años anteriores.
Timor-Leste	**Total**	Llegadas por vía aérea al aeropuerto de Dili.
Tonga	**Total**	Llegadas por vía aérea.
Trinidad y Tabago	**Total**	Llegadas por vía aérea.

NOTAS 2007 - 2011

2. Llegadas de visitantes no residentes en las fronteras nacionales, por nacionalidad

Albania	Total	Excluidos los nacionales residentes en el extranjero.
Argelia	Total	Incluidos los nacionales residentes en el extranjero.
Bahrein	Total	Excluidos los nacionales residentes en el extranjero.
Belice	Total	Incluidos pasajeros en tránsito y cruce de fronteras.
Colombia	Total	Llegadas de viajeros extranjeros por puntos de control del Departamento Administrativo de Seguridad (DAS). Excluidos los pasajeros en crucero y los viajeros no residentes llegados por zonas de integración fronteriza terrestre. Total de llegadas (en miles): 2007: 2.381 2008: 2.545 2009: 2.649 2010: 2.681 2010: datos según país de residencia.
Corea (República de)	Total	Incluidos los nacionales residentes en el extranjero y los miembros de las tripulaciones.
Ecuador	Total	Excluidos los nacionales residentes en el extranjero. 2011: datos provisionales.
Egipto	Total	Excluidos los nacionales residentes en el extranjero.
Guatemala	Total	2009-2011: datos compilados por país de residencia.
Italia	Total	Encuesta en fronteras. Excluidos los trabajadores estacionales y fronterizos.
Japón	Total	Excluidos los nacionales residentes en el extranjero.
Macao (China)	Total	Desde 2008, excluidos los datos sobre trabajadores no residentes, estudiantes, etc. Fuente de los datos: Fuerza de seguridad pública
Nigeria	Total	Fuente: "Nigerian Tourism Development Corporation (NTDC)"
Polonia	Total	2008-2011: Dado que Polonia se unió al espacio Schengen, el recuento preciso de tráfico entrante no es posible. Los datos presentados aquí se basan en encuestas realizadas por el Instituto de Turismo. Únicamente se cuenta con resultados aproximados de los principales países.
República Árabe Siria	Total	Encuesta del turismo receptor en 2004, 2006 y 2007.
	Iraq	Los nacionales de Iraq se incluyen únicamente a partir de 2008 y se han excluido en los años anteriores (desde principios de 2008, tienen que pedir un visado para entrar en Siria; si entraron anteriormente a esa fecha, se considera que han permanecido por un periodo superior a un año, convirtiéndose en residentes).
República de Moldova	Total	Visitantes que se beneficiaron de los servicios turísticos de las agencias de turismo y operadores turísticos (titulares de licencias turísticas). Excluido el margen izquierdo del río Nistru y la municipalidad de Bender.
Singapur	Total	Excluidas llegadas de los malasios por vía terrestre.
Turquía	Total	Incluidos los ciudadanos turcos residentes en el extranjero. Encuesta a la salida de los visitantes que se lleva a cabo en las puertas de embarque.

NOTAS 2007 - 2011

2. Llegadas de visitantes no residentes en las fronteras nacionales, por país de residencia

Australia	**Total**	Excluidos los nacionales residentes en el extranjero y los miembros de tripulaciones. Fuente: "Australian Bureau of Statistics"
Canadá	**China**	Incluido Mongolia y Tibet.
	Dinamarca	Incluido las Islas Feroe.
	Estonia	Incluido Letonia y Lituania.
	Francia	Incluido Andorra y Mónaco.
	Italia	Incluido San Marino, la Santa Sede y Malta.
	Suiza	Incluido Liechtenstein.
Finlandia	**Total**	Encuesta en las fronteras.
Hong Kong (China)	**Estados Unidos de América**	Incluido Guam.
	Francia	Incluidas Nueva Caledonia y la Polinesia Francesa.
	Nueva Zelandia	Incluidas las Islas Cook.
Israel	**Total**	Excluidos los nacionales residentes en el extranjero.
Letonia	**Total**	Salidas de no residentes. Encuesta realizada en los puestos fronterizos del país.
Macao (China)	**Total**	Desde 2008, excluidos los datos sobre trabajadores no residentes, estudiantes, etc. Fuente de los datos: Fuerza de seguridad pública
Mozambique	**Total**	Nota 2008: Cambio de metodología. Hasta 2007 los datos corresponden únicamente a 12 puestos fronterizos. A partir de 2008 se utilizan los datos de todos los puestos fronterizos del país.
Nueva Zelandia	**Total**	Los datos relativos a los movimientos de corta duración se obtienen de una muestra aleatoria de declaraciones de los pasajeros. Incluidos los nacionales residentes en el extranjero. Fuente: Estadísticas Nueva Zelanda ("International Travel and Migration").
Panamá	**Total**	Total de visitantes ingresados a Panamá por el aeropuerto internacional de Tocumen según domicilio permanente.
San Vicente y las Granadinas	**Total**	Llegadas por vía aérea.
Singapur	**Total**	Excluidas llegadas de los malasios por vía terrestre.
Sudáfrica	**Total**	2007,2008: Excluidos los nacionales residentes en el extranjero. Incluidas las llegadas por motivo de vacaciones, negocios, estudios, trabajo, tránsito, tráfico fronterizo y trabajadores con contrato. A partir de 2009 se aplicó una nueva metodología y por lo tanto la información no es comparable con años anteriores.
Suecia	**Total**	Datos para 2011 según una nueva encuesta nacional de fronteras (IBIS, visitantes que entran en Suecia). De 2004 a 2010 no se recopilaron datos. La nueva encuesta de fronteras (IBIS) se empezó a realizar en 2011. Fuente: Agencia Sueca de Crecimiento Económico y Regional.

NOTAS 2007 - 2011

3. Llegadas de turistas no residentes a los hoteles y establecimientos asimilados, por nacionalidad

Bolivia	**Total**	2007-2010: datos preliminares. Movimiento hotelero en las capitales de departamento.
Chad	**Total**	2010: Datos parciales.
Eslovenia	**Total**	2008: Nueva metodología de la encuesta de alojamiento.
Italia	**Total**	Llegadas a los hoteles únicamente.
Marruecos	**Total**	Llegadas en hoteles homologados, ciudades de vacaciones, residencias turísticas y Riad.
República Árabe Siria	**Total**	Encuesta del turismo receptor en 2004, 2006 y 2007.
	Iraq	Los nacionales de Iraq se incluyen únicamente a partir de 2008 y se han excluido en los años anteriores (desde principios de 2008, tienen que pedir un visado para entrar en Siria; si entraron anteriormente a esa fecha, se considera que han permanecido por un periodo superior a un año, convirtiéndose en residentes).
Turquía	**Total**	Llegadas a los establecimientos homologados incluidos: hoteles, moteles, pensiones, albergues, apartahoteles, ciudades de vacaciones y hoteles especiales. Resultados de la encuesta mensual realizada en ciertos establecimientos de alojamiento clasificados por el Ministerio de Turismo.

NOTAS 2007 - 2011

3. Llegadas de turistas no residentes a los hoteles y establecimientos asimilados, por país de residencia

Alemania	China	Incluido Hong Kong, China.
Austria	Total	Hoteles únicamente.
Cabo Verde	Bélgica	Incluido los Países Bajos.
Congo	Total	Fuente: "Direction Générale de l'Industrie Touristique", encuestas 2007 a 2010
Croacia	Total	Según el Reglamento sobre clasificación, normas mínimas y categorización de las instalaciones de alojamiento, los datos para los hoteles y establecimientos asimilados no incluyen hostales ni habitaciones con desayuno desde 2006.
Curaçao	Total	Grandes y pequeños hoteles, casas de huéspedes, apartamentos y bungalows.
Dinamarca	Total	Hoteles únicamente. 2011: cambio de metodología.
España	Total	Llegadas a hoteles y hostales.
Filipinas	Total	Llegadas por vía aérea.
	Nacionales residentes en el extranjero	Titulares de pasaportes filipinos que residen permanentemente en el extranjero; están excluidos los trabajadores filipinos.
Francia	Total	Fuente: "INSEE", "DGCIS", socios regionales. Encuesta de ocupación hotelera ("EFH"). Incluidos hoteles sin clasificar.
	Otros países Asia Oriental/Pacífico	Incluido la India.
Israel	Total	Llegadas a los hoteles de turismo en aquellos aun no homologados.
	Todos los países de América del Sur	Incluida América Central.
Luxemburgo	Total	Llegadas en hoteles, casas de huéspedes y albergues.
Macao (China)	Total	Fuente de los datos: Encuesta mensual de agencias de viajes
Nueva Caledonia	Total	Corresponde a los hoteles de Noumea.
Países Bajos	Total	Hoteles y pensiones.
Polonia	Total	Excluidos los hostales.
Puerto Rico	Total	Año fiscal de julio a junio. Hoteles endosados por la Compañía de Turismo de Puerto Rico.
	Otros países del Caribe	Se incluyen cifras agregadas de los turistas procedentes de las Antillas menores que no especificaron su país de procedencia.
	Otros países del Mundo	Incluye a los miembros de las tripulaciones.
Qatar	Total	Llegadas a los hoteles únicamente. 2007-2009: incluido el turismo interno.
	Todos los países de Europa	2010-2011: Europa y Américas
Rumania	Todos los países de África	Incluido Egipto y Libia.
Suiza	Total	Incluye los establecimientos de cura.
	Todos los países de África del Norte	Argelia, Libia, Marruecos y Túnez.
Togo	Burkina Faso	Incluidos Malí y Níger.

NOTAS 2007 - 2011

4. Llegadas de turistas no residentes en todo tipo de establecimientos de alojamiento, por nacionalidad

Eslovenia	**Total**	2008: Nueva metodología de la encuesta de alojamiento.
Hungría	**Total**	Establecimientos de alojamiento colectivo.
República Árabe Siria	**Total**	Se excluye el alojamiento privado. Encuesta del turismo receptor en 2004, 2006 y 2007.
República de Moldova	**Total**	Excluido el margen izquierdo del río Nistru y la municipalidad de Bender.
	Iraq	Los nacionales de Iraq se incluyen únicamente a partir de 2008 y se han excluido en los años anteriores (desde principios de 2008, tienen que pedir un visado para entrar en Siria; si entraron anteriormente a esa fecha, se considera que han permanecido por un periodo superior a un año, convirtiéndose en residentes).
Turquía	**Total**	Resultados de la encuesta mensual realizada en ciertos establecimientos de alojamiento clasificados por el Ministerio de Turismo.

NOTAS 2007 - 2011

4. Llegadas de turistas no residentes en todo tipo de establecimientos de alojamiento, por país de residencia

Alemania	**China**	Incluido Hong Kong, China.
Austria	**Total**	Únicamente alojamiento de pago; excluidas las estancias con amigos y familiares y las viviendas secundarias.
Bélgica	**Total**	Establecimientos hoteleros, terrenos de camping, centros vacacionales, ciudades de vacaciones y categorías específicas de alojamiento.
Croacia	**Total**	Excluidas las llegadas a puertos de turismo náutico.
Dinamarca	**Total**	Incluye el turismo no comercial. 2011: cambio de metodología.
	Otros países Asia Oriental/Pacífico	Incluido la India.
España	**Total**	Llegadas en hoteles, hostales, camping, apartamentos turísticos y alojamientos/casas rurales.
Filipinas	**Total**	Llegadas por vía aérea.
	Nacionales residentes en el extranjero	Titulares de pasaportes filipinos que residen permanentemente en el extranjero; están excluidos los trabajadores filipinos.
Luxemburgo	**Total**	Hoteles, albergues, casas de huéspedes, albergues de juventud, alojamientos turísticos privados, terrenos de camping y otros.
Malta	**Total**	Datos procedentes de las salidas por vías aérea y marítima. Fuente: "National Statistics Office".
Rumania	**Todos los países de África**	Incluido Egipto y Libia.

NOTAS 2007 - 2011

5. Pernoctaciones de turistas no residentes en hoteles y establecimientos asimilados, por nacionalidad

Bolivia	**Total**	2007-2010: datos preliminares. Pernoctaciones en las capitales de departamento.
Chad	**Total**	2010: Datos parciales.
Eslovenia	**Total**	2008: Nueva metodología de la encuesta de alojamiento.
Italia	**Total**	Pernoctaciones en los hoteles únicamente.
Madagascar	**Total**	Todos los establecimientos categorizados por estrellas (homologados y no homologados).
Marruecos	**Total**	Pernoctaciones en hoteles homologados, ciudades de vacaciones, residencias turísticas y Riad.
Noruega	**Total**	Pernoctaciones en los establecimientos homologados. Los datos cubren solamente los establecimientos con una capacidad de 20 o más camas.
República Árabe Siria	**Total**	Encuesta del turismo receptor en 2004, 2006 y 2007.
	Iraq	Los nacionales de Iraq se incluyen únicamente a partir de 2008 y se han excluido en los años anteriores (desde principios de 2008, tienen que pedir un visado para entrar en Siria; si entraron anteriormente a esa fecha, se considera que han permanecido por un periodo superior a un año, convirtiéndose en residentes).
Turquía	**Total**	Hoteles homologados, moteles, pensiones, albergues, apartahoteles, ciudades de vacaciones y hoteles especiales. Resultados de la encuesta mensual realizada en ciertos establecimientos de alojamiento clasificados por el Ministerio de Turismo.
Yemen	**Total**	Incluidos los nacionales residentes en el extranjero.

NOTAS 2007 - 2011

5. Pernoctaciones de turistas no residentes en hoteles y establecimientos asimilados, por país de residencia

Alemania	**China**	Incluido Hong Kong, China.
Austria	**Total**	Hoteles únicamente.
Cabo Verde	**Bélgica**	Incluido los Países Bajos.
Congo	**Total**	Fuente: "Direction Générale de l'Industrie Touristique", encuestas 2007 a 2010
Croacia	**Total**	Según el Reglamento sobre clasificación, normas mínimas y categorización de las instalaciones de alojamiento, los datos para los hoteles y establecimientos asimilados no incluyen hostales ni habitaciones con desayuno desde 2006.
Dinamarca	**Total**	Hoteles únicamente. 2011: cambio de metodología.
España	**Total**	Pernoctaciones en hoteles y hostales.
Francia	**Total**	Fuente: "INSEE", "DGCIS", socios regionales. Encuesta de ocupación hotelera ("EFH"). Incluidos hoteles sin clasificar.
	Otros países Asia Oriental/Pacífico	Incluido la India.
Israel	**Total**	Pernoctaciones en hoteles de turismo y apartahoteles.
	Todos los países de América del Sur	Incluida América Central.
Luxemburgo	**Total**	Pernoctaciones en hoteles, casas de huéspedes y albergues.
Macao (China)	**Total**	Fuente de los datos: Encuesta mensual de hoteles y establecimientos asimilados
Nueva Caledonia	**Total**	Corresponde a los hoteles de Noumea.
Países Bajos	**Total**	Hoteles y pensiones.
Polonia	**Total**	Excluidos los hostales.
Qatar	**Total**	Pernoctaciones en los hoteles únicamente. 2007-2009: incluido el turismo interno.
	Todos los países de Europa	2010-2011: Europa y Américas
Rumania	**Todos los países de África**	Incluido Egipto y Libia.
Suecia	**Total**	Pernoctaciones en los hoteles únicamente.
Suiza	**Total**	Incluye los establecimientos de cura.
	Todos los países de África del Norte	Argelia, Libia, Marruecos y Túnez.
Togo	**Burkina Faso**	Incluidos Malí y Níger.

NOTAS 2007 - 2011

6. Pernoctaciones de turistas no residentes en todo tipo de establecimientos de alojamiento, por nacionalidad

Eslovenia	Total	2008: Nueva metodología de la encuesta de alojamiento.
Hungría	Total	Establecimientos de alojamiento colectivo.
República Árabe Siria	Total	Encuesta del turismo receptor en 2004, 2006 y 2007.
	Iraq	Los nacionales de Iraq se incluyen únicamente a partir de 2008 y se han excluido en los años anteriores (desde principios de 2008, tienen que pedir un visado para entrar en Siria; si entraron anteriormente a esa fecha, se considera que han permanecido por un periodo superior a un año, convirtiéndose en residentes).
República de Moldova	Total	Excluido el margen izquierdo del río Nistru y la municipalidad de Bender.
Turquía	Total	Resultados de la encuesta mensual realizada en ciertos establecimientos de alojamiento clasificados por el Ministerio de Turismo.

NOTAS 2007 - 2011

6. Pernoctaciones de turistas no residentes en todo tipo de establecimientos de alojamiento, por país de residencia

Alemania	China	Incluido Hong Kong, China.
Austria	Total	Únicamente alojamiento de pago; excluidas las estancias con amigos y familiares y las viviendas secundarias.
Bahamas	Total	Pernoctaciones en todo tipo de alojamiento comercial.
Bélgica	Total	Establecimientos hoteleros, terrenos de camping, centros vacacionales, ciudades de vacaciones y categorías específicas de alojamiento.
Canadá	China	Incluido Mongolia y Tibet.
	Dinamarca	Incluido las Islas Feroe.
	Estonia	Incluido Letonia y Lituania.
	Francia	Incluido Andorra y Mónaco.
	Italia	Incluido San Marino, la Santa Sede y Malta.
	Suiza	Incluido Liechtenstein.
Croacia	Total	Excluidas las pernoctaciones en puertos de turismo náutico.
Dinamarca	Total	Incluye el turismo no comercial. 2011: cambio de metodología.
España	Total	Pernoctaciones en hoteles, hostales, camping, apartamentos turísticos y alojamientos/casas rurales.
Francia	Total	Fuente: "DGCIS", "Banque de France". Encuesta a los visitantes que vienen del extranjero ("EVE") - resultados 2009 revisados y 2010 provisionales
	China	Incluye Hong-Kong (China) y Macao (China).
	Suiza	Incluye Liechtentein.
	Todos los países de África del Norte	Argelia, Egipto, Libia, Marruecos y Túnez.
	Otros países Asia Oriental/Pacífico	Incluido la India.
Irlanda	Total	Incluidas pernoctaciones en alojamiento privado gratuito (casas de huéspedes y casas particulares).
	Reino Unido	Incluidos los residentes de Irlanda del Norte.
Jamaica	Total	Se ha obtenido la información multiplicando la duración media de estancia por el numero de turistas (stop-overs) procedentes de cada país de origen. Excluidos los nacionales residentes en el extranjero.
	Otros países de las Américas	América Latina.
	Todos los países de Europa	Reino unido y resto de Europa.
Malta	Total	Datos procedentes de las salidas por vías aérea y marítima. Fuente: "National Statistics Office".
Países Bajos	Total	Excluidas las pernoctaciones en instalaciones fijas (alquiladas anualmente o por temporada).
Rumania	Todos los países de África	Incluido Egipto y Libia.
Suecia	Total	2007: Pernoctaciones en hoteles, albergues juveniles, poblados de vacaiones y camping. 2008-2011: Pernoctaciones en hoteles, albergues juveniles, poblados de vacaiones, camping y alquiler, a través de agencias intermediarias, de casas de campo y apartamentos privados.

DATA SOURCES

Albania	Institute of Statistics – INSTAT
	http://www.instat.gov.al/
Algeria	Ministère de l'Aménagement du Territoire, de l'Environnement et du Tourisme and Office National des Statistiques
	http://www.ons.dz/-Tourisme-.html
Andorra	Ministerio de Turismo y Medio Ambiente and Ministerio de Finanzas
	http://www.estadistica.ad/serveiestudis/web/index.asp?lang=2
Angola	Ministério de Hotelaria e Turismo - Gabinete de Estudos, Planeamento e Estatística
Anguilla	Anguilla Statistics Department - Ministry of Finance, Economic Development, Investment, Commerce and Tourism
	http://www.gov.ai/statistics/cab_external.htm
Antigua and Barbuda	Ministry of Tourism
	http://www.tourismantiguabarbuda.gov.ag/tourism_programs/statistics.php
Argentina	Dirección de Estudios de Mercado y Estadística - Secretaría de Turismo de la Nación
	http://www.turismo.gov.ar/
Armenia	Tourism Department - Ministry of Trade and Economic Development
	http://www.armstat.am/en/
Aruba	Aruba Tourism Authority
	http://www.cbs.aw/cbs/do/home.html
Australia	Australian Bureau of Statistics
	http://www.abs.gov.au/
Austria	Statistics Austria
	http://www.statistik.at/web_en/statistics/tourism/accommodation/index.html
Azerbaijan	Ministry of Culture and Tourism and Statistical Committee
	http://www.azstat.org/statinfo/consumermarket/en/tur_en.shtml
Bahamas	Bahamas Ministry of Tourism
	http://www.tourismtoday.com/prelim/statistics/
Bahrain	Tourism Sector - Ministry of Culture and Information
Barbados	Barbados Tourism Authority
Belarus	State Committee of Frontier Troops and Ministry of Statistics and Analysis
Belgium	Institut National de Statistique
Belize	Belize Tourist Board
	http://www.belizetourism.org/content/view/248/295/
Benin	Direction du développement touristique - Ministère de la culture, de l'artisanat et du tourisme
Bermuda	Bermuda Department of Tourism
	http://www.gov.bm/portal/server.pt?space=CommunityPage&control=SetCommunity&CommunityID=227
Bhutan	Department of Tourism - Royal Government of Bhutan
	http://www.nsb.gov.bt/index.php?id=13
Bolivia	Instituto Nacional de Estadística
	http://www.ine.gov.bo/default.aspx
Bonaire	Tourism Corporation of Bonaire (TCB)
	http://www.tourismbonaire.com/contact_services/trade_section/statistical_info/
Bosnia and Herzegovina	Agency for Statistics of Bosnia and Herzegovina
	http://www.bhas.ba
Botswana	Department of Tourism - Ministry of Environment, Wildlife and Tourism
	http://www.mewt.gov.bw
Brazil	Ministério do Turismo
	http://www.dadosefatos.turismo.gov.br/dadosefatos/home.html
British Virgin Islands	The Development Planning Unit - Ministry of Finance
	http://dpu.gov.vg
Brunei Darussalam	Brunei Tourism - Ministry of Industry and Primary Resources

DATA SOURCES

Bulgaria	Ministry of Economy, Energy and Tourism and National Statistical Institute, Bulgarian National Bank http://www.nsi.bg/otrasalen.php?otr=57
Burkina Faso	Service de l'analyse statistique et de la Coopération touristique - Ministère de la Culture, des Arts et du Tourisme http://www.insd.bf/
Burundi	Office National du Tourisme
Cambodia	Ministry of Tourism http://www.tourismcambodia.org/mot/index.php?view=statistic_report#comp
Canada	Canadian Tourism Commission and Statistics Canada http://en-corporate.canada.travel/Corporate/Flyout.page?id=369&fid=376
Cape Verde	Instituto Nacional de Estatística Ministério da Economia, Crescimento e Competitividade http://www.ine.cv/indexBDeo.aspx
Cayman Islands	Cayman Islands Department of Tourism http://www.caymanislands.ky/statistics/
Central African Republic	Ministère du Développement du Tourisme et de l'Artisanat
Chad	Ministère du Tourisme et de l'Artisanat - Direction de la Planification et des Études Prospectives
Chile	Servicio Nacional de Turismo - SERNATUR http://www.sernatur.cl/institucional/htm_instit/estadisticas.html
China	National Tourism Administration http://en.cnta.gov.cn/
Colombia	Departamento Administrativo de Seguridad (DAS) Ministerio de Comercio, Industria y Turismo http://www.mincomercio.gov.co
Comoros	Direction Nationale de la Promotion du Tourisme et de l'Hôtellerie - Ministère du Transport, Tourisme, Postes et Télécommunications Banque centrale des Comores
Congo	Direction Générale du Tourisme et de l'Hôtellerie - Ministère du tourisme et de l'environnement
Cook Islands	Cook Islands Tourism Corporation Cook Islands Statistics Office http://www.stats.gov.ck/Statistics/Tourism/tournav.htm
Costa Rica	Banco Central de Costa Rica (BCCR) Instituto Costarricense de Turismo (ICT) Instituto Nacional de Estadística y Censos (INEC) http://www.visitcostarica.com/ict/paginas/modEst/estudios_demanda_turistica.asp?ididioma=1
Croatia	Central Bureau of Statistics http://www.dzs.hr/default_e.htm http://www.mint.hr/default.aspx?id=363
Cuba	Oficina Nacional de Estadísticas http://www.one.cu/sitioone2006.asp
Curaçao	Curaçao Tourist Board http://www.curacao.com/Corporate/Statistics
Cyprus	Statistical Service of Cyprus Cyprus Tourism Organization http://www.mof.gov.cy/mof/cystat/statistics.nsf/index_en/index_en?OpenDocument
Czech Republic	Czech Statistical Office, TSA Ministry for Regional Development http://www.czso.cz/eng/redakce.nsf/i/home
Democratic Republic of the Congo	Office National du Tourisme
Denmark	VisitDenmark http://www.dst.dk/HomeUK.aspx
Dominica	Discover Dominica Authority http://tourism.gov.dm/

DATA SOURCES

Dominican Republic	Secretaría de Estado de Turismo
	http://www.bancentral.gov.do/estadisticas.asp?a=Sector_Turismo
Ecuador	Ministerio de Turismo
	http://www.turismo.gov.ec/index.php?option=com_content&task=view&id=459&Itemid=95
Egypt	Ministry of Tourism
El Salvador	Corporación Salvadoreña de Turismo (CORSATUR) - Ministerio de Turismo
	http://www.elsalvador.travel/category/estadisticas/
Eritrea	Ministry of Tourism
Estonia	Estonian Tourist Board / Enterprise Estonia
	http://pub.stat.ee/px-web.2001/I_Databas/Economy/databasetree.asp
	http://visitestonia.com/en/additional-navigation/press-room/eas-views-on-tourism/estonian-tourism-statistics
Ethiopia	Ministry of Culture and Tourism
Fiji	Fiji Islands Bureau of Statistics
	http://www.spc.int/prism/Country/FJ/stats/Tourism/tourmigstats_index.htm
Finland	Tourism Statistics - Statistics Finland
	http://www.mek.fi/w5/mekfi/index.nsf/(pages)/Tutkimukset_ja_tilastot
France	DGCIS (Direction Générale de la Compétitivité, de l'Industrie et des Services)
	INSEE (Institut national de la statistique et des études économiques)
	http://tourisme.gouv.fr/
	http://www.insee.fr/fr/default.asp
French Polynesia	Service du Tourisme
	http://www.ispf.pf/ISPF/Chiffres/Tourisme.aspx
	http://www.servicedutourisme.gov.pf
	http://www.tahiti-tourisme.com/Partners/
Gambia	Gambia Tourism Authority
	http://www.visitthegambia.gm/index.php/en/publications
Georgia	Georgian National Tourism Agency - Ministry of Economy and Sustainable Development
	National Statistics Office of Georgia
	http://www.gnta.ge/?61/statistics/&lan=en
Germany	Statistiches Bundesamt
	http://www.destatis.de
Greece	Hellenic Statistical Authority (EL STAT.)
	http://www.statistics.gr/portal/page/portal/ESYE
Grenada	Grenada Board of Tourism
Guadeloupe	Comité du Tourisme des Îles de la Guadeloupe
Guam	Guam Visitors Bureau
	http://www.bsp.guam.gov
	http://www.visitguam.org
Guatemala	Instituto Guatemalteco de Turismo - INGUAT
	http://estadisticas.almadelatierra.com/
Guyana	Guyana Tourism Authority
Haiti	Ministère du Tourisme
	http://www.visithaiti.gouv.ht/page.php?id=4
Honduras	Instituto Hondureño de Turismo
	http://www.iht.hn/?page_id=27
Hong Kong, China	Hong Kong Tourism Board
	http://partnernet.hktb.com/pnweb/jsp/comm/index.jsp?charset=en
	http://www.censtatd.gov.hk/hong_kong_statistics/index.jsp
Hungary	Hungarian Central statistical Office
	http://portal.ksh.hu/portal/page?_pageid=38,119919&_dad=portal&_schema=PORTAL
Iceland	Hagstofa Íslands Statistics Iceland
	http://www.statice.is/Statistics/Tourism,-transport-and-informati

DATA SOURCES

India	Ministry of Tourism - Government of India http://tourism.gov.in/
Indonesia	Ministry of Culture and Tourism BPS Statistics Indonesia http://dds.bps.go.id/eng/aboutus.php?tabel=1&id_subyek=16 http://www.budpar.go.id/page.php?ic=621&id=180
Iran, Islamic Republic of	Iran Cultural Heritage and Tourism Organization (ICHTO)
Iraq	Iraqi Tourism Board
Ireland	Fáilte Ireland http://www.failteireland.ie/Home
Israel	Ministry of Tourism http://www1.cbs.gov.il/reader/?MIval=cw_usr_view_SHTML&ID=432
Italy	Banca d'Italia Istituto Nazionale di Statistica (ISTAT) http://www.bancaditalia.it http://www.istat.it
Jamaica	Jamaica Tourist Board http://www.jtbonline.org/statistics/Annual%20Travel/Forms/AllItems.aspx
Japan	Japan National Tourism Organization http://www.tourism.jp/english/statistics/index.php
Jordan	Ministry of Tourism and Antiquities http://www.tourism.jo
Kazakhstan	Agency of Statistics of the Republic of Kazakhstan http://www.eng.stat.kz/digital/Tourism/Pages/default.aspx
Kenya	Kenya Tourist Board
Kiribati	Kiribati National Tourism Office, Ministry of Communication, Transport and Tourism Development and PATA http://www.spc.int/prism/Country/KI/Stats/Tourism/tourism-index.htm
Korea, Republic of	Ministry of Culture and Tourism http://kto.visitkorea.or.kr/inout.kto?func_name=search
Kuwait	Central Statistical Office http://mopweb4.mop.gov.kw/
Kyrgyzstan	National Statistical Committee
Lao People's Democratic Republic	Lao National Tourism Administration and Tourism Development Department http://www.nsc.gov.la/Selected_Statistics.htm
Latvia	Transport and Tourism Statistics Section - Central Statistical Bureau http://www.csb.gov.lv/csp/content/?lng=en&cat=355
Lebanon	Ministère du Tourisme http://www.cas.gov.lb/index.php?option=com_content&view=frontpage&Itemid=28
Lesotho	Lesotho Tourism Development Corporation http://www.ltdc.org.ls/researchArrivalStats.php
Liechtenstein	Office of Statistics Liechtenstein. Tourism Statistics http://www.llv.li/amtsstellen/llv-as-tourismus.htm
Lithuania	Lithuanian State Department of Tourism http://www.stat.gov.lt/en/pages/view/?id=1638&PHPSESSID=0522a6cef6b6d204b72ec646d272a81f
Luxembourg	STATEC http://www.statistiques.public.lu
Macao, China	Macau Statistics and Census Service Macau Government Tourist Office http://www.dsec.gov.mo/Statistic/TourismAndServices/VisitorArrivals.aspx http://industry.macautourism.gov.mo/en/index.php
Madagascar	Ministère des Transports et du Tourisme http://www.mtoura.gov.mg/?page_id=603

DATA SOURCES

Malawi	Ministry of Tourism, Wildlife and Culture
Malaysia	Department of Statistics Malaysia Tourism Malaysia http://www.tourism.gov.my/corporate/research.asp?page=facts_figures
Maldives	Ministry of Tourism http://www.tourism.gov.mv/stat.php?statId=3
Mali	Office malien du tourisme et de l'hôtellerie (O.MA.T.HO)
Malta	Malta Tourism Authority National Statistics Office http://www.maltatourismauthority.com/page.aspx?id=105 http://www.nso.gov.mt/site/page.aspx?pageid=27
Marshall Islands	Marshall Islands Visitors Authority http://www.spc.int/prism/country/mh/Stats/index.htm
Martinique	Comité Martiniquais du Tourisme http://www.martiniquetourisme.com/martinique/Le-C.M.T/Les-donnees-sur-le-tourisme
Mauritius	Ministry of Tourism and Leisure http://www.gov.mu/portal/site/cso/menuitem.dee225f644ffe2aa338852f8a0208a0c/?content_id=52160fa67278c010VgnVCM1000000a04a8c0RCRD
Mexico	Secretaría de Turismo de México (SECTUR) Instituto Nacional de Estadística y Geografía (INEGI) http://www.gob.mx/wb/egobierno/egob_Estadisticas_del_sector_turismo http://www.inegi.org.mx/prod_serv/contenidos/espanol/biblioteca/Default.asp?accion=1&upc=702825224585
Monaco	Direction du Tourisme et des Congrès http://www.monaco.gouv.mc/devwww/wwwnew.nsf/1909$/b9d7989a41d6c875c1256f820057b766fr?OpenDocument&7Fr
Mongolia	National Tourism Center - Ministry of Nature, Environment and Tourism http://mongoliatourism.gov.mn/
Montenegro	Ministry of Sustainable Development and Tourism http://www.monstat.org/EngMeniGodisnjiPodaci.htm
Montserrat	Statistics Department Montserrat
Morocco	Ministère du tourisme http://www.tourisme.gov.ma/francais/5-Tourisme-chiffres/ArriveeTouristes.htm
Mozambique	Ministry of Tourism Instituto Nacional de Estatística http://www.ine.gov.mz/sectorias_dir/turismo/
Myanmar	Ministry of Hotels and Tourism http://www.myanmartourism.org/tourismstatistics.htm
Namibia	Ministry of Environment and Tourism Namibian Tourism Board http://www.namibiatourism.com.na/research-center/
Nepal	Nepal Tourism Board Ministry of Culture, Tourism and Civil Aviation http://www.tourism.gov.np
Netherlands	Statistics Netherlands http://www.cbs.nl/en-GB/menu/themas/vrije-tijd-cultuur/nieuws/default.htm
New Caledonia	Institut de la Statistique et des Études Économiques (ISEE) http://www.isee.nc/
New Zealand	Statistics New Zealand (SNZ) Ministry of Business, Innovation & Employment (MBIE) http://www.stats.govt.nz/ http://www.med.govt.nz/sectors-industries/tourism/tourism-research-data
Nicaragua	Instituto Nicaragüense de Turismo (INTUR) http://www.intur.gob.ni/estadisticas.php

DATA SOURCES

Niger	Ministère du Tourisme et de l'Artisanat Institut National de la Statistique http://www.stat-niger.org/statistique/
Nigeria	Nigerian Tourism Development Corporation
Niue	Statistics Niue http://www.spc.int/prism/country/nu/stats/Migration/Migration_index.htm
Northern Mariana Islands	Marianas Visitors Authority
Norway	Statistics Norway Institute of Transport Economics http://www.ssb.no/english/subjects/
Oman	Ministry of National Economy Ministry of Commerce and Industry Directorate General of Tourism - Ministry of Tourism http://www.moneoman.gov.om
Pakistan	Pakistan Tourism Development Corporation - Ministry of Tourism http://www.pakistantourism.gov.pk/downloads.php
Palau	Office of Planning and Statistics, Bureau of Budget and Planning - Ministry of Finance Palau Visitors Authority http://www.palaugov.net/stats/PalauStats/Tourism/tourism.htm http://www.visit-palau.com/publication/index.cfm
Palestine	Palestinian Central Bureau of Statistics http://www.pcbs.gov.ps/DesktopDefault.aspx?tabID=3039&lang=en
Panama	Autoridad de Turismo de Panamá http://www.atp.gob.pa
Papua New Guinea	Papua New Guinea Tourism Promotion Authority
Paraguay	Secretaría Nacional de Turismo - SENATUR http://www.senatur.gov.py/estadisticas.php?language=1
Peru	Dirección General de Migraciones y Naturalización (DIGEMIN) Ministerio de Comercio Exterior y Turismo (MINCETUR) http://www.mincetur.gob.pe/newweb/Default.aspx?tabid=141
Philippines	Department of Tourism http://www.tourism.gov.ph/Pages/TourismResearch.aspx
Poland	Institute of Tourism http://www.intur.com.pl/itenglish/institute_en.htm
Portugal	Turismo de Portugal, I.P. http://www.ine.pt/xportal/xmain?xpid=INE&xpgid=ine_princindic&contexto=pi&selTab=tab0
Puerto Rico	Junta de Planificación de Puerto Rico Compañía de Turismo de Puerto Rico http://www.jp.gobierno.pr/
Qatar	Qatar Statistics Authority http://www.qsa.gov.qa http://www.qix.gov.qa
Republic of Moldova	National Bureau of Statistics http://www.statistica.md/category.php?l=en&idc=293&
Reunion	Institut National de la Statistique et des Études Économique - INSEE Comité du Tourisme de la Réunion http://webpro.la-reunion-tourisme.com/connaitre2.php3?id_rubrique=71 http://www.insee.fr/fr/themes/theme.asp?theme=13&nivgeo=24
Romania	National Institute of Statistics https://statistici.insse.ro/shop/index.jsp?page=tempo2&lang=en&context=63
Russian Federation	Russian Federal Agency for Tourism www.russiatourism.ru
Rwanda	Rwanda Development Board http://www.rdb.rw/welcome-to-rwanda/tourism-research-and-statistics.html

DATA SOURCES

Saba	Saba Tourist Bureau Caribbean Tourism Organization Central Bank of the Netherlands Antilles
Saint Kitts and Nevis	Eastern Caribbean Central Bank http://www.eccb-centralbank.org/Statistics/index.asp#tourismdata
Saint Lucia	Saint Lucia Tourist Board http://www.stlucia.gov.lc/
Saint Vincent and the Grenadines	Ministry of Tourism and Culture http://www.discoversvg.com/index.php/es/about-svg/tourism-statistics
Samoa	Samoa Tourism Authority Statistical Services Division (Ministry of Finance) http://www.sbs.gov.ws/ http://www.mof.gov.ws/publish/economicreview.shtml
San Marino	Segreteria di Stato per il Turismo, lo Sport, le Telecomunicazioni, i Trasporti e la Cooperazione Economica http://www.statistica.sm/on-line/Home/DatiStatistici/docCat.14000570.1.10.1.html?Categoria=Afflusso turistico
Sao Tome and Principe	Direcçao do Turismo e Hotelaria
Saudi Arabia	The Saudi Commission for Tourism and Antiquities (SCTA) http://www.mas.gov.sa/
Senegal	Ministère du Tourisme et des Transports Aériens
Serbia	Statistical Office of the Republic of Serbia National Bank of Serbia http://webrzs.stat.gov.rs/WebSite/
Seychelles	National Bureau of Statistics Seychelles Tourism Board http://www.nbs.gov.sc/
Sierra Leone	National Tourist Board Statistics Sierra Leone http://www.statistics.sl/
Singapore	Singapore Tourism Board http://www.singstat.gov.sg/stats/themes/economy/tourism.html https://app.stb.gov.sg/asp/tou/tou02.asp#VS
Sint Eustatius	St. Eustatius Tourism Development Foundation
Sint Maarten	St. Maarten Tourist Bureau
Slovakia	Tourism Section – Ministry of Transportation, Construction and Regional Development Statistical Office www.mindop.sk www.statistics.sk
Slovenia	Statistical Office - Tourism Statistics, Structual Business Statistics, Statistical register of employment Bank of Slovenia http://www.stat.si/eng/tema_ekonomsko_turizem.asp
Solomon Islands	Solomon Islands National Statistics Office http://www.spc.int/prism/country/sb/Stats/Migration%20and%20Tourism/Tour-Index.htm
South Africa	Statistics South Africa South African Tourism http://www.statssa.gov.za/default.asp
Spain	Instituto de Estudios Turísticos Instituto Nacional de Estadística http://www.iet.tourspain.es/paginas/home.aspx?idioma=es-ES http://www.ine.es/inebmenu/mnu_hosteleria.htm
Sri Lanka	Sri Lanka Tourist Board http://www.sltda.lk/statistics
Sudan	Ministry of Tourism and Wildlife
Suriname	Suriname Tourism Foundation

DATA SOURCES

Swaziland	Swaziland Tourism Authority Ministry of Tourism, Environment and Communications
Sweden	Tillväxtverket - The Swedish Agency for Economic and Regional Growth http://www.tillvaxtverket.se/english http://www.scb.se/Pages/Product____11830.aspx
Switzerland	Swiss Federal Statistical Office http://www.bfs.admin.ch/bfs/portal/fr/index/themen/10.html
Syrian Arab Republic	Ministry of Tourism
Taiwan (Province of China)	Planning Division Tourism Bureau - Ministry of Transportation and Communication http://admin.taiwan.net.tw/english/statistics/release.asp?relno=6
Tajikistan	Committee of Youth Affairs, Sports and Tourism under the Government of the Republic of Tajikistan
Thailand	Ministry of Tourism and Sports http://www.tourism.go.th/2010/th/statistic/tourism.php
The Former Yugoslav Republic of Macedonia	State Statistical Office http://www.stat.gov.mk/english/glavna_eng.asp?br=110#Tourism
Timor-Leste	Direcçao Nacional de Estatística http://dne.mof.gov.tl/publications/index.htm
Togo	Ministère de l'Environnement, du Tourisme et des Ressources Forestières
Tonga	Tonga Visitors Bureau http://www.spc.int/prism/tonga/index.php/tourism-statistics
Trinidad and Tobago	Tourism Development Company Limited http://www.tdc.co.tt/stopover_statistics.htm
Tunisia	Ministère du Tourisme - Office National du Tourisme Institut National de la Statistique http://www.ins.nat.tn/indexfr.php
Turkey	Ministry of Culture and Tourism http://sgb.kulturturizm.gov.tr/belge/1-90750/turizm-istatistikleri.html http://www.turkstat.gov.tr/PreTablo.do?tb_id=51&ust_id=14
Turks and Caicos Islands	Turks and Caicos Tourist Board
Tuvalu	Ministry of Foreign Affairs, Trade, Tourism, Environment and Labour http://www.spc.int/prism/Country/TV/Stats/Tourism_migration/tour_index.htm
Uganda	Ministry of Tourism, Trade and Industry Uganda Bureau of Statistics http://www.ubos.org/?st=pagerelations2&id=19&p=related%20pages%202:Migration%20and%20Tourism%20Statistics
Ukraine	State Statistics Committee of Ukraine http://www.ukrstat.gov.ua/operativ/operativ2007/tyr/tyr_e/arh_vig_e.html
United Kingdom	VisitBritain Office for National Statistics http://www.visitbritain.org/insightsandstatistics/keystats/index.aspx http://www.statistics.gov.uk/statbase/Product.asp?vlnk=1905&More=N
United Republic of Tanzania	Tourism Division - Ministry of Natural Resources and Tourism National Bureau of Statistics http://www.mnrt.go.tz/index.php/documents-a-publications/category/8-tourism
United States of America	Office of Travel and Tourism Industries (OTTI) http://tinet.ita.doc.gov/ http://www.ahla.com/content.aspx?id=3448
United States Virgin Islands	Bureau of Economic Research http://www.usviber.org/publications.htm
Uruguay	Ministerio de Turismo y Deporte http://www.mintur.gub.uy
Uzbekistan	National Company "Uzbektourism"

DATA SOURCES

Vanuatu	Vanuatu National Statistics Office
	http://www.vnso.gov.vu/
Venezuela	Ministerio del Poder Popular para el Turismo
	http://www.mintur.gob.ve/estadisticasTur.php
Viet Nam	Viet Nam National Administration of Tourism
	General Statistics Office
	http://www.vietnamtourism.com/e_pages/news/index.asp?loai=1&chucnang=07
	http://www.gso.gov.vn/default_en.aspx?tabid=491
Yemen	Ministry of Tourism
	Central Statistical Organization
	http://www.yementourism.com/statistics/
	http://www.cso-yemen.org/content.php?lng=english&pcat=131
Zambia	Ministry of Tourism, Environment and Natural Resources
Zimbabwe	Zimbabwe Tourism Authority – ZTA
	http://www.zimbabwetourism.net/index.php?option=com_zoo&view=category&Itemid=199
	http://www.aitbase.co.zw/zta/index.php?option=com_docman&task=cat_view&gid=105&Itemid=183